THE OXFORD HISTORY OF
HISTORICAL WRITING

THE OXFORD HISTORY OF HISTORICAL WRITING

The Oxford History of Historical Writing is a five-volume, multi-authored scholarly survey of the history of historical writing across the globe. It is a chronological history of humanity's attempts to conserve, recover, and narrate its past with considerable attention paid to different global traditions and their points of comparison with Western historiography. Each volume covers a particular period, with care taken to avoid unduly privileging Western notions of periodization, and the volumes cover progressively shorter chronological spans, reflecting both the greater geographical range of later volumes and the steep increase in historical activity around the world since the nineteenth century. *The Oxford History of Historical Writing* is the first collective scholarly survey of the history of historical writing to cover the globe across such a substantial breadth of time.

Volume 1: Beginnings to AD 600
Volume 2: 400–1400
Volume 3: 1400–1800
Volume 4: 1800–1945
Volume 5: Historical Writing since 1945

THE OXFORD HISTORY OF HISTORICAL WRITING

Daniel Woolf

GENERAL EDITOR

The Oxford History of Historical Writing

VOLUME 3: 1400–1800

José Rabasa, Masayuki Sato, Edoardo Tortarolo,
and Daniel Woolf

VOLUME EDITORS

Ian Hesketh

ASSISTANT EDITOR

OXFORD
UNIVERSITY PRESS

OXFORD
UNIVERSITY PRESS

Great Clarendon Street, Oxford OX2 6DP

Oxford University Press is a department of the University of Oxford.
It furthers the University's objective of excellence in research, scholarship,
and education by publishing worldwide in

Oxford New York

Auckland Cape Town Dar es Salaam Hong Kong Karachi
Kuala Lumpur Madrid Melbourne Mexico City Nairobi
New Delhi Shanghai Taipei Toronto

With offices in

Argentina Austria Brazil Chile Czech Republic France Greece
Guatemala Hungary Italy Japan Poland Portugal Singapore
South Korea Switzerland Thailand Turkey Ukraine Vietnam

Oxford is a registered trade mark of Oxford University Press
in the UK and in certain other countries

Published in the United States
by Oxford University Press Inc., New York

British Library Cataloguing in Publication Data

Data available

Library of Congress Cataloging in Publication Data

Data available

Typeset by SPI Publisher Services, Pondicherry, India
Printed in Great Britain
on acid-free paper by
MPG Books Group, Bodmin and King's Lynn

ISBN 978–0–19–921917–9

1 3 5 7 9 10 8 6 4 2

The Oxford History of Historical Writing was made possible by the generous financial support provided by the Offices of the Vice-President (Research) and the Provost and Vice-President (Academic) at the University of Alberta from 2005 to 2009 and subsequently by Queen's University, Kingston, Ontario.

General Editor's Acknowledgements

The *Oxford History of Historical Writing* has itself been the product of several years of work and many hands and voices. As general editor, it is my pleasure to acknowledge a number of these here. First and foremost, to the volume editors, without whom there would have been no series. I am very grateful for their willingness to sign on, and for their flexibility in pursuing their own vision for their piece of the story while acknowledging the need for some common goals and unity of editorial practices. The Advisory Board, many of whose members were subsequently roped into either editorship or authorship, have given freely of their time and wisdom. At Oxford University Press, former commissioning editor Ruth Parr encouraged the series proposal and marshalled it through the readership and approvals process. After her departure, my colleagues and I enjoyed able help and support from Christopher Wheeler at the managerial level and, editorially, from Rupert Cousens, Seth Cayley, Matthew Cotton, and Stephanie Ireland. I must also thank the OUP production team and Carol Carnegie in particular.

The series would not have been possible without the considerable financial support from the two institutions I worked at over the project's lifespan. At the University of Alberta, where I worked from 2002 to mid-2009, the project was generously funded by the Offices of the Vice-President (Research) and the Provost and Vice-President (Academic). I am especially grateful to Gary Kachanoski and Carl Amrhein, the incumbents in those offices, who saw the project's potential. The funding they provided enabled me to hire a series of project assistants, to involve graduate students in the work, and to defray some of the costs of publication such as images and maps. It permitted the acquisition of computer equipment and also of a significant number of books to supplement the fine library resources at Alberta. Perhaps most importantly, it also made the crucial Edmonton conference happen. At Queen's University in Kingston, Ontario, where I moved into a senior leadership role in 2009, funding was provided to push the project over the 'finish-line', to transfer the research library, and in particular to retain the services of an outstanding research associate, Assistant Editor Dr Ian Hesketh. I am profoundly grateful for Ian's meticulous attention to detail, and his ability ruthlessly to cut through excess prose (including on occasion my own) in order to ensure that volumes maintained editorial uniformity internally and together with other volumes, not least because the volumes are not all being published at once. A series of able graduate students have served as project assistants, including especially Tanya Henderson, Matthew Neufeld, Carolyn Salomons, Tereasa Maillie, and Sarah Waurechen, the last of whom almost single-handedly organized the complex logistics of the Edmonton conference. Among the others on whom the project has depended I have to thank the Office of the Dean of Arts and Science for providing project space at Queen's University, and the Department of History and Classics at Alberta. Melanie Marvin at Alberta and Christine Berga at Queen's have assisted in the management of the research accounts, as has Julie Gordon-Woolf, my spouse (and herself a former research administrator), whose advice on this front is only a small part of the support she has provided.

Foreword

Daniel Woolf, General Editor

Half a century ago, Oxford University Press published a series of volumes entitled *Historical Writing on the Peoples of Asia*. Consisting of four volumes devoted to East Asia, Southeast Asia, the Middle East, and South Asia, and based on conferences held at the School of Oriental and African Studies, University of London, in the late 1950s, that series has aged surprisingly well; many of the individual essays are still being cited in our own day. The books were also remarkably ahead of their time since the history of historical writing was at that time firmly understood as being the history of a European genre. Indeed, the subject of the history of history was itself barely a subject—typical surveys of the early to mid-twentieth century by the likes of James Westfall Thompson and Harry Elmer Barnes, following Eduard Fueter's paradigmatic 1911 *Geschichte der Neueren Historiographie* [History of Modern Historiography], were written by master historians surveying their discipline and its origins. The Oxford series provided some much needed perspective, though it was not followed up for many years, and more recent surveys in the last two or three decades of the twentieth century have continued to speak of historiography as if it were an entirely Western invention or practice. Since the late 1990s a number of works have been published that challenge the Eurocentrism of the history of history, as well as its inherent teleology. We can now view the European historiographic venture against the larger canvas of many parallel and—a fact often overlooked—interconnected traditions of writing or speaking about the past from Asia, the Americas, and Africa.

The Oxford History of Historical Writing is conceived in this spirit. It seeks to provide the first collective scholarly history of historical writing to span the globe. It salutes its great predecessor of half a century ago, but very deliberately seeks neither to imitate nor to replace it. For one thing, the five volumes collectively include Europe, the Americas, and Africa, together with Asia; for another, the division among these volumes is chronological, rather than by region. We decided on the former because the history of non-European historical writing should, no more than that of its European counterpart, be viewed in isolation. We chose the latter in order to provide what amounts to a cumulative narrative (albeit with well over a hundred different voices), and in order to facilitate comparison and contrast between regions within a broad time period.

A few caveats that apply to the entire series are in order. First, while the series as a whole will describe historical writing from earliest times to the present, each individual volume is also intended to stand on its own as a study of a particular period in the history of historical writing. These periods shrink in duration as they approach the present, both because of the obvious increase in extant materials and known authors, but also because of the expansion of subject matter to a fully global reach (the Americas, for instance, do not feature at all in volume 1; non-Muslim Africa appears in neither volume 1 nor volume 2). Second, while the volumes share a common goal and are the product of several years of dialogue both within and between its five editorial teams and the general editor, there has been no attempt to impose a common organizational structure on each volume. In fact, quite the opposite course has been pursued: individual editorial teams have been selected because of complementary expertise, and encouraged to 'go their own way' in selecting topics and envisioning the shapes of their volumes—with the sole overriding provision that each volume had to be global in ambition. Third, and perhaps most importantly, this series is emphatically neither an encyclopedia nor a dictionary. A multi-volume work that attempted to deal with *every* national tradition (much less mention every historian) would easily spread from five to fifty volumes, and in fact not accomplish the ends that the editors seek. We have had to be selective, not comprehensive, and while every effort has been made to balance coverage and provide representation from all regions of the world, there are undeniable gaps. The reader who wishes to find out something about a particular country or topic not included in the *OHHW*'s more than 150 chapters can search elsewhere, in particular in a number of reference books which have appeared in the past fifteen or so years, some of which have global range. Our volumes are of course indexed, but we have deemed a cumulative index an inefficient and redundant use of space. Similarly, each individual essay offers a highly selective bibliography, intended to point the way to further reading (and where appropriate listing key sources from the period or topic under discussion in that chapter). In order to assist readers with limited knowledge of particular regions' or nations' political and social contexts, certain chapters have included a timeline of major events, though this has not been deemed necessary in every case. While there are (with one or two exceptions) no essays devoted to a single 'great historian', many historians from Sima Qian and Herodotus to the present are mentioned; rather than eat up space in essays with dates of birth and death, these have been consolidated in each volume's index.

Despite the independence of each team, some common standards are necessary in any series that aims for coherence, if not uniformity. Towards that end, a number of steps were built into the process of producing this series from the very beginning. Maximum advantage was taken of the Internet: not only were scholars encouraged to communicate with one another within and across volumes, but draft essays were posted on the project's website for commentary and review by other authors. A climactic conference, convened at the University of Alberta in Edmonton, Canada, in September 2008, brought most of the editors and just over half the authors together, physically, for an energizing and exciting two days during which matters of editorial detail and also content and substance were discussed. A major 'value-added', we think, of both conference and series, is that it has introduced to one another scholars who normally work in separate national and chronological fields, in order to pursue a common interest in the history of historical writing in unique and unprecedented ways. As the series' general editor, it is my hope that these connections will survive the end of the project and produce further collaborative work in the future. Several key decisions came out of the Edmonton conference, among the most important of which was to permit chronological overlap, while avoiding unnecessary repetition of topics. The chronological divisions of the volumes—with calendrical years used instead of typical Western periods like 'Middle Ages' and 'Renaissance'—remain somewhat arbitrary. Thus volume 1, on antiquity, ends about AD 600 prior to the advent of Islam, but overlaps with its successor, volume 2, on what in the West were the late antique and medieval centuries, and in China (the other major tradition of historical writing that features in every volume), the period from the Tang through the early Ming dynasties. Volumes 4 and 5 have a similar overlap in the years around the Second World War. While 1945 is a sensible boundary for some subjects, it is much less useful for others—in China, again, 1949 is the major watershed. Certain topics, such as the Annales School, are not usefully split at 1945. A further change pertained to the denotation of years BC and AD; here, we reversed an early decision to use BCE and CE, on the grounds that both are equally Eurocentric forms; BC/AD have at least been adopted by international practice, notwithstanding their Christian European origins.

It became rather apparent in Edmonton that we were in fact dealing with two sets of two volumes each (vols. 1/2 and 4/5), with volume 3 serving in some ways as a bridge between them, straddling the centuries from about 1400 to about 1800—what in the West is usually considered the 'early modern' era. A further decision, in order to keep the volumes reasonably affordable, was to use illustrations very selectively, and only where a substantive reason for their inclusion could be advanced, for instance in dealing with Latin American pictographic forms of commemorating the past. There are no decorative portraits of famous historians, and that too is appropriate in a project that eschews the history of historiography conceived of as a parade of stars—whether Western or Eastern, Northern or Southern—from Thucydides to Toynbee.

This, the third volume in the series (and fourth to be published), spans the gap between the first two volumes (covering antiquity and what is usually called—problematically in the case of South Asia and Islam—the 'Middle Ages') and volumes 4 and 5, which deal with modernity. The roughly four centuries covered in the present volume encompass a period of enormous change, including the Renaissance, Reformation, Enlightenment, and French Revolution in Europe, the Ming and early Qing dynasties in China, the rise and fall of the Mughal Empire in India, and the vicissitudes within the other main Islamic powers, the Persian and Ottoman Turkish empires. It is also the volume in which the Americas enter fully into the history of history, and both European and indigenous forms of historical writing are the subjects of several chapters; Africa, too, absent from the preceding volumes (with the exception of North African Islamic writers) receives its first extended treatment here. The editors of this volume have assembled an international roster of authors with expertise in a variety of different historical cultures, and they have also included thematic chapters, many with a strong comparative dimension, addressing some of the issues that arose over the period, from the application of philological techniques to historical evidence, to the emergence of 'antiquarianism' and the relations between history, myth, and fiction.

NOTE ON TRANSLATION AND TRANSLITERATION

Non-Roman alphabets and writing systems have been routinely transliterated using the standard systems for each language (for instance, Chinese using the Pinyin system). For the transliteration of Arabic, Persian, Turkish, and Syriac we have followed the rules set out by the *International Journal of Middle Eastern Studies*. Non-English book titles are normally followed (except where meaning is obvious) by a translated title, within square brackets, and in roman rather than italic face, unless a specific, published English translation is listed, in which case the bracketed title will also be in italics.

Contents

List of Maps

Notes on the Contributors

Guido Abbattista is Professor of Modern History at the University of Trieste (Italy). Among his recent publications are several essays on the politics and the ideology of empire in late eighteenth-century Britain, Edmund Burke's writings on empire, and the representation of 'otherness' in modern European culture; on this topic he has edited the volume *Facing Otherness: Europe and Human Diversities in the Early Modern Age* (Trieste, at the University Press, 2011).

David Allan is Reader in Scottish History at the University of St Andrews. His recent books include *A Nation of Readers* (2008), *Making British Culture* (2008), and *Commonplace Books and Reading in Georgian England* (2010).

Don Baker is Professor of Korean History and Civilization in the Department of Asian Studies at the University of British Columbia, Canada. Among his previous publications are *Korean Spirituality* (2008). He was a co-editor of *Sourcebook of Korean Civilization* (1996).

Elizabeth Hill Boone is Professor of Art History at Tulane University, New Orleans. Among her single-authored books are *The Codex Magliabechiano* (1983), *The Aztec World* (1994), *Stories in Red and Black: Pictorial Histories of the Aztecs and Mixtecs* (2000), and *Cycles of Time and Meaning in the Mexican Books of Fate* (2007).

Peter Burke was Professor of Cultural History, University of Cambridge, until his retirement in 2004 and remains a Fellow of Emmanuel College. His studies of historiography include *The Renaissance Sense of the Past* (1969) and *The French Historical Revolution* (1990).

Jorge Cañizares-Esguerra is the Alice Drysdale Sheffield Professor of History at the University of Texas-Austin. He is the author of *How to Write the History of the New World: Histories, Epistemologies, and Identities in the Eighteenth Century Atlantic World* (2001), *Puritan Conquistadors* (2006), and *Nature, Empire, and Nation* (2006).

William J. Connell is Professor of History and holds the Joseph M. and Geraldine C. La Motta Chair in Italian Studies at Seton Hall University. He recently edited (with Fred Gardaphé) *Anti-Italianism: Essays on a Prejudice* (2010).

Pamela Kyle Crossley is Professor of History at Dartmouth College in New Hampshire, United States. Among her previous publications are *The Wobbling Pivot* (2010), *What is Global History?* (2008), and *A Translucent Mirror* (1999).

Diogo Ramada Curto is Professor of History and Sociology at Univeridade Nova de Lisboa (Portugal). Among his previous publications are (co-ed.) *Portuguese Oceanic Expansion, 1400–1800* (Cambridge, 2007), *Cultura Política e Projectos Coloniais (1415–1800)* (Campinas, 2009), and *Cultura Política no Tempos dos Filipes (1580–1640)* (Lisbon, 2011).

Chantal Grell teaches history at the Université Versailles-Saint-Quentin. Among her previous publications on historiography are *Le dix-huitième siècle et l'antiquité en France, 1650–1789* (1995) and *Histoire intellectuelle et culturelle de la France de Louis XIV* (2000).

Ian Hesketh (**Assistant Editor**) is a research associate in the Department of History at Queen's University in Kingston, Canada. Among his publications are *Of Apes and Ancestors: Evolution, Christianity, and the Oxford Debate* (2009) and *The Science of History in Victorian Britain: Making the Past Speak* (2011).

Catherine Julien was Professor of History at Western Michigan University, Kalamazoo. She was the author of *Reading Inca History* (2000) and *Titu Cusi, History of How the Spaniards Arrived in Peru: Dual Language Edition* (2006). She died in 2011 after completing this chapter.

Donald R. Kelley is James Westfall Thompson professor of history, executive editor emeritus of the *Journal of the History of Ideas*, and author of many works, most recently a three-volume history of historical writing, *Faces of History* (1998), *Fortunes of History* (2003), and *Frontiers of History* (2006), and a survey of the history of intellectual history, *Descent of Ideas* (2002).

Howard Louthan is Professor of History at the University of Florida. His previous publications include *The Quest for Compromise: Peacemakers in Counter-Reformation Vienna* (Cambridge, 1997) and *Converting Bohemia: Force and Persuasion in the Catholic Reformation* (Cambridge, 2009).

Paul E. Lovejoy is Distinguished Research Professor, Department of History, York University, and holds the Canada Research Chair in African Diaspora History. His recent publications include *Slavery, Commerce and Production in West Africa* (2005), *Ecology and Ethnography of Muslim Trade in West Africa* (2005), *Slavery, Islam and Diaspora* (2009), and *Repercussions of the Atlantic Slave Trade* (2010).

Christoph Marcinkowski is Principal Research Fellow at IAIS, a policy and security think tank in Kuala Lumpur, Malaysia. Among his previous publications are *Mirza Rafi'a's Dastur al-Muluk* (2002), *Persian Historiography and Geography* (2003; trans. of a work by the late Bertold Spuler), and *Shi'ite Identities* (2010).

Peter N. Miller is a professor and Dean at the Bard Graduate Center in New York City. He is the author of *Peiresc's Europe: Learning and Virtue in the Seventeenth Century* (2000) and *Peiresc's Orient: Antiquarianism as Cultural History in the Seventeenth Century* (2011), and editor of *Momigliano and Antiquarianism: Foundations of the Modern Cultural Sciences* (2007).

Achim Mittag is Professor for Chinese Studies at the University of Tübingen. His special field of interest lies in Chinese historiography and intellectual history of early modern China. His latest publications include *Conceiving the 'Empire': China and Rome Compared* (jointly edited with Fritz-Heiner Mutschler, 2008).

On-cho Ng is Professor of History, Religious Studies, and Asian Studies at Pennsylvania State University. Apart from his co-authored book on Chinese historiography, *Mirroring the Past: The Writing and Use of History in Imperial China* (2005), he has published extensively on Confucian religiosity and Chinese hermeneutics.

Karen O'Brien is Professor of English Literature at the University of Warwick. She is the author of *Narratives of Enlightenment: Cosmopolitan History from Voltaire to Gibbon* (1997) and *Women and Enlightenment in Eighteenth-Century Britain* (2009). She is currently co-editing *The Cambridge Companion to Gibbon* and volume 2 of *The Oxford History of the Novel.*

Kira von Ostenfeld-Suske was recently awarded a Post-Doctoral Fellowship from the Social Science and Humanities Research Council of Canada which she will hold at Queen's University, under Prof. Daniel Woolf. Her post-doctoral project will investigate the political ideologies and methodologies behind the writing of 'world history' in sixteenth-century Spain and England.

Michael A. Pesenson is Assistant Professor of Slavic and Eurasian Studies at the University of Texas at Austin. He has written extensively on early East Slavic literature and culture. His forthcoming monograph is entitled: *The Antichrist in Russia: Visions of the Apocalypse in Russian Literature and Culture from the Middle Ages to the Revolution.*

José Rabasa teaches in the Department of Romance Languages and Literatures at Harvard University. His publications include: *Inventing America: Spanish Historiography and the Formation of Eurocentrism* (1993), *Writing Violence on the Northern Frontier: The Historiography of New Mexico and Florida and the Legacy of Conquest* (2000), and *Without History: Subaltern Studies, the Zapatista Insurgency, and the Specter of History* (2010).

David Read is Professor of English at the University of Missouri. His publications include *Temperate Conquests: Spenser and the Spanish New World* (2000) and *New World, Known World: Shaping Knowledge in Early Anglo-American Writing* (2005).

Asim Roy, former Director of Asia Centre, University of Tasmania, Hobart, Australia, is currently Fellow, School of History and Classics there. His previous publications include *The Islamic Syncretistic Tradition of Bengal* (1983), *Islam in South Asia* (1996), and (ed.), *Islam in History and Politics: Perspectives from South Asia* (2006).

Masayuki Sato was born in Japan. He read Economics, Philosophy, and History at Keio University and Cambridge University. After teaching in Kyoto, he was invited to the University of Yamanashi and is Professor of Social Studies in the Faculty of Education and Human Sciences. He was President of the International Commission for the History and Theory of Historiography (2005–10).

Karen Skovgaard-Petersen is research librarian at the Royal Library, Copenhagen, and is the managing editor of the Danish branch of the Danish-Norwegian digital editorial project, *The Writings of Ludwig Holberg (1684–1754)*. She is the author of *Historiography at the Court of Christian IV: Studies in the Latin Histories of Denmark by Johannes Pontanus and Johannes Meursius* (2002).

Jennifer B. Spock is Professor of History at Eastern Kentucky University in Richmond, Kentucky. Her previous publications focus on the socio-economic, religious, and cultural contexts of pre-Petrine Russian monasteries.

Baki Tezcan is Associate Professor of History and Religious Studies at the University of California, Davis, and the author of *The Second Ottoman Empire: Political and Social Transformation in the Early Modern World* (2010).

Edoardo Tortarolo is Professor of Early Modern History at the University of Eastern Piedmont, Italy. Among his previous publications are *L'Illuminismo: Ragioni e dubbi di una modernità europea* (1999) and *L'invenzione della libertà di stampa: Censura e scrittori nel Settecento* (2011).

Markus Völkel is Professor of European Intellectual History and Historical Methodology at the University of Rostock, Germany. Among his previous publications are *'Pyrrhonismus historicus' und 'fides historica'* (1987) and *Geschichtsschreibung: Eine Einführung in globaler Perspektive* (2006).

Geoff Wade is a historian with interests in Sino-Southeast Asian interactions and comparative historiography. Among his works are an online database of translated Chinese references to Southeast Asia (http://www.epress.nus.edu.sg/msl/), a six-volume compendium *China and Southeast Asia* (2009), and the chapter on Southeast Asia, 800–1500 in *The New Cambridge History of Islam* (2010).

Neil L. Whitehead is Professor of Anthropology at the University of Wisconsin-Madison. He is author of numerous works on the native peoples of South America and their colonial conquest, as well as on the topics of sorcery, violence, sexuality and warfare.

Daniel Woolf is Professor of History at Queen's University in Kingston, Canada. Among his previous publications are *A Global Encyclopedia of Historical Writing* (1998) and *The Social Circulation of the Past* (2003). His *A Global History of History* was published in 2011.

Advisory Board

Editors' Introduction

José Rabasa, Masayuki Sato, Edoardo Tortarolo, and Daniel Woolf

The period analysed by this, the middle volume of *The Oxford History of Historical Writing*, is a transitional one between the ancient and medieval eras covered by volumes 1 and 2, and the modern centuries after about 1800 which are the subject of volumes 4 and 5.[1] In keeping with the series plan, the temporal scale of this volume shifts down again, to cover a 'mere' four hundred years, with occasional glances ahead to the nineteenth century, and backward as far as the thirteenth and fourteenth centuries, since meaningful historiographical periods are not respecters of uniform and neat chronological boundaries. At the same time, the series' geographical scope here expands to embrace the Americas and Islamic West Africa.

The temporal span of this volume may be only four centuries, but it is still a long one, covering the period from Europe's late Middle Ages/early Renaissance to the end of its Enlightenment, from pre-Columbian America to the early post-Revolutionary era (in the United States) and the eve of independence for many Latin American nations, from the early decades of the Ming regime in China to the middle part of the successive—and final imperial—Qing dynasty. The European part of this story will already be familiar to many readers of this book and has featured prominently in histories of historical writing. Less well known, except to specialists, are the parallel—and, we assert, interlocking—stories in the rest of the world. Europe has its place in this volume, but we have deliberately de-centred it in our narrative, and have elected to follow the sun from east to west. As with the roster of chapters itself, we begin this introductory essay in East Asia.

'East Asia' is a historical concept, taken here to comprise the peoples and cultures of China, Japan, Korea, and sometimes expanded to include China's frequent satellite Vietnam (the last studied in this volume by Geoff Wade in his

---

[1] While the Introduction as a whole is the collaborative work of all four editors, the primary authors of the individual sections are Sato (East and Southeast Asia), Woolf (the Islamic world and Europe to c.1650), Tortarolo (Europe and the United States, 1650–1700), and Rabasa (the non-Anglophone continental Americas).

chapter on the neighbouring region of 'Southeast Asia'). Early modern East Asia revolved around the great, unified Ming (1368–1644) and Qing (1644–1912) empires, which were the political and cultural centre of gravity for the region at large. Cultural Sinocentrism was the *basso ostinato* of East Asia for more than a millennium: the classical Chinese language and writing system; ideological frames of the Confucian social and familial order; legal and administrative systems; Buddhism, which was transmitted to Korea, Vietnam, and China via Chinese translations of canonical texts and Chinese versions of Buddhist practice; and the art of historiography itself.

East Asia had been among the first regions of the world to produce written records of the past.[2] Well into modern times Chinese script, the common script across East Asia, served—with local adaptations and variations—as the normative medium of record-keeping and written historical narrative, as well as official communication. This was true, not only in China itself, but in Korea, Japan, and Vietnam. Just as shared use of the Roman alphabet and Latin classical corpus bound Western Europe together as a civilization, the Chinese script and classical corpus has mediated an East Asian ecumene for more than two millennia.

The technique of recording the past in writing has been shaped as well by environmental factors. The written records that bind civilizations together depend on a durable media complex—paper and ink—and technologies of dissemination. Both print technologies and the mass production of paper were already well established across East Asia by the fifteenth century, producing and responding to the demands of a vast population of educated people.

When speaking of 'historical writing' we tend to emphasize 'historians', the people who produce written 'histories'; but it is worth remembering that the existence of 'history readers' is equally crucial to the success of historical culture. Kenji Shimada has estimated that the number of books published—printed—in China alone prior to 1750 far exceeded the total world publishing output in all other languages combined up to that time; moreover, he notes, works of history were the most numerous of all genres in print.[3] In this respect, China experienced something like the same efflorescence of historical genres and their wider dissemination which occurred during the same period in other parts of the world. Even in the East Asian states on China's periphery, Japan and Korea, historical narrative was dominated by the language and norms of classical Chinese historical writing, much as medieval and early modern European intellectuals wrote in Latin. Some Japanese composed historical narratives and theoretical enquiry in Japanese (at this time written with Chinese characters but utilizing Japanese word order and pronunciation), but with a few exceptions, the major historical

---

[2] See coverage in Andrew Feldherr and Grant Hardy (eds.), *The Oxford History of Historical Writing*, vol.1: *Beginnings to AD 600* (Oxford, 2011); and Sarah Foot and Chase F. Robinson (eds.), *The Oxford History of Historical Writing*, vol. 2: *400–1400* (Oxford, forthcoming).

[3] Kenji Shimada, 'Chūgoku', in *Heibonsha hyakka jiten*, vol. 9 (Tokyo, 1985), 817–28.

narratives in the cultures on the Chinese periphery were written almost exclusively in the classical Chinese language.

While there are common features to history-writing across the globe, however, crucial differences must also be noted. In particular, the art of recording the past had developed along quite a different trajectory in East Asia than it had in the Graeco-Latin world of ancient and medieval Europe. European historical writing has, since Herodotus and Thucydides, been predominantly an individual endeavour, the product of a single author generally writing for an audience of atomized, individual readers (and sometimes for assembled audiences who would hear works read aloud) or, as in the example of monastic chronicles of medieval Europe, for the benefit of successive writers. In contrast, historical writing and the discipline or culture of 'history' in East Asia emerged from a culture of public historiography. The task of writing history was traditionally a state-run project. The dominant—and ideologically normative—mode of historical writing consisted in the collection and compilation of sources for the production of 'official histories', the subject of Achim Mittag's chapter in the present volume.

The corpus of official histories thus compiled, usually by committee, constituted the core of Chinese historiography, its bureaucratic organization more or less mirrored in Korea and in early Japan's *Rikkokushi* or Six National Histories (the lack of distinct dynasties in Japan made aspects of the Chinese model an awkward fit). The early modern era alone saw the compilation of official histories of the Yuan and Ming dynasties in China, the Koryŏ dynasty in Korea (contemporary historiography in which is examined in Don Baker's chapter), the *Đại Việt sử ký toàn thu* [Complete Annals of Dai Viet] (1479; expanded edn, 1697) in Vietnam, and the *Honchō tsugan* [Comprehensive Mirror of our Country] (1644–70) in Japan (the subject of Masayuki Sato's chapter), all under state sponsorship. In addition, the Chinese and Korean states compiled massive records of the day-to-day workings of the emperor or king and his court, in anticipation that an official history of the dynasty would be compiled in the future.

State-sponsored historical writing owed its status as the normative model in East Asian societies to certain deeply rooted cultural and ideological assumptions. In East Asia, historiography—both the writing and study of history—was the primary and hegemonic cultural undertaking. This is in stark contrast to European, Indic, and Islamic civilizations, where historical writing had not—to this point—been vested with dominant cultural power and authority. In East Asia, the purpose of historical writing was rooted in the Chinese philosophical premise that historical facts were the only certain and immutable reality, and in the corollary proposition that it was only by reflecting on history—metaphorically conceived as a 'mirror', after all—that one could approach ultimate truth.[4]

---

[4] The precise place of 'history' proper within the branches of Chinese learning varied somewhat over the centuries, the ancient historical texts such as the *Chunqiu* [Spring and Autumn Annals]

Chinese metaphysics was not premised on a revealed religion founded upon the transcendental existence of a unique and omnipotent deity, as in the Abrahamic religions. Rather, Chinese metaphysics took the world as mutable, conceived in the *Yijing* [Book of Changes or Classic of Changes] as an ever-changing set of phenomena, and therefore sought immutable reality in history, because people could not alter that which had already happened.[5] This belief made history the axis of Chinese civilization, the core discipline around which all others orbited. Despite being sponsored by the state, even official historiography set itself apart from political affairs, standing both outside and, in a sense, above day-to-day administration of state affairs, and established itself as the grounds for all human judgement. The historiographical tradition therefore demanded both historical objectivity and chronological accuracy; both these standards had been firmly established in China by the first century BC.

Many of the world's civilizations have sought the absolute through religion, in a transcendent identity beyond the human realm, beyond intellect, beyond space and time. By positing an omniscient and omnipotent deity or plane of immaterial existence, outside of time and space, they conceive of an eternal, absolute entity that exists in a continuous, changeless, and perpetual state. Such civilizations continually produced new perspectives for interpreting the past, reconceiving and re-re-conceiving it to reflect the observed changes in the physical and social world (when these were noted). History in such circumstances is simply a method for becoming conscious of the past, and a literary vessel for articulations of this consciousness.

The cultures of East Asia, by contrast, did not develop indigenous concepts of transcendental revealed religion; and while they encountered such belief systems—principally in the form of Buddhism—revealed religion was never able to attain the hegemonic epistemological status which the Abrahamic religions achieved in Europe and Western Asia. In the absence of a countervailing absolute, history itself became that absolute, that immutable truth on which one could rely. History, consequently, came to be endowed with a 'normative' function and, by extension, it became a source of authority that did not—at least in theory—permit revision or rewriting.[6]

---

sometimes losing ground, especially in periods of resurgent Neo-Confucianism of the sort associated with the twelfth-century philosopher Zhu Xi; but it was invariably near the top of the intellectual ladder.

[5] Masayuki Sato, 'The Archetype of History in the Confucian Ecumene', *History and Theory*, 46 (2007), 217–31.

[6] This was not always honoured in practice as the oft-repeated ancient tale of three historian-brothers, executed by a usurper who wished to efface their true report of his deeds, illustrates; and there are numerous instances, especially under the early Ming and early Qing, of imperial interference with the project of official history-writing. But the general principle still holds, its strength illustrated by the vigour of reaction against its violation.

By the ascent of the Ming in 1368, the focus of Chinese historiography had for nearly a millennium and a half centred on 'official history', with each successive dynasty compiling the history of its predecessor as a core enterprise of the state. Later generations have positioned Sima Qian's *Shiji* [Records of the Scribe], composed at the end of the second century BC, as the first of what became twenty-four 'official histories'; with the exception of the *Shiji*, each was compiled by scholars in service of a new dynasty to narrate the history of the predecessor dynasty. It was a critical characteristic of these official histories, following the example of the *Shiji*, that they had an encyclopaedic range. Sima Qian, that is, brought an entire civilization—indeed, all human history as he knew it—into a single, unified structure: not simply the culture, but its politics, economics, society, and technology, as well as accounts of all the peoples and states of the known world. The compilation and writing of history, which had developed into an art that comprehensively described an entire world system, remained the dominant paradigm and the trunk whence sprang other branches of knowledge in early modern East Asian civilization—though with distinct institutional forms and modes of practice specific to each of the local cultures of the region. In that sense, one might see historiography in East Asia as a 'primary cultural undertaking', perhaps equivalent to biblical exegesis and the *Corpus Iuris Iustanianus* in the West, the *Laws of Manu* in India, or the study of the Qur'an in the Muslim world.

The Chinese had developed their own way of creating—they would have said, 'recording'—an immutable past. In China and Korea, it became standard practice for each new dynasty to direct a historical compilation bureau (first founded by the Tang in China during the seventh century) to collect historical sources and to compile the official history of the immediately preceding dynasty. Upon completion of the official history, moreover, the bureau was supposed to destroy the sources it had collected, a practice designed to prevent others from revising or rewriting the official history, for once it had been published by the state, the history itself took on the character of sacred text. The surest way to endow the official history with unassailable authority, after all, was to destroy the sources on which it was based. This did not always occur in practice, and a variety of *Shilu* (the 'Veritable Records' of a particular emperor's reigns), supposedly transitory documents toward the final dynastic history, survived the Ming–Qing transition, along with many other forms of document, official and unofficial, such as the *fangzhi* or regional gazetteers.[7]

The various cultures comprising East Asian civilization preserved in this fashion the ideal of history as the sole immutable basis for human judgement.

---

[7] Timothy Brook, *Geographical Sources of Ming-Qing History* (2nd edn, Ann Arbor, 2002); Wolfgang Franke, 'The Veritable Records of the Ming Dynasty (1368–1644)', in W. Beasley and E. G. Pulleyblank (eds.), *Historians of China and Japan* (London, 1961), 60–77; and Franke, *An Introduction to the Sources of Ming History* (Kuala Lumpur, 1968).

The biographies that comprise over half the material in the official histories, maintained in their own way this tradition of objective narration. In the biographies, as in other sections of the official history, the compilers first set forth what they believed to be 'fact', and only then did they follow this with their own evaluation. This vast corpus of biographies, however, forces us to consider why East Asian historians believed biography to be a necessary part of any history: arguably, because the East Asian tradition lacks a unitary supreme being, it was only in the recorded lives of eminent individuals that one could find true sacred texts—sacred in the sense of being un-rewritable, unchangeable, and authorized.

An episode in the life of a fifteenth-century Korean historian is paradigmatic of the notion of the historian as exemplar. It is recorded that in 1431, as the compilation of the *T'aejong taewang sillok* [Veritable Records of King T'aejong] was nearing completion, T'aejong's successor, King Sejong, asked the compilers to show him their work in progress. 'In the previous dynasty', Sejong is quoted as saying, 'each monarch personally reviewed the *Sillok* of his predecessor; but [my predecessor] King T'aejong did not review the *Sillok* of [the Chosŏn dynastic founder] King T'aejo'. Sejong's senior ministers resisted, replying that, 'If Your Majesty were to review [the work in progress], future monarchs would surely revise [historians' drafts]. Were that to happen, then [future] historians would suspect that the monarch might look at their drafts and, [fearing royal displeasure] might fail to record the facts completely. How, then, could we transmit [facts] faithfully to future generations?' Upon hearing this, the king ultimately withdrew his request.[8]

In the traditional East Asian paradigm, therefore, the role of the past was to serve as a normative history, and as a template of exemplars, both positive and negative, for monarchs and ministers alike. Were historians to shade their narratives to fit the predilections of a monarch in their own day, the historical record they produced would fail to provide either a true picture of the past, or a reliable guide to future action. It would fail in its purpose. This forms an interesting contrast to historical practices in Europe, where, Masayuki Sato has argued, history had evolved as a 'cognitive' discipline, rather than as a normative one.[9] In the West, notwithstanding the strong appeal of historical exemplarity (that is, its utility as a source of moral and political wisdom) dating back to antiquity, the historian's *raison d'être* often lay in *rewriting* the past;[10] the practice of history evolved as a competition among the interpretations and approaches of

---

[8] Suiichiro Tanaka, *Tanaka Suiichiro shigaku ronbunshu* (Tokyo, 1900), 510–12. *Sillok* is the Romanized Korean rendering of the Chinese term *shilu*.

[9] Sato, 'The Archetype of History', 225.

[10] With certain exceptions: the great classicist Arnaldo Momigliano famously observed the reluctance of Renaissance humanist historians to tackle the task of rewriting ancient historians such as Tacitus and Thucydides, with whom they believed they could compete neither stylistically nor in terms of accurate knowledge of the period described. Momigliano, 'Ancient History and the Antiquarian', in *Studies in Historiography* (New York and Evanston, Ill., 1966), 1–39.

different historians engaged with a mutable past. This difference becomes increasingly apparent during the centuries covered in this volume, when the combination of competing Christian faiths, emerging new central monarchies, the impact of printing, a spreading readership, and the routine deployment of history as a political weapon rendered even the most apparently stable views of the past open to a process of revision and argument, especially during times of acute ideological, religious, and dynastic conflict, a frequent occurrence in the early modern world.

The Ming dynasty witnessed, in addition to the continued activity of official history-writing, an efflorescence in the composition of what is often called 'private' or 'unofficial' historiography (here treated by On-cho Ng). This tendency continued, along with the multiplication of genres (a feature once again observable in contemporary Europe) under the last imperial dynasty, the Qing, Manchurian conquerors who nonetheless adopted the historiographical traditions of the Han people they had subjugated. In the course of the later seventeenth and eighteenth centuries, the peak of Qing power, history became a tool of imperial expansion, as demonstrated in Pamela Kyle Crossley's chapter. Finally, something of the philological scholarship that is generally associated with Renaissance European humanism and late eighteenth- to early nineteenth-century German classical studies can be seen in the late Ming and Qing practice of *kaozheng*.[11]

Japanese historical writing, here described by Masayuki Sato, shared many features with Chinese, the influences of Confucianism and Buddhism among them, but the differences are nearly as profound. Official historical writing in a Chinese vein did not fit well with a political system that postulated only a single, uninterrupted dynasty (albeit one prone to schisms and, from the twelfth century virtually through to the mid-nineteenth, largely under the sway of a series of *bakufus* headed by shoguns). The late Middle Ages had left off the earlier practice of writing national histories, and generated a variety of different genres in both Chinese and Japanese. These included the series of 'Mirrors', such as the *Ōkagami* and *Azuma kagami* ('Mirror of the East', a late thirteenth-century chronicle written from the perspective of the shogunate), and the various literary works, in Japanese, such as the various classes of *monogatari*, prose or verse epics about fictional events but often in a historical setting.

During the seventeenth century, with the consolidation of power in the hands of the Tokugawa *bakufu*, historical writing continued, sometimes in the hands of the rulers themselves. A relative of the shogun named Tokugawa Mitsukuni personally oversaw a pro-imperial history, the *Dai Nihon Shi* [Great History of Japan], which had nearly 130 scholars working on it by the time Mitsukuni died in 1700; the work would only be presented in draft to the *bakufu* in 1720 and it

---

[11] Benjamin A. Elman, *From Philosophy to Philology: Intellectual and Social Aspects of Change in Late Imperial China* (Cambridge, Mass., 1984).

was not completed till the early twentieth century. Japan, too, produced its share of historians or scholars in the seventeenth and eighteenth centuries, such as Arai Hakuseki, mentor to a shogun, and the great eighteenth-century nationalist—and foe of Chinese influences upon his country—Motoori Norinaga, who sought to use philology to strengthen, rather than undermine, some of Japan's national myths and established a school of 'national learning' emphasizing the emotive aspects of Japanese culture at more or less the same time that Goethe and Schiller were exploring similar themes in the German *Sturm und Drang*.[12]

Moving westwards into Central and South Asia we encounter a very different historiographical culture in the three major Islamic empires of the early modern era, the Mughals of northern and central India, the Persian Safavid dynasty, and the Ottomans. A further variant, or family of variants, occurs in the Muslim parts of Africa—once previously thought to be 'without history' and here explored (in its West African manifestations) by Paul E. Lovejoy. The early modern African and Asian versions of Islamic historical writing were all heirs to an eight hundred-year-old tradition of Muslim historiography the formative and classical ages of which are treated in *OHHW* vol. 2. Each, however, spun history in directions that reflected Islamic values but were devoted primarily to the recording of the great deeds of the various rulers. In India, for instance, a series of royal *namas* or books were written to celebrate the reigns of successive Mughals from the founder, Babur, through Akbar the Great (under whose court historian, Abu'l Fazl, the genre matured) to the ill-fated Shah Jahan, builder of the Taj Mahal and an inveterate micro-manager of his own court historians. Under Akbar, in particular, historical writing became an explicit tool of empire and was employed by the emperor both to weaken the power of the Muslim religious elite and to recast Indian history in a more secular form.[13] Asim Roy's chapter focuses on this Persian-influenced imperial tradition of Indian historical writing. By tracing the Indo-Persian connection back into the Delhi Sultanate (a pre-Mughal state of the thirteenth to early sixteenth centuries), Roy

---

[12] John S. Brownlee, *Japanese Historians and the National Myths, 1600–1945: The Age of the Gods and Emperor Jinmu* (Vancouver and Tokyo, 1997), offers a good introduction; as does W. G. Beasley and Carmen Blacker, 'Japanese Historical Writing in the Tokugawa Period (1603–1868)', in Beasley and Pulleyblank (eds.), *Historians of China and Japan*, 245–63. See also Kate Wildman Nakai, *Shogunal Politics: Arai Hakuseki and the Premises of Tokugawa Rule* (Cambridge, 1988); and Nakai, 'Tokugawa Confucian Historiography: The Hayashi, Early Mito School, and Arai Hakuseki', in Peter Nosco (ed.), *Confucianism and Tokugawa Culture* (Princeton, 1984), 62–91. Shigeru Matsumoto, *Motoori Norinaga 1730–1801* (Cambridge, 1970) studies the pivotal figure in the 'National Learning' movement; and Masao Maruyama, *Studies in the Intellectual History of Tokugawa Japan*, trans. Mikiso Hane (Princeton, 1974), is a classic survey of the intellectual scene, with an emphasis on philosophical aspects, by one of Japan's leading modern historians.

[13] Mughal official historiography was not the sole mode of writing in the subcontinent, and recent works have examined the rich regional and local modes of historicity that existed. See, for instance, Velcheru Narayana Rao, David Shulman, and Sanjay Subrahmanyam, *Textures of Time: Writing History in South India 1600–1800* (New York, 2003).

demonstrates the many features shared by South Asian historical writing with that of its neighbour to the north-west. Persian had indeed long been a literary tongue for the pursuit of *adab* (literary and scientific scholarship as distinct from Qur'anic studies) and had become the dominant language for the writing of history within much of the later medieval Islamic world. Within Persia itself, the rule of the Safavids (the first native dynasty in Persia to reign as Shahs in nearly seven centuries) created a court culture of which history became a significant by-product, through the writings of chancery scribes and officials such as the munshi (or chancery scribe) Iskandar Beg. Christoph Marcinkowski here traces the development of Safavid historiography, once dismissed by orientalist scholars as dry and difficult to read, but in recent years the subject of renewed attention.[14]

The courtly historians of Persia and India are reminders that aspects of historical writing can transcend otherwise impermeable borders. The third great Islamic empire of the period, the Ottomans, regarded as the most potent enemy of Western Christendom from the fifteenth to the eighteenth century, had much in common historiographically with both its Muslim coreligionists in Persia and India, and their European neighbours to the west, where history was also used as an instrument of state power alike by monarchies (new and old) and republican regimes such as those of Florence and Venice. Solidifying their power in the fifteenth and early sixteenth centuries, the Ottomans sought to bestow a level of centralized order on the inherited frontier culture of their semi-nomadic past, captured in works such as the 'Chronicles of Osman'. By the mid-sixteenth century, with the empire expanding in several directions, court historians called *şehnāmeci* were being appointed by the sultans. Their name itself derived from Persian origins, and the holders themselves aspired to the highly literary style of medieval Persian epitomized by the great eleventh-century epic writer, Firdawsi (from whose great epic, the *Shah-nama*, they drew their title). Notwithstanding the close relationship that some of them, such as Seyyid Lokman, enjoyed with the sultans who appointed them, the *şehnāmeci* never entirely evolved into historians of the Ottoman state. In the course of the seventeenth and eighteenth centuries, they lost ground to a number of other official writers. These included leading civil servants or bureaucrats—often writing unofficially—such as the chancellor Mustafa Çelebi Celâlzade, the polymath Katib Çelebi, and the Hungarian-born Ibrahim Peçevi. By Peçevi's time, Ottoman historians were also growing familiar with the historical writings of the Christian nations to the west. As Baki Tezcan's chapter shows, a respectable quantity of Ottoman historical

---

[14] Sholeh A. Quinn, *Historical Writing during the Reign of Shah 'Abbas: Ideology, Imitation and Legitimacy in Safavid Chronicles* (Salt Lake City, 2000); the latter part of Bertold Spuler, *Persian Historiography and Geography*, trans. Christoph Marcinkowski (Singapore, 2003) (a translation of a much older work); R. M. Savory, '"Very Dull and Arduous Reading": A Reappraisal of the *History of Shah 'Abbas the Great* by Iskandar Beg Munshi', *Hamdard Islamicus*, 3 (1980), 19–37; and Felix Tauer, 'History and Biography', in Jan Rypka *et al.*, *History of Iranian Literature*, ed. Karl Jahn (Dordrecht, 1968), 438–61.

writing ranged beyond the house of Osman, or even the Turks themselves, to cover the pasts of the various subject and neighbouring peoples whom their armies and ambassadors had encountered.[15] By the early eighteenth century, Ottoman history had evolved further away from its courtly connection and become a truly official genre in the hands of *vak'a-nüvis*, state-sponsored historians whose version of Turkish imperial history could now be spread increasingly through the medium of that great European invention, printing.

As in other parts of the world, the year 1400 in Europe marks in itself no particular epoch nor any sharp break with the past. Historiographically, the enduring medieval practice of chronicling would remain for several more decades (longer still in northern Europe) not only the dominant but, for all intents and purposes, the only mode of representing the past, biography excepted (which, apart from saints' lives remained a relatively minor genre, and not always included under the umbrella of history). There were, however, some changes on the horizon. First and foremost, the traditional dominance of the monastic clergy in historical writing had begun to break down in the thirteenth century, as secular clerics and increasingly laity (such as the Crusader chroniclers Villehardouin and Joinville, or the aristocratic authors of French martial romances) began in increasing numbers to write about the past.[16] The laity wrote history of two different sorts, typically in the vernacular language of their homeland. The first comprised politically and militarily focused narratives (often but not always in conventional annalistic form) motivated by the martial struggles of the late medieval years, the period of the Hundred Years War in Western Europe, and, on the eastern borders, the looming presence of the Ottomans and the rapid decline (and by 1453, extinction) of the Byzantine Empire. The second type was the urban chronicle, frequently written by a socially inferior rank of person, typically the prosperous mercantile townsman or civic official, for instance Giovanni Villani of Florence.[17]

---

[15] Cemal Kafadar, *Between Two Worlds: The Construction of the Ottoman State* (Berkeley, 1995); Halil Inalcik, 'The Rise of Ottoman Historiography', in Bernard Lewis and P. M. Holt (eds.), *Historians of the Middle East* (London, 1962), 152–67; Cornell H. Fleischer, *Bureaucrat and Intellectual in the Ottoman Empire: The Historian Mustafa Ali* (Princeton, 1986); Lewis V. Thomas, *A Study of Naima*, ed. N. Itzkowitz (New York, 1972); V. L. Ménage, *Neshri's History of the Ottomans: The Sources and Development of the Text* (London, 1964); Gabriel Piterberg, *An Ottoman Tragedy: History and Historiography at Play* (Berkeley, 2003); Baki Tezcan, 'The Politics of Early Modern Ottoman Historiography', in V. H. Aksan and D. Goffman (eds.), *The Early Modern Ottomans: Remapping the Empire* (Cambridge, 2007), 167–98; and Christine Woodhead, 'An Experiment in Official Historiography: The Post of Sehnameci in the Ottoman Empire c. 1555–1605', *Wiener Zeitschrift für die Kunde des Morgenlandes*, 75 (1983), 157–82.

[16] See Gabrielle Spiegel, *Past as Text: The Theory and Practice of Medieval Historiography* (Baltimore, 1997); and Nancy Partner, *Serious Entertainments: The Writing of History in Twelfth-Century England* (Chicago, 1977) for two illuminating studies of this period. See also Foot and Robinson (eds.), *The Oxford History of Historical Writing*, vol. 2.

[17] On the transition from chronicle to history in Renaissance Florence see Louis Green, *Chronicle into History: An Essay on the Interpretation of History in Florentine Fourteenth-Century Chronicles* (Cambridge, 1972); on humanism and Florentine historiography see Donald Wilcox, *The*

As throughout the history of the world's historical writing, social and political, and not merely intellectual, change underlay shifts in the representation of the past. The advent of city chronicles represented not so much a revival of ancient and late antique *annales* so much as a curiosity, among a growing urban bourgeoisie, about the origins and illustrious histories of their cities, which over the previous several centuries had established themselves as semi-autonomous political entities within larger realms. Similarly, the first three centuries of our period would see considerable growth at the opposite end of the social ladder, among kings and princes, many of them of very new dynasties (Tudor, Habsburg, Hohenzollern, Valois and Bourbon, Romanov) as monarchs cementing their power at the expense of a feudal aristocracy (and, in Protestant lands, at the expense of the papacy and Holy Roman Empire) encouraged, influenced, and sometimes censored accounts of their own reigns and of those of their ancestors. The tangled relations of history, myth, and fiction across Europe, with glances further afield to Asia, are captured in Peter Burke's chapter.

Two significant developments of the early modern era were the related phenomena of humanist philology and antiquarianism. The former, which had roots in the study of both language and law, played a considerable part in the development of that sense of historical distance, and of anachronism, which has become a hallmark of modern Western historicity. Its development has a long history and Donald R. Kelley's chapter places it in the *longue durée* of European culture between the late medieval and modern, from the era of Lorenzo Valla, Angelo Poliziano, Guillaume Budé, and Joseph Scaliger, to that of the great Enlightenment and early nineteenth-century philologists, such as Barthold Niebuhr, and thus to the advent of 'disciplinary' history in the decades covered by *OHHW* vol. 4; its comparability, in broad terms, with Chinese *khaozheng* has been noted above. In the course of the fifteenth, sixteenth, and seventeenth centuries, philologists restored a number of ancient texts to something like their original forms, developed a critical apparatus for editing manuscripts and citing sources (the footnote originates at this time), and sent packing a number of celebrated textual frauds such as the medieval Donation of Constantine.[18] Antiquarianism (the main features of which are here summarized by Peter N. Miller) grew out of the same roots as philology, but it was also very much focused on the physical remains of the past, both man-made (coins, statuary, buildings, funerary urns) and natural (landscape features, fossils, and curiosities such as the skeletal remains of 'giants'). What began as the activity of aristocratic virtuosi, a collecting mania often satirized in contemporary literature and for a time excluded from narrative historiography, would evolve by the late

Development of Florentine Humanist Historiography in the Fifteenth Century (Cambridge, Mass, 1969).

[18] Anthony Grafton, *Forgers and Critics: Creativity and Duplicity in Western Scholarship* (London, 1990); and id., *The Footnote: A Curious History* (Cambridge, Mass., 1997).

seventeenth century into the foundation of both classificatory natural history (especially geology and biology) and of those erudite studies 'ancillary' to history such as numismatics, palaeography, and diplomatic.

A further consequence of this new scholarship was to cast doubt on some traditional explanations for the origins of particular peoples, while generating new ones that were sometimes equally implausible. Apart from historical writings on particular 'races' (further encouraged by the discovery of aboriginal populations in the Americas, and by increased contact with East Asia), the 'nation' as an organizing principle for historiography began to feature more prominently in the late medieval and early modern era. Reflecting this, much of the present volume follows political and often 'national' lines, acknowledging that the latter term really only works in the monarchies of Western and Northern Europe, especially England, Spain, France, and Russia, and that even these contained ethnic and linguistic minorities, frequently with divergent (and sometimes mutually inconsistent) historical traditions. Elsewhere, the map was divided into larger chunks, either great multinational empires (the Habsburgs or the Ottomans) or subordinated principalities and city-states. Italy is a case in point: it is permissible to speak of Italian historiography during this period if one understands that to mean writing *by* Italian-speaking persons (in the first half of the period, often writing in humanist Latin rather than the vernacular). Indeed, Italy has traditionally and deservedly occupied a central role in narratives of early modern Europe—despite the fact that throughout these centuries it was a fractured peninsula of republican city-states and minor monarchies, converted by the later sixteenth century into a slightly less fractured territory of larger principalities, mainly satellites of greater powers to the west, especially Spain.

Whatever its disunity, Italy's importance in European historiography is beyond dispute. It was on the peninsula, and especially in Florence, that the urban chronicles composed by the likes of the Villani family in the fourteenth century first metamorphosed into humanist historiography via a few key individuals of genius like Leonardo Bruni, Florence's sometime chancellor and one of its leading scholars through much of the early fifteenth century. William J. Connell's chapter recounts the story of Italian historical writing through the first half of this volume, paying close attention to its medieval precedents and revising the master narrative, set three decades ago by the late Eric Cochrane.[19] From Italy, the revival of classical methods of writing history spread first westward, to France, Spain, and Britain, north to the Habsburg lands (including the future Dutch Republic), Scandinavia, and Germany (where by the 1520s it engaged with another potent force, that of Lutheranism), and, rather later, eastward to the emergent Muscovite Empire. As Edoardo Tortarolo shows in his complementary chapter on the late seventeenth and eighteenth centuries,

---

[19] Eric Cochrane, *Historians and Historiography in the Italian Renaissance* (Chicago, 1981).

Italy continued to play an important role in the post-Renaissance age, its Enlightenment historical texts including the significant contributions of jurists, philologists, and philosophers such as Pietro Giannone and Giambattista Vico.

The *corso* followed by historical writing in Western Europe from the late Middle Ages through to the seventeenth century, from late medieval chronicling through early humanist experiments and ending in the grand tradition of neoclassicism in the late seventeenth and early eighteenth centuries, is perhaps most obviously typified in France, the subject of Chantal Grell's chapter. In the fifteenth century, France saw the growth of a politically attuned though not yet fully humanist narrative, epitomized in the historical writing of Philippe de Commynes. France was also one of the few Western monarchies to have developed a systematic Crown-sponsored historiography in the *Grandes Chroniques de France* [The Great Chronicles of France], produced at the pro-royalist abbey of Saint Denis.[20] The impact of humanism altered the style and structure of writing but not its general direction: as first the Valois and then the Bourbon kings cemented their power over the great aristocracy, the Estates General, and provincial *parlements* (culminating in the rule of the adult Louis XIV), the *Grandes Chroniques* tradition was easily converted into a much more highly bureaucratized system of *historiographes du roi* (and much less frequently appointed *historiographes de France*) that endured up to the age of the Revolution. In a sense, France was repeating, as were the contemporary Ottomans, a pattern observable in China centuries earlier, namely the transition from a monarch-focused official historiography to a more formalized bureaucratic system. To the south in Spain (from the late fifteenth century, the newly united crowns of Castile and Aragon, each with subordinate kingdoms), there was a much longer medieval tradition of royalist historical writing, including some ostensibly authored by the kings themselves. Kira von Ostenfeld-Suske traces Spanish official historical writing from the early years of Trastámara/Habsburg hegemony to the high point of Spanish imperial fortunes under Philip II. Her chapter links Europe to the various modes of historical writing (and some oral and pictographic forms of history) discussed in the final section of the volume. Across the Channel from France lay England and Scotland, the northern and southern halves of Britain (which until 1707 is a term that applies to a geographic space, the island, and not to an actual political entity). Both show roughly similar trajectories to that of France, with some important differences both from France and, notably, each other. We have treated them both jointly and separately at different points in the four-century period, because their historiographies, while overlapping, nevertheless reveal many different features. In many ways, Scotland, the less prosperous and more sparsely populated kingdom, was consistently the more innovative of the two with respect to history-writing, as illustrated in

---

[20] Gabrielle Spiegel, *The Chronicle Tradition of Saint-Denys: A Survey* (Brookline, Mass., 1978).

Daniel Woolf's and David Allan's respective chapters. While both Scots and English writers of the sixteenth century clung to late medieval mythologies concerning putative foundational monarchs, Scottish writers embraced continental humanism much more quickly in the form of Hector Boece and then George Buchanan. To the south, an abortive importation of classical models through the Italian Polydore Vergil and the humanist lawyer-minister turned Catholic martyr Sir Thomas More quickly faded before a resurgent chronicle, its fortunes briefly revived through the medium of print and the curiosity of an urban mercantile audience; a more robust humanist historiography would appear only in the last years of the sixteenth century. The Scottish willingness to depart from past patterns continued into the eighteenth century, in narrative historians such as William Robertson and David Hume and in philosophical, juridical, and socio-economic thinkers such as Adam Smith, Adam Ferguson, and John Millar. Against this must be weighed the considerably greater volume of English historical writing and—something that did not develop well in Scotland—the emerging practice of antiquarian scholarship. And, as Karen O'Brien demonstrates in her chapter on later eighteenth-century England, the southern kingdom experienced its own somewhat different historiographic Enlightenment, one in which Britannic Scots such as Hume featured prominently, and which was concluded in that most cosmopolitan of narrative historians, Edward Gibbon.

In Northern Europe, Latin humanism also had a significant impact, but it was the Reformation rather than the Renaissance that occasioned a sharper break with past historiographical practices as parts of Germany, Scandinavia (including Denmark and a newly independent and powerful Sweden), and the northern sections of the Low Countries successively migrated over to the Protestant side of Christendom's religious iron curtain. Karen Skovgaard-Petersen discusses the unfolding of this story in Denmark and Sweden while Markus Völkel offers a counterpart study of Germany between the Reformation and the age of Kant and Herder. In the predominantly but not exclusively Catholic central Europe of the Habsburg hereditary territories, including Austria, Hungary, and Bohemia, a Counter-Reformation historiography would emerge (as it had in late sixteenth-century Italy), which used much of the same philological and antiquarian methods that were employed by Protestant counterparts. Howard Louthan's chapter points to the complexities of writing history within a multi-lingual, multiethnic, and confessionally diverse empire. Another emergent empire during this period, one, like the Ottoman, wracked by persistent internecine quarrels and not infrequent assassination and deposition, was the Muscovite regime. Jennifer Spock and Michael A. Pesenson take the story of Russian and Ukrainian historical writing from the period of the great late medieval chronicles through the age of Ivan the Terrible (which may have produced the Procopian-style classic history ostensibly written by his friend-turned-foe-in-exile, Andrei Kurbskii), ending in the Western-influenced post-Petrine Enlightenment histories of

Vasilii Tatishchev and Mikhail Lomonosov, and of Germanic visitors such as August Ludwig Schlözer.

True to its transitional character, this volume features essays in which changes and transformations are crucial in establishing our perspective on the early modern European approach to the past. The contributions of Karen O'Brien, Guido Abbattista, and David Allan collectively focus on historiography in the period from the late seventeenth through the eighteenth century. This was an age that witnessed significant theoretical and political upheavals culminating in the French Revolution, the purgative event anticipated in some of the later French *philosophes*. These disturbances in turn reinforced each other in shaking up received wisdom and setting the stage for the dramatic innovations in nineteenth-century historical research and writing. The complexity of the 'historical age', as Hume famously called his own time, can be fully apprehended only through a nuanced investigation of the eighteenth century's major cultural trends. The phenomenon of the French Enlightenment, explored by Abbattista, was, despite the variety of its forms, committed to a radical revision of basic assumptions that left an enduring mark on the European notion of history-writing. Among the numerous shifts made by the historians of the French Enlightenment Abbattista stresses two innovations that became a part of European historical thought. In the eighteenth century historians—the French and Scots most famously—developed the need to articulate their self-perception as members of a society representing a stage in the incremental *progress* (a word that came to acquire its modern meaning principally in this era) of humankind. Parallel to this innovation the historians of the Enlightenment also revised the notion of civilization. They used it as a means to analyse the human world as a coherent set of social patterns, and argued for the greater significance of these patterns in comparison with the traditional focus of historiography on rulers, notables, and public institutions. In retrospect, this eventually proved to have been a process of self-clarification and experimentation in both the collecting and assessing of historical sources and the establishment of cognitive goals for the study of the past. 'Disenchanting the past' and freeing interpretation from the kind of providentialism epitomized in Bishop Jacques-Bénigne Bossuet's *Discours sur l'histoire universelle* [Discourse on Universal History] (1681) loomed large among many history writers' concerns at a time when the grip of religion in other spheres of knowledge, notably science, was beginning to loosen. The *philosophes* throughout Europe argued in fact that the history of human activity should be fully secularized; by the end of the eighteenth century they had been largely successful in shifting the cultural climate in this direction. The so-called stadial conception of human development, most commonly associated with certain among the Scottish *philosophes* and subsequently refined by late Enlightenment figures such as Condorcet, became increasingly incompatible with the biblical narrative. And the claim made by orthodox interpreters of the Bible (such as the seventeenth-century Irish archbishop James Ussher), that the earth had been created in less than a week only four millennia before Christ, was undermined if not yet thoroughly discredited by empirical findings which historians were beginning to incorporate in their narratives, including the accumulated antiquarian, geological, and archaeological discoveries of the previous two centuries. Providentialism was less and less invoked as an explanation for major developments, even if it continued to provide an accepted background for virtually all history textbooks used in schools. Visions of intellectual, civil, and political change often went hand in hand with new historical narratives, as the case of Voltaire shows. Voltaire's dream of a reforming and modernizing monarchical rule interacted with his own interpretation of French and Russian history.

While suggesting that there is no obvious connection between the American War of Independence and the adoption of secular categories, David Read shows in this volume that the impact of the political decisions taken in 1776 was remarkable among American historians. In the late colonial and early republican decades, general social and institutional changes made themselves felt in the way historians from different cultural backgrounds investigated the past in the second half of the eighteenth century. Trends in readership, detectable since at least the late sixteenth century, now picked up considerable momentum. An expanding public of non-specialist readers provided a market for histories that experimented with new modes of combining literary skills, new empirical knowledge, and innovations in philosophical outlook. Socially more diversified and including a growing participation of the middle classes in cultural life, especially within urban settings, this new public also included women both as readers of history books and, albeit still sporadically, as occasional authors, such as England's Catharine Macaulay and, later, America's Mercy Otis Warren.

The historians themselves reacted to these social trends by opting for forms of cultural history which elaborated on Voltaire's interest in the social past and which took up anew issues previously explored by nascent proto-disciplines such as political economy and anthropology. Aided by two centuries of European writings on the East (see Diogo Ramada Curto's chapter) and the non-English Americas (see below), and on the information provided by the booming genre of travel accounts, they also opened up to non-European peoples whose pasts and presents were integrated into a number of 'universal histories' very different from the providential accounts of earlier centuries.[21]

At the same moment when an expanding public was starting to influence the production of history books, state institutions in continental Europe became more and more interested in history as a practice and method (the word 'discipline' was not yet in vogue) essential to the education of the nobility and the administrators. The quality of the historical knowledge taught at colleges and universities had to be improved: the various regimes invested resources in

---

[21] Tamara Griggs, 'Universal History from Counter-Reformation to Enlightenment', *Modern Intellectual History*, 4 (2007), 219–47.

academies, focusing mainly or exclusively on research, and in teaching institutions, better to develop more reliable bodies of sources from which histories could be drawn. Under the aegis of absolute monarchies throughout Europe a new heyday for erudition commenced in the early eighteenth century, associated with editors like the Modenese Lodovico Muratori and with scholarly bodies patronized by Europe's princes. Decades later, in completing his impressive history of the *Decline and Fall of the Roman Empire* during the 1770s and 1780s, Edward Gibbon extensively profited from the erudite essays produced at the Académie des Inscriptions et Belles-Lettres in Paris, a research institution sponsored by the Bourbon monarchy, that set very high standards of accuracy.

The impressive revision of ancient history completed in Germany during the early nineteenth century (for which see *OHHW* vol. 4) was based in large measure on the 'philological turn' that took place at the university of Göttingen and elsewhere in the Holy Roman Empire during the second half of the eighteenth century (and which, again, parallels the similar move 'from philosophy to philology' in late Ming and early Qing China).[22] Late medieval and Renaissance forgeries, such as the infamous pseudo-Berossus of Annius of Viterbo or the Hermetic texts, did not disappear altogether—indeed, one or two such as *Ossian,* the alleged remnants of ancient Gaelic heroic poetry, became literary *causes célèbres.* But it became a shared doctrine that historians should not deliberately fabricate evidence to back up their narrative and that they ought to expose fakes when they became aware of them.

As a consequence of the changes and transformations sketched in the contributions for the European part of this volume, a distinctively Western notion of history emerged at the turn of the century. History came to be perceived, as famously noted by Reinhardt Koselleck, as a 'collective singular', a single process of development which at both the national and global level revealed a pattern of regularities.[23] This new understanding of history is clearly visible in the writings of such diverse historians as Condorcet, Herder, and Ferguson, all of whom wrote in the late eighteenth century.

As suggested above, a major feature of early modern historiography in its later decades was the increasing inclusion of the non-European past within its patterns of explanation. Diogo Ramada Curto's chapter illustrates this as it focuses on how European historical writing on Asia fits within this framework. While opening up to a more detailed, empirical, and less mythical knowledge of the Asian cultures, especially Japan, China, and India, European historians also

[22] See Elman, *From Philosophy to Philology.*
[23] Reinhart Koselleck, 'Historia Magistra Vitae: On the Dissolution of the Topos into the Perspective of a Modernized Historical Process', in *Futures Past: On the Semantics of Historical Time,* trans. Keith Tribe (New York, 2004), 26–42.

shifted their perspectives; they left behind the essentially religious concern of earlier missionary historians for the conversion of Asians to Christianity and adopted instead the language of commercial society that the major currents in European historiography had gradually developed over the previous century or so. If mere chronicling had not completely disappeared from European historical culture, it had now definitively been marginalized by a narrative approach that aspired to show the meaning of past events and even to suggest the course of future developments, instead of contenting itself with listing those events. Historiography became more inclusive of a variety of social, political, institutional, and cultural dimensions, and this in turn contributed to its success as the form of knowledge that characterized the nineteenth century. The price it paid for this achievement came in the form of a stronger emphasis on a Eurocentric and ultimately ethnic-national point of view that shaped the European approach to history-writing for a long time to come and which would eventually distance nineteenth-century European historians from their early modern predecessors.

The chapters on the Americas, coupled with the earlier chapter on Spain, offer three points of entry into the question of historical writing on a global perspective in the sixteenth century. The first examines the key figures in sixteenth-century Peninsular historiography (that is, works written about Spain itself) on the eve and aftermath of the 'discovery' of America; the second addresses the particular challenges writers faced in the description of New World phenomena and in providing ethical and juridical accounts of the conquering enterprises; the third addresses the paradox of speaking of simultaneous radically discontinuous historical forms of writing in Europe and the Americas. Whereas Peninsular historiography was neither bound nor often even affected by the 'discovery', the writing of New World histories manifested an autonomy with respect to the genre and political motivations that defined its Peninsular counterpart. The question of simultaneity takes us one step further away from Peninsular history in that the chapters take stock of writing traditions which coexisted—that is, shared a temporal moment—with European historical writing, but remained independent, clearly before the Spanish presence, and also in histories written during the colonial period. With respect to the specifically American historiography the chapters raise two main questions. The first is what was the impact of the discovery of a New World on European history? The second is how should we address the paradox of temporally simultaneous yet radically discontinuous historical forms of writing in Europe and the Americas?

The first question calls forth themes that include the production of new historical genres, the emergence of ethnography and ethnology, the transformation of European thought into Euroamerican, and the interface of American historians in the debates on the Enlightenment. Reading the participants in the 'disputes' of the New World, to borrow Antonello Gerbi's title, *The Dispute of the New World*,[24] makes us aware of the centrality of the Americas in European thought. Even when the main European participants in the debate denigrated American cultures and nature or undermined the significance of America in world history, their disparagements manifest their historical consciousness as inseparably bound to the place which the New World came to occupy in the articulation of European subjectivity and historical thought.

The second question regarding simultaneity poses issues that affect the conceptualization of the volume itself. This collection of chapters on historical writing from 1400 to 1800, perhaps inevitably, continues to privilege European dating systems even when committed to a view of historical writing from a global perspective. Thus 1400–92 defines a period in the production of history when Amerindian and European historians ignored each other and produced their texts independently, with no contact whatsoever. This is a very different situation from that of historical writing in Asia and Africa during the period 1400–1800 when historians in these different parts of the world were often aware of the existence of counterparts elsewhere, though perhaps not conversant with their distinctive ways of knowing and recording the past.

The volume includes two distinct essays on Spanish historiography of the Peninsula and the New World, both authored by Kira von Ostenfeld-Suske: the first, mentioned above, covers the connection between history and politics in Spain (c.1474–1600); the other, the production of new historical genres in the first hundred years of writing on the New World. In the first, which focuses on the 'official historians' of Spain and its monarchy, von Ostenfeld-Suske warns us against assuming that the histories she covers are representative of an era's character. She does underscore that these writings offer a lens through which one may survey early modern forms of constructing royal imagery, political ideology, and authority. For her, these concerns also fulfil a role in framing the historiographical project. It is noteworthy that these histories express little if any concern with the conquest of America. Von Ostenfeld-Suske's subsequent chapter on New World historiography covers the very different writings, during virtually the same period, of Columbus, Peter Martyr, Gonzalo Fernández de Oviedo, Juan Ginés de Sepúlveda, Bartolomé de las Casas, Fray Bernardino de Sahagún, José de Acosta, and Antonio de Herrera y Tordesillas. This list includes both writers who wrote without knowing the New World first hand and others who claimed epistemic privilege from the fact of being eyewitnesses. The chapter takes us through the difficulties faced in describing unheard of phenomena, the legacy and shortcomings of ancient histories, and the new political circumstances defined by legal issues concerning conquest and the incorporation of the new lands to Spanish sovereignty. Together with von Ostenfeld-Suske's Peninsular chapter, it testifies both to the uncertain impact

---

[24] Antonello Gerbi, *The Dispute of the New World: History of a Polemic, 1750–1900*, trans. Jeremy Moyle (Pittsburgh, 1973).

of the New World and to the creation of new genres that are a direct consequence of the so-called encounter of two worlds.[25] Beyond this simultaneity of Spanish historians writing histories independent of each other, her New World chapter also raises the question of indigenous history-writing during a time when both continents remained oblivious of each other. In analogous terms, we also speak of the uncertain impact of European indigenous historiography.

Elizabeth Hill Boone's chapter on pictographic histories before and after colonization makes particularly patent the need to consider simultaneity in reading Mesoamerican pictorial texts. Boone's analysis of pictographic history undermines the impact of the conquest and influx of European forms that painters adopt. Even when post-conquest pictographic histories often combine European and Mesoamerican forms, this shouldn't be reduced to responses or resistances to Spanish dominion, but rather taken as a historical continuum in which *tlacuiloque* (native painters/writers) produce pictorial vocabularies— consistent with Mesoamerican pictographic convention—for depicting new objects, institutes, and historical personages.[26] Indeed, Boone reminds us that the *tlacuiloque* continued to paint history without mention of the Spanish invasion or with negligible reference to this event. Even when bearing the imprint of Spanish colonization pictographic histories retain the Mesoamerican pictorial vocabularies, chronologies, and narrative genre.[27] The concept of simultaneity seeks to underscore that historical writing or inscriptions of memory coexisted under various chronologies; consider the simultaneity of the Mesoamerican year 4 House and AD 1453, but also consider that the equivalence tends to privilege *anno domini* accounts, even when in sixteenth-century Europe (if not before, as in Alfonso X's *Siete Partidas*) we already find systematic interrogations of the universality of Judeo-Christian chronologies such as in the French philologist Joseph Scaliger.

José Rabasa's chapter further elaborates on the question of simultaneity with Nahua alphabetical writings. The Nahua historians of the sixteenth and seventeenth centuries apparently adopted the *anno domini* chronology and inscribed within a history of salvation the narratives they collected on ancient Mesoamerica and the colonial world from community elders. However, Rabasa underscores that these historians systematically inscribe *both* systems of dating, thus allowing for possible reflections on Mesoamerican chronology independent of the translations to dates *anno domini*. Rabasa complements Boone's study of pictographic histories by examining the instances of the sorts of verbal performances that would have supplemented the pictorial histories. In this regard these alphabetical

[25] For the general thesis of an uncertain impact of the New World, see J. H. Elliot, *The Old World and the New, 1462–1650* (Cambridge, 1978).

[26] José Rabasa, *Tell Me the Story of How I Conquered You: Elsewheres and Ethnosuicide in the Colonial Mesoamerican World* (Pittsburgh, 2011).

[27] Elizabeth Hill Boone, *Stories in Red and Black: Pictorial Histories of the Aztecs and Mixtecs* (Austin, 2000).

histories also offer instances of speech and voice that retain continuity with ancient Mesoamerica and the characteristic narrative genre. Whereas in pictographic histories we find ourselves limited to saying someone spoke (chanted, dialogued, cried, and so forth) on a given occasion at a particular time, the Nahuatl alphabetical histories provide samples of these sorts of speech events. The collecting of Nahuatl historical accounts was conducted by Nahua members of the community who accumulated narratives articulated on a given reading of a pictorial history. Rabasa underscores that these narratives must be seen as collective verbal events rather than the recording of an individual member of the community. These alphabetical records also form part of the ethnographic efforts of missionaries who requested samples of the Mesoamerican speech genre from the community elders. The most well-known case, though hardly the only one, is the Franciscan Bernardino de Sahagún's monumental, *Historia general de las cosas de la Nueva España* [General History of the Things of New Spain] (*c*.1579). In the course of the sixteenth century one can observe the movement between the collection of speech genres performed by elders and informants to the writing of Nahuatl accounts that record daily events, as in Domingo Francisco de San Antón Muñón Chimalpahin Cuauhtlehuanitzin's *Diario*, also known in the English translation as *Annals of His Time*.[28] These Nahuatl texts offer particularly vivid examples of the creation of an alphabetical historical tradition in Nahuatl.

On a different line of enquiry, mainly because of the different kinds of sources available (the extreme rarity of histories written in Quechua or Aymara), the late Catherine Julien reads Spanish and native Andean histories to identify what she calls Inca historical forms. These forms include a wide range of objects (*khipus*, vases, textiles) that colonial historians used to write their histories. Thus, Julien documents the materials and the kinds of information recorded in the precolonial and colonial periods by indigenous historians. If this chapter takes Inca historical forms as a starting point, it also examines the interplay between Inca and European forms. Julien argues that the weight we may place on European versus Inca forms depends on the stance we take in reading the histories. For Julien the emphasis should reside in the attention we pay to the impact of an alien tradition on historical representation rather than showing how alphabetical writing became dominant in the colonial period. The project calls for attentive readings of Spanish narratives (by Spaniards, mestizo, and indigenous historians) that testify to the multiple non-alphabetical sources.[29] Her chapter identifies two main forms from which Spanish historians drew information: the use of paintings and tablets for recording genealogies and the use of *khipus* for life histories. These forms are

[28] *Annals of His Time: Don Domingo de San Antón Muñón Chimalpahin Quauhtlehuanitzin*, ed. and trans. James Lockhart, Susan Schroeder, and Doris Namala (Stanford, 2006).
[29] Catherine Julien, *Reading Inca History* (Iowa City, 2000).

of particular interest to Spaniards because of the similarities they bear with Spanish interest in genealogy and biography. Spaniards, however, were not able to recognize Inca forms of memory though they do record their existence and at times called for their extirpation. Julien gives particular attention to the sacred places or objects called *huacas*. The *huacas* included both natural and built objects. They correspond to ancient cult sites in nature (e.g. springs, rocks, or mountains) and built objects that commemorated events in the rule of particular Incas.[30] Furthermore, *khipus* recorded lists of *huacas* that bear a similarity to what modern scholars classify as geography or history. Once Julien's chapter has defined Inca forms of history, it proceeds to identify the key characteristics of three main historical moments corresponding to what she calls the 'short sixteenth century', the 'long seventeenth century', and the 'eighteenth century' *tout court.*

In a similar vein to von Ostenfeld-Suske's chapter on the New World, Neil L. Whitehead also points in the direction of identifying new forms of history though he emphasizes the multiple European nations and languages that represent the historical corpus of colonial Brazil. Whitehead discusses a wide range of writing on Brazil in Latin, Spanish, Portuguese, French, Dutch, and German. In tracing this corpus Whitehead provides a genealogy of the recurrent tropes on Brazil: e.g. cannibalism, nudity, voracious savage women, tropical lush vegetation, and so on. Whitehead reads these accounts with an eye for the ethnographic description of Brazil, and he evaluates them as early samples of ethnology. In addition to the written record, Whitehead underscores the value of the pictorial components that illustrated the accounts but which he reads as rich sources of information independent of the written sections they complemented visually. In closing his chapter, Whitehead expresses the hope that his inventory of historical writings on Brazil will 'stimulate a broader definition of what might come to constitute a more complete historiography of Brazil'. In this regard the historical records could turn into sources of information on historical practices that could be further illuminated by archaeological records—in Whitehead's terms, 'a mute source of historiography'.[31] This remains a future task that would further document the simultaneity which we have traced in the chapters by Julien, Boone, and Rabasa.

Jorge Cañizares-Esguerra focuses his chapter on the great debates over the New World in the eighteenth century. Cañizares-Esguerra's chapter traces the ways in which Spanish and American historians responded to Northern Europeans writing about the inferiority of New World cultures and nature.[32]

---

[30] Following a convention among Andean scholars, Julien uses the spelling *Inca* to refer to the civilization and its peoples and the form *Inka* for the rulers.

[31] Neil L. Whitehead, *Histories and Historicities in Amazonia* (Lincoln, 2003).

[32] Jorge Cañizares-Esguerra, *How to Write the History of the New World: Histories, Epistemologies and Identities in the Eighteenth-Century Atlantic World* (Stanford, 2001). Cf. Gerbi, *The Dispute of the New World*, cited above.

(It should be noted that his use of the word 'American' goes beyond the provincial use of this term to refer to the citizens and things belonging to the colonies which became the United States.) Cañizares-Esguerra finds in American, and to some extent also in Spanish historians a redefinition of the ideals of the Enlightenment. In fact, he argues that American historians were truer to the scientific spirit of the Enlightenment than their European counterparts. Cañizares-Esguerra traces how European historians could claim originality and newness, conveniently ignoring American historians while mining their books.

This introduction has brought us around the world from east to west, and the reader will have grasped by now the two central premises of the volume, and of the series within which it appears: first, that the modes of capturing the past which humans have employed are far more variable than Eurocentric histories of history have acknowledged; and second, that during these centuries the experience of encountering alien forms of historical thought and historical representation sometimes produced significant changes in both parties to the encounter, and at others the continued existence of cultural solitudes. As the eighteenth century ended, and on the eve of the great mid-nineteenth-century 'disciplining' of history, the rich global variety in Asian, European, and American forms of historicity had only just begun, through the process of intercultural contact, to narrow.

Chapter 1

Chinese Official Historical Writing under the Ming and Qing

Achim Mittag

THE SONG LEGACY: NEW CONFIGURATIONS IN LATE IMPERIAL HISTORIOGRAPHY

Chinese official historiography has become enshrined in the Twenty-Five Dynastic Histories (*Ershiwushi*), an unrivalled corpus of historical records over more than three thousand years, which forms the spine of Chinese pre-modern historical writing. These twenty-five histories are remarkably uniform in their composition. This is not to say, however, that Chinese official historiography developed along a similarly uniform trajectory. Thus, the period under discussion here, the Ming and Qing dynasties (1368–1644 and 1644–1911), is clearly set apart from earlier times, with the Song period (960–1279) constituting a watershed in historical thinking and writing.[1]

In the field of official historiography, a milestone was set by Sima Guang's monumental *Zizhi tongjian* [Comprehensive Mirror of Aid in Government] (1064–84). This great chronicle was imperially commissioned for use in the lectures held in the Classics Seminar (*jingyan*), yet it was compiled by a group of historians at Sima Guang's private mansion at Luoyang, and not by the Historiographical Office (*shiguan*).[2] This inaugurated a new era of official historiography beyond the narrow confines of the Historiographical Office.

Broadly speaking, Song and post-Song historiography were characterized by five major currents: (1) the expansion of non-official and private historiography; (2) the growth of a culture of reviewing, discussing, and reflecting on the past, paired with the unfolding of historical criticism (*shiping*); (3) an enormous increase of 'gazetteers', that is, historical works with a local or regional focus (*fangzhi*); (4) development of new forms of historical narration such as the 'historical novel' (*yanyi*); (5)

---

[1] Thomas H. C. Lee, 'Introduction', in Lee (ed.), *The New and the Multiple: Sung Senses of the Past* (Hong Kong, 2004), pp. vii–xxxii.

[2] Since the Song Dynasty, the Historiographical Office had been officially renamed as Imperial Office of History (*guoshi guan*), but it continued to be often referred to by its old name, which therefore will be used in the present chapter.

Map 1. East and Southeast Asia in the Seventeenth Century

change of the coordinate system of norms and values towards emphasizing ethical motives behind human action. The latter development is highlighted by the rise of Zhu Xi, the foremost proponent of Song Confucian thought, who during the Ming became regarded as the ultimate authority in historical matters, only second to Confucius. Concurrently, the notion of the 'moral constitution of the heart-and-mind' (*xinshu*) attained prominence. It implied the vigilant awareness of one's moral obligations within the Five Human Relationships (*wulun*), among them loyalty towards the sovereign in the first place.

The notion of the 'moral constitution of the heart-and-mind' entered historical discourse in the Yuan dynasty (1271–1368). When asked about the basic requirements for collaborators of the official history projects concerning the Song, Jin (1115–1234), and Liao (907/946–1125) dynasties, Jie Xisi counselled to employ historians not only by the criteria of erudition, talent in literary writing, and grasp of historical facts, but primarily also by the proper 'constitution of the heart-and-mind'.[3]

Increasingly oriented towards this notion of moral consciousness, Ming historical thinking grew in moral rigour. This trend also affected the debate on the issue of 'legitimate dynastic rule' (*zhengtong*), one of the most controversially debated issues in Chinese historiography. The Ming debate on 'legitimate dynastic rule' was shaped by the persisting threat posed by the Mongols and growingly strident anti-'barbarian' voices of an unbridgeable divide between Chinese civilization and the barbarians (*Hua/yi*); the most radical one even advocating exclusion of the Tang dynasty (618–907) from 'legitimate dynastic rule' on account of the Tang royal house being not purely of Chinese origin.[4]

With the Ming dynasty's decline and demise, the 'moralist' scheme of historical interpretation, and along with it, the militant advocacy of the concept of 'legitimate dynastic rule' began to lose ground against the 'pragmatist' scheme, which dominated historical thinking and writing for the next one and a half centuries.[5] Then, quite unexpectedly in the latter half of Emperor Qianlong's reign (r. 1736–95), another reversal occurred and the pendulum swung again in the other direction of the 'moralist' stance. The great revision to which the history of the Ming–Qing transitional period was subjected by Qianlong's decree, loses half its meaning unless one takes note of this second reversal.

Zhang Xuecheng, generally acknowledged as China's greatest historical thinker, was writing under the influence of this reversal. Reiterating Jie Xisi's earlier proposal and placing the individual historian at the nodal point of historiography, Zhang, in his essay 'On the historian's moral integrity'

---

[3] See Chen Guangchong, 'Jie Xisi lun shi', *Zhongguo shixueshi luncong* (1984), 365–8.

[4] See Thomas Göller and Achim Mittag, *Geschichtsdenken in Europa und China* (Sankt Augustin, 2008), 80–5.

[5] A formidable example of the 'pragmatist' criticism of the *zhengtong* concept is provided by the eminent Ming loyalist Wang Fuzhi; see ibid., 86–93.

('*shi de*'), asserts that the 'moral constitution of one's heart-and-mind' is the most essential requirement of a good historian (*liangshi*).[6]

Zhang's celebrated essay may serve as a corrective to the stereotypical view of a completely impersonal Chinese state historiography, which presumably only produced histories devoid of any literary qualities and filled with trivial, unimportant details. This stereotype has long hampered research, along with a limited access to a sizeable number of Ming and Qing works classified as 'official historiography'. Fortunately, this situation has greatly changed in the past thirty years and considerable progress has been made in the field.

THE COMPILATION OF THE OFFICIAL YUAN HISTORY AND THE VERITABLE RECORDS

Compilation of the Yuan official history (*Yuanshi*) was ordered by Emperor Taizu (r. 1368–98), founder of the Ming dynasty, in early 1368. Under the directorship of Song Lian and Wang Hui, who headed a staff of sixteen and fourteen collaborators respectively, the project was rushed to completion in 332 days. To rationalize the extreme haste, Song Lian pointed to the great Emperor Tang Taizong (r. 626–49), who, upon having gained control over the empire, saw to the compilation of the preceding dynasties' histories.

Another certain motive was the desire to allure former Yuan scholars into the service of the new dynasty. Their loyalty to the Mongol dynasty, regardless of its 'barbarian' origin, is, for example, manifested by Wei Su, who, upon the Ming army's entrance into Dadu (Beijing), could only be stopped from drowning himself in a well by a monk who exclaimed that, 'There is no one as knowledgeable as you about the empire's history. If you die, it all will be lost.'[7] Through Wei Su the new regime attained the Veritable Records of the Yuan emperors' reigns from Chinggis (Ghengis) Khan's (r. 1206–27) rise to power down to the enthronement of the last Mongol emperor, that is, from 1206 to 1332. Missing from it were only the records of the last emperor's long reign from 1332 to 1368.[8]

The extreme hastiness of the Yuan official history's compilation has ever since been the main point of criticism. Traditionally known as 'the most careless' among the Twenty-Five Dynastic Histories,[9] it nevertheless is esteemed by

---

[6] Achim Mittag, 'What Makes a Good Historian: Zhang Xuecheng's Postulate of "Moral Integrity" (*shi de*) Revisited', in H. Schmidt-Glintzer, Mittag, and J. Rüsen (eds.), *Historical Truth, Historical Criticism, and Ideology: Chinese Historiography and Historical Culture from a New Comparative Perspective* (Leiden, 2005), 365–6, 373–82.

[7] *Mingshi* (1997, 6th edn, Zhonghua shuju), 285/7314.

[8] Luo Zhonghui, 'Mingchu shiguan he *Yuan shi* de xiuzuan', *Zhongguoshi yanjiu* (1992), 1, 144–53.

[9] For early critics, see Huang Zhaoqiang, *Qingren Yuan shixue tanyan—Qingchu zhi Qingzhongye* (Banqiao, 2000), 409.

modern researchers mainly for two reasons: First, it preserves an abundance of historical sources without intrusive editorial rewrites as was often the case with other official histories. Second, some of its treatises (*zhi*) rank among the best of all twenty-five dynastic histories, specifically the treatises on astronomy and the calendar, on geography and on rivers and waterways.

Since the establishment of the Historiographical Office as a separate court office in 629 under the Tang dynasty, the compilation of the preceding dynasty's official history (or its complete revision), had been its most important and prestigious task. Yet it was not until the late sixteenth century that the procedures for producing the historical record took on a more systematized form. Moreover, throughout the Ming and early Qing, diverse editorial activities and compilations, such as that of the monumental *Yongle dadian* [Yongle Encyclopedia], were undertaken by the Historiographical Office.[10]

The Office's second most important task was the compilation of the Veritable Records (*shilu*) for each successive reign. Drawing upon various sources produced by the central bureaucracy, first and foremost the Diaries of Activity and Repose (*qijuzhu*),[11] supplemented by the Daily Calendar (*rili*) and a multitude of documents from the Six Ministries (*liubu*) and other governmental agencies, the Veritable Records constituted the spine of any future official history.

It has been estimated that about one thousand people were involved in the compilation of the Ming Veritable Records (*Ming shilu*), including two large-scale revisions, from the supervisor (*jianxiu*), usually an elder statesman who served as a figurehead of the compilation project, and the directors-general (*zongcai*) down to the copyists and proofreaders.[12] With the exception of some minor losses, the Ming Veritable Records are the first to be handed down in their entirety, providing an unusually rich collection of historiographical material.

In the course of the Ming dynasty, considerable thought was given to the preservation of the Veritable Records. Following the completion of each preceding emperor's reign, two manuscript copies were presented to the ruling emperor in a solemn ceremony. While the duplicate copy (*fuben*) was deposited for reference in the Grand Secretariat (*neige*), the original (*zhengben*) was put under seal for its safekeeping, after 1534 in a specially constructed building known as the Imperial Historical Archives (*huangshicheng*). In another ceremony

---

[10] Not until 1765 was the Historiographical Office made into a permanent institution exclusively in charge of historical matters.

[11] Instituted under the first Ming emperors, the practice of recording Diaries of Activity and Repose was given up in the Xuande era (1426–35), before being reintroduced in 1575; see Wolfgang Franke, *An Introduction to the Sources of Ming History* (Kuala Lumpur, 1968), 12; Wolfgang Franke, 'Historical Writing during the Ming', in Frederick W. Mote and Denis Twitchett (eds.), *The Cambridge History of China*, vol. 7: *The Ming Dynasty, 1368–1644*, Part I (Cambridge, 1988), 737–8; and Xie Gui'an, *Ming shilu yanjiu* (Taipei, 1995), 218–19.

[12] Xie, *Ming shilu yanjiu*, 101–207.

all drafts and other materials were then burnt. Moreover, the whole set of existing Veritable Records were copied twice, in 1534–6 and in 1588–91; both copies were also deposited in the Imperial Historical Archives.[13]

However, all these measures could not prevent two major cases of large-scale revision to the Veritable Records. One concerned the Veritable Records of Taizu, the other the Veritable Records of the month-long reign of Emperor Taichang (r. 1620). In the first case, it was the emperor himself—Emperor Yongle (r. 1402–24)—who twice ordered a revision of his father's Veritable Records, in order to legitimize his uprising against his nephew (and Taizu's legitimate successor), known as the Jianwen Emperor (r. 1399–1402). In the second case, the emperor played only a passive role: the twice-repeated alteration in 1625–8 and 1628–30/1 were the outcome of bitter strife between the eunuch clique and the followers of the Donglin party, who occupied the moral high ground and had earlier supervised the compilation of the Veritable Records completed in 1623. From about the 1580s onward, the Ming Veritable Records in general were increasingly subjected to criticism and some voices even called for a revision of the most distorted records.[14]

This indicates an increasingly vibrant historical discourse, which in contemporary parlance was referred to as the 'discourse that holds to the general norm' (*gonglun*). The idea of such a public hearing of historical cases culminated with the Ming national history (*guoshi*) project. Under the directorship of Jiao Hong this project was initiated in 1594, but came to an abrupt end two years later. As we can learn from a memorandum by Jiao Hong, this project aimed to render full recognition of the two originally excluded emperors Jianwen and Jingtai (r. 1449–57), supplementing biographical entries for those who had previously been considered troublemakers unworthy of historical remembrance, and revising existing biographies in which the subjects were treated unfairly.[15]

This bold proposal signalled, after Sima Guang's eleventh-century *Zizhi tongjian*, a second milestone in the transformation of official historiography in late imperial China. Never before had the influence of the educated elite outside of the Historiographical Office been so strong. This all changed with the Ming dynasty's demise and the rise of the Manchu-Qing Empire.

---

[13] Franke, *An Introduction to the Sources of Ming History*, 9–10, 20–2; Franke, 'Historical Writing during the Ming', 737–40, 744–5; and Xie, *Ming shilu yanjiu*, 330–4.

[14] Franke, 'Historical Writing during the Ming', 748–52; and Xie, *Ming shilu yanjiu*, 34–41, 80–6, 380–3.

[15] Edward T. Ch'ien, *Chiao Hung and the Restructuring of Neo-Confucianism in the Late Ming* (New York, 1986), 52–5.

THE FORMATION OF STATE HISTORIOGRAPHY
UNDER THE QING AND THE WRITING OF THE
HISTORY OF THE OFFICIAL MING DYNASTY

Following the creation of the Manchu script in 1599, record-keeping offices and state archives were subsequently established under the Later Jin dynasty (1616–35), the forerunner state of the Qing dynasty proclaimed in 1636. In 1633, Abahai (r. 1627–43), son and successor of the Manchu state's founder Nurgaci (sometimes written as Nurhaci), decreed the recording of his deceased father's deeds. The outcome was the first version of the Veritable Records of Nurgaci's reign, completed in 1643, accompanied by an illustrated account of his campaigns. This was the starting point of Qing official historiography.[16]

Yet it was not until 1690 that a regular Historiographical Office was established. After having been dissolved twice, it was re-established on a permanent basis in 1765, serving as a primary agency of Qianlong's many historiographical projects in the latter half of his reign, certainly the Office's heyday. Apart from the Historiographical Office, there were four other offices dealing with historiographical matters: the Office of Military Documentation (*fanglve guan*),[17] the Office of the Diaries of Action and Repose (*qiju guan*),[18] the Veritable Records Office (*shilu guan*),[19] and the Office of Collected Statutes (*huidian guan*)—the first two offices of which were even made into permanent institutions during the Qing. All five historiographical offices were more or less loosely attached to the Grand Secretariat, the Hanlin Academy, or, in the case of the Military Archive, to the Grand Council (*junji chu*). Principally headed by a high-ranking director-general, they enjoyed the privilege of being allowed directly to correspond with the emperor.[20] In addition, there were a few ad hoc commissions set up for specific historiographical projects, the most prestigious being the one for the compilation of the official Ming history (*Mingshi*).

Among the Twenty-Five Dynastic Histories the *Mingshi* is in size second only to the *Songshi* [History of the Song Dynasty] and its compilation took the longest time—ninety-five years, from 1645 to 1739. Even after completion it underwent a

---

[16] Qiao Zhizhong, *Zhongguo guanfang shixue yu sijia shixue* (Beijing, 2008), 73–4.

[17] Beatrice S. Bartlett, *Monarchs and Ministers: The Grand Council in Mid-Ch'ing China, 1723–1820* (Berkeley, 1991), 225–8; Qiao, *Zhongguo guanfang shixue*, 94–5; and Peter C. Perdue, *China Marches West: The Qing Conquest of Central Eurasia* (Cambridge, Mass., 2005), 654, n. 4. See also ch. 2 by Pamela Kyle Crossley in this volume.

[18] Established in 1671 under the supervision of the Grand Secretariat (*neige*), the Office of Diaries of Action and Repose produced more than 12,000 volumes (*ce*) in Manchu and Chinese up until the end of the Qing dynasty; Qin Guojing, *Ming Qing dang'an xue* (Beijing, 2005), 287–9.

[19] The Veritable Records Office also oversaw other historiographical projects such as the compilation of the 'sacred edicts' (*shengxun*) willed by each emperor from Kangxi onward.

[20] Qiao, *Zhongguo guanfang shixue*, 90–6.

lengthy revision from 1775 to 1789. It is estimated that altogether 200–300 people were involved; yet the one person who has always been singled out for outstanding contribution is Wan Sitong, a student of the eminent scholar Huang Zongxi. Because of his staunch Ming loyalist stance, Wan rejected official appointment and salary. For most of the time during his nineteen years at Beijing, he was lodged at the private mansions of two directors-general, Xu Yuanwen and Wang Hongxu.

Wan Sitong is credited with having produced a complete draft manuscript of the Ming history in 416 chapters (*Mingshi [gao]*). On this basis, the aforementioned Wang Hongxu submitted a first draft version of the biographical part in 202 chapters in 1714, followed by a complete draft version in 310 chapters in 1723. Still, Emperor Yongzheng (r. 1723–35) set up a new commission in the same year. Its primary task was to provide all the evaluative comments, which were lacking in Wang Hongxu's draft version.[21] After Qianlong's enthronement, the finalized draft version was ready to go into print at the Imperial Printing Office housed in the Wuying Hall (the so-called Palace edition, published in 1739).

This was not yet the final act, however. In 1775 and again in 1777, in the context of the various revisions of Ming history works, the Palace edition was ordered to be revised. After years of cumbersome collation the final version was eventually included in the *Siku quanshu* [Complete Library of the Four Treasuries] in 1789. Circulation of this recension was very limited and, hence, it has received little attention.[22]

Apart from a sizeable quantity of textual emendations and corrected transliterations of Mongol and foreign names,[23] there are some changes which, though minimal, affect the whole picture. An illuminating example is provided by the account of Jianwen's 'abdication' (*xunguo*) and his presumed escape out of the besieged Nanjing.[24] Another blunt reversal of the Palace edition's evaluation occurs in the 'appraisal' (*zan*) of Emperor Yingzong (r. 1436–49 and 1457–64), whose earlier and rather positive evaluation is dismissed with scorn; the reason is that for Qianlong, Yingzong did not live up to the 'heroism' (*ying*) alluded to in his posthumous name, but was plainly a great loser, just the opposite of Qianlong.[25]

---

[21] A manuscript fragment offers valuable insight into the reworking process; see Xu Qingsong and Zhou Zheng, '*Mingshi* cangao jieshao', *Zhongguo lishi bowuguan guankan*, 4 (1982), 101–5.

[22] See Qiao, *Zhongguo guanfang shixue*, 287–99.

[23] By and large, these changes are already documented in Wang Songwei's *Ming shi kaozheng junyi* (first published in 1894); see Qiao, *Zhongguo guanfang shixue*, 294, 296–8.

[24] See Harold L. Kahn, *Monarchy in the Emperor's Eyes: Image and Reality in the Ch'ien-lung Reign* (Cambridge, Mass., 1971), 44–6.

[25] *Yupi lidai tongjian jilan* (edn, Hefeishi, 1996), 105/6473–4 (upper margins); cf. Qiao, *Zhongguo guanfang shixue*, 292–3.

An eminent feature of the *Mingshi* must be seen in its broad treatment of non-Chinese peoples and foreign countries. The first draft of these chapters was compiled by You Tong,[26] who worked in the Ming History Commission from 1679 to 1683. With few slight changes and additions, this draft was then incorporated in the *Mingshi* draft manuscript prepared by Wan Sitong, yet underwent another revision in the next stage of the *Mingshi*'s compilation supervised by Zhang Tingyu.

Building on this comprehensive survey in the *Mingshi*, another outstanding project of ethnographic writing was undertaken with the compilation of the *Huang-Qing zhigong tu* [Illustrations from the Office of Receiving Tribute under the August Qing Dynasty]. Begun in 1751, this ethnographic encyclopedia of the world grew over the years to a large collection of 550 illustrations, two for each ethnic group represented, one man and one woman, with glosses on its history, its exchanges with the Chinese court, and its traditional costumes.[27] This work was the crowning piece of a cherished tradition of illustrated descriptions of foreign peoples, which can be traced to at least the sixth century. It surpasses similar works of earlier times in size and in scope, extending the idea of all foreign peoples partaking in the Chinese Empire's beneficial world-order through bringing 'tribute' (*gong*), in order to 'get under the sway of our policies aimed at (moral) transformation' (*shucheng xianghua*), as Qianlong declared in his 1751 edict, by which the *Huang-Qing zhigong tu*'s compilation was ordered.[28]

GAZETTEER HISTORIOGRAPHY

In China, as in pre-nineteenth-century Europe, geography has always been an integral part of historiography. Since Ban Gu's *Hanshu* [History of the Han] every full-blown official history contains a treatise on the administrative geography of the empire. In addition, the focus of the spatial dimension gave early rise to a historiographical genre known as 'gazetteers' (*fangzhi*), the origins of which are commonly traced to antiquity.[29]

In spite of the gazetteer genre's long pedigree, gazetteers began to occupy an important place in historiography only in late imperial China, not only on account

---

[26] Later separately published under the title of *Mingshi waiguo zhuan* (originally in *Xitang yuji*, preface 1691).
[27] This collection was expanded in 1763, 1771, 1775, and *c*.1790. On the several printed and hand-copied versions, which partly differ from one another, see Hartmut Walravens, '"Tribute-Bearers in Manchu and Chinese": A Unique 18th-Century Source for East and Central Asian History', *Acta Orientalia Academiae Scientiarum Hungaricae*, 49 (1996), 395–406.
[28] Translated by Walravens, 'Tribute-Bearers in Manchu and Chinese', 396–7; and Laura Hostetler, *Qing Colonial Enterprise: Ethnography and Cartography in Early Modern China* (Chicago, 2001), 46.
[29] Huang Wei *et al.*, *Fangzhixue* (Shanghai, 1993), 88–104; and Pierre-Étienne Will, *Chinese Local Gazetteers: An Historical and Practical Introduction* (Paris, 1992), 7.

of the sheer number of produced gazetteers, which amounts to about 2,800 and more than 5,000 for the Ming and Qing periods, respectively,[30] but also on account of the progress made in gazetteer historiography—the scope of the subject matter broadened, the organization of the material became more refined, and research into the source material was carried out with ever greater diligence. All these advances went along with the emergence of 'gazetteer studies' (*fangzhixue*) associated with such eminent scholars as Dai Zhen and, above all, Zhang Xuecheng.

Unlike in Song and pre-Song times, when gazetteers were primarily compiled *by* and *for* the bureaucracy, Ming and Qing gazetteers below the provincial level were usually produced collectively by a group of local officials, members of the local gentry, and the educated elite. Through compiling a gazetteer, this group 'strove to project an image of local conformity to state requirements'.[31] Hence, officially compiled gazetteers, regardless of their relatively small number, had an enormous impact on Ming and Qing gazetteer historiography in general. This is especially true for the 'all-under-one-rule' or 'national gazetteers' (*yitongzhi*); their compilation was accompanied by the state's frequent encouragement to initiate or update provincial and local gazetteers and efforts to standardize their format.[32]

The first such national gazetteer was produced under the Mongol conquerors. Sensible to the need for geographical knowledge as the basis of the installed postal and overland transport system, Qubilai Khan accepted the advice of the Persian astronomer and geographer Jamal al-Din and, in 1286, decreed the compilation of the *Da-Yuan da yitongzhi* [Great All-Under-One-Rule Gazetteer of the Great Yuan Dynasty]. First completed in 1291, it was later continuously expanded, eventually amounting to 600 fascicles (*ce*) and 1,300 chapters.[33] Structured around the surveys of the eleven newly established provinces, the *Da-Yuan da yitongzhi* provided the basis not only for the official Yuan history's 'Geographical Treatise', but also for the national gazetteer decreed by Ming Taizu in 1370. Although not finalized under Taizu, its first draft was supplemented by a large map,[34] which may well have served as a draft for the illustrious 'Universal Map of the Great Ming Dynasty' (*Da-Ming hunyi tu*).[35]

---

[30] Numbers refer to gazetteers above township level only; the number of Ming gazetteers includes lost and extant works (1,786 and 928, respectively); the exact number of Qing gazetteers (only extant works) amounts to 4,819 items. Cf. Huang Wei *et al.*, *Fangzhixue*, 176, 184–5, 187–8, 212, 220. Including township gazetteers and gazetteers for institutional and topographical sites such as e.g. monasteries and mountains, there are close to 7,000 extant Ming and Qing gazetteers; see Timothy Brook, *The Chinese State in Ming Society* (London, 2005), 15.

[31] Ibid., 162.

[32] This is especially true for gazetteer historiography in the Kangxi and Yongzheng periods, i.e. 1662–1735; see Qiao, *Zhongguo guanfang shixue*, 248–54.

[33] *Zhongguo xueshu mingzhu tiyao: Lishi juan*, ed. Jiang Yihua (Shanghai, 1994), 660–2.

[34] An inspection of this map by Emperor Taizu in 1385 is reported in *Jin yan* (edn. Beijing, 1984) 1/28–9.

[35] Wang Qianjin, Hu Qisong, and Liu Ruofang, 'Juanben caihui Da-Ming hunyi tu yanjiu', in *Zhongguo gudai dituji*, 3 vols., ed. Cao Wanru *et al.* (Beijing, 1990–7), ii. 51–5 and fig. 1.

After his usurpation Emperor Yongle showed great concern for the National Gazetteer project as well as for gazetteer writing in general. Thus, in 1412 and 1418, he called on prefectures, sub-prefectures, counties, and commanderies (*tusi*) to compile gazetteers; his decrees were appended by 'Directives for the Compilation of Gazetteers' (*Xiuzhi fanli*), which specified twenty-four categories for treating the subject matter. However, the National Gazetteer project was brought to completion only decades later. In 1456 the *Huanyu tongzhi* [Comprehensive Gazetteer of All the Regions] was finalized, but before being printed, it was amended, supplemented by seventeen maps, and re-edited in 1461 under the title of [*Da-Ming*] *Yitongzhi* [All-Under-One-Rule Gazetteer of the Great Ming Dynasty].[36]

A conspicuous development took place beneath the level of National Gazetteer historiography: after a handful of provincial gazetteers (*tongzhi*) had already been compiled under the Yuan dynasty, provincial gazetteer historiography began to flourish under the Ming, with the number of produced works amounting to sixty-nine (including updates and revisions). Significantly, the three provinces at the empire's southern and south-western frontier zone—Yunnan, Guangxi, and Guizhou—which bore the brunt of late imperial inner-Chinese migration, produced the most provincial gazetteers (each 9 resp. 10 items).[37] This indicates how gazetteer historiography and the gradual southward expansion of the Chinese Empire fed on each other. Thus, gazetteers became a powerful instrument for affecting 'moral transformation' (*jiaohua*), to use the key notion in Ming and Qing colonizing ideology.[38]

Provincial gazetteer writing signifies a remarkable extension of Chinese late imperial official historiography: as the centres of state historiography multiplied, nuclei of expertise and professionalization grew in the provinces. This process continued and intensified under the Qing, culminating in the prohibition of *private* gazetteer writing in 1766. In the early Qing, the process of standardizing provincial gazetteers is connected with the name of Jia Hanfu, who, as Governor of Henan and Shaanxi, successively initiated and supervised the compilation of gazetteers for these two provinces. In 1672 they were promulgated empire-wide as models, together with imperial 'Directives' for the compilation of gazetteers, which incorporated Jia Hanfu's earlier guidelines.[39]

However, the compilation of a Qing national gazetteer did not proceed smoothly. Entangled in a faction struggle, Xu Qianxue, one of the directors-general originally appointed to the National Gazetteer Commission in 1686, was allowed to transfer the commission to his villa at Dongting Island on Lake Taihu.

---

[36] Huang Wei *et al.*, *Fangzhixue*, 177; and Franke, *An Introduction to the Sources of Ming History*, 237 (8.1.1. and 8.1.2).

[37] Huang Wei *et al.*, *Fangzhixue*, 178, 184–5.

[38] Cf. Hostetler's exemplary study of ethnographic writing in Guizhou, 1560–1834; *Qing Colonial Enterprise*, 127–57.

[39] Huang Wei *et al.*, *Fangzhixue*, 864 and 213–15.

Xu was joined by a *pléiade* of great scholars, but after his death in 1694, his team was dispersed and the draft manuscript was left unfinished.[40] With an eye turned towards the national gazetteer project, Emperor Yongzheng in 1729 decreed that provinces, prefectures, sub-prefectures, and counties were each to compile a gazetteer every sixty years. However, as with the official Ming history, completion of the national gazetteer project was not achieved until 1743, early in Qianlong's reign.

In subsequent decades the focus of gazetteer historiography shifted to the north and north-west, the capital region of Beijing, the Manchu homeland, and the newly conquered Northwestern territories. In the aftermath of the Qing conquest of Chinese Turkestan, Qianlong decreed the revision and expansion of the *Xiyu tuzhi* [Illustrated Gazetteer of the Western Regions], compilation of which had already begun in 1756.[41] Work on this project was accompanied by a string of successively commissioned gazetteers of locations with high symbolic significance for the imperial mystique, namely the gazetteers of Beijing and the metropolitan region (*Rixia jiuwen kao*; decreed 1774); Shengjing (i.e. Shenyang), the capital of the Manchu homeland (*Shengjing tongzhi*; decreed 1779); and Rehe, the summer residence north-east of Beijing (*Rehe zhi*; decreed 1781). These gazetteers were part and parcel of a 'historiographic and inscriptional machinery [which] occupied not only the Chinese textual space but nearly all of the Manchu and Mongolian spaces as well'.[42]

To integrate the sacralized spaces of the north and the north-east into the spatial order of All-under-Heaven (*tianxia*), Qianlong ordered the National History Office to expand the national gazetteer in 1764. Completed in 1784, it was destined to comprise 500 chapters, in obvious reference to the classical concept of All-under-Heaven's expanse being laid out in nine concentric squares of 500 miles (*li*) each. However, contrary to the claim in its preface as well as in the pertinent entry of the Annotated Imperial Library Catalogue (*Siku quanshu zongmu tiyao*), the revised edition ended up with only 424 chapters.

Its subsequent enlargement (*Jiaqing chongxiu yitongzhi*), completed in 1842, after more than thirty years of editorial work, was the largest project of official historiography in nineteenth-century China. Qianlong's grand vision of creating an imperial space of 'all-under-one-rule' is neatly visualized by this edition's map on the two front pages. Doubling the width of the traditionally longish format, this map shows the Qing Empire as consisting of four macro-regions—Manchuria-Eastern Mongolia, China Proper, Western Mongolia-Chinese Turkestan, and Qinghai-Tibet—which each take up about one-fourth of the land mass (with China proper occupying the smallest part).

---

[40] Qiao, *Zhongguo guanfang shixue*, 244–8.
[41] Ibid., 270–86.
[42] Perdue, *China Marches West*, 494.

IMPERIAL GRANDEUR AND GRAND HSTORY: THE APOGEE OF OFFICIAL HISTORIOGRAPHY UNDER EMPEROR QIANLONG

The Qianlong era (1736–95) was one of the longest and most formative in Chinese history. It also saw the apogee of official historiography in late imperial China. Historical works that were imperially commissioned amounted to a record number of more than sixty.[43] They all were part and parcel of Qianlong's conception and self-aggrandizing image of emperorship, which matured in the second half of his reign, i.e. from the 1760s onwards.

With one exception, all ten campaign histories that recorded the emperor's major and minor campaigns, were compiled in this period. They substantiated the aged emperor's self-congratulatory assessment of his military achievements, entitled 'Ten Steps to Full Accomplishment' (*Shi quan*), by which the definitive image of Qianlong the warrior king was cast. Moreover, Qianlong's Manchu khan identity was enhanced by the compilation of the [*Qinding*] *Manzhou yuanliu kao* [Researches on Manchu Origins] (1777–83), the crowning piece among various historiographical projects concerning the Manchu 'nation' or 'state'.[44]

At the centre of all historiographical activities in the second half of Qianlong's reign, however, lay the reinterpretation of the Ming–Qing transition and thence the recasting of Chinese history from its beginning.[45] The Ming–Qing transition's reinterpretation was closely connected with the posthumous rehabilitation of Dorgon, the 'throne regent' (*shezheng wang*) on behalf of the boy emperor Shunzhi. Although Dorgon must be credited with the swift conquest of Ming China, he fell into disgrace soon after his premature death. He has especially been known through his famous correspondence with Shi Kefa, the great Ming loyalist general, who, up to his last breath, defiantly refused to surrender. Qianlong prided himself at having retrieved this later document, often anthologized, from the archives.[46] Its importance is due to the fact that the two opponents, Dorgon and Shi Kefa, each from their own point of view, discuss the question of the rightfulness of the imminent Manchu-Qing conquest and the legitimacy of the Southern Ming dynasty, which, under Prince Fu, had been established in 1644 at Nanjing.[47]

---

[43] Qiao, *Zhongguo guanfang shixue*, 80. Lynn Struve, *The Ming-Qing Conflict, 1619–1683: A Historiography and Source Guide* (Ann Arbor, 1998), 60, gives a number of 55 works. For the wider context, see also Qiao, *Zhongguo guanfang shixue*, 188–204; and He Guanbiao, *Ming Qing renwu yu zhushu* (Hong Kong, 1996), 146–82.

[44] See ch. 2 by Pamela Kyle Crossley in this volume.

[45] Qiao, *Zhongguo guanfang shixue*, 205–18.

[46] *Yupi lidai tongjian jilan* 106/7172–4 (upper margins).

[47] See ibid.; intro. and trans. Hellmut Wilhelm, 'Ein Briefwechsel zwischen Durgan und Schï Ko-fa', *Sinica*, 8 (1933), 239–45.

Qianlong's judgement crystallized in the years from 1775 to 1777.[48] Recognizing the legitimacy of the short-lived Southern Ming regime until Prince Fu's capture in 1645, Qianlong judged all other regimes of Ming pretenders unrightful, yet, as a gesture of magnanimity, stipulated that the records of the two princes Tang and Gui be preserved in an appendix. Striking the pose of an impartial yet generous-minded arbiter, Qianlong thus declared, with solemnity, that 'the empire (*tianxia*) belongs to the whole world and not to a single ruling house'.[49]

These stipulations had far-reaching repercussions for various other historiographical projects. The first work ordered to be revised was a chronicle of the Ming dynasty (*Yuding Zizhi tongjian gangmu sanbian* [Imperially Directed Comprehensive Mirror of Aid in Government Arranged under Main Headings and in Subsections, Third Part]), which was the first major historical work that Qianlong had commissioned early in his reign.[50] Concurrently, a work was produced in which short entries were given to more than 3,500 men who had died out of loyalty to the fallen Ming dynasty, and thus posthumously granted the distinction of martyrdom. This work entitled [*Qinding*] *Shengchao xunjie zhuchen lu* [Record of Various Subjects Who Died Out of Loyalty to the Defeated Dynasty] (completed in 1776) has justly been characterized as 'the epitome of high-Qing emphasis on righteous death'.[51] Ranked highest among the honoured loyalists was Shi Kefa, the lionization of whom began at this time.

Once the rewriting had moved into full swing, Qianlong ordered the creation of a new biographical category for the prospective Qing dynastic history—the 'twice-serving officials' (*erchen*).[52] To prepare this new section, 120 figures were selected for biographical portrayal. The biographies were then arranged in two groups—the meritorious and the unmeritorious—which were each subdivided by three ranks. Under Qianlong's stern supervision, the compilation was completed in 1785 and published separately ([*Qinding guoshi*] *Erchen zhuan*), accompanied by a compilation comprising biographies of forty-one rebels and treacherous elements ([*Qinding guoshi*] *Nichen zhuan*).[53]

---

[48] A set of three pertinent edicts is translated by Luther Carrington Goodrich, *The Literary Inquisition of Ch'ien-lung* (New York, 1966), 138–40, 144–55. See also Struve, *The Ming-Qing Conflict*, 60–4; He, *Ming Qing renwu yu zhushu*, 257–80 *passim*; and Qiao, *Zhongguo guanfang shixue*, 188–204.

[49] *Yupi lidai tongjian jilan* 116/7121 (upper margin). Cf. He, *Ming Qing renwu yu zhushu*, 264, n. 60.

[50] Ibid., 245–56.

[51] Struve, *The Ming-Qing Conflict*, 63.

[52] The pertinent edict is translated by Goodrich, *The Literary Inquisition of Ch'ien-lung*, 154–6.

[53] Wing-ming Chan, 'Qianlong Emperor's New Strategy in 1775 to Commend Late-Ming Loyalists', *Asia Major*, 3rd ser., 13 (2000), 1, 109–37; and Pamela Kyle Crossley, *A Translucent Mirror: History and Identity in Qing Imperial Ideology* (Berkeley, 1999), 291–6.

Moreover, revision was ordered for the *Yupi lidai tongjian jilan* [Imperially Annotated Synopsis of the Comprehensive Mirror Throughout the Ages],[54] a world chronicle, which encompassed 4,559 years from the sage-emperor Fuxi until the Ming dynasty's demise.[55] Having first been completed in early 1768, its revised version (with documented amendments in 1782 and 1794) included Qianlong's own numerous marginal comments. Intended 'to instruct rulers and officials alike for a myriad of generations',[56] the *Yupi lidai tongjian jilan* was meant to provide the essential repertoire of Chinese history. The organizational principle around which it was structured is the imperially sanctioned scheme of 'legitimate dynastic rule'. According to this scheme, thirteen dynasties—apparently juxtaposed with the Thirteen Classics—were specified as legitimate; the main alteration vis-à-vis the standard Ming scheme being the acknowledgement of the Qin and Yuan as fully legitimate dynasties.

The *Yupi lidai tongjian jilan* was the apex of Qianlong's historiographical projects, which, as we have seen, encompassed various fields of historical writing, namely geography, military history, and biography. Mention must finally be made of the achievements in institutional historiography. In 1747 two commissions were set up, which both operated for twenty years (until 1767); one extended and added on the *Da-Qing huidian* [Collected Statues of the Great Qing Dynasty], a collection of documents originating with the court administration, the Six Ministries (*liubu*) and the other offices of the central government, which saw altogether five editions in the Qing. The other commission produced a continuation of Ma Duanlin's *Wenxian tongkao* [Comprehensive Investigations of Records and Documents] from the Yuan period (fourteenth century). Incorporating an earlier work by Wang Qi, this great work of institutional history covers the period of more than 400 years from the late Southern Song to the end of the Ming (*Xu Wenxian tongkao* [Continuation of the Comprehensive Investigations of Records and Documents]). In 1767, the commission was ordered to produce similar continuations for the other two of the Three Comprehensive Institutional Histories (*san Tong*), Du You's *Tong dian* [Comprehensive Collection of Statutes] and Zheng Qiao's *Tong zhi* [Comprehensive Records]. On their completion in 1783 and 1785 respectively, the commission moved on to compile within two years a continuation of each of the three institutional histories for the Qing dynasty up to the year 1786.[57]

---

[54] See He, *Ming Qing renwu yu zhushu*, 265–72; and Qiao, *Zhongguo guanfang shixue*, 256–69, 330–2.

[55] Though praising the chronicle earlier commissioned by Kangxi as the epitome of annalistic historiography, Qianlong dismissed it as the basis of the *Yupi lidai tongjian jilan*; see He, *Ming Qing renwu yu zhushu*, 258.

[56] 'Tongjian jilan xu', in *Yupi lidai tongjian jilan*, front page.

[57] *Zhongguo xueshu mingzhu tiyao: Lishi juan*, 574–83.

'EVIDENTIAL RESEARCH' AND CONCLUDING REMARKS

In the late Qianlong and early Jiaqing periods *kaozheng* ('evidential research') scholarship came into full bloom. Along with it, the dominant view of history-writing changed and a major shift in the valorization of authorities in historiography—away from Zhu Xi and back to Sima Guang—took place.[58] The penchant for critical enquiry reached its apogee in three outstanding works, respectively published in 1782, 1787, and 1800; all three brimmed with copious research notes on the official histories, yet differed in the acuteness of their critical comments on historical events.[59] These works were written privately, yet two of their authors—Qian Daxin and Zhao Yi—had had first-hand acquaintance with official historiography after having previously served in various historiographical offices in the capital.

However, official historiography's influence on the unfolding and profusion of *kaozheng* scholarship went beyond personal affiliation with state historiographical institutions in three respects. First, the search for Manchu identity generated a stream of linguistic, geographic, and genealogical studies. A case in point is Qianlong's 'Preface' to the *Manzhou yuanliu kao*, in which the emperor himself strikes the pose of a *kaozheng* scholar.[60] Another field of study concerned the corrections and unification of personal names, place names, official titles, and other transliterations that occur in the official histories of non-Chinese dynasties. Activities in this field culminated with the revision of the three official histories of the Liao, Jin, and Yuan dynasties;[61] the emendations were documented in the [*Qinding*] *Liao Jin Yuan shi guoyu jie* [Explanations of the Occurrences of Home Language in the Three Official Histories of the Liao, Jin, and Yuan Dynasties] (1781–5). Such linguistic studies also provided the basis for the flourishing of Mongol-Yuan studies, notably championed by the aforementioned Qian Daxin.[62]

Second, the compilation of the Annotated Imperial Library Catalogue (*Siku quanshu zongmu tiyao*) had an enormous influence on the rise of *kaozheng* scholarship in general. Similarly, historical research was greatly enhanced by the critical reviews of 1,564 works from the History Section (*shibu*), which were produced for the Annotated Imperial Library Catalogue. Among the many reviewers involved, mention must be made of Shao Jinhan, who contributed the draft reviews of all twenty-two standard histories, in addition to seven other historical works.[63] In the

---

[58] See Mittag, 'What Makes a Good Historian', 394.
[59] See ch. 3 by On-cho Ng in this volume.
[60] See Crossley, *A Translucent Mirror*, 299–311, esp. 302.
[61] He, *Ming Qing renwu yu zhushu*, 215–40.
[62] Huang, *Qingren Yuan shixue tanyan*, 73–182.
[63] R. Kent Guy, *The Emperor's Four Treasuries: Scholars and the State in the Late Ch'ien-lung Era* (Cambridge, Mass., 1987), 122, 124–40.

larger context of the *Siku quanshu* project, a sizeable number of historical works, which were previously thought to have been lost, resurfaced or could be retrieved from the Yongle Encyclopedia. Contemporary historians swiftly made use of these newly available materials. A foremost example is provided by the *Xu Zizhi tongjian* [Continuation of the Comprehensive Mirror of Aid in Government] (completed in 1792), which extended Sima Guang's great work into the Song and Yuan periods, i.e. from 960 to 1368.[64] Compiled by a group of renowned historians under the directorship of Bi Yuan, this chronicle amasses an abundance of historical sources, including miscellaneous notes on historical matters (*biji*), local gazetteers, and reports of diplomatic missions, not only on the history of the Song and Yuan, but also on the Liao, Jin, and Xia dynasties. Following Sima Guang's model, the *Xu Zizhi tongjian* includes an appendix, which discusses in more than 1,500 entries the differences between the sources used (*Kaoyi*). However, the *Xu Zizhi tongjian* lacks the discussions (*lun*) that are a hallmark of Sima Guang's original *Zizhi tongjian*.

Third, one reason why the *Xu Zizhi tongjian*'s author(s) thought it wise to abstain from any comments, reflections, and interpretive disquisitions might have been the fear of falling into conflict with the emperor's opinions. Claiming to have read, corrected, and commented upon during the evening what his historians had compiled the day before, Qianlong took an active part in the revision of the *Yupi lidai tongjian jilan*. As the number of his commentarial glosses grew, it was proposed in 1771 to compile them separately. The outcome was the *Yuzhi ping jian chanyao* [Imperially Edited Comments on the Comprehensive Mirror and Elucidations of the Key Issues] with 798 entries, for three-tenths of which Qianlong claimed authorship. Depicting this work as holding 'the jade yardstick for the study of history', the Annotated Imperial Library Catalogue's reviewers were quick to place Qianlong on the Olympus of historical criticism.[65] In fact, the *Yuzhi ping jian chanyao* is one of China's most comprehensive works of historical comment. Without doubt, it contributed to directing historians to engage in ever-more detailed *kaozheng* research and cumbersome compilations that circumvented the risks of an opinionated historiography.

This timidity set the course for Chinese official historiography during the 'long' nineteenth century (1795–1911). It is characterized by the paper-producing routine work of the various historiographical offices and some huge large-scale compilations, which lacked the unifying vision of Qianlong's universal monarchy and, hence, failed to lend new significance to the contemporary history of China's troubled encounter with the rising imperial powers of the West and Japan. Against this backdrop, the great scholar and reformist Liang Qichao would set forth his explosive criticism of Chinese historiography in 1902.[66] This criticism

[64] *Zhongguo xueshu mingzhu tiyao: Lishi juan*, 162–5.
[65] Cf. He, *Ming Qing renwu yu zhushu*, 169–78.
[66] Cf. On-cho Ng and Q. Edward Wang, *Mirroring the Past: The Writing and Use of History in Imperial China* (Honolulu, 2005), 262–3.

would in turn have an enormous influence on the shape of twentieth-century views of Chinese traditional, in particular official, historiography. It is time to reread Liang's essay with fresh eyes, in order to rediscover the richness of Chinese historical writing and to develop a better understanding of the inner dynamics of late imperial official historiography.

TIMELINE/KEY DATES

1206 Chinggis (Ghengis) Khan rises to power

1271 Qubilai Khan proclaims the Yuan dynasty

1368 Zhu Yuanzhang captures Dadu (Beijing) and establishes the Ming dynasty

1399–1402 A civil war ends with Emperor Yongle's usurpation

1405–33 Seven expeditions sent under admiral Zheng He to Southeast Asia, into the Indian Ocean, the Persian Gulf, and to the East African coast

1421 Capital moved from Nanjing to Beijing

1449 Ming defeat in the battle at Tumu; Emperor Yingzong is captured by the victorious Mongols

1508 Spiritual 'enlightenment' of Wang Yangming, who renovates the prevailing Song Confucianism centred on Zhu Xi and the Four Books

1567 Ban on private overseas trade lifted

1578 Altan Khan adopts Lamaism; the Mongols assume protecting power over the Dalai Lama

c.1580–1630 Extensive wall-building results in the Great Wall

1583 The Italian Jesuit Matteo Ricci enters China

1644–5 Demise of the Ming dynasty; the Southern Ming dynasty is established at Nanjing and is soon overturned by the Qing

1664–5 Trial against the Jesuit missionary Johann Adam Schall von Bell

1689 Treaty of Nerchinsk between Qing China and Russia

1750 A revolt in Lhasa leads to a more rigorous Qing protectorate over Tibet

1793 Lord Macartney's Embassy to Beijing and Rehe

1799 Death of Emperor Qianlong; the fabulously corrupt chief minister Heshen is convicted and forced to commit suicide

KEY HISTORICAL SOURCES

[*Da-Ming*] *Yitongzhi* (Beijing, 1461).

Da-Qing huidian (Beijing, 1690, 1733, 1763, 1818, and 1899).

Da-Qing yitongzhi (Beijing, 1743 and 1784).

Huang-Qing zhigong tu (Beijing, 1751–90).

Jiaqing chongxiu yitongzhi (Beijing, 1842).

Ming shilu (rpt. Beijing, 1940).

Mingshi (Beijing, 1739 and 1789).

Mingshi [*gao*] (Beijing, *c.*1710).

[*Qinding*] *Liao Jin Yuan shi guoyu jie* (Beijing, 1785).

[*Qinding*] *Shengchao xunjie zhuchen lu* (Beijing, 1776).

Rehe zhi (Beijing, 1781).

Rixia jiuwen kao (Beijing, 1785).

Shengjing tongzhi (Beijing, 1778).

Siku quanshu zongmu tiyao (Beijing, 1781).

Xiyu tuzhi (Beijing, 1782).

Xu Wenxian tongkao (Beijing, 1767, printed in 1782–4).

Xu Zizhi tongjian (Beijing, 1792).

Yuanshi (Beijing, 1370).

Yuding Zizhi tongjian gangmu sanbian (Beijing, 1775; printed in 1782).

Yupi lidai tongjian jilan (Beijing, 1782, resp. 1794).

Yuzhi ping jian chanyao (Beijing, 1771–*c.*1782).

BIBLIOGRAPHY

Brook, Timothy, *The Chinese State in Ming Society* (London, 2005).

Crossley, Pamela Kyle, *A Translucent Mirror: History and Identity in Qing Imperial Ideology* (Berkeley, 1999).

Franke, Wolfgang, *An Introduction to the Sources of Ming History* (Kuala Lumpur, 1968).

—— 'Historical Writing during the Ming', in Frederick W. Mote and Denis Twitchett (eds.), *The Cambridge History of China*, vol. 7: *The Ming Dynasty, 1368–1644*, Part I (Cambridge, 1988), 726–82.

Göller, Thomas and Mittag, Achim, *Geschichtsdenken in Europa und China: Selbstdeutung und Deutung des Fremden in historischen Kontexten. Ein Essay* (Sankt Augustin, 2008).

Guy, R. Kent, *The Emperor's Four Treasuries: Scholars and the State in the Late Ch'ien-lung Era* (Cambridge, Mass., 1987).

He Guanbiao, *Ming Qing renwu yu zhushu* (Hong Kong, 1996).

Hostetler, Laura, *Qing Colonial Enterprise: Ethnography and Cartography in Early Modern China* (Chicago, 2001).

Huang Wei *et al.*, *Fangzhixue* (Shanghai, 1993).

Ng, On-cho and Wang, Q. Edward, *Mirroring the Past: The Writing and Use of History in Imperial China* (Honolulu, 2005).

Qiao Zhizhong, *Zhongguo guanfang shixue yu sijia shixue* (Beijing, 2008).

Struve, Lynn, *The Ming-Qing Conflict, 1619–1683: A Historiography and Source Guide* (Ann Arbor, 1998).

Will, Pierre-Étienne, *Chinese Local Gazetteers: An Historical and Practical Introduction* (Paris, 1992).

Chapter 2

The Historical Writing of Qing Imperial Expansion

Pamela Kyle Crossley

Historians of China have long recognized a distinction between 'official' (*guan*) and 'public' (*gong*) views of events.[1] In the case of the Qing, records derived from the Ming Empire, the Joseon royal government of Korea, the Chakhar khaghanate, and the earliest Qing state are all 'official' sources, but the views they present do not suggest a coherent official view. Previously, I have introduced, without much elaboration, the metaphor of the 'main sequence'.[2] By the 'main sequence' I mean a narrative emerging from a variety of sources, and over time acquiring sufficient mass to generate the heat and light necessary to dominate all other views. One might in this respect think of stars as born in nebulosity, then either aborting because of insufficient mass or beginning the consumption of internal resources that incorporates them into the main sequence. Different historical narratives and their interpretation emerged from the same chronological field, but those that eventually collapsed into coolness, darkness, and isolation due to insufficient mass I call the 'off sequence' narratives. The most obvious way for a narrative to outshine others is to have the power of the state, and particularly state publishing, behind it. But a main-sequence narrative is unlikely to respect such delimitations as 'private' and 'public'. Its dominance is such that it permeates all dimensions of discourse, informing public and private writing and interpretation equally. This chapter examines the backbone of the Qing main sequence in the narration of its history of conquest.

---

[1] See Harold Kahn, *Monarchy in the Emperor's Eyes* (Cambridge, Mass., 1971). In 'Boundaries of the Public Sphere in Ming and Qing China', *Daedalus*, 127:3 (1998), 167–89, Frederic Wakeman, Jr., discussed these two zones of opinion in relation to a third, the 'private' (*si*) dimension of ostensible self-interest and small-mindedness.

[2] The original inspiration was astronomy, but in adapting the analogy to historiography I have done a bit of violence to the original. I used this metaphor casually in *A Translucent Mirror: History and Identity in Qing Imperial Ideology* (Berkeley, 1999) but wish to expand it here. Astronomers will recognize that my 'star' incorporates the dynamics of a proto-star (as described before the use of the Hubble space telescope), and conflates variations on main-sequence types.

BEFORE THE MAIN SEQUENCE

The Qing Empire, founded in 1636, was preceded by local political orders whose history might be most meaningfully traced to 1587. In that year Nurgaci (often written as Nurhaci or Nurhachi), credited by Qing historians as the founding ruler, established a capital of sorts for himself and promulgated a law code.[3] He used these to govern a mixed population composed mostly of Jurchens but including communities and individuals of Korean, Northeast Asian,[4] Mongol, and Chinese descent. From that time to 1616 (the year Nurgaci declared himself khan and may have announced the name of his state as Jin), the history of this ancestral regime is gleaned primarily from the records of the Ming Empire in China and the Joseon (Yi) kingdom of Korea.[5] Each had regular contact with Nurgaci's organization as both a trading partner and an intermittent military challenge.

From the early seventeenth century, as the Nurgaci state began to evolve, it also began to generate a historiographical infrastructure. This may have awaited the creation of a script, the predecessor of the Manchu script, in 1599, though there is no logical reason why it would need to. There was a phonographic medieval Jurchen script, which Nurgaci's followers appear to have avoided.[6] Chinese and Mongolian were used throughout Northeast Asia for long-distance written communications, and the Nurgaci-era Jurchens had evidently used it in the past. However, literate men in general were in short supply. The creation of a standard syllabic script for the writing of Jurchen expanded the opportunities for learning to write the language, allowed Nurgaci more choices of scribes upon whom he could depend, and created the literary medium through which the earliest history of the state is now filtered.

When annalistic activity began is uncertain, though the pattern of surviving information suggests that it dates only from shortly before the declaration of Nurgaci's khanate in 1616. Records before that time allowed Qing historians to reconstruct a sketch of Nurgaci's campaigns of conquest, but the years between

---

[3] The name occurs only in the genealogical records; it is, however, amply attested via transliteration in contemporary Chinese and Korean records. See Tak-sing Kam, 'The Romanization of Early Manchu Regnal Names', *Studia Orientalia*, 87 (1999), 133–48.

[4] The region called 'the Northeast' in English-language scholarship on modern China (an exact translation of the Chinese term *dongbei* normally used to refer to it) was once called 'Manchuria' in English-language writing on China.

[5] From the Korean side, most important is *Joseon sillok*. There are also important mentions of early Jurchen leaders in *Yongbi eo'cheonga*, which is the court-commissioned saga of the ancestral rise of the Yi royal family of Joseon. See Peter H. Lee, *Songs of Flying Dragons: A Critical Reading* (Cambridge, Mass., 1973). See also ch. 5 by Don Baker in this volume.

[6] It is nevertheless the source of some of our knowledge of Jurchen political origins as they touched embassies to the Ming court. See Gisaburo Kiyose, *A Study of the Jurchen Language and Script: Reconstruction and Decipherment* (Kyoto, 1977).

1582 and 1615 are notable primarily for the contrast between the wealth of action and the paucity of records generated by the Jurchens themselves. Lists of slaves, lands, gifts, dependants and ancestors, and soldiers enrolled in the banners— these were the matters that constituted the early documentary concerns of what would become Nurgaci's state. Writing in Chinese and Mongolian was important to Nurgaci because it allowed him to communicate with the Ming and Joseon when he so desired. But his pool of literate men in these years was small, and their cataloguing duties were heavy. The establishment of a scribal capacity in the state, which also established a civil, literate, bureaucratic identity, allowed Nurgaci simultaneously to refine his control over the resources at his command and to regulate a certain amount of social and economic activity among his subjects. Beginning in 1616 there was a dramatic upswing in the density of documentation for Nurgaci's khanate. One reason is the existence of the khanate itself, and the increasing need to foster offices of documentation.

In the case of the Ming, information about the earliest history of the Qing ancestral regime comes through the redacted annals, the official provincial histories of Liaodong, Jilin, and Heilongjiang, the records of the offices connected with foreign embassies and patent trade, and a handful of important personal memoirs. The Ming records, particularly for the Wanli period (1573–1620), portray the early leaders of what would become the Qing Empire as ambitious seekers of trade patents and political favour. The Jianzhou Jurchens, the group from whom Nurgaci emerged, were recorded by the Ming as federated tribesmen on the Northeastern frontier. They participated in Ming military campaigns (as when repelling the Hideyoshi invasion of Korea from 1592 to 1598), petitioned for permission to sell their dogs, horses, pearls, furs, and agricultural goods in the Ming markets of Liaodong province, and on occasion came to Beijing to pay respects to the Ming, and court and collect their gifts of cash and clothing. Nurgaci himself made such an embassy to the court in 1609, and in Ming eyes this secured his status as a vassal. When he declared war on them in 1618 and seized a portion of Liaodong province in 1621, Ming historians unanimously recorded it as the perfidious act of an unscrupulous and dangerous client.

For the Joseon state in Korea, redacted annals are the primary source on their relations with the Jurchens. They include what is accepted as the text of some personal testaments, such as the official Sin Chung-il, of which the originals have been lost.[7] In the Joseon records, the Jurchen group from which Nurgaci emerged had a distinct history with relation to the dynasty. When the Yi regime

---

[7] Sin's uniquely valuable report has been briefly summarized by Giovanni Stary, 'Die Struktur der Ersten Residenz des Mandschukhans Nurgaci', *Central Asian Journal*, 25 (1981), 103–9. The manuscript was discovered in 1938 by Yi Yinseong, and the next year was reproduced in *Xingjing er dao hezi jiu lao cheg*, a publication of the Manzhouguo daxue (Manchukuo University in Mukden). It was afterwards published under the title *Konjeu gicheong dorok*, in Korea. In 1977 a new, corrected, and partially restored edition by Xu Huanpu was published (in jiantizi). It appears that

was consolidating its territories in the very late fourteenth century, it did so by driving Jurchens north of the Yalu; many fled farther north, while those who fell into Joseon hands swelled the ranks of the agricultural slave class (*nobi*). For their part, Jurchens of the fifteenth and sixteenth centuries made continuous raids into Korean territory to abduct farmers to work the growing Jurchen farming enterprises north of the Yalu; at the same time, leaders of the Jurchens visited the Joseon court to demand trading rights and cash for the cessation of hostilities. When Nurgaci declared war on the Ming in 1618, the Joseon court was outraged, but undertook no serious military action to aid its traditional ally. By 1627 Nurgaci's successor, Hung Taiji, had forced Joseon to accept a client relationship with his khanate, and this was reaffirmed after the creation of the Qing Empire in 1636. After removal of the Qing imperial capital from Mukden to Beijing, embassies of Korean officials, students, and merchants travelled almost continuously over the land routes through the Northeast to Beijing and back again.[8] But the official view—or, the view of officials—in Korea remained as hostile to the Qing as the early Joseon had been to their Jurchen ancestors. They looked forward to an end to barbarian rule in China, and a restoration of the righteous Ming.[9]

A third, though fragmentary, source is from various Mongol records of contact with Nurgaci and his government.[10] The Chakhar khaghanate under Lighdan (r. 1604–34) saw itself as the direct heir of the Mongol imperial legacy of Chinggis and Khubilai. It maintained a capital at Köke khoto (present-day Hohhot in Inner Mongolia) that was by far the largest city north of Beijing. Lighdan ran a complex operation of religious and historical printing there. His determination to suppress the growth of Jurchen power led him to confront Hung Taiji in 1632, resulting in Lighdan's defeat and death in 1634. Hung Taiji proceeded to meld the organization, rituals, aristocracy, and historical voice of the Chakhar khaghanate and the Jurchen khanate into one entity, the Qing Empire, which declared on the lunar new year's day of 1636. Two Mongolian chronicles of the later seventeenth century, *Sira tuyuji* [The Yellow History] of unknown authorship and *Erdeni-yin tobci* [Precious Summary] by Saghang Secen Khongtayiji (Ssanang Setsen Chungtaidji), focus heavily on the Chakhar khanate and on Lighdan personally. The former emphasizes the importance of Lighdan's descent from Chinggis Khaghan, his correct relationship with Buddhist clergy,

the original manuscript was lost long ago, but the text was entered into the *Joseon sillok* (Seonjo reign, 1567–1608).

[8] The travel diaries generated by this phenomenon are the subjects of extensive scholars in Korean and in Chinese. English readers know them primarily through Gari Ledyard, 'Korean Travelers in China over Four Hundred Years, 1488–1887', *Occasional Papers on Korea*, 2 (1974), 1–42.

[9] See also ch. 5 by Don Baker in this volume.

[10] See also Nicola di Cosmo and Dalizhabu Bao, *Manchu–Mongol Relations on the Eve of the Qing Conquest: A Documentary History* (Leiden, 2003).

and the role of the Mongol aristocracy in preserving Mongolia's integrity and independence before the onslaught by Hung Taiji. The latter work portrayed Lighdan as fragmenting the solidarity of Mongolia, thus creating the opportunity for Hung Taiji's victories. Saghang Secen nevertheless was no Qing apologist, and his narrative clearly espoused the right of Chinggisid descendants to rule Mongolia independently—a right which, the narrative suggests, may have been permanently encroached upon by the Qing.[11]

THE EMPIRE GENERATES THE MAIN SEQUENCE

Qing history, as later written, narrates the Nurgaci period and the invasion of Liaodong as the beginning of the 'great enterprise' (called the 'rise of the dragon' in the court narratives). There are certainly elements of Nurgaci's state building that adumbrate distinctive themes in Qing institutional and political history. But the conceit also requires that the conquest of Liaodong be seen as the initiation of the conquest of China, the view later established in the imperial narrative through the publishing enterprises of the Qianlong court. The actual scope and impetus of Nurgaci's campaigns are suggested better by the off-sequence materials still found in the records of Ming, Joseon, and early Manchu materials that for some reason were not swept up in later revision. Both Ming annals collated in Beijing and surviving provincial market records for the late sixteenth century clearly portray Nurgaci and his direct ancestors as growing wealthy on the trade in Ming border markets. They were eager to gain and retain mono-polies on the most lucrative goods, and to that end entered into complex relationships with Ming provincial authorities in order to undermine the com-mercial prominence of other local Jurchen lineages and federations. Even the incident that led to the death of his father and grandfather in 1582 (the two were killed under murky circumstances while collaborating in an attack by Ming authorities on a rival Jurchen leader) did not, in fact, prevent Nurgaci from continuing to curry favour with the Ming government, and he attended court to perform the rituals of a loyal subordinate in 1609. Only in 1618, after his declaration of a state and experiencing the sting of Ming border officials who intended seriously to undermine his wealth and influence, did Nurgaci declare war; still, his avowed goals were to achieve recompense for wrongs done to him by the Ming, not to wrest from them control of either Liaodong or of China as a whole. Nurgaci's conquest of Liaodong is most aptly seen as a plan to seize the towns where he did his trade, and overthrow the Ming monitoring and taxing of those stations. There is evidence that while he was fierce in his attack on those commercial regions at his borders, he had no very passionate determination to

[11] Shagdaryn Bira, *Mongolian Historical Writing from 1200 to 1700*, trans. John R. Krueger, 2nd edn (Bellingham, Wash., 2002), esp. 184–214.

conquer western Liaodong. The taking of Shenyang (in Manchu, Mukden) in 1621, it appears, was the culmination of Nurgaci's career of conquest, and was seen as such by him; further expansion was undertaken to secure his base against Ming invasion, and he died in 1626 attempting to secure his western perimeter. Ming failures in the management and defence of Liaodong made it a vacuum into which a local magnate such as Nurgaci could advance. But there is no historical reason to see this as the beginning of empire.

In all those respects, Nurgaci's career is a very striking contrast to that of his son and successor, Hung Taiji.[12] For ten years Hung Taiji ruled as khan of the Jin state. And then, in 1636, he changed everything—consciously, systematically, and with a cosmically pretentious rhetoric that suggested a change in the fabric of reality. For the first ten years after his father's death, Hung Taiji ruled as a khan. As such he was bound by the traditions of collegial rule that forced him to acknowledge the patrimonial rights of his brothers and a cousin—all called by the traditional rank of *beile*—that made them co-commanders of the military, granted them the slave-holding rights peculiar to the ruling class of the khanate, and made them all eligible to succeed him as khan (*han*). Hung Taiji set about undermining or eliminating the power of the princes, and by 1631 he had succeeded in displacing or silencing all his rivals.

The key to imperial status, however, lay in defeat of the Chakhar khanate on Hung Taiji's Northwest, and destruction of its ruler, Lighdan Khaghan. Lighdan was the direct descendant and heir of Chinggis Khaghan and Khubilai Khaghan. The lineage were not merely khans, but khaghans—khans of khans, supreme rulers, emperors. Lighdan had a powerful and sophisticated government and military. He intimidated not only the Ming, but the Mongols to his east, who wished to remain free of his control (and had appealed to Nurgaci for alliance and leverage), and the Oyirods to his west. Beginning *c*.1630 Hung Taiji turned all his energies towards the destruction of Lighdan. By 1634 he had captured Lighdan's capital, absorbed all his military forces, incorporated the Chakhar princes as new members of his Jin aristocracy, and forced Lighdan's survivors to transport all the paraphernalia of the Mahākāla cult—including a massive gold statue of the Mahākāla emanation—from Kökö khoto to Mukden. This was the literal threshold of Hung Taiji's ascendance to emperorship. His new Qing Empire, when announced in 1636, was an articulation of the Jin khanate (which

---

[12] Fragmentary Manchu annals for the period before 1616 indicate that he was normally referred to as 'Fourth Prince' (*Duici beile*), but Joseon records suggest that as early as 1619 he was referred to as Hung Taiji. Kam Taksing points out that the proper spelling should be Hong Taiji or Xong Tayiji. I choose to continue my use of 'Hung Taiji' for the simple reason that 'Hong Taiji' is indistinguishable from the Chinese romanization for the characters involved; 'Hung Taiji', while technically incorrect, is clearly Manchu. See also Kam, 'The Romanization of Early Manchu Regnal Names', esp. 90. For many decades scholarship in Western languages referred to Hung Taiji as 'Abahai', based on Erich Hauer's translation of the *Kaiguo fanglve* (see below), which was mistakenly derived. See Giovanni Stary, 'The Manchu Emperor "Abahai": Analysis of an Historiographical Mistake', *Central Asiatic Journal*, 28:3–4 (1984), 296–9.

in many forms persisted) and the Chakhar khaghanate (which in virtually all its forms persisted). Finally, in 1636, Hung Taiji was enthroned as 'emperor' (*huangdi, hūwangdi*), and announced the creation of a new empire, the Qing ('pure'). Unlike his father, Hung Taiji delighted in informing Ming officials (whom he hoped to recruit) that he intended to fight and defeat the Ming for control of the Northeast and part of Mongolia. Beyond that he left his ambitions less explicit (though they tended to be expressed in cosmic terms and to invoke the 'mind of Heaven'—*tianxin, abka i mujilen*); in fact he spent more time leading campaigns against tribal peoples and a few Russian interlopers in the Amur River region than in fighting on the western front that faced China. He died in 1643, at the age of fifty-two, of natural causes. Less than a year later, Qing forces entered Beijing.

Hung Taiji's reign marks the establishment of a main sequence in Qing historical narrative. One of the first priorities of the new empire was the authoring of an interpretation that both legitimated Hung Taiji's emperorship and justified Qing wars against Chakhar and Ming. The 'Documentary Offices' (*wenguan*), initiated in 1629 as the khan's bureau, had by 1636 (the year the empire was created) become the 'Three Imperial Offices' (*sanyuan*). By 1635 the production of documentation in Chinese, Jurchen (soon to be 'Manchu'), and Mongolian had become a routine function of this bureaucracy. The first of the 'Three Imperial Offices' as they were composed in 1636 was the Imperial Office of History (*guo shi guan*), an organ fundamental to the articulation of imperial legitimacy and prerogatives in the Jurchen polity. It was this office that assumed responsibility for the writing of the annals for the Nurgaci years. An illustrated version of the Nurgaci annals in both Chinese characters and in Manchu script was completed in 1635, and included illustrations of the mounted, mustachioed, hook-nosed Nurgaci leading his troops into battle at various celebrated encounters. The next year the first formal narrative, in the Chinese style, of the Nurgaci reign was completed: *Taizu Wuhuangdi shilu* [Annals of the Martial Emperor of the Qing] was an indispensable source for the eighteenth-century completion of a grand story arc of Qing origins and Qing conquests.

The Qing conquest of China is usually dated to 1644, giving a rather neat appearance to a process that was actually long and uncertain. The Ming Empire was destroyed in 1644 by the convergence of two enormous rural uprisings in Central and in North China. In April 1644 the leader of one of the rebellions entered Beijing and declared himself emperor of a new dynasty after the Ming emperor hanged himself. In the ensuing months, Ming restorationists in various parts of South China attempted to coordinate military resources for recapture of the capital, and as part of the plan they fatally invited the Qing to send troops to Beijing. The Qing Empire's 'Eight Banner' (*Baqi, Jakūn gūsa*) forces quickly drove the rebel dynasts out of Beijing, and instead of restoring the Ming proceeded to establish their own young emperor on the throne. Consolidating a hold over North China did not take the Qing long, but as the conquest moved towards the Yangtze River and attempted to push into South China, resistance became heavy. The court (under the domination of regents because Hung Taiji's son Fulin, the Shunzhi emperor, was still in his early teens) decided to dispatch three Northeastern Chinese generals to pacify the region by establishing occupation governments at the provincial level. In exchange, these new military governors were given extraordinary discretion in their methods, including the right to retain their own tax revenues. The Shunzhi emperor died young, and his own son Xuanye was only seven years old when he became the Kangxi emperor in 1661. In 1669 the emperor attained personal rule, and within a few years had accused the occupation governors of the South of having dynastic ambitions. One of the governors rose in rebellion, initiating a war of nearly ten years in length, which resulted not only in destruction of Ming pretenders (and their courts) in Southern China and the establishment of local government in the south controlled from Beijing, but also the crushing of a pirate dynasty on Taiwan and the incorporation of Taiwan into an empire based in China for the first time in history. Only after this 'Rebellion of the Three Feudatories' (*Sanfan zhi luan*) concluded in 1683, and the South was secure, was the empire on a footing to expand into territories that the Ming had never ruled.

The Rebellion of the Three Feudatories provided the inspiration for an official history that established a distinct genre of Qing historical presentation. In 1682 the emperor commanded that his edicts and reports both from bureaucrats and from generals relating to the campaigns be collated, in chronological order, and printed with a long explanatory introduction. This work, *Pingding sanni fanglve*[13] [Strategic Narrative of the Pacification of the Three Traitors], was completed in 1686. The genre of 'strategic narrative' (*fanglve, bodogon-i bithe*) was the first compilation of documents about a campaign, organized and edited by the generals who ran the campaign, all under court commission. The few authors who have given attention to the emergence of this genre have suggested that *fanglve* is, in the words of Peter Perdue, 'officially commissioned military campaign history'.[14] Certainly, most of the *fanglve* we have relate to military topics, but not all. The great official Jin Fu, for instance, was honoured to have the compendium of documents relating to waterworks he presented to the Yongzheng court in 1727 officially re-titled as *Zhihe fanglve* [Strategic Narrative on Water Control],[15] and we have no reason to believe this was unique.

---

[13] In modern Chinese romanization, the umlaut-u sound is transliterated 'v' in order to distinguish it from the normal u-sound without the use of diacriticals.

[14] Peter C. Perdue, 'The Qing Empire in Eurasian Time and Space: Lessons from the Galdan Campaigns', in Lynn A. Struve (ed.), *The Qing Formation in World-Historical Time* (Cambridge, Mass., 2004), 75. See also Beatrice S. Bartlett, *Monarchs and Ministers: The Grand Council in Mid-Ch'ing China, 1723–1820* (Berkeley, 1991).

[15] J. C. Yang, 'Chin Fu', in Arthur W. Hummel (ed.), *Eminent Chinese of the Ch'ing Period* (Washington, 1943), 163. Neither *fanglve* nor *bodogon* denote anything military; both terms refer to a plan or a strategy—a long-term coordinated action.

Fanglve are probably best understood as compendia of selected documents on topics of great strategic importance to the Qing court—and military campaigns were clearly of the highest importance. From the campaigns against the Three Feudatories onwards, the prosecution of a campaign proceeded apace with the generation and collation of documents describing the campaign; leading generals in the campaign were expected to appear among the editors commissioned to complete the *fanglve*. In 1749 the Qing created a new Office of Military Documentation (*fanglve guan, bodogon-i bithe kuren*), named for the genre (not the other way around). The genre was the primary venue through which the imperial court shaped its narrative of conquest, and, as Perdue suggests, the impact of the collective military narratives of the *fanglve* still control our perception of Qing imperial expansion. This is evident in the Kangxi choices of military *fanglve* topics: the Three Feudatories and Oyirods were huge strategic problems solved through vigorous military action, resulting in the annihilation of the enemy. They were the subject of *fanglve*. But Tibet, though put under military occupation in the Kangxi years, was never the subject of a *fanglve*. Tibet was a matter of complex significance to the Qing, quite apart from the strategic importance of the Tibetan plateau. From the historical point of view of the Qing court, it was not an enemy, not an object of a military campaign, and not under Qing military occupation.

The Kangxi emperor was even more deliberate in his creation of *Pingding shuomo fanglve* [Strategic Narrative of the Pacification of the Oyirod]. Soon after the conclusion of the campaign against the Three Feudatories, the Kangxi emperor had turned his eyes towards Mongolia. The region had been a constant worry to the Ming, but it was a more complex problem to the Qing. Mongol headmen had been the first to grant Nurgaci his status as khan, and Mongolia was the venue through which the Qing mediated much of the spiritual and genealogical sources of their legitimacy. The Qing relied upon leaders of at least some of the Mongol population, but feared military or commercial interference from the rest. In addition, the Mongols appeared always vulnerable to manipulation by the Russian Empire, which was already challenging the Qing for control of parts of the Northeast. The emperor decided to present the Khalkha—the most numerous and most centrally located of the Mongol groups—a virtual ultimatum to accept his rule. After a great deal of debate the Khalkha were ready to agree, but Galdan—leader of the Oyirod, a distinct people of partly Mongol origin to the west of Khalkha—objected, insisting that the Khalkha should submit to him instead. Having concluded a treaty with Russia in 1689, the Kangxi emperor implied his sovereignty in Mongolia by attempting to intervene on behalf of the Khalkha. The result was that between 1690 and 1697 the Qing and the Oyirod were at war. In the latter stages of the conflict the emperor himself led his troops in pursuit of Galdan, who was finally abandoned (and perhaps poisoned) by his own followers. *Pingding shuomo fanglve* was commissioned in 1699 to celebrate the victory, and completed in 1708.[16] Like the earlier *fanglve*, it was titled in Chinese, and its front matter and reflective essays were written in Chinese, but it contained a great deal of Manchu documentation, including personal letters written by the emperor to his son Incheng (Yinreng), who led the government in Beijing while his father was in the field.

Another facet of the Kangxi emperor's literary production constituted a cornerstone of the main sequence. In 1677 the Kangxi emperor commissioned Umuna to lead an expedition to Mount Changbai (*Changbaishan*, [*Golmin*] *Šanggiyan-alin*) near the border between the Northeast and Korea. The young emperor explained to Umuna that no one knew the 'exact spot' of the origin of the Qing imperial lineage; Umuna's mission was to find it, and to sacrifice to its gods. The mission was difficult, not least because Umuna was being sent into a literal wasteland (by its name, a place of perpetual winter) of thousands of square miles of unexplored territory. But he understood the unvoiced purpose of the mission as well: to establish a Qing familiarity with the region and its geographical features that would be useful in delimiting boundaries with Korea (to the south of Mount Changbai) and Russia (to its east). After some misadventures Umuna and his mission miraculously achieved the top of Mount Changbai, and accurately described its crater lake and the five prominences around it. These and other descriptions were combined in the work, *Feng Changbaishan* [Finding Mount Changbai], first presented to the court later in the year.[17]

The Kangxi emperor was sensitive to the need to parallel his military incursions into Mongolia with a cultural campaign. In addition to attempting to communicate and coordinate with the Dalai Lamas (there was a transition during the Galdan War), the Kangxi emperor continued at Beijing the same publishing programmes of religious liturgies that Lighdan had initiated in the days of the Chakhar khaghanate; the intended effect was to represent himself as both a patron of Tibetan Buddhism and a *čakravartin*, incarnating the legacy of Buddhist monarchs back to King Ašoka. Though the Kangxi period witnessed a rich history of resistance to or rebellion against the Qing by Mongol aristocrats (including Burni, a grandson of both Hung Taiji and Lighdan), by the time of the war against Galdan the emperor had made himself credible as a ruler of the Khalkha Mongols (in addition to the Mongols who had capitulated earlier). In the period of the Kangxi wars in Mongolia, Mongolian historical

---

[16] The work was printed again soon after with *qinzheng* added to the title (in recognition of the emperor's own command in the field), and with a separate Manchu version (*Beye wargi amargi babe necihiyeme toktobuha bodogon-i bithe*) appended. For further comment, including an analysis of the content and the impact of this work, see Perdue, 'The Qing Empire in Eurasian Time and Space: Lessons from the Galdan Campaigns', in Lynn A. Struve (ed.), *The Qing Formation in World-Historical Time* (Cambridge, Mass., 2004).

[17] On the relationship between Feng Changbaishan and the [*Qinding*] *Shengjing fu*/Han-i araha Mukden i fujurun bithe (see below) see Crossley, *A Translucent Mirror*, 297–8; and Mark C. Elliot, 'The Limits of Tartary: Manchuria in Imperial and National Geographies', *The Journal of Asian Studies*, 59:3 (2000), 603–46; for details of the Umuna mission see ibid., 612–13.

writing—which had become more secular and slightly topical in the earlier seventeenth century—turned back to the themes of Chinggis biography, Chinggisid genealogy, and clerical history. The Qing invasion and the war against Galdan are omitted from nearly every known historical narrative produced in Mongolian in the later seventeenth and eighteenth centuries, except for the briefest references.[18] Historians who have searched for extended historical comment from Mongols in the eighteenth century have usually quoted Lomi, a Chinggisid and high-ranking officer in the Mongol Eight Banners, whose history of the Chinggisid (Borjigid) lineage, written between 1732 and 1735, very strongly suggested that Chinggisid legitimacy had passed to the Qing, and that hopes for the unity and peace of Mongolia would henceforth reside with the Qing emperors. Lomi's work, for this reason, lies on the main sequence, even though it is written by a Mongol in Mongolian.[19]

THE ZENITH OF THE MAIN SEQUENCE

The reign of the Qianlong emperor (r. 1736–96) was marked by the comprehensive, energetic pursuit of a documentary legacy for the Qing Empire that would integrate origins, identity, righteous conquest, and the fate of civilizations into a coherent imperial narrative. The undertaking relied heavily upon development of the *fanglve* genre, complemented by administrative histories, historical compendia, and lyric meditations through the media of poetry, architecture, landscaping, curating, and ritual performance. The administrative histories were compiled by the same method as the *fanglve*: a central office coordinated the process (even if the office had to be created for this purpose), gathered relevant records from other imperial offices if necessary, and published them together with genealogical charts, a series of forewords documenting the imperial commissioning of the work, a table of contents, and the introduction written by the editors themselves. From the Yongzheng period (when the *Baqi Tongzhi* [*chuji*]/*Jakūn gūsai tong jy sucungga weilehe bithe* [General History of the Eight Banners] (1739) was commissioned in 1727), such compilations were normally produced both in Manchu and in Chinese.

The major conquest campaigns of the Qianlong period were the subject of numerous *fanglve* commissioned very soon after the military engagements were completed. In 1745 the Qianlong emperor decided to press Qing conquests in Mongolia westward to destroy the remaining Oyirods, who now called themselves and their regime by the name 'Dzungar'. The result was not only eradication of the Dzungar leaders and the greater part of the Dzungar population, but

---

[18] Bira, *Mongolian Historical Writing*, 169–70.
[19] On Lomi contemporaries with similar views see Joseph F. Fletcher, Jr., 'A Source of the Erdeni-yin Erike', *Harvard Journal of Asiatic Studies*, 24 (1962–3), 229–33.

the Qing invasion of Eastern Turkestan. The Dzungar Empire had ruled Eastern Turkestan in Galdan's time, and the Qing plan was to usurp all the Dzungar lands. This was accomplished in 1755, after which Muslim Eastern Turkestan was often called by the Qing court the 'new frontier' (*xinjiang, ice jecen*), though in state documents it was normal to refer to the region as 'the Northwest'.[20] In retrospect this can be seen as the last phase of Qing conquest, and it is possible that the court never had any intention of extending farther than the outer reaches of Dzungaria, the limits of its strategic concerns. The court documented this war in a large *fanglve, Pingding Zhungar fanglve/Jungar-i babe necihehiyeme toktobuha bodogon-i bithe* [Strategic Narrative of the Pacification of the Dzungars], which was commissioned immediately after the war ceased, in 1755, and published for the first time in 1770. The publication was, in fact, a multimedia event, since it was accompanied by the completion of both silk paintings and copper engravings of triumphant battle scenes from the campaign, for display in a principal hall in the Forbidden City.[21] The extravaganza inspired a parallel genre of private war narratives, sometimes by officials with a connection of some degree to the events. Most of the *fanglve* inspired illustrated editions (*zhantu*) that were privately printed and marketed.

The Qianlong period marked a profound transition for the empire, from expansion to stability. This did not mean, however, that *fanglve* as a genre of imperial compendia withered. Indeed, the number of *fanglve* produced after 1755 outnumbered those produced before that date. But subsequent *fanglve* were inspired by internal conquests, particularly against rebel kingdoms. The Tibetan-related rebels of Jinchuan in Sichuan province were a recurrent problem of the Qianlong period, and imperial forces were frequently mustered to suppress uprisings in the region. Optimistically, the court commissioned the *fanglve* of their suppression in 1743; but troubles recurred in the area before the work was completed and published in 1780,[22] and continuing warfare at Jinchuan necessitated a new edition of the work in 1800 (after the Qianlong emperor's death). From the beginning of the nineteenth century, the empire was troubled by increasingly widespread, organized, and recurrent disorders, culminating in the Taiping War of 1850–64 and the coinciding war against the Nian rebels in

---

[20] The term 'Northwest' is being used here, as with 'Northeast', as both a reflection of current practices in English-language scholarship on modern China and as an exact translation of the normal Qing terms (*xibei, wargi amargi*). The value of this is that in its Qing imperial context the term encompassed territories both inherited from the Ming as Northwest China (western Shaanxi and Gansu provinces) and newly acquired territories such as Eastern Turkestan (Xinjiang).

[21] The Jesuits Castiglione, Attiret, Sichelbarth, and Sallusti were responsible for most of the illustrations; for details of their involvement and the fate of the copper plates see Lothar Ledderose, 'Chinese Influence on European Art, Sixteenth to Eighteenth Centuries', in Thomas H. C. Lee (ed.), *China and Europe: Images and Influences in Sixteenth to Eighteenth Centuries* (Hong Kong, 1991), 226–7.

[22] *Yuzhi Pingding liang Jinchuan fanglve/Zanla cucin-i babe necihiyeme toktobuha bodogon-i bithe* (Beijing, 1780).

Northern China, not concluded until 1868. The largest and most threatening of them were commemorated in *fanglve*: the White Lotus rebellion (1796–1804) in *Jiaoping sansheng xie fei fanglve* [Annihilation of the Heretical Bandits in Three Provinces] (1810); the capture and execution of the Muslim rebel Jehangir in 1828 in *Pingding Huijiang jiaoqin niyi fanglve* [Strategic Narrative of the Pacification of the Frontier Muslims and the Punishment of the Traitor] (completed 1830; published in 1833); victory over the Taipings in *Jiaoping Yuefei fanglve* [Strategic Narrative of the Annihilation of the Bandits of Guangdong Province] (1872); the Nian in *Jiaoping Nianfei fanglve* [Strategic Narrative of the Annihilation of the Nian Bandits] (1872); the Panthay sultanate in Yunnan province, active from 1856 to 1873, in *Pingding Yunnan Hui fei fanglve* [Strategic Narrative of the Pacification of the Muslim Bandits of Yunnan] (1896); and the defeat of Yakub Beg, who had tried to establish an independent state of Kashgar in the 1870s, as well as loosely connected Muslim uprisings in the Northwest in *Pingding Shaan Gan Xinjiang Huifei fanglve* [Strategic Narrative of the Pacification of Muslim Bandits in Shaanxi, Gansu, and Xinjiang] (1896).

The Qianlong court was not satisfied with shaping the narrative of its contemporary events. It was during this era that the empire undertook the most comprehensive rewriting and reshaping of the entire arc of its origins, its legitimacy, and its conquests. This began with a complete revision and repackaging of the annals of the Nurgaci era, now re-titled *Manzhou shilu* [Manchu Annals], printed in 1740 and as a special illustrated edition in 1781.[23] Grander in concept and in execution was *Kaiguo fanglve (Huang Qing kaiguo fanglve/Han-i araha fukjin doro neihe bodogon-bithe)* [(Imperially Commissioned) Strategic Narrative of the Founding of the Nation], commissioned in 1774 and first published in 1786. In this work, the emergence of the Qing imperial lineage, the rise of Nurgaci, and the early campaigns against the Ming are narrated. The treatment features a remarkable alteration of the facts as they appear in the off-sequence materials. In the Qianlong narrative, the Manchus originated at Mount Changbai; in fact, it is clear from Ming and Joseon records that while the early leaders of the Jurchen federations (the ancestors of the Qing imperial lineage) had resided for a time north of the Yalu River, in Jilin province, by the time of Nurgaci's grandfather they had moved east and lived on the boundary of the Ming province of Liaodong.[24] The *fanglve* of the founding as recast by Qianlong-era scribes traces Qing imperial ancestry back to a supernaturally endowed hero (appropriated from the folk tales of the tribal peoples of the Mount Changbai region, many of whom had been Qing subjects since the time of Hung Taiji) who was

---

[23] After the Hung Taiji era revisions (see above), these chronicles were revised again for the Kangxi printing, *Qing Taizu gao huangdi shilu* of 1686. In the Qianlong period, they were reprinted in 1740 and in 1781 as *Manzhou shilu tu* and *Taizu shilu tu* respectively. The 1636 edition was reproduced under the auspices of the Japanese-sponsored Manchukuo publications office in 1932.

[24] Details of eighteenth-century impositions upon historical sources from the previous century are extensively examined in Crossley, *A Translucent Mirror*.

more or less drafted by the early Jurchens to lead them after an internal power dispute. Both the illustrated *Manzhou shilu* and the *Kaiguo fanglve* include narratives and illustrations of Nurgaci's campaigns against Ming that make him the enduring personal image of the righteous pursuit of power against a corrupt, decaying, and arrogant empire. To reinforce the message of these historical works, the Qianlong court supplied a rich lyrical complement, most outstanding [*Qinding*] *Shengjing fu/Han-i araha Mukden i fujurun bithe* [Ode to Mukden], which drew heavily upon the details of the report provided by the Kangxi emperor's expedition to Mount Changbai.[25]

This general understanding of the motives and history of Qing conquest pervaded not only Qianlong revisions in the annalistic and *fanglve* genres but newly commissioned works on Manchu and Mongol origins,[26] detailed descriptions of shamanic ritual, and a critical study of early Chinese collaborators with the Qing that cast doubt on the motives of those who abandoned the Ming in order to serve the Qing conquerors.[27] These new works were published and distributed in the context of an ongoing literary inquisition, which resulted not only in a purge of undesirable writing (primarily works that appeared critical of the Manchus, no matter how indirectly) but also in the elevation of works the Qing saw as enhancing their own cultural depth and political standing. These included the newly revised histories of the Liao, Jin, and Yuan empires, from whom the Qianlong emperor felt the Qing derived much of their civilized status independent of any connections with China. In sum, the works reinforced a central conceit: that Manchu state and society were the culmination of millennia of political and cultural development in the Northeast, that the lineages and spiritual practices of the Manchus were the connection to this independent heritage and political legitimacy, and that this legitimacy was universally translatable to Chinese, Mongolian, and Tibetan as well as Northeastern civilizations. In total these works present a self-referential and—in an ideological sense— coherent imperial narrative, not very surprising since in their present form they were issued by, or directly derived from, works issued by the Imperial Office of History (see above).

---

[25] On [*Qinding*] *Shengjing fu/Han-i araha Mukden i fujurun bithe* see Crossley, *A Translucent Mirror*, 268–9, 283; and Elliott, 'The Limits of Tartary', 614–17.

[26] *Manzhou yuanliu kao* was completed in 1783. For a detailed description of the contents see Pamela Kyle Crossley, '*Manzhou yuanliu kao* and Formalization of the Manchu Heritage', *Journal of Asian Studies*, 46:4 (1987), 761–90.

[27] *Erchen zhuan* was published without preface, and most of the document's intentions must be inferred from its evolution and the context of other publication programmes proceeding concurrently, all of which come under the larger umbrella of the Four Treasures (*siku quanshu*) projects. For further discussion see Pamela Kyle Crossley, 'The Qianlong Retrospect on the Chinese-martial (hanjun) Banners', *Late Imperial China*, 10:1 (1989), 63–107. For general background on the Four Treasures see R. Kent Guy, *The Emperor's Four Treasures: Scholars and the State in the Late Ch'ien-lung Era* (Cambridge, 1987).

THE MAIN SEQUENCE IMPLODES

A coda to the main sequence (to mix metaphors) is provided by consideration of the story of the *Pingding Luocha fanglve* [Strategic Narrative of the Pacification of Russia]. Its name suggests its relationship to the model of the *fanglve*, but it began as a private work. In 1860 the scholar He Qiutao was granted an imperial audience, at which he presented a huge masterwork entitled *Shuofang beisheng* [Documents on the North]. The story of the 'pacification' of Russia was contained within it. The Xianfeng emperor was delighted with He's offering. The empire was still deep in the throes of the Taiping civil war, and Britain and France were on their way to invade China. Still, the history of Qing rivalry with the Russian Empire remained a bright spot. Not only had the Qing fought Russia to a standstill in the seventeenth century, leading to two major treaties that defined both the border between them and its management, but Qing banner forces had consistently denied Russia's wish to control the lower Amur River, and the Pacific coast to its east. A narrative of the 'pacification' of Russia certainly seemed a just companion to the earlier imperial works on the conquest of Mongolia and Eastern Turkestan. The court awarded the work the status of *fanglve* and ordered it published as a royal commission. Unfortunately shortly afterward the British and French troops arrived in Beijing, and among the many casualties of their looting and burning was the *Pingding Luocha fanglve*, which was burned when the palace was sacked. An acquaintance of He's had a copy of the work and arranged to have it copied. But before it could be accomplished, his own house was burned and the copy lost.[28] For good measure, the Russians threatened to join Britain and France in the military assault, and wrested from the Qing a treaty that finally, after two hundred years of struggle, awarded Russia the lands east of the Amur, creating the Maritime Province (Primorkii Krai). Almost twenty years later He's son delivered to the Qing court a manuscript that he claimed was a copy of a copy of a copy of the original work. But the provenance was never proved, and the *Pingding Luocha fanglve* remained the unachievable end of the main sequence. In the death of the genre as in its birth, the fate of the *fanglve* and the campaign it was intended to describe were inextricably intertwined.

TIMELINE/KEY DATES

1587   Nurgaci establishes capital of multilingual regime
1599   Adaptation of the Mongolian script to Manchu

---

[28] Tu Lien-che, 'Ho Ch'iu-t'ao', in Hummel (ed.), *Eminent Chinese of the Ch'ing Period*, 283.

1616 Nurgaci establishes khanate (Jin)
1627 Hung Taiji succeeds to khanate, moves towards monarchical rule
1634–6 defeat of Lighdan Khaghan, declaration of Qing Empire
1644 Qing capture of Beijing
1673–83 War of the Three Feudatories, conquest of Taiwan
1686–97 Kangxi campaigns in and conquest of central Mongolia
1718–20 Qing war against Dzungars in Tibet and military occupation of Lhasa
1747 First of intermittent Jinchuan wars
1755 Defeat and annihilation of the Dzungars, military occupation of East Turkestan (*xinjiang, ice jecen*)
1771 Cessation of Jinchuan wars
1796–1804 White Lotus Rebellion
1828 Capture and execution of Jehangir
1850–64 Taiping War
1865–8 Nian Rebellion
1856–73 Panthay Rebellion
1865–77 Yakub Beg secession

KEY HISTORICAL SOURCES

Baqi manzhou shizu tongpu (Beijing, 1745).
Baqi Tongzhi [chuji]/Jakōn gōsai tong jy sucungga weilehe bithe (Beijing, 1739).
Huang Qing kaiguo fanglve/Han-i araha fukjin doro neihe bodogon-bithe (Beijing, 1786).
Jakōn gōsai manjusai mukōn hala be uheri ejehe bithe (Beijing, 1745).
Jiaoping Nianfei fanglve (Beijing, 1872).
Jiaoping sansheng xie fei fanglve (Beijing, 1810).
Jiaoping Yuefei fanglve (Beijing, 1872).
Konjeu gicheong dorok (Seoul, 1597).
Manzhou jishen jitian dianli/Manjusai wecere metere kooli bithe (Beijing, 1776).
Pingding Huijiang jiaoqin niyi fanglve (Beijing, 1830).
Pingding sanni fanglve (Beijing, 1686).
Pingding Shaan Gan Xinjiang Huifei fanglve (Beijing, 1896).
Pingding Yunnan Hui fei fanglve (Beijing, 1896).
Pingding Zhungar fanglve/Jungar-i babe necihehiyeme toktobuha bodogon-i bithe (Beijing, 1770).
[Qinding] Baqi tongzhi (Beijing, 1799).
[Qinding] Manzhou yuanliu kao (Beijing, 1783).
[Qinding] Shengjing fu/Han-i araha Mukden i fujurun bithe (Beijing, 1743).
[Qinzheng] Pingding shuomo fanglve (Beijing, 1708).
Yuzhi Pingding liang Jinchuan fanglve/Zanla cucin-i babe necihiyeme toktobuha bodogon-i bithe (Beijing, 1780).

BIBLIOGRAPHY

Bartlett, Beatrice S., 'Books of Revelations: The Importance of the Manchu Language Archival Record Books for Research on Ch'ing History', *Late Imperial China*, 6:2 (1985), 25–33.

——*Monarchs and Ministers: The Grand Council in Mid-Ch'ing China, 1723–1820* (Berkeley, 1991).

Bira, Shagdaryn, *Mongolian Historical Writing from 1200 to 1700*, trans. John R. Krueger, 2nd edn (Bellingham, Wash., 2002).

Cimedorji, Jaga and Weiers, Michael, *Indices zum Daicing gurun-i fukjin doro neihe bodogon-i bithe and zum Huang Qing kaiguo fanglue* (Berlin, 2000).

Crossley, Pamela Kyle, '*Manzhou yuanliu kao* and Formalization of the Manchu Heritage', *Journal of Asian Studies*, 46:4 (1987), 761–90.

——'The Qianlong Retrospect on the Chinese-martial (hanjun) Banners', *Late Imperial China*, 10:1 (1989), 63–107.

——*A Translucent Mirror: History and Identity in Qing Imperial Ideology* (Berkeley, 1999).

—— and Rawski, Evelyn Sakakida, 'A Profile of the Manchu Language in Ch'ing History', *Harvard Journal of Asiatic Studies*, 53:1 (1993), 63–102.

Elliott, Mark C., 'The Limits of Tartary: Manchuria in Imperial and National Geographies', *The Journal of Asian Studies*, 59:3 (2000), 603–46.

——'The Manchu-Language Archives of the Qing Dynasty and the Origins of the Palace Memorial System', *Late Imperial China*, 22:1 (2001), 1–70.

——*The Manchu Way: The Eight Banners and Ethnic Identity in Late Imperial China* (Stanford, 2001).

Fletcher, Jr., Joseph F., 'A Source of the Erdeni-yin Erike', *Harvard Journal of Asiatic Studies*, 24 (1962–3), 229–33.

——'Manchu Sources', in Donald Leslie *et al.* (eds.), *Essays on the Sources for Chinese History* (Canberra, 1973), 141–6.

Kam, Tak-sing, 'The Romanization of Early Manchu Regnal Names', *Studia Orientalia*, 87 (1999), 133–48.

Puyraimond, Jenne-Marie, *Catalogue du fonds manchou* (Paris, 1979).

Stary, Giovanni, 'The Manchu Emperor "Abahai": Analysis of an Historiographic Mistake', *Central Asiatic Journal*, 28:3-4 (1984), 296–9; orig. pub. in *Cina*, 18 (1982), 157–62.

Tieliang *et al.*, [*Qinding*] *Baqi tongzhi* 1977 (Taibei repr., 1966).

Wang, Chen-main, 'Historical Revisionism in Ch'ing Times: The Case of Hung Ch'eng-ch'ou (1593–1665)', *Bulletin of the Chinese Historical Association*, 17 (1985), 1–27.

Wilkinson, Endymion Porter, *The History of Imperial China: A Research Guide* (Cambridge, Mass., 1973).

Yang Lien-sheng, 'The Organization of Chinese Official Historiography', in W. G. Beasley and E. B. Pulleyblank, *Historians of China and Japan* (Oxford, 1961), 44–59.

Chapter 3

Private Historiography in Late Imperial China

On-cho Ng

Late Imperial China produced an unsurpassed amount of historiography outside the official ken of the *zhengshi* (standard histories), *shilu* (veritable records), and other court-sponsored compilations, even though the compilers of the private works might well be officials, including the aspiring, inactive, and retired ones. Freed from the stylistic and substantive restraints of bureaucratized undertakings, a wide array of texts of a historical nature came into being: panoramic dynastic histories, historical criticisms and redactions, family chronicles, local gazetteers, epic sagas, historical romance, and narrative histories. Not only did the literati write their own histories but they also reprinted and edited old ones. Moreover, the consumption of history spread to the masses as literacy grew, facilitated by advances in printing and the distribution of books. The fact that the Veritable Records (hitherto classified archives) became open to public circulation also aided the growth of private historiography. Readership, unlike that in the Tang and Song, was no longer confined to the scholarly elite. Reading materials became far more accessible as commercial outlets reprinted court-produced works, such as the classical canon, standard histories, legal codes, and so on. Personal libraries burgeoned and book collecting became all the rage.[1] It was in this context of ferment that private historiography in Ming–Qing China from the fifteenth through the eighteenth century evolved. Although the quality of the private writings varies, many of them display judicious assemblage and critical use of sources, innovative narrative structure, unconventional coverage, and astute historical analysis. Breaking loose from the strictures of official format and spurred on by the dissatisfaction with historiographical orthodoxies, private writers creatively and rigorously undertook the task of ordering the past. This

---

[1] Wolfgang Franke, 'Historical Writing during the Ming', in Frederick W. Mote and Denis Twitchett (eds.), *The Cambridge History of China*, vol. 7: *The Ming Dynasty, 1368–1644*, part 1 (Cambridge, 1988), 726–7.

chapter, by examining a host of significant authors and their works, sheds light on the heretofore under-studied private historiography of late imperial China.

The late Lien-sheng Yang remarked that by the time of the Ming (1368–1644) many of the historiographic conventions had become ossified, such that, for instance, the *lunzan* (comments) sections became cosy places for eulogies rather than contentious sites of doubts and questions.[2] On the other hand, Wolfgang Franke posited that historical writing had made great strides in the Ming, especially after the fifteenth century.[3] Indeed, the Ming witnessed both the rehearsing of established ways and the breaking of new ground. The *Yiwen zhi* [Bibliography of (Ming) works] in the *Mingshi* [Ming History] (1739) provides a picture of tremendous variety and volume. Apart from official histories, there were *zashi* (miscellaneous histories), *shichao* (sundry historical recordings), *gushi* (anecdotes), *dili* (geographies), *pudie* (genealogies), *zhuanzhi* (biographies), *zhiguan* (works on the bureaucracy), *yizhu* (rites and ceremonies), and *xingfa* (penal codes), amounting to some 27,547 fascicles.[4] The proliferation of private histories was duly noted by contemporary commentators. Tan Qian marvelled that 'there were so many private unauthorized histories and family chronicles that the oxen bearing them perspired and . . . they filled the house to the rafters, unaccountably numerous'.[5] Much was the stuff of popular history with deliberate mass appeal—loosely based on historical documents, they were more fiction than history. One prime example is Luo Guanzhong's *Sanguo yanyi* [Romance of the Three Kingdoms] that inspired much emulation. There were also many private works that examined events of the Ming, many of which were first-person accounts of dubious trustworthiness. Wang Shizhen dismissed them on grounds of their partiality.[6] Yet, leaving aside the question of quality, there is no doubt that since the mid-Ming, private historical productions thrived.[7]

One notable fifteenth-century historian was Qiu Jun, who participated in such court-mandated compilations as the Veritable Records. Inspired by the moral didacticism of the Song dynasty *Tongjian gangmu* [Outlines and Details Based on the Comprehensive Mirror] by the *daoxue* (Learning of the Way) master, Zhu Xi, Qiu produced *Shishi zhenggang* [The Correct Bonds in Universal History] (1481), which aimed to redress moral degeneration by appealing to historical lessons, 'making manifest the changes in the world and recording the geneses of

[2] Lien-sheng Yang, 'The Organization of Chinese Official Historiography: Principles and Methods of the Standard Histories from the T'ang through the Ming Dynasty', in W. G. Beasley and E. G. Pulleyblank (eds.), *Historians of China and Japan* (London, 1971), 53.
[3] Wolfgang Franke, *An Introduction to the Sources of Ming History* (Kuala Lumpur, 1968), 4.
[4] Tao Fanbing, *Zhongguo gudai shixueshi lue* (Changsha, 1987), 389–90.
[5] Quoted in Xiaoshu Li, 'Fengjian chuantong shixue de muluo yu tongsu shixue de xingsheng—Mingdai shixue tanlun', *Beijing shehui kexue*, 1 (1999), 91–6.
[6] Ibid., 93–4.
[7] Franke, 'Historical Writing during the Ming', 756–60.

events'. Most important, for Qiu, history demonstrated three universal bonds: distinction of the Chinese from the barbarians; interactions between the ruler and his ministers; and relations between father and son. Knowing the past meant applying the historiographic principle of praise and blame to criticize the violation of these bonds and laud their preservation.[8]

Qiu was preoccupied with the question of *zhengtong*, or the legitimate and orthodox transmission of the authority of the dynasties. To denote legitimacy, or the lack thereof, he employed a graphic system that readily indicated his judgements. In the text, the dynasties that inherited the orthodox line of succession are each placed within a circle. Names of the illegitimate dynasties are not entered but are simply represented by an empty circle. The most illegitimate was the Mongol Yuan dynasty, marked as a dark solid circle that signified the baleful pervasion of the dark *yin* forces when China fell completely into barbarian hands. The cosmological *yin* and *yang* forces manifested themselves as the alternation of peace and disorder. Qiu identified China and the morally superior men as *yang*, Heaven's principle. When the bright *yang* forces held sway, moral leaders predominated and brought peace; such was the rule of history.[9] His historical view no doubt reflected the geopolitical realities of the day. To distinguish rigidly between China and the barbarians was to celebrate restoration of native Chinese rule under the Ming. Qiu lived in a time of grave external threats. In 1449 Emperor Yingzong personally led an army of half a million to do battle with the Mongols. Disastrously, the Ming forces were overwhelmed and the emperor was captured, which was followed by the Mongol onslaught on the capital, Beijing. Qiu espoused the universal historical principle of the separation between the Chinese and barbarians as a means to confront the present with the past.[10]

Further evidence of the flourishing of private historiography abounds. Writers such as Zhu Yunming and Qu Jingchun, keenly aware of history as an independent subject, concentrated on historical criticism. Zhu authored the provocatively titled *Zhuzi zuiyan lu* [Master Zhu's Records of Wrongful Knowledge], which questioned conventional views of historical events and figures. For instance, he debunked the myths surrounding the founders of the Shang and Zhou dynasties, King Tang and King Wu, commonly admired as sagely rulers who received the Mandate of Heaven owing to their virtues. Zhu argued instead that they gained power through brute force, vanquishing the previous dynasty as a result of bloody campaigns. He also questioned the cultural authority of the iconic Confucian figure Zhu Xi, contending that while the Song master could be praised as a grand synthesizer of learning, he should not be viewed as an irreplaceable paragon whose shoes could never be filled. Just as history changed, so should the reception of Zhu Xi's teachings.[11]

[8] See Li Zhuoran, 'Qiu Jun zhi shixue', *Mingshi yanjiu zhuankan*, 7 (1984), 163–208; and Du Weiyun, *Zhongguo shixueshi*, vol. 3 (Taipei, 2004), 165–8.

[9] Ibid., 176–90.

[10] Ibid., 196–8.

[11] Quoted in Yang Yangqiu, 'Ming zhonghouqi de sixue sichao', *Shixueshi yanjiu*, 2 (2001), 36–7.

Qu Jingchun wrote *Gujin shixue deshi* [On the Merit and Demerit of Historical Learning from Past to Present] that interrogated the standard histories and canonical works. He pinpointed the goals and methods of history, claiming that a historian had *sishi* (four responsibilities): focusing on the task at hand; cultivating patience and perseverance; nurturing a sense of professional devotion; and conscientious marshalling of sources—and was devoted to the *wuzhi* (five purposes) of history: arriving at the moral Way and its meanings; announcing the laws against transgressions; comprehending the connections between past and present; illuminating achievements and sacrifices; and making manifest the upright and talented. Last, there were the *sanke* (three rules) of historical deliberation: narrating the evolution and development of events from beginning to end; illuminating the wicked and evil deeds; and making manifest the meanings of the calamities and prodigies.

The prevailing trends in the private composition of history continued in the late Ming period, from the Wanli reign that began in 1573 to the end of the dynasty in 1644. The opening of the Veritable Records to the public obviously contributed to the growth of private historiography. It is instructive to examine several major private compilations that have roughly the same chronological coverage of the official *Mingshi*, and bring into relief the differences between the unofficial versions and the official one. A private history that covers much of the span of the Ming (*c.*1368–1572) is He Qiaoyuan's *Mingshan cang* [Hidden Treasures in the Celebrated Mountains] (1993 [1640]), also known as *Ming shishan chao yishi* [Forgotten History of the Thirteen Reigns of the Ming].[12] He places his materials in thirty-five *ji* (records), which include what are similar to the 'annals', 'biographies', and 'monographs' of the standard histories. The *Dianmo ji* [Records of Model Design], for instance, resembles the official 'imperial annals'. Separate 'records' are the equivalents of the 'monographs'. Yet other records are very much like the 'comments' (*lunzan*) in the official histories, but the *Mingshan cang* is notably different in that all the biographies are clearly categorized. For example, the biographies of the comrades of the Ming founder are placed within the 'Records of the Origins of the Heavenly Dynasty', thereby acknowledging their key roles in the regime's founding. The *Mingshi*, by contrast, accords these personages' biographies no special status. Correspondingly, the rivals of Taizu are undermined by placing their biographies in 'Records of the Expulsions by the Heavenly Dynasty', stressing their destruction. Moreover, the *Mingshan cang* explores foreign relations and peoples with far greater latitude. Instead of eschewing the story of the homeland of the Manchus, it covers the rise of Manchu power in the 'Records of Imperial Enjoyment', together with information on the other 'barbarians'. The Jurchen Manchus are classified as the

---

[12] For a brief biography of the author see L. Carrington Goodrich and Chaoying Fang (eds.), *Dictionary of Ming Biography, 1364–1644* (New York, 1976), 507–9.

'northeastern barbarians'. In fact, the author pointedly referred to the threats from the north and called for strengthened defence.

He Qiaoyuan also wrote about the writing of the history of the contemporary dynasty. In addition to the practice of *jihui* (avoiding things tabooed), he lamented the general lack of reliable and substantive sources, even with the release of the veritable records from the imperial archives. Interestingly, in a preface to the *Mingshan cang* by Li Jiantai (*jinshi* 1625), Li exposed the flaws and inadequacies of the Veritable Records, which tended to be uncritical commendation of the court, and as the focus was on the official matters of the court, what took place in society got short shrift. Thus, we may say that dissatisfaction with the Veritable Records actually stimulated private historiography.[13]

Another well-regarded private history of the Ming, written in the annalistic style, is *Guoque* [Evaluations of (the Events of our) Dynasty] (1653) by Tan Qian.[14] The section covering the years from 1628 to 1645 was compiled during the early Qing, but because Tan saw himself as a surviving Ming subject, he did not avoid reference to the names of the Qing rulers, and he referred to the Manchus as *Jianlu* (slavish subjects of Jianzhou). The writing of this mammoth work was prompted by the widespread existence of bad histories of the Ming, including the Veritable Records. Tan was aggrieved by the compromise of the *shiquan* (authority of history) in official and commissioned histories, as the compilers were beholden to the throne and often succumbed to the whims of emperors.[15] He was determined to produce a thorough and truthful history, insofar as 'a regime may be destroyed, its history must not be destroyed'. He travelled extensively to collect materials, consulting a wide range of sources (including local gazetteers), and collecting statutes, inscriptions on stones and steles, pruning from them errors and biases. In all, Tan spent thirty-six years on the project, employing some 270 different sources and rewriting the project six times.[16]

With its annalistic format, Tan's work is obviously different from the *Mingshi*. Moreover, Tan liberally commented on events and personalities. Notably, the comments are not always placed at the end of a fascicle but interspersed throughout the texts, thereby weaving his judgements into the narrative fabric. Apart from his own comments, which number more than 900, he included those of others, which amount to no fewer than 1,200.[17] Tan's work also differs considerably from the Veritable Records. For example, the Ming compiled no

---

[13] On-cho Ng, 'Private Historiography of the Late Ming: Some Notes on Five Works', *Ming Studies*, 18 (1984), 47–50.

[14] For biographical information on Tan and a brief history of the work's compilation see Goodrich and Fang (eds.), *Dictionary of Ming Biography*, 1239–42; and Jin Zhezhong, 'Tan Qian *Guoque* chutan', *Zhonghua wenhua fuxing yuekan*, 22:1 (1989), 43–6.

[15] Ibid., 46; and Ng, 'Private Historiography of the Late Ming', 51–2.

[16] Ibid., 49–51; and Jin, 'Tan Qian *Guoque* chutan', 46–7.

[17] Ibid., 48–9.

separate Veritable Records for the problematic reign of the Jianwen emperor, who was deposed by Yongle. The records of this reign were absorbed into those of the Yongle reign, and they were tellingly entitled, 'Records of the Events of the Removal of Troubles by Order of Heaven', which affirmed the legitimacy of the actions of Yongle. Moreover, the next eight fascicles continued the use of the reign title of Hongwu. In the Veritable Records of Taizu, the reign title of Hongwu was used until the thirty-fifth year, although in reality, the reign lasted only thirty-one years.[18] Tan restored the reign of Jianwen and its rightful place in history, remarking that the Han dynasty did not tamper with the Imperial Annals because of the illegitimate rule of Empress Lü, and the Tang dynasty did not distort the Veritable Records with the usurpation of Empress Wu. He went so far as to endorse the persecuted officials loyal to the Jianwen emperor as moral exemplars.[19]

Yanshantang beiji [A Special Anthology from the Yanshan Studio] (1590) by Wang Shizhen, an anthology of *kao* (treatises or investigations) on sundry subjects, also commands attention.[20] Like Tan Qian, Wang was satisfied with neither the Veritable Records nor the voluminous private writings. His mission was to set the record straight.[21] Some of the treatises are similar to sections in the *Mingshi*. One treatise of significance is *Shisheng kaowu* [A Critical Treatise on the Errors in Historical Works], the opening salvo of which summarily dismissed Ming official historiography: 'The national historiography never failed in its task to such an extreme degree as under our dynasty.' Political expediency always trumped historical accuracy, as evidenced by the practice that the compilation of the veritable records only took place after the death of the emperor, for fear of offending the living emperor. Wang also chafed at the use of inadequate sources. There was too much reliance on the memorials from the Censorate that supervised the Six Ministries, supplemented by files from the Bureau of Remonstrance. It did not help that the Ming, unlike other dynasties, failed to compile the *Guoshi* (National History) and the *Qijuzhu* (Diary of Activity and Repose), both detailed first-hand recordings of the goings-on in the court, which could have served as corroborating materials.[22] Private historical works did not fare better, falling victim to hearsay and rumours, and appealing to the bizarre and extraordinary.[23] Yet both official and unofficial historiographies are useful in their own ways:

---

[18] Franke, *An Introduction to the Sources of Ming History*, 16; and Franke, 'Historical Writing during the Ming', 748.

[19] Ng, 'Private Historiography of the Late Ming', 50–3.

[20] Goodrich and Fang (eds.), *Dictionary of Ming Biography*, 1399–1405.

[21] Gu Cheng, 'Wang shizhen de shixue', *Mingshi yanjiu luncong*, 2 (1983), 337–9; Du, *Zhongguo shixueshi*, vol. 3, 179–83.

[22] Quoted in Franke, *An Introduction to the Sources of Ming History*, 19.

[23] Ng, 'Private Historiography of the Late Ming', 54.

The official historians are unrestrained and are skilful at concealing the truth; but the memorials and laws they record and the documents they copy cannot be discarded. The unofficial historians express their opinions and are skilful at missing the truth; but their verification of right and wrong and their abolition of taboo of names and things cannot be discarded. The family historians flatter and are skilful in exceeding the truth; but their praise of the merits of [the] ancestors and their manifestations of their achievements as officials cannot be discarded.[24]

Appreciative of the lessons of history, Wang Shizhen valued change and innovation. The late Song dynasty was enervated by its obdurate continuation of received learning, uncritically accepting the classical canon. Wang turned to events in history rather than the ideals in the classics: 'Within and between Heaven and earth, there is nothing that is not history'.[25] The classics were, nevertheless, a sort of history—a history of moral principles.

While He Qiaoyuan, Tan Qian, and Wang Shizhen purposefully broke the yoke of official history, the most iconoclastic views are found in the works of Li Zhi. His *Cangshu* [A Book to be Concealed] (1599), completed late in his life, encapsulated his main ideas on history. Largely organized in the composite style of the standard histories, but without tables and monographs, the work covers the period from the Warring States (403–221 BC) to the end of the Yuan in 1368, with more than 800 biographical entries. It has a sequel that contains some 400 Ming biographies, in addition to *Shigang pingyao* [Commentary on the Essentials of the 'Outline of History'], which was meant to be another supplement. Li's *Fenshu* [A Book to be Burned], albeit being a collection of letters, essays, and poems, also conveys views on historical events and the writing of history.[26]

At the outset, *Cangshu* sets up the premise of Li's historical endeavours: 'Human judgments are not fixed quantities; in passing judgments, men do not hold settled views.'[27] For him, right and wrong were like the alternation of night and day, so that what was right yesterday could well be wrong today.[28] He took strong issue with the orthodoxy of the 'Learning of the Way'. Zhu Xi's and Confucius's teachings, along with the classics, could not be taken as timeless guides and ideals. Even the praises and condemnations in the *Chunqiu* [Spring and Autumn Annals] could not be permanent judgements, as the text was a history of a specific time. The Six Classics were indeed histories that showed that

---

[24] Quoted in Franke, 'Veritable Records', 67–8.
[25] Quoted in Yang, 'Ming zhonghouqi de sixue sichao', 44.
[26] Peng Zhongde and Li Lin, 'Li Zhi de shilun ji qi yingxiang', *Zhongguo wenhua yuekan*, 261 (2001), 36–7; Hok-lam Chan, *Li Zhi 1527–1602 in Contemporary Chinese Historiography: New Light on His Life and Works* (New York, 1980), 3–5, 20–5, 155–6, 163, 164, 167–8; and Wm. Theodore de Bary, 'Individualism and Humanitarianism in Late Ming Thought', in de Bary (ed.), *Self and Society in Ming Thought* (New York, 1970), 201–3.
[27] Quoted in Goodrich and Fang (eds.), *Dictionary of Ming Biography*, 811.
[28] Peng and Li, 'Li Zhi de shilun ji qi yingxiang', 39; Yang, 'Ming zhonghouqi de sixue sichao', 37.

'the Way is repeatedly moving, changing and transforming'.[29] Li thus repudiated the idea of *zhengtong* (legitimate political succession) because each dynasty had to be judged by its merit and not some ideal notion of succession.[30] Historical judgements had to be passed in accordance with accomplishments rather than norms. A good ruler should be praised for confronting the problems of his time, even if his policies diverged from moral conventions. Learning was for the grand purpose of *jingshi* (ordering and management of the world); otherwise, it was just empty talk. Li embraced the so-called immoral and unscrupulous figures in history, so long as they benefited the country. Therefore, he lauded the first emperor of the Qin for unifying China and creating a centralized state, notwithstanding the coercive and severe nature of his regime. Ignoring the Confucian unease with the pursuit of wealth and profits, he showed that history lent credence to the fact that utility and material well-being were a part of life. In brief, Li's historiography rejected moral conceptions of the past with their *dingli* (established principles) and *sangang wuchang* (Three bonds and Five Constant Relations), and supplanted them with the expediency of usefulness and function.[31]

The domain of private historiography in the Qing dynasty was similarly fecund and innovative. From the Ming–Qing transition in the seventeenth century through to the eighteenth, many historical works espoused views of the past that revealed a keen sense of anachronism and an awareness of the differences between time periods. They also placed a premium on evidence, reading sources with the utmost care. Interests in speculative metaphysics and spiritual introspection were replaced by the rage for concrete and practical learning. History figured prominently as scholars endeavoured to understand current problems by probing the past.[32]

The eminent scholar Huang Zongxi assiduously studied the Ming veritable records his family owned and compiled the mammoth *Ming shi'an* [Case Studies of Ming History] in 240 fascicles, which regrettably is no longer extant.[33] Huang's greatest work was undoubtedly *Mingru xue'an* [Intellectual Lineages of Ming Confucians] (1667) in sixty-two fascicles, an intellectual history of the Ming. Huang placed some 308 Ming scholars under nineteen intellectual lineages and divided the dynasty's intellectual developments into three major periods.[34] Repelled by the partisanship of earlier works, he rose above narrow sectarian

---

[29] Quoted in Qian Miaowei, 'Lun Li Zhi dui yili shixue de xitong pipan', *Xueshu yuekan*, 7 (1999), 82–3.

[30] Ibid., 82–3; Yang, 'Ming zhonghouqi de sixue sichao', 41.

[31] Qian, 'Lun Li Zhi dui yili shixue de xitong pipan', 84–8; Peng and Li, 'Li Zhi de shilun ji qi yingxiang', 43.

[32] Hao Chang, 'On the *Ching-shih* Ideal in Neo-Confucianism', *Ch'ing-shih wen-t'i*, 3:1 (1974), 36–61.

[33] Deng Lequn, 'Huang Zongxi de shixue tezheng', *Xueshu yuekan*, 7 (1999), 89; and Du, *Zhongguo shixueshi*, vol. 3, 231–4.

[34] Thomas A. Wilson, *Genealogy of the Way: The Construction and Uses of the Confucian Tradition in Late Imperial China* (Stanford, 1995), 184–92.

affiliations,[35] and based his work on primary sources. For each intellectual lineage, Huang first described its origins and principal ideas. He then selected a roster of representative scholars, providing their biographies, excerpts of their writings, and then his own comments. He abandoned the customary references to the sages' teachings as the wellspring of the lineages because he believed that a dynasty and its institutions were worthy subjects in their own right.[36] Huang's work may be regarded as the first true Chinese intellectual history, and it remains a valuable resource for our study of Ming thought. Huang also took on the writing of the intellectual history of the Song and Yuan dynasties, but wrote only the preface and seventeen fascicles before he died. The work, entitled *Song Yuan xue'an* [Intellectual Lineages of Song-Yuan Confucians], was eventually completed by Quan Zuwang in 1754.[37]

Gu Yanwu, another towering figure of the Ming–Qing transition, compiled two massive works of historical importance: *Tianxia junguo libing shu* [A Treatise on the Merits and Demerits of Territorial Administrations] (1652), a systematic institutional, social, and economic history of the Ming, and *Rizhi lu* [Records of Knowledge (Acquired) Daily] (1676), an assemblage of writings on multifarious subjects, not the least of which was history.[38] For Gu, history must be constituted from primary sources. In writing a biography, all the works by the subject must be read, taking into account the contexts of the subject's life. Thus, an author writing about a court official must know the court's history. By the same token, writing about a local official required knowledge of local history and conditions. Moreover, sources included more than written texts—a great practitioner of oral history, Gu visited not only celebrated places and large cities but also neglected lands and abandoned towns.[39]

Gu claimed that historical pursuit requires humility, by which he meant respecting and acknowledging one's debts to sources. Not to register the use of others' works amounted to denying these authors their rightful place in history. Humility also bred impartiality. Gu loathed the all-too-common practice of manipulating the 'Imperial Annals' in order to legitimize transmissions of political authority. Often the 'Annals' of illegitimate reigns were discarded or placed under the calendars of the so-called orthodox dynasties. For Gu, the histories of the post–Han Northern and Southern dynasties, the Five Kingdoms following the Tang, and the Liao and Jin dynasties of conquest, should all be

[35] Wilson, *Genealogy of the Way*, 167–84.

[36] Wm. Theodore de Bary, 'Enlightenment', in de Bary (ed.), *The Unfolding of Neo-Confucianism* (New York, 1975), 197–8; and Julia Ching (ed.), *The Records of Ming Scholars: A Selected Translation from Huang Tsung-hsi's Ming-ju hsueh-an* (Honolulu, 1987), 12–20.

[37] Deng, 'Huang Zongxi de shixue tezheng', 89–90; and Du, *Zhongguo shixueshi*, vol. 3, 244–8.

[38] Fu Yongke, 'Gu Tinglin zhi shilun', *Zhonghua wenhua fuxing yuekan*, 20:6 (1987), 31–9.

[39] Gu Weiying, 'Zhongguo chuantong zhishi fenzi dui lishi zhishi de taidu—yi Gu Yanwu wei zhongxin', *Shixue pinglun*, 11 (1986), 53–4; and Du, *Zhongguo shixueshi*, vol. 3, 210–12.

recorded with their own dynastic calendars.[40] Most important, for Gu, historical knowledge provided guidance for the present: 'Historical books are composed to mirror what happened in the past so as to provide lessons for the present.'[41] It could 'illuminate the Way' by 'recording of the affairs of the state, revealing the concealed [sufferings] of the people, and the joyful disquisition on the goodness of humanity'.[42] In fact, history was statecraft: 'To refer to the past in deliberations about the present is scholars' practice of statecraft to order the world.'[43] Knowing the succession of dynasties meant knowing the universal principles of management of the world, especially safeguarding the welfare of the people. Therefore, there must be institutional reforms to better people's lives, as laws and institutions had to change with circumstances, and if not, 'there can be no salvation' of culture.[44]

Wang Fuzhi wrote several well-known histories: *Du Tongjian lun* [On Reading the *Comprehensive Mirror*] (1687), a critical reflection on Sima Guang's Song dynasty masterpiece, *Zizhi tongjian* [The Comprehensive Mirror of Aid in Government] (1084); *Song lun* [On the Song] (1687), a trenchant attack on factionalism in the late Ming by analysing sectarian politics in the Song; and *Yongli shilu* [Veritable Records of the Yongli Reign] (1651–61). For Wang, history was instrumental to the enterprise of ordering the world. Wang contended that Sima Guang's metaphor of *a mirror* referred specifically to useful and practical reflections on dynastic success and failure.[45] History provided pragmatic moral lessons, established usable precedents, and revealed the factors for the effectiveness and inefficiency of rulership. However, there were no perennial patterns or unchanging answers. A historian must imaginatively enter the minds of historical personages and fathom how one might act were one placed in a similar situation, paying due attention to the changed contexts and circumstances. Praise and blame were crucial parts of history, but they came only after much study and questioning. They should be couched in limpid language, not florid verbiage, in order that facts and interpretations might be woven together into a coherent narrative. In so doing, the dynamics of history would be laid bare, revealing the interplay between time and circumstance that accounted for the rise and fall of governments, policies, and events.[46]

Wang's historical views were based on the metaphysical idea of the inevitability of change in an ancient text, the *Yijing* [Classic of Changes]. Insofar as the *zhi* (substance) of all things changed even when outward forms appeared constant,

[40] Fu, 'Gu Tinglin', 39–42; and Du, *Zhongguo shixueshi*, vol. 3, 212–24.
[41] Quoted in Gu Weiying, 'Zhongguo', 54.
[42] Quoted in Tao Fanbing, *Zhongguo gudai shixueshi lue* (Changsha, 1987), 433–4.
[43] Gu, 'Zhongguo', 54.
[44] Quoted in Tao, *Zhongguo gudai shixueshi lue*, 435–6.
[45] S. Y. Teng, 'Wang Fu-chih's Views on History and Historical Writing', *Journal of Asian Studies*, 28:1 (1968), 118, 120, 122.
[46] Ibid., 118–19; and Du, *Zhongguo shixueshi*, vol. 3, 250–76.

Wang embraced a dynamic view of history, regarding institutions of every dynasty and period as *sui generis*.[47] He theorized that humans descended from animals that were bipeds and walked upright; even the Chinese were barbarians in the times of Yao and Shun. Just as *shi* (circumstances and conditions) changed, so history was a process of cultural progress and accumulation. There were no *li* (eternal principles) in that all principles must be in tune with the times and circumstances.[48] Heaven was not some transcendent being of pure possibilities; it was the natural order of things, and the minds and hearts of the people. History repeatedly demonstrated one simple fact of effective governance: promoting the welfare of the people through benevolent and public-minded government.[49]

Wang's thought was at odds with the cosmological idea of dynastic change as the displacement of one cosmic agent by another. In traditional Chinese historiography, the notion of *zhengtong* was often explained in terms of the esoteric belief in the movement of the yin-yang forces and the corresponding five agents of earth, wood, metal, fire, and water. Wang disputed such supernatural connection between political changes with cosmological alternations. He was no supporter of the ideal of legitimate successions, arguing that rulers and regimes came to power by brute force. *Zhengtong* was merely justification of victory and defeat. Wang's views of *zhengtong* were coloured by his thinking on the relationship between China and the surrounding barbarians. He contended that there were two *defang* (great defensive embankments) that distinguished one group of human beings from another: first, the separation between the profound persons of moral superiority and the mean folk of inferior moral constitution; and second, the distinction between the Chinese and the barbarians who were so inferior that rules of human relations need not apply to them. The Manchu conquest of China no doubt contributed to his pejorative characterization of the barbarians. As a Ming loyalist, Wang rejected the legitimacy of the Qing dynasty and begrudged their manipulation of the notion of *zhengtong* to fabricate orthodox status. Furthermore, he did not recognize dynasties as the most useful units in the study of China's past, opting to periodize Chinese history into epochs. Wang adopted a seven-epoch periodization that began with the Shang and Zhou and ended with the beginning of the Ming.[50]

In short, during the seventeenth century, a time of momentous dynastic transition, the study of history was considered a most valuable form of solid and practical learning. It came to be functionally linked with the endeavour of

---

[47] Teng, 'Wang Fu-chih's Views on History and Historical Writing', 113–15; and Ian McMorran, 'Wang Fu-chih and Neo-Confucian Tradition', in de Bary (ed.), *The Unfolding of Neo-Confucianism* (New York, 1975), 447–58.

[48] Du, *Zhongguo shixueshi*, vol. 3, 259–76.

[49] Teng, 'Wang Fu-chih's Views on History and Historical Writing', 115–17; McMorran, 'Wang Fu-chih and Neo-Confucian Tradition', in de Bary (ed.), *The Unfolding of Neo-Confucianism*, 447–58; and Du, *Zhongguo shixueshi*, vol. 3, 253–9.

[50] Teng, 'Wang Fu-chih's Views on History and Historical Writing', 115, 117–18.

jingshi (ordering the world).[51] Scholars increasingly approached the world historically, favouring the particularistic and dynamic nature of things rather than timeless universals and unchanging principles.[52] A sort of historicity or historical-mindedness thus emerged; it valued time-bound contingencies over timeless norms.[53] This is not to say that early Qing thinkers completely abandoned universal norms, such as those enshrined in the classics. But for many of them, given inevitable change as a rule of history, expedient reforms and adjustments were as much a part of the Confucian moral order as were universal values.[54]

Eighteenth-century China saw the growth and maturation of the *kaozheng* (evidential research) learning, through which scholars engaged in exegetical and philological investigations of the classics and histories. Care with evidence, breadth of sources, and meticulousness in reading applied equally to classical and historical studies. Moreover, the tight rein that the throne placed on historical production seemed to have goaded scholars into focusing on exposing errors in existing works and verifying their accuracies.[55] Instead of producing new histories, they rewrote old ones.[56] The *kaozheng* approach was typified by the historical endeavours of Qian Daxin, who compiled *Ershi'ershi kaoyi* [Critical Notes on the Twenty-Two Histories] (1782) and rewrote the *Yuanshi* [Yuan History].[57] For Qian, praise and blame could only be rightly assessed when facts were recorded without bias, concealment, and embellishment.[58] He contended that historical method must be based on *shishi qiushi* (looking for truths in actual facts and events). Qian therefore used the best editions of existing historical works, if at all possible, which would then be corroborated and complemented by wide ranges of materials such as topography, rituals, astronomy, phonetics and linguistics, and inscriptions on bronze and stones.[59] He also investigated genealogies and biographies, geography, and the origins and evolutions of institutions. For Qian, history shed light on right and wrong, and functioned as a concrete guide to rulership. As such, it was morally didactic. In that sense, histories and

---

[51] Chang, 'On the *Ching-shih* Ideal in Neo-Confucianism', 36–61.

[52] See Willard Peterson, *Bitter Gourd: Fang I-chih and the Impetus for Intellectual Change* (New Haven, 1979), 12.

[53] On-cho Ng, 'A Tension in Ch'ing Thought: "Historicism" in Seventeenth- and Eighteenth-Century Chinese Thought', *Journal of the History of Ideas*, 54:4 (1994), 561–7.

[54] Ibid., 572.

[55] On-cho Ng and Q. Edward Wang, *Mirroring the Past: The Writing and Use of History in Imperial China* (Honolulu, 2005), 239–43.

[56] Du, *Zhongguo shixueshi*, vol. 3, 311–25.

[57] Du Weiyun, 'Qingdai shixue zhi diwei', *Shixue pinglun*, 6 (1983), 1–13; and Du, *Zhongguo shixueshi*, vol. 3, 352–5.

[58] Benjamin A. Elman, 'The Historicization of Classical Learning in Ming-Ch'ing China', in Q. Edward Wang and Georg G. Iggers (eds.), *Turning Points in Historiography: A Cross-Cultural Perspective* (Rochester, 2002), 129–30.

[59] Zeng Yifen, 'Qian Daxin de lishi wenxian xue', *Shixueshi yanjiu* 1 (1998), 64–71; and Du, *Zhongguo shixueshi*, vol. 3, 331–46.

classics were comparable since the knowledge contained in each led to moral regeneration.[60]

While Qian's historiography saw sociopolitical betterment in moral terms, his contemporary, Zhao Yi, cautioned reducing history into moral judgement, even though he also saw the need for praise and blame. Zhao wrote *Nian'ershi zhaji* [Notes on the Twenty-Two Standard Histories] (1796), with which he distilled larger patterns of social and institutional developments from seemingly disjointed and unrelated details. Methodologically, Zhao investigated issues in the dynastic histories by first gathering all pertinent evidence and studying all relevant facts, followed by the inductive construction of his theses. For him, history was at the service of statecraft and so he ascribed great importance to institutional history. History informed Zhao that bureaucratic centralism—with strong imperial rule—was crucial for maintaining national strength and forging communal unity.[61]

In the main, eighteenth-century China witnessed not so much the production of full-fledged histories as the pursuit of historical criticism and revision, propelled by the *kaozheng* evidential methodology. In the process of reconstructing the past by scrutinizing the ancient past, antiquity and its texts came to be historicized. Questions were asked of the authenticity of the classics. As antiquity and the classics became historical objects of investigation, the fundamentalist end of ascertaining universal truths of the classics came to be tempered by the historical effort of establishing what really happened and what was genuine. As a result, the classics were increasingly seen as histories.[62]

The historicist ethos found eloquent expression in the works of Zhang Xuecheng, who systematically espoused views on the nature and practice of history. His groundbreaking *Wenshi tongyi* [General Principles of Literature and History] (1770) opened with the proclamation that 'the Six Classics are all history', to the extent that 'the ancients never ever talked of principles in separation from affairs. The Six Classics are the statutes and records of the ancient rulers' government.'[63] History was the story of institutions and laws of antiquity, and because the classics were the records of antiquity, they were also historical texts. Accordingly, the Way that could be distilled from them was not universal but historically specific. The classics shed light on what took place once

---

[60] Du, *Zhongguo shixueshi*, vol. 3, 347–51; Huang Qihua, 'Qian Daxin de shixue shulun', *Guoshiguan guankan*, 16 (1994), 1–35; and Wei Hong, 'Qian Daxin lishi kaozheng fangfa shulun', *Shixueshi yanjiu*, 4 (1998), 53–60.

[61] Quinton G. Priest, 'Portraying Central Government Institutions: Historiography and Intellectual Accommodation in the High Ch'ing', *Late Imperial China*, 7:1 (1986), 27–49; and Du, *Zhongguo shixueshi*, vol. 3, 485–502.

[62] Elman, 'The Historicization of Classical Learning in Ming-Ch'ing China', 102–4, 127–34; Du, *Zhongguo shixueshi*, vol. 3, 202–4; Luo Bingliang, 'Qingdai Qianjia shijia shixue piping fangfalun de jige wenti', *Hebei xuekan*, 2 (1999), 90–4; and Liu Zhonghua, 'Shixi Qingdai kaojuxue zhong yizi zhengjingshi de fangfa', *Qingshi yanjiu*, 1 (2001), 85–6.

[63] Quoted in Li Shimin, *Shixue sanshu xinquan* (Taipei, 1997), 184–5.

upon a time, but 'as to the development of events which occurred thereafter, the classics could not have anything to say'.[64] Zhang understood the Way to be a naturalistic one in the flow of history. The Way was simply the *suoyiran* (why and wherefore) of events and things, and not some normative ideal of *dangran* (what things ought to be).[65] The classics enshrined not the incorporeal *dao* but expressed the experiential *qi* (material force), just as Confucius regarded the ancient classics as the material expression of the concrete Way, made tangible by *qi* (implements), a homonym of *qi*-qua-material force, that is, institutions. The Way could be known through tracing the evolution of things in history.[66] In ancient times, as Zhang informed us, history was recognized as *the learning* that illuminated human affairs and in the end, revealed Heaven's Mandate. Through the enterprise of history, theory and practice were unified, *zhi* (rulership) and *jiao* (teaching) became mutually complementary, and a coherent Way came into being.[67] For Zhang, the *dao* evolved in history with different meanings and characteristics, and could not have been apprehended once and for all by the sages. He therefore valued contemporary history and the study of the institutions of the current regime, especially those that governed human relations and daily utilities. History was practical learning based on careful documentation of the social and political institutions at all levels—central, regional, and local—and he wanted to adapt the form of the standard dynastic histories to the compilation of local histories.[68] Zhang concluded that 'historical scholarship is employed to manage the world. It is certainly no composition and narration of empty words.'[69]

But Zhang's historicism had its limits. In the end, he did not see history as parades of relative spaces and times; he found the universally normative in the ancient past and the classics. Just as there was the evolving *dao*-in-history, so there was the transhistorical Way in the classics—the *daoti* (essential Way) embodied in the *mingjiao* (illustrious moral teachings) of the sages, which formed the basis of order and prosperity for all times.[70] Zhang never challenged the authority of the ancient classical texts, even if they were histories. For him, history threw into sharp relief the profound Way that shot through and unified time—this authoritative Way was thoroughly expounded in the classics, whose

[64] Quoted in David S. Nivison, *The Life and Thought of Chang Hsueh-ch'eng (1738–1801)* (Stanford, 1966), 201–2.

[65] Ibid., 140–4.

[66] Ibid., 150–1; and Li, *Shixue sanshu xinquan*, 70–2.

[67] Nivison, *The Life and Thought of Chang Hsueh-ch'eng*, 60–2; and Jiang Yibin, 'Zhang Xucheng "lijing jieshi" de yizhi', *Huagang wenke xuebao*, 16 (1988), 175–82.

[68] Nivison, *The Life and Thought of Chang Hsueh-ch'eng*, 144–50, 216; Ng, 'A Tension in Ch'ing Thought', 576–7; Li, *Shixue sanshu xinquan*, 146–51; and Du, *Zhongguo shixueshi*, vol. 3, 426–430.

[69] Quoted in Li, *Shixue sanshu xinquan*, 181.

[70] Zhou Qirong and Liu Guangjing, 'Xueshu jingshi: Zhang Xuecheng zhi wenshilun yu jingshi sixiang', in Zhongyang yanjiuyuan jindaishi yanjiusuo (ed.), *Jinshi Zhongguo jingshi sixiang yantaohui lunwenji* (Taipei, 1984), 127–33.

import was as brilliant as the sun and moon; the events of the Three Dynasties were guides for the ensuing hundred ages, and Confucius and the Duke of Zhou established the Way that required no subsequent additions. Such conception of ultimacy and finality trumped the historical process and watered down Zhang's historicism.[71]

In short, even though Zhang saw the past as a continuum of differentiated times, he ultimately appealed to the universal values and enduring principles identified with antiquity. Moreover, he did not develop conceptions of periodization—notions of epochs with defining traits and characteristics—as did some other scholars, especially those who studied the *jinwen* (New Script) classical commentaries.[72] The New Script tradition, developed around the *Gongyang zhuan* [Gongyang Commentary] of the *Chunqiu*, espoused particular views on the political and dynastic successions in the ancient past, from the Xia, through the Shang, to the Zhou. Zhuang Cunyu, for example, expounded the principal New Script historical notions of *cun santong* (preserving the Three Systems) and *zhang sanshi* (unfolding of the Three Ages). The former affirmed the legitimacy of the Heaven-mandated dynastic succession of the Xia, Shang, and Zhou. As a result of the dual alternation of *zhi* (simplicity) and *wen* (refinement)—two different modes of cultural orientation—institutions of the three dynasties came into being, developing their own calendar and cosmic colour. The notion of 'unfolding the Three Ages' referred to the phraseological manipulations necessary for the conveyance of Confucius's nuanced treatment of historical events and personages in different ages. The three ages were, namely: the period of which Confucius heard through transmitted records, the period of which he heard through contemporary accounts by living elders, and the period of which he personally witnessed. With subtle use of varying language, Confucius narrated events belonging to these different periods and in so doing highlighted their significance, simultaneously assessing praise and imposing blame. This notion of 'unfolding the Three Ages' also referred to the historical development from the 'Age of Disorder', through the 'Age of Approaching Peace', to the 'Age of Universal Peace'.[73]

Gong Zizhen, the famous statecraft thinker, embraced and modified such New Script historicism by developing his schematic 'Three Ages' based on his unique understanding of the *Chunqiu*. He wrote of the *sandeng* (three classes) of ages: the age of orderly rule, age of disorder, and age of decay, each characterized

---

[71] Zhou and Liu, 'Xueshu jingshi', 128–30; and Ng, 'A Tension in Ch'ing Thought', 578.

[72] On the origins and salient features of the New Script commentarial tradition see Ng and Wang, *Mirroring the Past*, 76–9, 250–1; and Benjamin A. Elman, *From Philosophy to Philology: Intellectual and Social Aspects of Change in Late Imperial China* (Cambridge, Mass., 1984), 177–80.

[73] Zhang Shou'an, 'Gong Ding'an yu Changzhou Gongyangxue', *Shumu jikan*, 13:2 (1979), 3–4; On-cho Ng, 'Mid-Ch'ing New Text (*Chin-wen*) Classical Learning and Its Han Provenance: The Dynamics of a Tradition of Ideas', *East Asian History*, 8 (1994), 10–18; and Chen Qitai, *Qingdai Gongyangxue* (Beijing, 1997), 64–8.

by its *cai* (talents), or the lack of them. While the conventional New Script scheme was a progressive one in the sense of improvement, Gong's was regressive in that it pointed to the descent from order to decay. He regarded his own time as an age of disorder and counselled scrutiny of the problems so as to return to the ages of 'approaching peace' and 'universal peace'. In his later writings, Gong developed the notion of the Three Ages as a progressive development from disorder to peace. But his goal remained the same: to provide a model of inspiration for reform and change. The succession of the Three Ages was connected by the Way, even though every era had specific problems, of which there were three categories—the first involved the livelihoods of people; the second the establishment of institutions; and the third the knowledge of moral nature and the way of Heaven. Every age had its particular besetting problems and challenges that varied, and so there could not be one universal remedy. The idea of the Three Ages provided Gong with a pattern of historical time defined by changing problems.[74] History revealed that in the age of disorder, people's livelihood was the central problem that should command the foremost attention of the government. When people's livelihood was secured, the Age of Approaching Peace arrived, and the regime must then proceed to establish the proper rites and rituals, which would usher in the Age of Universal Peace. In this age, scholars were honoured as valued guests and teachers, who undertook the profound moral project of realizing human nature and the Way. This was the age that witnessed the ultimate political and cultural achievement: installing the institution of universal rule, which dissolved the barriers between the core and periphery— the barbarians and Chinese—as all-under-Heaven came to be unified.[75]

Wei Yuan wrote on scores of diverse subjects, offering sobering thoughts on current problems by producing several notable historical works. He was co-editor of a voluminous anthology on statecraft, *Huangchao jingshi wenbian* [Anthology of Essays on Statecraft in the Imperial Dynasty] (1826), an assemblage of writings on subjects such as institutions, agriculture, military affairs, laws, and the like. He compiled *Mingdai bingshi erzheng lu* [A Record of the Two Administrations of the Military and Economy in the Ming Period] (1855) that addressed the causes of the decline of the Ming dynasty. His assiduous study of the West yielded the justly famous *Haiguo tuzhi* [Illustrated Gazetteer of Maritime Nations] (1852), the first systematic Chinese investigation of the European countries. He also edited and revised the hastily compiled *Yuanshi*.[76] Wei was not merely a compiler of history but was also a philosopher of history. Appealing to the New Script

---

[74] Zhang, 'Gong Ding'an yu Changzhou Gongyangxue', 16–17; Ng, 'A Tension in Ch'ing Thought', 245–56; and Xu Guansan, 'Gong Wei zhi lishi zhexue yu bianfa sixiang', *Zhonghua wenshi luncong*, 1 (1980), 69–104.

[75] Zhang, 'Gong Ding'an yu Changzhou Gongyangxue', 12–16; Xu, 'Gong Wei zhi lishi zhexue yu bianfa sixiang', 80–4; Chen, *Qingdai Gongyangxue*, 170–9.

[76] Wang Jiajian, 'Wei Yuan de shixue yu jingshi shiguan', *Taida lishi xuebao*, 21 (1993), 155–63; Chen, *Qingdai Gongyangxue*, 254–60.

notions of the alternation between 'simplicity' and 'refinement', and the succession of the 'Three Systems', Wei suggested that his own time was poised for change. For him, the notion of the 'Three Ages', which explained how Confucius recorded events of different 'ages' with proper language, also revealed the universal way of governance. The 'Three Ages' represented three different worlds: the age of 'attained peace' that Confucius knew through transmitted records; the age of 'arising peace' that he knew through the contemporary accounts of living elders; and the age of 'universal peace' that Confucius experienced himself. This New Script schema was the basis of Wei's conceptions of historical movement.[77] He further claimed that all beings inevitably had their polar opposites with whom they were dialectically engaged, thereby accounting for the dynamism of history. Both the cosmic and human worlds were propelled by *qihua* (the transformative material force), and hence the inexorability of change. Just as stars perished, rivers altered courses, and flora and fauna evolved, so too human cultures—diet, attire, music, dance, punishment, institution, military strategy— changed. The universe from antiquity to the present was a great chess game, and history represented the myriad moves. What was historically constant was the fact that as old institutions outlived their usefulness, reforms became necessary.[78] As with Gong Zizhen, Wei indentured the project of history to the enterprise of ordering the world.

In sum, the Ming and Qing worlds of private historiography might not have produced major comprehensive historical works, but there was no dearth of diversity, creativity, and innovation. The Ming scholars, highly critical of a degenerate official historiography, sought improvement by pursuing private projects. In the Qing, many historians were guided by a discriminating sense of anachronism, as the *kaozheng* methods pushed them into rigorous interrogations of the past. For a host of writers and compilers of history in late imperial China, the past was neither an unchanging domain defined by the perennial values and events of a golden antiquity, nor a transient realm governed by the expedient concerns and problems of a particular time. For many, the classics were indeed histories; but history, far from being a relativized, contingent space, also manifested the constant Way of human deeds and heavenly mandate. The past was not merely a dispassionate record of time-bound human deeds, it was also a well-stocked storehouse of enduring moral and political lessons.

---

[77] Wu Ze, 'Wei Yuan de bianyi sixiang he lishi jinhua guannian', *Lishi yanjiu*, 9:5 (1962), 44–50; On-cho Ng, 'Worldmaking, *Habitus* and Hermeneutics: A Re-reading of Wei Yuan's (1794–1856) New Script (*chin-wen*) Classicism', in William Pencak (ed.), *Worldmaking* (New York, 1996), 61–8; Xu, 'Gong Wei zhi lishi zhexue yu bianfa sixiang', 72–4, 85–8; Chen, *Qingdai Gongyangxue*, 238–41.
[78] Wang, 'Wei Yuan de shixue yu jingshi shiguan', 155–72; Wu, 'Wei Yuan de bianyi sixiang he lishi jinhua guannian', 34–9; and Xu, 'Gong Wei zhi lishi zhexue yu bianfa sixiang', 87–94.

TABLE OF MING AND QING EMPERORS
AND PERIODS, 1368–1820

1368–1644 Ming Dynasty

1368–98 Hongwo period; reign of Zhu Yuanzhang
1399–1402 Jianwen period; reign of Zhu Yunwen
1403–24 Yongle period; reign of Zhu Di
1425 Hongxi period; reign of Zhu Gaochi
1426–35 Xuande period; reign of Zhu Zhanji
1436–49 Zhetong period; reign of Zhu Qizen
1450–5 Jingtai period; reign of Zhu Qiyu
1457–64 Tianshun period; reign of Zhu Qizhen
1465–87 Chenghua period; reign of Zhu Jianshen
1488–1505 Hognzhi period; reign of Zhu Youtang
1506–21 Zhengde period; reign of Zhu Houzhao
1522–66 Jiajing period; reign of Zhu Houcong
1567–72 Longqing period; reign of Zhu Zaihou
1573–1620 Wanli period; reign of Zhu Yijun
1620 Taiching period; reign of Zhu Changluo
1621–7 Tianqi period; reign of Zhu Youxiao
1628–44 Chongzhen period; reign of Zhu Youjian

1644–1911 Qing Dynasty

1644–61 Shunzhi period; reign of Aisin-Gioro Fulin
1662–1722 Kangxi period; reign of Aisin-Gioro Xuanyue
1723–35 Youngzheng period; reign of Aisin-Gioro Yizhen
1736–96 Qianlong period; reign of Aisin-Gioro Hongli
1796–1820 Jiaqing period; reign of Aisin-Gioro Yongyan

KEY HISTORICAL SOURCES

Gu Yanwu, *Rizhi lu* (Taibei, 1958).
—— *Tianxia junguo libing shu* (n.p., 1900).
He Qiaoyuan *Mingshan cang* (Beijing, 1993).
Huang Zongxi, *Mingru xue'an* (Taibei, 1965).
Li Zhi, *Cangshu* (Shanghai, 2002).
Qian Daxin, *Ershi'ershi kaoyi*, in *Jiading Qian Daxin quan ji* (Nanjing, 1997).
Qiu Jun, *Shishi zhenggang* (Jinan, 1996).
Tan Qian, *Guoque* (Beijing, 1958).

Wang Fuzhi, *Du Tongjian lun*, in *Chuanshan quanshu* (Changsha, 1988).
——*Song lun*, in *Chuanshan quanshu* (Changsha, 1988).
Wang Shizhen, *Yanshantang beiji*, in *Wang Shizhen quanji* (Jinan, 2007).
Zhang Xuecheng, *Wenshi tongyi* (Shanghai, 2008).
Zhao Yi, *Nian'ershi zhaji* (Beijing, 1987).

BIBLIOGRAPHY

Du Weiyun, 'Qingdai shixue zhi diwei', *Shixue pinglun*, 6 (1983), 1–13.
——*Zhongguo shixueshi*, vol. 3 (Taibei, 2004).
Elman, Benjamin A., 'The Historicization of Classical Learning in Ming-Ch'ing China', in Q. Edward Wang and Georg G. Iggers (eds.), *Turning Points in Historiography: A Cross-Cultural Perspective* (Rochester, 2002).
Franke, Wolfgang, *An Introduction to the Sources of Ming History* (Kuala Lumpur, 1968).
——'Historical Writing during the Ming', in Frederick W. Mote and Denis Twitchett (eds.), *The Cambridge History of China*, vol. 7: *The Ming Dynasty, 1368–1644*, part 1 (Cambridge, 1988).
Gu Cheng, 'Wang shizhen de shixue', *Mingshi yanjiu luncong*, 2 (1983), 337–46.
——'Qian Daxin de shixue shulun', *Guoshiguan guankan*, 16 (1994), 1–35.
Jiang Yibin, 'Zhang Xucheng "lujing jieshi" de yizhi', *Huagang wenke xuebao*, 16 (1988), 175–87.
Jin Zhezhong, 'Tan Qian *Guoque* chutan', *Zhonghua wenhua fuxing yuekan*, 22:1 (1989), 43–53.
Li Shimin, *Shixue sanshu xinquan* (Taibei, 1997).
Li Zhuoran, 'Qiu Jun zhi shixue', *Mingshi yanjiu zhuankan*, 7 (1984), 163–208.
Ng, On-cho, 'Private Historiography of the Late Ming: Some Notes on Five Works', *Ming Studies*, 18 (1984), 46–68.
——'A Tension in Ch'ing Thought: "Historicism" in Seventeenth- and Eighteenth-Century Chinese Thought', *Journal of the History of Ideas*, 54:4 (1994), 561–83.
——'Worldmaking, *Habitus* and Hermeneutics: A Re-reading of Wei Yuan's (1794–1856) New Script (*chin-wen*) Classicism', in William Pencak (ed.), *Worldmaking* (New York, 1996), 57–97.
——and Wang, Q. Edward, *Mirroring the Past: The Writing and Use of History in Imperial China* (Honolulu, 2005).
Nivison, David S., *The Life and Thought of Chang Hsueh-ch'eng (1738–1801)* (Stanford, 1966).
Peng Zhongde and Li Lin, 'Li Zhi de shilun ji qi yingxiang', *Zhongguo wenhua yuekan*, 261 (2001), 35–47.
Priest, Quinton G., 'Portraying Central Government Institutions: Historiography and Intellectual Accommodation in the High Ch'ing', *Late Imperial China*, 7:1 (1986), 27–49.
Qian Miaowei, 'Lun Li Zhi dui yili shixue de xitong pipan', *Xueshu yuekan*, 7 (1999), 82–8.
Teng, S. Y., 'Wang Fu-chih's Views on History and Historical Writing', *Journal of Asian Studies*, 28:1 (1968), 111–23.

Wang Jiajian, 'Wei Yuan de shixue yu jingshi shiguan', *Taida lishi xuebao*, 21 (1993), 155–72.

Wei Hong, 'Qian Daxin lishi kaozheng fangfa shulun', *Shixueshi yanjiu*, 4 (1998), 53–60.

Wu Ze, 'Wei Yuan de bianyi sixiang he lishi jinhua guannian', *Lishi yanjiu*, 9:5 (1962), 33–59.

Xu Guansan, 'Gong Wei zhi lishi zhexue yu bianfa sixiang', *Zhonghua wenshi luncong*, 1 (1980), 69–104.

Yang, Lien-sheng, 'The Organization of Chinese Official Historiography: Principles and Methods of the Standard Histories from the T'ang through the Ming Dynasty', in W. G. Beasley and E. G. Pulleyblank (eds.), *Historians of China and Japan* (London, 1971), 44–59.

Chapter 4

A Social History of Japanese Historical Writing

Masayuki Sato

The period from 1400 to 1800 was the age in which Japan produced a character-istic culture, rooted deeply in the past, that continues to the present. From 1400 to 1600 battle tales such as the *Ōninki* [The Chronicles of the Ōnin Wars] (*c.* early sixteenth century) constituted the most common form of historical writing. After the end of this era, which still retains a strong medieval flavour, Japan entered a period of national unification under the Tokugawa regime, a *pax Japonica* lasting from 1603 to 1867. During this age, almost all legitimacy of official institutions was based on precedent. Thus, all aspects of history were traced as far back as possible. At a collective level, the desire to root things in the past produced history books, records of origins, family trees, and chronologies. On a more individual level, the historical consciousness of the era manifested itself in forms of ancestor worship that spread to the common public. As Christianity was forcefully eliminated and all Japanese citizens were made to register with the Buddhist temple of the village to which they belonged, even individual commoner families found their history recorded.[1]

From the start of the Tokugawa period, several important types of historiog-raphy emerged. One kind was typified by Hayashi Razan,[2] who edited the official history of the Tokugawa government, the *Honchō tsugan* [Consp-ectus of Our Land] (1644–70). A second was that associated with Tokugawa Mitsukuni, who initiated the *Dai Nihon shi* [Great History of Japan] (1657–1906). The compilation of this history, which greatly influenced later historians, continued until the second half of the nineteenth century. A third type

---

[1] In this system of family registries (*shūmon aratame-chō*) compiled by Buddhist temples, the name, age, marriage, and death of Japanese individuals are recorded in small booklets. Countless numbers of these records, corresponding roughly to the parish registers of Europe, are extant and contributed greatly to the study of historical demography popular in the 1970s. See Akira Hayami, *The Historical Demography of Pre-Modern Japan* (Tokyo, 2001).

[2] Japanese names are given in Japanese order: surname, given name. Before the Meiji period, intellectuals, artists, and other notables were referred to by given names or an appropriate pseudonym. I have followed this practice below.

is exemplified by Arai Hakuseki, whose autobiography, *Oritaku shiba no ki* [Told Round a Brushwood Fire] (1716), is replete with historical insights and an acute consciousness regarding historical research. Other examples include the works of Ogyū Sorai and Motoori Norinaga, both of whom included many profound historical observations regarding Japanese tradition in their work. Fourth, the blind historian Hanawa Hokiichi, known as the 'Japanese Milton', emphasized the need to preserve the past. He succeeded in compiling and editing the *Gunsho ruijū* [Classified Collection of Japanese Classics and Documents], a massive work of 1,851 fascicles in 1,860 volumes. An example of the fifth type of historical work can be seen in Rai San'yō's *Nihon gaishi* [Unofficial History of Japan] (1827), which relies greatly on the author's own interpretive powers and insights. Finally, the great variety of chronological tables and genealogies published in this period highlights the rich historical consciousness of Tokugawa Japan.

HISTORICAL NARRATIONS OF AN AGE OF TURBULENCE, 1400–1600

In order to comprehend the past we use systems of periodization. The period from 1400 to 1600 in Japan was a period of continuous internal conflict. In an effort to make sense of this period, historians of Japan use various periodization techniques. The four periods most commonly identified are: (1) the Muromachi period (1336–1573), so named because the Ashikaga shogunate was located in the Muromachi section of Kyoto during this period; (2) the Nanboku period (1336–92), in which the two factions of the bifurcated imperial household were at war; (3) the Warring States period (1467–73), so called because all of Japan was in a constant state of civil war; and (4) the Azuchi-Momoyama period (1573–1603), which is named after the respective castles of Oda Nobunaga and Toyotomi Hideyoshi, who succeeded in conquering all of Japan during this period. Another convention is to group the Azuchi-Momoyama and Edo periods together as the 'early modern period' (1568–1867), because this was the period in which the unification of power was achieved. However, generally speaking, the Edo period (1603–1867) alone is understood as the period of 'early modern' Japan, though the 'Tokugawa period' is mostly used instead of 'Edo period' in English. The period before this is referred to as Japan's 'medieval period', which was a period of widespread civil war. The very fact that there are so many different periodization systems is evidence of just how turbulent was this era in Japanese history.

In the midst of this era of turmoil, the emergence of a world among the social elite based on the ideals of *wabi* and *sabi* (literally: austere refinement and quiet simplicity)—perhaps best represented in the Noh drama, tea ceremony, and Japanese gardens—contrasted sharply with the ravages of war. While battle records and war chronicles narrate the turbulent history of this period, this culture of transcendence emerged as an important counter-history to the brutal realities of war.

Two texts that illustrate this abstract concept of transcending reality are *Gukanshō* [The Jottings of a Fool] (1220) and *Jinnō shōtoki* [Chronicle of the True Succession of the Divine Sovereigns] (1339), although it should be noted that both of these texts were written before 1400. Beginning in the fifteenth century, the orientation towards a spiritual world that transcended historical time was achieved not through the metaphysical writing of history, but rather was expressed in the spiritual culture of the tea ceremony, the abstract aesthetic of Noh, the transcendent beauty of the Japanese garden, the practice of Zen, and the Buddhist desire for enlightenment. In other words, this aesthetic world served as an important counterbalance to the realities of a world ravaged by war.

STANDARD HISTORICAL NARRATION, 1400–1600

Numerous war chronicles appeared during this medieval period, the most famous of which is the *Ōninki*. This text, the authorship of which is unknown, describes the war that took place in the area around Kyoto, the capital at the time, from 1467 to 1477. Kyoto was in ruins and the text concludes: 'The capital of Kyoto as well as the outlying rural areas, both have become Asura.' 'Asura' is a Buddhist term meaning 'scene of carnage', and 'Ōnin' is the name of the era and refers to the year in which the battle began, 1467–8. The basic outline of the text begins with internal family disputes among the Ashikaga shogunate family, the Hatakeyama clan, and the Shiba clan, among others, and goes on to chronicle the cause of the conflict and describe the scene in Kyoto, as well as the deaths of the central figures Hosokawa Katsumoto and Yamana Sōzen.

This kind of historical narrative falls into the genre known as 'war tales' (*gunki monogatari*), which first appeared in the late twelfth century, but this text is the only notable example of this genre from the period 1400 to 1600. In fact, while numerous war chronicles were produced, historical narratives that tell the story of this period did not appear until the seventeenth century, after the civil wars had come to an end. Some notable texts include Ōta Gyūichi's *Shinchō kōki* [Chronicle of Lord Nobunaga] (c.1596–1613), a history of Oda Nobunaga, who governed Japan from 1568 to 1582, and Oze Hoan's *Taikōki* [Records of the Regent] (1626), a biography of Toyotomi Hideyoshi, who unified Japan in 1590. During the Tokugawa period medieval battles were also the subject of *kōdan* (storytelling), *bunraku* puppet and kabuki plays, and novels, all of which played a fundamental role in educating Japanese people about history.

Other notable examples of historical narratives from this period include Zuikei Shūhō's three-volume *Zenrin kokuhōki* [A Record of the National Treasure of Good Relations with Our Neighbours], which was completed in 1470 and was Japan's first diplomatic history. This text is an historical account of foreign diplomacy, together with a collection of diplomatic papers documenting travels from Japan to China and Korea. Zuikei was a Buddhist monk from the Rinzai sect in the mid-Muromachi period, when monks were the primary figures responsible for compiling and organizing government and diplomatic papers.

Ichijō Kanera, a court noble in the mid-Muromachi period, was active as a politician and became chief adviser to the emperor in 1447. Among his numerous writings, his *Kujikongen* [Origin of Court Ceremonies] (1422–43) describes proceedings for events in the imperial court based on the phases of the moon, including their origin, development, and specific details, and the author demonstrates a clear historical consciousness in this text. Ichijō's later *Nihonshoki sanso* [Commentaries on the Chronicle of Japan] (1455–7) is evidence that the *Nihon shoki* [Chronicle of Japan] (720) was already being read as a classic among intellectuals at that time.

Yoshida Kanetomo was an important scholar of hereditary learning and Shinto doctrine. As an historian he wrote *Shinsen sangoku unsū fugōzu* [A Synchronized Chronological List of India, China, and Japan]. This text is a chronology that synchronizes four different calendars: the Chinese astrological calendar, the Chinese calendar, the Buddhist calendar, and the Japanese calendar. Yoshida boasts in his preface that he came up with this synchronized table on his own. In the early sixteenth century, this text established the roots of a standard historical temporal consciousness and, by situating Japanese history within a global context (for sixteenth-century Japanese, the world consisted only of Buddhist India, China, and Japan), helped lay the foundation for an historical spatial consciousness as well.

NOH AS HISTORICAL NARRATIVE

Developed in the fourteenth century, Noh drama continues to be one of Japan's most refined performing arts. It expresses the metaphysics of human nature, and actors perform on a simple stage wearing masks and elaborate costumes. Nearly all of the stories that are performed in Noh are historical or quasi-historical narratives. They are often quite literally a performance of history.

Fūshi kaden [The Flowering Spirit] (1406) is the first theoretical work written by Zeami that addresses the question of what Noh is. Zeami is widely recognized as the founder of Noh. Put in the language of Aristotle, Zeami's philosophy of Noh demonstrates a desire to produce a sense of catharsis in the audience. Interestingly, Zeami himself attempted to explain the essence of Noh in historical terms. The prologue of this text begins:

If we try to establish the origins of the life-extending art of *sarugaku*, we find that it has been transmitted either from the land of Buddha (India) or from the Age of the Gods. Yet time has passed, and with the interpretation of the ages it no longer lies within our abilities to learn how it first appeared. This art, which recently so many people take pleasure in, dates from the reign of Empress Suiko (592–628), when the regent Prince Shōtoku Taishi ordered Hada no Kokatsu to create sixty-six pieces of entertainment—either to promote peace in the nation or for public enjoyment—that he called *sarugaku*. Over the generations, writers have used the scenery of nature as a medium for this entertainment. Later, Kokatsu's descendants passed this art down the line of succession, as priests at either the Kasuga Shrine in Yamato or the Hie Shrine in Ōmi. Thus, the performance of religious rites at both of these shrines thrives to this day. Thus, when 'studying the old and admiring the new', you should not treat this elegant art with any trace of distortion. We can perhaps say that someone who understands this art has become accomplished simply because his speech is respectful and his form subtly elegant. The person who wishes to follow this Way should practice no other. The only exception that may quite reasonably apply is the Way of poetry, which will further enrich this life-extending art by adorning it with elements from nature.[3]

In this passage, Zeami's reference to 'studying the old and admiring the new' is taken from Confucius's *Analects*. This phrase has been used for centuries in East Asia as a standard response to the question: What is history? The notion of using an historical explanation to describe the spiritual world is an indication of how deeply ingrained historical consciousness was in Japan at the time. The narrative structure of Noh epitomizes this principle. The vast majority of stories in Noh invariably include interaction between the living and the dead. In most cases, the living ask what happened to the dead and the dead provide answers. This notion of living along with the dead is a reflection of the period of continuous war in the fourteenth and fifteenth centuries in Japan. Zeami's basic structure of 'history-telling by the dead', which sought to establish a direct link to the past by allowing the dead to speak, is a reflection of the Japanese historical way of thinking. In other words, in contrast to the Christian tradition in which the meaning of history is anchored in an Almighty God, in Japan it is anchored in historical events themselves.

Noh remained a highly refined art, but in the seventeenth century, *kabuki* emerged as a flashier form of entertainment that contrasted sharply with the more subdued tone of Noh. Like Noh, however, *kabuki* plays were sometimes historical narratives and formed sources of historical knowledge in the Tokugawa period.

EMAKI AS HISTORIOGRAPHY

Emaki (literally: picture scrolls) are historical narratives that come in a variety of forms, including stories, tales, biographies, and shrine and temple histories. They

---

[3] Zeami, *The Flowering Spirit: Classic Teaching on the Art of No*, trans. William Scott Wilson (Tokyo, 2006), 61–2.

combine text with images to depict scenes and narratives. The form of the scroll was originally introduced from China, but the technique of using pictures and words to tell a history was developed independently in Japan. More than 400 kinds of *emaki* are extant today and more than 600 scrolls appear to have been produced during this period.

Typical *emaki* alternate text with corresponding images, they are roughly 30 cm wide and 10 m long, and collections range in size from as few as one, two, or three scrolls to as many as forty-eight. When they were read, they were held with both hands and unrolled naturally in sections of 50–60 cm so that as one read a block of text one could see the corresponding images. Thus, the story was told in such a way that as one moves little by little from right to left, the reader experiences both a spatial and a temporal change. In contrast to reading from left to right, as is common practice in European culture, Japanese is written from top to bottom in volumes that are read right to left. *Emaki* was a form that truly made the most of this spatial layout of narration.

The first *emaki* were produced in about the ninth century, but the Japanese style of *emaki* did not appear until the tenth century, and the historical narrative form of *emaki* developed in the twelfth century. Beginning in the late fourteenth century large numbers of *emaki* were produced, and were distributed even to the common people. One such example of a historical narrative is *Dōjō-ji engi* [The

FIG 4.1 *Dōjō-ji engi* [The legend of the Dōjō-ji] (http://www.dojoji.com/). Reproduced with permission from the Dojoji temple.

legend of the Dōjō-ji Temple], a sixteenth-century story of a young monk and a girl that is presented on two hand scrolls made of coloured paper. This kind of scroll was commonly used to depict historical narratives—about the origins of a temple—in pictures.

The last scene from *Dōjō-ji engi* demonstrates the typical form of historical representation in *emaki*, in which the image is of primary focus and the text is written alongside it (see Fig. 4.1). The *emaki* tradition continued until the nineteenth century and earned a position within Japanese culture as a common form of historical expression. Today, some regard *emaki* as the origin of contemporary Japanese comics (*manga*).

THE HISTORIOGRAPHY OF *PAX JAPONICA*, 1603–1867

In China, the practice of historical compilation was typically carried out by the government, and Japan eventually adopted a similar practice. In ancient China, when a change of dynasty occurred, one of the first tasks undertaken by the new dynasty was to compile a history of the previous dynasty in order to establish the legitimacy of its own rule. The notion that the government had the authority to record the past formed the core of Chinese historical culture and spread to other parts of East Asia, finally making its way to Japan in the sixth century and continuing for more than a thousand years.

In Japan, however, the compilation of 'standard' histories took on a slightly different form than it did in China. Japan did not have dynastic change. Rather than corresponding with the changing dynasties, the basic format in Japan was structured politically around the emperor and the shogun (who was appointed by the emperor).[4] This political structure is reflected in how history was compiled. Since the twelfth century, Japan maintained a system in which the warrior class was in power, at least in principle, but the power to rule was dependent upon official appointment by the emperor. Even Tokugawa Ieyasu, who established the Tokugawa shogunate and maintained a firm grip on political power, was nominally appointed shogun by the emperor. This system continued until the Meiji Restoration (1868), when the emperor himself assumed direct rule. The Japanese political structure naturally shaped the historical narratives produced by the state, which are usually structured around the emperor.

Historical narratives that were produced on a state scale fall into two narrative styles: *kiden-tai* (Chinese: Jizhuan-ti; important emperors' annals, chronological tables, treatises, eminent rulers' annals, and eminent peoples' biographies); and *hen'nen-tai* (Chinese: Biannian-ti; historiography based on official histories with events presented in chronological order). No matter what form historical

---

[4] Ronald P. Toby, 'Contesting the Centre: International Sources of Japanese National Identity', *International History Review*, 7:3 (1985), 347–63.

compilations took in East Asia, all narrative styles were imported from China. Two great state-sponsored histories from the Tokugawa period, mentioned earlier, illustrate these two types of historical narrative: Hayashi Razan's *Honchō tsugan* employed the *hen'nen-tai* style, while Tokugawa Mitsukuni's *Dai Nihon shi* was in the *kiden-tai* style.

Below, I shall treat six of the most important Tokugawa-period historians who had a lasting effect on succeeding generations. The reason for taking up these historians is to show both the variety of historical research common in this period as well as the diversity of backgrounds from which historians emerged. These men were, respectively, the sons of tradesmen, farmers, samurai, physicians, merchants, and scholars, and included a grandson of the first Tokugawa shogun. This diversity indicates that scholarship was something that transcended social status and constituted something that could be held in common by people of different social classes. Even though Tokugawa-period society was one constituted by strict social status, some individuals, albeit a small minority, demonstrated that learning could help overcome the barriers of social class.

HAYASHI RAZAN AND TOKUGAWA OFFICIAL HISTORY

Hayashi Razan was born in Kyoto as the son of a tradesman. He entered a Zen monastery as a youth but left to study Chinese classics at the Zhu Xi Neo-Confucian School of Interpretation. In 1605 Razan began working in the service of Tokugawa Ieyasu, the first Tokugawa shogun, thus marking the start of a long career as the house scholar of the first four shoguns of the Tokugawa period.

In 1630 Razan founded a school in Edo for the teaching of Zhu Xi's doctrines, which would become state orthodoxy by the end of the eighteenth century. This school, later named the *Shōheikō* after the birthplace of Confucius, became the shogunal Confucian academy. As an historian, Razan initiated, on shogunal orders, the compilation of the *Honchō tsugan*. As a result of this project, Razan is sometimes called the father of Tokugawa historiography.

Honchō tsugan was written in classical Chinese and covers the history of Japan from pre-modern times to the early seventeenth century. For the years prior to 887 the text draws primarily from the *Rikkokushi* or Six National Histories, which consists of the *Nihon shoki* [Chronicle of Japan] (720), *Shoku nihongi* [Continued Chronicle of Japan] (797), *Nihon kōki* [Latter Chronicle of Japan] (840), *Shoku nihon kōki* [Continued Latter Chronicle of Japan] (869), *Nihon montoku tennō jitsuroku* [True Record of Japanese Emperor Montoku] (879), and *Nihon sandai jitsuroku* [True Record of Three Generations] (901). In spite of the breadth of this project, Razan's attitude towards history, which is clear in this work, became an *idée fixe* for the remaining two centuries of the Tokugawa period.

Hayashi Gahō, who worked together with Razan in compiling the *Honchō tsugan*, expressed his editorial policy by noting that 'when historical events are described as they really were, based on actual facts, the facts speak for themselves of virtues and vices'.[5] Razan's purpose in compiling this history was to record Japan's periods of war and peace based on the method of restructuring the histories in chronological order as first used by Sima Guang in *Zizhi tongjian* [Comprehensive Mirror for Aid in Government] (1065–84). Razan also wished to discuss the virtues and vices of sovereigns and subjects following the practice introduced by Zhu Xi in *Zizhi tongjian gangmu* [A Condensed Comprehensive Mirror for Aid in Government] (1172).

Hayashi Razan was interested in promoting the Confucian notion that history is both a moral lesson and a method of historical compilation based on historical facts. This method would later develop into the discipline of *kōshōgaku* (historical study based on textual criticism of historical documents). *Honchō tsugan* is little read today, but at the time it was an important indicator that early modern Japanese historiography would take its models from neo-Confucianism. It was also the first work of early modern Japanese historiography not bound by speculative approaches to history, which marked a significant departure from medieval Japanese practices of historiography.

The Hayashi family was not the usual group of individuals connected by blood, but rather by adopting sons and sons in law. By such means it succeeded in maintaining its position as the head of a scholarly academy in Tokugawa Japan over a period of 265 years. Razan's text inspired the monumental Mito historical project of *Dai Nihon shi* [History of Great Japan] (1657–1906), initiated by Tokugawa Mitsukuni and destined to become a major ideological force from the mid- to late Tokugawa period.[6]

TOKUGAWA MITSUKUNI AND AN ALTERNATIVE OFFICIAL TOKUGAWA HISTORY

In addition to Razan's *Honchō tsugan*, Tokugawa Mitsukuni's *Dai Nihon shi*, which was compiled continuously through the end of the nineteenth century, was one of the most influential texts of its time. Tokugawa Mitsukuni was the grandson of Tokugawa Ieyasu and became the second lord of the Mito domain (r. 1661–90). His emphasis on civil administration made him a popular ruler, and as a result he continues to be a popular subject of contemporary television

---

[5] Hayashi Gahō, 'Introduction to *Honchō tsugan* Continued', *Honchō tsugan*, vol. 1 (Tokyo, 1920), 5.

[6] Kate Wildman Nakai, 'Tokugawa Confucian Historiography: The Hayashi, Early Mito School, and Arai Hakuseki', in Peter Nosco (ed.), *Confucianism and Tokugawa Culture* (Princeton, NJ, 1984), 62–91.

dramas in Japan today. A devotee of the Zhu Xi school of neo-Confucianism, he made himself a master of learning, employing as his teacher Zhu Shunshui, a scholar who fled China after the fall of the Ming dynasty (1368–1644) in order to avoid serving under the new regime.

Tokugawa Mitsukuni's greatest historical achievement was to initiate the compilation of the *Dai Nihon shi*, a monumental text of early modern Japanese historical scholarship. This project involved dozens of scholars over two and a half centuries and had immense influence thereafter on both Japanese historical scholarship and ideology. The significance of Mitsukuni's contributions is described in his epitaph, which reads: 'He [made manifest] the legitimacy of the Imperial Line, discussed the rights and wrongs [committed by] subjects, collected [these facts], and established himself as an authority.' Mitsukuni's primary objective in compiling the *Dai Nihon shi* was to define the relationship between sovereign and subject in Japanese history according to the neo-Confucian conception of history. In fact, the text was a moral lesson written in opposition to Razan's *Honchō tsugan*, which was compiled by order of the shogun and thus privileged state interests. In 1657 Tokugawa Mitsukuni established the Historiographical Institute in Edo (now Tokyo), into which he invited many distinguished historians. The bureau was renamed the *Shōkōkan* (Hall of Elucidation [of the Past] and Consideration [of the Future]) and was moved to Mito in 1829.

The *Dai Nihon shi* is written in *kanbun* (classical Chinese) and is comprised of four parts in the style of *kiden-tai*. Working on the premise that historical research should be carried out on the basis of accurate historical materials, Tokugawa Mitsukuni concentrated his efforts on locating, gathering, and accumulating historical materials, criticizing them textually, and ascertaining accurate historical evidence. As part of this process, he even sent enquiries overseas, seeking information from Korea and China, and consulted Japanese who were known to have travelled abroad. Mitsukuni emphasized the importance of objectivity in historical description; he attempted to narrate historical events without editorializing them and he was careful to indicate which sources he used in each section.

As the emphasis throughout *Dai Nihon shi* is on legitimizing imperial rule and on documenting how moral rectitude is reflected in historical events themselves, the Mito historical project started by Tokugawa Mitsukuni had a significant impact on the rediscovery of the emperor as the focus of Japanese loyalty during the Tokugawa period. Mitsukuni is said to have adopted the same position that Kitabatake Chikafusa took in his fourteenth-century text, *Jinnō shōtōki* [Chronicle of the True Succession of the Divine Sovereigns] (1339). The dynastic schism of the fourteenth century split the imperial house into a northern and a southern line, and Chikafusa took to heart the Confucian principle that, 'In Heaven there are not two suns; on earth there are not two kings.'[7] In this way, he posited the southern line as legitimate, and the northern line as usurpers. The *Honchō tsugan*, by contrast, had reflected the policies of the Tokugawa shogunate and legitimized the northern line.

Tokugawa Mitsukuni's historical project had a substantial influence on the movement to restore imperial rule in the mid-nineteenth century, and on the eve of 1868, Meiji Restoration provided a theoretical background of the *son'nō-jōi* movement, which advocated the reverence for the emperor and the expulsion of foreigners.

HANAWA HOKIICHI AND *MONUMENTA JAPONICA HISTORICA*

The existence of archives cannot be overlooked as a necessary prerequisite for historical research. One might even argue that the principal reason historical research developed in Western Europe and East Asia was that extensive written records were available. In East Asia, historical records were recorded on a variety of materials, including paper, silk, stone, and woodblocks. The collection of these materials, and the production of archival collections, was indispensable to the establishment of historical research as a discipline. In Japan the preservation of historical records was highly developed, and primary resources were deliberately and carefully preserved. For example, at Kyoto's Reizeike (the house of the Reizei family of aristocrats), one can still find primary materials and old family registers that have been preserved for 800 years. These materials have been protected against war and other disasters for posterity's sake and have become a kind of family treasure.[8]

One person who was highly significant in the collection, compilation, revision, and publication of historical records in the Tokugawa period was Hanawa Hokiichi. Although Hokiichi was blind, he possessed an extraordinary memory and was able to memorize many Japanese family records and other historical materials. He classified and organized these records in his *Gunsho ruijū*. It is fair to say that Hokiichi was single-handedly responsible for organizing Japan's unique system of classification, which had its early roots in the thirteenth century and is still in use today. Of the many historical texts discussed throughout this chapter, Hokiichi's text is probably the most accessible.

Hanawa Hokiichi was the son of a farmer in the hinterlands of Edo, and went blind at the age of five. He travelled to Edo and worked as an acupuncturist while embarking on a career as a scholar, and relied on his extraordinary

---

[7] Confucius, *Raiki* (*Zhou-li*) (Tokyo, 1976), vol.1, 492–4.
[8] Reizei Tamehito, *Kyōto Reizeike no 800 nen* (Tokyo, 2005).

powers of memory in his study of *kokugaku* (national learning), Japanese history, classics, and ancient institutions.

Hokiichi believed that the study of the past should be based on reliable historical materials that would be subject to careful, textual criticism, and analysed with academic rigour. Recognizing the need for a classified collection of reliable texts of Japanese classics and other historical documents, Hokiichi embarked on his plan to publish the *Gunsho ruijū* in 1779. He issued the first volume of this collection in 1786. In 1793 he received aid from the shogunate to establish the Wagaku Kōdansho (Institute for Japanese Studies), where he continued compiling and publishing the *Gunsho ruijū*. The first series, consisting of 1,270 titles in 530 volumes, was completed in 1819; the second series, of 2,103 titles in 1,150 volumes, appeared in 1822, following his death.

Gunsho ruijū includes documents from ancient times to the early seventeenth century. They are classified according to Hokiichi's schema of twenty-five categories: Shintōism, emperors, official appointments, genealogies, biographies, official posts, ordinances, public affairs, apparel, literature, letters, poetry, linked-verse poetry, stories, diaries, travelogues, music, *kemari* (a court pastime similar to football), falconry, pastimes, food and drink, battles, warriors, Buddhism, and miscellaneous. The classification system is in itself an interesting historical topic for Japanese historical studies.

The *Gunsho ruijū* was the single greatest collection of historical source materials in early modern Japan, exhibiting high standards of bibliographic and philological scholarship, and remains a major reference work for historians today. *Gunsho ruijū* is the forerunner to numerous important modem collections and compendia of historical source materials, including the *Dai Nihon shiryō* [Historical Sources of Great Japan] (1901–), *Dai Nihon komonjo* [Historical Documents of Great Japan] (1901–), and other series of the Historiographical Institute (shiryō hensanjo) founded in 1869 by the Japanese government.

Beginning in 1789, Hanawa Hokiichi also participated in the compilation of Mitsukuni's *Dai Nihon shi*. He also compiled *Keiyō shō* [Collection on Foreign Affairs] (1811) and *Shiryō* [Historical Sources] (1808–21). His conviction that the historian should let historical sources speak for themselves laid the foundation for much subsequent historical scholarship in Japan, where the tradition of quoting extensively from primary sources remains strong.[9]

ARAI HAKUSEKI AND POSITIVISTIC HISTORY

Arai Hakuseki was the son of an obscure masterless samurai. Despite strained financial circumstances, Hakuseki devoted himself to learning and, in 1683, was

---

[9] Ota Yoshimaro, *Hanawa Hokiichi* (Tokyo, 1966).

taken into service by a minor *daimyō* (feudal lord). Following the *daimyō*'s downfall in 1685, however, Hakuseki found himself once again unemployed. He joined the school of Kinoshita Jun'an, an outstanding Confucian scholar of the day, who in 1693 recommended Hakuseki as a tutor to Tokugawa Tsunatoyo, lord of Kōfu and nephew of the childless shogun. When Tsunatoyo was chosen to succeed as the sixth Tokugawa shogun, reigning as Ienobu (1709–12), Hakuseki accordingly served as Confucian lecturer and policy adviser to the new shogun, helping to usher in a period of civilian administration often referred to as 'the peaceful era of Shōtoku' (1711–16). After the sudden death of Ienobu and his infant successor in 1716, Hakuseki devoted himself entirely to writing about history, politics, linguistics, and international relations.

Hakuseki set forth his idea of history in *Koshitsū* [Study of Ancient History] (1716): 'History is the science of describing historical events based on actual facts; this gives lessons to readers and calls for their sincere reflection.'[10] He was a distinguished source-based historian, whose methods of rigorous documentation were backed by his critical intellect and strict rationalism. In *Koshitsū* he denied the mythical conception of the 'age of the gods', arguing that 'gods are nothing but men'.[11] He wrote a history of ancient Japan as a history of the human world at a time when a countermovement was taking shape that accepted literally the accounts of the 'age of the gods' in the *Kojiki* [Record of Ancient Matters] (712) and *Nihon shoki*. In *Tokushi yoron* [Obiter Dicta on Reading (Japanese) History] (1712–16), Hakuseki draws from lectures he gave to Ienobu in 1712 on Japanese history from the eighth to the seventeenth century. He discusses the rise of the warrior class, proposing an original periodization of Japanese history aimed at justifying the legitimacy of warrior governance and the ruling Tokugawa shogunate. This work seeks to understand Japanese history as one large stream that is intellectually comprehensible in its unity. As such it is a unique narrative history of the country, the style of which would eventually influence Rai San'yō's *Nihon gaishi* [Unofficial History of Japan] (1827).

Arai Hakuseki's most widely read book, the earlier mentioned *Oritaku shiba no ki*, is considered the first autobiography in Japan as well as being a narrative of what the author, who stood at the centre of politics during his age, saw going on around him. Other historical works include *Hankanfu* [A List of Daimyō Family Trees] (1702), a narrated genealogy of 337 feudal lords, and *Seiyō kibun* [Notes on What I Heard about the West (Europe)] (1715), in which he reported on what he learned of Europe from his conversations with Giovanni Battista Sidotti, a captured Jesuit priest.

---

[10] *Arai Hakuseki zenshsū*, ed. Imaizumi Sadasuke, vol. 3 (Tokyo, 1906), 212.
[11] Ibid., 219.

OGYŪ SORAI AND JAPANESE HISTORICISM

While historicism, as a mode of historical thinking, developed in late eighteenth-century Europe, a similar process was taking place in early eighteenth-century Japan. Ogyū Sorai explains the importance of history in his *Gakusoku* [Instructions for Students] (1715):

To be sure, past and present *are* different. Wherein can we see their differences? Only in their physical realities. Physical realities change with the age; ages change with physical realities . . . Physical realities exist already; one must study them with the aid of the various histories and so see their differences. One must use these differences to shed light on both sides, and only then can he 'have converse with their world'. Unless one does this, then it is all too easy to set up his own fixed standards and use them to slander the hundred ages. This is to set oneself straight and not to worry about the age. In that case, of what use are the histories? The man who desires to know the present must be versed in the past. He who desires to be versed in the past must study history.[12]

Ogyū Sorai was the son of a physician to the shogun. At age fourteen, Sorai moved to Kazusa Province (now Chiba Prefecture) with his exiled father and stayed there for twelve years, absorbing himself in study.[13] On returning to Edo in 1696, he entered the service of Yanagisawa Yoshiyasu, the shogun's intimate and chief adviser, and in this capacity sometimes served as an unofficial brain trust for the shogun. In 1709 Sorai started the private academy, the 'Ken'en', where he educated many disciples who came to be known as 'the Ken'en School'.

Among his most important works are *Bendō* [Distinguishing the Way] (1717), *Taiheisaku* [A Policy for Great Peace] (1719–22), and *Seidan* [Discourses on Government] (1727). One of the greatest men of ideas and letters in early modern Japan, Sorai was a firm historicist *avant-la-lettre*. Sorai was not so much a *writer* of history as a great *interpreter* of history. The interpretation of history was Sorai's primary interest—as it was for most scholars in early modern Japan. To 'learn history' was not to explore the facts of the past *per se*, but rather to become conversant in the historical books of the successive Chinese dynasties and to make them thoroughly and completely one's own.

Most scholars in early modern Japan could be called historians in some sense, because even those Chinese classics that were not overtly 'historical' were filled with references to historical events from which the scholar then had to extract meaning based on his interpretation. With regard to the necessity of such interpretive history, Sorai stated that:

---

[12] Richard H. Minear, 'Ogyu Sorai's Instructions for Students: A Translation and Commentary', *Harvard Journal of Asiatic Studies*, 36 (1976), 22–3.

[13] Olof Lidin, *The Life of Ogyū Sorai: A Tokugawa Confucian Philosopher* (Lund, 1973).

The path into scholarship is a knowledge of one's letters, and for this one should employ the study of history . . . For [histories] contain the facts of the successive dynasties, the Way for governing the country, the facts of the [great] military campaigns and the goings-on of the world at peace, as well as the accomplishments of loyal ministers and dutiful officials. Rather than [merely] hearing about Principles [governing the world], nothing will move one like observing the effects [of actions and events, through reading history].[14]

Sorai believed that the mere reconstruction of the facts of the past was not the primary purpose of history, and he cast his net widely to include texts both ancient and modern as the basis of his many works. On the surface, most of these texts were concerned with subjects relating to philosophy, politics, or linguistics, but underlying all of them are Sorai's ideas about the *interpretation* of history. This is also explicit in his definition of his own scholarship as that of *Fukko-gaku* (classical study through a return to the original ancient texts rather than studying the later commentaries). His method of returning to original texts encouraged a concern for philology and linguistics, both of which were techniques necessary for recovering the meaning of ancient texts in their own time. In this sense, Sorai provoked the transformation of historical methodology in eighteenth- and nineteenth-century Japan. He opposed the neo-Confucian idea that the purpose of history was moralistic, encouraging good and punishing evil. Rather, his view of history is summed up in the phrase 'actions speak louder than words'.

MOTOORI NORINAGA AND PHILOLOGICAL HISTORIOGRAPHY

Motoori Norinaga was the son of a wealthy wholesale merchant specializing in cotton goods. In addition to taking lessons in Chinese medicine, in 1752 he began studying both Chinese and Japanese classics in Kyoto. He returned home in 1757, and although he had already become a medical practitioner by vocation, he began intensive study of the Japanese classics. Norinaga would later give informal lectures on these subjects at his home.

Norinaga was largely responsible for bringing the philological study of the Japanese classics to its culmination. His primary interest in this work was to search for the true spirit of ancient Japan, undistorted and unembellished by (alien) Buddhism and Confucianism. The *kokugaku* (national learning) movement emerged in opposition to Confucianistic Chinese studies in the eighteenth century and became the dominant academic school in Japan at that time.[15] During his six-year stay in Kyoto, Norinaga was awakened to the importance of antiquity studies by Ogyū Sorai, and he learned how to apply philological

---

[14] Ogyū Sorai, 'Taiheisaku', in *Ogyu Sorai* [*Nihon shiso taikei*], vol. 36 (Tokyo, 1973), 485.
[15] *Kokugaku* is the textual and exegetical study of Japanese classical histories, literatures, and poems.

methods to the Japanese classics from Keichū, founder of *Kokugaku*. Norinaga later established his own field of scholarship, *Kogaku* (ancient studies), which was based on the critical adoption of the works and methods of Sorai and Keichū.

In 1764, inspired by Kamo no Mabuchi, a *Kokugaku* scholar and devotee of the 'ancient Japanese spirit', Norinaga began annotation of the *Kojiki*, which was originally compiled by Ōno Yasumaro in 712. This project took Norinaga thirty-five years to complete. The fruit of those labours, the forty-four-volume *Kojiki den* [Annotation of the Records of Ancient Matters] (1790–1822) is both his magnum opus and the foundational text of the *Kokugaku* school. The significance of Norinaga's achievement cannot be overemphasized. The language of the *Kojiki*, though a form of Japanese, was so archaic and obscure that the meaning of the text had been lost until Norinaga's explications recovered it. Thereafter, the *Kojiki* became a canonical text in modern Shintō nationalism.

Norinaga's attitude towards learning was to approach the classics himself, rather than to draw the classics to him, as is clear in this passage: 'Classical learning is the study of illuminating ancient things as they were by direct examination of the classical texts themselves, leaving all subsequent theories aside.'[16] His methodological premise was that word, deed, and mind were linked together but that among the three, word was the most important because the deeds of the ancients, bequeathed in history, had been put into words: 'word is tantamount to deed'. By elucidating the meanings and expressions of ancient words, Norinaga eventually aimed to throw light on the minds of the ancients and on facts as they were. That was why Norinaga chose *Kojiki*. This work contained records of archaic Japanese language and descriptions of the bounteous life of the ancient Japanese under the gods and their imperial descendants, without reference to moralistic principles, and so was more valuable than *Nihon shoki*, which was the oldest official history of Japan but was written in classical Chinese. The choice also reflected Norinaga's sense of revulsion against Chinese ways of thinking and the moralistic Chinese outlook.

In all of Norinaga's works, annotation characterizes his philological method: 'When your study advances to a certain degree, it shall be your next work to annotate the ancient texts: Annotation contributes in every respect to the advancement of your study.'[17] But ultimately Norinaga went too far in identifying what was written in the histories with historical facts and in expounding his vision of the path of duty based on those facts, for he then stepped from the world of learning into the world of faith. In his learning, these two contradictory ideas were unified: an objective and rigorous philological method and an attitude of faith towards ancient Japan. The former contributed to the development of Japanese philology and later produced historians such as Hanawa Hokiichi. The

---

[16] Motoori Norinaga, *Uiyamabumi*, in *Motoori Norinaga zenshū*, ed. Motoori Kiyozō, vol. 9 (Tokyo, 1902), 479.
[17] Ibid., 482.

latter was elaborated by Hirata Atsutane as the ideological character of national-ism and later used as an ideological framework for the emperor-centred nation-alism of nineteenth- and twentieth-century Japan.[18]

RAI SAN'YŌ AND THE PHILOSOPHY
OF HISTORICAL CHANGE

Rai San'yō grew up in Aki Province (now Hiroshima Prefecture) as the son of a Confucian scholar. In 1797 he went to Edo to study at the earlier-mentioned official shogunal Confucian academy, the Shōheikō, founded by Hayashi Razan. He returned to Aki the following year. In 1811 San'yō moved to Kyoto, where he founded a private academy and spent the rest of his life as an historian, writer, and poet. San'yō is best remembered as the author of the *Nihon gaishi*, the most widely read and influential work of history in nineteenth-century Japan. It became a touchstone for the political activists of the mid-nineteenth century who sought to overthrow the Tokugawa shogunate and restore direct imperial rule.

Nihon gaishi, a history of Japan from the tenth to the eighteenth century, begins with the rise and fall of national military regimes from the Genji and Heike families that took secular power in the early medieval period, and ends with the founding and flourishing of the Tokugawa shogunate, the warrior administration under which San'yō himself lived. *Nihon gaishi* is written in a Japanese version of classical Chinese and is modelled on the style of Sima Qian's *Shiji* [Records of the Scribe] (109–91 BC). It is also informed by the ethical interpretations of the Zhu Xi school of neo-Confucianism. Although in many places the text is historically inaccurate, San'yō captivated his readers with his concise, lucid narration and his florid literary style. His personal judgements about historical events, inserted parenthetically throughout the text, inspired his reader to imperial loyalism.

San'yō also published *Nihon seiki* [Political Account of Japan] (1845), which is an historical text that begins with Emperor Jinmu, the mythical founder of Japan, and ends with Emperor Goyōzei, who reigned from 1586 to 1611. In addition, he wrote poetry and essays in classical Chinese on a wide range of subjects in Japanese history.[19]

---

[18] H. D. Harootunian, 'The Consciousness of Archaic Form in the New Realism of Kokugaku', in Tetsuo Najita and Irwin Schemer (eds.), *Japanese Thought in the Tokugawa Period: Methods and Metaphors* (Chicago, 1978), 63–104.

[19] W. G. Beasley and Carmen Blacker, 'Japanese Historical Witting in the Tokugawa Period (1603–1868)', in Beasley and R. G. Pulleyblank (eds.), *Historians of China and Japan* (Oxford, 1961), 245–63.

CHRONOLOGICAL TABLES AND GENEALOGY AS HISTORIOGRAPHY

The development of history as a narrative form has been particularly strong in Europe, where chronologies and genealogies have been used as a foundation upon which historical narratives are based, and where this kind of history-as-narrative is highly valued. This privileging of narrative history is clear from the origin of the very term 'history'.[20] In contrast, in East Asia chronologies and genealogies are the preferred styles of history. The historiography known as *hen'nen-tai*, or the deliberate rewriting and recompilation of historiographies in chronological order, has come to be viewed as the ultimate form of historical expression. A typical example of this is Chinese historian Sima Guang's *Zizhi tongjian*. This text is essentially a reorganization of all of the *kiden-tai* style official histories since Sima Qian's *Shiji*. But translating the historical form of *hen'nen-tai* into English as 'chronicle' or 'annals' is inaccurate. Borrowing an expression once used in conversation by the German historian Jörn Rüsen, a more accurate term to describe this style of historiography would be 'non-narrational narrative'.

In *Genkō shakusho* [A History of Japanese Buddhism], written by Kokan Shiren in 1322, Kokan explains his theory of historical compilation this way:

Long ago, when Confucius wrote *Chunqiu* [Spring and Autumn Annals] he employed the time-based narrative style (*hen'nen-tai*), based on months and dates. Sima Qian revised this method and produced the classification style (*kiden-tai*). Since then, historians have employed Sima's method when compiling history. In the time-based narrative style, time is the primary axis of historiography, for biographic style it is classification. Even fools can follow a historical narration based on classification, but history that centres on time is difficult to comprehend even for common people. This is one of the primary reasons for changes in historical narration. When I compiled this text [*Genkō shakusho*], I intended to do so in the same fashion as *Chunqiu*, but I thought that this might be difficult for ordinary people to understand. I suppose there was no other choice [than to go with the biography-based narrative], but I still had a lingering attachment to the style used in *Chunqiu*.[21]

The strength of the time-based narrative (*hen'nen-tai*) lies in the fact that it excludes the judgement of the historian in the reporting of historical facts and, compared to the narrative style (*kiden-tai*), it is both a highly objective and relatively unfiltered form of expression.[22] This method of keeping historical records was introduced to Japan in the sixth century and developed into an independent format over the course of the early modern period. From 1400 to

---

[20] Masayuki Sato, 'Historiology and Historiography', in Q. Edward Wang (ed.), *Many Faces of Clio* (New York, 2007), 262–76.

[21] Kokan Shiren, *Genkō shakusho* (Tokyo, 1965), 289.

[22] Masayuki Sato, 'The Archetype of History in the Confucian Ecumene', *History and Theory*, 46 (2007), 217–31.

1800, a total of sixty-nine historical chronologies were written and published, forty of which appeared after 1600. This was an important form of historical narration.

Another reason why historical chronology developed as one style of historical narration is that it helped to synchronize the various calendars used throughout East Asia. The Japanese calendar combined the era name and the sexagesimal cycle rather than using a linear way of counting years, as in the Christian calendar. This type of calendar was used throughout East Asia, including China, Korea, and Vietnam, so it was necessary to synchronize all of the different era names that were used for each year in each country. A synchronized historical chronology was something that every intellectual had on his desk, and this indispensable tool effectively increased their historical consciousness and raised their overall interest in history.

Mimura Sogen's *Wakan nenkei* [Synchronized Chronology of Japan and China] (1798) was among the most widely read historical chronologies. This text was updated regularly and a total of seven editions were published. In terms of content, there were quite literally three levels of text: the top margin, an upper column, and a lower column. In the margin was a timetable that summarized historical events relating to the emperor and shogun, in the upper column were events relating specifically to Japan, and the lower column listed events relating to China. In other words, this table synchronized three separate chronologies. While readers typically tend to focus on historical events, if we read this table chronologically we can clearly see that although the imperial line remained unbroken in Japan, imperial rule was not continuous because the emperor appointed shogun to govern the country in each period. In this sense, the timetable clearly reflects the 'shape of the country' and ultimately laid the groundwork for the Meiji Restoration, in which an emperor-centred political system was restored.

The 250 years of the Tokugawa period was an era in which there was very little internal strife within the Japanese archipelago. In addition, because Japan was isolated from the outside through political fiat there was also little exchange with the Asian continent, and travel to foreign countries was heavily restricted. As a result of these policies mobility was severely limited, not only for the ruling class but also for commoners. When people are limited in their spatial mobility, they have no option but to look back in time. These conditions produced the thinking that the further back in time one can trace something, the more value it had. This is the origin of the kind of historical culture that persists in Japan today, and these are the circumstances out of which Japan's historical culture arose. Genealogy is the form that perhaps best represents this stereotypical historical consciousness.

As a preliminary step in the writing of *Honchō tsugan*, the Tokugawa shogunate ordered Hayashi Razan and his son Hayashi Gahō to compile the *Kan'ei shoke keizu den* [Genealogies of All Daimyō and Hatamoto Houses in 1641–3]. This document classified the samurai elite into four groups: the Seiwa Minamoto clan, the Fujiwara clan, the Taira clan, and all other clans. In order to ensure accuracy, the 1,530-volume *Kansei chōshū shoka fu* [Genealogies of All Daimyō, Hatamoto, and Other Tokugawa Retainer Houses in 1799–1812] was also compiled in 1812. Beginning with daimyō and feudal lords, this text traces the history of high-ranking samurai through 1798. Arai Hakuseki's *Hankanfu* [A List of Daimyō Family Trees] (1702) is another well-known genealogy that traces the exploits and origins of 337 daimyō families, and Tokugawa Mitsukuni's *Shoka keizu den* (1692) is a record of the genealogies of various daimyō. Even Hanawa Hokiichi's *Gunsho ruijū* has genealogical sections.

Inspired by this kind of state-level genealogical compilation, other daimyō families and vassals compiled their own family histories or genealogies. As a result, nearly every family of the samurai class compiled genealogies in the Tokugawa period. This temporal way of thinking in which a family traces its history back to its ancestors or traces back its roots as far as possible helped spread the notion that the justification for power is to be found through history.

Most of the samurai class can be traced back to the medieval Minamoto (Genji) clan, connecting all warrior families to the emperor, but the oldest portions of these genealogies are largely false. There were even people who travelled to daimyō homes in the countryside to manufacture false genealogies. This was true not only for the ruling class but also for wealthy farming families in the countryside and prosperous merchants.

The fact that there were forged genealogies meant that historical evidence was necessary in order to determine the veracity of these documents. This led to the development of the discipline of genealogy, which was an important contribution to historical research in Japan. Generally speaking, genealogy is thought to have developed in sixteenth-century France and Germany, but a discipline of genealogy also developed in Japan in the seventeenth century, spearheaded by the Tokugawa shogunate's compilation of family histories.

Important in the development of genealogy as one form of historical narration was the continuous *ie* (household/family) system, which was set in place in early modern Japanese society. This system began in 1603 with a registration system similar to the one in which all Japanese people were required to register with their local Buddhist temple. This system was originally developed by the Tokugawa shogunate in an effort to prevent Christianity from entering Japan, but it would eventually become a nationwide registration system that recorded births, marriages, and deaths. Buddhism in Japan was different from that in India in that it was more like ancestor worship disguised as Buddhism.[23] This ancestor worship was protected by both the government and the Buddhist temples and strengthened the thinking that legitimacy was to be found through tracing one's history back in time.

---

[23] Kaji Nobuyuki, *Jukyō toha nanika* (Tokyo, 1990).

In the Tokugawa period, more than 80 per cent of the population was agrarian and because they were engaged in rice farming their living was tightly bound to their rice paddies. In addition, Japan was divided into more than 500 administrative units, and because people's ability to move freely outside of those units was largely restricted, people tended to be born, get married, and die in a single location. Because people's lives were tied to the land their motto became 'one life, one place' (*issho kenmei*).[24] People had an unusual attachment to their homes/ families. With this as the backdrop in early modern Japan, Japanese people had a strong concern for the past and this helped both to shape and to characterize Japan's historical culture.

TIMELINE/KEY DATES

1392 Unification of rival Northern and Southern imperial courts, ending fifty-six-year dynastic schism

1467 Outbreak of Ōnin War begins century of civil war (Sengoku era)

1542 Portuguese introduce firearms (*arquebus*) to Japan

1549 Francisco Xavier arrives in Japan, begins Jesuit mission

1573 Oda Nobunaga deposes last Ashikaga shogun, ending Muromachi bakufu (1336–1573)

1582 Akechi Mitsuhide assassinates Oda Nobunaga in Kyoto

1590 Battle of Odawara: Toyotomi Hideyoshi unifies Japan after 120 years of civil war

1592 Toyotomi Hideyoshi's invasion of Korea; Ming China enters war

1598 Death of Toyotomi Hideyoshi; Japanese forces withdraw from Korea

1600 Battle of Sekigahara: victory of Tokugawa Ieyasu establishes his national supremacy

1603 Emperor Goyōzei appoints Tokugawa Ieyasu 'Shogun'; Ieyasu establishes bakufu (government) in Edo (now Tokyo)

1614 Tokugawa Ieyasu bans Christianity

1633–41 Tokugawa Iemitsu (third shogun) proscribes Christianity, expels missionaries; forbids all overseas voyages by Japanese, designates Nagasaki the sole port for foreign trade (limited to Chinese and Dutch)

1650s–80s Edo and Osaka emerge as engines of national money and commercial economy

1680–90s 'Genroku culture' (flourishing of arts and literature): fiction, poetry (haiku), drama (kabuki and puppet theatre), ukiyoe prints; painting

1780s Tenmei Famine, mass starvation, urban food riots

---

[24] This is the origin of the term 'one life, one company', which was the standard mantra of Japanese companies in the period of rapid economic growth in the mid-twentieth century.

1787–93 Kansei Reforms: in response to Tenmei crisis, a programmatic attempt to reinvigorate bakufu, restore finances, and impose ideological control with neo-Confucianism

1792–3 Russian demands for trade sparks long-term sense of international threat and crisis

KEY HISTORICAL SOURCES

Arai Hakuseki zenshū, 6 vols. (Tokyo, 1977).
Dai Nihon kokiroku, comp. Shiryō Hensanjo, 28 titles in 121 vols. to date (Tokyo, 1952–).
Dai Nihon shiryō, comp. Shiryō Hensanjo, 384 vols. (Tokyo, 1901–).
Gunsho ruijū, comp. Hanawa Hokiichi, 30 vols. (Tokyo, 1959–60).
Hayashi Razan, *Hayashi Razan bunshū*, 2 vols. (Tokyo, 1979).
——— et al., *Honchō tsugan*, 18 vols. (Tokyo, 1918–20).
Motoori Norinaga zenshū, ed. Ōno Susumu and Ōkubo Tadashi, 23 vols. (Tokyo, 1968–93).
Nihon nenpyō senshū, comp. Hioki Eigō, 8 vols. (Tokyo, 2005).
Nihon shisō taikei, ed. Ienaga Saburō et al., 67 vols. (Tokyo, 1970–82).
Ogyū Sorai zenshū, ed. Imanaka Kanji et al., 6 vols. (Tokyo, 1973–8).
Rai San'yō zensho, ed. Kizaki Aikichi and Rai Seiichi, 8 vols. (Tokyo, 1931–2).
Shintei zōho Kokushi taikei, ed. Katsumi Kuroita et al., 62 vols. (Tokyo, 1929–64).
Tenri Toshokan zenpon sōsho wahon no bu, 80 vols. (Tenri-shi, 1972–86).
Tokugawa Mitsukuni et al., *Dai Nihon shi*, 5 vols. (Tokyo, 1900–18).
Waseda Daigaku zō shiryō eiin sōsho, 48 vols. (Tokyo, 1984–95).
Zoku Gunsho ruijū, comp. Hanawa Hokiichi, 86 vols. (Tokyo, 1957–72).

BIBLIOGRAPHY

Baxter, James C. and Fogel, Joshua A. (eds.), *Writing Histories in Japan: Texts and Their Transformations from Ancient Times through the Meiji Era* (Kyoto, 2007).
Beasley, W. G. and Pulleyblank, E. G. (eds.), *Historians of China and Japan* (Oxford, 1961).
Brownlee, John S., *Japanese Historians and the National Myths* (Vancouver, 1997).
Gomi Fumihiko, *Shomotsu no chūseishi* (Tokyo, 2003).
Hakuseki, Arai, *Lessons from History: Arai Hakuseki's* Tokushi yoron, trans. Joyce Ackroyd (Tokyo, 1982).
Hall, John W. et al. (eds.), *The Cambridge History of Japan*, 6 vols. (Cambridge, 1988–99).
Igi Hisaichi, *Nihon komonjogaku* (Tokyo, 1976).
Kaji Hiroe, *Chūsei rekishi jojutsu no tenkai* (Tokyo, 1999).
Kubota Osamu, *Kinsei shigakushi ronkō* (Ise, 1968).
Kuroda Hideo, *Kaiga shiryō de rekishi o yomu* (Tokyo, 2004).
Maruyama, Masao, *Studies in the Intellectual History of Tokugawa Japan*, trans. Mikiso Hane (Princeton, 1974).

McEwan, J. R., *The Political Writings of Ogyū Sorai* (Cambridge, 1962).

Nakai, Kate Wildman, *Shogunal Politics: Arai Hakuseki and the Premises of Tokugawa Rule* (Cambridge, Mass., 1988).

Noguchi Takehiko, *Edo no rekishika* (Tokyo, 1979).

Ozawa Eiichi, *Kinsei shigaku shisōshi kenkyū* (Tokyo, 1974).

Sakamoto Tarō, *Nihon no shūshi to shigaku* (Tokyo, 1958).

Sato Masayuki, *Rekishi ninshiki no jikū* (Tokyo, 2004).

—— 'The Archetype of History in the Confucian Ecumene', *History and Theory*, 46:2 (2007), 218–32.

Shigakkai (ed.), *Honpō shigakushi ronsō*, 2 vols. (Tokyo, 1939).

Toby, Ronald P., 'Contesting the Centre: International Sources of Japanese National Identity', *International History Review*, 7:3 (1985), 347–63.

Webb, Herschel, 'What is the Dai Nihon Shi?' *Journal of Asian Studies*, 19:2 (1960), 135–49.

Chapter 5

Writing History in Pre-Modern Korea

Don Baker

On a map of Northeast Asia, Korea appears to be overshadowed by China, Japan, and, in recent centuries, Russia. Yet Korea has survived in the shadows of those giants, maintaining political autonomy and a separate and distinct cultural identity for most of the last two thousand years. It has done this by cultivating a collective memory of the Korean state and the Korean people as different from the states and peoples that surround it. Writing histories has been a major tool for nurturing and promoting such memories.

For most of the more than five centuries of the Chosŏn dynasty (1392–1910), Koreans proudly declared that they had created a cultural replica of China on their small peninsula. To a certain extent, that assertion is understandable. Though the Korean language is genetically as different from Chinese as Arabic is from English, and although by the middle of the fifteenth century Koreans had an indigenous writing system they could use to write in Korean, Classical Chinese continued to be the preferred language for both government records and respectable literature, both of which followed Chinese models. In government institutions Korea also closely resembled China, on the surface. Aside from the fact that the ruler was called a king rather than an emperor, the government of Chosŏn Korea looked like a small-scale version of the Chinese government. Korean Confucian civil-service examination passers filled bureaucratic posts with titles and responsibilities similar to those of their Chinese counterparts. And, as in China, a landowning class of Confucian scholars dominated local society, with Confucian academies overshadowing the Buddhist temples that shared the countryside with them.

Histories written in Korea resembled histories written in China. Official histories, and most un-official histories as well, followed the format seen in histories produced by Confucian scholars in China. Nevertheless, writing history in Korea was not the same as writing history in China. Though Koreans followed Chinese guidelines for what a history should look like, they wrote their histories to establish a separate and distinct political and cultural history for Korea, using techniques borrowed from China in order to assert the distinctiveness of the Korean identity.

Koreans wrote Chinese-style histories also to serve other Korean ends. The court produced official histories to legitimize lines of succession to the throne within the dynasty, and to legitimize the Chosŏn dynasty within the broader sweep of Korean history. Private individuals wrote unofficial histories for a much greater range of reasons. Some wrote histories to settle the question of whether the founder of the Korean nation was from China or was a native Korean. Others wrote histories of ancient Korea in order to claim Manchuria for Korean history. Still others wrote histories justifying the role of their particular faction in earlier political battles. And some wrote of particular traumatic events, such as the Japanese invasions of the 1590s and the killing of the crown prince in the mid-eighteenth century, in order to clarify or glorify the role played by their ancestors or their factional colleagues in those incidents.

This chapter surveys the wide variety of history texts produced in Korea from the fifteenth century through the eighteenth, how—and why—they were produced. The focus will be on the Korean use of history written in the Chinese style to define a distinctive Korean identity, and to settle Korean political scores. In Chosŏn Korea, writing history was usually a political act. That was as true at the founding of the dynasty in the late fourteenth century as it was four hundred years later, when that dynasty was moving into its final century.

In 1400 the Chosŏn dynasty was only eight years old and still seeking legitimacy. In 1388 General Yi Sŏng-gye had marched his troops into the capital of the Koryŏ dynasty (918–1392) and deposed the king, declaring him illegitimate. After placing a couple of pliable children on the throne, in 1392 he declared them illegitimate as well and seized the throne for himself, announcing that the Koryŏ dynasty was over and that a new dynasty, called Chosŏn, had taken its place. His overthrow of the Koryŏ dynasty was a blatant violation of the core political virtue of loyalty to one's sovereign, and had somehow to be explained away, both to gain legitimacy in the eyes of the Korean political elite and to gain recognition from Ming China as a legitimate government.

History-writing was one of the weapons Yi and his descendants wielded in their fight for legitimacy. Yi Sŏng-gye had to show both his subjects and the Chinese emperor in Beijing that his overthrow of the previous dynasty was not a usurpation of power but was instead a justifiable transfer of the right to rule, which Koreans, like the Chinese, called the Mandate of Heaven. He had to commission histories that argued that his immediate predecessors on the Korean throne had lost their right to rule because they had failed to govern in the virtuous manner required of legitimate holders of the Mandate of Heaven. He also needed histories that strengthened his claim to legitimacy by arguing that the last occupants of the Koryŏ throne were not direct biological descendants of legitimate Koryŏ kings and therefore they did not share in the legitimacy of their predecessors.

Yi's descendants also had to ensure that the histories of their immediate predecessors supported their right to sit on the Korean throne. Sometimes princes fought over which one of them would wear the Chosŏn dynasty crown. The eventual victor, then, needed to produce histories to legitimize his victory over his sibling and show why he, instead of his rival, had been given the Mandate of Heaven. Theoretically, a king who was not a legitimate wielder of royal power could be removed from his throne by an order from the Chinese emperor. Though the emperor in Beijing never exercised his power to declare a king in Seoul ineligible to wield royal authority, two times during the five centuries of the Chosŏn dynasty kings were dethroned by their own officials and replaced by a sibling. Chosŏn kings, therefore, were well aware of the need for acceptance by both the Chinese emperor and their own subjects. Writing histories as a way of asserting legitimacy was not a new idea in Korea. The Yi could draw on precedents from previous kingdoms on the peninsula. Koreans began writing dynastic histories during the period they call the era of the Three Kingdoms, which ended in 668. In fact, it is possible that one of those three kingdoms, Paekche, produced a dynastic history as early as 375.[1] However, none of those early histories were extant at the end of the fourteenth century. The oldest Korean histories that could be used by Chosŏn dynasty Koreans as models for writing a history of Korea were the *Samguk sagi* [Historical Records of the Three Kingdoms], written in the twelfth century, and the *Samguk yusa* [Memorabilia of the Three Kingdoms], written in the thirteenth century. However, those two books provided dramatically different models of how history should be written.

A Koryŏ Confucian official of Silla descent, Kim Pu-sik, is given credit for the *Samguk sagi*. He and the official historians who worked under his direction produced a sober history. Modelled after Sima Qian's *Shiji* [Records of the Scribe] (109–91 BC), the *Samguk sagi* provides a basic annalistic chronicle of the three early kingdoms of Silla, Paekche, and Koguryŏ, as well as treatises on such aspects of official culture before the Koryŏ dynasty as ritual, music, clothing, and vehicles, followed by biographies of men of military, literary, and ethical distinction.[2] Dating the foundation of Silla back to the unlikely early year of 57 BC (thus making Silla the first of the three kingdoms to emerge—an assertion historians today deny), the *Samguk sagi* covers almost ten full centuries of Korean history, going all the way up to 935, when the last Silla king stepped down. However, Kim ignores the existence of another kingdom to the north, which ruled over most of what had been Koguryŏ territory during what South Koreans today call the Unified Silla period (668–935). This lack of concern for the kingdom of Parhae (698–926), even though Silla only controlled the lower two-thirds of the Korean

---

[1] Song Kiho, 'Ancient Literacy: Comparison and Periodization', *Seoul Journal of Korean Studies*, 20:2 (2007), 149–92 at 172.

[2] Jonathan W. Best, *A History of the Early Korean Kingdom of Paekche: Together with an Annotated Translation of the Paekche Annals of the Samguk sagi* (Cambridge, Mass., 2006), provides the most comprehensive glimpse of the *Samguk sagi* in English.

peninsula and Parhae had the rest, brought Kim criticism from Korean historians in the second half of the Chosŏn dynasty, even though Kim was not alone in excluding Parhae from Korean history.

The *Samguk yusa* appeals to more nationalistic students of Korean history. It was written by Iryŏn, a Buddhist monk who was also of Silla descent (and therefore it is equally Silla-centric). Though Buddhism was no more native to Korea than was Confucianism, Buddhist-oriented histories of Korea are often considered more nationalistic than Confucian-oriented ones, probably because they were often filled with tales of miraculous events on the Korean peninsula that made the land appear to be sacred, and because they did not emphasize as much as Confucian histories Korea's subordinate role within the Sino-centric world order. The *Samguk yusa* is no exception to this generalization. However, the primary reason it appeals to later nationalists, aside from the fact that it has a brief (very brief) essay on Parhae, is that it pushes Korean history much farther back than that in the *Samguk sagi*.

The *Samguk yusa* is the oldest extant Korean history that identifies the first Korean kingdom as emerging in 2333 BC, only a few years after the first legendary Chinese emperor, Yao, ascended his throne. It follows a brief discussion of that first kingdom, Tan'gun Chosŏn, with a discussion of Kija Chosŏn, which supposedly was established a little more than one thousand years later by a former official of the defunct Shang dynasty of China. A thousand years after that, Wiman Chosŏn replaced Kija Chosŏn in northern Korea soon after the Han dynasty arose in China. The *Samguk yusa* goes on to claim that the last king of Kija Chosŏn fled to the southern part of the peninsula, where he established a legitimate successor to Tan'gun Chosŏn and Kija Chosŏn, known as Mahan. Though much of the basic chronology of early Korea established by the *Samguk yusa* became the standard chronology for both official and non-official histories of Korea written during the later Chosŏn dynasty, the overall approach of the *Samguk yusa* was not adopted.[3]

Though like the *Samguk sagi* it drew on Chinese models and relied on Chinese source materials, because the *Samguk yusa* emphasized Buddhism over Confucianism and because it emphasized local lore rather than highlighting Korea's place within the Sino-centric world order, it was seen as less rational and less civilized.[4] For most of the Chosŏn dynasty, to be civilized was to be like, though not exactly the same as, the Confucian elite of China. Moreover, the Chosŏn dynasty was staunchly Neo-Confucian, particularly the educated elite who wrote Korea's histories. Iryŏn devoted much of his history of Korea to telling the

---

[3] There is a readable, but not academically rigorous, English translation. See *Samguk Yusa: Legends and History of the Three Kingdoms of Ancient Korea*, trans. Ha Tae-Hung and Grafton K. Mintz (Seoul, 1972).

[4] For a discussion of Chinese sources used in the *Samguk yusa* see Richard McBride, 'Is the *Samguk yusa* Reliable? Case Studies from Chinese and Korean Sources', *Journal of Korean Studies*, 11 (2006), 163–89.

history of Buddhism on the peninsula, including many tales of Buddhist miracles that contradicted the Neo-Confucian assumption that the world was rational and governed by moral principles rather than supernatural personalities.

However, perhaps the primary reason the *Samguk sagi* provided the model for history-writing during the Chosŏn dynasty rather than the *Samguk yusa* is that history-writing was a political activity—and politics during the Chosŏn dynasty was Confucian politics. For example, the royal family of the Chosŏn dynasty relied primarily on Confucian principles for legitimizing their rule. The Korean royal family had an even greater need for legitimation through Confucian historical writing than did the imperial families of China. There are two reasons for that. First, the Korean king needed to be recognized by China as a legitimate king. Theoretically, the authority exercised by a Korean king was delegated by the emperor of China. The narrative of how a particular king came to the throne had to satisfy the Chinese criteria for legitimate succession or that king would be denied the imperial Chinese cachet of approval essential to acceptance by members of the Korean elite. The two dynasties that ruled China while the Yi family was on the throne in Korea both governed according to Confucian principles. Therefore Korean kings had to present a story—that could be justified in Confucian terms—of how they assumed the throne.

Second, Korean kings were much more dependent on their bureaucracy than Chinese emperors were on theirs. Over the course of the five centuries of Yi family rule, two kings were removed from the throne by their officials and replaced by another member of the royal family. A primary criterion for legitimacy that Korean officials applied to the throne, in addition to appropriate parentage, was conformity to Confucian norms. The kings of Chosŏn were often not as rigidly Confucian as were their officials. There are many instances of kings supporting the publication of Buddhist texts and the building of Buddhist temples. However, if those same kings were to maintain legitimacy in the eyes of the officials they depended on to run their kingdom, and to stay on their throne, they had to act like a Confucian monarch. One way to do so was for the king to commission the writing of a Confucian history of his immediate predecessor, and to allow Confucian officials to maintain detailed records that would be used after his death to write a history of his reign. One of the more urgent acts of the new dynasty was to show that the Yi overthrow of the Wang family that had ruled Koryŏ was justified in Confucian terms, even though it might appear on the surface to be an act of disloyalty. That required the production of an official history of the Koryŏ dynasty showing that the Koryŏ had lost its claim to legitimacy by 1392.

It took more than half a century after the Yi family seized power before an official Confucian history of the entire Koryŏ dynasty was approved by the government. The *Koryŏsa* [History of the Koryŏ Dynasty] appeared in 1451. Government historians, all of them Confucian scholars, pored over the voluminous court records left by the previous dynasty and extracted from them data for annalistic accounts of the reigns of thirty-four kings. They then added to those annals the same sort of treatises and biographies that the *Samguk sagi* had included, such as genealogies of the royal family and treatises on natural calamities, ritual, music, and official clothing, as well as fifty volumes of biographies. The Confucian bias of the compilers is clear in both what was included in that official history and what was left out. For example, in those fifty volumes of biographies, there are no biographies of famous Koryŏ monks, though Buddhism was the state religion of Koryŏ and the court appointed a national preceptor.[5] Moreover, in those biographies they provided more favourable evaluations of civilian officials than military officials, displaying the Confucian belief that scholar-officials outranked warriors.[6]

However, the clearest example of distortion occurs in the treatment of the last two kings of Koryŏ. Kings U and Ch'ang, the kings whom General Yi Sŏng-gye overthrew, are not even listed in the chapters on royal family members. Instead, they are discussed in the section of the biographies reserved for rebels.[7] As the dedication to the *Koryŏsa* explains, 'We recorded the loyal and deceitful officials as well as the evil and the upright individuals under separate categories . . . Only by probing into the past can we be sure of achieving the impartiality of historical writings; only by exhibiting the illustrious mirror of history can we ensure that the consequences of good and evil acts shall not be forgotten by posterity.'[8] The *Koryŏsa* was written to argue that the Yi had not overthrown the Koryŏ dynasty but had only stepped in after the Wang family had had their throne taken from them by the real rebels, men whom the *Koryŏsa* described as the illegitimate descendants of a power-hungry monk named Sin Ton.

Soon after the *Koryŏsa* was published, a second official history of Koryŏ appeared. The *Koryŏsa chŏryo* [Abridged Essence of Koryŏ History], as its name suggests, was shorter than the *Koryŏsa*. However, it was not simply an abridged version. It left out the treatises and the biographies and concentrated instead on providing a chronology of Koryŏ history in annals form. Moreover, it includes some events not mentioned in the *Koryŏsa*.[9] More important, it includes many evaluations of royal behaviour. For this reason, some modern historians have argued that the *Koryŏsa chŏryo* represents a reaction against the king-centred approach of the *Koryŏsa*, by providing ample examples of virtuous scholar-officials pointing out instances in which a king had not acted as virtuously as he should have.[10]

---

[5] See Sin Hyŏng-sik, *Han'guk sahaksa* (Seoul, 1999), 141.
[6] See Chŏng Tu-hŭi, 'Chosŏn hugi ŭi yŏksa inshik', in Han'guksa yŏn'guhoe (ed.), *Han'guk sahaksa ŭi yŏn'gu* (Seoul, 1985), 105–27 at 114.
[7] See the discussion in Tai-Jin Kim, *A Bibliographical Guide to Traditional Korean Sources* (Seoul, 1976), 108–12.
[8] Translation from Peter H. Lee *et al.* (ed.), *Sourcebook of Korean Civilization*, vol. 1: *From Early Times to the Sixteenth Century* (New York, 1993), 533.
[9] Kim, *A Bibliographical Guide to Traditional Korean Sources* (Seoul, 1976), 113–18.
[10] Chŏng, 'Chosŏn hugi ŭi yŏksa inshik', 113; and Sin, *Han'guk sahaksa* (Seoul, 1999), 143–53.

This difference in emphasis between the king-centred approach of the *Koryŏsa* and the greater attention paid to Confucian scholar-officials in the *Koryŏsa chŏryo* is just one manifestation of the tension that existed throughout the dynasty between the Chosŏn kings and the officials who were supposed to serve them, and which often influenced how histories were written. Kings clearly preferred histories in which they were the final arbitrators of what was righteous behaviour and appropriate Confucian policy, while officials often saw themselves as guardians of Confucian ethical and political orthopraxy. If a king was strong, he would tell his officials what to do, and what to write in the histories of his reign and the reigns of his predecessors. If a king was weak, scholar-officials would often lecture him on the proper behaviour of a Confucian monarch and would show in the histories they authored that the best king was one who followed the advice of his officials.

Often the struggles for supreme power between kings and officials were fought by using the language of *sadae* and of *myŏngbun*. *Sadae* means 'serving the great', a reference to the subordinate role Korea was supposed to play within the Sino-centric world order. If officials were displeased with a particular policy a king adopted towards China, they might accuse him in memorials, and in histories of his reign, of not displaying a proper *sadae* attitude. In one instance, accusations of failing to show proper deference to China led to civilian officials overthrowing King Kwanghaegun (r. 1608–23), who had angered his officials with his refusal to provide unwavering support for Ming China against Manchu rebels.

Myŏngbun involved recognizing that different social classes had different social responsibilities. For example, scholars had a responsibility to point out to a king when he had wandered from the proper Confucian path; and a king had a responsibility to listen to his scholar-officials. Also, it was important that names reflect Confucian ethical assumptions rather than remain neutral. For example, both Kwanghaegun and Yŏnsan'gun (r. 1494–1506), another king who was overthrown by his own officials, were denied the title of king in the official histories. Instead, they are referred to only as princes, since they were accused of not acting like true kings.

The royal family tried to offset challenges to their authority by enlisting history on their side. In addition to commissioning histories that showed that their seizure of power from the Wang family was legitimate, the Yi family also tried to show that they were just the latest in a long line of legitimate dynasties in Korea. They commissioned the compilation of a history of Korea from its beginning to the end of the dynasty that immediately preceded theirs, a display of respect for their predecessors that they believed would enhance their own legitimacy.

In 1485 that comprehensive history, the *Tongguk t'onggam* [Comprehensive Mirror of the Eastern Country], was published. For the next four centuries, it remained the definitive official history of Korea, 'the only officially sanctioned work that covered all of Korean history from Tan'gun through the fall of the

Koryŏ dynasty'.[11] Modelled on the *Zizhi tongjian* [Comprehensive Mirror for Aid in Government] (1065–84) of Sima Guang, it adopted the same general chronology as that introduced by the *Samguk yusa*.

Compiling the *Tongguk t'onggam* began under a king who had reached the throne under questionable circumstances. King Sejo (r. 1455–68) usurped the throne from his supposedly undeserving teenage nephew. The strongmen who had helped Sejo seize power were entrusted with the responsibility for producing a comprehensive history of Korea that emphasized the absolute authority of the king. However, the *Tongguk t'onggam* was finished under another king, one who ascended the throne the usual way, relying on the support of Confucian officials. That king was more willing to listen to such officials. He, therefore, allowed them to include elements in the *Tongguk t'onggam* that emphasized the need for a proper Confucian monarch to heed advice from his scholar-officials, and for his officials to offer their king criticism if they thought it was warranted. The fifty-seven volume *Tongguk t'onggam* thus includes competing views of the relationship between a king and his top officials.[12]

Nevertheless, the *Tongguk t'onggam* does not abandon the moralistic orientation so characteristic of Confucian historiography. Like all Confucian histories, it highlighted personalities and episodes from the past believed to provide lessons for the present and future. As the preface to the *Tongguk t'onggam* says:

We have tried to narrate in a straightforward manner the unity and disunity of national strength, the good and weak points in national fortunes, the beneficial and evil rules of kings, and successful and failed administrations in governing the state for fourteen hundred years. We have been particularly strict in emphasizing the rectification of names, in respecting loyalty and uprightness, in condemning rebels, and in punishing evil and deceitful men in the hope that these will provide lessons for the encouragement and admonition of prosperity.[13]

These histories were available to the general public, or at least to those educated few who were comfortable reading Classical Chinese. However, Korea's most notable accomplishment in the field of historical writing during the Chosŏn dynasty was not available to the general public. Nevertheless, the *Sillok* [Veritable Annals] represent in the eyes of many Koreans today one of their proudest cultural achievements. The complete set of the annals for all but the last two of the twenty-seven kings of the Chosŏn dynasty is Korea's National Treasure number 151.

There was one set of annals for each king, produced after that king died. They were supposed to provide a day-by-day record of issues discussed and decisions

---

[11] Yong-ho Ch'oe, 'An Outline History of Korean Historiography', *Korean Studies*, 4 (1980), 1–27 at 11–12.

[12] Chŏng, 'Chosŏn hugi ŭi yŏksa inshik', in Han'guksa yŏn'guhoe (ed.), *Han'guk sahaksa ŭi yŏn'gu* (Seoul, 1985), 120–2; and Sin, *Han'guk sahaksa* (Seoul, 1999), 164–74.

[13] Peter H. Lee *et al.* (eds.), *Sourcebook of Korean Civilization*, vol. 1: *From Early Times to the Sixteenth Century* (New York, 1993), 535.

made in that king's court, and to also include the moral judgements of the historians on those discussions and decisions. This record was then put aside for later generations to read and draw the appropriate moral lessons from.

While a king was alive, two low-level civil servants bearing the title of 'official historian' would shadow him, whenever and wherever he was engaged in official business, taking notes on everything he and those he conversed with said. After he died, a committee of high-level Confucian officials especially formed for the task would use the notes taken by the historians, along with other official documents, to compile the annals of that king's reign. The next king was not allowed to look at those annals for fear he might try to alter what they contained. Of particular concern were any changes a king might want to make to judgements of the behaviour of his predecessor.

Serving as an official historian was not risk free. Even though the king was not supposed to know how they recorded his behaviour, there were a few instances in which a historian's notes were revealed either to a king or to an official displeased with the historian's records. Over the more than five hundred years of the Chosŏn dynasty, there were a few instances (not many, but some nonetheless) of historians being executed for the notes they took. That happened, for example, in 1498 when King Yŏnsan'gun discovered that an official historian had implied in his notes that Sejo, Yŏnsan'gun's direct ancestor, might not have been a legitimate occupant of the throne.[14]

Who were these historians, that they dared to risk their lives in the defence of what they felt was truth in history? They were from the group Koreans called *yangban*. The *yangban*, the high-ranking civil servants of Chosŏn Korea, resembled the Confucian literati of China, in that they had to be well educated in the Confucian classics as well as the hegemonic philosophy of neo-Confucianism. Moreover, in most instances, if they wanted a bureaucratic post, they had to pass a series of civil-service exams testing their knowledge of Confucianism. However, unlike their literati counterparts in China, who gained their positions primarily through high scores on civil-service examination, the *yangban* were members of a hereditary class. Only those with *yangban* ancestors could hold a public office such as official historian.

The *yangban* often divided into factions that fought for control of the bureaucracy. Sometimes those battles turned deadly. For example, in the middle of the sixteenth century, some officials were executed when they were accused of bias in the preservation of historical records.[15] Moreover, sometimes when one faction gained power after a while in the political wilderness, they would alter the supposedly sacrosanct annals, not by erasing what was recorded in them but by

[14] Edward W. Wagner, *The Literati Purges: Political Conflict in Early Yi Korea* (Cambridge, Mass., 1974), 42–8.
[15] Suematsu Yasukaze, 'Introduction to the Ri Dynasty Annals', *Memoirs of the Research Department of the Toyo Bunkoi*, 17 (1948), 120.

supplementing them—adding new material to the old, supposedly already complete, annals. They were not so much concerned about the factual data included in those annals as they were about the moral judgements added by historians.

Because the original annals were kept along with the supplementary annals, it is easy to identify such struggles over control of the documentary record. For example, a faction known as the Southerners controlled the annals for King Hyŏnjong (r. 1649–74) and therefore his original annals, which were finished in 1677, reflected the Southerner evaluation of his reign. However, their rivals the Westerners gained control of the government soon afterwards and, in 1682, added a supplement to the Hyŏnjong annals, reflecting their different evaluation. In a similar dispute over history, the original annals for the short-lived King Kyŏngjong (r. 1720–4) were completed in 1732, but those who disagreed with what those annals said had to wait until Kyŏngjong's half-brother and successor, King Yŏngjo (r. 1724–76), had died before they could add their interpretation of King Kyŏngjong's reign to the official record.[16]

The historians respected the need for accuracy in the annals in that they at least did not destroy the records they disagreed with. In fact, annals might contain contradictory moral judgements, as when a king is cited as praising the moral character of a particular official and later the historian adds a negative moral assessment of the behaviour of that same individual. However, respect for historical accuracy did not mean that all historically relevant information was included in the annals. The annals are centred on the court and do not tell us much about what is going on outside the halls of government, unless it is discussed within those halls. In addition, some more embarrassing facts are either ignored or alluded to without explicit articulation. The most prominent example of such a gap in the official record is the lack of any detailed discussion of the mental problems of the crown prince Sado, who was put to death by his father King Yŏngjo in 1762.[17]

Nevertheless, the *Sillok* are generally comprehensive and were intended to preserve the unvarnished truth, as historians on the scene saw it. Such reverence for history was necessary for a Confucian government to be considered legitimate. However, the Chosŏn royal family also needed a way to spread the message that they were not just legitimate but also wise, virtuous, and benevolent monarchs. To do that, they produced an expurgated version of the annals for public consumption. The first *Kukcho pogam* [Treasured Mirror of Our Dynasty] was published in 1459. A century later a second edition, adding coverage of most of the kings since the first edition, was published. Updated editions continued to appear regularly. The last edition was published in 1909, only two years before the fall of the dynasty.

---

[16] JaHyun Kim Haboush, *A Heritage of Kings: One Man's Monarchy in the Confucian World* (New York, 1988), 247–9.
[17] Ibid., 250.

The *Kukcho pogam*, unlike the *Sillok*, was intended to be widely read. It became the primary resource for Chosŏn Koreans who wanted to learn the history of their own dynasty. However, it was a biased source, more propaganda than accurate history. For example, it skips the reigns of the two most controversial kings, Yŏnsan'gun and Kwanghaegun, though the former sat on the throne for twelve years and the latter for fifteen. The 1762 incident in which the crown prince was put to death by his father is also left out of what represented itself as a comprehensive account to Yi family rule. This contrasts sharply with the annals, which leave out some unsavoury details but nonetheless gives an account of that 1762 tragedy and includes day-by-day records for deposed kings, though it labels those records 'diaries' rather than the more respectable term 'annals'.

A similar piece of propaganda, but one with greater aesthetic value, is a song hailing the virtue and military prowess of the Yi royal family. *Yongbi ŏch'ŏn'ga* [Songs of the Dragons Flying to Heaven] was commissioned by King Sejong (r. 1418–50) to honour his father, his grandfather (the founder of the dynasty), and their progenitors for four generations back.[18] King Sejong ordered his top scholar-officials to collect accounts of the great deeds of his ancestors by both combing official records and by talking with eyewitnesses about some of the seminal events in which they took part. (Two of the three officials in charge of that project also worked on compiling the *Koryŏsa*, so they were experienced historians.) As they were gathering data for this family history-in-verse, the king had another group of scholars invent the Korean alphabet (*han'gŭl*) so that Koreans could write songs and poems in their own language instead of having to use Classical Chinese, a language they did not speak. (A phonetic alphabet for Korean was necessary because Classical Chinese is written with logographs rather than phonetic symbols and therefore could not be easily used to reproduce the sounds of Korean.) In 1447 when this song was performed in public for the first time, and hundreds of copies were distributed to members of the ruling elite, it was the first significant literary creation in the Korean alphabet, serving to legitimize the Yi family both in terms of their ancestry and in terms of their concern for the distinctiveness of Korean culture.[19] Though there are some supernatural stories in this long poem, most of the events it relates are actual events, though somewhat embellished.[20] Therefore, despite its unusual form, the *Yongbi ŏch'ŏn'ga* should be included in a list of works of history produced during the Chosŏn dynasty.

A more orthodox approach to historical writing, but one that mixes geography and history, appears in the few studies of foreign countries that Koreans produced during the Chosŏn dynasty. They tended not to write about the China of

[18] *Songs of the Dragons Flying to Heaven*, trans. James Hoyt (Seoul, 1971).
[19] Peter H. Lee (ed.), *A History of Korean Literature* (New York, 2004), 151–2.
[20] James Hoyt, *Soaring Phoenixes and Prancing Dragons: A Historical Survey of Korean Classical Literature* (Seoul, 2000), 179.

their day as that would have been considered presumptuous. Instead, they wrote about their less powerful neighbours. One of the earliest examples of this sort of historical writing is *Haedong chegukki* [A Record of the Various Countries in the Eastern Sea]. Compiled by royal order in 1471, it surveyed the geography and history of Japan as well as the Kingdom of the Ryūkyūs to the south. It contains a chronological summary of the events that occurred during the reigns of various Japanese emperors from the legendary Jimmu to the reigning emperor in 1471, and it also lists the various shoguns who had ruled Japan at various times.[21]

The *Haedong chegukki* is an official history, commissioned by the court. However, some Confucian scholars produced histories on their own, particularly after 1600. When they did so, they tended to write about their own country. These histories adopted the same basic pattern as the official histories: they were more concerned with telling *what* happened rather than *why* it happened. The emphasis was on annalistic narration rather than analysis. Moreover, they generally were court-centred, focusing on the king and his officials. And they were written more to influence the present than to shed light on the past *per se*.

One way history was used to influence the present was either to strengthen one side's claims to political legitimacy, or weaken an opposing side's claim. Another way was to identify instances from the past of appropriate or inappropriate behaviour that could serve as guidelines for conduct in the present, and in the future. By the middle of the Chosŏn dynasty, in the early seventeenth century, the Yi family's claim to the Chosŏn throne was firmly established and no longer needed support from legitimizing histories. New historical issues arose, stimulated by the ascension of the Manchu from just above Korea's northern border to rule over all of China and by the fragmentation of the ruling elite in Korea into hereditary antagonistic factions. Histories were written to re-fight factional battles or to suggest indirectly how Korea should view the Manchu's Qing dynasty. Such issues were usually dealt with not in official histories but in histories written privately, primarily by members of the *yangban* Confucian scholar elite.

The Chosŏn dynasty had considered the Manchu to be only one step above ordinary barbarians. Before Manchu tribes united into a force powerful enough to conquer China in the seventeenth century and establish the Qing dynasty, Manchu tribal leaders had acknowledged the superior position of the Chosŏn dynasty in the Sino-centric international order by offering ritual tributary gifts to the Korean court, just as Korea had recognized Chinese superiority by offering tributary gifts to the emperor of China. Koreans therefore found it difficult to accept the Manchu overthrow of the Chinese Ming dynasty in 1644, and to

---

[21] Kim, *A Bibliographical Guide to Traditional Korean Sources*, 144–7.

accord the Manchu Qing dynasty legitimacy.[22] Though it was dangerous to question directly the legitimacy of the Qing dynasty, Koreans could indirectly challenge the Qing by writing histories centred on political legitimacy in Korea's ancient past, or by expanding the scope of Korean history to include ancient kingdoms that were based in what later became the Manchu homeland.

The first influential Chosŏn history raising the question of legitimacy in ancient Korea was *Tongguk t'onggam chegang* [The Basic Framework of the Comprehensive Mirror of Korea], by Hong Yŏ-ha. Hong denied legitimacy to the kingdom of Wiman Chosŏn, which was established in the northern part of the peninsula in the second century BC. Instead, Hong maintained that the kingdom it was believed to have conquered, Kija Chosŏn, remained the only legitimate government on the peninsula even after it was forced to move to the peninsula's southern half. An Chŏng-bok in his *Tongsa kangmok* [Annotated Account of Korean History] and Han Ch'i-yun in his *Haedong yŏksa* [Encyclopedic History of Korea] followed Hong's example. By denying full legitimacy to Wiman Chosŏn, these historians indirectly suggested that a later northern regime, that of the Manchu, was also of doubtful legitimacy.

Another approach to implicit criticism of the Manchu was to claim that the Manchurian homeland was actually part of Korean history. Starting in the last quarter of the eighteenth century, a number of historians claimed for Korean history the kingdom of Parhae, which had controlled Manchuria and much of the northern half of the Korean peninsula when Silla ruled unchallenged in the south. The first to make this assertion was Yu Tŭk-kong in his *Parhae-go* [Study of the Parhae Kingdom]. When Yu wrote 'The fact that Koryŏ did not assume its rightful responsibility of writing a history of Parhae shows us that Koryŏ failed in its responsibility to assert its authority in our corner of the world',[23] his Korean readers understood that he was lamenting that Korea had allowed the tribes in Manchuria to gain more autonomy and power than was legitimate.

Besides the issue of the legitimacy of the Qing dynasty in China, historians also addressed the issue of the legitimacy of the particular political factions that monopolized official posts at various times in the dynasty. Since the faction in power usually determined how the policies and actions of its members were depicted in the *Sillok*, scholars who were members of out-of-power factions wrote unofficial histories, such as *Haedong Yaŏn* [Unauthorized Tales of Korea] by Hŏ Pong, to ensure that their faction's stances were presented in the best possible light. In the late eighteenth century, one out-of-office Confucian scholar, Yi Kŭng-ik, decided to rise above the factional fray and produce a history of the

---

[22] JaHyun Kim Haboush, 'Contesting Chinese Times, Nationalizing Temporal Space: Temporal Inscription in Late Chosŏn Korea', in Lynn Stuve (ed.), *Time, Temporality, and Imperial Transition: East Asia from Ming to Qing* (Honolulu, 2005), 115–41.

[23] Translation from Peter H. Lee *et al.* (ed.), *Sourcebook of Korean Civilization*, vol. 2: *From the Seventeenth Century to the Modern Period* (New York, 1996), 230.

Chosŏn dynasty that simply reproduced what participants and eyewitnesses had reported, without stating which reports he considered more reliable, even though those reports often contradicted each other. His *Yŏllyŏsil kisul* [Narrative from the Yŏllyŏ Studio] is now considered one of the best sources for studying the politics at court during the Chosŏn dynasty.

Yi's history is an example of a greater self-conscious concern for accuracy—for identifying 'what really happened' in Korea's past—that emerged in historical writing in the second half of the Chosŏn dynasty. Korea's Confucian historians tried to be as accurate, realistic, and objective as they could be within the confines of a moralistic historiography. The official annals were supposed to be an accurate reflection of what the official historians observed. Even the moral judgements historians recorded were supposed to be unbiased applications of universal moral principles rather than an expression of a particular historian's individual ethical preference. In the latter half of the dynasty, however, a new trend appeared alongside the traditional concern for the unbiased extraction of moral lessons from history. Private historians, such as An Chŏng-bok and Han Ch'i-yun, begin comparing documents to determine which narrative of the distant past was more reliable.

In addition, we begin to see unofficial accounts of specific important events in Korea's history by eyewitnesses. One of the better known such histories is the *Chingbirok* [The Book of Corrections] by Yu Sŏng-ryong.[24] Yu combined memorials and other official documents from the period when Korea was resisting a Japanese invasion in the last decade of the sixteenth century with his own personal account of what he, a high-ranking government official at that time, experienced. Another important personal record is the *Hanjungnok* [A Record Written in Sorrow] of Lady Hyegyŏng, who was the wife of the crown prince who was put to death by his own father, King Yŏngjo.[25]

Hanjungnok is unusual in that not only is it a personal memoir, it was written by a woman. Almost all histories written during the Chosŏn dynasty were written by men. The only exceptions are memoirs and diaries of palace women. Besides *Hanjungnok*, there are a couple of important other accounts of palace intrigue that were written by women. However, both the *Kyech'uk ilgi* [Diary of the Year of the Black Ox, 1613] and *Inhyŏn wanghu chŏn* [Life of Queen Inhyŏn] straddle the line between history and fiction. They both were written to distinguish clearly between the good and the evil participants in palace battles over the legitimacy of royal consorts and, therefore, the legitimacy of their offsprings' claims to the throne. The events they describe are real, yet the characters they portray are caricatures.

---

[24] Yu Sŏngnyong, *The Book of Corrections: Reflections on the National Crisis during the Japanese Invasion of Korea, 1592–98*, trans. Choi Byonghyon (Berkeley, 2002).

[25] *The Memoirs of Lady Hyegyŏng: The Autobiographical Writings of a Crown Princess of Eighteenth-Century Korea*, trans. JaHyun Kim Haboush (Berkeley, 1996).

As Korea entered the nineteenth century, the types of histories Koreans were producing as well as the types of questions historians sought to answer were more varied than they had been four centuries earlier. Nevertheless, historical writing in Korea in 1800 remained traditional. Historians continued in most cases to see history as a series of moral lessons, to be mined for lessons to heed in the present. And historians continued to focus on power struggles among the ruling elite rather than on the lives of the average Korean. History was by definition political history. It was not until the twentieth century, after Koreans embarked on their march to modernity, that Korean history would expand to include social history, economic history, cultural history, and the history of the Korean people as a whole.

TIMELINE/KEY DATES

2333–1122 BC Tan'gun Chosŏn (legendary)
1122–194 BC Kija Chosŏn (legendary)
194–108 BC Wiman Chosŏn
57 BC–AD 668 Three Kingdoms period
      57 BC–668 Silla
      37 BC–668 Koguryŏ
      18 BC–660 Paekche
668–935 Unified Silla period
      698–926 Parhae
918–1392 Koryŏ dynasty
      1270–1351 Mongol rule over Korea
1392–1910 Chosŏn dynasty
      1592–98 Japanese Invasions
      1627–1637 Manchu invasions

KEY HISTORICAL SOURCES

An Chŏng-bok, *Tongsa kangmok* (1778; Seoul, 1977–80).
Chosŏn wangjo sillok (Seoul, 1984).
Haedong chegukki (Seoul, 1471; P'aju, 2004).
Han Ch'i-yun, *Haedong yŏksa* (1823; Seoul, 1982).
Hong Yŏ-ha, *Tongguk t'onggam chegang* (Sangju, 1786; Seoul, 1986).
Hyegyŏng, Lady, *Hanjungnok* (1805; Seoul, 2001).
Iryŏn, *Samguk yusa* (Kaesŏng, 1281; Seoul, 1973).
Kim Pu-sik, *Samguk sagi* (Kaesŏng, 1145; Seoul, 1985).
Koryŏsa (1451; Seoul, 1983).
Koryŏsa chŏryo (1451; Seoul, 1983).

Kukcho pogam (1909; Seoul, 1980).
Tongguk t'onggam (1485; Seoul, 1974).
Yi Kŭng-ik, *Yŏllyŏsil kisul* (1797; Seoul, 1968).
Yongbi ŏch'ŏn'ga (1447; Seoul, 1971).
Yu Sŏng-ryong, *Chingbirok* (1647; Seoul, 1960).
Yu Tŭk-kong, *Parhae-go* (1784; Seoul, 1976).

BIBLIOGRAPHY

Ch'oe, Yong-ho, 'An Outline History of Korean Historiography', *Korean Studies*, 4 (1980), 1–27.
Cho Sŏng-ŭl, *Chosŏn hugi sahaksa yŏn'gu* (Seoul, 2004).
Cho Tong-gŏl, Han Yŏng-u, and Pak Ch'an-sŭng, *Han'guk ŭi yŏksaga wa yŏksahak* (Seoul, 2007).
Han Yŏng-u, *Chosŏn chŏn'gi sahaksa yŏn'gu* (Seoul, 1981).
—— *Chosŏn hugi sahaksa yŏn'gu* (Seoul, 1989).
Pak In-ho, *Han'guk sahaksa taeyo* (Seoul, 1996).
Sin Hyŏng-sik, *Han'guk sahaksa* (Seoul, 1999).
Sohn, Pow-key, 'The Concept of History as Seen by Korean Yangban', *Korea Journal*, 17:9 (1977), 4–17.
Suematsu, Yasukaze, 'Introduction to the Ri Dynasty Annals', *Memoirs of the Research Department of the Toyo Bunko*, 17 (1948), 97–166.
Yi Sŏng-mu, *Chosŏn wangjo sillok ŏddŏn ch'aegin'ga* (Seoul, 1999).

Chapter 6

Southeast Asian Historical Writing

Geoff Wade

The huge geographical, cultural, and historical diversities of Southeast Asia make discussion of the region as an entity almost impossibly daunting. Extending from South Asia, across the major massifs, rivers, and plains that constitute the southeast extension of the Eurasian landmass, and incorporating the archipelagos of the Philippines and Indonesia/Malaysia, the Southeast Asian region must necessarily be discussed in a succession of categories. This is even more the case given the range of the religious, linguistic, and historical influences that affected different parts of the region at various times and to differing degrees.

This chapter examines how and why accounts of the past were transmitted in Southeast Asian societies from about 1400 to the beginning of the nineteenth century. The adoption of 1400 as the date with which to begin this overview derives from the fact that the fifteenth century was a watershed in the region's history. It was a period when the classical kingdoms had seen decline, and when both South Asian and Chinese influences on the region were burgeoning. Anthony Reid has described the period from about 1400 to the middle of the seventeenth century as the Southeast Asian 'Age of Commerce', which produced revolutions in various spheres, including commerce, urban structures, religious affiliations, military modes, and statecraft.[1] Victor Lieberman, a Southeast Asia historian as well as a Eurasia comparativist, shares the opinion that the fifteenth century was a crucial age for the mainland Southeast Asian polities and societies.[2] He sees, beginning in the fifteenth century, a process of territorial consolidation in mainland Southeast Asia, resulting in a reduction in the number of polities that existed, accompanied by administrative centralization and strengthened social regulation (including regulation of religious organizations) by these polities.[3]

---

[1] Anthony Reid, *Southeast Asia in the Age of Commerce*, 2 vols. (New Haven, 1988–93).

[2] Victor Lieberman, 'An Age of Commerce in Southeast Asia? Problems of Regional Coherence: A Review Article', *Journal of Asian Studies*, 54:3 (1995), 796–807; and Lieberman, *Strange Parallels: Southeast Asia in Global Context, c. 800–1830*, vol. 1: *Integration on the Mainland* (Cambridge, 2003).

[3] Ibid., 28–36.

Thisproduced a sixteenth century where Toungoo Burma, Ayutthaya, and Đại Việt controlled much of mainland Southeast Asia. The integration was also marked by a growing uniformity of religious, ethnic, and other cultural symbols, and the emergence of stronger core ethnies.[4] Additionally, rising literacy saw growth in vernacular as well as religious literatures. Correlated to this was an increased interest and need for the writing of histories. At both ends of the Eurasian continent during this period, then, we see a great burgeoning of history-writing, as a constituent element of a global early modern age.

We will end our survey at the beginning of the nineteenth century, an ending determined by both the great domestic turmoil within the region and the global change that marked the period. The changes wrought in worldviews by the late eighteenth-century rebellions and invasions experienced in the Toungoo Empire in Burma, the late Ayutthayan Empire in Siam, and the Nguyễn and Lê/Trịnh principalities in Vietnam,[5] were epoch-defining. So, too, were the changes that took place later in the nineteenth century: the vast increases in the mobility of people, ideas, and capital in Southeast Asia, with steamships, the opening of the Suez Canal, the coming of the telegraph, new British settlements in the Malay peninsula and Burma, the extension of Dutch administration throughout the Indonesian archipelago, and French colonies being created in the Southeast Asian mainland. Another hugely important element of change in this period was the expansion of Chinese commerce and immigration throughout the region.[6] Ann Kumar suggests that a new historiography emerged from this period in Java,[7] and there are sufficient intimations of change in the historiographies of other Southeast Asian societies to warrant choosing 1800 as the point of closure for the present survey.

While it is a common assumption—and sometimes even a definition—that 'history' began only with writing, it was certainly the case that many Southeast Asian societies long used, and in some cases continue to maintain, oral histories that provide family, village, and district histories that extend often for many centuries. In Eastern Indonesia, these are sung or recited in usually exclusively male village ceremonies. Perhaps the best studied of these societies is that of Roti, an island in Eastern Indonesia where oral histories include the genealogies of the families in each domain, and in many cases individuals are familiar with not only their own histories, but also those of their *manek* or domain lord. James Fox

---

[4] Lieberman, *Strange Parallels*, 37–52.

[5] For which see Victor Lieberman, 'Mainland-Archipelagic Parallels and Contrasts c. 1750–1850', in Anthony Reid (ed.), *The Last Stand of Asian Autonomies: Responses to Modernity in the Diverse States of Southeast Asia and Korea* (Basingstoke, 1997), 27–56.

[6] For which see Anthony Reid, 'A New Phase of Commercial Expansion in Southeast Asia, 1760–1840' and Carl Trocki, 'Chinese Pioneering in Eighteenth-Century Southeast Asia', ibid., 57–82, 83–102.

[7] Ann Kumar, 'Java: A Self-Critical Examination of the Nation and its History', ibid., 321–43, on 338.

claims that 'the historical narratives of each domain constitute a dynastic chron-icle', on the basis that the Roti narratives, while being genealogies, also explain the founding of the domain and the successes and failures of the ruling lines.[8] Robert Barnes has recorded similar traditions among peoples of the Solor archipelago in Eastern Indonesia.[9]

The introduction of writing to Southeast Asia, first through the use of Chinese graphs in what is today northern Vietnam and later through Indic scripts, in island and then mainland Southeast Asia, brought the capacity for written histories. There is a wide range of inscriptional texts detailing polity histories, lines of descent, and religious affiliations from both mainland and island polities over the period 400–1400, but these texts fall beyond the scope of the present study.

HISTORICAL WRITING IN ĐẠI VIỆT/VIETNAM

In order to situate Vietnamese historical writing from the fifteenth century, it is perhaps necessary to begin this survey with a thirteenth-century text—the *Đại Việt Sử Ký* [Historical Annals of Đại Việt], which was completed in 1272. This work followed the annalistic form of Chinese historian Sima Guang's *Zizhi tongjian* [Comprehensive Mirror of Aid in Government], written in Classical Chinese, and which covered the period from Triệu Đà of the third century BC to the end of the Lý dynasty in 1225. The author of this history, Lê Văn Hưu, was an official of the Trần court (1225–1400), and he lived during the Mongol invasions of Đại Việt between 1257 and 1288. It was the Mongol threat that induced the Trần ruler to order the creation of a national history to solidify Trần power and retain their independence from the Mongols. Lê Văn Hưu thus concentrated his history on representing a polity that was equal to China. The *Đại Việt Sử Ký* thus stressed the legitimacy of both Triệu Đà of the third century BC, as well as Đinh Bộ Lĩnh, who assumed the title of emperor as restorer of Nam Việt's independence in 966. To support the validity of Viet independence, the history depicts Vietnam's golden age in terms of cultural excellence and imperial independence when the Viet court was an equal counterpart of the Chinese court. In his history, Hưu indirectly attacked Buddhism on the grounds that it weakened the court and wasted revenue and manpower, and criticized past rulers from a Confucian ethical viewpoint. In this way he was endorsing both the rule of the Trần court and Confucian values. Lê Văn Hưu's work, although now

---

[8] James J. Fox, 'Standing in Time and Place: The Structure of Rotinese Historical Narratives', in Anthony Reid and David Marr (eds.), *Perceptions of the Past in Southeast Asia* (Singapore, 1979), 17.

[9] Robert H. Barnes, 'Time and the Sense of History in an Indonesian Community: Oral Tradition in a Recently Literate Culture', in Diane Owen Hughes and Thomas R. Trautmann (eds.), *Time: Histories and Ethnologies* (Ann Arbor, 1995).

lost, is cited and quoted repeatedly in later works and in some ways provided a template for later Vietnamese histories.

The creation of works of history justifying the independent existence of the Viet state continued in the fourteenth century, with the writing of the *Việt Điện U Linh Tập* [Compilation of the Departed Spirits in the Realm of Việt], a non-state-sponsored text, inspired instead by Mahayana Buddhism. Compiled by Lý Tế Xuyên, a thirteenth-century court official, this work detailed historical figures, as well as the roles they subsequently played as spirits, and the titles accorded to them. This was written during and after the Mongol invasions, so it was undoubtedly intended as a form of national strengthening.

A separate tradition of Buddhist history can be observed in Vietnam from this time. Buddhism was a significant force during the Lý and Trần dynasties. *Thiền Uyển Tập Anh* [Compendium of Outstanding Figures of the Zen Garden] details the formation of the three Zen schools in the Viet area. This was composed around 1337 and, like similar Chinese texts, recorded the biographies of sixty-five eminent monks. It was 'intended to be a record of the Zen lineages in Việt Nam which, at least according to its compiler, have their roots in China'.[10]

Ming China's invasion and occupation of the Vietnamese polity from 1406 to 1427 was to have profound effects on mainland Southeast Asia. One of the most obvious was the change it induced in the political topography of Vietnam. By expanding the borders of their new province of Jiao-zhi, particularly to Champa territory in the south, the Ming left the resurgent Đại Việt with a larger polity than it comprised formerly. By attempting to eliminate Vietnamese culture, the Ming also ensured that the Vietnamese would incorporate and adopt those aspects of Chinese elite culture they found useful, including Confucian justification of their expansion. During the invasion and occupation, many books, histories, and other materials were destroyed by the Ming forces. Thus, when the Ming were forced out of the country in 1427, there was a need for a new state history reflecting expanded territory and new relations vis-à-vis Ming China.

It may well be that an annalistic work entitled *Việt Sử Lược* [Historical Annals of Viet] was written in the fourteenth–fifteenth centuries, although some consider it to be a later work. The work remains extant, but the author is unknown. Comprising three chapters, the first begins with earliest antiquity and ends at the equivalent of 1009 when the Lý dynasty was founded. The second and third chapters cover the period of the Lý dynasty ending in 1225. There is then appended a list of rulers of the Trần dynasty, suggesting to some that this was simply a condensed version of the *Đại Việt Sử Ký* with the list of Trần kings added.

Subsequent to the Ming occupation, scholars began studying their society's antiquity (mainly as it existed in the Chinese classics) and, following the earlier example of Chu Văn An, the Sinic antiquity was incorporated and became a

---

[10] Cuong Tu Nguyen, *Zen in Medieval Vietnam: A Study of the Thiền Uyển Tập Anh* (Honolulu, 1997), 85.

Vietnamese antiquity.[11] The many vestiges of bureaucratic forms and ideological structures that were left following the withdrawal of Ming forces included new ways of writing history. In 1460, the emperor Lê Thánh Tông (r. 1460–97) ordered Confucian officials to compile an official national history. One of the compilers, named Ngô Sĩ Liên, participated initially in the project, but later withdrew because of his father's death. However, Ngô Sĩ Liên later went on to write his own version of the national history under the title *Đại Việt sử ký toàn thư* [Complete Annals of Dai Viet], which was presented to the emperor in 1479. Today, the official history that was compiled at this time has been lost, but the *Toàn Thư* has come down to us. Like Lê Văn Hưu, Ngô Sĩ Liên exhibited an anti-Buddhist sentiment in his work, almost a necessity for a neo-Confucian historian.[12] The inclusion of Nguyễn Trãi's *Bình Ngô Đại Cáo* [Great Proclamation upon the Pacification of the Ngô] in its entirety into the *Toàn Thư* was significant in that this asserted that Đại Việt was an independent civilized country different from China, and with a history as long as that of China. Through such writing, the Vietnamese were looking in very new ways at their polity—a polity that had also been expanding southwards into Champa and, during the fifteenth century, pushing westwards into the Lao lands. In addition to the recording of events, Ngô Sĩ Liên (like Lê Văn Hưu before him) expressed his personal opinions on the historical events and figures detailed, through 170 personal commentaries. Yu Insun suggests that Ngô Sĩ Liên wrote the *Toàn Thư* because he felt the need to promote Confucian ideology and dynastic stability in the place of Buddhist ideas.[13]

Ngô Sĩ Liên's work provided the basis for national histories over the next few centuries. In 1511 Vũ Quỳnh completed the *Việt giám thông khảo* [Complete Study of the History of Viet], which comprised a reorganization of the basic and peripheral records. This became the standard version of the national annals. In 1665 there were further revisions carried out by Phạm Công Trứ as a 'continued compilation' of events up to 1662, and this work was printed under the title *Đại Việt Sử Ký Toàn thư Tục biên* [Continued Compilation of the Complete Book of the Historical Records of the Great Viet]. Copies of this edition are extant today.

In the middle of the eighteenth century, Lê Qúy Dôn created a new form of Vietnamese history when he compiled his *Đại Việt Thông Sử* [Complete History of Dai Viet], otherwise known as *Lê Triều Thông Sử* [Complete History of the Lê Dynasty]. Completed prior to 1752, it was centred on the biographies of kings, queens, and ministers. Lê Qúy Dôn also innovatively provided his own ideas on how history should be written and the wide range of sources from which it

---

[11] John K. Whitmore, 'Chu Văn An and the Rise of "Antiquity" in Fourteenth-Century Đại Việt', *Vietnam Review*, 1 (1996), 50–61.
[12] Yu Insun, 'Lê Văn Huu and Ngô Sĩ Liên: A Comparison of Their Perception of Vietnamese History', in Nhung Tuyet Tran and Anthony Reid (eds.), *Viet Nam: Borderless Histories* (Wisconsin, 2006).
[13] Ibid., 57.

should be drawn. Li Tana considers this work 'a milestone marking a new era in Vietnamese historiography', and it was certainly influential on subsequent Vietnamese historians.[14]

HISTORICAL WRITING IN BURMA

The historiographical traditions of the areas now controlled by the modern state of Burma/Myanmar are diverse, with Burmese, Mon, Shan, and a range of other histories having been produced over time. Early Pyu, Mon, and Burman inscriptions occasionally provided historical aspects by including prophecies of the Buddha as elements of historical origins. The great Kalyāni inscription of 1479, created by the Mon king Rāmādhipati (Dhammaceti), is a Pali and Mon inscription incised on ten stelae. This provides an account of the history of Buddhism to the end of the fifteenth century, and recounts the dispatch of monks to Sri Lanka and their reordination. This action was intended as a means of validating control over his polity and a purged sangha.

Works of historical relevance were already appearing by the fourteenth century. The *Zambu Kungya Po Yāzā Mū haung* [Ancient Actions of Kings] is attributed to Po Yāzā, tutor to Min Khaung, crown prince in the late fourteenth century.[15] However, it is the chronicular tradition that attracts most attention in the sphere of history-writing. The Burman tradition of chronicles (*yazawin* from Sanskrit *rajavamsa*, literally 'Genealogy of Kings') began by at least the fifteenth century, as the earliest extant chronicle, the *Yazawinkyaw* [Celebrated Chronicle of Kings], written by Shin Thilawuntha in the 1520s, cites from earlier chronicles. This work was based on the *Mahāvamsa* [Great Chronicle], a Pali history of Buddhism and politics in Sri Lanka to the fifth century, and thus also harks back to the Buddhist kings of India and Sri Lanka. It then continues with lists of kings in Pagan, Pinya, and Sagaing, and thus provides a Theravada Buddhist genealogy of the Burman rulers. Other local chronicles, also generally compiled by monks, include the Tagaung Chronicle, the Tharehkittara Chronicle, and the Pagan Chronicle that detailed kings, their lineages and their activities, woven around the local history of Buddhism. The Burman chronicles also drew on the earlier Mon texts and their historical styles. In the middle of the sixteenth century, Binnya Dala, a Mon officer at King Bayinnaung's court, translated *Rajadarit Ayedawpon* [Chronicle of the King of Kings] from Mon to Burmese, and this was to have quite some influence on later Burmese historical writing.

---

[14] Li Tana, 'Le Quy Don', in Kelly Boyd (ed.) *Encyclopedia of Historians and Historical Writing*, vol. 1 (London, 1999), 710.
[15] U Tet Htoot, 'The Nature of the Buddhist Chronicles', in D. G. E. Hall (ed.), *Historians of South East Asia* (London, 1961), 53.

The most famed history of Burma is U Kala's *Mahayazawin* [The Great Chronicle], completed in 1724. U Kala was, unusually, not a monk but almost a full-time chronicler, being the first to record systematically the dynasties after the fall of Pagan in the thirteenth century, and in effect was thereby the first to write a history of the early modern nation-state of Burma. The work is divided into three parts, the first two detailing the origin of the universe and the Buddhist kings of ancient India. The third part relates the founding of Tharehkittara and Pagan, and proceeds to provide accounts of the Pinya, Sagaing, Ava, and Toungoo dynasties, and takes history down to his own time (the reign of Taninganwe Min [1714–33]).

Three versions of the chronicle exist—the *Mahā Yazawin Gyi* [The Great Chronicle in Twenty-One Volumes], *Yazawin Lat* [The Shorter Chronicle in Ten Volumes], and *Yazawin Choke* [The Brief Chronicle in One Volume]. In a colophon to the shorter version, U Kala, about whom little is known, says that he collected the materials for the chronicle from various *thamaings* and *mawguns* (accounts of founding of cities, temples, etc.). A salient characteristic of U Kala's work is its composite character: the chronicle is a pastiche of legends, local histories, biographies, and detailed court records, but Lieberman suggests that the second half of the work covering the Toungoo period *c.*1530 enjoys a comparative degree of accuracy.[16]

A further Burman historical literary genre is that known as *Ayedawbon Kyan*, important historical texts that supplement the main Royal Chronicles.[17] In its archaic meaning, *Ayedawbon* referred to an 'historical account of a royal campaign'. There are seven *Ayedawbon kyan* known today, five of which are centred on the achievements of individual Burman kings—Rajadirit (r. 1385–1423), Bayinnaung (r. 1551–81) and his son King Nyaungyan (r. 1559–1605), and Alaungpaya (r. 1752–1760) and his son Bodawpaya (r. 1782–1819). Two relate to Arakan kings. These texts consistently portrayed the rulers as *cakravartin* (universal ruler) who listened to the counsel of their ministers and generals before undertaking any military campaign.

The Arakanese polity, which had been subject to Bengali and Islamic influences and was incorporated into the modern Burmese state in the late eighteenth century, also possessed an independent history-writing tradition. The earliest attested works include *Man raja-kri Ayedawbon* [Chronicle of Man Raja-kri] and *Kyauk-ro thamaing* [Chronological Account of Kyauk-ro]. The rewriting of Arakan history began almost immediately on Burmese conquest, with the Burman monk Danyawadī Sayadaw, who had been sent to control the local clergy, compiling *Danyawadī Ayedawbon* [Danyawadī's Chronicle] in 1787. This

---

[16] Victor B. Lieberman, 'How Reliable is U Kala's Burmese Chronicle? Some New Comparisons', *Journal of Southeast Asian Studies*, 17 (1986), 236–55.

[17] U Thaw Kaung, 'Ayedawbon Kyan, an Important Myanmar Literary Genre Recording Historical Events', *Journal of the Siam Society*, 88:1–2 (2000), 21–33.

recorded, in a pro-Buddhist and anti-Islamic manner, the history of Arakan down to its conquest by King Bodawpaya and incorporation into Burma.

Another major polity incorporated by the Burmese state was the Mon state of Pegu (Bago), which had burgeoned since the fourteenth century. During the efflorescence of Pegu under King Dhammaceti (r. 1472–92), there was a burgeoning of inscriptions, suggesting some increased concern with memory and history. Michael Aung-Thwin also proposes that it was during this period that Dhammaceti invented an earlier eleventh-century Mon Theravada Buddhist tradition of Thaton, 'to which he then linked his reign and dynasty, thereby legitimating the pre-Pagan antiquity of "orthodox" Ramaññadesa'.[18]

The three Mon historical literature traditions—*rājāwan* (genealogies of kings), *dhātuwan* (histories of relic pagodas), and *pum* (biographies or stories of specific monarchs)—mirror in some ways the literary categories in Burman society. It has been noted by Shorto that these *rājāwan*, genealogies of kings, were used politically to legitimate the kings, while the *dhātuwan*, recording histories of relic pagodas, assisted in legitimating the regime religiously.[19] One of the earliest extant *rājāwan* is *Nidāna Ārambhakathā* [Preface to the Legend], but the nature or extent of earlier Mon works is unclear given the cultural destruction and incorporation by the Burmans over the sixteenth to eighteenth centuries.[20] The *Nidāna Ārambhakathā* comprises a likely seventeenth-century text entitled *Rāmañ'-uppatti-dīpaka* [An Explanation of the Origins of Ramaññadesa], which includes a Mon genealogy of kings and polity history (including Thaton and Hamsāwatī /Pegu) up until soon after the death of Dhammaceti. The dating of the various Mon histories, including the royal chronicle *Slapat rajawan datow smim ron* [The History of Kings] and the *Lik smin asah* [Account of the Founding of Pegu], is however fraught with difficulty.

HISTORICAL WRITING IN SIAM/THAILAND

Since the establishment of the first central 'Thai' kingdom of Sukhothai (*c.*1238–1438), the Thais have been recording their histories in diverse forms. The area over which the Thai state has extended has also been frequently expanded and this has required a continual rewriting of histories in order to include the newly incorporated regions. The earliest texts are inscriptional and the most famous of

---

[18] Michael Aung-Thwin, 'Lower Burma and Bago in the History of Burma', in Jos Gommens and Jacques Leider (eds.), *The Maritime Frontier of Burma: Exploring Political, Cultural and Commercial Interaction in the Indian Ocean World, 1200–1800* (Leiden, 2002), 49.

[19] H. L. Shorto, 'Mon Genealogy of Kings: Observations on the *Nidāna Ārambhakathā*', in Hall (ed.), *Historians of South East Asia*, 63–72, on 69.

[20] Michael Aung-Thwin has recently called into question the entirety of Ramaññadesa Mon history prior to the fifteenth century in *The Mists of Rāmañña: The Legend that was Lower Burma* (Honolulu, 2005), 67–78.

these is perhaps the controversial Ramkhamhaeng stele, which purports to bear the earliest Thai inscription, describing the establishment of the polity by King Ramkhamhaeng. Much controversy surrounds this claim, with some describing it as a fake.[21]

The pre-modern historical texts of Siam can be divided into *tamnan* (which mainly record the past in a distinctly Buddhist framework) and *phongsawadan* (which record the histories of political, military, and other developments of specific kingdoms). The *tamnan* were more common in the north of Siam, including Sukhothai, but they were also written in Ayutthaya. They are intimately associated with Buddhism and its institutions, beginning with Gautama Buddha, continuing with the Buddhist kings of India and Sri Lanka, and subsequently with the history of the Buddhist polity, religious institution, or relic that is the subject of the text. These *tamnan* were thus composed to legitimize their subjects by showing how they were linked to the Buddha. That is to say, they were local histories but were tied to a universal history. These works were generally written in Pali, but sometimes Thai, Northern Thai, Lao, or Khmer. There is a concept of change through time implicit within, with Buddhism as the moving force, and the *tamnan* is designed to record that force. *Tamnan* history-writing declined in the seventeenth century but continued in a lesser form into the last half of the eighteenth century. An example of late *tamnan* is the *Sangitiyavamsa* [Chronicle of the Buddhist Councils], which was an attempt to follow the *tamnan* tradition, and was written by Somdet Phra Wannarat, a leading monk during the reign of Rama I (r. 1782–1809). The *Sangitiyavamsa*, dated 1789, was important for Rama I as it recorded his efforts to restore royal patronage of Buddhism as a corrective to his predecessor Taksin's mysticism and abuse of the monkhood. The chronicle details in its eighth chapter the gathering of Buddhist monks known as the Tripitaka Revision Council held in Bangkok in 1788, and which was aimed at compiling a listing of Pali texts and producing an authentic canon. It is claimed that in its selection of events and its account of the relationship between monarchy and sangha, the chronicle is similar to the Sri Lankan chronicle *Mahāvamsa*.

While the *tamnan* dealt with 'universal' Buddhist history, the *phongsāwadāns* provided accounts of dynastic or kingly history, including the deeds of the successive rulers. This was the most important type of history-writing in Siam from the seventeenth to the nineteenth centuries. Such histories were written by scribes or officials at court rather than Buddhist monks, and by playing this role, the historians were serving a court or a ruler rather than the Buddhist *sangha*. It has been suggested that the chronicle created for a ruler was considered part of his legitimating regalia. This form of writing appears to have developed in the seventeenth century, possibly during the reign of Narai (r. 1657–88) of

---

[21] James F. Chamberlain (ed.), *The Ramkhamhaeng Controversy: Selected Papers* (Bangkok, 1991).

Ayutthaya. At this time, kingship had attained a prominent role, and people were assuming affiliations other than their religion. The *Pharatchaphongsawadan Krung Si Ayutthaya chabap Luang Prasoet* [The Luang Prasoet Chronicle of Ayudhyā] of the seventeenth century was compiled by a royal astrologer and was written in Thai, a more secular language than the Pali in which the *tamnan* were written. The chronicles of Ayutthaya are the major manifestation of this genre, and these exist in multiple versions: (a) Luang Prasoet (LP) edition—dated 1680, with events in the existing version up to 1605; (b) the chronicle of the 1157 tradition—dated to 1795 and composed on orders of Rama I; (c) the chronicle included in the 1789 religious history *Sangitiyavamsa*, which was recorded by Jeremias van Vliet;[22] (d) the 2/k.125 fragment that details the period from 1441 to 1444. This includes accounts of Ayutthayan relations with the Cambodians and relations with the north. Following study of all versions, Michael Vickery concludes that 'the LP, the earliest but one of the extant texts, was composed from true records, and all the other Ayudhyan chronicles, except *Sangitiyavamsa*/van Vliet and 2/k.125 derive from it, and the Cambodian chronicles for the period between 1346 and the early sixteenth century were composed artificially under the influence of the new chronicles of Ayudhya'.[23] Vickery also considers that many of the Thai chronicles were written as parts of royal restorations and were therefore considered as elements of the regalia.

A further genre of Thai historical writing in the mainstream canon is that of poetry. One of the most famous historical poems is the *Yuan Pâi* [Defeat of the Yuan], which was likely written in the early sixteenth century in Ayutthaya,[24] but none of the currently extant manuscripts date earlier than the nineteenth century. The work relates fifteenth-century battles between the rulers of Ayutthaya and Lan Na, and was obviously written by a pro-Ayutthaya author, who depicted the Lan Na ruler as a villainous madman.

To the south, over time, the Thai polity incorporated other polities of diverse ethnicities that also had their own historical traditions. Nakhon Sithammarat has been a key port linking this region to the major sea routes east and west for centuries, and there are traditions that Buddhism came to the Thai people through here. Both *Tamnan Muang Nakhon Si Thammarat* [A Religious History of Nakhon Si Thammarat] and *Tamnan Phraboromathat Muang Nakhon Si Thammarat* [A Religious History of the Phraboromathat Chedi at Nakhon Si Thammarat] assign the region a key role in terms of the introduction of Buddhism to an earlier, possibly Mon, polity. Both speak of a tooth relic of the Buddha that was

---

[22] Jeremias van Vliet was a Dutch employee of the VOC, based at Ayudhya in the 1640s. His *Cort Verhael van't naturel eijnde der volbrachte tijt ende successie der Coningen van Siam . . .* was a short history of Siam based on a Thai history. It has been published in English as *The Short History of the Kings of Siam*, trans. Leonard Andaya and ed. David K. Wyatt (Bangkok, 1975).

[23] Michael Vickery, 'Cambodia after Angkor: The Chronicular Evidence for the Fourteenth to Sixteenth Centuries', Ph.D. dissertation, Yale University, 1977, p. 150.

[24] According to Chanthit Krasaesin, in his 1970 version of the poem.

buried at the beach where the city of Nakhon Sithammarat was founded, and its later recovery and the establishment of a reliquary to house it.

Further south, at Phattalung on the Songkhla Lake, the historical accounts of the region consist of two types of document—the *tamra* or royal decree dealing with monastic endowments, and the accompanying history or *tamnan*. The *tamra* was considered protective of the local community, while the *tamnan* also had a protective role for the community in validating why the *tamra* was granted. It was a community text proving their tax exemption rather than a regional text, and thus provided a social history.[25] These local histories date from the late seventeenth century, with some having been copied in the eighteenth century. The monasteries centred on Wat Phra Kho were the subject of the Wat Phra Kho manuscripts, which were essentially historical accounts of the monasteries and the endowments provided to them. The *Phongsawadan Muang Phattalung* [Chronicle of Phattalung] concerns the story of Nang Lüad Khao (Lady White Blood) and the endowment of Phattalung's monastery. This work was apparently recopied at Ayutthaya in AD 1698 at the request of the local monks of Phattalung.[26]

At Patani, a Malay polity that had been incorporated by the Thai state, the *hikayat* tradition of history-writing remained in place. The *Hikayat Patani* [Story of Patani] falls within the Malay historiographical tradition, is written in the Malay language with Jawi script, and appears to have been created in the eighteenth century, deriving from an original text that included the genealogy of Raja Hujan and death of Raja Kuning.[27] The work is divided into six parts, the first three of which relate to the Inland dynasty that founded the city of Patani, with the later chapters detailing the Kelantan dynasty and outlining the legal code of Patani. The stories included are essentially accounts of the rajas of Patani with the earliest recorded events dating from the late fifteenth century.

HISTORICAL WRITING IN LAN NA AND OTHER NORTHERN TAI SOCIETIES

There is a long and rich tradition of history-writing in Lan Na (a region that included today's northern Thailand) and its neighbouring polities, and in fact much of the Ayutthayan historical writing borrowed heavily from the texts of this area. The epigraphic tradition begins in the early fourteenth century, while the major history-writing tradition of this region is that of the *tamnan*, histories centred on the

---

[25] Chuleeporn Virunha, 'Historical Perceptions of Local Identity in the Upper Peninsula', in Michael J. Montesano and Patrick Jory (eds.), *Thai South and Malay North: Ethnic Interactions on a Plural Peninsula* (Singapore, 2008), 39–70.

[26] Lorraine M. Gesick, *In the Land of Lady White Blood: Southern Thailand and the Meaning of History* (Ithaca, 1995).

[27] See *Hikayat Patani: The Story of Patani*, trans. A. Teeuw and D. K. Wyatt (The Hague, 1970).

Buddhist past. The major *tamnan* can be said to be of the *Mahāvamsa* tradition. The *Mūlasāsanā* [History of the Origin of the Religion], which is dated to the 1420s, was written in the Tai Yuan language by Phra Phuttaphukam and Phra Puttayan. This work provides a history of Buddhism until its arrival in Chiang Mai. The *Ratanabimbavamsa* [Chronicle of the Emerald Buddha] also likely dates from the 1420s. Another famed fifteenth-century text is the *Cāmadevīvamsa* [Chronicle of Cāmadevī].[28] This history was written in Pali by Bodhiransī of Chiang Mai, and relates the founding of Hariphunjaya (Lamphun) by the Mon Queen Cāmadevī within the broader context of the history of the religion. Perhaps the most famous of these Lan Na *tamnan* is the *Jinakālamālīpakaranam* [Sheaf of Garlands of the Epochs of the Conqueror], completed in 1516. Written in Pali by *Ratanapañña* of Chiang Mai, the work relates the history of the spread of Buddhism in India, Sri Lanka, and eventually to Chiang Mai.

The *Tamnan phün müang Chiang Mai* [Religious Account of Chiang Mai] holds a special position in northern Thai historiography. Hundreds of versions of the anonymous chronicle exist, as opposed to only a dozen versions of the Chronicle of Ayudhyā. An interesting element of this chronicle is that it was rewritten to follow the political centre of Lan Na as it moved. David Wyatt has observed that the contents of the Chiang Mai chronicle of 1827 down to the early eighteenth century were based almost entirely on a 1741 version written by Suryavamsa Bhikkhu in Chiang Saen. However, more recent sections had been adjusted to reflect the position of Chiang Mai and Lan Na's new relations with Bangkok. The kingdom of Nan, sometimes independent of Lan Na, also had its own chronicles, including *Phra Khanan Khantha*, dating to the early eighteenth century. In addition to these regional histories, most polities and many *wat* in this region, and in the contiguous Tai polities that are now parts of Burma, Laos, China, and Vietnam, have their own histories,[29] but determining which of these existed prior to 1800, and in what form, is an exercise fraught with difficulty. The chronicle of Chiang Khaeng, a Lü kingdom that occupied much of present-day north-west Laos and some of modern Burma, includes events dating from the late 1400s, with the extant texts being compiled in the late 1700s or early 1800s.

HISTORICAL WRITING IN LAOS

One of the polities of the northern Tai world that has maintained an independent status and become a modern nation-state is Laos. The kingdom of Lān Xāng emerged, at least according to its own chronicles, in the fourteenth century.

---

[28] For a translation see *The Legend of Queen Cama: Bodhiramsi's Camadevivamsa, a Translation and Commentary by Bodhiransi*, trans. Donald K. Swearer (New York, 1998).
[29] Often 'downgraded' to *tamnan* by modern Thai scholars of the Damrong generation, by denying them the name *phongsawadan* or *phra ratcha phongsawadan*.

Under the name 'Lao-wo', it first appears in the annals of Ming China in 1402, as the new Yong-le emperor pushed outwards in his quest for political hegemony and domestic legitimacy. The earliest known historical work in Laos is a chronicle entitled *Nithān Khun Bôrom* [The Story of King Bôrom],[30] with the earliest version in verse dating to 1422, and another in prose dated 1479. The longest and best-known version dates from the early sixteenth century. Beginning with the semi-divine King Bôrom, legendary progenitor of the Tai-speaking peoples, sending out his sons to take possession of new lands, the account continues with the eldest son Khun Lo assuming control of Luang Phrabāng. This claimed descent from the eldest son of King Bôrom allows the Lao people to claim precedence over other Tai speakers. The account then details the dynasties prior to Fā Ngum, and then recounts the rise of Fā Ngum (r. *c.*1353–73), and his conquests and establishment of the capital at Lān Xāng.

A second group of texts relate to this new capital and are generically entitled *Phongsāvadān Lān Xāng* [Chronicle of Lān Xāng]. This court chronicle dates possibly from the sixteenth century but the earliest version available today is dated 1656. The common aspects of the accounts within these chronicles are that the story of *Khun Bôrom* is shortened as is that of Fā Ngum and more dates are given in the Culasakkarāt era. Early law codes are included as appendices. Sounet Phothisane has collected forty different versions. Other chronicles exist for Champāsak and Xiang Khvāng, as detailed by Charles Archaimbault, and for Luang Prabang, as recorded in *Phongsāvadān meuang luang phabāng*.

As in other traditions, Lao chronicles had a legitimizing function and they were read aloud as court entertainment at evening gatherings during the coronation period, which lasted a few days. They were also treated as sacred texts, insofar as monks gained merit from copying them.

HISTORICAL WRITING IN CAMBODIA

The end (or at least profound decline) of the great Khmer Empire centred on Angkor, sometime in the early fifteenth century,[31] was to have deeply felt effects on both Cambodian political organization and the way in which the rest of mainland Southeast Asia was structured at the time. This is, however, one of the least-recorded periods in Khmer history, due to the apparent total absence of Cambodian inscriptions between the middle of the fourteenth century and the beginning of the sixteenth.[32] We are thus left with only later chronicles as

---

[30] As in the Mon texts, the preferred term for this historical account derives from the Sanskrit/Pali *nidāna* meaning 'primary source', 'cause', 'origin', while the term in Thai, Lao, and Khmer means 'story'.

[31] Some authors have proposed the abandonment of Angkor in the 1440s.

[32] David P. Chandler, *A History of Cambodia* (Colorado, 1992), 77.

histories of this period. The chronicles we have are compilations of either the eighteenth or nineteenth centuries. There are two major traditions of the chronicle—one of which is known as the *Nong* tradition, as represented by the 1818 'Nong Chronicle', which was composed by Okna Vongsa Sarapech (Nong) at the court of King Ang Chan (r. 1806–35). The period covered by the text extends from 1414 to 1800, this forming the basis for Francis Garnier's translation in *Journal asiatique* (1871–2). The other tradition is known as Version II, and is represented by the Ang Eng fragment, presented to King Rama I of Siam by his Cambodian protégé Ang Eng (r. 1795–7) in 1796 and extant only in Thai translation. This text nominally covers the period 1346 to mid-fifteenth century. Another fragment presented to the Thai court in 1808 is also available only in Thai translation and covers the period 1570–1628.

The chronologies presented in these two traditions vary enormously and remain highly controversial. They also differ in terms of composition, with Version II having much more detailed accounts in the fifteenth and sixteenth centuries. Michael Vickery suggests that fourteenth-century Cambodian history is actually sixteenth-century history moved backwards, opining that 'the first 150 years of Cambodia's post-Angkor history are thus entirely artificial and the reason must have been to imitate the Ayutthayan chronicles, of which new versions had been prepared just before the date attributed to Ang Eng, and to make Cambodia's written history as long as that of its neighbour'.[33] Vickery stresses the importance of composition of a new chronicle as an integral part of any royal restoration. This seems to have occurred in the mid-eighteenth century and again in the first few years after 1806 when Ang Chan came to the throne.

The whole tortuous process of revision in the eighteenth and nineteenth centuries was to force Cambodian records into the Ayutthayan model . . . Thus the Cambodian writers accepted that their country had been a weak vassal of the Thai from nearly the beginning of recorded history and the only special thread I see running through the whole account is a picture of Cambodian kings who brought the kingdom back together after times of trouble, as men who had established a special relationship with the Thai court, and who had received Thai aid in regaining the throne against local opposition.[34]

HISTORICAL WRITING IN SUMATRA
AND THE MALAY WORLD

It is difficult to distinguish sharply the histories or the historiographies of Sumatra from those of the peninsula that is separated from that island by the Straits of Melaka. The Malay histories look back to Bukit Seguntang in Sumatra

---

[33] Vickery, 'Cambodia after Angkor', 151.
[34] Ibid., 154.

as their homeland, with flight to and then colonization of the peninsula by Malay people featuring only in the period post-1400. We can thus treat the Malay history-writing of Sumatra and the peninsula as part of a single historiographical tradition. The two major forms of history-writing within this tradition are the *hikayat* (usually rendered as 'story' or 'romance', and often intended to be read aloud) and the *sejarah* (more usually 'history' or 'annals'), while the poetic forms of literature are often grouped under the rubric of *syair/shair*. It should be noted that each of these terms is derived from Arabic, suggesting something of the influences on the evolution of the forms.

Widely considered the oldest chronicle of this tradition is the *Hikayat Raja-Raja Pasai* [Story of the Kings of Pasai], a history of Samudera-Pasai in northern Sumatra, written by accretion between 1350 and 1524. The work reveals *Mahabharata* and *Ramayana* influences, and certainly in turn influenced the later *Sejarah Melayu* and other *sejarah*. Constituting probably the most influential historical work in Malay literature, the *Sejarah Melayu* or Malay Annals, also known as *Sulalat al-Salatin* [Genealogy/Descent of Kings], written at the end of the fifteenth century or early in the sixteenth century, is concerned with dynastic legitimation of the Sultans of Melaka and, in some ways, the preservation of Malay ceremonial tradition. The Malays, who moved to Melaka, and then beyond, needed an ideological basis for their new polities. Leonard Andaya suggests that, for Melaka, in order to 'create the glory of Srivijaya on the peninsula, it was necessary not only to re-establish the conditions for favourable trade, but also to promote itself actively as the new centre of the Melayu':

An interesting contest thus ensued not on the battlefield but in the creation of rival texts. It would have begun in the fifteenth century when the Melaka court asserted its centrality in the Melayu world through a court document entitled *Sulalat al-Salatin*...The writing of the *Sejarah Melayu* was intended as a reaffirmation of its central position in Melayu.[35]

The *Sejarah Melayu* is represented in a number of versions (although none of the extant manuscripts predate the nineteenth century); and a succinct account of these has been given by Roolvink.[36] There are two major traditions that differ markedly. In the earlier and shorter version, often known as the 1536 version, the author acknowledges his debt to *Hikayat Iskandar* [The Story of Iskandar] and in fact begins the work with a paraphrase of the Iskandar story. That is to say, borrowings were made from *Hikayat Iskandar Zulkarnain*, an account describing the military conquest of the East by the Macedonian king Alexander the Great and his meeting with the 'king of India'. The Islamic specialist Marrison notes Persian influences in the *Sejarah Melayu*—with its division into chapters, Persian

[35] Leonard Y. Andaya, 'The Search for the Origins of Melayu', *Journal of Southeast Asian Studies*, 32:3 (2001), 315–30.
[36] R. Roolvink, 'The Variant Versions of the Malay Annals', *Bijdragen tot de Taal-, Land- en Volkenkunde*, 123:3 (1967), 301–24.

loan words, and occasional Persian citations.[37] The later version, edited in Johor in 1612 by Tun Seri Lanang, sees many changes to the text and added prestige for the family of the Bendahara or prime ministers of Johor, who succeeded the last Melaka sultan in 1699. It includes a paraphrase of *Hikayat Iskandar*, but with a fuller account of Alexander's descendants down to Raja Suran Padshah.

Let us return now to Sumatra, where an influential history-writing tradition developed in Aceh between the beginnings of the state in the late fourteenth century and its apogee in the first half of the seventeenth century. Aceh had close links with Muslim India and based its bureaucracy on the administrative structure of the Mughal Empire. There is evidence that the Malay language versions of the Persian works popular in the Mughal court date from this period.[38] The most famous work to emerge from this milieu was *Hikayat Aceh* [The Story of Aceh], eulogizing Aceh's greatest ruler, Iskandar Muda (r. 1607–36). This was an attempt to mimic *Akbar-nama*, a biography of the Mughal emperor Akbar (r. 1556–1605), and was likely compiled *c.*1630. Seventeenth-century manuscripts of the work still exist, and the standard modern text and analysis is that by Teuku Iskandar.[39]

Anthony Johns believes that the *Hikayat Aceh* draws on the tradition of 'penglipur lara' (soother of cares) folk tales, which also often involve genealogies with supernatural origins. In the *Hikayat*, Iskandar Muda's descent is traced to two brothers, one of whom starts his line with a princess found in a bamboo grove, while the other brother marries a flying princess who has deserted from Heaven. The king, as the stabilizing fulcrum of the realm, is the hero of the *Hikayat Aceh* story, in the same way as the hero of a folk romance provides the principle of order in the episodes told about him.[40] 'This is not to argue that either structurally or imaginatively a chronicle is simply a special form of folk story—only that the chronicles and the folk stories come from the same cultural matrix and reflect a common perception of the shape of the world.'[41]

History-writing in Aceh during this post-sixteenth-century period was also influenced by the various Islamic *tarīkas* (Sufi sects), which flourished in Aceh and were renowned for their mystical literature. Hamzah Fansuri was a famed writer, but his works were later deemed heretical and were burned with the death of the Aceh ruler Iskandar Muda in 1636 and the arrival of Nuruddin al-Raniri from Gujarat in 1637. Al-Raniri's most famous historical work was *Bustan al-Salatin* [The Garden of Kings] (*c.*1643), a universal history that examined the history of the Muslim kings of Melaka and Pahang, and those of Aceh, as well as

---

[37] A. H. Johns, 'The Turning Image: Myth and Reality in Malay Perceptions of the Past' in Reid and Marr (eds.), *Perceptions of the Past in Southeast Asia*, 43–67, esp. 46; G. E. Marrison, 'Persian Influence in Malay Life', *Journal of Malaysian Branch of the Royal Asiatic Society*, 28 (1955), 52–69.

[38] Ibid., 47.

[39] Teuku Iskandar, *De Hikajat Atjeh* (The Hague, 1958).

[40] Johns, 'The Turning Image', 52.

[41] Ibid., 55.

various religious teachers in Aceh prior to and during the seventeenth century. It placed these accounts in a much longer historical stream, beginning with the creation of Heaven and Earth, stories of the prophets from Adam onwards, the kings of Egypt up to the time of Alexander, the kings of Nejd and Hijaz until the time of Muhammad, the history of Muhammad and the first four caliphs, the Ummayads, the Abbasids, and the history of the Muslim kings of Delhi. Much of the historical writing by the Sufis during this period was informed by the attitudes to history-writing in Muslim India, and while being histories in many ways, these works were also warnings to the faithful to beware heterodox mysticism of the *Wujūdiyya.*[42]

There is a range of other Malay history texts, which were likely initially created prior to 1800, associated with locations extending through much of insular Southeast Asia. However, the fragility of paper manuscripts in the tropics has meant that only the most recent survive, which creates major problems with dating or verifying dates provided in these texts. The sultans of Brunei still trace their origins through the *Salasilah Raja-Raja Brunei* [Book of Descent of the Kings of Brunei], compiled in the 1730s. The *Hikayat Merong Mahawangsa* [The Story of Merong Mahawangsa] provides an account of the origins of the polity of Kedah. Dismissed by Richard Winstedt as a 'farrago of folk-tales', it has been the subject of a major study of literature and history by Henk Maier.[43] *Hikayat Bandjar* [The Story of Banjarmasin], which describes the origin of the Sultanate of Banjarmasin in southern Borneo, appears to have been compiled mainly in the sixteenth century during the reign of the first Islamic ruler, Sultan Suryanu'llah, but extant copies are all of the nineteenth century. The more recent histories, such as *Misa Melayu*, a contemporary account of the state of Perak over the period 1742–78, written by Raja Chulan, showed a new historiography emerging, manifesting more distinctly modern sensibilities. This new historiography was to burgeon later in the nineteenth century with works such as *Tuhfat al-Nafis* [The Precious Gift].

HISTORICAL WRITING IN JAVA

Similar to some of the mainland Southeast Asian polities, Java has a rich inscriptional heritage, extending from the eighth to the fifteenth century. In general, however, these were not records of political events, ruling family histories, or local accounts, but rather were concerned with the recording of diversions of land tax to religious foundations and the establishment of *sima* (monastic boundaries). Javanese versions of Indian texts—such as the *Kakawin*

---

[42] A. H. Johns, 'Muslim Mystics and Historical Writing', 45.
[43] Henk Maier, *In the Center of Authority: The Malay Hikayat Merong Mahawangsa* (Ithaca, 1988).

Rāmâyana [Ramayana in Kakawin Metre] began to appear in the ninth century, but it was not until the fourteenth century that a major historical epic appeared. The earliest historical Javanese text that has come down to us is the *Nāgarakrtāgama* or *Désawarnana* [The Description of the Regions], completed in 1365 by Prapañca.[44] This work describes the Majapahit realm during the reign of Hayam Wuruk (r.1350–89). It provides a brief dynastic history, including King Kertanagara, the grandfather of Hayam Wuruk, and describes the regions visited by the latter during his royal progress throughout his kingdom. The form of the text is *kakawin*, a work written in verse form with rhythms and metres derived from Sanskrit literature. C. C. Berg sees this work as 'the starting point of Javanese historiography', and considers that it was intended as a new basis for Majapahit's ritual activity, with Prapañca aiming to re-establish certainty and order in the ritual sphere.[45]

The next work of major note is the sixteenth-century *Pararaton* or *Pustaka Raja* [Book of Kings], the sole Old Javanese work that can be considered to resemble a chronicle.[46] The work was clearly historiography in the service of the ruler's legitimacy. *Pararaton* relates the stories of the East Javanese kingdoms of Singhasari and Majapahit up until 1481. The work begins with an earlier incarnation of Ken Arok, the founder of the Singhasari kingdom (1222–92), but proceeds to shorter narrative fragments in a chronological succession. Many of the events recorded here are dated, and have been correlated with inscriptions and other sources. The earliest extant manuscript dates from 1600.

The canonical form of *babad* literature, established during the reign of Sultan Agung (1613–45), characterized Javanese historical writing from the seventeenth century onwards.[47] The *Babad Tanah Jawi* [Chronicle of Java], which likely saw its earliest codification in the seventeenth century, is a history of Java seen from the court of Mataram, from the time of the first man, Adam, through a genealogy of various Hindu gods and Muslim prophets. It describes the descent of all the kings of Java from the Pandawas, and provides genealogies of the kings of Kediri, Pajajaran, Majapahit and the later courts of Demak, Pajang, and Mataram.

The prolegomena of the *Babad*, which was written in a strictly metrical form, is more complex than that of the *Pararaton*. It begins with the founding of the central Javanese state of Mataram by Senapati in 1582, and continues through till the new state reaches its apogee under his grandson Agung. Anthony Johns

[44] For translations of this text see Theodore G. Th. Pigeaud, *Java in the 14th Century: A Study in Cultural History—The Nagara-Kertagama by Rakawi, Prapanca of Majapahit, 1365 A.D.*, 5 vols. (The Hague, 1960–3); and Mpu Prapanca, *Desawarnana (Nagarakrtagama)*, trans. Stuart Robson (Leiden, 1995).

[45] C. C. Berg, 'Javanese Historiography—A Synopsis of its Evolution', in D. G. E. Hall (ed.), *Historians of South East Asia* (London, 1961), 13–23.

[46] For a Dutch translation of the text see J. L. A. Brandes, *Pararaton (Ken Arok) of het Boek der Koningen van Tumapel en van Majapahit* (Batavia, 1920).

[47] Anthony H. Johns, 'The Role of Structural Organisation and Myth in Javanese Historiography', *The Journal of Asian Studies*, 24:1 (1964), 94.

considers that the Mataram *babad* grew out of an earlier Demak *babad*, which in turn derived from a Pajang *babad*, being revised and rewritten for the new rulers on each occasion.[48] This supports the claim by Charles Archaimbault that, as in mainland Southeast Asia, chronicles in Java were considered an element of royal regalia.[49]

By the eighteenth century, a different form of *babad* had developed, with the *Babad Balambangan* of 1773–4 being a Javanese account of the Dutch conquest of the Javanese kingdom of Balambangan and the Malang-Lumajang region. It is different in language and style from the earlier *babad* and certainly presaged new ways of writing Javanese history.

HISTORICAL WRITING IN BALI

Located just to the east of the much larger island of Java, Bali has long been affected by the political changes in, and cultural influences of, Java. Bali has an inscriptional tradition extending back to the ninth century, but history-writing on the island is a much more recent phenomenon. The fourteenth and fifteenth centuries saw Majapahit attacks on Bali and subsequently the flight of Javanese to Bali when Majapahit faced its own decline. Majapahit then became, ironically, a legitimizing icon in the histories of Bali.

As in Java, the *babad* form occupies a key position in the historiography of Bali. Often defined as a chronicle or a dynastic genealogy, it encompasses a wide range of historical, literary, and religious elements. As in Java, the *babad* were essentially used to legitimate political control. The three earliest texts appear to be *Babad Dalem*, *Usana Bali*, and *Usana Jawi*, in all of which Balinese royal families trace their origins to persons originating in Majapahit. These texts generally date to the eighteenth century, a period of great political upheaval as power shifted from the Gelgel dynasty, which had held (or at least is represented to have held) supreme power from the fourteenth to the seventeenth century, to the new Klungkung dynasty. In some ways, *Babad Dalem* can be considered Klungkung's official legitimating chronicle. It was partly due to the existence of this legitimating text (and diverse satellite texts), and the ruling family's claims of descent from Majapahit, that Klungkung, despite its size, was able to dominate in Bali until Dutch conquest of the island in 1908. The *Babad Dalem* offers a reasonably chronological account of the major ruling dynasties and elite families of Bali, and is as much about the lesser nobility as the core Gelgel dynasty. Helen Creese notes that:

---

[48] Ibid., 98.
[49] Charles Archaimbault, 'Les annals de l'ancien royaume de S'ieng Khwang', *Bulletin de l'École français d'Extrême-Orient*, 53:2 (1967), 557–674.

It is written as a series of interwoven fragments moving from one descent group to another in a bewildering array of interconnecting lineages interspersed with narrative and mythical events. The structure and elliptic language of the text have implications for the interpretation and reinterpretation of the text itself through the generations, providing a fluidity that Western chronological historical writing lacks.[50]

The idea of Majapahit origins was also adopted by other families as a legitimating trope, and the importance of the *Babad Dalem* is underlined by the fact that such works, in claiming a hereditary connection through Klungkung and Gelgel, incorporate passages from Klungkung's *Babad Dalem.*

Adrian Vickers has also brought to attention the Balinese genre of *Pangéling-éling* (Commemorations), which are often attached to 'literary texts', including courtly romances, and provide details of events that occurred in the eighteenth and nineteenth centuries, and which in some ways have consonance with the content of the text they are attached to. These are often related to events in the kingdoms of Karangasem and Bulèlèng. Some of these 'commemorations' suggest the 'past as pattern' by noting crucial events that occurred at the same time as other major events or which recall important ancestors in people's memory.[51]

HISTORICAL WRITING IN EASTERN INDONESIA

One of the Southeast Asian areas least well served by written histories is the region known today as Eastern Indonesia. However, despite the general dearth of histories, the Makassar and Buginese people of the southern Sulawesi are famed for the keeping of diaries—both court documents and personal accounts, and it is these which were used as the basis of the existing chronicles. The chronicles of Sulawesi are written in an Indic-derived script, suggesting perhaps that the writing of such began before the introduction of Islam and Arabic script in 1605. The fact that Portuguese names are used for months of the year also suggests strong European influence prior to the arrival of Islam.

The chronicles of Goa and Tallo', which are state narratives deriving from genealogies, are written in simple prose and are not strictly chronological, but devote sections to individual princes of ruling dynasties, their families, and their achievements. In the chronicle of Goa, there is some obvious concern for chronology, and the year AD 1511 when the Portuguese took Melaka is the first synchronic date that can be established. The chronicles begin with mythical elements sometime prior to AD 1500, with the first king of the dynasty, the *manurang*, descending from Heaven. Other versions have a beautiful woman (or

---

[50] Helen Creese, 'Chronologies and Chronograms: An Interim Response to Hägerdal', *Bijdragen tot de Taal-, Land- en Volkenkunde,* 151:1 (1995), 125–31.

[51] Adrian Vickers, 'Balinese Texts and Historiography', *History and Theory,* 29:2 (1990), 158–78.

a girl and her six elder brothers) descending from Heaven to a river, inducing a local federation of chieftainships.

The various early chronicles extend up to the seventeenth century, with the Tallo', Bone, Goa, and Wadjo' chronicles ending with dates equivalent to 1641, 1660, 1670, and 1650 respectively, but none of the actual texts can be dated that early. The chronicles are continually being revised, and in Wadjo', there are four great chronicles: one from the seventeenth century, two from the eighteenth, and one completed just before the Second World War. Comparison of these various texts provides an excellent example of the processes of chronicle revision through time.

The chronicles are generally descriptive, with little commentary or judgement on events or why they are included in the history. However, it has been noted that chronicles were written 'because it is feared that the old princes would be forgotten by their posterity'.[52] Anthony Reid suggests that the Goa history is indicative of a burgeoning early modernity in the region, as it identifies with each reign of the ruling Makassar house not only battles and royal marriages, but also advances in technology and statecraft.[53] It needs to be stressed how different are these Sulawesi chronicles from those of the Malay/Javanese traditions, and there seem to be no direct influences from the latter. There are no prolegomena as seen in the Javanese or Malay traditions and rather there seems to be a concern for 'facts'.

That is not to say that the islands have not been affected at all by the Malay/Javanese history-writing tradition. One early work in this tradition worthy of mention is the *Sy'air Perang Mengkasar* [Rhymed Poem of the Makassar War] written in Malay verse by Entji' Amin, official writer of the Sultan of Goa (Makassar), a contemporary history describing the fall of Makassar to Dutch-led troops in the 1670s.

HISTORICAL WRITING IN THE PHILIPPINES

The writing of Philippine history was essentially a colonial period enterprise. No pre-Hispanic document of uncontested authenticity has ever been identified.[54] The Spanish records left to us from the sixteenth century note a widespread literacy amongst Filipinos at least from the mid-sixteenth century, but at the same time it was stated in various texts that the Filipinos used their script only for letters and messages.[55] Some Visayan oral epics were recorded by Spanish friars

---

[52] J. Noorduyn, 'Some Aspects of Macassar-Buginese Historiography', in Hall, (ed.) *Historians of South East Asia*, 24–36, on 34.

[53] Anthony Reid, *Southeast Asia in the Early Modern Era: Trade, Power and Belief* (Ithaca, NY, 1993), 8.

[54] William Henry Scott, *Prehispanic Source Materials for the Study of Philippine History* (Quezon City, 1984), 63.

[55] William Henry Scott, *Looking for the Prehispanic Filipino and Other Essays in Philippines History* (Quezon City, 1992).

but their historicity remains moot. There are, of course, thirteenth- and fourteenth-century Chinese texts that record places and people in the Philippines, as well as their visits to China,[56] but in terms of indigenous written texts, the earliest extant appear to be the *tarsilas* or *salsilas*—the royal genealogies—of the rulers of Sulu and Mindanao in what is today the southern Philippines. Najeeb M. Saleeby[57] has provided us with a translation of the 'Genealogy of Sulu', a Malay text, the extant copy of which dates from the mid-nineteenth century, but which details the genealogy of the Sulu sultans supposedly from the fourteenth century, noting their origins in the Minangkabau area of Sumatra.

Like the Sulu *tarsila*, the *tarsila*s of Mindanao/Magindanao are genealogies tied together with the history of Islam on the island. These are sometimes written in Malay, but others are in the language of Mindanao. Extant manuscripts are all quite late, with none appearing to predate the nineteenth century, although eighteenth-century visitors to the islands report the existence of such genealogies at that time, and there is no reason to suggest that they did not exist even earlier. The contents of individual *tarsila* are diverse, with the 'Genealogy of Kabungsu-wan', for example, beginning with the Prophet Muhammad, proceeding to references to a princess born of a bamboo stalk, and ending with Mindanao figures otherwise historically attested.[58] A further *tarsila* collected by Saleeby includes the descent of the sultans of Magindanao,[59] very similar to the *salisilah* of Brunei mentioned above, and in fact, a common genre with the *Sejarah Melayu* of Melaka.

Spanish histories written in the islands include the *Sucesos de las Islas Filipinas* (1609), edited by António Morga. It records the Spanish history of the islands from the time of Magellan in 1521 until the beginning of the seventeenth century, and includes details of links with Japan, China, and other areas with which the Spanish in Manila had trade or other contacts. Subsequent histories were to incorporate major aspects of Spanish historiographical influence.

CONCLUDING REMARKS

The diversity of the historiographical traditions noted above almost precludes any formal conclusion. The difficulty of synthesizing the ideas that generated these diverse histories, written over a period of 400 years—and across hugely different societies, political systems, and economic structures, and in a range of languages and scripts—will be immediately apparent. What can be suggested are a number of commonalities within some of the traditions and the influences that

---

[56] William Henry Scott and Go Bon Juan, *Filipinos in China before 1500* (Manila, 1989).
[57] Najeeb M. Saleeby, *The History of Sulu* (Manila, 1963).
[58] Najeeb M. Saleeby, *Studies in Moro History, Law, and Religion* (Manila, 1905), 21–5.
[59] Ibid., 36–40.

either gave rise to or changed those traditions. In his thesis on the evolution of polities in the Southeast Asian mainland over the period from 800 to 1800, Victor Lieberman suggests that during the fifteenth century, many western and central mainland polities were characterized by a 'decentralised Indic adminis-tration, manifested as a loose solar polity, with semi-independent tributaries, autonomous viceroys, reduced economic and social role for temples and still modest administrative and manpower control'.[60] They lacked the autonomous religious institutions and temple complexes that characterized earlier 'charter polities'. We might thus posit that the newness felt by the Southeast Asian polities and societies about what was happening in the fifteenth century was reflected in a new attention to history.

The traditions of recitation or singing of genealogical descent and social histories, still practised in Eastern Indonesia, were likely the precursor of many of the forms of historical writing detailed above. The public reciting of histories continued into the period of literacy with Lao chronicles being read aloud during coronation celebrations. Shorto has in fact suggested that '[i]t is possible that a preoccupation with the genealogical theme is one of the autochthonous elements in Southeast Asian culture'.[61]

The most common aspect that runs throughout almost all the histories is that of confirmation of legitimacy—religious and political. In many ways, by providing appropriate genealogies, the histories justified the social arrangements in place, the existing religious structure, and the legitimacy of the ruling line or individual. The Vietnamese histories were intended to justify the independent existence of a Viet polity alongside China. It also appears that the writing of new histories after periods of disorder was important in re-establishing a social/political order and new legitimacy. That is why the histories were often consid-ered a part of the royal regalia in both mainland and island Southeast Asia. 'By their very composition, chronicles testified to the new ruler's ability to promote orthodox culture and thus to stabilize society. Stilling confusion in the world might quell disorder in the world.'[62] In fourteenth-century Java, *Nāgarakrtāgama* provided a new basis for Majapahit's ritual activity, while the later *Pararaton* (sixteenth century) and *Babad Tanah Jawi* (seventeenth century) are clearly histories written in the service of the ruler's legitimacy. In Bali, the *Babad Dalem* was drawn on by a range of dynastic lines to provide them legitimacy extending back to Majapahit in Java. The 'Genealogy of Sulu' provides a genealogy of the Sulu sultans supposedly from the fourteenth century, suggesting origins in the Malay homeland of Sumatra.

---

[60] Lieberman, *Strange Parallels*, 33–5.
[61] Shorto, 'Mon Genealogy of Kings', 67.
[62] Lieberman, 'How Reliable is U Kala's Burmese Chronicle?' 253.

By putting forward specific territorial or dynastic claims, chronicles could legitimate the ambitions or existing territory of their patrons. For example, Siamese chronicles were sponsored by usurpers-cum-restorers Prasat Thong (r. 1629–56) and Rama I, which projected back to earlier periods Ayutthayan hegemony over Cambodia, Sukhothai, and Chiang Mai—periods when those polities were actually independent. Rewriting of the Arakan chronicles was an integral part of Burman incorporation of that polity into the Burmese realm. Conversely, it has been suggested that the Cambodian court adopted Thai chronicles wholesale as a means of assuming some legitimacy.

Some legitimations were very local. We see in southern Thailand the issuing of *tamrā*[63] or royal decrees dealing with monastic endowments, and the writing of accompanying history or *tamnan* of the monastery. The history had a protective role for the community in validating why the *tamra* was granted. It was thus essentially a community text (rather than a regional text) proving their tax exemption.

In Southeast Asian histories, a supernatural origin—as well as other supernatural events—are often *de rigeur*. Accounts of persons born from bamboo stalks are found frequently in these histories as well as in much folklore of the region, while descent from Heaven is also a common motif, as in the Sulawesi chronicles. The semi-divine King Bôrom, legendary progenitor of the Tai-speaking peoples, can also be found in a wide range of Tai chronicles. Anthony Johns suggests of Javanese histories that, as the function of the ruler in Java is to connect the present with the past and the future, and to give human life its place in the cosmic order, two principles are of concern—the cosmic function of the king, and his innate divinity.[64] This necessarily demands accounts of supernatural events and portents to validate the divinity of the ruler.

Obviously there was a range of external religious influences on the histories written in different regions of Southeast Asia in different periods. Most of these came from or via South Asia, but the obvious Chinese influence on the Vietnamese annals cannot be ignored. The South Asian influences included both Buddhist and Hindu aspects, and vestiges of Hindu classics such as *Mahabharata* and *Ramayana* can be seen in the earlier Acehnese and Malay histories. The impact of Buddhism on Southeast Asian history-writing has been immense, with the entire historical canons of most of the mainland Southeast Asian states being premised on religious descent from Gautama Buddha. They are also infused with Buddhist iconography and historiographical forms, mainly derived from the *Mahāvamsa*, the Sri Lankan chronicle of the Theravada tradition. This model

---

[63] Sometimes written in an unusual form of Khmer.
[64] Johns, 'The Role of Structural Organisation and Myth in Javanese Historiography', 93.

was particularly important in ancient Siam and Burma and continued to be followed until the seventeenth and eighteenth centuries. It has been suggested that in order to justify the writing of stories of kings, ministers, and generals, Buddhists need the moral justification that they are showing the impermanence of all things. The Burmese historian U Kala noted this justification in his exordiums as rationale for writing them.[65] In an astute observation on the nature of Buddhist and Hindu influence on societies (and by implication history-writing) in Southeast Asia, H. L. Shorto noted:

It is characteristic of Buddhism in its later forms that, while its social ethic certainly assists political stability, it is, with its repudiation of caste and consequent neutrality towards status-systems generally, singularly lacking in doctrine designed to regulate the institution of monarchy. This in Southeast Asia was necessarily provided from Hindu sources, a development which led to a syncretism always nominally Buddhist but incorporating without embarrassment many Hindu elements, especially in the political field, as well as residues of the autochthonous animism of the region.[66]

The advent of Islam in the archipelago was also hugely influential on the forms of history written throughout maritime Southeast Asia, not only with the newly introduced Arabic script being employed, but with a wide range of religious and literary conventions being incorporated within the rewritten histories of the regions. We have few examples of pre-Islamic histories from the maritime realm, which makes it difficult to assert specifically how texts were changed in this process, but the change was certainly thorough, with the adoption of new origin stories, new religious iconography, and new ideas of a global *ummah* being manifested to some degree in the histories. The Javanese, Bugis, and Balinese continued to use their own scripts, even though the histories of the first two mentioned were rewritten in accordance with the new religious affiliation. In Java, the *babad* tradition, with its central narrative of legitimation of rulers, was created by the Islamo-Javanese courts during the transition to Islam, yet *Babad Tanah Jawi*, an account of the state of Mataram in Central Java, begins with a syncretic genealogy of Hindu gods and Muslim prophets.[67] The *Hikayat Aceh*, eulogizing Aceh's greatest ruler, Iskandar Muda, was more exclusively Islamic, drawing its pattern from a Mughal text.

A further characteristic that is manifested throughout Southeast Asia during this period is the continual rewriting of histories. Few texts were considered classics and thus retained or copied. Rather, the chronicles or other histories were

[65] Lieberman, 'How Reliable is U Kala's Burmese Chronicle?' 236–55.
[66] Shorto, 'Mon Genealogy of Kings', 67.
[67] Johns, 'The Role of Structural Organisation and Myth in Javanese Historiography', 92.

continually reworked to incorporate the newest religious, political, and social phenomena, or indeed a new regime. It appears that the *Babad Tanah Jawi*, which legitimized the Mataram state, grew out of an earlier Demak *babad*, which in turn derived from a Pajang *babad*, being revised and rewritten for the new rulers on each occasion. A range of elements was often incorporated to aid the rewriting and the continuity. Michael Aung-Thwin notes of Burmese histories that the 'Prophecies, omen and dialogue bridged the ideological gap between the ever-changing events of narrative history (and belief in the Law of Imperma- nence) and the persistent traditions and institutions of custom-valued society (and the desire for continuity). To put it another way, the discontinuity of text was embellished to serve the continuity of context.'[68]

From the nineteenth century, a new period in Southeast Asian history-writing began. Anthony Johns suggests that this indeed constituted a break from the past and that European dominance weakened or suppressed altogether the Southeast Asian mechanisms for adaptation and change. As a result, and in competition with the Western traditions of secular history, Southeast Asian history-writing had to create new forms of representing the past.

KEY HISTORICAL SOURCES

Archaimbault, Charles, 'Les annals de l'ancien royaume de S'ieng Khwang', *Bulletin de l'École français d'Extrême-Orient*, 53:2 (1967), 557–674.

Brandes, J. L. A., *Pararaton (Ken Arok) of het Boek der Koningen van Tumapel en van Majapahit* (Batavia, 1920).

Chamberlain, James F. (ed.), *The Ram Khamhaeng Controversy: Selected Papers* (Bangkok, 1991).

Cheah Boon Kheng and Abdul Rahman Haji Ismail (eds.), *Sejarah Melayu: The Malay Annals* (Kuala Lumpur, 1998).

Chen Ching Ho (ed.), *Đại Việt sử ký toàn thư*, 3 vols. (Tokyo, 1986).

The Chiang Mai Chronicle, trans. David K. Wyatt and Aroonrut Wichienkeeo (Chiang Mai, 1995).

The Glass Palace Chronicles of the Kings of Burma, trans. Pe Maung Tin and G. H. Luce (Oxford, 1923).

Halliday, Robert, 'Slapat rajawan datow smim ron', *Journal of the Burma Research Society*, 13:1 (1923), 1–67.

---

[68] Michael Aung-Thwin, 'Prophecies, Omens and Dialogue: Tools of the Trade in Burmese Historiography', in David K. Wyatt and Alexander Woodside (eds.), *Moral Order and the Question of Change: Essays on Southeast Asian Thought* (New Haven, 1982), 100.

Hikayat Patani: The Story of Patani, trans. A. Teeuw and David K. Wyatt (The Hague, 1970).

Hill, A. H., 'Hikayat Raja-Raja Pasai: A Revised Romanised Version', *Journal of the Malaysian Branch, Royal Asiatic Society*, 33:2 (1960).

Kala, U., *Maha Yazawin-gyi*, ed. U Khin Soe (Yangon, 1960–1).

Mpu Prapanca, *Desawarnana (Nagarakrtagama)*, trans. Stuart Robson (Leiden, 1995).

The Nan Chronicle, trans. and ed. David K. Wyatt (Ithaca, 1994).

Olthof, W. L. (ed. and trans.), *Babad Tanah Djawi in proza: Javaansche geschiedenis*, 2 vols. (The Hague, 1941).

Pigeaud, Theodore G. Th., *Java in the 14th Century: A Study in Cultural History—The Nagara-Kertagama by Rakawi, Prapanca of Majapahit, 1365 A.D.*, 5 vols. (The Hague, 1960–3).

Putu Phalgunadi, I. Gusti, *The Pararaton: A Study of the Southeast Asian Chronicle* (New Delhi, 1996).

Roolvink, R., 'The Variant Versions of the Malay Annals', *Bijdragen tot de Taal-, Land- en Volkenkunde*, 123:3 (1967), 301–24.

The Royal Chronicles of Ayutthaya, trans. Richard D. Cushman, ed. David K. Wyatt (Bangkok, 2000).

Saimong Mangrai, Sao, *The Pādaeng Chronicle and the Jengtung State Chronicle Translated* (Ann Arbor, 1981).

Saleeby, Najeeb M., *The History of Sulu* (Manila, 1963).

The Sheaf of Garlands of the Epochs of the Conqueror: Being a Translation of Jinakā-lamālīpakaranam of Ratanapañña Thera, trans. N. A. Jayawickrama (London, 1968).

Sila Viravong, Maha, *History of Laos* (New York, 1964).

Souneth Photisane, 'The Nidān Khun Bôrom: Annotated Translation and Analysis', Ph.D. dissertation University of Queensland, 1997.

Vickery, M., 'Cambodia after Angkor: The Chronicular Evidence for the Fourteenth to Sixteenth Centuries', Ph.D. dissertation, Yale University, 1977.

BIBLIOGRAPHY

Aung-Thwin, Michael, 'Burmese Historiography Chronicles (*Yazawin*)', in D. R. Woolf (ed.), *A Global Encyclopedia of Historical Writing* (New York, 1998), 417–19.

Berg, C. C., 'Javanese Historiography—A Synopsis of its Evolution', in D. G. E. Hall (ed.), *Historians of South East Asia* (London, 1961), 13–23.

Coedès, G., 'Documents sur l'histoire politique et religieuse du Laos occidental', *Bulletin de l'Ecole française d'Extrême-Orient*, 25 (1925), 1–201.

Cowan, C. D. and Wolters, O. W. (eds.), *Southeast Asian History and Historiography: Essays Presented to D. G. E. Hall* (Ithaca, NY, 1976).

Creese, Helen, 'Balinese Babad as Historical Sources: A Reinterpretation of the Fall of Gelgel', *Bijdragen Tot de Taal-, Land- en Volkenkunde*, 147:2–3 (1990), 236–60.

Dutton, George, 'The *Hoang Le Nhat Thong Chi* and Historiography of Late Eighteenth-Century Đại Việt', *Journal of Southeast Asian Studies*, 36:2 (2005), 171–90.

Frasch, Tilman, 'Der Buddhismus im Jahr 1000', *Periplus: Jahrbuch für Außereuropäische Geschichte*, 10 (2000), 56–72.

Gesick, Lorraine M., *In the Land of Lady White Blood: Southern Thailand and the Meaning of History* (Ithaca, NY, 1995).

Hall, D. G. E. (ed.), *Historians of South East Asia* (London, 1961).

Johns, Anthony H., 'The Role of Structural Organisation and Myth in Javanese Historiography', *The Journal of Asian Studies*, 24:1 (1964), 91–9.

Langlet, Philippe, *L'ancienne historiographie d'Etat au Vietnam* (Paris, 1985).

Lieberman, Victor B., 'How Reliable is U Kala's Burmese Chronicle? Some New Comparisons', *Journal of Southeast Asian Studies*, 17 (1986), 236–55.

Lorrillard, Michel, 'Les Chronique royales du Laos: essai d'une chronologie des règnes des souverains lao (1316–1887)', Ph.D. dissertation, École Pratique des Hautes études, 1995.

Maier, H. M. J., *In the Center of Authority: The Malay Hikayat Merong Mahawangsa* (Ithaca, NY, 1988).

Ras, J. J., 'The Genesis of the Babad Tanah Jawi: Origin and Function of the Javanese Court Chronicle', *Bijdragen tot de Taal-, Land- en Volkenkunde*, 143 (1987), 343–56.

Reid, Anthony, 'Historiography and Historical Thought: Southeast Asia', in Neil J. Smelser and Paul B. Baltes (eds.), *International Encyclopedia of the Social and Behavioural Sciences* (New York, 2001), 6808–13.

——and Marr, David (eds.), *Perceptions of the Past in Southeast Asia* (Singapore, 1979).

Reynolds, Craig, *Seditious Histories: Contesting Thai and Southeast Asian Pasts* (Seattle, 2006).

Scott, William Henry, *Prehispanic Source Materials for the Study of Philippine History* (Quezon City, 1984).

——*Looking for the Prehispanic Filipino and Other Essays in Philippines History* (Quezon City, 1992).

Shorto, H. L., 'Mon Genealogy of Kings: Observations on the *Nidāna Ārambhakathā*', in Hall (ed.), *Historians of South East Asia*, 63–72.

Taylor, K. W., *The Birth of Vietnam* (Berkeley, 1983).

——'Looking Behind the Vietnamese Annals: Ly Phat Ma and Ly Nhat Ton in the *Viet su luc* and the *Toan thu*', *Vietnam Forum*, 7 (1986), 47–69.

Teeuw, A., 'Hikayat Raja-Raja Pasai and Sejarah Melayu', in J. Bastin and R. Roolvink (eds.), *Malayan and Indonesian Studies* (Oxford, 1964), 222–34.

Thaw Kaung, U, 'Ayedawbon Kyan, an Important Myanmar Literary Genre Recording Historical Events', *Journal of the Siam Society*, 88:1–2 (2000), 21–33.

Vickers, A., 'Balinese Texts and Historiography', *History and Theory*, 29:2 (1990), 158–78.

Vickery, Michael, 'The Composition and Transmission of the Ayudhya and Cambodian Chronicles', in Reid and Marr (eds.), *Perceptions of the Past in Southeast Asia*, 43–67.

Wang Gungwu, 'South and Southeast Asian Historiography', in David L. Sills (ed.), *International Encyclopedia of the Social Sciences* (New York, 1968), 420–28.

——'The Study of the Southeast Asian Past', in Reid and Marr (eds.), *Perceptions of the Past in Southeast Asia*, 1–9.

Wolters, O.W., 'Lê Văn Hưu's Treatment of Lý Thần Tôn's Reign (1127–1137)', in Cown and Wolters (eds.), *Southeast Asian History and Historiography*, 203–26.

Worsley, P. J., *Babad Buleleng: A Balinese Dynastic Genealogy* (The Hague, 1972).

Yu Insun, 'Lê Văn Huu and Ngô Sĩ Liên: A Comparison of their Perception of Vietnamese History', in Nhung Tuyet Tran and Anthony Reid (eds.), *Viet Nam: Borderless Histories* (Wisconsin, 2006).

Chapter 7

Indo-Persian Historical Thoughts and Writings: India 1350–1750

Asim Roy

This chapter explores Indo-Persian historical thoughts and writings spanning the 400 years (1350–1750) of the late medieval and early modern centuries.[1] A historiographical study of its kind on India as a component of a global project of history-writing cannot overlook issues of approach and perception. Most histories of history-writing produced in the West in modern times, with some exceptions in recent decades, evince a hegemonic pre-eminence of forms, ideas, and values of the Western historical tradition, and a corresponding failure to involve the non-Western historical traditions. This unfortunate situation has been largely attributed to Western colonial dominance and its 'cultural, linguistic, and economic influences', giving rise to 'a thoroughly decontextualized and celebratory grand narrative of the rise of modern method that has only been challenged in recent years'. Most regrettably, the 'global dominance of Western academic historical practices' has tended to generate a feeling in non-Western

---

[1] A few points should be noted at the outset. The first and most obvious is that the analysis here begins in 1350, about fifty years earlier than most chapters of this volume. This was done because by the mid-fourteenth century much of the early development of Indo-Persian historiography had been formulated and consolidated enough to generate the confidence of historians such as 'Isami, a major Indo-Persian author of a versified history in 1350, who declared his ambition to rival the legendary Persian model of Firdawsi's *Shah-nama*. Also, 1357 saw the production of an outstanding historical work by Ziya al-Din Barani, widely considered as the finest of historians in the period of the Delhi Sultanate. Second, as I have adopted a thematic rather than a chronological approach, especially regarding the two critical and final sections of the chapter, I have found it essential at times, in order to provide adequate context, to refer back to earlier pre-1350 developments in Indo-Persian historiography. Finally, I have limited myself here to one family of traditions in South Asian historical writing—albeit the most prominent and well-known—during this time. Given constraints of space, this seemed preferable to a wider-ranging but more superficial survey of all forms of late medieval and early modern Indian historical writing. Consequently, I have omitted here many types of historical discourse that developed in other languages elsewhere on the subcontinent. For a study of some of these other varieties of historical thinking and narrative see Velcheru Narayana Rao, David Shulman, and Sanjay Subrahmanyam, *Textures of Time: Writing History in South India 1600–1800* (New York, 2003).

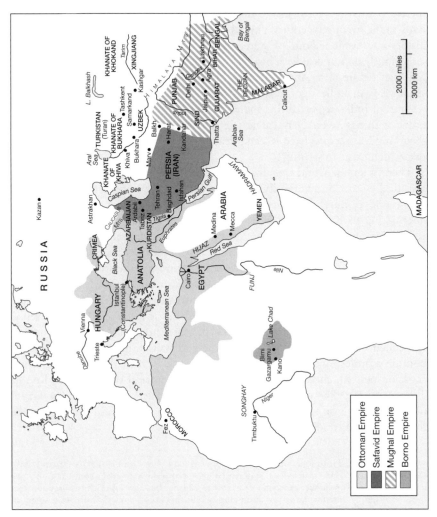

Map 2. The Muslim Empires of Cental and Southern Eurasia and Northern Africa
*c.*1700

quarters that 'not just history, but historiography' has been 'written by the victors'.[2]

Early India's sense and consciousness of the historical past have long been questioned. That it supposedly 'lacked historical writing and, by implication therefore, a sense of history' was, until very recent times, almost 'taken as given'.[3] Early in the twentieth century a noted British scholar asserted that ancient Indian history was 'fashioned out' of 'purely religious and priestly' compositions, which 'notoriously do not deal with history' and 'totally lack the historical sense'.[4] Nine centuries before him, Abu Raihan al-Biruni, a celebrated Muslim scholar who spent years in India rigorously undertaking critical studies of various arts and sciences of India, regretted that the Hindus paid little attention to the 'historical order of things', were 'very careless in relating the chronological succession of their kings', and considered it 'canonical only that which is known by heart, not that which exists in writing'.[5]

There is sporadic and tantalizing evidence from early India indicative of its historical essence and antiquity, such as a Buddhist sculptural representation of the second century. This depicts a scene with 'three wise men' engaged in interpreting to King Shuddhodhana and Queen Maya, future parents of the yet unborn Buddha, the legendary 'dream' of Queen Maya in Buddhist tradition that portends the Buddha's ensuing birth. The important point for us in this is the depiction of a scribe sitting down and 'recording' the interpretation.[6] Regardless, there has been a broad sense of recognition among leading historians of early India of the relative scarcity of the standard chronographic and sequential narratives of conventional annal, regnal, and dynastic forms. Early India's sense, image, quest, and representation of the past are, however, deeply and widely embedded in the profusion of oral bardic and written genealogical traditions, both on a professional level. Besides, there 'are many texts that reflect historical consciousness which later became the basis for historical traditions', as Romila Thapar affirms. The concern today, she contends, is less with the absence of historical writing in early India and more with the 'nature and assumptions of these [historical] traditions'.[7]

---

[2] Daniel Woolf, 'Historiography', in M. C. Horowitz (ed.), *New Dictionary of the History of Ideas* (New York, 2005), 1. He concludes that 'any new survey of historical writing' must not only pay serious attention to non-Western types of historical writing, but also reject the assumption that these are 'simply inferior forms awaiting the enlightenment of modern European-American methodology'. Ibid.

[3] Romila Thapar, 'Historical Traditions in Early India: *c.*1000 BC to *c.* AD 600', in Andrew Feldherr and Grant Hardy (eds.), *The Oxford History of Historical Writing*, vol. 1: *Beginnings to AD 600* (Oxford, 2011), 553.

[4] F. E. Pargiter, *Ancient Indian Historical Tradition* (London, 1922; repr. edn, Delhi, 1962).

[5] Al-Biruni, *Kitab al-Hind* (n.p., 1030); ed. and trans. Edward C. Sachau as *Alberuni's India*, 2 vols. (repr. edn, New Delhi, 1964), i. 10–11. For full bibliographic details of this and all other primary sources cited in the endnotes, see relevant entries in the lists of 'Key Historical Sources'.

[6] Sculptural artefact from Nagarjunakonda, 2nd century AD (National Museum, New Delhi).

[7] Thapar, 'Historical Traditions in Early India', 553.

GROWTH AND STANDING OF ISLAMIC
HISTORIOGRAPHY BEFORE THE INDIA CONNECTION

Despite the contested sense and notion of the ancient Indian past, the perception of the tradition of Muslim historical writing in medieval India is altogether different. A broad sense of recognition, at least among the more informed, of the significant growth and strength of the Islamic historical tradition is a possible reason behind a frequently posed question: 'Did Muslims bring history-writing with them to India?' The earliest extant Muslim historical work in South Asia however, answers this question in the negative. The particular work (title and authorship unknown) on the subject of the Arab conquest of Sind (711–12), written in Arabic and completed in the ninth century, has come down to us only in its Persian translation under the title *Chach-nama* [The Book of Chach] (*c*.1217). It includes an account of the pre-conquest ruling Hindu dynasty under Chach, its Brahmin ruler. Significantly, this Perso-Arabic account clearly acknowledges a local source in Sanskrit for the Hindu dynasty—a clear attestation to the fact that the early Muslim historians in India did not operate in a historiographically virgin land.

Islamic historical tradition has long been recognized as one of the three major traditions of historical thought and writing, along with the Chinese and the Western, the latter being a combined product of classical Greek, Roman, and Judeo-Christian influences. The total span of Muslim conquests and rule in India extended from the early eighth century (Arab conquest of Sind and Multan) through the thirteenth to the early sixteenth centuries of the rise and fall of the Delhi Sultanate (1206–1526), to the final phase of the rise and fall of the Mughal Empire (1526–1857). It is important to keep in mind that the entire period under study overlapped and corresponded with the substantive and clearly earmarked phases of historiographical developments in Islam from which Indo-Persian historiography derived its inspiration, life, and form. The 'formative' period (from the death of the Prophet Muhammad in 633 to the ninth century) in particular, and in a more limited sense, the 'classical' period (*c*.tenth–fourteenth centuries) of Islamic historical tradition remain outside the scope of this chapter. The significant period of the sultanate, nonetheless, overlapped with both the classical and early medieval centuries of the Islamic historical tradition. The subsequent period (1526–1750) belonging to the Mughals remained co-extensive with the 'later medieval' and 'early modern' periods of Muslim historiography. One of the most important facts to emerge from the growth of Islamic historical tradition was that it had already reached, by the beginning of the fifteenth century, a rather significant level of development comparable to the contemporaneous historical tradition in the West.

Islamic historiography has indeed been characterized by its outstanding productivity, fullness, and attention to detail, reflected in an unprecedented bibliomania evident from its beginnings. A tenth-century bookseller and writer in Baghdad, Ibn al-Nadim, produced a valuable list of books, *al-Fihrist* [The Catalogue of Books] (988), which includes one hundred authors and over a thousand titles of historical and historiographical import. A library in Cairo of the late tenth century, with an enormous collection of books, held multiple copies of 'what had by then become standard histories'. What is more, according to Chase Robinson, 'Nothing in the contemporaneous Christian world, East or West, compared with this bibliomania, nor had Greece or Rome produced anything on its scale.'[8]

In its formative stage of development, Islamic historiography drew on various Arab and non-Arab, especially Persian, resources. Those traditions possessed indigenous forms of popular oral as well as written genealogical and historiographical traditions about stories of battles (*akhbār*, sing. *khabar*),[9] and also a specific tradition among Persians of royal and priestly narratives of an historical nature. Underlying the major developments in the classical centuries was the central issue of the steady Islamic expansion beyond the Arab world, embracing the vast regions between the Guadalquivir in the West and the Indus in the East. The phenomenal enhancement of non-Arab elements in the Muslim population, their cultures and overall position, began with the influence of Persian culture. Subsequently, the whole-hearted adoption of Persian culture by the steadily rising Turkish powers was the determining factor in the relative weakening of the influence of Arabic language and culture, outside the sphere of religious fundamentals, in comparison with the growing popularity, strength, and eventual dominance of Persian language and literature—with their moral-ethical (*adab*), intellectual, and political ideas and practice. The special patronage of the Ghaznavid rulers (Persianized rulers of Turkic origin based in the new and growing city of Ghazni in Afghanistan) made seminal contributions, in the eleventh and twelfth centuries, towards this process of the growing Persianization of the Islamic world of learning and culture in the north, east, and south. The impact of such developments had direct bearings on India, as the late twelfth and the early thirteenth centuries saw the Turko-Afghan contingents move towards India, culminating in the establishment of the Sultanate of Delhi. The interactions of Perso-Arabic and other historical traditions had contributed significantly to the development of classical Islamic historiography, which, in its Persian-Turko-Afghan formulation, thus found a new, prosperous, and enduring home

---

[8] Chase F. Robinson, *Islamic Historiography* (Cambridge, 2003), 6–7. See also Franz Rosenthal, *A History of Muslim Historiography* (2nd edn, Leiden, 1968), 196.

[9] The old battle-day narrative in pre-Islamic Arabia (*khabar*; pl. *akhbār*) is the oldest form of Islamic historiography which absorbed its oral literary tradition. See Rosenthal, *Muslim Historiography*, 68.

in India, thanks to Turko-Afghan and Turko-Mongol conquerors and patrons, for the next few centuries.

The new Persian historical tradition underwent adaptation and change. To begin with, the popular pre-Islamic Persian tradition of verse epic, which continued as late as 1010, when Firdawsi produced his epic and magnum opus, *Shah-nama* [Book of Kings], steadily yielded place to the chronologically orient-ed new Persian Muslim literary court histories. This new chronographic tradi-tion, combined later in the fifteenth century with the Herat–Afghanistan-based imperial Timurid chronicle tradition, set the dominant pattern for the subsequent Muslim historiography of the Safavid Empire (1501–1736) as well as that of the Delhi Sultans and the Imperial Mughals in India.[10] There was a noticeable trend in this evolving Persian historiographic tradition of gradually moving away from rigid adherence to the hadith- and religion-centred historical discipline. Also, the liberating influence of the humanizing and secularizing principles of the Persian version of *adab* is believed to have paved the way for the emergence between the tenth and fourteenth centuries of a new breed of Muslim historians of great repute, including al-Biruni and the peripatetic Ibn Battuta, both of whom had substantial Indian connections.

Scholars dealing with the origins of Islamic historiography have traced some of its forms to the influence of the Persian tradition such as the broad 'dynastic' principle of historical periodization and the ruler/regnal scheme of historical presentation. Though the latter was an old tradition and used in Eastern and Greco-Byzantine historiographies, its Persianized Islamic form was differentiated by a particular concern with ethical issues and political administration. The same ruler scheme, along with ruler-ethics and concern with political administration, was most likely to have been influenced by Persian national historiography. Some writers have also contrasted the Arab and Persian historical traditions for their 'opposed ideals and methods' in regard to their notions of historical representa-tion of people. Given the strength of the historically entrenched Persian monar-chical tradition, historians, according to this view, virtually treated 'history as a biography of kings', focusing on the 'life of the governing classes to the exclusion of all other sections of population'. In contrast, the Arab tradition, rooted in tribal values, was not averse to 'the life of the common man'.[11]

INDO-PERSIAN HISTORIOGRAPHY, 1350–1750

Evidently, a major feature of late medieval and early modern Indo-Muslim historical writing is its high level of convergence with classical Islamic histori-ography, especially in its Persian formulation. India's exposure to the rich legacies

---

[10] See ch. 8 by Christoph Marcinkowski in this volume.
[11] Khaliq Ahmad Nizami, *On History and Historians of Medieval India* (New Delhi, 1983), 6.

of the wider world of Islamic historiography began centuries before the founding of the Delhi Sultanate (1206), through the Arab, Ghaznavid, and Ghurid conquests between the eighth and twelfth centuries. The Muslim conquerors opened the doors for the diverse agencies that would spread Islamic knowledge and learning throughout India: career seekers of both religious and secular persuasions, fortune hunters and adventurers, travellers, Islamic religious preachers, seekers and practitioners of mystic knowledge and discipline, and so on. The polymathic Muslim scholar al-Biruni (mentioned above in a different context), was an iconic pioneer for the spread of Islamic knowledge in India.

The most striking areas of convergence between the two historiographic traditions—the Indo-Persian and its extra-Indian classical Islamic paradigm—relate to the forms, genres, and sources. The chronographical and biographical forms of history-writing have been the oldest and most universal across the Muslim world. The basic form of medieval Indo-Persian historical writing was chronographic, and the popular genres of chronicles and annalistic, regnal, and dynastic schemes were in conformity with their classical Islamic paradigmatic model. In the earlier centuries the Indo-Muslim writers also toyed with the ideas of the so-called universal as well as regional and local histories. In the course of its natural progression, political narratives emerged and continued as the most dynamic and enduring genre of Indo-Persian historical writing throughout the medieval period.

An extended version of the literature of political narratives in the form of fully versified history (*mathnawi*) was introduced to India by Amir Khusrau and, later, 'Isami. *Mathnawis* are generally of two forms, one predominantly based on historical contents and the other essentially romantic. These 'versified histories' may not always be treated as an analogue of 'history', but this voluminous *mathnawi* literature is a rich quarry of information for later historians.[12] Another curious feature of the Indo-Persian chronological narratives is that they are often interspersed with verses woven around celebratory or sad themes and occasions. Such compositions, contrasted with the wholly versified histories of Amir Khusrau and 'Isami are often unrelated to the theme of the particular historical narrative, and of much less historical significance than literary. Why would this be? Admittedly, history in the early phase of its development occupied a much lower social standing in the medieval world of Muslim learning, compared with theology and law, or even philosophy and literature.[13] The *akhbārīs* (historians)

---

[12] For the reign of 'Ala' al-Din Khalji (r. 1296–1316), for instance, Khusrau's *Khaza'in* remains the only contemporary source. See *Khaza'in al-Futuh* (1312; Aligarh, 1927); his *Qiran al-Sa'dayn* (1289; Aligarh, 1918), 30–9, 43–4, 52, 56–61, 66–72; and his *Nuh Sipihr* (n. p., 1318); ed. *Bibliotheca Indica* (Calcutta, 1950), 76–80. Finally, 'Isami's versified history contains useful information on the Deccan, especially the Bahmani sultanate. See his *Futuh al-Salatin* (n.p., 1350), ed. A. S. Usha (Madras, 1948).

[13] Robinson, *Islamic Historiography*, 92, 103, 112. Islamic historiography was not, however, an exceptional case in this respect. It is highly interesting to note that 'it was not until 1850 that history

were drawn into locking horns with the custodians of those popular disciplines. In this competitive environment, it is plausible that the historical verse compositions represent the historians' calculated intervention in displaying their 'literary' skills.

The popularity and dominance of political narratives in medieval India went hand in hand with a plethora of political-administrative notes and documents of an enormously diverse nature, preserved in the Indian archives and dating especially from Mughal times.[14] Archival materials of this nature were vital components of political and administrative history, comprising *firmāns* (royal decrees), *nishāns* (royal seals/signets), *parwānas* (official orders/permissions), *bakhars* (memoirs), and similar types of documents. Two sets of material form a great bulk of the archival holdings. One is the popular and very useful system of official newsletters (*akhbarāt*). Official news writers—*akhbar-nawīs* or *waqi-nawīs*—were entrusted with the responsibility of keeping the ruler reasonably informed through brief and regular news reports covering the major parts of the kingdom or empire. *Dastūr al-ʿAmal* (Manual of Customary Regulations) is another category of administrative guidance and instruction for officials, especially during the Mughal period. A very small proportion of the collections of this mass of documents is available in edited form; both among the edited and unedited collections, Hindu authorship is noted.[15]

The extensive volume of material in the Persian language is well-supplemented by an abundant body of historical sources in the regional languages, especially Rajasthani, Marathi, Punjabi, Sindhi, and Bengali. Over and above the Persian and Indian regional languages, some relevant information since the late medieval period can also be gleaned from records in European languages—apart from English, especially French, Portuguese, and Dutch.[16]

Medieval Indo-Persian historiography is richly endowed with both political and non-political sources. The totality of Indo-Persian biographical literature of various kinds is overwhelming. The dominant form of Indo-Persian biographical writings is biographical memoir (*tazkira*). The popularity of *tazkira* literature (see below) is easily explained by the wide flexibility of its usage. The Indo-Persian writers of biographical memoirs were generally attracted to the lives of popular poets (*shāʿir*) as their subjects, followed by that of the well-known Sufi

---

was given a place in the [Oxford] university curriculum. The University had existed without it for more than seven hundred years.' R. W. Southern, *History and Historians: Selected Papers of R. W. Southern*, ed. R. J. Bartlett (Oxford, 2004), 120.

[14] See Sri Ram Sharma, *A Bibliography of Mughal India, 1526–1707 A.D.* (Bombay, 1938); and V. D. B. Taraporevala and D. N. Marshall, *Mughal Bibliography* (Bombay, 1962).

[15] Nanda Ram Kayath, *Siyaq-nama* (Lucknow, 1879); and Jawahar Nath Baikas Sahaswani, *Dastūr al-ʿAmal* (Aligarh Muslim University Library, Subhanullah Collection, 554).

[16] For a brief but authentic illustration of such archival material in Indian and European languages see Nizami, *Historians of Medieval India*, 38–9; and J. F. Richards, *Mughal Administration in Golconda* (Oxford, 1975), 320–9 ('Select Bibliography').

mystic teachers and preceptors. However, there was no dearth of authors whose *tazkiras* focused on theologians and jurists ('ulama'; sing. *'alim*), or those who, away from the religious personages and poets, turned to the distinguished members of the ruling elites (*umara*; sing. *amir*). Some writers sought to produce, instead of an individual biography, a biographical dictionary of a kindred group of poets, or Sufis, or 'ulama', or *umara*, or even a composite biographical dictionary of more than one of these groups together, a good example of the last category being a large collection of biographical notices of poets, Sufis, and 'ulama' by Amin bin Ahmad Razi.[17] Another form of biographical dictionary of non-religious people embraces the nobility. Shaykh Farid Bhakkari's *Tazkira* (1651) covered many Mughal nobles, and another of Hindu authorship by Kewal Ram (completed 1728) also dealt with the Mughal nobility of the period between the two padishahs (emperors), Akbar (r. 1556–1605) and Aurangzeb (r. 1657–1707). The most comprehensive, authoritative and popular biographical records of a large number of Indian nobles from Akbar's time to the eighteenth century is the work of Shah Nawaz Khan (work commenced 1742).[18] Historians find this diverse literature informative and valuable for the depiction of the social and cultural life of contemporaneous India.

The Sufi saints and 'ulama' of medieval India constitute another large core segment of the Indo-Persian *tazkira* literature, and the trail of this tradition was laid by a noted mystic authority, Shaykh Farid al-Din Attar. Attar's early and famous *Tazkirat al-Awliya* [Biographies of the Saints], a prose work written in the early thirteenth century, contained accounts of nearly seventy Sufi saints of the first three Islamic centuries as well as some later saints.[19] But the most popular and significant *tazkira* on the Indian saints was left by Saiyid Muhammad bin Mubarak Alawi Kirmani (alias Mir Khurd). The book contains biographical notices of saints of the Chishti Sufi order, written during the reign of Sultan Firuz Shah Tughluq (r. 1351–88).[20] Another highly popular biographical dictionary of 225 Indian saints in medieval India came from a very learned Islamic scholar, Shaykh 'Abd al-Haq Muhaddis Dihlawi.[21]

Autobiographical compositions, another distinctive genre of biographical literature in Indo-Persian, are of a much smaller proportion than other forms of biographical literature. Usually originating with the rulers or the ruling and the noble families, two autobiographies from the Sultanate period are respectively attributed to Muhammad Shah Tughluq (r. 1325–51) and Firuz Shah

---

[17] Razi, *Haft Iqlim* (n.p., 1594).
[18] Bhakkari, *Zakhirat al-Khawanin* (n.p., 1651); Kewal Ram, *Tazkirat al-Umara* (n.p., 1728); and Shah Nawaz Khan, *Ma'asir al-Umara* (n.p., c.1742); ed. and trans. H. Beveridge; 'revised, annotated & completed', Baini Prashad, Bibliotheca Indica, 2 vols. (Calcutta, 1941–52); repr, 2 vols. (2003).
[19] Farid al-Din Attar, *Tazkirat al-Awliya* (London, 1905–7).
[20] Mir Khurd, *Siyar al-Awliya* (Delhi, 1885).
[21] 'Abd al-Haq Muhaddis, *Akhbar al-Akhyar* (Delhi, 1914).

Tughluq.[22] The supposed autobiography of Muhammad Shah, available only in few pages, is assumed to be a part of his autobiography now lost. A dubious attribution of this nature remains unconvincing. Firuz Shah's autobiography, on the other hand, was originally inscribed on the walls of Jami‘ Masjid of Delhi. Mughal imperial rule, representing the height of Indo-Persian literary and cultural attainments, found the padishahs and the imperial family often leading from the front. Zahir al-Din Muhammad Babur (r. 1526–30), the founder of the Mughal dynasty, has left us a universally acclaimed reflective and perceptive memoir in the Turkic language.[23] His writings clearly reveal his total identification with the ideals of all Timurid princes—the pursuit of the power of both the pen and the sword. His keen interest in chronology and history and deep knowledge of geography are recurrent themes in his memoirs. Gulbadan Begum, Babur's daughter, wrote her memoirs of the reign of her brother, the second Mughal Emperor Humayun, at the request of Emperor Akbar, Humayun son and successor, and her nephew. The original version of her memoir, subsequently known as *Humayun-nama*, ranged beyond Humayun himself to include material on Akbar, but, curiously and regrettably, those sections are missing in all the extant copies of the manuscript.[24] Given the global rarity of accomplished women writers in that age, Gulbadan's well-known command of the Persian language and her direct, unadorned, and forceful style have been widely acclaimed. Her work remains very rich on the social side, particularly from an elite woman's perspective of the lives of high Mughal society, especially its *harem* life. Nur al-Din Muhammad Jahangir (r. 1605–27), Akbar's son and heir, followed in the footsteps of his great grandfather to write a memoir and adopted a rather innovative methodology.[25] Having covered initially the first twelve years of his reign, he had copies of the draft bound and circulated among relations, friends, and officials, inviting comments and suggestions. Thereafter, the revised drafts were re-presented successively in the seventeenth and the nineteenth years, leading to the final version of the manuscript.

In the whole corpus of medieval Indo-Persian religious literature, the impact of the two specific Sufic traditions (leaving aside the biographical genre of *tazkira*), remained very significant. These are *malfuzat* (collections of Sufi discourse or conversation) and *maktubat* (collections of letters or correspondence). History of the Indo-Persian *malfuz* literature begins with the pioneering effort of Amir Hasan Sijzi, whose compilation of the discourses of his celebrated spiritual mentor, Shaykh Nizam al-Din Auliya, earned him the praise of the

[22] See K. A. Nizami, 'The So-Called Autobiography of Muhammad bin Tughluq', in Nizami, *Historians of Medieval India*, 198–204. See also Firuz Shah Tughluq, *Futuhat-i Firuz Shahi*, ed. and trans. S. A. Rashid (Aligarh, 1943).

[23] Babur, *Tuzuk-i Baburi* or *Babur-nama* (n.p., 1530).

[24] Gulbadan Begum, *Humayun-nama* (n.p., 1603).

[25] Jahangir, *Tuzuk-i Jahangiri* or *Jahangir-nama*, ed. Saiyid Ahmad Khan (Ghazipur/Aligarh, 1863–4).

legendary Persian poet Jami, an enviable distinction for a Persian writer from India.[26] It is hardly surprising that Sijzi's masterly work quickly became a model not only for the Chishti order, but for all other major Sufi orders as well. Numerous contributions to the *malfuz* literature appeared in quick succession from various parts of India. Another important contribution on the discourses of an eminent Chishti Sufi, Shaykh Nasir al-Din Chiragh-i Dihlawi, attained considerable popularity.[27] The total volume of the *malfuz* literature far outweighs its *maktub* counterpart. Additionally, the details of the *maktubat* collections are generally less than adequate. The *maktubat* collections of Shaykh Sharaf al-Din Yahya Maniyari were particularly treated with honour and respect by a wide cross-section of society, especially the mystic circle.[28]

The entire corpus of mystical literature, ranging from biographical material to the discourses and letters of the Sufi masters, forms a significant component of the sources for medieval Indian history. The world of the courtier-writers and that of the Sufi *khanqas* (hospices), which drew people from all walks of life, could not have presented greater contrasts. The relationship between the king and the Sufi was never an easy one, and the critical issue underpinning this was bluntly expressed by some leading Sufis: 'If you desire elevation in your spiritual ranks, do not mix with princes of the blood.'[29] In fact mystic records have often been used as a tool for moderating and countering the elite viewpoints projected from the throne or the army camp. In short, the historical information derived from such diverse sources proved useful for historians in striking a balance with conflicting historical information. No discerning student of history could, none-theless, afford to overlook certain negative aspects of the mystic literature, especially its hagiographical stream with its highly exaggerated eulogy. A major portion of the *malfuz* and *maktub* literature attributed to early Sufi saints is considered to consist of fabrications. Despite the enormous importance attached to the mystical literary sources, extreme caution is an imperative in the utilization of such materials as tools of history.

The foregoing analyses of the sources and genres is intended to provide a broad understanding of the patterns and processes of Indo-Persian historiographical development. Because of the very nature and salience of the early developments in the pre-Mughal stage, the particular and seminal contributions of the Mughals, especially in the reign of Emperor Akbar, have not always found appropriate focus. The Mughal period, especially in the sixteenth to mid-eighteenth centuries, is not unreasonably held to be the most glorious, prolific, and creative epoch of Indo-Persian historiography. India's contribution to medieval historical

---

[26] Amir Hasan Sijzi, *Fawaʾid al-Fuʾad* (Delhi, AH 1302).

[27] Hamid Qalandar, *Khayr al-Majalis* (Aligarh, 1959).

[28] *Maktubat-i Yahya Maniyari* is a rare collection of his 151 letters: Hermann Ethé, *Catalogue of Persian Manuscripts in the India Office Library* (Oxford, 1903; repr. edn, London, 1980).

[29] Mir Khurd, *Siyar al-Auliya*, 75; also 204, 295.

literature in Persian had not been insubstantial in the Sultanate period, as we have seen, but during the Mughal period, Indo-Persian literature became a dominant force not only in South Asian historiography but also in the Persian-language historiography produced elsewhere. In C. A. Storey's well-known survey of historical literature in Persian, it is revealing that 475 items are assigned to India alone and 299 to Persia and other countries put together. It is also significant that much of this Indo-Persian historical literature was written during the Mughal period.[30]

The vast corpus of this historical literature is also protean in variety. The literature embraces in its fold chronographic accounts and narratives of all descriptions and all known genres, forms, and sub-forms—chronicles, annals, regnal, and dynastic; histories of all varieties—universal, general, regional, and local; historical gazetteers, compilations of official correspondence and administrative documents; memoirs, biographies, autobiographies, and biographical dictionaries; geographical-travel accounts, and so on. It is nonetheless, important to stress that the significance of the Mughal phase in Indo-Persian historiography is not merely an issue of the greater variety and diversity of genres and sources in this period, though the sheer magnitude of the volume of archival material on Mughal India is a compelling argument. The historiographical importance of the Mughal era has had other major facets.

An outstanding feature of Mughal government under Akbar was the revolutionary concept, in the context of medieval India, of appropriating history for the imperial vision and purpose. Given the massive accumulation of historical resources since the Sultanate period, Akbar's creative genius saw in this a brilliant opportunity and a powerful tool to exploit history in the service of his imperial vision and ambition. Of the two major components of the new imperial vision— the concepts of the new monarchy and the new history of India—the former is directly linked to the policy and strategy of Akbar and Abu'l Fazl of weakening the 'ulama'. This particular objective was partly achieved through the religious debates of the 'Ibadat Khana (a religious assembly founded 1575), in which they sought to expose the parochialism and hollowness of the chief theologians at court. The goal was fully achieved, in 1579, with the promulgation of the decree of *mahzar*, making the emperor final arbiter in disputes concerning theological issues and scriptural law. Seeking to build a national platform on the pillars of political and cultural accord, and also tolerance and unity, Akbar came to realize the necessity of transcending the religious divide.

'Official history' proper, first introduced to Indo-Persian literature during Akbar's reign, under the guiding hands of the emperor and Abu'l Fazl, became the focal point of this new history and historical methodology. The new history is marked by its intellectual and rationalist approach, rather than its seeking to offer

---

[30] C. A. Storey, *Persian Literature: A Bio-bibliographical Survey*, vol.i, pt. 1 (London, 1927–39); and pt. 2 (London, 1953).

religious and traditional explanations. More often than not, the views projected in these new historical writings are secular and pluralist. The importance attached to Hindu religious-cultural tradition, as clearly embodied in the pages of the official histories, is poignantly symbolic of this new concept of history. Both Akbar and Abu'l Fazl rejected out of hand the assumptions of the Indo-Persian historians of the pre-Akbar age that history concerned Muslims alone and that the central dynamic of Islamic history in India was a perennial conflict between Hindus and Muslims. In the new history of India, the real conflict was between the Mughal Empire, on one hand, epitomizing the motto of *sulh-i kul*—peace and harmony—as well as stability and good government for all, and those who opposed and challenged the empire among Muslims and Hindus, on the other. The new history also represented a broader view than the court–camp-centred history. The scope of history was considerably widened, with the incorporation of a mass of material beyond the political, relating to social, economic, and religious-cultural life of people other than Muslim.

With the blueprint of Akbar's new historical project in place, his historians brought to bear certain common and distinctive methodological principles on their task. First, historical research came to be grounded squarely on a systematic use of the vast amount of archival material. For his monumental historical projects *Akbar-nama* [The Book of Akbar] (1596) and *A'in-i Akbari* [Rules of Akbar] (1599), Abu'l Fazl was assisted by a large team of researchers; historians such as Nizam al-Din Ahmad Bakhshi and Firishta listed numerous historical works that were used in preparing their own narratives.[31] Second, a number of key historical personages were commissioned by the government to write memoirs intended to facilitate research and writing by the historians. The first and fourth Mughal rulers, Babur and Jahangir, and Babur's daughter, Gulbadan Begum, wrote their memoirs, as noted above. Third, going beyond the idea of commissioned memoirs, historians were also commissioned to write historical narratives, perhaps intended to facilitate the production of a master narrative of the new history of India—a vision that the genius of Abu'l Fazl was patiently engaged in sketching out in the *Akbar-nama*. Abbas Khan bin Shaykh 'Ali Sarwani produced a popular commissioned narrative of its type.[32] Fourth, Abu'l Fazl's rather modern research methodology of critical examination, comparison, and assessment of the extant sources in order rationally to extrapolate the truth was another seminal development in Indo-Persian history-writing, dating from this time. Finally, the creative spirit awakened in this exciting environment of cultural and intellectual ferment soon found some new directions in

---

[31] Nizam al-Din cited twenty-nine works of earlier writers. See Nizam al-Din Ahmad Bakhshi, *Tabaqat-i Akbari* (n.p., 1594). Firishta used thirty-two earlier studies. See Firishta (alias Muhammad Qasim Hindu-Shah Astarabadi), *Gulshan-i Ibrahimi* or *Ta'rikh-i Firishta* (1606–7; Lucknow, AH 1281).

[32] Sarwani, *Tuhfa-i Akbar Shahi* (n.p., compiled in 3 recensions, c.1579–86).

history-writing such as the writing of a 'general history of India'. Nizam al-Din Ahmad Bakhshi and Firishta wrote the first and second general histories of India respectively. Another innovative historical product of this new spirit was Akbar's own bold initiative in introducing a daringly new concept of Islamic chronography and writing a new millennial Islamic history, *Ta'rīkh-i Alfī* [History of the Millennium], beginning from the death of the Prophet Muhammad (*Rihlat*) in AD 632, instead of the traditional Hijri era beginning in AD 622. This change, however, proved unpopular. The wide public interest in history generated by Akbar and his direct appeal and invitation to people of the imperial establishment to write or dictate their reminiscences and impressions drew eager response from some lower-ranking servants of the imperial household. Two such contributors, Jawhar Aftabchi, Emperor Humayun's ewer-bearer, and the physically disabled elderly, Bayazid Biyat, the Superintendent of the Royal Kitchen, have been of much interest.[33]

INDO-PERSIAN HISTORIOGRAPHY AS REPRESENTATION

Though the idea of representation is embedded in the very notion of history, the contours of this discourse have changed over time, often rather dramatically, and still are changing. For centuries, concerns with representation revolved essentially around 'cosmetic' issues of forms, genres, branches, sub-branches, and so on. Historiography has moved away from these early considerations and even from some of its later concerns with the 'philosophy' of history and 'objectivity'. Even the least controversial popular notion of historical representation—that it is a conscious effort to recover knowledge of the past—does not hold much water. The crucial question today is much less concerned with *how* the past is represented than with the ultimate *end* or *purpose* of historical representation. This, in turn, is integrally linked with the central concept of 'power' in the sense of knowledge being the source of 'power'. The history of history in much of the world at virtually all periods is littered with glaring instances of the use and abuse of perceptions of and writings about the past.[34] Indian history is no exception, though the stage for the most blatant abuses has been limited to colonial and post-colonial times. Even the history of pre-colonial India with its Muslim rulers has seen such abuses by some modern and contemporary historiographical efforts, rather ideologically motivated, seeking to reinterpret medieval Indian history, as discussed below.

---

[33] Jauhar Aftabchi, *Tazkirat al-Waqi'iat* (n.p., commenced 1556); trans. Major Charles Stewart (London, 1832); and Bayazid Biyat, *Tazkira-i Humayun wa Akbar*, ed. M. Hidayat Husain, in *Bibliotheca Indica* (Calcutta, 1941).

[34] See Antoon de Baets, 'Censorship and History since 1945', in Axel Schneider and Daniel Woolf (eds.), *The Oxford History of Historical Writing*, vol. 5: *Historical Writing since 1945* (Oxford, 2011), 52–73.

The phenomenal growth of the Islamic historiographical tradition through its formative and classical centuries of development has drawn wide academic attention and recognition. Critical students of this historiography cannot, however, help juxtaposing its positive features with certain paradoxical and ambivalent aspects of such historiographic developments within the Islamic world. The past is valued in all cultures for a variety of reasons, most importantly for its critical bearings on their self-identity. Muslims in history have been no exception, having invested so much value in their past as to hold it up as a model for the present. The bibliomania and popularity of historical literature in Islamic culture have been a natural outcome of developments of this nature. Paradoxically, the value attached to historiography as a source of knowledge and learning remained disproportionate to its popular esteem through the early centuries, including the classical. As noted above, history lacked, in the world of medieval Islamic learning, the prestige and standing of the other branches of knowledge, such as theology, law, and even philosophy. Largely seen as a branch or sub-genre of literature, history's claim to truth belonged to a lower plane given that it was not derived from 'revelation'. The ruling elites were primarily interested in those areas of learning that promoted traditionalist values and institutions. Naturally enough, Prophetic biography and other religious biographies appealed to them, beyond theology and law, while non-Prophetic biography and autobiography were marginalized by the traditionalists because of the former's concern with a particular past that did not matter to them. Both contemporary biography and contemporary history remained virtually proscribed as impudent and impious.

The classical period nonetheless witnessed a significant transformation in the production of chronographic works. A more self-confident narrative tradition gradually took its own place. Given particularly the sceptical and ambivalent outlook of the traditionalists, the outstanding success of the chronographic tradition in universal and post-Prophetic history has been a dominant feature of Islamic historiography that calls for adequate explanation. Some reasonable answers have been sought in Islam's spectacular success in 'political missionizing' and creating a 'broader culture of politics and learning' that gave rise to a burgeoning group of princes, administrators, bureaucrats, scribes, secretaries, and patrons of various sorts, amongst whom 'all varieties of historical narrative were in great demand'. 'As great imperialists', therefore, 'Muslims became great historians.'[35] Indeed, the encouragement and patronage of the kingly and princely courts proved vital not only for the promotion of the cause of historical narratives, but also enhanced the status of the historians. Moreover, one could scarcely overlook that the historians lacked the economic benefits and support of the institutions of higher education (*madrasa*) dominated by the religious/legal establishment. They utilized this new opportunity of royal patronage by writing

---

[35] Robinson, *Islamic Historiography*, 104.

books to teach lessons of history for good governance to bureaucrats and aspiring office-holders. It did not take very long for this readership to extend beyond the court, establishing historical knowledge and intellectual sophistication as the mark of *adab* for the men of culture and learning in the cosmopolitan medieval Islamic world. Also, the emergent new elites in search of leading roles in the changing world around them, and the new states, eager to draw and build on the support of this growing power base, were thrown into each other's arms. The educated elites—writers and historians—could make 'representations of the past', 'exemplify truths and provide models', and 'set standards' to compare and uphold or discredit the contemporary rulers, as required. Learning on an extensive scale depended, on the other hand, on urban networks of knowledge, the protection of which was incumbent on the state.[36]

Even a cursory look at the social and political forces propelling the growth and development of Islamic historiography in the classical and post-classical centuries reveals similar thrusts underlying the corresponding Indian developments. Ghur, Ghazni, and Dehlawi (Delhi) clearly represented a continuum of the process of new empire-building as well as creating the state culture of politics and learning, accompanied by the emergence of new clusters of princes, bureaucrats, secretaries, scribes, and so on, with an appetite for historical narratives that provided lessons of good governance or exemplified good and bad models for princes, bureaucrats, or would-be bureaucrats. The new state and the elite of the sultanate and padishahi were drawn together by the bond of mutual interests—patronage at one end and legitimation of power and authority through 'historical representation' at the other. It is particularly important to note that Persian history placed special emphasis on imparting appropriate lessons and setting up a model for its didactic function.

The encouragement and patronage by both Delhi sultans and Mughal padishahs as well as the regional princely courts proved vital to the promotion of historical narratives. During the Sultanate and Mughal periods the preponderance of political narratives and other relevant writings were authored largely by the courtiers patronized by the rulers, the courtiers to-be, or others with close contacts with the rulers and the core of the ruling classes. Correspondingly, a large proportion of such historical products were either directly written for and dedicated to particular rulers or members of the ruling class or at least subsequently presented to such people. Hailing from a noble and scholarly family in Persia, Sadr al-Din Hasan Nizami is the first known Indo-Persian historian to have received royal patronage from the first Delhi Sultan, Qutb al-Din Aibak (r. 1206–10).[37] Nizami was followed by many other historians of noble origins, who maintained contacts with the ruling families and the courtiers, even if they

---

[36] Ibid., 188–9.
[37] Sadr al-Din Hasan Nizami, *Taj al-Maʾasir* (n.p., 1217).

were not courtiers themselves. Minhaj al-Din bin Siraj al-Din Juzjani,[38] with his connection to the ruling houses of Ghur and Ghazni, high educational attainments, and patronage of Sultan Shams al-Din Iltutmish (r. 1211–36) and his son, Sultan Nasir al-Din Mahmud (r. 1246–65), saw himself crowned with the highest judicial position of the Chief Qazi of Delhi and the far more exalted title of *Sadr-i Jahan* (Chief Justice of the World). Amir Khusrau, who inherited an aristocratic and bureaucratic heritage from both his parents and enjoyed the confidence and support of the Khalji and Tughluq sultans, was the first and the most prolific author of versified history in Indo-Persian. Ziya al-Din Barani belonged to a highly respectable family of Saiyids,[39] who were for long in the service of the Khalji rulers.[40] A luminous figure, Barani is recognized by many as the finest Indo-Muslim historian of the Sultanate period.[41] Shams al-Din bin Siraj al-Din ʿAfif, like Barani and other historians mentioned above, was closely associated with the ruling house, in his case the Tughlaq dynasty.[42] Yahya bin Ahmad bin ʿAbd Allah al-Sirhindi chose to write about the ruler of the Saiyid dynasty (1414–51), Mubarak Shah (r. 1421–33), to whom the author dedicated the work.[43]

This proximity to the royal house and the court made these historians privy to the high politics revolving around the centre of power, and consequently it became a natural assumption that those narrators offered a more truthful and insightful version of history, as suggested by the distinguished British historian Henry Dodwell. Writing in the 1930s about Muslim chronicles in India, he observed that Islam began a great tradition of Indian chronicles and that Muslim chronicles were 'far superior to our own medieval chronicles' since the former were 'written for the most part not by monks but by men of affairs, often by *contemporaries who had seen and taken part in the events they recount*'.[44]

Given the circumstances of these historians, writing from their vantage position stationed at the centre of events, Dodwell's logical expectations embrace at once the most central and the hardest question for students of this historiographical literature. Did Indo-Persian historiography indeed live up to these high expectations? With virtually any form of historical writing, issues concerning its 'truth', veracity, and purpose, as well as the manner in which, as a literary work, it represents past events, emerge as very critical. In Islamic history authored by Muslim historians these issues are of prime importance, since the historiographical

[38] Minhaj al-Din, *Tabaqat-i Nasiri* (n. p., 1259).
[39] Saiyids traditionally claimed a distinctive position in Muslim society by tracing their descent from the Prophet.
[40] See his *Taʾrīkh-i Firuz Shahi* (n.p., 1357); and *Fatawa-i Jahandari*, ed. A. Salim Khan (Lahore, 1972).
[41] M. Athar Ali, 'History in Indo-Muslim Tradition', in id., *Mughal India: Studies in Polity, Ideas, Society and Culture* (Delhi and Oxford, 2006), 364.
[42] Afif, *Taʾrīkh -i Firuz Shahi* (n.p., completed after 1398).
[43] Al-Sirhindi, *Taʾrīkh-i Mubarak Shahi* (n.p., 1434).
[44] H. Dodwell, *India*, 2 vols. (London, 1936), i. 22 (emphasis mine).

problems, for them, essentially stem from a wider Islamic belief of the absolute, omnipotent, and sovereign position assigned to God. As already observed, since truth, in Islam, originates with God and not historians, and also since history as an Islamic discipline is not rooted, unlike hadith, theology, and law, in the Prophetic revelations, it should be clear why history remained marginalized in relation to those disciplines. The special nature of man's standing in relation to God based on the latter's total omnipotence lies at the core of Islamic perceptions of the making and writing of history.

INDO-PERSIAN HISTORIANS' PURPOSE AND TRUTH

In approaching the prime historiographical question relating to historians' purpose and truth we need to begin with a clear understanding of two significant matters raised above. One relates to the notion of 'truth' itself—that it originates with God and not with historians. The other follows from the first that Muslim historians did not seek to absolve themselves of their own responsibilities as historians simply by placing God at the centre of historical knowledge. Confronted with the challenge of making sense of the past, the vast majority of Muslim historians did not emerge as indifferent to their tasks. On the contrary, a number of historians entertained rather exalted notions of the 'science of history' and practised their craft with considerable seriousness. In the words of one Mughal historian, 'Abd al-Qadir Badayuni, 'The science of history is essentially a lofty science and an elegant branch of learning.'[45] Other prominent historians held similar views. A good measure of the importance attached to history was a strong and quite common belief that *ilm al-ta'rikh* (the science of history) and *ilm al-hadith* (the science of hadith) were to be seen almost as 'twins'. Most medieval historians making reference to this close relationship between the two 'sciences' neither attached any religious significance to this association nor equated *ta'rikh* with hadith as a religious science. Historians, however, zealously pursued, as the guiding principle of their own historical enquiries, the remarkable technique and methodology of *isnad* used in the authentication and compilation of the hadith tradition—a system of character verification of all persons in a chain of sources involved in the transmission of a Prophetic tradition. Although it is inconceivable that such methods could be applied to all kinds of historical enquiries, the methodology as such was not unscientific, and more importantly, was characteristically marked by a genuine concern with establishing the 'truth'.

In dealing with the sources for their historical works, Indo-Persian historians often spoke of 'reliable' or 'trustworthy witnesses' or simply named them in their narratives. When faced with a lack of, or inadequate, or conflicting evidence,

---

[45] Badayuni, *Muntakhab al-Tawarikh* (n.p., 1596); trans. G. S. A. Ranking, vol. 1 (Calcutta, 1895–9), 4.

those historians commonly resorted to statements such as 'Truth is known to God alone' or 'God alone knows'. They apparently developed a working code of professional conduct based on religious and moral principles, inculcating devotion to truth and arguing against its suppression, or hiding the darker side of a regime and a ruler, while glorifying their brighter aspects. The clarion-call for Indo-Persian historiography was sounded by its towering figure, al-Biruni, who invoked the religious-moral authority of the Qur'an and the Bible in support of the call for honesty and integrity of the historians. In the preface of his book on India, he quotes the Qur'anic verse: 'Speak the truth, even if it were against yourselves' (Sura 4.134), and also the Gospel: 'Do not mind the fury of kings in speaking the truth. They only possess your body, but they have no power over your soul' (Matt. 10.28; Luke 12.4). Al-Biruni himself pledged: 'I shall place before the reader the theories of the Hindus *exactly as they are*, and I shall mention in connection with them similar theories of the Greeks in order to show the relationship existing between them.'[46]

Al-Biruni's was followed over a period of time by other emphatic pronouncements on the truth in relation to history and historians. Ziya' al-Din Barani brought a fresh approach. The singularity of his contribution is laid out in the preface to his major work, in which, *inter alia*, the issues of the truth in history and the importance of history take precedence.[47] History, he writes, is 'based on truth' and historians should be 'just and truthful'. To be truthful is a 'religious obligation' and 'accountable on the Day of Judgment'—'the lying historian' can be expected to be condemned with the harshest of punishments. Barani's strong conviction of the historian's truth is also borne out by his willingness to compromise on the question of dealing with uncomfortable truth regarding 'contemporaries', but he urged historians to be 'honest' and 'truthful' in respect of 'past events'. The world of Islamic learning had perhaps never been so frontally challenged by an Indo-Persian historian before Barani's supremely confident and emphatic assertion: 'I have not seen as many benefits in any other form of learning or practical activity as I have in the sciences of history.' He outlined the various benefits, arguing that the consequences of both 'good deeds' and 'wickedness' are revealed through history and that histories of the prophets and of unjust and oppressive rulers provide the faithful with necessary knowledge and wisdom. Barani's rather practical conception of the value and role of history that teaches by example has already been discussed above. Following Barani, the Timurid historian Mir Khwand, grandfather of the later Indo-Persian historian Khwandamir (1475–1534/7), exhorted his fellow historians to 'describe all aspects of everyday affair' and just as they recount 'the merits, charities,

---

[46] Al-Biruni, *Kitab al-Hind*, i. 4–5, 7 (emphasis mine).
[47] Ziya al-Din Barani, *Ta'rikh-i Firuz Shahi* (Calcutta, 1862/91), 1–18, esp. 9–13.

justice and mercy of great men', similarly they 'should describe, and not seek to hide, their wicked and mean acts'.[48]

In practice such prescriptive standards posed insurmountable difficulties for historians in medieval India, most of whom were closely connected to the court, and therefore unable to write what they felt and knew to be true. Very often they wrote to justify the ruler's confidence and expectations of them and to please and zget rewards from their patrons, or, worse still, to deliver a command performance. Most political narratives embraced contemporary history and were undertaken at the requisition of the reigning monarch either to glorify his individual or dynastic achievements, or to leave behind an enduring record of some major events of the reign. The court historians were often constrained to work under the pressure of competing with court poets or other writers in extolling and glorifying the ruler. They were also challenged to boost the image of the ruler as the champion of religious orthodoxy and the extirpator of infidelity, especially in the eyes of the 'ulama'.

Nonetheless, we could hardly overlook those historians who struggled to unburden their conscience and reveal their inner thoughts. Here, again, Mir Khwand boldly spoke his mind to his fellow historians and others: 'If he [the historian] considers it prudent, he may describe his [ruler's] "wicked acts" openly; if not, he should resort to hints, insinuations and indirect remarks. A hint to the wise is enough.'[49] Historians devised various other forms of diplomatic devices for getting around the problem of discussing 'unpalatable' and even 'hazardous' truth. Mir Khwand recommended the practice of extravagant praise, flattery, and adulation to convey to the readers just the opposite impression. Amir Khusrau, while glorifying 'Ala' al-Din Khalji's victories in Southern India, found himself pained by the consequent destruction of life and property. He inserted a cryptic note: 'And you saw bones of men and animals.'[50] Sometimes, silence proved as effective as discretion. Abu'l Fazl as a friend, admirer, and devotee of Emperor Akbar, often remained conspicuously silent or ambivalent about many controversial aspects of Akbar's liberal religious and cultural policies. Further, Abu'l Fazl often resorted to overly involved, ornate, and florid language with a view to hiding or obfuscating his own stance on a particular issue. Yahya bin Ahmad Sirhindi, while exploring the causes of unrest and conflicts in the highly controversial reign of his patron, Muhammad bin Tughlaq, chose to turn away from this uncomfortable topic with the remark that it was 'improper' to narrate 'the errors of the great'.[51]

---

[48] Mir Khwand, *Rauzat al-Safa*, English trans. (Allahabad, 1960), 130.
[49] Ibid.
[50] Khusrau, *Khazaʾin al-Futuh*, trans. M. Habib as *The Campaigns of ʿAla-ud-din Khilji* (Madras, 1931), 152.
[51] Al-Sirhindi, *Tarikh-i Mubarak Shahi*; see also Hardy, *Medieval Historians*, 60.

In drawing conclusions with respect to the overall position of the Muslim historians in relation to the question of truth and honesty, it is necessary to steer clear of the twin potholes of 'intemperate censure' and 'uncritical acclaim' to which they have at times been subjected.[52] Distinguished European scholars have bestowed their accolades on medieval Islamic, including Indo-Islamic, historiographical traditions, especially with respect to that of political narratives.[53] Such scholarly appreciation and endorsement stand in sharp contrast with that of the apologists of the British colonial empire. More recently, having taken their cue from British colonialist writers, contemporaneous champions of militant Hindu zealotry have sought to denigrate and vilify the medieval Muslim world in India.

The politics of the Hindu supremacists has been assiduously built with an intent to devalue and often 'smear' Muslim rule and rulers in pre-British India. This strategic political consideration underlying the anti-Muslim prejudice and hostility of the Hindu hegemonists is a clear legacy of earlier British colonial thinking and writing on India. The former drew on literary and epigraphical materials from the English translation of Persian historical writings, of which the most readily accessible collection was the eight-volume *History of India as Told by its Own Historians*, edited by Henry Elliot and John Dowson (1867). Hindu extremists found this 'most useful', since those British colonial authors shared the same political objective of disparaging the Muslim rulers as 'fanatics' and 'tyrants', contrasting Muslim rule with the so-called enlightened and efficient British governance based on the 'Rule of Law', with their ultimate objective of winning over the Indian subject people to 'progressive' and 'benevolent' British rule. The colonial mode of historical representation of 'Muslim rule', glibly appropriated by Hindu chauvinists, was riddled with problems, resulting from a combination of tendentious political motivations of the writers and a grossly selective and lopsided use of translated Persian material from the Elliot and Dowson volumes.[54]

It is apparent, therefore, that medieval Indo-Persian historians, at least those with some better understanding of the nature of contemporaneous historical science, had a significant level of awareness of the issues of historical truth. Occasional compromise with the truth, often eliciting stretched and strained

---

[52] Chase Robinson's depiction of Islamic historiographical experiences since the classical period offers some grounds for seeking parallels in Indo-Persian historiographical developments in our period. Robinson, *Islamic Historiography*, 143.

[53] See H. Dodwell, *India*, 2 vols. (London, 1936), i. 22; Bernard Lewis, 'The Periodization of History—Excerpts', *Hudson New York*, February 2009, p. 4; Rosenthal, *Muslim Historiography*, 196; and Robinson, *Islamic Historiography*, 6–7.

[54] For a fuller exploration of the politics of medieval Indian historiography of British colonial and Indian, especially the Hindu hegemonist, authorship, see Asim Roy, '"Living Together in Difference": Religious Conflict and Tolerance in Pre-colonial India as History and Discourse', in *South Asia: Journal of South Asian Studies*, New Series, Special Issue, 33:1 (2010), 33–60; and Roy, 'Introduction', in Mushirul Hasan and Roy (eds.), *Living Together Separately: Cultural India in History and Politics* (New Delhi, 2005), 1–25.

justifications from the historians concerned, may very well be taken as a vicarious affirmation of their recognition of and faith in the norm and the system. Indo-Persian historians, in sum, set themselves a laudable goal in the context of the time and the world they lived in, namely to uphold the ethical and didactic purpose of history-writing. Regardless of their inadequacies, shortcomings, and failings, almost all of them stood their ground.

TIMELINE/KEY DATES

1186–1206 Reign of Mui'zzuddin Muhammad, Sultan of Ghur, whose military successes in north-western India directly contributed to the establishment of the Turko-Afghan Sultanate of Delhi

1206 Foundation of the Delhi Sultanate under Qutb al-Din Aibak (r. 1206–10)

1206–1526 Rule of the Delhi Sultanate under five largely Turko-Afghan dynasties

1236–40 Reign of Raziyya, the first female Muslim Sultana in India and in the Muslim world

1398 Timur's invasion and plunder of India

1501–1736 Persian Safavid Empire

1526–1857 Mughal imperial rule (Padishahi)

1526–30 Reign of Zahir al-Din Muhammad Babur, the founder of the Mughal Padishahi

1530–40, 1555–6 Reign of Humayun, Babur's son and successor, who was temporarily overthrown by the Afghan Sur dynasty (1540–55) of Sher Shah Suri (r. 1540–5)

1555–6 Humayun's Restoration

1556–1605 Reign of Emperor Jalal al-Din Muhammad Akbar, Humayun's son and heir

1605–27 Reign of Nur al-Din Muhammad Jahangir, Akbar's son and heir

1658–1707 Reign of Padishah Aurangzeb (also known as Alamgir), whose orthodoxy countered the earlier Mughal liberal policies

1707–1857 Decline of the Mughal Empire under the later Mughals, and its eventual overthrow by the British (1857)

KEY HISTORICAL SOURCES

Abu'l Fazl, *Akbar-nama* (n.p., 1596), in *Bibliotheca Indica*, 3 vols. (Calcutta, 1873–87); trans. H. Beveridge, in *Bibliotheca Indica*, 3 vols. (Calcutta, 1902).

——*A'in-i Akbari* (n.p., 1599); ed. Saiyid Ahmad Khan (Delhi, AH 1272); trans. H. Blochmann *et al.*, in *Bibliotheca Indica* (Calcutta, 1868–94).

ʿAfif, Shams al-Din bin Siraj al-Din, *Taʾrikh-i Firuz Shahi* (n.p., completed after 1398); ed. Maulavi Vilayat Husain as *The Tarikh-i Firoz Shahi of Shams Siraj ʿAfif*, in *Bibliotheca Indica* (Calcutta, 1891).

Al-Biruni, Abu Raihan, *Kitab al-Hind* (n.p., 1030); ed. and trans. Edward C. Sachau as *Alberuni's India*, 2 vols. (repr. edn, New Delhi, 1964).

Al-Sirhindi, Yahya bin Ahmad bin ʿAbd Allah, *Taʾrikh-i Mubarak Shahi* (n.p., 1434); ed. M. Hidayat Hosain as *Tarikh-i Mubarak Shahi of Yahya bin Ahmad b. ʿAbdullah As-Sihrindi*, in *Bibliotheca Indica* (Calcutta, 1931); trans. K. K. Basu as *The Tarikh-i-Mubarakshahi of Yahya bin Ahmad bin ʿAbdullah As-Sirhindi* (Baroda, 1932).

Babur, Zahir al-Din Muhammad, *Tuzuk-i Baburi* or *Babur-nama* (n.p., 1530); trans. Annette S. Beveridge as *Baburnama*, 2 vols. (London, 1921; repr. edn, New Delhi, 1979).

Badayuni, ʿAbd al-Qadir, *Muntakhab al-Tawaʾrikh* (n.p., 1596); ed. W. N. Lees *et al.*, in *Bibliotheca Indica*, 3 vols. (Calcutta, 1865–9); trans. G. S. A. Ranking, vol. 1 (Calcutta, 1895–9); W. H. Lowe, vol. 2 (Calcutta, 1884–98; repr. edn, 1925); T. W. Haig, vol. 3 (Calcutta, 1899–1925).

Bakhshi, Nizam al-Din Ahmad, *Tabaqat-i Akbari* (n.p., 1594); ed. B. De, in *Bibliotheca Indica*, 3 vols. (Calcutta, 1911; repr. edn, 1973).

Barani, Ziyaʾ al-Din, *Taʾrikh-i Firuz Shahi* (n.p., 1357); ed. Saiyid Ahmad Khan *et al.* as *The Tarikh-i Feroz-shahi of Ziaa al-Din Barni*, in *Bibliotheca Indica* (Calcutta, 1862/91).

——*Fatawa-i Jahandari*, ed. A. Salim Khan (Lahore, 1972); trans. Muhammad Habib and Afsar Khan as *The Political Theory of the Delhi Sultanate* (Allahabad, n.d.).

Firishta (alias Muhammad Qasim Hindu-Shah Astarabadi), *Gulshan-i Ibrahimi* or *Taʾrikh-i Firishta* (1607; ed. 2 vols. Bombay, 1832).

Gulbadan Begum, *Humayun-nama* (1603; London, 1902); trans. Annette S. Beveridge as *The History of Humayun* (London, 1902; repr. edn, Delhi, 2006).

Ibn Battuta, *Rihla*, ed. and trans. H. A. R. Gibb as *The Travels of Ibn Battuta, AD 1325–1354* (London, 1958).

ʿIsami, *Futuh al-Salatin* (n.p., 1350); ed. Agha Mahdi Husain (Agra, 1938).

Jahangir, Nur al-Din Muhammad, *Tuzuk-i Jahangiri*, ed. Syed Ahmad Khan (Ghazipur/Aligarh, 1863–4); ed. and trans. A. Rogers and H. Beveridge as *Memoirs of Jahangir*, 2 vols. (London, 1909–14).

Khusrau, Amir (Dehlawi), *Khazaʾin al-Futuh* (n.p., 1312); ed. S. Moinul Haq (Aligarh, 1927); trans. M. Habib as *The Campaigns of ʿAla-ud-din Khilji* (Madras, 1931).

Kufi, Muhammad ʿAli bin Hamid, *Chachnama* (n.p., *c.* AH 613 /*c.*1216–17), ed. Umar bin Muhammad Daudpota (Hyderabad, 1939).

Minhaj al-Din bin Siraj al-Din Juzjani, *Tabaqat-i Nasiri* (n.p., AH 657–8/1259–60); ed. W. N. Lees *et al.*, in *Bibliotheca Indica* (Calcutta, 1863–4); trans. H. B. Raverty (Calcutta, 1873–81).

Mir Khurd (alias Sayid Muhammad Mubarak Kirmani), *Siyar al-Auliya* (Delhi, AH 1302).

Mir Khwand (alias Muhammad bin Khwand Shah), *Rauzat al-Safa fi Sirat al-Anbiya waʾl Muluk waʾl Khulafa* (Lucknow, AH 1270–4; Bombay, 1845); partial trans. E. Rehatsek (London, 1891–93).

Sarwani, Abbas Khan bin Shaykh 'Ali, *Tuhfa-i Akbar Shahi* (n.p., compiled in 3 recensions, *c*.1579–1586).

Tughluq, Firuz Shah, *Futuhat-i Firuz Shahi*, ed. and trans. S. A. Rashid (Aligarh, 1943).

BIBLIOGRAPHY

Ali, M. Athar, *Mughal India: Studies in Polity, Ideas, Society and Culture* (Oxford, 2006).

Ashraf, Kunwar Muhammad, *Indian Historiography and Other Related Papers*, ed. Jaweed Ashraf (New Delhi, 2006).

Chandra, Satish, *State, Pluralism, and the Indian Historical Tradition* (Oxford, 2008).

—— *Historiography, Religion, and State in Medieval India* (New Delhi, 1996).

Chatterjee, Kumkum, *The Cultures of History in Early Modern India: Persianization and Mughal Culture in Bengal* (Oxford, 2009).

Habib, Irfan, *Interpreting Indian History* (Shillong, India, 1988).

Habib, M. and Khan, A. U. S., *The Political Theory of the Delhi Sultanate* (Allahabad, 1960).

Habibullah, A. B. M., 'Re-evaluation of the Literary Sources in Pre-Mughal History', *Islamic Culture*, 15:2 (1941), 207–16.

—— 'Medieval Indo-Persian Literature Relating to Hindu Science and Philosophy, 1000–1800 A.D.', *Indian Historical Quarterly*, 14:1 (1938), 167–81.

Hardy, Peter, *Historians of Medieval India: Studies in Indo-Muslim Historical Writing* (London, 1960).

Hasan, Mohibbul and Mujeeb, Muhammad (eds.), *Historians of Medieval India* (Meerut, India, 1968).

Hasan, Nurul, *Religion, State and Society in Medieval India: Collected Works of S. Nurul Hasan*, ed. Satish Chandra (Oxford, 2005).

Husain, Mahdi, 'Critical Study of the Sources for the History of Medieval India (1320–1526)', *Islamic Culture*, 31:4 (1957), 314–21.

Husaini, Syeda Bilqis Fatema, *A Critical Study of Indo-Persian Literature during Sayyid and Lodi Period, 1414–1526 A.D.* (Delhi, 1988).

Mukhia, Harbans, *Historians and Historiography during the Reign of Akbar* (New Delhi, 1976).

Nizami, Khaliq Ahmad, *On History and Historians of Medieval India* (New Delhi, 1983).

Robinson, Chase F., *Islamic Historiography* (Cambridge, 2003).

Rosenthal, Franz, *A History of Muslim Historiography*, 2nd edn. (Leiden, 1968).

Roy, Asim, *Islam in South Asia: A Regional Perspective* (New Delhi, 1996).

—— 'Being and Becoming a Muslim: A Historiographic Perspective on the Search for Muslim Identity in Bengal', in Sekhar Bandyopadhyay (ed.), *Bengal: Rethinking History: Essays in Historiography* (New Delhi, 2001), 167–229.

—— 'Introduction', in Mushirul Hasan and Roy (eds.), *Living Together Separately: Cultural India in History and Politics* (Oxford, 2005), 1–25.

Sarkar, Jadu Nath, *Mughal Administration* (Calcutta, 1920).

Sen, Sudipta, 'Imperial Orders of the Past: The Semantics of History and Time in the Medieval Indo-Persianate Culture of North India', in Daud Ali (ed.), *Invoking the Past: The Uses of History in South Asia* (Oxford, 2002), 231–57.

Waseem, Shah Mohammad (ed.), *Development of Persian Historiography in India from the Second Half of the Seventeenth Century to the First Half of the Eighteenth Century* (New Delhi, 2003).

Chapter 8

Persian Historical Writing under the Safavids (1501–1722/36)

Christoph Marcinkowski

The establishment of the Safavid dynasty in 1501 marks a significant turning point in Persian history during the Islamic period, as well as in the history of Islam at large.[1] Under their rule, through the efforts of Shah Isma'il I—the adolescent head of the militant Shi'ite *Safawiyyah* Sufi order—Twelver Shi'ism was elevated to what is often referred to as 'religion of state' in Persia, originally a centre of Sunni 'orthodoxy'.[2] This was the first time since the advent of Islam that a major Islamic state had taken this step. The later rise of the country's Shi'ite clerics—in particular during the post-Safavid period—would be difficult to conceive without an awareness of the foundations that were laid during the early sixteenth century.[3] Moreover, the (most probably Turkic-speaking) Safavid shahs understood themselves as heirs or revivers of the patterns set by traditional Persian kingship with clear references to certain pre-Islamic traditions, as reflected in their commissioning of magnificently illustrated versions of Firdawsi's *Shah-nama* [Book of Kings] (c.1000). As staunch Shi'ites, the Safavids saw themselves (and Persia) surrounded by potentially hostile Sunni powers, such as the Ottomans, the Mughals, and the khanates in Central Asia. Their rule can thus be considered a synthesis of Shi'ite Islam and 'Persian revivalism'.[4]

In terms of historical writing, the Safavid contribution is usually considered a continuation of the splendid fifteenth-century Timurid chronicle tradition,

---

[1] For overviews of this period see Roger Savory, *Iran under the Safavids* (Cambridge, 1980); and Andrew J. Newman, *Safavid Iran: Rebirth of a Persian Empire* (London, 2006).

[2] Twelver Shi'ism is the largest denomination within Shi'ite Islam. Its adherents are most commonly referred to as 'Twelvers', which is derived from their belief in twelve divinely ordained successors of the Prophet of Islam as leaders (or Imams) of the Muslim community. Today, they are most prominent in Iran, Azerbaijan, Iraq, parts of Saudi Arabia, the Arab countries at the southern Persian Gulf shores, Lebanon, and parts of the Indian subcontinent.

[3] For a good overview see Kathryn Babayan, 'The Safavid Synthesis: From Qizilbash-Islam to Imamite Shi'ism', *Iranian Studies*, 27:1–4 (1994), 135–61.

[4] A still useful account of this transition period is Walther Hinz, *Der Aufstieg Irans zum Nationalstaat im fünfzehnten Jahrhundert* (Berlin, 1936).

which under the Safavids at times assumed the colouring of a kind of 'history of salvation', in the light of the rulers' self-consciousness as devout defenders of Twelver Shi'ism. Safavid power reached its climax under Shah 'Abbas I the Great, a level of power and prosperity never before achieved in Persia's Islamic history, and Iskandar Beg Munshi's chronicle *Tarikh-i 'Alam-ara-yi 'Abbasi* [World-Illuminating History of 'Abbas] (1628–9) is certainly the most eminent contribution of Safavid historical writing, which was almost entirely composed in Persian. Other historical accounts of that period address the quasi-mythical rise of the Safavids, dealing in particular with the dynasty's founder, Shah Isma'il I, and his claim to religious legitimacy, as the Safavids rank as one of the more malleable ruling families in terms of self-legitimization, cloaking themselves with a variety of genealogies, titulature, and religio-political claims.

Administrative literature—although little of it has come down to us—has to be considered an important part of Safavid historical writing as well. Already in the 1940s, the early eighteenth-century state manual *Tadhkirat al-Muluk* [Memorial of the Kings] had been made accessible to the world of scholarship. *Dastur al-Muluk* [Regulations of the Kings], a more detailed version of the latter, was translated for the first time into English by this writer.[5] As in the case of the chronicles, both manuals bear witness to the 'multicultural' character of the Safavid state and society. This feature is reflected in their application of Persian, Arabic, Turkic, and Mongolian terminology—the latter two in particular in terms of military technology.[6]

Historical writing in the wider sense also includes geographical and travel literature. A particularly splendid example of this genre and of how 'the Other', the outside world, was perceived during that period, is *Safinah-yi Sulaymani* [The Ship of Sulayman], a late seventeenth-century account of an official Safavid embassy to Siam, home to an influential community of Persian 'expatriate' merchants.

The Safavid era was at times idealized as an age of stability and glory in the memory of subsequent generations, as reflected in the historiographical works of

---

[5] Christoph Marcinkowski, *Mirza Rafi'a's Dastur al-Muluk: A Manual of Later Safavid Administration. Annotated English Translation, Comments on the Offices and Services, and Facsimile of the Unique Persian Manuscript* (Kuala Lumpur, 2002); see also id., 'Mirza Rafi'a's *Dastur al-Muluk*: A Prime Source on Administration, Society and Culture in Late Safavid Iran', *Zeitschrift der Deutschen Morgenländischen Gesellschaft*, 153:2 (2003), 281–310; and id., 'Mirza Rafi'a's *Dastur al-Muluk* Again: Recently Discovered Additions to the Persian Manuscript', *Zeitschrift der Deutschen Morgenländischen Gesellschaft*, 157:2 (2007), 395–416. A. B. Vil'danova published the first annotated translation of *Dastur al-Mulik* (in Russian; Tashkent, 1991). Unfortunately, her painstaking work has so far not received the attention of international scholarship. For another recent English translation see Willem Floor and Mohammad H. Faghfoory, *Dastur al-Moluk: A Safavid State Manual* (Costa Mesa, Calif., 2007).

[6] Gerhard Doerfer's *Türkische und mongolische Elemente im Neupersischen, unter besonderer Berücksichtigung älterer neupersischer Geschichtsquellen, vor allem der Mongolen- und Timuridenzeit*, 4 vols. (Wiesbaden, 1963–75) gives a good impression as to the extent of Mongolian loanwords in Persian.

the subsequent Zand and early Qajar periods. As an example as to how the Safavid claim to religiously sanctioned rule was perceived during the 'Time of Troubles', following the collapse of Safavid rule in 1722, reference shall be made to *Zayn al-'Arifin* [Embellishment of the Gnostics] (before 1733), a piece of the advice (*naṣīḥat*) genre which has a long-standing tradition in Islamic literature.

Before proceeding, it should be mentioned that Persia under the Safavids was also home to Jewish as well as Armenian and Georgian Christian communities. Although they, too, left invaluable accounts which are important sources, this chapter shall solely be concerned with Safavid historical writing by Muslims. Due to the limits set to this contribution, the same applies to the important observations penned by seventeenth-century Western travellers to the Safavid dominions. Their writings are particularly rich as they serve as important correlatives when studying the period under consideration here. It can only be noted in passing that Safavid Persia also exercised a certain fascination on French eighteenth-century authors as reflected, for instance, in Montesquieu's fictitious *Lettres Persanes* [Persian Letters] (1721).[7]

SAFAVID CHRONICLES

In spite of the fact that the coming of the Safavids marked the beginning of a new chapter in Persian history—which is mainly due to their promotion of Twelver Shi'ism—historical writing during that period still followed in the tradition of the dynasty's predecessor in the east, the empire of the Timurids, which was centred in Herat, in what is now Afghanistan.[8]

This becomes evident when considering the circumstance that many Safavid historians themselves lauded the works of their Timurid predecessors as valuable patterns. This is particularly well reflected in Ibrahim Amini's *Futuhat-i Shahi* [The Royal Conquests], the earliest work of Safavid historical writing, finalized in Safavid Herat around 1530, during the reign of Shah Tahmasp I. Especially in his preface, Amini refers directly to Sharaf al-Din Yazdi's *Zafar-namah* [Book of Conquests], a work dedicated to the history of the Timurid dynasty, completed around 1425. As late as about a century after Amini, Iskandar Beg Munshi, too, in his chronicle *Tarikh-i 'Alam-ara-yi 'Abbasi* [World-Illuminating History of 'Abbas], considers himself obliged to earlier Timurid predecessors. Timurid

[7] Overview in Olivier H. Bonnerot, *La Perse dans la littérature et la pensée française au XVIIIe siècle: De l'image au mythe* (Paris, 1988).

[8] See Sholeh A. Quinn, 'The Timurid Historiographical Legacy: A Comparative Study of Persianate Historical Writing', in A. J. Newman (ed.), *Society and Culture in the Early Modern Middle East: Studies on Iran in the Safavid Period* (Leiden, 2003), 19–32; and Maria Szuppe, 'L'évolution de l'image de Timour et des Timourides dans l'historiographie Safavide du XVIe au XVIIIe siècle, *Cahiers d'Asie Centrale*, 3–4 (1997), 313–31.

historiography was firmly rooted within the Persian literary tradition of official court histories of the post-Mongol period.

Aside from the eastern, Timurid tradition, Safavid historiography is also indebted—although to a lesser degree—to certain 'western' influences, that is to say, Persian historical writing that had been produced under the Turcoman dynasties, such as the Aq-Quyunlus, the immediate predecessors of the Safavids. In this regard, Abu Bakr Tihrani's *Kitab-i Diyarbakriyyah* [A History of the City of Diyarbakir] (late fifteenth century) and Fadl-Allah Khunji Isfahani's *Tarikh-i 'Alam-ara-yi Amini* [World-Illuminating History of Amini] (completed after 1491) had been particularly important sources for the Safavid chroniclers. While it developed a distinct tradition of its own, Safavid historiography can thus also be seen as a merging of the 'western' (Aq-Quyunlu) and 'eastern' (Timurid) traditions.

Let us first turn to Amini's work and the 'eastern tradition'. As mentioned earlier, Amini completed his *Futuhat-i Shahi*—a general history, which also includes accounts on the twelve Shi'ite Imams, the *Safawiyyah* Sufi order, and ultimately the rise to power of its leader, Isma'il I—in 1530, during the reign of Isma'il's successor, Tahmasp I, the second Safavid king. However, as a matter of fact, he had started working on this chronicle ten years earlier, as it had been Shah Isma'il himself who had commissioned it. Amini produced a version in prose as well as in verse. Originally, Amini must have been a Sunni, for he had served earlier as *sadr* (head of the administration of justice and religious affairs) under the last Timurids. After the Safavid takeover of his city in 1510, Shah Isma'il entrusted Amini with the compilation of *Futuhat-i Shahi*. Amini, who lived in Herat, is thus a particularly good exponent for exemplifying the transition period from (Sunni) Timurid to (Shi'ite) Safavid rule. He was a product of the Timurid scholarly tradition, in which he continued to work under his new patrons. In spite of his originally Sunni background, he apparently had no difficulties in switching his religious allegiances, for he seems to have relied in his account of the early *Safawiyyah* on *Safwat al-Safa* [The Quintessence of Purity], a hagiography (*manaqib*) started by Ibn Bazzaz in 1334, the year of the death of Shaykh Safi al-Din, the founder of that order, and completed around 1358.

Amini is not the only example of that transition process from Timurid to Safavid rule. Ghiyath al-Din Khwandamir, a contemporary of Amini, who, too, was originally based in Herat, and who had also previously been in the service of the Sunni Timurids, is the author of *Habib al-Siyar* [The Friend of Biographies], a general history, completed in 1524, the year of the death of Shah Isma'il. *Habib al-Siyar* is an account of Muslim 'world history', with a geographical survey of the then known world and its curiosities. The most valuable third volume deals with the reigns of the Timurid Sultan Husayn Bayqara (r. 1469–1506) and Shah Isma'il. Khwandamir, who dedicated his work to a high-ranking Safavid official, was a grandson of the celebrated Timurid historiographer Mirkhwand, to whose gigantic work *Rawdat al-Safa* [Garden of Purity] (completed 1498) he is largely indebted in terms of style and structuring, and the last volume of which he actually wrote himself. Khwandamir thus gains in significance as the most important historian of the transition period. Similar to Amini, Khwandamir, too, relied heavily on Ibn Bazzaz's *manāqib* when dealing with the early history of the Safavids.

During the reign of Shah Tahmasp I, the historiographical tradition continued in Khwandamir's family with his son Amir Mahmud, who was also based in Herat. Amir Mahmud wrote *Tarikh-i Shah Isma'il-i Awwal wa Shah Tahmasp*, a history of the first two Safavid monarchs, which is also known as *Dhayl-i Habib al-Siyar* [Continuation of the Friend of Biographies]. The second half of this work, extending to about the year 1550, contains valuable original material for the reign of Tahmasp.

As a matter of fact, the long reign of Tahmasp (especially its later part) witnessed the full blossoming of Safavid historical writing with the appearance of several major works. Among them are Qadi Ahmad Ghaffari's *Nusakh-i Jahan-ara* [World-Illuminating Leaves] (1564–5) and 'Abdi Beg Shirazi's *Takmilat al-Akhbar* [Completion of News] (*c.*1570), both of whom followed the earlier patterns set by Amini and Khwandamir, and who worked at the Safavid capital Qazvin, which had replaced Tabriz. Shah Tahmasp himself is the only Safavid monarch to write their memoirs, which also constitute a valuable source.[9]

Historiography during the time of Isma'il I and Tahmasp I was characterized by the prevalence of general histories. Aside from the already mentioned works by Khwandamir and Ghaffari, Yahya Qazwini's *Lubb al-Tawarikh* [Essence of the Histories] (*c.*1542) also falls into this category. Qazwini was eventually executed by the Safavids for being a crypto-Sunni. With the progression of time, and the rulers of the dynasty felt they were firmly established, dynastic histories became more prominent, particularly during the reign of 'Abbas I.

The year 1577, which marked the end of the very short reign of Shah Isma'il II, who attempted unsuccessfully to bring Persia back into the fold of Sunni Islam, saw the completion of the voluminous *Ahsan al-Tawarikh* [Best of Histories] by Hasan Beg Rumlu, an ethnic Turk and Safavid military officer, an important source which has come down to us only in part. The intermezzo of Isma'il II was followed by his successor Muhammad Khudabandah, who followed again a Shi'ite course, but who seems not to have officially commissioned any historical works.

The reign of 'Abbas I the Great, who brought the internal civil war-like situation to an end, is usually considered the apex of Safavid power. During his rule, several territories, previously taken by the neighbouring Sunni Ottomans and Uzbeks, were reconquered, among them Iraq with its Shi'ite shrine cities. 'Abbas is particularly remembered by his countrymen to this day as a

---

[9] Paul Horn (ed.), 'Die Denkwürdigkeiten des Šah Tahmasp von Persien', *Zeitschrift der Deutschen Morgenländischen Gesellschaft*, 44 (1890), 563–649; 45 (1891), 245–91.

devout Shi'ite and for making Isfahan the capital city of his realm, transforming it into one of the most magnificent centres of the Islamic world at that time. In terms of historiographical output, one of the first works completed under the rule of this able monarch was *Khulasat al-Tawarikh* [Summary of Histories] (*c*.1591) by Qadi Ahmad Qumi, whose work was the result of his own initiative rather than that of a patron.[10]

By the beginning of the seventeenth century and at the zenith of Safavid royal power under Shah 'Abbas the Great, the majority of chroniclers—although not all of them—wrote dynastic histories.[11] Among them are partial dynastic accounts, such as Mahmud bin Hidayat-Allah Afushta'i Natanzi's *Nuqawat al-Athar* [Selection of Antiquities] (1598), dealing with the transition period from the end of the rule of Tahmasp I to that of 'Abbas the Great, or complete histories of the Safavid dynasty, such as Fadli Isfahani's *Afdal al-Tawarikh* [The Best of the Histories] (1639).[12] Certainly the most significant work of that period, however, is *Tarikh-i 'Alam-ara-yi 'Abbasi* by Iskandar Beg Munshi, an ethnic Turkish member of the military and student of Qumi. Iskandar Beg's dynastic chronicle, completed in 1629, is available to the English reader in Savory's magnificent translation.[13] Qumi's and Iskandar Beg's works became standard models for subsequent chronicles as they both trace back the genealogical origins of the ruling dynasty to the family of the Prophet of Islam, along with outlining its 'spiritual' beginnings as a Sufi order. Iskandar Beg also began writing a continuation of his own chronicle during the first years of the subsequent monarch, Shah Safi I. The successful military exploits of the Safavid armies against the Ottomans, Portuguese, and Uzbeks during that period provided historians with ample opportunity to glorify 'Abbas the Great, as reflected in Siyaqi Nizami's *Futuhat-i Humayun* [Imperial Conquests] (1611), which is devoted to the 1598 campaign of that ruler against the Uzbeks.

Another eminent historian during the time of the most successful Safavid ruler was Jalal al-Din Munajjim Yazdi, a court astrologer, who completed his *Tarikh-i*

[10] See Hans Müller, *Die Chronik Hulasat at-Tawarih des Qazi Ahmad Qumi: Der Abschnitt über Schah 'Abbās I* (Wiesbaden, 1964); and E. Echraqi, 'Le *Kholasat al-Tawarikh* de Qazi Ahmad connu soues le nom de Mir Monshi', *Studia Iranica*, 4:1 (1975), 73–89.

[11] On the 'ideological' setting of those works see Sholeh A. Quinn, *Historical Writing During the Reign of Shah 'Abbas: Ideology, Imitation, and Legitimacy in Safavid Chronicles* (Salt Lake City, 2000).

[12] On this work see Alexander H. Morton, 'The Early Years of Shah Isma'il in the *Afzal al-tavarikh* and Elsewhere', in Charles Melville (ed.), *Safavid Persia: The History and Politics of an Islamic Society* (London, 1996), 27–50; and Charles Melville, 'A Lost Source for the Reign of Shah 'Abbas: The *Afzal al-tawarikh* of Fazli Khuzani Isfahani', *Iranian Studies*, 31:2 (1998), 263–6.

[13] Iskandar Beg Munshi, *History of Shah 'Abbas the Great (Tarih-e 'Alamara-ye 'Abbasi)*, trans. Roger M. Savory, 2 vols. (Boulder, Col., 1978). See also Roger Savory, '"Very Dull and Arduous Reading": A Reappraisal of the History of Shah 'Abbas the Great by Iskandar Beg Munshi', *Hamdard Islamicus*, 3 (1980), 19–37.

'Abbasi [History of 'Abbas] in 1611. Due to the importance ascribed to his profession, Yazdi was permanently in the company of his master, a circumstance which provided him with valuable information to be recorded in order to cast horoscopes or to come out with predictions. He applies highly technical wording throughout his work, which perhaps is evidence to the fact that he must have had access to administrative manuals and official documents. His work was continued by his son, Mulla Kamal, under the title *Zubdat al-Tawarikh* [Cream of the Histories], completed in 1652, under the rule of 'Abbas II.[14]

Like their predecessors, the historians of the time of 'Abbas the Great also covered the events of earlier periods in their works. However, when dealing with Safavid historiography since the early seventeenth century, which witnessed the consolidation of royal power both internally and externally, the works tend to focus on purely Persian events, while neglecting the general course of Islamic history. An exception is *Khulasat al-Tawarikh* [Summary of the Histories], a universal history following the patterns of the earlier mentioned Yahya Qazwini's *Lubb al-Tawarikh*, written by an anonymous author who was flourishing during the time of 'Abbas II. The reason for this shift of emphasis could be seen in the fact that the transition from Sunnism to Twelver Shi'ism as 'religion of state' in Persia from the time of 'Abbas I onwards can be considered more or less permanent and irreversible. Persia was now seen at the forefront, facing her Sunni 'opponents' (the Ottomans, Mughals, and Uzbeks), letting her appear in the minds of the authors as the suffering and victimized 'centre of the universe'— at least as far as Islam is concerned. This attitude towards 'the Other' is even discernible in subsequent generations of Persians.

Following the rule of 'Abbas the Great, the fortunes of the Safavids began to decline under his successor, Shah Safi I, and this is perhaps best exemplified by the Ottomans' recapture of Baghdad in 1638. Although there was temporary relief under Shah 'Abbas II, the rest of the dynasty's rulers up to the collapse of 1722 are usually considered to have been ineffective. In spite of this, Safavid historical writing continued to grow. Wali-Quli Shamlu, for instance, in writing his *Qisas al-Khaqani* [Imperial Stories] (compiled 1664–74), consciously emulated the standards that had been set by Iskandar Beg's chronicle. Other authors of that period tried deliberately to distance themselves from it, such as Mirza Beg Junabadi, the author of *Rawdat al-Safawiyyah* [Safavid Garden] (1625–6), who stands in the tradition of the Timurid Herat school of embellished historiography, or Muhammad Ma'sum bin Khwajagi Isfahani, whose *Khulasat al-Siyar* [Summary of Biographies] (*c.*1642) followed a simpler style, different from that to be found in *Tarikh-i 'Alam-ara-yi 'Abbasi.*

---

[14] Ali Asghar Mossadegh, 'La Famille Monajjem Yazdi', *Studia Iranica*, 16:1 (1987), 123–9.

The reign of Shah Sulayman, the penultimate Safavid monarch, who was brought up in the harem and thus had no experience of the world outside, was markedly unsuccessful. His rule is usually considered the beginning of the irreversible decline of Safavid power. Sulayman, suffering from poor health and said to have been an alcoholic, was thus unable to deal with the series of natural disasters and devastating Cossack, Uzbek, and Kalmyk raids that his country was facing at that time. He developed little interest in the business of government, preferring instead to retreat to the harem, leaving decision-making to his grand viziers or to a council of harem eunuchs. Corruption became widespread and military discipline decreased dramatically. Persia was thus unable to make appropriate use of the weakness of her Ottoman rival in the aftermath of the failed 1683 siege of Vienna.

In terms of historiographical output, however, Shah Sulayman's reign was particularly fruitful, although none of the works attempt to present an account of the (indeed non-existent) achievements of his reign. More than during the preceding period, the works produced during this time come in various shapes and types: *Shahanshah-namah* [Book of the King of Kings] (late seventeenth century), for instance, by an unknown author, is a versified approach to the Safavid period, whereas Shamlu's already mentioned *Qisas al-Khaqani* is a florid narrative, following the patterns to be found in Shaykh Husayn Pirzadih Zahidi's *Silsilat al-Nasab-i Safawiyyah* [Safavid Genealogy] (1679), which offers a comprehensive genealogical treatment of the dynasty's origins as the *Safawiyyah* Sufi order. The same period also saw a kind of nostalgic interest in accounts of the early Safavid rulers (especially Ismaʿil I and Tahmasp I), who were perhaps considered as (positive) 'antipodes' to the then prevailing plight. This particular interest—as exemplified by the survival of several, for the most part anonymous, heroic and partly fictitious accounts of Shah Ismaʿil—might perhaps be considered the *only* manifestation of some sort of 'social criticism', though veiled, on the part of historians in the Safavid period, aside from the *Zayn al-ʿArifin*, to be discussed in the closing section of this chapter.

Under the feeble, albeit long reign of Shah Sultan Husayn, the last ruler of the dynasty before the Afghan invasion, the number of historiographical works decreased again, although some might have perished in the subsequent 'Time of Troubles'. Among the works from this period that have come down to us are Mir Muhammad Saʾid Mushiri Bardasiri's *Tadhkirah-yi Safawiyyah-yi Kirman* [Safavid Memorial of Kirman] (late seventeenth century), Muhammad Ibrahim bin Zayn al-ʿAbidin Nasiri's *Dastur-i Shahriyaran* [Regulations of the Rulers] (1692–1700), and Husayn bin Murtada Husayn Astarabadi's *Tarikh-i Sultani* [Royal History] (1703–4).

REGIONAL HISTORIES AND ADMINISTRATIVE LITERATURE

In spite of the fact that Safavid authors were more concerned with the events that unfolded at the royal capital and with the rulers' biographies and military campaigns—the vast majority of their material being commissioned works—some of them also produced regional histories, although their output in this genre was numerically less when compared with previous periods. Shams al-Din 'Ali Lahiji's *Tarikh-i Khani* [History of the Khans], completed in 1516, is the earliest specimen of this genre for the Safavid period. His work deals with the history of the Caspian region of Gilan in the period between 1475 and 1514, prior to its Safavid conquest. About 1630, 'Abd al-Fattah Fumani wrote another history of this region, the *Tarikh-i Gilan* [History of Gilan], which is particularly valuable as it describes the local resistance to the silk monopoly that had been established by Shah 'Abbas the Great. The history of the central Persian city and region of Yazd is covered by Muhammad Mufid Yazdi's *Jami'-i Mufidi* [Compendium of Mufid], written around 1679. The fortunes of Fars province in southern Persia (the ancient 'Persis') are covered by Muhammad Mirak bin Mas'ud Husayni's *Riyad al-Firdaws* [Gardens of Paradise], completed around 1681, which is particularly important for the history of Shi'ism in that region in the seventeenth century. Malik Shah Husayn bin Malik Ghiyath al-Din Mahmud's *Ihya' al-Muluk* [Revival of the Kings], written in 1619, focuses on the history of the eastern Persian region of Sistan, the home of the *Sacae* of the Ancients. Most of the works mentioned in this category also contain important source material in terms of pre-Safavid, medieval history, including the Islamization period.

Administrative literature was also an important part of Safavid historical writing. This genre contains invaluable information on culture, as well as fiscal, administrative, and religious practices, which are often only dealt with in a rather cursory manner by the chronicles. Moreover, as in the case of the chronicles, this genre continued earlier traditions.[15]

Dastur al-Muluk [Regulations of the Kings] is a manual of administration in Persian from the very end of the Safavid period which, nevertheless, appears also to contain material from the sixteenth century. It was composed by Muhammad Rafi' Ansari (known as Mirza Rafi'a), an 'insider', who had the title of *Mustawfi al-Mamalik* (accountant-general), a high-ranking position in the central administration at Isfahan (the then capital of Safavid Persia). Together with a similar work, *Tadhkirat al-Muluk* [Memorial of the Kings], the two books provide much

---

[15] For a particularly impressive documentation see Heribert Busse, *Untersuchungen zum islamischen Kanzleiwesen an Hand turkmenischer und safawidischer Urkunden* (Cairo, 1959).

information on the administrative structure and social conditions prevailing in Persia at that period. They are in fact the only two surviving administrative manuals from the end of the Safavid period, aside from Nasiri's later work, *Alqab wa Mawajib-i Dawrah-yi Safawiyyah* [Nomenclatura and Pensions during the Safavid Period] (*c.*1730). *Tadhkirat al-Muluk* should be considered a derivative of *Dastur al-Muluk*, although thanks to the well-known bilingual edition by Vladimir Minorsky,[16] *Tadhkirat al-Muluk* has attracted more scholarly attention and is far better known. According to the late Persian scholar M. Danishpazhuh, *Dastur al-Muluk* served as an update of a 'directive sample' which 'had been compiled at the beginning of the Safavid period, and . . . which was constantly updated in the course of time' and whose 'preface was always written anew in the name of the [respective] shah'.[17]

Both *Dastur al-Muluk* and *Tadhkirat al-Muluk* describe in a succinct style and without artifice the practical duties of the offices of the religious, military, and civil administration towards the end of the Safavid period, from the high officials (whether those at the imperial capital or in the provinces) to the lower staff, such as those at the palace kitchens. Both manuals are written in Persian, but because the subject necessitates extensive use of technical terms, they require the reader to have some knowledge of the complicated mechanism of Safavid bureaucracy. Besides, both texts draw heavily on Persian, Arabic, Turkish, and Mongolian technical administrative terms. These borrowings, as well as the insertion of other loanwords from Turkish and Mongolian, are also interesting in the more general context of the historical development of the Persian language. The wording of the two manuals is very similar and, at times, almost identical. *Dastur al-Muluk* appears in general more detailed and contains more information on offices of lower rank, such as those connected with the supplies to the palace. Some of these minor figures do not appear at all in *Tadhkirat al-Muluk*. In this respect *Dastur al-Muluk*, much more than *Tadhkirat al-Muluk*, is a valuable source of information on the daily life of the lower strata of Safavid society.

Moreover, the various geographical and etymological characteristics contained in *Dastur al-Muluk*, as well as the wealth of information on minor offices and services, give the work its special significance. In addition, the application of a technical terminology in both manuals which is based on four languages, and related to that the utilization of (Azeri-)Turkish as the court language until the very end of the Safavid period (for which there is plenty of evidence), cannot be emphasized enough.[18]

---

[16] Vladimir Minorsky (ed. and trans.), *Tadhkirat al-Muluk: A Manual of Safavid Administration (circa 1137/1725) Persian Text in Facsimile (B.M. Or. 9496)* (London, 1943).

[17] Muhammad Rafiʿ Ansari [Mirza Rafiʿa], *Dastur al-Muluk*, ed. M. Danishpazhuh, *Majallah-yi Danishkadah-i Adabiyyat waʿUlum-i Insani-yi Danishgah-i Tihran* (July 1968), 484.

[18] Tourkhan Gandjei, 'Turkish in the Safavid Court of Isfahan', *Turcica*, 21–3 (1991), 311–18. See also Christoph Marcinkowski, 'The Reputed Issue of the "Ethnic Origin" of Iran's Safavid Dynasty

The overall impression with regard to *Tadhkirat al-Muluk*, in turn, is that it was arranged as a 'practical' manual, for the benefit of the Sunni Afghan conquerors of Persia, since it omits any mention of offices bearing special Shi'ite implications, such as the custodians (*mutawallis*) of the various shrines of Shi'ite Imams, saintly persons, and tombs of the members of the royal family, which would be of no relevance to the Sunni Afghans. Therefore, *Tadhkirat al-Muluk* might well be considered a 'revision' or 'modification' of *Dastur al-Muluk*, which would suggest that it was compiled later. In my view, a date of composition between 1722—the year of the ultimate collapse of Safavid rule under the onslaught of the Afghans—and 1726—during the Afghan occupation of Persia—might be accurate. The factors that contributed to the 1722 breakdown (i.e. the historical background for the composition of *Dastur al-Muluk*), have been dealt with elsewhere and from different angles. This in itself appears to give evidence to the fact that Safavid patterns—similar to the case of the Timurid models emulated during the early Safavid period—prevailed also during the post-Safavid period, up to the early Qajar era.

GEOGRAPHICAL AND TRAVEL LITERATURE

Numerically speaking, what has come down to us in terms of geographical and travel literature from the Safavid period is not impressive, in spite of the fact that during the Safavid period in particular, Persia was deeply involved in diplomatic activities with various European (Christian) powers in order to counterbalance the Ottoman threat. The Safavids, however, were also in close contact with other Shi'ite powers of the time, such as the Qutbshahs on the Indian Deccan, where many Shi'ites from Persia—merchants, scholars, military—were living and employed in various functions. The Qutbshahs, in turn, were in contact with the Buddhist kingdom of Ayutthaya (Siam, present-day Thailand), where resident Shi'ite Persian 'expats' had also been highly influential in court and society since the late sixteenth century.[19] The Safavids entertained diplomatic contacts with Ayutthaya under Shah Sulayman, although those contacts might even have reached back to the early seventeenth century.

The last embassy sent by the Safavid Shah Sulayman to Ayutthaya was documented by Ibn Muhammad Ibrahim's travel account *Safinah-yi Sulaymani* [The Ship of Sulayman] (after 1685), an outstanding document for the historical

---

(907–1145/1501–1722): Reflections on Selected Prevailing Views', *Journal of the Pakistan Historical Society*, 49:2 (2001), 5–19.

[19] The history of those Siamese–Safavid contacts is discussed in Christoph Marcinkowski, *From Isfahan to Ayutthaya: Contacts between Iran and Siam in the 17th Century* (Singapore, 2005).

and cultural presence of Persia in the eastern Indian Ocean region.[20] From it we learn that Persian-speaking dignitaries at the Siamese court, in turn, served as Ayutthaya's ambassadors to the shah, a circumstance that was also recorded by Engelbert Kaempfer, who visited Safavid Persia and Siam.[21] *Safinah-yi Sulaymani* also refers to the religious life in the resident Persian Muslim community of Ayutthaya, such as the public performance of Shi'ite mourning ceremonies (*ta'ziyyih*s), for which we also have a detailed eyewitness account from the French Catholic missionary Guy Tachard, who was present at the same time in the Siamese capital.[22]

Generally speaking, *Safinah-yi Sulaymani* is contemptuous of Siamese customs and beliefs, evincing its author's complete lack of understanding of, and sympathy for, the country and its hospitable people.[23] The author refers constantly to a supposed cultural superiority of Persia and its religion, Shi'ite Islam. There are, however, no traces of 'ethnic bias' in the text. Finally, Thai expressions, when Ibn Muhammad Ibrahim bothers to refer to them, appear mostly in a corrupted and at times unintelligible form.

Safinah-yi Sulaymani consists of four main parts, referred to as 'gifts', *tuhfah* in the Persian text. The first gift (and in fact the whole account) is written in a highly embellished style and reports on the first part of a journey aboard an English vessel, which started on 25 Rajab 1096 (27 June 1685), from the Persian Gulf port Bandar 'Abbas, via Muscat in Oman, to Madras in India. The second gift elaborates on the voyage from India to the then Siamese port of Tenasserim in present-day Burma, by crossing the Gulf of Bengal, and from Tenasserim via land first to Ayutthaya and then to Lopburi, at that time the residence of the Siamese king Narai. The third gift amounts to what can be called a report on the internal affairs of the Kingdom of Siam. It 'comments' on Siamese religious practices, the legal system, as well as holidays and festivals, marriage and funeral rites, official titles, criminal investigations, and varieties of punishments. The fourth gift concerns itself in a rather general fashion with an account of some of Siam's neighbours, such as the then Spanish Philippines, the Dutch possessions in what is now Indonesia, and even China and Japan, mostly based on hearsay, since the author did not visit these countries himself. This is followed by a detailed 'Appendix' on the Mughal conquest of Hyderabad on the Deccan—the

---

[20] For the English translation see Ibn Muhammad Ibrahim [Muhammad Rabi'], *The Ship of Sulayman*, trans. John O'Kane (New York, 1972).

[21] Walther Hinz (ed. and trans.), *Am Hofe des persischen Grosskönigs (1684–85): Das erste Buch der Amoenitates Exoticae* (Leipzig, 1940; repr. Tübingen/Basel, 1977), 199; and Jean Aubin, 'Les Persans au Siam sous le règne de Narai', *Mare Luso-Indicum*, 4 (1980), 121–2.

[22] Guy Tachard, *A Relation of the Voyage to Siam, Performed by six Jesuits, sent by the French King to the Indies and China, in the Year 1685* (1688; 3rd repr. Bangkok, 1999), part 2, 214–15.

[23] Christoph Marcinkowski, '"Holier Than Thou": Buddhism and the Thai People in Ibn Muhammad Ibrahim's 17th-Century Travel Account *Safineh-yi Sulaymani*', *Zeitschrift der Deutschen Morgenländischen Gesellschaft*, 156:2 (2006), 407–19.

capital of the Golconda kingdom, ruled by the Shi'ite Qutbshahs—which actually happened on 21 September 1687.

Safinah-yi Sulaymani closes with the mentioning of the escape of the Mughal prince Akbar (not to be confused with his namesake, the famous Mughal emperor) to the court of Safavid Persia, which took place in 1682. Substantial also are Ibn Muhammad Ibrahim's observations on the activities of Western powers in the Indian Ocean region, in particular the Dutch, the British, and the waning fortunes of the Portuguese.

From the perspective of Persian as well as Southeast Asian and Thai studies, the account is particularly rich in information on Siam's late seventeenth-century Persian community, providing a kind of 'who's who' for it. It is a source of prime importance since it constitutes the only extant Persian source on those contacts.

THE 'WORLDVIEW', METHODOLOGIES, AND ETHNIC AND SOCIAL BACKGROUNDS OF SAFAVID HISTORIANS

As stated above, the standards that were set in the fifteenth century by Timurid historiography continued to hold their grip on Safavid authors. In terms of 'worldview', however, the Safavid period also brought something new. One of those new features that came to the forefront—in particular during the long reign of Shah Tahmasp I—was that history began to be rewritten in order to cast it into a 'politically correct' Twelver Shi'ite mould, the result of the establishment of Twelver Shi'ism as the official creed of the land in 1501.[24] This can already be exemplified by looking at prefaces (*dibachas*) during that period,[25] which now omit the mentioning of the Four Rightly Guided Caliphs of Sunni Islam, replacing them with references to the Twelve Imams of Shi'ism. In addition to this, almost all chronicles that had been written under the Safavids had made an attempt to trace back the origins of that dynasty to the family of the seventh Shi'ite Imam, Musa al-Kazim (d. 799), which would make the monarchs descendants of the Prophet, thus providing them with a saintly aura of legitimacy, vis-à-vis their Sunni neighbours. Moreover, as most of the chronicles were royal commissions, they are devoid of any theories in terms of philosophy of history or social criticism on the part of their authors. Again, the main purpose of the job had been to promote the 'rights' of the ruling dynasty and to focus attention on the king's actions—his campaigns, hunting trips, internal politics, personal piety, and promotion of the 'orthodox' Shi'ite faith.

---

[24] Sholeh A. Quinn, 'The Dreams of Sheikh Safi al-Din in Late Safavid Chronicles', unpublished paper presented at the Sixth Biennial Conference of Iranian Studies, 3–5 August 2006, at the School of Oriental and African Studies (SOAS), London.

[25] Sholeh A. Quinn, 'The Historiography of Safavid Prefaces', in Charles Melville (ed.), *Safavid Persia: The History and Politics of an Islamic Society* (London, 1996), 1–25.

As briefly mentioned earlier, in terms of methodology, the 'eastern' models from the Timurid and early sixteenth-century 'transition' period that were considered particularly worthy of emulation were Mirkhwand's *Rawdat al-Safa* and Khwandamir's *Habib al-Siyar*, and Safavid historians largely tried to imitate their style. For instance, a Safavid author would often select, or even incorporate, an earlier text as a model which he would then bring 'up to date' by adding changes in terms of style or political 'correctness'. Today, this practice would be considered plagiarism by some, whereas Safavid authors would have thought otherwise as they tried to underscore the importance of, and respect felt towards, an admired archetype. The most obvious example of this approach is perhaps Khwandamir's *Habib al-Siyar*, when dealing with the 'transition period' from Sunni Timurid to Shi'ite Safavid rule. As a matter of fact, such changes—some might call them 'cosmetic'—could have been a question of life and death to the author, as the fate of Yahya Qazwini demonstrates most drastically (he was eventually executed by the Safavids).

Most of the historical works written during the Safavid period followed annalistic patterns or focused on a particular subject. Some of them tried to link both approaches. Iskandar Beg, for instance, gave first a general account of the earlier Safavid monarchs, before—when dealing with his hero, Shah 'Abbas the Great, of whom he was a contemporary—proceeding with his narrative year by year.

There were, however, also several novelties. One of these is the inclusion of biographical sections following the historical narrative. Some authors, for instance, among them Iskandar Beg, added sections on eminent scholars, men of letters, artists, bureaucrats, or religious figures, in order to enliven the picture drawn by them on a particular period. The first Safavid historian who employed this method was Khwandamir in his *Habib al-Siyar,* and subsequent authors followed his example.

The quasi 'multicultural' character of Persia under the Safavids—a Twelver Shi'ite state, its official language of administration being Persian, Azeri-Turkish the spoken language of the rulers, while tracing back its roots in terms of administration to the Arabic (Abbasid) and Turco-Mongol heritage—is perhaps particularly well attested when considering the methods of chronology applied by the historians writing under them. Safavid chroniclers applied a variety of dating systems in their works. Some of them used the Islamic calendar, applying the *hijri* years—either lunar or solar—whereas others referred to the respective ruler's regnal years (something which we also encounter in Mughal historical writing). Several writers, however, used the Turco-Mongol 'animal' calendar—which, in turn, is based on the Chinese model—a remainder from Persia's Mongol intermezzo. Iskandar Beg Munshi's work is a particularly striking example of this method. Sometimes, we meet different dating systems in one and the same work, which makes the life of the modern historian studying Persian history not easy.[26]

This 'multicultural' character of the Safavid period is also reflected in the historiographers themselves, who hailed from a variety of milieus, both in terms of their social standing and their ethnic background. As we have seen, some of them were bureaucrats, secretaries, or high-ranking government officials, such as the compilers of the state manuals *Dastur al-Muluk* and *Tadhkirat al-Muluk*. Other authors were clerics or were employed as court astrologers, as was the case with Jalal al-Din Munajjim Yazdi and his son. Most members of this category— by far the largest group among Safavid historical writers—were ethnic Persians, reminiscent of the 'Men of the Pen' class of classical medieval Islamic civilization. As most of them were based at the royal capital and the court, they usually had access to official records and documents, and were often also eyewitnesses of the events they recorded. At times, several generations of the same family were involved in historical writing, again as in the case of Jalal al-Din Munajjim Yazdi, or that of Khwandamir, who witnessed the transition of rule from one dynasty to another.

However, 'Men of the Sword' (again, a term and concept from medieval Islam), that is to say, members of the military class, also contributed considerably to Safavid historical writing. Most, but not all, of them were ethnic Turks. To this category belong Hasan Beg Rumlu, Wali-Quli Shamlu, and, above all, Iskandar Beg Munshi, but perhaps also Ibn Muhammad Ibrahim, the author of the travel account *Safinah-yi Sulaymani*. This trend actually increased after Shah 'Abbas the Great had reduced the power of the Turkic tribes, largely by way of his multifaceted military reforms.

In line with this development, ethnic Georgian or Armenian members of the new army units established by Shah 'Abbas I also became involved in historical writing. Most members of this group were converts from Christianity to Twelver Shi'ite Islam. Perhaps the best-known example from this group is Bizhan, the seventeenth-century author of the *Tarikh-i Rustam Khan* [History of Rustam Khan] (1680s) and the *Tarikh-i Jahangusha-yi Khaqan* [World-Conquering History of the Emperor] (1680s), which is also known as *Tarikh-i Shah Isma'il*.

EPILOGUE

Following the 1722 collapse and the Afghan conquest of Isfahan, Persian historiography throughout the eighteenth century reflected the significant political and social changes that took place in Persia after the fall of the Safavids. However, the prevailing reverence of the population for the Safavids continued, a fact to which

---

[26] Robert D. McChesney, 'A Note on Iskandar Beg's Chronology', *Journal of Near Eastern Studies*, 39 (1980), 53–63.

numerous post-1722 uprisings in favour of supposed scions of that royal line may bear witness. This circumstance, along with what could have been perceived as a 'lack of religious legitimacy', might have determined the subsequent short-lived Afsharid and Zand dynasties to rule 'in the name' of Safavid *rois fainéants*, whom—needless to say—they themselves had previously placed on the throne. Although Safavid rule 'proper' ended in 1722, patterns set by Safavid historical writings continued far into the eighteenth century.

A much neglected document of the time, which brings a bit more colour into the picture than chronicles usually do, is *Zayn al-ʿArifin* [Embellishment of the Gnostics], a piece of the classical 'advice' genre. A kind of memorandum, which does not, however, name a specific addressee or patron, *Zayn al-ʿArifin* constitutes a remarkable original analysis of the ethical crisis of the times, which had become manifest due to the prevailing political chaos. *Zayn al-ʿArifin*, only recently edited and translated in English and presumably composed before 1733, is a work in Persian by Sayyid Muhammad Sabzawari, a loyalist to the Safavids and member of the Shiʿite clergy.[27] In his work, Sabzawari laments the lack of pious, capable, and learned religious leaders. He blames this on his colleagues, who did not encourage righteousness among the believers, thus encouraging others to commit sins. Furthermore, and quite remarkably, he condemns those who were too closely associated with worldly affairs and dependent on the rulers. He finds fault with their refusal to take advice from those not attached to the court, reprehending their disregard of the virtuous scholars. Concerning the degree of responsibility for the regnant plight, he mentions the clerics, the military commanders and governors, and the subjects—in that order—one responsible for the fault of the next. It is remarkable that Sabzawari did not enumerate on the required qualities of his champions, the Safavid rulers. His general attitude with regard to the reasons for the sad situation in his country at the time he composed this work might therefore be seen as proof of the still prevailing popular reverence towards the deposed dynasty.

Although Afsharid (and Zand) court histories were to a large extent indebted to long-established Safavid patterns in terms of their structuring and wording, they nevertheless differed from them in several important ways. For the Afsharid period (1736–96), this can be exemplified by the work of Mirza Muhammad Mahdi Khan Astarabadi, the official historiographer of Nadir Shah (r. 1736–47) and author of the bombastic chronicle *Tarikh-i Jahangusha-yi Nadiri* [World-Conquering History of Nadir]. Astarabadi started his work during Nadir Shah's lifetime, but finalized it several years after his master had been assassinated. Temporarily, his work enjoyed relative popularity, even beyond the borders of Persia; a circumstance that is not so much due to its rather difficult style, but rather to Nadir Shah's military campaigns, which brought the Persian armies to

[27] Sayyid Muhammad bin Sayyid Quraysh Sabzawari, *Islamic Political Thought in Safavid Iran: Zayn al-ʿArifin*, trans. and ed. Sayyid Hasan Amin (Tehran, 1989).

Mughal India. In his chronicle Astarabadi follows the embellished style of the Timurid period and his work displays an annalistic arrangement similar to that encountered in Safavid historiographical works. However, several descriptive sections of *Tarikh-i Jahangusha* could rightly be considered as 'baroque', going far beyond the usual Safavid-era models.

In the aftermath of the Afsharids' failed attempt to establish themselves as the 'legitimate' successors of the Safavids, the Zand dynasty (1750–94)—based in Fars province—was able to stabilize parts of the country and to create a limited period of relative stability during the second half of the eighteenth century. The main exponents of Zand historiography, such as Muhammad Sadiq Nami and Mirza Muhammad Abu-l-Hasan Ghaffari Kashani, followed the archetypal tradition of Safavid chronicles that had been in vogue since the late seventeenth century. However, Zand chroniclers had to face the problem of how to reconcile the claim to legitimacy of their rulers with the still prevailing popular respect shown towards the Safavids. They were still around as puppet rulers, for in 1757 Karim Khan Zand, the new ruler, had placed the infant Isma'il III, the grandson of the last Safavid shah, Sultan Husayn, on the throne in order to add legitimacy to his claim. Isma'il was a mere figurehead, and the real power was with Karim Khan. Throughout his rule, Karim Khan never referred to himself as *shah* ('king'), and later Zand rulers continued to honour the Safavid claim of ancestral connection to the Shi'ite Twelve Imams. Zand historical writers were thus not in a position to refer to their masters in the traditional terms of Persian historiography.

To conclude, the eighteenth century can be considered the end of the dominance of traditional chronicles written as justification for the country's dynasties in terms of 'history of salvation'. The changing styles of eighteenth-century chronicles thus heralded a move towards a transformation in Persian historiography which continued well into the nineteenth century. In addition to this, one has to consider the fact that the number of historical accounts increased during the seventeenth and eighteenth centuries. We may, however, assume that this was essentially the result of the fact that the historical works written during that time have survived up to the present day, whereas many more works from previous periods have perished.

Perhaps one of the last reminiscences of the cherished memory of the bygone Safavids comes from Muhammad Hashim Asif's (also known as Rustam al-Hukama') *Rustam al-Tawarikh* [Rustam of the Histories], an entertaining history of Persia in the late eighteenth century. Rustam al-Ḥukamā', who wrote at the beginning of the Qajar period, held that certain influential Shi'ite clerics were at least indirectly responsible for the acceleration of the Safavid decline by having made the absurd claim that the Safavid Empire would exist until the Mahdi's 'reappearance' at the 'end of times', and thus having tempted Shah Sultan Husayn and his courtiers to become careless in governmental matters.[28]

---

[28] Birgitt Hoffmann, *Persische Geschichte 1694–1835 erlebt, erinnert und erfunden: Das Rustam al-Tawarikh in deutscher Bearbeitung*, 2 vols. (Berlin, 1986), i. 97–8, 221–2, 306.

TIMELINE/KEY DATES

1501–24 Isma'il, leader of a militant sufi order, unifies Persia and is declared Shah of Persia (1501); replacement of Sunni Islam as official creed of Persia

1524–76 Reign of Tahmasp I; 'import' of Shi'ite clerics from Iraq, Lebanon, and Arabian Peninsula; civil war-like struggle between rival Turcoman groups and factions

1576–7 Reign of the mentally unstable Shah Isma'il II; he tries unsuccessfully to revert to Sunnism and is eventually assassinated

1578–88 Shah Muhammad Khudabandah is deposed by his son 'Abbas (I); substantial weakness of the empire; Uzbek raids occur

1588–1629 Reign of Shah 'Abbas I the Great; apogee of Safavid power; Isfahan becomes capital (1598); increased diplomatic and commercial contacts with Europe

1629–42 Reign of Shah Safi I; loss of Baghdad (1638); unfavourable Treaty of Qasr-i Shirin with Ottomans

1642–66 Reign of Shah 'Abbas II; temporary stabilization and extension of trade

1666–94 Reign of Shah Sulayman; weak ruler; general decline; 'harem politics'

1694–1722 Reign of Shah Sultan Husayn; nadir of Safavid power; Sunni Afghan tribesmen take capital, Isfahan, killing the shah; Ottomans and Russians invade Persia

1736 Safavid rule is effectively terminated; Tahmasp-Quli (assass. 1747) assumes power in his own name as Nadir Shah, founding the Afsharid dynasty; several real (or imaginary) royal princes and pretenders continue to exist in parts of the country (even beyond the subsequent Afsharids and Zands)

KEY HISTORICAL SOURCES

Afushta'i Natanzi, Mahmud bin Hidayat-Allah, *Nuqawat al-Athar*, ed. I. Ishraqi (Tehran, 1971).

Amir Mahmud bin Ghiyath al-Din Khwandamir, *Tarikh-i Shah Isma'il wa Shah Tahmasb-i Safawi (Dhayl-i Tarikh-i Habib al-Siyar)*, ed. M. Jarrahi (Tehran, 1991).

Anon., *Jahangusha-yi Khaqan (Tarikh-i Shah Isma'il)*, ed. A. Muztarr (Islamabad, 1986).

Fumani, 'Abd al-Fattah, *Tarikh-i Gilan*, ed. M. Sutudih (Tehran, 1970).

Ibn Bazzaz, Darwish Tawakkuli bin Isma'il al-Ardabili, *Safwat al-Safa*, ed. Gh. Tabataba'i-Majd (Tabriz, 1994).

Isfahani, Faḍlī, *Afdal al-Tawarikh*, partial trans. S. Abrahams as 'A Historiographical Study and Annotated Translation of Volume 2 of the *Afdal al-Tavarikh* by Fazli Khuzani al-Isfahani', Ph.D. dissertation, University of Edinburgh, 1999.

Isfahani, Muhammad Ma'sum bin Khwajagi, *Khulasat al-Siyar*, trans. G. Rettelbach as *Hulasat al-siyar: Der Iran unter Schah Safi (1629–1642)* (Munich, 1978).

Iskandar Beg Munshi, *History of Shah ʿAbbas the Great (Tarih-e ʿAlamara-ye ʿAbbasi)*, trans. Roger M. Savory, 2 vols. (Boulder, Col., 1978).

Junabadi, Mirza Beg bin Hasan, *Rawdat al-Safawiyyah*, ed. Gh. Tabatabaʾi-Majd (Tehran, 1999).

Khunji-Isfahani, Fadl-Allah Ruzbihan, *Tarikh-i ʿAlam-ara-yi Amini*, trans. Vladimir Minorsky as *Persia in A.D. 1478–1490* (London, 1957).

Khwandamir, Ghiyath al-Din bin Humam al-Din, *Habibuʾs-siyar*, trans. and ed. W. M. Thackston, 2 vols. (Cambridge, Mass., 1994).

Marcinkowski, Christoph, *Mīrzā Rafīʿāʾs Dastur al-Muluk: A Manual of Later Safavid Administration. Annotated English Translation, Comments on the Offices and Services, and Facsimile of the Unique Persian Manuscript* (Kuala Lumpur, 2002).

Mirkhwand, Muhammad bin Khwandshah, *Rawdat al-Safa*, trans. E. Rehatsek as *Rauzat-us-safa or Garden of Purity*, ed. F. F. Arbuthnot, 3 vols. (London, 1891).

Qazwini, Yahya, *Lubb al-Tawarikh*, ed. J. Tihrani (Tehran, 1937).

Qumi, Qadi Ahmad, *Khulasat al-Tawarikh*, ed. and trans. E. Glassen as *Die frühen Safawiden nach Qāzi Ahmad Qumi* (Freiburg im Breisgau, 1970).

Rumlu, Hasan Beg, *Ahsan al-Tawarikh*, ed. and trans. C. N. Seedon as *A Chronicle of the Early Safawis*, 2 vols. (Baroda, India, 1931–4).

Shamlu, Wali-Quli, *Qisas al-Khaqani*, ed. H. Sadat-i Nasiri, 2 vols. (Tehran, 1992–5).

Shirazi, ʿAbdi Beg, *Takmilat al-Akhbar*, ed. A. Nawaʾi (Tehran, 1990).

Tihrani, Abu Bakr, *Kitab-i Diyarbakriyyah*, ed. N. Lugal and F. Sümer, 2nd edn, 2 vols. in 1 (Tehran, 1977).

BIBLIOGRAPHY

Browne, Edward Granville, *A Literary History of Persia*, vol. 4: *Modern Times (1500–1924)* (Cambridge, 1924).

Horn, Paul (ed.), 'Die Denkwürdigkeiten des sah Tahmasp von Persien', *Zeitschrift der Deutschen Morgenländischen Gesellschaft*, 44 (1890), 563–649; 45 (1891), 245–91.

Marcinkowski, Christoph, *Persian Historiography and Geography: Bertold Spuler on Major Works Produced in Iran, the Caucasus, Central Asia, India and Early Ottoman Turkey* (Singapore, 2003).

Matthee, Rudi (ed.), 'Historiography and Representation in Safavid and Afsharid Iran', special issue of *Iranian Studies*, 31: 2 (1998), 143–7.

Mitchell, Colin P. (ed.), *New Perspectives on Safavid Iran, Majmuʿah-i Safaviyyah in Honour of Roger Savory* (London, 2009).

Newman, A. J., *Safavid Iran: Rebirth of a Persian Empire* (London, 2006).

Pfeiffer, Judith, and Quinn, Sholeh A. (eds.), *History and Historiography of Post-Mongol Central Asia and the Middle East: Studies in Honor of John E. Woods* (Wiesbaden, 2006).

Savory, Roger, *Persia under the Safavids* (Cambridge, 1980).

——'Is There an Ultimate Use for Historians? Reflections on Safavid History and Historiography', *The Annual Noruz Lecture Series*, Foundation for Iranian Studies, Washington, DC, 16 March 1995, available online at http://www.Iranchamber.com/history/articles/reflections_safavid_history_historiography1.php (accessed 10 June 2011).

Chapter 9

Ottoman Historical Writing

Baki Tezcan

The oldest extant literary sources on the formative period of the Ottoman Empire are in Arabic, Greek, and Persian, and are products of Mamluk, late Byzantine, and medieval Anatolian historiography. The earliest extant examples of Ottoman historical writing produced by Ottomans themselves are anonymous royal calendars in Persian and Turkish, brief sections of longer epics in Turkish verse dating from the early fifteenth century, battle accounts, and holy-heroic tales.

Royal calendars appear to have commenced during the fourteenth century,[1] but the oldest surviving examples date from the early fifteenth. These works were astrological rather than historiographical, yet their introductions included a temporal record of significant events in the past, ordered chronologically, beginning with God's creation of Adam and noting dates in relation to the present: 'It has been 6,984 years since the creation of Adam (peace be upon him).'[2] While the record of the more recent past found in such calendars helps one establish some of the important dates of fourteenth-century Ottoman history and was most probably used by chroniclers who had access to them, the dates determined in accordance with them are not always consistent with one another.[3] A thorough and comparative study of these calendars has yet to appear.[4]

The oldest extant Ottoman narrative accounts of their own history date from the early fifteenth century. This may sound somewhat surprising as the Ottomans had been around since the end of the thirteenth century and their founder

---

[1] Victor Louis Ménage, 'A Survey of the Early Ottoman Histories, with Studies of Their Textual Problems and Their Sources', Ph.D. dissertation, University of London, 1961, 19–20.

[2] [Nihal] Atsız (ed.), *Osmanlı Tarihine Ait Takvimler* (Istanbul, 1961), 12.

[3] Compare, for instance, the dates ascribed to the 'origin' of Osman Bey, the founder of the dynasty; ibid., 49, 81, 120.

[4] Osman Turan, *İstanbul'un Fethinden Önce Yazılmış Tarihî Takvimler* (Ankara, 1954), reproduces sections from two Ottoman calendars produced for 1445–6 and 1446–7. Atsız studies three calendars prepared for 1421, 1431–2, and 1439–40 in his *Osmanlı Tarihine Ait Takvimler*; he worked on two other calendars from 1452 and 1454 in his 'Fatih Sultan Mehmed'e sunulmuş tarihî bir takvim', *İstanbul Enstitüsü Dergisi*, 3 (1957), 17–23; and 'Hicrî 858 yılına ait takvim', *Selçuklu Araştırmaları Dergisi*, 4 (1975), 223–83, respectively.

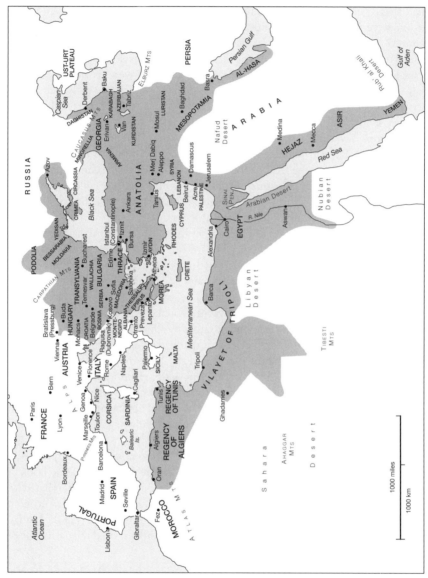

Map 3. The Ottoman Empire *c.*1675

had already entered Byzantine chronicles at the beginning of the fourteenth.[5] Yet if one were to consider the relative position of the early Ottomans in the larger context of the Islamic world to which their rulers belonged, this absence may be understandable. The Ottoman political enterprise was founded as a frontier vassalage in the outer orbit of the Mongol Ilkhans, who were centred in Azerbaijan, around the time when the Mongols had decided to dispense with their Seljuk vassals in central Anatolia (*c.*1300). Even though this frontier attracted many a soldier of fortune, it was not, at least not initially, a hub for written cultural production. Yet things started to change towards the end of the fourteenth century when Bayezid I succeeded in establishing an empire of respectable size. He could now attract the likes of Ibn al-Jazari, a major Arab scholar-jurist from the Mamluk Empire, to his capital. Although Bayezid's empire collapsed after his defeat at the hands of Timur (1402), once Timur left Anatolia the courts of his sons attracted many contemporary men of letters.

The two oldest extant pieces of Ottoman historical writing were produced in the post-Timurid era as segments of epics in Turkish verse that were presented to the sons of Bayezid I. Ahmedi's *İskender-nâme* [Book of Alexander] was the first one. It was presented to Prince Süleiman and includes an account of the Ottomans from their beginnings to the time of composition. The second one was Abdülvasi Çelebi's *Halîl-nâme* [Book of Abraham], which was presented to Mehmed I in 1414, after the latter had secured his succession to his late father by eliminating all of his competing brothers, and includes the account of a battle that had taken place between Mehmed I and his brother Prince Musa the previous year.[6] Thus the oldest genre in which Ottomans recounted their own history was epic verse. Historically, this need to tell their own story in a heroic fashion seems to have dawned on the Ottomans right after their very existence had been threatened by Timur, and while they were still in the midst of a civil war during which brothers were fighting against each other and thus needed to justify their claims.

Battle accounts, such as the one found in the *Halîl-nâme*, eventually came to constitute a genre in Ottoman historiography called the *gazavât-nâme*, or 'book of exploits', which was marked by a mixture of facts and conventions related to heroic epics. One of the earliest extant examples of this genre, written in Ottoman Turkish prose, was about Murad II's victory at the Battle of Varna (1444).[7] Unlike the calendars and epics mentioned above, this genre did not need the patronage of

---

[5] The occasion was the Battle of Bapheus that took place around 1302; Halil İnalcık, 'Osman Ghazi's Siege of Nicaea and the Battle of Bapheus', in Elizabeth Zachariadou (ed.), *The Ottoman Emirate (1300–1389): Halcyon Days in Crete* (Rethymnon, 1993), 77–99.

[6] For the section on Ottoman history in the first book see Tace'd-din İbrahim bin Hızır Ahmedi, *History of the Kings of the Ottoman Lineage and their Holy Raids against the Infidels*, ed. and trans. Kemal Silay (Cambridge, Mass., 2004). For the battle account in the latter see Dimitris J. Kastritsis, *The Sons of Bayezid: Empire Building and Representation in the Ottoman Civil War of 1402–1413* (Leiden, 2007), 33–4, 221–32.

[7] For an English translation, see Colin Imber, *The Crusade of Varna, 1443–45* (Aldershot, 2006), 41–106.

the royal court to develop. The military accomplishments of one of the Ottoman lords of the marches, Mihaloğlu Ali Bey (d. 1507), for instance, were recounted by a provincial author, Suzi Çelebi of Prizren, who worked as a secretary for Mihaloğlu Ali Bey and—later—his son, in a versified book of exploits.[8] Books of exploits continued to be written well into the nineteenth century, either on specific battles or on the military exploits of a single character, and their particular mixture of facts, fiction, and conventions, still continues to produce intriguing questions for further study.[9]

A very similar genre in which fact, fiction, and conventions are mixed is the *menâkıb-nâme*, or the 'book of glorious deeds'. While one would be justified in calling some examples of this genre hagiography and others legend, neither of the terms does justice to the *menâkıb-nâme* genre as a whole because some *menâkıb-nâmes* have also been treated as historical chronicles. Most *menâkıb-nâmes* indeed focus on the life of a Muslim holy man, such as Ahmad Aflaki's *Manāqib al-ʿārifīn* [The Glorious Deeds of the Sages], which was produced in Persian within the vicinity of early Ottoman realms, on the life of Rumi (d. 1273).[10] But there were also other *menâkıb-nâmes* that centred on heroes who were better known as warriors than saints. The anonymous *Battâl-nâme* [Book of Battal]—a legend based on the life of the Muslim warrior Battal—is one of them. Battal had probably lived in the late seventh and early eighth centuries and fought for the Umayyads against the Byzantines on the Anatolian frontiers. While his stories must have circulated orally for centuries, the oldest extant manuscripts of the legend date from the first half of the fifteenth century.[11] Another similar legend, *Dânişmend-nâme* [Book of Danişmend], based on the life of Danişmend, who was a Turkish leader in late eleventh-century eastern and central Anatolia, the political leadership of which was passing from Byzantine to Anatolian Seljuk hands, was redacted in this period as well. Neither Battal nor Danişmend appear as mere warrior-heroes in their legends. Both of them, but especially Battal, are described as possessing supernatural powers, and both fight in the name of Islam. They are holy heroes of the frontiers.[12] While their legends may not qualify as works of history, it is important to remember that the oldest known narrative of Ottoman origins, which only survives in the form it was incorporated into the chronicle of Aşıkpaşazade in the late fifteenth century, was also known as a *menâkıb*, the *Menâkıb-ı âl-i ʿOsmân* [Menâkıb of the House of Osman].

---

[8] Agâh Sırrı Levend, *Gazavat-nameler ve Mihaloğlu Ali Beyʾin Gazavat-namesi* (Ankara, 1956); and Altay Suroy Recepoğlu (ed.), *Prizrenli Suzi'nin 500. Yılı: Bildiriler, Bilgiler, Belgeler* (Prizren, 2000).

[9] See, for instance, Claire Norton, 'Fiction or Non-Fiction? Ottoman Accounts of the Siege of Nagykanizsa', in Kuisma Korhonen (ed.), *Tropes for the Past: Hayden White and the History / Literature Debate* (Amsterdam, NY, 2006), 119–30.

[10] Eflâkî, *Menâkıbü l-ʿârifîn: Metin*, ed. Tahsin Yazıcı, 2 vols. (Ankara, 1959–61).

[11] Hasan Köksal, *Battalnâmelerʾde Tip ve Motif Yapısı* (Ankara, 1984).

[12] Ahmet Yaşar Ocak, *Kültür Tarihi Kaynağı Olarak Menâkıbnâmeler: Metodolojik bir Yaklaşım*, 2nd edn (Ankara, 1997), 20–1, 24–5, 57.

The *Menâkıb-ı âl-i ʿOsmân* was written by Yahşi Fakı, the son of the imam of Orhan (d. 1362), the second ruler of the Ottomans. It covered early Ottoman history up to the reign of Bayezid I (1389–1402). Yahşi Fakı must have composed it by 1413 when Aşıkpaşazade read it at the author's home in Geyve. Given the use of the term *menâkıb*, it is clear that early fifteenth-century contemporaries of Yahşi Fakı perceived the anecdotes about early Ottomans very similarly to the way they perceived the legendary stories about Battal or Danişmend. This should not be surprising, since, just like these heroes, Osman and his followers were fighting along the frontiers of Islam to open lands for new Muslim settlements. They were not devoid of supernatural forces, either.[13] The *menâkıb-nâme* genre continued to thrive in Ottoman letters throughout the fifteenth and sixteenth centuries with biographical works on sheiks, legendary heroes, and even statesmen who came to be seen retrospectively as holy.[14]

MATURATION

The royal calendars, epics, books of exploits and glorious deeds, and oral traditions were used by Ottoman men of letters of the mid- to late fifteenth century to produce some of the first composite works on Ottoman history. Having conquered Constantinople, the Ottomans found they had established a great empire, and so they sat down to record how it all came about.

Some of the earliest composite works were short accounts devoted to the Ottomans in universal histories and remind us of the debt that Ottoman historiography owes to Arabic and Persian historiographies in which universal history was developed as a major field.[15] The earliest Ottoman example of this kind, the *Bahjat al-tawārīkh* [Joy of Histories], was written in Persian by Şükrullah, an Ottoman diplomat and man of letters, in the 1460s. Şükrullah's work consists of thirteen parts. The first part covers a wide range of subjects from the creation of the world to a history of ethnic groups, such as the Chinese, Turks, Greeks, Arabs, Indians, and Ethiopians. The second part covers the histories of fourteen prophets from Adam to Jesus, who is regarded by Muslims simply as a prophet. The next five parts deal with Muhammad's ancestors, his life, his family, his ten disciples, and his other companions. In the eighth part, one reads about such Muslim scholars as the four jurists who are regarded as the founders of the four Sunni legal schools and the six scholars who compiled the

---

[13] See the supernatural anecdotes cited by V. L. Ménage, 'The *Menāqib* of Yakhshi Faqīh', *Bulletin of the School of Oriental and African Studies*, 26 (1963), 50–4.

[14] Halil bin İsmail, *Sımavna Kadısı oğlu Şeyh Bedreddin Menâkıbı*, ed. Abdülbaki Gölpınarlı (Istanbul, 1967); A. Yaşar Ocak, *Sarı Saltık: Popüler İslâm'ın Balkanlar'daki Destanî Öncüsü (XIII. Yüzyıl)* (Ankara, 2002); and Theoharis Stavrides, *The Sultan of Vezirs: The Life and Times of the Ottoman Grand Vezir Mahmud Pasha Angelović (1453–1474)* (Leiden, 2001).

[15] See ch. 8 by Christoph Marcinkowski in this volume.

most trusted collections of Muhammad's traditions. The ninth part is devoted to Sufi sheiks, while the tenth part is on Greek philosophers. Pre-Islamic kingdoms are covered in the eleventh part. The twelfth part deals with the Umayyads, Abbasids, Fatimids, and Seljuks—four major dynasties of the Muslim past. Finally, the thirteenth part is reserved for Ottoman history.[16] Clearly, this is an Islam-centred universal history, and all Şükrullah's sources are from the Islamic literary tradition.[17] Nevertheless, it is important to note that this tradition afforded some space—however limited it may be—to non-Muslim history and peoples.

Non-Muslim history became central to some Ottomans who dealt with the history of Constantinople after this imperial capital changed hands in 1453. Rather than relying on Byzantine sources and simply translating them, however, they first chose to create their own version of the history of Constantinople, as a starting point getting some help from the Arab tradition, which included Byzantine influences. According to the late Stefanos Yerasimos, this version was meant to be an anti-imperialist treatise that was written in response to Mehmed II's (1451–81) policies, which were meant to transform the Ottoman enterprise into a centralized empire. Yerasimos suggests that the imperialist party responded with their own version of a Constantinopolitan legend of Byzantine origin on the foundation of the Hagia Sophia. Thus began a duel between two different stories about Constantinople that continued well into the times of Süleiman the Magnificent, whose reign was another intense period for empire-building.[18] Interestingly, some of the earliest versions of the imperialist version were written in Persian,[19] which remained the imperial language of historical expression for a while to come.

The prestige of Persian was contested from very early on, though. While Şükrullah's history and the early imperialist version of the Constantinopolitan stories were in Persian prose, another historical work from this period, the history of Karamani Mehmed Pasha, was in Arabic, whereas a third one, the *Düstûr-nâme* [The Constitutional Book (for Ottoman History)] of Enveri, was a universal history in Turkish verse.[20] This trilingual growth of Ottoman historiography continued both in prose and verse well until the seventeenth century, even though Ottoman Turkish became the dominant language of historiographical expression

---

[16] Şükrullah's history remains unpublished. Here I rely on Joseph von Hammer, *Geschichte des osmanischen Reiches*, 10 vols. (Pest, 1827–35), ix. 177–9.

[17] For his sources, which he lists in his introduction, see ibid., ix. 179–80.

[18] Stefanos Yerasimos, *La fondation de Constantinople et de Sainte Sophie dans les traditions turques* (Paris, 1990).

[19] Félix Tauer, 'Les versions persanes de la légende sur la construction d'Aya Sofya', *Byzantinoslavica*, 15 (1954), 1–20.

[20] Karamanlı Nişancı Mehmed Paşa, 'Osmanlı Sultanları Tarihi', trans. Konyalı İbrahim Hakkı, in Çiftçioğlu N. Atsız (ed.), *Osmanlı Tarihleri* (Istanbul, 1949), 321–69; and Enverî, *Düstûrnâme-i Enverî* (Istanbul, 1928–9).

outside court circles in the late fifteenth and early sixteenth centuries, thanks to a boom in the production of *tevârîh*, or 'chronicles'.

The *Tevârîh-i al-i ʿOsman* [Chronicles of the House of Osman], is a title shared by many chronicles in the late fifteenth and early sixteenth centuries. It would be futile to discuss these works in detail as the questions they pose are too complex to be dealt with in an introductory chapter, and more importantly, there are several accessible scholarly articles written on them which have recently been crowned by Cemal Kafadar's historiographical study.[21] Simply put, the reign of Mehmed II signified the closing of an era for the enterprising lords of the marches, soldiers of fortune, and unruly dervishes who had led the expansion of the Ottoman realms in Anatolia and the Balkans for almost two centuries. Mehmed II was interested in building a centralized empire that taxed people and controlled land resources much more closely than the looser administrative structure ruled by his ancestors. Thus people burst into writing of the past as a bygone age, romanticizing it as a time of heroism, and contrasting it—mostly implicitly—with the present.[22] Although not everyone had the same ideas about every aspect of the past, they shared common sources. Halil İnalcık and V. L. Ménage have shown that the many chroniclers of the mid- and late fifteenth century may be divided into two groups based on the sources they used, many of which remained anonymous.[23] Finally, Neşri, who wrote a history around 1490, brought them together, interweaving them in the Ottoman history section of his universal history, the *Jihân-nümâ*, the '[Book] that shows the whole world', or as idiomatically rendered by Ménage, *Cosmorama*.[24]

After this long series of the *Tevârîh-i al-i ʿOsman* most of which were not dedicated to a particular sultan or vizier, one witnesses the development of a royal tradition of historiography starting during the reign of Bayezid II (1481–1512), who commissioned several works of history. Among them were two major works, the *Hasht bihisht* [Eight Paradises], written by Idrīs Bidlīsī in Persian, and the *Tevârîh-i al-i ʿOsman* by Kemalpaşazâde, who produced in this work an example of what cultivated literary expression was supposed to sound like in Ottoman Turkish. Thus the tone was set for the growth of Ottoman historiography in the sixteenth century, which was enriched by the political tension between court patronage and the relatively more independent historiographical production

---

[21] Cemal Kafadar, *Between Two Worlds: The Construction of the Ottoman State* (Berkeley, 1995).

[22] That is how Halil İnalcık interprets Aşıkpaşazade; see his 'How to Read ʿĀshık Pasha-zāde's History', in Colin Heywood and Colin Imber (eds.), *Studies in Ottoman History in Honour of Professor V. L. Ménage* (Istanbul, 1994), 139–56.

[23] For an excellent introduction to these texts see Halil İnalcık, 'The Rise of Ottoman Historiography', in Bernard Lewis and P. M. Holt (eds.), *Historians of the Middle East* (London, 1962), 152–67; and V. L. Ménage, 'The Beginnings of Ottoman Historiography', ibid., 168–79.

[24] V. L. Ménage, *Neshri's History of the Ottomans: The Sources and Development of the Text* (London, 1964), p. xv.

outside the court circles.[25] Although there were times when these two traditions were not so much in contact with each other, as exemplified in the absence of the works of the court historiographer Seyyid Lokman among the sources of Ottoman historians outside the court,[26] they grew closer in the eighteenth century. Naʿima, who is usually regarded as the first occupant of the position of *vak̟ʿa-nüvis* (or *vekâyiʿnüvis*, the 'writer of events'), which may be translated as the official historiographer of the state (rather than the court), relied heavily on Katib Çelebi, who, despite his association with the state bureaucracy, produced his historical works relatively independently.[27]

Not all histories written by Ottoman historians concerned the House of Osman, even though that topic first comes to mind today. As mentioned above, the Ottomans felt a cultural and intellectual belonging to the Islamic world and produced many universal histories in the Islamic tradition, such as the *Bahjat al-tawārīkh*.[28] They also authored and translated works devoted to particular periods of pre-Islamic and Islamic history from Old Testament prophets to the Anatolian Seljuks. For instance, as early as the first half of the fifteenth century—before most of the Ottoman chronicles discussed above were written—Yazıcızâde Ali, a court official of Murad II (1421–51), translated and expanded the Anatolian Seljuk history of Ibn Bībī.[29] Even though not as numerous as their works on the history of the Islamic world, the Ottomans also produced works on European history. Commissioned by Chancellor Feridun Bey, the *Tevârîh-i Pâdishâhân-i Frânçe* [Chronicles of the Kings of France] (1572), is a compilation-translation from several French sources done by Hasan bin Hamza and Ali bin Sinan, the first a translator and the latter a scribe, both of whom were probably employed by the Ottoman chancery. The work starts with the biography of Pharamond, the legendary king of the Franks, and ends with the reign of Charles IX (1550–74), who was the ruler of France at the time of the composition.[30] In the seventeenth century, İbrahim Mülhemi devoted a chapter to French history in his universal history entitled *Murâd-nâme* [Book of Murad

---

[25] On this tension and how it played out in the early modern period see Baki Tezcan, 'The Politics of Early Modern Ottoman Historiography', in Virginia H. Aksan and Daniel Goffman (eds.), *The Early Modern Ottomans: Remapping the Empire* (Cambridge, 2007), 167–98.

[26] On Seyyid Lokman and Ottoman court historiography see Christine Woodhead, 'Reading Ottoman *şehnames*: Official Historiography in the Late Sixteenth Century', *Studia Islamica*, 104–5 (2007), 67–80.

[27] On this position and some of its occupants see Bekir Kütükoğlu, *Vekâyiʿnüvis: Makaleler* (Istanbul, 1994); on Naʿima, his works, and his debt to Katib Çelebi, see Lewis V. Thomas, *A Study of Naima*, ed. Norman Itzkowitz (New York, 1972); for a short autobiography of Katib Çelebi see Katib Chelebi, *The Balance of Truth*, trans. G. L. Lewis (London, 1957), 135–47.

[28] For a limited bibliography of such works composed in Ottoman Turkish see Maarif Vekilliği Kütüphaneler Müdürlüğü Tasnif Komisyonu, *İstanbul Kütüphaneleri Tarih-Coğrafya Yazmaları Katalogları* (Istanbul, 1943–62), 1–101.

[29] Yazıcızâde Ali, *Tevârîh-i Âl-i Selçuk*, ed. Abdullah Bakır (Istanbul, 2009).

[30] Jean-Louis Bacqué-Grammont (ed. and trans.), *La première histoire de France en turc ottoman: chronique des padichahs de France, 1572* (Paris, 1997).

(IV)], and Katib Çelebi wrote another work on Europe, the *İrşâdü'l-hayârâ ilâ ta'rîhi'l-Yûnân ve'n-Nasârâ* [Guide of the Perplexed towards the History of the Greeks, the Byzantines, and the Christians].[31]

Another field in which Ottoman men of letters authored historiographical works was biography. Inheriting the long-standing Islamic tradition of biographical dictionaries, Ottoman men of letters produced them for such men as Muslim saints (*evliyâ*), poets, scholar-jurists, Sufi sheiks, viziers, ministers of finance, chancellors, and chief eunuchs. Chronologically, the earlier biographical dictionaries concentrated on men of law, religion, and scholarship. Some major examples that have been published are Taşköprüzade's Arabic biographical dictionary of scholars and men of religion from the sixteenth century,[32] Nev'izade Ata'a's seventeenth-century continuation of it,[33] and Aşık Çelebi's biographical dictionary of poets.[34] In the eighteenth century, with the consolidation of the early modern Ottoman state, the administrative cadres of the state and dynasty became the focus of biographical dictionaries, such as Ahmed Ta'ib Osmanzade's *Ḥadīqat ül-vüzerā* [Garden of Viziers],[35] and Ahmed Resmi's biographical dictionaries of chancellors (*re'îsü'l-küttâb*) and chief eunuchs.[36] What is interesting to note about biographical dictionaries in Ottoman Turkish is that neither the earlier period in which men of religion and scholarship were in the foreground, nor the later one that showcased bureaucrats, reserved any space for commoners. This was not the case in contemporary Ottoman historiography in Arabic, mainly produced in the Arab provinces.[37] Ottoman historiography in Arabic was also rich in regional and local histories, a genre of which Ottoman Turkish historiography produced fewer examples.[38]

There are no independent theoretical works about history as a genre or form of enquiry—comparable to Western European *artes historicae*—though some Ottoman historians addressed these matters within larger works. For Taşköprüzade, for instance, the purpose of history was 'to become acquainted with the conditions of the past'. 'The usefulness of history is (the opportunity that it affords) to learn from those conditions, to seek advice in them, and to form the habit of

[31] İbrahim Mülhemi, *Murâd-nâme*, Süleymaniye Kütüphanesi, MS Esad 2149; and V. L. Ménage, 'Three Ottoman Treatises on Europe', in C. E. Bosworth (ed.), *Iran and Islam: In Memory of the Late Vladimir Minorsky* (Edinburgh, 1971), 421–33.

[32] Taşköprüzade Ahmed, *Eş-Şekā'iku n-nu'maniye fi 'ulemā'i d-devleti l-'osmaniye*, ed. Ahmed S. Furat (Istanbul, 1985).

[33] Nev'izade Ata'i, *Hadā'iku'l-hakā'ik fi tekmileti'ş-şakā'ik*, 2 vols. (Istanbul, AH 1268).

[34] Aşık Çelebi, *Meşā'ir üş-şu'arā, or Tezkere of 'Aşık Çelebi*, ed. G. M. Meredith-Owens (London, 1971).

[35] *Ḥadīqat ül-vüzerā (Der Garten der Wesire)* (repr. edn, Freiburg, 1969).

[36] Ahmed Resmi, *Halîfetü'r-rü'esâ*, ed. Mücteba İlgürel (Istanbul, 1992); Ahmed Resmi, *Hamîletü'l-küberâ: Darüssaade Ağaları*, ed. Ahmet Nezihi Turan (Istanbul, 2000).

[37] See, for instance, al-Ḥasan ibn Muḥammad al-Būrīnī, *Tarājim al-a'yān min abnā' al-zamān*, ed. Ṣalāḥ al-Dīn al-Munajjid, 2 vols. [incomplete] (Damascus, 1959–63).

[38] For Arabic historiography during the Ottoman period, see Laylá 'Abd al-Laṭīf Aḥmad, *Dirāsāt fī ta'rīkh wa-mu'arrikhī miṣr wa'l-shām ibbān al-'aṣr al-'uthmānī* (Cairo, 1980).

experience through acquaintance with the vicissitudes of time. This will serve as a protection against damages similar to those reported (from the past) and as a means to produce similar benefits.'[39] Katib Çelebi explicitly endorsed this definition.[40] Anticipating Leopold von Ranke by several centuries, he stated that the task of history was to express the events of the past in the way they actually happened.[41] Çelebi's follower, Na'ima, added that historians 'must prefer the reliable, documented statements of men who knew how to record what actually did happen'.[42] Again not unlike Ranke, however, Katib Çelebi and Na'ima were products of their own age, and thus, like all historians, their works represented their own position and values in society.[43]

Prosopographically, it is difficult to make generalizations about Ottoman historians, as exhaustive studies of historians have so far not been done. Franz Babinger's study of Ottoman historians and their works is very much outdated and yet still indispensable.[44] Even though it might be premature to state—given the relative absence of biographical and bibliographical studies that would provide a reliable basis for such a statement—it seems that bureaucrats and scholar-jurists dominated Ottoman historiography as authors. Two examples of the former group, Mustafa Âli and Ahmed Resmi, have been studied by Cornell Fleischer and Virginia Aksan, respectively.[45] Representatives of less educated groups have also written historical works. One of them, a retired janissary, for instance, wrote a chronicle on the regicide of Osman II that shaped the Ottoman historiography on the subject.[46] Perhaps a more striking example is that of a Damascene barber from the eighteenth century who wrote a chronicle of his lifetime.[47] Prosopographic analyses will be better made once the *Historians of the Ottoman Empire* (*HOE*), an online project led by Cornell Fleischer, Cemal Kafadar, Hakan Karateke, and an international team of

---

[39] Quoted (and translated) by Franz Rosenthal, *A History of Muslim Historiography*, 2nd edn (Leiden, 1968), 531.

[40] Katib Çelebi quotes Taşköprüzade in two of his Arabic works; see *Keşf-el-zunun*, ed. Şerefettin Yaltkaya and Kilisli Rifat Bilge, 2 vols. (Istanbul, 1941–3), i. c. 271; and *Fadhlakat aqwāl al-akhyār fī 'ilm al-ta'rīkh wa'l-akhbār*, excerpt trans. Orhan Şaik Gökyay, in Orhan Şaik Gökyay (ed.), *Kâtip Çelebi'den Seçmeler* (Istanbul, 1968), 187–8.

[41] Katib Çelebi, *Fezleke*, 2 vols. (Istanbul, AH 1286–7), ii. 9.

[42] Quoted (and translated) by Thomas, *A Study of Naima*, 113.

[43] For an example of personal bias from Katib Çelebi's work see Baki Tezcan, 'The 1622 Military Rebellion in Istanbul: A Historiographical Journey', *International Journal of Turkish Studies*, 8 (2002), 25–43 at 34–5.

[44] Franz Babinger, *Die Geschichtsschreiber der Osmanen und ihre Werke* (Leipzig, 1927).

[45] Cornell H. Fleischer, *Bureaucrat and Intellectual in the Ottoman Empire: The Historian Mustafa Âli (1541–1600)* (Princeton, 1986); and Virginia H. Aksan, *An Ottoman Statesman in War and Peace: Ahmed Resmi Efendi, 1700–1783* (Leiden, 1995).

[46] Gabriel Piterberg, *An Ottoman Tragedy: History and Historiography at Play* (Berkeley, 2003); and Baki Tezcan, 'The History of a "Primary Source": The Making of Tûghî's Chronicle on the Deposition of Osman II', *Bulletin of the School of Oriental and African Studies*, 72 (2009), 41–62.

[47] Dana Sajdi, 'A Room of His Own: The "History" of the Barber of Damascus (fl. 1762)', *The MIT Electronic Journal of Middle East Studies*, 4 (2004), 19–35.

advisers, is completed.[48] The *HOE* project has already revolutionized the way in which Ottoman historiography is understood—by including historians who wrote in languages other than Arabic, Persian, and Turkish. The present chapter follows their example.

OTHER HISTORIES

Some of the earliest sources on Ottoman history were produced by their neighbours, who (or their offspring) eventually became Ottomans themselves. These works were written in such regional languages as Arabic, Armenian, and Greek—languages that continued to be used by Ottoman subjects to produce Ottoman histories well after the establishment of Ottoman Turkish as the primary language of literary expression for the imperial elite. In the period covered in this volume, one also finds examples of Ottoman historical writing in Hebrew, Latin, Persian, Romanian, and Slavic languages. They should all be regarded as an integral part of Ottoman historiography. Below I focus on some examples from Greek, Armenian, and Persian.

Some of the oldest extant literary sources on the formative period of the Ottoman Empire are in medieval Greek.[49] While these works should be considered as examples of Byzantine historical writing written mostly in classical style, a historiographical tradition in both classical and vernacular Greek was continued by the Greek subjects of the Ottoman Empire as well. The most well-known Greek author of Ottoman historical writing is Michael Kritoboulos, a member of the nobility of Imbros, an Aegean island. He wrote a history of Mehmed II, the conqueror of Constantinople, covering the first seventeen years of the sultan's reign (1451–67).[50] This work, however, could not have had much of an influence on Ottoman historiography, either in medieval Greek—since its only known manuscript remained in the library of the Ottoman imperial palace until the nineteenth century—or in Ottoman Turkish, since it was only translated into Turkish in the early twentieth century.[51]

Marios Philippides suggests that there were 'two traditions in Greek historiography in the sixteenth and early seventeenth centuries'.

One was centered in Istanbul in areas that were directly under Ottoman control and the jurisdiction of the Patriarchate; this 'school' produced histories and works with a heavy

---

[48]   http://www.ottomanhistorians.com (accessed 30 May 2011).

[49]   For examples in English translation, see Doukas, *Decline and Fall of Byzantium to the Ottoman Turks: An Annotated Translation of 'Historia Turco-Byzantina'*, trans. Harry J. Magoulias (Detroit, 1975); and George Sphrantzes, *The Fall of the Byzantine Empire: A Chronicle by George Sphrantzes, 1401–1477*, trans. Marios Philippides (Amherst, 1980).

[50]   Kritovoulos, *History of Mehmed the Conqueror*, trans. Charles T. Riggs (Princeton, 1954).

[51]   Ibid., p. ix; and Kritovulos, *Tarih-i Sultan Mehmet Han-i Sani*, trans. Karolidi (Istanbul, 1912).

ecclesiastical emphasis, more or less in the Byzantine tradition . . . The second 'school' flourished in the Greek communities of Italy or in areas in the Greek mainland that were still under Italian control.[52]

An important example of the first school is the Κατάλογος Χρονογραφικὸς τῶν Πατριαρχῶν Κωνσταντινουπόλεως [History of the Patriarchs of Constantinople] (*c.*1572) by Damaskenos the Stoudite.[53] Makarios Melissourgos-Melissenos's expansion of Sphrantzes's history to produce the *Chronicon Maius* is an example of the second school.[54] Philippides published English translations of two anonymous chronicles, each one of which represents one of these two traditions.

Although I cannot possibly provide an exhaustive survey of Ottoman-Greek historiography here, I should mention the ongoing tradition of short chronicles, many of which have been edited by Peter Schreiner.[55] A major example of the Byzantine local chronicle tradition is the seventeenth-century chronicle by Synadinos, a priest from Serres in modern Greece, who refers to the Ottoman sultan in the Byzantine fashion as the *basileus*, never calling into question his legitimacy of rule.[56]

Unlike Ottoman-Greek historiography, Ottoman-Armenian historical writing was both geographically and temporally removed from an independent Armenian political entity as the last such state, the Armenian Kingdom of Cilicia, had ceased to exist in 1375. The resulting loss of cultural patronage may well be responsible for the relative lack of history-works in Armenia in the fifteenth century.[57] Notwithstanding this relative absence of independent works of history, there is a rich tradition of historical writing in colophons from this period.[58] As for the sixteenth century, according to Kevork Bardakjian, '[t]here are simply no historians from this age; at least, no histories are extant'.[59] The seventeenth century, however, is quite different in both Armenia proper and in the Armenian diaspora, especially Istanbul.

---

[52] Marios Philippides (trans.), *Byzantium, Europe, and the Early Ottoman Sultans, 1373–1513: An Anonymous Greek Chronicle of the Seventeenth Century (Codex Barberinus Graecus III)* (New Rochelle, 1990), 11.

[53] Marios Philippides (ed. and trans.), *Emperors, Patriarchs and Sultans of Constantinople, 1373–1513: An Anonymous Greek Chronicle of the Sixteenth Century,* (Brookline, 1990), 17.

[54] Philippides, *Byzantium, Europe, and the Early Ottoman Sultans,* 11.

[55] Peter Schreiner, *Die byzantinischen Kleinchroniken,* 3 vols. (Vienna, 1975–9); the title is misleading in that Schreiner's collection includes many chronicles produced during the Ottoman period as well.

[56] Paolo Odorico (ed. and trans.), *Conseils et mémoires de Synadinos, prêtre de Serrès en Macédoine (XVIIe siècle)* (n.p., 1996).

[57] For an example of Armenian historiography from this period see Tovma Metzopetsi, *History of Tamerlane and His Successors,* ed. and trans. Robert Bedrosian (New York, 1987).

[58] Avedis K. Sanjian (trans.), *Colophons of Armenian Manuscripts, 1301–1480: A Source for Middle Eastern History* (Cambridge, 1969).

[59] Kevork B. Bardakjian, *A Reference Guide to Modern Armenian Literature, 1500–1920, with an Introductory History* (Detroit, 2000), 43.

While the fall of Constantinople was a source of sorrows for at least some contemporary Armenians,[60] it became the historical foundation for a new and relatively prosperous Armenian community in Istanbul. For them it was, at least partially, the blessing of Hovakim, the Armenian bishop of Prusa [Bursa], that had empowered Mehmed II to conquer Constantinople. According to Mik'ayēl Ch'amch'yants', an Armenian historian from the eighteenth century, Mehmed II had promised Hovakim to take him to Istanbul and make him the leader of Armenians there, hence the Armenian Patriarchate of Istanbul that was founded in 1461.[61] The immigration of Armenians from the eastern provinces of the empire to the imperial capital, seeking refuge from the havoc created by the Jalali rebellions as well as the Ottoman–Safavid wars during the early seventeenth century, contributed to the development of a populous and diverse Armenian community in Istanbul. Not surprisingly, this community, whose members were engaged in various crafts and professions, also produced a rich literary culture both in Armenian and Armeno-Turkish, or Turkish written in Armenian letters.[62] Armenian-Ottoman historiography flourished in this socio-cultural context.

The first major Armenian chronicler of the seventeenth century was Vardapet Grigor Kamakhets'i, who was born in Kamakh (modern Kemah in eastern Turkey), grew up as an orphan, studied at a monastery in Armenia, and was created *vardapet*, a celibate priest who is also a doctor of theology, in 1603. After a pilgrimage to Jerusalem in 1604, Grigor travelled to Istanbul to help his half-sister and her daughter. There he got involved in the affairs of the Armenian community and became a major actor in the rivalries over the patriarchal throne in the first half of the seventeenth century. His commitment to the Armenian community took him to all corners of the empire, ending his days as the prelate of Rodosto (modern Tekirdağ in Turkish Thrace). His *Zhamanakagrut'iwn* [Chronology] is a rich source of information for Ottoman social history as well as the history of the Armenian Church and community.[63]

There are several Armenian historians in the seventeenth and eighteenth centuries, some of whom lived in the Ottoman Empire while others were Safavid subjects.[64] The ease with which they could operate in both of these empires is truly remarkable.

---

[60] Avedis K. Sanjian, 'Two Contemporary Armenian Elegies on the Fall of Constantinople, 1453', *Viator*, 1 (1970), 223–61.

[61] Kevork B. Bardakjian, 'The Rise of the Armenian Patriarchate of Constantinople', in Benjamin Braude and Bernard Lewis (eds.), *Christians and Jews in the Ottoman Empire: The Functioning of a Plural Society*, 2 vols. (New York, 1982), i 89; compare Markus Rahn, *Die Entstehung des armenischen Patriarchats von Konstantinopel* (Hamburg, 2002).

[62] For an example of Armeno-Turkish literature see Avedis K. Sanjian and Andreas Tietze (eds.), *Eremya Chelebi Kömürjian's Armeno-Turkish Poem: The Jewish Bride* (Wiesbaden, 1981).

[63] Grigor's *Zhamanakagrut'iwn* was published with various other writings of his by Mesrop Nshanean in Jerusalem in 1915; Bardakjian, *A Reference Guide*, 67–8, 354; Hrand D. Andreasyan, 'Türk tarihine aid Ermeni kaynakları', *Tarih Dergisi*, 1/1–2 (1949–50), 95–118, 401–38 at 426–8.

[64] For an overview see Bardakjian, *A Reference Guide*, 68–73, 87–94.

Abraham Kretats'i, for instance, was born an Ottoman subject in Crete, was primate of the Armenians of Thrace, and then, while visiting monasteries in Armenia, he found himself elected Catholicos in Etchmiadzin in 1734. His *Patmut'iwn* details the last years of the Safavids and the election of Nadir, an able commander from the Afshar tribe, to the kingship of Persia in 1736 in the aftermath of his victories against the Ottomans.[65] As members of a community that lived in multiple polities, Armenians wrote cosmopolitan histories that paid equal attention to both Ottoman and Safavid realms. A prime example of this wide scope is found in the *Patmut'iwn* [History] of Vardapet Arak'el Dawrizhets'i, whose work covers various events that happened in the Ottoman Empire although he was a Safavid subject.[66] Their works also display a clear awareness of historiographical traditions in languages other than their own. Eremia Chelebi K'eomiwrchean's history of the Ottoman sultans in verse, for instance, makes use of various chronicles in Ottoman Turkish.[67] Incidentally, Eremia Chelebi also wrote a history of the Armenians in Armeno-Turkish, specifically to educate his contemporaries who could not read Armenian, which became a source for a world history written by an Ottoman historian in Arabic.[68]

The Kurds constituted another community, the members of which lived in both Ottoman and Safavid empires and were thus well versed in the affairs of both. Some of them, like Idrīs Bidlīsī, mentioned above, or Shukrī,[69] produced Ottoman histories in Persian or Turkish for the Ottoman court. Kurdish started to become a literary language in the late seventeenth century, a process that is marked by Ahmad Khānī's composition of *Mem u Zîn*, a Kurdish epic based on the love story between the two characters of Mem and Zîn, in 1692 in Kurdish.[70] Yet Ottoman Kurdish historiography predates the development of Kurdish as a literary language, as exemplified by the monumental work of Sharaf Khān of Bidlis, the *Sharaf-nāmeh*, composed in 1597 in Persian. This two-volume work is also a summary of the political state of the Kurds. While the well-known first volume is about Kurdish tribes of Kurdistan, the second volume is an annalistic history of the Ottoman Empire and the Persian realm to the east that starts around 1290 and ends in 1596. For every year, Sharaf Khān records the important events in both realms.[71] Not unlike the author, who changed

---

[65] Abraham Kretats'i, *The Chronicle of Abraham of Crete* (Patmut'iwn *of Kat'oghikos Abraham Kretats'i)*, trans. George A. Bournoutian (Costa Mesa, Calif., 1999).

[66] Arak'el Dawrizhets'i, *The History of Vardapet Arak'el of Tabriz*, trans. George A Bournoutian, 2 vols. (Costa Mesa, CA, 2005–6), see esp. chs. 51 (on Ottoman sultans) and 56 (on chronology).

[67] Bardakjian, *A Reference Guide*, 61.

[68] Sanjian and Tietze (eds.), *Eremya Chelebi Kömürjian's Armeno-Turkish Poem*, 35, n. 97. The historian in question is Müneccimbaşı, whose work was translated to Turkish in the eighteenth century by the famous poet Nedim; *Sahâ'ifü'l-ahbâr*, 3 vols. (Istanbul, AH 1285).

[69] Shukrī, *Selîm-nâme* [in Turkish verse], Topkapı Sarayı Müzesi Kütüphanesi, MS Hazine 1597–98, f. 276b.

[70] Ahmed Khani, *Mem and Zin*, trans. Salah Saadalla (Istanbul, 2008).

[71] Sharaf Khān, *Scheref-nameh, ou Histoire des Kourdes*, ed. V. Véliaminof-Zernof, 2 vols. (St Petersburg, 1860–2); and *Chèref-nâmeh, ou Fastes de la Nation Kourde*, trans. François Bernard Charmoy, 4 parts in 2 vols. (St Petersburg, 1868–75).

allegiance from the Ottomans to the Safavids and then back to the Ottomans, his book symbolizes the Kurdish political experience in between two imperial powers.

A CASE STUDY

In the earliest examples of Ottoman universal histories, such as the works of Şükrullah and Enveri, 'Ottoman history occupied a modest place as a continuation of Islamic history, and the Ottoman Sultans were presented as *ghazis* on the frontiers of the Muslim world'.[72] The reign of Süleiman witnessed the first efforts to create narratives of world history that would take the Ottoman sultans from the frontiers to the centre of the Islamic world. One of these narratives, started by Arifi and continued by his successors in the office of the *şehnāmeci*, the '*Shāh-nāmeh*-writer', was the *Zübdetü't-tevârîh* [Quintessence of Histories], which was originally written on a scroll that came to be known as the *Tomar-ı hümâyûn* [Imperial Scroll].[73]

The *Zübdetü't-tevârîh* is a history of the world that starts with the creation of the heavens and the earth. Once it gets to Adam, it turns into an annotated genealogy of illustrious men and women, including prophets, caliphs, and kings. The length of the annotations varies. The stories of prophets are much longer than the notices that surround the names of kings. Yet once the Ottomans enter the stage of history, annotations become a little more detailed; when the scroll gets to the reign of Süleiman, the annotations are transformed into a full-blown chronicle.

The invocation section of the introduction with which the scroll begins sets the tone for the aim of the work, and is worth quoting here at length:[74]

In the name of God, most-benevolent, ever-merciful. All praise be to God who created the heavens and the earth, and ordained darkness and light. (Q 6:1)

May abundant praises and thanks, and limitless thanksgivings and eulogies, be on that Sultan, the Creator of the Worlds and the non-obliging Maker—*May His glory be sublime and exalted, may His favours become all-embracing and continuous!*

Who wrote and registered all of the creatures and every one of the creations in the register of construction and innovation with the pen of His preordainment in accordance with the

---

[72] İnalcık, 'The Rise of Ottoman Historiography', 166.

[73] Topkapı Sarayı Müzesi Kütüphanesi, MS A 3599; Sinem Eryılmaz, 'The *Shehnameci*s of Sultan Süleyman: 'Arif and Eflâtûn and Their Dynastic Project', Ph.D. dissertation, University of Chicago, 2010.

[74] For the significance of this section in Ottoman literary introductions, see Baki Tezcan 'The Multiple Faces of the One: The Invocation Section of Ottoman Literary Introductions as a Locus for the Central Argument of the Text', *Middle Eastern Literatures*, 12 (2009), 27–41. The italicized parts are originally in Arabic; Q refers to the Qur'an, followed by the number of the chapter and that of the verse from which the quotation comes.

felicitously designed notion that '[God] *created every thing and determined its exact measure;'* (Q 25:2)

Who spread the seven lands, adorned with rivers, seas, trees, and mountains, according to the sense of [the statement] '*It is God who made the earth a dwelling for you, and the sky a vaulted roof;*' (Q 40:64)

Who made [all] kinds of plants grow from those lands for the whole of the creation, as the saying goes '[A]*nd We made every kind of splendid thing to grow upon it;*' (Q 50:7)

Who created the heavens, adorned with revolving spheres of stars, suspending above those lands and covering each other, according to the notion that [God] '*created the seven skies one above the other;*' (Q 67:3)

Who made the provisions of all the existing things descend from those heavens [in accordance] with [the statement that God] '*sends you food from the heavens;*' (Q 40:13)

Who, with the good tidings of [His words:] '*I am placing a trustee on the earth,*' (Q 2:30) leavened the substance of Adam with His hand of might in accordance with [His expression:] '*I leavened the substance of Adam with my hands for forty mornings;*' (H.Q.)[75]

Who designed and drew [Adam] in the best of appearances [in accordance] with the miracle of [His statement:] '*Surely We created man of finest possibilities;*' (Q 95:4)

Who sent the Munificent Book [i.e. the Qur'an]—that must be revered—to the Apostle who is a messenger and an admonisher, and the leader of the two worlds—the corporeal and the spiritual—and the two races—the humans and the jinn;

Who, for the precise execution of the rules of the religion of Islam and for the system of the order of the affairs of all the mankind, made in every age those, submission to whom is incumbent (for the rest of the humankind), obedient and subjugated to the command of an emperor who is the defender of the faith.[76]

God speaks so much in this section that even the non-Qur'anic statements start to acquire a divine aura. These statements all lead, however, to a very worldly argument: God renders His creation subjugated to an emperor in every age. This is such an emperor that even those who enjoy the submission of the rest of mankind have to submit to him. 'Those, submission to whom is incumbent (*efrad-ı lazımü'l-inkıyad*)' could refer to authorities of religion or lesser kings. It does not matter really; they are all subjugated to the 'emperor who is the defender of the faith'.

The section of praise to God also mirrors the contents of the *Tomar-ı humayun* [Imperial Scroll], which further helps one to comprehend the motive for the scroll's production. The first part, which accounts for slightly more than one tenth of the scroll, is devoted to the creation of the heavens and the earth and a detailed description of them. Most of the text is written around two large illustrations. One has to rotate the scroll in order to read the text as it surrounds these illustrations in a number of columns that go in different directions. Then

[75] H.Q. is short for *hadīth qudsī*, a Muslim tradition in which Muhammad is believed to have been quoting divine speech.

[76] Topkapı Palace Library, A. 3599, lines 1–7; the translation is mine with the exception of the quotations from the Qur'an, which are based, with some minor modifications, on *Al-Qur'an: A Contemporary Translation*, trans. Ahmed Ali (rev. edn, Princeton, 1988).

comes the creation of Adam, followed by the prophets sent by God to mankind. In this section, various genealogical lines that start with Adam and Eve continue through tens of generations, connecting everyone whose name is mentioned with everybody else. Including the life story of Muhammad and the first four caliphs, this section comprises about one-fifth of the scroll.

These divine and prophetic parts are followed by the genealogies of the rulers of the Muslim world up to the Ottomans. These genealogies run vertically throughout the scroll. The lines are dotted with circles in which names are recorded, the assumption being that the man in the circle above is the father of the one below. At any point there may be a number of lines running parallel to each other, such as the Turkish forefathers of the Ottomans and the Mongol khans. Hardly anything is recorded for most of them, only a few sentences that may be called 'subtitles' are written down around the names of the prominent ones. The 'subtitles' are hard to follow as they go in different directions around the names, depending on the availability of open space between the circles surrounding the names. This section covers less than one-tenth of the scroll.

Finally, of course, come the Ottomans, dominating the last part of the scroll. The first nine sultans, Osman through Selim I, are introduced with brief sections around the adorned circles that surround their names. The coverage of individual reigns starts to become more detailed with that of Süleiman. His reign and those of his son and grandson—the latter two were added to the scroll in later stages— cover the second half of the scroll, which ends with the mention of the enthrone-ment of Mehmed III, Süleiman's great grandson, in 1595. Not surprisingly, the prominent place accorded to the Ottomans, especially to Süleiman, is fore-shadowed in the introduction. In the section in which the author, who must be Arifi, talks about the work and its contents, Süleiman is introduced with the Qur'anic quotation from 3:110: '*Of all the communities raised among men you are the best, enjoining the good, forbidding the wrong.*' Just as the Muslims constitute the best community, Süleiman is superior to all other sultans and khans.[77]

Thus the *Tomar-ı humayun* was a project to construct a monumental world history in Turkish prose that culminated in Süleiman. In this perception of world history, Süleiman's exploits were to parallel God's creation of the universe. The space devoted to each is more or less equal. God's creation of the heavens and the earth starts the text, and Süleiman's conquests were to end it. All of the genealogical lines that start with Adam and Eve eventually disappear. Only one line is left, that of the Ottomans. And that line was to end with Süleiman, the ultimate ruler of the world whose empire came to encompass every other one. That is why, perhaps, the first author of the text thought of the title the *Zubdetü't-tevarih*—the 'Quintessence of Histories'. It was not just a summary

---

[77] A. 3599, line 18.

providing the history of the world in a kernel. It was the channel in which all histories ran to the ultimate one, to that of Süleiman.

The medium chosen for the project, a long scroll, was perfect for the purpose. Arifi had already produced a multi-volume project in Persian verse, lavishly illustrated in codices.[78] This was going to be different. The text was intended not to be read from beginning to end but rather to be looked at for effect. What really mattered was that the text included the genealogies of major Islamic dynasties that one could easily recognize. Their histories were reduced to some circles, surrounding the names of their kings, and following or running parallel to each other, only to disappear.

The dynasties they represented were now all gone, assimilated into the empire of Süleiman, who was the last remaining ruler of the world. Their stories were not important in and of themselves. They had simply been a means for the history to reach the Ottomans, and especially Süleiman. With Süleiman came the end of history at last. Long before Francis Fukuyama,[79] one of Süleiman's court historians—most probably Arifi—had declared the end of history. Or perhaps it was Süleiman's own idea to shape the format that way. The *Tomar-ı humayun* was to become a monument for posterity, not a mere book.[80] Needless to say, though, history had not come to an end with Süleiman, just as it did not end—as Fukuyama would suggest—with the collapse of the Soviet Empire.

Ottoman historians continued to produce works of history well up to the end of the Ottoman Empire in 1922.[81] It is obviously impossible within the confines of the present chapter to do justice to the four centuries of Ottoman historical writing between 1400 and 1800. The historians and genres of historical writing mentioned, however, should give a clear idea about the diversity of historiographical expression in this period, which may well be the most important feature of Ottoman historiographical tradition.

TIMELINE/KEY DATES

*c.*1300 Osman appears in Bithynia as a warlord
1326 Ottoman conquest of Bursa (Prusa)
1361 Conquest of Edirne (Adrianople)

---

[78] See Esin Atıl, *Süleymanname: The Illustrated History of Süleyman the Magnificent* (Washington, 1986).

[79] Francis Fukuyama, 'The End of History?' *National Interest*, 16 (Summer 1989), 3–18.

[80] Süleiman's scroll was later rendered into a codex form during the tenure of Seyyid Lokman as the court historian of Murad III; see Tezcan, 'The Politics of Early Modern Ottoman Historiography'.

[81] See Cemal Kafadar and Hakan T. Karateke, 'The Late Ottoman and Early Republican Turkish Historical Writing', Stuart Macintyre, Juan Maiguashca, and Attila Pók (eds.), *The Oxford History of Historical Writing*, vol. 4: *1800–1914* (Oxford, 2011), 559–77.

1402 Defeat at the Battle of Ankara against Timur's forces
1453 Conquest of Istanbul (Constantinople)
1514 Selim I defeats the Safavid shah Ismail at Çaldıran
1516–17 Conquest of Egypt, and the greater Syria; submission of the Hejaz
1521 Conquest of Belgrade
1529 Siege of Vienna
1534 Conquest of Baghdad
1571 Defeat at the Battle of Lepanto
1578–90; 1603–39 Wars with Persia
1622 Regicide of Osman II
1648 Regicide of İbrahim
1683 Siege of Vienna
1687 Deposition of Mehmed IV
1699 Treaty of Carlowitz (Ottomans lose territories in Europe)
1703 Deposition of Mustafa II
1730 Deposition of Ahmed III
1774 Treaty of Küçük Kaynarca (Ottomans lose Crimea)
1798 Napoleon invades Egypt

KEY HISTORICAL SOURCES

Abdülvasi Çelebi, *Halilname*, ed. Ayhan Güldaş (Ankara, 1996).

Ahmedi, *İskender-nāme: İnceleme-tıpkıbasım*, ed. İsmail Ünver (Ankara, 1983).

Anonymous, *Gazavât-ı Sultân Murâd b. Mehemmed Hân: İzladi ve Varna Savaşları üzerine anonim gazavâtnâme*, ed. Halil İnalcık and Mevlûd Oğuz (Ankara, 1978).

Arif Ali (Tokatlı), *La geste de Melik Danişmend: Etude critique du Danişmendname*, ed. Irène Mélikoff, 2 vols. (Paris, 1960).

Aşıkpaşazade, 'Tevârîh-i Âl-i 'Osman', ed. Çiftçioğlu N. Atsız, in *Osmanlı Tarihleri* (Istanbul, 1949), 77–319.

Kemalpasazade, *Tevârih-i Âl-i Osman—I. Defter*, ed. Şerafettin Turan (Ankara, 1970); *II. Defter*, ed. Şerafettin Turan (Ankara, 1983); *IV. Defter*, ed. Koji Imazawa (Ankara, 2000); *VII. Defter*, ed. Şerafettin Turan (Ankara, 1957); *VIII. Defter*, ed. Ahmet Uğur (Ankara, 1997); *X. Defter*, ed. Şefaettin Severcan (Ankara, 1996).

Mik'ayēl Ch'amch'yants', *History of Armenia by Father Michael Chamich, from B.C. 2247 to the year of Christ 1780, or 1229 of the Armenian era to which is appended a continuation of the history by the translator from the year 1780 to the present date*, abridged trans. Baron John Avtaliantz, 2 vols. (Calcutta, 1827).

Na'ima, *Tarih-i Na'ima*, 6 vols. (Istanbul, AH 1281–3).

Nesri, *Gihannuma: Die altosmanische Chronik des Mevlana Mehemmed Neschri*, ed. Franz Taeschner, 2 vols. (Leipzig, 1951–5).

Sukrullah, 'Der Abschnitt über die Osmanen in Sukrullah's persischer Universalgeschichte', ed. Theodor Seif, *Mitteilungen zur osmanischen Geschichte*, 2 (1923–6), 63–128.

BIBLIOGRAPHY

Aksan, Virginia H., *An Ottoman Statesman in War and Peace: Ahmed Resmi Efendi, 1700–1783* (Leiden, 1995).

Babinger, Franz, *Die Geschichtsschreiber der Osmanen und ihre Werke* (Leipzig, 1927).

Fleischer, Cornell H., *Bureaucrat and Intellectual in the Ottoman Empire: The Historian Mustafa Âli (1541–1600)* (Princeton, 1986).

Kafadar, Cemal, *Between Two Worlds: The Construction of the Ottoman State* (Berkeley, 1995).

——Karateke, Hakan, and Fleischer, Cornell H. (eds.), *Historians of the Ottoman Empire*, at http://www.ottomanhistorians.com (accessed 30 May 2011).

Kütükoğlu, Bekir, *Vekâyiʿnüvis: Makaleler* (Istanbul, 1994).

Lewis, Bernard and Holt, P. M. (eds.), *Historians of the Middle East* (London, 1962).

Ménage, Victor Louis, 'A Survey of the Early Ottoman Histories, with Studies of Their Textual Problems and Their Sources', Ph.D. dissertation, University of London, 1961.

Piterberg, Gabriel, *An Ottoman Tragedy: History and Historiography at Play* (Berkeley, 2003).

Thomas, Lewis V., *A Study of Naima*, ed. Norman Itzkowitz (New York, 1972).

Chapter 10

Islamic Scholarship and Understanding History in West Africa before 1800

Paul E. Lovejoy

The historical scholarship indigenous to West Africa was closely associated with the Islamic sciences, including history and geography, which flourished in such places as Timbuktu for centuries before 1800.[1] The importance of history was displayed in such writings as 'Abd al-Rahman al-Sa'di's *Tarikh al-Sudan* [History of the Sudan] (*c.*1655) and *Ta'rikh al-fattash fi akhbar al-buldan wa'l-juyush wa-akabir al-nas* [The Chronicle of the Researcher into the History of the Countries, the Armies, and the Principal Personalities], attributed to Mahmud Ka'ti and continued after his death, with the surviving version ending in AH 1074 (AD 1654–5). The legal tradition was also historical in orientation because of the practice of citing previous fatwa in issuing opinions on contemporary legal questions. The intellectual tradition of quoting the Qur'an and the hadith privileged historically documented chains of authority in the construction of arguments and establishing legitimacy. Among Muslims, there was the scholarly tradition of *isnād*, which traced an individual's intellectual and religious pedigree with reference to one's teachers and, in turn, their teachers. The identification with a chain of authority that was historical established specialization and knowledge of a specific curriculum. The Ibadi scholarship in the Mzab, various Saharan oases, and other Berber enclaves sustained a learned tradition that was autonomous from Sunni orthodoxy but nonetheless committed to an equally intellectual discipline. In addition, the consolidation of the Qadiriyya sufi brotherhood in Morocco and then elsewhere spread a system of education that enhanced this appreciation of history.

[1] This chapter was originally presented as the inaugural William A. Brown Memorial Lecture on Islam in West Africa at the University of Wisconsin, Madison, on 12 March 2009. William Brown inspired my interest in Islamic West Africa. His advice on my Ph.D. research was fundamental. His insistence on the erudition of scholarship in the Muslim centres of West Africa presaged many of the discoveries of recent years. I wish to thank Jan Vansina and Thomas Spear for inviting me to present the inaugural lecture in his honour, and the Canada Research Chair in African Diaspora History for its support. I also wish to thank Feisal Farrah and Yacine Daddi Addoun for their assistance.

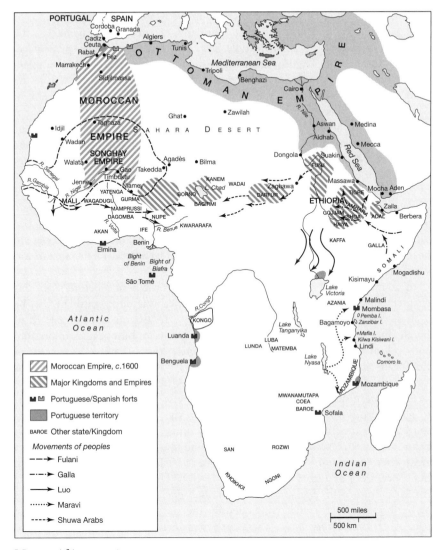

Map 4. Africa to *c.*1600

In summary, the tradition of scholarship in the western and central regions of what was known as Bilad al-Sudan, 'the land of the blacks', paralleled the traditions of the Maghreb and Middle East, connected by literacy, pilgrimage, trade, and migration. Dahiru Yahya makes the useful reminder of the complexities of intellectual and political currents within the Islamic world, despite the fundamental opposition between Christianity and Islam in the Mediterranean world.[2] Within this setting, the strong influence of Andalusia on sub-Saharan Africa should be noted; the influences across the Mediterranean and Sahara went both ways, reflecting the vitality of linkages rather than isolation because of the vast desert. Moreover, in the sixteenth century, the consolidation of Ottoman control as far west as Algeria extended new influences across the Sahara, especially to Borno. The autonomy of the Ibadi enclaves, along with the influence of Andalusia, and the Ottoman penetration, provided the context for a dynamic local tradition of historical writing and scholarship, not only in Timbuktu but ultimately in scores of towns in the sahel and savanna, in which Muslims were to be found in great numbers. The many libraries that have survived in Saharan and sub-Saharan Africa reflect these linkages.

In examining how Africans perceived history in the period before 1800, this chapter draws on an extensive scholarship. Africa was once considered to be a classic example of a region 'without history'. In the oft quoted remark of Hugh Trevor-Roper, Africa had no history prior to European 'exploration' and 'colonization'. According to Trevor-Roper, 'there is only the history of Europeans in Africa. The rest is darkness . . .'; he later refers to Africa as 'unhistoric'.[3] In fact, local scholars in West Africa, Ethiopia, and elsewhere were writing histories and documenting history well before the rise of Europe to global prominence after the sixteenth century. There are extensive written sources from the fifteenth century and continuing into the nineteenth century, before European 'exploration' or imperial conquest. This is not only in Muslim areas where writing in Arabic was common, and Islamic scholarship flourished, but conceptions of history were also well developed elsewhere, as with the literate Amharic culture in Ethiopia and at various enclaves where Christians were to be found. Literacy and, consequently, the survival of written records, are part of African history. From these surviving documents it is possible to gain some understanding of how people tried to interpret history, well before the Portuguese and, later, other Europeans circumnavigated Africa. Indeed Islamic scholarship flourished during the seventeenth, eighteenth, and early nineteenth centuries, during the period when the trans-Atlantic slave trade grew to enormous proportions.

---

[2] Dahiru Yahya, *Morocco in the Sixteenth Century: Problems and Patterns in African Foreign Policy* (Atlantic Highlands, NJ, 1981).

[3] Hugh Trevor-Roper, 'The Past and Present: History and Sociology', *Past and Present*, 42 (1969), 6; and Trevor-Roper, *The Rise of Christian Europe* (New York, 1965), 9.

Any attempt to assess the history of 'understanding history' in Africa cannot be a synthesis or overview of the whole continent: there is too much research currently being undertaken to attempt such an approach here, which would inevitably be filled with significant gaps in coverage. Rather, this chapter has approached the problem of historical perspective through examples of how contemporaries in the period under review viewed their ethnography and history. Although there were large parts of Africa where there were no indigenous written records and often only vague (if any) references in external sources, the focus here is on western and central Sudan (i.e. the savanna, sahel, and Sahara Desert of West Africa). In these extensive areas there was a literate class of Muslim scholars, some of whom wrote about their history, that extends back to the period AD 1000–1300 and the Muslim state of Ghana and the Almoravid conquests of the Maghreb and Andalusia. By concentrating on western and central Sudan, this chapter analyses perceptions of history of the Muslim intelligentsia in the period from the fourteenth century to the early nineteenth century. Moreover, the forms of oral tradition that have survived also enable a reconstruction of how history was conceptualized in a mythological form that was indigenous and that can be documented to have been important alongside the literary tradition. In addition to the literate tradition, there were professional sages, known as *griots*, who staged performances that were historical in both content and intent, and that were closely tied to the political leadership of the Muslim states, especially Mali.

Several themes that focus on changes and developments in the various areas of Africa dominate the historiography of the continent from 1400 to 1800. These themes are divided both geographically and in terms of the relative importance of external influences on change. The regions in which Islam was an important factor had already been consolidated in the sahel and Sahara by the fourteenth century, from the Red Sea and along the east coast of Africa westward across the Nile valley, the Lake Chad basin, the inner Niger River to the Senegal River in the west. Many areas had been introduced to Islam as early as the eleventh century, and hence it is erroneous to think of Islam as a 'foreign' or alien religion and culture, much as it would be to suggest that Christianity was a new introduction to north-west Europe in this period.

The interpretation of the history of Islamic areas of Africa is likely to be an ongoing process for years to come. This prediction is based solely on the materials that have been identified in John Hunwick's massive compendium of Arabic and *ajami* script texts in the different regions of Black Africa. The Hunwick inventories are informative of the vastness of these sources, which are clearly more extensive than is often thought.[4] The Timbuktu repository at the

---

[4] John Hunwick *et al.* (eds.), *Arabic Literature of Africa*, vol. 2: *The Writings of Central Sudanic Africa* (Leiden, 1995); and vol. 4: *The Writings of Western Sudanic Africa* (Leiden, 2003). See also Hunwick, 'Toward a History of the Islamic Intellectual Tradition in West Africa down to the Nineteenth Century', *Journal of Islamic Studies*, 17 (1997), 9.

Ahmad Baba Centre alone includes more than 15,000 manuscripts dating to the period before the seventeenth century. Similar collections that pertain to sub-Saharan Africa are to be found in Morocco, the Mzab, and other parts of Algeria, Libya, Egypt, the Nilotic Sudan, and the Hijaz. There are similarly important private and public archives in other places, such as Sokoto, Agadez, and the major Saharan oases.

The context of this scholarship in western and central Sudan was fundamentally religious, with a keen appreciation of the life and times of the Prophet Muhammad. The focus of various Islamic sciences was essentially historical. The range of scholarship can be appreciated with respect to the holdings of libraries in West Africa and the Maghreb. A survey of libraries demonstrates both the basis of a core curriculum that was taught widely, and the extent of knowledge that was based on books and manuscripts brought from different parts of the Islamic world, whether from Andalusia and the Maghreb, the Ottoman domains, or the Hijaz and the pilgrimage trails. Moreover, there was the Ibadi tradition that influenced much of the Sahara wherever Berber populations were to be found. Ibadi traced their origins to 'Abd Allah bin Ibad al-Murri 'l-Tamimi, while the Qadiriyya sufi brotherhood traced its origins to Shaykh 'Abd al-Qadir al Jilani.

The range of subjects that were studied in West Africa over several hundred years before 1900 included Qur'anic studies (recitation, exegesis), Arabic language (lexicons, lexicology, morphology, syntax, rhetoric, and prosody), and studies of the Prophet Muhammad, including biography, devotional poetry, the hadiths, and, by extension, history. Other areas of concentration included theology (*tawḥid*), mysticism (*taṣawwuf*), and law (sources, schools, didactic texts, legal precepts, and legal cases and opinions). While the concern here is with historical reconstruction and historical perspective, the focus of Islamic scholarship on the life and times of the Prophet, on language, and on religious themes, establishes a context for understanding the purpose of history, which essentially was to inform the political, scholarly, and spiritual elite. The legal tradition following the Maliki school of jurisprudence placed West Africa in the dominant legal tradition within Islam, along with the Maghreb and Andalusia, in which the importance of precedence in law was fundamental. The issuance of fatwa (legal opinions) required an appreciation of historical tradition, since reference to earlier legal opinions was essential in order to establish authority. Ibadi tradition was similar in terms of requiring accurate citations of the scholarly and legal literature; thereby displaying an appreciation of history.

The categories of legal materials to be found in the libraries of West Africa included sources of jurisprudence (*uṣūl al-fiqh*); schools of thought (*madhhab*), including foundational texts and *fiqh* manuals, didactic texts, legal precepts and maxims (*al-qawā'id al-fiqhiyya*); as well as legal cases and opinions, such as *al-Mi'yar al-mu'rib wa 'l-Jami' 'l-Mughrib fi fatawa Ifriqiya wa 'l-Andalus wa 'l-Maghrib* [Criteria for the Collection Containing the Fatwa of the People of

Ifriqia, Andalusia, and Maghreb] of al-Wansharisi, a massive collection of fatwa from the Maghreb and Andalusia from the ninth to the fifteenth century that was finished in 1496. Abdullahi dan Fodio cites the collection of Egyptian al-Ujhuri in establishing his understanding of law. Attitudes towards ethnicity, race, and gender are thereby revealed in the sources of the period, especially in discussions of issues arising from slavery and enslavement. Ahmad Baba specifically wrote a treatise, *Mi'raj al-su'ud* [The Ladder of Ascent towards Grasping the Law Concerning Transported Blacks] in 1613 on the legitimacy of enslavement in West Africa, in which he cites legal opinion and historic arguments to disprove any presumed association between racial features, such as being black skinned, and the legitimacy of enslavement.[5]

As the collection of books and manuscripts in the various libraries of West Africa demonstrate, influence flowed to the Sudan along three main axes, perhaps the strongest influence being from Andalusia and the Maghreb, and following trans-Saharan routes from Ottoman domains from the sixteenth century, with the influence of the pilgrimage route to Mecca always important. An overview of the books and manuscripts that are held in the various libraries of West Africa demonstrates what books were in circulation, at least in some places. Bruce Hall and Charles Stewart have examined seventy-two libraries in Nouakchott and Boutilimit in Mauritania, comprising a total of 4,600 items. In Shinqit and Wadan, twelve libraries hold about 1,100 manuscripts, while the library that belonged to al-Hajj 'Umar Tall and his family, now housed in Bamako, comprises 4,100 manuscripts. At Timbuktu, there are other libraries, including that of Bou 'l-Araf that forms the basis of the collection at the Ahmed Baba Institute. Similarly, there are important and substantial libraries in Kano, Sokoto, Agades, and elsewhere. The 'Umar Falke library has 3,030 items that were originally in Kano but are now located at Northwestern University.[6]

History was a recognized discipline of the Islamic sciences in West Africa. Ahmad Baba, for example, quoted Ibn Khaldun's *Muqaddima* [The Introduction] (AH 776; AD 1375) and *Kitab al-'Ibar* [The Universal History] (AH 780; AD 1379). 'Abd al-Rahman al-Sa'di bin 'Abd Allah's *Tarikh al-Sudan* [History of the Sudan] and *Tarikh al-khulafa* [History of the Caliphs], of al-Suyuti, as well as various abridgements and versifications, were well known and perhaps circulated widely. 'Abdullahi dan Fodio's autobiography and account of events leading to the Sokoto jihad is another example, although dating to the early nineteenth century.[7] There are many histories that were written since at least the late fifteenth century. The Mamma Haidara library

---

[5] Bruce Hall and Charles Stewart, 'The Historic "Core Curriculum" and the Book Market in Islamic West Africa', in Graziano Kratli and Ghislaine Lydon (eds.), *One Thousand Years of Trans-Saharan Book Trade* (Leiden, 2011), 109–74.

[6] Ibid.

[7] 'Abdullahi dan Fodio, *Idā' al-nusūkh man akhadhtu 'anhu min al-shuyūkh*, in Mervyn Hiskett, 'Material Relating to the State of Learning among the Fulani before their Jihad', *Bulletin of the*

contains 4,000 manuscripts that belong to all fields of Islamic studies: Qur'an, hadith, jurisprudence, literature, astrology, grammar, and sufism. In addition, it contains 1,000 documents of historic value, including fatwa on daily religious matters, commercial relations, and public issues. The correspondence between traders and scholars reveals the extent of international relations among Islamic countries, and again an appreciation of the past. The Mamma Haidara library was established in the middle of the nineteenth century at Bimba village and is still regarded as one of the best libraries in Mali.[8] The Centre de Documentation et de Recherches Historiques Ahmed Baba in Timbuktu contains 355 titles in *fiqh* alone, with many documents on sufism and 150 titles on history. The oldest manuscript dates to the seventh century AH (that is, the thirteenth century). While there are many manuscripts that derive from the central Islamic lands, predominant in the collection are local scholars from West Africa and the Sahara.[9]

The way that history was perceived is revealed in the various chronicles, which were essentially political in their dimension and within a perspective that records the filtered history of the Muslim community. The analysis of history as revealed in contemporary chronicles distinguishes among several periods. These chronicles are referred to as *tarikh*, in Hausa as *tarihi*, which is translated as 'history'— as distinct from stories, known in Hausa as *tatsuniyoyi*, which include historical memories as well as fanciful stories of animals, and relations between people and the supernatural.[10] The conscious recourse to historical documentation reflects an awareness of history as a documentable form of knowledge. In Islamic science, history and geography were distinguished, although geographical accounts, such as those of Ibn Battuta or the less well known Muhammad bin 'Umar al-Tunusi, contain important historical information and analysis. There are *mahram* and *diwan* that date to the fourteenth century and earlier for Borno and Kanem.[11] There are also histories that appear to rely on oral traditions, such as the *Asl al-Wangariyyin*, the Wangarawa Chronicle (*c.*1650), and the so-called Kano Chronicle, which dates to the end of the nineteenth century but clearly builds on earlier texts.[12]

School of Oriental and African Studies, 19:3 (1957), 550–73. See also Hall and Stewart, 'The Historic "Core Curriculum" and the Book Market in Islamic West Africa'.

[8] *Catalogue of Manuscripts in Mamma Haidara Library*, vols. 1–4, ed. Ayman Fuad Sayyid (London, 2000).

[9] *Handlist of Manuscripts in the Centre de Documentation et de Recherches Historiques Ahmed Baba, Timbuktu, Mali,* vols. 1–5, ed. Julian Johansen (London, 1995).

[10] See, for example, Frank Edgar, *Litafi na tatsuniyoyi na Hausa*, 2 vols. (Belfast, 1911).

[11] Dierk Lange, *Le Diwan des Sultans du (Kanem) Bornu: Chronologie et Histoire d'un Royaume Africain* (Wiesbaden, 1977). See also H. R. Palmer (ed.), *Sudanese Memoirs, Being mainly Translations of a Number of Arabic Manuscripts Relating to the Central and Western Sudan*, 3 vols. (Lagos, 1928).

[12] Paul E. Lovejoy, Abdullahi Mahadi, and Mansur Ibrahim Mukhtar, 'C. L. Temple's "Notes on the History of Kano"', *Sudanic Africa: A Journal of Historical Sources*, 4 (1993), 7–76; Lovejoy, 'Alhaji Ahmad el-Fellati ibn Dauda ibn Muhammad Manga: Personal Malam to Emir Muhammad Bello of Kano', in Femi J. Kolapo and Kwabena Akurang-Parry (eds.), *African Agency and European*

Muslim West Africa operated within a broader Islamic context, especially as focused on Morocco and by extension Andalusia. It is not possible to separate the scholarship of the Maghreb, Andalusia, and the Sudan; and Cordova and Timbuktu were within the same orbit of intellectual interaction. As Andalusia collapsed, the changes reverberated across the Sahara. This interpretation of history is evident in the accounts of numerous Muslim scholars. The writings of al-Maghili, Ibn Battuta, al-Hasan bin al-Wazzan al-Zayyati (Leo Africanus), Ahmad Baba, Muhammad Bello, and others uncover a vast scholarship that was a disciplined and annotated study of the past and contemporary society through history and geography.[13] How the long interaction across the Sahara shaped this intellectual environment and how deep into the savanna and forests to the south of the Sahara this knowledge and approach to history and geography penetrated is still being determined.

In addition there are chronicles from Gonja, in the middle Volta Basin, and various histories from central Sudan, such as the mid-seventeenth-century *Asl al-Wangariyyin* from Kano. Later histories, such as the Kano Chronicle, probably compiled in the late nineteenth century, attest to the existence of king lists and oral testimonies that were undoubtedly recounted publically in praise of previous rulers for several centuries.[14] The Wangarawa Chronicle is unique in that it recounts the migration of a community of Muslim merchants from western Sudan to the Hausa cities, and in doing so correlates historical events with other indigenous documentation.[15] What this local tradition demonstrates is an appreciation of history as a means of establishing legitimacy. Scholars felt the need to document events and information that was considered significant. The 'Wangara' were associated with Ibadi tradition, at least in this early period, rather than the sufism that would become dominant by the eighteenth century in many places.

The ways in which history was understood is also evident in oral traditions and myth, as in the Sunjiata epic of Mali. The epic recounts events that occurred between the twelfth and fifteenth centuries and that were fundamental to the charter of the Mali Empire, which fell to Songhay in the fifteenth century. There are at least seventeen variants of the legend. The scholarship that focuses on understanding the relevance and process of transmission of the tradition demonstrates that the tradition of historical reconstruction and historical commentary extends back into the past. The caste of professional minstrels and court

---

Colonialism: Latitudes of Negotiations and Containment: Essays in Honour of Sydney Kanya-Forstner (Trenton, NJ, 2007); and John Hunwick, 'A Historical Whodunit: The So-Called "Kano Chronicle" and its Place in the Historiography of Kano', *History in Africa*, 21 (1994), 127–46.

[13] 'Abd-al-'Aziz 'Abd-Allah Batran, 'A Contribution to the Biography of Shaikh Muhammad Ibn 'Abd-al-Karim ibn Muhammad ('Umar-A'mar) al-Maghili, al Tilimsani', *Journal of African History*, 14:3 (1973), 381–94; and John Hunwick, *Shari'a in Songhay: The Replies of al-Maghili to the Questions of Askia al-Hajj Muhammad* (London, 1985).

[14] Lovejoy, Mahadi, and Mukhtar, 'Temple's "Notes on the History of Kano"', 7–76.

[15] Paul E. Lovejoy, 'Notes on the *Asl al-Wangariyyin*', *Kano Studies*, 1:3 (1978), 46–52.

historians, the *griots*, had the task of performing and presenting traditions to audiences that were well versed in the lore and had critical expectations of how the traditions were represented. Structured traditions were maintained and even enhanced alongside a literate tradition of scholarship that was as well developed as the Latin of medieval Europe. The considerable texts that were written in the several centuries before *c*.1820 demonstrate how people saw themselves and how they interpreted their history.

The epic of Sunjiata dates to the period of Mali ascendancy in West Africa, most notable during the reign of Mansa Musa (d. 1337). The period is perhaps best symbolized by the influence of Abu Ishaq al-Sahili, the Andalusian poet and architect. Having returned to western Sudan with Mansa Musa's pilgrimage in 1324, al-Sahili was associated with the construction of the Great Mosque (Dyingere Ber) at Timbuktu, an audience chamber for Mansa Musa at his palace in the capital, Niani, and the royal residence for the kings of Mali at Timbuktu, as well as possibly a mosque in Gao.[16]

Local scholars wrote about this history and documented its importance in terms of an understanding of the Muslim world. Jurists referred to historic precedents and quoted earlier scholarship in addressing issues of enslavement and ethnicity, in a form that was historical in reconstruction. Libraries were maintained, and an institutionalized instruction was sustained at the mosques, and most especially at the mosques in Timbuktu, where different disciplines were taught, from law, to divination, history, numerology, and geography. The method of instruction was through the analysis of texts and mastering the literature of instruction, including the Qur'an, the hadiths, the Shari'a and Maliki legal interpretation, and other texts shared with the Muslim world.

THE 'RECONQUEST' OF IBERIA AND EMIGRATION FROM THE LANDS OF ANDALUSIA

The conquest of Granada in 1492 coincided with an uprising and *coup d'état* in Songhay, far to the south, that led to the ascendancy of Askia Muhammad and an avowedly more orthodox Muslim government, replacing the regime of Sunni 'Ali, himself a Muslim but considered to be not sufficiently strict, and supposedly tolerating non-Muslim practices.[17] Thus the year 1492 stands out as a watershed, both with respect to the expulsion of Muslims from Granada, the Songhay *coup d'état*, leading to the emergence of Askia Muhammad and the reinforcement of Muslim scholarship, and the arrival of Christopher Columbus in the Americas

---

[16] John Hunwick, 'An Andalusian in Mali: A Contribution to the Biography of Abu Ishaq al-Sahili, *c*.1290–1346', *Paideuma*, 36 (1990), 59–66.

[17] John Hunwick, 'Songhay, Bornu and Hausaland in the Sixteenth Century', in J. F. Ade Ajayi and Michael Crowder (eds.), *History of West Africa*, vol. 1, 3rd edn (London, 1985), 205–12.

and the opening of the Iberian overseas migration that paralleled the Andalusia diaspora across the Sahara. What is often not appreciated is that the expulsion of Muslims from Iberia was the final phase of a movement to Morocco and beyond, including to Songhay and the Muslim areas of West Africa, that had been under way for at least two centuries and continued through the sixteenth century. Clearly the impact and timing of migration differed, but the association with Iberia/Andalusia is certain.[18]

Even before the movement of Portuguese and Spanish peoples across the seas, there was a steady migration of Muslims from Andalusia across the Sahara. This migration culminated in the invasion of Songhay at the end of the sixteenth century, at the same time that the Spanish and Portuguese had united their monarchies in consolidating their conquest of vast parts of the world. These parallel trajectories were interrelated, it is argued here; only the Muslim trajectory of expansion from Andalusia has hitherto been recognized by a limited number of specialists.[19] While there is an understanding of the significance of the Iberian world and its overseas expansion, the parallel impact across the Sahara has escaped the attention of most scholars of European expansion. In fact, sugar plantations using African slave labour were first developed in southern Morocco, in the area between Marrakesh and Essaouira on the coast.[20] Slave labour from sub-Saharan Africa maintained irrigation works that enabled the production of sugar, much of which was sent to England in the early sixteenth century. Hence slave-based sugar production was developed between Marrakesh and the coast well before the earliest sugar plantations in the Americas, or indeed on São Tomé, in the Gulf of Guinea. The sugar plantations of Morocco may not have served as the model for the forms of sugar production using slave labour in the Americas, but 'European' enterprise in developing plantations in the Americas was not unique, as has often been thought in the scholarship of the Americas and Europe.

The connections between western Sudan and Andalusia have been well documented.[21] For example, 'Ali bin Ziyad al-Quti, the grandfather of Muhmud

[18] Ismaël Diadié Haïdara, *L'Espagne musulmane et l'Afrique subsaharienne* (Bamako, 1997); and Haïdara, *Jawdar Pasha et La Conquête Saâdienne du Songhay (1592–1599)* (Rabat, 1996).

[19] P-P. Rey, 'La jonction entre réseau ibadite berbère et réseau ibadite dioula du commerce de l'or, de l'Aïr à Kano et Katsina au milieu du 15e siècle, et la construction de l'Empire songhay par Sonni Ali Ber', *Revue de Géographie Alpine*, 1 (1994), 111–36; and Rey, 'L'influence de la pensée andalouse sur le rationalisme français et européen', in Doudou Dienne (ed.), *Les Routes d'al-Andalus: patrimoine commun et identité plurielle* (Paris, 2001), 111–18.

[20] P. Berthier, *Les anciennes sucreries du Maroc et leurs réseaux hydrauliques* (Rabat, 1966), 233–9. See also Michel Abitol, *Tombouctou et les Arma: De la conquête marocaine du Soudan nigérien en 1591 à l'hégémonie de l'Empire Peul du Macina en 1833* (Paris, 1979), 42–3. Hence one of the reasons for the invasion of sub-Saharan Africa was to acquire more enslaved workers, as well as soldiers.

[21] S. M. Cissoko, 'L'intelligentsia de Tombouctou aux XVe et XVIe siècles', *Bulletin de l'IFAN*, 31 (1969), 927–52; Cissoko, 'L'université de Tombouctou au XVIe siécle', *Afrika Zamani*, 2 (1974), 105–38; Ismaël Diadié Haïdara, *L'Espagne musulmane et l'Afrique subsaharienne* (Bamako, 1997); John Hunwick, 'Fez and West Africa in the Fifteenth and Sixteenth Centuries:

Ka'ti, author of *Tarikh al-fattash*, came from Toledo, and moved to Tuwat, in the Sahara, in 1468, apparently reaching Timbuktu within a year or two after that, where he married a local woman of Soninke origin.[22] Although Toledo had come under Christian rule in 1085, Muslims continued to live in the city at least until 1502, when a royal decree ordered conversion or exile. As Muhmud Ka'ti's grandfather's migration demonstrates, Muslims were moving to sub-Saharan Africa before the fall of Granada in 1492, and the emigration from Andalusia continued long into the sixteenth century. Muhmud Ka'ti was a contemporary of Askiya al-Hajj Muhammad, who ruled Songhay from 1493 to 1529.

The travels of al-Hasan bin al-Wazzan al-Zayyati show the extent of interaction between Andalusia and West Africa. Like al-Sahili, Al-Hasan was from Granada, only some 250 years later.[23] In writing about his travels, al-Hasan demonstrates his awareness of historical and geographical themes of Islamic scholarship. He referred to Ibn Khaldun and other authorities, whom he had read, and he learned of al-Maghili, who was in Kano c.1493, only seventeen years before his own visit to Kano c.1510. Al-Maghili crossed the Sahara to Kano during the reign of Muhammadu Rumfa (1463–99), before travelling on to Songhay. The city of Kano from that time became a religious, economic, and political centre. Rumfa consciously introduced royal-wife seclusion and expanded the institution of concubinage—in a direct attempt to conform to what was perceived to be Islamic norms in North Africa and later the Ottoman Empire.[24]

Because al-Hasan was not an historian but rather a diplomat and pilgrim, his knowledge of history is probably indicative of the importance of history in the thinking of many intellectuals. Al-Hasan was aware that al-Sahili had been instrumental in the construction of the Timbuktu mosque, which reveals knowledge of the history of relations between Andalusia and the Sudan for more than 250 years. The reference to Ibn Khaldun and Ibn Battuta clearly establishes the line of authority based on historical chronicles. Local historical texts, such as the Wangarawa Chronicle of Kano, which also refers to al-Maghili, demonstrate that this sense of history was deep-rooted.[25] Despite the controversy over the authorship and dating of the compilation of the Kano Chronicle, the information in

Scholarly and Sharifian Networks', in *Fès et l'Afrique: relations économiques, culturelles et spirituelles* (Rabat, 1996), 57–71; and Elias Saad, *Social History of Timbuktu: The Role of Muslim Scholars and Notables* (Cambridge, 1983).

[22] John O. Hunwick, 'Studies in *Ta'rikh al-fattash*, III: Ka'ti Origins', *Sudanic Africa*, 11 (2001), 111–14.

[23] Natalie Zemon Davis, *Trickster Travels: A Sixteenth-Century Muslim between Worlds* (New York, 2006).

[24] Murray Last, 'From Sultanate to Caliphate: Kano, 1450–1800 A.D.', in Bawuro M. Barkindo (ed.), *Studies in the History of Kano* (Kano, 1983), 67–91. See also Heidi J. Nast, 'Islam, Gender, and Slavery in West Africa Circa 1500: A Spatial Archaeology of the Kano Palace, Northern Nigeria', *Annals of the Association of American Geographers*, 86:1 (1996), 44–77.

[25] Muhammad A. Al-Hajj, 'A Seventeenth-Century Chronicle of the Origins and Missionary Activities of the Wangarawa', *Kano Studies* 1:4 (1968), 7–42.

that text associates history with the periods of reign of the various *sarki* (kings) of Kano, and hence with political authority and legitimacy.

This tradition of scholarship that connected Andalusia, the Maghreb, and western Sudan became associated with an indigenous class of Muslim scholars in western and central Sudan who were known locally by various names. Those associated with the Saghanughu clan were part of the diaspora of Juula (Dyula) merchant communities in western Sudan and sahel.[26] The pervasiveness of this class of Muslim scholars and teachers can be seen with reference to Muhammad Kaba Saghanughu, who was enslaved in 1777 and sent to Jamaica. Although a young man, he was well educated and claimed to have been on his way to Timbuktu to study law when he was kidnapped and sold. In about 1820, he saw fit to write two related manuscripts, which have been entitled *Kitab al-Salat* [The Book of Praying], which provides details of his educational experiences in West Africa before 1777 and which reflects accurately the Qadiri curriculum of the Saghanughu towns of Futa Jallon and its interior.[27] The history of the Kaba clan, and specifically the Saghanughu clerics, has been reconstructed through the compilation of *silsila*, literally the chain of transmission, collected by Ivor Wilks, among others. Individuals received an *ijaza* or diploma that certified the knowledge received from a specific scholar, including the books studied and the chain of teachers. Wilks published one such document that provides an intellectual pedigree back to Muhammad al-Mustafa Saghanughu.[28]

Therefore historical observation largely arose in documenting pedigree and hence focused on and reflected the major political events of the period. The expulsion of Muslims from Andalusia influenced the transmission of scholarship south of the Sahara. The fall of Granada in 1492, the emergence of a Sharifian dynasty in Marrakesh, and the conquest of Songhay in 1591, provided context for this influence. The extension of Ottoman rule across North Africa and into the Sahara resulted in an alliance with Borno, thereby maintaining links with the central regions of Islam. The predominance of sufism, specifically the Qadiriyya, which developed a major intellectual and spiritual centre in Fez, furthered the interest in historical authority. The jihad of the late seventeenth and eighteenth centuries, culminating in the Sokoto jihad of 1804–8, were legitimized with reference to the initial jihad of the Prophet and subsequent efforts, both spiritual and military, to purify Islam. The history of this period strongly influenced

---

[26] Ivor Wilks, 'The Transmission of Islamic Learning in the Western Sudan', in Jack Goody (ed.), *Literacy in Traditional Societies* (Cambridge, 1968), 162–97.

[27] Yacine Daddi Addoun and Paul E. Lovejoy, 'Muhammad Kaba Saghanughu and the Muslim Community of Jamaica', in Lovejoy (ed.), *Slavery on the Frontiers of Islam* (Princeton, 2004), 201–20; and Daddi Addoun and Lovejoy, 'The Arabic Manuscript of Muhammad Kaba Saghanughu of Jamaica, *c.* 1820', in Annie Paul (ed.), *Creole Concerns: Essays in Honour of Kamau Brathwaite* (Kingston, 2007), 313–41.

[28] Wilks, 'The Transmission of Islamic Learning in the Western Sudan', 162–97.

Muslim scholars to write about their times and the political history of the Islamic regimes.

The expulsion of Muslims from the Iberian peninsula, especially after 1492, punctuated what can be thought of as the 'Andalusia period' from the perspective of western and central Sudan. The period reached its peak during the century of Songhay dominance of western and central Sudan, culminating in the fall of Songhay to Moroccan invasion in 1591–2, during the reign of Sultan al-Mansur of Marrakesh. It should be noted that these events occurred in the year AH 1000; the 1st of Muharram AH 1000 corresponds to AD 19 October 1591. Andalusian influence continued but there was a considerable shift, of historic proportions, with the consolidation of the trans-Atlantic slave trade in the seventeenth and eighteenth centuries. A consideration of African history from the perspective of contemporary reflection and study provides an insight into global history that corrects a major bias and distortion in our understanding of the rise of the 'Atlantic world' and the origins of slavery in the Americas. Through an examination of contemporary Africa's understanding of their own history, it can be seen that the Iberian explosion across the Atlantic was matched by an Iberian explosion across the Sahara into western and central Sudan, with reverberations that are as complex as those in the African diaspora of the Americas.

Despite the fall of Songhay, the tradition of scholarship flourished, first evident in the writings of Ahmad Baba in defence of Songhay and its legitimacy but eventually providing for a movement of jihad that would intensify Muslim scholarship even more. 'Abd al-Rahman al-Sa'di discussed the main texts being studied in Timbuktu, demonstrating both the continuation of scholarship after the fall of Songhay in 1592 and explicitly recounting the most important texts that were read during the sixteenth century. His *Tarikh al-Sudan* is a history of Songhay that also describes what has been called 'the classical, 17th-century Sudanese tradition of Islamic learning'.[29]

It was once thought that the fall of Songhay led to a political crisis in western Sudan, which in turn resulted in the collapse of Islam, yet the thrust of recent research has demonstrated that this was not the case. There was a spread of the sufi brotherhood of the Qadiriyya and its curriculum, reformed in the middle of the eighteenth century, which was an example of the ongoing tradition of scholarship.[30] Qadiri training and scholarship promoted political action and advocacy of jihad to establish regimes that would conform to the shari'a and perhaps even usher in the millennium. Qadiri teaching was based on interpreting history, drawing on the original jihad for inspiration on how to purge society of

---

[29] Hall and Stewart, 'The Historic "Core Curriculum" and the Book Market in Islamic West Africa'. See also John Hunwick (ed.), *Timbuktu and the Songhay Empire: Al-Sa'id's Ta'rikh al-sudan Down to 1613 and Other Contemporary Sources* (Leiden, 1999), 1–270; and Hunwick, 'Studies in the Ta'rikh al-fattash* II: An Alleged Charter of Privilege Issued by Askiya al-hajj Muhammad to the Descendants of Mori Hawgaro', *Sudanic Africa*, 3 (1992), 133–48.

[30] Wilks, 'The Transmission of Islamic Learning in the Western Sudan'.

wrongdoing and institute a regime of equity for Muslims. Of particular note was the emergence of the Kunta family in Mauritania and the area as far east as Timbuktu in the late eighteenth century, and continuing into the nineteenth century.[31] Sayyid al-Mukhtar bin Ahmad bin Abi Bakr al-Kunti al-Kabir, in his *al-Minnah fi I'tiqad Ahl al-Sunnah* [The Gift of the Followers of the Path of Muhammad], examines the history of Songhay and discusses important questions of Islamic law that arose in the administration of empire, including the status and rights of women and children in Muslim society.

The ongoing historical tradition is evident in the biographical accounts collected and collated by al-Talib Muhammad al-Bartili, whose *Fath al-shakur fi ma'rifat a'yan 'ulama' al-Takrur* [The Key Provided by (God) Most-Rewarding for the Knowledge of the Most Learned Scholars of Takrur] is a biographical dictionary of the scholars at Walata, in the sahel to the west of Timbuktu. Al-Bartili summarized the qualifications of each scholar according to the books each had studied. As Chouki El Hamel has demonstrated, al-Bartili provides an overview of the scholarly tradition for at least one part of West Africa for the seventeenth and eighteenth centuries.[32] We can see the tradition in the writings of the founders of the Sokoto Caliphate, Sheikh 'Uthman dan Fodio, his brother, 'Abdullahi dan Fodio, and his son, Muhammad Bello, among many others. 'Abdullahi, who described his training in *Ida' al-husukh man akhadhtu 'anhu min al-shuyukh* [Clarification of the Ambiguous about the Shaykhs with Whom I Studied] reveals an extensive exposure to the scholarship of West Africa, the Maghreb, and the classical Islamic texts.[33] His education was similar to that of his brother. His nephew, Muhammad Bello, wrote a history of the Sokoto jihad, *Infaq al-maysur fi tarikh Bilad al-Takrur* [Dispensing the Wisdom of the History of the Land of Takrur] in 1813, after the jihad had been successfully consolidated in the Hausa heartland and already was extending the frontiers through an aggressive campaign.[34] Not only do these texts recount the history of the times, but a considerable amount about the intellectual context in which these histories were conceived is revealed in the texts.

[31] Charles Stewart and E. K. Stewart, *Islam and Social Order in Mauritania: A Case Study from the Nineteenth Century* (London, 1973); and Hall and Stewart, 'The Historic "Core Curriculum" and the Book Market in Islamic West Africa'.

[32] Chouki El Hamel, *La vie intellectuelle islamique dans le Sahel Ouest-Africain (XVIe–XIXe siècles): Une étude sociale de l'enseignement islamique en Mauritanie et au Nord du Mali (XVIe–XIXe siècles) et traduction annotée de Fath ash-shakur d'al-Bartili al Walati (mort en 1805)* (Paris, 2002).

[33] Hiskett, 'Material Relating to the State of Learning among the Fulani before their Jihad', 550–78. See also 'Abdullah ibn Muhammad dan Fodio, *Diya' al-sultan wa ghayrihi min al-ikhwan fi ahamm ma yutlab 'ilmuhu fi umur al-zaman*, in Muhammad Sani Zahradeen, "Abd Allah ibn Fodio's Contributions to the Fulani Jihad in Nineteenth-Century Hausaland', Ph.D. dissertation, McGill University, 1976, 13–14; and Abdullahi ibn Fodio, *Tazyin al-Waraqat* (Ibadan, 1963).

[34] *The Infaq al-Maysur of Sultan Muhammad Bello written 1227 A.H. 1812/3 A.D.* (Legon, Ghana, 1964).

THE QUESTION OF SLAVERY AND HISTORY

Ahmad Baba's treatise of 1613, *Mi'raj al-su'ud*, was a determining influence in setting the course of trans-Atlantic slavery by codifying limitations on the participation of the Muslim interior in the sale of slaves to Christians.[35] The hidden parallel to the Andalusian and Iberian spheres of expansion revolved around issues of slavery—who could be enslaved, and who could not be enslaved. The focus of Andalusia and Iberia were different, the first across the Sahara, the second across the Atlantic. The slavery issue was confusing. Christians and Muslims in the Mediterranean enslaved each other, but most often for purposes of obtaining a suitable ransom, not for the purpose of acquiring labour or service. In the Muslim context, the question of who could be enslaved and who could not was often based on historical interpretation.

Ahmad Baba's career corresponded with the Moroccan conquest and occupation of Songhay after 1591, which intensified the debate about the legitimacy of enslavement and about who could legally be held as a slave and who should be freed from captivity on religious grounds.[36] Although both Morocco and Songhay were Muslim states, Morocco's subjugation of Songhay revealed that legal opinion could be overridden for political reasons. The expulsion of Muslims from the Iberian peninsula in the late fifteenth century, and the ongoing conflict between Spain and Portugal on the one hand, and the Muslim states of North Africa on the other, has been studied extensively. The conflict among Muslims in the Maghreb was an integral part of this larger picture. The expansion of the Ottoman Porte to the western Mediterranean involved the conquest of Muslim states in an attempt to establish a pan-Islamic empire, but the Ottomans faced resistance from many Muslims, including the Sharifian dynasty of Morocco that was centred in Marrakesh.[37] The dynasty claimed descent from the Prophet Muhammad (as reflected in their designation as *shurfa*, pl. *sharif*), and hence they claimed to be the inheritors of the 'caliphate' of the Prophet. On this basis, the regime not only resisted Ottoman hegemony and opposed the Qadiriyya sufi brotherhood for its support of the Ottomans, but also developed a strategy to obtain the support of Muslim governments south of the Sahara, or otherwise overthrow any governments that opposed their claims to the caliphate.

---

[35] John Hunwick and Fatima Harrak, *Mí'raj al-su'ud: Ahmad Baba's Replies on Slavery* (Rabat, 2000). For a brief biography see John Hunwick, 'Further Light on Ahmad Baba al-Tinbukti', *Research Bulletin*, 2:1 (1966), 19–31; and Mahmoud A. Zouber, *Ahmad Baba de Tombouctou (1556–1627): sa vie et son oeuvre* (Paris, 1977).

[36] In addition to the *Mi'raj al-su'ud*, Ahmad Baba also wrote *Nayl al-ibtihaj bi-tatriz al-dibaj and Taj al-din fi ma yajib 'ala al-muluk*; see Hunwick and Harrak, *Ahmad Baba's Replies on Slavery*.

[37] The attempt to unify Morocco was partially a response to the crisis in Iberia in the fifteenth century. Initially promoted by Imam al-Djazuli (d. 1465), the movement advocated no cooperation with Christians and from a dozen *zawiya* and *ribat* resisted Portuguese encroachment after the conquest of Ceuta in 1415 and Tanger in 1437; see Abitol, *Tombouctou et les Arma*, 35–9.

According to Michael Abitol, the intention was to establish a large Muslim state in the west that stretched from Borno in the region of Lake Chad to the Atlantic and northward to include the Maghreb.[38] In resisting Ottoman encroachment from Algiers, the Sharifian dynasty at times found an ally in Spain and, after the defeat of the Spanish armada in 1588, from England.[39] Particularly ominous for the development of trans-Atlantic slavery, the Sharifian dynasty, for much of its foreign exchange (as noted above), relied on the export of sugarcane that was produced on plantations worked by black slaves in the region of Sous.

As a member of the Timbuktu 'ulama', Ahmad Baba was adamantly opposed to the Sharifian invasion of Songhay. Because he was also associated with the rival Qadiriyya, he was imprisoned and removed to Morocco along with other captives who without doubt were devout Muslims. Though he was eventually released and returned to Timbuktu in 1615, his experience in captivity under conditions of dubious legality made him uniquely qualified to write on the historical context of slavery, which is perhaps one reason that his opinions weighed so heavily in subsequent Muslim scholarship in West Africa. Morocco's subjugation of Songhay pitted Muslim state against Muslim state, and through captivity Ahmad Baba undoubtedly came into contact with enslaved people of diverse backgrounds, an experience that must have informed his commentary. Moreover, Songhay had promoted enslavement of non-Muslims as state policy in the sixteenth century, especially under Askia Dawud (1549–82), who settled large numbers of enslaved people on agricultural estates along the middle Niger River, as well as exporting slaves to North Africa.[40] In both Morocco and Songhay, therefore, the employment of slave labour on agricultural estates, erstwhile plantations, was part of state policy. The importance of slave labour in state policy means that the legal opinions on who could be legitimately enslaved had special meaning, especially in understanding the role of ethnicity in identifying who was protected and who was not. The arguments were based on history.

Ahmad Baba drew upon a long tradition of commentary on the subject of slavery, and he was well aware of the importance of slavery to the economies of both Songhay and Morocco. Muslim scholars in West Africa, as well as in North Africa, whom he quotes or summarizes, had already examined the issue of legitimacy in enslavement. This legal tradition predated European slaving on

---

[38] As *shurfa*, they claimed to possess *baraka*, or blessing, that could only be inherited by blood from the Prophet; the *shurfa* had been invited to Drāʿ in Morocco in the twelfth century and were widely respected; see Abitol, *Tombouctou et les Arma*, 35.

[39] Abitol, *Tombouctou et les Arma*, 40–6.

[40] On the slave estates of Songhay see especially John Hunwick, 'Notes on Slavery in the Songhay Empire', in John Ralph Willis (ed.), *Slaves and Slavery in Muslim Africa* (London, 1985); and N. G. Kodjo, 'Contribution à l'étude des tribus dites servile du Songai', *Bulletin de l'IFAN*, 38:4 (1976), 790–812. See also Paul E. Lovejoy, *Transformations in Slavery: A History of Slavery in Africa*, 2nd edn (Cambridge, 2000), 31–2.

the African coast and the rise of the trans-Atlantic slave trade, and of course involved relations between Christians and Muslims, especially in the Mediterranean. Some scholars, and Ahmad Baba was one of them, argued that the non-Muslims in sub-Saharan Africa, although not Christians, should be treated in a similar fashion. That is, they were subject to enslavement, unless they were protected through the payment of a discriminatory tax (*jizya*). It is argued here that this debate helped shape the contours of the European trade along the African coast, which resulted in the settlement of enslaved Africans in the Americas. The connection between sugar production in southern Morocco in the region of Sous and the export of sugar to England especially has been noted above.

Ahmad Baba was of the opinion that people from Muslim countries in sub-Saharan Africa, including Borno, Songhay, and the Hausa cities, should not be enslaved, and if individuals from these states were found in a state of captivity they should be freed without reservation. He based this fatwa on the basis of history, that people who had been long under Muslim government were protected by law. Ahmad Baba's relative, Mahmud bin ʻUmar bin Muhammad Aqit, who was the qadi of Timbuktu between 1498 and 1548, issued a legal opinion that any Muslim who had been enslaved and who came from a country that was considered to have embraced Islam voluntarily should be freed. Again, historical precedent of citizenship was the determining factor.[41] These scholars wrote at a time when Songhay and Borno dominated much of the West African interior and were actively raiding in the quest of slaves who were clearly not Muslims. But in North Africa there was considerable confusion as to whether or not colour of skin was enough to identify those who could be enslaved. As would later be true for the trans-Atlantic slave trade, those who had been enslaved were often identified with the place where they were first traded, in this case Songhay and Borno, which made it difficult to determine whether or not the enslaved were actually from those places or from somewhere else and only passing through these states. These early fatwa attempted to address the questions of legitimacy over who had been enslaved in terms of whether or not they had come from countries that had been historically Muslim.[42]

In the seventeenth and eighteenth centuries, Islamic schools across West Africa taught the principles of history that conceptualized slavery in ethnic terms that derived from Ahmad Baba and the scholars to whom he referred. This considerable continuity in thinking about the relationship between ethnicity and slavery in West Africa derived from the educational system associated with the Qadiriyya

---

[41] Lovejoy, *Transformations in Slavery*, 46.

[42] Paul E. Lovejoy, 'The Context of Enslavement in West Africa: Ahmad Baba and the Ethics of Slavery', in Jane Landers (ed.), *Slaves, Subjects, and Subversives: Blacks in Colonial Latin America* (Albuquerque, 2006), 9–38; and John Hunwick, 'Islamic Law and Polemics over Race and Slavery in North and West Africa (16th–19th Century)', in Shaun E. Marmon (ed.), *Slavery in the Islamic Middle East* (Princeton, 1999), 45–6.

brotherhood with which Ahmad Baba identified.[43] In the eighteenth century, the Tuareg scholar Jibril bin 'Umar relied on this earlier tradition in advocating jihad to confront injustices arising from the violation of the free status of Muslims through their enslavement. Jibril's student 'Uthman dan Fodio, along with his son, Muhammad Bello, and his brother, Abdullahi dan Fodio, were strongly influenced by this literary tradition, and in their turn revitalized the arguments of Ahmad Baba in justifying jihad to protect Muslims from wrongful enslavement and to sanction the enslavement of the enemies of jihad, even if those enemies were Muslims. The many references in the writings of the Sokoto leadership reveal the extent of the intellectual and ideological debt to the tradition of scholarship epitomized by Ahmad Baba.[44] This scholarly tradition had profound consequences for the later imposition of Islamic rule. Governments that were in fact ruled by Muslims were declared apostate, just as Askia Muhammad had earlier pronounced Sunni 'Ali's regime in Songhay in 1492–3 and al-Mansur had denounced the government of Songhay in 1591. These charges were based on historical interpretation, whether or not military action was ultimately justified. Interpretations of history were fundamental to the justification of state action.

Ethnicity and the political discourse of enslavement and legitimacy in Islamic context reflected an historical perspective and sense of geography and ethnicity that are well portrayed in the extant literature of the centuries before *c*.1800. Citizenship was associated with free status and being Muslim, both of which were confirmed with reference to history. Arabic was the common language, although the lands of Islam incorporated people who spoke many languages, from Berber to Songhay, Mande, Hausa, and Kanuri. The resulting multi-linguistic setting forced the intelligentsia and merchant class at least to speak more than one language and to varying degrees to be literate in Arabic. The question of citizenship was contested, however. The 'Alawi sultan of Morocco, Mawlay Isma'il, who reigned from 1672 to 1727, enacted a decree in 1699 that enslaved all blacks in Morocco on the assumption that they had once been slaves or were descended from slaves. In this way, Isma'il amassed a large slave army, based on the re-enslavement through conscription of young blacks in southern Morocco and the purchase of slaves from south of the Sahara.[45] He also confronted history by denying the rights of *haratin* to free status, and the subsequent opposition to his decree was based on historical argument.

---

[43] Wilks, 'The Transmission of Islamic Learning in the Western Sudan'.

[44] The literature is extensive, but see Zahradeen, ''Abd Allah ibn Fodio's Contributions', 13–14, 20; Shehu Yamusa, 'Political Ideas of the Jihad Leaders: Being Translation and Edition of Diya 'l-hukkam and Usul al-Siyasa', MA thesis, Ahmadu Bello University (1975), 270–85.

[45] Chouki El-Hamel, '"Race", Slavery and Islam in Maghribi Mediterranean Thought: The Question of the *Haratin* in Morocco', *Journal of North African Studies*, 7:3 (2002), 29–52.

CONCLUSION

A perspective on how Africans viewed their own history in the period 1400–1800 necessarily draws upon known documentation and the ability to date oral narratives and myths, and how these might or might not have changed over time. Moreover, the coverage here, focusing on the interior of West Africa, is not intended to be comprehensive, even with respect to Muslim areas of Africa, and the chronicles of Coptic Ethiopia demonstrate that a literary tradition was not only confined to Muslim records. Chronologically, there is no particular logic to begin this discussion in 1400 or to end it in 1800. While the focus has been on this period, where necessary or appropriate earlier and later time periods have been assessed to demonstrate continuities or disjunctures of relevance to an assessment of how people conceptualized the past.

TIMELINE/KEY DATES

1324 Mansa Musa of Mali performs pilgrimage to Mecca
1330s Construction of Great Mosque (Dyingere Ber) in Timbuktu
1350 Ibn Batuta visits Mali
1464 Sonni Ali becomes ruler of Songhay
1492 Fall of Granada
1554 Sharifian rule established in Marrakesh
1492–1528 Askia Muhammad
1492–8 al-Maghili in Kano
1463–99 Reign of Muhammad Rumfa of Kano
1482 Portuguese build Elmina Castle
1525 Ottoman occupation of Algiers
1549–82 Askia Dawud, ruler of Songhay
1564 Mai Idris Alooma, ruler of Borno
1579–1603 Ahmed al-Mansur, ruler of Marrakesh
1591 Morocco invasion of Songhay
1713 Bambara state of Segu established
1725 Jihad of Futa Jallon
1804–8 Jihad of Uthman dan Fodio

KEY HISTORICAL SOURCES

'Abdullahi dan Fodio, *Idā' al-nusūkh man akhadhtu 'anhu min al-shuyūkh*, in Mervyn Hiskett, 'Material Relating to the State of Learning among the Fulani before their Jihad', *Bulletin of the School of Oriental and African Studies*, 19 (1957), 550–78.

—— *Tazyīn al-Waraqāt*, trans. Mervyn Hiskett (Ibadan, 1963).

Ahmad Baba, *Mi'raj al-su'ud*, in John Hunwick and Fatima Harrak (eds.), *Mi'raj al-su'ud: Ahmad Baba's Replies on Slavery* (Rabat, 2000).

Al-Hajj, Muhammad A., 'A Seventeenth Century Chronicle of the Origins and Missionary Activities of the Wangarawa', *Kano Studies*, 1:4 (1968), 7–42.

'Abd al-Rahman al-Sa'di bin 'Abd Allah, *Tarikh al-Sudan*, in John Hunwick (ed.), *Timbuktu and the Songhay Empire: Al-Sá'di's* Tarikh al-Sudan *Down to 1613 and Other Contemporary Sources* (Leiden, 1999).

Conrad, David C., *Sunjata: A West African Epic of the Mande People* (Indianapolis, IN, 2004).

Edgar, Frank (ed.), *Litafi na tatsuniyoyi na Hausa*, 2 vols. (Belfast, 1911).

El Hamel, Chouki, *La vie intellectuelle islamique dans le Sahel Ouest-Africain (XVIe–XIXe siècles): Une étude social de l'enseignement islamique en Mauritanie et au Nord du Mali (XVIe–XIXe siècles) et traduction annotée de* Fath ash-shakur *d'al-Bartili al Walati (mort en 1805)* (Paris, 2002).

Hunwick, John, *Shari'a in Songhay: The Replies of al-Maghili to the Questions of Askia al-Hajj Muhammad* (London, 1985).

—— *et al.* (eds.), *Arabic Literature of Africa*, vol. 2: *The Writings of Central Sudanic Africa* (Leiden, 1995); vol. 4: *The Writings of Western Sudanic Africa* (Leiden, 2003).

Lange, Dierk, *Le Diwan des Sultans du (Kanem) Bornu: Chronologie et Histoire d'un Royaume Africain* (Wiesbaden, 1977).

Le Sourd, Michel, 'Tarikh el Kawar', *Bulletin de l'I.F.A.N.*, ser. B, 8 (1946), 1–54.

Levtzion, Nehemia and Hopkins, J. F. P. (eds.), *Corpus of Early Arabic Sources for West Africa* (Cambridge, 1981).

Levtzion, Nehemia and Spaulding, Jay (eds.), *Medieval West Africa: Views from Arab Scholars and Merchants* (Princeton, 2003).

Mahmud Ka'ti, *Ta'rīkh al-fattāsh fī akhbār al-buldān wa 'l-juyūsh wa-akābir al-nās*, ed. and trans. O. Houdas and M. Delafosse (1913; Paris, 1964).

Palmer, H. R. (ed. and trans.), *Sudanese Memoirs, Being mainly Translations of a Number of Arabic Manuscripts Relating to the Central and Western Sudan*, 3 vols. (Lagos, 1928).

Urvoy, Yves, 'Chronique d'Agades', *Journal de la Sociétés Africanistes*, 4 (1934), 145–77.

'Uthman dan Fodio, *Bayan wujub al hijra 'ala 'I-'ibad* (1804); ed. and trans. F. H. El Masri, *The Exposition of Obligation of Emigration upon the Servants of God* (Khartoum, 1978).

BIBLIOGRAPHY

Abitol, Michel, *Tombouctou et les Arma: De la conquête marocaine du Soudan nigérien en 1591 à l'hégémonie de l'Empire Peul du Macina en 1833* (Paris, 1979).

Ajayi, J. F. Ade and Crowder, Michael (eds.), *History of West Africa*, vol. 1, 3rd edn (London, 1985).

Cissoko, Sekene Mody, *Tombouctou et l'Empire Songhay: Epanouissement du Soudan Nigerien aux XVe–XVIe siècles* (Dakar, 1975).

Davis, Natalie Zemon, *Trickster Travels: A Sixteenth-Century Muslim between Worlds* (New York, 2006).

Dienne, Doudou (ed.), *Les Routes d'al-Andalus: patrimoine commun et identité plurielle* (Paris, 2001).

Haïdara, Ismaël Diadié, *L'Espagne musulmane et l'Afrique subsaharienne* (Bamako, 1997).

Hall, Bruce and Stewart, Charles, 'The Historic "Core Curriculum", and the Book Market in Islamic West Africa', in Graziano Kratli and Ghislaine Lydon (eds.) *One Thousand Years of Trans-Saharan Book Trade* (Leiden, 2011).

Levtzion, Nehemia, 'A Critical Study of "Tarikh al-fattash"', *Bulletin of the School of Oriental and African Studies*, 34, 3 (1971), 571–93.

——*Islam in West Africa: Religion, Society and Politics to 1800* (Aldershot, 1994).

——and Pouwels, Randall L. (eds.), *The History of Islam in Africa* (Oxford, 2000).

Lovejoy, Paul E. (ed.), *Slavery on the Frontiers of Islam* (Princeton, NJ, 2004).

Martin, B. G., 'Mai Idris of Bornu and the Ottoman Turks, 1576–78', *International Journal of African Historical Studies*, 3:4 (1972), 470–90.

Mauny, Raymond, *Tableau geographique de l'Ouest African au Moyen Age, Moyen les sources ecrites, la tradition et l'archeologie* (Dakar, 1961).

Moumouni, Seyni, *Vie et oeuvre du Cheik Uthmân Dan Fodio (1754–1817): De l'Islam au soufisme* (Paris, 2008).

Parry, J. H., *The Age of Reconnaissance* (New York, 1963).

Saad, Elias, *Social History of Timbuktu: The Role of Muslim Scholars and Notables* (Cambridge, 1983).

Wilks, Ivor, 'The Transmission of Islamic Learning in the Western Sudan', in Jack Goody (ed.), *Literacy in Traditional Societies* (London, 1968), 162–97.

Willis, John Ralph (ed.), *Slaves and Slavery in Muslim Africa*, 2 vols. (London, 1985).

Yahya, Dahiru, *Morocco in the Sixteenth Century: Problems and Patterns in African Foreign Policy* (Atlantic Highlands, NJ, 1981).

Zouber, Mahmoud A., *Ahmad Baba de Tombouctou (1556–1627): sa vie et son oeuvre* (Paris, 1977).

Chapter 11

Philology and History

Donald R. Kelley

Philology refers to the critical study of literary texts with regard to style, structure, and historical meaning. In this connection it has been associated for centuries with the study of history, understood especially in the sense of the past of Western (and by extension non-Western) culture through its written remains, and with the human sciences more generally. 'The modern conception of history', declared Eugenio Garin, 'appeared on the terrain of humanist "philology" at just the point where the "consciousness" of the "novelty" of humanism arose.'[1]

In Renaissance Europe history was regarded as one of the humanities (*studia humanitatis*) and in that connection had close relations with both grammar and rhetoric and so philology. On the one hand, the art of writing history was virtually identified with rhetoric; on the other hand, 'history' referred to the most basic, literal mode of interpretation; and philology represented the critical study of texts developed out of this. 'History' (*historia*) began as a narration of discrete but causally connected facts and then of words, and as such, ever since Aristotle, it has been contrasted with poetry and so with philosophy—though in its narrative form it was celebrated as 'philosophy teaching by example'. In more general usage history was defined in the early modern period as the 'knowledge of what exists' (*cognitio quod est*) and 'knowledge of singulars' (*cognitio singularium*), thus reinforcing the notion of neutral 'things', 'particulars', and 'facts', and independent of theoretical or formal considerations. As a modern commentator on Aristotle and author of an essay on 'the art of history' put it, 'poetry speaks more of universals, history of singulars'.[2] By implication, as Rodolfus Goclenius wrote, 'history is the study of particulars, theory of universals' (*historia particularis notitia est, theoria universalis*).[3]

Philology as the criticism of texts has a long history, going back to ancient Greek, Roman, and Byzantine practices, although it has since been extended to other

[1] Eugenio Garin, review of Franco Simone, 'La coscienze del rinascimento francese', *Rinascimento*, 1 (1950), 97.

[2] Antonio Riccobono, 'De poetica', in E. Kessler (ed.), *Aristotles Latine interpretibus variis* (Berlin, 1995), 744.

[3] Rodolfus Goclenius, *Lexicon philosophicum* (Frankfurt, 1613), 626.

languages. Textual self-awareness is already apparent in Homer, but it was the Alexandrine 'grammarians' and 'critics' who defined a scholarly field of textual study. Eratosthenes in particular coined the term *philologus* to indicate the encyclopaedic student of literature (rather than the loquacious, disputatious *philologus* of Plato), and he called his discipline 'many-sided philologia'. Its convergence with the art of history was based on its utility in the study of documentary and literary sources, and in the course of time it became one of the principal auxiliary sciences (*Hilfswissenschaften*) of history. This was the link between the modern science of history and Renaissance 'method', as reflected especially in the handbook of Jean Bodin, by which the 'method of history' succeeded the Italianate 'arts of history' (*artes historicae*), and similar books by French and German authors.[4] Bodin criticized the old imperial scheme of the four world monarchies ending with the contemporary 'Holy Roman Empire of the German Nation', and the equally parochial claims of other nations about their native origins, and he studied the order of reading historians and their sources. Even more important than Bodin's controversial work was the foundational book by Joseph Justus Scaliger, *Opus novum De emendatione temporum* [Study on the Improvement of Time] (1583), which offered a systematic criticism of Western historical chronology; Scaliger was joined by other humanist scholars in the recovery, editing, and criticism of ancient texts in the 'age of erudition'.[5]

But the humanist canon is much older. There was some tenuous continuity in the Middle Ages, for example in Martianus Capella's *De nuptiis Mercurii et Philologiae* [On the Marriage of Mercury and Philology], which represented the aforesaid seven arts as handmaidens to *philologia*. Philology and history in particular met in the work of the 'father' of Renaissance humanism, Francesco Petrarca, or Petrarch. His sense of history came from his living emotionally in another and better age, Roman antiquity, and his devotion to philology came from his desire to imitate precisely the words and thought of ancients such as Cicero, whose private letters he sought to emulate.[6] Leonardo Bruni, an early disciple, wrote that 'Francesco Petrarch was the first with a talent sufficient to recognize and call back to light the ancient elegance of the lost and extinguished style'.[7] As Petrarch himself wrote,

Among the many subjects that interested me, I dwelt especially upon antiquity, for our own age has repelled me, so that, had it not been for the love of those dear to me, I should have preferred to have been born in any other period than our own. In order to forget my own time,

[4] Jean Bodin, *Methodus ad facilem historiarum cognitionem* (Paris, 1566); trans. Beatrice Reynolds, *Method for the Easy Comprehension of History* (New York, 1945).

[5] Anthony Grafton, *Joseph Scaliger: A Study in the History of Classical Scholarship*, 2 vols. (Oxford, 1983–93).

[6] Donald R. Kelley, *Renaissance Humanism* (Boston, 1991).

[7] Quoted ibid., 1.

I have constantly striven to place myself in spirit in other ages, and consequently I delighted in history.[8]

This ambition was realized in Petrarch's *De Viris illustribus* [On Illustrious Men]. He possessed a manuscript of Homer, though he could not read it. Yet there was a Christian aspect to his attitude, for it was the reading of Augustine that led him 'from the contemplation of space to that of time'.[9] This view reinforced the sense of discrimination underlying Petrarch's historical criticism, which enabled him, for example, to expose the forged 'Habsburg donation' which the Emperor Charles IV gave him to examine. This was the first of many examples of the applications of philology to historical scholarship.

Other humanists carried on the search, criticism, and eventually publication of the literary remains of antiquity, including classical historians. Translation from Greek into Latin was crucial in the determination of historical and cultural differences. Lorenzo Valla's Latin versions of Herodotus and Thucydides, and translations by other scholars from the Greek, appeared early on in the age of print, as did editions of Livy, Tacitus, and other Latin historians. Vernacular translations followed in quick succession, such as Claude de Seyssel's renderings of Valla's Latin translations, while national, urban, and family histories and biographies were published along classical lines, though Latin continued to be the main vehicle of transmission. Leonardo Bruni established a long tradition of Florentine historiography on the model of Livy,[10] while Flavio Biondo surveyed the downfall of the Roman Empire and the rise of modern Europe, and his work was built on by various later scholars.[11] Textual criticism proceeded apace, and scholarship became cumulative as well as more widespread.

In the first half of the fifteenth century humanist book hunters, following Petrarch and Coluccio Salutati, extended their searches and connections across what Francesco Barbaro called the 'republic of letters' (*respublica litterarum*).[12] Like Jerome, Salutati defended the 'New Learning', pagan literature, against changes of anti-Christian bias, and indeed he argued that 'Christian doctrine must, by a kind of necessity, begin with grammar'.[13] Manuscripts of Cicero's letters and orations were discovered, as were the works of Tacitus and many others, including Greek manuscripts from before the time of Manuel

---

[8] Petrarch, 'Familiar Letters', in *Petrarch: The First Modern Scholar and Man of Letters*, ed. and trans. James Harvey Robinson (New York, 1898), 64–5.

[9] Petrarch, 'The Ascent of Mt. Ventoux', in Ernst Cassirer, Paul Oskar Kristeller, and John Herman Randall, Jr. (eds.), *The Renaissance Philosophy of Man* (Chicago, 1948), 42.

[10] See ch. 17 by William J. Connell in this volume.

[11] Eric Cochrane, *Historians and Historiography of the Italian Renaissance* (Chicago, 1981); and Donald J. Wilcox, *The Development of Florentine Humanist Historiography in the Fifteenth Century* (Cambridge, Mass., 1969).

[12] Poggio Bracciolini, *Two Renaissance Book Hunters: The Letters of Poggius Bracciolini to Nicolaus de Niccolis*, trans. Phyllis Gordon (New York, 1974), 199.

[13] Coluccio Salutati, 'De Tyranno', in Ephraim Emerton (ed.), *Humanism and Tyranny: Studies in the Italian Trecento* (Cambridge, 1925), 351.

Chrysoloras, teacher of Bruni, who was the translator of Plato and Aristotle. The early books of Livy were sought largely in vain, and the conjectures of Valla did little to restore them. Many other manuscripts were the object of an endless quest extending over several centuries and uncounted languages. Tacitus was one of the most remarkable and influential discoveries. Medieval sources were also included in the chase, and in 1425 Poggio Bracciolini reported the discovery not only of some Tacitus but also a copy of Vincent of Beauvais's *Speculum*. He and Barbaro corresponded extensively over the business of book-hunting. Among other Italian scholars, Angelo Poliziano (Politian) studied Homer, Aristotle, Roman law, and Hellenistic literature, and his *Miscellanies* contained emendations and corrections of many classical authors and the *Digest* (a sixth-century compendium of Roman law). The collection and support of private and then public libraries also enhanced the work of humanists.

The fall of Constantinople brought a growing tide of Byzantine scholars to Italy, though a few had fled earlier.[14] These included Chrysoloras, George Gemistos Pletho, his pupil (later Cardinal) Basilios Bessarion, and George Trapezuntius, bringing with them the old debate about Plato versus Aristotle, although soon historical criticism diverted the debate away from doctrine to scholarship, especially through the Greek editions of Aldo Manuzio. The influence of Greek thought was enhanced by translations into Latin, such as those by Bruni of Aristotle and those by Marsilio Ficino of Plato, and into French, as for example those by Claude de Seyssel. Of particular importance were the scientific treatises of Galen and others which joined the intellectual tradition. Natural science in the Renaissance was primarily a bookish and therefore a philological pursuit, although empirical methods came to predominate even before Francis Bacon's time.[15] Yet Bacon himself defended the history of books, of 'literature', as a necessary complement to the history of nature itself.[16]

In the fifteenth century, roughly contemporaneous with the invention of printing, Italian humanism revolutionized textual scholarship by shifting from medieval commentary to grammatical, or philological, annotations. Filippo Beroaldo, Ermolao Barbaro, Niccolò Perotti, and especially Angelo Poliziano, among many others, published 'observations' on classical texts, discussing questions of both fact and method. Poliziano's *Miscellanea*, for example, followed the classical precedent of Aulus Gellius's *Noctes atticae* [Attic Nights] in presenting small erudite essays on points of historical and biographical fact, and he had disciples in France and Germany as well as Italy.

---

[14] N. G. Wilson, *From Byzantium to Italy* (Baltimore, 1992).

[15] Nancy Siraisi, *History, Medicine, and the Traditions of Renaissance Learning* (Ann Arbor, 2007).

[16] Francis Bacon, 'Advancement of Learning', in James Spedding (ed.), *Philosophical Works* (London, 1905), 130.

These notes were also often filled with personal polemic and invective, for such was the style of the 'gladiators of the Renaissance', fashioned just in time for the printed book. Most important, as Anthony Grafton has shown, were the scholarly practices of Angelo Poliziano and his followers, which represented the beginning of a 'new philology', including not only conjectural emendation and the establishing of critical editions of ancient texts but also forgeries, as with the pseudo-Ciceronian *Consolatio* published in 1583 by Carlo Sigonio. As Grafton says, 'Forgery and philology fell and rose together, in the Renaissance as in Hellenistic Alexandria'.[17]

One aspect of the humanist method, besides its historical orientation, was its comparative tendencies, which were inherent in the art of translation. In his essay 'On the Correct Way to Translate', Leonardo Bruni noted the importance of knowing both languages—Greek and Latin—to understand cultural and linguistic difference; and he distinguished between literal meaning and intellectual sense and gave many examples of the mistakes of medieval translators, adding that 'there has never been anything said in Greek that cannot be said in Latin'.[18] Valla wrote extensively on the 'elegances' (*elegantiae*) of the Latin language, with critical comments on biblical translation continued by Erasmus. 'Who does not know', asked Valla, 'that when the Latin language flourishes, all studies and disciplines thrive, as they are ruined when it perishes?'[19] Hence the urge toward both 'restitution' and 'imitation', which at its most naive produced that (potentially anti-Christian) Ciceronianism debated by Erasmus, Julius Caesar Scaliger, Etienne Dolet, Carlo Sigonio, and other humanists. Hence, too, the temptation to compose works in the style of one ancient author or another was itself a sign of a growing mastery of 'elegant' Latin.

From his base in Latin rhetoric—and on the 'authority of antiquity'—Valla applied his critical methods to canon and Roman law, and biblical scholarship as well as the classics. His *Elegantiae Latinae linguae libri sex* [Elegancies of the Latin Language] (1444) represented a basis for critical historical method as well as being a handbook of classical literature, and he contributed to history itself with his study of Ferdinand of Spain. Valla's critique of Aristotelian philosophy, rejecting the transcendentals and categories for correct and ordinary usage, raised history above philosophy.[20] His most famous accomplishment was in exposing the 'Donation of Constantine' as a forgery. Many forgeries were committed as well as uncovered not only in the Renaissance but also in the Middle Ages, and indeed

---

[17] Anthony Grafton, *Defenders of the Text: The Traditions of Scholarship in an Age of Science, 1450–1800* (Harvard, 1991), 103.

[18] Leonardo Bruni, 'On the Correct Way to Translate', in Gordon Griffiths, James Hankins, and David Thompson (eds.), *The Humanism of Leonardo Bruni: Selected Texts* (Binghamton, NY, 1987), 217–29, at 228.

[19] Lorenzo Valla, *Elegantiae Latinae linguae libri sex* (1444), bk. 1, preface, in *Opera omnia*, ed. E. Garin, vol. 1 (Turin, 1962), 4.

[20] Kelley, *Renaissance Humanism*, 20–50.

canon lawyers necessarily became adept at detecting false documents used against the Church. Forgery and textual criticism developed hand in hand in this period. In this same age of confessional conflict and the printed book, classical scholarship also advanced to higher levels of insight and emendation, especially in the work of such masters of the Renaissance 'art of criticism' (*ars critica*) as Henri Estienne, Joseph Justus Scaliger (son of the aforementioned Julius Caesar Scaliger), Justus Lipsius, and Isaac Casaubon, who carried Erasmus's and Budé's project of 'restitution' beyond the limits of the Western tradition.[21]

Erasmus, who was first to publish Valla's notes on the New Testament, went on to publish a new critical edition of the Bible to rival the Vulgate, wanted to see Scriptures translated into vernacular languages, and, with Martin Luther among others, took up the charge for Germany. 'I do not think that even Theology herself, the queen of all sciences', Erasmus wrote, defending Valla's work, 'will consider it beneath her dignity to be handled and be given due attention by her maid, Grammar.'[22] With this came the development of a theory of translation and interpretation, which was formulated by Matthias Flacius Illyricus in his seminal treatise on sacred hermeneutics. Drawing on the rhetorical and exegetical traditions, Flacius founded a systematic science of biblical interpretation. 'It is one thing to understand a proposition in itself,' wrote Johann Chladenius in the eighteenth century, 'and another to understand it as being presented and asserted by someone.'[23] The hermeneutical tradition shifts emphasis from abstract reason to cultural meaning, from the sacred to the profane, and so to the various levels of language from the literal to the analogical and allegorical to cultural context. The philological method reached its first height in Richard Simon's *Histoire critique du Vieux Testament* [A Critical History of the Old Testament] (1678), who then extended his criticism to the New Testament, and it was continued through the works of the neologists of the eighteenth century.[24] For Simon and his followers the Bible was a flawed human document, composed by many hands, and needed external evidence to enable it to be corrected. Along with this came a sceptical view of miracles and the assumption of the superiority of the Judaic tradition.

In France the major follower of Valla, and rival of Erasmus, was Guillaume Budé, who wrote a learned essay on the praise of philology, annotations on the *Digest*, including remarks on the Bible, and his *De Asse et partibus ejus* [On the Pound and its Parts] (1514), a study of ancient coinage.[25] Most important was his *Comentarii linguae graecae* [Commentaries on the Greek Language] (1529), which

---

[21] Jean Jehasse, *La Renaissance de la critique* (Lyon, 1976).

[22] Hans Hillerbrand (ed.), *Erasmus and His Age* (New York, 1970).

[23] Chladenius, 'On the Concept of Interpretation', in Kurt Mueller-Vollmer (ed.), *The Hermeneutics Reader* (Oxford, 1985), 56.

[24] W. Neil, 'The Criticism and Theological Use of the Bible, 1799–1950', in S. L. Greenslade (ed.), *The Cambridge History of the Bible*, vol. 3: *The West from the Reformation to the Present* (Cambridge, 1963), 238–93.

[25] Donald R. Kelley, *Foundations of Modern Historical Scholarship* (New York, 1970), ch. 2.

provided the foundation of Greek lexicography down to the present day. 'Once an ornament', wrote Budé, 'philology is today the means of revival and restoration.'[26] Like other French scholars, he argued that the 'lamp' of learning, especially the new humanist jurisprudence, had passed in the reign of Francis I from Italy to France; indeed, it was Valla's *Elegantiae* that had led Budé to his study of the *Digest* and his criticisms of interpolations by both the medieval commentator Accursius and the Byzantine editor Tribonian. Valla's sense of history through stylistic change was intensified by Budé, who had an informal threefold periodization (antiquity, a dark middle age, and the modern age). For Budé the ultimate aim of *philologia*—which he called his 'cause' and even his 'second wife'—remained the same: the 'restitution' (*restitutio*) not only of passages in corrupt texts but of 'letters' and of 'antiquity' as a whole. History for Budé was not only the 'interpretation of antiquity' but also the 'mistress of life' (according to Cicero), which led to his comparisons between Roman and French institutions and the whole tradition of legal and institutional history.[27] After Budé the great triumvirate of humanists of the first rank were, according to Ulrich von Wilamowitz-Moellendorf, Joseph Scaliger, Isaac Casaubon, and Casaubon's father-in-law, the great scholar-printer Henri Estienne; and they were accompanied by lesser lights, including Adrien Turnèbe, Denis Lambin, and Marc-Antoine Muret. By the later seventeenth century French was beginning to replace Latin as the language of scholarship, as seen in the *Dictionnaire historique et critique* [Historical and Critical Dictionary] (1695–7) of Pierre Bayle and the proliferation of learned journals.

PHILOLOGY AND RELATED 'DISCIPLINES'

Allied to philology in the West was the science of chronology, which had its roots in lists of ancient kings and Christian attempts to synchronize their tradition, based on the Old Testament, with that of the Greeks and Romans.[28] Eusebius's *Chronicon* was the foundational text in this tradition, and of later efforts culminating in Joseph Justus Scaliger's *Opus novum De emendatione temporum*, which exploited classical texts in correlating dates, including recorded historical as well as astronomical events. He was given the first wholly research professorship at the new University of Leiden, where Justus Lipsius, Hugo Grotius, and G. J. Vossius also taught, so that the Netherlands came to replace France as the leader of the scholarly world. The major work of Lipsius centred on his editions of Tacitus, which, since the rediscovery of the latter's works in the fifteenth century, had

---

[26] Guillaume Budé, *De Philologia*, in *De studio litterarum* (Basel, 1533), 351.
[27] Guillaume Budé, *De asse et partibus ejus* (Lyon, 1551), fol. 141.
[28] Donald J. Wilcox, *The Measure of Times Past* (Chicago, 1987).

accumulated a large amount of commentary, especially on *Germania*.[29] Among Vossius's significant works was a history of Greek and Latin historians.[30]

Meanwhile, in Europe, historiography—in the sense of the writing of narrative histories—was being pursued along official and especially national lines, so that history became both a form of ideology and a government-supported endeavour. Yet hired *historiographes du roi* (or *de la ville*), often trained and employed as lawyers, were open to the growing practice and theory of historical criticism. What Bruni had done for Florence and Flavio Biondo for Italy as a whole, Paolo Emilio tried to do for France, Polydore Vergil for England, Beatus Rhenanus for Germany, and other followers of Flavio Biondo for the rest of the 'barbarian' nations established on the ruins of the ancient Roman Empire. The most famous myth, accepted by humanist historians like Paolo Emilio and Polydore Vergil, was that of Trojan origins, which bestowed a spurious antiquity on the French and English monarchies, and other fables were exposed in the wake of national and religious pride and bias, such as Charlemagne's founding of the University of Paris. The students of Jacques Cujas introduced the methods of legal humanism into the study of national history. These included the brothers Pierre and François Pithou and Etienne Pasquier, who began to study the antiquities of France and French literature. Jean du Tillet brought archival sources into the realm of official historiography. Criticism became hypercriticism as the Jesuit Daniel Papebroch challenged the authenticity of documents that showed the supposed antiquity of the Benedictine order. This charge was refuted by Jean Mabillon, a monk of that order, who, in his foundational *De re diplomatica* [On the Science of Diplomatics] (1681), formulated the proper rules for the criticism of medieval documents on the basis of historical philology as well as palaeography and diplomatics.

In the seventeenth century Gottfried Wilhelm Leibniz praised the elder Christian Thomasius for treating the history of philosophy and not merely of philosophers. Unfortunately the same could not be said of philology as late as the twentieth century, which continued to be the chronological story of the great philologists. There has been some agreement about relative importance, but the fact is that achievement in textual criticism has been the product of individual judgement of quantity and perceived quality, based on changing standards of literal correctness rather than conceptual schemes. Historians of philology have given lists of men (and later women) and their works and critics, with attention to biographical context, but little to the presumed disciplinary projects. The seventeenth century was 'the age of erudition', and the roster of memorable

---

[29] Donald R. Kelley, 'Tacitus Noster', in T. J. Luce and A. J. Woodman (eds.), *Tacitus and the Tacitean Tradition* (Princeton, 1993).

[30] See Nicholas Wickendon, *G. J. Vossius and the Humanist Concept of History* (Assen, the Netherlands, 1993).

scholars is vast, but the upshot has been largely bibliographical.[31] However, in the eighteenth century erudition was caught at the centre of a campaign for idealist philosophy against 'useless' erudition, best represented by Kant and Hegel. According to Arnaldo Momigliano, Edward Gibbon was one of those who tried to bridge this gap between philosophy and 'pedantry'.[32]

In England the leading figures in the new philology were Isaac Casaubon and John Selden, who studied national history as well as the classics, biblical tradition, and oriental languages. Casaubon exposed as a later creation the semi-legendary work of Hermes Trismegistus. Henry Savile produced, among other works, a translation of Tacitus's works and an edition of Chrysostom, and many other classical scholars contributed to the new philology.[33] The 'quarrel between the Ancients and the Moderns', associated in France with Bernard de Fontenelle and Charles Perrault, came to England in the later seventeenth century, with William Temple representing the Ancients and William Wotton the Moderns; the battle was accompanied by the critical study of the Greeks and a growth in historical method.[34] Wotton argued the superiority of the Moderns not just in science but in philology, referring to the work of Scaliger, Casaubon, and Selden. In this spirit Richard Bentley exposed as forgeries the letters of Phalaris (a sixth-century BC Greek tyrant), and he edited the works of Homer, which became the centre of later discussions. Bentley was at the forefront of many scholarly projects as well as polemics, and his reputation was Europe-wide.

PHILOLOGY AND THE WORLD BEYOND CHRISTIAN EUROPE

Like Christianity, both Judaism and Islam were 'religions of the book', and they developed techniques of reading designed to preserve their textual tradition, the Jews through rabbinic scholarship and the Arabs through methods derived from their Latin translators of the Qur'an. As with all translations, the choice was between reading word-for-word and reading according to the sense. The former was the more common method but the latter (derived from the twelfth-century *Lex Mahumet pseudoprophete* [Law of Muhammad the False Prophet] by Robert of Ketton) was used in order to refute the sacrilegious as well as to make the text clear in the context of Latin culture (*Latinitas*). According to Thomas Burman, both techniques remained faithful to philology as well as to Christianity.[35] These

---

[31] Blandine Kriegel, *L'Histoire à l'âge classique*, 4 vols. (Paris, 1979).
[32] Arnaldo Momigliano, 'Ancient History and the Antiquarian', *Journal of the Courtauld and Warburg Institutes*, 13 (1950), 285–315.
[33] John Edwin Sandys, *A History of Classical Scholarship*, 3 vols. (Cambridge, 1908), ii. 333.
[34] Joseph M. Levine, *Humanism and History* (Ithaca, 1987).
[35] Thomas E. Burman, *Reading the Qur'an in Latin Christendom, 1450–1560* (Philadelphia, 2007).

methods were followed down to the sixteenth-century edition of Egidio da Viterbo, progressing in a fashion parallel to biblical studies.

In the late eighteenth century the 'Oriental Renaissance' extended the reach of Western philology to the Far East, especially India, and translations from Sanskrit were carried out by William Jones. Sanskrit texts had an enormous influence on Romantic writers—Schelling, Fichte, Hegel, Schlegel, and others—and soon began to be taught in European universities, first in Germany and France and later in England, culminating in the work of Friedrich Max Müller at Oxford.[36] This was the 'era of decipherings', of which that of the Egyptian hieroglyphs by Jean-François Champollion was the most famous, followed by that of the cuneiforms, and later others, including Mayan script. In this context, too, appeared the notion of 'comparative philology' as well as linguistics, both of which established an alliance with evolutionary thought and Indo-European ideas.

According to many scholars, at least up to the eighteenth century, 'philology' was an exclusive product of the Western classical tradition, but textual and even historical criticism was by no means limited to European scholarship. As Benjamin Elman writes, 'the transition in China from Neo-Confucian Philosophy to Ch'ing [Qing] philology, for example, demonstrates that changes in social norms are frequently responsible for new approaches to knowledge'. In the eleventh century there emerged a 'wave of skepticism and of attacks on the authenticity of classical texts', and scholars followed this up in the next century.[37] In the genre of 'critical essays' (*pien*), Qing philology rejected the rational and universalizing habits of neo-Confucianism in favour of a more concrete and 'evidential' method. This was reinforced by the eighteenth century in the development of 'Han learning', which emphasized original texts, native traditions, and in effect historical perspective, itself intensified by Jesuit influence. By this time, too, printed texts, libraries, catalogues, and other apparatus of erudition, as well as classifications of knowledge, contributed to the growth of humanistic learning in China. And in the seventeenth century this method of research was also transmitted to Japan and Korea, among other countries.

KEY HISTORICAL SOURCES

Bodin, Jean, *Methodus ad facilem historiarum cognitionem* (Paris, 1566); trans. Beatrice Reynolds, *Method for the Easy Comprehension of History* (New York, 1945).

Bracciolini, Poggio, *Two Renaissance Book Hunters: The Letters of Poggius Bracciolini to Nicolaus de Niccolis*, trans. Phyllis Gordon (New York, 1974).

---

[36] Raymond Schwab, *The Oriental Renaissance*, trans. G. Patterson-Black and V. Reinking (New York, 1984).

[37] Benjamin A. Elman, *From Philosophy to Philology: Intellectual and Social Aspects of Late Imperial China* (Cambridge, Mass., 1984), 38, 41.

Bruni, Leonardo, 'On the Correct Way to Translate', in Gordon Griffiths, James Hankins, and David Thompson (eds.), *The Humanism of Leonardo Bruni: Selected Texts* (Binghamton, NY, 1987), 217–19.

Budé, Guillaume, *Comentarii linguae graecae* (Paris, 1529).

Chladenius, 'On the Concept of Interpretation', in Kurt Mueller-Vollmer (ed.), *The Hermeneutics Reader* (Oxford, 1985), 55–64.

Goclenius, Rodolfus, *Lexicon philosophicum* (Frankfurt, 1613).

Mabillon, Jean, *De re diplomatica* (Paris, 1681).

Petrarch, 'The Ascent of Mt. Ventoux', in Ernst Cassirer, Paul Oskar Kristeller, and John Herman Randall, Jr. (eds.), *The Renaissance Philosophy of Man* (New York, 1948), 36–46.

Scaliger, Joseph Justus, *Opus novum De emendatione temporum* (Paris, 1583).

Simon, Richard, *Histoire critique du Vieux Testament* (Paris, 1678).

Valla, Lorenzo, *Elegantiae Latinae linguae libri sex* (1444).

BIBLIOGRAPHY

Cochrane, Eric, *Historians and Historiography of the Italian Renaissance* (Chicago, 1981).

Burman, Thomas E., *Reading the Qur'an in Latin Christendom, 1450–1560* (Philadelphia, 2007).

D'Amico, John F., *Theory in Renaissance Textual Criticism* (Berkeley, 1988).

Grafton, Anthony, *Joseph Scaliger: A Study in the History of Classical Scholarship*, 2 vols. (Oxford, 1983–93).

—— *Forgers and Critics* (Princeton, 1990).

Hillerbrand, Hans (ed.), *Erasmus and His Age* (New York, 1970).

Jehasse, Jean, *La Renaissance de la critique* (Lyons, 1976).

Kelley, Donald R., *Foundations of Modern Historical Scholarship* (New York, 1970).

—— *Renaissance Humanism* (Boston, 1991).

Kriegel, Blandine, *L'Histoire à l'age classique*, 4 vols. (Paris, 1979).

Levine, Joseph M., *Humanism and History* (Ithaca, 1987).

Momigliano, Arnaldo, 'Ancient History and the Antiquarian', *Journal of the Courtauld and Warburg Institutes*, 13 (1950), 285–315.

Pomata, Gianna and Siraisi, Nancy (eds.), *Historia: Empiricism and Erudition in Early Modern Europe* (Cambridge, Mass., 2005).

Salutati, Coluccio, 'De Tyranno', in Ephraim Emerton (ed.), *Humanism and Tyranny: Studies in the Italian Trecento* (Cambridge, 1925), 70–116.

Sandys, John Edwin, *A History of Classical Scholarship*, 3 vols. (Cambridge, 1908), ii.

Schwab, Raymond, *The Oriental Renaissance*, trans. G. Patterson-Black and V. Reinking (New York, 1984).

Siraisi, Nancy, *History, Medicine, and the Traditions of Renaissance Learning* (Ann Arbor, 2007).

Wickendon, Nicholas, *G. J. Vossius and the Humanist Concept of History* (Assen, the Netherlands, 1993).

Wilcox, Donald J., *The Development of Florentine Humanist Historiography in the Fifteenth Century* (Cambridge, Mass., l969).

Wilson, N. G., *From Byzantium to Italy* (Baltimore, 1992).

Chapter 12

Major Trends in European Antiquarianism, Petrarch to Peiresc

Peter N. Miller

Writing a history of antiquarianism is difficult because so many of the key figures are still not studied. But writing such a history is also difficult because there is little agreement on what antiquarianism means. There is, of course, the narrow view that antiquarianism is carried out by antiquaries whose subject is antiquities— from the Latin *antiquitates*. But since this word derived from the title of an encyclopedic study of Rome produced by a first-century Roman, Marcus Terrentius Varro, *Antiquitates rerum divinarum humanarumque* [Divine and Human Antiquities], it also licensed a much broader interpretation. *Antiquitates* could refer, as it did for Varro, to the entire lived culture of a people or a period. This, in turn, meant that it could be tracked down through philology, law, natural history, and politics, among other things.

The narrower approach, which is closely bound up with our understanding of the revival of antiquity, first in Italy and then across the Alps, has already borne many fruits, even though our knowledge remains limited to a small number of the texts produced by a small percentage of those who concerned themselves with antiquity. The broader approach, which might prove crucial to understanding the shape of learning in the late Renaissance (or early Enlightenment), has been adopted less, perhaps because most of those who study antiquarians and antiquarianism are art historians—and are interested first and foremost in the objects being studied rather than *how* they were being studied.

But whether we choose the narrower or the wider field of view, writing a history of early modern antiquarianism at this point, despite being a desideratum of the highest degree, remains impossible. Arnaldo Momigliano, more than fifty years ago, at just this point in an essay, acknowledged, 'I wish I could simply refer to a History of Antiquarian Studies. But none exists.'[1] This statement remains true today, despite the real renewal of studies in early

---

[1] Arnaldo Momigliano, 'Ancient History and the Antiquarian', in *Contributo alla storia degli studi classici* (Rome, 1955), 69.

modern antiquarianism.[2] There are occasional efforts to plumb national traditions of antiquarianism, especially for northern Europe. But on the whole many of the histories of antiquarianism that we do possess—histories written of, by, and for antiquaries—are those we might not wish to read. The outline of what such a comprehensive history would look like is clear enough. It would begin with Petrarch, not as an ideologist of antiquity but as a student of its material remains, especially in verbal form (manuscripts, epigraphy, numismatics). The next highpoint—though perhaps this judgement is a function of the limited scholarship on the intervening period—occurs a century later, in the 1440s, with Poggio Bracciolini, Flavio Biondo, and Cyriac of Ancona. A century later still, the lead is taken by a group of scholars circling around the household of Cardinal Alexander Farnese, including Pirro Ligorio and Onofrio Panvinio. Their breakthrough, towards an intensive engagement with ancient visual and material culture in its fullest extent, was picked up in the next generation by the Frenchman Peiresc and his colleagues in the circle of Cardinal Francesco Barberini. With Peiresc it is possible to see the outlines of that 'broader' history of European antiquarianism, as it intersects with natural history, medicine, and astronomy, as well as oriental languages and literature. Some of Peiresc's wide interests were shared by the great contemporary northern antiquaries, William Camden and Ole Worm, as well as by some of the students of biblical antiquities, such as Jean Morin and William Lightfoot. Another aspect of Peiresc's focus on material evidence was carried on through Mabillon and on towards Gatterer's creation of a curriculum for the *historische Hilfswissenschaften* (Auxiliary Sciences of History). The Italian tradition of object-based studies led on towards Winckelmann through Bellori and Bianchini, but also towards Caylus and Barthélemy in Paris. Then there would be a fascinating, long, and rich coda that would carry us on into what Donald R. Kelley once termed 'the old cultural history' of the 1840s and 1850s.[3] And, finally, there would be the complex question of the relationship of the old cultural history to the newer forms created by Jacob Burkhardt and Karl Lamprecht in the next decades. Without any sense of the morphology of antiquarianism the history of cultural history will remain an exercise in genealogy only.

Big stories require solid foundations, and even the narrow definition of antiquarianism and the antiquarian age requires careful examination: is antiquarianism the study of antiquities, the fascination with antiquity, or the inspiration by antiquity? Each of these takes us in a very different direction, and each is significant to an understanding of early modern European cultural life. But even these broad

[2] Momigliano's second-best source was K. B. Stark's *Handbuch der Archäologie der Kunst* (Leipzig, 1880). On Stark see Peter N. Miller, 'Writing Antiquarianism: Prolegomenon to a History', in Miller and François Louis (eds.), *Antiquarianism and Intellectual Life in Europe and China, 1500–1800* (Ann Arbor, 2012).

[3] Donald R. Kelley, 'The Old Cultural History', *History and the Human Sciences*, 9 (1996), 101–26.

categories admit of significant omissions, in particular the relationship between antiquarianism and history. Bacon was only the most famous of those who distinguished between history and antiquities. The latter he described as 'history defaced, or remnants of history which have casually escaped the shipwreck of time'. These remnants took different forms, and Bacon's catalogue bespeaks a more intimate familiarity than the tone of disparagement might otherwise suggest.

Antiquities, or remnants of histories, are (as was said) like the spars of a shipwreck: when, though the memory of things be decayed and almost lost, yet acute and industrious persons, by a certain perseverance and scrupulous diligence, contrive out of genealogies, annals, titles, monuments, coins, proper names, and styles, etymologies of words, proverbs, traditions, archives, and instruments as well public as private, fragments of histories scattered about in books not historical,—contrive, I say, from all these things or some of them, to recover somewhat from the deluge of time; a work laborious indeed, but agreeable to men, and joined with a kind of reverence; and well worthy to supersede the fabulous accounts of the origins of nations; and to be substituted for fictions of that kind.[4]

It might be simpler to follow Bacon in positing a sharp division between 'ancient historians' and 'antiquarians', but Anthony Grafton's recent work on the *ars historica*, and in particular on the works of François Baudouin and Francesco Patrizi, suggests that any hard-and-fast division between silver-tongued historians and club-footed antiquaries is misleading.[5]

On the other hand, one may fairly ask whether 'antiquarianism' actually belongs in a history of historical writing, not because it isn't intimately related to history, but because its written expression is extrinsic to its identity. That is to say, literary style, *per se*, is not central to the practice of antiquarianism in the way that it was for history. (Thus, by extension, there could be no Hayden White for antiquarianism.) Research methods, evaluation of evidence, questions—these were more characteristic of antiquarianism, and better guides to its practice. Perhaps the metaphor would be the comparison between a traditional building, with an attractive 'skin' or curtain wall, and the Pompidou Centre or Lloyd's Building, with no skin hiding the machinery of the building from its spectators. The historian of antiquarianism must be a connoisseur of questions and tools,

---

[4] Francis Bacon, *De Augmentis Scientiarum* (1623), bk. 2, ch. 6. Bacon's words—and Cyriac of Ancona's thoughts—remained current, and perhaps even commonplace, at the end of the seventeenth century. See John Aubrey: 'These Remaynes are *tanquam tabulata naufragii* (like fragments of a Shipwreck) that after the Revolution of so many yeares and governments have escaped the teeth of Time and (which is more dangerous) the hands of mistaken zeale. So that the retrieving of these forgotten things from oblivion in some sort resembles the Art of a Conjuror who makes those walke and appeare that have layen in their graves many hundreds of yeares: and represents as it were to the eie, the places, customs and Fashions, that were of old Time. It is said of Antiquaries, they wipe off the mouldinesse they digge, and remove the rubbish.' Quoted in Stan A. E. Mendyk, *'Speculum Britanniae': Regional Study, Antiquarianism and Science in Britain to 1700* (Toronto, 1989), 174.

[5] Anthony Grafton, *What Was History? The Art of History in Early Modern Europe* (Cambridge, 2007).

rather than literary style. Perhaps this is why the revival of the study of antiquarianism has coincided with a rising interest in history of scholarship rather than, more generally speaking, intellectual history.

With so much still unknown, still unexplored, there is a logic to establishing, in so far as it is possible, the beginnings. Much has been said about Petrarch's antiquarianism—probably more has been said about him on this subject than he actually wrote himself. Of Petrarch, we could do worse than begin with Peter Burke, who observed that despite being a poet and tuned in to words, 'he was, one might say, the first modern antiquarian, in the sense of someone who is interested in the reconstruction of the past from its physical remains'.[6] Yet Petrarch's interest in the other chief sorts of remains, though real, was superficial and very imperfectly acted upon.[7] And because it is often forgotten that he began his career as a lawyer—or at least this was his father's vision for him—it is almost always forgotten that he was a contemporary of the great Bartolus. At a time when lawyers paid no attention to the fact that the Roman law they were implementing had been made in and for a different Rome, Petrarch was chiding that 'it never occurs to them that the knowledge of arts and of origins and of literature would be of the greatest practical use for their very profession'.[8]

The main loci for Petrarch's antiquarian ventures are *Rerum Familiarium* [Letters on Familiar Matters] (*c.*1366) (V.4) on Roman ruins in the bay of Naples, *De remedis utriusque fortunae* [Remedies for Both Kinds of Fortune] (*c.*1366) on ancient buildings destroyed by time, *Rerum Familiarium Libri* (XIX.3) on Roman coins, and, especially, *Rerum Familiarium Libri* (VI, 2 of 1341), which we will have more to say about, as well as Book 8 of his *Africa* (*c.*1351) epic. Yet the reconstruction of Carthage in the latter was entirely from books while the reconstruction of Rome in *Rerum Familiarium Libri* (VI.2) affects the pose of autopsy only in order to deny its power relative to books.

Petrarch, like most everyone else in his day, and certainly before—and most since, too—simply preferred literary to material sources. He found them easier to work with, of more meaningful content, and more familiar. On top of that, what had survived was often broken, or at least so damaged as to require exquisite powers of remediation. Books, by contrast, seemed to come more whole. 'Seek in books and you will find authorities. Explore the entire city and either you will find nothing or the tiniest signs of great works.'[9]

---

[6] Peter Burke, *The Renaissance Sense of the Past* (London, 1969), 23.

[7] Roberto Weiss, 'Petrarch the Antiquarian', in Charles Henderson, Jr. (ed.), *Classical, Medieval and Renaissance Studies in Honor of Berthold Louis Ullman*, 2 vols. (Rome, 1964), 199–209 at 207; and Angelo Mazzocco, 'The Antiquarianism of Francesco Petrarca', *The Journal of Medieval and Renaissance Studies*, 7 (1977), 203–24.

[8] Burke, *The Renaissance Sense of the Past*, 24.

[9] *De remediis utriusque fortunae* (Bern, 1605), i. 118, pl. 350; quoted in Angelo Mazzocco, 'Petrarca, Poggio, and Biondo: Humanism's Foremost Interpreters of Roman Ruins', in Aldo Scalgione (ed.), *Francis Petrarch, Six Centuries Later: A Symposium* (Chapel Hill, 1975), 353–63.

What the physical remains of the past did for Petrarch, however, was provide him with the food his imagination needed. And so it was less the learned, precise reconstruction of ancient Rome that he sought—not, of course, that it would have been possible at that time—so much as to use the remains that were there to evoke and stimulate interest in a Roman past that was much richer than just the physical survivals.[10] This is the way to understand the importance of Petrarch's famous description of a walk in Rome, sent to Francesco Colonna in 1341 or 1337. Indeed, few walks have ever had such an impact. For, strolling across a landscape hallowed by memory, loss, and survival, Petrarch saw physical Rome as a gigantic kind of looking glass: reconstructing it from its broken fragments was a form of self-examination.

And so, in that famous letter to Francesco Colonna, it was 'not so much because of what I actually saw, as from the recollection of our ancestors, who left such illustrious memorials of Roman virtue so far from the fatherland'.[11] Indeed, Petrarch actually feared the consequences of too great a familiarity with the 'real' remains of the ancient world: 'fearing that what I had imagined in my mind my eyes would belittle at the moment of reality, which is always injurious to a reputation'. In fact, he continues, 'Rome was greater, and greater are its ruins than I imagined'.[12]

Nevertheless, in making space, and the movement through space, the axis of his quest, Petrarch was creating a new way of studying and thinking about the past. The *locus classicus* for the spatialization of history, at least for the European Renaissance, might well be in Cicero's *De Finibus*: 'Such powers of evocation are inherent in those places . . . And in this City there is no end to them: wherever we go we walk over history.'[13] The topos of movement through space was, then, more than just a literary tool; the spatialization of antiquity, not just as scattered pieces but the vision of a whole fabric, provided a model for reconstruction. Petrarch might have been a great manuscript hunter, but ancient manuscripts, wherever they were found, were found decontextualized. By contrast, spatializing antiquity created a model for its reconstitution which would shape the study of the past to the present day.

These two lines of access to the ancient world launched by Petrarch had rich *fortunae* afterwards: space as a prompt for the learned imagination, and words on monuments as the preferred kind of antiquity (favouring numismatics and epigraphy). In the decades after Petrarch some followed him in these interests. But actually they were few in number. And they complained about the difficulty of the work, even of reading inscriptions in a language they thought they knew.

---

[10] Mazzocco, 'The Antiquarianism of Francesco Petrarca', 208.
[11] These words are actually drawn from *Rerum Familiarium Libri*, 1.5, writing about his daytime and nighttime wanderings around Cologne.
[12] *Rerum Familiarium Libri* (2.14), trans. Aldo S. Bernardo, 3 vols. ([1975] New York, 2005), ii. 14, iii. 113.
[13] Cicero's *De Finibus*, V.i.2

The difficulties experienced by Odofredus with the 'lex de imperio' show this. Likewise, for Magister Gregorius, who couldn't read inscriptions, namely 'In hac tabula plura legi, sed pauca intellexi'.[14] Or Buoncompagno da Signa, author of *Formula litterarum scholasticarum* [The Rule of Learned Letters], who noted the marvels of ancient epigraphy 'which today we cannot clearly read or under-stand'.[15] Giovanni Dondi, a doctor and friend of Petrarch in his old age, wrote that on the triumphal arch 'are sculpted many letters but they are read with difficulty'.[16] Yet it was also during this time that people began to make the first collections of inscriptions (*syllogae*).[17] Truth be told, we still know very little about the century between Petrarch and the three giants of the fifteenth century generally credited with the real beginning of antiquarianism in Europe: Cyriac of Ancona, Poggio Bracciolini, and Flavio Biondo.[18]

Poggio is the figure singled out as key by both Roberto Weiss and Anthony Grafton.[19] But Grafton also gave Poggio credit for creating the model of a community of collaborating scholars, the so-called *Respublica literaria*, or Republic of Letters.[20] Poggio follows Petrarch in using the convention of the walk through Rome—the topographical framing of time—as a way of presenting the fruits of his study of Roman inscriptions in Book 1 of *De Varietate Fortunae* [On the Variability of Fortune] (1448).[21] But from our perspective what is interesting about this project is that it is *not* dedicated to antiquarian study. It is *not* a volume about Roman antiquities, even though its fame has come to be identified very much with that Book 1.[22] In fact, this book is followed by three others, one illustrating changing fortune by looking at the period 1377–1431 and the death of Pope Martin V, the next giving a short history of the pontificate of Eugenius IV (1431–47) and attempts to create a union of the Eastern and Western Churches, concluding with a discussion of Eastern Christians (those

[14] Quoted in Angelo Mazzocco, 'Biondo Flavio and the Antiquarian Tradition', Ph.D. dissertation, University of California, Berkeley, 1973.

[15] Cited by G. B. De Rossi, *Le prime raccolte d'antiche iscrizioni compilate in Roma tra il finire del secolo XIV e il cominciare del XV* (Rome, 1852); and quoted in Roberto Weiss, *The Renaissance Discovery of Classical Antiquity* (Oxford, 1969), 18.

[16] 'sunt multae literae sculptae, sed difficiliter leguntur', quoted in Mazzocco, 'Biondo Flavio and the Antiquarian Tradition', 219.

[17] Weiss, *Renaissance Discovery of Classical Antiquity*, 145.

[18] Ibid., 207: 'The Renaissance antiquarians were the Descartes of archaeology. A new methodology was introduced by them into their field of study, which was really the new methodology pursued in the various provinces of humanist learning.'

[19] Weiss, *Renaissance Discovery of Classical Antiquity*, 64; and Anthony Grafton, *Leon Battista Alberti: Master Builder of the Italian Renaissance* (Oxford and New York, 2000), 229.

[20] Grafton, *Leon Battistta Alberti*, 229.

[21] Twenty-three of the fifty-two inscriptions copied out by Bracciolini, and preserved in a sylloge that passed through the hands of Cyriac and Coluccio Salutati before eventually finding a place in the Vatican Library, were used in the first book of *De Varietate*. Poggio Bracciolini, *Les Ruines de Rome: De varietate fortunae*, bk. 1, ed. Philippre Coarelli and Jean-Yves Boriaud, trans. Jean-Yves Boriaud (Paris, 1999), p. xiii.

[22] So much so that this recent bilingual French edition *only* included Book 1.

living under Islamic rule) then in Italy, including Armenians, Copts, and Ethiopians. The final book discusses the lands beyond Islam, Poggio's famous retelling of Nicolò Conti's tales of India and Ethiopia.

The section on India rearranges Conti's narrative into a structural presentation, not so different from what people were asking at that time about ancient Rome. What are the categories discussed? The geographical division of India, inhabitants, buildings and furniture and lifestyle, food manners, hairstyle, sleep style, shoes, ornament, funeral rites and mourning rites, priests and Brahmins, navigation techniques, shipping, gods/idols and their rites including a section on self-sacrifice to the gods, weddings, legends about where diamonds come from, calendar, zodiac, money, weapons and technology, writing, languages, slaves, penal practices, and diseases. This is a long and fascinating list. Many of these areas of interest were the same ones that caught the eye of Poggio the epigrapher.

But perhaps even more important, at least from the point of view of his impact on what came later, was Flavio Biondo. He copied inscriptions and visited Rome, but used it all virtually to reconstruct the lost city. His *Roma Instaurata* [Rome Restored] (1444–6) 'is a book of fundamental importance in the history of historical thought. It is a topographical account of ancient Rome' describing all the monuments and buildings, using literary sources as well as information from walking the site.[23] What we might say of this project is that it represents the formalizing into *scientia* of what Petrarch began as a frame for the imagination, and which still survived as such, in part, in the work of Poggio. In Biondo, by contrast, the imaginative, personalized, and reflective context is gone, but the vision of Rome from a walker's perspective is retained, though now filled in and overwhelmed by a great body of facts. This is historical chorography, and as such influenced Conrad Celtis and William Camden in the two centuries that followed, but it is also what we might term today 'cultural geography'. The physical space provides the setting and the prompts for the telling of that story.

But we might add to Peter Burke's judgement that *Roma Triumphante* [Rome Triumphant] (1453–59) represents the point of departure from the Petrarchan tradition in that it shifts from reconstruction based on spatial to one based on conceptual apperception. In other words, instead of being modelled on a possible perambulation through the physical city, it reflects an abstract division of Rome by function, with parts of the book devoted to religion, public administration, the military, private institutions, and triumphal marches. Each large category serves as the rubric for an occasionally—and inevitably—overlapping but ambitiously encyclopedic survey of Roman public, private, military, and religious matters.[24] Yes, sometimes Biondo is led to discuss Roman institutions in the

---

[23] Burke, *The Renaissance Sense of the Past*, 25.

[24] Some commentators, such as Georg Voigt, also recognized the unprecedentedness of this work, though for other reasons: Voigt, for example, emphasized the *Roma Triumphans* and saw it as an unprecedented work. See his *Il risorgimento dell'antichità classica ovvero il primo secolo*

Instaurata, just as he sometimes presents archaeological data in the *Triumphans*, but these exceptions to form confirm his general effort to adopt distinct vantage points in the two projects.

With his new fourfold division into public, private, military, and sacred antiquities, Biondo also broke with Varro's way of chopping up the encyclopedia. Varro had thought and organized in terms of human and divine matters, and then divided these big rubrics into people, places, times, and things, or institutions. Perhaps Biondo even thought he was following Varro, so close are they in point of fact. But Biondo has shifted still further away from narrative history (Varro's 'people'), signalling a movement that would have real consequences over the subsequent three hundred odd years.

We can presume Biondo's thorough acquaintance with physical Rome—he was a member of the Curia for many years, after all—but *autopsia* figures less often than one might expect in these works. More typical is the text-driven vision of the city, even in the *Roma Instaurata*. Its three books are divided into the physical space of Rome, its aqueducts, arenas, and even its churches.

Interestingly, in the discussion of Rome's physical space in *Roma Triumphante* Biondo signals his awareness of what he was facing. He writes that 'having described those parts of the city of Rome for which we possess the terms that name and capture it, it will be necessary that in describing the rest we take another way. Because who can give an account of things of such great age, and of almost infinite parts and buildings? We will therefore take this path', and will divide what follows into discussions rather of categories than of space: what pertains to religion, public administration, spectacles, and, fourth, more specialized matters.[25]

But in Book 3, when entering the abandoned quarters of the ancient city, where only modern buildings lay, Biondo acknowledged feeling insecure,

> because not having for them neither the testimonies, nor any certainty, because to see with the eyes, or only with the mind, what is today very inhabited in Rome, one would say that I haven't touched anything, which did not occur because of any negligence of ours, nor by accident, but for not wanting to affirm what we do not know . . . without ancient testimonies, worthy of faith.[26]

Archaeology does not appear to satisfy this condition of a trustworthy testimony since it is so little drawn upon. Even in the fascinating account of Roman villa life in Book 9 of the *Roma Triumphante*, the entire discussion of decorative

---

dell'umanesimo, trans. Diego Valbusa, 2 vols. (Florence, 1888–90), ii. 491, quoted in Mazzocco, 'Biondo Flavio and the Antiquarian Tradition', 8.

[25] Flavio Biondo, *Blondi Flavii forliviensis de Roma Triumphante Libir Decem, priscorum scriptorum lectoribus utilissimi, ad totiiusque Romanae antiquitatis cognitionem pernecessarii* (Basel, 1531), bk. 2, 245–6, no. xxxix.

[26] Ibid., 270.

arts, domestic objects, useful objects, glass, marble, porphyry, architecture—everything—is culled from literary sources.

And yet, lest we feel that Biondo should be demoted from his position of honour alongside Cyriac and Poggio, there is also the fact that he preserves for us, in several different versions, the most elaborate account of an archaeological 'dig' that has survived from the fifteenth century. This is the fascinating narrative of the underwater excavations at Lake Nemi, south-east of Rome, in 1447, an expedition made with Alberti. After a long description of the excavation and then of the ship itself, down to how they figured out from the remains themselves how it was originally built (the fusing of clay and iron 'just as today we make a sealant of brick and iron'), Biondo then gives Alberti's views on the relationship between the pipes found at the bottom of the lake and the springs nearby—that water was piped in for the houseboats on the lake.[27] Grafton has made this episode the key to defining not only part of the early modern antiquarian venture, but also the signal contribution of the multi-talented Alberti:

> In studying the way the ship's hull was made, the bonds between the pieces of lead pipe, and the forms of the letters on them, Biondo—whose forte lay in the analysis of texts—adopted an object-oriented approach. It seems altogether likely that he reported, in such passages, exactly what Alberti told him. It also seems probable that Alberti inspired Biondo's effort to compare modern ships with those of the Romans in his later *Rome Triumphant*.[28]

For Grafton, Alberti emerges as an ideal of antiquarianism, alongside his many other talents. It is Alberti who in fact presents himself as the modern antiquary, in learning from direct contact with the physical remains of the past. Though others before him, like Donatello and Brunelleschi, and many others after, would turn to physical remains for information and inspiration, what Alberti offered was a combination of interest in ancient material culture *and* in the 'expressive capabilities of ancient sculpture', as Grafton terms it.[29]

The *Italia illustrata* [Italy Illuminated] (*c.*1453) was the first work begun by Biondo and the last to be finished. Technically, it is chorography, including a genealogy of ruling houses of each settlement, their chronology, antiquities, local history, and topography. It is a mostly bookish treatment, though Biondo's personal acquaintance with the topography of Italy is on display in almost every section, even if not quite as hands-on as in the dig at Lake Nemi.[30] There are accounts of human history drawn from ruins, as at Ostia, and accounts

---

[27] Flavio Biondo, *Italy Illuminated*, ed. and trans. Jeffrey A. White (Harvard, 2005), no. 49, pp. 191–3.

[28] Grafton, *Leon Battista Alberti*, 251.

[29] Ibid., 232.

[30] Ottavio Clavuot, in the only monograph-length study of *Italia illustrata*, devotes the greatest part of his efforts to discussing Biondo's use of the literary sources. See Clavuot, *Biondos 'Italia Illustrata'—Summa odern Neuschöpfung? Über die Arbeitsmethoden eines Humanisten* (Tübingen, 1990).

of human history drawn from the appearance of the landscape, as at Incisa in the Val d'Arno.[31] There are discussions of the customs of local people, as in the two means of fowling practised throughout the year near Anzio and much more, showing the depth of Biondo's knowledge.[32] There is also a kind of self-consciousness about space that is very intelligent. In describing Lazio, Biondo explained,

> we shall not be able to adhere to the plan used in other regions, orienting ourselves by the mouths, sources and course of rivers. We shall adopt another method (one suited to this region alone) which will meet our needs better, by proceeding along three roads, the Appian, Latin, and Tiburtine which lead in different ways to the river Liri and to Sinuessa and Gaeta.

And so, oriented in this way, he begins a section with, for example, 'present-day travellers from Rome to Terracina come first to . . .'.[33] We will want to note again the similarity to Chinese geographies, though perhaps all this demonstrates is the inevitability of choosing amidst a limited number of chorographic options.

In addition to the physical space, Biondo also retells some of the events that occurred within that space, as he explains: 'So this work will be not just a description of Italy, but also a catalogue of her famous and outstanding men, as well as a summary of no small part of Italian history.'[34] Biondo marks a crucial transition in what a history of antiquarianism would look like were it ever written. Through his *Roma Instaurata* we can trace the impact of Petrarch's imaginative convention of the movement through the physical space of Rome as a mnémotechnique. But with *Roma Triumphante* Biondo advances the situation, moving starkly away from the individual experience as vector for the propagation of knowledge, and towards a predigested, predetermined form. It was this decision that changed the shape of antiquarian studies in the centuries to come. We can trace this immediately in the titles of works that were produced in the sixteenth century, both through the use of the term *antiquitates* and in the selection of a particular subject to investigate.

The third great figure of these decades was Cyriac of Ancona, a larger-than-life merchant made larger, paradoxically, by the near-complete disappearance of his literary corpus, of which only fragments and copies survive. The first period of his life covers forty-five years, from 1391 to 1435—a period covered in Scalamonti's *Vita*.[35] We know of his middle period (1435–43) from two extensive excerpts from his travel diaries that were printed in the seventeenth and eighteenth centuries from now-lost manuscripts and letters.

---

[31] Biondo, *Italy Illuminated*, no. 22, p. 63 and no. 36, p. 79.
[32] Ibid., no. 7, pp. 127–9.
[33] Ibid., no. 19, p. 149.
[34] Ibid., no. 10, p. 19.
[35] Francesco Scalamonti, *Vita Viri Clarissimi et Famosissimi Kyriaci Anconitani*, ed. and trans. Charles Mitchell and Edward W. Bodnar (Philadelphia, 1996).

Cyriac's letters are extraordinary. But what contemporaries read most carefully, and copied out even more attentively, were his transcriptions of inscriptions,
and his architectural drawings with inscriptions. Cyriac is recognized so widely as
the founder of epigraphy because of this influence. Mommsen said that his
manuscripts were snapped up by princes and then disintegrated. De Rossi said
it was not the book, but the *excerpta* that Cyriac had made for friends that spread
so widely. Sabbadini said the *Commentaria* were destroyed in a fire at the Sforza
library at Pesaro in 1514. There is evidence from the 1660s of a project in Rome,
begun by Holstenius under Barberini's inspiration, and then taken over by Carlo
Moroni, Holstenius's follower as keeper of the Barberini library, to edit the
inscriptions of Cyriac of Ancona. But the manuscript, if it ever reached that
stage, has since disappeared.

In Europe, the next key step in consolidating the century of antiquarian
exploration after Biondo occurred more than a full century later. Johannes
Rosinus's *Romanorum antiquitatum libri decem* [Ten Books on Roman Anti-
quities] (1583) is organized in terms of subjects that Biondo had separated out
into *Roma Instaurata* and *Roma Triumphante*. It is also true that Rosinus's
handbook was almost totally untouched by archaeology, with few illustrations,
all from coins.[36] His ten books are divided into the City and Populace; Gods,
Temples; Priests; Calendar; Games and Rituals; Nobility; Magistrates; Laws;
Judges; and Militia. According to Mazzocco, this represents a shift away from
Biondo's fourfold classificatory system and a closer identification with the
approach of sixteenth-century scholars such as Panvinio, Sigonio, and Lipsius.[37]

What is especially important about Rosinus is his self-consciousness. He
understood his place in the history of the study of *antiquitates*. And so, for
instance, in his dedicatory letter to the Dukes of Saxony, Rosinus points to the
ancient Romans, who wrote 'so that the origins and causes of the old ways, rites,
and ceremonies' would be understood by posterity. The figure of Varro loomed
large for Rosinus. He enumerated what he took to be the content of the latter's
'Human Antiquities': 'Concerning Roman cities and their parts, on patricians
and plebians, patrons, clients, on tribes, curia, ports and centuries, on the city,
the Senate, rostrum, fora, stadiums and other buildings, on the counting of years,
months, days, and their divisions, auspicious and inauspicious days, assemblies,
warriors; on peace and war, the committees, magistrates, laws, judges, games,
etc.'[38] But after the death of Varro, 'the study of antiquities and of humane
letters' dwindled, until Flavio Biondo 'rescued it out of darkness'. Many have
since followed him 'so that the study of antiquities as if buried have been called

---

[36] Ingo Herklotz, *Cassiano dal Pozzo und die Archäologie des 17. Jahrhundert* (Munich, 1999),
248.
[37] Mazzocco, 'Biondo Flavio and the Antiquarian Tradition', 119 n. 20.
[38] Johannes Rosinus, *Romanarum Antiquitatum Libri Decem: Ex variis Scriptoribus summa fide
singuarique diligentia collecti* (Basel, 1583), (2v-)(3r).

back to life'—attributing to a whole field of study what Cyriac spoke of for individuals.[39]

Rosinus explained that he diligently studied four classes of material that tended all to the same end: scholarship and imagination facilitating reconstruction. He compared monuments of ancient writing with manuscripts, 'and pulled out many vestiges of antiquity from the darkness and brought them into the light'. He also read various writers. And, finally, he described how he '[i]nvestigated the other ancient monuments, stones, coins, trophies, buildings, etc. and in this way the image of ancient Rome was known, as if placed before our eyes'.[40]

Rosinus's publisher had high hopes for the volume. Beyond simply referring to his author as 'the new Varro of our age' ('novo nostro aetatis Varrone'), Johannes Freigius even imagined Rosinus as having 'brought antiquarian learning into the form of some kind of ars' ('antiquitatis cognitionem in quandam artis formam redigi'). 'I hope', Freigius continued, 'for a future in which among the liberal arts of Grammar, Rhetoric, Logic, Arithmetic, Geometry, Music, Astronomy and others, the knowledge of antiquities will be placed as an art.' Nor was it necessary to add to what others had noted so much, that is, the utility of antiquarian knowledge for poets, historians, and legists. Thus, he concluded, 'to the other liberal arts is added the science of antiquities'.[41]

But for all the publisher's claims of novelty, Rosinus himself, writing to his readers, starts from the very familiar foundation of pedagogy: when young eyes read Cicero they encounter many terms and concepts 'which without knowledge of the histories and antiquities of the Romans cannot be understood'.[42] He gathered up all this material to assist teachers in their task.[43] Rosinus therefore represents a real turning point in the story we have been examining so far. On the one hand, his ten-book survey picks up where Biondo had left off, in scope and in organization. It represents the climax of the earlier Petrarch-to-Biondo moment, the crystallization of a vision of *antiquitates* in which careful and wide reading of texts, combined with some familiarity with material remains is used to present the panorama of ancient Roman culture—though with categories which themselves emerged from that textual tradition. And Rosinus would have an impact on the future too. For his approach is nominally embodied in the same tradition of the *Handbucher* that would become so prominent in the nineteenth century.

But in between—and this is where Rosinus does seem more an end than a beginning—and especially in Southern Italy and among independent scholars rather than school teachers, we see the dominance of a different kind of study of antiquities, one that is just as well-read but much more attentive to material culture, and much more interested in the information-laden character of images. Rosinus, for all his reading, has very few images, and nearly all of them come from coins, and nearly all relate to public life, such as altars, weapons, and clothing.

---

[39] Ibid., (3r).   [40] Ibid., (3v).   [41] Ibid., [)(6]r.
[42] Ibid., [)(D6v].   [43] Ibid., [)(6]v.

Rosinus really does represent one line of development, one that can trace itself back through Biondo to Petrarch and which, while making a gesture towards the material reality of the ancient world, is actually drawn substantially from the textual. And really, this represents the bulk of what antiquarianism in Europe was: extrapolating from texts in order to enable the reconstruction of diverse aspects of ancient life. The single best treatment of this line of development comes in the second half of Ingo Herklotz's masterly study of Cassiano dal Pozzo 'and archaeology in the seventeenth century'.

It is against this backdrop that the achievements of the antiquarians in the Farnese group in the sixteenth century, and the Cassiano group in the seventeenth, really stand out. For it is with them that images and objects emerge as key documents in themselves. (From Herklotz's perspective, indeed, which focuses most closely on the study of *mores et instituta*, Cassiano represents the very climax of the sixteenth-century project.[44]) Yes, it is certainly true that very often these scholars approached their artefacts with questions derived from texts, questions that they were seeking to answer in new ways with new evidence, but still questions from texts. But sometimes it was the direct encounter with the puzzling newness of an artefact—either disinterred or translated from another place—that provoked the questioning. And this, too, was new.

The big, new, visual turn came from Pirro Ligorio, in the first instance, and then from Onufrio Panvinio, Girolamo Mercuriale, Fulvio Orsini, and Alfonso and Pedro Chacón. The actual courtiers were Mercuriale, Panvinio, and Orsini, but the others were part of the circle. All of them represent the flowering of antiquarianism in the protective shelter of Cardinal Alexander Farnese. It was the presence of such a volume of remains in Rome, especially, but also elsewhere in Italy, that gave Italian scholars such a leg up over their northern competitors and partners. In his *Advis pour dresser une bibliothèque* [Instructions for Making a Library] (1627), Gabriel Naudé wrote that one could buy Chacón, Panvinio, Agustín, and Mercuriale with one's eyes closed, their work was that good.[45]

Herklotz argues, however, that around 1600 failing patronage and Counter-Reformation narrowness worked against the newly developing union of textual and visual material. This was true in Rome and in Padua and led to a turn back towards new textual material—though he adds, of course, that this shifting of gears appears more abrupt and less gradual from our perspective than it would have seemed from theirs.[46]

Having said all that, we must not undersell the contemporary awareness and self-consciousness about the power of objects. Philip Rubens, the painter's brother and Lipsius's star student, wrote, 'It's incredible how much the study of coins, epigraphy and other ancient monuments adds to the fuller

---

[44] Herklotz, *Cassiano dal Pozzo*, 225.
[45] Quoted ibid., 225.
[46] Ibid., 232.

understanding of antiquity. Indeed, I would dare to assert that these things, scarcely able to be grasped from ancient writers, can be properly understood from these physical sources and indeed well explained.'[47]

Herklotz argues that Biondo's *Roma Triumphante* was so ambitious—we might say: such a break from the relatively new spatial structure—that nobody followed it for a century. But then, first Robertello tried to reach back to Roman ways in his *De vita et victu populi romani* [On the Life and Manners of the Roman People] (1559), and then later, Rosinus. Pirro Ligorio tackled it in his giant opus of fifty manuscript books. But with Ligorio, a practising architect and autodidact as opposed to a philologist or *érudit*, the importance of the art object moves to the centre. With him, and with various vicissitudes up through the present, deciphering the specific languages of prior artworks emerges as a key way of accessing the past. No antiquary of the century put text and image closer together than did Ligorio. His early fifty-volume project was followed, at the end of his life, by an eighteen-volume one, this organized purely alphabetically, as if a gazetteer of ancient art. His approach had no followers.

Ligorio's impact on his contemporaries was great. It was Ligorio who inspired Panvinio's plan for an *Antiquitatum romanarum*, which grew from sixty books in 1565, to eighty, and then to one hundred. Book 1 was devoted to topography; Book 2 to four classes of institutions—private (including domestic life, speech, coins, metrology, libraries, transport, baths, medicines), public (including estates, representatives, offices), religion, and, finally, the circus and games; and Book 3 was devoted to 'Imperii Romani extra urbem declaratio'. Interestingly, in all this presentation of Roman institutions of empire, there is only one chapter on the military—compared with Biondo, it appears much less important to Panvinio. Book 4 was devoted to inscriptions, and Book 5 to chronology.

The scholars of the Farnese circle present us with a model of antiquarian scholarship. Were we to believe that the 'narrower' vision of antiquarianism was, in fact, all that there was to say about antiquarianism, then our story would end here. But it is not. Indeed, across the threshold of the seventeenth century we find scholars building on the techniques and research agendas of these very Romano-centric and reconstruction-oriented scholars to ask very broad questions about the shape and meaning of ancient, but also distant, societies. Herklotz, in his landmark study of Cassiano dal Pozzo, who sat at the heart of the great Barberini *équipe* of the 1620s and 1630s, casts this scholarship in terms of the study of culture—*mores et instituta*—through visual imagery—*illustratione*.[48]

Probably the best example of the possible reach of the antiquary into the domain later colonized as cultural history is provided by the work of Fabri de Peiresc. A lawyer, astronomer, and naturalist as well as a numismatist and historian, Peiresc's interests and questions ranged further and wider than those

---

[47] Philip Rubens, *Electorum Libri II* (Antwerp, 1608), 20, quoted in Herklotz, *Cassiano dal Pozzo*, 253.
[48] See Herklotz, *Cassiano dal Pozzo*, ch.13.

of many contemporary antiquaries. What he may have sacrificed in depth—publishing almost nothing in his lifetime—he more than made up for in breadth, and for cultural history, breadth is key. (This is one of the reasons why historians of more easily masterable subjects have always been somewhat sniffy about 'cultural history': for them breadth equals shallowness.) For Peiresc, this range had direct methodological consequences. It led him to rely on the art of comparison. Peiresc learned from the numismatists and philologists of the ancient world (perhaps most of all from Joseph Scaliger) who used texts to make sense of objects and objects to make sense of texts. But Peiresc extended this practice to other material, places, times, and things. His archive shows him comparing the orbital tracks of Jupiter's satellites over time, the ritual processions at French funerals, different versions of medieval maritime law, among others. Comparison, for this scholar, as for others in his wider circle with more libertine philosophical pursuits, opened up new worlds of questions.

If we can indeed think about antiquarianism as a 'philology of things' (*Sachphilologie* was an aspirational term coined by August Boeckh in the first half of the nineteenth century, but a practice already in existence in the sixteenth and seventeenth centuries), then we can immediately perceive how it could also link up with the broader cultural historical impulses of the sixteenth, seventeenth, and eighteenth centuries. From an epistemological point of view we find parallels in the antiquarian approach to antiquities, and the contemporary jurist's approach to law, or the doctor's to medicine.[49] The Peiresc who studied the past, nature, and peoples was not unique in early modern Europe; he rested on the shoulders of figures like Ulisse Aldrovandi, he was inspired by Francis Bacon, imitated Galileo, and created Pierre Gassendi and Jacob Spon.[50] This story, too, takes us out of Italy, and all the way to places like Franklin's Philadelphia or, even, Goethe's Frankfurt.

But the line from Peiresc forward also takes us to figures such as Mabillon, whose diplomatics were founded on close reading, but which opened up wider horizons of social and political change, and on to Vico, who saw history in mythology, to Montesquieu, who built a history of society and social change out of close reading of legal history, and on to Caylus, Winckelmann, Gibbon, and Dégérando. Within this trajectory we can track the slowly spiralling union of *antiquitates* and *historia*.

---

[49] Donald R. Kelley, *Foundations of Modern Historical Scholarship: Language, Law and History in the French Renaissance* (New York, 1970); and Nancy Siraisi, *History, Medicine, and the Traditions of Renaissance Learning* (Ann Arbor, 2007).

[50] Peter N. Miller, 'Description Terminable and Interminable: The Past, Nature and Peoples in Peiresc's Archive', in Nancy Siraisi and Giana Pomata (eds.), *'Historia': Empiricism and Erudition in Early Modern Europe* (Cambridge, Mass., 2005), 355–97. For more on Peiresc in particular, and the seventeenth-century world of erudition in general, see the references in the above essay and in Miller, *Peiresc's Europe: Learning and Virtue in the Seventeenth Century* (New Haven, 2000).

The long century from Peiresc to Winckelmann—not the years from Colocci and Raphael to Peiresc—was the one that Momigliano, so many decades ago, referred to as 'the Age of Antiquaries'.[51] Élisabeth Décultot's fine study of Winckelmann as a humanist reader confirms Momigliano's judgement of the age, and reveals that its hero was a reader of Peiresc's manuscript letters, as well as Kircher's and Pietro della Valle's published works.[52] Scholarship has still clustered on the earlier period, but for our understanding of the wider implications of the new methods of historical research for the emergence of the historical and cultural sciences, it is antiquarianism in the age of enlightenment, ironies, awkwardnesses, and all, that marks the next frontier of research.

KEY HISTORICAL DATES

Bacon, Francis, *De Augmentis Scientiarum* (1623).
Bracciolini, Poggio, *De varietate fortunae* (Basel, 1538).
Biondo, Flavio, *Blondi Flavii forliviensis in Romae Triumphantis* (Brixia, 1482).
——*Blondi Forliviensis viri praeclari Romae Instauratae* (Verona, 1482).
——*Biondi Flavii Forliviensis in Italiam illustratam* (Verona, 1482).
Cyriac of Ancona, *Later Travels*, ed. and trans. Edward W. Bodnar with Clive Foss (Cambridge, Mass., 2003).
Gassendi, Pierre, *Viri Illustris Nicolai Claudii Fabricii De Peiresc, Senatoris Aquisextiensis, Vita* (Paris, 1641).
Petrarca, Francesca, *Rerum familiarum libri* (Venice, 1492).
——*De remediis utriusque fortunae* (Bern, 1605).
Rosinus, Johannes, *Romanarum Antiquitatum Libri Decem: Ex variis Scriptoribus summa fide singuarique diligentia collecti* (Basel, 1583).
Scalamonti, Francesco, *Vita Viri Clarissimi et Famosissimi Kyriaci Ancontinanti*, ed. and trans. Charles Mitchell and Edward W. Bodnar (Philadelphia, 1996).

BIBLIOGRAPHY

Burke, Peter, *The Renaissance Sense of the Past* (London, 1969).
Clavuot, Ottavio, *Biondos 'Italia Illustrata'—Summa odern Neuschöpfung? Über die Arbeitsmethoden eines Humanisten* (Tübingen, 1990).
Décultot, Élisabeth, *Johann Joachim Winckelmann: Enquête sur la genèse de l'histoire de l'art* (Paris, 2000).
De Rossi, G. B., *Le prime raccolte d'antiche iscrizioni compilate in Roma tra il finire del secolo XIV e il cominciare del XV* (Rome, 1852).
Ferrary, Jean-Louis, *Onofrio Panvinio et les antiquités romaines* (Rome, 1996).

---

[51] Momigliano, 'Ancient History and the Antiquarian', 68.
[52] Élisabeth Décultot, *Johann Joachim Winckelmann: Enquête sur la genèse de l'histoire de l'art* (Paris, 2000).

Grafton, Anthony, *Leon Battista Alberti: Master Builder of the Italian Renaissance* (Oxford and New York, 2000).

—— *What Was History? The Art of History in Early Modern Europe* (Cambridge, 2007).

Herklotz, Ingo, *Cassiano dal Pozzo und die Archäologie des 17. Jahrhundert* (Munich, 1999).

Kelley, Donald R., *Foundations of Modern Historical Scholarship: Language, Law and History in the French Renaissance* (New York, 1970).

Mazzocco, Angelo, 'Petrarca, Poggio, and Biondo: Humanism's Foremost Interpreters of Roman Ruins', in Aldo Scalgione (ed.), *Francis Petrarch, Six Centuries Later: A Symposium* (Chapel Hill, 1975), 353–63.

—— 'The Antiquarianism of Francesco Petrarca', *The Journal of Medieval and Renaissance Studies*, 7 (1977), 203–24.

Mendyk, Stanley G., *'Speculum Britanniae': Regional Study, Antiquarianism and Science in Britain to 1700* (Toronto, 1989).

Miller, Peter N., *Peiresc's Europe: Learning and Virtue in the Seventeenth Century* (New Haven, 2000).

—— 'Writing Antiquarianism: Prolegomenon to a History', in Miller and François Louis (eds.), *Antiquarianism and Intellectual Life in Europe and China, 1500–1800* (Ann Arbor, forthcoming, 2012).

Momigliano, Arnaldo, 'Ancient History and the Antiquarian', in *Contributo alla storia degli studi classici* (Rome, 1955), 67–106.

Siraisi, Nancy, *History, Medicine, and the Traditions of Renaissance Learning* (Ann Arbor, 2007).

Stark, Karl Bernhard, *Handbuch der Archäologie der Kunst* (Leipzig, 1880).

Stenhouse, William, *Reading Inscriptions and Writing Ancient History: Historical Scholarship in the Late Renaissance* (London, 2005).

Weiss, Roberto, 'Petrarch the Antiquarian', in Charles Henderson, Jr. (ed.), *Classical, Medieval and Renaissance Studies in Honor of Berthold Louis Ullman*, vol. 2 (Rome, 1964), 199–209.

—— *The Renaissance Discovery of Classical Antiquity* (Oxford, 1969).

Chapter 13

History, Myth, and Fiction:
Doubts and Debates

Peter Burke

For 'scientific' historians of the nineteenth and early twentieth centuries, the three central concepts around which this chapter is organized were obviously distinct. 'History' was a true story, 'fiction' an invented story presented as such, and 'myth' an invented story presented as a true one. Today, matters no longer seem so simple. We have learned that in different cultures and in different periods, the boundary between what we call 'history' and what we call 'fiction' has been drawn in different places as well as with different degrees of precision. It is therefore imperative to translate these concepts into the terms—themselves changing—that were employed in the four centuries under discussion.

In the Middle Ages, some writers made a distinction between 'history' and what they called 'fable' (*fabula*), while some chroniclers criticized others for telling 'lies', as William of Newburgh criticized Geoffrey of Monmouth. All the same, the boundary between history and fiction was an extremely open one.[1] For medieval readers, texts that we might place on the 'fiction' side of the boundary, such as stories about the siege of Troy or King Arthur, were apparently works of history.

THE RENAISSANCE AND THE REFORMATION

In the Renaissance, as in the Middle Ages, explicit distinctions between history and 'fable' were sometimes made. The invention of speeches and the fabrication of documents were denounced by some scholars. In his *Methodus ad facilem historiarum cognitionem* [Method for the Easy Comprehension of History] (1566), Jean Bodin criticized the Italian historian Paolo Giovio for these

---

[1] Peter G. Bietenholz, *Historia and Fabula: Myths and Legends in Historical Thought from Antiquity to the Modern Age* (Leiden, 1994), 62–145.

practices, while the translator Jacques Gohory compared Giovio's work to the once-famous romance of chivalry, *Amadis de Gaule* (1508).

All the same, there were many instances of what now appear to be blatant transgressions of the boundary between history and fiction. Homer was still taken seriously as an historian. Following classical models, the fabrication of speeches placed in the mouths of ambassadors or commanders was a common practice in the historical works of humanists from Leonardo Bruni to Francesco Guicciardini.

A large number of what might be called 'foundation myths' were in circulation in this period. There were stories about the origins of dynasties such as the Habsburgs (supposedly descended from Jason and Noah) and the Tudors (who claimed descent from King Arthur); cities such as Rome (supposedly founded by Romulus) or Padua (by the Trojan Antenor); and other institutions such as religious orders, the English Parliament, and the universities of Oxford and Cambridge.

Most important of all were the stories about the origins of peoples. France and England claimed to have been founded—like ancient Rome—by the Trojans, and the Scots to be descended from the Egyptians, the Swedes from the Goths, the Poles from the Sarmatians, and the Hungarians from the Huns. Some of these stories were challenged by humanist scholars, particularly foreign humanists who had not invested in this kind of symbolic capital and had nothing to lose if the stories were shown to be false. Polydore Vergil, for example, was an Italian whose *Anglica Historia* [English History] (1534) dared to deny the Trojan origins of the British and even the existence of King Arthur, and was roundly attacked by indigenous scholars.

The documents adduced in support of such stories sometimes turned out to be fabrications in their turn. In the Renaissance, as in the Middle Ages, a number of texts in circulation proved to be inauthentic, among them the correspondence between St Paul and the Roman philosopher Seneca; the treatises attributed to 'Dionysius the Areopagite' (a pagan philosopher with whom St Paul conversed in Athens); the so-called hermetic writings attributed to the Egyptian sage Hermes Trismegistus; and the 'Donation of Constantine', a kind of charter conferring on Pope Sylvester and his successors the lands later known as the States of the Church.

New forgeries were added during the Renaissance, among them the texts attributed to the ancient Babylonian writer 'Berosus' but actually produced by a sixteenth-century Italian friar, Annius of Viterbo, and the so-called lead books discovered in Granada in 1588.[2] These texts were usually intended to justify something, as in the case of the papal claim to the States of the Church, or to prove something, such as the Egyptian origins of civilization, in the case of Annius, or the long tradition of Christianity among speakers of Arabic in Andalusia, in the case of the lead books.

---

[2] Anthony Grafton, *Defenders of the Text* (Princeton, 1991), 76–103; and Julio Caro Baroja, *Las falsificaciones de la historia* (Barcelona, 1992), 49–158.

The critique of the authenticity of material objects such as the lead books developed in this period in reaction to the fabrication of fakes to meet the growing demand from collectors of antiquities. Books about antiquities, notably Enea Vico's *Discorsi sopra le medaglie de gli antichi* [Discourse on Ancient Medals] (1555), offered collectors clues to forgery detection.[3] Exposures of forged documents were an offshoot of the process of 'textual criticism', the attempt by humanists to reconstruct texts as their original authors (usually ancient Greeks or Romans) had written them, texts which had been corrupted by copyists over the centuries. In the course of 'emending' texts in this way, it was obviously necessary to consider whether or not a given text had been correctly attributed to its author. The critique of the Donation of Constantine by the Roman humanist Lorenzo Valla, who showed conclusively that the text had been written centuries later than it purported, is simply the most famous of a series of such demonstrations by leading humanists from Petrarch onwards.[4]

The *Pyrrhōneioi hypotypōseis* [Outline of Scepticism] by the ancient philosopher Sextus Empiricus, which argues against the possibility of knowing the past, was rediscovered by the humanists in the course of their hunt for classical texts.[5] At much the same time, general discussions of the problem of historical knowledge are recorded for the first time since classical antiquity. In one of his *Della historia dieci dialoghi* [Ten Dialogues on History] (1560) the Italian philosopher Francesco Patrizzi included a discussion of 'the truth of history', focusing on the problem of contradictory accounts of the same event. Sir Philip Sidney's *Apology for Poetry* (1595) against the critics of poetry included a pre-emptive strike on history, mocking the historian as someone 'loden with old mouse-eaten records', yet 'for the most part authorising himself on the notable foundations of hearsay'.[6]

Other debates focused on specific texts. Fernando Gonzales de Oviedo contrasted his own 'true history' based on observation with the 'fables', derived from books, of his rival Pietro Martire d'Anghiera. In similar fashion, the soldier Bernal Díaz called his own account of the conquest of Mexico a *historia verdadera*, distinguishing it from a rival history by Lopez de Gómara.

Again, the biography of the Roman emperor Marcus Aurelius by the Spanish Franciscan preacher and moralist Antonio de Guevara, *Reloj de principes* [The Dial of Princes] (1529), was criticized by a certain Pedro de Rua for including invented details. Guevara defended himself by claiming that reading history was little more than a pastime, since so far as secular histories were concerned 'we have no certainty that some tell the truth more than others'. Rua's reaction to Guevara's conclusion, or more exactly to his refusal to reach a conclusion, was

---

[3] See also ch. 12 by Peter N. Miller and ch. 11 by Donald R. Kelley in this volume.

[4] Franco Gaeta, *Lorenzo Valla: filologia e storia nell'umanesimo italiano* (Naples, 1955); and Donald R. Kelley, *Foundations of Modern Historical Scholarship* (New York, 1970), 19–52.

[5] Richard Popkin, *The History of Scepticism from Savonarola to Bayle*, 3rd edn (1960; Oxford, 2003), 17–43.

[6] Philip Sidney, *Apology for Poetry*, ed. Geoffrey Shepherd (Manchester, 1973), 105.

to compare his adversary with Pyrrho of Elis and other 'sceptical philosophers'. Whether or not Guevara's letter is authentic (and this matter, too, is disputed), fray Antonio was indeed sympathetic to scepticism and liked to quote the remark attributed to the ancient Roman Pliny that 'Nothing is more certain in this life than that everything is uncertain.'[7]

In his classic study of the history of modern scepticism, Richard Popkin argued that sceptical attitudes were encouraged by the Reformation, since both Catholics and Protestants proved more skilful at undermining each other's arguments than at supporting their own. Protestants subverted the traditional trust in tradition, while Catholics undermined the authority of Scripture. The sceptical Calvinist Pierre Bayle had already made a similar point, describing both tradition and the Bible as 'noses of wax' that could be twisted in different directions, 'good arguments for historical pyrrhonism'.[8]

This argument may be given a historiographical twist, focusing on Catholic and Protestant historians of the Church, notably the Protestant team known as the 'Centuriators of Magdeburg' on one side and Cardinal Baronio on the other.[9] For example, Valla's exposure of the Donation of Constantine was printed for the first time by the German reformer Ulrich von Hutten, and employed by the Centuriators in their attack on the Pope. On the other hand, the Centuriators and other Protestants accepted the story of a female pope, 'Papesse Jeanne' or 'Pope Joan', a story that was rejected as mere 'fable' by the Catholics.[10]

The debate over the Reformation also encouraged awareness of the problem of partiality or bias in historical writing. Two historians, the German humanist Johannes Sleidanus in his *De statu religionis et reipublicae, Carolo Quinto, Caesare, commentarii* [Commentaries on the State of Religion and the Commonwealth in the Reign of the Emperor Charles] (1545) and the Frenchman Henri La Popelinière in his *La vraie et entière Histoire de ces derniers troubles* [The True History of the Late Troubles] (1571), presented themselves as impartial narrators, concerned only, in the phrase that Leopold von Ranke would later make famous, with 'what actually happened': in the words of Sleidanus, *prout res quoque acta fuit*, or as La Popelinière put it, *réciter la chose comme elle est advenue*. The problem of bias would attract still more attention in the seventeenth century.

---

[7] William Nelson, *Fact or Fiction: The Dilemma of the Renaissance Storyteller* (Cambridge, Mass., 1973), 35–6.

[8] Popkin, *The History of Scepticism*, 3–17. Bayle quoted in Hubert Bost, 'Histoire et critique d'histoire chez Pierre Bayle', *Revue d'histoire et de philosophie religieuses*, 70 (1990), 69–108, at 99.

[9] Heinz Scheible, *Die Entstehung der Magdeburger Zenturien* (Gütersloh, 1966); and Stefano Zen, *Baronio storico: controriforma e crisi del metodo umanistico* (Naples, 1994).

[10] Bietenholz, *Historia and Fabula*, 97–107; and Alain Boureau, *The Myth of Pope Joan*, trans. Lydia G. Cochrane (Chicago, 2001).

THE SEVENTEENTH-CENTURY CRISIS

In a famous study, Paul Hazard vividly described what he called the European 'crisis of consciousness' of the late seventeenth century.[11] It included what might be called a 'crisis of historical consciousness', in the sense of increasingly frequent and radical criticisms of traditional historical practice. There was a reaction against the use of rhetoric in works of history at this time and especially against invented speeches. In the preface to his *Annals* (1615–27), William Camden declared that he had 'thrust in no orations but such as were truly spoken; or those reduced to fewer words; much less have I feigned any'. The Venetian friar Paolo Sarpi excluded orations from his *Istoria del Concilio Tridentino* [History of the Council of Trent] (1619), a decision all the more remarkable because speech-making was one of the major activities of the Council. Sarpi summarized these discourses in indirect speech.[12]

More radical than the reaction against rhetoric was the critique of historical knowledge formulated in the course of the epistemological debates of the seventeenth century. Three French philosophers in particular played an important part in the articulation of this debate: René Descartes, François La Mothe Le Vayer, and Pierre Bayle. The discussion of historical scepticism or 'pyrrhonism' became an international one and continued well into the eighteenth century.[13]

The problem was the failure of historical knowledge to measure up to strict standards of certainty, notably the epistemological standards formulated by René Descartes. In his search for firm foundations for knowledge in his *Discours sur la methode* [Discourse on Method] (1637), Descartes dismissed both written history (*les histoires*) and fiction (*les fables*) on similar grounds. The problem with fables is that they 'make one imagine events as possible that are not'. As for history,

> Even the most reliable histories, even if they do not change or augment the value of what happened, to make it more worthy of being read, at least they almost always omit the lowest and least illustrious circumstances. As a result, what is left does not appear as it is, so that those people who model their conduct on the examples that they take from it are liable to fall into the exaggerations of the paladins of our romances, and to make plans that they are not capable of carrying out.[14]

[11] Paul Hazard, *The European Mind (1680–1715)* (London, 1953).
[12] Peter Burke, 'The Rhetoric and Anti-Rhetoric of History in the Early Seventeenth Century', in Gerhard Schröder *et al.* (eds.), *Anamorphosen der Rhetorik: Die Wahrheitspiel der Renaissance* (Munich, 1997), 71–9.
[13] Carlo Borghero, *La certezza e la storia: cartesianesimo, pirronismo e conoscenza storica* (Milan, 1983); Markus Völkel, *'Pyrrhonismus historicus' und 'fides historica': Die Entwicklung der deutschen historischen Methodologie unter dem Gesichtspunkt der historischen Skepsis* (Frankfurt, 1987); and cf. Martin Mulsow, 'Cartesianismus, Pyrrhonismus und historische Kritik', *Philosophische Rundschau*, 42 (1995), 297–314.
[14] René Descartes, *Oeuvres philosophiques*, ed. Ferdinand Alquié (Paris, 1963), 574. My translation.

In other words, Descartes rested his case on the harmful results of following the traditional principle of the 'dignity of history'. The reference to the 'paladins' echoes the mockery of romances of chivalry by Cervantes, and may even be intended as an allusion to *Don Quixote*.

Descartes thus focused attention on the relation between content and form, raising the crucial problem of the criteria according to which historians select or omit information. A critique of historical knowledge was also offered by Descartes's contemporary Gassendi and his follower Malebranche. However, the undermining of what, following Descartes's architectural metaphor, he called the 'great building of history' was carried still further by La Mothe Le Vayer and also by Bayle.

François La Mothe Le Vayer, a member of the group of so-called *libertins érudits* in Paris, admirers of Michel de Montaigne, wrote a *Discours de l'histoire* [Discourse on History] (1638, a year after Descartes's *Discourse on Method*) later amplified and re-titled *Du peu de certitude qu'il y a en histoire* [The Uncertainty of History] (1668). Like Descartes, La Mothe criticized literary conventions that required the omission of whatever could not be discussed in an elegant manner. He also noted contradictions between different accounts of the same event, such as the battle of Pavia.[15] As for Pierre Bayle, a Protestant pastor in exile in Rotterdam, scepticism was central to his famous *Dictionnaire historique et critique* [Historical and Critical Dictionary] (1695–7), a work of reference which might better be described as a contribution to ignorance than as a contribution to knowledge, since Bayle's main aim was to show the unreliability of received accounts of the past, such as the ones in the historical dictionary compiled by his predecessor, Louis Moréri.[16]

By the early eighteenth century, the debate on historical knowledge had come to involve scholars and thinkers in the Netherlands, England, Italy, Spain, and especially Germany.[17] The same basic arguments were put forward again and again, so that we may summarize the arguments theme by theme. Following the traditional analogy between history and law, we might imagine Clio in the dock. The prosecution rested its case on two principal problems, bias and forgery.

THE PROBLEM OF BIAS

In their own time, ancient historians (notably Herodotus) were sometimes criticized for distorting the truth, and these criticisms had been revived at the

---

[15] Popkin, *The History of Scepticism*, 80–7; Borghero, *La certezza e la storia*; and V. I. Comparato, 'La Mothe dalla critica storica al pirronismo', in Tullio Gregory (ed.), *Ricerche su letteratura libertina e letteratura clandestina nel seicento* (Florence, 1981), 259–80.

[16] Ruth Whelan, *Anatomy of Superstition: A Study of the Historical Theory and Practice of Pierre Bayle* (Oxford, 1989).

[17] Völkel, '*Pyrrhonismus historicus' und 'fides historica'*.

Renaissance. Modern historians were attacked for the same reasons. The general problem these criticisms illustrate is that of partiality or bias. Montaigne's essay 'Des livres' (On Books) (1580) criticizes historians who like to draw a moral lesson from the past and cannot avoid 'distorting and twisting the story according to this bias'.[18]

'Bias' is a metaphor derived from the game of bowls, to which the dons of Oxford and Cambridge were particularly addicted in the seventeenth century. Perhaps this is how the term came to be applied to deviations from the true path in politics and religion. The accusation of bias might refer to conscious manipulation, but the term was also used to suggest that our passions and our interests prevent us from seeing beyond our own Church, nation, or political 'party'—a term that was beginning to come into use in the seventeenth century, as in the English case of Whigs versus Tories.

In similar fashion to Montaigne, the scholar Gabriel Naudé noted that historians, 'with the exception of those who are quite heroic', never represent things as they are, but 'slant and mask them according to the image they wish to project'.[19] La Mothe also had much to say about the problem of bias. What would our image of the Punic Wars be today, he asked rhetorically, if we had access to an account from the Carthaginian point of view as well as that of the Romans? How would Caesar's Gallic wars now appear if Vercingetorix rather than Caesar had been the one to write his *Commentaries*?

A concern with modern examples often underlay the quotation of ancient ones. La Mothe, who worked for Cardinal Richelieu, was especially concerned with the bias of Spanish historians. He criticized Prudencio de Sandoval, official historian to Philip III, for 'calumny' and 'partiality', including the attribution of valour to the Spanish troops alone in their conflicts with the French. Widening his criticisms, La Mothe pointed out that biographers such as Eusebius and Eginhard had flattered the emperors about whom they wrote, Constantine and Charlemagne.

One of the readers delighted by La Mothe's attack on Sandoval and others was the sceptical philosopher Pierre Bayle: 'How I love to see someone mock the bias of historians', he wrote. 'There is no greater deception (*filouterie*) greater than that which can be exercised on historical monuments.' 'I hardly ever read historians with the intention of discovering what has happened', Bayle confessed, 'but only to learn what is said in each nation and in each party.'[20]

In Germany, Gottfried Wilhelm Leibniz, who like Bayle combined interests in philosophy and history, was interested in the problem of bias and distinguished three kinds: 'from venality' as in the case of Giovio; 'from ambition', as in the

---

[18] Montaigne, *Essays*, ed. Maurice Rat, 3 vols. (Paris, 1962), bk. 2, ch. 10.
[19] Gabriel Naudé, *Apologie* (Paris, 1625), 18.
[20] Bayle, *Critique générale de l'histoire du calvinisme* (1682), quoted in Arnaldo Momigliano, 'Ancient History and the Antiquarian' (1950), in *Studies in Historiography* (London, 1966), 1–39, at 10.

case of the French historian Scipion Dupleix; and the bias to be found in the sources themselves. Again, in a study with the unforgettable title, *De Charlataneria eruditorium* [On the Charlatanry of the Learned] (1717), the German scholar J. B. Mencken, an acquaintance of Bayle's, emphasized the diversity of the judgements made by the classical historians themselves. 'Ammianus Marcellinus and Montanus commend Julian [Roman emperor, nicknamed 'the Apostate'] as a paragon of virtue; others censure him as a monster of vice. Dio condemns the deeds of Brutus and Cassius; Plutarch extols them. To Paterculus, Sejanus is a lovable man; to many others, he is odious.'[21]

The problem of bias was often discussed in a religious context. As we have seen, the ideal of narrating 'what actually happened' was put forward in the context of the religious wars. Bayle's remarks on bias were occasioned by the publication of an anti-Calvinist history of Calvinism published shortly before Louis XIV decided to expel Protestants from his kingdom.[22] For their part, Catholics drew attention to the bias of Paolo Sarpi's notoriously anti-papal *Istoria del Concilio Tridentino*. The German Protestant Gottfried Arnold offended almost everyone by what he called his 'unpartisan' (*unparteyische*) history of Christianity, which attempted to be fair to the orthodox and heretics alike.[23] The debate continued into the eighteenth century, when a German scholar, Johann Friedrich Burscher, produced a formula close to Ranke's, declaring that the historian *muss die Sache so vorstellen, wie sie Geschehen ist* (must present a fact just as it happened).[24]

Voltaire was not saying anything radically new but summing up more than a century of debate when his essay *Le Pyrrhonisme de l'histoire* [Historical Pyrrhonism] (1769) discussed the bias of Whigs against Tories and Roman historians against Carthage. 'In order to judge fairly it would be necessary to have access to the archives of Hannibal's family.'[25] Being Voltaire, he could not resist wishing that he could see the memoirs of Pontius Pilate.

The problem of bias was particularly topical in the seventeenth century thanks to the prevalence of religious wars and the formation of centralized states. Each 'party', religious or political, tried to present its own version of recent events and to 'unmask' the misrepresentations in the enemy version. The case of the 'Anhalt Chancery' vividly illustrates the process. After the defeat of the Calvinist prince Frederick V by imperial forces at the battle of the White Mountain in 1621, the papers of his follower Christian of Anhalt fell into the hands of the imperialists. They instantly produced a pamphlet, called *The Anhalt Chancery*, in order to pin the 'war-guilt' on to their enemies. The following year, one of the generals on the

[21] J. B. Mencken, *Charlataneria* (New York, 1937), 128.

[22] Bost, 'Histoire et critique'.

[23] Gottfried Arnold, *Unparteyische Kirchen- und Ketzer-historie* (Frankfurt, 1699).

[24] Quoted in L. E. Kurth, 'Historiographie und historischer Roman: Kritik und Theorie im 18. Jht', *Modern Language Notes*, 79 (1964), 337–64, at 340.

[25] Voltaire, *Le pyrrhonisme de l'histoire* (Paris, 1769), 54.

Protestant side, Ernst von Mansfeld, captured an imperial courier, and a rival and opposing pamphlet called *The Spanish Chancery* duly appeared, blaming the Habsburgs for the war.[26] Whether or not the couriers and their documents ever existed, the rise of this technique of persuasion is worth noting.

These circumstances encouraged the rise of official history. Official historians were not uncommon in the Renaissance, working for the republics of Florence and Venice and for new dynasties from Portugal to Hungary, but their numbers multiplied in the seventeenth century. Assemblies, such as the Dutch States-General, and religious orders, such as the Jesuits, commissioned accounts of their activities. So, above all, did monarchs. James I employed Camden, Louis XIII Scipion Dupleix, and Louis XIV Boileau and Racine (among others). The emperor Leopold, Charles II, and the rulers of Prussia and Sweden all commissioned histories. Awareness of these commissions and of the pressures on official historians to show their masters in a glorious light encouraged scepticism about earlier accounts of past events.

THE PROBLEM OF AUTHENTICITY

The second major argument for the prosecution was even more fundamental than the argument for bias. Historians were accused of basing their accounts of the past on forged documents, and writing about characters who never existed and events that never took place. As we have seen, the humanists of the Renaissance had already exposed a number of forged documents, as well as producing some more. New texts of this kind were produced in the seventeenth century, especially in Spain, including the chronicle of the monk 'Haubertus', published in 1667.[27] However, the seventeenth-century critiques were more serious than earlier ones in the sense of challenging the credibility of more and more texts, including some that were fundamental to the classical and Christian traditions. Indeed, the term 'critic'—etymologically related to 'crisis'—came into use at this time, partly to refer to these exposures.[28]

For example, the so-called hermetic writings attributed to the Egyptian sage Hermes Trismegistus were shown by the French Protestant scholar Isaac Casaubon to have been written after Christ, not before.[29] The letters of a Greek despot were exposed as forgeries by the classical scholar Richard Bentley in his *Dissertation on the Epistles of Phalaris* (1697).[30] The history of Carthage attributed to Sanchoniathon,

---

[26] R. Koser, *Der Kanzleienstreit* (Halle, 1874).

[27] Caro Baroja, *Las falsificaciones de la historia*, 97–102.

[28] Jean Jehasse, *La Renaissance de la critique: l'essor de l'humanisme érudit de 1560 à 1614*, 2nd edn (Paris, 2002).

[29] Grafton, *Defenders of the Text*, 145–61.

[30] Joseph Levine, *Ancients and Moderns* (Ithaca, 1991).

and even the records of the magistrates and pontiffs of ancient Rome, fell victim to critics.

Among the most powerful arguments employed by these critics was the argument from 'anachronism', a new word in the seventeenth century. The anachronisms exposed ranged from the language of the forged documents to references to people or events about which the supposed authors could not have known. Casaubon, for instance, pointed out that the hermetic writings referred to the sculptor Phidias, who lived centuries after the texts were supposed to have been written.

The same criteria were applied to the Bible. Baruch Spinoza and Thomas Hobbes both challenged the attribution of the Pentateuch to Moses on the grounds that his death is recounted in the text. Some writings attributed to the Fathers of the Church were also called into question, notably by the Calvinist scholar Jean Daillé. So were some medieval documents, including papal decretals, Icelandic sagas, and charters issued by the Merovingian kings.

A French Jesuit named Jean Hardouin went so far as to claim that the majority of classical texts were forgeries. It was in 1693 that he began, he wrote, 'to scent fraud' in texts attributed to St Augustine, a fraud perpetrated 'about four hundred years ago' by what he called 'the criminal faction' (*scelerata grex*), who anticipated the Calvinists and Jansenists. The monasteries of Corbey, Fleury, and Bobbio were centres of this 'conspiracy', while the great period of forgery extended from the fourteenth to the sixteenth century. The conspirators forged not only the Fathers but also Cicero and Virgil, 'imaginary adversaries, decrees, canons and charters'.[31]

As in the case of the Reformation debates, seventeenth-century religious controversies such as the battle between Jesuits and Jansenists, encouraged scepticism. The Jansenists, who believed that only a minority of Christians would be saved, appealed for support to the writings of St Augustine, while Hardouin began to scent fraud, in 'Augustine and his contemporaries', before he extended his scepticism backwards to include classical texts. Hardouin has been called 'pathological' and would now be diagnosed as paranoid—after all, he believed in a conspiracy to forge texts—but he was only an extreme example of a general trend.[32]

THE CRISIS

The example of Hardouin shows how these specific challenges might have a cumulative effect. No wonder that in 1700 an Italian scholar, Gianvicenzo Gravina, described his own time as the 'age of criticism', or that the word

---

[31] Jean Hardouin, *Prolegomena* (Amsterdam, 1729).

[32] Jean Sgard, 'Et si les anciens étaient modernes . . . le système du P. Hardouin', in Louise Godard de Donville (ed.), *D'un siècle à l'autre* (Marseille, 1987), 209–20; and Anthony Grafton, 'Jean Hardouin: The Antiquary as Pariah', *Journal of the Warburg and Courtauld Institutes*, 62 (1999), 241–67.

'critical' became a fashionable one for book titles, especially in France: the *Histoire critique du Vieux Testament* [Critical History of the Old Testament] (1678) by the Oratorian priest Richard Simon, for instance, Bayle's previously mentioned *Dictionnaire historique et critique*, or the *Histoire critique des pratiques superstitieuses* [Critical History of Superstitious Practices] (1702) by another Oratorian, Pierre Lebrun.

An increasing amount of what had been accepted as true history—the foundation of ancient Rome by Romulus, for example, the lives of certain saints, or the foundation of the French monarchy by Pharamond, was now being dismissed as invention. Did Pharamond exist, scholars asked? Did Romulus exist? Did Aeneas ever go to Italy? Did the Trojan War take place, or was it just the subject of Homer's 'romance'? The debate on early Roman history was particularly vigorous in the early eighteenth century, the main forum being the French Academy of Inscriptions, where a paper 'on the uncertainty of the first four centuries of Roman history' stirred up a major controversy.[33]

Stories about national origins came under particularly heavy fire. La Mothe noted the absurdity of Sandoval's genealogy of the Habsburgs, which went back to Adam. The Protestant scholar Samuel Bochart remarked on the 'folly' of tracing the French and other modern peoples back to Troy. Giambattista Vico generalized from examples such as these when he formulated his famous axiom in the *Scienza Nuova* [New Science] (1725) about the 'conceit of nations' (*boria delle nazioni*): 'Every nation . . . has the same conceit that it before all other nations invented the comforts of human life.'[34] Following in the footsteps of Descartes and his systematic doubt, some scholars went still further, at least in their thought-experiments. Did Charles V exist? Did Augustus exist? Did the siege of La Rochelle really take place?

RESPONSES TO CRISIS

Historians had either to find an answer to sceptics or go out of business. They did find an answer, or, to be more exact, they found a number of different answers which between them permitted what has been called the 'rehabilitation' of history or, as contemporaries put it, 'the trustworthiness of historians' (*fides historica*).[35]

One of the apparent exits from the crisis turned out to be a blind alley, and to be perceived as such by some scholars of the period. This was the geometrical

[33] Mouza Raskolnikoff, *Histoire romaine et critique historique dans l'Europe des Lumières* (Paris, 1992).
[34] Vico, *Scienza Nuova*, section 125.
[35] Judith Shklar, 'Jean D'Alembert and the Rehabilitation of History', *Journal of the History of Ideas*, 42 (1981), 643–64.

method, so prestigious in the late seventeenth century. Pierre-Daniel Huet, for instance, tried to establish the truth of Christianity as an historical religion on the basis of 'axioms' such as the following: 'Every historical work is truthful, if it tells what happened in the way in which the events are told in many books which are contemporary or more or less contemporary to the events narrated.'[36]

A Scottish theologian, John Craig, formulated *Rules of Historical Evidence* (1699) in the form of axioms and theorems. Unfortunately these axioms and theorems turned out to be rather banal, using the language of mathematics and physics to restate commonplaces, for example the principle that the reliability of sources varies with the distance of the source from the event recorded. As Nicolas Fréret pointed out early in the eighteenth century, Craig was pursuing the illusion of a perfect certainty which cannot be found in morals, politics, or history.

SOURCES

More productive and more useful than the geometrical method was the emphasis on original documents. Reviewing Thomas Rymer's *Foedera* (1704), a collection of the original text of treaties, the critic Jean Leclerc made the point that compilations of this kind were a means of refuting pyrrhonism.[37]

The critique of documents had a positive side as well as a negative one. Responding to the Jesuit Papebroch, who had questioned the authenticity of royal charters in early medieval France, the great Benedictine scholar Jean Mabillon produced a treatise, *De re diplomatica* [On the Science of Diplomatics] (1681), discussing the methods of dating such documents by the study of their handwriting, their formulae, their seals, and so on, showing in this way how forgeries might be detected and the authenticity of other charters vindicated. This was not the first work to discuss medieval charters in this way, but it was by far the most systematic. Mabillon convinced his opponent, as the latter was generous enough to admit.[38] There was no single definitive reply to Hardouin as there was to Papebroch, and perhaps there was no need for one, but Le Clerc's *Ars Critica* [Art of Criticism] (1697) laid out the rules of textual criticism, classical and biblical.

The techniques elaborated by Mabillon and others have become known as 'source criticism'. Renaissance humanists such as Erasmus frequently spoke of the need to return 'to the sources' (*ad fontes*), while the English scholar John

---

[36] April G. Shelford, 'Thinking Geometrically in Pierre-Daniel Huet's *Demonstratio Evangelica*', *Journal of the History of Ideas*, 63 (2000), 599–618.

[37] Jean Leclerc, *Bibliothèque Choisie* (Amsterdam, 1703–13).

[38] David Knowles, 'Jean Mabillon', *Journal of Ecclesiastical History*, 10 (1959), 153–73; and Blandine Barret-Kriegel, *La défaite de l'érudition* (Paris, 1988).

Selden used to refer to the 'fountains'. A similar idea was that of 'originals', as in the proud phrase of Bernard de Montfaucon in the preface to his history of the French monarchy: 'I have composed this history on the basis of the originals themselves'.[39]

In the course of the seventeenth and eighteenth centuries, the language of historians came to include more and more references to 'proofs', 'pièces justificatives', 'pièces authentiques', 'monuments' (in the sense of ancient texts), 'evidence', and 'testimony'. The legal language of 'eyewitnesses' and 'testimony' is worth noting. Thomas Sherlock's *The Trial of the Witnesses of the Resurrection of Jesus* (1729) was presented as if in a court of law, while the Jesuit Henri Griffet made an elaborate comparison between the task of an historian and that of a judge. Linked to the increasing awareness of the need for evidence was the rise of the reference, whether footnote, endnote, or marginal note.[40]

Witnesses needed to be cross-examined and some scholars, such as Jacobus Perizonius, in his *Animadversiones historicae* [Truth of Histories] (1685), offered rules for the detection of bias, suggesting that the trustworthiness of a text depended on the age, nationality, education, and character of its author and distinguishing unreliable writers like Louis Maimbourg and Antoine Varillas from trustworthy historians such as Thucydides and Commynes.

Another response to the sceptics was to emphasize the relative reliability of the evidence from material culture, notably inscriptions, coins, and medals. Montfaucon, for instance, edited ten volumes entitled *L'Antiquité expliquee, et représentée en figures* [Antiquity Explained and Represented in Images] (1719–24). When he reached the eleventh century, Montfaucon discussed and illustrated the Bayeux Tapestry. In the field of material culture, the notorious Hardouin was not a sceptic but an enthusiast, who believed that the only way of establishing a satisfactory chronology of ancient history was from coins rather than the assertions of ancient writers. Inscriptions, coins, and medals could of course be forged, as we have seen, but as in the case of texts, rules for the detection of such forgeries could be worked out, and an Italian scholar, Scipione Maffei, wrote an *Ars Critica Lapidaria* [Art of Lapidary Criticism] (1765). Thus the debate with the sceptics had the unintended consequence of encouraging historians to make increasing use of non-literary sources, not only for ancient history but for the Middle Ages as well.[41]

---

[39] Bernard de Montfaucon, *Les monumens de la monarchie françoise*, 5 vols. (Paris, 1729–33), i. preface.

[40] Anthony Grafton, *A Short History of the Footnote* (Cambridge, Mass., 1997).

[41] Francis Haskell, *History and Its Images: Art and the Interpretation of the Past* (New Haven, 1993).

THE REHABILITATION OF MYTH

Yet another response to the challenge of pyrrhonism was what has been called the 'rehabilitation of myth'. The meaning of myths, generally known in this period as 'fables', was discussed with renewed interest and often in a comparative framework. For example, in his *L'Origine des fables* [Origin of Fables] (1724), Bernard de Fontenelle described Greek mythology (which he compared with the Chinese and the 'American', in other words the myths of the Incas) as a mass of falsehoods, but he also noted that fables were both the history and the philosophy of those 'rude ages' (*siècles grossiers*). Similar views, expressed in more detail and with more sympathy for early times, were put forward by Giambattista Vico in Naples and Christian Gottlob Heyne in Göttingen.

Vico was a sceptic in the sense that he considered all accounts of the origins of nations to be uncertain, apart from that of the Jews. However, Vico was an anti-sceptic in the sense that he believed that myths were originally 'true stories' in the sense that they expressed 'the mode of thought of whole peoples'. As Bayle had read historians for evidence of prejudice, so Vico read myth for evidence of changing mentalities. In similar fashion Heyne presented what he called 'fables' or 'mythical discourse' (*sermo mythicus*) as both true and rational, the philosophy and the history of the childhood of humanity.[42] This view, still unorthodox, would become the new conventional wisdom after 1800, especially among the German Romantics.

TOWARDS A RESOLUTION

Drawing on more specific studies, a number of general refutations of historical pyrrhonism appeared in the late seventeenth and early eighteenth centuries.[43] The key argument against the sceptics was the one about 'degrees of assent' put forward by John Locke in his *Essay Concerning Human Understanding* (1690): 'When any particular matter of fact is vouched by concurrent testimony of unsuspected witnesses, there our consent is . . . unavoidable.' For example, 'that there is such a city in Italy as Rome; that about 1700 years ago there lived in it a man, called Julius Caesar; that he was a general, and that he won a battle against another, called Pompey'.[44]

---

[42] On Vico see Joseph Mali, *The Rehabilitation of Myth* (Cambridge, 1992); and on Heyne see Luigi Marini, *I maestri della Germania: Göttingen 1770–1820* (Turin, 1975), 254–70.

[43] Borghero, *La certezza e la storia.*

[44] John Locke, *Concerning Human Understanding*, ed. John Yolton, 2 vols. (London, 1961), ii. 257 (bk 4, ch. 16).

Like Locke, Gerhard Patje (or his academic supervisor, Friedrich Bierling), in his dissertation *Historical Pyrrhonism* (1707), distinguished levels of certainty or probability in history, three in all, from the maximum (that Julius Caesar existed) via the middle level (the reasons for the abdication of Charles V) to the minimum (the problem of the complicity of Mary Queen of Scots in the murder of her husband, or of Wallenstein's plans in the months before his assassination).

Again, Fréret's critique of what he called 'the historical pyrrhonism which is so fashionable in our time' depended on the distinction between 'different degrees of probability'. His rehabilitation of history included arguments in favour of 'unwritten tradition' (*la tradition non écrite*).[45] Fréret was well aware of oral tradition's propensity to change and he granted it a lesser degree of reliability than texts, but he defended it all the same. The rediscovery of oral tradition by historians began long before our own time.

By the middle of the eighteenth century, at the latest, the crisis of historical consciousness was considered to be resolved. Voltaire's contribution to the debate, however entertaining, came rather too late to be useful. From the scholar's point of view, the merit of the sceptics had been to provoke scholars to distinguish different degrees of probability, to formulate practical rules for the criticism of different types of source, and to be more suspicious of 'empty conjectures' about hidden motives, in the style of the secret histories.

SECRET HISTORIES, GAZETTES, AND NOVELS

The crisis of pyrrhonism had consequences beyond the domain of historical scholarship. It is scarcely surprising to find that the relation between history and fiction—discussed in the Renaissance, as we have seen—was examined with particular interest during the crisis. For some scholars, the distinction between history and fiction was clear and distinct, so that describing a colleague as a writer of 'romances' was a way of rejecting his work. Like Gohory on Giovio (discussed above), Leibniz compared the legend that Britain had been founded by Brutus the Trojan to the romance *Amadis de Gaule*. A historian of the Reformation, Gilbert Burnet, condemned the French historian Varillas because 'his books had too much the air of a romance', only to be denounced in his turn for exactly the same failing. In 1710 a man from Padua was denounced to the Inquisition for calling the Bible a 'holy novel' (*sacro romanzo*).[46]

There was also a minority view that historians had something to learn from novelists. Maimbourg, whose history of Calvinism provoked Bayle's critique,

---

[45] Nicolas Fréret, 'Réflexions générales sur l'étude des anciennes histoires' (1724), in *Mémoires académiques* (Paris, 1996), 73–126, at 87.

[46] Quoted in Federico Barbierato, *Politici e ateisti: percorsi della miscredenza a Venezia fra Sei e Settecento* (Milan, 2006), 167.

hoped that his work would give his readers 'the pleasure of a romance'. Even Leibniz wished for 'a little of a romance' (*un peu de roman*) in historical writings, especially when motives were being discussed.[47]

The authors of the so-called secret histories, a new genre which proliferated in the late seventeenth century, certainly gave Leibniz what he wanted. The name 'secret history' was borrowed from the sixth-century Byzantine historian Procopius, whose scandalous account of the doings of the empress Theodora had been published in 1623. Like the modern gossip column, these histories made use of the idiom of intimacy. Their claim to authority was based on their supposed ability to go behind the scenes of public life.[48]

Among the most famous French secret histories were two studies of Florence under the Medici, Varillas's *Les Anecdotes de Florence, ou l'Histoire secrète de la Maison de Medici* [Anecdotes of Florence, or Secret History of the House of Medici] (1685) and Eustache Lenoble's *Histoire secrète de la conjuration des Pazzi* [Secret History of the Pazzi Conspiracy] (1697). In England, Mary Manley's *The Secret History of Queen Zarah* (1705)—in other words Queen Anne's favourite, Sarah Churchill—dared to be more topical, like a series of works by Daniel Defoe, including *The Secret History of the October Club* (1711).

Secret history was, among other things, a response to the weaknesses of humanist history, written in the high style and emphasizing high motives and the effectiveness of political and military leaders. These weaknesses were pitilessly exposed by Descartes, as we have seen. The secret historians, on the other hand, claimed that great events had petty causes, a claim discussed at a general level in an essay by the novelist Saint-Réal and brilliantly summarized in Pascal's epigram 'Cleopatra's nose, had it been shorter, the whole face of the world would have been changed'.[49] Secret history may also be regarded as an antidote to 'official history', which was becoming increasingly important, as we have seen. It was obvious that official historians were not telling the whole truth. Authors and publishers alike realized that there was a market for alternative stories, unofficial versions of the past, whether they were presented as histories or romances.

The unofficial or secret historians were sometimes described with more or less contempt as mere journalists or as novelists, and the relations between all three genres were close. The late seventeenth century was a time when periodicals were increasing in numbers and importance, including unofficial journals which gave an independent account of recent events. Some 'journalists' (a term coined at this time) also wrote history in book form.

Although awareness of the discrepancy between different accounts of the same event is nothing new—think of the problem of reconciling the four

[47] G. W. Leibniz, *Opuscules* (Paris, 1903), 225–6.
[48] Peter Burke, 'Publicizing the Private: The Rise of "Secret History"', in Christian Emden and David Midgley (eds.), *Changing Perceptions of the Public Sphere* (Oxford, forthcoming, 2012).
[49] Pascal, *Pensées*, no. 180.

Gospels—this awareness was surely made more acute by the rise of journals, since divergent accounts of the same event might be published in different newspapers on the same day, or in the same paper on successive days as more information came to light. One of Pierre Bayle's arguments for pyrrhonism was precisely the fact that gazettes were unreliable and that there are many 'bad historians' who produce their books simply by stitching together these 'poor pieces'.[50]

While some historians and journalists were producing semi-fiction, writers of fiction were moving closer to history. As Huet remarked in his essay *Traité de l'origine des romans* [On the Origins of Romances] (1669), in classical antiquity the difference between the genres of history and fiction was one of degree rather than kind, on one side 'truths mixed with a few falsehoods' and on the other 'falsehoods mixed with some truths'. In England, Defoe produced both fiction and secret history, while Manley's *Secret History of Queen Zarah* might equally well be described as a contribution to either genre.

The late seventeenth century also saw the rise of the historical romance, in the sense of a story that was not only set in the past but also introduced real people and offered interpretations of historical events. The most famous examples came from the pen of César de Saint-Réal, whose *Dom Carlos*, published in 1672, bore the subtitle 'nouvelle historique', a term that soon became fashionable in France. Another well-known historical novel of the time was Pierre de Boisguilbert's *Marie Stuart* (1675). In order to give readers the impression that these texts were historical sources, Saint-Réal included footnotes, while Boisguilbert claimed to be telling the 'truth' about Mary Queen of Scots, not writing a 'romance'.

At a time when novel-writing was under attack from moralists for telling lies as well as stimulating the passions, Nicolas Lenglet Dufresnoy, who worked on both sides of the boundary between history and fiction, argued in *De l'usage des romans* [The Use of Romances] (1734) that 'the imperfection of history ought to make us esteem romances', which made no claim to be true and which gave their due place to women, who 'hardly appear in histories' despite their essential role in 'great affairs'.[51] Pierre Bayle might well have agreed, since he enjoyed both *Dom Carlos* and other seventeenth-century historical romances. However, he disliked the 'impudence' of writers who published what claimed to be memoirs but which were actually 'a mixture of truth and fable'.[52]

From the late seventeenth to the late eighteenth century, invented memoirs were a fashionable literary genre in France, among them the *Mémoires de M. d'Artagnan* (which inspired *The Three Musketeers* of Alexandre Dumas), and the

---

[50] Brendan Dooley, *The Social History of Skepticism: Experience and Doubt in Early Modern Culture* (Baltimore, 1999), esp. 9–44.

[51] Georges May, *Le dilemme du roman au 18e siècle* (New Haven and Paris, 1963), 139–61, at 141; and cf. Geraldine Sheridan, *Nicolas Lenglet Dufresnoy and the Literary Underworld of the Ancien Regime* (Oxford, 1989).

[52] Quoted in Faith E. Beasley, *Revising Memory: Women's Fiction and Memoirs in Seventeenth-Century France* (New Brunswick, 1990), 162.

memoirs of the Mancini sisters, close to the young Louis XIV (the memoirs of Hortense Mancini may well have been written by Saint-Réal).[53] The fashion spread abroad, the obvious English examples being Daniel Defoe's *Memoirs of a Cavalier* and his *Journal of the Plague Year*, the latter complete with official documents and statistics to give the texts what used to be called verisimilitude and what modern critics would describe as a stronger 'reality effect'. Contemporary readers appear to have taken the *Journal* to be a work of history, and it continued to be cited as a historical source in the nineteenth century.[54]

In other words, at the very time that scholars were giving more attention than ever before to distinguishing fact from fiction, other writers were making successful attempts to blur the genres. Ideas and techniques such as the sense of anachronism, the use of footnotes, and the practice of quoting documents supported the verisimilitude of new semi-fictional genres such as secret histories and historical romances as well as works of scholarship. The interaction between written histories and works of fiction is a long-term phenomenon, running from the ancient world to our own time, and this chapter has presented only a few twists and turns in a much longer story.

CHINA AND JAPAN

In the early modern Islamic world, the long-standing interest in philology does not seem to have led to a general discussion of either unreliable histories or forged documents, though new research may modify this conclusion. In early modern China or Japan, however, as in Europe, lively debates on these topics took place. The tradition of official history was a particularly long and strong one in China, but unofficial or 'secret history' (*mi shi*) also existed, focusing, like the work of Procopius and his early modern followers, on the sex lives of rulers.[55] As early as the Song dynasty (960–1279) some Chinese scholars were expressing criticisms of earlier histories, while a 'school of evidential learning' (*kaozhengxue*) developed in the seventeenth and eighteenth centuries and spread to Japan.

As in the case of the European Renaissance, there were many scholars in China who hoped for a 'return to antiquity' (*fugu*). The Neoplatonism and the neo-Aristotelianism of the Middle Ages and the Renaissance had a Chinese parallel, the neo-Confucianism associated with the Song scholar Zhu Xi. As in the cases of Plato and Aristotle in Europe, the revival of Confucius led to a movement to strip away later commentaries and return to what the master had originally said, or at

---

[53] Vivian Mylne, *The 18th-Century French Novel* (Manchester, 1965); and Marie-Thérèse Hipp, *Mythes et réalités: enquête sur le roman et les mémoires, 1660–1700* (Paris, 1976).

[54] R. Mayer, 'The Reception of the *Journal of the Plague Year* and the Nexus of Fiction and History in the Novel', *English Literary History*, 57 (1990), 529–56.

[55] Harold L. Kahn, *Monarchy in the Emperor's Eyes: Image and Reality in the Ch'ien-Lung Reign* (Cambridge, Mass., 1971), 50.

least to earlier interpretations of his philosophy, suggesting in the process that one canonical text, the *Shenjing* [Documents Classic] contained forged material.

By the time of the transition from the Ming to the Qing dynasty in the middle of the seventeenth century it is possible to speak of a school or schools of evidential learning. Scholars associated with these schools criticized their predecessors for lack of concern with evidence and failure to cite sources.

The parallels between the history of scholarship in China in the seventeenth and eighteenth centuries and scholarship in Renaissance and post-Renaissance Europe are striking. There was a similar concern with 'sources' and a similar concern to replace classical texts in their original historical contexts, as in the case of Dai Zhen or Zhang Xuecheng who went so far as to say that the Confucian classics 'were histories'.[56]

Like Valla in Italy, Yan Ruoju used philological methods, noting that linguistic anachronisms offered valuable clues to 'the detection of forgery' (*bianwei*). Like Renaissance humanists, some of these scholars supplemented the evidence of dynastic histories with that of epigraphy, in their case inscriptions on stone slabs and bronze vessels. Also like the humanists, some of these scholars, including Dai Zhen, were antiquarians, concerned with objects ranging from bells to ancient vehicles. As in Renaissance Europe, this interest in the history of material culture grew out of the fashionable pursuit of collecting antiques, which led to the production of fakes and consequently to the formulation of rules for detecting them.[57]

In Japan, too, there was a movement of evidential learning (*kōshōgaku*), including a philological turn and a historicization of canonical texts, whether Buddhist or Confucian. Tominaga Nakamoto emphasized the difficulty of discovering what the Buddha and Confucius had actually taught, while Ōta Kinjō pointed out that the neo-Confucianism of Zhu Xi included elements of Buddhism and Daoism and so needed to be purified.[58]

In a more original development out of the *kōshōgaku* movement, some Japanese scholars dared to criticize their foundation myths. As we have seen, European humanists had criticized the myths of origin of many peoples, like the claim of the British to descend from Brutus the Trojan. In similar fashion, if somewhat more tactfully, Hayashi Razan doubted the traditional stories of the foundation of Japan by the gods and the descent of the first emperor, Jinmu,

---

[56] See ch. 3 by On-cho Ng and ch. 1 by Achim Mittag in this volume.

[57] Benjamin A. Elman, *From Philosophy to Philology: Intellectual and Social Aspects of Change in Late Imperial China*, 2nd edn (1984; Los Angeles, 2001); Craig Clunas, *Superfluous Things: Material Culture and Social Status in Early Modern China* (Cambridge, 1991); and On-cho Ng and Q. Edward Wang, *Mirroring the Past: The Writing and Use of History in Imperial China* (Honolulu, 2005), 243–50.

[58] Tetsuo Najita, *Visions of Virtue in Tokugawa Japan* (Chicago, 1987), 101–21; and Benjamin A. Elman, 'The Search for Evidence from China: Qing Learning and Kōshōgaku in Tokugawa Japan', in Joshua A. Fogel (ed.), *Sagacious Monks and Bloodthirsty Warriors: Chinese Views of Japan in the Ming-Qing Period* (Norwalk, Conn., 2002), 158–82.

from the sun goddess, although he did not express these doubts in public, while Arai Hakuseki suggested that stories about the gods should be interpreted in human terms. In the early nineteenth century, the militant rationalist Yamagata Bantō dismissed earlier accounts of the age of the gods as absurd and emphasized the unreliability of oral traditions as evidence for distant events, declaring that 'without documentation, there is darkness'.[59]

Indeed, approaching each culture with categories taken from the other, we might speak of Chinese and Japanese 'humanism', or of Western *kaozheng* or *kōshōgaku*. The Asian movement appears to have been smaller in scale than the Western one and led to no 'crisis of pyrrhonism', but the similarities between the two are clear enough.

KEY HISTORICAL SOURCES

Bayle, Pierre, *Dictionnaire historique et critique* (Rotterdam, 1695–7).
Defoe, Daniel, *Journal of the Plague Year* (London, 1722).
Fontenelle, Bernard de, *De l'origine des fables*, ed. J. F. Carré (1724; Paris, 1932).
La Mothe Le Vayer, François de, *Du peu de certitude qu'il y a dans l'histoire* (Paris, 1668).
Lenglet Du Fresnoy, Nicolas, *L'histoire justifiée contre les romans* (Paris, 1735).
Saint-Réal, César de, *Dom Carlos, nouvelle historique* (Amsterdam, 1672).
Vico, Giambattista, *Scienza Nuova*, 3rd edn (Naples 1744); trans. Thomas G. Bergin and Max H. Fisch as *The New Science of Giambattista Vico* (Ithaca, 1948).
Voltaire, *Le pyrrhonisme de l'histoire* (Paris, 1769).

BIBLIOGRAPHY

Bietenholz, Peter G., *Historia and Fabula: Myths and Legends in Historical Thought from Antiquity to the Modern Age* (Leiden, 1994).
Bizzocchi, Roberto, *Genealogie incredibili: scritti di storia nell'Europa moderna* (Bologna, 1995).
Borghero, Carlo, *La certezza e la storia: cartesianesimo, pirronismo e conoscenza storica* (Milan, 1983).
Brownlee, John S., *Japanese Historians and the National Myths 1600–1945: The Age of the Gods and Emperor Jinmu* (Vancouver, 1997).
Elman, Benjamin A., *From Philosophy to Philology: Intellectual and Social Aspects of Change in Late Imperial China*, 2nd edn (1984; Los Angeles 2001).
Grafton, Anthony, *Forgers and Critics* (Princeton, 1990).
—— *Defenders of the Text* (Princeton, 1991).
Haskell, Francis, *History and Its Images: Art and the Interpretation of the Past* (New Haven, 1993).

---

[59] John S. Brownlee, *Japanese Historians and the National Myths 1600–1945: The Age of the Gods and Emperor Jinmu* (Vancouver, 1997), 42–60. See also ch. 4 by Masayuki Sato in this volume.

Hipp, Marie-Thérèse, *Mythes et réalités: enquête sur le roman et les mémoires, 1660–1700* (Paris, 1976).

Mali, Joseph, *The Rehabilitation of Myth* (Cambridge, 1992).

Momigliano, Arnaldo, *Studies in Historiography* (London, 1966).

Ng, On-cho and Wang, Q. Edward, *Mirroring the Past: The Writing and Use of History in Imperial China* (Honolulu, 2005).

Popkin, Richard, *The History of Scepticism from Savonarola to Bayle*, 3rd edn (1960; Oxford, 2003).

Chapter 14

Historical Writing in Russia and Ukraine

Michael A. Pesenson and Jennifer B. Spock

The one-thousand-year-old tradition of historical writing in Russia emerged in the medieval culture of Kiev under the Riurikid dynasty and survived the destruction and fragmentation caused by the Mongol conquests.[1] An important part of the rich local and dynastic textual culture of Muscovy, historical writing burgeoned in the fifteenth century. Slowly, its forms and traditions moved towards a unified national voice simultaneously with the transformation of the state into imperial Russia. From 1400 to 1800 historical writing in Russia was tied closely to political circumstances, the ideology and structure of the Moscow and St Petersburg courts, and to the development of the Russian Orthodox Church as an independent branch of Eastern Orthodoxy, after the fall of Constantinople. These three conditions affected four areas of historical writing: chronicles (*letopisi*) and chronographs (*khronografy*) that eventually led to personal historical accounts, hagiographical saints' lives (*zhitiia*), which in time overlapped with the genres of autobiography and biography, official state historiographies, and researched histories.

The Mongol conquests of Eastern Europe in the thirteenth century caused Kievan Rus' to disintegrate into regional principalities whose princes struggled for dominance. At the start of the fifteenth century, Moscow's princes ruled as heads of the Riurikid dynasty in name only. However, by the early 1500s the grand princes in Moscow had managed to consolidate most north-eastern Rus' territories to create the centralized state of Muscovy. The metropolitan of Moscow helped to incorporate the new territories of the grand princes and tsars into the religious and political narrative of the new polity. From 1400 to 1600 historical texts were produced in princely and episcopal courts and monasteries, and were largely based on earlier prototypes.[2] Writers copied from earlier texts, adding information as needed. The sixteenth century saw Muscovy

---

[1] Jennifer Spock would like to thank Charles J. Halperin and Donald Ostrowski for their counsel early in the process of drafting this chapter.
[2] See Jonathan Shepard, 'The Shaping of Past and Present, and Historical Writing in Rus', *c.* 900–*c.*1400', in Sarah Foot and Chase F. Robinson (eds.), *The Oxford History of Historical Writing*, vol. 2: *400–1400* (Oxford, forthcoming), particularly for the origins of the chronicle tradition in Russia.

expand beyond traditional Rus' borders in the east. The seventeenth century was ushered in by the Time of Troubles (*Smuta*),[3] which fractured political unity. The *Smuta* ended soon after the election of Michael Romanov in 1613 and its impact galvanized individuals to compose more personal histories, while State and Church became increasingly interested in standardizing texts. Under the Romanovs, Russia expanded to the west, south, and east, and Peter I (the Great) and Catherine II (the Great) encouraged Russia's adoption of Western culture. By Catherine's death in 1796, historical writing in Russia had become strongly influenced by the Enlightenment and scholars searched for primary documents to illuminate and analyse the past. However, Westernization primarily affected elites, for the bulk of Russia's population, the peasantry, remained illiterate— bound to tradition by law and custom. The desire to place Russia within the history of Orthodoxy and the history of the world, and a developing urge to frame a national narrative, influenced the development of historical writing which remained in elite control to 1800.

CHRONICLES, CHRONOGRAPHS, AND HISTORIES

Russia's chronicles are one of its most valuable primary sources, providing an enormous text base for fifteenth- to seventeenth-century Moscow and other major principalities such as Novgorod, Tver', and Pskov.[4] The chronicles mixed brief annual entries of princely activity or parochial human interest, of extraordinary or mundane events—battles, the birth of an animal, the arrival of a new bishop, or a particularly bad harvest—with extended tales of significant events, such as the 1380 Battle of Kulikovo.[5] Extensive tales were usually inter- polated long after the original event to craft a political ideology. Thus, events which now appear significant, such as the battles of Prince Alexander Nevsky against the Swedes and Livonian Knights in the early 1240s, received no mention in the *Ipat'evskaia letopis'* [Hypatian Chronicle] (end of the thirteenth century).[6] In their entries for 1380, Moscow chronicles of the fifteenth century described Prince Dmitrii Donskoi's victory over the Mongols at Kulikovo in rich detail, while for the same year the *Pskovskaia letopis'* [Pskov II Chronicle] (after 1486) stated laconically: 'Grand Prince Dmitrii and all the princes of Russia fought

---

[3] The *Smuta* is usually dated from 1605 to 1613, but some scholars date the start of the Troubles earlier from 1598 or 1604.

[4] A number of Russia's chronicles have been published in the multi-volume *Polnoe sobranie russkikh letopisei*, 43 vols. (St Petersburg, 1841–2002) (hereafter, *PSRL*).

[5] East Slavic, Byzantine, and other Orthodox calculations for the biblical beginning of the world differed: see *The Nikonian Chronicle: From the Beginning to the Year 1132*, vol. 1, ed. Serge A. Zenkovsky (Princeton, NJ, 1984), pp. xxxvii–xl.

[6] For the year 6750 (1241/42) the chronicler entered: 'nothing happened' (*ne bys nechto zh*), *PSRL* (repr. edn, Moscow, 1998), ii. col. 794. Dates after chronicle titles indicate the last dated entry in the text.

with the Tatars on the Don'.[7] Russia's chronicle tradition included extensive compilations (*svody*, singular *svod*) such as the massive *Nikonovskaia letopis'* [Nikonian Chronicle] (1520s–30s) as well as shorter family and local chronicles appearing in the seventeenth century.[8] Titles were assigned to the chronicles later by scholars to designate their place of production, where they were found, a well-known owner, or when they were created. However, unravelling the 'genealogies' of each text and its interrelations with other chronicles is a lengthy, complex, and ongoing process. Chronographs, which attempted to recount the history of the world and Russia's place in it, were a related form of historical writing, but organized differently by regions and episodic narratives.

A. A. Shakhmatov generated seminal critical analyses of the older Kievan and Muscovite chronicles in which he hypothesized not only the existence, but also the content, of earlier works: templates of the surviving manuscripts.[9] His scholarship so influenced the study of Russian chronicle-writing (*letopisanie*) that almost seventy years later V. I. Buganov wrote of 'pre-Shakhmatov' and 'post-Shakhmatov' research. Subsequent scholars have disagreed with Shakhmatov's findings, but most have merely corrected or refined his conclusions rather than altered his methodology.[10]

FIFTEENTH CENTURY

The fifteenth century marked an important phase in Russian chronicle-writing because despite the genre's origins in earlier centuries, no manuscripts before the 1400s are extant. The chroniclers of the fifteenth century used, and therefore preserved in part, previous texts to recreate historical narrative while adding passages to provide contemporary witness, resulting in a plethora of composite texts. Scholars have shown that the *Novgorodskaia I letopis'* [Novgorod I Chronicle] (late fourteenth to early fifteenth century), the *Sofiiskaia I letopis'* [Sofia I Chronicle] (1418 and 1471), and the *Troitskii svod* [Trinity Compilation] of 1409 were based on earlier works and copied by later compilers.[11] Certain chronicles were favoured in Moscow as models; for example, in addition to those listed above, various redactions of the *Simeonovskaia letopis'* [Simeonov Chronicle] (1493), the

---

[7] 'Pskovskaia vtoraia letopis'', in *PSRL* (1851), v. 1–46, at 16.

[8] For brief overviews of the shorter chronicles, see M. N. Tikhomirov, 'Maloizvestnye letopisnye pamiatniki', *Istoricheskii arkhiv*, 7 (1951), 207–53; and A. A. Zimin, 'Kratkie letopistsy XV–XVI vv', *Istoricheskii arkhiv*, 5 (1950), 3–39.

[9] A. A. Shakhmatov, *Razyskaniia drevneishikh russkikh letopisnykh svodov* (St Petersburg, 1908). Ia. S. Lur'e urged caution while researching chronicles in *Dve istorii Rusi 15 veka: Rannie i pozdnie nezavisimye i ofitsial'nye letopisi ob obrazovannii Moskovskogo gosudarstva* (St Petersburg, 1994), 12.

[10] V. I. Buganov, *Otechestvennaia istoriografiia russkogo letopisaniia: Obzor sovetskoi literatury* (Moscow, 1975), 321–6.

[11] The 1409 *svod*, the earliest Moscow chronicle, burned in 1812 and is known today only through N. M. Karamzin's work. See Lur'e, *Dve istorii*, 13.

Rogozhovskaia letopis' [Rogozhov Chronicle] (1412), the *Novgorodskaia IV letopis'* [Novgorod IV Chronicle] (1437 and 1447), and the 1479 *svod* were copied in part or in whole into later works.

Innovation in the fifteenth century took the form of so-called grand princely (*velikokniazheskie*) chronicles compiled in Moscow that began with the 1472 and 1479 *svody*. Compilers constructed new interpretations of Muscovite political conditions, occasionally altering facts to support the prince's position.[12] As part of Moscow's creation of a new political identity, chroniclers downplayed the Mongols as overlords even as they highlighted Mongol ruthlessness.[13] Nevertheless, many chronicles reported that a prince 'went to the Horde' or 'returned from the Horde' as grand prince: in 6940 (1432) 'Grand Prince Vasilii Vasil'evich arrived at the grand princedom from the Horde and with him [came] Tsarevich Mansyr Ulan, who set him in the grand prince's position'.[14] Although compilers often hesitated to acknowledge explicitly that the grand princes received their titles from the khan, mention of their journeys confirmed grand princely authority.[15] Eventually, the differences among regional texts lessened in significance as Ivan III's (r. 1462–1505) compilers wove local texts into a single history linking the grand princes of Kievan Rus' to the Moscow royal line. D. S. Likhachev argued that Ivan consciously crafted an 'all-Russian' (*obshcherusskii*) narrative that recounted events in the territories of the grand princes from the Baltic to the Black Seas.[16] Thus, Alexander Nevsky's successes against Western aggression and Donskoi's victory at Kulikovo confirmed Moscow's position as defender of Russia. The reworked narrative of Vasilii II's reception of the charter to rule and his conquest of Nizhnii-Novgorod, along with many other entries in successive chronicles, pointed to Moscow's hegemony over other Russian principalities.[17]

Simultaneously with the revival of the chronicle tradition in the fifteenth century, Russian bookmen compiled chronographs based on Byzantine works by Hamartolos, Malalas, and Constantine Manasses and inserted the stories of Kievan and Muscovite Russia. Likhachev argued that Russia's tradition of historical writing bears witness to an evolution in literary language and that the *Russkii Khronograf* [Russian Chronograph] was consciously focused on literary presentation and moral teachings. He averred that the embellished language of the *Khronograf* influenced Muscovite and provincial chronicles to become more

---

[12] D. S. Likhachev, *Russkie letopisi i ikh kul'turno-istoricheskoe znachenie* (Moscow, 1947), 360.

[13] Charles Halperin, *Russia and the Golden Horde: The Mongol Impact on Medieval Russian History* (Bloomington, Ind., 1985), 61–74.

[14] 'vyide iz ordy kniaz' velikyi Vasilei Vasil'evich na velikoe kniazhenie, a s nim posol Man'syr' Ulan tsarevich', tot ego posadil na velikoe kniazhenie.' 'Sofiiskaia pervaia letopis'', in *PSRL* (1851), v. II–275, at 264.

[15] Lur'e, *Dve istorii*, 79.

[16] Likhachev, *Russkie letopisi*, 289–93.

[17] Lur'e, *Dve istorii*, 57–81.

episodic, developing plot lines within their basic chronology.[18] The 1512 version of the *Khronograf* contained a lengthy account of Emperor Constantine of Rome including a rendering of the emperor's baptism, the baptism of Armenia, and the creation of Constantinople.[19] It could not fail to remind Muscovites of Emperor Basil II who helped to baptize Russia through its first Christian ruler St Vladimir, thus linking the Muscovite Church to the spiritual power of ancient Byzantium. Thus, the chronograph manuscripts influenced the style of later chronicle compilations and presented a narrative of world history in keeping with Orthodox beliefs.[20]

SIXTEENTH CENTURY

Moralizing and commentary abound in the *Russkii khronograf*, but that did not mean that the chronicles lacked moral teachings or a Christian worldview, for an eschatological vision in which God punished sin and rewarded virtue existed in the manuscripts. In late works such as the Novgorod *svod* (1539), the chronicler interpreted Ivan III's 1471 campaign against Novgorod in moral terms. Rather than referring to 'Grand Prince Ivan Vasil'evich' as had been the norm in earlier chronicles, the compilers described Ivan III as 'noble' (*blagorodnyi*), 'pious' (*blagochestivyi*), and 'righteous' (*blagovernyi*), thus demonstrating ties to Church teachings and to the moral tone of the *Khronograf*. Meanwhile, the inhabitants of Novgorod who opposed his rule and sought aid from Lithuania were denounced as 'witless' (*bezumnye*) and influenced by the devil.[21] Not surprisingly, this episode received similar treatment in the *Nikonovskaia letopis'* and the *Stepennaia kniga* [Book of Degrees] (1560s), both produced in Moscow's metropolitan court.

Metropolitan Daniel (r. 1522–39) was directly involved in the composition of the *Nikonovskaia letopis'*. An enormous 'all-Russian' work, it exhibited systematic Church influence: the use of Church festivals to mark dates, constant references to God and Moscow as his favoured city, and elaborate language.[22] The *Nikonovskaia letopis'* was a direct prototype for the *Stepennaia kniga*, which was incorporated into the *Velikie minei chetii* [Great Menology] (1540s) produced

---

[18] Likhachev, *Russkie letopisi*, 308–48.

[19] *Russkii khronograf*, in *PSRL* (1914), xxii. part 2, 82–92.

[20] The notion of Muscovy as the Third Rome has been a staple of general texts on Russian history with respect to Muscovy's 'self-image'. Although the idea existed in sixteenth-century Muscovy, it was limited to ecclesiastical circles, and overshadowed politically by the concept of Moscow as the New Jerusalem. See Daniel B. Rowland, 'Moscow—The Third Rome or the New Israel?' *Russian Review*, 55:4 (October 1996), 591–614, at 594–6.

[21] *Novgorodskaia letopis' po spisku P. P. Dubrovskogo*, in *PSRL* (2004), xliii. 189. See also Likhachev, *Russkie letopisi*, 331, 344, 352–3.

[22] Ibid., 352; and B. M. Kloss, *Nikonovskii svod i russkie letopisi XVI–XVII vekov* (Moscow, 1980), 112–30.

at the court of Metropolitan Makarii (r. 1542–63).[23] The *Stepennaia Kniga* was organized by the regnal periods of grand princes and metropolitans, thus reflecting a structural link between Crown and Church, and it in turn became a template for the *Litsevoi svod* [Illustrated Compilation] (1560s–80s), an invaluable, ornately illuminated manuscript.[24]

In addition to more elegant language and increasing religious references and interpolations, the chronicles of the later fifteenth and sixteenth centuries such as the 1479 *svod* and the *Nikonovskaia letopis'* inserted copies of Moscow court documents. Entire letters were copied into the texts as well as lists of names and petitions from the records of the diplomatic chancellery (*posol'skii prikaz*).[25] In this way, the chancellery structure and the ideology of the grand prince's court influenced the content and structure of historical texts, lending them a more authoritative voice.

Not all texts, however, were Moscow-centric. The *Ipat'evskaia letopis'* has become the focus of studies by Ukrainian scholars who refer to its *Khlebnikovskii* compilation (sixteenth century) and other redactions based on earlier south-western texts such as the *Galitsko-Volynskaia letopis'* [Galicia-Volhynia Chronicle].[26] Other sixteenth-century texts were produced in western regions that were ultimately absorbed by the Russian tsar, and these compilations sometimes contained chronicles of both the eastern Russian and Lithuanian grand princely dynasties. Texts such as the *Vilenskii spisok* [Vilno Copy] focused on the narrative of the Lithuanian princes.[27]

Finally, the second half of the sixteenth century and early seventeenth century witnessed the advent of personal history-writing. Prince Andrei Mikhailovich Kurbskii (*c.*1528–83), a disaffected and exiled member of Ivan IV's (the Terrible, r. 1533–84) court, is supposed to have written a polemical history of Ivan's reign, denouncing his erstwhile sovereign. This *Istoriia o velikom kniaze Moskovskom* [History of the Grand Prince of Moscow] (*c.*1573[?]) abounds with biblical and patristic references and pious judgements of the tsar.[28] Although its attribution and dating have been challenged, the writer's polemics strongly influenced the

---

[23] Attributed to Makarii, this extensive work was compiled by a group, some of whom are known: 'Velikie minei chetii', *Slovar' knizhnikov i knizhnosti drevnei Rusi, vtoraia polovina XIV–XVI*, vol. 1: *A–K*, ed. D. S. Likhachev (Leningrad, 1988), 126–33, at 130.

[24] Kloss, *Nikonovskii svod*, 206–52. See also S. O. Shmidt, *Rossiiskoe gosudarstvo v seredine XVI stoletiia: Tsarskii arkhiv i litsevye letopisi vremeni Ivana Groznogo* (Moscow, 1984).

[25] Likhachev, *Russkie letopisi*, 354–70.

[26] For historiographical and textual disputes relating to the *Ipat'evskaia letopis'* and its variants see *Galitsko-Volynskaia letopis': Tekst, kommentarii, issledovanie*, ed. and comp. N. F. Kotliar (St Petersburg, 2005).

[27] *PSRL* (1907), xvii contains twenty-two fifteenth- to seventeenth-century texts from western Russian and Polish-Lithuanian lands.

[28] A clear and succinct discussion, with useful references, of the most important elements of the disputes over the attribution of the *Istoriia o velikom kniaze Moskovskom* and other writings of Andrei Kurbskii and Tsar Ivan IV can be found in Carolyn Pouncy, 'Missed Opportunities and the Search for Ivan the Terrible', *Kritika: Explorations in Russian and Eurasian History*, 7:2 (2006), 309–28.

historiography of Ivan IV's reign as he wondered how so 'good and distinguished' a tsar who 'enjoyed good renown from all' could transform into so vile a prince. Among others he blamed the 'sorcerous' wives of the Riurikid clan, citing John Chrysostom on evil women, and throughout the text he railed against Ivan's 'wicked' advisers, who 'drove him from the vicinity of God'.[29] The author focused heavily on Ivan's campaigns against Kazan' and the Livonians, as well as on his treatment of servitors during the notorious *oprichnina* period (1565–72).

SEVENTEENTH CENTURY

In the seventeenth century, chronicles increasingly focused on personal and regional tales as the court relied more heavily on formal administrative documentation for its historical needs. The Time of Troubles played a role in this transformation, as did Russian expansion into Siberia in the seventeenth and eighteenth centuries. During the Troubles, literate Muscovites began to write their own historical texts, committing to paper their personal experiences as part of the flow of Muscovite history. With the traumatic events fresh in their minds, Muscovite writers, eyewitnesses, and sometimes participants in the turmoil struggled to understand, and come to terms with, the disastrous occurrences that had led Russia to the brink of the abyss. Four texts in particular stand out as the most significant historical works composed in the aftermath of this, one of the bloodiest periods in Russian history—Avraamii Palitsyn's *Istoriia v pamiat' predidushchim rodom* [History to be Remembered by Future Generations] (1620), Ivan Timofeev's *Vremennik* [Annals] (1616–19), Ivan Khvorostinin's *Slovesa dnei i tsarei i sviatitelei moskovskikh* [Account of the Days of the Tsars and Prelates of Muscovy] (1620s), and Semyon Shakhovskoi's *Letopisnaia kniga* [Book of Bygone Years] (1620s). These texts, influenced by the popular medieval models of the military tale and the chronicle, are best classified as historical tales (*istoricheskie povesti*), combining memoir, chronicle narrative, and polemical treatise. Exhibiting a conceptual and thematic unity largely absent in the earlier chronicle tradition, these tales indicate a new direction in the writing of history in Russia, one focused on relating and critically analysing specific events or themes freed from a strictly chronological narrative.

These tales were products of writers from different backgrounds espousing diverse political views, united by a common feeling of patriotism and concern for Russia's future lest chaos and carnage resurface. They asserted that calamity had engulfed Russia as punishment for her sins, whether these had been the excesses of Ivan the Terrible's *oprichnina*, the intrigue and corruption of the Boyars, the cupidity and lust for power of Boris Godunov, the popular support for lowly

---

[29] *Prince A. M. Kurbsky's History of Ivan IV*, ed. and trans. J. L. I. Fennell (Cambridge, 1965), 3, 9, 155.

apostate foreign-sponsored pretenders (a succession of False Dmitriis), the weakness of Vasilii Shuiskii, or Russia's capitulation to mob rule. Russia had suffered terribly, but was now cleansed of both her enemies and her sins and thus stood poised to rise again under a new legitimate monarch, Michael Romanov, who by 1618 had finally restored order, unity, and peace.

While these tales were grounded in the medieval Russian conception of providential history, the authors allowed their heroes a certain degree of agency whereby men were increasingly deemed responsible for their actions. For example, both Palitsyn and Timofeev chastised themselves and others for cowardice in failing to oppose Boris Godunov's 'treachery' in the murder of Dmitrii Ivanovich and the exile of the Romanovs.[30] Timofeev and Shakhovskoi, both of whom discerned the origins of the Time of Troubles in the excesses of Ivan IV, faulted the tsar for betraying his God-anointed calling in instituting the *oprichnina*, seeing in it the seeds of the divisiveness, cronyism, and depravity that had brought Muscovy to her knees.

The few chronicles produced in the seventeenth century are also noteworthy for their commentary on the Troubles; these are the *Khronografy* of 1617 and 1620, which represent a substantial reworking of the *Russkii Khronograf* of 1512, and the *Novyi letopisets* [New Chronicle] written in 1630. The *Khronograf* of 1617 continued where the first chronograph left off, shortening entries on world history while expanding chapters on Russia through the coronation of Michael Romanov.[31] While neither as colourful nor as detailed as the historical tales in its depiction of the Time of Troubles, the *Khronograf*'s account was significant in that it presented in condensed form the earliest overview of Russian history from the death of Ivan IV to 1613. As part of the larger (and official) chronograph narrative, it was widely circulated and may have been consulted by the writers of the historical tales themselves.

The *Khronograf* of 1617 was also important for the new information it provided on the history of Europe through the middle of the sixteenth century, taken primarily from the influential *Kronika swiata* [Universal Chronicle] of Marcin Bielski (1551–64, translated into Russian in 1584), introducing Muscovites to the history of the Reformation and the great discoveries of the New World. The *Khronograf* of 1620 further expanded Russian knowledge of the world by including Bielski's chapters on cosmography, themselves based on the famous *Cosmographia* [Cosmography] of Sebastian Münster (1644).[32]

---

[30] *Skazanie Avraamiia Palitsyna*, ed. L. V. Cherepnin, prep. and comm. O. A. Derzhavina and E. V. Kolosova (Moscow, 1955), 105–10; and *Vremennik Ivana Timofeeva*, ed. V. P. Adrianova-Peretts, trans. and comm. O. A. Derzhavina (Moscow, 1951; repr. edn, St Petersburg, 2004), 234–52.

[31] For the excerpt from the *Khronograf* of 1617 on the Time of Troubles see 'Iz Khronografa 1617 goda', in *Pamiatniki literatury drevnei Rusi: Konets XVI–nachalo XVII vekov*, 218–357.

[32] For discussion of Bielski's *Kronika* and its influence on the *Khronograf* see N. A. Kazakova, *Zapadnaia Evropa v russkoi pis'mennosti XV–XVI vekov* (Leningrad, 1980), 230–56.

Unlike the bulky, all-encompassing *Khronograf* of 1617, the *Novyi letopisets* compiled in 1630 was concerned only with the Time of Troubles.[33] It offered a final assessment of the events, while promoting a theory of absolutism that would ideologically and politically prop up the young Romanov dynasty. Thus, it viewed the Time of Troubles as a punishment from God for the Muscovites' betrayal of the legitimate dynasty, with the main villain, Boris Godunov, murdering the rightful heir, Dmitrii Ivanovich, and exiling or imprisoning the Romanovs, who claimed succession to the throne through Ivan IV's first marriage to Anastasia Romanov. The chronicler insisted that since the tsar could only be chosen by God, Godunov had transgressed against Divine will in his ruthless pursuit of power. Thus, Godunov's illegitimate actions against God's chosen dynasties provoked God's retribution, which only subsided when legitimacy was restored to the throne through Michael Romanov. Since Michael had been elected to the throne by the National Assembly, and had only a tenuous claim as a descendant of the Riurikids, the chronicler went to great lengths to justify his rule. Unlike earlier ('fraudulent') elections of Boris Godunov and Vasilii Shuiskii, who, the writer contended, had been supported by few people, Michael's appointment resulted from an outpouring of national desire 'reflecting the will of the people guided by the grace of God'.[34]

Polish-Lithuanian texts narrated their own versions of the clashes with Russia in the early seventeenth century. Although texts such as the *Kievskaia letopis'* [Kievan Chronicle] (1241–1621) covered the events of 1605–13, these were for some writers less traumatic than internal struggles such as those depicted in the *Letopis' sobytii v iuzhnoi rusi L'vovskogo kanonika Iana Iuzefovicha* [Chronicle of the Events in Southern Russia by the L'viv canon Joannis Josephowicz] (Latin, published with the Russian title, covering 1608–1700 but compiled in 1769). The chronicle described extensively upheavals of the 1640s and 1650s, during which Zaporozhian Cossaks led by Bogdan Khmelnitskii clashed with Polish magnates.[35]

HAGIOGRAPHY

The chronicles of the fifteenth to seventeenth centuries recounted the activities of many prominent holy men and Church administrators whose written saints' lives became major literary pieces. The audiences for Muscovy's hagiographic works undoubtedly viewed them as historical texts, a type of biographical writing providing

---

[33] For the complete text, see 'Novyi letopisets', in *PSRL* (1910), xiv.

[34] L. V. Cherepnin, *Russkaia istoriografiia do XIX veka* (Moscow, 1957), 124.

[35] *Sbornik letopisei otnosiashchikhsia k istorii iuzhnoi i zapadnoi Rusi izdannyi kommissiei dlia razbora drevnykh aktov* (Kiev, 1888), 113–212. This volume contains sixteen texts originating from regions that now belong to modern Ukraine or Poland.

that exempla. A saint's life recounted the history of an individual in the contexts of the world of man and the divinity of God. Without the backdrop of the world and its struggles, the meaning and achievements of a saint's life were lost. Just as an icon reflected the visage of a saint as he or she existed in heaven, a written life reflected the ideal history of a saint's activity. Consequently, although the lives were not always founded on historical reality, they represented a worldview for the Muscovite audience and the modern researcher, for they primarily documented historical conditions or views.

Russian hagiography became more complex in the late fourteenth and early fifteenth centuries. Balkan monks and churchmen transmitted texts with Byzantine, especially Athonite, forms to north-eastern Europe as part of the Second South Slavonic Influence, bringing a new model of elegant prose known as 'word-weaving' (*pletenie sloves*). Monks and scribes wrote or rewrote the lives of major Russian saints into formulaic narratives employing flowery language. As Muscovy incorporated new lands in the sixteenth and seventeenth centuries, more and more holy men in distant cloisters were honoured with lives, but these local texts could be less formal, shorter, or focused on only a few years that had been witnessed by the writer or his informants.

The diverging trends of elaboration and simplification attest to the success of the Muscovite Church on two fronts. On the one hand, the embellishment of saints' lives showed the metropolitans' ability to raise up Russian holy men as patterns of virtue and place them on an equal footing with Byzantine saints, their written lives serving as examples of sophisticated Orthodox culture. On the other hand, one sees the Church's tremendous headway in incorporating the provincial parishes and bringing their saints' cults into the lives of monks and lay believers.

Ivan III's annexation of Novgorod in 1471–84 and Ivan IV's annexation of Kazan' in 1552 extended the Church's influence considerably. The archbishop of Novgorod and the elite townsmen were no longer the leaders of the Novgorod territories; that role belonged to the tsar. The Moscow metropolitan became undisputed leader of the Church despite an attempt by the author of the *Povest' o belom klobuke* [Tale of the White Cowl] (second half of the sixteenth century) to increase the prestige of the Novgorodian see. In fact, Metropolitan Makarii included in the *Velikie minei chetii* not just the traditional Byzantine and Russian saints' lives organized by their calendrical festivals; he also included new Russian wonder workers from the centre and outlying regions. The creation of the *Velikie minei chetii* coincided with an attempt to support monastic cults and if not intentionally, at least ultimately helped tie adherents of the northern cults more strongly to Moscow.[36]

Two of Muscovy's most renowned hagiographers, Epifanii Premudryi (the Wise) and Pakhomii Logofet, were purveyors of the Second South Slavonic

---

[36] Paul Bushkovitch, *Religion and Society in Russia: The Sixteenth and Seventeenth Centuries* (New York, 1992), 88–9.

Influence who transformed Russian hagiography into grandiloquent works considered more representative of the extraordinary spirituality of the saints. Epifanii's *Slovo o zhitii i uchenii sviatogo ottsa nashego Stefana* [The Tale of the Life and Teaching of Our Holy Father Stefan of Perm] (early fifteenth century) not only documented Russian attitudes towards the non-Christian northern tribes and the history of Stefan's (d. 1396) missionary work, but also became a prototype for later written lives.[37] Epifanii also composed the *Zhitie Sergiia Radonezhskogo* [Life of St Sergius of Radonezh] (1417–18), one of Russia's most beloved saints and founder of its most important cloister, the Trinity-St Sergius Monastery.[38] The *Zhitie* ('Life') of St Sergius (d. 1392) exhibited many recognizable medieval hagiographical *topoi* such as Sergius's humility and ability to see visions, but it also attempted historical description. Epifanii recounted Sergei's relations with his brother, also a monk, and imagined Sergei's communication with Dmitrii Donskoi before his famous campaign against the Mongols. Unlike the chronicles, these lives were character-driven histories of Russia's spiritual journey.

Pakhomii further illustrated Russia's spiritual journey in his *Zhitie pr. Kirilla Belozerskogo* [Life of St Kirill of the White Lake] (1460s).[39] In the *Zhitie*, *umilenie* (the gift of tears, deep emotion) became an important part of the Russian hagiographical lexicon, while the quest for quietude (*hesychia*) and the use of the Jesus prayer became widely taught. In this way, the Byzantine monastic movement of *hesychasm* entered Russia indirectly through the narration of idealized lives rather than theological texts.[40] Pakhomii wrote a number of other major hagiographic works including a second redaction of Epifanii's *Zhitie Sergiia Radonezhskogo*.[41]

By the end of the sixteenth century and in the early seventeenth century, Ivan IV's turbulent reign had ended but the Time of Troubles was beginning and institutional traditions were being challenged. One saint's life that was written to pursue an historical political agenda was that of Metropolitan Filipp II (Kolychev, r. 1564–6). Deposed and incarcerated in 1566 by Ivan IV, Filipp had been *hegumen* (abbot, father superior) of Solovki Monastery from 1544 to 1564. The *Zhitie i podvizi . . . Filippa mitropolita Moskovskogo* [Life and Deeds of Filipp . . . Metropolitan of Moscow] was written no earlier than the 1590s and possibly as late as the 1610s. Both redactions expressed the monastic teachings of quietude, obedience, and humility, but focused on Filipp's role as metropolitan, fabricating conversations in which Filipp challenged Ivan IV's violent policies. Like many of

[37] An English introduction with Old Russian text is in *Zhitie sv. Stefana episkopa Permskogo*, photomechanic reprint with an introduction by Dmitri Čiževskij [Chizhevskii] (Heidelberg, 1959).

[38] 'Epifanievskaia redaktsiia zhitiia prepodobnogo Sergiia', in *Die Legenden des heiligen Sergij von Radonez: Nachdruck der Ausgabe von Tikhonravov mit einer Einleitung und einer Inhaltsübersicht*, ed. Ludolf Müller (Munich, 1967), 3–144.

[39] *Pachomij Logofet Werke in Auswahl: Nachdruck der Ausgabe von V. Jablonskij*, ed. Dmitrij Tschizewskij [Chizhevskii] (Munich, 1963), pp. i–lxiii.

[40] Paul Bushkovitch, 'The Limits of Hesychasm: Some Notes on Monastic Spirituality in Russia 1350–1500', *Forschungen zur osteuropäischen Geschichte*, 38 (1986), 97–109.

[41] Two redactions of the *Zhitie* by Pakhomii are in *Die Legenden*, part 2, 3–100.

the extended episodes in the chronicles, Filipp's direct speech promoted a political stance. The Church used its textual traditions to assert the evil consequences of disobedience to the rightful metropolitan,[42] and just as Kurbskii's *Istoriia o velikom kniaze Moskovskom* affected the historiography of Ivan IV, so too did the *Zhitie sv. Filippa* by painting the tsar in dark colours.

The Solovki Monastery, one of Russia's largest cloisters, housed a library with examples of pious lives written far from Moscow and recounting local histories, often with a deliberate message.[43] Some saints' 'lives' were actually about their deaths or the discovery of their remains. Others were about the lives of near non-entities, buried within the pages of miscellanies without the flourishes of a fully articulated saint's life.[44] It was not unusual for seventeenth-century lives to focus on a particular incident in the life of a holy person as in the *Zhitie . . . Irinarkha byvshego igumena* [Life . . . of the Former Hegumen Irinarkh] (*c*.1638). Irinarkh (d. 1628) had been hegumen of Solovki Monastery and his *Zhitie* consisted of a short narrative of events surrounding his retirement after he had prophesied a period of disorder and the name of his eventual successor.[45] The *Zhitie* then turned from Irinarkh and focused on the internal uproar that followed as two opposing factions struggled to select a new leader. The *Zhitie* attempted to bolster the position of one Makarii, who was eventually chosen as hegumen by the brothers after a failed bid to elect Eleazar of Anzer (d. 1656), leader of a small satellite community. Although presented as a prophecy and its fulfilment, the *Zhitie . . . Irinarkha byvshego igumena* crafted an official historical narrative of events within Solovki.

In the seventeenth century, two trends emerged within the hagiographical tradition. One was a movement towards autobiography and biography, the other a move towards standardization. Eleazar of Anzer wrote an autobiographical work, *Svoeruchnaia khartiia* [Note by My Own Hand] (1636–8), that told of the founding of the Anzer Skete, the building of its first church, his relations with hegumen Irinarkh of Solovki, and his visions of the Mother of God. Eleazar's brief work reads much like a traditional saint's life and monastic founding tale in its language and Eleazar's selection of events. Yet, it was written in the first person by a living witness.[46] Personal histories had begun to emerge during the Time of Troubles, and autobiography was part of this seventeenth-century trend.

---

[42] Paul Bushkovitch, 'The Life of St Filipp: Tsar and Metropolitan in the Late Sixteenth Century', in Michael S. Flier and Daniel Rowland (ed.), *Medieval Russian Culture*, vol. 2 (Berkeley, 1994), 29–46, at 34.

[43] Jennifer B. Spock, 'The Solovki Monastery 1460–1645: Piety and Patronage in the Early Modern Russian North', Ph.D. thesis, Yale University, 1999, chs. 5–6.

[44] See the 'Life' of Nikifor of Solovki, Russian National Library, Manuscript Division (hereafter RNB-OR), *fond* 717, MS 205/205, ff. 408r–12v. A portion is published: *Opisanie rukopisei Solovetskogo monastyria, nakhodiashchikhsia v biblioteke Kazanskoi dukhovnoi akademii*, vol. 2 (Kazan', 1881–98), 242–3.

[45] RNB-OR, *fond* 717, MS 238/238.

[46] E. V. Krushel'nitskii (ed.), *Prepodobnyi Eleazar, osnovatel' Sviato-Troitskogo Anzerskogo skita*, prepared for publication by S. K. Sevast'ianova (St Petersburg, 2001), 48–56, 109–18.

The drive for standardization entered political and religious thought most particularly during the reign of Tsar Aleksei (1645–76). The tsar founded an academy in Moscow and with Patriarch Nikon (r. 1652–66) began to examine Church texts in Muscovy and newly conquered territories around Kiev for consistency with the see of Constantinople. The move to standardize was in part transmitted via Orthodox churchmen from the Polish-Lithuanian Commonwealth who had been trained during the Polish Counter-Reformation. Eventually this led to the Old Belief schism in Russia, which further galvanized the state to print standardized editions of religious material.

Dmitrii, bishop of Rostov (r. 1700–9), oversaw the compilation of the most important menology in Russia since Makarii's *Velikie minei chetii*, consisting of elaborate and sometimes late redactions of saints' lives. These versions, which contained newly manufactured elements, became the Russian Orthodox Church's standard published texts of saints' lives. Subsequently, new lives were written in the official Church, but rarely new redactions of the old texts.

OFFICIAL STATE HISTORIOGRAPHY OF THE SECOND HALF OF THE SEVENTEENTH CENTURY

Legitimizing and strengthening the rule of the Romanovs while promoting absolutism and autocracy in Russia became the central theme of a number of official Muscovite historical texts in the second half of the seventeenth century. One such example was the *Istoriia o tsariakh i velikikh kniaziakh zemli Russkoi* [History of the Tsars and Grand Princes of the Russian Lands] (1669), written by Fedor Griboedov at the request of Tsar Aleksei Mikhailovich as a textbook for his children. Basing his work on the sixteenth-century *Stepennaia kniga* [Book of Degrees], the *Khronograf* of 1617, the Time of Troubles tales, and other documents pertaining to genealogy, Griboedov created a dynastic history that sought to prove a link between the Riurikid and Romanov dynasties. Following the lead of his sources, which proclaimed the Riurikids to be descendants of the Roman Emperor Augustus, Griboedov maintained a Roman lineage for the Romanovs as well to reinforce their authority and international standing.[47]

Another writer charged with promoting and buttressing the power of the Romanovs was the Moldavian-born Nicolae Milescu Spafarii, who worked for many years (from 1671) in Moscow as a chief translator and diplomat at the Diplomatic Chancellery. His works not only reinforced the rightful succession of the Romanovs to the throne, but also proclaimed the Russian tsar to be the successor to both Roman and Byzantine emperors. Thus, Spafarii's *Vasiliologion* [Book of Rulers] (1674) declared that the tsar's rule was derived from God, and

---

[47] For further discussion, see Cherepnin, *Russkaia istoriografiia*, 129–30.

that consequently the tsar was God's representative on earth. The work presented short histories of famous rulers culminating with Aleksei Mikhailovich. Michael's and Aleksei's inclusion in the company of such illustrious predecessors as Ivan IV, Dmitrii Donskoi, and Alexander Nevsky, the Byzantine emperors Constantine and Theodosius, and the Roman emperors Augustus and Julius Caesar, revealed much about the political message of the work. Notably, the only other Russian ruler discussed was the feeble-minded Fedor Ivanovich, who paled in comparison with the other great monarchs. However, his inclusion was necessary for Spafarii to maintain the theme of dynastic continuity.[48]

Another text by Spafarii, the *Khrismologion* [Book of Prophecy] (1672), exhibits most clearly the writer's panegyric to the Russian monarchy.[49] Examining ancient and medieval exegesis on Daniel's prophecy of the Four Kingdoms, Spafarii argued that Russia was the only true successor to Daniel's Fourth Kingdom—Rome, through its historical connection to Constantinople.[50] Indeed, claimed Spafarii, only Muscovy was explicitly given the right of Roman succession, not the Holy Roman Empire.[51] In his conclusion Spafarii summarized his principal points:

The Westerners claim that the Greek kingdom was replaced by the German. Similarly, the Turks say that according to God's will the Greek kingdom was bequeathed unto them. We insist that the Russian monarchy is the only successor to the Greek, not only due to its piety but also because of the monarch's direct descent from Anna of Constantinople; and as the prophecies write: the Turkish kingdom will be vanquished and the Greek monarchy restored in its piety to the throne of Constantinople.[52]

Spafarii's reference to Princess Anne of Constantinople (sister of the Byzantine Emperor Basil II), who married Vladimir, the first Christian Grand Prince of Kiev, reinforced not only the strong historical bond that he perceived between Byzantium and Russia, but also the important dynastic connection between the Riurikid Prince Vladimir and the Romanov Tsar Aleksei Mikhailovich.

Promoting and justifying the political union of Russia and Ukraine by underscoring the strong historical links between Kievan Rus' and Moscow was the goal of the Ukrainian historian Innokentii Gizel, archimandrite of the ancient Kievan Caves Monastery, who in 1674 published his *Sinopsis ili kratkoe sobranie ot razlichnykh letopistsev* [Synopsis or Short Summary from Different Chronicles], commonly regarded as the first history textbook in Russia and reprinted into the nineteenth century.[53] An impressive effort at a constructive, unified historical

---

[48] The *Vasiliologion* is unpublished. A well-preserved manuscript is in the Library of the Academy of Sciences (St Petersburg), Arkhangel'skoe collection, MS 129.

[49] The *Khrismologion* is unpublished. A well-preserved manuscript is in the State Historical Museum in Moscow, Synodal Library collection, MS 192.

[50] Ibid., f. 101.

[51] Ibid., f. 29v.

[52] Ibid., f. 308v.

[53] *Mechta o russkom edinstve: Kievskii sinopsis (1674)*, ed. O. Ia. Sapozhnikov and I. Iu. Sapozhnikova (Moscow, 2006).

narrative focusing on the Kievan principalities and utilizing Polish and Russian sources, the work served as a springboard for eighteenth-century Russian historiography. Gizel's underlying message was the continuity between the Kievan and the Muscovite states. Gizel claimed that virtually all the attributes of Muscovite tsardom could be traced back to Kievan Rus'; he discussed the Mongol invasion and sacking of Kiev, followed by chapters describing and extolling Prince Dmitrii Donskoi's 'liberation' of Russian lands from the Tatar yoke. The defeat of the Mongols, the transfer of the capital from Kiev to Moscow, and the consolidation of Moscow's power were, for Gizel, the culmination of the great national idea begun in Kievan Rus'. Gizel's goal was to affirm for Tsar Aleksei that Kiev was his 'true and eternal patrimony' and must be united to the Muscovite lands. In that, Gizel's history succeeded. However, by barely touching on the history of the Muscovite state and ignoring the history of Russia's important north-western principalities such as Novgorod and Pskov, Gizel's work left much to be desired. A more complete and rigorous history of Russia, one liberated from medieval biblical chronology, annalistic models and patterns, and questionable sources, had to await the Westernizing reforms of Peter the Great.

EIGHTEENTH-CENTURY HISTORIOGRAPHY AND THE BEGINNING OF CRITICAL STUDIES OF HISTORY

Modern Russian historiography is said to begin with Vasilii Tatishchev, a Westernizer and true disciple of Peter I, who in 1739, after twenty years of diligent and painstaking labour, produced the first comprehensive, critical history of Russia. A pioneering endeavour, Tatishchev's five-volume *Istoriia Rossiiskaia s samykh drevneishikh vremen* [Russian History from the Earliest Times] (1739) was a new type of historical work in Russia, one based on a thorough critical study of the sources that Tatishchev had scrupulously collected during his years travelling throughout Russia and Europe as a military engineer and regional governor.[54]

In writing his history, Tatishchev was motivated by a sense of patriotism and pride. He wanted to produce a modern, serious history to prove to Russians and foreigners alike that Russia had a worthy and honourable past. Moreover, he claimed, Russian history should not be viewed in isolation from the history of other peoples. Illustrating these ideas in his work, he rejected the narrow Russo-centric focus of earlier historical writings and devoted considerable space to narrating the histories of the non-Russian peoples of the growing empire.[55]

---

[54] Vasilii Tatishchev, *Istoriia Rossiiskaia*, 3 vols. (Moscow, 2003).
[55] Ibid., 5–28. See also Cherepnin, *Russkaia istoriografiia*, 174–9.

Tatishchev utilized an unprecedented number of historical sources, many put into circulation for the first time. These included chronicles, historical tales, diplomatic correspondence, personal letters, and widely scattered archival material. While some scholars claim that Tatishchev had trouble organizing this material properly and evaluating it thoroughly, the sheer volume of new information that he was able to extract from these texts speaks highly of his scholarly abilities.[56]

The first part of Tatishchev's study differed in form and content from the rest of the volumes, consisting of diverse chapters examining various problems of early Slavic history. The other three parts rendered political history in a curious amalgamation of chronicle narrative and analytical writing. Among the main points raised by Tatishchev in the first volume were the growth of literacy in Kievan Rus' and the spread of Christianity, both of which Tatishchev viewed as significant to the development of the first Russian state. Tatishchev also weighed in on the 'Normanist Controversy', the contentious historiographical debate surrounding the calling of the Varangian Rus' princes in 862 and the allegedly Scandinavian (Norman) origins of the Russian state.[57] Writing a decade before the dispute boiled over after a confrontational speech given at the Academy of Sciences in St Petersburg by German-born historian Gerhard Friedrich Müller, Tatishchev supported the idea that Riurik and his brothers came from the area of present-day Finland, where Riurik was leader of the Varangian Rus'. However, Tatishchev sought to find a compromise between the two sides, discovering in one source mention of a local northern Slavic prince, Gostomysl', allegedly Riurik's maternal grandfather, who proclaimed Riurik as successor upon his death. Thus, according to Tatishchev, the calling of Riurik was simply a matter of succession to the throne, and Riurik, though Varangian, was also a Slav. Tatishchev's main task in recounting the story (as throughout his work) was to underscore Russia's need for a strong and uninterrupted monarchy.[58] Tatishchev was unable to publish his *Istoriia Rossiiskaia s samykh drevneishikh vremen* during his lifetime, as he was in the process of revising it when he died. It was published only posthumously through the efforts of Gerhard Müller and subsequent historians (1768–1848).

Müller has been described as a tireless compiler and gatherer of texts to whom future historians of Russia owe a tremendous debt. He was one of the first German-born historians to settle in Russia permanently and the one who,

[56] Anatole G. Mazour, *Modern Russian Historiography* (Westport, Conn., 1975), 31.

[57] The 'Normanist Controversy' erupted in 1749, and involved an acrimonious debate between German members of the Academy of Sciences, who argued that Kievan Rus' was founded and organized by Norse (Varangian) settlers, and their Russian-born colleagues, who insisted that the Rus' were descendants of Slavic tribes living south of Kiev. For more see Omeljan Pritsak, 'The Origin of Rus'', *Russian Review*, 36:3 (1977), 249–73.

[58] Rudolph L. Daniels, *V. N. Tatishchev: Guardian of the Petrine Revolution* (Philadelphia, 1973), 93.

among his fellow countrymen, had perhaps the greatest impact on the study of Russian history. He is best known for his impressive two-volume *Istoriia Sibiri* [History of Siberia] (1751–64), which remains to this day a valuable source of documents and information. Remarkable in its scope, the work stemmed from Müller's exhaustive travels through remote Siberian towns in search of historical and archival documents, all previously unknown to Russian scholarship. The astounding amount of material he brought back to St Petersburg after ten years of difficult fieldwork became known as 'Müller's Portfolios', which remain a treasure trove of sources on Siberia even today. Previous knowledge of Siberian history had been based on scattered and often unreliable chronicle accounts. Müller supplemented these with government charters, orders, decrees, official and private correspondence, and various statistical data pertaining to ethnography and geography. He was also the first Russian historian to examine and incorporate previously unknown Mongol and Tatar sources.[59]

Müller invited to Russia a young and ambitious German historian, August Ludwig von Schlözer, to assist him in writing a comprehensive Russian history (never completed). Schlözer soon had a falling out with his patron, as Müller felt increasingly threatened by Schlözer's ambition, while Schlözer felt contempt for what he considered to be Müller's lack of erudition and proper historical training. Unfortunately, these strained relations ended his access to Müller's 'Portfolios'. Schlözer's stay in Russia was regrettably cut short; however, he managed to remain in St Petersburg for six years, was appointed a professor of Russian history and an ordinary member of the Academy of Sciences in 1765, and managed to collect enough material from sources outside Müller's purview to produce important works devoted to Russian history after his return to Germany.

Schlözer maintained that 'history must be universal, embracing more than mere political development; the historian must therefore abandon his academic isolation and seek a closer acquaintance with the wide world of reality'.[60] He urged historians to flush out all possible sources: 'The painter of history . . . ought to have all the bare facts at his disposal. Second, he ought to know all the historical material in existence touching upon his subject so as to be able to select what is relevant. He ought to know everything that belongs to his field.'[61] Furthermore, these sources must be reliable and should be studied without any prejudice or bias, something Schlözer felt was sorely lacking at the Petersburg Academy during the height of the 'Normanist Controversy'.

Thus, Schlözer believed that it was too early to write a complete history of Russia, since every available source had not yet been gathered and properly

---

[59] Mazour, *Russian Historiography*, 38.
[60] Cited ibid., 40–1.
[61] Cited in Helmut D. Schmidt, 'Schlözer on Historiography', *History and Theory*, 18:1 (1979), 44.

examined. He advocated on behalf of a critical edition of every known Russian chronicle.[62] Such a study would have to include a discussion of Byzantine, Arabic, Scandinavian, and other European sources from which the Russian chronicles may have taken their accounts. Schlözer began ambitious work in this direction soon after he returned to Germany, publishing two studies on Russian chronicles in 1768 and 1769, and culminating in his masterful five-volume translation and critical edition of the *Nestor Russisch Annalen* [Nestor's Russian (Primary) Chronicle] (1802–9).

A principal reason for Schlözer's decision to leave Russia in 1767, apart from his falling out with Müller, was the continued bitterness and tension in the Academy of Sciences between its German and its Russian members over the 'Normanist Controversy'. The leader of the anti-Normanist camp, Mikhail Lomonosov, the great Russian scientist and Renaissance man, felt so offended by the Normanist claims, particularly those of Müller, that without much previous study he plunged into Russian history to prove his thesis that the Russians had a well-developed state long before the arrival of the Varangians, and that contrary to the Normanist position, Russia's past 'equals that of ancient Greece and Rome, except for the absence of historians to prove it'.[63]

In his polemics with Müller, Lomonosov ridiculed the German historian's interpretation of sources, maintaining that he was unable to distinguish fable from truth. Lomonosov further criticized Müller for undue reliance on foreign sources and for sweeping aside anti-Normanist evidence found in Russian documents, thereby tailoring his documentation to fit his thesis. Considering himself a worthier scholar of Russian language and grammar than his opponent (he had, after all, written the first scholarly Russian grammar in 1755), Lomonosov took issue with Müller's derivations of Russian princely names from the Scandinavian. Lomonosov also relied on linguistic evidence, but to argue the anti-Normanist position. Thus, he listed a number of Slavic names of rivers, towns, and villages in areas the Varangian Rus' allegedly had inhabited, suggesting that the Varangians were Slavs. Moreover, he contended that had the Varangians spoken a Scandinavian tongue and had much influence in early Russian society, it would have left a mark on the development of the native Slavic language, as was the case with the Mongols. Yet no Scandinavian borrowings into Slavic were to be found.[64]

In 1758 Lomonosov produced the first volume of a projected four-volume history of Russia, which focused on the most contentious period from the earliest history of the Slavs to 1054.[65] Unfortunately, Lomonosov's *Drevniaia rossiiskaia istoriia* [Ancient Russian History], although based on an impressive array of

---

[62] Mazour, *Russian Historiography*, 43.
[63] Cited ibid., 46.
[64] Cherepnin, *Russkaia istoriografiia*, 196–200.
[65] Lomonosov, Mikhail, *Drevniaia rossiiskaia istoriia ot nachala rossiiskogo naroda do konchiny velikogo kniazia Iaroslava Pervogo ili do 1054 goda* (St Petersburg, 1766).

historical documents, suffered from an excess of patriotic zeal, especially in the peculiar linguistic arguments it used to defend the anti-Normanist position. Nonetheless, Lomonosov did argue persuasively that (1) the Slavs had a well-developed culture and society well before the Normans arrived and (2) the term *rus'/ros* could just as easily come from Slavic derivation as from Scandinavian. Both arguments are widely accepted by historians today.

The last decades of the eighteenth century saw the continuation of the great strides the study of Russian history had taken since the publication of Gizel's *Sinopsis*. Under the patronage of Catherine the Great (r. 1762–96), an avid admirer of the history of her adopted country, amateur and professional historians discovered and published an increasing number of historical documents, expanded areas of historical enquiry to incorporate Russia's vast regions (V. V. Krestinin), and included little-studied subjects such as the history of commerce (M. D. Chulkov) and of law (S. E. Desnitskii). Eighteenth-century historians laid a solid foundation for the serious, critical study of Russian history, unearthing a treasure trove of previously unknown historical sources in the process. Yet historical writing in the eighteenth century was still the domain of aristocratic enthusiasts whose main goal was to exalt Russia's grand imperial present by finding its noble and illustrious roots in the past. It would remain up to the great Russian historians of the nineteenth century to make the study of history in Russia a truly scientific discipline that would have made August Ludwig Schlözer proud.

TIMELINE/KEY DATES

1462–1505 Reign of Grand Prince Ivan III (the Great)

1478 Novgorod annexed to Moscow

1505–33 Reign of Grand Prince Vasilii III

1533–84 Reign of Tsar Ivan IV (the Terrible)

1569 Formation of the Polish-Lithuanian Commonwealth

1584–98 Reign of Tsar Fedor, last of the Riurikids

1598/1605–13 Time of Troubles (*Smuta*)

1613–45 Reign of Tsar Michael, first of the Romanovs

1645–76 Reign of Tsar Alexei

1652–66 Patriarch Nikon of Moscow

1660s–70s Start of the Old Belief schism

1667 Treaty of Andrusovo: Kiev annexed to Moscow by treaty

1682–89 Regency of Tsarina Sophia

1682–1725 Reign of Tsar Peter I (the Great)

1700–21 Great Northern War

1725–7 Reign of Empress Catherine I

1730–40 Reign of Empress Anna

1741–61 Reign of Empress Elizabeth

1761–2 Reign of Emperor Peter III
1762–96 Reign of Empress Catherine II (the Great)
1772–95 Partitions of Poland

KEY HISTORICAL SOURCES

Die Legenden des heiligen Sergij von Radonez: Nachdruck der Ausgabe von Tikhonravov mit einer Einleitung und einer Inhaltsübersicht, ed. Ludolf Müller (Munich, 1967).

Griboedov, Fedor, *Istoriia o tsariakh i velikikh kniaziakh zemli Russkoi*, ed. S. F. Platonov and V. V. Maikov (St Petersburg, 1896).

Lomonosov, Mikhail, *Drevniaia rossiiskaia istoriia ot nachala rossiiskogo naroda do konchiny velikogo kniazia Iaroslava Pervogo ili do 1054 goda* (St Petersburg, 1766).

Mechta o russkom edinstve: Kievskii sinopsis (1674), ed. O. Ia. Sapozhnikov and I. Iu. Sapozhnikova (Moscow, 2006).

Pachomij Logofet Werke in Auswahl: Nachdruck der Ausgabe von V. Jablonskij, ed. Dmitrij Tschizewskij [Chizhevskii] (Munich, 1963).

Pamiatniki literatury drevnei Rusi, 11 vols. (Moscow, 1982–94).

Polnoe sobranoe russkikh letopisei, 43 vols. (St Petersburg, 1841–2002).

Sbornik letopisei otnosiashchikhsia k istorii iuzhnoi i zapadnoi rusi izdannyi kommissiei dlia razbora drevnykh aktov (Kiev, 1888).

Skazanie Avraamiia Palitsyna, ed. L. V. Cherepnin, prep. and comm. O. A. Derzhavina and E. V. Kolosova (Moscow, 1955).

Tatishchev, Vasilii, *Istoriia Rossiiskaia*, 3 vols. (Moscow, 2003).

Velikie minei chetii: Sobraniia vserossiiskim metropolitom Makariem, 12 vols. (St Petersburg, 1868–1915).

Vremennik Ivana Timofeeva, ed. V. P. Adrianova-Peretts, trans. and comm. O. A. Derzhavina (Moscow, 1951; repr. edn, St Petersburg, 2004).

BIBLIOGRAPHY

Cherepnin, L.V., *Russkaia istoriografiia do XIX veka* (Moscow, 1957).

Hoffmann, Peter, *Gerhard Friedrich Müller (1705–1783): Historiker, Geograph, Archivar im Dienste Russlands* (Frankfurt, 2005).

Kliuchevskii, V. O., *Drevnerusskie zhitiia sviatykh kak istoricheskii istochnik* (1871; repr. edn, Moscow 1989).

Kuzmin, A. P., *Tatishchev* (Moscow, 1981).

Likhachev, D. S., *A History of Russian Literature 11th–17th Centuries*, trans. K. M. Cook-Horujy (Moscow, 1989).

Mazour, Anatole G., *Modern Russian Historiography* (Westport, Conn., 1975).

Miliukov, P., *Glavnye techeniia russkoi istoricheskoi mysli*, vol. 1 (Moscow, 1898).

Slovar' knizhnikov i knizhnosti drevnei rusi, 3 vols. (Leningrad, 1987–2004).

Swoboda, Marina, 'Tradition Reinvented: The Vision of Russia's Past and Present in Ivan Timofeyev's "Vremennik"', Ph.D. thesis, McGill University, Montreal, Canada, 1997.

Ursul, D. T., *Milesku Spafarii* (Moscow, 1980).

Peshtich, S. L., *Russkaia istoriografiia XVIII veka*, 3 vols. (Leningrad, 1961–71).

Chapter 15

Austria, the Habsburgs, and Historical Writing in Central Europe

Howard Louthan

For those foolish enough to attempt a survey of the history of historical writing in the Habsburg lands in the late medieval and early modern periods there are a number of significant methodological problems. Anyone who examines historical writing in this era must first acknowledge that history as we understand the discipline today did not exist. There were 'histories', of course, as well as an extensive and sophisticated body of literature on the *ars historica*, but it was not until the eighteenth century that History emerged as an independent field of study with its own set of conceptual problems and questions.[1] Likewise, there are difficulties studying historical writing within a specific geographic context. Arguably, the most important historian of Central Europe in the Late Middle Ages was an Italian, and with the growth of the Republic of Letters the writing of history became an even more cosmopolitan and international pursuit. A Benedictine historian in eighteenth-century Austria would have shared more intellectually and culturally with his colleagues in France and Italy than with the townsmen down the hill from his abbey. Such problems, though, are common for anyone studying the evolution of historical writing in pre-modern Europe. Central Europe, however, presents the scholar with a number of special challenges.

Central Europe has always been a contested region of ambiguous geographic boundaries. The situation was particularly complicated at the beginning of the fourteenth century as the lines of local dynasties that had ruled much of this territory for generations failed. The Arpads, Piasts, and Přemysls were replaced by Angevins, Jagiellonians, Luxemburgs, and Habsburgs. These new families, whose holdings extended across the continent, came to their respective thrones with a more cosmopolitan outlook making the cultural world, of which historical writing was a part, correspondingly more complex. Politically, the situation was

[1] For an introduction to this earlier period and the *ars historica* in particular see Anthony Grafton, *What Was History? The Art of History in the Early Modern Period* (Cambridge, 2007). I would like to thank Markus Völkel for his suggestions and critique of an earlier draft of this chapter.

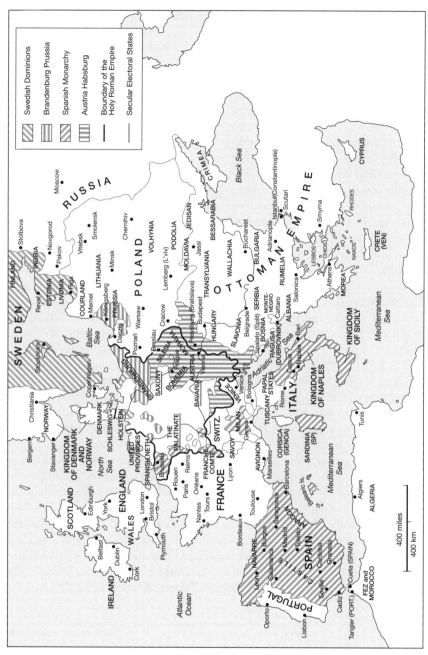

Map 5. Europe, 1648

equally convoluted, with the region's long-standing traditions of decentralized governance perhaps best epitomized by R. J. W. Evans's characterization of the Habsburg Empire as a 'mildly centripetal agglutination of bewilderingly heterogeneous elements'.[2] Diffuse political authority resulted in rival centres of power and culture that also affected the writing of history. Additionally, there was the issue of ethnicity. No other region in Europe could match the diversity of peoples and languages. A city such as Cracow in the sixteenth century was populated by substantial groups of ethnic Poles, Germans, and Italians. During this period the university that had the greatest impact shaping and training Poland's elites was actually outside the kingdom altogether, south of the Alps in Padua. This transnational view of Central Europe and its historical culture was distorted in the nineteenth and twentieth centuries by scholars who frequently used history as a tool for nation-building, thus dividing the region along anachronistic political lines. A figure such as the humanist Conrad Celtis confounds such artificial divisions, for this scholar, so critical in any discussion of historical writing in Central Europe, had a broad impact across the region. He established the *Sodalitas Litterarum Vistulana* in Cracow, the *Sodalitas Litterarum Hungaria* in Hungary, and the *Sodalitas Litterarum Rhenana* in Heidelberg before moving to Vienna, where he had perhaps his greatest influence.

As this chapter focuses primarily on historical writing in the lands of the Austrian Habsburgs, a few comments should be made on yet another problematic term, Austria. To the great frustration of modern scholars, the words Austria and Austrian cannot be traced back through time to a single meaning and uniform usage. The noun and adjective have been used historically in a variety of contexts with overlapping meanings: the Archduchy of Austria, the House of Austria, the Austrian Monarchy, and the Hereditary Emperor of Austria. The first two terms developed in the Middle Ages, with the former corresponding more narrowly to the specific territory that today essentially conforms to Upper and Lower Austria, while the latter referred to the more complicated family conglomerate of possessions and capital that extended far beyond the archduchy and even the hereditary lands (*Erblande*). As Grete Klingenstein has noted, by the beginning of the eighteenth century 'the "House of Austria" represented a complex array of rights and claims, on which Leopold I and his sons established their position in Europe not only as heads of their own House but also as Holy Roman Emperors'.[3] To understand the development of historical writing in this context, then, we will need to range over a broad territory that includes the Austrian lands proper, Bohemia, Hungary, Poland (at least peripherally), and the

---

　　[2]　R. J. W. Evans, *The Making of the Habsburg Monarchy* (Oxford, 1979), 447.
　　[3]　Grete Klingenstein, 'The Meanings of "Austria" and "Austrian" in the Eighteenth Century', in Robert Oresko, G. C. Gibbs, and H. M. Scott (eds.), *Royal and Republican Sovereignty in Early Modern Europe* (Cambridge, 1997), 423–78, at 473; and Alphons Lhotsky, 'Was heißt "Haus Österreich"', in Hans Wagner and Heinrich Koller (eds.), *Aufsätze und Vorträge*, 5 vols. (Vienna, 1970), i. 344–64.

Holy Roman Empire which extended not only across a wide swathe of Central Europe but also over the Alps into Reichsitalien.[4]

With these caveats in mind, let us begin by considering developments in the Austrian lands during the Late Middle Ages. Before the advent of print, historical writing was normally local in nature. It was rare for an historical work to cross regional boundaries and become known by a broader 'national' or even 'European' readership. Within this more insular setting, Austrian historical literature was comprised primarily of the standard late medieval genre of annals and chronicles. Typical were figures such as the fourteenth-century Cistercian abbot Johannes von Viktring, who as an adviser of princes emphasized the importance of objectivity in research, and the Franciscan Johann von Winterthur, who though less critical than Viktring vividly captured the impact of the plague in Vorderösterreich. One of the most remarkable texts of the period was the *Chronik von den 95 Herrschaften* [Chronicle of the 95 Rulers] of Leopold of Vienna. In this collection of fact and fantasy, the Augustinian friar laid out one of the earliest outlines of a primeval Austrian age with a genealogy of eighty-one mythical princes. This search for a mythical primordial age here had parallels elsewhere in the larger territories of the Reich.[5] A significant historiographical turning point came in the next century in the person of Thomas Ebendorfer. Ebendorfer recognized the importance of non-written sources and enlisted them in his work. He visited battlefields, sought out grave sites, and uncovered forgotten monuments all in an effort to represent the past more accurately in his writings.[6] He is also significant as an early court historian. Emperor Frederick III commissioned a number of works from him, and though the relationship between the two was never smooth, the emperor established a pattern that was exploited more successfully by his son Maximilian.

As the Ebendorfer example suggests, the winds of change that were transforming the writing of history were blowing primarily through the princely courts of Central Europe. Moreover, this steady breeze was coming from the south. In fourteenth-century Bohemia Emperor Charles IV cultivated critical cultural links with Italy. The Roman firebrand Cola di Rienzo visited the kingdom, albeit as an unwanted guest. The Luxemburg prince was more assiduous in his efforts to attract Petrarch to his court. Although these early Renaissance stirrings were cut short by the Hussite wars, Italian influence did penetrate the kingdom though often mediated through its distinctive religious culture. Ties with Italy were even more direct in Hungary. The kingdom's Angevin princes with their Neapolitan roots kept Hungary embroiled in Italian affairs. In the late fourteenth century the

---

[4] Karl Otmar von Aretin, *Das Reich: Friedensgarantie und europäisches Gleichgewicht, 1648–1806* (Stuttgart, 1986), 76–163, 268–89.
[5] For historical writing in the Holy Roman Empire, see ch. 16 by Markus Völkel in this volume.
[6] Alois Niederstätter, *Das Jahrhundert der Mitte: An der Wende vom Mittelalter zur Neuzeit* (Vienna, 1996), 391; and Alphons Lhotsky, *Thomas Ebendorfer: ein österreichischer Geschichtschreiber, Theologe und Diplomat des 15. Jahrhunderts* (Stuttgart, 1957).

Hungarian king and Holy Roman Emperor Sigismund I helped transform Buda into an important cultural centre with a vibrant Italian community. The humanist statesman Pier Paolo Vergerio lived in Hungary for nearly three decades. This cultural trajectory reached its peak under Matthias Corvinus, when in terms of historical writing the Italian humanist Antonio Bonfini set the standard with his *Rerum ungaricarum decades* [Ten Volumes of Hungarian Matters], composed in a style that consciously followed Livy. Bonfini's work superseded the late medieval chronicle of János Thuróczy. Fifteenth-century Poland had a distinguished historical tradition best represented by the Cracow churchman Jan Długosz and his ten-volume *Annales seu cronicae inclitii Regni Poloniae* [Annals or Chronicles of the Famous Kingdom of Poland] (1455). Italian influence came with the humanist exile Filippo Buonaccorsi (Callimachus), who had been caught up in a conspiracy against Pope Paul II. An influential member of the royal court, Callimachus wrote a history of the Jagiellonian king Ladislaus III and influenced future generations of historians including the sixteenth-century Prince-Bishop of Warmia, Martin Kromer.

The most influential Italian active in fifteenth-century Central Europe was the colourful humanist and future pope Aeneas Sylvius Piccolomini. Though Aeneas Sylvius is best remembered for his *Commentaries*, his colourful autobiography that captures the drama and politics behind his election to the Holy See as Pius II, he spent significant time in Central Europe on papal business. He was active at the Council of Basel and later enjoyed the patronage of Frederick III through whose offices he was named poet laureate. His *Historia Gothorum* [History of the Goths] (1453), *Historia Australis* [Austrian History] (1453), *Germaniae descriptio* [Description of Germany] (1457), *Historia Bohemica* [Bohemian History] (1458), and *Historia Friderici III* [History of Frederick III] (1458) helped shape the contours of Central European historiography during the Renaissance, either through imitation or in reaction.[7] Following the model of Leonardo Bruni, Aeneas Sylvius paid close attention to the political developments of the period though there was an underlying polemical message to his work. He argued that the region's prosperity and good fortune were dependent on its allegiance to the Roman Church. Once that bond was broken, as was the case with the Hussites, catastrophe would follow.[8] Not surprisingly, such assertions prompted a patriotic backlash. Historical writing within the Empire generally did not follow the model of Hungary or Poland, with the Italian humanist hired to celebrate the glories of a particular region. The Alsatian Beatus Rhenanus, a friend of Erasmus,

---

[7] Rolando Montecalvo, 'The New *Landesgeschichte*: Aeneas Sylvius on Austria and Bohemia', in Z. R. W. M. von Martels and Arie Johan Vanderjagt (eds.), *Pius II: 'El più expeditivo pontefice': Selected Studies on Aeneas Sylvius Piccolomini, 1405–1464* (Leiden, 2003), 55–86; and Alphons Lhotsky, 'Aeneas Silvius und Österreich', in Wagner and Koller (eds.), *Aufsätze und Vorträge*, iii. 26–71.

[8] Markus Völkel, *Geschichtsschreibung* (Cologne, 2006), 211–12; and Eric Cochrane, *Historians and Historiography in the Italian Renaissance* (Chicago, 1981), 45–7.

put forward a very different model in his *Rerum Germanicarum libri tres* [Three Books of German Matters] (1531), which traced the development and growth of German civilization independent of Rome. A careful and critical historian, Rhenanus developed an early form of historicism. Unlike many of his contemporaries whose understanding of a present German *natio* was based on a genealogy that could be traced back without break or interruption to the Roman era, the past for him was located in 'antiquity', an epoch clearly separated from the present. Along with the Swiss humanist Joachim Vadianus, Beatus Rhenanus was one of the first Central European historians to employ the phrase 'middle ages', albeit in a more limited way than it is understood today.[9]

In yet another response to Aeneas Sylvius, Conrad Celtis drew his inspiration from a branch of Italian humanism that approached the past in a manner significantly different from that of Bruni. As opposed to the Florentine, whose fame rests on his masterful analysis of political developments, the antiquarian Flavio Biondo came to his subject by seeking the material remains of past cultures. His *Italia illustrata* [Italy Illuminated] (1448–53) was a topographical history of eighteen Italian provinces and was immensely influential north of the Alps.[10] Following Biondo as his model, Celtis put forth his own plans for a *Germania illustrata*. Celtis, whose interests were primarily literary, also edited an important edition of Tacitus's *Germania* (1500). Celtis may have been most significant, however, as an organizer and teacher. In 1512 Beatus Rhenanus put together a list of Germany's most important humanists. Nearly half of them were alumni of Celtis's sodalities.[11] He was a friend of Callimachus in Cracow and the teacher of both Vadianus and the Bohemian historian Johannes Dubravius. His most important pupil was the Bavarian humanist Johannes Turmair or Aventinus. An assiduous collector of documents, Aventinus wrote a highly praised history of Bavaria that helped establish the genre of *Landesgeschichte*.[12]

The highpoint of Celtis's career came when he was called to Vienna by Frederick III's son, Maximilian. The enterprising Celtis encountered an equally energetic and enthusiastic patron. To enhance the prestige of the university Celtis convinced Maximilian to establish a separate college for poets and mathematicians. Such plans were representative of the ambitious prince who worked so hard to secure the imperial crown and then schemed to acquire both the papal tiara and the Byzantine imperial title. He was the first Habsburg to unite the family's territorial holdings in more than a century, and his appetite for power and success helped make the imperial court an important centre of historical

---

[9] Peter Schaeffer, 'The Emergence of the Concept *Medieval* in Central European Historiography', *Sixteenth Century Journal*, 7 (1976), 21–30.

[10] See ch. 12 by Peter N. Miller in this volume.

[11] Lewis Spitz, *Conrad Celtis* (Cambridge, Mass., 1957), 62.

[12] Gerald Strauss, *Historian in an Age of Crisis: The Life and Work of Johannes Aventinus, 1477–1534* (Cambridge, Mass., 1963).

research.[13] During this period, three major distinctives emerged that would characterize historical writing at the Habsburg court through the seventeenth century. Maximilian elevated the importance of genealogical research to new heights. The work of his scholars directly complemented his aggressive marital diplomacy. Most representative was the *Fürstliche Chronik* [Princely Chronicle] (1518) of Jakob Mennel, a student of Johannes Nauclerus. At Maximilian's urging, Nauclerus had composed a famous *Weltchronik* [World Chronicle] (1516). This, of course, was the great age of the world chronicle of which the most famous exemplar was that of Hartmann Schedel produced in Nuremberg.[14] Not to be outdone by Nauclerus, Mennel in his chronicle displayed his genealogical ingenuity by buttressing Maximilian's claims to the imperial throne with a family tree traced back to the Trojans. He secured his rights to Byzantium by working out a similar ancestry with the Greeks, and to place him in line for the kingdom of Jerusalem he highlighted his genealogical connection with Noah.

A second development that reinforced and strengthened the programme of Maximilian's genealogists was the emergence of print. It was not simply the ability to reproduce texts that, in the end, proved transformative. The media revolution also facilitated the inclusion of illustrations, and the historical culture of the Habsburg court became highly visual. Albrecht Dürer's magnificent *Ehrenpforte* [Triumphal Arch], with its depiction of the emperor's illustrious forebears, was the visual equivalent of Mennel's *Fürstliche Chronik*. Maximilian was keen to preserve his memory in suitable fashion, and towards that end he worked with his councillors to produce a series of autobiographical texts that glorified his reign. The three most important of these projects, *Weißkunig*, *Theuerdank*, and *Freydal*, combined image and text effectively. The *Theuerdank*, which was published in Augsburg in 1517, included 118 woodcuts. While Maximilian's fantastic genealogical schemes were not the products of a critical humanist culture, there was a more sober strain of scholarship within the imperial circle that points us to a third distinctive of historical literature at the Habsburg court, a serious engagement with the imperial legacy. Representative here is the diplomat and historian Johannes Cuspinianus. Early in his career Cuspinianus edited the work of Cassiodorus and then later composed *De Caesaribus et Imperatoribus* [On the Caesars and Emperors] which, in its original version, followed the imperial past up through Frederick III, with special attention to the Eastern Roman Empire. His work was characterized by a close attention to, and a keen analysis of, political developments, perhaps best represented in his sketch of Frederick III and his struggle to consolidate power at the

---

[13] For an overview of the literary activity at Maximilian's court including historical writing, see Jan-Dirk Müller, *Gedechtnus: Literatur und Hofgesellschaft um Maximilian I* (Munich, 1982).

[14] Kurt Gärtner, 'Die Tradition der volkssprachigen Weltchronistik in der deutschen Literatur des Mittelalters', *Pirckheimer-Jahrbuch*, 9 (1994), 57–71.

expense of the estates.[15] The search for a Roman and imperial past should be contrasted with a parallel tradition that sought to uncover specific links with a Germanic heritage. Here the work of Ferdinand I's court historian, Wolfgang Lazius, comes to the fore. His *De gentium aliquot migrationibus* [On the Migrations of Peoples] (1547) followed the migrations of the barbarian tribes into Central Europe.[16]

In the sixteenth and seventeenth centuries the writing of history in Central Europe reflected broader political and social developments of the period. The Turkish conflict in Hungary, the struggle between the Habsburgs and the local nobility in Bohemia, and the crisis of oligarchy and the estate system in Poland were among the major themes of the day. More specifically, as we trace the evolution of historical literature in the Habsburg lands, two factors had a particularly critical impact shaping this work: the territorial complexity of the family holdings and the religious changes of the Protestant and Catholic Reformations. Though by the time of Maximilian I the Habsburg domains were a complex chequerboard of territories, matters became even more complicated with the accession of his grandson, Ferdinand I, who added the Hungarian and Bohemian lands to the family legacy. In the context of decentralized governance, historical writing was a multi-polar phenomenon where competing centres of power frequently turned to the past in an effort to preserve and memorialize their respective rights and privileges. The most important foil to the court was the local estates.

The sixteenth century was the golden age of *Landesgeschichte* in the Habsburg lands.[17] In the Austrian archduchies the dominant figure was the native Viennese, Wolfgang Lazius, who, apart from his duties at court, was a doctor, university professor, and cartographer. For two decades he laboured on a massive history of the Austrian lands that was published only in part and remained unfinished at his death. This influential work by a zealous Catholic crossed confessional lines and served as the basis of many provincial histories such as Michael Gothard Christalnick's *Annales Carinthiae* [Carinthian Annals] (1612). For Tyrol there was Marx Sittich, while in Upper Austria the Lutheran Reichard Streun von Schwarzenau composed a significant regional history. In the seventeenth century the polymath Johann Weickhard von Valvasor, a member of England's Royal Society, wrote the massive *Ehre des Hertzogthums Crain* [Honour of the Duchy of Carniola] (1689), which weighed in at fifteen volumes and

---

[15] Paul Joachimsen, *Geschichtsauffassung und Geschichtsschreibung in Deutschland unter dem Einfluss des Humanismus* (Berlin, 1910), 209–18; and Hans Ankwicz-Kleehoven, *Der Wiener Humanist Johannes Cuspinian* (Graz, 1959).

[16] Michael Mayr, *Wolfgang Lazius als Geschichtsschreiber Österreichs* (Innsbruck, 1894).

[17] The following discussion on both the court and the estates draws from Thomas Winkelbauer, 'Ständische und höfische Geschichtsschreibung und Geschichtsbilder', in Winkelbauer, *Ständefreiheit und Fürstenmacht: Länder und Untertanen des Hauses Habsburg im Konfessionellen Zeitalter*, 2 vols. (Vienna, 2003), i. 227–81.

included more than five hundred illustrations![18] The local histories of Hungary reflected the complex nature of this region. The humanist bishop Nicholas Oláh composed two works, *Hungaria* (1536) and *Athila* (1537), which presented an idealized view of the kingdom, contrasting its past glories with its present sufferings. One of the most fascinating figures of the period was the anti-Trinitarian Gáspár Heltai, who established an important printing house in Transylvania and composed the first history of Hungary in Magyar.

Members of the estates produced histories of their particular regions, and powerful magnates commissioned formal accounts of their families' past. In a competitive age when nobles jostled with each other for position and power, a chronicle of illustrious ancestors was yet one more way to secure the dignity of one's household and fashion a pedigree worthy of high rank. Families such as the Liechtensteins, whose fortunes reached new heights in the seventeenth century, engaged teams of antiquarians to work through genealogical records to celebrate the accomplishments of their house. As time progressed, the results of such genealogical exercises became correspondingly more spectacular. The Hungarian Esterházys proudly pointed to Attila the Hun as their progenitor, while the Bohemian Sternbergs even more ambitiously found a connection with the Three Magi. Cities, too, were centres of historical research and produced histories of their respective municipalities both as a means to memorialize traditional freedoms and as an expression of civic pride.[19] Once more, it was the busy Wolfgang Lazius who set the pace with his *Vienna Austriae* (1546), with others following suit.

Though these different genres of *Landesgeschichte*, family chronicles, and urban histories did represent the interests of various constituencies in the Habsburg lands, it would be a mistake to see such writings set in simple opposition to each other. Admittedly, these histories could reflect conflicting agendas between the court and the provinces, but a figure such as Lazius, who worked across these boundaries, illustrates that the situation was decidedly more complicated. A form of convergence could develop over time. Families increasingly represented themselves as loyal to the emperor, and certain scholars endeavoured to craft *Landesgeschichte* in a manner that was congenial to the imperial cause. In Silesia the humanist Joachim Cureus wrote a history that focused on the region's integration into the Habsburg conglomerate while ignoring its political and social ties with Poland. A century later in *Croatia rediviva* (1700), Paul Ritter-Vitezović expressed the dream of a new Illyricum that united the south Slavic lands under Habsburg leadership as a shield against both the Turks and the Venetians.

---

[18] Branko Reisp, *Kranjski polihistor Janez Vajkard Valvasor* (Ljubljana, 1983).

[19] Susanne Rau, *Geschichte und Konfession. Städtische Geschichtsschreibung und Erinnerungskultur im Zeitalter von Reformation und Konfessionalisierung in Bremen, Breslau, Hamburg und Köln* (Hamburg, 2002); and Peter Johanek (ed.), *Städtische Geschichtsschreibung im Spätmittelalter und in der frühen Neuzeit* (Cologne, 2000).

Historical writing at the imperial court, in contrast, evinced a more international and cosmopolitan outlook. When Maximilian married Mary of Burgundy, the Habsburgs acquired not only new territorial holdings but also inherited a rich set of cultural traditions that included the long-established position of court historian. From Ferdinand I to Maria Theresa this position was rarely ever vacant, and throughout the period the office reflected Italian, Netherlandish, and Spanish influence. Though the pretensions of Ferdinand I were more modest than those of his grandfather, the archducal courts were also important centres of historical writing and research. Foremost was Innsbruck. Ferdinand of Tyrol's librarian, Gerard van Roo, began working on a history of the Habsburg family which was completed by the archduke's secretary, Konrad Dietz von Weidenberg. Jacob Schrenk von Notzing, personal secretary of the archduke, compiled what may be considered one of the first museum catalogues in the Habsburg lands, an annotated register of Ferdinand's famous armour collection at Ambras Castle. With its large-scale copperplate portraits and short histories of those represented in the armoury, the *Armamentarium Ambrasianum Heroicum* [Ambras Armoury of Famous Commanders] (1601) harkened back to the age of Maximilian I and was, at least in part, an imitation of Italian developments best represented in the work of Paolo Giovio.[20] Even more significant were the efforts of the Swiss historian Franz Guillimann who, at the court of Ferdinand's successor, Archduke Maximilian III, began a mammoth project on the *Casa Austria* which had a global reach.

In the seventeenth century Emperor Ferdinand II consolidated the family holdings, and the imperial court once more emerged as the centre of historical research. The nature of court histories, however, was changing as there was a shift away from genealogical surveys to chronicles that focused on contemporary events. Representative is the *Annales Ferdinandei* [Annals of Ferdinand] of Count Franz Christoph Khevenhüller, published posthumously in twelve volumes in 1721–6. After serving many years as a diplomat in Spain, Khevenhüller returned to Vienna, where he composed a history that examined political, diplomatic, and military events during the era of Ferdinand II. The high point of Habsburg court history came during the reign of Emperor Leopold I (1658–1705).[21] In Vienna, the dynastic image was carefully cultivated and strategically deployed, with history playing a significant role in this calculated campaign of imperial propaganda. When a sixteenth-century manuscript, the *Oesterreichische Ehrenwerk* [Austrian Book of Honour] of an Augsburg archivist, came to the attention of the Habsburgs, it was painstakingly vetted by censors, purged of its Protestant references, and reissued in Nuremberg as the handsome folio volume,

---

[20] E. Scheicher, 'Historiography and Display: The Heldenrüstkammer of Archduke Ferdinand in Schloß Ambras', *Journal of the History of Collections*, 2 (1990), 69–79.
[21] Nana Eisenberg, 'Studien zur Historiographie über Kaiser Leopold I', *Mitteilungen des Instituts für Österreichische Geschichtsforschung*, 51 (1937), 359–413.

Spiegel der Ehren des höchstlöblichsten Kayser- und Königlichen Erzhauses Oester-reich [Mirror of the Honour of the Praiseworthy Imperial and Royal House of Austria]. The profile of the court historian was also changing. The influential insider (a priest or political adviser) was being replaced by the historian and biographer. Count Galeazzo Gualdo Priorato had written several studies for Mazarin before coming to Vienna to compose a series of imperial biographies. Gottlieb Eucharius Rinck, a professor of law at Altdorf and biographer of Louis XIV, was commissioned to produce a history of Leopold I.

The second major factor that transformed historical writing in the Habsburg lands during the sixteenth and seventeenth centuries was religion. The Protestant and Catholic Reformations had a profound effect on shaping scholarly under-standings of the past. Most influential among the Protestants was Philipp Melanchthon, who took the insights of Luther and applied them to history. Reworking Johann Carion's popular *Chronicon* (1532), he added a theological gloss to this account of world history. One of the greatest achievements of Melanchthon's circle was the renewal of Christian universal history based on the prophecies of Daniel. Johannes Sleidan's *De quatuor summis imperiis* [On the Four Greatest Empires] (1556) charted the European past by applying Daniel's vision of four successive world empires. Confident interpretations of these puzzling apocalyptic prophecies gave German Protestants a sense of self-confidence as they saw themselves as members of a renewed and purified Church living in the last of the four great empires. Such an understanding was bolstered by the most important historical project directly inspired by the Lutheran Reformation, the *Magdeburg Centuries* (1559–74). The chief of the Centuriators was Matthias Flacius Illyricus, a fervent Lutheran who brooked no compromise with his theological opponents. The Centuriators divided Church history into hundred-year periods that they then proceeded to examine from a doctrinal perspective. They traced the Church's decline under Rome and identified the new Protestant movement as the recrudescence of an ancient and unblemished Christian community.[22]

Ironically, the Habsburg court lent early support to the *Magdeburg Centuries* through the sympathetic offices of the privy councillor and librarian Caspar von Nydbruck. A more official Catholic response was far less equivocal and in the end was instrumental in redirecting historical writing across the Catholic lands of Central Europe. The answer to the *Magdeburg Centuries* was Cesare Baronio's twelve-volume *Annales ecclesiastici* [Ecclesiastical Annals] (1588–1607). Baronio and his collaborators sought to rebut the charges of the Magdeburg Centuriators by demonstrating that the key doctrines the Church held as orthodox in the present day had not changed from the first century. To support their contentions

---

[22] Heinz Scheible, *Die Entstehung der Magdeburger Zenturien* (Gütersloh, 1996); and Ronald Ernst Diener, 'The Magdeburg Centuries: A Bibliothecal and Historiographical Analysis', Th.D. thesis, Harvard Divinity School, 1978.

they drew from an immense body of documentary, philological, and antiquarian evidence. Despite the criticism of scholars such as Isaac Casaubon, the *Annales* was a great success, particularly in Central Europe, where it was quickly translated into German and Polish. The Protestant scholar Justus Calvinus was purportedly so impressed by the work that it led not only to his conversion but also prompted a name change. He returned from a trip to Rome with the new name Justus Calvinus-Baronius.[23]

More significant than the actual reception of the *Annales* in Central Europe was the response it elicited from the Catholic scholarly community. The Jesuit Jakob Gretser and the law professor Heinrich Canisius were key figures here. Both Baronio and the Centuriators compelled the historian to rethink the fundamental relationship between Church and State. Not surprisingly, debates quickly developed on key moments of the medieval past: the coronation and reign of Charlemagne, the investiture controversy, and the struggle between Frederick Barbarossa and Pope Alexander III. Gretser, whose main opponent was the Swiss Protestant Melchior Goldast, devoted substantial energy to defending Baronio and revalidating the Catholic Middle Ages. Highly critical of Goldast, whom he saw as an advocate of a universal monarchy from which ecclesiastical authority ultimately derived, he consistently argued for the strict separation of spiritual and secular authority. Heinrich Canisius, on the other hand, was more active as an editor of medieval texts. Influenced by the *mos gallicus*, he brought his legal expertise to the study of the past, as he and his colleagues scoured the libraries of Southern Germany for suitable material. There were other centres of research as well. The Carthusian community of Cologne was particularly active. Due in part to their efforts Cologne became Central Europe's most important publishing centre of Catholic literature before the Thirty Years War. Somewhat independent of these developments was a growing antiquarian movement. Interest in monuments and other physical remains of the past that may initially have been stimulated by a curiosity in the Roman era was also growing in respect to the region's ecclesiastical heritage. In Central Europe these two strands came together in the seventeenth century and formed the foundation upon which Catholics responded to the Protestant challenge.[24]

In sum, the Protestant and Catholic Reformations contributed to the confessionalization of historical writing in Central Europe as a whole and the Habsburg lands in particular. In Hungary Nicholas Oláh, who had once corresponded with Erasmus, abandoned his irenic convictions and became an increasingly strident supporter of Counter-Reform policies. His *Compendiarium suae aetatis Chronicon* [Abridged Chronicle of the Age], an examination of the kingdom from Matthias Corvinus to the present day, included a detailed account

---

[23] Stefan Benz, *Zwischen Tradition und Kritik: Katholische Geschichtsschreibung im barocken Heiligen Römischen Reich* (Husum, 2003), 47.
[24] Benz, *Zwischen Tradition und Kritik*, 79–99.

of his efforts to renew the Catholic Church. Similar changes were occurring in Bavaria. Though Aventinus's *Annales* was long considered a model of *Landesgeschichte*, the humanist history was confessionally out of step in an increasingly Catholic Bavaria. Many believed that Aventinus harboured Lutheran sympathies, and Church authorities eventually placed the *Annales* on the index. More suitable was Matthäus Rader's *Bavaria sancta* [Holy Bavaria] (1615–27), an account that highlighted the duchy's saints and glorified its princes.[25] A final testament to the region's rising confessional tensions was a rich variety of martyrological literature. Flacius wrote *Catalogus testium veritatis* [Catalogue of Witnesses of Truth] (1556) as part of his historical attack on the Catholic Church, while a Swabian Lutheran, Ludwig Rabus, compiled an influential matryology that helped galvanize the Protestant community in south-west Germany. In the seventeenth century, Jesuits such as the Tanner brothers in Prague responded with accounts of the heroic deaths of their members at the hands of heretics and heathens. Much of this literature, however, was produced by those religious groups most vulnerable and exposed to state coercion. Moravian Hutterites compiled manuscript accounts of the sufferings of their community. The Unity of Czech Brethren (Unitas Fratrum), a conservative offshoot of the Hussite movement, carefully preserved the records of their Church through long years of exile. Their bishop, John Amos Comenius, had initially begun work on the *Historia persecutionum ecclesiae Bohemicae* [History of the Persecutions of the Bohemian Church] (1648) as a contribution to Foxe's *Acts and Monuments*.[26] Finally, there were individual accounts. The Slovak Protestant Juraj Láni recounted in lurid detail the miseries of his imprisonment during the Counter-Reformation, while his countryman Štefan Pilárik retold a harrowing story of Turkish captivity.

A closer examination of the Bohemian kingdom may help illustrate in greater detail the major features of historical writing of the Habsburg conglomerate in the sixteenth and seventeenth centuries. The first history of Bohemia printed in the Czech lands was, appropriately enough, a vernacular translation of Aeneas Sylvius's *Historica Bohemica* (1510). Three more histories of the kingdom appeared in quick succession once it was demonstrated there was a popular market for this material. These three vernacular chronicles were decidedly different, reflecting the territorial and religious complexity of the region in the early sixteenth century.[27] First was the *Kronyka czeská* [Czech Chronicle] (1537) of

---

[25] Trevor Johnson, 'Holy Dynasts and Sacred Soil: Politics and Sanctity in Matthaeus Rader's *Bavaria Sancta* (1615–1628)', in Sofia Boesch Gajano and Raimondo Michetti (eds.), *Europa sacra* (Rome, 2002), 83–100; and Alois Schmid, 'Geschichtsschreibung am Hofe Kurfürst Maximilians I. von Bayern', in H. Glaser (ed.), *Um Glauben und Reich: Kurfürst Maximilian I. Beiträge zur bayerischen Geschichte und Kunst 1573–1657* (Munich, 1980), 330–40.

[26] Most generally see A. G. Dickens and John Tonkin, 'Weapons of Propaganda: The Martyrologies', in Dickens and Tonkin, *The Reformation in Historical Thought* (Cambridge, Mass., 1985), 39–57.

[27] Winkelbauer, 'Ständische und höfische Geschichtsschreibung', 235–7.

the Utraquist priest Bohuslav Bílejovský, who used the text to defend the religious rites and rituals of the Hussite Church. Bílejovský maintained that the practice of receiving the Eucharist in two kinds (*sub utraque*), the Church's most prominent feature, could be traced back to the ninth-century era of Cyril and Methodius. The humanist poet and townsman Martin Kuthen wrote his *Kronika o založení země české* [Chronicle of the Founding of the Czech Lands] (1539) from an entirely different perspective. Dedicating his history to the city council of Prague's Old Town, Kuthen approached the past with a pronounced anti-German bias and highlighted the political privileges of Bohemia's urban centres that were being challenged by both the nobility and the Crown. The last of these histories, Václav Hájek's *Kronika česká* [Czech Chronicle] (1541), was far and away the most successful and written from yet another vantage point. A Catholic convert, Hájek became known as the Bohemian Livy for his dramatic retelling of the myths and legends of Czech antiquity. He defended both the kingdom's Catholic legacy and the social and political organization of the traditional *Ständestaat.*

To complicate the situation even further, there were also successful Latin histories. The *Historia regni Bohemiae* [History of the Bohemian Kingdom] (1552) of Johannes Dubravius reflected the humanist's Erasmian sensibilities. Less well publicized are the histories in the kingdom's other vernacular, German. Matthäus Aurogallus (Matthäus Goldhahn), a native of Chomutov/Komotau and professor of Hebrew at Wittenberg, wrote *Chronik der Herzöge und Könige von Böhmen* [Chronicle of the Dukes and Kings of Bohemia], and at the end of the century Johann Sandel produced a popular German translation of Hájek's chronicle. Finally, one should not forget the work of Jewish historians. With nearly 10,000 inhabitants in 1600, the Prague ghetto was one of the largest Jewish settlements in Europe. Home to a lively intellectual community, the ghetto was also an important publishing centre. The most significant historical work that came off its presses was the Hebrew *Zemah David* [Offspring of David] (1592–3) of David Gans. Gans included two parallel but distinct histories in this volume. The first covered the sacred Jewish past from the creation of the world to the present, while the second was dedicated to a chronology of general history.[28]

After the defeat of the Czech estates at White Mountain in 1620, historical writing became substantially more polarized. Pavel Stránský's *Respublica Bohemiae* [Bohemian Republic] (1634), an eloquent late humanist history of a Bohemian exile, was at least in part a response to the work of Melchior Goldast, who defended the absolutist claims of his Habsburg patrons. Stránský, in contrast, described the political traditions of a Bohemian 'republic'. Though political traditions were important, the matter of religion was an even greater point of contention among historians. Count Vilém Slavata, one of the victims of

---

[28] Rachel Greenblatt, 'A Community's Memory: Jewish Views of Past and Present in Early Modern Prague', Ph.D. thesis, Hebrew University of Jerusalem (2006).

the famous 1618 defenestration, wrote an account of the Bohemian revolt that reflected a distinct Catholic perspective. At the same time, Protestant exiles were busy producing their own histories. Apart from the work of Stránský and Comenius, there was the martyrology of Jan Rosacius Hořovský and a history of Ondřej Habervešl of Habernfeld, an officer in the army of Bohemia's ill-fated Winter King. Within Bohemia, however, the religious debate was settled definitively and a new type of confessional history was emerging. At its forefront was the prolific Jesuit scholar Bohuslav Balbín. Balbín brought together the perspective of Baronio with a pronounced set of antiquarian sensibilities. The key for Balbín and his colleagues was to demonstrate that the disturbances of the Hussite era and Reformation were an historical anomaly. Towards that end they sought to unearth (both literally and figuratively) the artefacts of a vibrant Catholic culture that had existed before the appearance of the schismatics. Balbín's unfinished *Miscellanea historica regni Bohemiae* [Historic Miscellany of the Bohemian Kingdom] (vol. 1, 1679), an encyclopedic overview of the kingdom's history and culture, included a separate volume examining the holy men and women of a *Bohemia sacra*. The work of Balbín was replicated many times over on a local level. In this golden age of ecclesiastical antiquarianism, forgotten pilgrimage shrines, neglected monasteries, and ruined churches, all found their eager chronicler.[29]

The notion that Catholicism slowed, stunted, or even stopped the penetration of Enlightenment thought in Central Europe has a long pedigree. Though scholars have challenged this stubborn stereotype, the image of German Catholic principalities as 'highly ornamental baroque troughs, in which epicurean prelates happily if sleepily wallowed' still persists in the popular imagination.[30] In terms of historical writing there has been a pronounced tendency to focus on Protestant innovations while underplaying or even ignoring developments in Catholic regions from 1648 to 1789. All, however, was not dark in the Habsburg lands during this period. A truer assessment of historical writing must begin by re-evaluating the intellectual links that this scholarly community maintained with the broader Catholic world. The first connection to note is with the Bollandists. The work of these Jesuits from the Low Countries grew out of the Catholic historical renaissance centred on Cologne before the Thirty Years War. Their tentacular reach eventually extended across Central Europe's broad expanse. In Bohemia Bohuslav Balbín's life of the fourteenth-century priest John Nepomuk was intended for the *Acta Sanctorum*. In the early eighteenth century the Bollandists appropriated the work of Gábor Hevenesi, who, a generation earlier, had spearheaded a movement to collect sources on Hungarian ecclesiastical history.

---

[29] Howard Louthan, 'Finding a Holy Past: Antiquarianism and Catholic Revival', in Louthan, *Converting Bohemia: Force and Persuasion in the Catholic Reformation* (Cambridge, 2009), 115–45.

[30] T. C. W. Blanning, 'The Enlightenment in Catholic Germany', in R. Porter and M. Teich (eds.), *Enlightenment in National Context* (Cambridge, 1981), 118.

The links with the French Maurist community were even more substantial. These Benedictines, who so eagerly collected and edited medieval manuscripts, worked with like-minded houses to create a network of what were essentially ecclesiastical learned societies. In Austria the Maurist connection extended beyond the important Benedictine outposts of Vienna, Melk, Göttweig, and Kremsmünster. The Alsatian Johann Christoph Bartenstein, an adviser of Charles VI and Maria Theresa, had studied with the Maurists in Paris and once in Vienna sought to establish a programme that would regularly have sent a select group of young Benedictines for an extended period of study to Saint-Germain-des-Prés.[31] Though Charles VI's Jesuit confessor ultimately scuttled this plan, the Jesuits could not dampen Maurist influence elsewhere. At Göttweig, Abbot Gottfried Bessel produced a counterpiece to Jean Mabillon's *De re diplomatica* [On the Science of Diplomatics] (1681). His *Chronicon Gottwicense* [Göttweig Chronicle] (1732) was a comprehensive treatment of German diplomatics. Up the river at Melk, the Pez brothers were transforming their abbey into a serious centre of historical research. When not sparring with the Jesuits, Bernhard Pez endeavoured to create a *Bibliotheca Benedictina* [Benedictine Library], a collection of manuscripts from the order's major houses in Central Europe, France, and Italy. Along with Bartenstein he planned to establish a Benedictine academy in Vienna following the model of Saint-Germain-des-Prés. His brother Hieronymus compiled the three-volume *Scriptores rerum austriacarum* [Writers on Austrian Matters] (1721–45), a thick edition of medieval Austrian manuscripts now transcribed and accessible to a broader audience.[32]

The tensions that had developed between the Benedictines and Jesuits were indicative of broader changes transforming the intellectual world of Catholic Central Europe. The historical challenge of the Protestant Reformation had initially prompted a more unified response from Catholic scholars in this region. With Jesuits assuming the lead and inspired by the Baronian watchwords, *semper eadem*, they produced a formidable body of scholarship that demonstrated the doctrinal consistency of the Catholic Church from Christian antiquity, through the Middle Ages, and into their present day. After 1648, however, this apparent unity slowly gave way to a more factionalized scholarly community. The rise of Jansenism had a profound effect on Catholic scholarship. Its success in the Southern Netherlands loosened the region's intellectual ties with the Empire, while a Jansenist party within the Habsburg lands gradually grew in power and influence. The emergence of a Benedictine school further complicated the situation and contributed to a growing antipathy to the Jesuit domination of learning in general and university education in particular. In the early eighteenth century a new challenge to Catholic unity appeared in Italy. Its impact was

---

[31] Eduard Winter, *Frühaufklärung* (Berlin, 1966), 127–8.
[32] Jan and Meta Niederkorn-Bruck, 'Hochbarocke Geschichtsschreibung im Stift Melk', in Ernst Bruckmüller (ed.), *900 Jahre Benediktiner in Melk* (Melk, 1989), 399–403.

quickly felt across the Alps as it affected both religious life and historical scholarship.

Ludovico Antonio Muratori, the librarian and archivist of the Dukes of Modena, was an early opponent of baroque Catholicism. His *Della carità cristiana* [On Christian Charity] (1723) was dedicated to Charles VI. Censuring the extravagance of baroque religiosity, he advocated a form of Catholicism characterized by simpler practices of piety. His ideas found purchase in Vienna and contributed to the reform agenda of Maria Theresa and Joseph II. As an historian, Muratori developed an approach to the past that was similar to the Maurist programme.[33] In 1708 he became involved in a nettlesome dispute between Rome and Vienna over the harbour town of Comacchio, which had been seized by imperial troops. An outraged pope aggressively asserted his rights of temporal jurisdiction over the area. In response Muratori composed a masterful defence of Habsburg claims, supporting his argument with a thick compilation of genealogical material.[34] Muratori's most important work was his twenty-eight-volume *Rerum italicarum scriptores* [Writers on Italian Matters] (1723–51), a collection of Latin and vernacular histories from the peninsula. In contrast to Baronio, Muratori demonstrated the possibility of studying the Middle Ages from a more secular vantage point. Hagiographical excess typical of the *Annales ecclesiastici* was generally absent, while voices antagonistic to Rome and the Church were included in the series.

In Vienna these ideas were especially well received in the circle that had developed around Austria's great hero, Eugene of Savoy. Assisted by his free-thinking adjutant, Baron von Hohendorf, the well-read prince built up a celebrated library of rare books and valuable manuscripts that attracted visitors from great distances. Giambattista Vico dedicated an early work to Eugene and took special care to send him one of the first printed copies of the *Scienza Nuova* [New Science] (1725). Prince Eugene was particularly interested in one of the most radical historians writing in Habsburg territory, Pietro Giannone.[35] Like Vico, Giannone was from Naples. He had originally studied law and combined legal and historical interests in his remarkable *Storia civile del Regno di Napoli* [History of the Kingdom of Naples] (1723). Written for the new Habsburg rulers of Naples as a blueprint for reform, the text reviewed the Neapolitian past from a pronounced anti-papal perspective. Giannone's outspoken anti-clericalism led him to exile in Vienna, where he began writing the *Triregno*, a history of civilization with a pointed critique of ecclesiastical power.

---

[33] See ch. 18 by Edoardo Tortarolo in this volume.

[34] Eleonore Zlabinger, *Lodovico Antonio Muratori und Österreich* (Innsbruck, 1970), 73–7.

[35] For connections with Reichsitalien in the eighteenth century see Elisabeth Garms-Cornides, 'Reichsitalien in der habsburgischen Publizistik des 18. Jahrhunderts', in M. Schnettger and M. Verga (eds.), *L'impero e l'Italia nella prima età moderna* (Bologna, 2003), 461–97.

At the same time, the imperial library was also becoming an important locus of historical research and activity. A series of Italian librarians, B. Gentilotti, P. N. Garelli, and Nicola Forlosia, were at the centre of an extensive correspondence network that included Muratori and the Pez brothers. Under Garelli's supervision Fischer von Erlach drew up the plans for the library's magnificent *Prunksaal*, while Forlosia continued one of Giannone's projects to publish the letters of Petrus de Vinea, the adviser to Emperor Frederick II (1220–50) who had worked with his patron to strengthen imperial power at the expense of the papacy. The most significant member of this circle in terms of historical writing was Gottfried Philipp Spannagel. Spannagel spent many years in Italy as a Habsburg publicist. He was eventually called to Vienna by Charles VI, who appointed him court historian, librarian, and tutor to the young Maria Theresa. The prolific Spannagel left behind a significant body of work. His *Histoire civile autrichienne* [Austrian History], an examination of the dynasty from Ferdinand I to Ferdinand III, as well as an eight-volume biography of Charles VI, remained in manuscript form. His most important work, a nine-volume study of Joseph I, though never completed, reflected a thoroughgoing Gallicanism that made no concessions to Rome.[36]

These scholarly circles and networks in time developed into more formal associations. The new learned societies were yet another factor that influenced the writing of history in the Habsburg lands. Instrumental here were the efforts of Central Europe's great polymath, Gottfried Wilhelm Leibniz, who lived in Vienna from 1712 to 1714. A tireless advocate of scientific institutions, he had long urged the Habsburgs to establish an association along the lines of the Royal Society and the Paris Academy. He saw the imperial residence of Vienna as an ideal location for an institute that would bring all forms of knowledge together. As part of his grand scheme, Leibniz, who was the long-standing court historian of the Welf family, envisioned the creation of a scholarly series, 'Annalen des Deutschen Reiches'. A specific proposal for this grand undertaking was drawn up, with the Lutheran Christian Wolff as the academy's director. In the confessionally sensitive environment of Charles VI's Vienna, however, this plan faltered and ultimately failed. There was more success elsewhere in the region. Encouraged by Muratori, who himself had dreamed of a *Repubblica letteraria d'Italia*, a group of scholars in Salzburg formed a small association that looked across the Alps for inspiration. A similar institution was formed in Innsbruck specifically dedicated to the study of history. In 1738 a group of churchmen and scholars with ties to the Bollandists and Maurists founded a society that eventually became known as the *Academia Taxiana*. Among its members were the historian and reformer Paul Joseph Riegger and Christoph Anton Migazzi, the future cardinal and archbishop of Vienna. Once more, Muratori's influence was substantial.

---

[36] Benz, *Zwischen Tradition und Kritik*, 418–21.

Joseph von Sperg made liberal use of his *Rerum italicarum scriptores* to compose a critical history of Tyrol.[37]

In Bohemia these societies had an even greater impact on the writing of history. The *Societas eruditorum incognitorum in terris austriacis*, the first academy officially recognized by the state in the Habsburg lands, was organized in the Moravian city of Olomouc in 1746. Its co-founders, a former aide-de-camp of Prince Eugene and an Italian churchman whose father was the Modenese ambassador in Vienna, established the society with two explicit goals: the elevation of the German language and the study of history. Appropriately enough, its early members included both Johann Christoph Gottsched and Hieronymus Pez. Somewhat later, in Prague, a group of natural scientists and historians founded the 'Private Learned Society'. One of its principal backers was the Piarist priest Gelasius Dobner. Dobner, an important representative of a new critical approach to the Bohemian past, initiated what became the first scholarly controversy in modern Czech historiography by attacking Hájek's popular history and challenging his claims of ethnogenesis. He dismissed as mythical fabrication Hájek's contention that the original inhabitants of the region were followers of the ancient chieftain Čech. Another Piarist member of the society, Mikuláš Adaukt Voigt, systematized the study of numismatics, while his closest collaborator, František Martin Pelcl, helped produce the first modern edition of Czech historical sources, *Scriptores rerum Bohemicarum* [Writers on Bohemian Matters] (1783–4).[38]

In many respects, historical writing in the Habsburg lands of the eighteenth century was heading in two directions. At the centre a more coherent and cohesive picture of the Habsburg dynasty and its territory was emerging, perhaps best reflected in the work of Marquard Herrgott, the last of a great line of Benedictine historians active in the Austrian baroque.[39] A native of Vorder-österreich, Herrgott studied in Strasbourg, Rome, St Gallen, and Melk before being sent off to Paris to complete his training. Initially employed as the librarian of the St Blasien Abbey, Herrgott eventually attracted the attention of Charles VI, who commissioned him to produce a history of the imperial family. The first volume of Herrgott's *Genealogia diplomatica Augustae Gentis Habsburgicae* [Diplomatic Genealogy of the Venerable Habsburg Family] (1737) marked a significant turning point for this genre and served as a model for other dynastic histories of the period. Herrgott did not place the genealogical emphasis on the ancient past. He did not engage in a search for Roman or Trojan predecessors. Instead, he carefully traced the links between the Habsburg and Lorraine families in an effort to secure their territorial claims. Herrgott's expertise in diplomatics

---

[37] Zlabinger, *Lodovico Antonio Muratori*, 47.

[38] Milan Kudělka, *Spor Gelasia Dobnera o Hájkovu Kroniku* (Prague, 1964); and B. Slavík, *Od Dobnera k Dobrovskému* (Prague, 1975).

[39] Josef Peter Ortner, *Marquard Herrgott (1694–1762)* (Vienna, 1972).

was thus of critical importance and indicative of a new and more pragmatic approach to genealogy. Such concerns were widespread in the era of the Pragmatic Sanction, with the Habsburgs facing a series of territorial challenges from their political rivals. While historians at the imperial court endeavoured to present a coherent and unified vision of the Habsburg domains, there was a countervailing dynamic on the periphery. Though there was a long tradition of vernacular histories in the Habsburg lands, their character changed as the eighteenth century progressed. The leading figure of the Bohemian Enlightenment was the patriotic Josef Dobrovský, whose efforts as a Czech philologist equalled his accomplishments as an historian.[40] In Hungary the Protestant Mátyás Bél and Jesuit György Pray helped develop a school of national history, while the Slovaks began to draw attention to a history that was distinct from the Hungarian past. A creative tension persisted between the centre and the periphery throughout the eighteenth century, but over time the balance slowly shifted towards the latter. The story of Herder's *Volksgeist*, growing nationalist sentiment, and the spread of vernacular histories, however, is beyond our scope and in its totality belongs to another century.

TIMELINE/KEY DATES

1316–78 Charles IV of Bohemia (r. 1346–78)

1415 Council of Constance and the execution of Jan Hus

1443–90 Matthias Corvinus of Hungary (r. 1458–90)

1459–19 Maximilian I (r. 1493–1519)

1500–58 Charles V (r. 1519–56)

1526 Battle of Mohács; Ferdinand I elected king of Bohemia and Hungary

1555 Peace of Augsburg

1569 Union of Lublin uniting Kingdom of Poland with the Grand Duchy of Lithuania

1618–48 Thirty Years War

1620 Battle of White Mountain

1630–1705 Leopold I (r. 1658–1705)

1648 Peace of Westphalia

1683 Ottoman invasion of Habsburg lands; siege and relief of Vienna

1685–1740 Charles VI (r. 1711–40)

1699 Peace of Karlowitz; Ottomans cede significant portions of Hungary, Transylvania, and Slavonia to the Habsburgs

1701–14 War of the Spanish Succession

---

[40] Zdeněk Fiala, 'Josef Dobrovský a počátky historické kritiky u nás', *Československý časopis historický*, 1 (1953), 257–71.

1714 Peace of Rastatt with France; Habsburgs acquire Naples, Milan, Sardinia, and the Southern Netherlands
1717–80 Maria Theresa (r. 1740–80)
1740–8 War of the Austrian Succession
1782 Joseph II issues the Edict of Toleration

KEY HISTORICAL SOURCES

Balbín, Bohuslav, *Miscellanea historica regni Bohemiae* (Prague, 1679–88).
Bessel, Gottfried, *Chronicon Gottwicense* (Tegernsee, 1732).
Bílejovský, Bohuslav, *Kronyka czeská* (Nuremberg, 1537).
Bonfini, Antonio, *Rerum ungaricarum decades* (Frankfurt, 1581).
Cuspinianus, Johannes, *De Caesaribus et Imperatoribus* (Strassburg, 1540).
Hájek, Václav, *Kronika česká* (Prague, 1541).
Khevenhüller, Franz Christoph, *Annales Ferdinandei* (Leipzig, 1721–6).
Lazius, Wolfgang, *Vienna Austriae* (Basel, 1546).
—— *De gentium aliquot migrationibus* (Basel, 1547).
Leopold of Vienna, *Chronik von den 95 Herrschaften* (*c.*1390).
Piccolomini, Aeneas Sylvius, *Historia Australis* (1453).
—— *Historia Bohemica* (1458).
Rader, Matthäus, *Bavaria sancta* (Munich, 1615–27).
Rhenanus, Beatus, *Rerum Germanicarum libri tres* (Basel, 1531).
Scriptores rerum Austriacarum (Leipzig, 1721–45).
Scriptores rerum Bohemicarum (Prague, 1783–4).
Stránský, Pavel, *Respublica Bohemiae* (Leiden, 1634).
Valvasor, Johann Weickhard von, *Ehre des Hertzogthums Crain* (Laibach, 1689).

BIBLIOGRAPHY

Antoljak, Stejpan, *Hrvatska historiografija* (Zagreb, 2004).
Benz, Stefan, *Zwischen Tradition und Kritik: Katholische Geschicthsschreibung im barocken Heiligen Römischen Reich* (Husum, 2003).
Birnbaum, Marianna, *Humanists in a Shattered World: Croatian and Hungarian Latinity in the Sixteenth Century* (Columbus, 1986).
Brendle, Franz, Mertens, Dieter, Schindling, Anton, and Ziegler, Walter (eds.), *Deutsche Landesgeschichtsschreibung im Zeichen des Humanismus* (Stuttgart, 2001).
Collins, David, *Reforming Saints: Saints' Lives and Their Authors in Germany, 1470–1530* (Oxford, 2007).
Coreth, Anna, *Österreichische Geschichtschreibung in der Barockzeit* (Vienna, 1950).
Evans, R. J. W., *Austria, Hungary and the Habsburgs* (Oxford, 2006).
Helmrath, J., Muhlack, U., and Walther, G. (eds.), *Diffusion des Humanismus: Studien zur nationalen Geschichtsschreibung europäische Humanisten* (Göttingen, 2002).

Joachimsen, Paul, *Geschichtsauffassung und Geschichtsschreibung in Deutschland unter dem Einfluss des Humanismus* (Berlin, 1910).

Johanek, Peter (ed.), *Städtische Geschichtsschreibung im Spätmittelalter und in der frühen Neuzeit* (Cologne, 2000).

Kersken, Norbert, 'Entwicklungslinien der Geschichtsschreibung Ostmitteleuropas in der Frühen Neuzeit', in J. Bahlcke and A. Strohmeyer (eds.), *Die Konstruktion der Vergangenheit* (Berlin, 2002), 19–53.

Kutnar, F. and Marek, J., *Přehledné dějiny českého a slovenského dějepisectví* (Prague, 1997).

Lhotsky, Alphons *Österreichische Historiographie* (Vienna, 1962).

——*Quellenkunde zur mittelalterlichen österreichischen Geschichte* (Graz, 1963).

Polman, P., *L'élément historique dans la controverse religieuse du XVIe siècle* (Gembloux, 1932).

Strauss, Gerald, *Historian in an Age of Crisis: The Life and Work of Johannes Aventinus, 1477–1534* (Cambridge, Mass., 1963).

Strohmeyer, Arno, 'Höfische und ständische Geschichtsschreibung', in Josef Pauser, Martin Scheutz, and Thomas Winkelbauer (eds.), *Quellenkunde der Habsburgermonarchie (16.–18. Jahrhundert)* (Vienna, 2004), 881–97.

Szegedi, Edit, *Geschichtsbewusstsein und Gruppenidentität: die Historiographie der Siebenbürger Sachsen zwischen Barock und Aufklärung* (Cologne, 2002).

Tropper, Peter, *Urkundenlehre in Österreich vom frühen 18. Jahrhundert bis zur Errichtung der 'Schule für Österreichische Geschichtsforschung' 1854* (Graz, 1994).

Vardy, Steven, *Modern Hungarian Historiography* (Boulder, Col., 1976).

Winkelbauer, Thomas, 'Ständische und höfische Geschichtsschreibung und Geschichtsbilder', in Winkelbauer, *Ständefreiheit und Fürstenmacht: Länder und Untertanen des Hauses Habsburg im Konfessionellen Zeitalter*, 2 vols. (Vienna, 2003), i. 227–81.

Chapter 16

German Historical Writing from the Reformation to the Enlightenment

Markus Völkel

STRUCTURE AND OUTLINES OF HISTORICAL CONSCIOUSNESS

The 'Holy Roman Empire'—an unfortunate translation of 'Heiliges Römisches Reich deutscher Nation'—might possibly be the most underrated commonwealth in history. This is first of all due to its self-perception as the 'Fourth World Monarchy' sanctioned by the biblical Book of Daniel. This conception did in fact free it from purely political interpretations and set its ending almost completely into a lofty theological and apocalyptical perspective. But the year 1806 proved fatal. By then every major European power—Prussia and Austria included—thought the Holy Roman Empire politically obsolete. It could not stem the tide of the French Revolution, and it was an obstacle to the Industrial Revolution. The catastrophic events of the nineteenth and twentieth centuries have put this kind of political assessment to shame. Once the nation-state was enforced in Middle and Eastern Europe it proved to be a focus of permanent political instability. Thus by its very absence the Holy Roman Empire has attested to its own apocalyptic status: the combined political wisdom from Bismarck to Stalin, from Roosevelt to Masaryk has failed to compensate for the loss of this enigmatic entity.

The Holy Roman Empire was a sovereign state, but a state whose sovereignty was shared by the head and the members of the 'body politic' in a highly unusual manner. Every 'estate'—and more than 1,000 territorial unities claimed to be an estate—was acknowledged as the bearer of an autonomous political will. This will, in order to act, had to be mediated by different styles of communication and institutional resolutions.

Politically speaking the Empire was a modus operandi, a way of acting, which members could and in fact could not adopt. Opting in and opting out of the Reich was a trivial affair. So it is scarcely surprising that the Empire neither had nor needed a clear consciousness of its borders, of its language, of its constitution, and even, after 1555, of its religion. Borders could be defended but need not be expanded; German was the language of the majority but no vernacular was ever favoured by Imperial Law (*Reichsabschied*), Latin functioning as the privileged media of public life. As it proved impossible to agree upon a formal constitution for the Empire and equal rights for the three major Christian denominations, the leading estates retreated to historical deadlines combined with an historical interpretation of 'the Imperial Law'. So the Peace of Westphalia stipulated that the year of 1624 should set the demarcation line of the de facto exercise of a local cult. History and law (*Reichsrecht, Reichherkommen*) would act together to compensate for the many loopholes and inconsistencies of the Imperial Law.

Clerical sovereign estates by the end of the Middle Ages had disappeared everywhere in Europe except the Papal States (Patrimonium Petri) and, within the Empire, the Imperial Bishops and Abbots (*Reichsbischöfe, Reichsäbte*). The Imperial Church (*Reichskirche*) had renounced its foremost office to provide the emperor with funds and manpower for an effective imperial 'foreign policy' by the fourteenth century. Yet during the early modern period the *Reichskirche* still operated as the most faithful clientele of the emperor.

In the sixteenth century the Empire was still an important player in the financial market of Europe. It lost its position definitively during the Thirty Years War, but it upheld substantial economic and technological power to push the Ottoman Empire out of Central Europe and to finance a rich and variegated system of education. So the Holy Roman Empire was among the first European states to establish a public postal service and consequently encouraged the advent of monthly, weekly, and daily newspapers. Two book fairs, respectively at Frankfurt-am-Main and Leipzig, served as a meeting ground for the European printing industry. Woodcut and copperplate engravings 'made in Augsburg, Frankfurt, or Nuremberg' enabled the publishers to sell their illustrated books all over the continent and also to the Americas. Modernity did not bypass the Empire, although the complete set of tokens of 'sovereignty' could be displayed only by the few larger territories. Even its few acknowledged central institutions, the Imperial Diet, the Imperial Aulic Council in Vienna (*Reichshofrat*), the Imperial Chamber Court (*Reichskammergericht*), and the Imperial Army were able to adapt to new challenges even though very slowly.

Modern research on the Empire argues that its over-complexity of structure and atomization of power were at least partially balanced by the performative and historic aspects of its day-to-day politics. Ceremonial and history did in fact weld the *Reichsstaat* (Imperial State) together. Thus 'history' was primarily viewed as 'public acting' and 'historical truth' accordingly as 'publicly perceived acts', the historian as 'public notary' of socially relevant facts, and 'historical sources' as vestiges of public administration. 'Ceremonial' was understood as the precise re-enactment of this knowledge.

Until the advent of humanism around 1450 the Empire knew next to nothing of its Germanic roots. The *Annolied* (before 1100) called the Franks descendants of the Trojans, while Caesar, after having defeated the four German tribes (Franks, Saxons, Swabians, and Bavarians) then formed an alliance with them, thus founding the Roman Empire. Then the 'Tacitean Revolution' took place: the 'theodisci' ('those belonging to the people') could be identified with the ethnic groups described in his *Germania*. At last an 'ethnic pool' was established enabling the Germans to take over the Roman Empire (the medieval *translatio imperii*) as well as classical knowledge (*translatio studii*).

After the Reformation this 'double translation' resulted in two different ways of dealing with the 'Roman reference'. The Protestants, the real inventors of 'Legal Imperial History', stressed the biblical foundations of the Empire together with its Germanic and aristocratic roots, unremittingly exposing the centrality of the 'German liberties' (*Deutsche Freiheiten*). The medieval Church and the papacy were put into parentheses, as a period of corruption but also of germination of the true Church. The Catholics referred to the civilizing role of the Church and the sacramental character of Empire and emperor for which the exclusive source was the pope. The majority of the Catholic Party being comprised of clerical estates, the 'holiness' of the Empire obliged the emperor and the secular Catholic estates to guarantee their status. Correspondingly the Peace of Augsburg (1555), intended originally as nothing more than a short-term truce between the antagonists, produced in the long run two quite different 'historical cultures' defined along confessional lines. Catholic historical culture was oriented towards the Roman centralizing tradition of the Empire, the performing arts, and the religious rites. The Protestant variant turned towards the single territorial state, hermeneutical analysis, encyclopedism, and secular values. Both types were capable of developing critical insights into historical method, 'historical critique' being nourished as well by the destruction of Roman 'tradition' as by the destruction of verbal inspiration.

A major consequence of having two confessional historical cultures was the frustration of any attempt to produce a 'master narrative' for the Empire. Christian universal history, the first candidate for this role, before assuming the shape of pragmatic interconnected history (*Pragmatische Historie*) after 1750, could only be used as a rigid metaphysical scheme. It caused the negative side effect of isolating the *Reichsstaat* from its neighbours. Imperial history fluctuated helplessly between the territorial state and the integrated Empire whose continued existence soon became a matter of urgent reform. But the direction of this reform could never be agreed upon. Even emotionally successful operations like the Turkish Wars and the fight against Louis XIV, or shared disasters like the Schmalkaldic League, the Thirty Years or the Seven Years Wars, produced no universally accepted national history. Late Enlightenment efforts to nationalize the Reich as an 'Empire of the German people' came to nothing.

As in every other European society sufficiently equipped with printing and literacy, history attracted a comparatively large part of the national audience. But readerships rarely overlapped. Universities, secondary schools, courts, cities, and monastic orders all educated different sorts of readers. Confessional borders within the book market were strongly pronounced, harbouring considerable linguistic and orthographic differences, for instance, 'Protestant Hochdeutsch' and 'Catholic Oberdeutsch'. A society based on estates and birth strictly recommended the reading of histories to those who could 'learn from it' when performing their public duties; persons of lesser rank and no power should confine their attention to morally edifying treatises. This does not imply that historiographical information (and disinformation) could not circulate widely, but it did so mainly in the forms of the broadsheet, the pseudohistorical romance, or the even more unconsolidated form of the 'yearly reports' drawn from the periodical press or published by the provincial of a Jesuit college. Something of a 'wild historical knowledge', that is, a knowledge produced from 'below' rather than by experts, may be assumed within greater sections of the population, even the rural ones; but we still know very little of it.

Even when they acknowledge an extremely rich field of published texts, of methodological talent, and archival treasures, modern historians of historiography have to plough very deeply in order to uncover the background to the later historiographical triumphs of nineteenth-century Germany. The reason for this, ironically, can be detected in the reductionist attitude of this 'German School' itself: it rejected the Holy Roman Empire because it had betrayed the national aspirations of the Germans. Consequently it had also to reject the Empire's historiographical feats, because they had not contributed to an adequate historical consciousness of the people. Adequacy was thought to be equivalent to 'historical success'. Whether the Holy Roman Empire was a failure is still an open question; the fecundity of its historiographical heritage for modern objectives leads, however, in the opposite direction.

GERMAN HUMANISM

The ascendancy of German humanism, focused evenly on the Empire and the 'German nation', was short-lived. It lasted from 1480 until 1520 and was then overcome by the Reformation. So in order to speak of the historiography of German humanism one should first separate it from its long afterlife under the religious influence of the Reformation and second, from its own rich medieval heritage. Third, early German humanism as a network of printing and discussion was largely a regional phenomenon situated in the south-west of the Empire: Alsace, the Palatinate, the Habsburg Vorlande, and the northern parts of the emerging Swiss Confederation. Although many of its major figures focused their gaze on Emperor Maximilian I, that extravagant monarch neither directed this loose association nor did much to finance it.

Schlettstadt, situated 40 kilometres south-west of Strassburg, was a major centre of humanist historiography. An important secondary school (Lateinschule) served as a meeting place for a regional elite keen on arousing 'national attention'. Jacob Wimpfeling in his *Epithoma rerum Germanicarum* [Digest of German History] (1501) wrote the first exclusively 'German' history. It started with the five Germanic tribes, repudiated any foreign descent, and lavished praise on the nation. This of course is 'nationalism' (in its pre-modern sense), a cultural as well as political plea for the autonomy of the Empire, but the *Epithoma* is also a rhetorical book of common places where the 'nation' serves as a topos where an author should gather all the relevant materials gleaned from the sciences, and from profane as well as ecclesiastical literature.

How futile it is to identify an author with his most famous book is proved by the case of Beatus Rhenanus (Beat Bild). He is commonly remembered for his *Rerum Germanicarum libri tres* [Three Books on German History] (1531), often labelled the first 'critical history' of the Germans. Rhenanus was an expert in philology and antiquarianism, but he was no follower of the 'Four Monarchies' theory of history, nor did he subscribe to the doctrine of *translatio imperii*. His empire is definitively a German one and the title 'Roman' a purely honorary tribute by the pope. In order to evaluate this achievement one should reconsider the philological activity of Rhenanus. He edited the works of the Church Father Tertullian (1521), and the *Autores historiae ecclesiasticae* [Authors of Ecclesiastical History] (1523), a group comprising Eusebius, Theodoret, Sozemenos, and Socrates, and of greatest importance, Tacitus's *Historiae* (1519) and the surviving sections of Livy (1535). Placed within this context the *Rerum germanicarum* could be viewed rather differently than they had been during the Middle Ages. At the same time, while Tacitus's *Germania* enabled the consciousness of the Germans as a chosen people, the Germanic historical achievement of 'universal nationalism of the Empire' could be reduced to an 'endogenous monogenetic nationalism'.[1] The 'new history of the humanists', that is the creation of a universally interconnected history, based on the ancients but integrating and subordinating the medieval authors, enlarged the 'Germanic horizon' to unknown dimensions, while at the same time reducing it to the then-present Empire or even smaller regional units. This remarkably efficient combination of universalism (spatial and temporal) with localism (also both spatial and temporal) compensated for its unsuitability for the production of a readable German history in the manner of Paolo Emilio's *De rebus gestis Francorum libri IX* [On the Exploits of the Francs, IX Books] (1517), the Empire being the sole major kingdom in Latin Europe not to import Italian humanists for this office.[2]

---

[1] Jörn Garber, 'Vom universalen zum endogenen Nationalismus: Die Idee der Nation im deutschen Spätmittelalter und in der frühen Neuzeit', in Helmut Scherer (ed.), *Dichter und ihre Nation* (Frankfurt, 1993), 16–37.

[2] Markus Völkel, 'Rhetoren und Pioniere: Italienische Humanisten als Geschichtsschreiber der europäischen Nationen. Eine Skizze', in Peter Burschel (ed.), *Historische Anstöße: Festschrift für Wolfgang Reinhard zum 65. Geburtstag* (Berlin, 2002), 339–62.

In his preface to Procopius's *De rebus Gothorum, Persarum ac Vandalorum libri VII* [On the History of the Goths, Persians, and Vandals, VII Books] (1531), Rhenanus follows the migrations of the Goths throughout Europe, marking a worldwide 'German space' into which their contemporary descendants have to settle themselves. So it comes as no surprise that Matthias Ringmann, committed to the very humanistic task of translating the ancients and editor of the first German *Corpus Caesareum* [Book of Caesars] (508), is the same person who in 1507 authored the *Cosmographiae Introductio* [Introduction into Cosmography] as an explanation of Martin Waldseemüller's famous world map exhibiting for the first time the name of 'America' on a new fourth continent.[3] The same range of historical topics can be discovered in Sebastian Münster, author of the best-selling *Cosmographia* [Cosmography] (1544, 1550). His description of the new expanded globe is still centred on Germany, while the main language humanists have to learn is Hebrew.

Consequently German humanism from the universal background of ancient history and topography reaches out to individual zones within the Empire. Albert Krantz, professor at Rostock and later deacon at the Hamburg dome, was a northern exponent of this tradition. Krantz's *Wandalia* (1519), *Saxonia* (1520), and his *Chronica regnorum aquilonarium Daniae, Suetiae, Norvagiae* [Chronicle of the Danish, Swedish, and Norwegian Kingdoms] (1548) rest on the concept of a 'Germania magna' where space defines ethnic affiliations. Here 'Germans' and 'Slaves' are without a doubt conflated. Accordingly an 'inner German space' is required marked 'Saxonia'. This special region is thus prepared to become the cradle of the future Reformation. Krantz prepared the paradigm of a future Protestant outlook of German history.

Other than might be expected by its perpetual 'Roman reference' (Roman Church, Roman antiquity, Roman character of the Empire), German humanistic historiography cultivated the medieval heritage of the Empire. One could almost speak of a kind of 'retrospective syndrome' around 1500 from which the quixotic memorial projects of Emperor Maximilian I stand out as the most visible examples. Medieval literature, Latin as well as vernacular, and written source material of any kind were collected and edited.

THE TWOFOLD PROTESTANT PARADIGM

Around 1520 the development of historiographical writing within the Empire had arrived at a crossroads. To combine the already reduced 'Germanic and

---

[3] Franz Joseph Worstbrock, 'Zur Einbürgerung der Übersetzung antiker Autoren im deutschen Humanismus', *Zeitschrift für deutsches Altertum*, 99 (1970), 45–81; and Dieter Wuttke, 'Humanismus und Entdeckungsgeschichte 1493–1534', in Wuttke, *Dazwischen: Kulturwissenschaft auf Warburgs Spuren* (Baden-Baden, 1996), 483–537.

polycentric' character with a political purpose, a kind of reason of state, did not seem impossible. On the other hand, Church and State were drifting towards a crisis: with the end of days seemingly near, history would finish and thus a new general design for its writing was needed.

Philipp Melanchthon, grandnephew of the famous Hebraist Johannes Reuchlin, was the first to achieve a durable synthesis of the two currents. Melanchthon's education first made him a man of letters and only after Luther's intervention did he become a theologian at the University of Wittenberg. History for Melanchthon was all-important for the true Christian because it passed on the morally effective examples of human agency while at the same time delimiting the temporal space of this agency (*historia universalis*) in the face of God. Historical acts occur in order to illustrate God's intentions towards mankind, and history itself is thus both an ethical and a linguistic phenomenon, a continuous lesson everybody should heed at every moment. In keeping this didactic view, Melanchthon's great historical books are manuals of instruction. He started with a little German-language book entitled *Chronica durch Magistrum Carion vleissig zusamen gezogen* [Chronicle Diligently Compiled by Master Carion] (1532), which hardly covered the ground until the coronation of Charlemagne. In the end his son-in-law Caspar Peucer had compiled a massive Latin outline of universal history covering all the ground up to Emperor Charles V, the *Chronicon Carionis* [Chronicle Commenced by Master Carion] of 1558.

The *Chronicon Carionis* may well be the most influential historical manual ever written. Its outstanding achievement was to make history essential for the Christian way of life. However, its considerable flaws have to be acknowledged. Although a fervid exponent of rhetoric, Melanchthon's 'idea of history' was anchored in the plain style of the biblical accounts and, even more dangerous, it depoliticized history. For Melanchthon concrete power had no human genesis but only divine origins and its true end must always be the spiritual salvation of man. So Melanchthon left a divided legacy as to how 'Christian history' should be written.

The political as well as the Machiavellian side of Reformation historiography is highlighted in Johann Sleidan's *Commentariorum de statu religionis et reipublicae Carolo V. Caesare libri XXVI* [Twenty-Six Books of Commentaries on the Condition of Religion and the State under the Emperor Charles V] (1555). An official historiographer to the Protestant Schmalkaldic League since 1552 and close friend of important Strassburg diplomats, Sleidan could make use of the official and at times even secret papers of the Protestant party. His commentary covers thirty-eight years and is the only German history of the sixteenth century that betrays traces of the influence of purely political historiography such as the *Mémoires* of Philippe de Commynes. Sleidan's *Commentarii* proved a European bestseller and provided the foundation on which Jacques-Auguste de Thou and Paolo Sarpi would later build their respective histories of the French religious wars and the Council of Trent.

While Sleidan surpassed Melanchthon on the political level, the *Magdeburg Centuries* tried to reformulate orthodox Lutheran theology in historical terms. They thus corrected Melanchthon's concept of keeping dogma and history strictly separate. The *Ecclesiastica historia, integram Ecclesiae Christi ideam . . . complectens* [Church History Comprehending the Perfect Idea of the Church of Christ] (13 vols., 1559–74) is the first collectively produced historiographical work in European history. The Magdeburgians refused to narrate: instead, they arranged their materials under sixteen thematic—mostly dogmatic—headings within each *Centuria.* Accordingly the book presented itself as a history of Christian dogma structured by a rigid chronology. The 'Magdeburg Centuriators'—Matthias Flacius the inspiring force and Johann Wigand and Matthäus Judex its executors—thus created a Protestant sentiment of historical superiority. In order to arrive at this result a double movement was necessary: the outward continuity of the visible Church had to be broken, while the inner continuity of true dogma and its tradition had to be upheld by the strongest historical proofs.

Impressive as this achievement seems, it was scarcely the most radical Protestant position concerning the importance of history. The priest-turned-printer Sebastian Franck of Donauwörth reversed the epistemological status of human history. His *Chronica, Zeytbuch und geschychtbibel* [Chronicle, Book of Times and History-Bible] (1531, 1536) established history written by human authors of all times as a 'second revelation' and a necessary supplement of the Bible. History in the end becomes the tombstone of dogma and opens a space for an individualistic following of Christ.

THE FRAGMENTED REICH AND THE EXUBERANCE OF HISTORY

The period following the Augsburg Religious Peace witnessed an astonishing increase in historiographical productions of all sorts, sacred as well as profane. For the first time, historiography composed in German successfully asserted itself on the book market. An expanding reading public was longing for more detailed information on its various territories or cities. Yet the interest in the Empire, the origins of its laws, and its eschatological dignity persisted, albeit increasingly confined to the officers and bureaucrats of the imperial institutions and the authors of schematic school manuals. The only figure to stimulate 'national interest' was the emperor himself, but the Habsburg family (except Emperor Maximilian I), until the end of the Reich, obstinately rejected the biographical approach. They conceived of the emperor as a bearer of public office, a link in the genealogical chain, and discouraged every attempt at psychological penetration and emotional identification.

The following presentation of a relevant choice of historiography starts in the south-west of the Empire, and ends in its far east. It proceeds by clusters based on the internal cooperation of groups of varied origin (confessional, local, rank, kinship, and patronage). Historical legitimization was its principal focus but was closely followed by the unaccomplished demands of German humanism: the *Germania illustrata* [Germany illustrated] envisioned by Conrad Celtis in 1492 still had to be written. Furthermore, its Christian traditions had to be redefined, predominantly in regional terms. The historical traditions of landscapes and Germanic tribes had to be merged with the genealogy of princely families. Likewise the constitutional and religious equilibrium of the cities, imperial or not, had to be readjusted by new chronicles. Old and new families outside the princely sphere strove to consolidate their 'historical standing', a concept not to be fulfilled without the commemoration of great individuals. Naturally the Imperial Church (*Reichskirche*), in its numerous institutional manifestations, participated in every development mentioned above.

Although the Swiss Confederation (*Eidgenossenschaft*) had loosened its ties with the Empire it did not relinquish its legal affiliations until the Peace of Westphalia. So Swiss historiography, while strengthening local identity, still reflects the reality of the Reich and partakes in its political interpretation. Around Zurich a first historiographical cluster can be identified, the anchoring figure of which was the reformer Heinrich Bullinger. Bullinger built up a vast Protestant information network that was of great use to him when he turned to history towards the end of his life. Of his three major works, the *Reformationsgeschichte* [History of the Reformation] (1564), the *Geschichte der Eidgenossenschaft* [History of the Swiss Confederation] (1575), and the *Tigurinerchronik* [History of Zurich] (1574), only the first was printed and not until 1840. But this does not imply that it would not be read in the form of manuscript copies. In the early modern Empire, as elsewhere in the world, unprinted matter circulated, was commented upon, and was sometimes even continued by other authors. Bullinger's close collaborator, Johannes Stumpf from Bruchsal, produced the first comprehensive Protestant chronicle of the confederation.[4] His vivid and graphic 'Oberdeutsch' makes good reading even today. Stumpf, on his part, relied on information provided by Bullinger. Supra-denominational teamwork was still possible, so the reformed Stumpf cited many charters unearthed by his great Catholic opponent Aegidius Tschudi in order to authorize his magnificent *Chronicon helveticum* [Chronicle of the Swiss] (1534–6). This conservative masterpiece laid the corner-stone of the Swiss political myth: a lawful rebellion within the Empire, within traditional Catholicism, and within the framework of the rural elites of the original (founding) cantons.

The Swiss authors and compilers cultivated a hybrid genre of historiography. According to their own tradition of the 'Illustrated Chronicle' they lavishly illustrated their works, they collected legends, and they incorporated official docu-

---

[4] Johannes Stumpf, *Gemeiner loblicher Eydgenossenschafft Stetten, Landen und Voelckeren Chronick wirdiger thaaten beschreibung* (Zurich, 1547).

ments. Stumpf was famous for his maps (*Landtafeln*), which were widely copied. A simple town chronicle like Christian Wurstisen's *Baßler Chronik* [Chronicle of the City of Basle] from 1580 could thus combine the genres of topography, genealogy, and archival documentation. Histories of Imperial Cities could easily become exemplary histories of the Empire as well as of its municipal representatives. Christoph Lehmann's *Speyerer Chronik* (1612) was the most widely read chronicle of this type. Based on the still complete archival records of Speyer, it deals with the medieval foundations of its law and everyday life, as well as with its political relations with the emperor. Many readers welcomed this book as a kind of substitute for the missing popular *Reichsgeschichte*. The German public thus responded to the irresistible transformation of this genre into a legal discourse.

Wurstisen himself had edited two massive compilations of medieval historians in 1585. Yet he was but one of the many Protestant lawyers and collectors of German antiquities and constitutions like Simon Schardt, Reiner Reineccius, Marquard Freher, Melchior Goldast, Justus Reuber, and Erpold Lindenbrog, including an occasional Catholic convert like Johannes Pistorius the Younger, confessor to Emperor Rudolf II. They were all from the same south-western German territories which looked towards the court of the Palatinate at Heidelberg with its strong ties to the Imperial Chamber Court at Speyer and to the ruthless printers at Frankfurt like Sigmund Feyerabend or Andreas Wechel. This first 'School of Historians of the Empire' (*Reichshistoriker*) combined the narrative sources of the Reich with its charters and the resolutions of the Diet. Their outlook was strictly legal and by concentrating on medieval sources they set off one of the many phases of 'medievalism' in the Reich, the first being a phenomenon of the reign of Emperor Maximilian I.

Yet noteworthy historians could be found in the most insignificant corners of the Empire. Mindelheim, 60 kilometres south of Augsburg, harboured Adam Reissner. He acted as a clerk to the great captain Georg von Frundsberg, returning with him from Rome as an eyewitness of the Sack of Rome. After 1531 he was a follower of the mystic Caspar Schwenckfeld. His *Historia Herrn Georgen und Caspar von Frundsberg* [Lives of the Knights Georg and Caspar Frundsberg] (1568) proves that German had by this time evolved into a language fit to deal with dramatic contemporary events. *Jerusalem die alte Haubtstadt der Juden* [Jerusalem, the Ancient City of the Jews] (1569–74), written by Reissner in an apocalyptic vein, is the first historical monograph on this sacred city. As the Empire never had an acknowledged centre there are virtually no 'peripheral' authors. This is why the historical ambitions of the local gentry deserve to be taken seriously.

During the sixteenth century a conspicuous number of noble or not so noble houses succeeded in climbing up the social hierarchy of the Empire. Consequently their family history had to be rewritten according to their future ambitions. Chronicles like the *Truchsessenchronik* [Steward's Chronicle], Sebastian Küng's *Chronik der Herzöge von Württemberg* [Chronicle of the Dukes of Württemberg], the *Zimmerische Chronik* [Chronicle of the House of Zimmern] drafted by Count Christoph Froben himself, and the superbly illustrated

Zollernchronik [Chronicle of the House of Zollern] all laboured to fuse pragmatic truth, genealogical fiction, and literary genres (autobiography, anecdote, tales) into a unified account. The results were hybrid texts which allowed story to comment on history, and image to illuminate diverging or even shocking morals. This often contradictory 'literarization' of history could easily be beaten by excessive artistic investment. This way was chosen by the Tucher family of Nuremberg who spent more than 2,000 gold ducats on a parchment copy of their massive *Geschlechterbuch* [Book of Lineage] (1590–1606).

It took the Tuchers only sixteen years to accomplish their prestigious enterprise. Herein they proved the efficiency of civic engagement and financing. In contrast, many histories and chronicles encouraged by princes remained in an unfinished state. Thus the most important chronicle of the Ernestine House of Saxony, written by their trustee Georg Spalatin and illustrated by the Cranach workshop, remained a fragment. The political decline of the Ernestine line prevented it from publishing a history of lost splendour. On the other hand, chronicles restricted to manuscript versions could still work efficiently to stabilize exponents of the beleaguered *Reichskirche*. Lorenz Fries's *Würzburger Bischofs-chronik* [Chronicle of the Bishops of Würzburg] was never printed. Yet Prince-Bishop Julius Echter, an eminent reformer, had the original version recopied, enlarged, and illustrated, and thus turned into a kind of 'expanding collective memory' until it was finally printed in 1713.

Before the Thirty Years War almost every historical writer was involved in some kind of confessional dispute. The Swiss were exemplary in this, but also inside the Empire this kind of antagonism was difficult to avoid. Marcus Welser of Augsburg, one of the two mayors of this Imperial City, was a universally respected member of the European Res Publica Litteraria. Privately he was a partisan of Catholicism and worked hard to consolidate an uninterrupted urban Catholic tradition harmoniously stretching back to the Roman founding fathers. Significantly, his writings deal with his city and the contiguous duchy of Bavaria in parallel ways. While the *Chronica der . . . Reichs Statt Augsburg* [Chronicle of the Imperial City of Augsburg] (1595–6) praises the citizen's devotion to its local saints, his *Bayrische Geschicht* [Bavarian History] (1605) outlines the early history of Bavaria. Both histories were originally written in Latin only to be translated into German without delay for the sake of the local Catholic elite.

It makes sense to confront the sedentary Marcus Welser with the militant and itinerant Protestant pastor Cyriacus Spangenberg. Clinging stubbornly to Flaccian positions he was driven from town to town by suspicious authorities. From his prolific writing stand out his *Adelsspiegel* [Mirror of Nobility] (1591–4) and two regional chronicles.[5] These histories obviously aim at educating an independent lesser nobility who could, in turn, defend religious dissenters. It was in that

---

[5] *Mansfeldische Chronica* (Eisleben, 1572); and *Hennebergische Chronica* (Strassburg, 1599).

middle ground that the German Reformed Church struck root. Region, territory, and landscape are thus drawn into an irresistible process of confessionalization and are usually combined with the *origines* (descent) of German tribes and the genealogy of the great reigning dynasties. The *Genealogia und Chronica... der Fürsten zu Anhalt* [Genealogy of the... Princes of Anhalt] (1556) by the Mayor of Merseburg, Ernst Brotuff, may stand for many others. This genre was to be productive until the beginning of the eighteenth century.

Admittedly, 'regions' within the Empire were not bound exclusively to dynastic or confessional identity. Martin Crusius, a distinguished professor of Greek at Tübingen, published a monumental compilation on his Suevian 'Heimatland'.[6] Here the Germanic tribe of the 'Allamani', together with the idolized dynasty of the Hohenstaufen and the Imperial Circle of Suevia, served as a strong focus of a 'Suevian Patriotism'. Crusius's close correspondent David Chytraeus, at Rostock on the Baltic Sea, shared his interest in the Orthodox Churches. Chytraeus developed his own concept of a 'historical space' synonymous with his repeatedly continued chronicle *Saxonia* (1593ff). The land of the Saxons was the heir to Krantz's *Vandalia*, the heartland of the Reformation which Chytraeus understood to be the intellectual centre of the Nordic Protestant Churches and the bulwark of the true German language. Chytraeus's vast network of information in the north of the Empire equals that of Bullinger in the south and it led to similar results: the intensification of regional historical research in order to integrate those autonomous parts into a coherent Protestant community. Thus Chytraeus continued the benchmark *Historia Rerum Prussicarum* [History of Things Prussian] of his pupil Caspar Schütz until the end of the sixteenth century and he encouraged his correspondent Paul Oderborn at Kowno to write the first contemporary life of Ivan IV 'the Terrible'.[7] The geographic borders of the Empire were but loose ends to which new histories could easily be attached.

WARS AND ENLIGHTENMENT, SCIENCE AND LITERATURE

The Thirty Years War did not destroy the Holy Roman Empire nor did it deter its elite from writing history. One might even have expected that by creating an 'imaginary community of suffering' the already existing protonational sentiment could have been turned into some kind of active political solidarity. But this was not the case. The war in fact did retard vital processes: the use and perfection of the German language, the merging of the still isolated two 'national book markets' (Catholic versus Protestant), the effective advancement of the new natural sciences,

---

[6] Martin Crusius, *Annales Suevici*, 3 vols. (Frankfurt, 1595–6).
[7] Paul Oderborn, *Ioannis Basilidis Magni Moscoviae Ducis vita* (Wittenberg, 1585).

and, most of all, the advent of a supra-regional, supra-denominational, and non-corporative social ideal capable of reflecting power and politics within accepted literary forms. In short: Enlightenment never achieved its universal synthesis in the Empire. The period stretching from 1648 to 1740 is illustrative of this kind of process.

The long war first took the shape of broadsheets, of diaries and journals, subsequently changed to almanacs, and when it had reached the threshold of literary composition it had already lost its creative momentum. The standard works of Franz Christoph von Khevenhüller, Peter Lotichius, Leonhard Pappus, and Everhard Wassenberg, surprisingly all pro-Catholic except the one written by the Swedish client Boguslav Philipp von Chemnitz, were read well into the next century but could not claim excessive literary or critical value. When it dawned upon the Protestant historians that they could not control definitively the long-term memory of the war they turned towards the historical interpretation of the Imperial Constitution. Friedrich Hortleder's attempt to base the constitutional position of the Lutheran party on the legitimacy of the Schmalkaldian War (1546–7) could not be repeated.[8]

Thus a second *reichshistorische Schule* entered the scene. From the first moment on, its lecture halls served the defence of those venerable 'German liberties' as was proved by the eminent scholar Professor Hermann Conring at Helmstedt. Following the foundation of the University of Halle in 1694, the *Reichshistorie* expounded by academic celebrities like Peter Ludewig and Hieronymus Gundling became a fashionable field of study, replacing theology as the leading science. Halle in 1737 was displaced by Göttingen as the dominant German university. The traditional course of *Reichshistorie* was complemented by auxiliary sciences such as numismatics, geography, statistics, and diplomatics. *Reichsgeschichte* in a way facilitated the advent of a future genuine academic discipline that would later be called *Geschichtswissenschaft*.

Traditional imperial historiography, from its very beginning, had absorbed an enormous amount of solid historical knowledge based on official documents and other written narratives, or derived from various forms of German antiquarian scholarship. *Reichsgeschichte*, in alliance with biblical hermeneutics and philosophical ethics, even played a significant role in overcoming the sceptical attacks of the 'historical pyrrhonists' on historical truth. Obvious contradictions passed on in histories and traditions could be reconciled by the simple means of naturalizing human action. The verifying power in history was taken away from the witness and handed over to the historian, who constructed history simply by narrating it. All a 'perfect historian' had to do was to submit to the ethical imperative of human society which was made coherent by 'reasonable faith'.

---

[8] Friedrich Hortleder, *Von den Ursachen des Teutschen Kriegs Kaiser Carls des V* (Frankfurt, 1617–18).

While the exponents of *Reichsgeschichte* were productive in promoting histor-ical methodology, and even slowly introduced German as the language of teaching and writing, they exerted very little influence on the literary develop-ment of historiography. They did nothing to establish history as an aesthetical and political agenda outside the legal or academic sphere. The case of Gottfried Wilhelm Leibniz is instructive in this respect. In its most noble version Friedrich Meinecke idealized German historicism by invoking Leibniz as its intellectual godfather. But what was the result of Leibniz's lifelong labours as the official archivist and historian to the House of Hanover? Leibniz endorsed the use of German for historical writing but he did not himself set an example for this. When Ludolf Hiob, the founder of Ethiopian studies, suggested the formation of a National Academy for History (*Historisches Reichskolleg*), Leibniz immediately adopted the idea. But as often happens, circumstance turned against this initia-tive. None among the most illustrious fellow historians of his time felt inclined to re-launch the history of the Empire in the manner of Cesare Baronius's *Annales ecclesiatici* [Annals of the Church] (1588–1607). The emperor, for his part, was reluctant to appoint Leibniz to the office of *Reichshofrat* and to take over the protectorate of the *Reichskolleg*. So what appears on Leibniz's balance sheet are his *Codex juris gentium diplomaticus* [Code of the Charters of Public Law] (1693–1700), his *Scriptores rerum Brunsvicensium* [Writers of the History of Brunsvic] (1707–11), plenty of dispersed remarks on historical method, and tricky legal issues concerning his historico-antiquarian works which, until recently, nobody had the nerve to collect and comment on.[9]

It should therefore come as no surprise to see the ingenious Leibniz vanquished in the public domain by his rival Samuel von Pufendorf. Rightly famous as a philosopher of natural justice, Pufendorf gained a lasting reputation with two voluminous accounts of the recent history of Sweden and Brandenburg-Prussia.[10] Pufendorf was proud of his archival diligence and even more so of his outspoken impartiality. Pufendorf scored yet another lasting triumph. He published the first successful manual on the history of the modern state, the famous *Einleitung zu der Historie der vornehmsten Reiche und Staaten von Europa* [*Introduction to the History of the Principal Kingdoms and States of Europe*] (English edn, 1699).

While the growth of the new absolutist state abroad and at home provoked prudent responses from the Empire's historians, what mattered to them was the history of the Protestant Church. When the French Jesuit Louis Maimbourg published his *Histoire du Luthéranisme* [History of Lutheranism] in 1680 the erstwhile councillor to Duke Ernst the Pious of Sachsen-Gotha, Veit Ludwig von

---

[9] Gottfried Wilhelm Leibniz, *Schriften und Briefe zur Geschichte*, ed. Malte-Ludolf Babin and Gerd van den Heuvel (Hanover, 2004).

[10] Samuel Pufendorf, *Commentariorum de Rebus Suecicis libri XXVI* (Utrecht, 1686); and *De rebus gestis Friderici Wilhelmi Magni, Electoris Brandenburgici, commentariorum: libri novendecim* (Berlin, 1695).

Seckendorf, stepped in. In his *Commentarius Historicus et apologeticus De Lutheranismo* [Historical and Apologetic Commentary on 'Lutheranism'] (1692) he first translated the French text into Latin, then broke his text down into paragraphs and went on to refute it methodically. This method was as simple as it was effective, retelling the whole story of the Reformation using the 422-volume documentation preserved at Weimar dealing with the years between 1517 and 1546. Thus the only person to write an authentic history of the Reformation was to be the chancellor of the Protestant Prince, the direct heir to the men who wrote those 'true letters'.

Seckendorf's 'Public Lutheranism' is decidedly distinct from Gottfried Arnold's *Unparteyische Kirchen- und Ketzerhistorie* [Impartial History of the Church and all Heresies] (1699–1703). According to Arnold the true dignity of Christianity rests in its beginnings, that is, on the equation of origin with perfect faith. The salient sense of history, then, is one of 'decline' and apostasy. Yet this sentiment could be overcome by the venerable concept of the 'invisible Church'. Sebastian Franck, in his *Zeytbuch* [Book of Times] (1531), had already told its story and given history the positive sense of 'probation of the believer'. Nothing could be more adverse to Seckendorf's 'diplomatic defence' of the true Church.

Situated in a 'prophetic perspective', the two columns of future German *Geschichtsphilosophie* can be identified by the positions of Seckendorf and Arnold: historical realization of the Ideal versus its withdrawal into the self or towards a future utopia. In a way, this antagonism describes the status of historiography in the Empire in the middle of the eighteenth century. Once the 'origins' could clearly be identified, the shape of a perfect history began to emerge. Lorenz von Mosheim thus earned a European reputation by his *Institutiones historiae ecclesiasticae antiquioris et recentioris* [On the Institutions of the Ancient and Recent Church] (1726–55), dealing for the first time with the Church as an entirely worldly institution. As the 'origins of true art' could positively be identified with classical Greece, Johann Joachim Winckelmann felt free to draw up his sensational *Geschichte der Kunst des Altertums* [History of Ancient Art] (1764). This was not the first attempt at an historical treatment of the arts, but the first based on emphatic language styled to invoke the inner experience of a 'contemplating historian'. It bordered on scandal that the German language, by common European decree declared to be rude and incapable of expressing delicate affections, should be thought equal to this task.

Unfortunately, the 'myth of origins' could not be applied to the Holy Roman Empire itself. In Göttingen, academic 'history of the ancient constitution' flourished until the end of Empire but failed miserably to produce a German 'Whig' version of history. Leibniz never moved beyond the period of the Salic emperors. The leading enlightened *Reichshistoriker* such as as Johann Jakob Mascov and Count Heinrich von Bünau stopped at the Merovingian or Carolingian kings. The Empire obviously defied all attempts to turn its past into a hegemonic master narrative. But this inability should be read as the consequence of the slow disintegration of the Empire following the War of the Spanish Succession.

Almost all of the great German Houses had, by this point, succumbed to the temptation to 'opt out of the Reich', that is, to start European careers. The Hohenzollern electors had been the trendsetters in 1657 (Duchy of Prussia); the Habsburgs followed in 1683 (Hungary); the Wettiner in 1697 (Poland-Lithuania); the Welfen in 1714 (United Kingdom); and Hessen-Kassel in 1720 (Sweden). As late as 1778 the Wittelsbachs were eager to exchange Bavaria for Belgium. In contrast, the great European powers rediscovered the Empire as a convenient battlefield and operational ground for political hegemony. The Empire should therefore accurately be called the 'vanishing mediator' of the redistribution of modern state power on a global scale.

This meta-story was of course an enciphered history, out of reach of any German historian of that period. Consequently, the last resort of the historically minded German intellectual was irony. Johann Gottfried Herder, when considering the fate of *Reichsgeschichte* in 1769, resigned himself to the following: 'The history of Germany ought to be such an original as its constitution.' And would this German 'libertinism', in former times called 'liberty', not necessarily entail 'dry accuracy, a stiff proceeding from charter to charter?'[11] Ending on the most advanced note of enlightened historical thought, the young Herder stripped the 'genius of the Germans' of its historical insignia. Ten years later he offered much more than a simple replacement in his revolutionary theory which made of peoples and languages the core of history. Following Herder's advice German historiography cut its ties with the inconclusive paradigm of the Holy Empire.

THE EIGHTEENTH CENTURY: FROM EMPIRE TOWARDS NATION

The situation of historical writing within the German-speaking territories in the second half of the eighteenth century was not altogether different from the state of affairs in Western Europe. Once again the historiography of the ancients became exemplary. The style of the classics, their emotional impact and potential for political criticism, appealed intensely to German authors. Though the 'big battles' of 'Romanism versus Germanism' were fought in France and Great Britain, in the spheres of *parlements* and parliament the meaning of a 'Germanic Past' was equally researched within the boundaries of the Empire.

At the end of the eighteenth century it emerges that no 'big historical question' of the German nation could actually be tied to the development of existing

---

[11] Johann Gottfried Herder, 'Über die Reichsgeschichte: Ein historischer Spaziergang', in Herder, *Kritische Wälder* (Riga, 1769), 166.

political institutions. German historical interest desperately lacked a clear focus. Antiquarianism still had a strong following and proved fruitful among philologists as well as textual critics. For this illustrious circle may stand Christian Gottlob Heyne of Göttingen, who expanded his concept of 'literary myth' into a cultural history of religion. Enlightened theologians like Johann Salomo Semler of Halle, in a kind of parallel action, 'historicized' Christianity, the Early Church, as well as the biblical canon or any concrete realization of religious institutions. Philosophical thinking was inexorably heading towards a total confrontation with history. Kant drew on Hume for his radicalization of the constructivist character of knowledge. Herder turned to the whole flock of French, British, Spanish, and Italian cultural historians and anthropologists in order to reconcile the dynamic diversity of mankind with the unifying forces. So, beyond religion and history there loomed something larger than a 'German state', a 'German political subject', or even 'German culture'.

Hegel was the legitimate heir to these potentially extreme positions which he tried to bring into one comprehensive, though at times violent, synthesis. His mediator of reality, the 'absolute spirit', was totally historic, yet in order to realize its absolute unity the 'historical' ought to be pronounced exclusively by the philosopher. Thus the 'German patriot' was caught in a predicament: he could either turn to the 'empirical world' and become a specialist or resort to the absolute unity of mankind and strive to be a citizen of the world. What was left blank was the 'historical middle ground', the concrete nation, the language of everyday life and their historical presuppositions. As the liberal critic Carl Gustav Jochmann remarked bitterly, Germany lacked a public sphere where free speech would produce free political acts. Until its very end the German Enlightenment produced a situation for historiography as theoretically sophisticated as it was pragmatically oppressive.

The question of who should write German history was still largely unsettled. As the number of professors slowly increased, the quality of the academic teaching of history, systematic as well as pragmatic, had reached levels unknown to the rest of Europe.[12] Yet the academic community produced but few *Geschichtsschreiber*. Against this background Justus Möser was widely acclaimed as the exception that proves the rule. For more than twenty years he acted as unofficial prime minister to Frederick Augustus, Duke of York, who had become Prince-Bishop of Osnabrück at the age of six months in 1764. Möser directed this unusual political entity with great skill, combining his administrative duties with the composition of its history, the *Osnabrückische Geschichte* [History of Osnabrück] (1768, 1780). Möser, possibly not unaffected by English Whiggism, chose an unexpected yet solid subject: the freeholders of Saxon Westphalia. Thus the evolution of liberty and property led to the historical analysis of a whole

---

[12] Hans Erich Bödeker, Georg G. Iggers, Jonathan B. Knudsen, and Peter H. Reill (eds.), *Aufklärung und Geschichte* (Göttingen 1986).

composite estate, grounded on professional use of documents, decidedly focused on social life, and written in an almost elegant German. Möser had more in mind than just his own little principality. He wanted to set an example: every 'socio-historical landscape' in the Empire should be the subject of a comparable history 'from below', and in the end these histories would grow together in a unified patriotic history of the Reich. Möser, as a defender of the 'German liberties', almost inevitably entered into argument with the most illustrious exponent of Enlightenment absolutism, King Frederick II of Prussia.

Besides being his own commander-in-chief, minister, philosopher, and musician, Frederick took over the writing of the history of his own reign. His historiographical works combine most skilfully parts of the classical heritage with Enlightenment morals and Machiavellian traditions. Frederick's first, the *Mémoires pour servir à l'Histoire de la Maison de Brandebourg* [Memoirs on the History of the House of Brandenburg] (1751), reads like a modest compendium for a future Prussian king, informing him discretely of the scarce physical and mental resources of this territory. His second work, the posthumously published *Histoire de mon temps* [History of My Time] (1787), covers the king's actions during the first and second Silesian Wars. Although highly partisan and apologetic, this work could have provided a major incentive for the development of German historical writing. Yet this auspicious opportunity was missed: first, the *Histoire de mon temps* was published too late and, worse, as part of the flawed edition of the *Oeuvres postumes*. Second, it was written in French, thus combining the impression of foreignness with the obsolescence of a past absolutist regime. In a sentimental age Frederick's astute distancing from morals and non-professional political values fell into an emotional void. The most popular history of the Seven Years War, Johann Wilhelm von Archenholz's *Geschichte des Siebenjährigen Krieges* [History of the Seven Years War] (1793), proves this in a strained blend of heroism and patriotism. After all, since 1760 it was a common belief in the Holy Roman Empire that history should either 'warm hearts' and stir them to virtuous deeds or provide purely practical knowledge. So the future agenda was already directed towards the synthesis of sentiment, more precisely 'language', with pragmatics. But unhappily this synthesis was never achieved in the eighteenth century.

'Pragmatic historiography' (*Pragmatische Historie*) was the academic answer to the challenge of 'philosophical history'. Its stronghold was the University of Göttingen and its prophets were Johann Christoph Gatterer and August Ludwig Schlözer. According to the Göttingen School the causal connection (*nexus rerum*), a concept already well known to humanist historiographers, was the key to 'rational history' (*vernünftige Geschichte*). As every event caused appropriate subsequent events and was itself produced by earlier incidents, so every single sequence of facts should be coordinated with all other detectable cause–event sequences in universal history. Arriving at the maximum of interconnectedness, the maximum degree of rationality of history could be grasped. Instead of the humanistic exemplum, the principles of history could be the foundation of practical behaviour for every member of civil society, not just the powerful. The only remaining question was this: how could this total pragmatic history be written and what was its relation to language, above all the German language? Gatterer, Schlözer, and their academic followers failed to put forward this history. They presented little more than dry blueprints to the hungry German public. Pragmatic history before long became a rapidly fading project, incapable of producing concrete 'historical sense' and of turning total interconnectedness into narration.

Thus in order to reach the 'philosophical level' of historiography the long overdue 'language turn' finally took place. To achieve this aim the universal *nexus rerum* had to be sacrificed, or at least surrendered, to the new transcendental philosophers. But the nation and its new 'master narrative' could make up for the predictable loss of coherence, and narration would finally deliver a common understanding of German history. So the German language movement, having now attained historiographical ground, was diverted into two separate if still communicating channels: historiography conceived as the literary expression of the 'science of history' (heuristics, critique of sources, and interpretation) and philosophy of history. Yet, immediately, two foundational problems arose: should scientific historiography still belong to the 'beautiful sciences' (*beaux arts*) and should historiography be permanently subordinated to philosophy?

Confronted with the excessive demands of doing justice to the 'two historical geniuses', to the genius of the people and the genius of the historical author, a profound disillusion soon spread among the German public similar to the impatience of the British public with the state of historical writing before the appearance of Hume, Gibbon, and Robertson. In the realm of German literature only Friedrich Schiller and Johannes von Müller could live up to the 'great expectations' of classical historical writing. First, a worthy plot had to be found and turned into a distinct fable, then scenic dramatization should follow; characters were to be formed according to the principles of liberty and world historical significance whereas aesthetic principles should add to visibility (*Anschaulichkeit*) and moral insight. Schiller's *Geschichte des Abfalls der vereinig- ten Niederlande* [History of the Rebellion of the Netherlands] (1788) and his *Geschichte des Dreissigjährigen Krieges* [History of the Thirty Years War] (1790) were the fruit of his four-year term as Professor of History in Jena. These works earned him considerable praise, but instead of proceeding with the task of the historian Schiller returned to drama writing and reached the apex of his historical insights in his massive three-part *Wallenstein* (1799). As Schiller exclaimed in 1788, alluding to his failed project to write an epic poem on Frederick II of Prussia: 'I feel incapable of undertaking this gigantic task of idealization!'[13]

---

[13] Friedrich Schiller, *Nationalausgabe*, vol. 26: *Briefwechsel. Schillers Briefe. 1.3.1790–17.5.1794* (Weimar, 1992), 114.

Inveterate idealization may account for the success of Johannes Müller's widely acclaimed *Geschichten Schweizerischer Eidgenossenschaft* [Swiss History] (1786–1808). The Swiss Confederation he painted had experienced an impressive development of liberal institutions. Only after a long and painful process had Müller adopted German, instead of French, as the language of his historical representations. Presumably he was the first and only historian in the late Holy Roman Empire to be able to live by his pen. Müller ended his life as a tragic figure. In the wake of his *Geschichten Schweizerischer Eidgenossenschaft* it was expected that his next work would be the long-desired German history, a messianic literary masterpiece designed to include the nation in the universal process of enlightened liberty. Müller frustrated all hopes, so what the nation finally received was the eleven-volume *Geschichte der Deutschen* [History of the German People] (1778–94) by the Catholic imperial lawyer Michael Ignaz Schmidt, Director of the Habsburg Central Archive in Vienna since 1780. This was a respectable work, integrating cultural with institutional history and cautiously appealing to the 'people' as the hidden agent of its history. Schmidt did not live long enough to see the end of the Empire or the completion of his history. The Holy Roman Empire vanished without having produced a history that would have inscribed its form into the Enlightenment discourse of mankind and thus would have secured the continuity of German historical consciousness.

TIMELINE/KEY DATES

1495 Imperial Diet at Worms; Reform movement culminates in the foundation of Imperial Chamber Court and Public Peace (*Landfrieden*)

1517 Martin Luther publishes his 95 Theses at Wittenberg

1519 Charles of Burgundy is elected Emperor

1530 Surrender of the *Confessio Augustana* by the German Protestant Estates

1546–7 Charles V defeats his Protestant opponents in the Schmalkaldic War

1546 Martin Luther dies at Eisleben; half a million German 'Luther Bibles' circulating in the Empire

1555 Peace of Augsburg, provisional political-juridical settlement of the Reformation

1564 First book catalogue of the Frankfurt book fair

1568 Imperial Diet at Speyer; Emperor and Catholic Estates accept the Tridentine decrees

1577 Acceptance of the *Formula Concordiae* by a majority of the Protestant Estates

1576–1612 Emperor Rudolf II; demise of the institutions of the Empire

1605 First newspaper (*Zeitung*) to appear at Strassburg

1617 Founding of the *Fruchtbringende Gesellschaft*, first German language society

1618–48 Thirty Years War

1654 Imperial Diet at Regensburg; reform of the Imperial Court and militarization of the great German Estates

1700 Gottfried Wilhelm Leibniz, first President of the new Academy of Sciences at Berlin

1701 Elector Frederic III of Brandenburg crowns himself 'King in Prussia' at Königsberg, beginning of the Austro-Prussian 'dualism' in the Empire

1733–5 Polish War of Succession wrecks Austrian financial and military strength

1756–63 Seven Years War further weakens the Imperial Constitution

1803 *Reichsdeputationshauptschluß* at Regensburg, secularization of the German Imperial Church and incorporation of smaller estates

1806 French Emperor Napoleon I forces Franz I of Austria to abdicate the Imperial Dignity

KEY HISTORICAL SOURCES

Archenholz, Johann Wilhelm von, *Geschichte des siebenjährigen Krieges in Deutschland von 1756 bis 1763* (Frankfurt, 1793).

Arnold, Gottfried, *Unparteyische Kirchen- und Ketzerhistorie* (Frankfurt, 1699–1703).

Brotuff, Ernst, *Genealogia Vnd Chronica des Durchlauchten Hochgebornen Königlichen vnd Fürstlichen Hauses der Fürsten zu Anhalt Graffen zu Ballenstedt vnd Ascanie Herrn zu Bernburgk vnd Zerbst auff 1055. Jar in sechs Büchern mit viel schönen alten Historien Geschichten Königlichen vnd Fürstlichen Wopen gezieret vnd beschrieben. Mit einer Vorrede Herrn Philippi Melanthon* (Leipzig, 1556).

Chyträus, David, *Dauidis Chytræi chronicon Saxoniæ et vicinarum aliquot Gentium: Ab Anno Christi 1500. usque ad M.D.XCIII: Appendix scriptorum certis Chronici locis inserendorum* (Leipzig, 1593).

Crusius, Martin, *Annales Suevici*, 3 vols. (Frankfurt, 1595–6).

Franck, Sebastian, *Chronica, Zeytbuch und Geschychtbibel* (Strassburg, 1531–6).

Fries, Lorenz, *Chronik der Bischöfe von Würzburg 742–1495*, ed. Ulrich Wagner, 6 vols. (Würzburg, 1992–2004).

Gatterer, Johann Christoph, 'Vom historischen Plan, und der darauf sich gründenden Zusammenfügung der Erzählungen', in *Allgemeine Historische Bibliothek*, vol. 1 (Halle, 1767).

Hegel, G. W. F., *Vorlesungen über die Philosophie der Geschichte* (Frankfurt, 1970).

Hortleder, Friedrich, *Von den Ursachen deß Teutschen Kriegs Kaiser Carls des V* (Frankfurt, 1617–18).

Krantz, Albert, *Chronica regnorum aquilonarium Daniae, Suetiae, Norvagiae* (Strassburg, 1548).

Leibniz, Gottfried Wilhelm, *Scriptores Rerum Brunsvicensium* (Hanover, 1707–11).

Melanchthon, Philipp (ed.), *Chronica durch Magistrum Carion vleissig zusamen gezogen* (Wittenberg, 1532).

Mosheim, Lorenz, *Institutionum historiae ecclesiasticae antiquioris et recentioris libri IV* (Helmstedt, 1726–55).

Pufendorf, Samuel, *Commentariorum de Rebus Suecicis libri XXVI* (Utrecht, 1686).

—— *De rebus gestis Friderici Wilhelmi Magni, Electoris Brandenburgici, commentariorum: libri novendecim* (Berlin, 1695).

Matthias Ringmann, *Mathias, Julius der erst Römisch Keiser von seinen Kriege(n)* (Strassburg, 1508).

Schütz, Kaspar, *Historia Rerum Prussicarum* (Zerbst, 1592).

Seckendorf, Veit Ludwig, *Commentarius Historicus et apologeticus De Lutheranismo* (Frankfurt and Leipzig, 1692).

Sleidan, Johann, *Commentariorum de statu religionis et reipublicae Carolo V. Caesare libri XXVI* (Strassburg, 1555).

Stumpf, Johannes, *Gemeiner loblicher Eydgenossenschafft Stetten, Landen und Voelckeren Chronick wirdiger thaaten beschreybung* (Zurich, 1547–8).

Tschudi, Aegidius, *Chronicon helveticum* (Basel, 1734–6).

Welser, Marcus, *Chronica Der Weitberuempten Keyserlichen Freyen vnd deß H. Reichs Statt Augspurg in Schwaben Von derselben altem Vrsprung Schöne... Gebäwen vnnd... gedenckwürdigen Geschichten: in acht vnderschiedliche Capitul... abgetheilt / Auß deß ... Marx Welsers... acht Büchern... gezogen vnd... in vnser teutschen Spraach in Truck verfertiget* (Frankfurt, 1595–6).

—— Bayrische Geschicht (Augsburg, 1605).

BIBLIOGRAPHY

Aretin, Karl Otmar von, *Das Alte Reich 1648–1808*, 4 vols. (Stuttgart, 1933–2000).

Bödeker, Hans Erich (ed.), *Aufklärung und Geschichte. Studien zur deutschen Geschichtswissenschaft im 18. Jahrhundert* (Göttingen, 1986).

Bollbuck, Harald, *Geschichts- und Raummodelle bei Albert Krantz (um 1448–1517) und David Chyträus (1530–1600)* (Frankfurt, 2006).

Fuchs, Thomas, *Traditionsstiftung und Erinnerungspolitik: Geschichtsschreibung in Hessen in der Frühen Neuzeit* (Kassel, 2002).

Fulda, Daniel, *Wissenschaft als Kunst: Die Entstehung der modernen deutschen Geschichtsschreibung 1760–1860* (Berlin and New York, 1996).

Hirschi, Caspar, *Wettkampf der Nationen: Konstruktionen einer deutschen Ehrgemeinschaft an der Wende vom Mittelalter zur Neuzeit* (Göttingen, 2005).

Huttner, Markus, *Geschichte als akademische Disziplin: Historische Studien und historisches Studium an der Universität Leipzig vom 16. bis zum 19. Jahrhundert* (Leipzig, 2007).

Pohlig, Matthias, *Zwischen Gelehrsamkeit und konfessioneller Identitätsstiftung: Lutherische Kirchen- und Universalgeschichtsschreibung 1546–1617* (Tübingen, 2007).

Rau, Susanne, *Geschichte und Konfession: Städtische Geschichtsschreibung und Konfessionalisierung in Bremen, Breslau, Hamburg und Köln* (Hamburg, 2002).

Repgen, Konrad, 'Über die Geschichtsschreibung des Dreißigjährigen Krieges: Begriff und Konzeption', in Konrad Repgen (ed.), *Krieg und Politik 1618–1648* (Munich, 1988), 1–84.

Schnettger, Matthias (ed.), *Imperium Romanum—Irregulare Corpus—Teutscher Reichs-Staat: Das Alte Reich im Verständnis der Zeitgenossen und der Historiographie* (Mainz, 2002).

Völkel, Markus and Strohmeyer, Arno (eds.), *Historiographie an europäischen Höfen (16.–18. Jahrhundert)* (Berlin, 2009).

Chapter 17

Italian Renaissance Historical Narrative

William J. Connell

During the early Renaissance in Italy there took shape a distinctive narrative genre for the writing of history that is the ancestor of much of today's historical writing. Renaissance historians emphasized human rather than divine agency. They experimented with historical periodization, developing what would become the standard framework of 'ancient, medieval, and modern' still used in most retellings of European history. They also claimed to base their histories on the comparative, critical examination of sources, which included not only written narratives and the accounts of eyewitnesses but also archival documents, physical remains, and inscriptions. The most engaged and intelligent of the Renaissance narratives give evidence of a critical approach that continues to be the sine qua non of modern historical writing. Renaissance histories typically were not anonymous works, nor were they written collaboratively. During the Renaissance, history-writing came to be understood as an activity that offered a plausible path for persons seeking individual fame and fortune. A series of governments—both princely and republican—appointed official historiographers, who were situated in courts, chanceries, or (more rarely) universities. And the diffusion of printing by the late fifteenth century led to new readers and new streams of revenue.

The formal literary aspects of Renaissance histories are less recognizable in modern histories, although they probably survive in more ways than is generally realized. The self-deprecating dedicatory letters that writers addressed to patrons have made a comeback in the form of lengthy 'Acknowledgements'. The division of the narrative into numbered books and chapters remains important to modern authors, although today's segmentation is usually believed to depend on the material, whereas Renaissance writers were often more concerned with slicing the unruly matter of history into manageable, well-proportioned sections. Along with an account of events and their causes, Renaissance readers expected to find in their histories rhetorical ornaments that included introductory moral essays, character sketches, digressions on topography, battle-pieces that provided excitement if not much practical instruction, excursuses on foreign peoples, and the juxtaposition of similar or contrary elements. There was a greater expectation that history might really improve the people who read it: so aphorisms intended to supply moral and political wisdom were sprinkled throughout the text, and speeches attributed to historical actors but composed by the historians were actually collected and published separately for use by future statesmen. Against a background production of thousands of lesser histories and chronicles, the Italian Renaissance gave birth to a series of impressive and still readable narrative histories that were written by an honour roll of Italian authors who continue to be remarkable guides to the early modern period in both Italy and the wider world.

Modern historians have yet to come up with an explanation that is entirely satisfactory for the new way of writing about the past that developed during the early Italian Renaissance. Medieval Italy had the richest tradition of chronicle-writing of any part of Europe.[1] Competing imperial and papal claims to universality meant that individual city-states had a material interest in constructing durable records in the form of city chronicles that recounted past alliances, privileges, constitutions, and religious traditions and controversies. Some of the most impressive medieval chronicles and historical works, such as those by Salimbene of Parma, were written by Franciscan friars. Franciscan piety seems to have afforded authors a perspective *supra partes* and independent of the commune from which they were able to pass judgement in the first person on contemporary events, although their chronicles could not pretend to be critical history.[2] It has also been argued that the Black Death, which struck Italy especially hard in 1348 and returned every decade or so thereafter until the end of the seventeenth century, prompted an intense, community-wide interest in commemoration and preserving the past. This seems to have been the case especially after the plague's first recurrence in 1361–3, when it became clear that the disease was not a one-off catastrophe, but rather something whose possible recurrence would have to be taken into account when planning for the future. There was thus a new understanding of the fragility of all things human and a new care for preserving their memory, whether through the construction of funeral chapels or the keeping of written records.[3]

The existence of a highly literate, urban mercantile culture, with a developed vernacular literary tradition, was certainly a factor in the creation of an appreciation for history. According to the chronicler Giovanni Villani the literacy rate in fourteenth-century Florence was nearly 70 per cent—a figure confirmed by a recent study of fifteenth-century records.[4] In Florence more than elsewhere there developed in the fourteenth century a tradition of family chronicle-writing in the

---

[1] Sharon Dale, Alison Williams Lewin, and Duane J. Osheim (eds.), *Chronicling History: Chroniclers and Historians in Medieval and Renaissance Italy* (University Park, Pa., 2007).

[2] Bernard Guenée, *Histoire et culture historique dans l'Occident médiéval* (Paris, 1980), 58; and Robert Brentano, 'The Chronicle of Francesco Venimbeni da Fabriano', *Memoirs of the American Academy in Rome*, 48 (2003), 159–70.

[3] Samuel K. Cohn, Jr., *The Cult of Remembrance and the Black Death: Six Renaissance Cities in Central Italy* (Baltimore, 1992); and Renée Neu Watkins, 'Petrarch and the Black Death: From Fear to Monuments', *Studies in the Renaissance*, 19 (1972), 196–223.

[4] Robert Black, *Education and Society in Florentine Tuscany: Teachers, Pupils and Schools, c. 1250–1500*, vol. 1 (Leiden, 2007).

vernacular. Originally an offshoot of mercantile accounting practice, books of *ricordi* or *ricordanze* or *memorie* were kept for the recording of matters important to the writer or his family.[5] These included births, deaths, marriages, offices held, property leases, court judgments, private vendettas, recipes for food dishes and medications, items loaned or borrowed, and insults and injuries suffered. Sometimes they included full-blown accounts of historical events.[6] Vernacular chronicles and record books would exert a strong influence on Renaissance historiography from the mid-fifteenth century onward, but the more immediate impulses that led to a Renaissance revolution in historical writing came from the world of Latin letters. In northern Italy literary practices independent of university study and of the communal chancery tradition resulted in early efforts to imitate the style of Latin antiquity, first in poetry, and, by the second decade of the fourteenth century, in the historical prose-writing of Albertino Mussato of Padua, whose two most important works covered the *Kronungsfahrt* of Henry VII of Luxembourg in 1310–14 and the period after Henry's death to 1321.[7] Although they showed a new concern for eloquence, these were still examples of the kind of Sallustian narrative that was common in the Middle Ages.[8]

Writing a generation later, in the mid-fourteenth century, Francesco Petrarca, known to the English-speaking world as 'Petrarch', exhibited an historical sensibility that was quite different. Style was important to Petrarch, as it was for Mussato, but his ideas about historical time represented something altogether new. Most importantly, in works like his historical epic *Africa* and his biographical treatise *De viris illustribus* [On Illustrious Men], Petrarch broke with a pattern set by the late antique historian Orosius, whose *Historiae contra paganos* [Histories Against the Pagans] were the most popular historical text in the Middle Ages. Orosius had maintained, in the face of much evidence to the contrary—including the Sack of Rome in AD 410—that ever since the coming of Jesus the world of men had been improving. Where Orosius denounced the slaughter of the Punic Wars as an example of the cruelty of pagan times, Petrarch thought this the most heroic period of Roman history.[9] And where Orosius

---

[5] Philip Jones, 'Florentine Families and Florentine Diaries in the Fourteenth Century', *Papers of the British School at Rome*, 24 (1956), 183–205; Angelo Cicchetti and Raul Mordenti, 'La scrittura dei libri di famiglia', in Alberto Asor Rosa (ed.), *Letteratura italiana*, vol. 3:2 (Turin, 1984), 1117–59; and William J. Connell, '*Libri di famiglia* and the Family History of Florentine Patricians', *Italian Culture*, 8 (1990), 279–92.

[6] Giovanni Ciappelli, 'La memoria degli eventi storici nelle "ricordanze" fiorentine del Tre-Quattrocento', in C. Bastia, M. Bolognani, and F. Pezzarossa (eds.), *La memoria e la città: Scritture storiche tra Medioevo ed età moderna* (Bologna, 1995), 123–50.

[7] Albertino Mussato, *De obsidione domini Canis Grandis de Verona ante civitatem Paduanum*, ed. Givanno M. Gianola (Padua, 1999); and Ronald G. Witt, *In the Footsteps of the Ancients: The Origins of Humanism from Lovato to Bruni* (Leiden, 2001), 139–56.

[8] Beryl Smalley, 'Sallust in the Middle Ages', in R. R. Bolgar (ed.), *Classical Influences on European Culture, A.D. 500 to 1500* (Cambridge, 1971), 165–75.

[9] Giuliana Crevatin, 'Roma aeterna', in Roberto Cardini and Donatella Coppini (eds.), *Petrarca e Agostino* (Rome, 2004), 131–51, at 148.

thought Adam, 'the first sinner', was the source of 'the miseries of mankind', Petrarch praised him as the progenitor of so many examples of human virtue.[10] Far from accepting the idea that Christianity had improved the condition of humans in this world, Petrarch expressed repeatedly the idea that an age of continuing decline had set in, either after the conversion of Constantine, or after the reign of Titus, when emperors of non-Roman extraction acceded to the throne. Petrarch thus divided history into two periods, antiquity, which was the time before the decline of the empire, and his own time, a time of 'shadows', which had come after.[11] Petrarch's own writings and studies, he declared, would concern only antiquity: 'For what is all of history but the praise of Rome?'[12] Thus was born in Western Europe the idea that the fall of Rome marked a turning point more definitive, at least for the *civitas terrena*, than did the Year One.

Petrarch was also a formidable textual critic. He did important work on the text of Livy, and he was able to use surviving texts from the time of Julius Caesar to expose for Emperor Charles IV two forged charters purportedly issued by Caesar and Nero.[13] His younger friend and correspondent, Coluccio Salutati brought this set of interests and skills to Florence, where he became chancellor. Although Salutati, like Petrarch, wrote no narrative history, he studied historical evidence with a critical eye, determining the priority of the available texts and judging their accuracy accordingly.[14] Salutati helped bring Greek studies to Florence, and it was the reading of the Greek historians, especially Thucydides and Polybius, that seems to have had a decisive influence on Salutati's friend, Leonardo Bruni, who would write the narrative that became the model for subsequent Renaissance historiography.[15]

Leonardo Bruni's *Historiae Florentini populi* [History of the Florentine People], begun in 1415 and completed by 1442, had a powerful impact on contemporaries. Like Livy's history of Rome, Bruni's history of Florence begins with the city's founding and continues down to his own times. (Bruni's *Historiae* ended in 1402 with the death of Florence's Milanese arch-enemy, Giangaleazzo Visconti.) Both histories tell the story of republics riven by internal conflict which became

---

[10] Riccardo Fubini, *Storiografia dell'Umanesimo in Italia da Leonardo Bruni ad Annio da Viterbo* (Rome, 2003), 98–9.

[11] Theodor E. Mommsen, 'Petrarch's Conception of the Dark Ages', in his *Medieval and Renaissance Studies*, ed. Eugene F. Rice, Jr. (Ithaca, 1959), 106–29.

[12] Petrarch, *Invectives*, ed. and trans. David Marsh (Cambridge, Mass., 2003), 60.

[13] Giuseppe Billanovich, 'Petrarch and the Textual Tradition of Livy', *Journal of the Warburg and Courtauld Institutes*, 14 (1951), 137–208; and E. B. Fryde, *Humanism and Renaissance Historiography* (London, 1983), 13.

[14] Ronald G. Witt, *Hercules at the Crossroads: The Life, Works and Thought of Coluccio Salutati* (Durham, NC, 1983); and Daniela De Rosa, *Coluccio Salutati: il cancelliere e il pensatore politico* (Florence, 1980).

[15] Udo Klee, *Beiträge zur Thukydides-Rezeption während des 15. Und 16. Jahrhunderts in Italien und Deutschland* (Frankfurt, 1990), 23–58.

great by conquering their neighbours. They include bold prefaces, battle-pieces, and speeches by historical figures. Bruni's Latin style is Livy's.

But there the similarities end. While other humanists, including Bruni's contemporary, Lorenzo Valla, continued to work over the text of Livy's history,[16] Bruni undertook the more fundamental task of correcting Livy's method. Livy preserves myths and legends that he confesses not to believe, but Bruni announces straightaway that concerning the founding of Florence he will reject 'some commonly held but mythical beliefs' which he does not even bother to repeat.[17] Livy's speeches tended to be mere oratorical exercises, but Bruni's, sometimes based on real documents, explained the causes of things. Bruni also investigated Livy's sources. Rather than follow one writer for a certain set of events, and another for the next, as Livy had done, Bruni set the available sources for individual events side by side and he determined on the basis of the evidence what he thought must really have happened. When his history approached more recent times and there were no more chronicles to use, he consulted chancery records and the private papers of Florentines. History for Bruni was all about human causation. 'History . . . requires at once a long and connected narrative, causal explanation of each particular event, and the public expression of one's judgment about every issue.'[18]

Bruni's periodization of history was configured more precisely than Petrarch's had been. He attacked the traditional idea of a divine convergence under the rule of Augustus, when Jesus was born and supposedly Florence was founded. Wasting no time, the *Historiae* open with the statement that Florence was founded several decades earlier by Roman veterans who had served with Lucius Sulla. The implication, understood by contemporaries, was that the evidence showed that Florence was founded under the Roman Republic, rather than the Principate, and that this was appropriate for the Florentine Republic, which (along with a number of other Italian cities) liked to consider itself the heir of Rome. Then, for Bruni, Roman decline did not set in slowly, as Petrarch had put forward, beginning with Titus or Constantine. Instead it was caused directly by the Germanic invasions, culminating with the overthrow of Romulus Augustulus in AD 476.[19] And where Petrarch had only distinguished antiquity from his own time, an age of 'shadows', Bruni introduced a second major caesura, at the year 1250, to distinguish his own more fortunate time from the period of Germanic domination. By 1250 the Holy Roman Empire had lost its hold over Italy, allowing the Italian city-states ample room to act independently, and in Florence the Guelf government of the Primo Popolo triumphed over the Ghibellines. For

---

[16] Fryde, *Humanism and Renaissance Historiography*, 18.

[17] Leonardo Bruni, *History of the Florentine People*, ed. and trans. James Hankins, 3 vols. (Cambridge, Mass., 2001–7), i. 7.

[18] Ibid., 5.

[19] Bruni, *History of the Florentine People*, 89.

Bruni that year inaugurated a new period of freedom after a period of decline and external domination. Thanks to this tripartite division of history, 'Bruni may be said to be the inventor of the earliest political conception of the Modern', as one historian recently put it.[20]

The first use of the actual phrase 'middle age', to describe the intermediate period between antiquity and a later period comprising fifteenth-century Italy, belonged to the historian Flavio Biondo of Forlì. Biondo is often described as the founder of modern antiquarian studies on account of his *De Roma instaurata* [Rome Restored] (1444–6), a detailed reconstruction of Roman topography, and his *Roma triumphans* [Rome Triumphant] (1459), a study of the sacred and civil institutions of ancient Rome. He also composed a geographic description, or chorography, of the Italian peninsula, his *Italia illustrata* [Italy Illuminated] (1458; published 1474), which proceeded, region by region and town by town, to explain the etymologies of names and give brief histories of each place. But the work that earned him lasting fame as Europe's first 'medievalist' was his *Historiarum ab inclinatione Romanorum imperii decades* [Decades of History from the Decline of the Roman Empire], written between 1439 and 1453. Biondo began his history with the sack of Rome by the Visigoths in AD 410. The fall of Rome he considered the greatest catastrophe that had ever befallen mankind. With the passing of Rome, the age of universal empire was over and a 'middle age' had begun. Italy, albeit not unified as a state, was one of the 'nations' that succeeded the Roman Empire, and Biondo, who had ties to several Italian milieux but was rooted in no particular city, was more cosmopolitan than most of his fellow humanists. With literary skill and critical acumen Biondo charted the histories of rulers up and down the peninsula, but he paid attention to Italian culture as well. Biondo's history thus comprised arts and letters as well as politics, and he determined that the revival of good letters, which he dated to 1410—one thousand years after the sack of Rome—marked the beginning of a new cultural age that corresponds rather closely to our modern understanding of the Renaissance.[21]

Biondo's conception of an Italy that, despite its division into multiple states, shared a common cultural inheritance and geographical identity was an idea that would resurface periodically down to the nineteenth century. But it hardly corresponded with the realities of the first half of the fifteenth century. The century after the Black Death was marked by the subjugation of hundreds of independent communes by a few larger, expansionist city-states. In Tuscany, Florence tripled its size through the acquisition of Arezzo (Bruni's hometown) and Pisa, along with a series of smaller centres. Milan under the Visconti took over much of the Po Valley and Genoa, while threatening to expand southward into Tuscany and the Papal States. In the first half of the fifteenth century Venice

---

[20] James Hankins, 'Introduction', ibid., p. xviii.
[21] Denys Hay, 'Flavio Biondo and the Middle Ages', *Proceedings of the British Academy*, 45 (1959), 97–128.

changed its traditional policy, which had been directed towards its maritime empire in the eastern Mediterranean, and carved out an extensive dominion on the terra firma. Meanwhile, in 1442, the year of the completion of Bruni's *Historiae*, Alfonso V of Aragon conquered the Kingdom of Naples, which he united with Sicily under the crown of Aragon.[22] The establishment of these territorial states, which were substantially different from the communes of the Middle Ages, had significant repercussions on historical writing. Bruni and his followers, as history-writers in Florence and in the other Italian states, had adopted a new critical approach to their sources, and their narrative style was more coherent and eloquent than that of the medieval chronicle, yet their histories were hardly ideologically neutral.[23]

Bruni's *Historiae* are frequently read today as an attempt to legitimize Florence's hegemony over Tuscany's other, newly subject communes. That it was read this way by his contemporaries is evident from a history written by one of Bruni's Florentine humanist friends, Giannozzo Manetti, which was in many ways a response to Bruni's work. Manetti composed a history of the subject town of Pistoia, which he began while he was governor there in 1446–7 and completed several months later.[24] The *Historia Pistoriensis* [Pistoiese History] harkens back to the age of communal autonomy. Manetti assigns value to the traditional sources for Florentine history, including Dante's *Commedia* and Villani's *Chronicle*, which Bruni had dismissed. Manetti corrects Bruni on numerous details although he also paraphrases him repeatedly. In the interest of accuracy Manetti consults archival documents and inscriptions, but portents, too, loom large, and he wears his providentialism on his sleeve. The Pistoiese, Manetti writes, having yielded their liberty to the Florentines, no longer produce great scholars or poets or statesmen. Manetti encouraged the Pistoiese to defend their rights and privileges—he even found a lawyer to represent them in the capital city. But Manetti was swimming against the same statist current that had already swept up his friends in Pistoia. Enemies in Florence raised his tax assessment to an unbearable level and he moved to Naples.[25]

Naples under Alfonso V became a major centre for history-writing, largely because Alfonso himself enjoyed history.[26] Lorenzo Valla was the most famous of

---

[22] See Giorgio Chittolini (ed.), *La crisi degli ordinamenti comunale e le origini dello stato del Rinascimento* (Bologna, 1979).

[23] Fubini, *Storiografia dell'Umanesimo*, 3–38.

[24] Giannozzo Manetti, *Historia Pistoriensis*, in *Rerum Italicarum Scriptores*, vol. 19 (Milan, 1731); with a critical edition edited by Barbara Aldi and Stefano Ugo Baldassarri, with historical commentery by William J. Connell forthcoming; and Connell, 'The Humanist Citizen as Provincial Governor', in Connell and Andrea Zorzi (eds.), *Florentine Tuscany: Structures and Practices of Power* (Cambridge, 2000), 144–64.

[25] Raffaella Maria Zaccaria, 'Documenti su Giannozzo Manetti', in Stefano Ugo Baldassarri (ed.), *Dignitas et Excellentia Hominis: Atti del convegno internazionale di studi su Giannozzo* (Florence, 2008), 333–45.

[26] Eric Cochrane, *Historians and Historiography in the Italian Renaissance* (Chicago, 1981), 147–50. See also Jerry H. Bentley, *Politics and Culture in Renaissance Naples* (Princeton, 1987).

the humanists at Alfonso's court, but his attempt to write a history of the conquest of the kingdom had to be cut short, becoming the biography of Alfonso's father, the *Gesta Ferdinandi regis aragonum* [The History of Ferdinand, King of the Aragonese], composed in 1445–6. It was Valla's only work of narrative history. While it lived up to his rigorous standard for historical truth, which was accompanied by a penchant for telling truth to power—'[s]ince', as one modern historian writes, 'Ferdinando did in fact snooze during the speeches of ambassadors and since he did in fact use extraordinary means to provoke erections'[27]—its significance was diminished by its subject. Valla's substantial contribution to historical practice lay instead in the criticism of ancient and (forged) medieval texts (such as the Donation of Constantine), in the study of the historical evolution of language, and in his influential translations into Latin of Thucydides and Herodotus, which would remain standard for several centuries.[28]

At Naples Valla had a famous argument with another court humanist, Bartolomeo Facio, about the role of the historian vis-à-vis his subject matter. For Valla what mattered was accuracy, regardless of what would please the dedicatee. Facio instead argued that the historian's role is to create 'monuments'—to commemorate great deeds and persons, but to shroud matters deemed inappropriate with circumlocutions or polite silence. Ironically, Facio proved a better historian than this in his valuable and much-read *Rerum gestarum Alfonsi regis libri* [History of King Alfonso] (1563), in ten books, an account of contemporary affairs that continued to be printed and praised in the sixteenth century.

The papacy did not assert itself territorially until the 1490s and the first decades of the 1500s, when under Popes Alexander VI, Julius II, and Leo X (who conquered Urbino) it did so with a vengeance. But the mid-fifteenth-century return of the papacy to Rome after the Councils of Constance and Basel meant that the popes had every reason to establish their credentials locally and internationally by capitalizing on the Roman past. The papal Curia attracted humanists from all over Italy, and two of them, Nicholas V and Pius II, became pope. Nicholas established the Vatican Library and commissioned an important series of translations of the Greek historians (including Valla's), while Pius II (the former Aeneas Sylvius Piccolomini) was himself an impressive historian. His many works include a history of Bohemia, a work *On Europe* (1453) that is often considered the first work of 'European history', a treatise on Germany, a biographical collection *De viris illustribus* [On Illustrious Men] (1450), and an abridgement of Biondo's *Decades* (1463).[29] He is most famous, however, for his *Commentarii* (1458–64; published 1584), an autobiographical account written in the third person which, after rapidly recounting his early career, gives fascinating

---

[27] Cochrane, *Historians and Historiography in the Italian Renaissance*, 149.
[28] See ch. 11 by Donald R. Kelley in this volume.
[29] Barbara Baldi, 'Enea Silvio Piccolomini e il *De Europa*: umanesimo, religione e politica', *Archivio storico italiano*, 161 (2004), 619–83.

detail about his papal election and his years as pontiff.[30] In the 1470s, Bartolomeo Platina, then prefect of the Vatican Library, reworked and supplemented with many other sources the *Liber pontificalis*, writing his engaging and often scandal-filled *Vitae pontificum* [Lives of the Popes].

Among the historians of the major Italian territorial states, those from Milan have probably fared the poorest in the eyes of modern historians, a judgement surely overdue for revision. One scholar has read them as debasing the superior tools of humanist historiography, departing from the epistemological clarity of Bruni and Biondo for self-interested motives.[31] Another describes the Milanese school as oblivious to change as a positive factor, obsessed with the idea of a golden age destined to return during the lifetime of whatever duke happened to be ruling at the moment.[32] Bernardino Corio, the author of a massive vernacular history of Milan that extended from the city's founding down to the sixteenth century, has been criticized for his pleasant characterization of Ludovico Sforza il Moro, and for his descriptions of the festivals and banquets held at Milan in the years before the French invasion of 1494. Yet Corio was one of the first historians to realize the enormity of the changes that ensued from the French invasion of 1494,[33] and recent research has shown he was a more substantial character than the court flunky portrayed by hostile modern critics.[34]

At Venice there was a rich, cumulative tradition of chronicle-writing which stood in the way of the development of humanist historiography before the middle of the fifteenth century. Moreover Venice, as a republic, was also controlled by a series of powerful committees. So when Biondo proposed to Doge Francesco Foscari that he be hired as official historian in 1454, there surfaced a series of other proposals from leading citizens, including one involving Lorenzo Valla. The upshot was a long delay in the writing of a humanist history for Venice when compared with other major Italian cities.[35] Bernardo Giustiniani took up the task in 1478, claiming Thucydides as his model. His *De origine urbis Venetiarum rebusque ab ipsa gestis historia* [History of the Origin and Accomplishments of the City of Venice], did not quite live up to its announced model, but it dismissed a goodly series of legends concerning

---

[30] Pius II, *Commentaries*, ed. Margaret Meserve and Marcello Simonetta, vols. 1 and 2 (Cambridge, Mass., 2004–7), with further volumes on the way.

[31] Gary Ianziti, *Humanistic Historiography under the Sforzas: Politics and Propaganda in Fifteenth-Century Milan* (Oxford, 1988).

[32] Cochrane, *Historians and Historiography in the Italian Renaissance*, 116.

[33] Felix Gilbert, *Machiavelli and Guicciardini: Politics and History in Sixteenth Century Florence*, 2nd edn (New York, 1984), 259.

[34] Stefano Meschini, *Uno storico umanista alla corte sforzesca: Biografia di Bernardino Corio* (Milan, 1995) offers raw biographical details, but Meschini's article 'Bernardino Corio: storico del medioevo e del Rinascimento milanese', in Paolo Chiesa (ed.), *Le cronache medievali di Milano* (Milan, 2001), 101–73, does the significant work of re-evaluating Corio.

[35] Felix Gilbert, 'Biondo, Sabellico and the Beginnings of Venetian Official Historiography', in John Gordon Rowe and W. H. Stockdale (eds.), *Florilegium Historiale: Essays Presented to Wallace K. Ferguson* (Toronto, 1971), 275–93.

the city's founding. It also justified Venetian rule over her maritime empire and her *Terrafirma* state by arguing that the exceptional domestic concord of Venice's citizens imposed on them the duty to rule other people who were not so blessed.[36]

Giustiniani's *De origine urbis Venetiarum rebusque ab ipsa gestis historia* was only published posthumously, in 1492, and in the meantime another humanist, the non-Venetian Marcantonio Coccio, known as Sabellico (because he came from the Sabine hills), managed to compose, present to the government, and even obtain the first known copyright or printing privilege for, his *Rerum venetarum ab urbe condita libri XXXIII* [Thirty-Three Books of Venetian Affairs from the City's Founding], which was published in 1487.[37] Sabellico's work with the sources was not at all critical, but the book did the job of covering the city's history down to his own times, and it was written in an elegant style that won many Venetian admirers, who arranged a professorship for him in the Scuola di San Marco, so that he became something like an official historian. By 1488 he was already at work on his second major historical work, grandly titled *Enneades sive Rhapsodia historiarum* [A Rhapsody of Histories in Enneads from the Creation of the World] (part 1 published in 1498; part 2 in 1504). The *Enneades* aimed to comprise within a single historical account both biblical and pagan classical sources when treating the early periods of human history, and to continue the story down to the present. It was written in Livian style (but in 'enneads' of nine books, rather than decades of ten), and it helped much that material covering the same period had been conveniently gathered and published in 1485 in a commercially successful volume of humbler prose, the *Supplementum chronicarum* [Supplement to the Chronicles] of an Augustinian friar from Bergamo, Jacopo Filippo Foresti. That Sabellico expected to outdo Foresti by 'redoing' him is suggested by an ingratiating letter sent by the former to the latter in 1493, in which Sabellico informed Foresti that he had already reached the sixteenth book of his *Enneades* (Foresti's work comprised fifteen), and he asked to be named among the literary greats of their times in some subsequent edition of Foresti's work—a favour granted in Foresti's 1502 edition, where Sabellico duly appeared among the worthies of the decade of the 1490s.[38] Sabellico's work, like Foresti's, too, would become a success in the sixteenth century in both Catholic and Protestant mi-

[36] Cochrane, *Historians and Historiography in the Italian Renaissance*, 81. On Giustiniani, see Patricia H. Labalme, *Bernardo Giustinian, a Venetian of the Quattrocento* (Rome, 1969). On the modern historiography of the myth of Venice in relation to the territorial state, see James S. Grubb 'When Myths Lose Power: Four Decades of Venetian Historiography', *Journal of Modern History*, 58 (1986), 43–94.

[37] Ruth Chavasse, 'The First Known Author's Copyright, September 1486, in the Context of a Humanist Career', *Bulletin of the John Rylands University Library of Manchester*, 69 (1986–7), 11–37.

[38] Marcantonio Sabellico, *Opera* (Venice, 1502), fol. 9v ('M. Antonio Foresio Suo'), with commentary in Giovanni Mercati, *Ultimi contributi alla storia degli umanisti*, 2 vols. (Vatican City, 1939), ii. 11–13.

lieux.[39] In an age of religious controversy people no doubt found it comforting to possess a continuous history, supported by texts, both Christian and classical, that reached all the way back to the Creation.

After Sabellico's death (of disfiguring syphilis) in 1506, Venice had no official or quasi-official historian until 1516, when Andrea Navagero was appointed to the position, but Navagero's work did not survive, since, when he died in 1529, the draft of his history was burned at his own request. Cardinal Pietro Bembo succeeded Navagero in 1529. His *Historiae Venetae libri XII* [History of Venice] (1551) begins where Sabellico's left off, in 1487, and continued to 1513, with the accession of Leo X to the papacy. Although he treats events that were catastrophic for Italy or for Venice—the French invasion of 1494, the defeat at Agnadello, and the subsequent terra firma revolt in 1509—Bembo's work does not really do them justice. The *Historiae Venetae*'s best-remembered passage, true to the author, albeit an escape from the military and diplomatic affairs he recounts, is the description at the end of Book 1 of a new diversion in Venice: a boat race in which all the rowers were women.[40] 'Venice was evidently still unable to support a mature historiography,' wrote one modern historian commenting on Bembo's inadequacies.[41]

The style of history-writing that had crystallized elsewhere in Italy in the years around 1500, but which was lacking in Venice, had been prompted by the French invasions of 1494 and 1499 and the Spanish invasion of 1502.[42] In the famous words of Machiavelli's *Prince*, Italy found herself 'without a head, without order, beaten, despoiled, torn, pillaged, and having suffered ruin of every sort'.[43] In some respects it marked a return to writing history in the manner of Leonardo Bruni. As with Bruni, it was a historiography that cared about political and military action. And divine agency mattered little if at all. But Bruni had succeeded in finding other causes, mostly human, where the historians of the post-1500 generation often could find none. In place of a benevolent God, fortune (*fortuna*) or chance (*occasio*) took on a new, powerful role, seeming to govern those things (and there were many of them) over which mankind exercised no control. Bruni's 'Florentine People' had been destined for great

---

[39] Cecil Clough, 'The Significance of the Illustrations in Thomas Mürner's 1530s Translation into German of Sabellico's *Enneades*', *Mediaevalia* (2001), 185–226; and Gaetano Cozzi, 'Intorno all'edizione dell'opera di M. A. Sabellico curata da Celio Secondo Curione e dedicata a Sigismondo Augusto re di Polonia', in L. Cini (ed.), *Venezia e la Polonia nei secoli* (Venice, 1965), 165–77.

[40] Pietro Bembo, *History of Venice*, ed. and trans. Robert W. Ulery, Jr., 3 vols. (Cambridge, Mass., 2007–9), i. 77. Compare, interestingly, the race in Thucydides, *History of the Peloponnesian War*, 6.32.

[41] William J. Bouwsma, *Venice and the Defense of Republican Liberty: Renaissance Values in the Age of the Counter Reformation* (Berkeley, 1968), 138.

[42] David Abulafia (ed.), *The French Descent into Renaissance Italy: 1494–95: Antecedents and Effects* (Aldershot, 1995), gives the background. Gilbert, *Machiavelli and Guicciardini*, remains invaluable.

[43] Niccolò Machiavelli, *The Prince*, trans. William J. Connell (Boston, 2005), ch. 26, p. 120.

things. There were no winners in the new histories—just battle after battle, the sackings of cities, and a great many violent changes of regime. The historians did a sometimes superb job in imposing narrative order on the events they described, but the direction in which those events were moving remained fundamentally uncertain.

The most influential historians of 'Generation 1500' came from Florence, where there had been less historical writing than might have been expected in the wake of Bruni's innovations. To be sure, in the decades after Bruni's death there had been histories written by two Florentine chancellors: Poggio Bracciolini, whose *Historiae Florentini populi* [History of the Florentine People] covered foreign affairs during the century from 1355 to 1455, and Bartolomeo Scala, whose incomplete *Historia Florentinorum* [History of the Florentines] began with the city's founding and reached only to 1264; but the first was a restrained recounting of military actions, while the second readmitted many of the Florentine legends Bruni had excluded. The increasing power of the Medici family, whose rise to quasi-princely status began slowly in 1434, imposed reticence on Florence's otherwise prolific writers when it came to treating past history and more recent events. Lorenzo de' Medici requested that the city's 'annals' be written, but the project went nowhere.[44] What was produced for public consumption was instead a series of works of Sallustian brevity that glorified the family that held the state in its grasp while the more interesting writing was done in private.[45]

But after the French invasion and the exile of the Medici in 1494 there took place a snowballing in Florentine history-writing. Only a few of the Florentine works were in Latin, like the perceptive *De bello italico commentarius* [Commentary on the Italian War], which Bernardo Rucellai wrote in 1506–9 while in self-imposed exile in France. The Florentine practice of keeping private *ricordi*, the widespread use of the *volgare* in diplomacy, and a switch in Florence towards the recording of laws in the *volgare* that occurred in 1494 were factors that contributed to the shift to the vernacular. One of the two greatest historians of Generation 1500, Niccolò Machiavelli, served from 1498 to 1512 as the chancery official in charge of Florence's *volgare* correspondence, and when in 1520 he was appointed Florence's official historiographer no one would have expected that he would write in Latin. Machiavelli's *Istorie fiorentine* [Florentine Histories] were presented to Clement VII in 1525, but they were only published in 1531, four years after the author's death. Originally commissioned to write about the period from 1434 down to the papacy of Leo X, Machiavelli began much earlier, taking Biondo and Bruni as his models, so that he began with the barbarian invasions and stressed, like Bruni, the importance of 1250 for the decline of the

---

[44] Fubini, *Storiografia dell'Umanesimo*, 197.
[45] On the reticence, see Mark Phillips, *The 'Memoir' of Marco Parenti: A Life in Medici Florence* (1987; Toronto, 2000).

German emperors in Italy. The eight books of the *Istorie* are divided evenly about the year 1434, and while Machiavelli is revealing about internal politics in the period before that date, he followed precedent by writing with restraint about the Medici in the period from 1434 to 1492, when the work ends. Machiavelli continued to receive payments as historiographer after the presentation to Pope Clement, and the work remained unpublished, yet the *Istorie* as they now stand are a work so carefully organized it would not be correct to say it was incomplete.[46]

Other Florentine historians belonging to Generation 1500 included Piero Parenti, Francesco Vettori, Jacopo Nardi, and Filippo de' Nerli. Along with Machiavelli and Francesco Guicciardini they established a tradition of republican historiography that would extend into Florence's grand ducal period, in the works of Benedetto Varchi and Bernardo Segni, and that would also influence the historical writing in Venice of authors like Paolo Paruta, who could read the Florentines as offering examples, whether reassuring or alarming, of what republics ought not to do.[47] Non-Florentines in this generation included Girolamo Borgia, whose still unpublished *Historiae de bellis italicis* [Histories of the Italic Wars] were a useful source for Guicciardini,[48] and Paolo Giovio, who responded audaciously to the new realities not by burrowing into their causes (like his contemporary Guicciardini) but by broadening his field of description. Personality, anecdote, fashion, and humour were used to enliven his political history; and, since the direction of history was not at all clear, Giovio took into account even distant nations and peoples like the Russians, the Poles, the Turks, and the Iranians.[49] Yet another of the historians of 1500, albeit transplanted to England, was Polydore Vergil. A client of Alexander VI's assistant, Adriano Castellesi, and therefore no stranger to the realities of Italian politics, Vergil arrived in England in 1502, about the time that Cesare Borgia seized his native Urbino. Although the early books of the *Anglica historia* [English History] conform to the model of Bruni in their criticism of medieval legends, the descriptions of Thomas Wolsey in the later books reveal an author eminently conversant with the realities of the sixteenth century.[50]

Yet of all these historians it was Francesco Guicciardini of Florence who wrote the towering masterpiece of Renaissance narrative history. Guicciardini made

---

[46] Harvey C. Mansfield, *Machiavelli's Virtue* (Chicago, 1996), 140, points out that the year 1434 divides evenly not only the eight books but the 286 individual chapters. On Machiavelli as historian, see especially the second volume of Gennaro Sasso, *Niccolò Machiavelli: Storia del suo pensiero politico*, rev. edn, 2 vols. (Bologna, 1980).

[47] Jean-Jacques Marchand and Jean-Claude Zancarini (eds.), *Storiografia repubblicana fiorentina (1494–1570)* (Florence, 2003); Rudolf von Albertini, *Firenze dalla repubblica al principato*, trans. Cesare Cristofolini (Turin, 1970); and Bouwsma, *Venice and the Defense of Republican Liberty*, 154–292.

[48] Elena Valeri, *Italia dilacerata: Girolamo Borgia nella cultura storica del Rinascimento* (Milan, 2007).

[49] T. C. Price Zimmermann, *Paolo Giovio: The Historian and the Crisis of the Sixteenth Century* (Princeton, 1995).

[50] Denys Hay, *Polydore Vergil: Renaissance Historian and Man of Letters* (Oxford, 1952).

two substantial but incomplete efforts at histories of his native city, the *Storie fiorentine* [Florentine Histories] (written 1508–10), covering the period from 1382 to 1506, and his *Cose fiorentine* [Florentine Matters] (written 1527–34), which recounted the city's history from its founding down to the early 1300s. But it was in retirement, in the last three years of his life, that Guicciardini discovered the formula that made the best use of historical talents, as well as his extensive experience in papal government and service to the Medici. In writing a *Storia d'Italia* [History of Italy] (1537–40) that followed the fortunes of all of the major Italian powers simultaneously, Guicciardini advanced the idea of 'Italy' as a meaningful construct that was already present in Biondo's *Italia illustrata*, but which historians had hitherto failed to develop. Guicciardini's research was comprehensive. He possessed an extensive library and he used it well. He consulted government documents. As a trained jurist he made use of his knowledge of the law. But most especially, because he had met so many of his history's protagonists, he was able again and again, through quick character sketches, to provide psychological reasons for decisions that could not be explained by the simple calculation of interests. Because he was accounting for so many historical actors at the same time, history's causes and effects ceased to operate in a linear way. The historian was now the master of a grand web, revealing only bit by bit to the reader the directions of its threads and the points on which they were anchored.[51]

For a long time it was believed that Guicciardini's *Storia d'Italia* represented the end of the Renaissance and that subsequent Italian historical work was best described as something else, usually 'baroque'. Although other explanations were sometimes alleged—antiquarianism, for instance, or the Spanish hegemony, or the growth of an academic 'art of history' (*ars historica*) that supposedly killed off the real thing[52]—there was also implicit a belief that Counter-Reformation culture caused Renaissance narrative history of the sort that had thrived in the Renaissance to suffer during the baroque.[53] Yet with each passing decade the baroque label loses more of its specificity. Separating the Italian baroque from that in northern Europe is much harder to do now that historians are emphasizing converging cultural and social trends in Catholic and Protestant realms during a common age of 'confessionalization'.[54] This is particularly true of

---

[51] Gilbert, *Machiavelli and Guicciardini*, 271–301; Gennaro Sasso, *Per Francesco Guicciardini: quattro studi* (Rome, 1984).

[52] On the *ars historica*, see Anthony Grafton, *What Was History? The Art of History in Early Modern Europe* (Cambridge, 2007). For the argument that an excess of historical theory undermined historical practice, see Giorgio Spini, 'Historiography: The Art of History in the Italian Counter Reformation', in Eric Cochrane (ed.), *The Late Italian Renaissance* (New York, 1970), 91–133.

[53] Eric Cochrane, 'The Transition from Renaissance to Baroque: The Case of Italian Historiography', *History and Theory*, 19 (1980), 21–38, reviews the arguments and defends the category—unconvincingly. See now Caroline Gallard, *Le Prince et la République: Histoire, pouvoir et société dans la Florence des Médicis au XVIIe siècle* (Paris, 2007).

[54] See Heinz Schilling (ed.), *Die reformierte Konfessionalisierung in Deutschland—Das Problem der 'zweiten Reformation'* (Gütersloh, 1986).

Italian narrative history, for the masterpieces of the later sixteenth and early seventeenth centuries belonged clearly to a Renaissance lineage that passed from Bruni through Machiavelli and Guicciardini.

And the many readers of northern Europe who purchased Italian works, both in the original and in translation, seemed to understand that they were buying into a tradition of historical writing that was continuous with that of the Italian Renaissance.[55] Machiavelli's *Istorie fiorentine* were published and read as widely as *The Prince* and possibly more so.[56] Other books that were successful in northern Europe included Paolo Giovio's *Historiae sui temporis* [The History of His Own Times] (1550–2), Guicciardini's *Storia d'Italia*, Paolo Sarpi's *Istoria del Concilio Tridentino* [History of the Council of Trent] (1619), Enrico Caterino Davila's *Storia delle Guerre civili di Francia* [History of the Civil Wars in France] (1630), and Guido Bentivoglio's history *Della guerra di Fiandra* [Of the Flanders War] (1633–9). The importance for subsequent developments in European historiography of these narratives written by Italians of the later Renaissance was confirmed by none other than Edward Hyde, earl of Clarendon, who was arguably seventeenth-century England's greatest narrative historian. In an essay of the 1660s, 'On an Active and on a Contemplative Life', Clarendon singled out Davila and Bentivoglio for praise, while at the same time dismissing the ponderous *Annales et Historiae de rebus belgicis* [The Annals and History of the Low Country Wars] (1621) of the great Dutchman Grotius. He called the two Italians historians who 'worthily stand by the sides of the best of the ancients . . . Both their histories are excellent, and will instruct the ablest and wisest men how to write, and terrify them from writing'.[57]

TIMELINE/KEY DATES

1250 Death of Emperor Frederick II

1348 Black Death in Italy

1402 Death of Giangaleazzo Visconti of Milan

1406 Florence takes Pisa

1440 Lorenzo Valla publishes his treatise against the forged Donation of Constantine

1442 Alfonso I of Aragon conquers Naples

1453 Fall of Constantinople to the Turks

---

[55] Peter Burke, 'Translating Histories', in Burke and R. Po-chia Hsia (eds.), *Cultural Translation in Early Modern Europe* (Cambridge, 2007), 125–41.

[56] Sydney Anglo, *Machiavelli—The First Century: Studies in Enthusiasm, Hostility, and Irrelevance* (Oxford, 2005); and Giuliano Procacci, *Machiavelli nella cultura europea dell'età moderna* (Bari, 1995).

[57] Edward Hyde, Earl of Clarendon, *Essays Moral and Entertaining*, 2 vols. (London, 1815), i. 245, 246.

1454 Peace of Lodi
1494 French King Charles VIII invades Italy
1494 Medici family exiled from Florence
1499 French King Louis XII invades Italy
1509 Battle of Agnadello
1512 Florentine Republic falls to the Medici, who return to Florence
1513–15 Machiavelli writes *The Prince*
1527 Sack of Rome
1545–63 Council of Trent

KEY HISTORICAL SOURCES

Bembo, Pietro, *Historiae Venetae libri XII* (Venice, 1551); reprinted as *History of Venice*, ed. and trans. Robert W. Ulery, Jr., 3 vols. (Cambridge, Mass., 2007–9).

Bentivoglio, Guido, *Opere storiche del cardinale Bentivoglio*, 5 vols. (Milan, 1806–7).

Biondo, Flavio, *Historiarum ab inclinatione Romanorum imperii decades*, in *Opera* (Basel, 1531).

Bruni, Leonardo, *Historiae Florentini populi* (1415–42); reprinted as *History of the Florentine People*, ed. and trans. James Hankins, 3 vols. (Cambridge, Mass., 2001–7).

Corio, Bernardino, *Storia di Milano*, ed. Anna Morisi Guerra, 2 vols. (Turin, 1978).

Davila, Arrigo Caterino, *Storia delle guerre civili di Francia* (Venice, 1630), ed. Mario d'Addio and Luigi Gambino, 3 vols. (Rome, 1990).

Facio, Bartolomeo, *Rerum gestarum Alfonsi regis libri* (1563), ed. Daniela Pietragalla (Alessandria, 2004).

Giovio, Paolo, *Historiae sui temporis* (1550–2), ed. Dante Visconti and T. C. Price Zimmermann, 3 vols. (Rome, 1957–85).

Guicciardini, Francesco, *Storia d'Italia* (1537–40), ed. Silvana Seidel Menchi, 3 vols. (Turin, 1971).

Machiavelli, Niccolò, *Istorie fiorentine* (1531), ed. Plinio Carli, 2 vols. (Florence, 1927).

Nardi, Jacopo, *Istorie della città di Firenze*, ed. Agenore Gelli, 2 vols. (Florence, 1858).

Petrarch, *De viris illustribus*, ed. Silvano Ferrone and Caterina Malta, 2 vols. (Florence, 2006–7).

Rerum italicarum scriptores ab anno aerae christianae 500 ad annum 1500, ed. Lodovico Antonio Muratori, 25 vols. (Milan, 1723–51; repr. with an index, Bologna, 1977); new edn, ed. Giosuè Carducci and Vittorio Fiorini, 33 vols. (Città di Castello; then Bologna, 1900–75).

Sabellico [Coccio, Marcantonio], *Opera omnia*, ed. Celio Secundo Curione, 4 vols. (Basel, 1560).

Sarpi, Paolo, *Histoire du Concile de Trente* (1619), ed. Maria Viallon and Bernard Dompnier (Paris, 2002).

Storici e politici veneti del Cinquecento e del Seicento, ed. Gino Benzoni and Tiziano Zanato (Milan and Naples, 1982), includes Paolo Paruta, Nicolò Contarini, and Battista Nani.

BIBLIOGRAPHY

Black, Robert D., 'The New Laws of History', *Renaissance Studies*, 1 (1987), 126–56.

Burke, Peter, *The Renaissance Sense of the Past* (New York, 1969).

Cochrane, Eric, *Historians and Historiography in the Italian Renaissance* (Chicago, 1981).

Connell, William J., 'The Eternity of the World and Renaissance Historical Thought', *California Italian Studies Journal*, 2:1 [= 'Italian Futures', ed. Albert Ascoli and Randolf Starn] (2011).

Cutinelli-Rèndina, Emanuele, Marchand, Jean-Jacques, and Melera-Morettini, Matteo, *Dalla storia alla politica nella Toscana del Rinascimento* (Rome, 2005).

Dale, Sharon, Lewin, Alison Williams, and Osheim, Duane J. (eds.), *Chronicling History: Chroniclers and Historians in Medieval and Renaissance Italy* (University Park, Pa., 2007).

Fryde, E. B., *Humanism and Renaissance Historiography* (London, 1983).

Fubini, Riccardo, *Storiografia dell'Umanesimo in Italia da Leonardo Bruni ad Annio da Viterbo* (Rome, 2003).

Gilbert, Felix, *Machiavelli and Guicciardini: Politics and History in Sixteenth Century Florence*, 2nd edn (New York, 1984).

Grafton, Anthony, *What Was History? The Art of History in Early Modern Europe* (Cambridge, 2007).

Green, Louis, *Chronicle into History: An Essay on the Interpretation of History in Florentine Fourteenth-Century Chronicles* (Cambridge, 1972).

Guenée, Bernard, *Histoire et culture historique dans l'Occident médiéval* (Paris, 1980).

Ianziti, Gary, *Humanistic Historiography under the Sforzas: Politics and Propaganda in Fifteenth-Century Milan* (Oxford, 1988).

Kelley, Donald R., *Faces of History: Historical Inquiry from Herodotus to Herder* (New Haven, 1998).

Pertusi, Agostino (ed.), *La storiografia veneziana fino al secolo XVI: Aspetti e problemi* (Florence, 1970).

Phillips, Mark, *The Memoir of Marco Parenti: A Life in Medici Florence* (1987; repr. Toronto, 2000).

Witt, Ronald G., *In the Footsteps of the Ancients: The Origins of Humanism from Lovato to Bruni* (Leiden, 2001).

Zimmermann, T. C. Price, *Paolo Giovio: The Historian and the Crisis of Sixteenth-Century Italy* (Princeton, 1995).

Chapter 18

Italian Historical Writing, 1680–1800

Edoardo Tortarolo

Diversity was the outstanding feature of the Italian peninsula in the early modern age. Political fragmentation and the domination of foreign powers in large sections of the peninsula, particularly Spain until the War of the Spanish Succession (1700–14), and Austria until the *triennio repubblicano* (1796–9), went hand in hand with the flourishing of cultural centres like Naples, Florence, and Milan: writers and intellectuals in each of them could develop their own profile, negotiating the terms of their own cultural, historical, and political identity with Vienna or Madrid and profit from the support or the benign negligence of the local governments and of the local social and religious elites. The hegemony of foreign powers, to varying degrees Spain in Southern Italy (the Kingdom of Naples ceased to be a viceroyalty in 1734 but remained in the sphere of influence of Spain) and Austria in the north, while opening up cultural milieux to the interaction with cultural models abroad (the University of Pavia was under Austrian influence), contributed to the strengthening of regional intellectual peculiarities in those areas of Italy such as the Savoy Duchy, the Republics of Venice and Genoa, and the small political entities like Modena and Lucca, where political independence was preserved, at least formally. The Church State, itself a still remarkable political factor stretching from Bologna to Rome, from the Adriatic coast to the Tyrrhenian Sea, provided a firm basis for Catholicism as the only Italian religion and a powerful framework for any intellectual endeavour to be undertaken in the humanities and in the natural sciences. The private libraries of the powerful Roman cardinals were important rallying points for those who travelled to Rome, more so than the official institutions of higher education.

The development of the interest for the past in eighteenth-century Italy, as research and as narrative, is best understood when seen against this background in which the cultural diversity of Italy was reflected. In fact it was the peculiarity of the power politics on the peninsula, as well as the changing attitude towards the achievements of Roman Catholicism, that marked the various forms of history-writing in Italy. Factors like a powerful central government or a growing public of middle-class readers or the interest in a free religious debate might explain the increase in history books in other European countries such as France and England but can hardly account single-handedly for the actual output of very different sorts of historical works in the Italian states. Learned traditions interacted and clashed in this period and added to the multiplicity of models: the humanistic tradition of Niccolò Machiavelli and Francesco Guicciardini, the passionate moral indictment of Paolo Sarpi's *Istoria del Concilio Tridentino* [History of the Council of Trent] (1619), the controversialist history-writing of Ferrante Pallavicino, and the encyclopedic historiography of Emanuele Tesauro were all components of a historiographic tradition that no historian could disregard or ignore, no matter how negative one could assess their merits.[1] This diversity of attitudes and undertakings, and the contrast among competing approaches, has been misunderstood as the absence of an original contribution to the European-wide discussion about history in Italy: the classical work on modern historiography by Eduard Fueter barely mentions Italy and Italian historians in the late seventeenth and eighteenth centuries, and recent overviews reiterate a similar pattern.[2] In fact the Italian interest for a renewal of the historical investigations shows a peculiar way to absorb and reinterpret the main strands of the European discussion. The tension between erudition and philosophy, between the painstaking factual research about a limited topic and the understanding of a series of events connecting the past to the present, may provide us with a set of issues that challenged the Italian intellectuals throughout the eighteenth century in their approaches to past events. Political and cultural diversity endorsed a variety of responses to the desire of connecting to, emotionally re-enacting, or rationally assessing relevant portions of the past and expressed the peculiar Italian way to transcend the Counter-Reformation, a general phenomenon that opened up the peninsula to contact with the rest of Europe.

ANTIQUARIANISM

Historical erudition was a factor of the historical culture in Italy since the rise of humanism. It was also a crucial component of the religious identity and a key element of the political status of each town and region in terms of public law. The Renaissance witnessed in Italy a revival of antiquarianism that ran parallel to the great historical achievements of Machiavelli and Guicciardini. The historiography of the Counter-Reformation had an increasing impact on the ideological confrontation between a Catholic and a Protestant historiography which stifled the ideal of an unbiased search for factual truth, imposing a providentialist and hagiographic reading on the whole process of human history, as well as on the

---

[1] Sergio Bertelli, *Ribelli, libertini e ortodossi nella storiografia barocca* (Florence, 1973).
[2] Eduard Fueter, *Geschichte der Neueren Historiographie* (Berlin, 1911). See Markus Völkel, *Geschichtsschreibung: Eine Einführung in globaler Perspektive* (Cologne, 2006), 227–49 (only Giannone and Muratori are quoted).

assessment of particular events, epitomized in Cesare Baronio's *Annales ecclesiastici* [Ecclesiastical Annals] (1588–1607).[3] The religious, ideological, and political implications in such historical works were quickly detected as their main feature. Scepticism about the historian's capability to ascertain the truth was widespread, and the baroque reverence for secrecy in political matters and obscure phrasing contributed to the decline of history-writing as an intellectual endeavour to gain true knowledge independent from the ecclesiastical or government sanctions. If historians did bring out sound information about the past, they were subject to the approval of the ecclesiastical and civil power and, if necessary, had to reinterpret their findings according to the prevailing intellectual mood and their political and religious allegiance. Descartes's insistence on clear and distinct ideas, which was widely discussed in Italy, discredited historical research as inherently uncertain and inconclusive. Moreover, the princes and republics as a rule restrained access to their archives as repositories of records crucially important for international relations. The radical mistrust in the human capacity of ever reaching the truth about past events, which was expressed in Europe in the discussion about 'historical pyrrhonism', touched a sensitive nerve in Italy, especially because historical pyrrhonism undermined the certitude of sacred history, together with pointing to the inconsistencies of human history. Despite the obvious abundance of records and monuments of a very long history, Italian culture was unable to keep up with the progress that antiquarianism had made in Holland, in England, and especially in France, while the contradictions and insufficiency of history books were more and more apparent.[4]

Most Italian *eruditi* were painfully aware at the end of the seventeenth century that their own methodology of analysis was outstripped in terms of accuracy by the achievements of the French monastic orders that devoted themselves to working out new techniques in diplomacy, sphragistics (study of seals), numismatics, and chronology. The impact of Jean Mabillon, and to a lesser extent Bernard de Montfaucon, in Italy was deep. They visited Italy and met antiquarians in the different cities where they stayed to visit libraries and search monasteries and repositories for manuscripts and codes. The *Iter Italicum* [Italian Journey] (1687) and the *Museum Italicum* [Italian Museum] (1687–9) by Mabillon (who travelled in Italy in 1685 and 1686), and the *Diarium Italicum* [Italian Diary] (1702) by Montfaucon, reporting on his voyage in 1699–1702, bear witness to the reactions of the Italian *eruditi*. The revision of Church history that was the obvious consequence of their new approach to the past was a source of concern for the Roman hierarchy, and antiquarianism remained a dubious

---

[3] C. K. Pulapilly, *Caesar Baronius, Counter-Reformation Historian* (Notre Dame, 1975); and Stefano Zen, *Baronio storico della controriforma* (Naples, 1996).

[4] Brendan Dooley, *The Social History of Skepticism: Experience and Doubt in Early Modern Culture* (Baltimore, 1999); and Anthony Grafton, *What was History? The Art of History in Early Modern Europe* (Cambridge, 2007).

approach stressing as it did the human skills at ascertaining the truth about the past rather than the respect due to the tradition articulated by the Church. Mabillon, Montfaucon, and their Italian followers were convinced that truth would impose itself: true religion had nothing to do with medieval forgeries. In fact, the close scrutiny of the sources was constantly associated with a critical attitude that easily metamorphosed into disapproval of those practices of the 'popular devotion' that promoted devotion to saints whose existence was at best dubious, belief in miracles unsupported by sound evidence, and acknowledgement of power relations based on fake documents. Systematic diligence in checking documents went hand in hand with an austerity in religion that contrasted with the baroque piety. Italian *eruditi* in the early eighteenth century knew they were walking on thin ice when giving their curiosity about the past free rein.

The central personality of Italian antiquarianism of the eighteenth century was Lodovico Antonio Muratori. In many ways Mabillon's example and writings made Muratori's scholarly accomplishments possible. A short sketch of his biography and scholarly works shows that pursuing a career as a scholar meant also getting involved in religious disputes. It also indicates that erudition as a discipline was attracting young and brilliant scholars who were ready to follow its demanding methodology. A priest living most of his life as a librarian and a parish priest in Modena, Muratori was fully aware of the progressive character of the new antiquarianism. Establishing the documentary truth in Church history was a way to purify religion and foster a more rigorous behaviour of men in society. He became aware of the dangers of critical enquiries early on, at the time when he undertook the investigation of the history of Milan from late antiquity to the Middle Ages: sacred relics and the Iron Crown in Monza, allegedly containing a nail from the Holy Cross, were the subjects of his early writings, in which he made a serious effort to reject legends and false information on plain empirical data. Muratori made use of the antiquarian methods to fortify the position of his country when it came to a dispute with the papal state. The study of the public law of the Holy Roman Empire since its origins gave him the opportunity to defend his duke in the Comacchio dispute from 1708 on, and to develop his perspective on the past in his correspondence with Leibniz. Muratori sided with the emperor and provided historical documents to uphold the emperor's claims (and those of his duke) against papal demands for secular power in northern Italy.

Erudition, however important, was in itself just a premise for a new understanding of the past. Muratori was able to go beyond the limits of a *bellum diplomaticum*, a dispute based solely on the assessment of the authenticity of the official records (or *diplomi*) testifying the original donation of a territory by the emperor or the pope and feudal relationships. The question of the historical method appealed to him. As early as 1708 Muratori stressed in his *Riflessioni sopra il buon gusto nelle scienze e nelle arti* [Reflections on Good Taste] that 'good taste' depended on the interaction of 'erudition' and 'good critique': both are necessary.[5] Muratori believed that reason could support the *fides historica*, based on the appropriate understanding of monuments of the past and on the principle of non-contradiction between documents. Reason was not incompatible with a sincere and moderate Christianity. Despite his frequent disagreements with Rome, Muratori became the living evidence that an enlightened Catholicism was possible.

A few years after publishing the *Riflessioni sopra il buon gusto*, in the 1710s, Muratori planned to publish the original texts of the chronicles which would improve the knowledge of the local stories: the *Rerum Italicarum Scriptores* [Sources of Italian History] (the first volume was published in 1723, the last one in 1738; the twenty-four volumes dealt with the whole span of years from 500 to 1500) was a path-breaking collection of medieval writers (*veteres*), while research had focused so far on the fifteenth-century chroniclers (*recentiores*). For the first time a variety of details were made available to historians. The *Rerum Italicarum Scriptores* was more than a useful collection of sources: Muratori made clear that he intended to promote 'civil historiography' as an alternative to the narrow understanding of Italian history as merely an effect of Church rule, and to show that modern times were more civilized and made living happier, or at least less evil than past times. In the *Rerum Italicarum Scriptores*, as in his following collection of seventy-five dissertations, the *Antiquitates Italicae Medii Aevi* [Antiquities of the Italian Middle Ages] (1738–42), the crucial step was made to give priority to the interaction of the 'barbarians', the Germanic peoples who invaded Italy from the fourth century on, and the population that had long lived on the peninsula under Roman rule. Thinking about Italian history in terms of a cultural history of the Middle Ages was an innovative and daring enterprise that marked the eighteenth-century debate on national identity from the perspective of the relationships between the civil governments and the Catholic Church and influenced the romantic understanding of the Middle Ages.[6]

Collecting, critically analysing, and interpreting documents was Muratori's main contribution to the revised methodological foundations of Italian historical research. When he attempted to write a narrative of Italian history from the beginning of the Christian era to 1749, he chose the annalistic form. Despite his effort to write 'civil history', that is the history of secular institutions, of the 'events and deeds of princes and peoples who successively showed up in the theatre of the world',[7] excluding the ecclesiastical history (already written by

---

[5] Lodovico Antonio Muratori, *Riflessioni sopra il buon gusto nelle scienze e nelle arti* (1708), in Giorgio Falco and Fiorenzo Forti (eds.), *Opere di Lodovico Antonio Muratori*, vol. 1 (Milan, 1967), 222–85.

[6] Sergio Bertelli, *Erudizione e storia in Lodovico Antonio Muratori* (Naples, 1960), 364.

[7] Muratori, *Annali d'Italia dal principio dell'era volgare sino all'anno 1500* (1744–8), in Falco and Forti (eds.), *Opere di Lodovico Antonio Muratori*, vol. 1, 1023–5.

Baronio and Claude Fleury), he could not really overcome the fragmentation inherent in the annalistic approach and was eventually unable to reshape the wealth of information into a coherent plot. The *Annali d'Italia* [Italian Annals] was published in 1744 in nine volumes stretching to 1500; three additional volumes treating the most recent events were printed in 1749. Muratori spent most of his life in Modena as a librarian and archivist for the Dukes of Este, but managed to build up a network of *eruditi* throughout Italy: his correspondence shows that he quickly became the centre of an expanding circle of local historians interested in the critical treatment of the past that Muratori was championing.[8] By exchanging information and transcripts, by asking for advice and providing expertise on controversial documents, and by promoting a tolerant and comprehensive approach to human events, Muratori emerged as the leading figure of a renewed Italian historiography. A 'Muratori School', which combined scholarly accuracy, Catholicism, and alertness to reformist strategies in politics, spread in Italy and in the Habsburg territories, turning private *eruditi*, but also members of the clergy and of the monastic orders, into accurate and enthusiastic antiquarians collecting epigraphs, coins, manuscripts, and memoirs, and laying the foundations for a revision of Italian history. From Piedmont to Sicily, antiquarianism gained recognition and prestige, and could occasionally get public support from the princes and rulers. But erudition was mainly an affair of private individuals.

In this context Scipione Maffei was the first antiquarian who refined Mabillon's technique in an original way and corrected his achievements substantially. In Verona, where he was born into a noble family, Maffei found a number of early medieval manuscripts in the Biblioteca Capitolare in 1712. Maffei, a strong character with clear opinions about the Italian past and about how to reform the economy and government in Italy, saw the importance of collecting and editing epigraphs from the Roman age (he enlarged the Museum lapidarium in Verona, where engraved stones had been collected since the Renaissance) and eventually published the *Verona illustrata* [Verona Elucidated] (1732), in which the history of his city acquired a new dimension, as Maffei included in the narrative the data disclosed by his erudite researches. Patriotism and scholarly accuracy were both present as goals of Maffei's erudition: that 'foreigners have gone well beyond Italians in the sciences' was a lamentable fact, but Italians would soon catch up in the antiquarian quest.[9]

Local pride was indeed a reason motivating quite a few relevant local historians who followed Muratori's lead. For some of them a research period in Paris was decisive. Giovan Battista Caruso travelled to Paris as a young man and familiarized himself with the methodology of the French Maurins in the 1690s. A correspondent of Muratori's, Caruso published original chronicles of Sicilian history in the *Bibliotheca historica Regni Siciliae* [The Library of the History of

[8] Ezio Raimondi, *I lumi dell'erudizione: Saggi sul Settecento italiano* (Milan, 1989).
[9] Scipione Maffei, *Istoria diplomatica che serve d'introduzione all'arte critica in tal materia*, vol. 1 (Mantua, 1727), 113.

the Kingdom of Sicily] in 1723. While Muratori had focused on the Middle Ages, Caruso and most of the Sicilian *eruditi* developed a peculiar interest in the pre-Roman past: antiquarian research was considered a tool to prove that the local identity could boast an immemorial continuity from the earliest times of the Cyclopes and Sicans, the first inhabitants of Sicily.[10] For Caruso, as for P. Troyli, a Benedictine monk who wrote an *Istoria generale del reame di Napoli* [A Comprehensive History of the Kingdom of Naples] (1747–84), ascertaining the true development of Sicilian history belonged to the political commitment for the defence of Sicilian historical liberty. This combination of 'modern' antiquarianism, exemplified by Torremuzza's *Le antiche iscrizioni di Palermo* [The Ancient Inscriptions in Palermo] (1762), and the commitment to the ideological needs of the local government boosted rigorous investigations but also provided opportunities for forgers: the most daring and successful being the Maltese Giuseppe Vella, who made up documents allegedly dating from the eleventh century and proving the enduring Arabic influence on the Sicilian public law.[11] Vella's forgery was exposed by an outstanding scholar of Arabic literature, Simone Assemani, who taught Arabic literature at the Seminar and at the University in Padua. Born into a well-known Maronite family in Tripoli, Lebanon, and a priest, Assemani became the most knowledgeable Arabian expert in Italy. His *Saggio sull'origine culto letteratura e costumi degli Arabi avanti Maometto* [An Essay on the Origins, Worship, Literature, and Customs of the Arabs before Mahomet] (1787) was a milestone in this crucial and clearly under-researched field of Italian history in a country where the Arabs had settled for centuries. A similar contribution was made by Giovanni Bernardo De Rossi, a professor of oriental languages at the University of Parma, to Hebrew studies, a field that the Counter-Reformation theologians had discouraged: in the *Variae lectiones Veteris Testamentis* [On the Different Versions of the Old Testament] (1784–8) he systematically collected and edited the variants of the Hebrew text of the Old Testament.

Antiquarianism revitalized the historical research within the monastic orders and made possible a revision of the history of the ecclesiastical institutions at the local level. Yet, some research conditions in Italy compared unfavourably with France. Anselmo Banduri, born in Ragusa, then a republic under Ottoman control (now Dubrovnik, in Dalmatia), and a Benedictine monk in Florence around 1700, met Montfaucon in Florence and went to Paris on a fellowship granted by the Grand Duke of Tuscany to perfect his training in the new methodology of the Maurin fathers. He stayed in Paris to become one the most eminent historians of Byzantium and an editor of humanistic texts.[12]

[10] Giovan Battista Caruso, *Dizionario Biografico degli Italiani*, vol. 21 (Rome, 1979), 10–15.
[11] Paolo Preto, 'Una lunga storia di falsi e falsari', *Mediterranea*, 3 (2006), 11–38.
[12] *Dizionario Biografico degli Italiani*, vol. 5 (Rome, 1964), 739–50.

Antiquarianism could be used to investigate practical problems: this was the aim of another follower of Muratori, Filippo Argelati, who published a path-breaking collection of treatises on coins in Italian history, *De monetis Italiae* [On Italian Coins] (1751–2), written by various erudites on the monetary history of the Italian states since the Late Middle Ages. In fact, Argelati provided an overview of the development of the ups and downs of prices, and attempts were made to explain the correlation of prices, gold and silver content, and general economic conditions.[13] What, surprisingly, is missing in the antiquarian revision of Italian history in the eighteenth century is a sustained analysis of the Roman period and of the inner working of the Roman Empire and republic. When Louis-Jean Levesque de Poully, Nicolas Fréret, and Louis de Beaufort engaged in revising the foundations of early Roman history at the Parisian academies, a debate among erudites on the first centuries of Roman history did not take place in Italy.[14] The focus was not on Roman rule, and anti-Romanism was quite widespread. Maffei wrote a short treatise on Roman rule in the provinces (1720–2), and Francesco Algarotti, who spent most of his life abroad, in England, France, and Germany, wrote *Saggio critico del Triumvirato di Cesare, Pompeo e Crasso* [A Critical Essay on the Triumvirate of Cesar, Pompeus, and Crassus] in 1739–41, but never published it.[15] Algarotti's commentary on Montesquieu's *Considérations sur les causes de la grandeur des Romains et de leur décadence* [Considerations on the Causes of the Greatness of the Romans and Their Decline] (1721), rather than being an original piece of research, focused on the controversial relationship between religion and politics, and took in particular Julius Cesar as the symbol of a Machiavellian strategy in manipulating the religious beliefs of the lower uneducated classes. In taking this standpoint, Algarotti diverged from the mainstream attitude towards the Roman past, stressing how damaging Roman rule had been to the rest of Italy. In 1787 Francesco Mengotti, from Veneto, published a dissertation on the Roman trade from the First Punic War to Constantine which was in fact a manifesto against the exploitation of the provinces by the metropolis.[16]

A peculiar version of this interest in the non-Roman past of Italy was apparent in Tuscany, where the study of antiquities enjoyed a spectacular revival under the Lorenese rule: libraries, museums, archives, and academies were founded or revitalized so that modern historical research was made possible. No chair of history was active at the only Tuscan university in Pisa in the eighteenth century. A major feature was the interest in research on Etruscan history, based on the publication of Thomas Dempster's *De Etruria regali* [On Royal Etruria] (1723)

[13] Franco Venturi, *Settecento riformatore: Da Muratori a Beccaria*, vol. 1 (Turin, 1969), 463–8.

[14] Mouza Raskolnikoff, *Histoire romaine et critique historique dans l'Europe des lumières: la naissance de l'hypercritique dans l'historiographie de la Roma antique* (Rome, 1992).

[15] Franco Arato, *Il secolo delle cose: Scienza e storia in Francesco Algarotti* (Genoa, 1991), 81–110.

[16] Franco Venturi, *Settecento riformatore: L'Italia dei lumi, V*, vol. 2: *La Repubblica di Venezia* (1761–97; Turin, 1990), 433–49.

and on the *Tabulae Iguvinae* [Iguvine Tables], a text in an Umbrian pre-Roman dialect engraved on bronze tablets discovered near Gubbio (Iguvium in Latin) in 1444.[17] The Academy in Cortona changed its name to Accademia Etrusca and became a centre of *etruscheria*, as this passionate interest in things Etruscan came to be known. The antiquarian methods were used to prove the dignity and importance of Tuscany independent from the Roman domination. The major figure was Filippo Venuti, who used his antiquarian skills to investigate the sensational findings at Herculaneum near Naples in 1738: as he wrote, 'a new Antiquity' had emerged—not 'merely small remnants and fragments, but...an entire city, complete with magnificent and precious decorations, with theatres, temples, pictures and houses'.[18] A new possibility of reconstructing a civilization without the aid of written sources opened itself up to investigators.

In the late seventeenth and eighteenth centuries most of the ruling elites were educated in Jesuit colleges until the order was expelled from the Borbonic States and then abolished in 1773. In these colleges, history and geography were declared mandatory subjects for noble students in 1747: by then, both were considered to be 'knightly sciences' (*scienze cavalleresche*) appropriate to the education of young noblemen. Before 1747 history was taught as part of the curriculum based on the teaching of Latin literature and Roman history: orthodoxy and the transmission of examples of virtue adapted to the Catholic requirements were the major concern and original historical research was not encouraged in Jesuit colleges.[19] The most notable exception was Girolamo Tiraboschi's multi-volume *Storia della letteratura italiana* [History of Italian Literature] (1772–81), which expanded into a history of Italian culture from the time of the Greeks and Etruscans down to the eighteenth century, recounting 'the origin and advancement of all sciences in Italy'.[20]

UNIVERSAL HISTORY: AN OLD AND NEW SCIENCE

Like in the rest of Europe at the beginning of the eighteenth century, in Italy universal history was an important part of higher education, predominantly imparted by the religious orders, and was the arena where competing views of the most fundamental notions about man confronted each other. In the Italian cultural debate the Old Testament provided the chronological framework for the earliest times, and the canonical texts, officially accepted as such by the Church,

---

[17] Francesco De Angelis, 'L'Etruria regale, da Dempster a Buonarroti: Ricerca antiquaria e attualità politica in Toscana fra Sei e Settecento', *Rivista Storica Italiana*, 121:2 (2009), 497–542.

[18] Quoted in Eric W. Cochrane, *Tradition and Enlightenment in the Tuscan Academies 1690–1800* (Rome, 1961), 185.

[19] Gian Paolo Brizzi, *La formazione della classe dirigente nel Sei-Settecento* (Bologna, 1976), 242–4.

[20] Girolamo Tiraboschi, *Storia della letteratura italiana*, vol. 1: *Dagli Etruschi fino all'anno MCLXXXIII* (Milano, 1833), 5, Preface to the second edition Modena 1787–94.

were the source of the providential design that history books displayed to readers. The European controversy on the pre-Adamites and the chronology of the world was fundamentally rejected by Italian culture. *Historia sacra* had pride of place. The *Mappamondo istorico* [Historical World Map] (1690–4) by the Jesuit Antonio Foresti, a teacher of the humanities in many colleges for the nobility in northern Italy and eventually in the most important of them, the 'Seminarium nobilium' in Parma, epitomized the orthodox view on universal history: sacred history was the interpretative structure, and God's miraculous intervention in human affairs was taken for granted. Its European success is proved by its translation into German. It fitted so well with general assumptions of the time that a Venetian printing entrepreneur, Girolamo Albrizzi, reprinted it as the first part of a more comprehensive universal history completed by volumes on the history of the European states, Islam, and China.[21] Jacques-Bénigne Bossuet's *Discours sur l'histoire universelle* [Discourse on University History] (1681) was translated into Italian and printed several times. Innovations within the genre of universal history were hard to come by under such circumstances. The principle of history-writing as an enterprise to show the glory of God in things human was strong. Evidence for this is the *Storia universale* [Universal History] (1697) by Francesco Bianchini, the librarian of the Biblioteca Ottoboniana in Rome. Bianchini held on to the biblical chronology but carefully integrated into his narrative the findings of antiquarian research: he prized archaeological and numismatic sources, and information from etymology, ethnography, and iconology. He intended to disprove historical pyrrhonism and was interested in finding out what historical content myths were concealing about the ages unrecorded in written texts. Bianchini was clearly struggling with the doubts about the validity of historical knowledge *per se* that historical pyrrhonism and Jean Hardouin in particular had disseminated in earlier years.[22]

The most original attempt to reinterpret universal history and to reply to the claims of Descartes and the pyrrhonists came with the writings of Giambattista Vico and in particular with the *Scienza Nuova* [New Science] in three versions (1725, 1730, 1744; the last one was left unpublished), which gave a systematic form to the complex web of his thoughts. Vico accepted the distinction between sacred history and profane history and the biblical chronology (§ 23), but in fact radically revised the traditional orthodox approach to the study of history by rejecting the Cartesian dichotomy of *factum*, the result of human activity and therefore true (*verum*) and understandable, and *datum*, the effect of God's creation of nature. Vico limited providential design (*historia sacra*) to the history

---

[21] *Mappamondo istorico, cioe' ordinata narrazione dei quattro sommi imperi del mondo e della monarchia di Cristo da San Pietro primo papa sino a' nostri di'*, 7 vols. (Venice, 1715–16). The additional volumes were written by Apostolo Zeno, Domenico Suarez, and Vittore Silvio Grandi.

[22] Giuseppe Ricuperati, 'Francesco Bianchini e l'idea di storia universale "figurata"', *Rivista Storica Italiana*, 117:3 (2005), 872–973.

of the Jewish people and believed that the actual development of human events was revealed through philology, the crucial foundation of a true understanding of human nature in history. The histories of the gentile peoples follow different pattern rules from those of the elected peoples: the 'ideal-eternal history' has development regularities, but no preordained development. History is the realm of human knowledge because social activity is what humanity is all about. Within this approach Vico revised the notion of the stages of development and suggested that man is the creator of 'meanings embodied in institutions and practices'.[23] Through a highly innovative and imaginative analysis of Roman law and language, Vico argued that the course of history is based on nations and goes through the stages of gods, heroes, and men, which metaphorically indicate different forms of culture. The first, divine stage of the nations is characterized by poetry and unwritten customs: 'The first human nature was a poetic or creative nature produced by the powerful illusions of the imagination, which is most vigorous in people whose powers of reasoning are weakest' (§ 916). The theocratic governments rule through oracles, while the heroic stage expresses itself in history, prose, and written laws, enacted by aristocratic governments. The human stage is recognizable by the presence of 'the human law which is dictated by fully developed human reason' (§ 924). Vico's reinterpretation of Homer, whose 'supreme greatness as a poet was the product of his heroic nature' (§ 837), his insights into the metaphorical nature of language, and his reinterpretation of the feudal system as part of the development of societies had a deep impact as late as the twentieth century, but were ignored during his lifetime and in the second half of the eighteenth century outside Naples, where he spent his whole life. The only exception worth mentioning is Lorenzo Boturini Benaduce, an Italian priest who was in Mexico for many years. His *Idea de una nueva historia general de la América Septentrional* [Idea of a New Comprehensive History of North America] (1746) applied Vico's ideas to Mesoamerican history. Boturini Benaduce's perspective was also long neglected and gained recognition only recently.[24]

---

[23] Bruce A. Haddock, 'Vico and the Methodology of the History of Ideas', in Giorgio Tagliacozzo (ed.), *Vico: Past and Present* (Atlantic Highlands, 1981), 227–39; Giuseppe Giarrizzo, *Vico, la politica e la storia* (Naples, 1981); Paolo Rossi, *The Dark Abyss of Time: The History of the Earth and the History of Nations from Hooke to Vico* (Chicago, 1987); and Mark Lilla, *Giambattista Vico: The Making of an Anti-Modern* (Cambridge, 1994). Quotations are from Giambattista Vico, *New Science: Principles of the New Science, Concerning the Common Nature of Nations*, 3rd edn, trans. David Marsh (London, 1999).

[24] Franco Venturi, 'Un vichiano tra Messico e Spagna: Lorenzo Boturini Benaduce', *Rivista Storica Italiana*, 87:4 (1975), 770–84; and Jorge Canizares-Esguerra, *How to Write the History of the New World: Histories, Epistemologies and Identities in the Eighteenth-Century Atlantic World* (Stanford, 2001), 135–42.

HISTORY AND POLITICS: FROM PIETRO GIANNONE TO CONTEMPORARY HISTORY

Arnaldo Momigliano remarked that in their time Vico was a lonely figure, while Pietro Giannone wrote for and was listened to by all of Europe.[25] This contrasts indeed with the twentieth-century discussion about Vico, in which structuralist, Marxist, idealistic, linguistic, and analytic approaches have been used worldwide to unveil the true meaning of his philosophy, while the scholarly interest in Giannone has been lively but limited to Italy. Giannone's life was as dramatic as Vico's was uneventful. After writing his main historical work, the *Istoria civile del Regno di Napoli* [The Civil History of the Kingdom of Naples] (1723), Giannone fled Naples to eschew persecution from the Catholic Church, settled in Vienna, then left Vienna for Venice and Geneva. He was eventually captured by the Savoy authorities and imprisoned in 1736 for twelve years on the instigation of the pope. He became a symbol of the religious and political persecution in *ancien régime* Italy. Giannone was educated as a lawyer and used a juridical approach as the interpretative category of his history: by stressing that he had written a 'civil' history he meant that the public law in Southern Italy from Roman times to the Austrian rule from 1707 onwards was the main focus of his work. The title also meant that Giannone was writing a history of the secular institutions and of their distinction from and opposition to the encroachments of the papal Church, which achieved a dominant position in the feudal system. Giannone's history revealed the manipulation of jurisprudence that had nurtured papal power and had contributed to the decline of Southern Italy after the collapse of the Roman Empire. The secularization of political rule and the return of religion to its original purity and simplicity were vehemently advocated by Giannone. Through the narrative of Italian history, the concern for reform in public morals and for a 'national' dynasty supported by the productive classes, not just by the rapacious nobility, came to be expressed: according to Giannone, a strong absolutist monarchical rule was necessary to perform this radical change. Giannone's work was a strong indictment of the contemporary balance between the secular and the ecclesiastical powers as well as a detailed description of how this became possible. In Vienna, Venice, Geneva, and even as a prisoner in Piedmont, Giannone widened the scope of his historical view thanks to the books of the European debate he eventually had access to. The *Triregno* [The Triple Kingdom], unpublished during his lifetime, was an historical overview of the development of religion from the earthly stage of the Jews, who did not believe originally in the immortality of the soul, the celestial stage, in which the belief in eternal life

---

[25] Arnaldo Momigliano, 'Mabillon's Italian Disciples' (1958), in *Terzo contributo alla storia degli studi classici e del mondo antico* (Rome, 1966), 152.

was reached first in ancient Egypt, and the papal stage, in which the popes since Gregory VII could take from the clergy and the common people any influence in the Church, raise the papal authority above kings and emperors, and dominate the political arena for centuries and still interfere with the inner workings of the legitimate civil governments.[26] The *Istoria civile* exerted a significant influence on European historiography (on Gibbon as well as others)[27] and was cherished by those historians who were interested in using history as a weapon in their struggle to modernize and secularize Italy by curbing the exorbitant power of the Church.

In doing so Giannone joined a vigorous tradition of politically engaged historiography. In the first half of the eighteenth century public law was frequently invoked as an argument for or against political reform. In Sicily the erudite Caruso wrote a *Discorso istorico-apologetico* [A Historical and Apologetic Discourse] (published for the first time in 1863) at the command of Victor Amadeus II to support the short-lived Savoy rule after the end of the War of the Spanish Succession and, at the same time, plea for a government that would resist the pressure from the Church State in Rome, preserve the historical freedom of Sicily, and actively pursue the well-being of the people.[28] In the eighteenth century other historians kept alive the tradition of defending the legal position of their prince by recourse to a narrative that was supposed to show the rightfulness of one side against the encroachments of the opposing party. In some cases historians submitted their writings to the government whose legal position they were questioning. The history of Genoa, written by Francesco Maria Accinelli shortly after the War of the Austrian Succession, extolled the principle of republican freedom and cast doubts on the role played by the nobility in defending the republic. The oligarchic government condemned Accinelli's book to be burnt on the stake in 1752 for attacking the prestige of the republic.[29] Venice defended its own legitimacy through history: the republic focused on controlling the discourse about its origins, legal status, and prerogatives, and reacted to diverging interpretations.

The interest in contemporary history seems to have increased in the early eighteenth century. Despite their dubious epistemological status and their biased narrative, stories of the most recent wars that had ravaged the Italian territory, of dynastic changes, of tensions between the Church State and Italian governments,

---

[26] Giuseppe Ricuperati, *L'esperienza civile e religiosa di Pietro Giannone* (Milan, 1970).

[27] Hugh Trevor-Roper, 'Pietro Giannone and Great Britain', *Historical Journal*, 39:3 (1996), 657–75; also published in Roper, *History and the Enlightenment*, ed. John Robertson (New Haven and London, 2010), 34–53.

[28] Giambattista Caruso, *Discorso istorico-apologetico della Monarchia di Sicilia*, ed. G. M. Mira (Palermo, 1863); and Giuseppe Giarrizzo, *Illuminismo*, in Rosario Romeo (ed.), *Storia della Sicilia*, vol. 4 (Palermo, 1980), 713–815.

[29] Accinelli, *Compendio delle storie di Genova dalla sua fondazione sino all'anno 1750* (Lipsia, 1750).

flooded the book market. Diplomatic reports released confidentially, eyewitness information, plain gossip, and hearsay were the documentary foundation of this political history-writing that addressed a growing audience that was not attracted by, or could not understand the complexity of, antiquarian or juridical historiography. Overlappings with traditional cultural forms were possible, the most striking being Alberto Radicati di Passerano, a Piedmontese deist who lived in London and died as an exile in Rotterdam, after writing philosophical and religious treatises. Radicati tried his hand at contemporary history in a critical vein. His short history of the abdication, spectacular comeback, and final detention of the Savoy King Victor Amadeus II in 1729–30 became an instant bestseller, with a wide circulation in England and France as a pamphlet and in Italy as a manuscript where printed copies were forbidden. With a different audience in mind and a different political agenda than Radicati, even Vico wrote contemporary history. The history of the conspiracy of Macchia in Naples in 1701, *Principum neapolitanorum coniurationis anni MDCCI historia* [History of the Conspiracy of the Neapolitan Princes of 1701] (1701), and the biography of the Neapolitan Antonio Carafa, commander-in-chief of the imperial troops in Hungary in the 1680s, *De rebus gestis A. Caraphaei* [The Deeds of Antonio Carafa] (1713–15), were written in Latin echoing the classical model of Titus Livy and served mainly as evidence for Vico's political visions: the accuracy of the first-hand information he was able to gather should nonetheless be noted.

Contemporary history was rather the domain of controversial journalists and profit-seeking printers. Starting in the 1680s, books were published collecting news from gazettes and broadsides that reported the latest events about wars, natural catastrophes, dynastic changes, and variations in economic relationships, with a varying degree of interest in gossip, secret affairs, and conspiracies. Negotiations with the local censors in Italy were necessary to get those stories through the press and their authors often had a very hard time with the authorities. It is no surprise that many of these forms of contemporary history appeared abroad: the most famous (and notorious) of these authors, Gregorio Leti, converted to Calvinism and lived most of his life in Geneva, London, and in Amsterdam (where he died) as an official historiographer of the city. Leti was aware that the narrative of contemporary events had an impressive political relevance on the emerging public opinion that writers could utilize in order to exert pressure on governments.[30] Conditions in Italy were not favourable to the development of this sort of contemporary history. To meet the demand for information about recent events gazettes spread all over Italy, under the control of the censors and provided with state privilege. A series of annual works called *La storia dell'anno* [The Last Year's History] were published from 1738 onwards. They summed up the main events of the preceding year. Published in Venice, the

---

[30] Mario Infelise, *Prima dei giornali: Alle origini della pubblica informazione* (Laterza, 2002).

Italian printing capital in the eighteenth century, the *Storia dell'anno* usually gave a wide overview of the military and diplomatic events that had an influence on Italian affairs and did not comment nor put in perspective the developments under scrutiny, but indeed reflected the concerns of the Venetian government and in particular its economic and strategic interest in the Balkans and in Eastern Europe. One of the major contributors to the early volumes of the *Storia dell'anno*, Antonio Catiforo, wrote the *Vita di Pietro il Grande Imperador della Russia* [The Life of Peter the Great Emperor of Russia] (1748), an Italian parallel to Voltaire's *Histoire de Charles XII* [History of Charles XII] (1731), and worked on a critical edition of the *Bibliotheca* of the patriarch Photius which was published only recently. Catiforo's various accomplishments show how close philology, journalism, and history of contemporary events in fact were around 1750.[31]

THE HISTORICAL WRITING OF THE ITALIAN ENLIGHTENMENT

No major history of contemporary events came out in Italy, while an effort was made to translate into Italian historical works in foreign languages, including some of Voltaire's historical texts. In fact French became the lingua franca among the Italian literati, so that the lack of an Italian translation of a French text might mean that it was too daring for the civil and ecclesiastical authorities but by no means that it was unknown in Italy. Besides French historical works by Voltaire, Montesquieu, and Mably, models for a new historical narrative came from England, Scotland, and Germany. A post-Muratorian, updated Italian historiography reflected this variety of cultural inputs in the second half of the eighteenth century. With Carlo Denina and Carloantonio Pilati, crucial Enlightenment notions like progress, the identity of human nature, the importance of the political and social context for the development of civilization, a sense of good taste as a social regulator, and the superiority of civil society over ecclesiastical institutions became crucial. Denina's *Discorso sulle vicende della letteratura* [Discourse on Literary Matters] (1761) was the first interpretive overview of the European literature in Italian: literature included historical writing for which Montesquieu and Voltaire were critically discussed, and Denina linked the rise and decline of the different forms of literature to political events like transformations in the political structure. A quiet but distinct anti-despotic tone was implicit in Denina's numerous historical works. *Delle rivoluzioni d'Italia* [Revolutions in Italy] (1769–70), which Denina completed when still in Turin and before leaving for Berlin to become a distinguished member of the Prussian

---

[31] Margherita Losacco, *Antonio Catiforo e Giovanni Veludo interpreti di Fozio* (Bari, 2003).

Academy of the Sciences, was probably the most popular survey of Italian history from the very beginning through to the eighteenth century. Referring exclusively to published sources, Denina echoed the Enlightenment concern for civilization and the conditions of civil society, and a main focus of his historical perspective was on the degree of happiness in any given period. A moderate reformist attitude gave coherence to a long narrative that carefully respected the Catholic religion and its positive influence on Italian history.

Pilati, who was educated as a lawyer in Trent, an imperial city governed by the prince-bishop, connected with the anticlerical strand in the Enlightenment historiography. For him history served as a repository of arguments against his polemical target, the exorbitant power of the Church in Italy, which he exposed in *Di una riforma d'Italia* [On Reforming Italy] (1767) and *Le Riflessioni di un italiano* [Reflections of an Italian] (1768). The damaging influence of the Catholic clergy extended to the forgeries that disfigured the Italian past and its capacity to see the problems it faced. Pilati's *Istoria dell'impero germanico e dell'Italia* [History of the German Empire and of Italy] (1769–71, translated into German in 1771 and highly appreciated, not surprisingly, in Berlin by the thinkers associated with the German Enlightenment) was his most sustained effort to reconstruct the medieval origins of the peculiar and disastrous evolution of Italian culture into superstition, credulity, economic and political decline, and fragmentation that played into the hands of the pope and the clergy and kept Italy a backward country. Despite the obvious differences between Pilati's resolute neo-Machiavellian anticlericalism and Denina's prudent plea for social and economic reforms, they shared a widespread attitude among Italian literati to take stock of the increase of dependable and accurate information on Italian history that Muratori and the Muratori School had so far accomplished and capitalize on it: in the 1760s the urgent task seemed to be to write an interpretive synthesis carrying out the educational function that history-writing indeed should perform and contribute to the progress of Italian society. In Milan, where one of the most innovative groups of intellectuals gathered regularly, Alessandro Verri wrote a history of Italy that claimed to be both certain and useful and would follow Hume's example. Alessandro Verri completed his long essay but never published it (it was first published in 2001[32]): though unified by anti-Roman sentiment and by the development of the Church as an institution distinct from Christianity as a religion, Verri could not be persuaded that his work met the high standards he had set for himself. His brother Pietro, who was a successful reformer in the local government, wrote a history of Milan from a similar standpoint. Pietro Verri aimed at writing a philosophical narrative that would explain how civilization in the city had historically changed for the better, the cause being 'the progress of reason, the increase of the enlightenment,

---

[32] Alessandro Verri, *Saggio sulla storia d'Italia*, ed. Barbara Scalvini (Rome, 2001).

the reproduction of books, the genius of culture, that moderate and beneficial philosophical spirit that has dispelled ferocity and fanaticism'.[33] Verri printed the first volume of the *Storia di Milano* [History of Milan] in 1783, but death prevented him from completing the narrative up to his own time, as he had originally planned.[34]

In the 1760s and 1770s the Italian writers were particularly focused on the opportunities for a reform of the existing economic, institutional, and juridical conditions in the Italian territories. Denina, Pilati, and the brothers Verri, among others, expressed this fundamental position with varying nuances and interpretive intentions, in a constant dialogue with the diverse forms of the European Enlightenment. Similarly, writers in the Kingdom of Naples investigated the history of the visible dramatic decline of Southern Italy with an eye to the meaning that their historical works might have for political action: if the feudal system was perceived as the main obstacle to economic progress and social modernization, it was necessary to investigate how that system had established itself, how it could be eradicated, and how a return to the original, natural form of social and economic organization was possible. Giuseppe Maria Galanti was the most remarkable among the writers who investigated the global history of parts of Southern Italy in *Descrizione dello stato antico ed attuale del contado di Molise, con un saggio storico sulla costituzione del Regno* [Description of the Ancient and Present State of the Molise Region, with a Historical Essay on the Constitution of the Kingdom] (1781) and of the whole kingdom in *Nuova descrizione storica e geografica delle Sicilie* [New Description Historical and Geographical of the Sicilies] (1786–90). The *Annali del Regno di Napoli* [The Annals of the Kingdom of Naples] (1781–6) by Francescantonio Grimaldi was, despite its title, a history of the civilization of Southern Italy that reflected his reading of Ferguson, Gibbon, and d'Holbach: the stadial theory was applied systematically to make sense of its development.

At the end of the eighteenth century Italian historiography had absorbed most of the European debates about new categories that would make the investigation of the past in general, and of specific historical problems, more fruitful. In at least two instances (Muratori and Giannone), approaches typical of the Italian cultural and political setting were recorded positively in Europe, Vico being the exceptional case of a deep and long-lasting but delayed reception. Its contribution to a collective effort to establish an undisputable documentary basis for the study of ancient and medieval times had been remarkable, however uneven and faulty in many cases. It may be suitable to recall that the great nineteenth-century historian Theodor Mommsen thoroughly revised the whole work of the Italian antiquarians and rejected a substantial part of the sources still accepted by

---

[33] *Storia di Milano del conte Pietro Verri, colla continuazione del barone Custodi*, vol. 1 (Milan, 1850), 431.

[34] See now Pietro Verri, *Storia di Milano*, ed. Renato Pasta (Rome, 2010).

eighteenth-century antiquarians with varying degrees of scepticism. Ironically, Melchiorre Delfico, himself the author of *Memorie storiche della repubblica di San Marino* [Historical Memories of the Republic of San Marino] (1804), wrote a work entitled *Pensieri su l'Istoria e sull'incertezza ed inutilità della medesima* [Thoughts on History and on its Uncertainty and Uselessness] (1808). He drew on a century-long discussion about history-writing and rejected the notion of history when history meant a barren list of massacres and wars, and the uninspiring recounting of evil and ignorance. Delfico conceded emphatically that it is a rewarding effort to assess critically the past and integrate it, especially the most recent, into the human effort to achieve progress in the natural and social sciences and live a good life.

TIMELINE/KEY DATES

1700–13 War of the Spanish Succession ends with the Peace of Utrecht: the Duke of Savoy Victor Amadeus II, becomes king of Sicily; the Habsburgs of Austria are the hegemonic power in Italy

1720 Victor Amadeus II becomes king of Sardinia; Sicily is returned to the Kingdom of Naples

1726–7 Concordat between Victor Amadeus II and the pope

1733–8 War of the Polish Succession: as a consequence of the war the Austrians are expelled from Southern Italy; the Kingdom of Naples becomes independent under the tutelage of the Spanish monarchy

1740–58 Papacy of Benedictus XIV

1740–8 War of the Austrian Succession: the peace of Aquisgrana begins a long period of peace for the Italian states

1746 Insurrection of Genoa against the Austrian army

1748 Publication of Lodovico Antonio Muratori's *On Public Happiness*

1764 Publication of Cesare Beccaria's *Of Crimes and Punishments*

1764–6 The periodical *Il Caffè* is published in Milan

1765 Famine in Italy; the son of the Empress Maria Theresa, Peter Leopold, becomes duke of Tuscany

1768 In Lombardy, censorship is taken over by the civil authorities, who tighten their control on a variety of ecclesiastical functions

1768 Corsica is taken over by the French monarchy from the Republic of Genoa

1769–74 Papacy of Clemente XIV

1773 The Jesuit order is abolished by the pope

1775–99 Papacy of Pius VI

1780–90 Reforms of Emperor Joseph II in Lombardy

1796–9 French armies under Napoleon Bonaparte defeat the Italian states and reshape constitutional, social, and economic settings during the Jacobin Triennium

KEY HISTORICAL SOURCES

Algarotti, Francesco, *Saggio critico del Triumvirato di Cesare, Pompeo e Crasso* [written in 1739–41], *Opere*, 17 (Venice, 1794), 149–522.

Argelati, Filippo, *De monetis Italiae*, 4 vols. (Milan, 1751–2).

Assemani, Simone, *Saggio sull'origine culto letteratura e costumi degli Arabi avanti Maometto* (Padua, 1787).

Bianchini, Francesco, *Storia universale* (Rome, 1697).

Boturini Benaduce, Lorenzo, *Idea de una nueva historia general de la América Septentrional* (Madrid, 1746).

Dempster, [Thomas], *De Etruria regali*, 2 vols. (Florence, 1723).

Denina, Carlo, *Delle rivoluzioni d'Italia*, 3 vols. (Turin, 1769–70).

Foresti, Antonio, *Mappamondo istorico*, 4 vols. (Parma, 1690–4).

Galanti, *Nuova descrizione storica e geografica delle Sicilie*, 4 vols. (Naples, 1786–90).

Giannone, Pietro, *Istoria civile del regno di Napoli*, 4 vols. (Naples, 1723).

Grimaldi, Francescantonio, *Annali del Regno di Napoli*, 10 vols. (Naples, 1781–6).

Maffei, Scipione, *Verona illustrata*, 4 vols. (Verona, 1732).

Muratori, Lodovico Antonio, *Rerum Italicarum Scriptores*, 25 vols. (Milan, 1723–38).

—— *Antiquitates Italicae Medii Aevi*, 6 vols. (Milano, 1738–42).

—— *Annali d'Italia dal principio dell'era volgare sino all'anno 1500*, 12 vols. (Milan, 1744–8).

Pilati, Carlo Antonio, *Istoria dell'impero germanico e dell'Italia*, 2 vols. (Coira, 1769–71).

Tiraboschi, Girolamo, *Storia della letteratura italiana*, 10 vols. (Medina, 1772–81).

Verri, Alessandro, *Saggio sulla storia d'Italia*, ed. Barbara Scalvini (Rome, 2001).

Verri, Pietro, *Storia di Milano*, ed. Renato Pasta (Rome, 2010).

Vico, Giambattista, *New Science: Principles of the New Science, Concerning the Common Nature of Nations*, 3rd edn, trans. David Marsh (London, 1999).

BIBLIOGRAPHY

Arato, Franco, *Il secolo delle cose: Scienza e storia in Francesco Algarotti* (Genoa, 1991).

Bertelli, Sergio, *Erudizione e storia in Lodovico Antonio Muratori* (Naples, 1960).

—— *Ribelli, libertini e ortodossi nella storiografia barocca* (Florence, 1973).

Cochrane, Eric W., *Tradition and Enlightenment in the Tuscan Academies 1690–1800* (Rome, 1961).

De Angelis, Francesco, 'L'Etruria regale, da Dempster a Buonarroti: Ricerca antiquaria e attualità politica in Toscana fra Sei e Settecento', *Rivista Storica Italiana*, 121:2 (2009), 497–542.

Giarrizzo, Giuseppe, *Vico, la politica e la storia* (Naples, 1981).

Lilla, Mark, *Giambattista Vico: The Making of an Anti-Modern* (Cambridge, 1994).

Momigliano, Arnaldo, 'Mabillon's Italian Disciples' (1958), in *Terzo contributo alla storia degli studi classici e del mondo antico* (Rome, 1966).

Preto, Paolo, 'Una lunga storia di falsi e falsari', *Mediterranea*, 3 (2006), 11–38.

Pulapilly, C. K., *Caesar Baronius, Counter-Reformation Historian* (Notre Dame, 1975).

Raimondi, Ezio, *I lumi dell'erudizione: Saggi sul Settecento italiano* (Milan, 1989).

Raskolnikoff, Mouza, *Histoire romaine et critique historique dans l'Europe des lumières: la naissance de l'hypercritique dans l'historiographie de la Roma antique* (Rome, 1992).

Ricuperati, Giuseppe, *L'esperienza civile e religiosa di Pietro Giannone* (Milan, 1970).

——'Francesco Bianchini e l'idea di storia universale "figurata"', *Rivista Storica Italiana*, 117:3 (2005), 872–973.

Rossi, Paolo, *The Dark Abyss of Time: The History of the Earth and the History of Nations from Hooke to Vico* (Chicago, 1987).

Tagliacozzo, Giorgio (ed.), *Vico: Past and Present* (Atlantic Highlands, 1981).

Venturi, Franco, *Settecento riformatore: Da Muratori a Beccaria*, vol. 1 (Torino, 1969).

——'Un vichiano tra Messico e Spagna: Lorenzo Boturini Benaduce', *Rivista Storica Italiana*, 87:4 (1975), 770–84.

—— *Settecento riformatore: L'Italia dei lumi, V*, vol. 2: *La Repubblica di Venezia* (1761–97; Torino, 1990).

Chapter 19

History and Historians in France, from the Great Italian Wars to the Death of Louis XIV

Chantal Grell

In the second half of the fifteenth century, the past was the focus of unprecedented enthusiasm. The most popular of the classical historians were quickly published: Valerius Maximus, Titus Livius (Livy), Caesar, Flavius Josephus's *Antiquitatum Judaicarum* [Jewish Antiquities], Eusebius's *Ecclesiastical History*, as well as Herodotus, Thucydides, Tacitus, Suetonius, and Plutarch's *Lives*. The printing presses responded to the expectations of a public that included clerics, learned scholars, and, more and more, jurists, courtiers, even merchants and the bourgeoisie. These readers were not only interested in the classics, however; they appreciated medieval chronicles, annals, and traditional narratives. Vincent of Beauvais's *Speculum historiale* [Mirror of History] and the *Mare historiarum* [Sea of Histories] were reprinted several times. Gregory of Tours's *Historia* [History (of the Franks)], written, according to humanist standards, in poor Latin, was not forgotten either. The success of recent works was constant: the *Grandes Chroniques de France* [The Great Chronicles of France] was the first French book printed in Paris in 1476–7, by Pasquier Bonhomme. The *Annales et Chroniques de France* [Annals and Chronicles of France] by Nicole Gilles enjoyed dozens of print runs over the course of the century. The *Compendium* by Robert Gaguin was reprinted nineteen times in Latin between 1497 and 1586, and seven times in French between 1514 and 1538. The *Illustrations de Gaule et singularitez de Troye* [Illustrations of Gaul and Singularities of Troy] by Jean Lemaire de Belges was published from 1509 to 1549. The *Antiquités de Paris* [Antiquities of Paris] by Gilles Corrozet (1531) was revised several times throughout the century. The *Methodus ad facilem historiarum cognitionem* [Method for the Easy Comprehension of History] by Jean Bodin (1566) had eleven print runs between 1566 and 1650. Etienne Pasquier died in 1615 after having provided six different editions of his *Recherches de la France* [Research in French History] (1560, 1565, 1581, 1596, 1607,

1611) and having prepared the 1621 edition. The examples are endless. History was truly at the heart of humanist thinking and its success is confirmed throughout the next two centuries. As illustrated by Jean Bodin, however, it is appropriate to use the plural form. History was not a discipline identified as such, in spite of the presence of a new theoretical and critical way of thinking. Neither was it a recognized literary genre; it was not taught as a subject, except perhaps in the education of princes. Contemporaries, and first and foremost Jean Bodin in his *Methodus,* did not limit it simply to the 'true narration of past events'. Even leaving aside 'natural' and 'divine' history, simple 'human' history was very diverse and there were many ways of relating 'the actions of men living in society'.

THE REVOLUTION OF THE PRINTING PRESS

The printing press revolutionized historians' work and way of thinking, for in just half a century, it gave them access to a mass of texts and information that even the privileged few who had access to the very best libraries had had difficulty obtaining previously. Admittedly, before the printing press became widespread, a few important libraries possessed the main works of reference. But the Sorbonne, with 1,722 volumes in 1338, was exceptionally well endowed. Saint Denis possessed only 1,600 volumes in 1465. Thanks to the printing press, books became common, and working in one's personal library, surrounded by books, became the rule. Nicole Gilles, a notary and secretary to Louis XII, wrote his *Annales et Chroniques de France* with the help of books that he himself had collected. In 1499 he owned about one hundred works: forty or more manuscripts, around sixty printed works including about fifteen history books, classical pagan historians (Livy, Valerius Maximus), Christian historians (Josephus, Paulus Orosius), the great classics of the seventeenth century (Vincent of Beauvais's *Speculum Historiale,* the *Grandes Chroniques de France*), and even recent works such as Froissart's *Chroniques* or the *Mare historiarum,* all published in Paris between 1476 and 1496.

Printing presses became more widespread, initially in northern Italy and in the Rhine Valley, until Paris acquired its first workshops in 1470 and went on to become, twenty years later, the most important centre in the European printing industry. It is estimated that, in Europe, 5,000 incunabula were published before 1481; then more than 20,000 between 1481 and 1500, with runs of between 200 and 500 copies, but that figure would reach 1,500 copies by the end of the fifteenth century. The price of books decreased with the perfecting of techniques, accompanied by a decline in the price of paper and in format sizes. Thus Nicole Gilles's library, remarkable for the 1490s, would have been judged modest one century later. Jacques-Auguste de Thou put together a scholarly library between 1573 and 1617 that had 6,600 references in the catalogue established upon his demise, one of the best-stocked in Paris during the reign of Louis XIII. History books accounted for 1,045 entries, less than theology (1,447), belles-lettres (1,469), or science and the arts (1,369), but more than law (346).[1]

For a long time, French historical culture had been based on a dozen works written before AD 800: 'For a thousand years, the two works by Flavius Josephus, the *Church History* by Eusebius-Rufinus, the *Chronicon* [Chronicle] by Eusebius-Jerome, Orosius' *Historiarum* [History], Cassiodorus' *Historia tripartite* [Tripartite History], Isidore's *Chronicon* [Chronicle], and Bede's *Historia ecclesiastica gentis anglorum* [Ecclesiastical History of the English People] were, for Christian history, the very foundation of Western culture.'[2] For Cassiodorus in the 560s, these were for the most part the titles whose knowledge was considered essential for a theologian. In the fourteenth century, the common basis of historical works consisted of about twenty titles. In the fifteenth century, the spectacular comeback of the classics preceded the printing press, thanks to Valerius Maximus and Justin, and the decline of theological culture had begun. The prompt printing of most of the ancient sources and of numerous medieval texts paved the way for the development of a history that was political and secular, ancient and national.

Thenceforth historians disposed of a massive amount of documentation that was, above all, recent. As a result, there is a difference in nature—and not just in degree—between the work of an historian in the Middle Ages and that of a Renaissance historian. The arrangement of the pages, the material shape of the books, led to new practices in reading and working, and a new acquisition of knowledge facilitated by the chapters, the tables, the indices, and the notes that allowed the reader rapidly to locate information and avoid the need to read *in extenso*. The printed texts, too, were worthy of confidence, carefully reread, and corrected; it was possible to quote them, and anyone could consult them. Historians, henceforth, could provide proof to back up their assertions.

SCHOLARLY NETWORKING

The model of the princely library comes from Italy. The first King's Library was dismantled in England in 1429, after being bought by the Duke of Bedford. Louis XII built up a new one at Blois, based on the library of his father, Charles d'Orléans. Compared with the Italian libraries, this was a paltry collection that was later enriched by looting during the Italian Wars. In 1495 Charles VIII brought back from his Neapolitan expedition 1,140 manuscripts taken from the superb library of the Kings of Aragon, and Louis XII pillaged the treasures of the

---

[1] See Antoine Coron, '"Ut prosint aliis": Jacques-Auguste de Thou et sa bibliothèque', in Claude Jolly (ed.), *Histoire des bibliothèques françaises*, vol. 2: *Les bibliothèques sous l'Ancien régime, 1530–1789* (Paris, 1988), 101–25.

[2] Bernard Guenée, *Histoire et culture historique dans l'Occident médiéval* (Paris, 1980), 303.

Sforza and the Visconti from their castle in Pavia. Louis XII considered his manuscripts to be his personal property and although he engaged Claude de Seyssel to translate several classical historians—Xenophon's *Cyropaedia*, Appian's *Historia Romana* [Roman History], Justin's *Epitoma* [Epitome], Eusebius's *Ecclesiastical History*, Diodorus Siculus, and Thucydides—these were for his own personal use. The attitude of Francis I was completely different. Advised by Guillaume Budé, he saw humanist publications as a source of glorification. He founded the College of Three Languages (Hebrew, Greek, Latin), the future Collège de France (1530), to rectify the shortcomings of the Sorbonne University, and not only did he have Seyssel's translations printed, but he also instituted a policy of systematic acquisition of documents, strengthened by the institution of legal deposit, in 1537, for the new library of Fontainebleau, enriched in 1544 by the Blois collections. Moved to Paris in the middle of the sixteenth century, the Royal Library was pillaged during the Wars of Religion. It contained only 1,329 volumes in 1645, when the legacy of Jacques Dupuy (1656) enriched it by 9,223 volumes. Jean-Baptiste Colbert, who managed the Kingdom finances under the supervision of King Louis XIV as the controller general from 1665 to 1683, moved it to rue Vivienne in 1666. The system of classification for the books, developed by Nicolas Clément at the end of the seventeenth century, was based on a codification (still in use) by letters of the alphabet that allocated ten letters to history, four to religion, and four to philosophy.

The King's Library was only made accessible to the public around 1700, unlike the Bibliothèque Mazarine, which opened its doors in 1661. Under Louis XIV, the Colbertine was the most famous library. Colbert had entrusted its administration to Etienne Baluze, who acquired the De Thou collection, and tied his name to the Maurist enterprise that Colbert took over, for the good of the state, because of its vast campaigns for the copying of manuscripts in France and Europe. The Colbertine catered to scholars. Its collections were integrated with those of the King's Library in 1731. The Sainte-Geneviève collections were completely renewed as of 1619 and attained 15,000 volumes around 1690–1711. Saint-Germain had suffered less, but its collections were mainly enriched after 1640, reaching 7,000 volumes and 1,000 manuscripts in 1685.

Scholarly circles grew up around the libraries. Historians no longer worked in isolation. The religious congregations used entire teams. Those in the legal profession (*la noblesse de robe*) collected books and manuscripts, organized discussion groups, exchanged books and information. The religious wars and looting had put numerous manuscripts on the market, which in certain cases would be preserved thanks to collectors. Etienne Pasquier made his personal treasures available to his friends, and in turn consulted their rare works and manuscripts; thus we know that Claude Fauchet possessed a manuscript of Flodoard's *Annalium* [Annals], originating from the Abbey of Saint Victor. Pierre Pithou also lent Pasquier his manuscripts on the history of France before having them published.[3] Pasquier socialized with Jacques-Auguste de Thou, whose library was the rallying point for erudite Parisian society. De Thou was in contact with Joseph Justus Scaliger, and with Isaac Casaubon, Claude Dupuy and his three sons, Pierre Pithou and his two sons, Denis Petau, and the Sainte-Marthe brothers. Correspondence provided information on the most recent publications, and publishing houses sent orders all over Europe. Diplomatic or religious friends were given the mission to buy manuscripts or rare editions. A scholar from Provence, Nicolas Claude Fabri de Peiresc, an important figure in the Republic of Letters who was consulted all over Europe, had a library— scattered, alas, after his death—that was the subject of widespread admiration for its diversity, its constant updating, and its valuable and rare texts. The authoritarian policies of Richelieu were not well adapted to the first *académies*, like the Académie putéane, the Thursdays of Henri Justel, and the circle of the abbé de Longuerue, informal circles of scholars where the great philosophical questions of the day were freely discussed. Richelieu preferred the official *académies*, sponsored by the authorities, over which it was possible to exercise control. The French Academy was founded in 1635; Colbert founded the 'Petite Académie' in 1661, the ancestor of the Académie des inscriptions et médailles (the Royal Academy of Inscriptions and Medals) in 1701, which later (1717) became the Académie des inscriptions et belles-lettres, whose function it was to study testimonies from the past that were the most appropriate for glorifying the king. After the monarchical rule was seriously challenged during the uprisings known as the Fronde (1648–53), the Petite Académie was a way of engaging scholars who often already occupied positions such as director of a library, censor, or historiographer and who sometimes received regular stipends, so that they would work for the king and be diverted away from Jansenist, devout, or libertine networks.

INVENTORY OF RICHES

This new abundance of books made necessary the publication of specialized lists, with commentaries on the authors and the various editions.[4] In the tenth chapter of his *Methodus* (1566), Jean Bodin proposed a critical bibliography of historians, including their degree of credibility and the information they provided. Two *Bibliothèques françaises* [French Libraries] appeared simultaneously in 1584, produced by La Croix du Maine, a Protestant, and by Antoine du Verdier,

---

[3] *Annalium et Historiae Francorum* (1588); and *Historia Francorum, scriptores veteres* (1596).

[4] This was a pan-European phenomenon: in 1531 Juan Luis Vives, *De tradendis disciplinis*, bk. 5, gives an overview of historians; Sebastian Fox Morcillo, *De Historiae institutione dialogus* (Anvers, 1557), also includes bibliographies. In 1563 David Chytraeus of Rostock gives a catalogue of ecclesiastical history, to which the Jesuit Antonio Possevino responds in 1567.

Table 1. Number of History Titles

	La Croix du Maine	Du Verdier
Cosmography, chronology	25	41
Ecclesiastical History	24	84
Greek and Roman History	32	38
General History of France and	19	
in particular the Kings of France	24	42
History of the provinces and cities of France	38	35
Compilations of the History of France	20	50
History of the different European States	25	50
Histories of Asia, Africa, and the Americas	32	50
Historical compilations	21	38
Genealogy, heraldry	21	23

a gentleman in the Ordinary of the king's household. The tables put together by Rigoley de Juvigny[5] illustrate the success of a triumphant history that encompassed cosmology, geography, travel, and all disciplines of antiquity: chronology, heraldry, genealogy, as well as the study of institutions, societal mores, and customs (see Table 1).

In *Méthode que l'on doit tenir en la lecture de l'histoire, vrai miroir exemplaire en notre vie* [Method to be Used in the Reading of History, a True Exemplary Mirror in our Lives], published by Pierre Droit de Gaillard in 1579, the bibliography represents only ten pages out of 570. In 1599 La Popelinière mentions more than a thousand historians in his *Histoire des histoires* [History of Histories], an overview of a century of historiographic studies. In 1713 Pierre Nicolas Lenglet Dufresnoy's catalogue *Méthode pour étudier l'histoire... avec un catalogue des principaux historiens et des remarques sur la bonté de leurs ouvrages* [Method for Studying History... with a Catalogue of the Main Historians and Comments on the Goodness of Their Works] consists of 304 very dense pages. The first edition of the *Bibliothèque historique de la France, contenant le catalogue de tous les ouvrages tant imprimés que manuscrits qui traitent de l'histoire de ce royaume* [Historical Library of France, Containing a Catalogue of all the Works Printed or in Manuscript Form that Deal with the History of this Kingdom] appeared in 1719. Updated tools such as this facilitated research and provided information on texts, authors, the different editions of authors' works, and their

---

[5] Rigoley de Juvigny, *Les Bibliothèques françaises de La Croix du Maine et de du Verdier, sieur de Vauprivas, édition revue, corrigée et augmentée*, 6 vols. (Paris, 1772–3).

availability: conclusive proof, if ever there was, that there existed a (healthy) market for history books.

Despite this healthy market, even for official historians like historiographers, history was not a profession. Polymaths who tried to make a living from it were not very successful.[6] There were no professors of history. It was an activity, a curiosity. The study of the past was included within other disciplines: theology, belles-lettres, law, and political studies. The profiles of historians were therefore as diverse as their works. Nevertheless, the terms 'historiographer' or 'chronographer', rarely found in the Middle Ages, were becoming more widespread.

THE HISTORIAN, A MAN OF THE CHURCH

The memory of the past was perpetuated thanks to monks and men of the Church. But the science of writing annals was declining, with the notable exception of the Abbey of Saint Denis, the burial place and sanctuary of the Capetian dynasty. Suger, who was the abbot there from 1122 to 1151, began the habit of inscribing the history of each reign (the *Chroniques* of Saint Denis) in Latin; however, at the request of Louis IX, Primat wrote in the vernacular the *Roman des Rois* [Story of the Kings], a history of the French monarchy dating back to its Trojan origins (completed in 1274). The Hundred Years War had interfered with this collective endeavour, but Charles VII showed his dedication to it when, after regaining Saint Denis from the English (1435), he designated Jean Chartrier, cantor of Saint Denis, as the 'Chronicler of France', duly sworn in and appointed (1437). The monks thus continued the *Grandes Chroniques de France* until the reign of Louis XI, who progressively put an end to Saint Denis's monopoly in matters of official history.

The Italian Wars dealt a severe blow to historiography, which was too much under the control of the Church. In the Middle Ages the 'authenticity' of a text was dependent on the guarantee of a figure of authority (prince, bishop, canon), and the higher the authority (emperor, pope), the more the document was considered authentic.[7] Lorenzo Valla, by questioning the validity of the Donation of Constantine, and therefore the authority of the pope himself, asserted a totally new criterion: the historical validity of facts, of factual accuracy. Valla had first served Alfonso of Aragon, and composed his *De falso credita et ementita Constantini donatione declamatio* [Discourse on the Forgery of the Alleged Donation of Constantine] (1440) in order to denounce the abuses of a temporal power whose authority was based on a false document identifiable as such by its

---

[6] Steve Uomini, *Cultures historiques dans la France du XVIIe siècle* (Paris, 1998).

[7] Cf. Guenée, *Histoire et culture historique dans l'Occident médiéval*, 131–40. 'Authentic' means approved by an authority and 'worthy of faith', i.e. credible. An apocryphal text, in the eyes of a theologian, refers to a text that has not been certified by an authority.

contradictions, discrepancies, and linguistic anachronisms. Valla finished his career in the service of Pope Nicholas V (1447); his *declamatio* was therefore only printed in 1517, by Ulrich von Hutten, in the same year that Luther posted his ninety-five theses.

Criticism of the traditions of the Catholic Church then logically became the prerogative of the Protestants, who saw history as an awesome weapon to undermine the authority of Rome. Protestants experienced early on the need to apply the rules of critical philology to the Holy Scriptures and to all the authorities dear to the Roman Catholic Church. Obliged to proceed rapidly, they also discovered the virtues of collective research. The credit for this goes to a professor from Wittenberg and later from Magdeburg, Matija Vlačić (Flacius Illyricus), who sent to all his correspondents a *consultatio* (consultation) in which he explained the necessity of conducting a large-scale investigation to establish the continuity of the true faith, denounce the abuses of the Church, and legitimate the Reformation. The *Magdeburg Centuries* (1559–74), which covered the first thirteen centuries of the Church, provoked a prompt response from Cesare Baronio via his *Annales ecclesiastici* [Ecclesiastical Annals] (1588–1607). The matter was later taken up by Jacques-Bénigne Bossuet, who, in his *Histoire des variations des Eglises protestantes* [History of the Variations of the Protestant Churches] (1688), carried the debate into the field of theology, reflecting on the consequences of the Reformation. A theologian, Bishop of Meaux, and one of the great preachers of his century, Bossuet was also entrusted with the position of private tutor to the 'Grand Dauphin' for whom he wrote the *Discours sur l'histoire universelle* [Discourse on Universal History] (1681), the last great exposition of Christian theology on history, in the tradition of Eusebius and Orosius.

In the wake of the Tridentine Reform of the mid-sixteenth century, the religious orders endeavoured to occupy the stage of scholarly research and prevent the reformers from monopolizing it. The Jesuits soon entered the fray. Ardent defenders of the Roman Catholic Church, they would also respond on historical grounds. In 1607, in Anvers, Father Heribert Rosweyde inaugurated the project of the *Acta Sanctorum*, a collection of the lives of saints based on original documents. Father Jean Bolland later took over the enterprise with Father Daniel Papebroch, and publication began in 1643. The Bollandists saw themselves as the initiators of scholarly critical hagiography, and Papebroch prescribed rules of methodology in 'Sur le discernement du faux et du vrai dans les vieux parchemins' [On the Judgement between Falsehood and Truth in Old Manuscripts] (1675). The French responded. Founded in 1618, in Lorraine, the Congregation of Saint Maur had adopted as its main objective responding to the Protestants. Established in Saint-Germain-des-Près in 1631, it numbered 191 abbeys by the end of the seventeenth century. In the constitution of 1645, its first superior-general, Dom Grégoire Tarisse, with the support of Richelieu, defined an ambitious plan of study. With a view to defending the Catholic position in the controversy, the congregation, as of 1648, worked on an edition of the Greek and Latin Church Fathers, a history of the Church, and a history of the Order of Saint Benedict. This work took the form of a well-supervised collective inquiry that was based on the research and criticism of original documents.[8] Thirteen volumes of documents on the history of the congregation were published between 1665 and 1677, followed, as of 1668, by the *Acta sanctorum ordinis sancti Benedicti* [Acts of the Benedictine Saints] (1668–1701) and the *Historia rei literariae ordinis S. Benedicti* [Literary History of the Order of Saint Benedict]. The Maurists developed rules of criticism to counter those of the Bollandists. Dom Jean Mabillon, a native of Champagne who arrived at Saint-Germain-des-Prés in 1664, rapidly became the herald of historical scholarship with his *Brèves réflexions sur quelques règles de l'histoire* [Brief Reflections on Some Rules for Writing History] in 1677, his *De re diplomatica* [On the Science of Diplomatics], which founded the science of 'diplomatics', in 1681, and finally his *Traité des études monastiques* [Treatise on Monastic Studies] in 1691. On the basis of more than two hundred charters cited as examples, Mabillon defined the rules of prudence for scholarship and the critical criteria, both external (parchment, paper, ink, writing) and internal (language, formulas, dating, internal coherence, consistency with regard to known historical data), thus showing that history depended less on narration than on knowledge, less on style than on good judgement.

In the 1680s the Maurist organization was running very smoothly. The congregation had some three thousand monks in six different provinces. In each province, responsibilities were assigned according to a strict hierarchy. One monastery was selected for scholarly study, and the young postulants singled out for their ability were given five years of training in philosophy and theology before returning to their original monastery to work on classifying archives and libraries, putting together files, and deciphering manuscripts. This local research provided the material necessary for the most famous scholars assembled at Saint Denis or at Saint-Germain-des-Prés. The latter abbey was home to about fifty monks, but only a dozen worked on the most important collections, applying Mabillon's protocol: putting together proof, avoiding fraud, fighting pyrrhonism (see below). The Maurists, with their strong philological and humanist heritage, thus defined the principles of a scholarly methodology and renewed the history of their order as well as that of the French provinces by their recourse to documentary sources.

The Jansenists, of whom there were many within the Maurist ranks, also worked at collecting evidence in favour of their convictions. Sébastien Le Nain de Tillemont chose to hide behind what he considered worthy and reliable sources in order to rewrite the early history of the Church,[9] and *Mémoires pour servir à l'histoire ecclésiastique des six premiers siècles justifiés par les citations des auteurs*

---

[8] *Lettre circulaire au sujet des mémoires qu'on demande pour composer l'histoire de l'ordre* (1647).
[9] *Histoire des Empereurs et autres princes qui ont régné durant les six premiers siècles de l'Eglise*, 16 vols. (Bruxelles, 1692–1710).

originaux [Ecclesiastical Memoirs of the First Six Centuries, Made Good by Citations from Original Authors] (1693–1712). The Oratorian Richard Simon applied the same critical methodology to biblical exegesis. His *Histoire critique du Vieux Testament* [Critical History of the Old Testament] (1678) provoked the wrath of the censors; the work was prohibited by the king and by the Congregation of the Index (1683), and Simon was excluded from his order. The Church was not yet ready to accept this evolution, and judged the application of criticism to the Holy Scriptures to be dangerous. Thus the Bollandists were also condemned by the Holy See in 1695. Caution was essential at a time when historical proof, apparently so powerful, was weakened by Cartesian doubt as well as by the scepticism of freethinkers. The story of Father Jean Hardouin, a Jesuit, illustrates the dangers of a critical approach that degenerates into pyrrhonism. A Breton who entered the noviciate in 1660 and became a Jesuit in 1664, he moved to Paris in 1674 to serve as librarian at the College Louis Le Grand, as well as teaching positive theology. As a scholar, he was entrusted with editing Pliny the Elder's *ad usum Delphini* (1684). While working on chronologies and on the Church Fathers, he became convinced, between 1690 and 1692—as he himself states—that ancient history was nothing but the invention of forgers, dreamt up in its entirety in the secret of Benedictine monasteries of the fourteenth century, by hard-working but godless and atheistic monks who created a historical tradition to give legitimacy to their heresy by showing that nature and destiny had allegedly been worshipped in antiquity. These monks had even imagined an entire body of history by multiplying the writings of alleged Fathers of the Church. Trained in textual criticism, Hardouin had ended up by turning the argument of the unanimity of testimonies into proof of a conspiracy. A rational, logical man, he was profoundly disturbed by the idea of not being able to discover the truth, and expressed unequivocally his mistrust of human history, so corrupt, so unworthy of credence. The Jesuits demanded a retraction,[10] but without withdrawing their confidence in Hardouin. Hardouin's obsessions pay homage to Maurist and Jansenist scholarship, capable, if he were to be believed, of creating out of nothing a history based on a complex set of 'proofs'.

---

[10] In 1708: 'I condemn in good faith . . . that which I have said about an impious faction that would have invented over several centuries most of the ecclesiastical or profane works that have been accepted up to now as ancient classics. I am very grieved not to have realized this earlier.' See Carlos Sommervogel, *Bibliothèque de la Compagnie de Jésus*, vol. 4 (1893). The only ancient authors who were authentic in his view were Cicero (*Treatises and Speeches*), Pliny the Elder (*Naturalis Historiae*), Virgil (*Bucolica* and *Georgica*), Horace (*Satires and Epistles*), Herodotus, Plautus, and Homer.

THE HISTORIAN, A MAN OF LETTERS

Assiduous reading of Cicero's *De Oratore* [On the Orator] had convinced humanists that history was first and foremost a narrative, subject to stylistic rules and demands. The worst enemy of history, according to the time-honoured expressions *testis temporum, lux veritatis, magistra vitae, vita memoriae*, was falsehood. Along with this demand for truth came that of majesty of composition and nobility of style. One had to take care with the *ordo* and the *dispositio* in classifying one's material; then arrange (*disponere*), embellish (*excolere*), and polish (*perpolire*) the narrative.

In the France of the end of the fifteenth century, 'tormented by Italianomania',[11] New History seemed to be the only type of history appropriate for celebrating the campaigns of Charles VIII. Louis XII called for a history of France stylistically worthy of the best Italian models, and asked that it be done by an Italian. Thus Paolo Emilio, a native of Verona, summoned in 1499, came to rewrite the history of the French monarchy, and his *De rebus gestis Francorum* [History of France] (1516–19) is in fact the first humanist history of France written by a foreigner.[12] The job was difficult because France was proud of its *Grandes Chroniques*, a revised version of which had been published by Nicole Gilles in 1492. Rejecting the medieval tradition was like meddling with the monarchy. Paolo Emilio, however, had the benefit of a certain amount of freedom and was able to apply Bruni's principles, that is, patriotic intent, political and secular history, a high stylistic level, and even the critical use of sources and the rejection of legends. The Trojan origins, which had been presented as fact by Gaguin, Gilles, and Lemaire de Belges, were but a simple assertion in Emilio's narrative, and the Holy Ampulla, brought by a white dove at the baptism of Clovis, is not even mentioned. Paolo Emilio adorned his narrative, however, with the expected speeches. Seyssel, Louis XII's translator of Thucydides, had explained to the king that the '*concions*' (speeches) were the best possible examples of rhetorical eloquence.

The success of this 'foreign' history gave rise to a strong reaction, exacerbated by patriotism. The imitation of Cicero was denounced as an academic exercise. The historian proposed as a model of a simple style that is effective, direct, and without superfluous and vain ornaments was Philippe de Commynes, the 'French Titus Livius', whose work was edited in 1552 by Denis Sauvage under the new title of *Mémoires* (rather than *Chronique et histoire*).

---

[11] *Dix ans d'études historiques*, 'Notes sur quatorze historiens antérieurs à Mézeray', cf. R. Gaguin, *Oeuvres*, vol. 6 (Paris, 1856), 347.

[12] In England, in 1507, Polydore Vergil was given the mission by Henry VII of writing a History of England. The *Anglicae Historiae libri XXVI* was partially published in Basel in 1534, and the complete work in 1555.

Nevertheless, the monarchy continued to support the ideal of eloquent history as the official history that 'historiographers' should write. Louis XI, who had put an end to Saint Denis's monopoly in the field, left the title of King's Historiographer vacant, even twice refusing (1476, 1479) to give it to Robert Gaguin. Paolo Emilio received neither title nor pension. Only in the reign of Henry II was the office officially instituted (1554), and the first holder named was Pierre de Paschal, a Latin historiographer, who became the object of an offensive against eloquent history and the Ciceronian *vera et pura narratio*.[13] The title of King's Historiographer, but without a pension, was generously distributed, especially in the second half of the sixteenth century when it was distinguished by some of the greatest names in the field: André Thévet, François Hotman, François de Belleforest, Bernard du Haillan, and Claude Fauchet. Missing from this list, however, are Jean du Tillet, Etienne Pasquier, Loys le Roy, Jacques-Auguste de Thou, Jean Bodin, and Henri de la Popelinière. There were two offices: that of Historiographer of France, much rarer—eight commissions between 1550 and 1670—was considered the most prestigious. The office of King's Historiographer, on the other hand, was very liberally bestowed, especially by a power in search of legitimacy, or in need of building up new networks of loyalty. Sixty-two commissions as King's Historiographer were granted between 1550 and 1700. The importance of the office reached its peak between 1550 and 1640.

Bernard du Haillan was Paolo Emilio's successor. His *Histoire générale des rois de France* [General History of the Kings of France] (1576) presents the qualities of a 'Great History'. 'History' (with a capital H) is different from chronicles, which are inadequate, vacuous, vague, and written by ignorant, barbarian men. Du Haillan recognized only the historical model of antiquity, combined with the political and diplomatic considerations added by the Italians, and which, according to him, should only concern matters of state. Going back to Paolo Emilio's chronological framework, he added fragments of chronicles and speeches, in imitation of the writers of antiquity. Scipion Dupleix, François Eudes de Mézeray, and Father Gabriel Daniel continued the same tradition. These 'Great Histories' of France all present an uninterrupted succession of kings, from the mythical Pharamond, the first to ascend to the throne, to the predecessor of the ruling prince, and this according to a continuous numbering system that conceals any usurpations, even though the latter are discretely suggested by the succession of three different 'races' on the 'throne of the Lilies': the Merovingians, the Carolingians, and the Capetians. Without it being necessary to go back to the Great Flood or even to the siege of Troy, these histories, based on genealogies and chronologies, told the story of the oldest European monarchy, the first and most faithful ally of the Roman Church, thanks to Clovis's baptism. From one historian to the next, the narratives were not simply repeated, but

---

[13] *Nouvelle manière de faire son profit des lettres* (Paris, 1559).

were actually expanded.[14] The history of France, a patriotic manifesto, was a framework on which each historian could embroider.[15] Such a serious subject could only be written in a noble style, with speeches that constitute veritable masterpieces.

Eloquent history charms an elitist public such as might be found in Jesuit colleges, or among Cicero's followers. In opposition to the Maurists, who endeavoured to perfect a scholarly form of criticism, the Jesuits, like the Cartesians and the freethinkers, became detractors of a pedant and pretentious scholarship that accumulated insignificant details and useless proofs. Father René Rapin set the tone in his 'Comparaison de Thucydide et de Tite Live' [Comparison of Thucydides and Livy].[16] Learning does not allow one to appreciate beauty, nor to develop exquisite and delicate taste. Rapin's *Réflexions sur l'histoire* [Reflections on History] (1675) thus present the aesthetic principles of French classicism:

History must be eloquent so as not to be boring: this is mainly in what consists its art . . . The memoirs that are made available to the historian give him his material, but it is up to him to organize it . . . The narrative is perfect when nothing in it is superfluous. That, in a word, is the essence that will lead to the best possible perfection. This is exactly what Cicero and Quintilian advise in their precepts: after which I have nothing to add.[17]

Simplicity, grandeur, purity, truth, vigour, force, dignity, a natural style, these are the terms that flow freely from his pen. All the different figures are mentioned: the passions, descriptions, haranguing, portraits, reflections, and convictions. Judgement, reason, and wisdom share, however, in the beauty of the final product. As models, Rapin proposes not only Thucydides, whom he clearly prefers, but also Livy, Commynes, and Paolo Emilio.

THE HISTORIAN AS JURIST AND MAN OF THE ROBE

In *La Manière de lire l'histoire* [The Way to Read History] (1614), René de Lucinge lists the national stereotypes:

It would seem . . . that each nation has a particular gift for some science in which it outshines all the others. Nations are inhabited by people with different intellectual dispositions, inclined to write better in one profession than another. The French have given rise to great jurisconsults

[14] François Eudes Mézeray, *Histoire de France depuis Pharamond*, 3 vols. (Paris, 1685), folio, 3,316 pages. Gabriel Daniel, *Histoire de France depuis l'établissement de la monarchie française*, 10 vols. (Paris, 1729), quarto, 7,395 pages.

[15] Ph. Ariès, *Le Temps de l'histoire* (Paris, 1986), 159.

[16] René Rapin, 'Comparaison de Thucydide et de Tite Live' (1677), in id., *Oeuvres*, vol. 1 (The Hague, 1725).

[17] Id., *Oeuvres*, vol. 2, 233, 259, 308.

and, in their courts of *Parlement*, excellent lawyers whose praise has rung through the golden corridors of the seats of power, who rank among the best in eloquence and doctrine.[18]

Indeed, the figure of the legal historian became well known with the success of the French school of law—the *mos gallicus*—founded in Bourges at the beginning of the sixteenth century by Marguerite de France and Chancellor Michel de l'Hôpital. This had welcomed into its ranks prestigious professors such as the Milanese Andrea Alciato, François Hotman, and Jacques Cujas. French law, reacting against the Roman law tradition of Bologna, aimed to show the superiority of royal institutions, and gave great importance to philology and criticism of sources. The intellectual formation of *Parlementarians* thus emphasized all knowledge related to the past. This group of jurists would in turn have a profound influence both on authors and readers. An incredible number of historians received their education at this school. François Hotman studied law at Orléans, before teaching in Paris, Valence, Bourges, and Geneva. Jean Bodin studied in Toulouse before becoming a lawyer in Paris, secretary to the Duke of Alençon, then secretary to the king. Etienne Pasquier studied under Hotman and Baudoin, and at Toulouse under Cujas, before going to Pavia to hear Alciato. Claude Fauchet, after studying at Orléans, became a lawyer and adviser at the Châtelet, then president of the *Cour des monnaies* (monetary court). Jean du Tillet was registrar at the *Parlement* of Paris. Christophe, the father of Jacques-Auguste de Thou, was the first president of the *Parlement* of Paris. His son, first intended for the Church, studied theology then law; he became *maître des requêtes*, member of the Council of State and, in 1595, *président à mortier*. In Pasquier's view, only a jurist was capable of writing history since only he knew the legal practices of his time: 'A man should not undertake to take pen in hand to write history if he is not worthy to manage business in the same way'.[19]

Latin is the language of the law. Teaching in French was only introduced by Jean-Baptiste Colbert to deal with French law. Among jurists, history was therefore written in Latin: the *Methodus* [Method for the Easy Comprehension of History] by Bodin; the *Franco-Gallia* [French Gaul] by François Hotman (translated by Simon Goulart as *La Gaule franque*, 1574); the collections of sources from the eighth to the thirteenth centuries by Pierre Pithou (1539–96), *Annalium et Historiae Francorum* [Of the French Annals and History] (1588); *Historiae Francorum scriptores veteres* [Histories of the Franks by Ancient Authors] (1596). De Thou (Thuanus) wrote his *Historia sui temporis* [History of His Own Time] in Latin. Faithful to the humanist tradition, he Latinized the names of his contemporaries, thus necessitating, in 1634, the publication of a *Clavis historiae Thuanae* [Keys to the Thuanus History]. The first partial transla-

---

[18] *La manière de lire l'histoire*, ed. Michael J. Heath (Geneva, 1993), 144. The German, he adds, attained more glory through mathematics, and 'the Italians take the honours for writing History well, for their good judgement and their skill at expressing it solemnly'.

[19] 'Le Pourparler d'Alexandre', in *Recherches de la France* (Paris, 1611), 993.

tion into French, by Pierre du Ryer, is from 1659. Pasquier and Fauchet, however, chose to write in French for patriotic reasons, and each devoted long developments to this language and its literature.

The jurists also imposed the standard of proof. Historiography by those in the legal profession was based on the tradition of authenticated documents, quoted at length, and duly criticized. Pasquier, whose rule is 'never say anything important without it being based on proof', drew his information from the *Parlement* archives, the *Chambre des comptes* (Chamber of Accounts), the *Trésor des chartes* (Royal Archives), as well as the collections of the Châtelet and Saint Denis. De Thou had reports sent to him from abroad, he worked from primary diplomatic sources, and he applied a well-advised critical approach to doubtful documents. 'Let's recognize Paolo Emilio as the most eloquent historian since Livy', Fauchet writes, 'but not the most reliable'. Fauchet himself always based his work on witnesses, he compared contradictory documents, and he used every means available to 'shed light on anything obscure'. The list of sources consulted for his *Antiquités gauloises et françoises* [Gaulish and French Antiquities] covers several pages. Jurists who were historians were interested in the past (Fauchet, Pithou), or in the present (de Thou), but always as this related to the history of their own nation. Pasquier's *Recherches de la France* (1560) encompasses all aspects of France: its customs, institutions, power structure, law, society, private life, language, historical memory, education, and even its popular sayings. For Pasquier, it was not the kings who made France, nor their succession the history of France; the country exists on its own and the objective of the *Recherches* is to define its outline and identity in a way that no continuous narrative can capture. Thus the 'labyrinthine' plan of this project, composed of a succession of essays on the most varied subjects, never ceases to be enriched, year after year, by the objects of Pasquier's curiosity, producing a work that is unique, original, and a true monument to sixteenth-century historiography. So it is that jurists, magistrates, judges, lawyers, *parlementarians*, all men of the law, worked towards constructing a collective, national memory. Conscious of representing the ruling elite, they promoted their own role and gave legitimacy to their social and political ambitions, to their projects for reform, as well as to their desire to bring peace to a kingdom torn by civil wars and in danger of being split asunder.

THE MEMOIRS OF THE NOBILITY

Men of the Church, men of letters, men of the law: what then was the contribution of the *noblesse de l'épée*, the traditional aristocracy, to the writing of history? This group considered itself poorly treated by the kings, who relied on the *robe*, and poorly served by the historiographers, who ignored them. The *noblesse,* for their part, looked down upon historiographers, who were viewed as mercenary pens, people of low extraction, unfit to understand and report on the exploits of great men. Separated from power, and largely excluded from contemporary history, the nobility had their past, their memories, and their family archives. 'Memoirs' as a genre was born rather belatedly, around 1555–70—in 1569, to be more precise, with the *Mémoires* of Martin du Bellay and his brother Guillaume, edited by René du Bellay and dedicated to King Charles IX. These *Mémoires*, in practical terms, were first and foremost a case presented before the tribunal of posterity, with a scrupulous record of all their heroic acts, services rendered, and the blood tribute paid. Blaise de Monluc wrote in order to respond to the Court's ingratitude and clear himself of unjust accusations. His narrative was dedicated to King Charles IX, but also to the lords and captains (the *noblesse de l'épée*) 'so that my name will not be forgotten, nor that of so many courageous men whom I have seen in action, since historians only write for the honour of kings and princes'.[20] René de Lucinge invites noblemen to take up the pen: 'The story of our lives is the true portrait of our soul; it represents our lifestyle just as the brush represents the features of our face. Why shouldn't the aristocracy choose the best hands and the best minds of their age to engrave in history their acts so that they will be properly remembered by posterity?'[21]

Memoirs as a genre had two main models: the *Commentarii* by Caesar, who was the most popular Roman historian in France, and Commynes. They are linked together by Johann Sleidan: 'Caesar tells what he wants to say with naive simplicity, good grace, and without any stylistic affectation . . . he should serve as a model and formula for those who undertake to narrate their own deeds and accomplishments'. Commynes 'deserves to be imitated by all those who wish to write history honourably'.[22] The memoirs had their own rhetoric: *historia nuda, simplex, recta et omnibus detracta ornamentis*, a clear and genuine style, an unpretentious sobriety, free of glorification and blame, faithful to the facts.

Memoirs were a combative form of literature whereby the aristocracy settled a score with the king and the *robe*, as well as serving as a form of combat between Catholics and Protestants or between rival factions in general. While the *robe* also appropriated this new genre with the appearance of the first *parlementary* memoirs, the aristocracy used it to proclaim their freedom and their daring to be themselves. The *Mémoires de l'épée* (Memoirs of the sword) experienced their pinnacle between the Wars of Religion and in the aftermath of the Fronde, between the editions of Commynes and Jean-François-Paul Gondi de Retz, so between 1525 and 1680. The aristocracy thus told their true history, the history they themselves had made, from their point of view, instead of leaving to others the need to account for it. In this vehement appropriation, knightly heroism registered the last glorious moment of a tumultuous era. All the narratives,

---

[20] Blaise de Monluc, *Commentaires* (1521–76), ed. P. Couteault (Paris, 1964), 830.
[21] René de Lucinge, *La Manière de lire l'histoire*, 132.
[22] 'Epitre à très magnanime Prince Edouard, duc de Sommerset', in Philippe de Commynes, *Chronique et histoire faite par feu messire Philippe de Commynes*, 2nd edn (Geneva, 1596), 855, 857.

whether they be by Castelnau, Nangis, Tavannes, or others, evoke with nostalgia a passionate youth: the sun that shone during the Italian Wars, the joyous massacres of the religious wars, the mad adventures of the Fronde, the golden memories of an aristocracy drunk with power, passionate, colourful, violent, boisterous. Their time was already past under the reign of Louis XIV: most of these accounts would only see the light of day after 1715, some not until the nineteenth century. As of 1660, the decline of this genre, closely related to the vitality of a warrior aristocracy, was an accomplished fact.

With the heavy etiquette imposed by Louis XIV appeared the memoirs of life at Court, no longer indictments of the king, but celebrations. The world of the Court was a fixed one that gave rise to descriptions, scenes, or sketches, attentive studies of character; it was a world of code and etiquette that implied a constant game of learning and deciphering. A world of secrets. Almost all of the 259 memoirs listed by Émile Bourgeois and Louis André for the seventeenth century announce strange details and revelations.[23] Court memoirs are inseparable from evasive power, intimate or state secrets. The style of these memoirs has absolutely nothing in common with that of the warrior memoirs, except for the mark of the aristocracy. Saint-Simon, by the act of writing, asserts his identity and his freedom 'with the hope of being something and gaining, to the best of my ability, knowledge of the matters of my time'.[24] In this literature, the truth sought is not of a factual nature, nor is it associated with the authority of a witness; it is psychological. History teaches us knowledge about mankind.[25] Thus the boundary between history and the novel tended to become blurred. Did Saint-Réal and Varillas, both of whom conducted authentic research at the King's Library, write historical novels or romanticized history?

HISTORY OVER THE YEARS

To sum up: in the space of two centuries, history—historical knowledge and culture—and the relationship of the French with their past underwent profound transformations. Several phases of this evolution can be distinguished here. The first phase was that of the Italian Wars and the fascination with the Italian model. The amazing discovery of the Italian Renaissance and of the ancient Greek and Latin authors is not an isolated incident. The revelation of the New World led to an unprecedented curiosity and a hunger for information that even the printing press, which magically made writing available, could not satisfy. Works of ancient or modern history, travel narratives, cosmography, chronology, were all part of the 'buffet' (La Croix du Maine) of a history where time and space seemed

---

[23] Émile Bourgeois and Louis André, *Sources de l'histoire de France: XVIIe siècle* (Paris, 1913).
[24] Saint-Simon, *Mémoires*, ed. Yves Coirault, vol. 1 (Paris, 1983), 20.
[25] Saint-Réal, 'De l'usage de l'histoire', *Oeuvres*, vol. 2 (Paris, 1745), 513.

to merge. The world was opening up to men driven by curiosity, a thirst for learning, and a desire for escape. Contemporary knowledge was turned upside down and, along with it, the mental make-up, the cognitive framework, and the moral, religious, and civic foundations of society. The old theological and philosophical assumptions were put into doubt at a time when Christian Europe was being torn by the Protestant schism and living under the threat of an all-powerful Spain.

The second phase was that of a reaction against the once idolized Italy and the search for a 'French' way. The defeat at Pavia (1525) and the humiliation represented by the captivity of Francis I sparked a widespread reflection on national identity that affected jurists and men of the Church. France had to define itself with regard to two main models: the Italian model, whose most eminent claims to prestige were based on the Roman Catholic Church, antiquity, and the Renaissance; and the German model, imposed by the Reformation, supported by the Germanic myth, and the imperial myth. At a time when proving one's antiquity was equivalent, for the churches as well as for the monarchies, to reconstituting a lost unity and, above all, combating opposing claims by others, the debate over one's origins, consubstantial to humanism and the Reformation, privileged history. Between a Germanic Europe that had found its political expression in the Reformation and an Italy dominated politically by Spain (and, on the religious front, by the papacy), France sought its own path. The reaction against Italy was evident in all fields: in opposition to the Rome of the popes, France was Gallican; in opposition to ancient Rome, it glorified the Gauls; in opposition to Latin, it praised the French language (related, it was said, to Greek); in opposition to Roman law, it adopted the *mos gallicus*; in opposition to humanist history, it accentuated national traditions. This reflection on the 'French way' was already well under way before the premature death of Henry II (1559).

The third phase, which would last forty years, was marked by crisis. France, now more fragile, was no longer a conquering nation. The monarchy, entrusted to an Italian regent, Catherine de Medici, seemed weak and vulnerable. The kingdom's unity was threatened by the religious schism, and eight religious wars with their cortège of horrors ruined a kingdom already in a crisis over rights of succession, Henry III not having had any children. Forty tragic years that were decisive for history, were seen as the only tool capable of reuniting the French and overcoming their animosities. This resulted in an important effort to rethink and understand the past, a series of publications in the 1570s that were exceptional by their number, their variety, and their originality; this was an unprecedented success for history, seen as a sign of attachment to France, since it played a role of compensation and, in the minds of the *politiques*, provided the only remedy to avoid tragedy. The French were invited to rethink their relationship with the past, and a sort of collective memory developed which renewed the vision and the assessment that French society had of itself and its future.

History became everyone's business; the different social groups participated in the construction of a 'French nation' that no longer consisted of a simple succession of kings. Of course, traditional history still had the lion's share; but there were also a multitude of new works about civil and political institutions, offices, law, the magistracy, cities, and provinces. The pressing need to improve the internal situation had given a new meaning to history. Even if the political crisis was profound, a dynamic and open society could see the possibilities for change, and the quest for a national identity stimulated the construction of a rich and complex collective memory. The accession of Henry IV to the throne (1589) and the involvement of France in the Counter-Reformation marked the beginning of a new phase. History returned to the annalistic narrative, scholarly research became an end in itself, and philological analysis lost its pioneering fervour. The efforts of critical analysis from then on were concentrated on ecclesiastical and religious history. The needs of controversy, first against the Protestants, then against the Jansenists, led to a detailed study of the tradition and origins of institutions and beliefs. The 'New History' of the 1570s lost its place under the Bourbon monarchy. One sign of this was the spacing out of the reprints of Pasquier's *Recherches*: 1621, 1665. The interest in institutions, levels of power, or the law ceased to stimulate the reflection of the learned jurists: 'absolute' monarchy, soon to become monarchy by divine right, suffered no alternatives. The history of its exploits, the narrative of its wars were confined to praise: the *petite académie* (the little Academy) and the historiographers (like Racine or Boileau) could in no way compete with the chorus of panegyrics offered to the greatest of kings every 25 August, the feast day of Saint Louis, by the *Académie française* (French Academy). In this context, the French proved less anxious to meditate on their past than curious to learn the latest anecdotes from the Court. In intellectual circles, among members of the *robe,* the association between political engagement and historical reflection began to fade. As for the nobility, they were prisoners of their preoccupation with genealogy. In George Huppert's view, history, engaged in the glorification of the monarchy and in the service of the kingdom's hegemonic ambitions, was threatened by the double risk of official historiography degenerating into propaganda and learned scholarship becoming the hostage of passing conflicts of interest.[26] Above all, history had become the victim of a crisis of confidence: the repeated attacks by freethinkers and sceptics, the definitive condemnation by the Cartesians, combined with the manipulation of those in power, had discredited a discipline that even ended up losing, in the education of the young Louis XV, the privileged position that it had always been given, up to that point, by royal tutors.

Translated by Annette Hayward

---

[26] George Huppert, *L'idée de l'histoire parfaite* (Paris, 1963).

TIMELINE/KEY DATES

1429 End of Hundred Years War with England
1534 Beginning of French Reformation
1562 Start of Wars of Religion
1572 St Bartholomew's Day massacre
1589 Accession of Henri IV; beginning of the Bourbon dynasty
1598 Edict of Nantes; end of Wars of Religion
1614 Last meeting of Estates General before 1789
1643 Accession of Louis XIV
1648 The Fronde
1701–13 War of the Spanish Succession
1715 Death of Louis XIV
1756–73 Seven Years War
1789 French Revolution begins

KEY HISTORICAL SOURCES

Bayle, Pierre, *Dictionnaire historique et critique* (Rotterdam, 1693).
Belleforest, François de, *Histoire des neuf rois Charles de France* (Paris, 1568).
—— *L'Histoire universelle du monde* (Paris, 1570).
Bodin, Jean, *Methodus ad facilem historiarum cognitionem* (Paris, 1566).
Bossuet, Jacques-Benigne, *Discours sur l'histoire universelle* (Paris, 1681).
Commynes, Philippe de, *Chronique et histoire faite par feu messire Philippe de Commynes* (Paris, 1524).
Daniel, Gabriel, SJ, *Histoire de France depuis l'établissement de la monarchie française*, 10 vols. (1696; Paris, 1729).
Duchesne, André, *Antiquités et recherches de la grandeur et majesté des rois de France* (Paris, 1609).
Dupleix Scipion, *Histoire générale de France, avec l'état de l'Eglise et de l'Empire* (Paris, 1621–8).
Emilio, Paolo, *De Rebus Gestis Francorum libri IV* (Paris, 1517).
Fauchet, Claude, *Antiquités gauloises et françoises* (Paris, 1579).
Gaguin, Robert, *De Origine et gestis Francorum Compendium* (Paris, 1497); trans. as *Les Grandes Chroniques de France: excellents faits et vertueux gestes des très-Chrétiens rois et princes* (Paris, 1514).
Gilles, Nicole, *Les Chroniques et Annales de France depuis la destruction de Troie* (1492; Paris, 1525).
Haillan, Bernard Girard du, *L'Histoire générale des rois de France... ordonnée en vingt-quatre livres: Quatre livres de l'état et succès des affaires de France* (Paris, 1576).
Hotman, François, *La Gaule française* (Cologne, 1574).
La Popelinière, Sieur de, *L'Histoire des histoires avec l'idée de l'Histoire accomplie* (Paris, 1599).

Lelong, Jacques, *Bibliothèque historique de la France* (Paris, 1719).

Lenglet-Dufresnoy, Nicolas, *Méthode pour étudier l'histoire* (Paris, 1713).

Le Roy, Loys, *Considérations sur l'histoire française et l'universelle de ce temps* (Paris, 1567).

Mabillon, Jean, *Brèves réflexions sur quelques règles de l'histoire* (1677; Paris, 1990).

—— *De re diplomatica* (Paris, 1681).

Mézeray, *Histoire de France depuis Pharamond*, 3 vols. (Paris, 1643–51).

Pasquier, Etienne, *Les Recherches de la France* (1560; Paris, 1611).

Rapin, R., *Réflexions sur l'histoire* (Paris, 1675).

Scaliger, Joseph Justus, *De Emendatione Temporum* (Paris, 1583).

Serres, Jean de, *Inventaire général de l'histoire de France* (Paris, 1597).

Tarault, SJ, *Annales de France* (Paris, 1635).

Le Nain de Tillemont, Sébastien, *Histoire des Empereurs et autres princes qui ont régné durant les six premiers siècles de l'Eglise*, 16 vols. (Brussels, 1692–1710).

—— *Mémoires pour servir à l'histoire ecclésiastique*, 16 vols. (Paris, 1692–1712).

Tillet, Jean du, *La Chronique des Rois de France depuis Pharamond* (Paris, 1549).

—— *Mémoires et Recherches contenant plusieurs choses mémorables pour l'intelligence de l'état de France* (Rouen, 1578).

Vignier, Nicolas, *Sommaire de l'histoire des Français* (Paris, 1579).

—— *Bibliothèque historiale* (Paris, 1587).

BIBLIOGRAPHY

Amalvi, Christian (ed.), *Les lieux de l'histoire* (Paris, 2005).

Barret-Kriegel, Blandine, *Les historiens et le monarchie*, 4 vols. (Paris, 1988–9).

Bizzochi, Roberto, *Genealogie incredibili: Scritti di storia nell'Europa moderna* (Bologna, 1995).

Borghero, Carlo, *La certezza e la storia: Cartesianesimo, pirronismo e conoscenza storica* (Milan, 1983).

Collard, Frank, *Un historien au travail à la fin du XVe siècle: Robert Gaguin* (Geneva, 1996).

Desan, Philippe, *Penser l'histoire à la Renaissance* (Caen, 1993).

Dubois, Claude-Gilbert, *Celtes et Gaulois au XVIe siècle: le développement littéraire d'un mythe nationaliste* (Paris, 1972).

—— *La conception de l'histoire en France au XVIe siècle (1560–1610)* (Paris, 1977).

Espiner-Scott, Janet, *Claude Fauchet, sa vie, son oeuvre* (Paris, 1938).

Evans, W. H., *L'historien Mézeray et la conception de l'histoire au XVIIe siècle* (Paris, 1930).

Ferguson, Wallace, *La Renaissance dans la pensée historique* (Paris, 1958).

Fueter, Eduard, *Histoire de l'historiographie moderne* (Paris, 1914).

Fumaroli, Marc, 'Aux origines de la connaissance historique du Moyen Âge: humanisme, Réforme et gallicanisme au XVIe siècle', *Dix-Septième Siècle*, 114–15 (1977), 6–29.

Grell, Chantal, *L'histoire entre érudition et philosophie: Etude sur la connaissance historique à l'âge des Lumières* (Paris, 1993).

—— 'L'éducation de l'enfant roi', in Cardinal de Fleury, *L'Abrégé de l'histoire de France écrit pour le jeune Louis XV* (Versailles, 2004), 13–104.

Grell, Chantal (ed.), *Les Historiographes en Europe de la fin du Moyen Âge à la Révolution* (Paris, 2006).

Guenée, Bernard, *Histoire et culture historique dans l'Occident médiéval* (Paris, 1980).

Jolly, Claude (ed.), *Histoire des bibliothèques françaises*, vol. 2: *Les bibliothèques sous l'Ancien régime, 1530–1789* (Paris, 1988).

Ranum, Orest, *Artisans of Glory: Writers and Historical Thought in Seventeenth-Century France* (Chapel Hill, 1980).

Uomini, Steve, *Cultures historiques dans la France du XVIIe siècle* (Paris, 1998).

Vivanti, Corrado, 'Les Recherches de la France d'Etienne Pasquier', in Pierre Nora (ed.), *Les Lieux de mémoire*, vol. 1 (Paris, 1986), 215–47.

Chapter 20

The Historical Thought of the French *Philosophes*

Guido Abbattista

The French Enlightenment was an epoch in cultural history whose protagonists were men of letters, intellectuals, and authors sharing a common aspiration to make their mark in an innovative, critical, and generically liberal perspective, on a whole range of aspects of culture, as indeed of politics and society, in the France of their day. They confronted the traditional guardians of religious, civil, political, and social authority with new ideas on the objectives of human institutions, on the individual and collective means of pursuing them, and on the role to be fulfilled by the various social categories within the institutions. The contest of ideas—involving polemics, pressure campaigns, cultural debates, law suits, teaching activities, a new awareness of public opinion—was the sphere of action which the literati, conventionally referred to as *philosophes*, chose in order to disseminate their ideals. They sought direct personal confrontation with high-placed officials in the civil and religious institutions, from the monarch downwards; they ventured into every conceivable form of print, were active in publishing and journalism, and cultivated the social dimension of communication through letter writing and cultural gatherings. In all these contexts they disseminated a worldview based on the values of rational critique, liberty, and tolerance. Their aspiration to wield a wide-ranging and incisive cultural influence at all levels of society covered every domain of knowledge. That their aspiration consciously and profoundly affected the domain of historical knowledge can be seen in the production of numerous, innovative works of historiography, complete with philosophical and methodological reflections on the nature, conditions, and grounds of historical knowledge and the elaboration of an original and ambitious, even if contradictory, vision of history and the historical era.

The crucial importance of this overlap between the culture of the Enlightenment and the domain of history was for a long time underrated by interpretative traditions conditioned by Romanticism or idealism. Such traditions viewed the Enlightenment as a mentality with a theoretical approach based predominantly not on the perception of a historical individuality and sensibility but rather on the construction of a scientific image of the world, and on the abstract proposition of values defined rationally as criteria for interpreting the present which were also deemed valid for interpreting the past. Naturally such a view was unable to recognize the true scope of the relationship between the culture of the Enlightenment and the domain of history, the complexity and richness of the historiographical production with its philosophical and historical perspectives, and indeed the prominence that historiography had acquired in the context of the activities of the *philosophes*. Thanks to the enormous amount of research carried out above all in the second half of the twentieth century, there has been a radical change in the evaluation of the place of historiography in the cultural project of the Enlightenment and the value of the latter's specific reflection on history as a form of knowledge. Starting in the 1990s in particular, a series of factors have contributed to raising awareness of the interaction of the Enlightenment and the discipline of history: a greater attention to the literary, linguistic, and narrative aspects of historiography; a renewed interest in the close link between historiography and anthropological studies in the broad sense of the term (involving the interpretation of forms of society, worships, and customs); and a sensitivity towards the historical forms of reflection on 'otherness' and all the related phenomena (colonial expansion, imperial conquest and subjugation, slavery, commercial competition and global policies, evangelization) which collectively represent the specific connotations of Enlightenment culture. We are confronted by a remarkably rich and stimulating picture, in constant evolution by virtue of some very original contributions, which illustrates the extreme complexity of the relationship between the Enlightenment, in France in particular, and the representation of history. Correcting to some extent the received image of the nineteenth century as the 'century of history', this picture gives us a better understanding of what David Hume meant when he said of the eighteenth century: 'this is the historical Age'.[1]

What does it mean to refer to the relationship between the Enlightenment and historical knowledge as 'complex'? First and foremost there is the range of historical approaches taken by those among the exponents of the French Enlightenment who were most interested in theory, for it is impossible to contain such richness within a framework that is homogeneous, coherent, or in any way systematic. Historical knowledge involved the knowledge and interpretation of historical facts, a methodological reflection on historiographical forms, the representation of history in writing, and an overview of historical time, and in this as in other domains of intellectual enquiry, the culture of the Enlightenment produced nothing systematic: it did not yield the treatises, manuals, or methods that were to characterize the following century. Every attempt to outline the 'historical thought of the Enlightenment' runs up against the fact that this

---

[1] David Hume to William Strahan, August 1770, in *Letters of David Hume to William Strahan*, ed. G. Birkbeck Hill (Oxford, 1888), 156.

thought has to be pieced together from a whole range of expressions and formulations, on the part of different authors, and is certainly not there waiting to be identified in works or pronouncements with a comprehensive theoretical grounding. Thus, while the attempt to clarify the contents of a vision of history pertaining to the French Enlightenment may be considered legitimate, it must not be forgotten that this vision was the end product of all sorts of different contributors. The diversity and originality of their contributions is matched by their sometimes ambiguous right to inclusion in the category of *philosophes*: major authors such as Voltaire, Montesquieu, Fréret, Rousseau, and Condorcet alongside figures of lesser historiographical standing such as Mably, Turgot, Condillac, Raynal, Bailly, and Volney, together with a host of more obscure authors who nonetheless played a part in the historical and historiographical approach of the Enlightenment, from Millot to Roubaud, and Linguet to Court de Gébelin. Of all of them, it was Voltaire who was closest to being an 'historian', in the most original, continuous, and proper sense of the term, throughout his career. He came up with the most persistent, probing, and problematic reflections on the representation of history, historical knowledge, and the course of history.

What importance the culture of the Enlightenment in France attached to historical knowledge and how it tried to work out an original approach to history can be inferred by the emphasis on definition and self-definition. The *philosophes* would qualify their enquiries in an effort to give a specific, unmistakable, and contradistinctive connotation to their own version of historical knowledge: *histoire philosophique*, *histoire raisonnée* or *raisonnable*, and *histoire critique* were all locutions with which authors ranging from Voltaire to Raynal, Millot and Deslisle de Sales sought to ascribe new functions, objectives, methods, and ambitions to historical understanding. In doing this, they revealed how the characteristic Enlightenment encyclopedic propensity for neology applied also, and with particular effectiveness, to history and historiography, showing a will to appropriate this field of knowledge by investing it with peculiar attributes. Besides, the recourse to neologisms or alternatively to more specific and semantically richer uses of pre-existing words, was an explicit mark of the urge towards linguistic reform on the part of an epoch in the history of culture that—it is worth reminding—reflected on *néologismes* and ended with producing a dictionary called *néologie*, itself a word only entered in the fourth edition (1762) of the *Dictionnaire de l'Académie française* [Dictionary of the French Academy]. Traditional terms were used both to add a metaphorical value to the titles of historical enquiries and to convey the way in which the material was being organized: *discours, considérations, essai, esquisse, plan, tableau, vue, idée*, as loans from the vocabulary of the figurative arts or optics, all served to highlight the idea of synthesis, of the essential (as opposed to superfluous), of the general (rather than detail), use of selection, and the aspiration to introduce a scale of observation based not on events and incidental phenomena but on macro-changes over the long term. At the same time, however, these terms were intended to allude also to the idea of the provisory nature of the conclusions reached and the precarious nature of human enterprises, in keeping with an intellectual approach based on moderate scepticism and detachment.

We can mention one further aspect concerning the evolving vocabulary of what we refer to as the 'sciences of man'. The mid-century saw the appearance in French of two concepts in particular: *civilisation*, rich in analytical premises and interpretative implications, and soon in general use throughout Europe; and the kindred *perfectibilité*, much prized by Rousseau, Helvétius, and Condorcet and still presented as a *mot nouveau* in Jean-François Féraud's *Dictionnaire critique de la langue française* [Critical Dictionary of the French Language] (1787–8). The latter term was used to refer not only to man and his faculties but also to *l'espèce humaine* as a whole, expressing its historical and heuristic potential. Another key word in the language of the Enlightenment which, although not new, certainly acquired a greater semantic charge was *progrès*. From use in the domains of astronomy, philosophy, medicine, and military theory, it began to be used to conceptualize historical time, responding to the need to select, place in perspective, and order events. Another expression coined in the 1700s with a marked symbolic and conceptual meaning was *philosophie de l'histoire*. True, this was to take on some much more structured meanings in the course of the nineteenth century, but it was nonetheless a linguistic innovation used polemically by Voltaire to refer to his own critical and rational outlook with respect to the Christian historiographical tradition. And we can point to one final instance of the importance attached by the Enlightenment to the meaning of words, with nuances able to open up new conceptions of historical enquiry. Voltaire, who was himself both one and the other, was scrupulous in making the distinction between *historiographe* and *historien*. Both vocations responded to an instance of truth, but the former, even when not limited to serving the monarch as hagiographer, was nonetheless a man of letters in state employment, with duties established by official mandate. These duties resembled those of an annalist, and for Voltaire the position was comparable to employment collecting documentary materials. In contrast, *l'historien* had to confront *le public*, taking into account its requisites, and thus enjoyed greater scope, with more freedom to choose the register he found most appealing, the possibility of letting himself be guided by his own creativity, but also a clearer duty to denounce cases of injustice, prevarication, and public wrongdoing.

In the light of all this, one can surely recognize in the French Enlightenment a deliberate intent to intervene creatively in the profiles, modes, and registers of historical discourse. This highlights the central role of historiography in the effort made by the Enlightenment to review, recompose, or indeed 'recreate' the cultural universe. Towards the end of the century, moreover, the *Histoire des Deux Indes* [History of the East and West Indies] (1780) proclaimed, in a passage penned by Diderot, that at the climax of a succession of epochs, each of which had been characterized by a particular genre of knowledge and scholar, now at last a new phase was dawning in which pre-eminence was to be accorded to history, *une carrière immense* which he somewhat ungenerously qualified as still lacking the creative contribution of philosophy.[2]

To gain a proper understanding of the contribution made by the culture of the Enlightenment in the domain of historiography, we have to ask ourselves which were the most significant elements in the debate concerning history (*res gestae*) and above all historiography (*historia rerum gestarum*) to emerge at the start of the eighteenth century. Taken as a whole, these developments posed grave difficulties for historical knowledge as a distinct domain of knowledge. It was a highly charged debate, fuelled by three interrelated elements, which exacerbated the problem of redefining the status of historical knowledge. This status had been thrown into a general uncertainty, but at the same time, in the longer term, the way had been paved for a secularized vision of history on a par with natural history. The first element under discussion concerned the extent to which history could be 'known' on the basis of erudition, philology, and antiquarian studies, following on from the major contributions to methodology made by the Maurists and biblical criticism. This also involved discussion of the reliability of the Greek and Roman chronology of history, and more in general the criteria for validating sources. These were factors which, if on one hand they cast suspicion on erudition as being subordinate to the requirements of religious history and the interests of the Catholic Church, on the other they contributed to greater awareness of the questions of method underlying the work of historical reconstruction, expressing a clear tendency to overcome the constrictions of tradition, particularly with regard to the origins and chronology of the world and humankind. The second element was the so-called *querelle des anciens et des modernes*. This debate turned on topics betraying the wish to assign a value to historical time in terms of scientific/cultural and artistic/aesthetic acquisitions, or in general of the attributes of *civilisation*. This prompted a reflection on the comparative evaluation of a present whose superiority rested on the idea of the progress of *l'esprit humain* produced by the accumulation over time of scientific knowledge. A third element derived from the diffusion of a scientific-empirical-mathematical worldview based on Cartesian philosophy and above all on the implications of Newtonian science, resulting in the need for a well-grounded, rational knowledge of nature. The fundamental query as to how far such models of knowledge could be applied to the world of human and historical facts could not but undermine confidence—as can be seen in the theoretically reductive interpretation of erudition and history contained in d'Alembert's *Discours préliminaire* (1751) for the *Encyclopédie* (1751–72)—in a historical knowledge which nonetheless found positive input in the project of encyclopedic recom-

---

[2] *Histoire des Deux Indes*, vol. 3 (Paris, 1780d), 128–9; the passage is shown to be by Diderot by G. Goggi's edition of the *Pensées détachées*, 2 vols. (Siena, 1976), ii. 394.

position, comprehension, and control of nature fuelled by the scientific approach.

Our consideration of the evolution of history must look beyond the intellectual context. We cannot ignore how, at the turn of the century and in particular in the first two decades of the eighteenth century, a whole mosaic of historical events across Europe created the preconditions for a profound renewal of the ability to view the history of Europe and European civilization within Western culture. We have in mind the political, institutional, dynastic, and international stabilization of areas of conflict, albeit still with elements of precariousness (ranging from England, fresh from the Glorious Revolution and union with Scotland, to France, post-Louis XIV and the Regency; Spain, with the Bourbons newly on the throne, to Austria in the aftermath of the siege of Vienna and the peace of Passarowitz; and again Russia, victorious in the Great Northern War against arch-rival Sweden). Then there was a new phase of commercial, naval, and colonial activity on the part of the major European powers in America and the East, thanks also to the simultaneous decline of leading imperial players such as Spain in the New World, the Ottoman Empire in the Balkans and Eastern Mediterranean, and the Mughal Empire in the Indian subcontinent. This was accompanied by an intensification of relations and contacts between the European and non-European spheres through the mediation of civil and religious agents who found themselves the protagonists of intercultural experiences which had a profound impact on their respective homelands and on the *République des lettres* in general. These were macro-phenomena of global history which helped to determine a new approach to the collocation and role of Europe in the world and in history. In addition they exerted a powerful influence on the capacity for perception and historical thought in the context of the culture of the Enlightenment, in France in particular. Without all the elements we have evoked thus far it would be impossible to account for the typical propensity of the 'movement' or 'cultural era' which, above all in France, is referred to as the Enlightenment to elaborate a self-definition and self-awareness as a distinct historical epoch: surely this is an absolutely distinctive feature of the sensibility, reflection, and historical thought of the French Enlightenment. The perception of the self, the ability to classify objects of knowledge according to scales of priority established by utilitarian criteria, the claim, always tempered by a healthy scepticism, to a clear vision of the present reality, constantly poised between optimism, disillusionment, and pessimism, and the intellectual disposition to question the grounding of one's own identity, are all aspects of the mentality and culture of the Enlightenment which proved able to nurture historical thought and render it fertile.

What then were the more specific priorities, objectives, and requisites which went to orient the attitude of the French Enlightenment to history, as the key perhaps to what we may legitimately refer to as 'historical thought'? One of the salient features of the historical culture of the Enlightenment is the pronounced capacity for self-perception and the related urge to position oneself in the history of humankind and civilization. From this point of view the French Enlightenment set out to assert itself as a key moment in a centuries-old process involving the liberation of critical reason, the gradual acquisition of a scientific knowledge of the world, and revolt against tradition and the abuses perpetrated in its name. Thus a first level of historical thought and discourse can be seen precisely in the forms taken by this self-awareness. One particular example is the autobiographical, historical, and philosophical overview elaborated, with an eye to tracing the history of modern European culture, by some exponents of the Enlightenment, and notably in d'Alembert's *Discours préliminaire* and Turgot's *Plan du second discours sur les progrès de l'esprit humain* [Second Discourse on the Gradual Progress of the Human Spirit] (1750). This paved the way for Condorcet's *Esquisse d'un tableau historique des progrès de l'esprit humain* [Sketch for a Historical Picture of the Progress of the Human Mind] (1795), itself an example of how a work of cultural autobiography could evolve into a full-blown philosophy of history and civilization, representing a truly mature expression of the historical thought of the French Enlightenment. Nonetheless it is worth reminding ourselves that it was precisely the *Discours préliminaire* that provided one highly important aspect of the way in which the French Enlightenment strove to pin down its own original theoretical contribution and historical and cultural identity. This is the distancing from the tradition of the *érudits* which constituted one of the most characteristic features of the Enlightenment approach to historical knowledge. This involved a reconstruction of history based not on a mechanical, albeit systematic, accumulation of details, but on philosophy, reason, and a critical analysis of data from the real world, *in primis* man and the universe of his needs, passions, and psychology. Thus in erudition we can identify the first counter-distinctive element through which to define an idea of history capable of 'philosophical' knowledge, deriving that is from the rational pursuit of material causes independent of tradition, authority, and institutions whether civil or religious. With its implicit appeal to freedom of thought, this emerged as the most original and effective factor in connotating the historical epistemology of the Enlightenment and providing a conceptual tool for ensuring its autonomy from the historiographical tradition. Voltaire provides some particularly eloquent examples of this polemical stance vis-à-vis the knowledge of the *érudits*, never missing an opportunity to deride its sterility, lack of taste, and futility.

Nonetheless it would be a mistake to believe that the culture of the Enlightenment expresses a univocal rejection of erudition. The mathematician d'Alembert himself, in the *Encyclopédie* entry *Erudition*, identified the necessary functional relationship between erudition and historical knowledge, and stressed that the former was inseparable from the exercise of *la critique*, meaning that faculty which, striving to avoid 'deux excès . . . trop d'indulgence, et trop de sévérité' ['two excesses . . . too much indulgence and too much severity'], but also a facile recourse to *conjectures*, not only went to establish the exact meaning of texts but could also provide rules for verifying the degree of truthfulness among historians and truth in historical facts. This kind of erudition—which united knowledge of historical facts, knowledge of languages, and textual criticism—had to be distinguished from pedantry. Thanks to its contribution, d'Alembert goes on elsewhere to take a position, in the *querelle des anciens et des modernes*, that the moderns have been able to invent a *philosophical* or *critical* brand of history—'histoire raisonnée et approfondie'[3]—as distinct from history-as-chronicle devoid of any criticism, selection or taste, and pedantic erudition for its own sake.

At the same time we cannot mention erudition without recalling the importance of the methodological and procedural contribution deriving from the work of an *érudit* who is not immediately identified with the Enlightenment but who can surely be included among the *philosophes*, namely Nicolas Fréret. His most important theoretical contributions to the epistemology of history were *Réflexions sur l'étude des anciennes histoires et sur le degré de certitude de leurs preuves* [Reflections on the Study of Ancient History and the Degree of Certainty of their Evidence] (1724) and *Vues générales sur l'origine et le mélange des anciennes Nations, et sur la manière d'en étudier l'histoire* [General Views on the Origin and the Mixture of Old Nations, on How to Study their History] (1744). These writings stand as among the most significant examinations of the relationship between erudition, seen as being responsible from ancient times for undeniable progress in methods of investigation, and the discipline of history which had to be *philosophique*. Identifying rules and principles which could well have been formulated by any man of letters of the Enlightenment, Fréret argues that history can achieve such a 'philosophical' status by combining critical procedures, logical argumentation, and the urge to formulate and answer questions of a general nature, also with recourse to all the accessory knowledge acquired with the help of what we would call 'auxiliary disciplines'.[4] In spite of his declarations of the autonomy of profane history and his acceptance of chronologies, such as that proposed by the Chinese, which contradicted the biblical framework, Fréret's contribution actually had little or no impact on the Enlightenment debate concerning history. The same was true for the work of another leading *académicien*, Joseph de Guignes, who imported into Western historical knowledge the history of the nomad peoples of Central Asia, and who occupies a place of honour in the historiography of eighteenth-century France, even though he, too, is not traditionally considered an Enlightenment figure. In fact, recognition of the importance of his *Histoire des Huns, des Mongoles des Tartares* [History of

---

[3] *Réflexions sur l'histoire, et sur les différentes manières de l'écrire*, in *Oeuvres complètes de d'Alembert*, vol. 2, part 1 (Paris, 1821–2), 7.

[4] *Vues générales sur l'origine et le mélange des anciennes Nations, et sur la manière d'en étudier l'histoire*, in *Histoire de l'Académie Royale des Inscriptions et Belles-Lettres, avec les Mémoires de Littérature tirés des Registres de cette Académie, depuis l'année MDCCXLIV jusques et compris l'année MDCCXLVI*, vol. 18 (Paris, 1753), 49–71.

the Huns, Mongols, and Tartars] (1756–8) came not from the latter milieu but from Edward Gibbon, the historian who achieved a unique compendium of erudition and 'philosophical history' and who professed himself an admirer of both Fréret and de Guignes.[5]

It should be enough to mention these two leading historians from the Académie des Inscriptions to guard against making hasty and superficial contrasts between historiography and the Enlightenment idea of history, on the one hand, and the history of the *érudits* and *académiciens* on the other. Such a simplistic dualism inevitably risks disguising the fact that the latter—at least as it emerges from a close investigation of the activities of the Académie des Inscriptions during the eighteenth century—undoubtedly constituted an autonomous line of historical enquiry, upheld by methodological awareness and endowed with explicit programmes with universal historical aspirations. This involved in the first place the study of the origins of peoples and nations of antiquity through a reconstruction of genealogies and migrations, in a perspective which was clearly alternative to stadialist and conjectural philosophies of history, which recur in the subsequent historiography of the French Enlightenment. At the same time it risked providing corroboration for that caricature of erudition which had become a genuine *topos* in the polemics on history developed by the French Enlightenment, also for self-representation purposes.

For in fact nothing came in for more regular derision on the part of the *philosophes* than the arid, massive, suffocating compilations of men of learning which offended not only the critical sensibility but also the sense of stylistic and literary quality that characterized intellectuals who looked to historical writing for instruction, aesthetic pleasure, and communicative efficacy. This is what Voltaire had in mind when he complained that 'la France fourmille d'historiens et manque d'écrivains' ['France swarms with historians and is lacking in writers'] and declared his preference for being 'le peintre et non l'historien' ['the painter and not the historian']. And this was the point of Mably's comment: 'j'aime un historien qui m'a rendu philosophe, quand je ne songeois qu'à m'amuser' ['I love an historian who made me a philosopher whereas I just cared to amuse myself'].[6]

The insistence on the theme of choice, selection, and evaluation which recurs constantly in the reflections of the Enlightenment on the representation of history—in Voltaire first and foremost, right from the minor piece *Remarques sur l'histoire* [Remarks on History] (1742)—and which emerges, for example, in

[5] See Edward Gibbon, *History of the Decline and Fall of the Roman Empire*, ed. J. B. Bury, 7 vols. (New York, 1972), i. 218 n. 4; and *The Miscellaneous Works of Edward Gibbon*, ed. Lord J. Sheffield, 5 vols. (London, 1914), v. 67.

[6] Voltaire to Thieriot, July 1735, and Voltaire to Abbé d'Oliver, January 1736. Gabriel Bonnot, abbé de Mably, *De la manière d'écrire l'histoire. Second entretien. Des histoires particulières; quel en doit être l'objet: Observations ou règles communes à tous les genres d'histoire* (1783), in *Oeuvres complètes de l'abbé de Mably*, vol. 12 (Lyon, 1796), 321–500, online at http://www.eliohs.unifi.it/testi/700/mably/ecrire.html (accessed 15 July 2009). All translations are mine unless otherwise noted.

the opposition of a simplified and polemical image of erudition, reveals a will to produce a historical-historiographical construct in terms of both substance and form. This is an unequivocal indication that the attitude of the French Enlightenment to the subject matter of history and its literary expressions was anything but passive, but on the contrary highly creative and inventive. In fact this attitude was reflected in a conscious project of construction of historical knowledge, its contents, overall image, grammar and syntax, the vocabulary of its verbal and literary representation, and its modalities of discourse, with marked attention for the communicative aspect, for its public and the possible, and desirable, political, social, and educative function. The first and essential requisite for a sound historical knowledge was freedom from the command of religious orthodoxy. The biblical vision of the history of humankind and nations was identified as the chief rival in the competition for control over the constituent elements of universal history: chronology, genealogies, geography, global population, the destiny of humankind, the ultimate factors behind the various epochs in a historical progress traditionally subordinated to sacred history in the Hebraic-Christian mould, as set out in the classic *Discours sur l'histoire universelle* [Discourse on Universal History] (1681) by Jacques-Benigne Bossuet, bishop of Meaux and tutor to the Dauphin.

If, then, universal history was the first, fundamental frame that Enlightenment historiographers set out to reform in a secular, materialist sense, it was not only the framework that they intended to transform, but also the content. The universal historian of the French Enlightenment *par excellence*, Voltaire, was determined to propagate not only the transcending of the temporal limits of Christian theological history, dispensing with the trite disputes on biblical chronology and recognizing the possibility of peoples and civilizations pertaining to the vast domain of antiquity, borne out by astronomical observations, but also the need to widen the horizon, going beyond the Judaea-centred view based on the Mediterranean and Near East to include the New World and the great oriental civilizations which history could no longer sideline. The *Essai sur les moeurs et l'esprit des nations* [Essay on the Manners and Spirit of Nations] (1756) was Voltaire's second great historical project after the *Siècle de Louis XIV* [The Age of Louis XIV] (1751), whose composition took more than a quarter of a century (1745–75). It set out to be a model universal history, with the *Philosophie de l'histoire* [Philosophy of History] (1766) added by way of introduction, and not only for the markedly anti-Christian valence with which Voltaire responded to Bossuet's *Discours*. The revolutionary nature of the *Essai* consists not only in its complete dispensation with the theological/providentialistic schemes of historiography, adopting a wholly laical and temporal perspective, but also in the rejection of the literary persona of the courtier or panegyrist. Voltaire was not writing for princes or potentates: the work was addressed to a *lecteur philosophe*, and set out to meet the requisites of the latter in terms of understanding the world, literary tastes, and intellectual curiosity. To this end, as previously in the

Siècle, the title itself presents a clear choice concerning the object of history and what is of genuine significance: not a bare chronicle of facts, particularly if these are painful and cruel, testifying to the irrationality and all the worst vices of humankind, but rather the 'spirit' of peoples and nations and their 'customs', meaning whatever defines their character and constitutes their multiple quintessence. 'Nature', representing human passions and needs, provides a criterion of order and unity, combining with 'culture', meaning the totality of practical, scientific, and artistic acquisitions and elements (laws, commerce, finance, agriculture, population) to define—much more than the unhealthy ambitions of power and conquest that distinguish the tormentors of the human race—the true civilization of a nation. This does not mean that the narrative of the wicked deeds of former times no longer regards the historian; on the contrary, the knowledge of errors and evil is also indispensable to an understanding of an epoch. And then history remains nonetheless a tribunal and place of education: 'a whole people'—Voltaire observes, assigning to history a 'pre-emptive' function— 'find it right that the fathers' faults are expounded before their eyes; they like to condemn and believe to be better than them. The historiographer or the historian encourages this feeling of theirs; and going to the origins of the Fronde's wars and of the Wars of Religion, they prevent that they occur again.'[7] 'Historians'—according to Montesquieu—'are strict examiners of the deeds of those who have been living on earth and they are like those Egyptian magistrates who convened in judgement the souls of the dead'.[8] Diderot, in one of the typical apostrophes with which he subsequently enriched, or rather stuffed, the *Histoire des Deux Indes*, went even further, conveying a clear idea of history as a form of knowledge capable of exacting revenge: 'The moment is coming when reason, justice and truth will snatch from the hands of ignorance and flattery a pen which they have been holding for too long. Tremble you who nourish men with falsehoods or make them suffer under oppression. You'll be judged.'[9]

The historian, according to Voltaire, should also make a second sort of choice, which concerns the period of time he has to deal with: not the ancient world, which had to be stripped of a plethora of mystification, myth, and legend before it could be the object of plausible knowledge, nor medieval times, the uncontrasted dominion of superstition fuelled by the religious power of the Church and the interests of the potentates, but modernity, with its roots, its non-linear, and indeed laborious and contradictory emergence from the disorderly actions of men under the sway of passions, interests, spirit of initiative and adventure, and contrasted by the irrepressible force of fanaticism, ignorance, and abuse. Voltaire is categorical in this regard:

---

[7] 'Historiographe', *Dictionnaire philosophique*, in *Oeuvres complètes de Voltaire*, ed. L. Moland, 70 vols. (Paris, 1877–85), xix. 373.

[8] *Pensées* (Siena, 1976), 419 n. 1260.

[9] *Histoire des Deux Indes*, 129.

It seems to me that if one wanted to make the best of the present time, one would not spend his life to become infatuated with ancient fables. I would suggest to a young man to endow himself with a slight veneer of those remote times; but I would like that one started a serious study of history on those times when it becomes really interesting to us: and it seems to me that this happens about the end of the fifteenth century.[10]

Moreover, in a flash of his proverbial extremism, Voltaire maintained in the *Siècle de Louis XIV* that one could only legitimately speak of 'Frenchmen' from the age of Richelieu onwards, since prior to that time the nation's history was exclusively peopled with examples of crudeness and *barbarie*.[11]

Contents, space, and time: these are the coordinates which guided the selection and traced the profile of the chosen object of study for the historian of the Enlightenment: European identity, the *civilisation* of modern Europe, what defines its essence and role in the domain of history, politics, and the global relations of civilizations. Thus history has the demanding task of constructing an identity on the basis of a reflection on the benefits and losses, merits and demerits, the steps forward and the steps backward, or as we should say the mutations and the immunity to change recognizable in the different epochs. Rejecting forms of history based on insubstantial documentary bases (with their futile focus on details which have become meaningless with the passage of time) or those which were hidebound in their adhesion to the court circle, Voltaire took as the focus for his own enquiries exclusively the 'seules révolutions frappantes qui ont changé les moeurs et les lois des grands États' ['only astonishing revolutions which have changed the manners and the laws of the large States'].[12]

While in this connection one is likely to come face to face with the problem of history's 'utility', there is another opposition—to add to the one with sterile erudition and compilation devoid of discernment and focus—that helps to define the concept of history that characterized the Enlightenment in general, and Voltaire in particular. This is the opposition between history and invention or myth, meaning those 'fables' which inevitably obscure, and render unreliable, the versions of their own past elaborated by ancient peoples and nations.[13] All through his extraordinary intellectual life, Voltaire never ceased speculating on the value and meaning of history. Perhaps his most significant considerations on these 'fables' are to be found in the essay 'Histoire' commissioned for the *Encyclopédie* and printed in the *Questions sur l'Encyclopédie* [Questions on the Encyclopedia] (1771). To say that the fables of the ancients or indeed the historiography of medieval times cannot be relied upon in the pursuit of historical truth does not mean to say that they are useless. Without reneging

---

[10] *Remarques sur l'histoire* [1742], in *Oeuvres complètes de Voltaire*, xvi. 134–7, on 136.

[11] *Siècle de Louis XIV*, in *Oeuvres complètes de Voltaire*, vol. 11 (Oxford, 2012), par. 107–9.

[12] *Histoire de l'empire de Russie sous Pierre le Grand* (1759), in *Oeuvres complètes de Voltaire*, vol. 46 (Oxford, 1999), par. 47.

[13] See also ch. 13 by Peter Burke in this volume.

on his conviction that only whatever stands up to a modern critical sense can be accepted in a historical reconstruction, Voltaire saw them as being of great interest as sources for the *histoire des opinions*, or indeed of *la crédulité humaine* and of errors, but also for the history of beliefs and of a people's ways of thought: 'the roughness itself of these monuments [pseudo-histories dating from medieval times] shows us the spirit of the times when they were made, and there is nothing, including legends, which cannot teach us to know the manners of our nations'.[14]

Thus there can be no doubt that the Enlightenment attitude towards history was extremely demanding, requiring of the historian a major intellectual commitment which involved a critical reappraisal of the models of the classical and humanistic past. This was a history that had to be selective, discerning, and critical; a history that distinguished and judged and which proposed both teachings and models. But also, and above all, it was to be a history able to account for facts: the major facts from the past and those facts with an immediate bearing on understanding the present. The pursuit of a knowledge of the past able to identify causal relationships, necessary links, and mechanisms of change was a consequence of the scientific approach to the natural world. It was Montesquieu who applied this pursuit most rigorously in terms of historical analysis and economic, social, and juridical enquiry. He did so with reference specifically to the history of republican liberty in Rome and to the vicissitudes of the history of the French nation observed from the standpoint of the evolution of the forms of property, the law, and government; and more generally in his quest for a governing principle able to throw light on the functioning of human institutions right across the historical and geographical board. Undoubtedly Montesquieu's paramount interest was political, concerning the idea of liberty and the forms it took down the ages. He did not interrogate history as a man of letters, seeking a tale of events as provided by an historian-narrator. It was the dynamics of politics, of forms of government, and of laws in their interaction with the physical setting which inspired his historical outlook. This emerges in the *Considérations sur les causes de la grandeur des Romains et de leur décadence* [Considerations on the causes of the Greatness of the Romans and of their Decline] (1734), and grants him, backed up with an immense knowledge of sources and documents, a remarkable penetration into the innermost workings of historical causality, imbued both with elements pertaining to the material sphere and with that *esprit général* which involves complex political, religious, and cultural factors, as well as aspects of mentality, popular passions, and collective psychology.

Here we meet the problems of historical causality and historical change. What was the Enlightenment attitude towards these most crucial problems in historical

---

[14] *Essai sur les moeurs*, ed. R. Pomeau, vol. 1 (Paris, 1963), 298.

understanding and historical thought? Again, it is very difficult to give a simple, single answer. Enlightenment historians were not, on the whole, disposed any longer to admit the influence in human affairs of transcendent, providential causes, descending from an inscrutable divine will. This is not tantamount to saying that history was under the complete, effective control of human will and intentionality, however great the Enlightenment propensity for lawgivers and demiurgic figures in history. A strong sense of the impersonal forces acting and determining the historical course and events is what emerges from Enlightenment historiography. Such forces are variously represented by material, geographical, environmental, and economic circumstances which affect human societies and govern their inner working and change in history; but also by the inner dynamics of political regimes, governed by their own laws exactly as human and natural bodies are. Human intentionality, and the role of individuals in history cannot be appraised, as a consequence, without a full understanding of what may be best summarized by the key notion of 'circumstance'. It is around this concept that the great complexity of historical change is manifested in Enlightenment historiography, in its effort to combine conceptions of regularities or laws governing the course of collective historical entities such as states, societies, orders, classes, and peoples. This was a powerful perception of general, invisible historical forces which still allowed for the role of human genius, will or intentions, and, more generally, for historical individuality. 'Souvent les circonstances changent la nature des choses' ['Often circumstances change the nature of things'] is the new observation, neatly appraising the part due to 'circumstance', to be found in the 1762 edition of the *Dictionnaire de l'Académie* as an addition to the 1694 entry. This approach, most visible in a historiography so much devoted to great men's deeds—Henry IV, Louis XIV, Charles XII, Peter the Great, Muhammad—undoubtedly often results in a sceptical attitude with respect to the possibility of man's sound mastery of his and his fellows' destiny, and discloses an historical outlook inspired by what has been termed 'law of the heterogeneity of ends'.[15] Circumstances, material conditions, chance, and elusive impersonal forces often make history into something very different from the product of conscious human behaviour. This outlook may even concede the role of paradox, unpredictability, a disproportionate relation between causes and effects, and an erratic idea of historical change.

There was another typical element of innovation that distinguished the historical thought of the French Enlightenment, once again concerning both the contents of historical discourse and also its formal expressions. The definition of its own contents on the part of historiography and reflection on history focused on modern history, the history of *civilisation* and its achievements, but also on the errors and the horrors which have haunted the history of humankind

[15] Duncan Forbes, '"Scientific Whiggism": Adam Smith and John Millar', *The Cambridge Journal*, 7 (1954), 643–70.

and continue to beset it. *L'histoire philosophique* refers to all this with another expression which it introduced into common usage: *l'histoire de l'esprit humain*. This refers to an implicit idea of successive stages of perfection, emerging from the dark ages of barbarism with the gradual attainment of a civilized condition involving the refinement of man's material and intellectual capacities and, indeed, the realization of a full 'humanity'. In this sense *histoire philosophique* is both an anthropology and a philosophy of history which expresses itself in the form not of factual *narrations* but rather of succinct *representations*. It uses sweeping brushstrokes to depict epochs and phases of human history governed by a universal-historical providentialism within a secular framework, yet it is not necessarily mono-directional. In Turgot's *Plan* and Condorcet's *Esquisse* one is indeed confronted with a history of progress involving gradual ascent, in which the living conditions of people and (Western) societies are steadily improved, and everything is projected towards future achievements. But this can also take on the aspect of a stark account of facts and concrete historical allusions featuring a process of *involution*, with a loss of humanity and an inverse ratio of civilization, customs, and personal liberty, as in Rousseau's 'first' and 'second' *Discours* (1750 and 1755). Here we have typical expressions of an historical vision elaborated within the culture of the Enlightenment, even though the value to be assigned to the march of history is highly problematic. In spite of the fact that there is nothing expository about the context, it is nonetheless history which provides the backdrop to Rousseau's reasoning. Naturally history constitutes the temporal dimension for the evolution of the human condition, but for Rousseau it can be encapsulated in certain phenomena or essential concepts such as 'need', 'property', 'inequality', 'virtue', 'arts and sciences', 'luxury', 'corruption', 'subservience': these are as it were so many points dotted along a fateful and apparently inexorable trajectory that leads in directions greatly at variance with the rational and optimistic providentialism of the standard bearers of progress *à la* Condorcet.

If the distinctive traits of historiography and the conception of history in the Enlightenment can be identified as a construction of the object of enquiry in terms of both choice of subject and mode of observation, perspective, and aims, striving after an original expository style in view of communicating with a wide reading public, a militant view of historical writing as the vehicle for expressing political, social, and religious criticism and proclaiming values, and irreverence in the face of any form of political or religious authority, there is one work in particular which seems to sum up these features with particular efficacy. The *Histoire philosophique et politique des établissements et du commerce des Européens dans les deux Indes* [Philosophical and Political History of the Settlements and Trade of the Europeans in the East and West Indies] (1770–80) dates from the full maturity of the French Enlightenment, although since it does not conform to the canons of the genre, it does not qualify as an example of historiographical excellence. Its authorship is conventionally ascribed to Guillaume-Thomas

Raynal, but in fact it was the product of an extensive team effort, with Diderot playing a fundamental and decisive part in the operation. It had an extraordinary influence on contemporary historical and political culture, and can legitimately symbolize some of the most significant historiographical achievements that characterized the Enlightenment. At its heart is a twofold choice: thematic and functional. It is first and foremost a history of the origins of European modernity which, with the two adjectives that feature in the title, *philosophique et politique*, takes an explicit stand within a particular set of problems and aims at objectives belonging to the sphere not of scholarship but of politics. The history of the formation of modern Europe derives directly not from the political, military, and diplomatic history of the European states system, but rather the history of what are identified as the two constituent factors in the historical dynamic of modern Europe: large-scale commerce overseas, involving colonial expansion and the extension onto the global scale of the economic, political, military, religious, and cultural activities of both the individuals and states of Europe; and the setting-up of a new network of relationships with peoples and nations outside Europe which had acquired a direct role in the global equilibrium. The subject matter, which up until now had been predominantly the domain of the highly successful genre of travel literature, now emerges as the protagonist of a new historical reconstruction. This, without in the least obscuring its national dimensions, proposes a comparative reconsideration of the phenomena that have disrupted the patterns of existence and co-existence among European states. Even without the ability to narrate it, or to make a serious attempt to observe from the inside the history and condition of 'others', it was nonetheless through the recounting of European achievements, together with the facts and dynamics of colonization and the penetration of far-off lands, that historical writing became global in scope. A renewed sense of the prevailing interconnections and interdependence helped the writing of history abandon 'universal' history as a mere accumulation of facts and evolve towards the pursuit of explanatory schemes that tended to unify. This then represented the history of activities and classes that traditionally remained excluded from the 'noble' echelons of modern European societies, and which were seeking a definitive social and political legitimization; but it also encompassed the history of encounters with what was 'other' in natural, human, and social terms, stimulating new questions concerning the forms of power, cults, life in societies, culture, modes of subsistence, and relations with the environment. All this anthropological and ecological variety found its way into this encyclopedia of mercantile and expansionist modernity—not, however, without soliciting a profound reconsideration of the values which, at the culmination of an historical process extending over centuries, underpin the Western world and civilization. Thus historical reconstruction came to promote a severe criticism of the misdemeanours and conquests, the acts of violence, deception and injustice in trade, the artifices of the missionaries, the cruelty spawned by the greed for profit and the love of excess, and the horrors of slavery, resulting in unresolved questions concerning the absolute value of European *civilisation*, its relationship with nature, natural law, and the rights of humanity.

In methodological terms the *Histoire des deux Indes* was compromised by the absence of any indication of sources, which Edward Gibbon for one found particularly disturbing. It is undeniably an anomalous work, variegated and impossible to tie down with a univocal definition or a coherent set of ideas. It is in fact a compilation of pre-existing printed matter, rich in philosophical, political, anthropological, and religious digressions, a manifesto of values and proposals for reform in the best Enlightenment manner, an up-to-date encyclopedia of naturalistic information on non-European realities, some of it of extraordinary interest and originality. It is particularly useful on the politics accompanying the balance of power in a world in which civilizations, empires, and fledgling nations confronted each other during an era which has been labelled the 'crisis of the seaborne empires'.[16] Thus it is a work which brings together not only historical ideas but also all the contradictory values championed by the French Enlightenment. It undoubtedly represented a Eurocentric vision, informed by the positive acknowledgement of the acquisitions and progress made by Western Europe. But at the same time expressions of unease at the dehumanizing effect wrought by modernity on man's natural essence can be discerned. It is an apology of commerce as a vehicle of civilization, but also a critique of the corruption provoked by a commercial culture whose protagonists are impelled by the logic of profit and dominion to engage in a ruthless struggle involving far-off peoples and countries, drawing them into conflicts to which they were completely extraneous. It is a criticism of the violence and abuses of power perpetrated by European colonialism, including slavery, and a warning concerning the profoundly corrupting effects which imperial and colonial domination produce on liberty and morality in the metropolises and on the behaviour of European expatriates. At the same time it views colonialism and imperialism as an inalienable dimension of modern civilization, which may nonetheless be rectified by means of internal reform and corrections in a humanitarian and liberal perspective. On the subject of black slavery the editors pass from exhortations to revolt to projects of philanthropical reform with a reconciling, pacifying intent. America is at one and the same time the natural world of degeneration and immaturity as evoked by Buffon and Cornelis de Pauw and the land of the vindicated colonized, whose struggle for independence heralds a future of political and religious liberty. It is a diatribe against the worst aspects of society, politics, and morality which predominated in contemporary Europe. It freely expresses admiration for the simplicity and naturalness of uncivilized societies and for ancient non-European cultures, but at the same time propounds a monolithic idea of civilization for export to savages who are seen as potential

[16] J. G. A. Pocock, *Barbarism and Religion*, vol. 4: *Barbarians, Savages and Empires* (Cambridge, 2005), 229.

beneficiaries of a project of betterment involving the introduction of agriculture, the arts, and the Christian religion. Indeed all the contradictions, preoccupations, and ambiguities of the Enlightenment are to be found in the great historical fresco depicting the advent of modern Europe as an expanding civilization committed to progress and as the scenario of chronic political, social, judicial, and religious abuses, prior to a great salvific event which is clearly presaged in the pages of the *Histoire des deux Indes*.

This major achievement, linked with the names of Raynal and Diderot, actually highlights a series of contradictory elements which characterized the Enlightenment vision of history. It expresses the typical issues of the idea of progress, the vocation for civilization and cosmopolitan universalism, seen particularly clearly when it faces the new provinces of historical knowledge represented by the non-European countries, peoples, and cultures then being discovered in the wildernesses of America and Africa, in the nomadic barbarian populations of Central Asia, and in the great civilizations of the East. One of the keys to understanding the *Histoire des deux Indes* is undoubtedly the encounter with an 'alien' world, and its response was continuously fluctuating. The pursuit of constants in human nature and the proclamation of the universal nature of needs, passions, morality, and the fundamental laws governing the behaviour of an individual alone, in the family and in society, coexists with unstinting admiration, in a relativist mould, for the variety of cults, sexual customs, religious ideas, and forms of society and authority encountered. The idea of the unitary nature of the human race and the quest for cosmopolitan bases for resolving conflicts—in a universe rendered peaceful by exchanges and the play of properly acknowledged reciprocal interests—does not do away with the sense of the irreducibility of the differences; but neither can it produce an example of successful coexistence, except perhaps in the extreme form of the evangelical-communal experiments carried out by the Jesuits with the natives who were the object of their missions. The intellectual curiosity shown towards the non-European world, accompanied on the one hand by a frank admission of the faults of Western Christendom, and on the other by a recognition of the value of each and every historical form of civilization and culture, were not enough to overcome a deep-seated Eurocentrism. There remained a fundamental inability to speak of 'others' and write their history letting their voices be heard, or to narrate the historical facts irrespective of the encounter with Europeans, so that history continued irremediably to be a history of 'us', incapable of integrating that of the 'diverse'.

When it comes down to it, the interpretation and vision of history elaborated by the culture of the Enlightenment did not succeed in assuaging these uncertainties; rather, it acted as a telescope for observing how they determined the unpredictable fate of humankind. Such uncertainties did not lead univocally either to pessimism or optimism, but made for a perpetual oscillation between one and the other, while awaiting the advent of a regenerative event for which the late Enlightenment found abundant omens. In other contexts, thanks to different contributions and experiences, it proved possible to evolve methods, tools, and ideas able to overcome these limits or at least to lay down the cultural premises for doing so. This came about above all on the strength of specialist knowledge, the definition of new fields of enquiry, and new linguistic, philological, and anthropological skills which, from the 'Oriental renaissance' to the development of modern ethno-anthropology and comparative juridical studies, opened up new horizons and made it possible to look outwards and attempt a reconstruction on new bases of the historical existence of non-European civilizations or their integration in explicative models of socio-anthropological phenomenology. Nonetheless the creative tension between nature and history which stimulated and fuelled historical perception and thought in the French Enlightenment was destined to remain always active.

To conclude, it is worth reviewing some specific manifestations of the historiographical interests of the mature Enlightenment and the relative visions of history which emerge. They point to an area of overlap between the line of enquiry typically pursued by *académiciens* and *érudits* and the historical culture of the mature Enlightenment. This much emerges from the genuine curiosity Voltaire showed for these enquiries (albeit belatedly and in contradiction of previous pronouncements in which he had been suspicious of research into the origins of peoples, which he saw as straying into conjecture, if not legend and fable). These enquiries involved reflections and interpretations concerning the origins of the most ancient Asiatic civilizations, part of that line of intense historical interest in the civilizations of Eastern Asia which was a feature of the culture of the Enlightenment and of the eighteenth century as a whole. They are to be found in the *Recherches philosophiques sur les Egyptiens et les Chinois* [Philosophical Investigations on the Egyptians and the Chinese] (1773) by Cornelis de Pauw and in a series of works by Jean-Sylvain Bailly.[17] These works explored two topics which were commonly debated in the Académie des Inscriptions as a whole: the question of the descent of the Chinese civilization from Ancient Egypt, connected to the well-established idea of the Egyptian primacy in the historical course of civilization, taken up in two essays by Joseph de Guignes in 1758 and 1759 which gained the official endorsement of the Académie;[18] and the more general theme of the Asiatic, and in particular Indian,

---

[17] Such as *Histoire de l'astronomie ancienne* (Paris, 1775); *Lettres sur l'origine des sciences* (Paris, 1777); *Lettres sur l'Atlantide de Platon* (Paris, 1779); and *Traité de l'astronomie indienne et orientale* (Paris, 1787).

[18] Joseph de Guignes, *Mémoire dans lequel, après avoir examiné l'origine des lettres Phéniciennes & Hébraïques, &c. on essaye d'établir que le caractère épistolique, hiéroglyphique, & symbolique des Egyptiens se retrouve dans les caractères des Chinois, & que la nation Chinoise est une colonie Egyptienne*, in *Histoire de l'Académie Royale des Inscriptions et Belles-Lettres Avec Les Mémoires de Littérature . . .*, vol. 29 (Paris, 1764), 1–26; and *Essai sur le moyen de parvenir à la lecture & à l'intelligence des hiéroglyphes Egyptiens*, in *Histoire de l'Académie Royale des Inscriptions et Belles-Lettres*, vol. 34 (Paris, 1770), 1–55. On this topic there is a fundamental essay by Salvatore Rotta, 'Egiziani e Cinesi a confront: Intorno alle *Recherches philosophiques sur les Egyptiens et les Chinois* di Cornelius

primacy in the process of civilization, which had long been one of the pivotal points for the research conducted in the Académie des Inscriptions. Each of our authors had his own position but what interests here is the determination, common to the historical culture of both the *érudits* and the Enlightenment, to analyse the relationships between different civilizations in terms of temporal precedence and genetic relationships, the quest for an original centre from which cultures and knowledge radiated outwards, and the effort to resolve this problem by means of bold comparative analyses based on forms of language and writing. This undoubtedly points to the approach characterized as 'universal history', with its objective of reconstructing a plausible picture of the history of peoples and civilizations that was emancipated from the biblical version; the mere existence of such peoples and civilizations required the elaboration of new explanatory hypotheses, whereupon the ancient and modern civilizations in the West could be relocated within the new configurations. In the 1780s these topics fuelled discussions among a whole range of historians, *érudits* and *philosophes*, not only of course in France, from Rabaut de Saint-Etienne to Sainte-Croix, Court de Gébelin, d'Hancarville, and Poinsinet de Sivry, from Blumenbach to Herder, from Paolino di San Bartolomeo to Gianrinaldo Carli. And in this same decade the terrain was being prepared for William Jones, the British Indologist and Sanskritist, to formulate his theory of the Indo-European origins of the civilizations of both East and West which was to sweep away Bailly's 'Scythian system'. Meanwhile, however, in the France of the Enlightenment the influence of these hypotheses and broad interpretative frescoes, if all too often based on conjecture and impressionistic data, was very powerful, even among thinkers who, like Voltaire, had adopted scepticism as a methodology in rejecting the excesses of conjecture. The pressure of the need to collate the ever greater volume of data, however problematic its interpretation, which was pouring in concerning the remote cultures of the East, within new historical and genealogical schemes had become so overwhelming that Voltaire himself could not refrain from engaging in impassioned discussion of Bailly's hypotheses, ending with the unusual recognition that he was 'fort ébranlé et presque converti' ['much upset and almost persuaded'] by them: 'je sacrifie sans peine tous mes doutes ['I with no difficulty give up all my doubts']—he avowed to Bailly in February 1776, revealing in his words the new tensions and propensities seeping into the historical sensibility of the Enlightenment—'under your beam of lights. Your book [the *Histoire de l'astronomie ancienne* (1775)] is not only a masterpiece of understanding and genius, but one of the most likely systems'.[19]

de Pauw (1773)', in Domenico Ferraro and Gianna Gigliotti (eds.), *La geografia dei saperi: Scritti in memoria di Dino Pastine* (Florence, 2000), 241–67, online at http://www.eliohs.unifi.it/testi/900/rotta/rotta_pauw.html (accessed 21 July 2009).

[19] Voltaire to Bailly, 9 February 1776, in *Voltaire's Correspondence*, vol. 42 (Oxford, 1977), 393–5.

KEY HISTORICAL SOURCES

Alembert, Jean-Baptiste Le Rond, d', *Réflexions sur l'histoire, et sur les différentes manières de l'écrire*, in *Mélanges de littérature, d'histoire, et de philosophie*, vol. 5 (Amsterdam, 1767), 469–94.

Bailly, Jean-Sylvain, *Histoire de l'astronomie ancienne* (Paris, 1775).

—— *Lettres sur l'origine des sciences* (Paris, 1777).

Bossuet, Jacques-Benigne, *Discours sur l'histoire universelle* (Paris, 1681).

Condorcet, Nicolas de, *Esquisse d'un tableau historique des progrès de l'esprit humain* (Paris, 1795).

Guignes, Joseph de, *Histoire des Huns, des Mongoles des Tartares* (Paris, 1756–8).

Fréret, Nicolas, *Réflexions sur l'étude des anciennes histoires et sur le degré de certitude de leurs preuves* (Paris, 1724).

—— *Vues générales sur l'origine and le mélange des anciennes Nations, sur la manière d'en étudier l'histoire* (Paris, 1744).

Mably, Gabriel Bonnot, abbé de, *De l'étude de l'histoire* (Paris, 1775).

—— *De la manière d'écrire l'histoire* (Paris, 1783).

Montesquieu, *Considérations sur les causes de la grandeur des Romains et de leur décadence* (Paris, 1734).

Raynal, Guillaume-Thomas and Diderot, Denis, *Histoire philosophique et politique des établissements et du commerce des Européens dans les deux Indes* (Paris, 1770–80).

Rousseau, Jean-Jacques, *Discours sur les sciences et les arts* (1750).

—— *Discours sur l'origine et les fondements de l'inégalité parmi les homes* (Amsterdam, 1755).

Turgot, *Plan du second discours sur les progrès de l'esprit humain* (Paris, 1750).

Voltaire, *Siècle de Louis XIV* (Paris, 1751).

—— *Essai sur les moeurs et l'esprit des nations* (Paris, 1756).

——*Histoire de l'empire de Russie sous Pierre le Grand* (Paris, 1759, 1763).

BIBLIOGRAPHY

Barret-Kriegel, Blandine, *Les historiens et la monarchie*, vol. 1: *Jean Mabillon*; vol. 2: *La défaite de l'érudition*; vol. 3: *Les Académies de l'Histoire*; vol. 4: *La République incertaine* (Paris, 1988).

Broc, Numa, *La géographie des philosophes: Géographes et voyageurs français au XVIIIe siècle* (Paris, 1975).

Cassirer, Ernst, *Die Philosophie der Aufklärung* (Tübingen, 1932); trans. Fritz C. A. Koelln, *The Philosophy of the Enlightenment* (Princeton, 1951).

Croce, Benedetto, *Teoria e storia della storiografia* (Bari, 1917).

Dagen, Jean, *L'histoire de l'esprit humain dans la pensée française: De Fontenelle à Condorcet* (Strasbourg, 1977).

Duchet, Michèle, *Anthropologie et histoire au siècle des Lumières* (Paris, 1972).

Goodman, Dena, *The Republic of Letters: A Cultural History of the French Enlightenment* (Ithaca, 1996).

Goulemot, Jean-Marie, *Discours, révolutions et histoire: Représentations de l'histoire et discours sur les révolutions de l'âge classique au siècle des Lumières* (Paris, 1975).

Grell, Chantal, *L'histoire entre érudition et philosophie: Étude sur la connaissance historique à l'âge des Lumières* (Paris, 1993).

Mazauric, Simone, *Fontenelle et l'invention de l'histoire des sciences à l'aube des Lumières* (Paris, 2007).

Meinecke, Friedrich, *Die Entstehung des Historismus* (Berlin, 1936).

O'Brien, Karen, *Narrative of the Enlightenment: Cosmopolitan History from Voltaire to Gibbon* (Cambridge, 1997).

Pocock, J. G. A., *Barbarism and Religion*, 5 vols. to date (Cambridge, 1999–).

Trevor-Roper, Hugh, 'The Historical Philosophy of the French Enlightenment', *Studies on Voltaire and the Eighteenth Century*, 27 (1963), 1667–87.

Vyverberg, Henry, *Historical Pessimism in the French Enlightenment* (Cambridge, Mass., 1958).

Chapter 21

Writing Official History in Spain: History and Politics, *c.*1474–1600

Kira von Ostenfeld-Suske

Spain experienced unprecedented change between 1474 and 1600: the expulsion of the Moors and Jews from the Iberian peninsula, the consolidation of the foundations of a new nationhood, the discovery of the New World, and the creation of an empire. These events produced an assertion of power, legitimacy, and authority through the writing of history. While the histories of the New World that resulted will be discussed in a later chapter,[1] this chapter surveys how emerging Spanish power found expression in the writing of history, by focusing on the work of Spanish 'official historians' concerned with Spain and its monarchy, and by looking at how 'official' history-writing adapted and evolved according to the changing needs of the Spanish Crown. While these forms of history do not define an era's character, in the case of historical writing we begin to understand the histories, the historians, and their motivations. These writings provide an important lens through which to survey both the place of early modern historiography in the construction of royal imagery, political ideology, and authority, but also the role of such concerns in the framing of the historiographical project. Official history was designed to court public opinion, rally support for a particular programme or set of beliefs, or legitimize a ruler's claim to power. Whether it was to foster notions of national identity or enhance a ruler's power and prestige, political machinations influenced the redaction of such histories, revealing the influence that power, politics, and ideology have upon the writing of history, and which persist even to this day.

HISTORY UNDER THE CATHOLIC MONARCHS: UNITY, ANCIENT FOUNDATIONS, AND MYTH

From the fifteenth century onwards, history originating in the court was understood primarily as a means of defending the monarch and providing an official

---

[1] See ch. 27 by Kira von Ostenfeld-Suske in this volume.

account of events. For this purpose, most European monarchs, starting around 1400, set about institutionalizing the office of the chronicler, hoping to invest his work with an aura of trustworthiness (*auctoritas*) that other, non-official histories lacked. These official royal chroniclers were to craft texts that served as a kind of *apologia* favourable to the interests and image of the monarch, supporting the politics, and conserving the memory of the monarch's many great deeds. Furthermore, history was to assist government objectives, compiling and recording the material necessary to preserve and solidify claims to privilege, clarify boundaries, and define precedence. Thus, chroniclers became the official custodians of memory, preventing the monarch and vital information from falling into the abyss of *el olvido* (the forgotten).

With the accession of Ferdinand and Isabella, whose reign (1474–1516) brought new political motivations to the Iberian peninsula, the role of royal chroniclers (*cronistas del rey*), and the subject matter of official histories changed. While history had long been used to praise the personal qualities of rulers, the marriage of the Catholic Monarchs and the union of the Crowns of Aragon and Castile extended history's use from merely praising the Crown and the monarch to exalting the purposes and interests of the kingdom more generally. This created problems of authority, however, for as the monarchs attempted to unify the peninsula, and centralize royal power at the expense of local nobility, they encountered an unprecedented profusion of unofficial or private histories inimical to the Crown's interest, as nobles tried to reassert the legitimacy of their territorial claims and titles.[2] In response, the monarchy wished to establish a monopoly over historical writing; to this end, the reins of royal censorship were tightened, chroniclers appointed by their predecessors were dismissed, and the Catholic Monarchs appointed Lorenzo Galíndez de Carvajal as royal chronicler with the mandate to 'censor and judge' both the writings of earlier chroniclers and the works of his contemporaries.[3] Such measures brought a halt to the widespread dissemination of the dispersed and individual histories that challenged the Crown produced in the preceding years and while local and private histories that either supported regional or noble interests persisted, limitations placed upon their circulation and publication meant that the most widely read histories were official works, or those which emerged from or received official endorsement directly from the court. Indeed both the kind of government enforced by the Crown, and the limitations placed upon the publication of books, determined which texts went to press. This cemented the close relationship between history and power in Spain, rendering history-writing almost exclusively at the service of the monarchy, and using history to create a

---

[2] See Peter J. Linehan, *History and Historians of Medieval Spain* (Oxford, 1993).

[3] The Catholic Monarchs also endowed the office of royal chronicler (*cronista del rey*) with new prestige by granting its incumbent a regular yearly salary, thereby entrenching 'official' history in Spain. See José Luis Bermejo Cabrero, 'Orígenes del oficio de cronista real', *Hispania*, 40 (1980), 395–409.

unified vision of Spain's past that favoured the Crown's political interests. What lends historiographical importance to the reign of the Catholic Monarchs was the dramatic increase in the number of officially appointed historians, the need for official support in the publishing of historiographical texts, and the establishment of the official historian's role as censor.

As official chronicler, Galíndez de Carvajal was commissioned to 'write, declare, copy, and collect, all the information pertinent to the [chronicle of the reign]', and to this end he collected documents, compiled genealogies, and prepared a *Memorial o registro breve*—a carefully organized and highly polished vernacular annal of the noteworthy actions of the Catholic Monarchs from 1468 to 1516. Significantly, Galíndez prefaced this work with the first extensive commentary on the problems and aims of official historians. He believed the chronicler should only 'witness or scribe, and not judge or gloss the deeds, but only record them as they occurred'.[4] Despite this avowed impartiality, he impressed upon Ferdinand the need to commission histories to enhance the king's reputation abroad, and warned him of the dangers of unflattering accounts. Galíndez believed that the only guarantee of historical accuracy was for chronicles to be written by scholars attached to the court, thus establishing the role that official historians filled as providers of historical truth, but he emphasized precision and a conscious attempt to avoid prejudice and eulogy as prerequisites for the official task.

Galíndez played a vital role in fostering the political advantages of historical scholarship when he advocated the translation and dissemination of the work of fellow historian Fernando del Pulgar. Understanding the importance of the unification of Spain through the Catholic Monarchs' marriage, Pulgar sought to link the personal triumphs of the monarchs with the broader history of Spain itself, believing that the momentous events the peninsula had witnessed by 1492 ushered in a new era in Spain's history. In his *Crónica de los Reyes Católicos* [Chronicle of the Catholic Monarchs] (1493), Pulgar presented not only an account of the Granada campaign, which restored the whole of Spain to Christian rule and ended the 781-year presence of Islamic rule in Iberia, but also of the expulsion of the Jews and the discovery of the 'Indies' that positioned the reign of Ferdinand and Isabella as the dramatic climax of decades of strife and a portent of a glorious future. Pulgar's *Crónica* was much more than a traditional 'chronicle'; rather, it illustrated the impact of humanism, by turning to the histories of Livy and Sallust as models for the literary presentation of the past, adding rhetorical flourish and anecdotal touches to his work, and adopting the Roman patriotic ethos. For Pulgar, the Roman emperors had entrusted poet-philosophers with the glorification of their achievements, and he saw himself as heir to that tradition. Thus he designed his history to project an image of power and unity

---

[4] Translation mine. Lorenzo Galíndez de Carvajal, *Memorial o registro breve de los Reyes Católicos* (1523; ed. Juan Carretero Zamora, Segovia, 1992), 2.

for the Catholic Monarchs, and conceived the religious uniformity that they had achieved throughout the peninsula as the starting point of worldly power, supplying a unity of purpose for the Spanish people and encouraging Spain's Christianizing mission. For Pulgar, the expulsion of the Moors not only unified the entire peninsula, but also bolstered a Spanish sense of self, and purity of integrity, by eliminating external encroachments and alien influences. By abruptly rewriting Spain's history as one that hinged upon the arrival of the Catholic Monarchs, Pulgar, however, invented a Spain that buried its Islamic and Jewish pasts, combined the symbols of exclusionary salvation and political unification, and established a tradition of exclusionary history in Spanish historical writing. Accordingly, Galíndez promoted and cultivated Pulgar's history for the Catholic Monarchs, not only for its propagandistic utility in the effort to realize a unified peninsular identity, but ordered it to be translated into Latin in 1509 by Antonio de Nebrija as *Rerum a Fernando et Elisabe Hispaniarum felicissimis regibus gestarum decades duae* [Two Decades of Things Done by Ferdinand and Isabella, the Most Fortunate Monarchs of all the Spains], formally planned as ten books and also known as the *Decades Duae* [Two Decades] (1545), thus demonstrating the increased use of history in Latin as a means of communication and a tool to extend Spain's political influence and image beyond its borders.

The works of official historians became a cultural accompaniment to the expansionist ambitions of the Catholic Monarchs, especially as they began to wield political influence in Europe. As Spain stepped onto the stage of European politics, the Crown began to understand how building international esteem needed to become a significant factor in cultural life. Closer contact with the Italian court had revealed that Italian humanists not only saw themselves as the sole inheritors of the glory of Rome, but generally regarded Spaniards as the barbaric and culturally immature descendants of the marauding Visigoths. Thus, in order to achieve for Spain a past of equal renown, Spanish historians conceived a storied and glorious history commensurate with that claimed for Italy through their own revival of classical history. To this end, official historians eschewed the works of their medieval predecessors and their concern with Spain's Visigothic heritage, in favour of presenting a picture of Spain under the Greeks, Carthaginians, and Romans.[5] For them, medieval chronicles also lacked any systematic use of sources, critical assessment, and above all any sense of composition. Instead, they turned to the works of ancient geographers and historians such as Pliny, Polybius, Plutarch, Mela, Cicero, Sallust, and even the poets Virgil, Lucan, and Ovid. Moreover, Spanish historians came to preoccupy themselves increasingly not only with the style and composition of the work of the ancients, but with the antiquity of their sources, and insisted, whenever possible, on using the most ancient account available. This marked an increased humanist cultiva-

---

[5] For representations of Spain's Visigothic past see J. N. Hillgarth, 'Spanish Historiography and Iberian Reality', *History and Theory*, 24:1 (1985), 23–43.

tion of history in Spain, in which present glories were mediated by the vestiges of antiquity. Such connections were easy to establish, as *Hispania* had included some of the most Romanized provinces of the republic and empire. In their attempt to understand the mechanisms of the classical world, Spanish historians honed their skills in philology, searched for antiquities, and tried to match the statements of classical geography and places of ancient settlements with their contemporary counterparts. They imitated humanist forms of writing, and the *laudatio* (laudation) played a crucial role in the production of a humanist conception of ancient Iberia, emphasizing connections between the Roman Empire and contemporary Spain. The histories that emerged reveal a growing sense of 'patriotism' that reflects both the sort of patriotic humanism reminiscent of Leonardo Bruni's notable history of Florence,[6] but also the influence of royal patronage, and because of the involvement of the Crown in supporting these official projects, the humanist and the nationalist impulse became closely knit. For instance, the Union of Castile and Aragon became *Hispania Citerior* and *Ulterior*, reinforcing the idea of the lost unity of *Hispania* since the days of the Muslim invasion. Spanish historians also took great pains to point out that Italians were not the only ones who had great men in their past, and sought to emphasize the number of rulers the peninsula had given the Roman Empire. While some official historians sought to recognize Spain's debt and contribution to classical culture, others, however, sought to show that the antiquity and nobility of Spain yielded to none in grandeur, including Rome, and even attempted to depict the Spanish kingdoms as rivals to the empires of the ancient world. Therefore, while their techniques were those of humanists, their aim was the enhancement of the prestige of the Spanish peninsula by creating a past more spectacular than that of any other nation. Indeed, they wanted to propagate a civilized and cultured Spanish past pre-dating the arrival of the Romans, and sought to give Spaniards priority over the Greeks and Romans in cultural matters. Drawing from classical texts, historians claimed that the heroic deeds of ancient Spaniards even outshone those in the Iliad, and that Spanish poetry, letters, and moral philosophy preceded those of Greece by some eight centuries. Thus, Spanish historians responded to foreign criticism by constructing a past in which the antiquity of the Spanish dynasty was emphasized and Spanish grandeur legitimized, establishing Spanish renown in the same way, with the evidence of the great historians of Greece and Rome.[7]

This new phase of humanist-inspired Spanish historiography, and its search for the history of ancient Spain, first appeared with the work of Joan Margarit. Resenting the exiguous way that the late antique writers Trogus Pompeius and

---

[6] See Leonardo Bruni, *Historiae Florentini populi* (Florence, 1492).

[7] See Robert B. Tate, 'Italian Humanism and Spanish Historiography of the Fifteenth Century', *Bulletin of the John Rylands Library*, 34 (1951), 137–65. See also, Erika Rummel, 'Marineo Sículo: A Protagonist of Humanism in Spain', *Renaissance Quarterly*, 50 (1997), 701–22.

Paulus Orosius had treated ancient Iberia, Margarit turned instead to the histories and geographies of Strabo, Ptolemy, Livy, and Caesar, uncovering hitherto unavailable material from Diodorus Siculus and Herodotus to produce his *Paralipomenon Hispaniae* [The Forgotten History of Spain] (1483), his history from ancient times until the reign of Augustus, creating a venerable past for Spain that rivalled scholarly research in Italy. Using the work of Strabo, Margarit sought to uncover the Spanish towns destroyed by the Roman invasion, and personally visited the sites of many ancient ruins. Furthermore, with this work Margarit also contributed to the notion of a Spanish ethnicity antedating the Visigothic Kingdom. This more universalist history-writing intended to demonstrate the antiquity and grandeur of Spain was continued by the philologist and grammarian Antonio de Nebrija and the transplanted Italian scholar Lucio Marineo Sículo. Officially appointed by the Crown, these humanist scholars were tasked with documenting the Spanish *imperium*. To this end, Marineo Sículo's *De Hispaniae laudibus* [In Praise of Spain] (1497) celebrated the glories of Spain's ancient past in glowing Ciceronian Latin specifically for a wider European audience. His work emphasized Spain's debt to the Romans, and heralded the apotheosis of *Hispania* restored to its ancient borders, and embarking on a new age under the Catholic Monarchs. In particular, Marineo Sículo sought to bring Spain back into Roman history, and integrate Spain into the centrality of the European context. Meanwhile, Nebrija provided the last stage of political antiquarianism in his vernacular *Muestra de la historia de las antigüedades de España* [Account of the History of the Antiquities of Spain] (1499), providing Spain with a prehistory that had Iberian civilization beginning well before that of the Greek city-states, and which sought to demonstrate the antiquity of Spanish culture as well as its independence from Rome.[8]

The political ascendancy of Spain was also heralded in historiography by a profusion of mythological history. Key to this enterprise was Annius of Viterbo (Giovanni Nanni), who provided Spanish historians with the means to lay claim to a consecrated origin and descent. Writing as Berossus, a real Chaldean historian of the third century BC whose works had not survived, Viterbo invented a royal genealogy 'proving' that the Catholic Monarchs were directly descended from Tubal, grandson of Noah, and the legendary first ruler of Spain.[9] Though

---

[8] Similarly, Rodrigo Sánchez de Arévalo's *Compendiosa historia hispánica* (Rome, 1470), the first general history of Spain to be printed, drew evidence from newly available classical texts to extend the antiquity of Spain to before that of Rome, claiming that Hispanic civilization derived from the Trojans, and thus was more venerable than Rome. See A. D. Deyermond, *Historical Literature in Medieval Iberia* (London, 1996).

[9] Viterbo aligned Jewish history with classical mythology to demonstrate that Christ's earthly parents were descended from the same lineage as the pagan gods, and in particular the semi-divine Aeneas. This systematically erased the distinction between history and legend by transforming imperial chronicles into mere continuations of the vernacular legends of Troy. By the time Charles V came to power, these foundations would be used to trace a single line of descent from Noah-Janus through Christ-Aeneas to the contemporary imperial heir. Viterbo's list of mythical Spanish monarchs was included in his *Commentaria super opera diversorum auctorum de antiquitatibus*

quickly recognized by many scholars as a work of forgery, Viterbo's work wove together biblical history, ancient myths, and medieval Trojan legends in a single story, providing a line of kings that spanned the dark ages separating the time of Tubal from the arrival of the Romans, and allowed the Catholic Monarchs to claim that the Spanish monarchy was far older than that of their arch rivals, the Valois of France. Thus, despite the questionable nature of these mythical foundations, the political implications that they provided allowed them to persist well into the seventeenth century. Indeed, inspired by Annius, Nebrija combined these mythic origins with classical sources, including Flavius Josephus and those provided by the Carthaginians to create his above-mentioned *Muestra*. While Nebrija realized the difficulties in tracing the earliest history of Spain and warned the reader that his text might mix historical events with 'fabulous fictions', he justified their use with the fact that they were all that was available.[10] Not only was the need to rely on myth necessary in the absence of more concrete sources, but Nebrija claimed the myths of the past explained the glorious present—how the Catholic Monarchs defeated the Moors, unified the peninsula, and discovered the New World, establishing a geographic and political unity not seen since pre-Roman times. Moreover, for Nebrija, there was no contradiction between an apparently evidential history and one that invoked myth, legend, or scripture; archaeological discoveries or evidence from reliable authorities served to corroborate consecrated interpretations and understandings of events, the very antiquity of which had rendered them mythic or iconic. Thus, myth provided a backdrop and landscape to explain present events, and extended and enhanced the background of Spanish antiquity. The invocation of myth was also used to justify the origins of political privileges as much as the hereditary rights of the monarchy. To provide the basis for a classical ethnology for the Spanish monarchy, historians also turned to the myth of Hercules, who served much as did Brutus for the Britons and Francus for the Franks, to link ancient Spain to the myths of the classical world. According to these accounts, Hercules entrusted the entire peninsula to Hispanus, whom he chose for his qualities of virtue, resistance to vice, and presumption of honour and courage.[11] As in other parts of Renaissance Europe, this mythology served political and didactic purposes, facilitating the identification of a national past and the application of historic virtues and values with the improvement of the present, while enhancing the prestige and status of monarchs and dynasties. Thus, by the early 1500s, history-writing had established itself as a political instrument that forged a community's sense of its past, including

loquentium (1498). See Robert B. Tate, 'Mythology in Spanish historiography of the Middle Ages and Renaissance', *Hispanic Review*, 22:1(1954), 1–18.

[10]   See Carmen Codoñer, 'Tres cronistas reales: Alfonso de Palencia, Antonio de Nebrija y Lucio Marineo Sículo', *La corónica: A Journal of Mediaeval Hispanic Languages, Literatures and Cultures*, 37:1 (2008), 121.

[11]   B. Cuart Moner, 'Los romanos, los godos, y los Reyes Católicos', *Studia Historica: Historia Moderna*, 11 (1993), 61–87.

a collective name, a myth of origin and descent, and a shared history and purpose through interpretations of ancient myth, and careful choice of 'reliable' sources. This not only demonstrated a deep consciousness of the importance of the past, but these works also expressed royalist ideology that exploited the rich legacy of European myth and classical history to promote and legitimize current objectives.

HISTORY UNDER CHARLES V: IMPERIAL HISTORY, *RES GESTAE*, AND THE GENERAL HISTORY OF SPAIN

As the Catholic Monarchs' grandson, Charles I (r. 1516–56) took the reins of an empire as Charles V in 1519, history became a vital tool for promoting the imperialist cause. Indeed, Charles's election as Holy Roman Emperor in 1519 added a new emphasis to 'universal monarchy', and Spanish official history would provide the ideological foundations for universal empire. Official history became a way to link the Spanish Monarchy to the older Roman imperial vision of a single *orbis terrarum*. Official historian Fray Antonio de Guevara (appointed official historian in 1527) set out the abstract arguments for Charles's universal empire in his *Relox de Príncipes* [The Dial of Princes] (1529), a life of Marcus Aurelius, while his *Década de Césares* [The Lives of Ten Roman Emperors] (1539), in imitation of the manner of Plutarch and Suetonius, provided a guide to imperial and royal virtue, casting Charles as the ultimate successor to this imperial legacy. In these works, the 'recovery' of empire represented by Charles V provided Guevara with a living vehicle to whom all the rediscovered repertoire of the ancient world was applied. Other official works provided a history of empire itself. These were true imperial histories (*historia imperial*), providing a history of the empire that was, first, a journey through history from ancient Rome to Charles V, second, a spiritual journey from ancient paganism to the Christianity of Charles's empire, and, last, a reflection upon the political virtues of the Roman Empire, and Charles as its inheritor. Furthermore, as not only emperor but head of the Catholic Monarchy, Charles was depicted as the champion of Christianity. Similarly, Pedro de Mexía's *Historia imperial y cesárea* [Imperial History or Lives of the Roman Emperors] (1545), recounted the lives of all the Caesars, from the conquerors of Gaul until Charles V, offering an implicit denial of any radical break in historical continuity by depicting the Habsburg dynasty as the heirs of Charlemagne and Augustus, while Juan Ginés de Sepúlveda's *Historium de rebus gestis Caroli Quinti imperatoris et regis Hispaniae* [The History of Charles V] (1545) chronicled the first true history of imperial Spain and the emperor's attempt to achieve European hegemony under the aegis of Catholicism.[12] More than just

---

[12] See Richard Kagan, 'The Emperor's Chroniclers', in Pedro Navascués Palacio (ed.), *Carlos V Imperator* (Madrid, 1999), 38–46.

recounting the actions of the emperor, however, Sepúlveda aimed to recount all of the pertinent events that occurred in the empire during Charles's reign, including the great Church councils, and even the deaths of such notable figures as Erasmus. Sepúlveda, who had travelled with the emperor, drew both from his firsthand experiences, as well as the works of Paolo Giovio, Johann Sleidan, Luis de Ávila, and Pedro de Salazar, including lengthy excerpts of their texts into his work in his efforts to find the 'most authentic' accounts of events at which he was not present. What marks Sepúlveda's work historiographically is a genuine defence of empire, and an encomium to the whole enterprise of imperial Spain. Sepúlveda not only saw himself as a humanist historian, writing in Latin, and following Livy and Sallust when considering how the empire was established and what Roman virtues were to be imitated or shunned, but he was also very aware of the interdependence of imperial events and politics, offering, in imitation of Thucydides, a pragmatic history in the true sense of the word.

Charles not only showed an interest in promoting his empire, but also wished to promote his own reign through historiography, commissioning Mexía in 1548 to write a history focusing on his own deeds and accomplishments. Mexía's *Historia del Emperador Carlos V* [History of Emperor Charles V] outlined the emperor's illustrious genealogy and emphasized Charles's most noteworthy accomplishments: his defeat of the *Communidades*, his great victory at Pavia, and his imperial coronation at Bologna, all for the good of what Mexía called 'the public weal of my Country and Nation'.[13] Mexía rejected, however, the rhetorical devices that embellished humanist histories, opting for brevity and limiting his description of events to those in which Charles was personally involved. In his revival of the medieval panegyric to the king, Mexía envisioned Charles as a Burgundian monarch who rose to glory through chivalrous prowess, wartime valour, and service to the Catholic cause, not as the Renaissance prince epitomized by Guevara and Sepúlveda. Mexía emphasized the sacred character of the monarchy, together with the notion that Charles's actions had benefited from divine sanction and support. There were clear ideological objectives for this; Mexía characterized Charles as the apogee of the Catholic monarchy, whose task it was to bring Catholicism to an empire, depicting Charles as almost superhuman, and his monarchy limitless. Moreover, his depiction of the defeat of the *Communidades* supported divine-right and absolutist notions of monarchy. Thus, while Mexía's veneration for the monarch, as well as his absolute faith in the divine right of kings, damaged the objectivity of his work, it was a powerful vehicle for expressing royalist ideology. His work demonstrates how the older medieval chronicle and medieval assumptions, values, and expectations persisted, remaining valuable persuasive tools, and reveals how Spanish historical writing

---

[13] Translation mine. See Baltasar Cuart Moner, 'La historiografía áulica en la primera mitad del siglo xvi: los cronistas del Emperador', in C. Codoñer and J. A. González Iglesias (eds.), *Antonio de Nebrija: Edad Media y Renacimiento* (Salamanca, 1994), 39–58.

was a mixture of the old and new, and that Spanish readers and the printing press easily accommodated both.

Official works written under Charles V were understood to possess a specific political, pragmatic, and pedagogical purpose within the court. In fact, in terms of historiography, what lends importance to the reign of Charles was the dramatic increase in the use of history as an educational tool, and history as *magistra vitae*. Even Mexía's work was cast with pedagogical and moralizing elements when he dedicated his history to young prince Philip (the future Philip II), casting history as a branch of philosophy, and a discipline supposed to convey sound doctrine to the reader. As official historian, Juan Páez de Castro wrote, 'History [provides] the letters and lessons which are the most useful and convenient to Princes and Kings'.[14] History wove together events into a story and provided moral instruction and pragmatic guidance through exemplars, slowly coming to replace the 'mirror for princes' genre as the pre-eminent means to mould future monarchs, and help them avoid errors committed by others. In this spirit, Mexía cast Charles as a model to be imitated by his young son, and Gonzalo Fernández de Oviedo's *Libro de la Cámara Real del príncipe don Juan* [The Chamber of Prince Don Juan] (1548) similarly provided a manual of courtly conduct for Philip, using the life of the young Don Juan, the only son of the Catholic Monarchs, as a model of virtuous behaviour, worthy of emulation.

Moreover, recounting acts of monarchical valour in histories created a desire for emulation, which justified history's utility, especially for those who governed. This blended two essentially different conceits: a religious vision of kingship as divinely ordained, which echoed the medieval convention of sacerdotal kingship, and a concept of kingship as emblematic of classical virtues. This combined the medieval chivalric glorification with the Renaissance political historiographical tradition of the perfect statesman. Both Alonso de Santa Cruz, in his *Crónica del emperador Carlos V* [History of Emperor Charles V] (1551), and Luis de Ávila y Zúñiga, in his *Comentario de la guerra de Alemaña, hecha por Carlos V en 1546 y 1547* [Commentaries on the war in Germany under Charles V in the Years 1546 and 1547] (1548), drew from this influence, emphasizing Charles's chivalric ideals and military exploits, especially those in defence of the Catholic faith, with the qualities and virtues of the ideal Renaissance monarch.

Another significant historiographic development during Charles's reign concerns the revival of the writing of general histories of Spain, not seen since the *Crónica General*, begun in the thirteenth century under the auspices of Alfonso X. Historians saw the writing of general histories not only as a way to serve patriotic objectives, but as a means of furthering Spanish prestige and monarchical authority and grandeur, since demonstrating the peninsula's illustrious lineage, accomplishments, and heroic deeds, would spread abroad the 'fame' and

---

[14] Translation mine. Juan Páez de Castro, 'De las cosas necesarias para escribir la historia' (1545), reprinted in *Ciudad de Dios*, 28 (1892), 601–10; 29 (1892), 27–37, at 601.

'reputation' of Spain and its monarchy.[15] The first of such general histories was Marineo Sículo's, *De rebus Hispaniae memorabilibus* [On the Memorable Things of Spain] (1530), which combined political history with a systematic geographical and ethnographical survey. Marineo Sículo began with a physical description of place, then moved to an account of what Cicero called the true virtues, the qualities of the inhabitants of places, their dedication to the arts, their martyrs and saints, the great deeds of its people, and included the succession of kings from those of the first inhabitants up to the Catholic Monarchs. His was not a comprehensive account of all of the events of Spain's past but, rather, carefully selected episodes of the victories and defeats that ennobled the country. His mixture of Livian narrative history with the geographically organized history of Biondo united a geography of Spain, both ancient and modern, with an explanation of how Spanish cultural accomplishments proceeded from Roman ancestry.[16] Like most of the accounts emerging from the royal court, Marineo Sículo's work concentrated on events in Castile, the centre of Spanish power, and largely excluded the history of Navarre and Aragon, so his was not a true compendium of Spanish history. To ensure a more complete history, Charles established a new official post, that of 'Chronicler of Spain', and appointed Florián de Ocampo, a humanist and pupil of Nebrija, with the task of writing a *Crónica General de España* [General History of Spain].

The general histories that followed grappled with both an ideological and historiographical issue: how to produce an overarching narrative that could satisfy each of the constituent elements of the religiously, culturally, and socially diverse Spanish kingdoms, but also bring together a diversity of different histories, documents, and even archaeological evidence, and fit them into a single mould. Ocampo would marshal these sentiments around a single patriotic myth as a focus for loyalty and devotion, and sought to identify the prototype of peninsular unity in a mythical past. For Ocampo, the collective past was envisioned not in terms of geography or nation, but in ethnic or racial terms as a kind of genealogical filiation. Ocampo defined the notion of Spanish identity as a lineage by tying together the diversity and copiousness of the Spanish kingdoms' prehistory by binding the state to its monarchy through common descent as well as celebrating the nobility. Ocampo thus honoured the ideological needs of a

---

[15] Such works were complemented by more specialized municipal histories such as that produced for Toledo by Pedro de Alcocer, and whose *Historia o descripción de la imperial ciudad de Toledo* (1554) endeavoured to insert the long and illustrious history of the city into the broader national epic of Spain and its monarchy, and general histories of the various Spanish kingdoms such as that of Jerónimo de Zurita y Castro, whose *Anales de la corona de Aragón* (1563–78) provided the first national history of Aragon from the Moorish invasion in 711 to the death of King Ferdinand II (1516), and whose erudition and sound historical judgement provided a monumental account of the heroic action of Aragonese monarchs and the laws that established the basis for the kingdom's legal regime.

[16] See Teresa Jiménez Calvente, 'Teoría historiográfica a comienzos del siglo XVI', in Alfredo Alvar Ezquerra (ed.), *Imágenes históricas de Felipe II* (Madrid, 2000), 197–215.

dynasty for whom mythic, lineal descent was central to the claim of imperial status.[17] This became even more important since across Europe historiography had become a way to substantiate claims to antiquity, and to assert one monarchy's precedence over another. Furthermore, Ocampo's preoccupation with the nobility reflected the political and economic reality in Spain in which royal government could not function without noble support. Ocampo mixed mythology, biblical narratives, speculative etymologies, toponomy, and geography, blending different modes of early modern historical writing, including genealogy, chorography, chronicle, noble family history, and urban history. This mixing of genres was characteristic of historical writing in this period and Ocampo's interest in ethnicity and race was undoubtedly influenced by the emergent ethnography to be found in narratives of the New World. Moreover, Ocampo rediscovered the peninsula's Romance chronicles, and combined them with his classical sources. Ocampo knew that he wrote a new type of general history, distinct from traditional chronicles, conceiving of history as both *magistra vitae* and *opus oratorium maxime*, and concerned with *inventio, dispositio,* and *elocutio.* Yet despite his lofty Ciceronian aspirations, Ocampo's *Los cinco libros primeros de la crónica general de España* [The First Five Books of the General Chronicle of Spain] (1543) provided only a narrative that started with Spain's mythical creation by Tubal, and ended with the Roman conquest of Iberia and the Second Punic War in the third century, leaving the *Crónica General de España* incomplete.[18]

The project to construct a grand narrative of Spain's past continued through the sixteenth century with Ambrosio de Morales and Esteban de Garibay y Zamalloa. Their works were part of this new conception of great historical projects based on new criteria and techniques. They expanded the scope of historical writing and provided a more general *Laus,* by combining geography, religion, human and intellectual values, and political and military history.

Morales's *La Crónica general de España: Que continuaua Ambrosio de Morales natural de Cordoua, Coronista del Rey Catholico nuestro señor don Philipe segundo deste nombre* [The General Chronicle of Spain: Continued by Ambrosio de Morales, Native of Cordoba, and Chronicler of the Catholic King, His Majesty Philip II] (1574–86) was a history of Spain that began where Ocampo's had ended and continued through the eleventh century. Morales, a humanist scholar versed in Latin and Greek and professor at the University of Alcalá de Henares, began his history with Roman Spain not only because he did not want to replicate what Ocampo had accomplished, but because Morales believed that due to the lack of

---

[17] A. Samson, 'Florián de Ocampo, Castilian Chronicler and Habsburg Propagandist: Rhetoric, Myth and Genealogy in the Historiography of Early Modern Spain', *Forum for Modern Language Studies,* 42:4 (2006), 339–54.

[18] The use of the term 'chronicle' in the title here is typical of Spanish historical writing, where we begin to see the interchangeability of the use of the term 'chronicle' with 'history' (*historia*), or the implied authorship by someone who possessed the tools and learning needed in order to enquire into a subject and then place it within a universal context.

textual and material evidence available, a complete history of Spain could only be written beginning with the Romans and not before. Indeed, Morales dismissed remote antiquity as a useful field of historical study.[19] Whereas Ocampo's reference to Noah's descendants had served to help him locate Spanish identity within the framework of universal history, making Spain exemplify one strand in the history of the world, Morales reversed this method of explaining Spain. One no longer had to see the history of the world as the necessary context and foundation for understanding the particular history of the nation; instead, Morales began with the tangible evidence that had been left in Spain by the Romans to demonstrate that the particular history of Spain was intelligible in its own right, and sought to emphasize the historical continuities that could be found between Roman and medieval Spain. Published in three volumes, Morales's history began with a detailed narrative of Roman Spain that focused in good humanist fashion on important matters of governance and war. He further succeeded in highlighting the Spanishness of *Hispania* by dedicating several chapters to the key founding myths of Catholic Spain, among them James (Santiago) the Apostle's mission to the country in AD 37, and his burial in the city that would become Santiago de Compostela, and wrote extensively on the lives of Spain's martyrs and saints, whose lives, he believed, had served to ennoble Spain. His second volume was a history of Visigothic Spain, up to the Moorish invasion. Morales celebrated the sovereign glory that the Visigoths had established, and how they had created a spiritually and politically homogeneous state, up until the so-called destruction of Spain occasioned by the Arab conquest in 711. Morales assured the reader, however, that Christianity had survived the Muslim invasion, and used both demography as well as archaeological discoveries, including his unearthing of Christian tombstones, to support his findings. His final volume looked at Spain's history from the eighth to the eleventh century. Morales had no desire, however, to write of the accomplishments or actions of the Moors, but rather focused solely on the actions of Spaniards such as King Pelayo and his followers in Castile and Leon, and their determination to re-conquer the peninsula and turn back the tide of Islam.

Garibay's *Compendio historial de las chronicas y universal historia de todos los reynos de España* [Compendium of the General Chronicles and Universal History of all of the Kingdoms of Spain] (1571) was not a general history in the traditional sense, but rather a juxtaposition of the histories of the reigns of Castile, Aragon, and Navarre, along with a history of the Muslim kingdoms. It was, however, the first 'universal' history of the realms of Spain in that it was the first to extend beyond Roman times and the Early Middle Ages to encompass the reign of Ferdinand. Garibay did not look at the Iberian peninsula as ancient *Hispania*, which had included Portugal, but only as *España* (Spain), or those peninsular reigns that when he wrote his work were directly under the sovereignty of Philip II. *Hispania* was a geographical-

---

[19] Sabine MacCormack, 'History, Memory and Time in Golden Age Spain', *History and Memory*, 4:2 (1992), 38–68.

archaeological-mythical construction, whereas *España* was a geographical-political one, and one that accorded much more with reality. Garibay, who was Basque by origin, saw the history of the Spain in which he lived as a conjunction of the diverse histories of the different reigns, although he believed that all arose from the same origins. Furthermore, despite being a conjunction of particular histories, Garibay's purpose was a unitary and generalist one. For Garibay these individual histories had no meaning unless he explained how they had played a constituent role in the creation of the Catholic monarchy. By creating a series of separate and essentially parallel narratives of the 'particular' histories of the various kingdoms that made up the Spanish monarchy, Garibay constructed a nation by creating a common history that not only helped define Spaniards against citizens of other nations, but gave them a heritage around which they could rally. Garibay believed that his all-inclusive approach would enable all Spaniards, regardless of *patria*, to identify with a common supranational past. Finally, the celebrated classicist and political theorist Juan de Mariana, a Jesuit, provided a comprehensive, erudite, and readable narrative that emphasized the formative role of the monarchy in the creation of a unitary, Catholic, Spanish state in *Historiae de rebus Hispaniae* [History of Spanish Affairs] (1592), which he also translated into Spanish. Unlike Garibay, Mariana sought to craft a national history through a single harmonious narrative that transcended the individual histories of the peninsular kingdoms. To give order to what his predecessors had written, Mariana provided a comprehensive synthesis of all that had been published and much of what remained extant. Unlike his fellow classical humanists, however, he decided to incorporate ecclesiastical matters into his narrative, which gave his work not only originality, but cohesion, as he sought to meld the secular accomplishments of the monarchy with the ecclesiastical accomplishments of the Church. He acknowledged that the three elements that comprised Spain were the Church, the monarchy, and a sense of 'Spanish mission', and included both factual as well as more fabulous accounts. Mariana was an exacting chronologist and the first to attack Annius of Viterbo constructively, and in his work we see the development of that critical scepticism leading to the major histories of the eighteenth century. Nevertheless, Mariana did not go so far as to reject Tubal or Hercules. Even though Mariana was influenced by the revolution in the critical approach to historical sources, he still responded to cultural demands for an adequate national tradition, which led him to produce, within the compass of one work, visionary lucubrations and the fruits of meticulous research.

HISTORY-WRITING UNDER PHILIP II: REASON OF STATE HISTORY, AND THE POWER OF DOCUMENTS

The accession of Philip II (r. 1556–98) to the Spanish throne (but not the Empire) brought new political necessities to the writing of history in Spain, developing historical methodology that transformed history's utility as an instrument of state. This was accomplished with the help of the Greek philologist and biblio-phile Juan Páez de Castro, whom Philip inherited from his father as his first official historian. Páez set in motion two historiographical projects that helped define Philip's historiographical agenda. First, Páez envisioned a grand history of Spain grounded in the particular history of each locale, and devised a questionnaire that was sent to each town and city on the peninsula soliciting information on local history, 'antiquities', administration, laws, customs, litera-ture, arts, geography, and resources, a project that would become known as the *Relaciones geográficas*.[20] Oriented to detail and particularities, the accumulation of such information was linked to the monarchy's imperial pretensions that sought glory on a wider scale, and which sought to write a history of Spain that included all expressions of social life. Second, Páez impressed upon Philip the need to create official archives and libraries to facilitate the writing of history. The combined forces of the Counter-Reformation (Páez had been Charles's repre-sentative to the Council of Trent) and the Renaissance had impressed upon Páez the growing importance of documentary evidence when writing history, and the need to record and guard the papers that protected the 'rights of the King, his patrimony, and patronage', but also those of 'all of his subjects and vassals' across all of his domains.[21] Páez expressed his specific desire to see official historians use such 'papers of state' in the writing of their history in order to supplement their claims and justify political actions. Philip followed Páez's suggestion, creating the royal library at the Escorial, reorganizing the archive established by his father in Simancas, founding an archive relating to the Crown of Aragon in Barcelona, and establishing an archive at the Spanish embassy in Rome. Both projects entrenched official history in Spain under Philip as one based on documentary evidence, and key to political activity and power.

To help in the formation of the royal archive, Philip ordered official historian Ambrosio de Morales to journey through Asturias, Galicia, and Leon to locate and catalogue old Greek, Latin, and Arabic manuscripts, relics, and materials for the genealogies of the Spanish royal house, to determine their authenticity, and to assess whether they were worthy of being placed in the Royal Library at the Escorial.[22] These literary voyages not only demonstrate the Crown's renewed interest in finding new sources to document Spain's political and sacred history, especially as it related to the nation's conversion to Christianity, the lives of its early martyrs and saints, and church councils, but as a result of these travels, Morales published *Las*

---

[20] They were called the *Relaciones geográficas*, or geographic reports because they dealt with human history and geography. See Carmelo Viñas Mey and Ramón Paz Remolar (eds.), *Relaciones histórico-geográfico-estadísticas de los pueblos de España hechas por iniciativa de Felipe II* (Madrid, 1971).

[21] Juan Páez de Castro, 'Memorial del Dr. Juan Páez de Castro, dado al Rey Phelippe II al principio de su reinado' (1556), reprinted in *Revista de Bibliotecas y Museos*, 9 (1883), 165–78.

[22] Ambrosio de Morales, *Viaje de Ambrosio de Morales por orden del rey D. Phelipe II a los reynos de León, y Galicia, y principado de Asturias* [1595] (Madrid, 1765; facs. edn, Oviedo, 1985).

antigüedades de las ciudades de España [The Antiquities of the Cities of Spain] (1575), a compendium of Spain's Roman antiquities, which Morales claimed served 'both the history of Spain and the Monarch', and 'transform[ed] dead stones into live ones' by making ancient inscriptions available for moral instruction.[23]

Morales's philological and antiquarian investigations of Roman Iberia and medieval Castile applied a greater critical consciousness to his research than that of his predecessors and attempted to redefine the coordinates of evidence and authority, attaching great significance to a variety of archaeological remains, ranging from coins and the remains of everyday objects, to the layout of ancient roads. Morales's skilful use of non-literary remnants of the past reflected the growing antiquarian movement, which enhanced the scope of historiography, demonstrating the awareness of and importance attached to primary sources, and evoking a sense of the wholeness of past life. In his treatment of both Roman and medieval history Morales affiliated himself with a group of Italian scholars who emphasized the comparative study of human societies and evolved critical methods for reconstructing events and institutions of the ancient world. By embracing mid-sixteenth-century Italian historical and antiquarian studies, Morales reconfigured the practices of the professional, appointed historian in Spain, by providing powerful tools for critical historical research.[24] Morales also introduced a *Tabla y suma* at the end of his work, which provided indices of illustrious Spaniards, famous Romans and foreigners in Spain, and the country's topographical features. This not only reveals his attempts to bring together the tensions between history as chronological narrative and a temporal storehouse of themes and *exempla* by drawing together these two modes of reading history, but such anatomization reveals the non-linear ways in which such books were designed to be read and used.

Official historians at Philip's court brought to their histories not only the values of humanist scholarship, but also the concerns of political theorists of the time. Influenced by new political ideas, especially those of the Italian political theorist Giovanni Botero, who impressed upon monarchs the need to defend their reputations, Spanish historians sought new ways to preserve and enhance Philip's power and grandeur through the writing of history. Defending the king meant more than just writing favourable histories; it meant embedding within those histories the moral and political philosophy of the king and the Spanish nation. Official works were thus designed to enhance and preserve Philip's

---

[23] Cited in Richard Kagan, 'History and the *Cronistas del Rey*', in Pedro Navascués Palacio (ed.), *Philippus II Rex* (Lunwerg, 1999), 19–29, at 20.

[24] See Sebastián Sánchez Madrid, *Arqueología y humanismo: Ambrosio de Morales* (Córdoba, 2002). Katherine van Liere has rightly pointed out that despite his critical skills, Morales rarely questioned the validity of many of the myths surrounding Christian martyrs and saints, especially James, and rather reasserted the authority of tradition alongside scripture to support his claim that James had indeed visited Spain. Katherine Elliot van Liere, 'The Missionary and the Moorslayer: James the Apostle in Spanish Historiography from Isidore of Seville to Ambrosio de Morales', *Viator*, 37 (2006), 519–43.

historical reputation by emphasizing the grandeur, dignity, and authority of the Spanish monarchy as well as the Spanish political philosophy that underpinned its rule.

The work of official historian Antonio de Herrera y Tordesillas epitomized the kind of history envisioned by the Crown. By 1586 Herrera had begun to publish specific histories that justified Philip's activities and interventions in England, Scotland, and France on religious grounds and, in 1591, he published a work that justified Philip's decision to bring both Portugal and its empire under Spanish control on historical grounds. He also published a series of histories concerning Milan and the Low Countries, in this way encompassing and legitimizing Spanish actions in all of Philip's European domains.[25] Herrera sought to reveal the underlying causes of political events, and the complexities behind Spanish conduct. Unlike the Machiavellian characterizations of Philip and Spanish actions coming from abroad, official history became a way to demonstrate that the causes and intentions determining Spanish actions were the desire to maintain privilege, custom, and rights, and to uphold religion. This further strengthened the role that official history played in promoting such 'truth', for as Botero had reminded princes, since the prince alone enjoyed full knowledge of the reason and circumstance of his undertakings and their outcome, history should be written by someone who was supported by, and who collaborated with, the prince. Moreover, such works sought to show how Philip's 'prudent' rule and Spanish government had brought enviable benefits to 'subjugated' societies, something eventually carried over to New World imperial histories. Herrera benefited from vast political knowledge and experience, having served as secretary to Vespiano Gonzaga in Italy, and was the first to translate, at Philip's behest, Botero's *Reason of State*. For Herrera, history was clearly conceived of as an instrument of statecraft, a rhetorical weapon used to defend the reputation of the monarchy and the 'public good'. Herrera saw his role as an indispensable official, labouring for the monarchy and the *res publica*.

Criticism of Philip II and the Crown from abroad, however, required that the writing of history bolster its claims to incontrovertible truth. Inspired by sixteenth-century notions of 'perfect history' that equated historical veracity with documentary proof, official works came to be grounded directly in state papers, documents, and manuscripts to ensure the fundamental 'truthfulness' of the account. This brought new importance to the role of the official historian and his work, since only officials were granted privileged access to the documents and raw

---

[25] Among them, Antonio de Herrera y Tordesillas, *Cinco libros de la Historia de Portugal y la conquista de las Islas de los Açores, en los años de 1582 y 1583* (Madrid, 1591); *Historia de los sucesos de Francia desde el año 1585 que comenzó la liga Católica hasta en fin del año 1594* (Madrid, 1598); and *Comentarios de las alteraciones de Flandes* (Madrid, 1600). The best discussion of Herrera's work is provided by Richard Kagan, '"Official History" at the Court of Philip II of Spain', in Martin Gosman, Alasdair MacDonald, and Arjo Vanderjagt (eds.), *Princes and Princely Culture 1450–1650*, vol. 2 (Leiden, 2005), 227–48.

accounts held in royal archives. Spanish official historiography was tasked with melding a search for definitive, authoritative, and source-based history with Tacitean politic history. This required an integration of non-narrative legal anti-quarian research with narrative history. Official historians began to name the chronicles and classical sources they had used, and also referenced the archives that they had visited and the documents they had consulted which supported their claims, going so far as to attach lists and their locations.[26] Such exhaustive use of sources allowed official historians to claim that their narratives were 'truthful'—that is, grounded in documentary evidence—while others were based solely on ideology. In this context, royal historians increasingly came to understand the complex and sometimes contradictory nature of their responsibilities, not only to provide 'truthful history', as a humanist discipline was expected to convey, but also to serve political ends. This dichotomy was much discussed among Spanish official historians, underscoring the tension inherent in trying to write official works. This also explains the prevalence of theoretical tracts concerning historical method, reasoning, and the purposes to which history could be put in Spain, where the number of such writings exceeded comparable works anywhere else in Europe. Among the most notable of these are Juan Páez de Castro's *De las cosas necesarias para escribir Historia* [Of the Things Needed to Write History] (1545), Sebastian Fox Morcillo's, *De Historiae Institutione Dialogus* [Concept of History or Dialogue on the Teaching of History] (1557), Juan Costa's *De conscribenda rerum historia libri duo* [Method for History] (1591), Antonio de Herrera y Tordesillas's, *Discursos morales, políticos e históricos* [On Moral, Political and Historical Matters] (1608), and Luis Cabrera de Córdoba's *De historia, para entenderla y escribirla* [On the Importance, Understanding and Writing of History] (1611).[27] Like their European counterparts, Spanish historians questioned their ability to remain impartial, and continued the humanist quest for an authentic and complete history (*legítima y perfecta historia*). They understood that the injunction to glorify and exalt needed to be reconciled with the impartiality necessary for any true account. Ultimately, however, it was political necessity rather than methodological deficiency, or lack of a critical spirit, that provided the impetus behind official history, and historians understood the best 'truth' as that which protected the Crown, and the 'common good'.

---

[26] See Alfredo Alvar Ezquerra, 'La Historia, los Historiadores y el Rey en la España del Humanismo', in *Imágenes históricas de Felipe II* (Madrid, 2000), 217–54.

[27] Herrera's work (original held at the Biblioteca Nacional [Madrid], Ms. 1.035), includes a 'Discurso y Tratado de la Historia e Historiadores Españoles' which not only discusses the writing of history in Spain (the first historiography of sorts), and provides a catalogue of all Spanish historians since antiquity, but also includes a treatise on Tacitus as the ideal historian, and an admonishment of Viterbo and other 'false' writings. Esteban de Garibay also commented on historical writing and his role as royal chronicler in Pascual Gayangos (ed.), *Memorias de Garibay*, included in the series *Memorial Histórico Español*, vol. 7 (Madrid, 1854).

CONCLUSION

The Catholic Monarchs were the first to attempt to harness the writing of history to the interests of Spain, and they established a foundation whereupon Spain's successive rulers would come to use history to suit their various political needs. Indeed, changes in Spain's political culture determined the manner in which official history was both written and conceived. From personalized king-centred history, to the broader national epic of Spain and its monarchy and its more Livy-esque narrative centred on the achievements of the kingdom as a whole, official history-writing in early modern Spain became an instrument of royal policy, used to document actions, legitimize policies, justify imperial titles, defend claims to territories, and ultimately augment royal authority and legitimate rule. While this chapter has focused selectively on the chronicles and histories wrought in honour of both country and king, such focus allows one to see how history-writing was transformed into an instrument of state, and offered the means to demonstrate Spanish grandeur and importance. Throughout this period, official history provided the illusion, if not always the substance, of power, together with the means to enhance this image for future generations. While the larger practice of history—conducted by non-royalist historians, various scholars and writers, and even Church historians—provided a corrective to official histories, official history itself contributed to the way power was conceived and projected for centuries to come.

Official histories also provided a way for Spaniards to see Spanish purpose and its role in their world. Ultimately, official histories served to make Spanish readers into members of a community sharing a common past, worldview, and common ideals. In this way, a sense of patriotism and burgeoning nationalism came to be expressed in history. Because of their past, their accomplishments, and their values, Spaniards came to regard themselves in historical terms not only as distinct and superior to all other Europeans, but also unique.

Using new humanist tools and techniques, official history became a rhetorical weapon in defending the 'public good', and the reputation of the monarchy. Official history was characterized by an interest in erudition, practical and ethical ends, and a patriotic desire to promote civility and unity. For official historians, the truth that history provided was never separate from notions of the *res publica*. The official historians' role was to maintain reputation, whether it was linking Spain to a glorious Roman past, to prove Spain's antiquity and monarchical grandeur, or using documents as testament to the legitimacy of and justification for the Spanish imperial vision. Indeed, official historians crafted historical accounts that became effective tools for the state by managing the tension between political and ideological needs, and upholding necessary humanist methodology. Such developments reflect the political crucible within which the historiographical enterprise itself was conceived and executed from the late fifteenth to the early seventeenth century on the Iberian peninsula.

TIMELINE/KEY DATES

1469 Marriage of Isabella of Castile and Ferdinand II of Aragon lays the foundation for the unification of Castile and Aragon as Spain

1475–79 War of the Castilian Succession

1478 Spanish Inquisition established

1479 Ferdinand II and Isabella I unite the crowns of Aragon and Castile in Spain

1492 The final defeat of the Moors in Spain; Jews are forced to convert to Christianity; those who refuse are expelled from Spain; Columbus's 'discovery' of the New World

1504 Isabella of Castile dies

1516 Ferdinand II of Aragon dies; Charles I becomes King of Castile and Aragon

1519 Charles I elected Holy Roman Emperor (as Charles V); crowned in Bologna in 1530

1525 Revolt of the *Communidades* in Spain

1527 Sack of Rome, led by Charles V

1545–63 Council of Trent

1556 Charles V abdicates; succeeded as king of Spain by Philip II

1561 Philip II centralizes his court in Madrid

1568–1648 Dutch Revolt against Habsburg control of the Netherlands

1571 Victory of the Catholic League against the Turks at the Battle of Lepanto

1580 Iberian Union of the crowns of Aragon, Castile and Portugal, which lasts until 1640

1585–1604 Anglo-Spanish War

1588 Spanish Armada defeated in the English Channel

1598 Philip III succeeds Philip II

KEY HISTORICAL SOURCES

Garibay y Zamalloa, Esteban de, *Compendio historial de las chronicas y universal historia de todos los reynos de España* (Antwerp, 1571).

Mariana, Juan de, *Historiae de rebus Hispaniae* (Toledo, 1592).

Marineo Sículo, Lucio, *De Hispaniae laudibus* (Burgos, 1497).

Mexía, Pedro de, *Historia imperial y cesárea* (Seville, 1545).

Morales, Ambrosio de, *Las antigüedades de las ciudades de España que van nombradas en la crónica con las averiguaciones de sus sitios y nombres antiguos* (1575; Valencia, 2001).

Nebrija, Antonio de, *Muestra de la historia de las antigüedades de España* (Burgos, 1499).

Ocampo, Florián de, *Los cinco libros primeros de la crónica general de España* (Zamora, 1543).

Pulgar, Fernando del, *Crónica de los Reyes Católicos* (1493; Alicante, 2003).

Sepúlveda, Juan Ginés de, *Historium de rebus gestis Caroli Quinti imperatoris et regis Hispaniae* [1545], in *Obras Completas*, ed. B. Cuart Moner (Pozoblanco, 1996).

BIBLIOGRAPHY

Andrés Gallego, José and Blázquez, José María, *Historia de la Historiografía española* (Madrid, 1999).

Ballester y Castell, Rafael, *Fuentes narrativas de la historia de España durante la edad moderna (1474–1808)* (Valladolid, 1927).

Cirot, Georges, *Les Histoires Générales d'Espagne: entre Alphonse X et Philippe II (1284–1556)* (Bordeaux, 1904).

—— *Études sur l'historiographie espagnole: Mariana historien* (Paris, 1905).

Cortijo Ocaña, Antonio, *Teoría de la historia en el siglo XVI en Sebastian Fox Morcillo: De Historiae Institutione Dialogus-Diálogo de la Enseñanza de la Historia (1557)* (Alcalá de Henares, 2000).

García Cárcel, Ricardo (ed.), *Las escencias patrias: La construcción de las Historias de España* (Madrid, 2004).

Kagan, Richard, *Clio and the Crown: The Politics of History in Medieval and Early Modern Spain* (Baltimore, 2009).

Morel-Fatio, Alfred, *L'historiographie de Charles V* (Paris, 1913).

Sánchez Alonso, Benito, *Historia de la historiografía española*, vol. 1: *Hasta la publicación de la crónica de Ocampo (–1543)* (Madrid, 1942).

—— *Historia de la historiografía española*, vol. 2: *Ensayo de un examen de conjunto, De Ocampo a Solis (1543–1684)* (Madrid, 1944).

Tate, Robert B., *Ensayos sobre la historiografía peninsular del siglo XV* (Madrid, 1970).

Chapter 22

Historical Writing in Scandinavia

Karen Skovgaard-Petersen

Covering the entire early modern period, 1400–1800, this chapter will move a long way from late medieval Scandinavia—with few cultural centres and limited access to a limited number of manuscript texts—to the urbanized and literate Scandinavian society in the age of the French Revolution. The region also underwent extensive political changes. From 1397 to 1523 Denmark, Norway (with Iceland), and Sweden (with Finland) were united in the Union of Kalmar. After 1523 two monarchies, Sweden-Finland and Denmark-Norway (with Iceland) were established, both embracing Lutheran Protestantism and both strongly centralized.

The relationship between the two Scandinavian monarchies was marked by rivalry throughout the sixteenth and seventeenth centuries, often breaking out in open warfare. Until the first decades of the seventeenth century Denmark was the leading power of the region, but this position was taken over by Sweden during the reign of Gustavus Adolphus, and until the Great Northern War (1700–20) Sweden enjoyed the status of a great power. The constant rivalry between the two monarchies left its mark on contemporary historiography, though less so in the eighteenth century.

This chapter will focus on a limited number of works, and priority has been given to narrative syntheses. Since Scandinavian historians were primarily concerned with writing the history of their own country, I shall focus on the writing of national history. In spite of the profound societal changes in the course of the early modern period, it was a basic concern in Scandinavian historical writing to present native traditions to a European public—to describe the culture of the periphery in the literary language of the centre—thereby claiming that peripheral Scandinavia had a share in the major cultural trends of the time.

1400–REFORMATION

The Union of Kalmar (1397–1523) between Norway, Sweden, and Denmark was ruled by Danish kings. For most of the period strong oppositional forces in the Swedish nobility strove to obtain independence. In the mid-fifteenth century this led to the election of a king of Sweden, Karl Knuttson, who also faced internal opposition and only ruled for brief periods. The massacre of Stockholm carried out by the Danish king Christian II in 1520 in effect marked the end of the Union.

While national historical writing came relatively late to Sweden, the fifteenth century saw the appearance of a variety of writings on Swedish history. The first fully fledged prose history of Sweden was the *Chronica regni Gothorum* [Chronicle of the Realm of the Goths] written *circa* 1470 by Ericus Olai, canon and later dean at the archdiocese of Uppsala. His *Chronica* was the most ambitious of a number of historiographical enterprises at the Uppsala archsee in the fifteenth century. This late medieval Latin chronicle covers the period from the birth of Christ to about 1470.

The prologue presents the work as the history of the Swedish realm according to the succession of both worldly and ecclesiastical leaders. The theme of division between secular and ecclesiastical power is struck recurrently, arguably reflecting Ericus's concern for asserting the interests of the archdiocese in power struggles within the Swedish elite, the implied reader thus being a member of the local clergy in Uppsala.[1] The prologue establishes a strong focus on Uppsala as a divinely ordained centre of political and ecclesiastical power of the realm, a parallel to both Jerusalem and Rome. Swedish history is emphatically placed in the context of universal history. Ericus develops the medieval notion of Gothicism according to which the Goths, descendants of Noah's son Japhet, settled in Sweden and laid the foundation of an ancient and powerful empire.

By depicting Sweden as an old, independent nation Ericus contributed to the Swedish struggles for independence from Danish dominance from the 1470s and onwards. The Kalmar Union forms a sinister background to Ericus's narrative, and he strongly deplores the oppression suffered by Sweden under the rule of foreign monarchs.

Ericus based his account on a variety of texts. Among his native inspirations seems to have been the *Prosaiska krönika* [Prosaic Chronicle], a brief account in Swedish, probably compiled in the 1450s in circles close to the Swedish king, Karl Knuttson. Moreover, he had access to documents of the Uppsala archsee, some of which he inserted into his account, vernacular as well as Latin. The narrative is told in a plain, medieval Latin, unaffected by contemporary Renaissance ideals of the classicizing purity of the Latin language. The Bible is very much present throughout Ericus's history, which also bears witness to a European horizon of

---

[1] It has previously been suggested that Ericus's work was written at the request of Karl Knuttson, but this is unlikely in view of his rather critical attitude to the king. An ecclesiastical superior is more likely to have been the commissioner, but since no dedication or other information to this effect has been preserved, the issue remains unresolved. On Ericus Olai's chronicle, see Biörn Tjällén, 'Church and Nation: The Discourse on Authority in Ericus Olai's Chronica regni Gothorum (c. 1471)', Ph.D. thesis, Stockholm University, 2007.

texts encompassing not only late antique authors such as Jordanes and Augustine but also thirteenth-century writers.

A much more limited textual horizon is seen in the contemporary Swedish vernacular chronicles. Rhymed chronicles formed a prolific genre in late medieval Sweden (with German roots); they thrived particularly as vehicles to express royal interests. A sequence of chronicles came into being, beginning in the fourteenth century with the *Erikskrönika* [Erik's Chronicle] from *circa* 1330. Among them the *Karlskrönika* [Karl's Chronicle] tells of the period from the Danish Queen Margrete's taking of power in Sweden in 1389 until 1452 in the reign of Karl Knuttson, who, in opposition to the Danish Union king, had been proclaimed king of Sweden in 1448. In some versions the *Karlskrönika* was connected to the *Erikskrönika* and furnished with a prologue leading Karl Knuttson's genealogy back to S. Erik, in an attempt to strengthen Karl's claim to power. It is fairly certain that the chronicle was an official product. It was continued in the *Sturekrönikan* [Sture Chronicle] covering the period up to 1496. This sequence of chronicles was formerly referred to as *Store rimkrönikan* [The Long Rhymed Chronicle] to distinguish it from the *Lilla rimkrönikan* [The Brief Rhymed Chronicle], also dating from the 1450s, but later continued up to the 1520s. These chronicles are political statements with constant references to divine intervention.

Unlike the third-person chronicles that make up the *Store rimkrönikan*, the *Lilla rimkrönikan* consists of a series of monologues put into the mouths of the Swedish rulers from the oldest times and up to the 1440s. The *Lilla rimkrönikan* was probably written in circles close to Karl Knuttson. In the following decades it appears to have enjoyed popularity among the high nobility, and it was continued in the sixteenth century.

No Danish comprehensive history is known from the fifteenth century. In the ecclesiastical institutions annalistic writing took place, and the *Compendium Saxonis* [Compendium of Saxo] (an abbreviation of Saxo's *Gesta Danorum* [History of Denmark]) enjoyed some popularity. Nor does there appear to have been much historiographical activity in Norway in this period. An important text, however, was the Danish *Rimkrøniken* [The Rhymed Chronicle], a vernacular chronicle in verse covering Danish history from the earliest past and up to Christian I (r. 1448–81) on the basis of the *Compendium Saxonis* and its continuation the *Jutland Chronicle*.[2] Known through text witnesses of the late fifteenth century it is normally dated 1460–70s but an older date has been suggested. It was published in 1495. One version bears a dedication from 'brother Niels of Sorø' to Christian I, and this dedication can be dated to 1460–74, but Niels is now believed to have been an editor rather than an author.

---

[2] On *Rimkrøniken*, see Pernille Hermann, 'Politiske og æstetiske aspekter i Rimkrøniken', *Historisk tidsskrift*, 107:2 (2007), 389–410, with further references.

Rimkrøniken consists of monologues by each of the Danish kings, from the eponymous King Dan onwards. A link to biblical history is even established by the representation of Dan's father as descendant of Japhet, son of Noah—a parallel to Ericus Olai's claim that the Goths who settled in Sweden descended from Japhet. This monological form makes *Rimkrøniken* different from other late medieval rhymed chronicles, except the above-mentioned Swedish *Lilla rimkrönikan* whose date relative to *Rimkrøniken* is disputed. The monological principle has been stretched to the point that the kings relate their own death. They also display a tendency to make general moral observations on the basis of the events related. Despite the uncertainties surrounding the text, it seems safe to maintain that it was composed in circles close to royal and ecclesiastical power, the form of the royal monologues in itself, of course, securing a monarchical focus.

Relations to Denmark's German neighbour play a significant role as they do in the texts on which the chronicle is based. Moreover, the problematic relationship to Sweden in the reign of Christian I seems to have been emphasized in the redactions known through the surviving textual witnesses. Anti-Swedish passages are here found in the monologues of the earliest kings, and there are signs that they were interpolated.

In 1514 the great medieval work of Danish history, Saxo's *Gesta Danorum* (written *c*.1200), appeared in print in Paris, edited by Christiern Pedersen, an early Danish exponent of Renaissance humanism. Behind the publication of this edition were members of the highest aristocracy close to the king. Saxo's history may be seen as an emphatic statement about Denmark as a powerful nation with a long history, and this was a message well suited to support the present King Christian II (1513–23)—not least in his claim as ruler of the Kalmar Union, a position threatened by Swedish attempts to gain independence. Moreover, through its classicizing Latin and its echoes of Roman and biblical pasts, Saxo's history presented Denmark as a civilized nation with ancient traditions and an integral part of Latin, Christian Europe.[3]

No manuscript version of Saxo's *Gesta Danorum* older than the printed edition has been preserved. Had it not been for Christiern Pedersen's edition the text might not have survived. However, once printed it came to influence practically all succeeding national historiography, not only in Denmark but also throughout the rest of Scandinavia—and it secured Saxo a place in the canon of European national histories.

When Ericus Olai wrote his chronicle in about 1470, the art of printing had not yet reached Sweden. It was not printed until 1615, and its immediate impact is difficult to grasp. It did, however, have significant influence on the next great

---

[3] The political background to the publication of Saxo's history is discussed in Karsten Friis-Jensen, 'Humanism and Politics: The Paris Edition of Saxo Grammaticus's Gesta Danorum 1514', *Analecta Romani Instituti Danici*, 17–18 (1988–9), 149–62.

history of Sweden, written by Johannes Magnus in about 1530 and printed for the first time in 1554. Unlike Ericus's chronicle, Johannes Magnus's *Historia de omnibus Gothorum Sueonumque regibus* [History of all the Kings of the Goths and the Swedes] was deeply influenced by Renaissance humanism.[4] Written in classicizing Latin, it bears witness to the increased access to books that followed the spread of printing. An important inspiration, or rather provocation, for Johannes Magnus was the *editio princeps* of Saxo's history of Denmark.

Appointed archbishop in Uppsala in 1523 Johannes Magnus had to leave Sweden shortly afterwards with the advent of the Protestant Reformation under the new Swedish king, Gustavus Vasa. Magnus wrote his Swedish history during his exile years. It covers the period from the earliest beginnings up to about 1520. Building on the medieval notion of the Goths as descendants of Magog, grandson of Noah, Magnus traced the history of the Goths back to the Flood, depicting their advanced civilization, including their use of runic letters, which outdated Greek-Roman culture. Noah's grandson Magog settled in Sweden and inaugurated a Gothic Golden Age.

Magnus's celebration of the ancient Goths has much in common with the contemporary Germanist movement. Inspired by Tacitus's description of the Germans in the *Germania*, already printed several times before 1500, German humanists were able to describe the ways of living and the manners of the ancient Germans in positive terms, against the contemptuous accusations of barbarism from Italian humanists. Magnus's Goths share the German virtues, but Magnus went considerably further in his detailed constructions of the earliest past.

Hand in hand with the glorification of the Gothic/Swedish past went Johannes Magnus's contempt for all things Danish. He wrote his history against the backdrop of the break-up of the Kalmar Union in 1523, and throughout it the Danes are described as unreliable, cruel, and weak. A recurrent theme is the province of Scania (today the southern part of Sweden, until 1658 Danish), which in Magnus's view rightly belonged to Sweden and only illegitimately was reckoned as part of Denmark. Magnus saw the Kalmar Union as a struggle between Danish greed for power and Swedish love of liberty. As the *grand finale* of the whole work Magnus included a long speech *contra Danos*, 'against the Danes', pronounced in 1510 by a Swedish magnate; this summarizes the many historical reasons for Swedes to hold their Danish neighbours in contempt.

Johannes Magnus did not live to see his great work in print. His brother Olaus Magnus saw it to the press in 1554 in Rome. It gained a European public and laid the foundation for the national ideology of the Swedish Great Age of Empire in the seventeenth century. In 1555 Olaus Magnus himself published an ethnographical description of Scandinavia with particular focus on Sweden, *Historia de gentibus*

---

[4] The lives and works of Johannes Magnus and his brother Olaus Magnus are the subject of Kurt Johannesson, *The Renaissance of the Goths in Sixteenth-Century Sweden: Johannes and Olaus Magnus as Politicians and Historians*, trans. James Larson (Berkeley, 1991).

septentrionalibus [History of the Northern Peoples]. Strongly patriotic and full of folkloristic and exotic details about the peoples living in the far north and the nature surrounding them, Olaus Magnus's account is based on a wide reading of classical texts, in particular Pliny's natural history. Magnus's work would be widely read.

REFORMATION–1700

The break-up of the Kalmar Union was followed by the establishment of two stable monarchies, both embracing Lutheran Protestantism and both in practice hereditary. Administrative and governmental institutions were located in the capitals Copenhagen and Stockholm. Both monarchies instituted the practice of censorship, which gradually became systematized.[5] Particular attention was paid to the control of texts about religion and national history. National historiography was—as elsewhere in Europe—a political concern at the highest level. Both monarchies strove to have their history written in up-to-date versions by official historiographers engaged at the courts. The office of royal historiographer was created in Denmark in 1594 and in Sweden around 1640 (with some attempts earlier on), but in practice the kings and their governments had been commissioning national historical writings since the Reformation. The well-paid historiographers, who were also given access to archival material, wrote under the supervision of highly placed officials, and their works must therefore be regarded as expressions of governmental views which in turn were the result of internal negotiations about sensitive issues of national history.

The fact that several foreigners went into Swedish—and to a lesser extent Danish—service as historiographers in the seventeenth century is an indication of the international nature of official historiography in this period. The national histories that they were engaged to write—in Latin—were very much aimed at the international republic of learning where connections between scholars, diplomats, and politicians were close. The royal historian's task was primarily one of rhetorical adaptation, of creating a text that conformed to common European historical discourse.

They were complemented by court poets, who commemorated the events and heroes of national history, often in the prestigious classical epic form derived from Virgil's *Aeneid*. Historical poems served many of the same purposes as prose history. Written in Latin they could be read by well-educated foreigners; depicting the past from a national point of view, they were in themselves an advertisement to the world of the high level of humanistic culture that the Scandinavian countries had attained. On the other hand the poet had greater licence than the

---

[5] Only much later did some relaxation take place, in Sweden with the 1766 Ordinance for the Liberty of Printing, in Denmark (with the exception of the Struensee period 1770–2) not until 1849.

historian in his disposition of materials, and he was not expected to conduct extensive research. Poetical history, therefore, did not carry the same authority, nor did it fulfil the needs for a new national history. In the course of the period the distance between historical writing in prose and poetry widened, prose historiography moving gradually from the realm of classicizing and uniform *Kunstprosa* to that of scientific prose.

A particularly sensitive issue was the historical relationship between Denmark and Sweden. In 1570, after the Nordic Seven Years War (1563–70), defamatory writings between the two countries were forbidden, in recognition of their damaging influence before and during the war. The prohibition remained in force until the outbreak of the Scanian War in 1675. During this period the two governments respected this prohibition except in periods of open warfare; the persons engaged by the respective governments to review texts before publication saw to it that passages which might offend their neighbour were removed. However, no attempt was made to define what constituted defamatory writings, and it was thus left to political decision-makers and their advisers to judge whether a given statement might cause offence in the other kingdom, and to find a happy balance between praising one's own side and avoiding excessive insulting of the other.

With the Protestant Reformation, the Lutheran version of Renaissance humanism associated with Philipp Melanchthon came to dominate Scandinavian intellectual life. Melanchthon's view of history (succinctly expressed in his *Carion's Chronicle*[6]), his emphasis on the duty of the authorities to protect religion, and his Erasmian portrait of the good ruler as a *pater patriae* all had an immense impact on Danish historical discourse throughout the rest of the sixteenth century and well into the seventeenth. Indeed Melanchthon's portrayal of kings as God's vicars on Earth may be said to point ahead to the absolutist monarchies of the late seventeenth century.

In the 1530s, while the Catholic Johannes Magnus was writing his Latin history of Sweden during his Italian exile, another, very different, Swedish history was being composed in Sweden by one of the key figures of the Swedish Reformation, Olaus Petri.[7] Like Magnus's work, Petri's history was neither commissioned nor approved by Gustavus Vasa. Petri composed the first version of his history in the late 1530s. Written in Swedish, its intended audience was local and 'un-learned' as the author himself states—in line with his endeavours, also in other writings, to address the common man in the vernacular. The history focuses on the period after the Christianization of Sweden in the eleventh century until the massacre of Stockholm in 1520. In its general concept of the past, it is marked by a strong religious insistence on the *magistra vitae* view that history provides understanding

[6] For which see ch. 16 by Markus Völkel in this volume.

[7] Olaus Petri, *En Svensk Krönika*, in *Olavus Petri Samlade Skrifter*, ed. Bengt Hesselman, vol. 4 (Uppsala, 1914–17). Olaus Petri's Swedish history is the subject of Elisabeth Lundqvist, *Reformatorn skriver historia: en kontextuell analys av Olaus Petris svenska krönika* (Stockholm, 1998).

of God's ways with men, but divine intervention is rarely mentioned. In Old Testament tradition, Petri saw tyrants as God's punishment upon a sinful people, but he also stressed, following Erasmus and Melanchthon, the obligation of the prince towards his subjects. Interestingly, the work is free of the attacks on Catholic practices found elsewhere in the contemporary Protestant writings, including some of Petri's own.

At the same time Olaus Petri's history stands out for its critical awareness. Several established truths are questioned, such as the traditional 'Gothicist' view that the Goths had come to Sweden in the distant past and then conducted plundering expeditions in Europe. Indeed, Olaus Petri is sceptical towards the possibility of obtaining knowledge of Swedish history before the arrival of Christianity on account of the lack of written documents. In contrast to Ericus Olai and Johannes Magnus, Petri adopted a friendly attitude towards the Danish neighbour, pointing out that historians in both countries tended to glorify their own side.

Not surprisingly, Gustavus Vasa was displeased with Olaus Petri's history, even taking it as evidence that Olaus Petri wished to instigate a rebellion. Not only did the king prevent it from being printed, he also tried, in vain, to confiscate all manuscripts after Olaus Petri's death. But the history was widely read despite the fact that it was not printed until 1818.

The king found another writer, Bishop Peder Swart, willing to celebrate his deeds in print. Moreover, Swart composed, at the king's request, a polemical response to the Danish *Rimkrøniken* (re-edited 1555), focused on the tyranny exercised over Sweden in the Kalmar Union. Swart's rhymed chronicle was a vernacular contribution to the Danish–Swedish literary feud preceding the Nordic Seven Years War.

The last half of the sixteenth century saw intense efforts on the part of the Danish government to produce an up-to-date, Latin history of Denmark.[8] In the 1550s Hans Svaning set out to compose a history of Denmark acceptable to the government. When news reached Denmark that Magnus's history was being widely read abroad, Svaning was also commanded to compose a response. The result, *Refutatio calumniarum cuiusdam Ioannis Magni* [Refutation of a Certain Johannes Magnus's Slanders] (1561), answers one by one the accusations put forward in the speech *contra Danos* with which Magnus's history concludes. In the following decades Svaning worked on his history of Denmark, but in 1579 he was told to submit his manuscript to the censors. It was rejected, but the manuscript was kept in the Copenhagen University Library until it burned with the library in 1728. Enough of it survived, however, to give an impression of Svaning's intentions, which were to place Danish history within the frame of

---

[8] On Danish historiography in the period 1550–1600, see Karen Skovgaard-Petersen, *Historiography at the Court of Christian IV: Studies in the Latin Histories of Denmark by Johannes Pontanus and Johannes Meursius* (Copenhagen, 2001), ch. 4.

Melanchthonian universal history; he follows the list of kings found in Saxo but also creates links back to biblical times and to the Greek-Roman world.

As Johannes Magnus had written his Swedish history in response to Saxo's recently published medieval work, so Svaning's history was in turn provoked by Magnus's attacks on the Danes. In his history of Hans (r. 1481–1513), one of the Danish Kalmar Union kings, Svaning creates a picture of a noble, Danish king whose only fault is his tendency to think too well of the cunning Swedes. Magnus, by contrast, had described Hans as greedy and untrustworthy. Considering the prohibition against Danish–Swedish defamatory writings issued 1570, it seems likely that the anti-Swedish tendency of Svaning's work was part of the reason for its rejection in 1579.

After Svaning, Anders Sørensen Vedel, translator of Saxo into Danish (1575) and publisher of Adam of Bremen (1579), began working on a history of Denmark in agreement with the chancellor. Although he managed to write very little, his historiographical reflections are noteworthy. Echoing contemporary critical voices that were increasingly being raised throughout Europe, Vedel found the first part of Saxo's *Gesta Danorum* too full of fanciful elements to be trustworthy. Danish history in his view could not be traced back further than the beginning of written testimonies, *circa* AD 700. Moreover, he was probably the first Danish representative of the view—inspired by antiquarian studies of the Graeco-Roman past and by recent treatises on the *ars historica* (art of history)—that the proper subject of the historian should encompass a broad range of human activities, not only politics and wars.[9]

Not until the turn of the sixteenth century did a history of Denmark see the light in print: *Danmarks riges krønike* [Chronicle of Denmark] (1595–1604), written by the politically influential nobleman Arild Huitfeldt. Strictly annalistic, full of quotations of archival documents, and written in Danish it was meant to serve as a basis for a Latin reworking, not as a finished work in itself. Nevertheless, Huitfeldt's history marks a watershed in Danish historiography, distinguished as it is by the author's reflections and interpretations. The lessons he sees in history are of a political nature (inspired by Machiavelli among others), rather than instances of divine judgements in the Melanchthonian tradition. A firm supporter of the division of power between the king and the Privy Council, Huitfeldt stressed that Denmark had in the past been an elective kingdom. Less polemical than Svaning towards the Swedes, he nonetheless argued against Johannes Magnus on several issues, for instance the right to Scania.

It was on Huitfeldt's initiative, it seems, that the *Norske kongers krønicke* [Chronicle of Norwegian Kings] was published in 1594 in Copenhagen. It had

---

[9] The influence of the François Bauduin *De institutione historiae* (1561) on Vedel is discussed by Lars Boje Mortensen, 'The Influence of François Bauduin's *De institutione historiae* (1561): A Primary Text Behind Anders Sørensen Vedel's *De scribenda historia Danica* (1578)', *Symbolae Osloenses*, 73 (1998), 188–200.

been compiled already in the 1540s by Mattis Størssøn in Bergen, Norway, where a mainly vernacular humanist milieu flourished in the mid-sixteenth century. Its publication after half a century was a path-breaking event in Scandinavian historiography whereby medieval Norse literature became accessible in print for the first time. The chronicle consists of extracts from the medieval Norwegian-Icelandic kings' sagas, translated into Danish. Its main focus is the period after Norway's unification under Harald Fairhair (*c*.900). Another, more original history, *Om Norges rige* [On the Kingdom of Norway], which also contained a description of contemporary Norway, saw the light, though not in print, in 1567 in Bergen. The author, Absalon Beyer, here displays a sentimental patriotism and discreet regret of Norway's present dependence on Denmark, characterizing his own period as the 'old age' of Norway as opposed to the 'manhood' of the High Middle Ages.

In Sweden the latter half of the sixteenth century and the first decades of the seventeenth was a period with comparatively little historiographical activity. Johannes Magnus's history probably fulfilled the need though only covering the period up to the 1510s. The publication in 1595 of Huitfeldt's history of the Danish Reformation king Christian III provoked a Swedish riposte, a history of Gustavus Vasa written by Erik Jöransson Tegel at the request of Charles IX and printed in 1622, *Then stormechtighe, höghborne furstes och christelige herres her Gustaffs, fordom Sveriges . . . konungs historia* [History of the Mighty, Noble Prince and Christian Lord Gustaff, Former King of Sweden].

A central figure of Swedish intellectual history in the early seventeenth century was Johannes Messenius. Having distanced himself from his former Catholicism, he entered, in 1609, the service of Charles IX. As a professor, and later archivist, he published a variety of writings, including historical treatises and political pamphlets. One of them is a fierce answer, entitled *Retorsio imposturarum* [Retorsion of Impostures] (1612), to Svaning's *Refutatio calumniarum* (1561) (which had itself been a response to Johannes Magnus). No Swedish answer to Svaning had hitherto been published owing to the prohibition against Danish–Swedish defamatory writings in force since 1570. However, when in 1611 a new Danish–Swedish war broke out, the time was ripe. Messenius took up some well-known themes of the older Danish–Swedish polemics, arguing that Scania was rightfully Swedish and demonstrating how the Danish kings of the Kalmar Union had cunningly tricked the poor Swedes into servitude.

Messenius's favour with the government came to a sudden end. Accused of high treason, he spent the years 1616–35 in imprisonment in Finland. During this period, however, he managed to compose the *Scondia illustrata* [Scandinavia Described], a milestone work in seventeenth-century Scandinavian historiography.[10] The text reflects Messenius's wide reading of printed books as well as transcripts of documents.

---

[10] First published in an abridged form in 1700–5 by Johan Peringskiöld.

The *Scondia illustrata* consists of a chronological history of Sweden (and for the earliest period also of Norway and Denmark) and a second part contains supplemental materials, ecclesiastical history, and discussions of various subjects. The chronological narrative, which stretches from the earliest beginnings and up to Messenius's own day, itself only occasionally refers to other texts and rarely hints at uncertainties either in factual matters or in judgement. The oldest segments are written in the Gothicist tradition, beginning with Noah's sons and describing the Scandinavian peninsula as a *vagina gentium*, home to an old Gothic, literary culture. However, in one of the additional chapters Messenius distances himself from Johannes Magnus's—and Saxo's—fanciful and chauvinistic constructions of the oldest history. Most of the chronological narrative is concerned with medieval and later history. Regarding the Danish neighbour, Messenius, though much less aggressively than his own *Retorsio imposturarum*, generally follows the hostile tradition from Ericus Olai and Magnus, disagreeing, for instance, with arguments taken from the oldest history that Danish monarchs could legitimately use the title of King of the Goths.

After Messenius's death the Swedish government was interested in obtaining his manuscripts and having them prepared for publication. Even though nothing came of it at the time, this was a clear expression of the government's interest in having a new national history published at a time when Sweden was emerging as a great power.

Around the middle of the seventeenth century one can observe an energetic historiographical activity centred on the Swedish government. In Denmark a similar interest on the part of the government in having a national history composed and published in Latin had emerged during the reign of Christian IV (1588–1648), particularly in the 1620s when Denmark was trying to play a role on the European scene in the early stages of the Thirty Years War. Huitfeldt's epoch-making history of Denmark from *circa* 1600 could not fulfil the need. It was left to the Dutch-Danish Johannes Isacius Pontanus, royal historiographer from 1618 to his death in 1639, to adapt Huitfeldt's Danish work to a full-scale Latin history, the huge *Rerum Danicarum historia* [History of Denmark] (1631).[11] Pontanus was an exponent of the antiquarian branch of national historiography. He not only devoted a separate section to giving a thematic presentation of Denmark—topography, monuments, trade, language, origins, intellectual history, character, etc.—but also included these subjects in the chronological narrative.

This antiquarian approach must be seen within the context of an enormous increase in available texts in the wake of the spread of print. Antiquarian studies thrived with the growing possibilities of conducting systematic investigations 'across' a variety of texts. Pontanus's text was based on a huge quantity of classical, medieval, and contemporary texts, on which Pontanus conducted

---

[11] On Johannes Pontanus and his colleague Johannes Meursius (cf. below), see Skovgaard-Petersen, *Historiography at the Court of Christian IV*. This Johannes Pontanus should not be confused with the better-known fifteenth-century Italian historian Giovanni Pontano.

discussions and from which he elicited extensive quotations. Also in this stylistic respect, Pontanus's text was influenced by systematic antiquarian studies—he eschewed the classical historiographical ideal of a stylistically uniform narrative.

Pontanus's position as royal historiographer is reflected in his text. His monarchical focus is stronger than Huitfeldt's, and he even claims that Denmark is close to being a hereditary monarchy. He deals a blow to Johannes Magnus's construction of a glorious Gothic past by demonstrating that it rests on a false identification of two peoples in the ancient world, the Goths and the *Getae*. Rejecting the traditional early history derived from Saxo, he allowed Danish history to begin with the Cimbrians' march against Rome around 100 BC and then continued with the late antique and medieval migrations from Scandinavia of the Goths, Saxons, and others. While more acceptable from a scholarly point of view than the legendary tales in Saxo, this approach drastically foreshortened Danish history. But it did have a patriotic potential resembling Johannes Magnus's Gothicism through its focus on Danish influence abroad. Like Magnus, Pontanus was inspired by Tacitus's description of the noble Germans, and he shared Magnus's interest in emphasizing the high level of culture among the ancient Scandinavians.

In the same period another Dutchman, Johannes Meursius, was engaged as historiographer to Christian IV. His *Historia Danica* [Danish History] (1638) is much briefer than Pontanus's work and has none of its antiquarian features. Meursius's text is coloured by Christian moralism, in particular a Melanchthonian emphasis on rulers as God's vicars. This thematic unity also comes out stylistically. He adduces no quotations from other texts and only rarely discusses the information given. The point of his narrative is the judgements to be passed on historical actors and events, not the factual basis on which they rest.

Before publication both Pontanus's and Meursius's histories were controlled by the chancellor or persons he trusted. In particular the relationship with Sweden remained sensitive, and the chancellor would not risk transgressing the prohibition against Danish–Swedish defamatory writings. Consequently, both histories took a cautious line.

Pontanus's and Meursius's histories served as standard works on Danish history well into the eighteenth century. However, already in the 1660s another Latin history of Denmark was written at the request of the government. Vitus Bering's *Florus Danicus* [The Danish Florus] is a brief, stylistically coherent presentation of Danish history, inspired by the Roman historian Lucius Florus. Appointed shortly after the introduction of absolutist and hereditary monarchy in Denmark in 1660–1, Bering was commissioned to contribute to the historical legitimization of the new system by demonstrating that hereditary monarchy had old roots. Danish history had to be re-written in the light of the introduction of hereditary monarchy.

In Sweden the office of royal historiographer was formalized around 1640. Already in 1618, however, the Dutch scholar Daniel Heinsius had accepted the post of Swedish royal historiographer—an offer probably related to Pontanus's appointment as Danish historiographer, but Heinsius's engagement never materialized. In the early 1650s Johannes Loccenius was engaged as Swedish historiographer. He had previously published a pioneering description of medieval Sweden based on his research into Swedish law. In the first edition of his history, *Rerum Svecicarum historia* [History of Sweden] (1654), he waxed sceptical towards the possibility of obtaining knowledge of the pre-Christian period and began with the earliest Christian kings. This was a drastic reduction of the long Swedish past, and he later made up for this by adding an account of the earliest past in the Gothicist tradition. The narrative is limited to political history with occasional general observations of a political nature. Loccenius followed the tradition from Ericus Olai that blamed foreign rulers for Swedish calamities. He portrays the Kalmar Union as a dark period culminating in the monstrous tyranny of Christian II, after which Gustavus Vasa, founder of the ruling dynasty, was sent by God.

Antiquarian studies thrived during the seventeenth century. After the publication of Magnus's history, which claimed that runes had been invented by the Goths shortly after the Deluge, Danish scholars were keen to emphasize that runes were not a Swedish monopoly; in turn the Swede Johannes Bureus stressed the runes' Swedish origins. This challenge was taken up in Denmark by Ole Worm, who eventually published his comprehensive work on Danish runic inscriptions, *Monumenta Danica* [Danish Monuments] (1643). The atmosphere of rivalry thus inspired scholarship, while preventing both sides from recognizing the neighbour's part in the runes. However, they shared the basic interest in presenting the long, civilized traditions of their respective countries to a European audience.

The value of Icelandic saga manuscripts as testimonies of the Nordic past was gradually realized beginning in the late sixteenth century. Among Worm's publications was an edition of Snorre's kings' sagas (1633), translated into Danish by the Norwegian dean Peder Claussøn Friis. Worm shared his interest in Old Norse with Stephanus J. Stephanius. The latter's learned commentary on Saxo's history of Denmark demonstrates the importance of Norse medieval literature for the interpretation of Saxo, and it is in itself a testimony to Saxo's status as a canonical history within the European republic of learning.

A decisive inspiration to Worm's and Stephanius's Old Norse studies had come from the Icelander Arngrímur Jónsson. In *Crymogaea* [Iceland] (1609), the first history of Iceland written in humanist tradition, Arngrímur creates a parallel between medieval Icelandic history and the rise and fall of the Roman republic, as laid out by the French political and historical theorist Jean Bodin. Arngrímur celebrates the Icelandic language as the mother tongue of the north, placing it on par with ancient Latin and close to biblical Hebrew.[12]

The Icelandic saga manuscripts were studied in an atmosphere of competition between Sweden and Denmark. While Danish scholars took the lead in the first

---

[12] See Gottskálk Jensson, 'The Latin of the North: Arngrímur Jónsson's Crymogæa (1609) and the Discovery of Icelandic as a Classical Language', *Renaessanceforum*, 5 (2008). Available online at www.renaessanceforum.dk (accessed 27 March 2011).

phase—Iceland being part of the Danish realm—these studies were eventually given an institutional framework in Sweden with the establishment of the 'Antikvitetskollegium' (College of Antiquities) in 1667. From a Swedish point of view the sagas were a welcome opportunity to construct an early past independent of Saxo. Focusing on those saga texts that had a Swedish connection, the Antikvitetskollegium published editions and studies, the crowning achievement being Johan Peringskiöld's edition in 1697 of Snorre's *Heimskringla* [The Circle of the World] (comp. mid-thirteenth century). Peringskiöld presents the text as a monument of Swedish as well as of Norwegian history, a history of those 'born of Gothic blood'. This did not include the Danes. But Norway, though politically part of Denmark, was not encompassed by Swedish anti-Danish rhetoric; on the contrary, Johannes Magnus had already made a point of pitying the Norwegians for the unfair treatment they suffered from the Danish kings.

While the studies of runes, saga manuscripts, archaeological monuments, and other antiquities led to deepened insight into Scandinavian medieval history, they also, paradoxically, took Gothicist constructions to new fanciful heights. Among Swedish intellectuals the idea gained ground that not only had the Goths known the art of writing long before the Greeks and Romans, the latter even owed their civilization to the Goths; classical civilization had its roots in ancient Gothic society. The most fantastic expression of these visions was the *Atlantica* (1679–1702) of Olof Rudbeck, professor in Uppsala. Rudbeck here identified Plato's sunken ideal society Atlantis with the Gothic realm and also found veiled references to Sweden in other classical myths. His point of departure remained the Old Testament, and Rudbeck, like Johannes Magnus, regarded Japhet, son of Noah, as the ancestor of the Swedes. Rudbeck insisted on publishing the text in Swedish— to him the oldest and finest of languages—and only reluctantly agreed to add a Latin translation. The *Atlantica* was the monumental culmination of Gothicism, published at a time when the Swedish Empire was at its height. Highly acclaimed at home and abroad in its own day, critical voices were soon raised against it.

Historiography of a different sort was produced by the German philosopher Samuel von Pufendorf, who served as professor in the new University of Lund (in Scania) from 1670 and from 1677 as royal historiographer to the Swedish king until he left Sweden in 1688. As Swedish royal historiographer he wrote two comprehensive works of recent history, the *Commentarium de rebus Suecicis* [Commentaries on Swedish Affairs] (1686) and the *De rebus a Carolo Gustavo gestis* [Of the Deeds of Charles Gustavus] (1696). The narrative is based on original documents, which Pufendorf managed to adapt into a succinct and coherent narrative with a focus on political events.

Pufendorf's successor as royal historiographer, Clas Örnhielm, published a Swedish church history, *Historia Ecclesiastica* (1689), covering the period *circa* 800–1200. Strongly hostile towards medieval Catholic practice, Örnhielm even claimed that Charlemagne's brutal conversions in northern Germany, instigated by the pope, were the reason that Scandinavians, acting in self-defence, set out on their Viking raids.[13] As royal historiographer, Örnhielm was requested to write texts for the *Suecia antiqua et hodierna* [Sweden in Antiquity and Today], an illustrated description of Sweden. Only the copper-engraved planches were published (1716), but the project was a monumental expression of Swedish ambitions at a time when its sun was beginning to set.

Swedish Gothicism also inspired historical writing in the Finnish part of the Swedish realm. Humanist historiography had made its first modest appearance in the late sixteenth century when the Bishop of Turku, Paulus Juusten, wrote an expanded version of a late medieval chronicle of bishops in Turku.[14] In the mid-seventeenth century, Michael Wexionius-Gyldenstolpe, professor in Aabo/Turku, discussed the origin of the Finns in his *Epitome descriptionis Sveciae, Gothiae, Fenningiae* [A Short Account of Sweden, Gothia, Finland] (1650), expressing uncertainty as to which of Noah's sons should be reckoned a Finnish ancestor. Wexionius-Gyldenstolpe depicts Finland as a formerly independent kingdom and attempts a general, and flattering, description of the country and its inhabitants. The Gothicist perspective was retained by Daniel Juslenius, who dated the foundation of Aabo/Turku shortly after Magog's arrival in Finland and traced the Finnish language back to the Babylonian Confusion of Tongues.

Until the introduction of absolute monarchy in Denmark-Norway in 1660–1, Norwegian history, as has already been noted, had lived a shadowy life within Danish historiography. After the Lutheran Reformation in Denmark-Norway in 1536, Norway was in principle reduced to a Danish province although not completely in practice. One indication that Norway was not simply regarded as a Danish province, is the fact that Norwegian history did not figure in the histories of Denmark planned and written in this period.

After 1660–1 the status of the two realms became at least in principle equal; there was now political interest in producing a history of Norway. In 1682 Tormod Torfæus, an Icelander attached to the court in Copenhagen, became Norwegian royal historiographer, and almost thirty years later, in 1711, his monumental *Historia rerum Norvegicarum* [History of Norway], a Norwegian history up to 1387, appeared in print.[15] Norway is here depicted as having been a hereditary monarchy ever since Harald Fairhair's institution of monarchical rule (*c.*900). It seems clear that Torfæus, like Bering, was requested to contribute to legitimizing the newly established Danish-Norwegian hereditary monarchy.

---

[13] This is pointed out by Hans Helander, *Neo-Latin Literature in Sweden in the Period 1620–1720: Stylistics, Vocabulary and Characteristic Ideas* (Uppsala, 2004), 322.

[14] This was not published until the eighteenth century, see further below.

[15] A Norwegian translation of the first part of Torfæus's *Historia rerum Norvegicarum* was published in 2008. The points made here are elaborated in Karen Skovgaard-Petersen, 'The First Post-Medieval History of Norway in Latin: The *Historia Rerum Norvegicarum* (Copenhagen, 1711) by Tormod Torfæus', in Eckhard Kessler and Heinrich C. Kuhn (eds.), *Germania latina—Latinitas teutonica* (Munich, 2003), 707–20.

In its antiquarian orientation Torfæus's work resembles Pontanus's Danish history. But whereas Pontanus had rejected the traditional local account of the early past (Saxo), Torfæus was able to present early Norwegian history in a new shape based on local tradition, namely Icelandic medieval literature. He reworked this material into a coherent Latin history also taking into account a large number of Latin histories. Based on Snorre and some of the Edda poems, he constructed a Norwegian list of kings reaching back to Noah. Due to his trust in Old Norse literature, Torfæus displays none of Pontanus's scepticism regarding the possibility of obtaining knowledge of periods older than those described by classical authors. But like Pontanus, Torfæus writes in an argumentative style replete with quotations, making no attempt at a classicizing style. He even declares that this pedestrian writing better suited the Nordic people than artificial elegance. Torfæus's history is thus a statement, in Latin, of Norway's place in the civilized world while at the same time anchoring it to a non-Latin, independent medieval literary culture.

1700–1800

The eighteenth century witnessed the emergence of a new public sphere in Scandinavia as elsewhere, a development that strongly influenced historiography. National histories addressed to a general readership were published in print. New ideals of scholarly communication with a wider readership gained ground, as did the use of vernacular languages even within the academic community. Enlightenment ideas of utility, criticism of religion, tolerance, and rationalism also suffused contemporary historical writings. As professional writers, historiographers became less dependent on powerful patrons and more on their popularity with a wider audience of readers.

Even more than in the previous sections of this chapter, it is impossible to do justice to the richness of historiography during this period, and instead of brief references to many texts and authors, a few important texts have been selected. In Denmark, still under absolutist rule, the first decades of the eighteenth century saw a serious attempt at continuing official historiography. Pufendorf's widely acclaimed works on Swedish history posed a challenge. In 1722 Andreas Hoier was appointed royal historiographer and commanded to compose a history of the ruling monarch, Frederik IV.[16] At the death of Frederik IV in 1730, Hoier had taken his account up to 1711. This work was never published but it deserves mention as a pioneering effort to write contemporary history on the basis of

---

[16] On Hojer's and Holberg's historical works, see Torben Damsholt, 'Den nationale magtstat 1560–1760', in Søren Mørch (ed.), *Danmarks historie*, vol. 10 (København, 1992), 53–104; and Ellen Jørgensen, *Historieforskning og historieskrivning i Danmark indtil aar 1800* (Copenhagen, 1931), 160–86.

archival material. Written in German and intended to be translated into Latin, this work was aimed at a European public. In the early 1730s Hoier, no longer officially engaged as royal historiographer, wrote a briefer account of the reign of Frederik IV, *König Friedrich des IV glorwürdigstes Leben* (not published until 1829).

A key figure of the Scandinavian Enlightenment was the Norwegian-Danish Ludvig Holberg, whose multifaceted literary oeuvre included several historical works. In 1730 Holberg was appointed professor of history in Copenhagen, having published the year before a description of Denmark-Norway. In this capacity he published a history of Denmark.[17] His status as an independent writer did not, of course, free him from censorship, but the distance between historians and government had grown in comparison with the royal historiographers of the seventeenth century: national history was no longer primarily a governmental concern.

Holberg's history broke new ground. Written in Danish, its readership was the emergent Danish and Norwegian reading public, and Holberg strove to 'attract the reader's attention'. He shared the interests of the antiquarian historians in broadening the field of historical subjects. One of his inventions was a division of Danish history into five periods, each of which he characterized in separate surveys with a focus on religion, laws, economy, and similar themes. But he emphasized that the information must be useful and relevant, proclaiming a pragmatic approach with discussions of motives and a strong focus on internal affairs; historical writing, in his view, should inform about 'Morals, public law, and matters of the state', as he states in the introduction to the third volume of his history of Denmark.[18]

The earliest periods continued to pose special problems. Holberg did not trust Saxo's account of the ancient past with its supernatural elements; still less did he favour attempts to track Danish kings back to Noah. But he did have faith in classical and early medieval testimonies about the migrations of Goths, Anglo-Saxons, and Normans. Following Pontanus's *Rerum Danicarum historia*, Holberg began his account of Danish history with these migrations. But he did not echo Pontanus's (and other seventeenth-century historians') triumphalist celebration of these early medieval raids. Instead, he praised the kings who advanced beneficent activities such as commerce; he even softened the traditional judgement of Christian II as an arch-tyrant by suggesting that a more positive picture would emerge if the views of contemporary citizens of Copenhagen were included. Nor did Holberg share the older historians' negative attitude towards Sweden. His striving for impartiality is seen in his treatment of the Danish–Swedish discussions about the right to Scania, but a certain pro-Danish attitude colours his account of the Kalmar Union.

---

[17] Ludvig Holberg, *Dannemarks Riges Historie* (Copenhagen, 1732–5).
[18] Ibid., fol. c1r.

Though basing his account on a wide variety of texts, Holberg managed, in keeping with his wish to appeal to the general reader, to compose a coherent narrative in an entertaining style, sometimes striking a disrespectful tone very different from the solemnity of the older official historiographers. But Holberg was also aware of the limits posed by censorship. Realizing the difficulties of treating the more recent past without being subject to personal interests, he refrained from taking his account further than the death of Frederik III in 1670. Somewhat ambiguously he later, in his *Epistle* 447, declared that 'few histories subjected to public censorship have been written with more honesty'.[19] Holberg was the most important Scandinavian representative of the philosophical branch of historiography in the eighteenth century. His history of Denmark was republished twice in the eighteenth century and translated into German and Russian.

In Sweden the age of Enlightenment saw a transition from monarchical rule to a system where power lay with the estates, the so-called Age of Liberty (1719–72). Among the historiographers employed by the estates was Olof Dalin, who had established himself as a poet and editor of the journal *Den swenska Argus* when in 1744 he was commissioned to compose a history of Sweden. Three years later he published the first part, and the remaining parts appeared in 1750 and 1761–2.[20]

In style as well as in content Dalin was an exponent of enlightened ideas. Writing in Swedish about Swedish history up to 1611, Dalin addresses the general public with an explicit edifying purpose, emphasizing the utility of history with appeals to 'common sense'. In keeping with this broad implied readership and his didactic view of historical writing, Dalin, like Holberg, writes in a light and entertaining style. The learned apparatus has been assigned to footnotes, thus combining a fluent discourse with a heavy display of learning. The narrative itself rarely reveals uncertainty as to the information provided. The prominent narrator passes unwavering moral judgements upon persons and actions—for example, strongly criticizing the worldly power of the medieval Church—and sometimes deduces general observations from the events.

In a long chapter on the earliest times Dalin gives a broad description of religion, letters, and ways of life. This period looms significantly larger in Dalin than in Holberg. While both distanced themselves from traditional theories about the earliest past, there are important differences between their accounts: whereas Holberg refrained from voicing an opinion, Dalin launched his own theory. Employing new geological insights, together with archaeological and linguistic arguments, Dalin claimed that Sweden had consisted of scattered

---

[19] Ludvig Holberg, *Epistler, Tomus V* (Copenhagen, 1754), 18.

[20] Olof von Dalin, *Svea rikes historia ifrån des begynnelse til wåra tider, efter hans kongl. maj:ts nådiga behag på riksens höglofliga ständers åstundan författad af Olof Dalin* (Stockholm, 1747–62). On Dalin, see Nils Eriksson, *Dalin—Botin—Lagerbring: historieforskning och historieskrivning i Sverige 1747–1787* (Göteborg, 1973); and Peter Hallberg, *Ages of Liberty: Social Upheaval, History Writing, and the New Public Sphere in Sweden, 1740–1792* (Stockholm, 2003).

islands until shortly before Christ when water began to withdraw. The first inhabitants had arrived, he thought, about 500 BC, a drastic shortening of history compared with Johannes Magnus. In his introduction Dalin criticized Johannes Magnus for his long succession of kings that 'no sensible lover of the past can acknowledge'.[21]

However, Dalin was not a stranger to other features of Gothicism. The Goths were blessed with love of freedom, honour, etc., their laws influenced legislation in other parts of Europe, and the northern climate made them suited for mathematical studies. Citing the authority of Tacitus's *Germania*, Dalin, like earlier Scandinavian historians, stresses the high moral standards of the Goths. Another Gothicist reminiscence occurs in Dalin's insistence that the Danish neighbours cannot claim as long a history as the Swedes: the Danish islands, we learn, were not colonized until long after the arrival of the Goths in Sweden.

Dalin and Holberg agree in their support of enlightened, monarchical rule. Dalin praises the kings who have made useful laws and promoted peaceful prosperity, and he sees aggressive warfare as no mark of glory. The monarch who promotes research and science deserves particular respect. Although Dalin's history of Sweden was criticized for its informal style as well as for its curtailing of Sweden's early past—a threat to national dignity—it became widely popular, though most of its readers, judging from the lists of subscribers, belonged to the upper classes. It also appeared in German translation.

Along with Holberg's and Dalin's efforts to narrate national history in the vernacular, historians of antiquarian orientation continued to use Latin in their commentaries, their collections of *monumenta*, and their studies of particular subjects. These historians, with their emphasis on critical research, would be hailed in later times as fathers of Scandinavian historical science. An early eighteenth-century representative of this branch was the Swedish philologist and librarian Eric Benzelius. In Denmark, Hans Gram, also a philologist and librarian, wrote several path-breaking studies of Danish history; many of his best insights can be found in his extensive commentary on Meursius's history. The towering intellectual of eighteenth-century Finland, still under Swedish rule, was Henrik Gabriel Porthan. His fame as an historian rests on his edition of a medieval bishop's chronicle (expanded by Juusten in the sixteenth century), which he provided with an extensive critical apparatus.

A narrative synthesis of Icelandic history appeared in Latin as late as 1772–8, the *Historia ecclesiastica Islandiae* [Ecclesiastical History of Iceland] by Finnur Jónsson. This pioneering account deals with the political, cultural, and ecclesiastical history of the period 870–1740. Inspired by Arngrímur's earlier *Crymogaea*, Finnur Jónsson celebrated the period before Norwegian rule as a golden age of

---

[21] Olaf von Dalin, *Svea rikes historia ifrån des begynnelse til wåra tider, efter hans kongl. maj:ts nådiga behag på riksens högloflige ständers åstundan författad af Olof Dalin*, 4 vols. (Stockholm, 1747–62), i. fol.)( )(4v.

freedom, drawing, as had Arngrímur, a parallel with the Roman republic. In the same period the Norwegian historian Gerhard Schøning published his account—in Dano-Norwegian—of the early medieval history of Norway, emphasizing the peculiar qualities of Norwegians as strong and freedom-loving— a point of view at the same time related to and opposed to Swedish Gothicism.[22]

Like Schøning and Finnur Jónsson, Sven Lagerbring (born Sven Bring) combined antiquarian studies and editions with writing narrative history.[23] Professor of history in Lund since 1742, he wrote, late in his life, a history of Sweden covering the period up to 1460.[24] Unlike Dalin, Lagerbring wrote his history on his own initiative, a major incentive to his work being the short-comings that he found in Dalin's history. With a strong insistence on the principle that older sources must be preferred to more recent, he strove to remove the errors that had been allowed to creep into his predecessors' works. This critical approach (resulting in fresh views on traditionally negative figures such as the Danish Queen Margrete) has secured for his work an important position in the history of Swedish historiography.

Lagerbring wrote in Swedish. But his history was not, like Dalin's, explicitly written for the general public, nor did he insist on utility and relevance. Lagerbring's work is scholarly in style and argumentation. Its apparatus of notes is used for documentary quotations of sources, and debates with earlier historians loom large in the text itself. Lagerbring's implied readership is Scandi-navian intellectuals but, particularly in its abridged version, it also reached an international audience in German and French translations.

Lagerbring agrees with Dalin in stressing the trustworthiness of the Icelandic saga tradition, a point of view that was criticized as old-fashioned by some contemporary critics. He is no friend of Gothicism, and he does not echo Dalin's glorification of the ancient Swedes and their cultural achievements. The two historians are both in favour of a strong monarchy and both condemn medieval Catholicism. But Dalin presses this last point more forcefully. He blames, for instance, the clergy for being pro-Danish in the period of the Kalmar Union, whereas Lagerbring, in line with his general negative attitude towards the nobility, focuses on internal factions in the Swedish aristocracy.

Lagerbring treats the Danish neighbour with more respect than tradition prescribed. This attitude mirrors both political and cultural developments and Lagerbring's own contacts with Danish and Norwegian historians. Far from the old historiographical polemics, Scandinavian historians from the late eighteenth century onwards began to practise collaboration, and Lagerbring may be seen as

---

[22] Gerhard Schøning, *Norges Riiges Historie* (Sorø, 1771–81).
[23] On Lagerbring, see Eriksson, *Dalin—Botin—Lagerbring*.
[24] Sven Lagerbring, *Swea rikes historia, ifrån de äldsta tider til de närwarande* (Stockholm, 1769–83).

an exponent of a new phase of fruitful exchange between Swedes and Danes in the study of the past.

CONCLUSION

Early modern Scandinavian historiography participated, as we have seen, in common European developments. The dramatic increase of accessible texts that followed the invention of printing profoundly influenced historical writing. In particular, the rise of antiquarian studies widened the field of subjects—such as laws, institutions, customs, and languages—that could be treated even in narrative historiography. Scholars during this period developed new standards of documentation, quotations, and references, and they refined critical principles for the evaluation of evidence.

As long as Latin dominated national historical writing, its audience, implied and real, was the international world of learning and diplomacy. In the eighteenth century historians began to write for the growing local readership in the vernaculars, which gradually gained status as vehicles for scholarship. In this period the governmental control exercised since the establishment of centralized monarchies in the mid-sixteenth century also loosened, allowing for more independent interpretations of national history.

At the same time other features were particular to Scandinavian historiography. The ongoing political rivalry between Denmark and Sweden had a strong impact on historical writing especially in the sixteenth and seventeenth centuries. Even more fundamental was the tension running through most of the period between emphasizing participation in European culture and stressing independent local tradition. The Gothicist line of thought, variants of which were found in all the Scandinavian countries, was one way of claiming an ancient Scandinavian civilization superior to the Graeco-Roman. The growing awareness of the Old Norse literary heritage in the seventeenth century gave new impulses to the insistence on a specific Scandinavian cultural tradition, an interest that would be taken even further in the Romantic period with its fascination with pagan mythology and cult of linguistic and ethnic origins.

TIMELINE/KEY DATES

1397–1523 Union of Kalmar between Denmark, Norway, and Sweden
1523 Gustavus Vasa becomes king of Sweden (with Finland); Frederik I becomes king of Denmark and Norway
1527 Beginning of Lutheran Reformation in Sweden
1536 Lutheran Reformation in Denmark
1563–70 The Nordic Seven Years War between Denmark and Sweden

1611–13 The Kalmar War between Denmark-Norway and Sweden

1657–60 Dano-Swedish Wars; the province of Scania, hitherto Danish, becomes Swedish in the Peace of Roskilde in 1658

1660/1–1849 Absolute monarchy in Denmark

1672–1719 Absolute monarchy in Sweden

1675–9 The Scanian War between Denmark and Sweden

1700–21 Great Northern War between Sweden and Russia with Denmark and Poland

1719–72 Swedish Age of Liberty

1809 Finland gains independence from Sweden (1809–1917 united with Russia)

1814 Norway gains independence from Denmark (1814–1905 united with Sweden)

KEY HISTORICAL SOURCES

Arngrímur Jónsson, *Crymogaea sive Rerum Islandicarum Libri II* (Hamburg, 1609).

Dalin, Olof von, *Svea rikes historia ifrån des begynnelse til wåra tider, efter hans kongl. maj:ts nådiga behag på riksens höglofliga ständers åstundan författad af Olof Dalin* (Stockholm, 1747–62).

Ericus Olai, *Chronica regni Gothorum* (1615), ed. Jan Öberg (Stockholm, 1993–5).

Finnur Jonsson, *Historia ecclesiastica Islandiae* (Copenhagen, 1772–8).

Holberg, Ludvig, *Dannemarks Riges Historie* (Copenhagen, 1732–5).

Huitfeldt, Arild, *Danmarks riges krønike* (Copenhagen, 1595–1604; facs. edn, Copenhagen 1977).

Klemming, G. E. (ed.), *Svenska Medeltidens Rim-krönikor* (Stockholm, 1866).

Lagerbring, Sven, *Swea rikes historia, ifrån de äldsta tider til de närwarande* (Stockholm, 1769–83).

Loccenius, Johannes, *Rerum suecicarum historia* (1654; 2nd edn, Stockholm, 1662).

Magnus, Johannes, *Historia de omnibus Gothorum Sueonumque regibus* (Rome, 1554).

Messenius, Johannes, *Retorsio imposturarum, quibus inclytam Suecorum Gothorumque nationem, Petrus Parvus Rosefontanus eques Danus...insectatur; quam...elaboravit Janus Minor Suemensis* (1612).

—— *Scondia illustrata seu chronologia de rebus Scondiæ, hoc est Sueciæ, Daniæ, Norvegiæ, atque una Islandiæ, Gronlandiæque tam ecclesiasticis quam politicis; â mundi cataclysmo, usque annum Christi MDCXII, gestis primum edita, et observationibus aucta â Johanne Peringskiöld* (1700–5).

Petri, Olaus, *En Swensk Cröneka*, in *Olavus Petri Samlade Skrifter*, ed. Bengt Hesselman, vol. 4 (Uppsala, 1914–17). Available online at http://runeberg.org/opetri/ (accessed 25 March 2011).

Pontanus, Johannes, *Rerum Danicarum historia* (Amsterdam, 1631).

Porthan, H. G. (ed.), *M. Pauli Juusten Chronicon episcoporum finlandensium, annotationibus et sylloge monumentorum illustratum* (1784–1800).

Pufendorf, Samuel von, *Commentariorum de rebus Suecicis Libri 26 ab Expeditione Gustavi Adolfi Regis in Germaniam ad Abdicationem usque Christinae* (Utrecht, 1686).

Pufendorf, Samuel von, *De Rebus a Carolo Gustavo Sveciæ Rege gestis Commentariorum Libri 7* (Nürnberg, 1696).

Den danske Rimkrønike (Copenhagen, 1495). Digital facsimile at http://www.kb.dk/permalink/2006/manus/217/eng// (accessed 27 March 2011).

Rudbeck, Olof, *Atland eller Manhem* (Uppsala, 1679–1702).

Schøning, Gerhard, *Norges Riiges Historie* (Sorø, 1771–81).

Størssøn, Mattis, *Den norske krønike* (1594), ed. Mikjel Sørlie (Oslo, 1962).

Svaning, Hans, *Refutatio calumniarum cuiusdam Ioannis Magni . . . huic accessit Chronicon sive Historia Ioannis Regis Daniæ* (1561; published under the pseudonym Petrus Parvus Rosefontanus in 1560).

Torfæus, Tormod, *Historia rerum Norvegicarum* (Copenhagen, 1711); trans. into Norwegian as *Norges historie* (Bergen, 2008–).

BIBLIOGRAPHY

Damsholt, Torben, 'Den nationale magtstat 1560–1760', in Søren Mørch (ed.), *Danmarks historie*, vol. 10 (København, 1992), 53–104.

Eriksson, Nils, *Dalin—Botin—Lagerbring: historieforskning och historieskrivning i Sverige 1747–1787* (Göteborg, 1973).

Friis-Jensen, Karsten, 'Humanism and Politics: The Paris Edition of Saxo Grammaticus's Gesta Danorum 1514', *Analecta Romani Instituti Danici*, 17–18 (1988–9), 149–62.

Gottskálk Jensson, 'The Latin of the North: Arngrímur Jónsson's Crymogæa (1609) and the Discovery of Icelandic as a Classical Language', *Renaessanceforum*, 5 (2008). Available online at www.renaessanceforum.dk (accessed 27 March 2011).

Hallberg, Peter, *Ages of Liberty: Social Upheaval, History Writing, and the New Public Sphere in Sweden, 1740–1792* (Stockholm, 2003).

Helander, Hans, *Neo-Latin Literature in Sweden in the Period 1620–1720: Stylistics, Vocabulary and Characteristic Ideas* (Uppsala, 2004).

Hermann, Pernille, 'Politiske og æstetiske aspekter i Rimkrøniken', *Historisk tidskrift*, 107:2 (2007), 389–410.

Jensen, Minna Skafte (ed.), *A History of Nordic Neo-Latin Literature* (Odense, 1995).

Johannesson, Kurt, *The Renaissance of the Goths in Sixteenth-Century Sweden: Johannes and Olaus Magnus as Politicians and Historians*, trans. James Larson (Berkeley, 1991); orig. pub. as, *Gotisk Renässans: Johannes och Olaus Magnus som politiker och historiker* (Stockholm, 1982).

Jørgensen, Ellen, *Historieforskning og historieskrivning i Danmark indtil aar 1800* (Copenhagen, 1931).

Lundqvist, Elisabeth, *Reformatorn skriver historia: en kontextuell analys av Olaus Petris svenska krönika* (Uppsala, 1998).

Mortensen, Lars Boje, 'François Bauduin's De institutione historiæ (1561): A Primary Text behind Anders Sørensen Vedel's De scribenda historia Danica (1578)', *Symbolae Osloenses*, 73 (1998), 188–200.

Rona, Georg, Danstrup, John, and Karker, Allan (eds.), *Kulturhistorisk leksikon for nordisk middelalder fra vikingetid til reformationstid* (Copenhagen, 1956–78).

Schück, Henrik and Warburg, K., *Illustrerad svensk litteraturhistoria*, 3rd edn (Stockholm, 1926–49).

Skovgaard-Petersen, Karen, *Historiography at the Court of Christian IV: Studies in the Latin Histories of Denmark by Johannes Pontanus and Johannes Meursius* (Copenhagen, 2002).

—— 'The First Post-Medieval History of Norway in Latin: The *Historia Rerum Norvegicarum* (Copenhagen, 1711) by Tormod Torfæus', in Eckhard Kessler and Heinrich C. Kuhn, *Germania latina—Latinitas teutonica* (Munich, 2003), 707–20. Available online at www.phil-hum-ren.uni-muenchen.de/GermLat/Acta/SkovgaardPetersen.htm (accessed 13 March 2011).

Tigerstedt, E. N. (ed.), *Ny illustrerad svensk litteraturhistoria* (Stockholm, 1955–8).

Tjällén, Biörn, 'Church and Nation: The Discourse on Authority in Ericus Olai's Chronica regni Gothorum (c. 1471)', Ph.D. thesis, Stockholm University, 2007. Available online at http://urn.kb.se/resolve?urn=urn:nbn:se:su:diva-7176.

Chapter 23

Historical Writing in Britain from the Late Middle Ages to the Eve of Enlightenment

Daniel Woolf

Historical writing in Britain underwent extraordinary changes between 1400 and 1700.[1] Before 1500, history was a minor genre written principally by clergy and circulated principally in manuscript form, within a society still largely dependent on oral communication. By the end of the period, 250 years of print and steadily rising literacy, together with immense social and demographic change, had made history the most widely read of literary forms and the chosen subject of hundreds of writers. Taking a longer view of these changes highlights continuities and discontinuities that are obscured in shorter-term studies. Some of the continuities are obvious: throughout the period the past was seen predominantly as a source of examples, though how those examples were to be construed would vary; and the entire period is devoid, with a few notable exceptions, of historical works written by women, though female readership of history was relatively common-place among the nobility and gentry, and many women showed an interest in informal types of historical enquiry, often focusing on familial issues.[2]

Leaving for others the 'Enlightened' historiography of the mid- to late eighteenth century, the era of Hume, Robertson, and Gibbon, which both built on and departed from the historical writing of the previous generations, this chapter suggests three phases for the principal developments of the period from 1400 to

[1] I am grateful to Juan Maiguashca, David Allan, and Stuart Macintyre for their comments on earlier drafts of this essay, which I dedicate to the memory of Joseph M. Levine. For reasons of space, this chapter will exclude Ireland and the predominantly oral historical memory of Gaelic Scotland—though see Martin MacGregor, 'The Genealogical Histories of Gaelic Scotland', in Adam Fox and Daniel Woolf (eds.), *The Spoken Word: Oral Culture in Britain 1500–1850* (Manchester, 2002). For broader issues of historical thought, perceptions of the past, or the social circulation of historical knowledge, see my book *The Social Circulation of the Past: English Historical Culture, 1500–1730* (Oxford, 2003).

[2] Well-known exceptions include Lucy Hutchinson, discussed below, and Margaret Cavendish, duchess of Newcastle; for other examples see my essay 'A Feminine Past: Gender, Genre and Historical Knowledge in England, 1500–1800', *American Historical Review*, 102 (1997), 645–79.

about 1740. The obvious cautions apply that any such articulation is rough-edged, must allow for overlap as well as long transitions, and should not obscure other changes of relevance that can cross these rather arbitrary lines:

1) The first phase, from 1400 to about 1550, is dominated by dynastic and nationalist themes inherited from the royal/baronial and monarchical/papal struggles of the Later Middle Ages.

2) A 'Late Renaissance and Reformation' phase, c.1540–1660, is governed by the religious tensions that climaxed in rebellion in both kingdoms.

3) A 'Restoration and Early Eighteenth Century' phase, ending about 1740. During this phase historical writing adjusted itself to the permanent presence of ideological division, to the reality of a multi-denominational kingdom in England and of a Scotland increasingly dependent upon its wealthier southern neighbour, and to the tastes of a broader and more demanding readership.

DYNASTIC AND NATIONALIST HISTORIOGRAPHY, 1400–c.1550

The historical writing of the late medieval and early Renaissance era continued themes and tendencies of the previous several hundred years, including a concern with issues of succession, legitimacy, and royal power that would carry over into the early sixteenth century. Perhaps the most notable feature was the rapid growth of writing in English throughout the fifteenth century in a country increasingly conscious of its anti-French national identity. This tendency, and the exposure of history to a wider lay audience than was possible in previous centuries, would be accentuated by the advent of printing in England from the 1470s, and among the earliest titles to come from William Caxton's press were a number of histories. While there is no space here for a lengthy discussion of the impact of print there is no doubt that it was enormous, and previous research has demonstrated an almost exponential growth in history books, and their readers, between 1500 and 1730, with the most vigorous growth occurring after 1640.[3]

One can distinguish four varieties of historical writing in this early phase.[4] First, a long-standing tradition of clerical historiography, organized around the central role of the kings of England, had produced the monastic 'St Albans' chroniclers of the thirteenth and fourteenth centuries (the closest thing to a counterpart to the vernacular, Crown-sponsored 1476–7 *Grandes Chroniques de France* [The Great Chronicles of France]) or the rich tradition of medieval

---

[3] Daniel Woolf, *Reading History in Early Modern England* (Cambridge, 2000).

[4] Charles L. Kingsford's survey, *English Historical Literature in the Fifteenth Century* (Oxford, 1913), remains a serviceable if dated survey; cf. Antonia Gransden, *Historical Writing in England, c. 1307 to the Early Sixteenth Century* (Ithaca, NY, 1982); and Mary-Rose McLaren, *The London Chronicles of the Fifteenth Century* (Rochester, NY, 2002).

Spanish royal historiography. The St Albans authors found fifteenth-century heirs in a monk such as Thomas Walsingham, and in secular clergy such as Adam of Usk, author of a Latin chronicle covering English history from 1377 to 1421. The *Polychronicon*, a Latin world chronicle written in the 1340s by Ranulf Higden, a Chester monk, achieved greater readership in the fifteenth century through the 1387 English translation by John Trevisa.[5] Secondly, chivalric and militaristic historical writing, influenced by romances on Alexander, Charlemagne, or Richard I, as well as by the historiography of the Crusades, and originating in earlier adaptations (often in verse) of Geoffrey of Monmouth's mid-twelfth-century *Historia Regum Britanniae* [History of the Kings of Britain] had grown in popularity through historians of the Hundred Years War such as Jean Froissart, who would be translated into English in the 1520s. This type of writing was continued in the fifteenth and early sixteenth centuries by both clerical and lay authors. Examples include the *Liber Metricus de Henrico Quinto* [literally, 'A Poem about Henry V'], a Latin verse chronicle (completed *c.*1418) by the monk Thomas of Elmham, and the chronicle of John Hardyng beginning with Brutus, the Trojan refugee widely held to have first established a monarchy in Britain. Hardyng's chronicle, written in English in the 1450s, was rewritten in the 1460s in a pro-Yorkist version. Various versions of the anonymous, London-based chronicle *The Brut* also circulated, the continuations of this originally Anglo-Norman work being the first prose histories composed in English since the ninth-century *Anglo-Saxon Chronicle*.[6]

Thirdly, a number of biographies of notables were written. Humfrey, duke of Gloucester, employed the Italian Tito Livio Frulovisi to pen a life of the duke's brother, King Henry V (r. 1413–22).[7] A highly hagiographic encomium of the last Lancastrian monarch, Henry VI, would be written by his former chaplain, John Blakman (or Blacman) during the Yorkist regime and published early in the sixteenth century.[8] Fourthly, the growth of incorporated cities and towns, especially London, nurtured a modest tradition of urban chronicle writing. This followed the annalistic organization of ecclesiastical chronicles, but with a much more local focus, each annal usually listing the mayor and other officers and then adding in brief accounts of miscellaneous events of local and occasionally national significance. This group includes the anonymous *Great Chronicle of London* and an early Tudor specimen, Robert Fabyan's two-volume *Newe*

---

[5] John Taylor, *The 'Universal Chronicle' of Ranulf Higden* (Oxford, 1966).

[6] Chris Given-Wilson, *Chronicles: The Writing of History in Medieval England* (London, 2004), 140.

[7] Recent treatments have been less kind to this work than previous scholars since Kingsford: see David Rundle, 'The Unoriginality of Tito Livio Frulovisi's *Vita Henrici Quinti*', *English Historical Review*, 123 (2008), 1109–31.

[8] Roger Lovatt, 'John Blacman: Biographer of Henry VI', in R. H. C. Davis and J. M. Wallace-Hadrill (eds.), *The Writing of History in the Middle Ages* (Oxford, 1981), 415–44.

Cronycles of Englande and Fraunce (1516), which covered all of English history since Brutus but from a Londoner's perspective.

Dynastic or nationalistic themes run through much of the historical writing of the period, some of it even directly encouraged by court patronage, though nothing emerged like the conscious programmes of 'official' historiography in late medieval France or Spain and, slightly later, in the Italian city-states and principalities. Moreover, whereas the historical writing of the sixteenth and early seventeenth centuries would with few exceptions be unimpeachably pro-royalist, and its authors acutely wary of the likely penalties for presenting alternative views, it is notable that fifteenth-century writers seem to have worried less about their works falling into the wrong hands—the pro-Lancastrian chronicle of the Wars of the Roses attributed to one Warkworth, Master of Peterhouse, Cambridge, was completed under the Yorkist Edward IV.[9]

The advent of the Tudor dynasty in 1485 marked no watershed in historical writing. Although very little further monastic history was produced—even before Henry VIII (r. 1509–47) dissolved the religious houses in the 1530s—dynastic themes remained dominant. Henry VII, the first Tudor king, employed a number of foreign poet/historians such as the Frenchman Bernard André. The greatest of these imports, who arrived in England in 1501 and sojourned there for most of his long life, was Polydore Vergil, a papal functionary from Urbino. Vergil was the first to write a humanist history of England, the *Anglica Historia* [English History] (1534) in Renaissance Latin, organized by reigns instead of annalistically. Vergil challenged the historicity of the line of Galfridian (that is, derived from Geoffrey of Monmouth) British kings, and the myth of a Trojan foundation, only to incur the wrath of English and Welsh critics, many of them humanists themselves, in the first great English historical controversy of the print age.[10]

Scottish historical writing from the late fourteenth through to the early sixteenth century was virtually conceived in opposition to, or defence against, its English counterpart. Aside from the vernacular patriotic verse represented by such works as *The Bruce* and *The Wallace*, celebrating the thirteenth- and fourteenth-century struggles for independence, learned Latin historiography, too, had to contend with its English counterpart. The prominence of Galfridian views of a British past wherein Brutus's heirs had ruled the whole island provoked among the lowland Scots a parallel myth of Scotland's equally ancient foundation and continued independence. John of Fordun's fourteenth-century *Chronica Gentis Scottorum* [Chronicle of the Scottish People] (transplanted wholesale into the *Scotichronicon* by the early fifteenth-century abbot Walter Bower) had invested the early West

---

[9] Given-Wilson, *Chronicles*, 211.

[10] F. J. Levy, *Tudor Historical Thought* (San Marino, Calif., 1967); Denys Hay, *Polydore Vergil: Renaissance Historian and Man of Letters* (Oxford, 1952); and Peter Roberts, 'Tudor Wales, National Identity and the British Inheritance', in Brendan Bradshaw and Roberts (eds.), *British Consciousness and Identity: The Making of Britain, 1533–1707* (Cambridge, 1998), 8–42, esp. 15.

Highland Scots with an ancient monarchy while at the same time contrasting the barbarity of highlanders with the civility of lowlanders, and thereby giving rise to a long historiographic tradition distinguishing the two. The Scots had their own national mythology going back (via historical kings such as the ninth-century Kenneth MacAlpin, subjugator of the Picts) to the mythical Fergus MacFerquard. They even produced a countervailing foundational hero to Brutus the Trojan in the person of the Greek prince Gathelos and his Egyptian wife Scota—superior because the Greeks had, of course, vanquished the Trojans.[11]

Building on Fordun and Bower, the early Scottish humanist Hector Boece wrote a Latin *Scotorum Historiae a prima gentis origine* [Histories of the Scots from the Origin of the Race] (1527) complete with a full-fledged line of Scottish kings starting with Gathelos; the work achieved great popularity through the rather loose 1536 English translation by John Bellenden, who had previously translated parts of Livy's history of Rome. A much more pro-'British' history by John Mair or Major, the *Historia Maioris Britanniae* [The History of Greater Britain] (1521), its title a pun on the author's name, had already appeared a few years earlier. Mair was a Parisian-trained scholastic eager to promote Anglo-Scottish amity by downplaying past conflicts and stressing common origins. His sentiments ran very much against the fervently independence-minded temper of his contemporaries, and consequently it was Boece's perspective, not Mair's, that would influence George Buchanan, the most outstanding Scottish historian of the century. Buchanan was somewhat sceptical of the earlier bits of Boece,[12] and his philological training led him to reject Gathelos. Fergus, however, became in Buchanan's telling the founder in 330 BC of a line of forty-five fully independent kings, while his post-Roman descendant Fergus II had re-initiated a kingdom that survived all subsequent incursions, English or Norman.

But the Protestant Buchanan also had a quite separate interest in the first Fergus that went beyond older issues of national pride, and which makes him a figure of the Reformation as much as the Renaissance. His Fergus was elected by clan chiefs, who were themselves chosen by their followers, thereby providing historical evidence for Buchanan's radical political theory which imposed severe limits on a monarch. That such cases could be argued either way is illustrated by Buchanan's own royal pupil, James VI (r. 1567–1625; from 1603–25 also James I of England), who would turn Fergus into a precedent for unrestricted royal authority, and a ruler by conquest rather than election.

---

[11] Roger Mason, 'Scotching the Brut: Politics, History and National Myth in Sixteenth-Century Britain', in Mason (ed.), *Scotland and England 1286–1815* (Edinburgh, 1987), 60–84; and Steve Boardman, 'Late Medieval Scotland and the Matter of Britain', in Edward J. Cowan and Richard J. Finlay (eds.), *Scottish History: The Power of the Past* (Edinburgh, 2002), 47–72.
[12] Roger Mason, 'Civil Society and the Celts: Hector Boece, George Buchanan and the Ancient British Past', in Cowan and Finlay (eds.), *Scottish History*, 95–119.

LATE RENAISSANCE AND REFORMATION
HISTORIOGRAPHY

Whatever the partisan differences separating families with royal aspirations and their literary advocates, historical writing prior to the mid-sixteenth century was uncomplicated by genuinely ideological issues. The Reformation changed this profoundly by introducing religious divisions into the mix. In Scotland, which came to Protestantism slightly later and rather more abruptly than England, history was almost immediately linked to the development of a political theory that could support severe limits on royal power within a Presbyterian context that saw kings as leading members of, not heads of, a Calvinist Kirk. In England, where royal jurisdiction over religion was never in serious jeopardy before the 1640s, the majority of historians accepted episcopal Protestantism as a core derivative of monarchical authority. Here, the dissenting voice came less from puritan critics of episcopacy than from a tiny minority of (principally émigré or underground) Catholic writers such as Nicholas Sander and Robert Persons.[13]

There is also a discernible change in focus among historians in both realms. In England, the fixation on dynastic stability that dominated historical writing through the first flourishing of humanism shifted quite noticeably between 1530 and 1580 on to the need to provide a pedigree for a newly independent English church, only returning to dynastic and succession questions near the end of the sixteenth century as English poets, playwrights, and historians faced the grim prospect of a disputed succession following the death of the childless Elizabeth I (r. 1558–1603). North of the border, the driving force behind Buchanan's *De Jure Regni apud Scotos* [A Dialogue Concerning the Rights of the Crown in Scotland] (1579) and his *Rerum Scoticarum Historia* [History of Scottish Affairs] (1582) was neither simply love of scholarship nor his inherited Boecian nationalism, but the provision of intellectual foundations for a Reformation more radical than Stuart monarchs were prepared to contemplate. This was even truer of John Knox, whose vernacular *History of the Reformation of the Church of Scotland*, published in fragments in 1587, avoided the remote past of the ancient kings and began with Lollard persecutions. Knox's Catholic counterpart, John Leslie, Bishop of Ross, wrote his *History of Scotland* from 1436 to 1571 (1578) with similar religious concerns rather than older issues of Scottish independence or royal/noble relations, disputing with both Knox and Buchanan. By the early seventeenth century, hardening lines between Episcopalian and Presbyterian factions within the Scottish Kirk generated posthumously published rival histories by the Episcopalian Archbishop John Spottiswood (*History of the*

---

[13] Christopher Highley, '"A Pestilent and Seditious Book": Nicholas Sander's *Schismatis Anglicani* and Catholic Histories of the Reformation', in Paulina Kewes (ed.), *The Uses of History in Early Modern England* (San Marino, Calif., 2006), 147–67.

Church of Scotland [1655]) and the Presbyterian David Calderwood (*History of the Kirk of Scotland* [1842–9]), an abridged version of which appeared in 1646.

Much has been written about the influence of continental humanism on historical writing, and once again Scotland and England exhibit somewhat different patterns. There are similarities: both kingdoms had an underdeveloped tradition of 'official historiography'; and in neither kingdom had there emerged a very vigorous urban chronicling tradition—certainly not when compared with the contemporaneous town chronicles of Switzerland and Germany, the modern edition of which fills several bookshelves.[14] Yet Scottish historians, fewer in number though they were, embraced a humanist style of historical writing much more firmly and quickly than did England. There is a continuity of style and of Latin models from Boece through Buchanan, with very little by way of medieval annalistic survivals, though of course there was not much there to begin with, poetry and song having been the preferred noble genres of historical representation. This is much less obvious in England (despite its considerably greater volume of writing) where early attempts to write classical-style regnal history, represented by Vergil's *Anglica Historia* and by Sir Thomas More's biographical *History of Richard III*, failed for the moment to take root, despite the adoption of the regnal format in Edward Hall's *Union of the Two Noble and Illustre Famelies of Lancastre [and] York* (1548), the last of the major dynastically oriented histories. Printing, which affected the distribution and popularity of history much faster in England than in Scotland, was the occasion of first an Indian summer for, and then the rapid decline and virtual extinction of, the chronicle. A long series of writers from society's middling ranks, including Richard Grafton, John Stow, and the editorial teams associated with Raphael Holinshed's *Chronicles* (1577; expanded edn, 1587), put out book after book from the 1550s to the 1580s; reprints and revisions of Stow in particular appeared at intervals until the 1630s.

The reasons for this disparity in the shift to humanist models are not entirely clear, but the traditional links of Scotland with the continent and especially France were undoubtedly a factor (as two centuries later they would be in causing Scottish historians to embrace European philosophical history faster and more fervently than their southern counterparts). While English writers were certainly aware of humanist and ancient models they did not, Vergil and More aside, choose to follow them. In the 1580s this began to change, first with a small number of works offering prescriptions for the writing or reading of history. These would include an English adaptation by Thomas Blundeville of two Italian works as *The True Order and Methode of Wryting and Reading Hystories* (1576) and the witty, provocative critique of history contained in the *Defense of Poesy* (1595) by the courtier and poet Sir Philip Sidney. Particularly striking was the popularity at Cambridge University of the

---

[14] *Die Chroniken der deutschen Städte vom 14. bis in 16. Jahrhundert*, 38 vols. (Leipzig, 1862–1968); and F. R. H. Du Boulay, 'The German Town Chronicles', in Davis and Wallace-Hadrill (eds.), *The Writing of History in the Middle Ages*, 445–69.

French theorist Jean Bodin, whose *Methodus ad facilem historiarum cognitionem* [Method for the Easy Comprehension of History] (1566) marked the peak of the European tradition of *artes historicae.*[15]

An even more powerful influence on history-writing was the vogue for the Roman historian Tacitus, who offered political acuity in a terse and epigrammatic style, and without the negative associations then attached to another shrewd political observer, the Florentine Niccolò Machiavelli. Tacitus was translated in the 1590s, and a series of historians quickly abandoned the chronicle for histories of particular monarchs, whose stories were simultaneously being engraved on English consciousness through the plays of Shakespeare and his contemporaries. These 'politic' historians include the civil lawyer John Hayward (author among other works of a controversial history of the accession of Henry IV), William Camden (the reluctant historian of Elizabeth I's reign, arranged as Tacitean *Annales*), Sir Robert Cotton (author of a *roman à clef* on the reign of Henry III with obvious application to his own times), Francis Bacon (attempting to use his analysis of Henry VII's reign as a ticket back to royal favour following his disgrace in 1621), and Edward Lord Herbert of Cherbury, whose history of Henry VIII is a late entry in this group. Press restrictions combined with self-censorship by authors fearful of offending the Crown kept political opinions within a fairly narrow spectrum, but authors such as Bacon and Cotton, and many playwrights and poets would nevertheless use the past obliquely to criticize and comment on contemporary policy. Perhaps the most outstanding narrative was *The Collection of the Historie of England* (1618), the work of a Jacobean poet, Samuel Daniel, whose subtle sense of cultural, legal, and linguistic change suffuses his account of events from the Norman Conquest to the late fourteenth century.

Politics and religion were by now inextricably linked, and the renewed concerns for dynastic stability, magnified by emerging English imperial aspirations, were not simply a revival of early Tudor issues. Indeed, a strong and independent monarchy provided the natural defence in England (unlike Scotland) against assertions of papal suzerainty. The older Galfridian myths proved to be of limited utility in this context. Much more relevant were the historical Emperor Constantine (the future 'champion' of Christianity born in Britain, allegedly of a British mother), and the murky figure of 'King Lucius', an entirely supposititious first- or second-century monarch who was converted by the emissaries of an early (and thus uncorrupted) pope, Eleutherius.[16] Many writers in this phase used history as a weapon in the task of Reformation, but none more effectively, nor

---

[15] Scotland never developed an *ars historica*, and England adopted it relatively late, and then derived largely from continental authors. Anthony Grafton, *What Was History? The Art of History in Early Modern Europe* (Cambridge, 2007); J. H. M. Salmon, 'Precept, Example, and Truth: Degory Wheare and the Ars Historica', in Donald R. Kelley and David Harris Sacks (eds.), *The Historical Imagination in Early Modern Britain* (Cambridge, 1997), 11–36.

[16] Felicity Heal, 'What can King Lucius do for You? The Reformation and the Early British Church', *English Historical Review*, 120 (2005), 593–614.

with greater impact, than John Foxe. Exiled during the brief restoration of Catholicism under Queen Mary I, Foxe was heavily influenced by continental Protestant ecclesiastical historiography. He would write the single most widely read history book of his era, *Acts and Monuments*, first published in 1563 and continuously expanded in several further editions. Because of its focus on the pious lives and heroic deaths of his subjects, often informed by both documentary accounts and contemporary witnesses, Foxe has become known as a martyrologist in the tradition of contemporary continental Protestants such as Jean Crespin, and his work has very often been called simply the 'Book of Martyrs'. But it was simultaneously an account of medieval and recent English history, as well as a church history in the tradition of Eusebius and Orosius.

Religion did not, however, feature prominently in the work of the politic historians at the start of the seventeenth century; indeed, many preferred to sidestep it as dangerous terrain. An exception of sorts was the ill-fated adventurer Sir Walter Raleigh, who famously published a *History of the World* (1614) that owed something to the tradition of 'prudence' to be found in Tacitus and Machiavelli, but much more to Protestant continental histories. Raleigh's work ended in AD 130, and thus avoided engaging directly with the recent history of Christianity, but in its providentialism, organized around the convention of four empires or world monarchies (a periodization rejected by Jean Bodin), it exhibited an implicit apocalyptic element that hearkens back to Foxe. It also abutted on another important and neglected genre of historical writing, chronology. This was essentially the science of figuring out, from a comparison of accurately edited ancient texts originating in different cultures, the precise age of the world (feasible in a mental environment that took the Old Testament account of Creation literally) and the key dates of ancient kingdoms, pagan and Jewish. No easy task, this demanded mastery of multiple tongues and often complex mathematical calculations then necessary to use astronomical data. Already the subject of a number of Tudor writings (including a notable unpublished example by the cleric William Harrison, a contributor to Holinshed's *Chronicles*), specimens of this multiplied in the seventeenth century. Few English practitioners actually met the bar set by Europeans such as Joseph Justus Scaliger—Thomas Lydiat and John Marsham spring to mind, as well as the Anglo-Irish bishop, James Ussher, who famously dated the Creation to a specific evening in October, 4004 BC. Chronology would find practitioners in the next decades such as William Howell, and even the great Sir Isaac Newton. But the genre was rather more vigorously practised in Scotland, where, nurtured by Knoxian apocalypticism, it famously inspired the laird John Napier's invention of logarithms as a calculating tool.[17]

---

[17] For Napier see Williamson, *Scottish National Consciousness in the Age of James VI* (Edinburgh, 1979); on chronology more generally see Anthony Grafton, *Joseph Scaliger*, vol. 2 (Oxford, 1993). Chronology remained a critically important and highly specialized subfield of historical enquiry well

Religious issues ultimately proved the catalyst for twenty years of political instability across the British Isles as first the Scottish Calvinists and then their English puritan counterparts rebelled against an episcopal regime, suspiciously close to 'popery', supported by King Charles I (r. 1625–49). Successive civil wars fought in Scotland, England, and Ireland during the 1640s climaxed in the execution of the king in 1649 and the establishment of a godly republic in England and, in turn, its direct military governance of a Scotland that had belatedly thrown in with the king and his son, Charles II. The two decades of civil conflict and frequent regime change marked the climax of this phase in British historical writing—a time of 'Wars of Religion' on the continent, too— but also a transition to our next phase.

The collapse of government and clerical censorship combined with the prolif-eration of cheap printing in aid of the various sides' propaganda efforts also had other effects. Most obviously, there was an immediate and considerable increase in the volume of historical writing—much of it oriented towards the very recent past which had been largely skirted by earlier generations as politically delicate. This gradually redirected public attention to the past as *cause* of the present rather than merely *mirror* on the present and source of cautionary examples, as it had done in sixteenth-century Italy and France. Above all, it produced much more explicit ideological divisions into historiography than existed previously. Prior to 1640, with a very few outlying exceptions, English historical writing was almost uniformly royalist in tone. Religion had of course long occasioned heated disagreement—Foxe's *Acts and Monuments* is a testament to the intensity of anti-Catholic feelings—but this did not feature prominently in the main stream of narrative histories which (again, with some Catholic exceptions) tended to cleave to the church and royal authority insofar as they discussed religion at all. After 1640, the distribution of viewpoints—parliamentarian, royalist, republican, Presbyterian, independent—became much wider as historians debated responsi-bility for the current predicament.

As so often is the case, a crisis reinvigorated narrative historical writing, which had notably run out of things to say about the English past—most of the best politic histories were the product of James I's reign with relatively few being contributed in the 1630s. There is an interesting parallel to be drawn with the Italy of the 1490s, where several decades of increasingly repetitive humanist historiography was suddenly re-catalyzed by the crisis of the French and Spanish invasions, producing the likes of Machiavelli and Francesco Guicciardini.[18] It must be admitted that few of the works produced in the 1640s are remarkable examples of research or intellectual achievement. Indeed, a great majority are the lacklustre efforts of parliamentarian partisans such as Arthur Wilson or their

---

into the eighteenth century, as exemplified in the late works of Sir Isaac Newton. See Frank E. Manuel, *Isaac Newton, Historian* (Cambridge, Mass., 1963).

[18]   Eric Cochrane, *Historians and Historiography in the Italian Renaissance* (Chicago, 1981), 163.

royalist opponents such as Peter Heylyn. Nevertheless, the conflict, as such turmoil often does, provided a new set of issues for historians to sort out, amid desperate circumstances, and in the end it produced a few lasting gems. Thomas May, a parliamentarian and translator of the Roman historical poet Lucan, contributed a history of the then-current Long Parliament (1647) while the staunchly puritan Lucy Hutchinson, a rare female historian, penned a life of her republican husband, Colonel Thomas Hutchinson, which languished un-published until the nineteenth century.[19] The political philosopher James Har-rington, heir to late Renaissance republicanism and Machiavellian prudence, achieved a stroke of brilliance in his conceptualization of the civil wars as the culmination of a century of social and economic change that he traced back to the Tudor assault on aristocratic power and the redistribution of ecclesiastical lands by Henry VIII. Harrington's *Common-wealth of Oceana* (1656) fictionalized England ('Oceana') and its recent monarchs, but the history it recounts in its early pages is unmistakable. The other great philosopher of the time, Thomas Hobbes, one-time translator of Thucydides and author of the infamous political treatise *Leviathan* (1651), would eventually answer May with his own history (cast in dialogic rather than narrative form) of the Long Parliament, *Behemoth* (1679).[20] Finally, the moderate royalist adviser to Charles I (and sometime Lord Chancellor to Charles II), Edward Hyde, earl of Clarendon, who fled the realm in the 1640s and then again following his fall from power in 1667, used his exiles to pen the manuscripts that have become his celebrated *History of the Rebellion and Civil Wars in England* (1702–4). This fascinating combination of third-person recitation of events with autobiographical self-vindication is one of the greatest works of historiography in the English language regardless of its factual flaws and biases. It has immortalized its author, whose most fervent advocates in the next century would compare him with Thucydides. Clarendon's and many of these other works point ahead to (and often chronologically belong to) the Restoration, and they each anticipate one of the central concerns of the next few decades—how to explain the past conflicts in an increasingly partisan environment without inflaming further violence.[21]

---

[19] Devoney Looser, *British Women Writers and the Writing of History, 1670–1820* (Baltimore, 2000), 28–60.

[20] On civil war historians see R. C. Richardson, *The Debate on the English Revolution* (3rd edn, Manchester, 1998); Royce MacGillivray, *Restoration Historians and the English Civil War* (The Hague, 1974), esp. 15–47; and David Cressy, 'Remembrancers of the Revolution: Histories and Historiographies of the 1640s', in Kewes (ed.), *The Uses of History*, 253–64.

[21] This problem, and the relation between history and memory in a post-civil war context, is the subject of Dr Matthew Neufeld's recent thesis, 'Narrating Troubled Times: Making Sense of the Civil Wars and Interregnum in Memory and History, England 1660–1714', Ph.D. thesis, University of Alberta, 2008.

THE RESTORATION AND EARLY
EIGHTEENTH CENTURY

The historians of the Restoration and early eighteenth century inherited two problems, one political and social, the other intellectual and aesthetic. The first was the fallout of two decades of intense instability culminating in a previously unthinkable regicide. Explanation of the civil wars continued to provide the dominant subject of narrative among both triumphant royalists of various stripes and the defeated. The latter included Edmund Ludlow, a former army officer and radical in exile, and the poet and former republican official John Milton, who published an unfinished *History of Britain* (1670), largely written during the 1650s. Nominally about divine punishment of the ancient Britons for collective sin, it was really on the failure of godly rule in his own times.[22] Many others such as the parliamentary general Sir Thomas Fairfax (1699), the Cromwellian official Bulstrode Whitelocke (1682), the cleric Richard Baxter (1696), and the royalist Sir Philip Warwick (1701) authored posthumously published (and often heavily censored) memoirs of their experiences in the fashion of the fifteenth-century French historian Commynes. The Crown even created in 1661 a French-style office of Historiographer Royal, with expressly polemical purposes. None of its early occupants produced original historical work, and they were selected principally for their polemical skills or for their literary reputation and connections with the powerful. Their number included the poet John Dryden, whose major contribution was the translation of the French Jesuit Louis Maimbourg's *History of the League* (1684), really a thinly disguised attack on the Whig parliamentary leader the earl of Shaftesbury. The office was subject to partisan patronage and at the Glorious Revolution Dryden was out, succeeded by his long-standing foe, the playwright Thomas Shadwell.[23] A comparable office was also established in Scotland to similar ends, and unlike its English counterpart has survived to the present day.[24]

Though the violence had abated and a precarious stability returned, this was not the Britain of a generation earlier. This period has often been distinguished for the emergence of the first political parties, Whig and Tory, towards the end of the century and for the so-called rage of party that ensued early in the next. But long before any parties came into being the political landscape was already well and truly fractured. So, too, was the religious picture, as neither

---

[22] Nicholas Von Maltzahn, *Milton's History of Britain* (Oxford, 1991).

[23] Paulina Kewes, 'Acts of Remembrance, Acts of Oblivion: Rhetoric, Law, and National Memory in Early Restoration England', in Lorna Clymer (ed.), *Ritual, Routine, and Regime: Institutions of Repetition in Euro-American Cultures, 1650–1832* (Toronto, 2006), 103–31.

[24] Denys Hay, 'The Historiographers Royal in England and Scotland', *Scottish Historical Review*, 30 (1951), 15–29. Only in the next century did the English office begin to be awarded to men of principally scholarly, rather than literary, abilities.

the re-establishment of the Church of England nor a series of punitive laws against former puritans—now called 'dissenters' or 'nonconformists'—could eradicate the various denominations and sects that had emerged in the 1640s and 1650s.

The consequences for historiography were several: that historians now very explicitly wrote from a distinctive politico-religious perspective, even while outwardly claiming that they were presenting the unvarnished truth; that debate continued (even more acerbically despite the insistence of literary arbiters such as Joseph Addison on 'polite' learning); and that this in turn imposed a need for these historiographical combatants to prove both their own veracity, probity, and 'impartiality', and their opponents' moral defects, poor judgement, and partisan bias.[25] Borrowing a traditional technique of church history, the historians of the Restoration turned to the transcription and printing of documents and political tracts at length. John Rushworth, a former parliamentary official, published *Historical Collections* (1659–1701) consisting entirely of such documents, a work answered by the *Impartial Collection* (1682) of his royalist counterpart, John Nalson. This document-mongering (unsatisfactory in literary terms, but ultimately helpful to later generations of historians) would continue through to the early eighteenth century, on both political and religious history; an author such as John Strype virtually making a career out of the publication of documents combined with lives of Tudor prelates. Others adopted the Procopian genre, previously underutilized in Britain, of the 'Secret History', purporting to lay open in public the *arcana imperii* and the private scandals of great men.[26] By the century's end, the former royalist and parliamentarian positions of the 1640s to the 1660s had transitioned, more or less, into identifiable 'Whig' and 'Tory' interpretations of history, their differences discernible not only in descriptions of seventeenth-century troubles but in attitudes to a whole range of episodes in English history such as the Norman Conquest, the relation of the medieval kings to their parliaments and nobility, and the course of the Reformation itself.[27]

The second problem was a consequence of the first. Historians and some readers were deeply dissatisfied with the quality of narrative historiography. In part this can be attributed to a renewed popularity of the *ars historica*, especially though French authors such as Pierre Le Moyne, and new editions of older English works such as those of Degory Wheare (1623; translated from Latin 1685) and Matthias Prideaux, whose *An Easy and Compendious Introduction for Reading*

[25] Joseph H. Preston, 'English Ecclesiastical Historians and the Problem of Bias, 1559–1742', *Journal of the History of Ideas*, 32 (1971), 203–20.
[26] Eve Tavor Bannet, '"Secret History": or, Talebearing Inside and Outside the Secretorie', in Kewes (ed.), *The Uses of History*, 367–88; and Michael McKeon, *The Secret History of Domesticity: Public, Private, and the Division of Knowledge* (Baltimore, 2005), 469–73, 482–505.
[27] Mark Knights, 'The Tory Interpretation of History in the Rage of Parties', in Kewes (ed.), *The Uses of History*, 347–66; Blair Worden, *Roundhead Reputations: the English Civil Wars and the Passions of Posterity* (London, 2001); and Melinda S. Zook, 'The Restoration Remembered: The First Whigs and the Making of their History', *The Seventeenth Century*, 17 (2002), 213–29.

all Sorts of Histories (1648), the work of a student, had reached its sixth edition by 1682. These delivered stylistic canons for the writing of history, and criticism of past historians, which ran well beyond the more general advice of an ancient authority such as Cicero, whose dictum that history was *lux veritatis et magistra vitae* now evolved into a more narrow construction of history as 'the most admirable foundation for politicks'.[28] Virtually none of the previous century of English historians was deemed adequate, and the chroniclers in particular were by now well beyond the pale, though one notes the survival of the annalistic form in many unpublished parochial and town chronicles of the eighteenth century.[29] Partly this was because of a conviction, articulated by earlier writers such as Bacon and Raleigh but never much honoured before 1660, that in order to write proper history one had to be a man of experience, education, high birth, and public life. Few had the requisite standing and experience to write a general history of England in the style of Livy (whose stock rose anew in this era of neoclassicism), or a history of a particular event such as the civil wars, after Thucydides, easily the most admired of the ancients in the second half of the century given the urgent reorientation of historiography to the recent past. Nor could most come up to the mark set by two much-respected early seventeenth-century figures, the Italian cleric Paolo Sarpi, whose antipapal politics and critical *Istoria del Concilio Tridentino* [History of the Council of Trent] (1619) played very well in Protestant England, and the French politician Jacques-Auguste de Thou, whose *Historia sui temporis* [History of his Own Times] (1604–20, its negative portrayal of Mary, Queen of Scots having provided the spark for Camden's *Annales* in response) became a model for contemporary political history. Perhaps the most successful imitator of Thucydides, de Thou, and the Italian historian of the French wars of religion, Davila, was Clarendon himself, whose work was published by his Tory sons in 1702–4 to a generally positive reception.[30] The posthumously published *History of his own Time* (1724) by the Scottish-born Whig Bishop Gilbert Burnet (who had in 1679 received the thanks of parliament for the first volume of his *History of the Reformation* [1679–1714]) proved much more divisive, generally attracting derision from Tories and High Church clerics, and scathing reviews from such notable literary figures as Jona-

---

[28] The remark is that of John Dunton, a hack writer of the end of the century; quoted in Daniel Woolf, 'Narrative Historical Writing in Restoration England: A Preliminary Survey', in W. Gerald Marshall (ed.), *The Restoration Mind* (London, 1997), 207–51, at 208.

[29] Philip Hicks, *Neoclassical History and English Culture: From Clarendon to Hume* (Basingstoke, 1996), 1–22, on dissatisfaction with the writing of English history; for urban chronicles, see Rosemary Sweet, *The Writing of Urban Histories in Eighteenth-Century England* (Oxford, 1997), 74–99.

[30] Clarendon remains the best-studied of English historians from this period: see B. H. G. Wormald, *Clarendon: Politics, Historiography and Religion, 1640–1660* (Cambridge, 1951); Martine Watson Brownley, *Clarendon and the Rhetoric of Historical Form* (Philadelphia, 1985); and Paul Seaward, 'Clarendon, Tacitism, and the Civil Wars of Europe', in Kewes (ed.), *The Uses of History*, 285–306.

than Swift. Critics of historical writing focused much more squarely than their Tudor predecessors on stylistic issues, and the very documents and quotations deemed essential to prove a case were disruptive of narrative flow and offered a poor substitute for the dramatic set speeches of ancient historiography.

The Restoration also saw renewed and more acute concern over the history of English law, its predating of the Norman Conquest (for if a Conqueror such as William I could set aside all laws, what was to stop his modern-day Stuart successors?), and the antiquity of institutions such as parliament. These issues dated back to the early seventeenth-century scholarship of Selden and Spelman, and to subsequent polemics against a Norman 'yoke' by the radical Levellers of the 1640s, but they acquired a new urgency in the post-civil war era, a time in which fear of absolutism and 'universal monarchy', embodied in France's Louis XIV, accentuated older anti-Catholic feeling. Both the royalist Robert Brady, author of a high Tory *Complete History of England* (1685) and several other historical works, and his Whig critic James Tyrrell, author of a three-volume *General History of England* (1696–1704) covering history up to Richard II, embody a historiography that attended anew to the medieval past in as highly polemical a fashion as the innumerable accounts of the recent wars.[31] Religion remained similarly controversial, and it too generated scholarship in support of argument, in various forms. These included pan-insular explorations of the primitive church in Britain such as Bishop Edward Stillingfleet's *Origines Britannicae* (1685); full-scale narrative church histories in the mode of Thomas Fuller's *Church-history of Britain* (1655), and Jeremy Collier's *Ecclesiastical History of Great Britain* (1708); lives of bishops and archbishops (most notably Henry Wharton's collection, *Anglia Sacra* [1691]); new editions of medieval chronicles (the stock-in-trade of the Oxford Tory Thomas Hearne early in the eighteenth century);[32] and, in the work of a cleric such as George Hicks, superior philological and linguistic scholarship.

In many ways, these decades saw a kind of 'reclericalization' of history as, for the first time since the end of the Middle Ages, significant numbers of clergy of various ranks engaged either in narrative history (as in the case of the rural cleric Laurence Echard, whose general *History of England* appeared in instalments from 1707 to 1718), or antiquarian scholarship. The universities, themselves clerically dominated institutions, played a much more direct role in generating both historical scholarship and historical narrative than they had done earlier in the century. This culminated in 1724 with the establishment of Regius Professorships

---

[31] The indispensable account of these issues remains J. G. A. Pocock, *The Ancient Constitution and the Feudal Law* (Cambridge, 1957; rev. edn, Cambridge, 1987). Cf. Janelle Renfrow Greenberg, *The Radical Face of the Ancient Constitution: St Edward's 'Laws' in Early Modern Political Thought* (Cambridge, 2001).

[32] Theodor Harmsen, *Antiquarianism in the Augustan Age: Thomas Hearne, 1678–1735* (Oxford/ New York, 2000).

of Modern History ('modern' here beginning in late antiquity) at Oxford and Cambridge. This court-sponsored initiative produced little concrete history for the moment, but it marked a milestone in the association of historical writing with the culture of academe (following the establishment by Camden of a chair in ancient history at Oxford a century earlier and a short-lived counterpart professorship at Cambridge about the same time). Moreover, the argumentative tactics embraced by lay authors such as Brady and Tyrrell were often derived from sacred history, including the tendency to bury one's opponents in a sea of quotations and documents.[33]

Faced with the challenge of writing what Francis Bacon had once called 'perfect history',[34] many aspiring historians self-insured against public failure by adopting the old tactic of the antiquaries—asserting that they were in fact *not* historians but rather assemblers of the materials for some future history. Even a bold spirit like Henry St John, Lord Bolingbroke, a transitional figure to the Enlightenment and the quintessential creature of party, would eventually formu-late his reflections on history as *Letters* (1752) rather than as a history *per se*. Others abandoned their histories incomplete or half-baked. Sir William Temple, one of the most outspoken critics of modern historical writing, called for a new national history, but his own efforts stopped short with an *Introduction to the History of England* (1695) that got no further than the Norman Conquest. Swift, Temple's more illustrious secretary, tried to continue his employer's work but would lay down his quill at the mid-twelfth century.[35]

Those with strong views on the literary deficiencies of historians faced an even worse spectacle in the very rapid climb in history's popularity during these decades. No longer a minor literary form, history had arguably become by the early eighteenth century the single most commercially popular and fashionable published form of writing, a supremacy that would be rivalled in coming decades only by the fledgling novel—itself generally packaged as a 'history'.[36] Historical works also achieved much wider distribution, socially and geographically, than ever before and genres and formats proliferated as publishers and would-be authors cashed in on this success. Where early Stuart readers had available a limited selection of classics and new works, their Restoration and early eighteenth-century successors faced a bewildering array of choices between large and expensive works on the one hand and compendia, epitomes, chapbooks, broadsheet ballads, and chronologies on the other. The sufferings of English and Scottish dissenters under the Restoration regime were chronicled respectively

---

[33] Hicks, *Neoclassical History*, 36–9, 91–8.

[34] George Huppert, *The Idea of Perfect History* (Urbana, 1970).

[35] Hicks, *Neoclassical History*, 100–1. Swift did, however, contribute a history in *History of the Four Last Years of the Queen* about politics under Queen Anne, which would not be published until 1758.

[36] Karen O'Brien, 'History and the Novel in Eighteenth-Century Britain', in Kewes (ed.), *The Uses of History*, 397–413.

by Edmund Calamy and his Scottish correspondent, the Glaswegian-born minister Robert Wodrow.[37] Clever authors and booksellers simultaneously devised a new strategy for making expensive books affordable through serialization, the means by which the French-born Paul de Rapin-Thoyras published the popular English translation of his *Histoire d'Angleterre* [History of England] (written 1707–24; serialized in English 1728–32). Many others sought advance subscription for works tailored to a particular group or even political party.[38] The Whig John Oldmixon would sell his *History of England during the Reigns of the Royal House of Stuart* (1730) in this manner. An ambitious literary projector named John Hughes commissioned a *Complete History of England* (1706) consisting of two volumes of reprints of early and mid-seventeenth-century histories and a third volume of new material, written by the Whig cleric White Kennett, beginning with Charles I and running up to the present. The durability of the earlier works is in itself a comment on the perceived poverty of more recent efforts, and may in turn have been partially responsible for the relative dearth of new writing on the political history of the late medieval and Tudor centuries before the mid-1700s.[39]

ANTIQUARIANISM

While humanism had failed initially to take hold of narrative history, it proved more immediately successful with other forms of scholarship related to the past, in particular the several different activities that have collectively acquired the unflattering modern name 'antiquarianism'.[40] Its practitioners were linked by a love of learning and of the evidentiary fragments of the past that largely eluded most narrative historians. The antiquaries were not oblivious to present concerns, nor to useful lessons that the past could provide, but their hearts lay elsewhere. For some time, most of them self-consciously eschewed both the duties and the title of historian, even though from our present-day perspective they were engaged in historical research, organizing their works around particular places or topics rather than chronologically. Peter N. Miller's and Donald R. Kelley's chapters in this volume provide surveys of antiquarian and philological scholarship across this long period, permitting a briefer excursus here.

---

[37] Calamy's Tory counterpart, John Walker, answered with a comparable account of *The Sufferings of the Clergy* (London, 1714) an account of ministers persecuted during the civil wars and interregnum.

[38] W. A. Speck, 'Politicians, Peers and Publication by Subscription, 1700–1750', in Isabel Rivers (ed.), *Books and Their Readers in Eighteenth-Century England* (Leicester, 1982), 47–68; and Woolf, *Reading History*, 281–317.

[39] Woolf, 'Narrative Historical Writing', 212.

[40] May McKisack, *Medieval History in the Tudor Age* (Oxford, 1971), remains the best single account of Tudor antiquarianism.

The antiquaries initially fell into two distinct but not mutually exclusive groups, both to some degree resembling a pair of fifteenth-century progenitors, William Worcestre and John Rous, but descended more directly from the Henrician scholar John Leland. The first group operated in the grand tradition of continental Renaissance philology, their scholarship directed towards the recovery and restoration of ancient and eventually medieval texts. This was Leland's principal interest, and his charge from Henry VIII following the dissolution of the great monastic houses (custodians of much of the kingdom's medieval heritage) was to rescue and preserve from ruin the manuscripts within which evidence might be found for the historical independence of the English Church and king from papal interference. A line of philological antiquaries stretches from Leland at the beginning of the sixteenth century through Richard Bentley two hundred years later, and includes along the way Archbishop Matthew Parker (a collector of Anglo-Saxon manuscripts which could be adduced to support a Protestant inheritance), Sir Henry Savile (translator of Tacitus and editor of medieval chronicles), and an outstanding early Stuart student of legal and ecclesiastical antiquities, Sir Henry Spelman. The most remarkable antiquary of the period, and England's most celebrated scholar internationally, was Spelman's younger contemporary, John Selden. A lawyer, parliamentarian, and polyglot admirer of French philology, Selden brought unrivalled erudition and a sophisticated sense of change to the writing of historical works. In the first half of the seventeenth century he poured out a stream of volumes on the institutions of English law, on the history of social arrangements such as ranks and titles (*Titles of Honor* [1614]), and on the payment of tithes (*Historie of Tithes* [1618]), often within a comparative framework that drew on ancient and contemporary European examples.

The other major category of antiquarianism descended even more directly from Leland. Though he published very little in his lifetime, Leland's peripatetic *Itinerary* through England in the 1540s recorded both popular lore (eventually repudiated in the next century by increasingly document-oriented writers) and local topography and antiquities. His manuscripts circulated in subsequent decades and influenced several Elizabethan and early Stuart scholars beginning with William Lambarde, who in 1576 published a *Perambulation of Kent* describing that shire's topography, great families, and other features of interest. There followed a series of county surveys or 'chorographies', and one or two comparable studies of particular cities (including the chronicler Stow's detailed *Survey of London* [1598]). It also pushed Camden, the future historian of Queen Elizabeth, to write an island-wide survey of British antiquities, *Britannia*, which first appeared in 1586 (in Latin since his target audience included foreign scholars). He expanded it over several further editions up to 1594, and had it translated into English in 1610; through further posthumous editions it became both anchor and guiding light for two centuries of English genealogical and archaeological antiquarianism, which relied less exclusively on close analysis of textual change and rather more on observation of natural or man-made physical objects. Many scholars followed Camden, variously concerned with everything from Roman or Saxon coins, funeral monuments, or the origins of particular customs or traditions, to family ancestry, titles, and heraldry.[41] This early explosion of antiquarian activity, often patronized by the wealthy virtuosi who were simultaneously amassing collections of interesting objects, even gave rise to a short-lived society or 'college' of antiquaries (1586–1614).

The Restoration saw significant changes in antiquarianism, especially its peripatetic variant. The keen interest in matters of ancestry and genealogy had abated considerably, reflecting the loosening of social standards for the claiming of social 'gentility'. County chorography continued with even more counties being surveyed, but the tone and scope of the post-Restoration specimens differs markedly from that of Camden's time, even though his *Britannia* continued to provide a revered point of departure, and was modernized and retranslated by a team of editors, led by the future bishop Edmund Gibson (1695). The reputation and recognizable name of Francis Bacon, whose methods provided guidance for the enquiries into 'natural history' of the Royal Society, also affected antiquarianism, which now bestowed on natural specimens and topographical features the enthusiasm it already devoted to man-made antiquities such as coins and monuments. Some of these early efforts, by the likes of Robert Plot, were of limited success, and virtually all—including the often bizarre essays on the construction of Stonehenge or on the origins of the earth and the genesis of fossils—were circumscribed by the instinctive privileging of classical culture and by a biblically limited chronology of five or six millennia. But the trend towards direct observation and even maverick departure from guiding ancient texts is unmistakable in the writings of John Aubrey, the Welshman Edward Lhuyd (an outstanding philologist and pioneer in Celtic studies as well as an exemplary field archaeologist), and the most distinguished antiquary of the first third of the eighteenth century, William Stukeley.[42] The informal networks of the previous century were now augmented by more institutional connections, first through the Royal Society and then through a new Society of Antiquaries that began meeting informally in 1707; this process mirrored that occurring in the academies of continental Europe.

The changes on the philological side of antiquarianism are more subtle. The heirs of Selden practised their craft at an increasingly high and often more specialized register in support of the Church or royal authority, or in pursuit of a literary and aesthetic debate such as the notorious 'Battle of the Books' (an

---

[41] Woolf, *Social Circulation*, 73–137 (on genealogy and ancestry), 141–256 (on antiquarianism); and Jan Broadway, *'No Historie So Meete': Gentry Culture and the Development of Local History in Elizabethan and Early Stuart England* (Manchester, 2006).

[42] Michael Hunter, *John Aubrey and the Realm of Learning* (London, 1975); Stuart Piggott, *William Stukeley: An Eighteenth-Century Antiquary* (Oxford, 1950; rev. edn, 1985); Graham Parry, *The Trophies of Time: English Antiquaries of the Seventeenth Century* (Oxford, 1995).

episode in the longer running European *querelle* of ancients and moderns) that pitted newer-style philologists such as Bentley against champions of the superiority of antiquity like Temple, and others who thought ancient texts needed to be presented without modern emendations.[43] Others such as the palaeographer and bibliophile Humfrey Wanley improved the study of Anglo-Saxon, or prepared editions of medieval documents such as Thomas Rymer's *Foedera* (1704–35) or Thomas Madox's *Formulare Anglicanum, or a Collection of Ancient Charters and Instruments* (1702). Still others, such as the clergyman Henry Bourne, turned their attention to local traditions; his *Antiquitates Vulgares, or The Antiquities of the Common People* (1725) providing a bridge between the Tudor antiquaries who had first recorded these and the nineteenth-century rediscovery of 'folklore'. The ecclesiastical preoccupations that we have seen previously also informed a good deal of antiquarian enquiry as authors such as Browne Willis, a prolific Tory squire, and Kennett, a future Whig bishop, attempted surveys of parochial antiquities and studies of individual churches and cathedrals.

By now, antiquarian pursuits had stretched into Scotland, which, having largely missed the sixteenth-century wave, now produced in Sir James Balfour of Denmilne a keen collector of old documents. After the Restoration, the Scots began to catch up with important figures such as Sir Robert Sibbald (a contributor to the 1695 edition of *Britannia*) and Father Thomas Innes. The last-mentioned, a Catholic priest who spent much of his life in Paris, would become a disciple of current continental historical techniques (especially the pioneering diplomatic and palaeographic work of Jean Mabillon); he would employ these tools to begin the process of sceptically demolishing the mythic kings inherited from Hector Boece.

The engagement with both English and continental scholarship exhibited by this generation of Scots was a further harbinger of things to come following the legislative union of Scotland and England in 1707. While Bolingbroke's 1752 *Letters* (mainly written in the late 1730s) reflect older Renaissance traditions of didactic history and Augustan concerns for style, order, and the primacy of political advice,[44] they also point to the Enlightenment's philosophical consideration of history, characterized by a moderate scepticism towards received truth, an ability to step back from the particular and generalize, and an inclination to look for human commonalities rather than national differences. Style remained a critical concern of authors and readers, and historians such as Hume attended increasingly to securing appropriate reactions from their readers, addressing the inner lives of historical figures as well as their public selves, and striking a

---

[43] Joseph M. Levine, *The Battle of the Books: History and Literature in the Augustan Age* (Ithaca, NY, 1991).

[44] Isaac Kramnick, 'Editor's Introduction', in Bolingbroke, *Historical Writings*, ed. Kramnick (Chicago, 1972), pp. xi–liii; and Kramnick, 'Augustan Politics and English Historiography: The Debate on the English Past, 1730–35', *History and Theory*, 6 (1967), 33–56.

sympathetic or 'sentimental' chord.[45] If a satisfactory national history remained the
elusive grail, at least till Hume, its absence was less acute a concern, having been
displaced by interests that are less nationalistic and more cosmopolitan, and by a new
attention to the private over the public, the cultural, social, and economic over the
political, and the imaginatively conjectured over the strictly documentable. As early
as the 1720s Rapin-Thoyras's *Histoire*, the work of an outsider, had attempted to
integrate England into a wider European past, his William I, as Karen O'Brien has
noted, being virtually a prototype for his William III, 'a military hero who pushes the
insular English people into an international arena'.[46] Bolingbroke himself, retired
from party politics, even argued that among history's uses was its ability to purge,
rather than enflame, 'those national partialities and prejudices that we are apt to
contract in our education'.[47] The cosmopolitanism of eighteenth-century historiography is all the more remarkable given that the same period witnessed extended
territorial warfare among the great powers, a furnace in which a united Britain
achieved its sense of identity in opposition to—once again—French influence.

In this vein, we can close our account with an ambitious and bold project of the
mid-eighteenth century, an entry in the resurgent genre of 'universal history'. If not
quite the global history of today, neither was this simply a reincarnation of Eusebian
ecclesiastical history. Indeed, it was largely stripped of the religious focus that had
informed such works from late antiquity and the apocalyptic tone that marked more
recent versions from Sleidan to Sir Walter Raleigh. Like Holinshed's *Chronicles*
nearly two centuries earlier but on a much grander scale, the *Universal History* (1747–
68) was the work of many hands, among them the Arabic scholar George Sale and
the Scottish once-and-future Jesuit Archibald Bower.[48] This was remarkable for its
scope: it was a genuine attempt to grasp the histories of other countries beyond
Europe, and it had few British precursors. With some notable exceptions such as
Richard Knolles's *Generall Historie of the Turkes* (1603) or its Restoration extension
by Sir Paul Rycaut (1667), the accounting for other countries' pasts had consisted
very largely in translations or adaptations of foreign-authored histories. Universal
history points ahead to the encyclopedic interests and cosmopolitan and pan-
European values of much of the historiography of the Enlightenment, in Britain as
much as on the continent, the subject of chapters elsewhere in this volume.[49]
National histories of Scotland and of England continued to be written throughout

---

[45] Mark Salber Phillips, *Society and Sentiment: Genres of Historical Writing in Britain, 1740–1820*
(Princeton, 2000); McKeon, *Secret History of Domesticity*, esp. 547–87; and Victor G. Wexler, *David
Hume and the History of England* (Philadelphia, 1979), 14.
[46] Karen O'Brien, *Narratives of Enlightenment: Cosmopolitan History from Voltaire to Gibbon*
(Cambridge, 1997), 17.
[47] Ibid., 15; and see ch. 25 by Karen O'Brien in this volume.
[48] Guido Abbattista, 'The Business of Paternoster Row: Towards a Publishing History of the
Universal History (1736–65)', *Publishing History*, 17 (1985), 5–50; and Tamara Griggs, 'Universal
History from Counter-Reformation to Enlightenment', *Modern Intellectual History*, 4 (2007), 219–47.
[49] For an excellent account of the transitions in eighteenth-century historiography see
J. G. A. Pocock, *Barbarism and Religion*, vol. 2: *Narratives of Civil Government* (Cambridge, 1999).

the eighteenth century, along with accounts of other countries. Oldmixon's Whig and Echard's Tory histories, and Scottish counterparts such as Patrick Abercromby's *The Martial Atchievements of the Scots Nation* (1711–15) were echoed at mid-century by the Jacobite Thomas Carte's *General History of England* (1747–55),[50] and by general histories-for-hire produced by literary figures such as Oliver Goldsmith and Tobias Smollett. But the eighteenth century would belong to the conjectural, philosophical history of Robertson, Kames, Ferguson, Hume, and Gibbon, and to the study of manners and civility rather than national martial achievement or religious difference. This was a very different world than Boece or Buchanan, or Camden or Bacon—or even Clarendon or Burnet—could ever have imagined.

TIMELINE/KEY DATES

1399 Deposition of Richard II (England) and Lancastrian accession

1453 End of the 'Hundred Years War' between England and France

*c.*1455–85 Yorkist–Lancastrian 'Wars of the Roses' and Yorkist rule (1461–85) of Edward IV and Richard III

1485 Henry Tudor defeats Richard III to become first Tudor monarch

1530s Henry VIII breaks with Rome, inaugurating the first phase of England's Protestant Reformation; dissolution of monasteries and abbeys in England, 1536–40

1558 Catholic Queen Mary I dies, bringing an end to mid-century persecutions of Protestants; Elizabeth I succeeds

1560 Advent of Reformation in Scotland

1587 Execution of Mary Stewart (or Stuart), Queen of Scots (in English captivity since 1567)

1603 James VI, king of Scotland, son of Mary Stewart, succeeds Elizabeth I as king of England; 'union of crowns'

1625 Accession of Charles I as king of England and of Scotland

1642 Outbreak of civil war in England between parliament and king

1649 Execution of Charles I following a second civil war; England becomes a republic, eventually governed (1654–58) by Lord Protector Oliver Cromwell

1651–60 Scotland under English military government

1660 Restoration of Charles II to English and Scottish thrones

1678–81 Popish plot and Exclusion Crisis in England; emergence of early versions of Whig and Tory parties

1688 'Glorious' Revolution deposes Catholic King James VII of Scotland/James II of England; succeeded by William III and Mary II

---

[50] On Carte see Pocock, *Barbarism and Religion*, vol. 4: *Barbarians, Savages and Empires* (Cambridge, 2005), 65–78.

1707 Parliamentary Union of England and Scotland into United Kingdom of Great Britain

1714 George I becomes first Hanoverian king of Great Britain

1715, 1745 'Jacobites' (supporters of exiled Stuart claimants to the throne) unsuccessfully rebel

KEY HISTORICAL SOURCES

Bacon, Francis, *The History of the Reign of King Henry the Seventh*, ed. F. J. Levy (New York, 1972).

Boece, Hector, *The Chronicles of Scotland*, trans. John Bellenden, ed. Walter Seton, R. W. Chambers, and Edith C. Batho, 2 vols. (Edinburgh, 1938–41).

—— *Annales rerum Anglicarum et Hibernicarum regnante Elizabetha* (London, 1615–27); trans. Robert Norton, *The Historie of the Most Renowned and Victorious Princesse Elizabeth* (London, 1630).

Bolingbroke, Henry St John, Viscount, *Historical Writings*, ed. Isaac Kramnick (Chicago, 1972).

Brady, Robert, *A Complete History of England . . . unto the End of the Reign of King Henry III* (London, 1685).

Buchanan, George, *Rerum Scoticarum Historia* (Edinburgh, 1582).

Burnet, Gilbert, *Bishop Burnet's History of His Own Time*, abridged by Thomas Stackhouse (London, 1979).

Camden, William, *Britannia* (London, 1586); trans. Philemon Holland, *Britain* (London, 1610).

Clarendon, Edward Hyde, earl of, *The History of the Rebellion and Civil Wars in England Begun in the Year 1641*, ed. W. Dunn Macray, 6 vols. (Oxford, 1888).

Daniel, Samuel, *The Collection of the Historie of England* (London, 1618).

Foxe, John, *Acts and Monuments of these Latter and Most Perilous Days* (London, 1563).

Hardyng, John, *The Chronicle of John Hardyng . . . with the Continuation by Richard Grafton*, ed. Henry Ellis (London, 1812).

Higden, Ranulf, *Polychronicon Ranulphi Higden Cestrensis: Together with the English Translations of John Trevisa and of an Unknown Writer of the Fifteenth Century*, ed. Joseph Rawson Lumby, 9 vols. (London, 1865–6).

Hutchinson, Lucy, *Memoirs of the Life of Colonel Hutchinson*, ed. N. H. Keeble (London, 1995).

Milton, John, *The History of Britain* (London, 1670).

Newton, Isaac, *The Chronology of Ancient Kingdoms Amended* (London, 1728).

Raleigh, Walter, *The Historie of the World* (London, 1614).

Selden, John, *The Historie of Tithes* (London, 1618).

Stow, John, *A Survey of London*, ed. Charles L. Kingsford, 2 vols. (Oxford, 1908).

BIBLIOGRAPHY

Allan, David, *Virtue, Learning and the Scottish Enlightenment: Ideas of Scholarship in Early Modern History* (Edinburgh, 1993).

Cowan, Edward J. and Finlay, Richard J. (eds.), *Scottish History: The Power of the Past* (Edinburgh, 2002).

Douglas, David C., *English Scholars, 1660–1730* (2nd edn, London, 1951).

Ferguson, Arthur B., *Clio Unbound: Perception of the Social and Cultural Past in Renaissance England* (Durham, NC, 1979).

Gransden, Antonia, *Historical Writing in England, c. 1307 to the Early Sixteenth Century* (Ithaca, NY, 1982).

Hicks, Philip, *Neoclassical History and English Culture: From Clarendon to Hume* (Basingstoke, 1996).

Kewes, Paulina (ed.), *The Uses of History in Early Modern England* (San Marino, Calif., 2006).

Kidd, Colin, *Subverting Scotland's Past: Scottish Whig Historians and the Creation of an Anglo-British Identity, 1689–c. 1830* (Cambridge, 1993).

Levine, Joseph M., *The Battle of the Books* (Ithaca, NY, 1991).

Levy, F. J., *Tudor Historical Thought* (San Marino, Calif., 1967).

Looser, Devoney, *British Women Writers and the Writing of History, 1670–1820* (Baltimore, 2000).

McKisack, May, *Medieval History in the Tudor Age* (Oxford, 1971).

O'Brien, Karen, *Narratives of Enlightenment: Cosmopolitan History from Voltaire to Gibbon* (Cambridge, 1997).

Pocock, J. G. A., *The Ancient Constitution and the Feudal Law* (Cambridge, 1957; rev. edn, Cambridge, 1987).

—— *Barbarism and Religion*, 5 vols. to date (Cambridge, 1999–).

Woolf, Daniel, *The Idea of History in Early Stuart England* (Toronto, 1990).

Wormald, B. H. G., *Clarendon: Politics, Historiography and Religion, 1640–1660* (Cambridge, 1951).

Chapter 24

Scottish Historical Writing of the Enlightenment

David Allan

'This is the historical Age', observed David Hume in August 1770, 'and this the historical Nation'.[1] Hume's boastful *aperçu* to William Strahan has often been used simply in order to illustrate contemporaries' awareness of the Scots' distinguished contribution to the study of the past in the age of the Enlightenment. Despite its brevity, however, this particular comment, no public declaration but rather a complex judgement offered in a private letter to a friendly publisher, was actually much less straightforward—and also raises far more interesting questions about the origins and nature of eighteenth-century historiographical developments—than might initially appear.

In the first place, it should be noted that Hume's assessment was chronologically unspecific. This is in fact a key omission, because it makes it harder for us to be sure—given that a plausible case can be fashioned for each alternative—whether Hume's 'historical Age' was the previous decade in particular (during which he and his close friends William Robertson, Adam Ferguson, and Lord Kames had published several well-received works), the eighteenth century as a whole, or even the modern period in its entirety. Secondly, since Hume's country, following the 1707 Treaty of Union, now shared not only its government but also its statehood and national identity with England, it is no more obvious whether this 'historical Age' was to be conceived narrowly as the product exclusively of Scottish pens or whether (as seems more likely) it alluded also to the impressive activities of a wider community of recent historians throughout Britain and Europe. Finally, the reference to 'the historical Nation' (which does seem to have meant Scotland alone) appears to hint at some kind of continuing relationship between Enlightenment scholarship and the achievements of several previous centuries of research and writing in Scotland. This too is a thought-provoking feature of Hume's assessment. For there can be no doubt that Scottish historiography of the eighteenth century was the result of the country's turbulent

---

[1] *Letters of David Hume*, ed. G. Birkbeck-Hill (Oxford, 1888), 155.

past as much as it was a consequence of what during Hume's own lifetime had come to be recognized as the Scots' singular present predicaments.

THE 'LONG NIGHT OF GOTHIC BARBARISM'?

In a number of important senses it is now possible for us to appreciate how far, by the time that Hume's famous judgement was formulated, Scotland had long seen itself as the 'historical Nation'. Above all, its very existence as a political entity, successfully defended on the late medieval battlefield during the Wars of Independence against the English, had been vindicated by and through the writing of its own history. The chancery propagandists who manufactured the Declaration of Arbroath (1320) had ultimately managed to craft an incomparably resonant tale of their ancient political autonomy, and deployed it to devastating polemical effect in the court of international opinion. But succeeding scholars such as John of Fordun (compiler of the *Scotichronicon* [*c*.1384–7]), Walter Bower (who continued the same text up to 1437), Andrew Wyntoun, and Hector Boece had only helped further bolster the burgeoning sense of the Scots' separateness and uniqueness. Later carping, like that of the early nineteenth-century Edinburgh professor Dugald Stewart, that this period had actually been a 'long night of Gothic barbarism', an age of intellectual sterility which had really ended only at the verge of the eighteenth century, was therefore thoroughly misleading. Indeed, it may have been motivated principally by a desire to exaggerate the originality of 'that never to be forgotten change in literary taste of the eighteenth century'—especially those innovations associated with figures such as Ferguson and Robertson, whom Stewart had known and revered—rather than fairly to weigh the genuine strengths and lasting significance of the country's medieval learning.[2]

It is also now widely recognized that the Renaissance had not only elevated Scottish historiography onto a new intellectual level but also established important points of contact with the greatest achievements of contemporary European humanism. Boece's *Scotorum historiae* [Chronicles of Scotland] (1527) best reflected this shift, weaving the familiar story of autonomous Scottish development into a highly charged moral dissection of political affairs, viewed through the distorting prism of classical antiquity, that his distinguished Italian contemporaries Machiavelli and Guicciardini would doubtless have appreciated. The *Historia maioris Britanniae* [History of Greater Britain] (1521), written by John Mair (or Major), a French-trained scholastic logician from East Lothian who favoured *rapprochement* between the Scots and the English, was similarly path-breaking,

---

[2] Dugald Stewart, 'Dissertation Exhibiting a General View of the Progress of Metaphysical, Ethical, and Political Philosophy, Since the Revival of Letters in Europe', *Supplement to the 4th, 5th and 6th Editions of the Encyclopaedia Britannica*, vol. 1 (Edinburgh, 1815–24), 21, 44.

exploring the historical affinities between the two insular peoples in a far less mean-spirited way than had previously seemed possible. George Buchanan's *Rerum Scoticarum Historia* [The History of Scotland] (1582), however, which transformed the tales and triumphs related by Fordun and Boece into a veritable literary landmark, represented the culmination of this potent historiographical tradition. In fact, in providing a not-very-well-disguised justification for the doctrines of accountable government and legitimate regicide that everywhere fuelled the radical Protestant cause in the late sixteenth century, Buchanan's colourful and controversial account of his own nation's history also confirmed that Scottish scholarship was more than capable of attracting and holding the attentions of a concerned wider audience.

It has nevertheless been customary—in fact, it first became a rhetorical commonplace during the eighteenth century itself—to dismiss Scotland between the 1580s and the dawning of the Enlightenment in the 1740s as nothing more than a stagnant cultural backwater: it was, complained John Pinkerton, one of the most bombastic historians of the age of Robertson and Hume, a period marked by 'neglect of literature', when a retreating tide of civilization had allowed the Scottish scene to become overrun with 'weeds and vermin, which its ebb has left on the shore'.[3] Once again, however, this is much too harsh a judgement and, perhaps, not a little self-serving. Indeed, because the underlying aim of this interpretation was manifestly to denigrate the past in order to establish beyond doubt the superior intellectual credentials of late Enlightenment scholarship—of which the supremely self-confident Pinkerton was virtually alone in considering himself among the pre-eminent exponents—it ignores not only the continuing seventeenth-century legacy of the Renaissance across several disciplines, which in Scotland ranged from pastoral poetry and political philosophy to domestic architecture and landscape gardening, but in addition the significant new directions that historiography in particular had taken between the end of the sixteenth century and the beginning of the eighteenth.

On the one hand, the dominance achieved in Scotland by mature humanism of the kind represented above all by George Buchanan had encouraged the emergence of a highly characteristic style of writing. This, whether applied more narrowly to family genealogy or much more broadly to the Scottish people's story, had attained great heights of literary flair and analytical sophistication in works such as David Hume of Godscroft's *History of the Houses of Douglas and Angus* (1644), a noteworthy study which treated the past, just as the leading sixteenth-century French and Italian authors had done, primarily as didactic material for the moral education of its readers. On the other hand, the practical utility of historical evidence to those engaged in lively contemporary disputes was to be regularly demonstrated by Scottish writers. This was especially

---

[3] John Pinkerton, *An Enquiry into the History of Scotland*, 2 vols. (London, 1789), i. pp. xlvi, 123.

true for a series of rival ecclesiastical historians—Presbyterians including John Knox, David Calderwood, John Row, and Alexander Petrie, and Episcopalians such as John Spottiswood, archbishop of St Andrews and author of a much-admired posthumous *History of the Church of Scotland* (1655)—who disagreed passionately with one another over the long-term origins as well as over the continuing implications of the Scottish Reformation. Many writers from the late sixteenth century onwards, particularly those operating from a strongly Calvinist theological standpoint, also evolved an approach to the interpretation of historical events in which providential agency, allegedly at work in the advancement of their own cause, loomed predictably large.

This, then, was the rich and complex scholarly heritage that generally lay behind what is best seen as a phase of renewed methodological innovation, increased productivity, and expanding publication and readership that overtook Scottish historiography from the 1750s onwards. More specific legacies, however, must also be strongly underlined. It is no accident, for example, that the works of Fordun, Mair, and Buchanan were all republished in the decades after 1707, unambiguous proof of a quickening of public and professional interest in the nation's distinctive historiographical traditions—significantly, just as its actual political autonomy had been abruptly ended. At the same time it is important to remember a series of early eighteenth-century writers who were engaged in elaborate historical arguments over the precise nature of Scotland's relationship with England. These included James Anderson and Sir James Dalrymple, whose treatises on the ancient Scottish Church and Crown contributed to the frenzied public debate that surrounded the negotiation of the treaty of union before 1707. No less important in this period was Thomas Ruddiman, the Jacobite antiquarian, who produced a new edition of Buchanan's works in 1715 and who as late as the 1740s was at the centre of a scholarly dispute triggered by his criticism of the *Historia*. Such authors were clearly already helping feed the Scots' voracious appetite for historiography even before the onset of the Enlightenment first led this phenomenon to attract comment and admiration from outside the country.

Authorship of this relatively conventional kind also played an important part in reinvigorating eighteenth-century interest in some of the defining scholarly controversies of the sixteenth century. Its most tangible expression was probably the series of studies focusing on the career of Mary, Queen of Scots—collectively an immensely detailed footnote rebutting point by point Buchanan's savage attack on her character and conduct—which emerged at intervals between the 1750s and the 1790s and involved not only intellectual heavyweights such as Hume and Robertson, whose works introduced the queen to a new and much wider audience, but also less well-remembered writers such as Walter Goodall and William Tytler.

Other traditional preoccupations also prospered in the newly propitious conditions for speculative thinking ushered in by the Enlightenment. Thus, the abiding concern of many Protestant writers in explaining the deep-lying causes of large-scale historical processes remained very much a recognizable Scottish specialism, in due course leading on in the hands of scholars such as Ferguson, Robertson, and Adam Smith to some of the eighteenth century's principal theoretical achievements. Like Knox and Calderwood before them, they were pursuing a form of historical analysis that fulfilled Kames's description of an enquiry in which 'reason is exercised in discovering causes and tracing effects through a long chain of dependencies'.[4] Yet relations between new and old approaches to historiography were as often to be characterized by productive tension. Indeed, perhaps the single most important stimulus—appropriately enough in an age increasingly influenced by the reformist impulses that invariably characterized the Enlightenment project in the round—was a growing discomfort with the mixture of obdurate prejudice and shameless mischief-making that a more polite and progressive generation began to see as vitiating much of what had previously been attempted by Scotland's historians.

HISTORY IN AN AGE OF POLITENESS

Hume himself, 'le bon David', was, it goes almost without saying, the outstanding instance of a writer determined to bring Enlightenment principles to bear in order to help clarify the course of past events. It is also crucial to recognize, however, that he was by no means a lone pioneer in appreciating the need for a thoroughgoing reconsideration of what had hitherto passed for acceptable historical narrative. Rather it was *A Critical Essay on the Ancient Inhabitants of Scotland* (1729) by Thomas Innes—like Mair two centuries earlier, a resident of a Parisian college—which first signalled the increasingly sceptical turn. In this landmark work Innes took the diplomatic techniques that he had learned from his French colleague Jean Mabillon, together with the naturally more detached perspective of an émigré scholar and the specific reservations about Buchananite interpretations of the Scottish past that came intuitively to a Jacobite and a Catholic, and applied them systematically to the entertainingly lurid but empirically threadbare narrative of the country's early history. Innes's announcement that the traditional sequence of forty ancient reigns was merely a self-deluding patriotic fantasy, and his willingness, as he said, to 'contradict the common opinion of my countrymen' on such a touchstone question of national prestige and honour, was shocking to many and clearly called for considerable courage.[5] But as influential in purely technical terms was his forensic skill in revealing how late medieval propagandists, answering to very specific political needs, had had both motive and opportunity to practise a series of outrageous frauds upon a

---

[4] Lord Kames, *Historical Law Tracts*, 2 vols. (Edinburgh, 1758), i. p. vii.
[5] Thomas Innes, *A Critical Essay on the Ancient Inhabitants of Scotland*, 2 vols. (London, 1729), i. p. vi.

credulous and ill-informed audience. So conclusive was Innes's intervention that it helped set the next generation of scholars on a path towards greater commitment to truthfulness, impartiality, and improved methodological rigour.

Hume's multi-volume *The History of England* (1754–62), which, tellingly, was what eventually emerged from a work that had begun life as the *History of Great Britain* (1754–6), cannot therefore be regarded as the first of the aggressively revisionist historical studies of the eighteenth century to emerge from a Scottish hand. It was, however, to prove by some margin the most popular and the most influential. Hume's avowed purpose in writing, as he famously said in an essay in 1752, was actually to 'refute the speculative systems of politics advanced in this nation'.[6] And if he eventually failed in this breathtakingly ambitious aim, Hume's attempt at re-educating the public through the discussion of history did quickly come to be recognized as a canonical work of modern historiography, remaining for decades thereafter—until at least the time of Macaulay—the standard resource for any inquisitive reader, foreigner or native, who wished to know more, and above all to *understand* more, about Britain's past.

Even when considered only as a literary artefact, the *History*, as befitted an author who had evolved his technique in composing a series of popular essays on moral and political themes, was a triumph. Praised by many well-qualified judges on account of its refined manner, it was also lauded for its teasing wit and for Hume's consummately ironical voice. Psychologically, too, it greatly impressed. This was because it seemed to offer a new depth of insight into human motives and manners, a peculiarity that, at a time when the novel, with its intense focus on character and interiority, was beginning to capture the public's imagination, was obviously especially opportune. Moreover, by some distance the finest work of historical narration ever conceived by a moral philosopher, the *History* sought to present itself as penetrating behind the explanatory veil that had been painstakingly constructed from out of the honeyed words of the participants and the evasive cant of their subsequent apologists. Time and again this permitted the cool and judicious Hume to position himself to maximum rhetorical advantage, apparently able to disclose to his own readers—who were alternately amazed and appalled at his revelations—what he insisted were the real reasons why individuals, such as the European princes who had embraced the Reformation or the cabal of noble conspirators who had so dramatically unseated James II in 1688, had acted as they did.

Politics, however, remained central to what Hume was trying to achieve as an historian as well as to the contrasting responses of those who read the *History*. Indeed, it was his disdain for the partisan posturing and ideologically motivated mythologizing which in the eighteenth century still disfigured the discussion of Tudor and Stuart history in particular that—in a work that had actually begun

---

[6] David Hume, *Essays Moral, Political and Literary*, ed. Eugene F. Miller (Indianapolis, 1985), 488.

with the seventeenth century and whose reach was then gradually extended backwards, volume by volume—formed his main motivation. One result was that, then and since, much effort would be expended in trying to determine whether its elusive author was really of the Tory or the Whig persuasion. Broadly speaking, contemporaries, mostly Whiggish (in the sense that they generally embraced the Revolution of 1688–9) and so unable to see past his refusal to portray the Stuarts as a series of scheming tyrants, tended to identify Hume as a purblind Tory, not to say a covert Jacobite. Some of the most hostile readers, notably Horace Walpole and Charles Lee, went further, also holding his Scottishness against him and reckoning his supposed Toryism part of a fiendish Scottish plot to subvert England's liberties by sapping readers' confidence in their own nation's distinctive historical commitment to political freedom. Recent scholars, by contrast, have been much more taken with Hume's enthusiasm for commercial society and by his adept tactical deployment of a brilliantly sardonic scepticism. Accordingly they have preferred to think of him more as a philosophical progressive or 'scientific' Whig. Yet in some ways these attempts at labelling miss the real point. Worse, it is arguable that they simply confirm Hume's deepest suspicions about the games that historians play. For his aim was precisely to challenge this instinctive willingness to view the past teleologically— warping and corrupting it in the process—by means of categories that are as inflexible as they are anachronistic.

Probably reflecting the concerns of the other leading historians of the Scottish Enlightenment most clearly was the *History*'s attempt to counter the corrosive effects of religious enthusiasm. In fact, in pursuit not only of a fair-minded interpretation of the past but also of a more sober and rational approach to contemporary public affairs, Hume would undoubtedly have agreed with the Edinburgh historian Hugo Arnot who lamented in 1779 that 'nothing so deeply perverts the judgement, and corrupts the heart, as the fury of civil contention, when excited by religious bigotry'.[7] What Hume himself derided as 'the zeal for speculative opinions' had clearly played an excessively prominent part in Scotland's own depressingly bloody history, a stain on their nation that he and many of his eighteenth-century colleagues were anxious first to point out and then to begin to rectify.[8] In this context it was inevitably the Scottish Reformation— pre-eminently the work of Knox, a fanatic and rabble-rouser as well as a historian, whom a disapproving Hume would skewer as 'the rustic apostle'—that required the most careful re-appraisal.[9] The influence of the reformers and their rigid doctrines, it was now strongly hinted, had been pernicious. They had undermined respect for established authority and encouraged violence and hatred between citizens. As a result, the superior virtues of toleration had

---

[7] Hugo Arnot, *The History of Edinburgh* (Edinburgh, 1779), 166.
[8] David Hume, *The History of England*, 3 vols. (London, 1875), ii. 305.
[9] ibid., ii. 353.

regrettably to be learned the hard way. Ultimately they had only been inculcated—as Hume's friend Robertson said in relation to early modern Europe as a whole—by 'the long experience of the calamities of mutual persecution, the influence of free government, the light of humanity acquired by the progress of science, together with the prudence and authority of the civil magistrate'.[10]

That Robertson, of all people, should have offered such a judgement, and that he should be found adopting an essentially similar sceptical posture to the 'Great Infidel' when evaluating for public consumption a central and previously hallowed feature of his own country's religious heritage, speaks volumes for the power of the polite agenda in modifying the perspectives adopted by Scottish historiography. After all, simultaneously the leader of the Church of Scotland and principal of the University of Edinburgh by the 1760s, Robertson was, unlike so many other Enlightenment intellectuals—who could write from the comfort of their ivory towers or the safety of the salons—unmistakably and unapologetically distancing himself from his own professional predecessors. It is in this context, as a stout defender of the case for a more accommodating approach to honest religious disagreement, not only in the writing of history but also in contemporary public debate, that we should add to his laurels the fact that Robertson was also to be the only one of the Scottish Enlightenment's historians to require protective custody for his family in Edinburgh Castle—in 1779, as a result of the local mob taking violent exception to his courageous support of legal amelioration for Catholics.

Yet it was chiefly in *The History of Scotland* (1759) and *The History of the Reign of the Emperor Charles V* (1769) that Robertson sought to show a British audience how polite Scottish historiography might repudiate the blind dogmatism that had previously marked so much of Protestant scholarship. In its place he tried to put a studied even-handedness and moderate ecumenism that in turn demanded as its centre-piece a far more sympathetic treatment of Mary, Queen of Scots (here framed as 'A woman, young, beautiful, and in distress'), even as it also obliged greater scepticism as to the motivation and behaviour of unsettling and unyielding ideologues such as Knox and Andrew Melville.[11] Recent students of his writings, perhaps reacting against the tendency of subsequent liberal hagiographers to situate Robertson at the very heart of the Enlightenment revolution in interpretative attitudes and methodologies, have often emphasized how much he still had in common with his predecessors—including a willingness still to invoke providential agency in historical explanation (albeit now sometimes bent to the rather different contemporary purposes of the British state and the House of Hanover) as well as an obvious underlying partiality for the causes of Protestantism and Presbyterianism. Even so, there can be no doubt that Robertson's

---

[10] William Robertson, *The History of the Reign of the Emperor Charles V*, 2 vols. (Dublin, 1762–71), ii. 391.
[11] William Robertson, *The History of Scotland*, 2 vols. (London, 1759), i. 367.

contribution to the related progress made both by polite literature and by religious toleration in the middle decades of the eighteenth century demonstrated to his contemporaries the extent to which Scottish approaches to historical writing were indeed undergoing substantial re-evaluation.

'THEORETICAL OR CONJECTURAL HISTORY'

Another form of re-thinking about the nature and purpose of historiography to which it is fair to say that Robertson's contribution was to prove especially important was the elaboration of what, following the problematic terminology bequeathed to us by Dugald Stewart (who actually had Adam Smith's work chiefly in mind), has come to be known as 'Theoretical or Conjectural history'.[12] This description has usually been taken as connoting the attempt in Scotland to marry the conventional preoccupations of historical analysis with the interpretative techniques and conceptual categories of what were then the emergent social sciences—to form what Hume had in 1739 presciently envisaged as 'the Science of Man'.[13] This was to prove a fruitful relationship for both parties, for out of it emerged a set of far-reaching assumptions about the evolution of society through successive stages of development—'from rudeness to civilization', as Ferguson summarized the anticipated direction of travel.[14] What may have made this so-called stadial model also seem quite so 'conjectural' was not just the astonishing scope of its pretensions as a catch-all historical explanation. It was also the fact that the universal principles that it claimed to have deduced seemed to encourage the view that it would be legitimate to reconstruct lost aspects of a given society's history by allusion to better-documented instances that had apparently adhered to the same general rules of development.

If Robertson's *Charles V* was indeed, as it appears to have been from the evidence of sales and ownership, one of the eighteenth century's most widely read historical studies, then the extraordinary prologue to that work, which bore the title 'A View of Society in Europe', may have been the single most influential articulation of these assumptions. Certainly this lengthy introductory essay had much to recommend it as a popularization of 'stadial' history that sought to disseminate its principal tenets among the literate public. For it made no attempt to present the main features of conjecturalism as an abstract system complete in itself (an unenviable task which it would be left to others to tackle). Instead, Robertson, whose great gift as a writer was an exceptionally alert and engaging

---

[12] Adam Smith, *Essays on Philosophical Subjects*, ed. W. Wightman (Indianapolis, 1982), 293.

[13] David Hume, *A Treatise of Human Nature*, ed. P. H. Nidditch (2nd edn, Oxford, 1978), p. xv.

[14] Adam Ferguson, *An Essay on the History of Civil Society*, ed. Fania Oz-Salzberger (Cambridge, 1995), 7.

narrative style, chose to paint a colourful and convincing picture that put relevant parts of the theory to work in accounting for some of the most dramatic yet previously obscure developments in Europe's long history. Hence key historical processes such as the decadence and political over-reach of Rome (which 'degraded and debased the human species'), that empire's eventual subjugation by much more vigorous races of barbarians, and then the fitful progress of the disparate peoples of medieval Europe towards 'that civility and refinement by which they are now distinguished', were each described by Robertson as though they could be understood as natural consequences of the interaction between different aspects of human nature and particular material circumstances.[15]

Robertson's two final works showed him pushing to its furthest extent the vast interpretative potential that conjecturalism seemed to offer. In *A History of America* (1777), the first part of a projected multi-volume work that was brought out in order to benefit from heightened public interest following the Declaration of Independence, his attention was focused on the pre-Columbian history of the New World, together with the problematic relationship between the native peoples and their subsequent Spanish and Portuguese conquerors. Not surprisingly, this expansive tableau—a veritable clash of civilizations—gave ample opportunity to explore some of the most fundamental premises of stadialism. Here, after all, had been an authentically 'primitive' society, comprising people in something relatively close to their pristine natural state who, placed in splendid isolation from other societies, had apparently evolved in slow and steady accordance with the general laws of development. As Robertson observed, waxing characteristically philosophical as well as manipulating the universalism implicit in any stadial theory in order to encourage his readers to identify with the natives, 'A human being, as he comes originally from the hand of nature, is every where the same . . . the talents he may afterwards acquire, as well as the virtues he may be rendered capable of exercising, depend entirely upon the state of society in which he is placed'.[16]

This rude and unrefined society, however, had ultimately little chance. It had quickly been overwhelmed by the sudden (and, this liberal-minded but also very Protestant historian would make clear, thoroughly callous) intrusion of men from a quite different and much more advanced form of human society— represented by the explorers, soldiers, administrators, and missionary priests of Catholic southern Europe. A rather different tack on the contrasting stages of social development, though again one that combined Robertson's special interest in belief systems with his commitment to a form of stadialism, was taken in the *Disquisition Concerning the Knowledge Which the Ancients Had of India* (1791). Here Robertson was able to foreground the peculiar culture that had evolved in southern Asia, a civilization then of growing interest in view of its rapid

[15] Robertson, *Charles V*, i. 11, 64.
[16] William Robertson, *A History of America*, 2 vols. (London, 1777), i. 401.

contemporary penetration by European power. The result was an analysis that purposely raised some intriguing questions—the more pertinent because of increasing open-mindedness among progressive thinkers about different peoples and their creeds—in which certain parallels between Eastern and Western practices were placed suggestively to the fore.

It was Ferguson, however, who contributed the more substantial working out of the implications of stadial theory. Above all in *An Essay on the History of Civil Society* (1767), Ferguson, whose academic responsibilities at Edinburgh included teaching across the interconnected fields that would later be recognized as comprising history, politics, law, psychology, and ethics, offered a broad-ranging theorization of the relationship between human nature and the natural environment, from out of which that train of major events that we have learned to call history was, as he attempted to show, largely constructed. Deliberately organized along thematic lines, the *Essay* lacked any real chronological structure. With separate sections bearing philosophical-sounding titles including 'Of moral sentiments', 'Of the principles of union among mankind', and 'Of the question relating to the state of nature', it would have been clear to any knowledgeable reader that Ferguson was in fact addressing the cruxes of contemporary moral philosophy and social theory as these had been isolated and argued over by writers such as Francis Hutcheson, Hume, Montesquieu, and Rousseau. Certainly it failed to offer a continuous account of any single historical event or epoch.

The historical ramifications of Ferguson's theorization were indisputably immense—as Hume, who harboured serious reservations about the *Essay*, and most of his Scottish friends, who greeted it with unrestrained enthusiasm, were equally well aware. Man, according to Ferguson's panoptic account of human history, was an intrinsically questing and ambitious creature. He was compelled by his very nature, as Ferguson memorably claimed, 'from the earliest age of his being, to invent and contrive'.[17] This, the incurably restless and endlessly creative human character, was actually the real driving force behind progress. A concern for material betterment was, moreover, the specific object that was invariably in view: 'the care of subsistence', as Ferguson explained at one point in the *Essay*, 'is the principal spring of human actions'.[18] In other words, a peculiarly intense form of human instinct was the engine bringing both limitless potential energy and dramatic forward motion to the otherwise static and somnolent history of this particular species.

Neither in the *Essay* nor elsewhere in his published lectures, much less in the narrative *The History of the Progress and Termination of the Roman Republic* (1783) that was actually his own favourite work, did Ferguson properly answer a question of fundamental importance to any historian concerned with such a

---

[17] Ferguson, *Essay*, 12.   [18] Ibid., 35.

broad canvas: Why exactly does large-scale change arise at one moment rather than at another? Necessarily a key technical issue for any theory that posits the existence of a series of discrete developmental stages, the resolution of this problem of transition clearly required the identification of a mechanism by which the decisive movement from one level of social evolution to the next might be made to come about. This was in fact a matter to which Adam Smith would successfully apply his formidably versatile intelligence. And like Ferguson, his answers would be closely related to his professional concerns as an innovative and much-respected professor of moral philosophy. Indeed, it was Smith's work whilst teaching at Glasgow, where he developed a particular expertise in the origins of legal systems and in the emerging field of political economy, which proved seminal. For he would eventually conclude, as he seems to have revealed first in a series of lectures on jurisprudence, that the shift between different stages occurred primarily as a consequence of the pressures on resources that arise because of population growth.

A relatively orthodox stadialist, though one with a rare talent for detecting the deep-lying influence of recognizably economic factors, Smith saw the various stages of society's historical development as being characterized by their reliance upon specific modes of production—which is to say, hunter-gathering (giving rise to the 'savage' state), herding (sustaining a 'barbarian' society), settled agriculture (closely linked with the emergence of 'feudal society'), and, finally, more complex trading systems (the basis of what had come to be recognized as 'commercial society'). Not only relations between individuals, however, but also their very notions of property ownership, and consequently their legal codes and political structures too, had been constructed in response to these same changing material conditions. Yet the trigger point for a society's translation from one stage to another, when all of these distracting accretions had been stripped away, was at bottom a function only of the effectiveness of the means of subsistence in meeting the basic needs created by human appetites at work within increasingly unfavourable demographic contexts. In this sense, people are eventually *forced* to progress, being compelled to invent and to innovate in order to stay alive: 'They would be necessitated to contrive', Smith concluded in one of his Glasgow lectures, 'some other method whereby to support themselves'.[19] Progress was therefore ultimately a product of dysfunction, the practical outcome of successful adaptation in response to the fatal failure of older and simpler modes of existence.

It was in *The Wealth of Nations* (1776) that Smith fleshed out many of the other aspects of his reading of political economy as a critical factor both in shaping the familiar contours of everyday life and in forging large-scale historical change. Like Ferguson's *Essay*, of course, this landmark work of the Enlighten-

---

[19] Adam Smith, *Lectures on Jurisprudence*, ed. R. L. Meek, D. D. Raphael, and P. G. Stein (Indianapolis, 1982), 14.

ment can still only be considered partly historiographical in intent. After all, it clearly went far beyond the task of providing for contemporaries a coherent account of particular aspects of the human past. Yet it patently arose out of recognizably historical concerns. It profoundly influenced contemporaries' understanding of historical processes. And it was almost immediately recognized— by Hume on his deathbed as well as by growing numbers of scholars and politicians—as representing one of the eighteenth century's most persuasive accounts of mankind's development, delivered at a time of accelerating social and economic change in Scotland and Britain and also specifically intended to improve understanding of how and why such transformations occurred. Perhaps its most striking contribution in this regard was to be the impetus that it gave to the re-conceptualization of historical causation—as we have seen, a long-standing interest among previous generations of Scottish scholars who had grown accustomed to thinking in terms of the decisive effects of a presiding intelligence. Not surprisingly, however, given Smith's private religious doubts and the increasingly forgiving temper of the times, his treatment of this question was markedly less metaphysical in character, and also had considerably more progressive implications, than had been those of any of his predecessors.

Smith's preferred formulation relied instead upon what at one point he famously chose to call the 'invisible hand'.[20] This was a mechanism whose material embodiment was not the pointed index finger of some stern and omniscient deity but rather the entirely uncoordinated and often unwitting conduct of innumerable men and women engaged in steadfast pursuit of their own personal self-interests. It was this mass of essentially routine activities rather than the success of any single superintending design (whether this happened to originate on earth or in heaven) that, for Smith, really lay behind such seismic processes in human history as the emergence of the division of labour—which he argued was nothing other than 'the necessary, though very slow and gradual consequence of a certain propensity in human nature which has in view no such extensive utility'.[21] Other developments, such as the loosening of feudal ties and the gradual growth of modern liberty, were likewise the unintended consequences of disparate individual actions over long periods of time.

This, of course, meant that the natural appetites of human nature, so far from being necessarily damaging (as many historians as well as moralists and theologians had previously insisted), might actually serve wholly constructive purposes. As Smith's mentor Kames explained this startling challenge to traditional reasoning in *Sketches of the History of Man* (1774), 'a universal benevolence, were it a duty, would contribute to the general good perhaps less than absolute selfishness'.[22] Such a conclusion was also why, as later readers would

---

[20] Adam Smith, *The Wealth of Nations*, ed. Edward Cannan (London, 1904), IV, ii, 9.
[21] Ibid., II, i, 1.
[22] Lord Kames, *Sketches of the History of Man*, 2 vols. (Edinburgh, 1774), ii. 308.

not be slow to notice, what has come to be known as the 'theory of unintended consequences' or 'theory of spontaneous order', which in Smith's version in particular formed such an integral part of the explanatory system that conjectural history could be made to yield, was in fact to prove such a potent antidote to the self-aggrandizing claims of visionaries and legislators to effective control over the future direction of human development.

'PLEASURE AND PROFIT'

If the nature and implications of 'conjectural history' have concerned many modern scholars who have written about the Scottish Enlightenment, then other aspects of eighteenth-century Scottish historiography have tended to receive far less attention. This is unfortunate, since these areas of activity were often creatively intertwined with intellectual preoccupations that have come to be seen as definitively connected with the Enlightenment. Above all, they can legitimately be understood as logical corollaries of the 'Science of Man', involving the systematic extension of stadial theories of development to the investigation of a diverse range of human institutions, general phenomena, and particular eventualities. Moreover, the growth of these interests also points to an immensely important aspect of Enlightenment historiography, and indeed of eighteenth-century culture in the round, that has only recently begun to receive sufficient consideration. This is the extent to which the Enlightenment, especially in Britain, was actually concerned primarily with the greatly expanded public consumption of culture—in other words, with words and ideas now conceived essentially as commodities on open sale to a mass of anonymous but increasingly discriminating consumers. In this context, the unprecedented public demand for historical literature, and the interest of growing numbers of authors (and, crucially, readers) in what John Belfour in his *New History of Scotland* (1770) smugly described as the 'pleasure and profit which are derived from History', are facets of the Scottish experience at this time that should remind us of certain contemporary forms of scholarly activity that have not always been adequately appreciated.[23]

A number of scholars who were closely associated with Hume, Robertson, Ferguson, and Smith made important contributions to this broadening-out of the new methodologies to embrace subjects that had not previously been considered the province of the historian but for which there was clearly a voracious public appetite. Among the most intriguing was Lord Kames, the rather older friend of the leading Edinburgh literati among whom, as a much-loved *bon viveur* and genuine eccentric, he acted often as patron and sponsor. Kames's

[23] John Belfour, *A New History of Scotland* (London, 1770), p. iii.

career—lawyer, judge, and landowner rather than university professor or professional philosopher—shaped his own unique blend of intellectual interests. Above all in the *Historical Law Tracts* (1758), Kames made it clear that judicial systems and legal concepts were properly historical constructs, adhering to certain universal principles of development which in turn led them to reflect the different circumstances of communities at particular points in time: it followed, of course, that 'Law in particular becomes then only a rational study, when it is traced historically, from its first rudiments among savages, through successive changes, to its highest improvements in a civilized society'.[24]

Also important in the same field was Sir John Dalrymple, an advocate and laird, who attracted controversy with his *Memoirs of Great Britain and Ireland* (1771). Like Hume's great work, this menaced the self-satisfied Whiggish cult of English liberty and accordingly drew down much criticism upon its author's head. Intellectually even more daring, however, was Dalrymple's earlier treatise, *An Essay Towards a General History of Feudal Property* (1758). This demonstrated the interconnectedness of legal and economic systems, resulting in a complex legacy from the medieval period with which an age of Enlightenment, sponsored by a modern-minded generation of Scots lawyers and landowners, was still grappling. It also operated on the assumption that the study of the law was an integral aspect of a recognizably stadialist history of manners which would eventually illuminate, as Dalrymple speculated, 'how men arrived from the most rude to the most polished state of society'.[25]

The most innovative contributor to the study of the law as a cultural and historical artefact was probably Smith's brilliant pupil John Millar, who held the chair of civil law at Glasgow for much of the second half of the eighteenth century. Millar's guiding principle, as he explained it in the opening pages of his *Origin of the Distinction of Ranks* (1771), was that human institutions, whether the law or other inventions designed for purposes of social organization, develop slowly. They 'are only susceptible of those gentle improvements', he warned, 'which proceed from a gradual reformation of the manners, and are accompanied with a correspondent change in the condition of society'.[26] Such premises allowed him to sketch out one of the first systematic accounts of how substantial differences in status and power arise between individuals and groups. Millar's other main work, *An Historical View of the English Constitution* (1787), carried the trademark stadialist interest in the long-term evolution of legal forms over into the formal study of political structures, subjecting the system of government to careful scrutiny. If this was its principal intellectual justification, however, its chief ideological feature helped earn Millar a well-merited reputation as a

---

[24] Kames, *Historical Law Tracts*, i. p. v.

[25] Sir John Dalrymple, *An Essay Towards a General History of Feudal Property* (London, 1758), p. ix.

[26] John Millar, *Origin of the Distinction of Ranks* (London, 1771), p. v.

committed—and, by the time that the 1790s arrived, potentially subversive—advocate of constitutional reform in Great Britain.

Other historians melded identifiably conjecturalist assumptions with fluent narrative structures to cater in a less challenging way to the increasingly sentimental tastes of an ever-widening readership. Gilbert Stuart, a professional writer and, after his failure to obtain a chair at Edinburgh, Robertson's irreconcilable literary foe, represents this deliberately popularizing tendency better than almost anyone else. Predictably, perhaps, the increasingly lucrative subject of the Queen of Scots provided the fulcrum upon which Stuart was able to pivot a detailed account of his country's tumultuous past, *The History of Scotland from the Establishment of the Reformation Till the Death of Queen Mary* (1782). Here the most extreme sentimentality was the order of the day, as Stuart, whose Whiggery actually forbade sympathy with the queen's political strategies, nevertheless invited his tender-hearted readers to commiserate with her as a luckless and much-maligned woman. There was also the *Historical Dissertation Concerning the English Constitution* (1768), which flattered its English audience by identifying the origins of their national liberties amid the naturally egalitarian and irresistibly martial tribesmen of the Germanic woods and forests.

More overtly stadialist but also shot through with emotive appeals to the exquisite moral sensibilities of the late eighteenth-century public was Stuart's *A View of Society in Europe in its Progress from Rudeness to Refinement* (1782). Here he attempted to trump Robertson by offering a narrative in which, apparently with female readers again very much in mind, aspects of cultural development such as dress, chivalric literature, and changing courtship practices were given unusual prominence. In the hands of a determined and unscrupulous polemicist like Pinkerton, however, these increasingly diverse applications of conjecturalism to new problems and new agendas could also be shown to enable the complete recasting of the more remote parts of Scotland's history—hitherto, he mocked, 'a field of the blackest forgery, falsification, and perversion of all authorities'.[27] Like the more reliable scholars of the mainstream Enlightenment, he too would cling ostentatiously to the principles of stadial theory, affirming that 'similar stages of society will produce like manners among all mankind'.[28] But with Pinkerton it was actually twisted and warped beyond recognition in order to help justify his central proposition—as ridiculous as it was racist—that the ancient inhabitants of Scotland had been of vigorously Gothic or Germanic rather than inferior Celtic stock.

The dramatic popularization of historical writing after the 1750s, especially in a more or less conjecturalist vein, also led to attempts to bring its methods to bear upon concerns that, if considerably more palatable to the modern partaker than

---

[27] Pinkerton, *Enquiry*, i. 5.
[28] John Pinkerton, *A Dissertation on the Origins and Progress of the Scythians or Goths* (London, 1787), 131.

Pinkerton's rancid brew, were also to be somewhat more narrowly conceived—not to say parochial. In this respect the proliferation of town, county, and regional histories in Scotland was as much an expression of deference towards the best-selling work of the leading Edinburgh literati as it was a recognition of the recent outbreak of a positive epidemic of local historical studies elsewhere in Hanoverian Britain, again feeding a ravenous public hunger. A rather slight earlier Scottish tradition, represented by largely antiquarian works such as Sir Robert Sibbald's *History of Fife* and George Crawfurd's study of Renfrewshire (both 1710), was accordingly swept away by a torrent of studies couched in the new style.

It was in this context that the Berwickshire minister George Ridpath's posthumous *A Border History of Scotland and England* (1776) exploited the turbulent history of the district where he had lived. His Elgin colleague Lachlan Shaw similarly published *The History of the Province of Moray* (1775) while William Nimmo issued *The General History of Stirlingshire* (1777). For its part the merchant John Gibson's *History of Glasgow* (1777) offered a study of his city's development from medieval backwardness to commercial splendour that provided a kind of urban variation on the increasingly well-worn stadial theme, even though his frank aside that 'I do not expect that this work will be read by the learned' also unintentionally revealed how far Scottish historiography, now a major focus for trend-conscious literary consumerism, had become genuinely public property.[29] Small wonder that the *Monthly Review*, one of the arbiters of the British Enlightenment, could announce in 1791, clearly much impressed, that 'The fashionable study (for there are *fashions* in *study*,) of topography, poligraphy, and partial history, has begun to make its appearance in the northern capital of our island'.[30]

READINGS AND MISREADINGS

It is natural, perhaps, with an intellectual achievement such as the Scottish Enlightenment (particularly if one also accepts the sweeping historical perspective encouraged by its leading exponents), to wonder about its long-term implications. It will already be clear, however, that historiography took many distinct forms in eighteenth-century Scotland—many discernibly aligned with the values of the Enlightenment, not all of them completely reputable, but several at least with the potential to exercise a lasting influence over the theory and practice of studying and writing about the past. In seeking to gauge the subsequent impact of these activities, we could do worse than consider the case of Sir Walter Scott, pupil of Dugald Stewart, young admirer of the elderly

---

[29] John Gibson, *The History of Glasgow* (Glasgow, 1777), p. vii.
[30] *Monthly Review*, 5 (n.s.) (1791), 403.

Ferguson (who returned the compliment), and in many ways the greatest popularizer of stadialism that Scotland would produce. After all, it was less the moody Gothicism of so many of Scott's novels or their extraordinary pace and fluency (features arguably reminiscent of Robertson and Stuart) than his continual alertness to the distinctive manners and detailed mores of each historical era which made him such a prodigious propagandist for eighteenth-century historiographical approaches. Thus, in a work like *Waverley* (1814), with its dramatic counterpoising of residual Highland primitivism and thrusting Lowland commercialism, Scott was able to appropriate the assumptions of stadialism and make them the source of much of the dramatic tension that propelled his fictional narratives to unprecedented success.

Other near-contemporary readings of the Scottish historians' legacy were, however, considerably less sentimental than Scott's, though probably at least as far-reaching. German students, for example, ranging from Herder and Iselin, through Hegel and on to Marx and Engels, tended readily to assimilate some of the chief premises of stadial theory. In Marx's case the indebtedness extended even to his endorsing (though also exaggerating) the Scots' emphasis upon the material determination of each stage of development as well as their consciousness of the alienating effects upon individuals of an increasingly commercialized environment. But none of these admirers properly grasped crucial aspects of the conjecturalists' methodology that were absolutely essential to the Scottish Enlightenment's rounded historical vision—such as an awareness of the potential reversibility of human progress (to which Ferguson and Robertson, Presbyterian moralists both, were especially liable). This peculiar and highly partial reception in the nineteenth century by Romantic and proto-socialist thinkers is especially interesting, given that in the twentieth century it would be mainly politically conservative theorists who would assert ownership of parts of the same intellectual heritage. They too, moreover, would do so without properly appreciating its problematic implications. Above all, it is clear that attempts to co-opt the historians' version of 'unintended consequences' for the critique of corporatism and central planning and their contributions to the development of classical political economy and to the notion of 'civil society' for the cause of free market neo-liberalism have often ignored those aspects of their analysis that happen to fit less well with these latter-day concerns—Smith's bitter assault on the monopolistic tendencies of businessmen, for instance, or Ferguson's resolute hostility to constitutional reform and popular government.

Aside from these questionable ideological appropriations by political scientists and social theorists, it is clear that twentieth-century historians in particular came increasingly to recognize the historiographical achievements of the Edinburgh literati as one of the high points in Enlightenment intellectual culture. From the Second World War onwards, a series of major works, notably Gladys Bryson's *Man and Society: The Scottish Enquiry of the Eighteenth Century* (1945) and later Ronald Meek's *Social Science and the Ignoble Savage* (1976), began to shed new light on their collective output as a case study in the history of ideas. This tendency has continued in more recent years, although few current scholars, it should be said, would now regard the Scottish historians as models for direct emulation. They were, after all, radically present-minded in relation to the highly particular preoccupations and peculiarities of Hanoverian Britain. Furthermore, they took for granted the existence and understanding of general laws of historical development that it was their central task to delineate—a predilection that today sits ill with the ingrained empiricism of many if not most Anglophone practitioners. Yet the scholars of the Scottish Enlightenment did share one thing with modern historians: a burning desire to better know the past. Accordingly, they adopted a healthy scepticism, sometimes stunningly revelatory, in relation to the unfounded preconceptions of their predecessors. What most distinguished them as a group, however, was ultimately that several of them achieved an impact of the kind that many intellectuals crave but scarcely any attain. It is surely on this basis that we should feel able to appreciate them in their own right. Not only basking in but also actively shaping and forming what Gilbert Stuart himself greeted in 1780 as 'this enlightened age of philosophy and reflexion', Scotland's historians were a prominent feature in the intellectual landscape of the Enlightenment, successfully placing the study of the human past centre-stage as contemporaries sought to re-think and re-imagine the world in which they lived.[31]

TIMELINE/KEY DATES

1660 Restoration of Charles II

1679–85 The 'killing time'—conflict between the Scottish government and Presbyterians

1685 Accession of James VII of Scotland (and as James II of England)

1688–9 The Williamite Revolution in Britain

1702 Accession of Queen Anne

1707 The Treaty of Union between Scotland and England

1714 Accession of George I

1715 The Earl of Mar's Jacobite rebellion

1727 Accession of George II

1745 Bonnie Prince Charlie's Jacobite rebellion

1760 Accession of George III

1779 Catholic relief controversy

1780 Industrial Revolution begins in Scotland

1793–1815 French Revolutionary and Napoleonic Wars

1820 Accession of George IV

---

[31] Gilbert Stuart, *The History of the Establishment of the Reformation of Religion in Scotland* (London, 1780), 206.

KEY HISTORICAL SOURCES

Dalrymple, Sir John, *Memoirs of Great Britain and Ireland* (Edinburgh, 1771).

Ferguson, Adam, *An Essay on the History of Civil Society* (Edinburgh, 1767); ed. Fania Oz-Salzberger (Cambridge, 1995).

——*The History of the Progress and Termination of the Roman Republic* (London, 1783).

Hume, David, *The History of England* (London, 1754–62; London, 1875).

Innes, Thomas, *A Critical Essay on the Ancient Inhabitants of Scotland* (London, 1729).

Kames, Lord, *Historical Law Tracts* (Edinburgh, 1758).

——*Sketches of the History of Man* (Edinburgh, 1774).

Millar, John, *Origin of the Distinction of Ranks* (London, 1771).

Pinkerton, John, *A Dissertation on the Origins and Progress of the Scythians or Goths* (London, 1787).

——*An Enquiry into the History of Scotland* (London, 1789).

Ridpath, George, *A Border History of Scotland and England* (London, 1776).

Robertson, William, *The History of Scotland* (London, 1759).

——*The History of the Reign of the Emperor Charles V* (Dublin, 1769).

——*A History of America* (London, 1777).

Smith, Adam, *The Wealth of Nations* (London, 1776); ed. Edward Cannan (London, 1904).

——*Lectures on Jurisprudence*, ed. R. L. Meek, D. D. Raphael, and P. G. Stein (Indianapolis, 1982).

Stuart, Gilbert, *The History of the Establishment of the Reformation of Religion in Scotland* (London, 1780).

——*A View of Society in Europe in its Progress from Rudeness to Refinement* (Edinburgh, 1782).

BIBLIOGRAPHY

Allan, David, *Virtue, Learning and the Scottish Enlightenment: Ideas of Scholarship in Modern History* (Edinburgh, 1993).

——*Adam Ferguson* (Edinburgh, 2006).

Bryson, Gladys, *Man and Society: The Scottish Enquiry of the Eighteenth Century* (Princeton, 1945).

Emerson, Roger L., 'Conjectural History and the Scottish Philosophers', *Canadian Historical Association Historical Papers* (1984), 63–90.

Fearnley-Sander, Mary, 'Philosophical History and the Scottish Reformation: William Robertson and the Knoxian Tradition', *Historical Journal*, 22 (1990), 323–38.

Ferguson, William, *The Identity of the Scottish Nation* (Edinburgh, 1998).

Forbes, Duncan, *Hume's Philosophical Politics* (Cambridge, 1975).

Hamowy, Ronald, *The Scottish Enlightenment and the Theory of Spontaneous Order* (Carbondale, 1987).

Höpfl, Harro, 'From Savage to Scotsman: Conjectural History in the Scottish Enlightenment', *Journal of British Studies*, 17 (1978), 19–40.

Kettler, David, *Social and Political Thought of Adam Ferguson* (Columbus, 1965).

Kidd, Colin, *Subverting Scotland's Past: Scottish Whig Historians and the Creation of an Anglo-British Identity, 1689–c.1830* (Cambridge, 1993).

Lehmann, William, *John Millar of Glasgow* (Cambridge, 1960).

Mason, Roger, *Kingship and Commonweal: Political Thought and Culture in Renaissance and Reformation Scotland* (East Linton, 1998).

Meek, Ronald L., *Social Science and the Ignoble Savage* (Cambridge, 1976).

Mossner, E. C., 'Was Hume a Tory Historian? Facts and Reconsiderations', *Journal of the History of Ideas*, 2 (1941), 225–36.

O'Brien, Karen, *Narratives of Enlightenment: Cosmopolitan History from Voltaire to Gibbon* (Cambridge, 1997).

Phillipson, Nicholas, *Hume* (London, 1989).

Ross, Ian S., *Lord Kames and the Scotland of His Day* (Oxford, 1972).

Sher, Richard B., *Church and University in the Scottish Enlightenment: The Moderate Literati of Edinburgh* (Princeton, 1985).

Sweet, Rosemary, *The Writing of Urban Histories in Eighteenth-Century England* (Oxford, 1997).

Zachs, William, *Without Regard to Good Manners: A Biography of Gilbert Stuart, 1743–1786* (Edinburgh, 1992).

Chapter 25

English Enlightenment Histories, 1750–*c*.1815

Karen O'Brien

This chapter considers the histories written by English writers of the period 1750–*c*.1815 separately from those written by Scottish, Irish, or Welsh writers. In doing so it departs from a dominant tendency in our time to treat English historical writing as part of a British tradition dominated by the Scottish Enlightenment, of which the English historian Edward Gibbon is often seen as an honorary member.[1] Yet Gibbon was an Englishman, indeed, at a time of national crisis, a patriotic one: 'as much as a foreigner as you think me', he wrote to his closest friend, 'on this momentous subject I feel myself an Englishman'.[2] Gibbon absorbed and greatly accelerated the general transformation of English historical writing in this period towards a new, 'philosophical' conception of its purpose and scope. This transformation owed an enormous amount to the Scottish Enlightenment in general, and to David Hume's *History of England* (1754–62) in particular. But it also had its indigenous elements, and it addressed a specifically English imperative, in the late eighteenth century, to come to terms with the growing polarization of English political and religious culture in its various Whig, Tory, and radical, and Anglican, dissenting, and evangelical strands.

Gibbon's *The History of the Decline and Fall of the Roman Empire* (1776–88) is, undoubtedly, a culminating work of the European 'Enlightenment narrative', as J. G. A. Pocock has described it.[3] That narrative—of the rise of forms of civil government and of the slow waning of clerical power in state affairs—was collectively shaped by the leading historians of the Scottish, Italian, and French Enlightenments, among them Hume, William Robertson, Pietro Giannone, and Voltaire. Yet, the greater sophistication and scope of Gibbon's work consists, for Pocock, in the deeply absorbed tradition of Arminian thought that underpins it.

---

[1] Most notably, J. G. A. Pocock, *Barbarism and Religion*, 5 vols. to date (Cambridge, 1999–).
[2] Gibbon to Sheffield, 30 May 1792, in *The Letters of Edward Gibbon*, ed. J. E. Norton, 3 vols. (London, 1956), iii. 258.
[3] *Barbarism and Religion*, ii. 29–162.

Pocock records Gibbon's early immersion, during his time in Lausanne, in the scholarly and controversial works of Protestant, Arminian intellectuals, and the shaping influence of their preoccupation with the relationship between civil action and salvation, and with religious doctrine as the product of human culture.[4] This was, for Pocock, more decisive than his encounter with the philosophical intellectual environment of the French Enlightenment (as opposed to the erudite and critical world of Arminian scholarship, to adopt Arnaldo Momigliano's distinction), with its structurally oppositional stance towards clerical, aristocratic, and royal institutions.[5] In Calvinist Scotland, the Arminian strain of Enlightenment was less widespread; its roots were mainly in the north-east, and its preoccupations were, to some extent, sidestepped by Gibbon's Scottish Enlightenment contemporaries in favour of a new science of morals, but it had long been embedded in English intellectual life and in English debates about religious moderation and toleration.[6] As well as sharing this English and Protestant European intellectual ancestry, Gibbon's history can be also seen as a highly contemporary English work if we take into account the publication dates of its three instalments: 1776 at the height of the American crisis when Gibbon was sitting as an MP loyal to the North government; 1781 after the recent Gordon Riots had shown to Gibbon that the 'dark and diabolical fanaticism, which I had supposed extinct', and which he attributed to the early Christians, 'actually subsists in Great Britain';[7] and 1788 at a turning point for the British Empire after the loss of the American colonies, the introduction of Pitt's India Act, and the opening of the Hastings trial to which Gibbon came and heard himself publicly praised by Sheridan.

If Gibbon's *Decline and Fall* spoke vividly to the great political debates of late eighteenth-century England, it also answered to a desire, on the part of English readers, for an encompassing kind of philosophical history good enough to equal or surpass the works of Hume, Robertson, and other Scottish historians. Scottish Enlightenment history was enormously popular in England, but it did not fully satisfy English curiosity about subjects of increasing national interest:[8] the ethnic and cultural origins of the peoples south of the Scottish border, the peculiar

---

[4] *Barbarism and Religion*, i. and ii. ch. 2.

[5] Arnaldo Momigliano, 'Gibbon's Contribution to Historical Method', in *Studies in Historiography* (London, 1966), 40–55.

[6] J. G. A. Pocock, 'Clergy and Commerce: The Clerical Enlightenment in England', in *L'Età dei Lumi: Studi Storici sul Settecento Europeo in Onore di Franco Venturi*, 2 vols. (Naples, 1985), i. 523–61. More recently, David Jan Sorkin, *The Religious Enlightenment: Protestants, Jews and Catholics from London to Vienna* (Princeton, 2008), 54–7.

[7] *The Miscellaneous Works of Edward Gibbon*, ed. Lord Sheffield, 5 vols. (London, 1814), i. 547. See John Seed, '"The Deadly Principles of Fanaticism": Puritans and Dissenters in Gibbon's *Decline and Fall of the Roman Empire*', in James Moore, Ian Macgregor Morris, and Andrew J. Bayliss (eds.), *Reinventing History: The Enlightened Origins of Ancient History* (London, 2008), 87–112.

[8] On the popularity of Scottish histories in England, see David Allan, *Making British Culture: English Readers and the Scottish Enlightenment, 1740–1830* (London, 2008).

legacy of Rome in its English colony, and the distinctive developmental path of English (as opposed to Scottish) laws, political institutions, and cultural artefacts. Gibbon's history, however, gave considerable impetus and a scholarly European context to a growing body of work, in the late eighteenth century, on England's ancient British, Anglo-Saxon, and medieval heritage. And it redefined the terms in which the English thought of themselves in relation to their former imperial Roman masters.[9]

The English appetite for a more philosophical kind of history in the late eighteenth century must be understood in the context of England's distinctive, lively printing industry and in the institutional contexts of historical production. At a time when the Scottish printing industry was only just beginning to gather strength, the London book market was saturated with locally published historical works, including large-scale collaborative productions such as the *Universal History* (1736–65). Boundaries between 'high' and popular histories remained blurred within an innovative print culture of serial publication, multi-author productions, republications, and continuations.[10] Historical publication remained very much a matter of private enterprise, and funds were raised for bigger productions through subscription or through consortia of printers.[11] History as an academic profession was far less developed in England than it was in Scotland, and many English historians cultivated an image of history as a gentlemanly pursuit, including Gibbon himself, who was highly self-conscious and articulate about his own public 'character' as an historian.[12] The Regius chairs of modern history bestowed on Oxford and Cambridge in 1724 were mainly held by career clergymen and literary figures such as Thomas Gray or Joseph Spence rather than by historians. In the Dissenting Academies, modern history was an important part of the curriculum.[13] Some of the academic teaching of history there reached a more general public, most notably Joseph Priestley's lectures on history, delivered at the Warrington Academy in the late 1760s, and published in 1788 as the *Lectures on History and General Policy*. Even so, for the most part, historians' claims to historical expertise and philosophical-ness are best understood as acts of self-positioning within a primarily commercial context. A vogue for a Voltairean mode of philosophical history took hold in England in the 1750s–60s. This kind of history foregrounded a critical or sceptical authorial perspective on source materials, on the fanaticisms of the

[9] See Piers Brandon, *The Decline and Fall of the British Empire* (London, 2007), 171, 210, 227.

[10] Guido Abbattista, 'The Business of Paternoster Row: Towards a Publishing History of *The Universal History*, (1736–65)', *Publishing History*, 17 (1985), 5–50; and Jeremy Black, 'Ideology, History, Xenophobia and the World of Print in Eighteenth-Century England', in Black and Jeremy Gregory (eds.), *Culture, Politics and Society in Britain, 1660–1800* (Manchester, 1991), 207.

[11] See Karen O'Brien, 'The History Market', in Isabel Rivers (ed.), *Books and their Readers in Eighteenth-Century England: New Essays* (London, 2001), 105–134.

[12] David Womersley, *Gibbon and the Watchmen of the Holy City: The Historian and his Reputation* (Oxford, 2002).

[13] Paul Wood (ed.), *Science and Dissent in England, 1688–1945* (Aldershot, 2004), 2–3.

past, even on the value of history itself; and it weighed evidential probabilities against the known features of human nature and human motivation. As Daniel Woolf has noted in this volume, there was a more general resurgence, in the mid-eighteenth century, of European and global histories, including Voltaire's own *Essai sur les moeurs et l'esprit des nations* [Essay on the Manners and Spirit of Nations] published in 1756, the *Universal History*, the compilation *General History of the World* (1744–51), and William Russell's popular *A History of Modern Europe* (1779). Historians such as the Irish writer Oliver Goldsmith and the Scotsman Tobias Smollett were assiduous in their promotion of Voltaire and of an anglicized (and less irreligious) version of Voltaire's philosophical history to an English readership.[14] Nevertheless, few of the historians who declared their status as philosophical historians on the model of Voltaire sustained this much beyond prefaces and footnoted asides.[15]

At Edinburgh University, Hugh Blair credited Voltaire for greatly enlarging the compass of history by paying 'a more particular attention than was formerly given to laws, customs, commerce, religion, literature, and every other thing that tends to show the spirit and genius of nations. It is now understood to be the business of an able Historian to exhibit manners as well as facts and events.'[16] In the opinion of many English readers, Scottish historians took this transformation to a new level. The English success of Robertson's histories (and Robertson took care to secure English publishers for his works) showed the way to a somewhat different kind of philosophical history that set political events in a richer, broader context of legal and social developments, arts, sciences, and 'manners'.[17] The discursive appendices in Hume's *History* also greatly influenced subsequent English historians seeking to diversify political narrative without diluting it too much. Conventional political narratives, such as Catharine Macaulay's highly successful *The History of England from the Accession of James I to That of the Brunswick Line* (1763–83), continued to be a dominant feature of the English book market up to and beyond the end of this period, and not all of them featured subsections or appendices on laws, society, and 'manners'. Yet they inhabited a changed intellectual environment in which public views about the social importance of the kinds of knowledge that history embodied had clearly changed enormously since the early eighteenth century. The traditional view of history as a source of moral, practical, prudential lessons for the (male) conduct

---

[14] O'Brien, 'The History Market', 117–20.

[15] A. M. Rousseau, 'L'école historique anglaise de Voltaire', in *L'Angleterre et Voltaire, Studies on Voltaire and the Eighteenth Century*, 147 (1976), 754–851.

[16] *Lectures on Rhetoric and Belles Lettres* (published 1783, first delivered in 1759–60), ed. Harold F. Harding, 2 vols. (Illinois, 1965), ii. 288.

[17] Richard B. Sher, 'Charles V and the Book Trade: An Episode in Enlightenment Print Culture', in Stewart J. Brown (ed.), *William Robertson and the Expansion of Empire* (Cambridge, 1997), 164–95; and more generally Sher's *The Enlightenment and the Book: Scottish Authors and their Publishers in Eighteenth-Century Ireland, Britain and America* (Chicago, 2006).

of public life did not disappear, but was greatly augmented by a newer and more elevated view of history as the pre-eminent source of insight into human nature and behaviour. The reading of history imparted practical, useful knowledge, but it was also a cognitive activity allowing the individual to connect him- or herself to collective experience, in self-enhancing but less obviously useful ways.

This more contemplative view of the nature and value of historical knowledge certainly provided an entrée for female readers. Hester Chapone, in her widely read *Letters on the Improvement of the Mind* (1773), offered history to her female readers as 'the principal study I would recommend. . . . I know of nothing equally proper to entertain and improve at the same time, or that is so likely to form and strengthen your judgement—and, by giving you a liberal and comprehensive view of human nature, in some measure to supply the defect of that experience, which is usually attained too late to be of much service to us.'[18] In a later letter, she set out a programme of historical reading designed to show the connection of British history to wider patterns of European development (Robertson is particularly recommended here), and of Europe in the long-standing process of colonial exploitation of other parts of this world. Chapone's idea of history as a kind of mental furniture and a corrective to national prejudice updated Lord Bolingbroke's philosophical prescriptions for history in the *Letters on the Study and Use of History* (1752).[19] Bolingbroke was arguably the first writer to articulate an English Enlightenment historical programme (without producing a history himself) which incorporated a French attitude of scepticism towards received ideas and 'national partialities and prejudices', and which asserted the value of historical epistemology: 'Experience is doubly defective; we are born too late to see the beginning, and we die too soon to see the end of many things. History supplies both these defects.'[20] Bolingbroke's influence was acknowledged by few in this period, but his idea of history as 'philosophy teaching by examples' was widely echoed in many different arenas. Priestley, in his *Lectures on History and General Policy* (1788), made comparable claims for history as both an eradicator of national prejudice and as a virtual form of experience: it provides, he said, an 'anticipated knowledge of the world' which is a 'better guide to us, than anything we would have learned from our own random experience'.[21]

---

[18] *Letters*, in *Bluestocking Feminism: Writings of the Bluestocking Circle, 1738–1785*, ed. Gary Kelly *et al.*, 6 vols. (London, 1999), iii. 332. See D. R. Woolf, 'A Feminine Past? Gender, Genre and Historical Knowledge in England, 1500–1800', *American Historical Review*, 102 (1997), 645–79.

[19] See ch 23 by Daniel Woolf in this volume.

[20] Henry St John, Viscount Bolingbroke, *The Works of Lord Bolingbroke*, 4 vols. (London, 1967), ii. 183, 186.

[21] Priestley, *Lectures on History and General Policy* (1788), ed. J. T. Rutt (London, 1840), 38.

PARTY-POLITICAL HISTORY

Priestley's utopian model of historical knowledge as a means of arriving at universal human values, beyond the distortions of national and religious prejudice, was very different from Bolingbroke's. Yet both writers shared an Enlightenment impulse to occupy an authorial perspective 'above' and outside their own culture by claiming that it was the completeness of historical knowledge itself that made such a transcendence of subjectivity possible. Among Scottish historians, such claims of transcendence were often motivated by the need to negotiate a difficult and violent, sectarian religious legacy. Among English writers and those writing English history, they resulted far more from a need to cope with the legacy of political party, and the religious and dynastic politics embedded in party. If, as Woolf argues in this volume, the period from 1660 to 1740 was one in which historical writing 'adjusted itself to the permanent presence of ideological division' in British politics, then the period after 1745 was one in which historians of England tried to come to philosophical terms with the paradox of the apparent political stability produced by that division. For Hume, that stability was a desirable, if fragile, consequence of the enshrining of liberty within the English constitution in the late seventeenth century. For his radical rival Catharine Macaulay, this stability was merely the combined effect of aristocratic oligarchy and popular apathy.[22] Hume's *History* was persistently misunderstood as a biased, Tory work with its conspicuously sympathetic account of the Stuart monarchs. But it was not in his account of individuals or even parties that Hume felt that his philosophical impartiality lay, rather, in his clinical diagnosis of party allegiance and religious fervour as peculiar forms of political behaviour. Ever the political scientist, Hume regarded party as an epiphenomenon of a deeply rooted, English culture of liberty, and his real interest lay in the contours and history of that culture.

Hume's *History* had a number of competitors issuing from London-based printing houses. Tobias Smollett's *A Complete History of England* (1757–8) rewarded its enterprising publisher James Rivington with spectacular sales for a time, partly because it captured a public mood of patriotism, royalism, and expansionism during the early phase of the Seven Years War.[23] Oliver Goldsmith's *History of England* (1771), published in London by Thomas Cadell and others, enjoyed popularity comparable to Hume's work well into the nineteenth century, although this was largely because it reproduced and adapted portions of Hume, Smollett, and other historians.[24] More importantly, Hume's *History* had

[22] See Karen O'Brien, *Women and Enlightenment in Eighteenth-Century Britain* (Cambridge, 2009), ch. 4 ('Catharine Macaulay's Histories of England').

[23] O'Brien, 'The History Market', 114–15.

[24] Ibid., 119.

the paradoxical effect of encouraging other historians to refute him. In Ireland, Protestant and Catholic historians, such as Thomas Leland, John Curry, and Sylvestor O'Halloran, fashioned an Enlightened revisionist account of Irish history partly motivated by their disagreement with Hume's portrayal of Irish religious fanaticism and violence during the Rebellion of 1641.[25] In England, as John Seed has argued, Hume's account of seventeenth-century Puritanism sparked a revival in a tradition of dissenting history—a tradition stretching back to Daniel Neal's landmark *History of the Puritans* (1732–8) and beyond.[26] Among these dissenting historians were William Harris, author of *An Historical and Critical Account of the Life of Oliver Cromwell* (1762), and others linked to the circles of Thomas Hollis and the radical political groups who supported John Wilkes.

Catharine Macaulay was by far the most prominent and successful historian to come out of those circles. Her *History of England* adopted a rigorous and sustained 'Old' Whig perspective on precisely the same historical material covered by Hume in the two Stuart volumes of his history. For some years, her earlier volumes outsold and outgunned those of Hume.[27] She gave an uncompromising account of the English discovery of political liberty in the seventeenth century, the (in her view, justified) execution of Charles I, the constitutional establishment of liberty during the Commonwealth, and the loss of that liberty after Cromwell's *coup d'état* and the Stuart Restoration. In the final volume, she denounced the failure of the so-called Glorious Revolution to restore liberty, and in a companion volume, *The History of England from the Revolution to the Present Time* (1778), she charted the progressive entrenching of aristocratic oligarchy throughout the following decades: 'under the specious appearance of democratical privilege, the people are really and truly enslaved to a small part of the community'.[28] Macaulay was an active presence in English and transatlantic radical political networks. Her volumes came out periodically during a highly eventful political era and engaged indirectly throughout with the wider issues raised by the Seven Years War, the Wilkes affair, the American Revolution, and the American Federal Constitution. However, her allegiance to an Old Whig tradition of political liberty did not prevent her from adopting an advanced and, in many ways, Enlightenment approach to matters of source, method, and theme. In addition to the striking modernity of her bold self-promotion as a female historian and to the solid basis of much of her history in primary research, Macaulay adopted a philosophically sophisticated approach to questions of

---

[25] See Deana Rankin, 'Historical Writing, 1750–1800', in Andrew Hadfield and Raymond Gillespie (eds.), *The Irish Book in English, 1550–1800* (Oxford, 2006), 282–300.

[26] John Seed, *Dissenting Histories: Religious Division and the Politics of Memory in Eighteenth-Century England* (Edinburgh, 2008).

[27] Bridget Hill, *The Republican Virago: The Life and Times of Catharine Macaulay, Historian* (Oxford, 1992), 41–4.

[28] *The History of England from the Accession of James I*, 8 vols. (London, 1763–83), viii. 330.

historical causation and change. In her histories, she emphasizes the role of accident and unintended consequence almost as much as Hume, and she considers liberty not as an abstract ideal, but as an effect of economic change, as a feature of particular kinds of political culture, and as an historical process. Moreover, coming as she did from a wealthy City of London family, she was by no means hostile to commerce or inclined to harp exclusively upon its corrupting effects. Her distinctive, commercially minded civic republicanism went down very well in the American colonies, and her histories continued to sell well there long after they had started to appear too old fashioned, nostalgic, or radical to English readers.[29]

CLASSICAL HISTORIES AND EARLY CHRISTIANITY

The achievements of Hume and Macaulay went some way towards silencing the earlier chorus of complaint that there were no adequate histories of England written by British writers.[30] Before Gibbon, similar anxieties attached to classical history. For much of the century, the standard work was the *Histoire Romaine* [*The Roman History*] (1738–41; English trans. 1739–45) by the French writer Charles Rollin. This was partly replaced by Goldsmith's accessible précis of classical and modern sources, *The Roman History* (1769). In the domain of early Roman history there was Nathaniel Hooke's *The Roman History from the Building of Rome to the Ruin of the Commonwealth* (1738–71), with its overtly Tory sympathy for the Gracchi and Julius Caesar, which was in turn surpassed by Adam Ferguson's *The History of the Progress and Termination of the Roman Republic* (1783).[31] Original scholarship into the ancient world lagged some way behind France with its Académie des Inscriptions, and few English histories (with the possible exceptions of Conyers Middleton's *Life of Cicero* [1741], Thomas Blackwell's *Memoirs of the Court of Augustus* [1753–63], and Hume's essays) matched the depth of philosophical engagement with the history of Rome to be found in Montesquieu's *Considérations sur les causes de la grandeur des Romains et de leur décadance* [The Greatness of the Romans and Their Decline] (1734). Gibbon's apprenticeship as a classical historian, as Pocock has shown, was both scholarly and philosophical, and entailed a profound engagement with three centuries of European research and reflection.[32] Since Gibbon had few English rivals to face in the sphere of Roman history, it was against Tacitus rather than

---

[29] See Kate Davies, *Catharine Macaulay and Mercy Otis Warren: The Revolutionary Atlantic and the Politics of Gender* (Oxford, 2005).

[30] On this perceived crisis in English history, see Philip Hicks, *Neoclassical History and English Culture: From Clarendon to Hume* (New York, 1996).

[31] On Hooke, see Frank M. Turner, *Contesting Cultural Authority: Essays in Victorian Intellectual Life* (Cambridge, 1993), 237–9.

[32] *Barbarism and Religion,* i.

any modern historian that he implicitly measured himself when he chose to begin his work with an overview of the age of the Antonines (from AD 138), shortly after the point where Tacitus left off. This era he famously dubbed 'the period in the history of the world, during which the condition of the human race was most happy and prosperous', while strongly hinting in the opening three chapters at the underlying structural weakness of the Roman Empire and the fatal complacency of the Romans.[33]

The preface to the first instalment of *The Decline and Fall* (published in 1776) sketched out Gibbon's ambition to encompass the stories of both the Western and Eastern Roman Empires right up to the fall of Constantinople in 1453, although it would be many years more before he settled on the final shape of the history. The process of writing enlarged still further the geographical scope of his original project, and drew him into a global-historical engagement with the most advanced scholarship of his day on early Chinese history, Arab history, the history of the Steppe peoples, the Crusades, and much more.[34] Recent work on Gibbon has revealed the extent of his debt to Scottish Enlightenment historical thought, with its sophisticated sociology of developmental stages, attention to economic modes of production and their attendant forms of law, politics, and social life, and its analysis of social mores in relation to the stages of society. The story of the collapse of the Roman Empire gave Gibbon a fascinating opportunity to dramatize the (often violent and bewildering) encounter between peoples at utterly different stages of social development, as successive waves of primitive Goths, Huns, Vandals, and other barbarians pitted themselves against the sophisticated peoples of the Roman Empire. Scottish influences undoubtedly shaped the complex, thickly described nature of Gibbon's causal narrative. In chapter 26, for example, Gibbon gives an extraordinary, many-layered account of the defeat of the Eastern Roman Emperor Valens by the Visigoths at the battle of Hadrianople (AD 378). The chapter begins with an analysis of the society and manners of the Huns (a people at the 'pastoral' stage of development), their diet, dwellings, forms of political organization, and the demographic expansion which had caused them originally to invade China and, during the time of Valens, to begin the massive westward push which would drive the Goths forward to the frontier of the Roman Empire. There ensues a political crisis, during which the Eastern Romans agree to allow the displaced Gothic refugees to cross the Danube in their thousands but then abuse and exploit them to the point where they attack their Roman masters. The defeat at Hadrianople would not in itself have been so significant, Gibbon argues, were it not for the structural weakness of the empire, and also for the damaging effects of imperial court culture and besetting lack of

---

[33] *The History of the Decline and Fall of the Roman Empire*, ed. David Womersley, 3 vols. (Harmondsworth, 1994), i. 103.
[34] The scope of this engagement has been discussed in Pocock, *Barbarism and Religion*, iv.

self-belief among the Romans.[35] Larger forces of demography and global history, mutual suspicion and incomprehension between peoples at incompatible stages of society, the accidents of military history, the failure of Roman leadership, and strategic error conspire to turn a single battle into a watershed in the decline of the Roman Empire.

Throughout *The Decline and Fall*, Gibbon conveys a rich and multi-dimensional sense of causality. Low in the pecking order of the causes of decline are moral factors. Gibbon gained a Victorian reputation as a doomy and prescient moralist of imperial decline. Yet nowhere did he capitulate to the old clichés that the fall of Rome was owing to luxury, moral decadence, loose women, bread, and circuses. Like Hume and Smith, Gibbon was committed to the notion that luxury, far from being harmful, stimulates economic growth, and 'seems to be the only means that can correct the unequal distribution of property'; he consistently defended the value to cities 'which are the seat of commerce and manufactures' of 'the middle ranks of inhabitants . . . the most prolific, the most useful, and, in that sense, the most respectable part of the community'.[36] Moreover, Gibbon was for his time an historian of exceptionally broad and tolerant moral sympathies, reserving some of his most devastating satire for the early Christians with their perversely ascetic insistence on sexual self-denial:

Disdaining an ignominious flight, the [Christian] virgins of the warm climate of Africa encountered the enemy in the closest engagement; they permitted priests and deacons to share their bed, and gloried amidst the flames in their unsullied purity. But insulted Nature sometimes vindicated her rights, and this new species of martyrdom served only to introduce a new scandal into the church.[37]

A great deal of attention was and continues to be given to Gibbon's mordantly ironic accounts of the rise of the early Christian Church, deliberately positioned as they are in the final two chapters of the first instalment in ways that implied that this was the true 'slow and secret poison' in 'the vitals of the empire' alluded to at the beginning.[38] David Womersley has explored Gibbon's shock and his determined, tactical response to the torrent of clerical fury which initially greeted these chapters.[39] Gibbon was clearly concerned to protect his reputation from the kind of damage which Hume's had suffered. More than this, he did not wish to allow the controversy to detract from the seriousness of his philosophical analysis of the relationship between civil society, political culture, and religion across the whole of his projected story. The second instalment opened with a truly decisive moment in Roman history, the shift of the imperial capital to Constantinople which would become soon after, on the conversion of the emperor, the capital of the Christian Empire. This shift certainly marks for Gibbon a lower rung on the

---

[35] *The Decline and Fall*, i. 1062, 1074.
[36] Ibid., i. 80; ii. 181.   [37] Ibid., i. 481.   [38] Ibid., i. 83.
[39] Womersley, *Gibbon and the Watchmen of the Holy City*.

ladder of decline, but, in subsequent volumes, it becomes clear that Christianity is really one of a number of factors that bring about a shift from the old political culture of Rome to the Asiatic (as Gibbon characterizes it), degenerate, and stultified political culture of Byzantium: 'The distinct view of the complicated system of policy, introduced by Diocletian, improved by Constantine, and completed by his immediate successors, may not only amuse the fancy by the singular picture of a great empire, but will tend to illustrate the secret and internal causes of its rapid decay.'[40]

There is arguably more of Montesquieu than of Hume or Smith in Gibbon's analysis of the pathologies of despotism. The essence of the Byzantine despotism is that it replaces all allegiance to political institutions and heritage, along with the elective and hereditary honours, offices, and social gradations associated with them, with a two-dimensional relationship of power and dependency. Gone are the old distinctions between Patricians and Plebeians ('the proudest and most perfect separation which can be found in any age or country'[41]), the Patrician monopoly of the legal profession, the ceremonial, public religious function of the Roman elites, the independence of the Senate and its supervision of the army, and the restriction of military and civil offices to citizens, rather than barbarians with no education and no sense of investment in Rome's traditions and laws. Economic stagnation follows from political decline: the Byzantine state stifles commerce through its creation of a court service economy in which the cities supply the court and are themselves parasitically dependent upon the agriculture of the provinces. Amid a narrative amplified, to an unprecedented degree, by attention to economic, cultural, and geographical factors, Gibbon's story of decline is, in the final analysis, a political one centred upon the loss of a unique set of hierarchical political structures and traditions. Eastern Christianity, insofar as it embroils itself in obscure yet often turbulent neo-Platonic controversy, forms part of that story of political decline, and is of a piece with the mystifications of Eastern despotism.

Gibbon was unable or unwilling to recognize the Eastern Orthodox Church as in any way separate from the Byzantine state.[42] Yet he did acknowledge and explore the ways in which, in the long run, the Catholic Church in the West preserved and protracted the legacy of the Roman Empire, and brought about the 'similar manners, and common jurisprudence, which have distinguished, from the rest of mankind, the independent, and even hostile, nations of modern Europe'.[43] Gibbon's measured account of the early and medieval Catholic Church as a partial agent of revival and civilization did not mollify his more

[40] *The Decline and Fall*, i. 602.
[41] Ibid., i. 607.
[42] See Steven Runciman, 'Gibbon and Byzantium', in John Clive, Stephen Graubard, and G. W. Bowersock (eds.), *Edward Gibbon and the Decline and Fall of the Roman Empire* (Cambridge, Mass., 1977), 53–60.
[43] *The Decline and Fall*, ii. 433.

pious opponents. Indeed, Priestley threw down a gauntlet to him in his *An History of the Corruptions of Christianity* (1782) which Gibbon—perhaps wisely—declined to take up.[44] Priestley's history gave a radically different version of the rise of Christianity from that of chapters 15 and 16 of *The Decline and Fall*. He presented an originally pristine Christian faith and worship obscured by the irrational and self-serving dogmas of ambitious Church fathers and ecclesiastical politicians.[45] Yet Gibbon's balanced appraisal of the medieval Catholic Church did prove enabling to a subsequent generation of historians. Among these was the Catholic priest and historian John Lingard, whose *The Antiquities of the Anglo-Saxon Church* (1806) presented a church that, although firmly tied to Rome from the outset, functioned as an agent of national civility and cultural progress. Moderate, occasionally ironic in tone, and mildly sceptical about miracles and martyrs, Lingard's *Antiquities* and his later *History of England* (1819–30) bear witness to Gibbon's influence as an historian of the social dimensions of religious institutions.

Gibbon's seemingly effortless command of Greek source material pointed up the deficiencies of Enlightenment scholarship into classical Greek history. Gibbon may have encouraged his acquaintance William Mitford in the writing of his *The History of Greece* (5 vols., 1784–1818), which covered ancient Greek history from the earliest known times to the death of Alexander the Great. Mitford's essentially political narrative reflected few of the developments in contemporary Enlightenment historical practice. It was, however, a sufficiently authoritative synthesis of sources such as Herodotus and Thucydides to displace earlier works by Temple Stanyan and Goldsmith, and remained a standard work until George Grote felt moved by its shortcomings to write his landmark Greek history in the 1840s and 1850s.[46] Two of Mitford's volumes came out during the 1790s, and reflected his sense of alarm at contemporary radicalism and Jacobinism, although the nineteenth-century view of his history as distorted by his reactionary politics is not entirely fair.[47]

MANNERS ANCIENT, MEDIEVAL, AND MODERN

The combined legacy of Gibbon and Robertson provided the scholarly basis for a more general English historical movement to rehabilitate the non-Roman bar-

---

[44] Gibbon's exchange of letters with Priestley on this subject were first published as appendix 4 to Priestley's *Discourses on the Evidence of Revealed Religion* (London, 1794), 412–20.

[45] See Alison Kennedy, 'Historical Perspectives in the Mind of Joseph Priestley', in Isabel Rivers and David Wykes (eds.), *Joseph Priestley: Scientist, Philosopher and Theologian* (Oxford, 2008), 172–202.

[46] Temple Stanyan, *The Grecian History*, 2 vols. (London, 1707–39); and Oliver Goldsmith, *The Grecian History*, 2 vols. (London, 1774).

[47] Ian Macgregor Morris, 'Navigating the Grotesque; or, Rethinking Greek Historiography', in Moore, Morris, and Bayliss (eds.), *Reinventing History*, 247–90.

barian and medieval antecedents of Europe's peoples. As Colin Kidd has shown, the Gothic revival at this time was not nationalist but rather European in focus, and emphasized a common European heritage at a time of persistent Anglo–French military conflict.[48] Part of that project of rehabilitation entailed a remapping of Europe's ethnic heritage as a result of which sources for Celtic and Gothic history were separated, and England's Gothic heritage was more closely studied and preferred. This in turn paved the way for renewed interest in England's Anglo-Saxon past, including the ethnic characteristics of the Angles and the Saxons and the nature of the early Anglo-Saxon Church. After a heroic phase of Anglo-Saxon scholarship in the late seventeenth to early eighteenth centuries (led by George Hickes, William and Elizabeth Elstob, Edmund Gibson, and others), there had been little progress in this field. *The History of the Anglo-Saxons* (1799–1805) by the English lawyer and scholar Sharon Turner marked the beginning of a new phase. Turner's *History* is authentically Gibbonian in its remarkable scholarship (he rediscovered *Beowulf*), its sceptical handling of sources, its insistently European rather than insular focus, and its dramatization of the Anglo-Saxon invasions as a clash of stages of civilization. In the narrative, he characterizes the Saxons as nomadic and brutal like any barbarian people at the pastoral stage, and shows how they overwhelm the sophisticated ancient Britons, who are at the agricultural stage: 'As the agricultural state advances, and the comforts of civilization accumulate, provident industry secures regular supplies', and these are utterly disrupted by barbarian invasion.[49] Like Gibbon's barbarians, Turner's Saxons are civilized by Christianity and brought into the family of European nations through their contact with Latinate Catholic culture (Gibbon is likewise always very clear that the conversions of the various barbarians to Christianity softened their blows to the Roman Empire).[50] Aspects of Turner's work were at the cutting edge of his time. He read Thomas Malthus's *Essay on the Principle of Population* (1798), and used what he learned about population pressure as a driver of migration, conquest, and social change to refine his account of the stages and clashes of civilizations: 'It is a law of nature', he wrote, 'that the population of every country shall ever tend to exceed its supply. The augmented resources of subsistence from the harvest of the ocean multiplied the inhabitants of the Saxon states', and it was this that drove them to Britain's shores.[51]

Turner did not completely digest Enlightenment historical methods and sociological categories: his *History* begins by claiming that his Saxon genealogy

---

[48] Colin Kidd, *British Identities before Nationalism: Ethnicity and Nationhood in the Atlantic World, 1600–1800* (Cambridge, 1999).

[49] Turner, *The History of the Anglo-Saxons*, 2 vols. (2nd edn, London, 1807), ii. 73. Turner's *History* was much revised in its second edition from which this quotation is taken.

[50] *The Decline and Fall*, ii. 511.

[51] *The History of the Anglo-Saxons* (London, 1799), 170.

is consistent with biblical accounts.[52] In many ways his work typifies the hybrid and attenuated English historical Enlightenment of the later eighteenth century with its combination of Gibbonian ambition, moderate piety, antiquarian scholarship, and generous definition of historical subject matter. Mark Salber Phillips has written of the extraordinary broadening of history's thematic compass in the late eighteenth century, and the growing sense of the inherent interest of any aspect of the past—including medieval, Anglo-Saxon and Icelandic literature, the history of women, local history, art history, the history of domestic life, and much more—that could be counted as part of the history of manners.[53] Such histories took a less systematic and, in the case of works such as Thomas Warton's *History of English Poetry* (1774–90), a more discipline-specific approach to manners than Gibbon or Robertson had done. Remarkable among these are Clara Reeve's pioneering history of the novel, *The Progress of Romance* (1785), and the works of the English engraver, antiquarian, and novelist Joseph Strutt, including his illustrated *Sports and Pastimes of the People of England* (1801), a work that stayed in print until the early twentieth century.[54] Such works alluded to a general, evolutionary Enlightenment historical framework, but were then quickly absorbed by the specificity and detail of their subject matter. Urban histories, such as John Whitaker's *The History of Manchester* (1771–5) and William Hutton's *A History of Birmingham* (1781), became more popular and prevalent during this period, and they too generally alluded to an overarching but distant Enlightened narrative of wider European development.[55] Female historians profited in somewhat different ways from the mutation of cultural history into more diffuse and anecdotal accounts of manners. After Catharine Macaulay, a generation of female historians made a living, not from political narrative, but from a new kind of heavily contextualized historical biography which typically described the lives of queens and other notable personages and the culture of their times. Among these were Mary Hays (author of *Historical Dialogues for Young Persons* [1806] and *Memoirs of Queens* [1821]), Elizabeth Benger (the biographer of Mary, Queen of Scots [1823] and Anne Boleyn [1821]), Lucy Aikin (*Memoirs of the Court of Queen Elizabeth* [1818] and other studies of the courts of James I and Charles I), and Mary Berry (author of *A Comparative View of the Social Life of England and France* [1828]). As I have argued elsewhere, this flowering of women's history and the enduring nineteenth-century association between female historians and historical subgenres such as biography and art

---

[52] *The History of the Anglo-Saxons*, 2–3. On the persistence of biblical racial genealogies, see Colin Kidd, *The Forging of Races: Race and Scripture in the Protestant Atlantic World, 1600–2000* (Cambridge, 2006).

[53] Mark Salber Phillips, *Society and Sentiment: Genres of Historical Writing in Britain, 1740–1820* (Princeton, 2000).

[54] Ibid., 159–61. On antiquarianism in this period more generally, see Rosemary Sweet, *Antiquaries: The Discovery of the Past in Eighteenth-Century Britain* (London, 2004).

[55] Rosemary Sweet, *The Writing of Urban Histories in Eighteenth-Century England* (Oxford, 1997).

history, had its roots in the late Enlightenment development of unsystematic, encompassing histories of manners.[56]

In relation to political history there were also deep continuities between the historical culture of the Scottish and English Enlightenments and nineteenth-century liberal Whiggism which were established by the generation of intellectuals and reformers who either studied in Scotland or wrote for *The Edinburgh Review*.[57] The *Edinburgh* espoused an historical outlook, derived from Hume, Smith, Millar, and Gibbon, that identified 'modern European civilisation with the progress of commercial society'.[58] Some leading historians of the early nineteenth century emerged from this stable, including the Scottish utilitarian historian of India, James Mill, the Scottish Whig historian James Mackintosh, and the pre-eminent English historian of this period, Henry Hallam. Hallam's *Edinburgh Review* and Enlightenment background are clearly apparent in his first history, a *View of the State of Europe during the Middle Ages* (1818), a series of essays, on the model of Gibbon's and Robertson's work, about the feudal, ecclesiastical, and social organization of medieval Europe. Hallam's final chapter 'On the State of Society in Europe during the Middle Ages', though presented in a more apologetic tone than would have been usual in the eighteenth century, offers a genuinely broad overview of the agriculture, commerce, religious practices, and domestic life of the time. Hallam adopts Gibbon's sceptical but occasionally positive valuation of the medieval Catholic Church, and concurs with the late eighteenth-century view of chivalry as a civilizing influence and 'school of moral discipline'.[59] More innovatively, he discusses vernacular architecture under the heading of 'domestic manners', and (foreshadowing his important *Introduction to the Literature of Europe in the Fifteenth, Sixteenth and Seventeenth Centuries* [1837–9]) covers the literature of the period. Hallam further developed his interest in religious issues and in the medieval origins of parliamentary representation in his *A Constitutional History of England* (1827), an influential work which pressed the case for Catholic emancipation, the abolition of slavery, and moderate electoral reform. Enlightenment historical traditions informed and nurtured not only Hallam, but a great number of Whig historians of nineteenth-century England, even as Gibbon's *Decline and Fall* continued to be read, reprinted, and, in 1826, Bowdlerized.[60]

---

[56] O'Brien, *Women and Enlightenment in Eighteenth-Century Britain*, 210–22.

[57] For an overview, see Boyd Hilton, *A Mad, Bad and Dangerous People? England, 1783–1846* (Oxford, 2006), 346–53.

[58] Biancamaria Fontana, *Rethinking the Politics of Commercial Society: The 'Edinburgh Review' 1802–1832* (Cambridge, 1985), 183.

[59] Hallam, *View of the State of Europe during the Middle Ages*, 3 vols. (2nd edn, London, 1819), iii. 314–35, 478.

[60] *Gibbon's History of the Decline and Fall of the Roman Empire: For the Use of Families and Young Persons. Reprinted from the Original Text, with the Careful Omission of all Passages of an Irreligious or Immoral Tendency*, ed. Thomas Bowdler, 5 vols. (London, 1826).

TIMELINE/KEY DATES

1756–63 Seven Years War
1757 Robert Clive's victory at Plassey
1760 Accession of George III
1768 John Wilkes elected MP for Middlesex
1773 Boston 'tea party'
1775–83 War of American Independence
1776 Congress declares American Independence
1780 Gordon Riots
1783 William Pitt becomes prime minister
1784 Pitt's India Act
1787 American Federal Constitution drafted
1788–95 Trial of Warren Hastings
1788–9 Mental incapacity of George III and Regency Crisis
1789 Outbreak of French Revolution
1791 Act providing constitutions for Canadian colonies
1791 Slave rebellion in St Domingue
1793–1801 Britain at war with France/French Revolutionary War
1798 Irish Rebellion
1801 Irish Act of Union
1801 First census in Great Britain
1803–15 Napoleonic Wars
1807 Abolition of the Slave Trade

KEY HISTORICAL SOURCES

Aikin, Lucy, *Memoirs of the Court of Queen Elizabeth*, 2 vols. (London, 1818).

Benger, Elizabeth, *Memoirs of the Life of Mary, Queen of Scots*, 2 vols. (London, 1823).

Berry, Mary, *A Comparative View of the Social Life of England and France, from the Restoration of Charles II* (London, 1828).

Ferguson, Adam, *The History of the Progress and Termination of the Roman Republic*, 3 vols. (London, 1783).

Goldsmith, Oliver, *The Roman History . . . to the Destruction of the Western Empire*, 2 vols. (London, 1769).

——*The History of England from the Earliest Times to the Death of George I*, 4 vols. (London, 1771).

——*The Grecian History . . . to the Death of Alexander the Great*, 2 vols. (London, 1774).

Gibbon, Edward, *The History of the Decline and Fall of the Roman Empire* (1776–88), ed. David Womersley, 3 vols. (Harmondsworth, 1994).

Hallam, Henry, *View of the State of Europe during the Middle Ages*, 2 vols. (London, 1818).

——*A Constitutional History of England*, 2 vols. (London, 1827).

Harris, William, *An Historical and Critical Account of the Life of Oliver Cromwell* (London, 1762).

Hays, Mary, *Female Biography; or, Memoirs of Illustrious and Celebrated Women*, 6 vols. (London, 1803).

Hooke, Nathaniel, *The Roman History from the Building of Rome to the Ruin of the Commonwealth*, 4 vols. (London, 1738–71).

Hutton, William, *A History of Birmingham* (Birmingham, 1781).

Lingard, John, *The Antiquities of the Anglo-Saxon Church*, 2 vols. (Newcastle, 1806).

——*A History of England, from the first invasion by the Romans*, 8 vols. (London, 1819–30).

Macaulay, Catharine, *The History of England from the Accession of James I to That of the Brunswick Line*, 8 vols. (London, 1763–83).

Mitford, William, *The History of Greece*, 5 vols. (London, 1784–1818).

Neal, Daniel, *The History of the Puritans or Protestant Non-Conformists*, 4 vols. (London, 1732–8).

Priestley, Joseph, *Lectures on History and General Policy* (1788), ed. J. T. Rutt (London, 1840).

——*An History of the Corruptions of Christianity*, 2 vols. (Birmingham, 1782).

Russell, William, *A History of Modern Europe*, 2 vols. (London, 1779).

Smollett, Tobias, *A Complete History of England*, 4 vols. (London, 1757–8).

Stanyan, Temple, *The Grecian History*, 2 vols. (London, 1707–39).

Strutt, Joseph, *Glig-Gamena Angel-deod: Sports and Pastimes of the People of England* (London, 1801).

Turner, Sharon, *The History of the Anglo-Saxons*, 5 vols. (London, 1799–1805).

Whitaker, John, *The History of Manchester*, 2 vols. (London, 1771–5).

BIBLIOGRAPHY

Allan, David, *Making British Culture: English Readers and the Scottish Enlightenment, 1740–1830* (London, 2008).

Clive, John, Graubard, Stephen, and Bowersock, G. W. (eds.), *Edward Gibbon and the Decline and Fall of the Roman Empire* (Cambridge, Mass., 1977).

Hicks, Philip, *Neoclassical History and English Culture: From Clarendon to Hume* (New York, 1996).

Hill, Bridget, *The Republican Virago: The Life and Times of Catharine Macaulay, Historian* (Oxford, 1992).

Kennedy, Alison, 'Historical Perspectives in the Mind of Joseph Priestley', in Isabel Rivers and David Wykes (eds.), *Joseph Priestley: Scientist, Philosopher and Theologian* (Oxford, 2008), 172–202.

Momigliano, Arnaldo, *Studies in Historiography* (London, 1966).

O'Brien, Karen, 'The History Market', in Isabel Rivers (ed.), *Books and their Readers in Eighteenth-Century England: New Essays* (London, 2001).

——*Women and Enlightenment in Eighteenth-Century Britain* (Cambridge, 2009).

Phillips, Mark Salber, *Society and Sentiment: Genres of Historical Writing in Britain, 1740–1820* (Princeton, 2000).

Pocock, J. G. A., *Barbarism and Religion*, 5 vols. to date (Cambridge, 1999–).

Seed, John, *Dissenting Histories: Religious Division and the Politics of Memory in Eighteenth-Century England* (Edinburgh, 2008).

Sher, Richard B., *The Enlightenment and the Book: Scottish Authors and their Publishers in Eighteenth-Century Ireland, Britain and America* (Chicago, 2006).

Sweet, Rosemary, *The Writing of Urban Histories in Eighteenth-Century England* (Oxford, 1997).

——*Antiquaries: The Discovery of the Past in Eighteenth-Century Britain* (London, 2004).

Womersley, David, *Gibbon and the Watchmen of the Holy City: The Historian and his Reputation* (Oxford, 2002).

Woolf, D. R., 'A Feminine Past? Gender, Genre and Historical Knowledge in England, 1500–1800', *American Historical Review*, 102 (1997), 645–79.

Chapter 26

European Historiography on the East

Diogo Ramada Curto

In the early 1960s, a series of conferences held in London at the School of Oriental and African Studies proposed a systematic approach to the study of historical writing on the peoples of Asia.[1] The articles concerned with European historiography during the early modern period corresponded to a process that began in 'the period of early empires and literature' and ended in 'the age of Western dominance'. Charles Boxer contributed to the volume on historians of China and Japan, as well as to the one on Southeast Asia, but he also inspired what was written in the volume on historians of India, Pakistan, and Ceylon. Putting aside the volume concerned with the Middle East, I want to consider what were the main overlapping features of the analytical contributions of Boxer and his colleagues. What are the main differences between their approach to the theme of European historiography on the East and ours?[2]

By far the most embedded conception fifty years ago was an unquestionable acceptance that European historians working on Asia belonged to the larger process of Western dominance. This was a notion that intended to insufflate new life into Eurocentric traditions by highlighting the particular attention that has been paid to the study of the so-called peoples of Asia. Nowadays, this argument is no longer possible to sustain. Decades of reflection—including different trends of historical analysis—has contributed to questions about the notion of Western dominance, particularly in Asia; an image of a more multi-centred and less Eurocentric world; and led to a more problematic view of the relation between modern systems of knowledge (including works of history) and structures of power.

The existence of a grand narrative regarding the European historiography on the East is the second identifiable feature in what was written some fifty years ago.

---

[1] The conference papers were subsequently published in four volumes: C. H. Philips (ed.), *Historians of India, Pakistan, and Ceylon* (London, 1961); D. G. E. Hall (ed.), *Historians of Southeast Asia* (London, 1961); W. G. Beasley and E. G. Pulleyblank (eds.), *Historians of China and Japan* (London, 1961); and Bernard Lewis and P. M. Holt (eds.), *Historians of the Middle East* (London, 1962).

[2] Charles Boxer, *Opera minora*, vol. 2: *Orientalism*, ed. Diogo Ramada Curto (Lisbon, 2003).

This is valid not only in the contributions of Boxer and his colleagues, but in a parallel work by Donald Lach and Edwin J. Van Kley, *Asia in the Making of Europe* (3 vols., 1965–93). What were the main plot lines of that great narrative? It was said that Portuguese secular historians of the sixteenth century came on to the scene with claims of an imperial militant faith and a pioneer capacity to gather local information. They were followed by generations of Jesuits who occupied a central role, and almost monopolized the field of historiographical production, mostly in areas such as China and Japan. The different national traditions of Portuguese, Spanish, Dutch, French, Danish, and English historians were identified and treated one by one. However, their competing approaches did not affect the centrality ascribed to the Jesuits and to a sort of ecclesiastic historiographical culture represented also by Spanish Dominicans and Franciscans, as well as by Protestant Dutch priests such as Johannes Nieuhof and François Valentijn. It was only at the end of the eighteenth century when so-called amateur historians, either priests or laymen using simultaneously the pen and the sword, gave place to a generation of European professional Orientalists fully engaged in studying local societies.

Preliminary criticisms of that great narrative imply a better awareness of four main aspects of European historical writing on the East. First, the centrality attributed to the Jesuits in the writing of history constituted one of the elements of a general tendency to overemphasize the scholarly role of the Society of Jesus rather than their religious orientation. In contrast, more recent works on the Jesuits emphasize their militant and *édifiante* side, at the expense of what was once considered their *curieuse* one.[3] Second, the identification of national traditions in historical writing should be followed by more attentive work that pays attention to cross-cultural relations of competition, collaboration, and appropriation. Third, fifty years ago the main criteria for assessing works of history from the past was to verify their ability to re-create reality, including ethnographical descriptions of the different societies encountered by Europeans. Currently, historians are perhaps more sensitive to the rhetorical conventions and models—in particular rooted in the Renaissance of classical antiquity—associated with historical discourses. The delimitation of a discourse of history or the practice of an antiquarian has been established in parallel to other competing forms of writing such as travel accounts, descriptions, theatre, epic poems, or works of fiction.[4] Historians are nowadays much more influenced by literary scholars when dealing with specific discourses governed by their own rules and autonomy. In another and perhaps opposite direction, but also as a result of the same reflexive attitude, historians argue that the social memory of

---

[3] Liam Brockey, *Journey to the East: The Jesuit Mission to China, 1579–1724* (Cambridge, Mass., 2007).

[4] Arnaldo Momigliano, review of 'Historical Writing on the Peoples of Asia' series, *Bulletin of the School of Oriental and African Studies*, 28:2 (1965), 447–51.

the past can no longer be reduced to a single historiographical discourse, but rather that it implies a multiplicity of registers and social instances. The fourth and final criticism is that European histories on the East have to be placed in a more global framework, particularly once universal histories began to appear during the Renaissance, well before Voltaire's *Essai sur les moeurs et l'esprit des nations* [Essay on the Manners and Spirit of Nations] was published in 1756.

The criticism of a single great narrative opens the door to the construction of a better one, or perhaps instead to a fragmented picture of the times once covered by a great explanatory process. These two alternatives might be presented in opposition to each other. However, there are reasons to believe that if the criticism of a general process leads to a more fragmented vision of the past, it also requires the creation of a new general view encompassing a broader explanation of how European historiography about the East worked during the early modern period. Therefore, this chapter stresses a general argument: that works of history were only relatively important in the process of shaping European views about the East during the early modern period; that travel accounts, cartography, cosmography, geographical descriptions, biblical genealogies overlapping moral views, grammars or dictionaries, and a variety of other genres (including theatre, individual memories, official correspondence, printed letters, poetry, and epics) constituted competing and in most cases more efficient forms of representing the Orient in Europe (and having an effect on culture with an even greater impact); and, finally, that it was only during the eighteenth century that a European historical turn occurred and drastically influenced the perception of Asian societies—but even then the so-called scientific travel missions remained influential.

If a relativistic claim concerning the role played by European works of history on the East can be taken as a general argument, a variety of fragmented views should be evoked in order to take into consideration different national traditions from the eastern Mediterranean to the Far East, and from East Africa to the Indonesian archipelago or to Australia. It is important to understand that if the East was a career, to use Benjamin Disraeli's expression,[5] in the sense of there being a large range of opportunities offered to so many Europeans, the same East was never considered to be a unified block. The East was neither an empty space where European values and attitudes could aspire to be projected, nor a single mirror used to shape forms of European identity. On the contrary, the existence of multiple situations and interactions involving Europeans and people from many other societies are difficult to reduce to linear processes of change. Therefore, alliances, partnerships, mixed marriages, indigenous collaborations, models of social and political organization (including images of primitivism, barbarism, oriental despotism, exoticism, racism), territories for displaying male violent

---

[5] 'The East is a career' was Disraeli's phrase most famously reproduced as an epigraph to Edward Said's *Orientalism* (New York, 1978).

values rooted in chivalry or in opposition to feminized attitudes, and a variety of misunderstandings—these are only but a few of the possible situations encountered by Europeans in the East, which are impossible to reduce to a simple great narrative. The same impossibility of reducing to a single bloc or to a linear process of change applies to this geography of unstable frontiers—as will be demonstrated below. A first configuration is defined by the sixteenth century, and will be considered through an analysis of Antonio de León Pinelo's bibliography on the East Indies. A second configuration corresponding to the late seventeenth and early eighteenth centuries will take León Pinelo's largely revised second edition of the same work as a starting point for a more contextual exercise.

Antonio de León Pinelo was probably born in Valladolid (or maybe in Lisbon), to a Portuguese father whose Jewish origins were several times scrutinized by the Inquisition. He moved to Río de la Plata in 1604–5. In 1612, after he had lived for several years in Buenos Aires and Córdoba, he was sent to Lima, where he studied theology, canon law, and civil law. He was temporarily nominated to a Chair at the University of Lima, but in 1618 he started a legal practice. In the same year he published his first book in Lima: a poem dedicated to a public festival in honour of Our Lady, and the year after was nominated to provide juridical assistance to the *corregidor* of Potosí. His departure to Madrid has been explained as a result of his need to develop the project of compiling colonial laws, launched in 1618 during his conversations with Solórzano Pereira, who was already involved in a parallel task. It also appears that his father's commercial activities, including trade in slaves and contraband, required assistance in Madrid. At the moment of departure, the city of Buenos Aires delegated to him the responsibility of representing the city's interests at the Spanish court. Once in Madrid, from 1623 onwards, Pinelo published a series of small memorials directly related to his activities as a lawyer, containing the defence of family and group interests located in Buenos Aires. In the course of these negotiations, he dealt several times with the Council of the Indies. In 1625 his work *El Gran Canciller de Indias* [The Great Chancellor of the Indies]—written when the Count-Duke of Olivares delegated the same post to his son-in-law, the Duke of Medina de las Torres, to whom the manuscript is dedicated—demonstrates how involved León Pinelo was with the Council of the Indies in Madrid. His first nomination as a reporter of the Council of the Indies—with a special obligation to produce a compilation of the laws of the region—is dated February 1629. In 1636 the same post was given to him. León Pinelo had personally initiated his projects about colonial law in Lima, but it was within the bureaucratic context of the activities of the Council of the Indies in Madrid that he pursued the research. The same spirit of accumulation of archival documents related to juridical matters also motivated León Pinelo in bibliographical matters concerning the Indies: in fact, his *Epitome de la Biblioteca Oriental i Occidental, Nautica i Geografica* [Epitome of the Library, Oriental and Occidental, Nautical and Geographical] (1629) is an excellent demonstration of his activities as a collector and bibliographer. It is also important to note that Pinelo applied to serve as historian of the Indies, another position of the Council of the Indies, as early as 1625, but he had to wait until 1658 to get this prestigious title. In 1654 he was also nominated judge of the *Casa de Contratación* with the privilege to reside in Madrid in order to pursue his compilation of colonial laws.[6]

The *Epitome*—the work of a jurist, historian, and collector of books—was divided into four parts. The sections on the 'Biblioteca Oriental' and the 'Biblioteca Occidental' are by far the most extensive parts reflecting Olivares's great strategy of unifying Hispanic forces and resources on a global scale. The last two parts, concerning nautical and geographical matters, indicate the scientific orientation of the book, where questions of cosmography and navigation are central. The first part, about the East, is made up of sixteen chapters and follows criteria that are simultaneously chronological, geographical, and thematic. Voyages and information available in Europe prior to Vasco da Gama, and then after 'the discovery of India' are the starting point. From the life of Alexander to the voyages of Marco Polo, or from the voyage of Vasco da Gama to the letters of Giovanni da Empoli, it is evident that Giovanni Battista Ramusio's *Delle Navigationi et viaggi* [Navigations and Voyages], a compilation of travel accounts published in Venice in 1550, played a role in shaping this inventory of works. The series of travel accounts published after Ramusio (and Theodor de Bry's collection of the same genre), consist of many other works in Italian, English, and French, including two travel accounts well known by their fictional dimension: the *Peregrinação* [Peregrination] (1617) by Fernão Mendes Pinto, and the *Viage del Mundo* [World Voyage] (1616) by Pedro Ordoñez de Zevallos. Particular attention is paid to the voyage of Vasco da Gama as it was evoked in the epic poem of Luís de Camões, the 'prince of Lusitanian poetry and glory of his nation'.[7] The several editions in Portuguese and the translations in Latin and Castilian of the *Lusíadas* [Lusiads] (1572) are also considered a sign of the general acceptance of the work by a large audience.

After the reference to the voyages of discovery, a specific chapter is dedicated to the histories of India. Here, the most coherent works of history are of the Portuguese kings or of the conquest of India by João de Barros, Fernão Lopes de Castanheda, Damião de Góis, Jerónimo Osório, Diogo do Couto, Francisco de Andrade, João Baptista Lavanha, and António Pinto Pereira. From this list are

---

    [6] José Toribio Medina, *Biblioteca hispanoamericana* (Santiago, 1898–1907), vi. pp. xlix–cxi, 437–84; vii. pp. vii–xlv; Boleslao Lewin, *Los León Pinelo: la ilustre familia marrana del siglo XVII ligada a la historia de la Argentina, Perú, América y España* (Buenos Aires, 1942); Agustín Millares Carló, *El Epitome de Pinelo: primera bibliografía del Nuevo Mundo* (Washington, DC, 1958); id., *Tres estudios biobibliográficos* (Maracaibo, 1961), 63–113; and Raúl Aguirre Molina, 'La defensa del comercio del Río de la Plata por el Licenciado D. Antonio de León Pinelo', *Historia: Revista trimestral de historia Argentina, Americana, Española*, 26 (1962), 37–112.
    [7] 'Principe de la poesia Lusitana i gloria de su nacion', in León Pinelo, *Epitome...* (Madrid, 1629), 8.

absent the histories of the conquest of India by Gaspar Correia and the continuation of the *Décadas* [Decades] by António Bocarro, perhaps because they both remained in manuscript until the nineteenth century; also missing are the histories of Asia by Manuel de Faria y Sousa, which pursue the same tradition. All these histories were composed in the vernacular, with the exception of Osório's about the kingdom of Manuel I, which is considered 'a history of India as all the modern histories of that kingdom [of Portugal]'—meaning that the history of Portugal was mainly composed by the glorious conquest of India by Portuguese noble soldiers.[8]

León Pinelo is particularly attentive in compiling the inventory of all the translations into Castilian, Italian, and French respecting the *Asia* of Barros, and the *História do Descobrimento e Conquista da Índia* [History of the Discovery and Conquest of India] (1552–61) of Castanheda. The centrality of conquest in all these histories is developed in another series of books on sieges of Portuguese fortressed cities from India to Southeast Asia (Cambay, Diu, Goa, Chaul, Malaca). From epic poems to descriptions in vernacular, Castilian, or Latin, the glory and reputation of Portuguese noble captains is represented in violent actions against the infidel, and in sacrifices in the service of the Crown. An initial reference to a letter about India by Manuel I confirms the association between the memory of the monarchy and the celebration of the conquest of India. The *Comentarios* [Commentaries] (1557) of Alfonso de Albuquerque, published by his son, belonged to the same sphere, where the political language of virtue was used to portray the actions of noble captains at war; and the same can be applied to the writings of Dom João de Castro, another Portuguese noble captain, able to articulate nautical knowledge with military strategy. In comparison to the values of war and conquest—associated with king, nation, and Portuguese noble captains—claims about commerce, its discovery and monopoly, are not so visible inside the same works of history. In this respect, an exception is António Galvão's *Tratado dos descobrimentos* [The Discoveries of the World] (1563), which refers explicitly to spices and their routes.

If Portuguese histories of India are mostly about the reputation and glory of conquest, León Pinelo's inventory of books and manuscripts still integrates a heterogeneous list of books under the rubric of histories of India. One nucleus is composed by books written by religious authors. The tome of the Jesuit Giovanni Pietro Maffei, *Historiarum Indicarum Liber Duodecimus* [History of the East Indies] (1588), is perhaps one of the best examples of appropriation by the Jesuits of the tradition of narrating the Portuguese conquest of India. A response by a member of another religious order came from the Benedictine António de San Román, the author of *Historia general de la India Oriental* [General History of the East Indies] (1603). The archbishop of Goa, the Augustinian Aleixo de

---

[8] 'Es historia de la India, como son todas las modernas de aquel Reyno', ibid., 17.

Menezes, patronized the publication of a book on his Indian travels by António de Gouveia.[9] However, this book was again a response to another one published by the Jesuit Nicolau Pimenta in 1600, where the figure of the same archbishop had been diminished. Finally, four printed or manuscript descriptions of the Mughal state, the kingdom of Cambodja, and the one of Pegu—out of more than fifty included in the chapter on the histories of India—represented an interest in describing non-European political units.

In León Pinelo's bibliographical classification, histories of India concerning missionary activities are included in another chapter labelled 'missions for converting India'. This is the case of works written by three Jesuits.[10] However, in the same chapter, two other works (one of them in manuscript) by a Franciscan and a Dominican, respectively exhorting the propagation of the Catholic faith among the 'gentiles' and a hagiography, reminded readers that Jesuits were not alone in their missionary task.[11] They were always competing with other missionaries, and their historical projects were fully embedded on an *édifiante* mould. Hagiographies—starting by precocious efforts to canonize St Francis Xavier, which produced a celebrated result in 1622—and letters or annual reports sent from the missions, and then diffused in carefully edited compilations, were actually at the core of the Jesuit system of communication and self-justification, and more elaborate works of history clearly emerged from this system. The large inventory made by León Pinelo of Jesuit printed letters also showed that the above works of history could not be disconnected from that practice of letter writing.

In fact the history of Guzmán was continued in Portuguese by the large annual reports compiled by Fernão Guerreiro (1603, 1605, 1607, 1609, 1611), which were in turn translated by Cristóbal Suárez de Figueroa in a version that is presented as an adaptation from Portuguese into Castilian.[12] León Pinelo refers to them in a section called 'letters from the missions in India'. For Guzmán and Guerreiro, the printed book served the interests of Jesuit propaganda, and the same was the case in French with the quoted history by Pierre du Jarric. As Guerreiro indicates

[9] António de Gouveia, *Jornada do Arcebispo de Goa Dom Frei Aleixo de Menezes Primaz da India Oriental Religioso de S. Agostinho: Quando foi as Serras de Malauar en lugares em que morão os antigos Christãos de S. Thome* (Coimbra, 1606).

[10] Manuel da Costa, *Historia rerum a Societate Jesu in Oriente Gestarum* (Paris, 1572); Luís de Guzmán, *Historia de las Missiones que han hecho los religiosos de la Compañia de Jesus . . . em la India Oriental, y en los Reynos de la China y Japon* (Alcalá, 1601); and Pierre du Jarric, *Histoire des choses plus memorables advenues tant en Indies orientales, que autre pays de la decouverte des portugais, en l'etablissement et progrez de la foy chrestienne, et catholique* (Bordeaux, 1608–14).

[11] Geronymo Gracián de la Madre de Dios, *Stimulo de la fee, contiene el vinculo de hermandad entre los Padres descalços de nuestra Señora del Monte Carmelo y del Seraphico Padre Sant Francisco para ayudarse y fauorescer se en la conuersion de la gentilidad, y una exortacion para ellos* (Lisbon, 1586; 2nd edn, Brussels, 1609).

[12] Cristóbal Suárez de Figueroa, *Historia y Anual Relacion de las cosas que hizieron los Padres de la Compañia de Iesus, por las partes de Oriente y otras, en la propagacion del Santo Evangelio los años passados de 607 y 608* (Madrid, 1614).

in the preface to the first volume of his reports, it was important to state the advances of Christianity, that the 'news of the qualities of the lands, peoples and individuals' should be part of this edifying proposal. For example, when describing the territory of Salcette when speaking of Goa, what happens is an enumeration of the thirteen churches that were in the charge of the Society of Jesus, where about 33,000 Christians would meet, the hope being for an even greater number. The responsibility for this success, recorded in 1600, is attributed to a catechism drawn up by the priests in dialogue form that the children, particularly, knew by heart: 'and there are some so small that they cannot say anything else except their doctrine and their questions that they hear from the older ones'.[13]

Among the authors absent from the bibliography of León Pinelo was Fr Sebastião Gonçalves, who lived in India for twenty-five years (1594–1619) and planned to write a history of the Jesuit missions in the East from 1542 to 1605, including the mission in East Africa (Mozambique and Ethiopia), Mesopotamia, Hormuz, Persia, Socotra, India, Ceylon, Malacca, Moluccas, China, and Japan. His manuscript, which was planned as a general history of the missions, dedicates the first five books to the life of St Francis Xavier, and includes a series of biographies that were intended to promote his canonization. The remaining extant books, which form the first part of the work, written in Goa and sent in manuscript to Lisbon and Rome around 1615, concentrate on the missionary actions and organization of the various provinces from 1542 to 1570, with the emphasis on the arduous labours and the martyrdoms suffered by the Jesuits. The second part, of which we know the plan but have not discovered the actual volumes, deals with the history of St Thomas and the Christian communities along the coast of Coromandel, the activities of Fr Matteo Ricci in China and the voyage to Portugal and Rome of the Japanese princes, of the attempts at missions in Japan, and the resistance by the local political structures around 1600. In this most informative work, which acts as a form of Jesuit propaganda, it is in the ninth book of the first part that the author most nearly approaches a compendium of the uses, customs, and social organization of the Canarims and Brahmins of Goa.[14]

However, the interest that today we would call ethnographic occupies a very restricted place, and is immediately followed by a description of the forms and instruments used for religious conversions. The chapter dedicated to the foundation of the college at Salcette and to the 'manner in which we cultivate Christians' serves as an example of this aspect, and can be compared with the information given by Fernão Guerreiro referred to earlier:

---

[13] Fernão Guerreiro, *Relação anual das coisas que fizeram os Padres da Companhia de Jesus nas suas missões*, ed. Artur Viegas, 3 vols. (Coimbra, 1930–42), i. p. 4.

[14] Sebastião Gonçalves, *Primeira parte da História dos Religiosos da Companhia de Jesus*, ed. José Wicki, S.J., vol. 3 (Coimbra, 1962), 9–90.

In all the churches there is a school for reading and writing and counting. They learn the doctrine of Marcos Jorge which is adapted to the ability of the pupils, translated into Canarim, and they discuss this in the churches during the monsoon season. The children who live near to the churches go every day in the morning to doctrine and those who live a long way meet in the sheds that have been built for this purpose in the villages. In some churches there are pictures that teach the ignorant the mysteries of our holy faith, for the images are books from which the people learn.[15]

The more specific case of works on China presented by León Pinelo reiterates the point that history competed with other forms of written production, such as letters, political discourses, moral treatises, and works relating to linguistics. In this context, the writing and publication of letters and descriptions was perhaps more diffuse, and the Jesuits aspired to monopolize the production of history, also in relation to histories as contextualized by priests from other religious orders. The Dominican Gaspar da Cruz was a pioneer with the publication in Portuguese of the *Tractado em que cõtam muito por estenso as cousas da China cõ suas particularidades e assi do reyno dormuz* [Book Telling Extensively the Facts of China with all the Particularities as well as of the Kingdom of Ormuz] (1569). The description of China was parallel to political projects of conquest and to missionary attempts to convert the Chinese to Catholicism. Bernardino de Escalante proposed to send an ambassador to the emperor, asking for protection of the missionaries; in his mind the conquest was simply useless.[16] In this context, the Augustinian Juan González de Mendoza published his *Historia de las cosas mas notables, ritos y costumbres, del gran Reyno de la China* [History of the Most Notable Things, Rites and Uses of the Great Kingdom of China] (1585). Although designed as a work of history, a large part of the book was occupied by the travel accounts from Manila to China written by Martín de Rada, another Augustinian, and two Franciscans, Agustin de Tordesillas and Martín Ignacio de Loyola. Up until the end of the sixteenth century, thirty editions in different languages of this last work were published.

At the beginning of the seventeenth century, Jesuit priests launched a series of historiographical projects taking their missionary activities in China as the main object. Luís de Guzmán, for instance, dedicates a large part of his history to the provinces of China and Japan;[17] and Fr Diego de Pantoja, in his *Relacion de la entrada de algunos padres de Cõpañia de Iesus en la China* [Relation of the Arrival of Some Jesuit Fathers in China] (1605), concentrated on the first moments of the mission. However, the most widely circulated contribution of the Jesuits to the history of China came from the adaptation of the manuscripts of Matteo Ricci by

---

[15] Ibid., 100–1.

[16] Bernardino de Escalante, *Discurso de la navegacion que los Portugueses hazen à los Reinos y Prouincias del Oriente, y de la noticia q se tiene de las grandezas del Reyno de la China* (Seville, 1577); and Charles Boxer, 'Portuguese and Spanish Projects for the Conquest of Southeast Asia, 1580–1600', *Journal of Asian History*, 3 (1969), 118–36.

[17] Guzmán, *Historia de las Missiones que han hecho los religiosos de la Compañia de Jesus*.

Nicolas Trigault.[18] In the same sequence, Francisco Herrera Maldonado, clearly influenced by the Society of Jesus, published his *Epitome historial del Reyno de la China* [Historical Epitome of the Kingdom of China] (1620). All these histories were about missions and missionaries, directly reflecting the type of communication that was the basis of an institutional organization, notably correspondence. They were also oriented towards the celebration of the founding fathers, aspiring to become saints and martyrs, as in fact happened with St Francis Xavier.

León Pinelo's extensive list of titles about Japan confirms the Jesuit tendency to emphasize hagiography, correspondence, or annals. Missionary histories belonged to this mould but they were not the most important genre. Hagiographical works include biographies of St Francis Xavier and his companions (in Portuguese, Spanish, and Latin), but they also integrate other narratives of the martyrdoms suffered by Catholic priests and converted Japanese. Although hagiography and sacrificial martyrdom were at the core of the Jesuit missions, this was a contentious field once older religious orders such as the Franciscans and Dominicans made claims in the same terrain. Following the same line, the famous Spanish playwright Lope de Vega wrote *Triunfo de la fee en los reynos de Japon* [The Triumph of Faith in the Kingdom of Japan] (1618). The Jesuits organized spectacular visits to Spain and Rome of the so-called Japanese princes and ambassadors, developing a strategy that included the publication of several books. Alessandro Valignano also wrote some commentaries on Japan, elaborating on the possible methods of conversion. In any case, the writing and publication of letters from the Jesuit missions in Japan constitute the largest genre with respect to Japan. More ambitious historiographical projects, comparable to Sebastião Rodrigues's work on India, were not considered. For example, the Jesuit Fr Luís Fróis—who left in manuscript form the *História do Japão* [History of Japan]—is only quoted for his letters.[19] Finally, the manuscript history of Japan by João Rodrigues, who worked as an interpreter for the Japanese warlord and regent Hideyoshi (d. 1598), and was expelled to Macao in 1612, is not included in León Pinelo's inventory.[20]

In 1629 the catalogue of the 'Biblioteca Oriental' complemented the references to India, China, and Japan, with shorter chapters about 'Histories of Persia', 'Histories of the Tartars', 'Discoveries of India by the North', 'Histories of Ethiopia', and 'Shipwrecks in the Indian Seas'. The 'East' corresponded then to a composite geography, which had been shaped by previous works on navigations and cosmography, mostly the collections of texts and images already published by Ramusio, Jan Huygen van Linschoten, and Theodor de Bry,

---

[18] Nicolas Trigault, *De Christiana Expeditione apud Sinas* (Augsburg, 1615).
[19] Luís Fróis, *História de Japan*, ed. P. José Wicki, 5 vols. (Lisbon, 1976–84).
[20] Michael Cooper (ed.), *João Rodrigues's Account of Sixteenth-Century Japan* (London, 2001); and id., *Rodrigues the Interpreter: An Early Jesuit in Japan and China* (1974; New York 1994).

including for example the voyages of Cabot, and the more recent Portuguese literature on shipwrecks. Ramusio's *Navigationi* clearly shaped the inventory of travel accounts and histories of Persia. A set of more recent books revealed also a precocious interest in the translation of local histories.[21] Jesuits and Augustinians were again quarrelling, staking their reputations on converting Persia.[22] Following once more the classification of Ramusio, the history of the Tartars—an ambiguous and rather geographically diffuse group of people on the move across the Asian steppes—was written originally by an Armenian but was augmented by new contributions in a contemporary Spanish translation.[23] The history of Ethiopia was, first of all, perceived as a territory where forms of Christianity already in place needed to be assessed, in order to develop the right missionary strategy. This assessment was made by Francisco Álvares in a widely circulated work of history on the reign of the legendary Prester John of Ethiopia, based on a sort of antiquarian method.[24] However, it was only from the beginning of the seventeenth century that Jesuits and Dominicans openly competed in relation to their missionary achievements in East Africa.[25]

Natural history constituted another rubric in León Pinelo's classificatory system. Contradicting a clear division made by the sixteenth-century *ars historica* (the genre of writing about the various categories of history and historical writing), the inventory of customs, uses, political and social life, was brought together with the natural history of plants and natural phenomena. The Italian translation of the book of Duarte Barbosa in Ramusio's compilation, which is

---

[21] Pedro Teixeira, *Relaciones de . . . d'el origen descendência y succession de los Reyes de Pérsia* (Antwerp, 1610); William F. Sinclair and Donald Ferguson, *The Travels of Pedro Teixeira with his 'Kings of Harmuz', and Extracts from his 'Kings of Persia'* (London, 1902); and António de Gouveia, *Relaçam em que se tratam as guerras e grandes victorias que alcançou o grade Rey da Persia Xá Abbas do grão turco Mahometto, en seu filho Amete* (Lisbon, 1611).

[22] *Relaciones de Don Juan de Pérsia . . . Divididas en tres libros: Donde se tratan las cosas notables de Pérsia, la genealogia de sus reyes, guerras de Persianos, Turcos y Tártaros, y las que vido en el viaje que hizo à España: y su conuersion, y la de otros dos Caualleros Persianos* (Valladolid, 1604); and António de Gouveia, *Triunfo Glorioso de três mártires españoles* (Madrid, 1623).

[23] Amaro Centeno, *Historia de las cosas del Oriente primera y segunda parte: Contiene una descripcion de los Reynos de la Assia* [sic]. *La historia de los Tártaros y su origen y principio. Las cousas del reyno de Egipto. La Historia y sucessos del Reyno de Hierusalem* (Córdova, 1595).

[24] Francisco Álvares, *Verdadeira informação das terras do Preste João das Indias* (1540; Lisbon, 1883).

[25] João dos Santos, *Ethiopia oriental e varia historia de cousas notaveis do Oriente* (Évora, 1609); Luís de Urreta, *Historia eclesiástica, politica, natural y moral de los grandes y remotos reynos dela Etiópia, monarchia del emperador llamdo Preste Juan de las Indias* (Valencia, 1610); id., *Historia de la sagrada Orden de los Predicadores, en los remotos Reynos de la Etiopia* (Valencia, 1611); Fernão Guerreiro, S.J., *Relacion anual de las cosas que han hecho los padres de la Compañia de Iesus en la Índia Oriental y Iapon, en los años de 600 y 601*, trans. António Colaço (Valladolid, 1604); Nicolau Godinho, S.J., *De Abissinorum Rebus, déque Aethiopiae Patriarchis Joanne Nónio Barreto, et Andrea Oviedo* (Lyon, 1615); and Manuel da Veiga, S.J., *Relaçam geral do estado da Christandade de Ethiopia . . . en do que de nouo socedeo no descobrimento do Thybet, a que chamam, gram Catayo: composta e copiada das cartas que os Padres da Companhia de IESV escreveram da Índia Oriental dos anos de 624, 625, en 626* (Lisbon, 1628).

usually cited in recent works as a model of geographical description, together with the manuscript of Tomé Pires's *Suma Oriental*, describes people, products, and trade. This was the line of enquiry followed by the Portuguese historian João de Barros in his lost *Geographia*. In this sequence, León Pinelo concludes with the *Libro de las costumbres de todas las gentes del Mundo* [Book of the Customs of All the Peoples of the World], a Castilian translation of Johannes Boemus with a supplement by Francisco Tamara, published in Antwerp in 1556. In the two first parts of the book, Boemus had collected information by classical authors on the different peoples of the world, following the style of ethnogenetic histories, but in a third part Tamara compiled the news about the discoveries of India by 'our Hispanics', including here 'the other territories and Indies, islands and provinces discovered by Hispanic Portuguese in the East'.[26] If Barbosa and Boemus provided the frame, works of natural history occupy the centre of this chapter, including the Latin essays on the medical use of Chinese plants by Cardano and Vesalio. In any case, the most important work mentioned here seems to be Garcia da Orta's *Coloquios dos simples, e drogas e coisas medicinaes da India* [Colloquies on the Simples and Drugs of India] (1563), translated into Castilian by Cristóval de Acosta, and disseminated throughout Europe in the Latin edition published by Carolus Clusius.

For someone organizing a catalogue of books on the East Indies in Madrid in 1629, the inclusion of a chapter about the Dutch voyages was a sign of intellectual honesty, and more than a submission to court political interests about the Portuguese Empire in the East. Travel accounts collected by Linschoten and de Bry began with the voyage to India of the former between 1584 and 1592. A miscellaneous character was present in all these travel accounts, where individual experiences were mixed with descriptions and bits of history. These were texts circulating in different languages—Latin, Dutch, German, Italian (in the case of the supplement to Ramusio), French, and English—and passing from one collection to another. The political impact of all these voyages was also seen in a final reference to the discussion between the Dutch Hugo Grotius and the Portuguese Serafim de Freitas on the freedom of the seas. But again, either in the case of travel accounts or in political treatises about the *mare clausum*, history does not occupy a central role.

The analysis of the 'Biblioteca Oriental', the first part of León Pinelo's *Epitome*, leads to four main conclusions regarding the role of history in shaping European visions of the East in the sixteenth and seventeenth centuries. First, the historical genre was in competition with, and sometimes on the margins of, many other discourses. The status of history was by no means dominant in a hierarchy of discourses going from well-disseminated travel accounts and letters to epics, drama, and moral or political treatises. Portuguese chroniclers such as

---

[26] Johannes Boemus, *El libro de las costumbres de todas las gentes del Mundo*, trans. Francisco Tamara (Antwerp, 1556), fl. 28, 328.

Barros, or Jesuit historians and hagiographers such as Guzmán wrote histories mostly to promote either military actions accomplished by the nobility in the service of their king, or missionaries willing to sacrifice themselves in martyrdom for the sake of salvation. Noble captains and missionaries serving the Church Militant were the main heroes of these histories, which is all very Eurocentric from our modern perspective. Works of history dealt mostly with the politics of war or religious missions; ethnographical curiosity—in the sense of knowledge of non-European societies formulated through distance and placed in perspective—occupied a rather limited space. As noted at the start of the present chapter, in the language of the Jesuits of the eighteenth century, the *édifiante* side was always more important than the *curieuse* dimension. The writing of history corresponded to rhetorical conventions, as well as to the political and religious language of virtues; against Charles Boxer's claims about European histories of Asia, history was only marginally shaped by an ethnographical curiosity. This occurred only in few cases: the antiquarianism of Francisco Álvares, in his descriptive assessment of Ethiopia based on the study of material vestiges and a large range of costumes and rituals, can be seen as an instance of that kind of curiosity. Not coincidentally, the same qualities are to be found in some manuscript works regarding India, China, and Japan—most of them absent from the bibliography of León Pinelo. Fr Rodrigues's treatise on Japan constitutes only one of the examples of this kind. It is perhaps in the printed translations of Persian local histories that a historiographical discourse published in Europe was better articulated with an interest on the history of the East. Besides that, it is only in the relatively small field of natural history that it is possible to identify the most developed forms of curiosity, from Duarte Barbosa to Garcia da Orta.

A second conclusion concerns the quarrelling mould within which many of those histories should be placed. The evocation of different forms of patronage—either provided by the Crown or noble houses (in the case mainly of Portuguese chroniclers), or by religious orders such as the Jesuits—can distort the perception of the competition and conflicts affecting the written uses of the past. In fact, Portuguese noble houses clearly claiming the services of their ancestors in the *Estado da Índia* tried to mobilize historians for their own defence. By the same token, Jesuits were in competition with Dominicans, Augustinians, and Franciscans, and more occasionally with representatives of the regular clergy, in order to establish *édifiante* versions of their missionary work. In any case, the weight of Portuguese *Padroado* over the religious orders and their respective missionary histories was disrupted only after 1622, with the creation of the *Propaganda Fide*. Indeed, patronage, competition, and conflicts reflecting national, social, or religious bodies had a bearing on the writing of European histories of the East.

A third conclusion concerns the circulation of texts due to the formation of an international print market. Matteo Ricci's history of China was disseminated in Latin by Tricault. Francisco Álvares, the Portuguese antiquarian and historian of Ethiopia, was translated into many languages, and an adaptation of his work was included in Ramusio's *Navigazioni,* together with many other Portuguese books and manuscripts. Garcia de Orta's *Colóquios* came out for the first time in Goa, and was translated and adapted into many languages, Latin editions being the most common. Boemus's ethnographical book appeared in Latin, and more extensive versions were published in Italian and Spanish. All these cases followed a rising demand in the book market for works of history in Latin, Portuguese, Spanish, and Italian. The Jesuit missionary history by du Jarric, published in French, remained rather an exception among the Jesuit-authored editions of letters, relations, and histories. Collections of travel accounts, such as those organized by Ramusio, de Bry, and Linschoten, extended the range of languages to French and, in the case of the two last works, Dutch. Works in English were almost absent from León Pinelo's bibliography: Latin and south European vernacular tongues were at this juncture the basic languages of the international book trade.

A fourth and final conclusion concerns the geography of an imagined Orient, at least in regard to León Pinelo's classification system. India, China, and Japan took precedence, and were consistently identified in terms of what could be called a European approach. Conquest, trade, and missionary activities informed the most important European historical representations of those civilizations. In comparison to a gaze determined by notions of conquest and conversion to Catholicism, it is possible to define an ethnographic dimension mostly in relation to the kingdoms of Persia and Ethiopia, and to the Tartars. In fact, translations in European languages of historical works are mostly about these kingdoms and people (and not so much about India, China, and Japan). The main reason for this interest is related to the medieval European tradition of making alliances with the kings of Persia and Ethiopia, as well as a certain familiarity with warriors from the steppes, going back to Marco Polo and previous, late Roman times. In any case, it was mostly in terms of large political units—from empires to kingdoms—that the East was perceived. Natural history and a sort of social and political geography, praising commerce and commodities—much more than civil and ecclesiastical histories—expressed also an ethnographic angle. From this composite picture of the East, Southeast Asia, including the Indonesian archipelago and other continental territories, was simply excluded. Works on the Philippines—starting with the relations or histories of António Morga and Bartolomé Leonardo de Argensola—were considered by León Pinelo as belonging to the Spanish West Indies.[27] In any case, the composite geography of the East represented in the *Epitome* can hardly be reduced to a classification system

---

[27] António Morga, *Sucesos de las Islas Filipinas* (Mexico, 1609); and Bartolomé Leonardo de Argensola, *Conquista de las Islas Molucas* (Madrid, 1609). See Charles Boxer, 'Some Aspects of Spanish Historical Writing on the Philippines', in Philips (ed.), *Historians of South East Asia,* 200–12; and Joan-Pau Rubiés, *Travellers and Cosmographers: Studies in the History of Early Modern Travel and Ethnology* (Aldershot, 2007), ch. 10.

inspired by divisions proceeding from the Middle East to the Far East, without forgetting India and Sri Lanka, as well as Southeast Asia, which were the four main areas to conceive the study of Asian historiography in the 1960s.

More than a century after the 1629 publication of León Pinelo's *Epitome* in 143 pages, Andrés González de Barcia published a second and much larger edition in three impressive tomes in Madrid (1737–8).[28] The work of González de Barcia corresponded to a series of attempts made by several academies and to various efforts of classification developed during the same period, resulting in dictionaries, libraries, and encyclopedias. The large quantity of authors, books, and manuscripts added to this edition made it, in effect, a new work. What follows concerns the main changes, observable between the two editions, pertaining to the significance of works of history in the representation of the East.

Based on different compilations and bibliographical inventories published during the Enlightenment, what happened to history inside a hierarchy of European discourses . . . and representations on the East? Due to the expanding importance of travel accounts, it is possible to argue that history—at least until the publication of the great works by Voltaire, Raynal, and Robertson—continued to be secondary. As the French historian Paul Hazard argued many years ago, the 'crisis of European consciousness' that happened at the end of the seventeenth and beginning of the eighteenth century was, among many other factors, launched by the publication and large diffusion of travel accounts on a world scale, including those concerning the East.[29] In fact, in the first half of the eighteenth century, some publishing initiatives revealed the interest shown by the educated European public mostly in large-format travel accounts, such as the new edition of León Pinelo's catalogue. An example of this tendency, which was a continuation of writing and publishing practices originating in the sixteenth century, is the vast four-volume *Collection of Voyages and Travels* assembled and published by Awnsham and John Churchill in 1704. In France, Antoine Augustin Bruzen de La Martinière, who claimed the status of geographer to Philip V, organized the ten-volume *Grand Dictionnaire Géographique et Critique* [Great Geographical and Critical Dictionary] (1726–39).

Another example, perhaps the most meaningful in terms of size and display, is to be found in the highly illustrated *Cérémonies et coutumes religieuses de tous les peuples du monde* [Rituals and Religious Customs of all the World's Peoples] (11 vols., 1723–43). This is a collection of descriptions of apparently all the religions of the world, one in which the engravings of Bernard Picart deserve greater attention than the accompanying historical explanations by the abbots

---

[28] Jorge Cañizares-Esguerra, *How to Write the History of the New World: Histories, Epistemologies, and Identities in the Eighteenth-Century Atlantic World* (Stanford, 2001), 158, 166–7; and Jonathan Earl Carlyon, *Andrés González de Barcia and the Creation of the Colonial Spanish American Library* (Toronto, 2005).

[29] Paul Hazard, *La Crise de la conscience européenne* (Paris, 1935).

Banier and Le Mascrier. The universal coverage of this work can be seen as a step in the direction of cultural relativism or of religious tolerance. However, an analysis of Picart's themes and images reveals the recurrence of some stereotypes and representations of ceremonies considered to be exotic. Some examples of such images are present in the representation of *sati*, the ritual sacrifice of widows practiced in India. This interpretation corresponded to a broader, emerging interest in defining the study of religion as a social phenomenon.[30] The appearance of works willing to think historically about religion suggests the development of a new sense of distance between authors and their objects of enquiry. Therefore, it clearly contrasts with more militant ways of engaging with religious matters, as was the case with Protestant criticisms of the Goa Inquisition, made by Gabriel Dellon and others, as well as the intense debates opposing Jesuits and Dominicans with respect to the so-called Chinese Rites.[31]

In the eighteenth-century, commerce was perhaps more important than religion as a European tool for perceiving and representing societies on a global scale. For instance, in 1756 Charles de Brosses's *Histoire des Navigations aux Terres Australes* [History of Voyages to Australia] (1756), argued that the discovery of Australia—the greatest glory of modern times—could only have been achieved by a great sovereign, such as the king of France, or, alternatively, by the entire body of a commercial republic. Isolated individuals motivated by a simple business spirit did not have the ability to take on such a task. However, the principal justification of that project which, according to the author, would logically fall to the French and their sovereigns, would consist fundamentally in 'enrichir l'ancien monde de toutes les productions naturelles, de tous les usages utiles du nouveau' ['acquiring for the Old World all the natural products and useful practices from the new one'].[32] The discourse on the glory of the French monarchy was expressed through the political language of the defence of trade. With this approach the author intended to upset the British maritime hegemony worldwide.[33] This was far from being one of the idealized projects of conquest. Honour in acquiring territory had nothing to do with arms and military conquests but rather peaceful trade and geographical knowledge.[34]

Did historical analysis contribute to the spreading of commerce-based discourses, and the image of a prosperous and peaceful European society? Works of political economists such as Adam Smith's *Wealth of Nations* (1776), with their large sections on the history of trade, seem to suggest the affirmative. However, is it really possible to compare French and English histories of the Enlightenment

[30] Abraham Rogerius, *Le Théatre de l'idolatrie* (Amsterdam, 1670); David Hume, *Principal Writings on Religion*, ed. J. C. A. Gaskin (Oxford, 1993); and Charles de Brosses, *Du Culte des dieux fétiches* (1760), ed. Madeleine V.-David, 2 vols. (Paris, 1988).

[31] Gabriel Dellon, *Relation de l'Inquisition de Goa* (Leyden, 1687; Paris, 1688).

[32] Ibid., i. 5.

[33] Ibid., ii. p. iv.

[34] Ibid., ii. 369–70.

to Portuguese and Spanish histories of conquest and violence of the sixteenth century? Despite the distance between the centuries explaining the contrasting languages available for historical enquiries, it will never be enough to insist on the English fascination regarding Dutch models of militarization in the East since the end of the seventeenth century. Anglo-French territorial conflicts in India during the eighteenth century also promoted the figure of captains and soldiers. This explains perhaps the long-lasting figure of the 'noble captain' recurrent in the different forms of European imperial culture.

The works of Awnsham and John Churchill, La Martinière, Picart, Charles de Brosses, and the monumental second edition of León Pinelo's bibliography represent a change in terms of cultural geography. The previous centres of production for works in large format on the literature of voyages—Italy with Ramusio, Iberia with Jesuit annual letters, Holland starting wtih Linschoten, Germany with de Bry and, in part, England with the large travelogues organized by Richard Hakluyt and Samuel Purchas—have given way to a different config-uration centred on the political and economic rivalry between England and France, now the main protagonists in a European balance within which Spain still struggled to demonstrate its imperial strength. This generalization, from a restricted number of works, is arguable and would be incomplete without reference to the editorial initiatives of greater continuity regarding the spread, within a European language, of information on other civilizations. A work by the Jesuits, *Lettres édifiantes et curieuses, des missions étrangères* [Edifying and Curious Letters on the Foreign Missions], was translated and published in French, in several editions; the first, comprising thirty-four volumes, was published between 1702–3 and 1776. Assuming the same character of compilation, one should also consider the English *Universal History* (1736–65) and the *Histoire Générale des Voyages* [General History of the Voyages] by the Abbé de Prévost (16 vols., 1741–61).[35] It should be noted that with the publication of the *Lettres édifiantes*, a specifically editorial aspect cannot be ignored, namely the question of the format of books. The Jesuits, for example, who were prominent in the use of the quarto format, now resorted to smaller and less expensive sizes, in octavo and in duodecimo. By lowering the price of the books, the Jesuits were acknowledging new patterns of consumption and the expanding public interest in travel ac-counts. Thus, the second half of the eighteenth century gave preference to the use of small formats in circulating this type of literature. One of the examples of adaptation of the production to new reading habits can be found in Abbot Joseph de la Porte's *Le voyageur français* [The French Traveller], in forty-two volumes in duodecimo (1764–95).[36]

---

[35] Guido Abbattista, 'The Business of Paternoster Row: Towards a Publishing History of the *Universal History*', *Publishing History*, 17 (1985), 5–50.

[36] Roger Chartier, 'Les livres de voyage', in Chartier and H.-J. Martin (eds.), *Histoire de l'édition française*, vol. 2 (Paris, 1990), 266–8.

The *Essai sur les mœurs et l'esprit des nations* (1756) by Voltaire was one of the most significant works in opening up the world to a historiographic discourse that was traditionally directed at the description of dynastic occurrences and the activities of the elite classes, essentially political, diplomatic, or military. Any type of generalization regarding this historiographic discourse would need to consider the fact that its thematic limits were equally established by courtly or military settings, including those that occurred at the supposed frontiers of Christianity or imperial demarcation. It was, in fact, from within a world-history orientation that strong criticism of the atrocities committed by Portuguese expansion and other types of European colonialism were made. This was the case with the work of Abbé Raynal. Meanwhile, in more generic terms, criticisms of Eurocentrism were not merely the result of a historiographic mutation, for one could say that, above all, at their base lay inventive literary constructions developed through imaginary reports of voyages. This was the case with the works of Daniel Defoe and Jonathan Swift and, later, with the *Supplément au Voyage de M. Bougainville* [Supplement to the Voyage of Monsieur Bougainville] (1772) by Diderot. Alongside these works in which Europeans came into contact with 'good' natives and clever observers, it is possible to discover other early attempts at criticizing Eurocentrism. This was the case with the *Lettres Persanes* [Persian Letters] (1721) by Montesquieu and the praise of a wise 'Chinaman' in *The Citizen of the World* (1762) by Oliver Goldsmith. Besides this, China as the model of civilization, particularly in administration, was much in vogue throughout the eighteenth century.[37] However, one should not exaggerate this admiration for China, since authors such as Montesquieu, Defoe, Winckelmann, and Hume remained critical of such fascination.

The publication of European national histories inspired by overseas expansion and colonial projects cannot be isolated from the strong historiographical awareness throughout Europe of the continent's place in a much larger globe. But one must consider that this context of cosmopolitanism and universalism, so well represented by Voltaire, Raynal, and Robertson, gave way at the end of the eighteenth century to tendencies that were far more oriented towards a celebration of European values of the progress of European civilization. It is within this tendency, from Condorcet to Hegel, that more teleological concepts of human progress and great narratives of European development were aligned. While national histories reveal a consistent continuation in the models of writing adopted throughout the century, one should note that it is the most general framework—European and global, particularly the triumphalism of European hegemony—that was to be felt at the end of the eighteenth century, more precisely at the moment of the Napoleonic campaigns. In general terms, one

---

[37] Federico Chabod, *Stora dell'idea d'Europa*, ed. Ernesto Sestan and Armando Saitta (Roma, 1961), 82–121; and L. Dermigny, *La Chine et l'Occident: Le commerce à Canton au XVIIIe siècle, 1719–1833*, vol. I (Paris, 1964), 21–43.

might think that the creation of hierarchies of modernization and development, which throughout the nineteenth century were translated into criteria of racial division capable of granting hegemony to Europe, was preceded by a series of operations of hierarchical organization by kingdoms and the nation-states.

Any exercise to sum up what was the general meaning of European histories regarding the East faces two main problems. On the one hand, it is necessary to analyse the different languages, systems of classification, and main themes used in different periods. In this respect, the non-linearity of the different processes of change can be demonstrated through the analysis of various discursive tensions opposing religion (or the defence of an orthodoxy) to commerce; the celebration of European values of conquest to ethnographic curiosity (starting by the capacity to perceive the differences between so many political units); or values associated with the glorification of kingdoms and nations to more universal and cosmopolitan views of the world. On the other hand, any analytical exercise oriented towards the interpretation of the same histories should be concerned with a series of external factors, from the determinations of the book market to the different forms of engagement in political projects of conquest and European supremacy.

KEY HISTORICAL SOURCES

Awnsham and Churchill, John, *A Collection of Voyages and Travels* (London, 1704).

Banier, Antoine and Le Mascrier, Jean-Baptiste, *Cérémonies et coutumes religieuses de tous les peoples du monde*, 11 vols. (Amsterdam, 1723–43).

Boemus, Johannes, *El libro de las costumbres de todas las gentes del Mundo*, trans. Francisco Tamara (Antwerp, 1556).

Da Cruz, Gaspar, *Tractado em que cōtam muito por estenso as cousas da China cō suas particularidades e assi do reyno dormuz* (Évora, 1569).

González de Mendoza, Juan, *Historia de las cosas mas notables, ritos y costumbres, del gran Reyno de la China* (Rome, 1585).

Pinelo, Antonio de León, *Epitome de la Biblioteca Oriental i Occidental, Nautica i Geografica* (Madrid, 1629); ed. and rev. Andrés González de Barcia, 3 vols. (Madrid, 1737–8).

Ramusio, Giovanni Battista, *Delle Navigationi et viaggi* (Venice, 1550).

BIBLIOGRAPHY

Anquetil-Duperron, Abraham-Hyacinthe, *Considérations philosophiques historiques et géographiques sur les deux mondes (1780–1804)*, ed. Guido Abbattista (Pisa, 1993).

Burke, Peter, 'European Views of World History: From Giovio to Voltaire', *History of European Ideas*, 6 (1985), 237–51.

Duchet, Michel, *Anthropologie et Histoire au siècle des Lumières* (Paris, 1971).

Griggs, Tamara, 'Universal History from Counter-Reformation to Enlightenment', *Modern Intellectual History*, 4 (2007), 219–47.

Marshal, P. J. and Williams, Glyndwr, *The Great Map of Mankind: British Perceptions of the World in the Age of Enlightenment* (London, 1982).

Meek, Ronald L., *Social Science and the Ignoble Savage* (Cambridge, 1976).

O'Brien, Karen, *Narratives of Enlightenment: Cosmopolitan History from Voltaire to Gibbon* (Cambridge, 1997).

Osterhammel, Jürgen, *Die Entzauberung Asiens: Europa und die asiatischen Reiche im 18. Jahrhundert* (Munich, 1998).

Schwab, Raymond, *La Renaissance Orientale* (Paris, 1950).

Van Kley, Edwin, 'Europe's "Discovery of China" and the Writing of World History', *American Historical Review*, 76 (1971), 358–85.

Chapter 27

A New History for a 'New World': The First One Hundred Years of Hispanic New World Historical Writing

Kira von Ostenfeld-Suske

The 'discovery' of the New World in 1492 marked a watershed for Spain and Europe, signalling a change in the way Spaniards and other Europeans conceived of themselves. Spain faced not only the challenge of connecting Europe to the New World with the exploration of the Americas and the expansion of its empire, but placing the New World into official cosmographical, geographical, anthropological, and, ultimately, historical understandings. The subsequent conquest and colonization of the New World, however, produced new challenges for historical writing, providing a disorienting strangeness of lands and peoples, and confronting early modern Spanish New World history with problems of description and understanding. With no clear referents, those who began to write about the New World realized that they would need to create texts where none had previously existed, invent new genres, or adapt versions of old genres, and combine different forms of historical writing to create a new kind of writing, one that required new sources of authority. So while these works form part of the evolutionary path of Spanish historiography discussed in Chapter 21, they also distinguished themselves in their material, their novelty, and the authority they used to support their texts.

While other chapters by Catherine Julien, Jorge Cañizares-Esguerra, and José Rabasa variously discuss the work of mestizo, creole, and Indian historians, this chapter will chronologically survey the incipient histories of the New World by looking at how the Spanish conceived of New World history, and ultimately what these histories broadcast to Europe. These New World writings fall into four broad categories: eyewitness accounts of the 'discovery' and 'conquest'; the work of armchair historians (who never left Spain) who sought to make sense of the New World; ethnographies by the friars who carried out the spiritual conquest; and the great literature that fuelled the debate about the moral, philosophical, legal, religious, and ethnographic implications of the conquest, written by official historians and religious men, not all of whom had set foot in the New World. Many works bridge two or more of these categories, and change and evolve according to the nature of the enterprises they record. By examining the key texts of this New World historiography, and focusing on the themes and genres that these new kinds of works addressed, this chapter will trace how historical writing took part in the changing influences and image of the New World, revealing that the significance of these works resides more with the authors, methods, and purpose of the accounts than what they were relating.

NEW WORLDS, NEW REALITIES: THE FIRST NEW WORLD HISTORIES

The first report of the discovery of the New World was provided by Christopher Columbus to the Catholic Monarchs, Ferdinand and Isabella (r. 1474–1516), and should be seen as a reflection of Columbus's struggle with a barely fathomable reality. His *Diario de a bordo* [Diary of Christopher Columbus's First Voyage to America, 1492–3], detailed, generally day by day, the explorer's first travels to the New World in search of the Orient.[1] Columbus was not a learned humanist or man of letters but a sailor whose a priori models were the *mappa mundi*, and the medieval travel literature of John Mandeville, Marco Polo, and others that described the 'marvels of the East'. When Columbus failed to find the Orient and its riches, to cover his failure he marshalled a new 'language' of success, presenting the New World as innocent, generous, and peaceful, populated with good-looking Indians, who had neither property nor religion. Columbus scraped bare the reality of the New World, dismissing the Indians' customs, rites, and rituals, and creating a tabula rasa on which to inscribe a political and cultural reality of his own. To promote the riches of the New World he based his account on fantasy, presenting a terrestrial paradise, not a site of human history. Columbus's New World was a land of plenty, a prophesied promised land ready to be exploited by Europe, and the *new man* portrayed as a helpless Adamic figure ready to be Christianized. In this way, Columbus drew on fictional and familiar modes, attaching them to New World realities and, in doing so, tried to bridge the gap between what he saw and understood, and what he could communicate. Thus, unlike the typical travel log, which was more strictly technical in its writing, Columbus blended his account of his navigations with his own testimo-

[1] The original now lost, the *Diario* is available to us only through Bartolomé de las Casas's selective, yet copious transcriptions. For a modernized edition, see Luis Arranz Márquez, *Cristóbal Colón: Diario de a bordo* (Madrid, 1985).

ny of the subjective experience of what he encountered, thus making his accounts both about navigation *and* discovery.

Columbus's account of his voyage through the Indies was articulated as the experience of a geography profoundly resonant with the cultural, political, and economic ideologies of the late fifteenth century. Columbus portrayed the potential of these new lands, and how they could serve the Crown. He established an inexorable rhythm of improvement and promise, while at the same time insistently noted the presence of rivers, possible sources of gold or potential commercial ports, and the fertility of lands that were ripe for development. This combination of subjective information—some fantastic others affective— produced an array of information ready to be interpreted by European readers. It is this practical aspect of the 'otherness' of the New World that gave Columbus greatest pause in the *Diario*. His account produced new signs for registering unheard-of peoples and things, and offered a way to acknowledge the New World within a European cosmology, creating a New World that suited the ideas and needs of the Old, and captured Europe's imagination.

The Catholic Monarchs tried to make sense of the array of reports that came out of the New World, and the various foreign pamphlets concerning the New World that Columbus's account had inspired, and began to appreciate the need for an official Spanish account of events. They turned to a renowned tutor in their court, the Florentine scholar Pedro Martyr de Anglería, to produce an historical account of the events surrounding the discovery and conquest of the New World. Originally written in Latin in eight *Decades*, Martyr's *De Orbe Novo*, later translated as *Décadas del Nuevo Mundo* [The Decades of the New World] (1494–1525), became the first 'official' chronicle of Spanish activities in the New World.

Martyr, however, never visited the New World, but used his humanist erudition to guide his project. For Martyr, as for many of his fellow humanists, personal experience had nothing to do with the fitness of the historian to interpret his subject. Rather it was important to bear in mind the patterns of the ancients, the classical models of Herodotus, Pliny, and Aristotle. Thus Martyr revealed himself as a man of his time, a Renaissance historian, who refracted his understanding of America through the prism of the classics. He used classical analogies, for example, to interpret ancient Amerindian polities, using the Latin terms for Roman institutions in his description of the 'senatorial house' of the Aztecs, implicitly superimposing Roman scenery upon the American landscape. Ultimately his work concerned the events of the conquest, and to facilitate the writing of his work, the Catholic Monarchs gave Martyr direct access to all available accounts of early Spanish explorers and the material goods with which they returned. Furthermore, Martyr was empowered to seek new documents, and commanded written and oral accounts (*relaciones*) of all expeditions, even interviewing Columbus. Thus he wrote his history by editing interviews, letters, and missives, recapturing in an almost journalistic fashion the first days of 'discovery', and creating an epistolary chronicle of the momentous meeting of Europe and the New World. In this, his work remains of fundamental importance for understanding the depictions of the first European contacts with native American civilizations.[2] Although not a natural history, Martyr's work included descriptions of the natural surroundings, which he recorded as rich and varied, and it provided the first published account of the political organization of the inhabitants, their religious beliefs, and their customs and trades—in short, the first ethnography. Martyr still included, however, many of Columbus's and other travellers' 'fantastic' accounts, and essentially gave birth to a 'thesaurus of New World motifs' such as the noble savage, exotic fauna and flora, cannibalism, and others. As one of the few available treatises on the New World in the sixteenth century, it became a source upon which many European authors drew for compilation (as much subsequent work produced in Europe was derivative). Passages in which Martyr wrote about strange animals were eagerly quoted, plagiarized, and held as truth for more than two centuries, no matter how fantastic some of the passages were. Moreover, the Spanish Crown followed a fairly consistent policy of treating any kind of information about the New World as a state secret, which may account in part for the fact that many works remained for centuries in manuscript form, and which makes the published works by Martyr, and later Oviedo, Acosta, and Herrera all the more significant as they became the primary texts through which the New World was transmitted to European readers. Martyr's skilful humanist writing evoked the ambiguous atmosphere that the early modern pictorial imagination conveyed in images of tall Amerindians with feathery regalia and noble countenance set against landscapes of tropical forests and classical ruins. In this, perhaps more than any other history, it tells us as much about the expectations and anxieties of the sixteenth-century European mind as it does about the events it claimed to report.

Martyr's work was intended to justify Spanish actions, and inform a learned European audience—for the benefit of expansion—about what had occurred. With the help of classical style and precedent, Martyr told the story as a continuation of the European drive for empire. A neo-Platonist, he drew from Columbus's account when he characterized the indigenous peoples as a docile, if rather stupid, tabula rasa, waiting patiently for the imprint of the Christian faith. Martyr thus designed his work to present Spain's overseas adventures in providential terms, justifying the Christianizing mission. Furthermore, by 1516 when he addressed the newest edition of his book to Charles V (r. 1516–56), he conceived

---

[2] Edmundo O'Gorman, *Cuatro historiadores de Indias, siglo XVI: Pedro Mártir de Anglería, Gonzalo Fernández de Oviedo y Valdés, Fray Bartolomé de Las Casas, Joseph de Acosta* (Mexico, 1972), 17–56.

of the *Novus Orbis* as a basis of effective *de facto* power for establishing a universal dominion, and after praising the magnificence, richness, and vastness of the newly discovered lands, he urged the king 'chosen by the powers above' to embrace the New World, where he would find 'the instruments by which the whole world will obey you'.[3] Thus the 'discovery' of the New World was directly assimilated into, and indeed made the cynosure of, the epic story of the Spanish monarchies. The earthshaking event crowned a tradition of imperial claims and mythology enhanced by the glorious Reconquista and victory over Granada, making it a matter of intense national pride, involving the territorial pretensions of states, and claims to priority in the 'discovery' of a hemisphere and the shaping of modern global history.

SURPASSING THE ANCIENTS: NATURAL HISTORY AND NEW FORMS OF AUTHORITY

Gonzalo Fernández de Oviedo y Valdés was a court humanist and historian before he sailed to Santo Domingo in 1514, to become a colonial administrator. There, Oviedo was constantly updated, by a stream of informants, about each province of the empire. Accordingly, in 1532, he was commissioned to write a history of the Indies by Charles V. His monumental *Historia general y natural de las Indias* [General and Natural History of the Indies] (1535) provided an account of all known Spanish discoveries, conquests, and colonization to date, along with descriptions of the flora, fauna, and indigenous peoples encountered. Oviedo styled himself as the 'Pliny of the New World', and insisted that he modelled his work after Pliny's *Naturalis Historia* [Natural History]. In fact, Oviedo relied explicitly on Pliny in certain details, particularly for some puzzling identifications of animals and plants, and Pliny was the basis upon which Oviedo built a sense of 'continuity' between the two worlds. Further, Oviedo dedicated and wrote his work for Charles V, whom he insistently called 'Caesar' or 'His Caesarian Majesty', underscoring Pliny's dedication to soon-to-be Emperor Titus. For Oviedo, the historian's purpose was to serve the king by providing him with information about the New World, information that would help him to rule wisely and promote the imperial vision. Thus, Oviedo took upon himself the task of describing the flora, fauna, and peoples of the hemisphere, and then, more importantly, of narrating the complete history of its occupation by the Spaniards; his work was designed to serve both as an encyclopedia and as a universal history of the Indies.

---

[3] Translation mine. Quoted in Alberto Mario Salas, *Tres cronistas de Indias: Pedro Mártir de Anglería, Gonzalo Fernández de Oviedo, Fray Bartolomé de las Casas* (Mexico, 1986), 22–43, at 27.

Thus, an attempt at a systematic description appears with Oviedo, who saw the New World not as inferior, but different, and rather than minimize the differences between Europe and America, he constantly stressed the 'newness' of the New World. His 1535 edition was even illustrated with woodcuts of his own drawings of flora, fauna, and cultural objects, physically inserted adjacent to the description of the object, activity, plant, or animal about which he was writing. These offered the earliest eyewitness portrayals of New World reality, and the first images of American mammals and fruit known to Europeans, providing a compilation of the riches of the New World's natural resources.[4] By providing an inventory of plants and animals in the territories newly subjected to Spain, Oviedo's work was also ideologically in tune with the project of imperial expansion. The multitude, variety, and exotic strangeness of animals became a symbol of Charles's imperial power extending itself over the entire globe, and Oviedo's inventories became part of the scaffolding of paperwork that engorged and fuelled the legal machinery of the colonies. With Oviedo, knowledge became a valuable unit of exchange in the conquest of America, and his writing, and the unique information it provided, became itself a material commodity—his 'gold' and his service.

To describe and organize unknown flora, fauna, and physical phenomena, the Europeans used criteria based on their similarity to, or difference from, those of Europe—and in this way they assimilated the foreign and the exotic. While Oviedo was able to describe the diversity of flora and fauna with reasonable accuracy, he still qualified, for example, animals that looked similar—as if they were, in fact, identical: for him, pumas *were* lions, jaguars *were* tigers, and so on. Further, claiming that a new species was 'as in Europe', meant accepting it within the known and familiar world.[5]

When it came to describing the people of the New World, however, Oviedo understood that the problem became far more complex. He tried to find a place in relation to his own world for what he saw—and regarded the inhabitants of the New World in relation to a commonly held notion of the uniformity of human nature, a belief that required every race to conform, within certain broad limits, to the same 'natural' patterns of behaviour. When describing the inhabitants of the New World, most New World writers tried to classify the Indians according to the nature of their society, and sought to find elements that they thought integral to European society, such as systems of beliefs and government, marriage rituals, hereditary practices, sumptuary

[4] See Daymond Turner, 'Forgotten Treasures from the Indies: The Illustrations and Drawings of Fernández de Oviedo', *Huntington Library Quarterly*, 48:1 (1985), 1–46.

[5] See Antonello Gerbi, *Nature in the New World: From Christopher Columbus to Gonzalo Fernández de Oviedo* (Pittsburgh, 1985).

norms, and means of subsistence. This, of course, denied much of the reality of the New World, by imposing foreign categorizing structures and Spanish norms on New World inhabitants. So set was this schema that Oviedo admitted that describing the human inhabitants required skills which he lacked, asking 'what mortal could understand such a diversity of languages, habits and customs as those practiced by the Indian?'[6]

Such remarks of genuine frustration reveal that classical models and interpretative frameworks were inadequate to understanding and narrating the history of the New World and its relationship to Spain. Those who actually witnessed the New World began to understand that it created new problems for historiography—it offered material for which the precedent of classical theory, evidence, and knowledge no longer sufficed, revealing the limits of 'book learning' and the value of direct experience. While Oviedo tried to reconcile established histories with his own observations, and frequently cited the ancients, he became increasingly aware that the New World required a different kind of history and new rhetorical strategies. In fact, Oviedo proclaimed the superiority of modern conquests over ancient exploits, and declared that contemporary voyages and discoveries had rendered obsolete much classical geography and learning. Without the framework of theology or tradition, however, New World chroniclers would need new ways to lay claim to a privileged form of interpretation that they called 'truth'; they would need to appeal to the authority of the eyewitness. Thus, Oviedo justified his deviations from canonical texts and authorities by creating a central role for himself as the transcriber of his own eyewitness testimony and that of others.[7] In this way, Oviedo's first-hand experience of the New World provided his work with an authority unavailable to those such as Martyr, and later Herrera, who never set foot in the New World but claimed to provide authoritative accounts based solely on the accumulation of sources.

Faced with ongoing exploration, conquest, and colonization, with multiple and often competing reports from the field, with imaginative literature as well as broader philosophical and theological influences, and with an abundant new natural world, Oviedo attempted to provide the fullest possible account of the American territories, while also promoting these innovations in traditional historiographical methods. Oviedo advanced a notion of truth as the sum of diverse perspectives, and presented multiple versions of a particular event, suggesting that since no one but God held the key to absolute truth, his *Historia* functioned as a courtroom, which admitted the gamut of testimonies. Thus, while Oviedo's plan of natural history was admittedly moulded on classical models, the epistemological foundations and the criterion of truth

---

[6] Translation mine. Gonzalo Fernández de Oviedo y Valdés, *De la natural hystoria de las Indias* (1526; Chapel Hill, 1969), 5.

[7] Sarah H. Beckjord, *Territories of History: Humanism, Rhetoric and Historical Imagination in the Early Chronicles of Spanish America* (University Park, Pa., 2007), 43–86.

proclaimed were different from those endorsed by contemporary European authorities. To locate authenticity not in tradition but in individual vision, as Oviedo did, was to turn the medieval notion of *auctoritas* on its head. The New World had demanded the construction of a new discourse on natural history, and even new standards of belief, and had broadened the discussion from mere comparison with the classics to an insistence on first-hand experience and observation as the basis for all true knowledge. Although this did not mean that the classics ceased to provide the intellectual foundations for understanding the New World, these authors came to emphasize their own peculiar originality. Consequently, New World histories prompted discussion in Europe about the relationship between sight and truth, and between the writing of history and the attainment of knowledge, as well as about the role of visual epistemology.

HISTORY AND THE LEGALITY AND MORALITY OF CONQUEST

Oviedo's work was grounded in his belief in Spain's destiny to establish a universal Catholic empire and, therefore, his desire to testify to the validity of the Spanish conquest. In fact, the legitimacy of Spanish rule in the New World was at the heart of many New World chronicles. More importantly, Spain's desire to colonize the New World and justify Spanish actions explains why a history of the natives' past was deemed so important. It became necessary to demonstrate how the Indians had been enslaved or mistreated by others, and that their abominable customs demanded a purifying change of regime.

The specific rhetorical and epistemological grounds that underlay many New World histories were to a large extent political, moral, and religious. Rather than search for objective narrative truth, these works were part of a polemical incursion into the central debates of possession of territory and the disposition of native people.[8] Many New World texts echoed the preceding debates as persuasive narratives intended to affect policy and social practice on both sides of the Atlantic. In this, historical records no longer registered exemplary lives but were used instead to compare and measure the cultural level of the Indians, and thus used for the appropriation of new territories and the transformation of social realities. Colonial chroniclers, starting with Columbus, established a hierarchy that presented European culture as superior and, consequently, ready to absorb

---

[8] See Rolena Adorno, *The Polemics of Possession in Spanish American Narrative* (New Haven, 2008).

or impose itself on other peoples and spaces. These created new realms of reality for European readers that still prevail by emphasizing the superiority of Europeans and creating a Eurocentric worldview.[9]

For sixteenth-century Europe, which had very little knowledge and still less understanding of the peoples beyond its borders, there were few terms with which to classify non-Europeans. In European eyes, most non-Europeans, and nearly all non-Christians, even including such 'advanced' peoples as the Turks, were classified as 'barbarians'. Further, Aristotle had listed the areas of social life requisite for any 'true civilization'. As such, Europeans characterized themselves as 'civilized' because they were Christian, came from a civil community, and lived predominantly in cities governed by the rule of law, and had written language. Thus for the sixteenth-century historian, to write a history of a people not only required some evidence of an historical past, of which the Caribbean cultures witnessed had little, but also demanded that the historian consider the people he was describing, topographically at least, to be living in societies that were comparable to his own. Furthermore, the conviction that Indians had no histories because they did not have written accounts of their past (since non-literary forms of recording the past were seen not only as inferior but essentially non-existent), led missionaries and learned men to self-nominate themselves to write these histories.[10] It was within this framework that histories of the New World characterized the natives and native culture. Early Spanish chroniclers identified the natives prior to the conquest as either living in some vague period of human prehistory or, by analogy, as belonging to the same genre as the more familiar barbarians of the ancient world. Even Oviedo chose to compare the Amerindians with the barbaric behaviour attributed by Aristotle to Ethiopians, which allowed Oviedo to identify certain types of behaviour—polygamy, poly-andry, matrilineal descent—as common to both.

Debate raged as to why the indigenous peoples had developed in a way unlike Europeans, and the 'barbaric' nature of the natives, and their past, provided fodder to justify the imperial enterprise.[11] History-writing came to the service of imperial expansion in the work of the official historian Juan Ginés de Sepúlveda, who wrote between 1553 and 1558, from the confines of Spain, a history of the New World, *De rebus Hispanorum ad Novum Terrarum Orbem*

---

[9] See José Rabasa, *Inventing America: Spanish Historiography and the Formation of Eurocentrism* (Norman, Okla., 1993).

[10] European Renaissance philosophies of language and writing privileged European forms of recording as exclusive vehicles for knowledge, effectively excluding Amerindian ways of recording and knowing. In this way the European form of writing history, and emphasis on the written word, also became an instrument of colonization. See Walter D. Mignolo, *The Darker Side of the Renaissance: Literacy, Territoriality and Colonization* (Ann Arbor, 1995).

[11] The best discussion of these developments is Anthony Pagden's, *The Fall of Natural Man: The American Indian and the Origins of Comparative Ethnology* (Cambridge, 1982).

Mexicumque gestis, also known as *De Orbe Novo Historia* [History of the New World], that provided a controversial defence of the Spanish right of conquest in the New World, and of Charles's universalist claims. Sepúlveda was a theologian, trained classicist, and translator of Aristotle, and claimed that the pre-conquest state of the indigenous peoples was one without rulers or laws, and thus legitimately appropriated. Melding historical and legal ideas, Sepúlveda claimed that Spanish rule in America rested on an interpretation of natural law that legitimized the subjugation of 'uncivilized' peoples by any Christian nation, which granted dominion to 'civilized' peoples over all those who were 'not civilized'. Added to this was the Spanish use of the Roman claim that they had earned their empire by bringing civilization and the rule of law to a backward race. Sepúlveda thus compared Spanish actions with the precedent of Rome's acquisition of a supposed 'world empire', arguing that the Spanish title to the New World was derived from the universal dominion of the Roman Empire, to which Charles was considered heir.

By the second half of the sixteenth century, arguments such as those of Sepúlveda had begun to lose their persuasive stronghold, as Spaniards had witnessed a profound transformation in their knowledge of the New World. The discovery of the great 'empires' of Mexico and Peru, and their respective conquests by Hernán Cortés in 1519–22 and Francisco Pizarro in 1531–2, revealed to Europeans the existence of highly developed cultures, quite distinct from those of the Caribbean, which had recognizable polities ruled by nobility, an economy with markets, merchants and means of exchange, public revenues, and possessing a structured and ritualistic, although bloody and idolatrous, form of religion. This provided ample evidence for the Dominican friar Bartolomé de las Casas, who had witnessed such developments first-hand, to compose his *Apologética historia sumaria* [Apologetic History] (1559), which sought to defend the rationality of the natives against those, like Sepúlveda, who sought to portray them as examples of Aristotle's natural slaves. Las Casas set out to prove that before the conquest, the natives were capable of ruling their own individual passions, and their political communities. Moreover, he argued that Inca and Aztec societies were at least as sophisticated, politically and religiously, as classical ancient polities. Las Casas complemented this work with *Brevíssima relación de la destruyción de las Indias* [A Brief Account of the Destruction of the Indies] (1552), a compendium of the arguments he wielded in his outraged indictment of the excess he witnessed, and the ravages and atrocities of the conquest, and *Historia de las Indias* [History of the Indies] (1561), his authoritative version of events that took place in America during his lifetime. In the latter work, Las Casas recounted events of discovery to 1526 in grinding detail, sometimes day by day, stopping for excursions into nature or geography. In preparing this widely circulated manuscript, Las Casas drew not only from his own experiences, but also did extensive archival work. He followed Columbus's descriptions and his log book, and included lengthy excerpts of comprehensive accounts, such as the unpublished *Relación acerca de las antigüedades de los indios* [Account of the

Antiquities of the Indians] (1498) of Columbus's companion Ramón Pané, providing the only written evidence of this work to date. Most Renaissance historians contented themselves with a less exhaustive account of the facts, and following the precepts of rhetoric, carefully transmuted most raw documents into smooth artistic prose. Las Casas, by contrast, often let the documents speak for themselves, extracting them at length even though doing so entailed inelegant variations in tone, style, and pace. In his long preface he pointed out that Greek historians, though eloquent and entertaining, had often mingled myth with truth, and that the 'good historian' should avoid the Greeks' errors by reserving credence for stories preserved 'in the public archives of Kings or kingdoms or cities, and by publicly appointed persons'.[12] In this way, Las Casas presented his admonition of Spanish actions as that of a superior sort of historian, an archival researcher, whose probity was guaranteed by his religious status, his own eye-witness experience, and the documentary evidence of his sources.

Writing his work in the form of an urgent petition, and providing an account from a retrospective point of view, Las Casas evolved a new, highly effective way of writing the history of the Indians across fifty years of Spanish domination. Furthermore, his telescopic and persuasive mode of writing history accommodated the new moral, philosophical, and political concerns that had come to the fore, and in doing so, Las Casas's work sought to effect change in policies regarding the New World. Las Casas did not challenge the Crown's claims to sovereignty in the New World, but sought to use history to open debate as to the rights of the natives. In fact, the conflicting vows, and historical arguments, of Las Casas and Sepúlveda provoked a debate as to the legality and morality of the conquest, one that would cross the ocean to the halls of Spanish universities and Charles's court. In addition, their debate would mark either implicitly or explicitly the writing of the history of the New World for centuries to come.

THE NEW ETHNOGRAPHERS

Las Casas was among a group of priests and mendicant friars who produced systematic histories and memoranda on the beliefs and customs of the natives and the actions of the Europeans.[13] While these were the works of religious men who had travelled to the New World on an evangelizing mission, they provided a new dimension to histories of the New World by including a closer exploration of indigenous culture; their authors saw the study and understanding of indige-

---

[12] Bartolomé de las Casas, *History of the Indies*, trans. and ed. Andrée Collard (New York, 1971), 12.
[13] Besides those mentioned here are the works of Fray Toribio de Benavente Motolinía, Fray Diego Durán, Fray Jerónimo de Mendieta, and Fray Juan de Torquemada. An excellent overview of these early ethnographies appears in Roberto González Echevarría and Enrique Pupo-Walker (eds.), *The Cambridge History of Latin American Literature*, vol. 1 (Cambridge, 1996).

nous society prior to the conquest as a necessary antecedent to their evangelization. Theirs was a new type of history aimed at recording a rapidly disappearing indigenous culture and history before it was entirely lost. Thus, a fundamental shift was made as histories began to concentrate on indigenous cultures as part of the past, rather than the present.

One of the best known of the Franciscan ethnographers was Fray Bernardino de Sahagún, whose *Historia de la Nueva España* [History of New Spain] (1547–77) provides the first account of Mexican mythology and culture, and an account of the conquest from an indigenous perspective. Sahagún sought to reconstruct Nahua culture as it existed before the Spaniards arrived in the New World. Like Oviedo, Sahagún tried to legitimize his narrative by referring not to his use of texts, but to his method. He claimed that the canon did not provide him with the necessary foundations to write his description of various native tribes that he himself had not witnessed, and therefore was compelled to base his account on the careful selection and interrogation of 'reliable witnesses'. Conserved through oral tradition, Sahagún used his knowledge of Nahuatl language and culture to collate indigenous myths, and was helped by native informants who gathered data about a variety of cultural beliefs and practices. Looking at these additions to Sahagún's text provides a glimpse into how natives reconstructed their own culture and natural history, and can be seen as a critical source of information about the key features of Nahua conceptualizations of themselves and their world.[14] Sahagún's reliance on such fieldwork allowed him to provide a comprehensive account of Nahuatl language and culture. Yet within this desire to rescue indigenous knowledge from oblivion was the desire to codify the past in order better to understand and ultimately control the present, as the text's ultimate goal was to enable missionaries to decipher and control public behaviour.

Among these missionary historians was also the Jesuit José de Acosta, whose *Historia natural y moral de las Indias* [Natural and Moral History of the Indies] (1590) was the first 'philosophical history', or moral history, which outlined the *mores* of the New World. Acosta's account explained the origin of the native inhabitants, and provided a brief history of the Inca and Aztec empires. He claimed that there were already enough accounts of the beginnings and growth of the Spanish colonies and complained that these only included cursory glances at the natives. Acosta believed that much philosophical knowledge could be garnered from studying the New World and its 'barbaric' inhabitants; he saw the New World as a laboratory for studying 'non-Christian' man, with the lessons

---

[14] See José Jorge Klor de Alva *et al.*, *The Work of Bernardino de Sahagún: Pioneer Ethnographer of Sixteenth-Century Aztec Mexico* (Albany, 1988).

learned easily applied in India, China, and North Africa. Acosta graded the natives according to their civility and appropriate place on the scale of social evolution by examining their political institutions, religious beliefs, and linguistic sophistication. He did so on the basis of empirical data, foreshadowing later developments in ethnology. Acosta's work, like that of Oviedo, however, helped establish a new genre of history-writing, that of 'natural and moral', or 'natural and general' history, covering both the natural and the human world. This was their response to the challenge of conveying the whole reality of the New World to contemporary readers, articulating both natural and political history in works of sweeping scope.

Acosta was like many other religious men who were interested primarily in the catechism of the natives—while they came to the Indians' defence, they also sought to unveil Indian mythology. Acosta was respectful of Indian customs and beliefs, as long as they did not contradict Christian dogma, and he understood how knowledge of the Indians' past enhanced present understanding of the Indians. He included a section on indigenous idolatry to assist new missionaries in identifying and rooting out what he thought were demonically inspired Amerindian religions. He also included sections on Inca and Aztec customs and systems of government to help colonial magistrates govern the Amerindians according to their own legal and political institutions, which Acosta believed revealed considerable ingenuity and adaptation to local customs. In this Acosta revealed the point of the new history that, in Europe, Jean Bodin and others had called for, one which was to be practical, not theoretical. The greatness of Acosta's book, however, lies in its conceptualization of the 'Indies' within a larger philosophical context. Acosta confronted many of the cosmological and natural philosophical questions that arose from the encounter between the Aristotelian philosophy in which he had been educated, and the reality of the New World, and he always sought to explain phenomena by weighing cause and effect, observation and reason. Acosta's approach to knowledge and understanding was based on his concept of the moral and natural aspects of history represented in the intersection of philosophy and theology. For Acosta, philosophy involved understanding nature as more than a catalogue of plants and animals—rather as constituting the fundamental order of the universe. He likewise considered theology as a way of knowing and revering God in the nature created by the Divinity. For Acosta, just as the Roman Empire had preceded the Empire of Christ, the 'empires' of the Mexica and the Inca preceded the coming of the Spaniards. This interpretation of world history not only confirmed ancient and Christian historiography, but promised an explanation of the cultural distance between the Amerindians and the people of Europe. It also provided a justification for the conquest that suited the ambitions of both missionaries and the Crown.

THE CRONISTA MAYOR DE LAS INDIAS AND
THE SPANISH IMPERIAL SCHOOL

The Spanish Crown had become increasingly aware of the circulation of anti-Spanish works, inspired by the writings of Las Casas, which criticized the actions of Spaniards in the New World,[15] and of the growing popularity of the self-serving works of Spanish conquistadores, their secretaries, or those of other soldiers, who had sought to exaggerate and defend their exploits as a means of receiving royal favour.[16] Such works did not present Spaniards in a favourable light, and so in 1571, Philip II (r. 1556–98) created the lucrative position of official Chronicler of the Indies (Cronista Mayor de las Indias), to write 'a general, moral and particular history of the deeds, and momentous events that occurred and continue to occur in those regions'. Similarly, the methodology of this work was also made explicit: 'It is of utmost importance that the histories written are armed with truth, and based in documents, because if they are not then they will be quite inconvenient . . . this is the reason why this Office of the Chronicler of the Indies was created, so that this history will be written with great accuracy'.[17] This increased specification of the New World chronicler's task and the need to acquire and record document-based information also marked a new phase of colonial development: expansion, settlement, and political and administrative organization.

In response to the challenges to the legal basis of Spanish control, and inspired by the same burgeoning reason of state ideas on the Iberian peninsula, the Crown encouraged a historiographical tradition dedicated to demonstrating the tremendous benefits that the Spaniards had brought to the New World, including how the natives had voluntarily become Spanish vassals because of the benefits and honour it brought them. Thus, unlike the work of Las Casas, official Spanish works did not emphasize Spanish cruelty or violence; rather, reality was camouflaged by a narrative of colonial benevolence. Perfectly suited to this official enterprise was Antonio de Herrera y Tordesillas. Although Herrera had never been to the Americas, he was appointed official Chronicler of the Indies in 1594, as his

---

[15] These included works such as Venetian historian Girolamo Benzoni's *Historia del Mondo Nuovo* (Venice, 1565). See Richard Kagan, 'La Historia y la Crónica de las Indias durante el siglo XVII: Antonio de Herrera y Tordesillas', in Manuel Chust Calero and Víctor Mínguez (eds.), *El imperio sublevado: monarquía y naciones en España e Hispanoamérica* (Madrid, 2004), 37–56.

[16] Most notably Francisco López de Gómara, *Hispania Vitrix, Historia General de las Indias* (Zaragoza, 1552); Bernal Díaz del Castillo, *Historia verdadera de la conquista de Nueva España* ([S.l.], 1568); and the work of Pedro Cieza de León, see below.

[17] Translation mine. Archivo de las Indias, Indiferente General, 745 n. 227. For the period under investigation, the only comprehensive history of the 'Official Chronicles' of the New World is Romulo Carbia's, *La crónica oficial de las Indias occidentales: Estudio histórico y crítico acerca de la historiografía mayor de Hispano-América en los siglos XVI a XVIII* (La Plata, 1934). Carbia's work is supplemented by that of Francisco Esteve-Barba, *Historiografía Indiana* (Madrid, 1964).

previous work for the Crown had shown not only his loyalty, but also the effectiveness of his writing in providing a mouthpiece for Spanish imperial ideas. Herrera published his *Historia general de los hechos de los castellanos en las Islas i Tierra Firme del Mar Océano* [General History of the Indies], also known as the *Decadas*, in five parts between 1601 and 1615, providing a history of the New World from 1492 to 1554, or the pacification of Peru. Herrera's history of the Indies furthered Spanish interests by attempting to disseminate 'the piety, valour, and spiritual constancy that had guided the Spanish Crown in the discovery, pacification, and colonization of the New World'.[18]

For Herrera, foreigners alleged Spanish cruelty in the New World in order to denigrate Spanish actions. While Herrera did not categorically deny that negative actions might have occurred, he stressed that the actions of a few men could not undermine the exemplary behaviour of the majority who had done so much to bring benefits to the natives. In fact, he admitted the abuses of the conquerors so as to emphasize the efforts of the Crown to protect its native subjects. To support his claims, Herrera was to have consulted 'all available materials' on the New World, including the reports of the *Relaciones* and correspondence that had come from the New World held at the archive in Simancas, and works such as the first official history of Peru, by Pedro Cieza de León.[19] Herrera even included in his printed edition one of the most extensive lists of New World sources, from travel logs to even the extant writings of Las Casas, producing an incipient bibliography, one of the first of its kind.[20] In this way, Herrera claimed that although he had not been to the New World, he had created a true piece of historical research in 'the best contemporary manner'. His reference to atrocities was 'proof' of his faithful adherence to the sources, which later commentators regarded as testament to the 'objectivity' of his account. This, of course, added authority to his official work for the Crown, since it was source-based and 'carefully researched'. Moreover, by reason of its wealth of data, it immediately garnered recognition as the chief source and record of Spanish settlement for both Spanish and other European readers.

Despite having access to almost all available accounts of the New World, Herrera's focus was on the activities of Spaniards; the world of indigenous peoples remained a backdrop. His only descriptive use of the Indians was to show that they were barbarous and idolatrous, and thus instruments to demonstrate how the Spanish monarchy was fulfilling its role as outlined in the *Inter Caetera* of Alexander VI, which had ceded Indian sovereignty to the Spanish monarchy under the condition that they attended to 'above everything else...

---

[18] Translation mine. Antonio de Herrera y Tordesillas, *Historia general de los hechos de los castellanos en las Islas i Tierra Firme del Mar Océano* (Madrid, 1601–15), prologue.

[19] Pedro Cieza de León, *Crónica del Peru* (Seville, 1553).

[20] A full list of all the sources used by Herrera appears in Mariano Cuesta Domingo's edition of Herrera's *Historia general* (Madrid, 1991), 57–80.

the exaltation and propagation' of the Catholic faith among New World inhabitants. The discovery by Columbus, and the conquests of Mexico by Cortés, and of Peru by Pizarro, were placed within this context. Thus the various stages of New World history centred on the actions of Europeans—only Spaniards were the lead protagonists, and the 'discovery' of the New World was the triumph of European innovation and exploration. Herrera's purpose, however, was not to glorify conquerors such as Cortés, but rather to demonstrate the ever-vigilant concern of the Spanish Crown for the welfare of New World subjects through detailed discussion of Spanish imperial administrative organization, created to achieve 'order' and 'good government' in the New Word. Thus, Las Casas was incorporated into the authorized history of the Indies by outlining his campaign on behalf of the Indians, and the role he had played in the framing of the Laws of 1542, thus confirming the support of his efforts by Charles V, who at all times sought to procure the welfare of his native subjects. In this, Herrera's work reflects the ways in which the New World was subsumed under Spanish politics and administrative structures, in an attempt to govern and impose control. Even the way he describes the land is, in Spanish terms, not defined by Indian populations or empires and kingdoms but rather in terms of the newly established bishoprics, viceroyalties, and audiences. In short, the *Decadas* marked the culminating point of the 'imperial school' in New World history, initiated by Martyr and developed by Sepúlveda, and designed to confirm the justice and right of the Spanish Crown's claim to dominion over the New World. Herrera not only created a very popular, readable, and polished account of events, but garnered great royal favour for this work, and remained in the office of 'chief historiographical chronicler of the Indies' until his death in 1625, serving three Spanish kings. Furthermore, this work was translated into Latin, French, and Dutch in 1622, into German in 1624, and into English in 1706, becoming one of the major texts for more than two centuries through which the New World was transmitted to European readers, and ironically asserting the authority of Europeans as protectors of the Indians from exploitation.

CONCLUSION

Spanish New World historiography expanded the scope of early modern historical writing while innovating its methodologies. The New World was assimilated to the legal and historiographical categories of Europe and subject to its judgements, and in this sense, 'America' was not so much 'discovered' as 'invented'.[21] Adapting and refurbishing the literary genres of antiquity, New World historians created a new kind of discourse, an intellectual tool appropriate

---

[21] See Rabasa, *Inventing America*.

for the building of a body of knowledge about the New World. Through the adoption of new conceptual frameworks, New World historians systematized and organized vast amounts of information, made novel claims to reliability and truth, and transmitted to Europe the first images of American nature and peoples. Writing about the New World not only continued the process of writing the Spanish Empire into being, but this corpus of texts played a crucial role in shaping the European image of the Americas, and the European conception of New World natives, their culture and society, and their early colonial history, and demonstrates how the writing of history played a significant part in the long history of Spanish colonization in the Americas. These works framed the founding images and topics—of utopia, civilization, and barbarism—which would resonate in European and Latin American writings, and influence colonialist policies, for centuries to come. In creating this vision of the New World, historians compounded the idea of the superiority of European achievements, created an official discourse for colonizers, and largely wrote out the experience and participation of the Indian.

Whether in works of synthesis by humanist historians, eyewitness accounts and early ethnographies, or the vast polemical literature about the legal and moral implications of conquest, the framing and selection of material inescapably reflected a convergence of competing discourses, ideological concerns, stylistic considerations, and rhetorical gestures. Rather than being ancillary to action, history-writing was an essential form of action, and a sense of what their works would *do* weighed heavily upon these writers. Despite this, New World histories looked to provide 'truthful' history, and the spirit of enquiry present in the humanist tradition of reflection, debate, and experimentation was present in their works. Furthermore, although most New World historians did not write historiographical treatises on method, they nonetheless included reflections on how they wrote their work and on the evidence they used. Many authors also drew heavily from their encounters with New World peoples. Las Casas, Oviedo, Acosta, and Sahagún were eyewitnesses to the events, inhabitants, and cultures of the New World, giving their works new claims to authority through experience. In this they were able to develop forms of writing through which they cushioned the impact of the New World on European readers, and created the means to control, mediate, and possess the new reality, not only intellectually but ultimately politically.

TIMELINE/KEY DATES

1492 Columbus sets sail on his voyage of discovery
1494 Treaty of Tordesillas divides the New World between Spain and Portugal
1506 Columbus dies at Valladolid
1513 Ponce de Léon discovers Florida

1519–21 Hernán Cortez conquers Mexico

1524 Council of the Indies is established to help administer the new colonies

1532 Pizarro conquers Peru

1535 Printing press established in Mexico

1542 The Spanish Crown issues Las Nuevas Leyes (The New Laws) to protect the Indians

1551 The University of Mexico is founded

1570–1 The Inquisition is established in Lima and Mexico City

1571–2 Revolt of Tupac Amaru I in Peru

1585 Printing press is established in Peru

KEY HISTORICAL SOURCES

Acosta, José de, *Historia natural y moral de la Indias: en que se tratan las cosas notables del cielo, y elementos, metales, plantas y animales dellas* (Seville, 1590; Durham, NC, 2002).

Fernández de Oviedo y Valdés, Gonzalo, *Historia general y natural de las Indias, Islas, y Tierra Firme del Mar Océano*, 8 vols. (Seville, 1535).

Herrera y Tordesillas, Antonio de, *Historia general de los hechos de los castellanos en las Islas i Tierra Firme del Mar Océano*, 5 vols. (1601–15; Madrid, 1991).

Las Casas, Bartolomé de, *Apologética historia sumaria* (1559; Madrid, 1992).

Martyr de Anglería, Pedro, *Décadas del Nuevo Mundo*, 2 vols. (1494–1525; Madrid, 1989).

Sahagún, Bernardino de, *Historia de la Nueva España*, 13 vols. (1547–77; Barcelona, 2008).

Sepúlveda, Juan Ginés de, *De rebus Hispanorum ad Novum Terrarum Orbem Mexicumque gestis* (1563), in *Obras Completas*, ed. B. Cuart Moner (Pozoblanco, 1996).

BIBLIOGRAPHY

Arias, Santa, *Retórica, historia y polémica: Bartolomé de las Casas y la tradición intelectual renacentista* (Lanham, Md., 2001).

Bernand, Carmen and Gruzinski, Serge, *Histoire du Nouveau Monde: De la découverte à la conquête* (Paris, 1991).

Folger, Robert and Oesterreicher, Wulf (eds.), *Talleres de la memoria- Reivindicaciones y autoridad en la historiografía indiana de los siglos XVI y XVII* (Hamburg, 2005).

Iglesia, Ramón, *Cronistas e historiadores de la conquista de México*, 2nd edn (Mexico, 1972).

Kohut, Karl, *Narración y reflexión: las crónicas de Indias y la teoría historiográfica* (Mexico, 2007).

Murray, James C., *Spanish Chronicles of the Indies: Sixteenth Century* (New York, 1994).

Myers, Kathleen Ann, *Fernández de Oviedo's Chronicle of America: A New History for a New World* (Austin, 2007).

Rodríguez Prampolini, Ida, *Amadises de América: Hazaña de las Indias Como Empresa Caballeresca* (Mexico, 1990).

Sánchez Alonso, Benito, *Historia de la historiografía española,* vol. 2: *Hasta la publicación de la crónica de Ocampo (–1543)* (Madrid, 1942).

Sánchez Alonso, Benito, *Historia de la historiografía española: Ensayo de un examen de conjunto, De Ocampo a Solis (1543–1684)* (Madrid, 1944).

Chapter 28

Mesoamerican History: The Painted Historical Genres

Elizabeth Hill Boone

Like several of the other chapters in this volume, this one treats a corpus of historical production that challenges traditional or narrow definitions of written history. It has long been argued that the Aztecs and their neighbours in Mexico before the Spanish conquest of 1521 did not have history as it was usually defined, and that history as a literary and disciplinary enterprise arrived in this region with the Spaniards, when the Mexican peoples were drawn into the European historical tradition. Indeed, in most colleges and universities, the peoples, cultural expressions, and events of pre-Columbian Mesoamerica are still studied within the disciplines of anthropology, archaeology, and art history rather than history itself. It was never a question of whether the pre-Columbian Mesoamericans had records of their past, for all would agree that they did. Instead questions arose about the graphic nature of those records—which were painted in figures rather than being written in logo-syllabic signs, letters, or words—and about the truth-value of the records, which were said to be more mythical than actual.

However, as our study of the pictorial histories of Mesoamerica has increased over the last several decades, the discipline of history has broadened and expanded its purview to cover a greater range of historical production. It is now clear that the Mesoamerican phenomenon does belong within the category of historical writing and that the painted documents share many features with the historical productions of other peoples. An understanding of their graphic features and the stories they tell can help elucidate the nature of historical writing.

HISTORICAL PICTOGRAPHY

The outstanding feature of the painted histories of Mesoamerica, and what distinguishes them from almost all other historical writings (save perhaps

Map 6. The Indigenous Peoples of Pre-Conquest Latin America

Egyptian), is that they employ a figural and conventional system of graphic expression. It is an iconic script, which I call Mexican pictography. In this system the data of history—the persons, places, events, and temporal markers—are rendered as figural images that either picture or symbolize (by conventionally understood referents) what they signify. These images compose the semantic content, or vocabulary, of the system. The system's grammar or syntax is spatial, in that the arrangement of the figures on the two-dimensional surface structures the data into a specific historical expression. The narrative or presentation may proceed in a linear sequence from one painted event to another (as in a *res gestae* or chronicle) or from one year to another (as in an annals), and in these cases, the system most closely approximates the linear, sequential nature of alphabetic prose writing. However, the presentation may also assume a diagrammatic structure, in which complex spatial arrangements take precedence over linear sequencing, and the elements of the history are displayed as a tableau (as in a cartographic history). Often two of these structural paradigms are employed together.

An example that illustrates how these graphic elements record the facts of history is the well-known opening passage of the Codex Mendoza, which describes the founding of the Aztec-Mexica capital of Tenochtitlan and the early years in the city's history before it attained imperial greatness (see Fig. 28.1).[1] A border of rectangular cartouches containing sequent year-dates frames the events and dates them to the year 2 House (top left corner) and the fifty subsequent years up to 13 Reed (centre top): the years read down the left side of the page, across the bottom, and then up the right side.[2] It was on 2 House that Tenochtitlan was founded after a long migration. Prominent in the centre of the page is the place sign of Tenochtitlan, a stone (*tetl*) out of which grows a flowing nopal or prickly pear cactus whose fruit is named *nochtli*. The place sign functions phonetically to signal *te-noch*, but it is also ideographic, for the nopal cactus features prominently in the foundation story. Tenochtitlan's topography is visually described as a marshy area cut into quarters by canals and surrounded on all sides by water (Lake Texcoco). In this way the place is both named and physically characterized. Additionally, the appearance of an eagle on the cactus transforms the place sign into a sign for the actual event of foundation, for it was the sighting of a great eagle on the cactus that signalled to the Mexica that they had reached their destination and future home.

---

[1] *The Codex Mendoza*, ed. Frances Berdan and Patricia Anawalt, 4 vols. (Berkeley, 1992). I follow the usual usage of the term Aztec for the Nahuatl-speaking peoples who inhabited central Mexico in the fifteenth and early sixteenth centuries and the term Mexica for those Aztecs who lived in Mexico-Tenochtitlan.

[2] The years are designated by the combination of one of four signs (Rabbit, Reed, Flint, and House) and one of the thirteen numerals from 1 to 13. For the Aztec calendar, see the overview by Alfonso Caso, 'Calendrical Systems of Central Mexico', *Handbook of Middle American Indians*, 10 (Austin, 1971), 333–48.

FIG **28.1** Opening passage of the Codex Mendoza (2r) recording the foundation of Tenochtitlan (MS. Arch. Selden A.1, Bodleian Library, Oxford).

The ten men who led the migration are diagrammatically arranged around this place/event glyph. All are depicted in the seated pose of Aztec men, and all are accompanied by their name sign, a glyph that is attached to the head or shoulder by a line: for example, Lord Tenoch, who is sitting just to the left of Tenochtitlan's place sign, is identified by the stone and prickly pear cactus of his name sign. He is also distinguished as a priest by his black face paint, a red patch at his ear, and long hair. The reed mat on which he sits and his curled speech-scroll further signal his position as the ruler or speaker for the group. Indeed it was Tenoch who led the Mexica into Tenochtitlan. The building of the city is signalled by the structure just above the eagle and the skull rack to the right of the eagle. The militaristic nature of the Mexica and their acts of conquest that will follow are symbolized by the glyph of a round shield backed by spears, which is included just below Tenochtitlan's place sign. Thus by the use of appellatives as well as visual attributes, the significant characteristics of the people and the place of Tenochtitlan are recorded, and their presence together signifies the larger event, which is Tenochtitlan's founding.

Later events are recorded in the bottom third of the page, where it is told that the Mexica distinguished themselves by the conquest to two important polities, Colhuacan and Tenayuca. The event of conquest is signalled by a presumably Mexica warrior—replete with warrior's topknot, quilted cotton armour, weapon, and shield—capturing a smaller and weaponless enemy. This convention of conquest is paralleled by a second, complementary expression: a temple with its tall roof ajar and with flames and smoke pouring out, signifying its destruction. The locations of these conquests and the identities of the conquered are recorded by place signs. The one additional event recorded on this page is the binding of the years at the end of a fifty-two-year cycle and the drilling of the new fire that initiates a new cycle. These linked events are rendered with the year 2 Reed in the bottom right corner: by a small knotted cord that binds the Reed sign and by the picture of a drill and drilling board, complete with smoke, which is connected to the year-date by a line. This Mendoza presentation is largely diagrammatic, but within the diagram run sequences of year signs and conquests. The historian has successfully recorded the essential elements of the foundation story by combining figural representation and glyphic signification.

This kind of pictographic expression operates within the rules of its own system but, in most cases, independently from spoken language. Mexican pictography does reference the specific sounds of a particular language in appellatives—in personal names, titles, and place names—when the intended meaning could not otherwise be conveyed. Pictography, however, was largely intelligible across language barriers, as long as the reader was versed in the graphic vocabulary and grammar of the system, or, in other words, was literate in pictography. A history recorded by a speaker of Nahuatl (the Aztec language) could thus be read by historians who spoke Otomi, Popoluca, and other languages, and vice versa. Pictography's supra-linguistic nature made it perfectly appropriate for the multilingual world of late Postclassic Mexico.

THE PAINTED BOOKS

Before the conquest, the physical vehicle for pictographic writing was deer hide, *amate* paper (the inner bark of the fig tree, *Ficus petiolaris*), or cotton cloth. Hide and *amate* documents especially were configured as long strips that could run over thirteen metres in length and that were usually folded in the manner of a folding screen into individual pages; they are thus called screenfolds (see Fig. 28.2).[3]

---

[3] An average page would measure *c*.20 x 26 cm. The Codex Vienna is the longest extant historical screenfold, with fifty-two pages measuring 22 x 26 cm, to reach a total length of 1,352 cm. The

The several surviving examples that are painted on both sides of the strip (Codices Bodley, Vienna, Zouche-Nuttall) feature a separate but complementary historical account on each side. These long strips (*tiras*) and screenfolds were the preferred vehicle for the histories organized as *res gestae* (deeds done) and annals, because they particularly support a linear expression. For other structural paradigms, such as cartographies or land-based histories, the preferred vehicle was a large rectangular sheet of hide or paper or, even more commonly among the Mixtecs, Zapotecs, and their regional neighbours, a great sheet of cotton cloth (*lienzo*). Such *lienzos*, composed of multiple cotton strips sewn together, could measure as much as 375 x 425 cm (see Fig. 28.8).[4] Although the indigenous pictorial history was not conceptualized as a bound book (or codex), the term 'codex' is usually used to refer to Mexican manuscripts in the indigenous tradition that have a high pictorial content.

Four painted histories have survived from pre-conquest Mexico (Codices Bodley, Colombino-Becker, Vienna, Zouche-Nuttall). All are hide screenfolds from the Mixtec-speaking region of southern Mexico that recount the origin and genealogical history of the region's ruling dynasties. A fifth pre-conquest manuscript with historical content is the Codex Borgia, a religious-divinatory book that contains an eighteen-page narrative section that has most recently been interpreted as a cosmogony.[5] Indigenous histories continued to be painted in great quantity after the conquest, however. Some were painted on European paper for a European readership to record the history of the people they had conquered; such is the Codex Mendoza (see Fig. 28.1). Most others, however, continued to serve indigenous rulers, who marshalled the past to maintain their lands, titles, and privileges in the new colonial environment. The Spaniards also accepted these painted records as valid evidence in legal and political disputes, and indeed it was sometimes argued that the truest history was the ancient history, which, by definition, was a painted history. More than 160 of these early colonial histories have survived.

NATIVE HISTORICAL GENRES

Historical production in Mexico included cosmogonies, biographies, genealogies, dynastic histories, and histories of community kingdoms that were organized as annals and cartographies. One sees a fundamental divide between

---

physical properties of the historical documents are summarized in Elizabeth Hill Boone, *Stories in Red and Black: Pictorial Histories of the Aztecs and Mixtecs* (Austin, 2000).

[4] The largest extant *lienzo* is Coixtlahuaca Lienzo no. 2, or Lienzo Seler II, now in the Ethnologisches Museum in Berlin.

[5] Elizabeth Hill Boone, *Cycles of Time and Meaning in the Mexican Books of Fate* (Austin, 2007), 171–210.

the Aztec genres and the Mixtec genres, however, due largely to their different political systems. Aztec rulers were selected by a committee from a pool of eligible royal candidates, and although sons would often take office upon the death of their fathers, sometimes the rule passed from brother to brother, uncle to nephew, or cousin to cousin. In the Mixteca, rule was passed by primogeniture descent from father to first son, although families who controlled multiple communities would often divide control of these communities among several of their offspring. In the Mixteca, the specific lines of descent of the rulers—their birth order and the genealogies of both parents—mattered very much. One sees these differential Aztec and Mixtec concerns reflected in the histories.

Surviving Aztec histories tend to recount the events of the past that affected the *altepetl* or community kingdom as a corporate body, rather than the lives and deeds of individuals. Rulers, but not usually their wives or their children, are included in Aztec histories, because the specific facts of descent were not relevant to rule. This means that details of birth and genealogy were not as important as the actual accession to office. What was also important to the Aztecs was their long migration from a place of origin or an ancestral homeland to their subsequent capital; thus most Aztec histories treat their migration in some detail. The histories describe the founding of the capital (as in the Codex Mendoza), and then continue to cover the development and expansion of the community kingdom by noting conquests and other events of great import to the community as a whole. These Aztec stories, painted in the early colonial period, then continue to document the arrival of the Spaniards and subsequent colonial history.

The Mixtec histories, in contrast, tend to focus less on an individual community than on a dynasty of rulers, who may at various times control more than one polity. These histories emphasize lines of descent, such that husbands and wives feature equally, because both may bring control of important polities. In the genealogical histories, the birth order of inheriting children is always recognized. Mixtec stories begin not with a migration from afar but with a statement of local dynastic origin: either an account of descent from supernaturals who emerged locally from the heavens or earth, or the reception of rule from a more powerful local ruler. Whereas the Aztecs emphasize their travels before reaching their final destination, the Mixtec emphasize their deep, local roots.

COSMOGONIES

Most of the pictorial histories begin with a statement of origins, but both the Aztecs and Mixtecs, as well as their neighbours, seem also to have painted cosmogonies as separate historical accounts. These naturally reflect the differential concerns of their authors.

The fullest and most complex of these surviving cosmogonies is the obverse side of the Codex Vienna (see Fig. 28.2). As a Mixtec genesis, it focuses on the

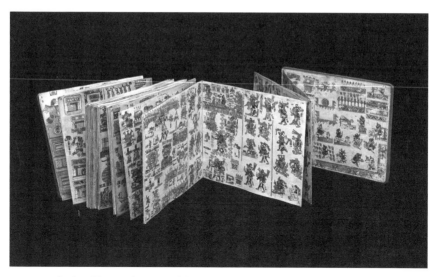

FIG **28.2** Codex Vienna (MS Vindobonensis Mexicanus I, Vienna) view of ADEVA facsimile.

formation of the physical and supernatural world out of a presumed void, the birth or appearance of supernatural entities, and the creation of all living things; it then explains significant rituals important to Mixtec cultural practice and details how the principles of polity and rulership were brought to the Mixteca. Its narrative is organized as a series of creation episodes, which move from the conceptually abstract to the more concrete and geographical as the account progresses. Like several of the other Mixtec screenfolds, the Vienna reads from the right to the left, generally in a vertical boustrophedon (back and forth) pattern, the registers defined by red lines. Its story opens in the heavens with the creation of such abstract fundamentals as song or prayer, offering, night, and day. At the bottom right of its first page (52) four unnamed human figures represent these concepts (see Fig. 28.3). They are a male with elaborate speech scrolls to signify song or prayer, followed by another who is bowing and offering powdered tobacco to indicate offerings, then a figure surrounded by twenty conventionalized stars, and a fourth bracketed by twenty conventionalized days; the sky band that frames the figures on the right and bottom of the page locates this action in the heavens before the birth of the sun.

    Thereafter the history records the birth of primordial couples, who in turn make offerings that generate a series of physical and cultural features, represented by pairs of named and unnamed figures; the birth of humans from a tree is pictorially described, as is the birth from a flint of the Mixtec culture hero Lord 9 Wind (see Fig. 28.4). The historian paints the hero attached to the great anthropomorphic flint by an umbilical cord (a statement of birth). The day of

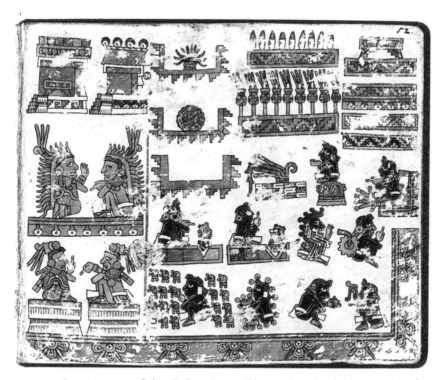

FIG 28.3 Opening page of the Codex Vienna Obverse (52): in the heavens, the first elements are song/prayer, offering, the twenty days, the twenty nights. Photograph courtesy of the Österreichische Nationalbibliothek, Vienna.

his birth is 9 Wind, which appears as nine discs and the Wind symbol (the buccal mask of the Wind God) just below the hero; he, like all Mixtecs, takes his birth day as his calendrical name. The year is 10 House, painted just to the right, with a trapeze-ray sign behind the House to indicate it is a year-date. This birth opens a long account of 9 Wind's successful efforts to bring the Mixteca and its ceremonial and political life fully into being in a series of nearly a dozen episodes. Lord 9 Wind carries down from the heavens the accoutrement of rule (see Fig. 28.5), brings into being some 200 named places, and orchestrates the creation of deities, ancestors, human conditions, things for human use, and, finally, ceremonies. The cosmogony then explains how the land was organized into coherent unities and polities. By the end of the story, the Mixteca has been created, populated, and politically organized for human use.

FIG 28.4 Lord 9 Wind is born from the great flint, Codex Vienna Obverse 49d. Drawing by John Montgomery.

No pre-conquest Aztec cosmogonies from the valley of Mexico have survived, but their features can be partially known through Nahuatl texts written alphabetically in the early colonial period, texts that surely record voicings of lost pictorials. Such are the *Historia de los Mexicanos por sus pinturas* [History of the Mexicans according to their Pictures], the *Histoire du Mexique* [History of Mexico], the *Leyenda de los Soles* [Legend of the Suns], and the beginning of the *Anales de Cuauhtitlan* [Annals of Cuauhtitlan], which variously tell of the creation and destruction of primordial ages, the birth of Aztec supernaturals, the creation of the sun and moon, the first counting of the calendar, and the origin of humans.[6] Pictorial fragments of lost cosmogonies are preserved in the Codex Vaticanus A/Ríos, a cultural encyclopedia made for European eyes, which contains paintings of heavenly and earthly layers, as well as the four primordial ages, all later annotated in Italian by one of the friars.[7]

Representing the tradition in the Puebla Valley is the pre-conquest Codex Borgia, a ritual-divinatory manuscript that seems to contain an eighteen-page

---

[6] A. María Garibay, *Teogonia e historia de los mexicanos* (Mexico City, 1979); and John Bierhorst, *History and Mythology of the Aztecs: The Codex Chimalpopoca* (Tucson, 1992).

[7] Ferdinand Anders and Maarten Jansen, *Religión, costumbres e historia de los antiguos mexicanos . . . Códice Vaticano A* (Graz and Mexico City, 1996).

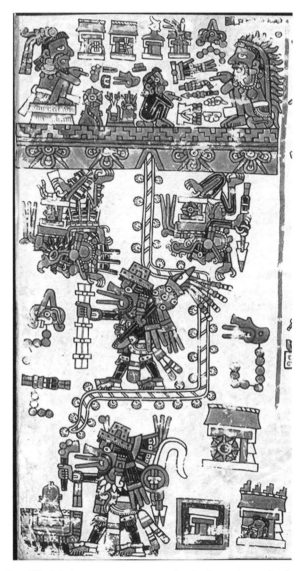

FIG 28.5 Lord 9 Wind brings accoutrements of rule down from the heavens, Codex Vienna Obverse 48c. Photograph courtesy of the Österreichische Nationalbibliothek, Vienna.

cosmogony. Its narrative is divided into eight episodes, each presented pictorially on a page or across a two- or four-page spread. These episodes begin with the first burst of creative energy and the establishment of fundamental concepts and essences, and include the beginnings of sacrality and cult, the sun, humans, maize (human sustenance), human sacrifice, and other ceremonies, ending with the drilling of new fire that initiates the world that humans will occupy.

One might consider these cosmogonies to be mythical rather than historical, but the Mesoamericans conceptualized them as being part of their historical past. Dennis Tedlock coined the useful term 'mythistory' for such creation stories as these and the *Popol Vuh*, a Maya genesis.[8]

MIXTEC GENEALOGICAL HISTORIES

The Mixtec histories created in the form of screenfolds are largely genealogical. They document the histories of the ruling families, describing the sources of their right to rule, the founding of polities, and, importantly, how rule was passed down through the generations. These histories trace the biological descent of the ruler from ancient (often supernatural) ancestors who emerge from the earth, trees, or the heavens; they then follow the family line to the then-present (contemporaneous with the manuscript's painting) or to some significant earlier period. Interspersed with these long genealogical passages are historical episodes about the military and diplomatic exploits of the rulers as they defend their communities or enlarge their territory through warfare and marriage. This combination of genealogy and *res gestae* accounting allows the histories effectively to explain in detail how the various royal families are interrelated and how rule is distributed among them.

The perspective of the histories is decidedly local. The stories they tell are not sweeping accounts of the Mixtec past but narrowly partisan records about an individual dynasty and its control over communities. For example, the Codex Colombino-Becker, painted for the ruler of Tututepec on the coast, tells a coastal version of the exploits and conquests of the great ruler Lord 8 Deer, whereas the Codex Selden from Jaltepec includes 8 Deer only as the parent of a wife who married into the Jaltepec line. Although the Selden history was painted after 1556, more than three decades after the Spanish conquest, it does not include the Spanish arrival or anything European, because these foreign elements were not part of the genealogical story.

These Mixtec screenfold histories are graphically organized into registers that may run horizontally across two facing pages or vertically, and the narrative can read bottom to top, left to right, or right to left in a boustrophedon pattern.

---

[8] *Popol Vuh: The Definitive Edition of the Mayan Book of the Dawn of Life and the Glories of Gods and Kings*, ed. and trans. Dennis Tedlock (New York, 1985), 64.

Events follow generally in temporal sequence, although they often proceed in chapters, which can jump forward or back in time, such that one chapter may carry one story to a certain point, and the next chapter may pick up a parallel story from its beginning and bring that story up to the same point. Two examples relating to the dynasty of Lord 8 Deer, from two different manuscripts, illustrate something of the range.

A genealogical passage from the Codex Zouche-Nuttall, which identifies 8 Deer's immediate ancestry, siblings, and offspring, has features typical of many genealogies (see Fig. 28.6). Here the narrative reads right to left in a vertical boustrophedon, beginning in the upper right, with the marriage statement of Lord 5 Crocodile (8 Deer's father) and Lady 9 Eagle, who sit facing each other in a palace. Immediately following such marriage statements the Mixtec histories always record the offspring: here they are two sons, 12 Movement and 3 Water, and a daughter, 6 Lizard. A second, partial marriage statement records 5 Crocodile's subsequent marriage to Lady 11 Water, who is pictured seated alone in a palace at the bottom of the page. This statement is again immediately followed

FIG **28.6** Genealogical record of the parentage and lineage of Lord 8 Deer, Codex Zouche-Nuttall 26. Photograph courtesy of the British Museum.

by offspring: the son 8 Deer and another son and daughter. With 8 Deer's immediate genealogy established, the historian then presents 8 Deer's own marriage statement on the left centre of the page, and immediately thereafter the births of his two sons. Although Lord 8 Deer and the other Mixtec persons who figure in the painted histories are primarily recognized historically by their calendrical names, each one also has a personal name, which can be manifest as a physical or costume attribute or an independent glyph. Lord 8 Deer's personal name is Jaguar or Jaguar Claw, and therefore he is often costumed in a jaguar pelt and has a jaguar's claw next to his image. In some of the genealogical histories, such successive statements of descent can be quite long.

Interspersed with genealogies are events that secure or increase territory or otherwise affect the dynasty's well-being. The exploits of Lord 8 Deer figure prominently in the Mixtec histories because he conquered a great number of other polities, killed many of the rulers, and himself married their wives and daughters. This meant that many of the subsequent ruling families traced their lines back to 8 Deer. A typical record of some of 8 Deer's conquests is in the Codex Bodley, the narrative of which is organized in horizontal registers (see Fig. 28.7). In the Bodley, the historian first presents the date of each event and then the event itself; the brief excerpt illustrated by Figure 28.7 thus begins in the lower right, dated with the year 6 Reed and day 13 Flower. The historian then records 8 Deer's conquest of a place or places identified by a compound toponym and the offering he makes to the supernatural Lady 9 Grass of Place of the Skull (Chalcatongo) (far left). Footprints then mark his subsequent travel to Apoala, where the rulers who sit facing him grant 8 Deer the lordship of the coastal community of Tututepec (Stone Bird), whose place sign is pictured just to the right. There the historian records 8 Deer seated on an attached platform, in a statement of rule.

FIG **28.7** Exploits of Lord 8 Deer, Codex Bodley 9cd (from *Codex Bodley*, ed. Alfonso Caso [Mexico City, 1960]).

The pattern in the Codex Bodley, as it is in most of the Mixtec genealogical histories, is to present the birth of a ruler, followed by his or her exploits that defend or increase the political holdings, and then to show the marriage and offspring, after which the narrative passes to the next generation. In the Mixtec histories, births are always shown, but deaths are omitted unless they were politically important.

These genealogical histories have linear, sequential character, where one event follows another. For each event, the particulars of person, place, act, and date are usually given, unless the date or place is assumed according to its narrative context. It was therefore quite easy for the historian to change any of these classes of data, to move from one person's actions to another's and to relocate the action. Being event-oriented histories, or what I call *res gestae*, these stories read like chronicles. They begin with a statement of emergence and usually end with the rule of the royal person whom we assume commissioned them.

LIENZOS AND *TIRAS* FROM OAXACA AND SOUTHERN PUEBLA

Histories painted on great cotton sheets (*lienzos*) and on long strips of hide or paper that is rolled rather than folded (*tiras*) together comprise another genre of historical production from Oaxaca and southern Puebla (see Fig. 28.8). Some of these documents refer to the same places, dynasties, and events as do the genealogical-historical screenfolds, and they are the products of the same and neighbouring people, but they focus less on genealogical details and personal action and more on the physical territory controlled by a ruling line. They are histories of an individual polity rather than an individual dynasty.

As these histories conceptualize it, a polity is composed of three principal things: a territory that has established borders, one or more lineages of rulers who successively inherit the territory or territories, and an origin story composed of a series of events that usually begin with supernaturals and end with the founding of the polity by the first rulers. These, then, are the features that make up the histories. The *tiras*, being linear, generally concentrate on the origin story (up to and including the foundation event) and on the lineage, whereas the *lienzos*, being physically broad and expansive, also link these features to a specifically delineated territory.

Compositionally, the *lienzos* and *tiras* are looser than the screenfold histories because they do not usually employ registers. The events that make up their stories are thus not confined to a tight linear sequence, which reads back and forth across pages. Instead, action and information can flow more easily over the sheets and rolls. Lacking the graphic denseness of the screenfolds, they concentrate on highlighting visually the most important events, which are the beginning

FIG **28.8** Lienzo of Tequixtepec 1. Photograph courtesy of Ross Parmenter.

and the foundation of the polity. These documents are intended to be displayed and read only when the cotton sheet or the roll is fully open, which means that readers can and must see the whole of the story at a single glance. Readers will thus have the broader perspective in mind as they read and interpret individual passages, which allows them to note and follow individual details but at the same time to understand how these episodes fit into the broader framework. The stories recounted on the *lienzos* and *tiras* therefore have a coherency and a narrative completeness that the *res gestae* screenfolds do not.

An example is the Lienzo of Tequixtepec 1 (see Fig. 28.8), which presents the polity of Tequixtepec (Hill of the Shell) as a cartographic entity in the top two-thirds of a great cotton sheet. The toponym of the town itself is centrally located and features the two ruling couples sitting on jaguar-skin thrones in a statement of rule. On the edges of the cloth, a cartographic rectangle links the place signs that define Tequixtepec's territory. The history and lineage of this town are recorded in the lower third of the sheet, beginning with the mythic past at the bottom, followed by the succession of ruling couples leading up to the map. In other *lienzos* these ruler lists are stacked vertically and read from bottom to top in a straight line, but the Tequixtepec historian may have felt that a horizontal arrangement allowed greater freedom to show the territory of Tequixtepec as a distinct entity.

Such *lienzos* are essentially town charters. They tell of the ancient, mythic history of the dynasty, the long succession of the rulers, and the geographic situation of the town itself, tying the present community to its sacred past and its rulers. The few towns, such as Tequixtepec, that are fortunate still to hold their sixteenth-century *lienzos*, guard and prize them as repositories of their ancient history and their rights to their land.

ACCOUNTS OF MIGRATION AND FOUNDATION IN THE CENTRAL VALLEYS

Cartographic histories were also produced in the central valleys of Mexico and northern Puebla. They share some features of the *lienzos* created to the south, for they are based on a broad cartographic presentation of territory, which is sometimes defined by a ring of boundaries. The historians either joined this cartograph to a *res gestae* narrative that leads up to it, or they wove the narrative into the cartograph itself. In both cases, a conceptual map is combined with a sequence or sequences of events related to it. Like the Oaxacan *lienzos*, the central Mexican map-based histories focus on the founding of polities.

The central Mexican histories, however, participate in the Nahuatl or Aztec historical tradition and express the political and historical concerns of those people. These are not stories of royal dynasties but stories about the people of the community kingdom, and they record the significant actions of the clan and tribal leaders and their followers. Generally there is little emphasis on genealogy or the display of long lists of rulers. Wives and children are largely absent except in the three Texcocan manuscripts (the Codex Xolotl, Mapa Tlotzin, and Mapa Qinatzin), and only the Mapa Tlotzin has a discrete list of rulers. Instead these cartographic histories describe the migration of people from a sacred or idealized place of origin, the perils and events along the journey to a new land, and their arrival at their final homeland. The histories then record how the people found the new polity, conquer enemies as needed, and consolidate and define their territory in order to create an independent *altepetl* or community kingdom.

The migrations originate in a sacred, earthly location. Most groups traced their origins to Chicomoztoc (Seven Caves), a legendary place of origin from which their clan leaders and ancestors emerged, and Chicomoztoc figures prominently in many migration accounts as a great, multi-pocketed opening in the earth. Concurrently, the Mexica Aztecs and a number of their neighbours traced their origins to the idealized homeland known as Aztlan, an island city in the middle of a lake—a place of abundance, and a home of reeds and herons. These two points of origin were not mutually exclusive, however, for several histories include Aztlan as the beginning point and Chicomoztoc as a secondary and subsequent place of emergence; some other histories merge the two. The stories reflect the generalized central Mexican understanding that their ancestors emerged from Chicomoztoc, but also that the Aztecs were special in originating from Aztlan. The essence of both variant stories is that these central Mexican people had migrated long distances, undergoing great hardships, to reach their present homelands.

Once this migration is recounted, the Mexican cartographies record the founding of polities. Usually the histories emphasize the place sign of the new community by enlarging it and locating it prominently, and they flank it with images of the leaders who led the people to that place. Such is the story told on the opening page of the Codex Mendoza (see Fig. 28.1). Occasionally the historians also encircle the presentation with the place signs of the territory's boundaries, joined together by a circuit of footprints to reference an act of delimiting territory.

The migratory journey is usually presented as a circuit or itinerary that follows a sequence of locations (represented by their place signs), the path marked by footprints. As with all itinerary projections, only those locations that were actually visited are included, because in these projections place only exists by virtue of the movement through it. When the destination is reached, however, the territory is often presented as a spatial abstraction, like a map in the modern sense, and any movement through this territory can be charted from one pre-existing location to another.

An example is the Mapa Sigüenza, which traces on a sheet of *amate* paper the migration of the Mexica Aztecs from their ancestral homeland of Aztlan to their new capital of Tenochtitlan (see Fig. 28.9). The right side of the sheet and the top third of the left side are devoted to the itinerary of the journey, which begins with Aztlan in the upper right and follows a footprinted path from place to place until the Valley of Mexico is reached on the left side. At this point, the historian foregoes the itinerary structure to offer a map of the wet and dry lands that surround Tenochtitlan. The place signs painted here are now in geographic relation to each other, and the lake itself is pictorially characterized as a swamp cut through by canals and dotted with rushes and reeds, with the place sign of Tenochtitlan at the centre.

The migration was a principal aspect of Aztec self-definition and was featured in almost all their accounts of the past. There was not just one migration, however, but many. Each group of people distinguished its own migration from the others. The Mexica Aztec accounts, for example, name the other communities who also left Aztlan, but they take pains to stress the different times of departure and the different routes they travelled. It was important that each community have its own, separate migration. Indeed in the colonial period, those polities that could successfully claim a separate migration were better able

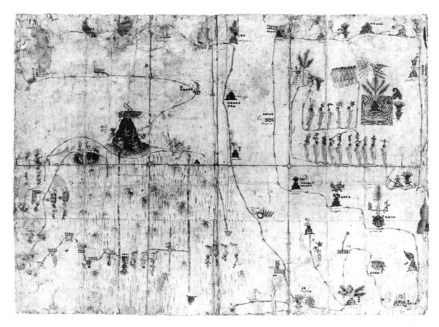

FIG **28.9** Mapa Sigüenza, tracing the Aztec migration from Aztlan to Tenochtitlan. CNCA.-INAH.-MEX; reproduced with permission of the Instituto Nacional de Antropología e Historia.

to maintain their independence and *altepetl* status, for they were thereby able to assert that they had been autonomous polities from the very beginning.

AZTEC ANNALS

The annals painted for Aztec *altepetl* differ structurally from all the other histories. Whereas the Mixtec genealogical histories are organized as tight sequences of events, and the cartographies link sequences of events to spatial geographies, the annals are driven by time. They present the passage of time as a continuous series of year-dates joined together side by side to form a year-count ribbon. This ribbon is the armature to which events are then linked: the events are recorded beside the appropriate year and are often graphically connected to the year by a line. The Aztecs called this history *xiuhpolhualli* (year count, year relation), *xiuhtlacuilolli* (year writing), *xiuhamatl* (year paper or year book), and *xiuhtonalamatl* (year day book). Physically the traditional indigenous annals were

FIG **28.10** Aztec imperial annals for the years 4 Flint through 13 House (1496–1505), Codex Aubin 39v-40r. Photograph courtesy of the British Museum.

created as long strips of paper (which could be rolled or folded as a screenfold), along the length of which the year count ran uninterrupted. Spatial economies, however, caused some annalists to cluster together in blocks those groups of years in which nothing notable occurred. Colonial annalists who painted on European paper arranged their year counts to fit the individual book pages (see Fig. 28.10). Regardless of the exact configuration of the year count, however, the year-dates were the foundation on which all the other information depended.

The history recorded in the annals could include both the migratory and imperial past as well as the more immediate situation after the arrival of the Spanish. Some annals begin their story with Aztlan and trace the migration, paralleling in a general sense the history in the Mapa Sigüenza, but focusing on the succession of place signs and the specific years these places were reached. Some, such as the Codex Mendoza, begin with the founding of Tenochtitlan and continue to record events leading up to the conquest; other annals include both. It is also in the annals in particular that one sees the painted historical record continuing past the conquest and into the second half of the sixteenth century. These latter annals, begun perhaps in the 1550s–70s, reflect back on a pre-conquest past that is fully completed but still carries political currency in the new colonial world. Many of the annals were amended over time: kept up to date and augmented with new information and sometimes altered with the knowledge of hindsight.

The information they contained was the kind of material that would have been of interest to the polity as a whole. The range of events included the accessions and deaths of the rulers, conquests, significant building programmes, the binding of the years at the end of a fifty-two-year cycle and the drilling of the new fire, extraordinary celebrations (such as the dedication of the Aztec Templo Mayor in 1486), and natural and climactic phenomena of a dramatic and far-reaching nature, such as drought, pestilence, earthquakes, floods, and eclipses. All of these are events that would have affected the community as a whole, for these annals are *altepetl* histories, rather than dynastic histories or personal histories. The personal exploits of rulers are rarely included unless they affected the polity as a whole. The rulers appear in the annals when they accede to the throne and when they die, but their births, marriages, and offspring are not included, except for the occasional birth statement (devoid of parents) in the Texcocan annals. Conquests are presented as statements of fact rather than the results of individual action on the part of a ruler.

Graphically the annals are more conventional than figural in their presentation of data. By this I mean that events are usually indicated succinctly by glyphic indicators rather than being illustrated by figures engaging in an activity. An example is the Codex Aubin, an early colonial annals painted on European paper *c.*1576 and subsequently annotated with explanatory glosses in Nahuatl (see Fig. 28.10). Here the conquest of an enemy polity is signalled by that polity's place sign accompanied by a shield and obsidian-edged club. The accession of a ruler is indicated by his seated pose on a reed throne, while wearing his pointed turquoise diadem. The death of a ruler is recorded by the appearance of his mortuary bundle. Most of the events in the annals are local, in that they are assumed to pertain to the place whose history it is; that place is rarely indicated because any reader would already know it. When an event occurs elsewhere, the location is identified by its place sign. In the annals, the most significant factor of each event is less its location than its timing. Each event is treated as if it had the same historical weight, for the annals are indifferent to causality or to the larger sweep of history.

The annals record the Spanish conquest as a series of events that occur over several years. A new set of actors and a slightly different range of events is introduced by means of new iconographic conventions, but the annals do not themselves change the way they treat history before and after the conquest. There is little sense that the end of an era has been reached; instead the annals effectively bring the Spaniards into what is still an Aztec story. The annalist of the Tira de Tepechpan (see Fig. 28.11), for example, documents the arrival of the Spaniards in the year 1 Reed by picturing a standing Cortés below the year sign and the cross and dove of the Holy Spirit above it. He next records the smallpox epidemic, the burning of Tenochtitlan, the sequent deaths and accessions of

FIG **28.11** Conquest events in the Tira de Tepechpan, 15. Photograph courtesy of the Bibliothèque Nationale de France, Paris.

Mexica rulers, and the acknowledgement of indigenous lands and rights by a seated Cortés (sitting in the hip chair of authority).

As these colonial annalists continue to record events in the sixteenth century, they document a gradual process of adjustment and hybridity. Indigenous lords come to be represented sitting in the hip chair rather than on a reed mat and they come to wear a European crown rather than the pre-conquest turquoise diadem. The Spaniards are represented speaking via speech scrolls, they are identified by name glyphs, and their figures are highly conventionalized. Conquest is still indicated by a shield and club or spears, but in the colonial period it is more often a European shield and a metal-tipped spear or metal sword. Mexican historical pictography expands and adjusts in order to accommodate the new reality. The annals continue uninterrupted until they simply break off at the time of their writing. There is no narrative closure, because such accounts are, theoretically, endlessly ongoing: they have no climax, no finale. Their fundamental message, if a single message can be read into them, is one of continuity. The Aztec world, which began at Aztlan or Chicomoztoc, continues to the present, and the Spaniards who arrived in 1519 are only part of the ongoing story.

PAINTED HISTORIES IN COLONIAL MEXICO

The pictorial history remained a valuable historical form throughout the six-teenth century and into the seventeenth, although there was a decline in produc-tion after the great epidemics of the 1570s. But those indigenous rulers who still possessed their old histories continued to update them. The annals of the Codex Aubin (see Fig. 28.10), for example, were updated with alphabetic entries as late as 1608. Pictorial histories carried semiotic and legal weight for indigenous communities for even longer, however. In the late seventeenth and early eight-eenth centuries—when towns in rural Mexico were in danger of being reduced via *composiciones*—some towns that had lost their painted histories had new ones fashioned: not quite fakes, but not quite authentically old either. Created on *amate* paper, these so-called Techialoyan codices contain pictures executed in an illusionistic style and alphabetic texts in an archaizing Nahuatl, which describe the towns' foundation, boundaries, and history. They were created to function as land titles, and their pictorial content was clearly important to their success. There are also instances in which pre-conquest histories were reworked in the colonial period in order to make of them distinctly new histories. The Codex Colombino-Becker, for example, is a pre-conquest Mixtec screenfold that was reconfigured and cut up in the sixteenth century for reuse by two separate polities. One set of fragments was brought forth in a boundary dispute in 1717, and the other set came to be presented as a land document in an 1852 case involving another town entirely. It was the pictorial nature and the antiquity of these documents that gave them their validity. Even in the twentieth century, towns that still have their pictorial histories look to them to document their land and autonomy. Although by this century historical pictography had long ceased to exist as a living graphic form, the concept of a pictorial history as a container of knowledge and truth has still remained valid.

TIMELINE/KEY DATES

1063–1115 Life of the Mixtec lord 8 Deer, Jaguar Claw of Tilantongo
1325 Traditional date of founding of Mexico-Tenochtitlan
1375 Acamapichtli becomes first *tlatoani* ('speaker' or king) of the Aztec Mexica
1428 Establishment of the Triple Alliance ('Aztec') Empire

1487 Dedication of renovated Templo Mayor (Great Temple) in Mexico-Tenochtitlan

1519 Hernando Cortés lands on Veracruz coast and begins invasion of Mexico

1521 Spanish conquest of Mexico-Tenochtitlan

KEY HISTORICAL SOURCES

Caso, Alfonso, 'El Mapa de Teozacoalco', *Cuadernos Americanos*, 47:5 (1949), 145–81.

—— *Interpretación del Códice Selden/Interpretation of the Codex Selden*, accompanied by a facsimile of the codex (Mexico City, 1964).

—— *Interpretación del Códice Colombino/Interpretation of the Codex Colombino*, accompanied by a facsimile of the codex (Mexico City, 1966).

Castañeda de la Paz, María, *Pintura de la peregrinación de los Culhuaque-Mexitin (El Mapa de Sigüenza)* (Zinacantepec and Mexico City, 2006).

Codex Bodley, ed. Maarten Jansen and Gambina Aurora Pérez Jiménez (London, 2005).

Codex en Cruz, ed. Charles Dibble, 2 vols. (Salt Lake City, 1981).

Codex Mendoza, ed. Frances Berdan and Patricia R. Anawalt, 4 vols. (Berkeley, 1992).

'Codex Mexicanus. Bibliothèque Nationale de Paris, Nos. 23–24', ed. Ernst Mengin, *Journal de la Société des Américanistes*, 41:2 (1951), 387–498, atlas.

Codex Telleriano-Remensis, ed. Eloise Quiñones-Keber (Austin, 1995).

Codex Zouche-Nuttall, British Museum, London (Add. MS. 39671) (Graz, 1987).

Códice Alfonso Caso: La vida de 8-Venado, Gara de Tigre (Colombino-Becker I), intro. Miguel León-Portilla (Mexico City, 1996).

Códice Azcatitlan, ed. Robert Barlow and Michel Graulich (Paris, 1995).

Códice Vindobonensis: Origen e historia de los reyes mixtecos, ed. Ferdinand Anders, Maarten Jansen, and Gabina Aurora Pérez Jiménez (Mexico City, 1992).

Códice Zouche-Nuttall. Cronica mixteca: El rey 8-Venado, Garra de Jaguar, y la dinastía de Teozacualco-Zaachila, ed. Ferdinand Anders, Maarten Jansen, and Gambina Aurora Pérez Jiménez (Mexico City, 1992).

Códice Xolotl, ed. Charles Dibble, 2 vols. (Mexico City, 1980).

Geschichte der Azteken: Codex Aubin und verwandte Dokumente, ed. and trans. Walter Lehmann and Gerdt Kutscher (Berlin, 1981).

Historia de la nación Mexicana: Reproducción a todo color del Códice de 1576 (Códice Aubin, ed. Charles Dibble (Madrid, 1963).

Historia Tolteca-Chichimeca, ed. Paul Kirchhoff, Lina Odena Güemes, and Luis Reyes García (Mexico City 1976).

Mohar Betancourt, Luz María, *Códice Mapa Quinatzin: Justicia y derechos humanos en el México antiguo* (Mexico City, 2004).

Tira de Tepechpan: Códice colonial procedente del valle de México, ed. Xavier Noguez, 2 vols. (Mexico City, 1978).

BIBLIOGRAPHY

Boone, Elizabeth Hill, *Stories in Red and Black: Pictorial Histories of the Aztecs and Mixtecs* (Austin, 2000).

——(ed.), *Painted Books and Indigenous Knowledge in Mesoamerica: Manuscript Studies in Honor of Mary Elizabeth Smith* (New Orleans, 2005).

Byland, Bruce and Pohl, John M. D., *In the Realm of 8 Deer: The Archaeology of the Mixtec Codices* (Norman, Okla., 1994).

Carrasco, David and Sessions, Scott (eds.), *Cave, City, and Eagle's Nest: An Interpretative Journey through the Mapa de Cuauhtinchan No. 2* (Albuquerque, 2007).

Caso, Alfonso, *Reyes y reinos de la Mixteca*, 2 vols. (Mexico City, 1977–9).

Corona Núñez, José, *Antigüedatdes de México, basadas en la recopilación de Lord Kingsborough*, 4 vols. (Mexico City, 1964–7).

Diel, Lori Boornazian, *The Tira de Tepechpan: Negotiating Place under Aztec and Spanish Rule* (Austin, 2008).

Glass, John B, 'A Survey of Native Middle American Pictorial Manuscripts', in Wauchope and Cline (eds.), *Handbook of Middle American Indians*, 3–80.

——with Robertson, Donald, 'A Census of Native Middle American Pictorial Manuscripts', in Wauchope and Cline (eds.), *Handbook of Middle American Indians*, 81–252.

Harvey, H. R., 'Techialoyan Codices: Seventeenth-Century Indian Land Titles in Central Mexico', in Victoria Bricker and Ronald Spores (eds.), *Handbook of Middle American Indians*, Supplement 4 (Austin, 1986), 153–64.

Jansen, Maarten, *Huisi tacu: studio interpretativo de un libro mixteco antiguo: Codex Vindobonensis Mexicanus I*, 2 vols. (Amsterdam, 1982).

——'The Search for History in the Mixtec Codices', *Ancient Mesoamerica*, 1:1 (1990), 99–112.

——Kröfges, Peter and Oudijk, Michel (eds.), *The Shadow of Monte Alban: Politics and Historiography in Postclassic Oaxaca* (Leiden, 1998).

Nicholson, H. B., 'Pre-Hispanic Central Mexican Historiography', in *Investigaciones contemporáneas sobre historia de México: Memorias de la Tercera Reunión de historiadores mexicanos y norteamericnos, Oaxtepec, Morelos, 4–7 de noviembre de 1969* (Mexico City, 1971), 38–81.

Pohl, John, *The Politics of Symbolism in the Mixtec Codices* (Nashville, 1994).

Robertson, Donald, *Mexican Manuscript Painting of the Early Colonial Period: The Metropolitan Schools* (New Haven, 1959).

——'Techialoyan Manuscripts and Paintings, with a Catalog', in Wauchope and Cline (eds.), *Handbook of Middle American Indians* (Austin, 1975), 253–80.

Smith, Mary Elizabeth, *Picture Writing from Ancient Southern Mexico: Mixtec Place Signs and Maps* (Norman, Okla., 1973).

——'Why the Second Codex Selden Was Painted', in Joyce Marcus and Judith F. Zeitlin (eds.), *The Caciques and Their People: A Volume in Honor of Ronald Spores* (Ann Arbor, 1994), 111–41.

Smith, Michael E., 'The Aztlan Migrations of the Nahuatl Chronicles: Myth or History?' *Ethnohistory*, 31:3 (1984), 153–86.

Wauchope, Robert and Cline, Howard F. (eds.), *Handbook of Middle American Indians*, vol. 14 (Austin, 1975).

Chapter 29

Alphabetical Writing in Mesoamerican Historiography

José Rabasa

According to an internal date in a history commonly known as the *Anales de Tlatelolco* [Annals of Tlatelolco], the Nahua from Central Mexico adopted the Latin alphabet as early as 1528. James Lockhart, however, has argued against this date on the basis that it took at least two decades before a system of alphabetical writing could have been devised for Nahuatl: 'The notion that by 1528 Spanish ecclesiastics could have learned the language well enough to have developed such a refined orthography, much less to train expert indigenous calligraphers capable of writing great amounts of complex prose, is so improbable as to verge on the ridiculous.'[1] Rafael Tena also questions this early date, but speculates that 'one or more eyewitnesses, knowledgeable of the ancient history, could have recorded some historical news that were later used by the final compilers'.[2] Tena's argument for a later date is based on the gothic script and the paper made of bark from *amate* trees, as well as the Nahuatl grammatical forms used in the different versions that have come down to us. Tena, however, also considers that the Nahuatl forms can be understood as interventions and modifications by the scribes and not necessarily as indications of the time of production. After all, Tena dates the manuscript—catalogued in the Bibliothèque Nationale de France as Ms 22 bis—towards 1620, and specifies that the 1528 date only appears in Section VI dedicated to the Spanish conquest. Compared to Lockhart's strident dismissal, Tena's dating is, indeed, more cautious.

We know that Fray Pedro de Gante, among other early Franciscan friars, taught young Nahua to write and read Spanish as early as 1523, but Lockhart assumes that the use of the alphabet for writing Nahuatl had to be developed first by the missionaries and then diffused among the Nahua. One wonders, however, if once the principle of phonological script was understood, it was not a matter of

---

[1] James Lockhart, 'Introduction', in *We People Here: Nahuatl Accounts of the Conquest of Mexico*, ed. and trans. Lockhart (Berkeley, 1993), 39.
[2] Rafael Tena, 'Presentación', in *Anales de Tlatelolco*, ed. and trans. Tena (Mexico, 2004), 14.

applying its principles to Nahuatl, especially given that in sixteenth-century central Mexico we find a proliferation of wild forms of literacy, that is, usages of the alphabet outside the supervision of missionaries and bureaucrats. Wild literacy suggests that alphabetical writing in sixteenth- and seventeenth-century Mexico was intimately bound to the recording of voice. Whether we take 1528 or sometime in the 1540s as the initial date of Nahuatl writings, the fact is that Lockhart also links usages of the alphabet to the recording of voice, in particular to regional accents and inflections. It is also important to note that the usage of Latin script did not mean the adoption of European historical genre, but rather the retention of forms of memorializing and narrating the past that can be traced in pictographic writing and the kinds of verbal performance they called forth.

Beyond the 'incorporation of America to Occidental culture', I propose a two-way street in which the circulation of cultural and material goods also entailed the incorporation of Europe into Mesoamerican culture.[3] It is not just the fact that this volume is part of a history of historical writing that leads us to address the question of the incorporation of Europe into Mesoamerica. Given the centrality of writing in processes of colonization, the adoption of the alphabet offers a particularly productive place for examining the limits of colonization and for questioning the tendency to assume that Nahua writers, by the mere fact of using the alphabet, would exemplify acculturated subjects. The concept of *echography* of voice offers a way to approximate recordings of speech in which one can isolate tone, timber, individual and collective authorship, internal thoughts, and cries.[4] The objective no longer concerns the differentiation of oral and literate culture, but rather seeks to identify categories that enable us to reflect on the spoken in the written, and beyond the stenographic record to isolate the internal voices exemplifying a distinct Nahuatl lettered culture. In speaking of echographies of voice in Nahuatl writing we have the opportunity to observe the ways in which a European technology was incorporated into Meso-america. Needless, to say this project also calls for a consideration of the ambiguity of such a process: are we considering one more modality of the incorporation of America into European culture? Do we face the task of developing a theoretical apparatus for understanding the presence of what is European in Mesoamerican semantic spaces? In addressing these questions, I concentrate on a few representative texts rather than offer an exhaustive approximation to the corpus. Suffice it

---

[3] See, for instance, Edmundo O'Gorman, *Fundamentos de la historia de América* (Mexico, 1942); and Serge Gruzinski, *The Conquest of Mexico: The Incorporation of Indian Societies into the Western World, 16th–18th Centuries*, trans. Eileen Carrigan (Cambridge 1993).

[4] I derive the concept of *echography* from Jacques Derrida and Bernard Stiegler, *Echographies of Television: Filmed Interviews*, trans. Jennifer Bajorek (Malden, Mass., 2002). In speaking of echographies of voice in Nahuatl writing we would trace the voice whose occasion remains lost, absent, yet accessible through multiple practices of reading and re-enactment. For a more elaborate discussion of the concept of echography and the Nahuatl histories I discuss in this chapter, see José Rabasa, 'Echografías de la voz en la historiografía nahua', *Historia y Teoría*, 25 (2006), 105–51.

to be known that hundreds of documents in Nahuatl remain dormant in archives in Mexico and in libraries abroad. In the 'key historical sources' section I provide a list of texts that complements those discussed in this chapter. In reading Nahuatl histories, this chapter places an emphasis on their significance as rhetorical and literary artefacts rather than on evaluating them as sources of information about the pre-Columbian or, for that matter, the colonial world.

Alphabetical histories in Nahuatl record a wide range of speech genre (dialogues, songs, narratives, itineraries, and myths) associated with the depicted events in pictographic histories. Whereas pictographic texts, which Elizabeth Hill Boone studies in Chapter 28 in this volume, tend to lack the verbal component in the performance of the pictographs, alphabetical texts tend to lack the pictographic grounds. This chapter examines the alphabetical records of voice in the *Historia tolteca-chichimeca* [History of the Totlteca-Chichimeca] (*c.*1547–60), Fernando Alvarado Tezozómoc's *Chronica mexicayotl* [Chronicle of Mexican Things] (1609), and Domingo Francisco de San Antón Muñón Chimalpahin Cuauhtlehuanitzin's *Relaciones and the Diario* (last entry is on 14 October 1615), among other texts by Chimalpahin, arguably the most accomplished Nahua historian. These authors belong to different locations and historiographical traditions (Quauhtinchan in the valley of Puebla, Mexico-Tenochtitlan, and Chalco on the edge of the volcanoes Ixtacihuatl and Popocatepetl in Mexico City). These texts enable us to trace multiple voices that range from stenographic-like recordings of speech-events to 'literary' texts in which Nahua 'authors' inscribe their internal voice. One of the main features in these histories, even in Chimalpahin, at least in his *Relaciones* (*c.*1620), is multiple authorship.[5] Even if we find instances of writing Nahuatl without reference to a speech event—that is, writing that records internal voice—in Tezozómoc and in a much more developed mode in Chimalpahin's *Relaciones*, it is in Chimalpahin's *Diario* where we find a sustained recording of and reflection on observed events that no longer refer to a verbal performance from which the written accounts originated. The non-conventional mode of producing entries and the hybrid nature of the *Diario* led its recent editors and translators into English to give it the title *Annals of His Time*. A most curious choice given that Chimalpahin, with the exception of a chronology of the history of Mexico-Tenochtitlan,

---

[5] These texts were never published in the sixteenth and seventeenth centuries when they were written. Note that the version of the *Chronica Mexicayotl* that I will use was found in 1983 among papers by Chimalpahin at the Bible Society Collection at Cambridge University, England. See Domingo de San Antón Muñón Chimalpahin Quauhtlehuanitzin, *Codex Chimalpahin: Society and Politics in Mexico Tenochtitlan, Tlatelolco, Texcoco, Culhuacan, and Other Nahua Altepetl in Central Mexico*, ed. and trans. Arthur J. O. Anderson and Susan Schroeder, 2 vols. (Norman, Okla., 1997). There is another edition of Fernando Alvarado Tezozómoc, *Crónica Mexicáyotl*, ed. and trans. Adrián León (Mexico, 1949). The spelling of names and titles of works lacks uniformity, thus Chimalpahin (as he wrote his name) is sometimes hispanicized by placing accents as in Chimalpaín and Chimalpáhin.

follows the days and inclusively marks the hours in some entries. I will return to the *Diario* below.

Before examining these great Nahuatl historical artefacts, I will briefly describe two collections of texts that further exemplify the diversity of writing comprising the corpus of colonial Nahuatl historiography. The *huehuetlatolli* (speech of the elders), which the great Franciscan ethnographer Fray Bernardino de Sahagún compiles in Book 6 of his *Historia general de las cosas de la Nueva España* [General History of the Things of New Spain] (*c.*1579), known as the Florentine Codex, offer an example of collective authorship. Observe that Sahagún's *Historia* consists of twelve books that collect forms of speech concerning the 'totality' of natural and cultural phenomena. Sahagún's collection of speech genre builds a corpus of authoritative Nahuatl text—to provide an equivalent to the classics in Latin antiquity—for the creation of grammars and dictionaries. In the *huehue-tlatolli* one finds instances of multiple voices and styles often in the space of a single discourse. The elder informants offer variations in intonation, in rhetorical form, and even in grammatical structures that suggest a collective utterance. As Frances Karttunen and James Lockhart have pointed out, 'in the tradition of oral literature, *huehuetlatolli* were created every time they were delivered'.[6] The utterance of a *huehuetlatolli* constituted a singular speech act determined by an immediate situation. Sahagún's ethnographic recordings of voice would have had an artificial character in that the speech of the elders lacked a real context—or better, the context is ethnographic. This artificial setting, however, does not alter the fact that they transcribe verbal performances. A typical example would include both the voices of men and women participants as well as those of the collectors. The compiling voices include Sahagún, the trilingual indigenous assistants, and the elders who reflect on the ethnographic situation as they articulated samples of speech genre.

We can trace a similar phenomenon in *Cantares Mexicanos* [Mexican Songs] (*c.*1585), where we can also trace various voices in one song and in some cases the juxtaposition of female (or at least men simulating women) and male voices. The juxtaposition of female and male voices can be observed, for instance, in the changes of the vocative suffices: *e* in the case of masculine speakers and its absence in female speakers. According to Horacio Carochi (1645): 'The women do not use this *e* in the vocative, but with a feminine affection they raise the last syllable of the noun a great deal'.[7] Consider the following line: 'Toznenexochiçaquanpa-palocíhuatl don palacisco iz ca moxochitzi ma xonmitotiya' [Oh, little parrot-flower-oriole-butterfly-woman! Oh, don Francisco! Here are your flowers,

---

[6] *The Art of Nahuatl Speech: The Bancroft Dialogues*, ed. and trans. Frances Karttunen and James Lockhart (Los Angeles, 1987), 9.

[7] Horacio Carochi, *Grammar of the Mexican Language with Explanations of its Adverbs* [*Arte de la lengua mexicana con declaración de los adverbios della*], ed. and trans. James Lockhart (Stanford, 2001), 45.

dance!].[8] The phrasing suggests that the reference to St Francis agrees in gender with 'little parrot-flower-oriole-butterfly-woman', and that his feminization corresponds to the fact that these were males—warriors, moreover—singing like women, a practice censured by the first bishop of Mexico, Fray Juan de Zumárraga, in the 1530s. The *Cantares* offers a spectral view of history that also can be found in the histories of Tezozómoc and Chimalpahin.

The examples I will examine in detail suggest that the range of alphabetical writing in Mesoamerica went from the stenographic use that records speech supplementing pictographic texts to the creation of a lettered Nahuatl culture, of which Tezozómoc and Chimalpahin would be two of its greatest representatives. The corpus would then encompass annals, songs, chronicles, *relaciones*, histories, and towards the end of the seventeenth and beginning of the eighteenth century, the *Títulos Primordiales* (Primordial Titles), hybrid pictographic and alphabetical texts produced in native paper that sought to create a *patina* of antiquity. These fascinating and complex *títulos* have given rise to disputes as to their authenticity, a topic we can only mention in this chapter.[9]

VOICE AND PICTOGRAPHY IN THE
HISTORIA TOLTECA-CHICHIMECA

The *Historia tolteca-chichimeca* is a unique document in the sixteenth century for it juxtaposes a pictographic text and an alphabetical record of a verbal performance that included multiple speech genre that traditionally supplemented the pictorial histories: dialogues, discourses, toponyms, onomasticons, and songs. The verbal component of the *Historia tolteca-chichimeca* also differs from the glosses that were written on the margins of pictographic inscriptions in colonial documents such as Codex Mendoza and Codex Telleriano-Remensis. Glosses for the most part reiterate the information contained in the pictography or annotate pertinent ethnographic information. The verbal recordings in the *Historia tolteca-chichimeca* do not reproduce the pictographic information with words— rather they record a singular speech event.

Scholars have argued that the recording of verbal expressions embalms a particular verbal expression and that consequently it leads to the destruction of oral traditions. If there is some truth that writing establishes one narrative among the many that could be told on the basis of a pictographic text, it is also

---

[8] *Cantares Mexicanos*, ed. and trans. John Bierhorst (Stanford, 1985), 274.

[9] See, for instance, Paula López Caballero, *Los títulos primordiales el centro de México* (Mexico, 2003); Stephanie Gail Wood, 'The Cosmic Conquest: Late Colonial Views of the Sword and Cross in Central Mexican Títulos', *Ethnohistory*, 38:2 (1991), 176–95; and 'The Social Against the Legal Context of Nahuatl *Títulos*', in Elizabeth Hill Boone and Tom Cummins (eds.), *Native Traditions in Postconquest World* (Washington, DC, 1998), 201–31.

worthwhile remembering that the recorded narratives, chants, and dialogues—among other speech genre—were intended for collective verbal performances that could very well have included music and dance. Improvisation, new contents, and variations could be a staple of the collective verbal performance of the *Historia*. Indeed, the *Historia* was only one source available to the community of Quauhtinchan.[10] The writers limited themselves to record voice, at least in the initial 'stenographic' moment, which eventually led to the version we know in which the layout, the pictographs, and the calligraphy manifest a second moment in the production of the manuscript. We must also discard the notion of an individual author who would have sat down to record the traditions of Quauhtinchan. Both the voices and the speech genre are multiple, and hence go beyond the knowledge of an individual in the community.

A note from the eighteenth century evidences the performance of the *Historia*: 'Come my uncle, sit on the chair// Come sit down// My grandfather, sit down// My grandfather, go with God// My uncle, drink a little// Oh, Tlatouani, go with God// Tomorrow Wednesday// Day after tomorrow Thursday// Book of conquest has fifty two folia'.[11] We face a bilingual text in Nahuatl and Popoloca. Several interpretations have been given as to the nature and reason for the production of the *Historia*, and the particular insertion in the eighteenth century of this summoning of the elders. However, the reasons for the bilingualism still elude us.[12] An explanation, perhaps the simplest, is that Popoloca speakers attended the event. It is evident that the invitation is in both languages and that it calls forth a collective participation in the re-creation of the narrative. We know the *Historia* was written between 1547 and 1560, and that it remained in the community of Quauhtinchan until 1718, when it became part of Lorenzo Boturini's collection of Mexican antiquities. We find it today in the Bibliothèque Nationale de France. Given its permanence in Quauhtinchan for close to two hundred years we can assume that it was produced for internal consumption rather than for arguing a case in Spanish courts. Towards the end of the manuscript, it mentions a boundary dispute between Quauhtinchan and Tepeyacac, and the visit by Judge Agustín Osorio, who, by the orders of Viceroy Antonio de Mendoza, had gone to Quauhtinchan to mediate between the parties. This notice is subordinated to the review of the boundaries that constitutes a memory for future generations.[13] Given the ritual nature of the *Historia*, it is not legitimate to reduce it to a document drafted for arguing a legal case.

---

[10] See David Carrasco and Scott Sessions (eds.), *Cave, City, and Eagle's Nest: An Interpretative Journey through the* Mapa de Cuauhtinchan No. 2. (Albuquerque, 2007).

[11] *Historia tolteca-chichimeca*, ed. and trans. Paul Kirchhoff, Lina Odena Güemes, and Luis García (Mexico, 1976), 131.

[12] See, for instance, Michael Swanton, 'El texto popoloca de la *Historia tolteca-chichimeca*', *Relaciones*, 86:22 (2001), 114–29.

[13] *Historia tolteca-chichimeca*, 232.

While there is not enough space here to examine the verbal sections of the
Historia in any detail it is worth noting that in the production of the verbal
components of the *Historia* we find a broad repertoire of speech genre that
included diverse voices, multiple authorship, and at least mention of a musical
component.[14] In the background of the alphabetical text we can picture the
participation of several members of the community who knew the narratives and
forms of speech presumably associated with this text and other pictographic
histories in the archives of Quauhtinchan. Alphabetical writing confers permanence to a series of speech acts that by definition are ephemeral. They disappear
in their articulation, leaving behind their memory in the traces of the letter. It is
worth remembering that each speech act is a singular, unrepeatable occasion. The
sounds of the voices and the music, the gestures, the apparel, the natural
surroundings, the fragrance of incense, and the historical context disappear in
the temporal flux. The echography of voice would limit itself to identifying the
traces of that event now contained in the written memory of what is gone. The
alphabetical record conveys that voice *was* (like a photograph that for Roland
Barthes captures a fragment of reality), even when we lack the certitude that we
are reading a 'pure' stenographic record.[15] Not unlike the manipulated photograph, the altered word would not stop being a testimony of a speech-event. The
recorded voice in turn can give place to multiple readings, to multiple inflections
with variants that could range from the present academic reading to a collective
performance in the community of Quauhtinchan.

THE COLLECTIVE AUTHOR IN TEZOZÓMOC'S
CHRONICA MEXICAYOTL

At the other end of the spectrum we find alphabetical texts from which we can
intuit a pictographic text that grounds the verbal performance. The different
voices recorded in Fernando Alvarado Tezozómoc's *Chronica mexicayotl* (1609)
point to a pictorial text and reproduce the genres of pictographic history. Codex
Chimalpáin, named after the famed Nahua historian from Chalco, Domingo de
San Antón Muñón Chimalpahin Quauhtlehuanitzin, gathered a series of narratives that included Tezozómoc's *Chronica*, who in turn identifies his sources
(singular verbal performances by individuals in some instances) and establishes
the collective character of the project. Tezozómoc and Chimalpahin differ from
the *Historia tolteca-chichimeca*, which provides scant information on its production, by including a metadiscourse that records an internal voice reflecting on the

---

[14] For a fuller discussion of the verbal components of the *Historia tolteca-chichimeca*, see Rabasa,
'Ecografías de la voz'.
[15] See Roland Barthes, *Camera Lucida: Reflections on Photography*, trans. Richard Howard
(London, 1981).

process of gathering narratives and the accuracy of the collected accounts of the pre-colonial and colonial worlds. In this regard, these Nahua writers assume the position of historians with the responsibility of creating an archive of voices that offer different versions of the past. In some places they judge the veracity of the sources but for the most part they limit themselves to recording voices or to copying transcriptions others had produced. They invariably mention the multiple participants who collaborate in the interpretation of pictographic texts.

The containment and enabling of voices in Tezozómoc and Chimalpahin lends multiple depths to the stories, to the murmur bound to disappear in an immemorial past when the accounts were passed on from generation to generation. Tezozómoc identifies the source of an account he intercalates in his narrative: 'Here ends the account of old Alonso Franco, whose home was here in the altepetl and city of Mexico Tenochtitlan and who died in the year 1602. He was a mestizo.'[16] We ignore who was the *mestizo* Alonso Franco, but the account of this *huehue*, of this elder, certainly carried sufficient weight to be included and for his name to be associated with a particular section of the *Chronica mexicayotl*. We cannot but wonder who was this *mestizo* with sufficient authority with the Tenochca community for telling the account of Mexitin Azteca Chichimeca's stay in Aztlan until they emerged to wander widely in *chichimecatlalpan*, all over chichimec land. Right after Franco's account Tezozómoc tells the story of Hutizilopochtli, of his sister Malinaxoch, of her abandonment, of her pregnancy with Copil, the eventual sacrifice of Copil, and of the defeat of the *Centzon-huitznahua* at the ball court, events that precede the first settlement of the Mexica in Tenochtitlan. In these stories the mythical and the historical—if we can separate them without incurring discursive violence—inflect each other's truths. Tezozómoc tells these foundational stories without mentioning specific sources. What is in Franco's story that might have revealed a singular point of view and the need to preserve his individualized voice? It is as if Tezozómoc wanted to testify to the power of alphabetical writing to retain the breath of speech that can be brought back to life by endless performances of Franco's words, but Tezozómoc also invokes the voice of his close relatives in a collective authorship, which even if lost in the anonymity of murmur remains no less memorable in the possibility of its re-enactment:

I have indeed heard their account from their very mouths as the highborn rulers and the highborn noblemen told them, they who came here to live, [who] later departed, they whom Our Lord God has effaced. Thus they agreed and told it among themselves, as they understood their ancient one's accounts. I listened to the rulers Don Diego de Alvarado Huanitzin, my dear parent, don Pedro Tlacahuepan, my uncle, don Diego de San Francisco Tehuetzquitizin, and other highborn noblemen who indeed rightly understood the ancient ones' accounts. Here I took their statements.[17]

---

[16] *Codex Chimalpahin*, i. 75. Hereafter all citation of the *Chronica Mexicayotl* will be listed as *Codex Chimalpahin*.

[17] *Codex Chimalpahin*, i. 65.

There is a difference in how Tezozómoc and Chimalpahin define their tasks. Chimalpahin inserts his voice in Tezozómoc's *Chronica mexicayotl* to question the veracity of Tezozómoc's version: 'But I who here tell my name, Domingo de San Antón Muñón Chimalpahin, have investigated and considered the year-count book of the Chalca as to the time when the Mexica were besieged in Chapultepec. It was in the year of Two Reed, 1299.'[18] Here and elsewhere Chimalpahin exposes a method of inquiry that enables him to write accounts that provide information on events that took place in multiple *altepeme* rather than the traditional practice of writing the *xiuhtlapohualli*, the count of the years, of a particular *altepetl*, in his case Chalco. I will return to this aspect of Chimalpahin's historiography later. For now, note that Tezozómoc also conceives his task as an historian of Tenochtitlan in a comparative vein: 'In order now to provide authentication and compare the accounts of any others as to what the first Christian neophytes mentioned above emphasized—they who indeed knew well how what they arranged was to appear, I now authenticate and affirm them in their accounts'.[19] Let us leave aside for now the reference to the first Christians, and just examine his method and criteria for the authentication of sources. If less systematic than Chimalpahin, who clearly positions himself in the Herodotean understanding of history as enquiry, Tezozómoc, who defines himself as a descendant and survivor, functions as an '*auctor*-witness'[20] by collecting narratives and testifying to their authenticity: 'They begot me; I am indeed their child, I who declare my name. I myself am the ancient ones' survivor, I who possess the accounts of the ancient ones, I whom our Lord God even now strengthens'. In his capacity as survivor and custodian of the ancient accounts, Tezozómoc constitutes the new archive that will be passed on to future generations: 'These accounts are indeed in our keeping. Therefore we too, but specially our sons, our grandsons, our offspring, those who will issue from us, they too will always guard them.'[21] Tezozómoc conceives his authorial function in the production of an archive that will eternalize the memory of antiquity for the descendants of Tenochtitlan.

---

[18] Ibid., 91; Susan Schroeder has noted that if the Chalca historian first arrived in Mexico City as Domingo Francisco, where the absence of a Spanish surname indicates his humble status, in his writings we find him assuming the name don Domingo de San Antón Muñon Chimalpahin Quauhtlehuanitzin evocative of high rank. See Schroeder, *Chimalpahin and the History of Chalco* (Tucson, 1991), p. xvi.

[19] *Codex Chimalpahin*, i. 65.

[20] In *Remnants of Auschwitz: The Witness and the Archive* (New York, 2002), Giorgio Agamben derives the concept of *auctor*-witness from the Latin *auctor*, which 'originally designates the person who intervenes in the case of a minor . . . in order to grant him the valid title it requires' (p. 148). In citing Agamben the objective is not to fold anachronistically the Jewish Holocaust with the invasion of the Americas, but to draw on Agamben's observations on the Latin term *auctor*, which may be extrapolated to Tezozómoc's historical vocation.

[21] *Codex Chimalpahin*, i. 63.

Tezozómoc's gift to the descendants of Tenochtitlan is filled with hope for a future in which the auguries looked dim at the time he produced the *Chronica mexicayotl* in 1609, when he lists don Juan Bautista as the last Indian judge-governor of Tenochtitlan. The last of the Tenochca judge-governors of Tenochtitlan had been don Luis de Santa Maria (d. 1565): 'With him the administration of Mexico Tenochtitlan in the midst of the waters by the highborn heirs of Tenochca rulers came to an end.'[22] Tezozómoc conceives the task of *auctor* in terms that suggest a Eucharistic understanding of alphabetical writing, one in which reading and performance would bring back, indeed resurrect, the voices of the elders that lay dormant in the letter: 'those children of the Mexica, those children of the Tenochca yet to live, yet to be born, will go on telling them, will go on celebrating them'.[23] It is as if Tezozómoc had in mind St Paul's dictum that the new law cancels yet retains the old law; the integration of the Nahuas into universal history would not exclude the memory of the ancients. Is it that Tezozómoc, to borrow Giorgio Agamben's term, called forth to continue Nahua forms of life in the mode of *as not*, 'as the revocation of every worldly condition, released from itself to allow for its use'?[24] From the tension between the old beliefs and the new Christian demands, Tezozómoc produces the memory of old, that is, a version of the foundational stories of Tenochtitlan as a remnant. The memorable past of Tenochtitlan and the speech of the elders will remain for all time in the universal history of Christianity, and yet will retain the possibility of a performance that would erase the reference to Christianity.

And yet Tezozómoc grounds the authority of the elders who provided reliable information in the fact that the Tenochca elite from which he descends were the first Christian neophytes. Their credibility has as much to do with their memorable status as highborn as with their status as first Christians. Tezozómoc is a grandson of Moteucçoma on his mother's side, doña Francisca de Moteucçoma, and lists his father, don Diego de Alvarado Huanitzin, as ruler of Tenochtitlan in 1536. Indian judge-governors played an indispensable role in the colonial administration of Tenochtitlan, at least during the first century. These figures could not have fulfilled this role unless they openly accepted their status as Christians. This does not necessarily imply that their Christianity was thoroughly engrained—a question that hardly concerns Tezozómoc, who proudly posed for a portrait bearing the signs of high status: Spanish dress, dagger, and sword. One would assume the right to ride a white horse as was given to don Juan Velasquez Tlacotzin, the first *cihuacoatl* after the hanging of Quauhtemoc in Huey Mollan: 'There [in Huey Mollan] the Spaniards gave him their clothing and a sword, a

---

[22] *Codex Chimalpahin*, i. 175.
[23] Ibid., i. 61.
[24] Giorgio Agamben, *The Time that Remains: A Commentary on the Letter to the Romans*, trans. Patricia Dailey (Stanford, 2005), 43.

dagger, and a white horse.'[25] In telling the story of his ancestors and highborn of Tenochtitlan as credible neophytes, he inscribes their account within the economy of salvation. This inscription suggests the structure of conversion in which Indian subjects were put in the position of accepting the missionaries' description of their deities as filthy, bloody, deceiving devils. Needless to say for Tezozómoc, as well as for the Spanish missionaries, these devils or, better, manifestations of the devil, had agency, even when qualified as false gods. But telling their story as manifestations of the devil, as false gods—as deceivers—saps their power. After all, who wants to believe in false gods, to live under deception? As such, Tezozómoc not only collects stories and writings for an archive of the ancient grandeur of Tenochtitlan, but also defines the rules for telling and retelling the stories from within a new institution of Mesoamerican writing.[26] The qualification of their deities as devils could be traced back to the speech of the elders who having being exposed to Christianity at the beginning of the Spanish invasion were forced to abhor their ancient rites and beliefs while retaining a memory of them.

SIMULTANEOUS HISTORICAL TIMES AND THE HISTORY OF THE PRESENT IN CHIMALPAHIN

One of the most striking features of Chimalpahin's history is the simultaneous recording of events from different locations in a given year. This practice distances him from the traditional recording of events in Mesoamerican local histories. In this regard he could not be farther from Tezozómoc's history centred on Tenochtitlan, which provides information on other locations only when relevant to the rise of the Mexica. We can picture Chimalpahin following several pictorial accounts, consulting alphabetical records from different sources and locations, and drawing from interviews of elders to provide a complete history of central Mexico and significant events in European history, even while privileging his native Chalco. On occasions he does provide the names of informants, most often connected to his relatives, but for the most part he speaks of female and male elders who told the stories.

In addition to the simultaneous citation of sources and events in a given year, Chimalpahin also draws from biblical sources to better situate the events in terms of the universal history, that is, the history of Christianity. Mentions of Judeo-Christian history span from the recurrent generic placement within *anno domini*: '3 Tecpatl [flint]. Then 1300 years had passed since birth of Jesus Christ our Lord'

---

[25] *Codex Chimalpahin*, i. 169.
[26] In this regard he exemplifies the etymology of the word archive in *commencement* and *commandment* in Jacques Derrida, *Archive Fever: A Freudian Impression*, trans. Eric Prenowitz (Chicago, 1998).

to the correction of dates for such events as the Tower of Babel: 'This account that was given by the ancient Tlacochalcas is very hard to believe; for if it is true that tongues were confused, but by the year the ancients say their tongue was confused many years had gone by since the confusion of the tongues as it appears and is written in the Christian book of god.'[27] Chimalpahin intercalates a brief account of Babel, Nemrod, and Noah to illuminate the account of how the Nonohualcas Teopixcas Tlacochalcas first emerged from a place named Tlapal-lan Nonohualco, which according to the *ymamatlacuilolpan in tliltica tlapaltica* (their books written in black and red) from which he derived the information, it was there where the ancients became mute: 'They were given the name of Nonohualca because they became mute when this occurred.'[28]

If the chronology is doubtful and difficult to believe, 'cenca ohuititica momatiz' (Alonso de Molina defines *mati*: 'pensar dudando si sera assi o no' [to think wondering if it is like this or not]),[29] the story remains fascinating not only because it goes back to a time before the arrival of the Tlacochalcas at Chico-moztoc, a time before their migration, perhaps before their historical time, but also because Chimalpahin goes on to mention Josephus and the poets of Graeco-Roman antiquity, whom he characterizes as the pagan tricksters of words (*tlahtolchichiuque*, the *enlabiadores* according to Molina), in particular Ovid's story of how the giants, the *tlacahueyaque*, constructed towers to reach the heavens and destroy the gods. Chimalpahin concludes with the laconic statement that Ovid expressed himself in different terms, 'because he was an idolater and did not know the one sole God'.[30] In the end, Chimalpahin casts doubt on the ancient accounts that would have placed Tlapallan near Babylon by alluding to evidence provided by the ancient count of the years, the *huhuexiuhtlapohualli*, which gives a much more recent date, and to the fact that it does not agree with the Bible, 'amo quinamiqui yn christiano xiuhpouhualli'.[31] Note the incorpora-tion of the scriptures into Mesoamerican categories and historical genre, 'yn christiano xiuhpouhualli', the Christian count of the years. After casting doubt on the correspondence between the loss of a common language in Mesoamerica with the biblical account of the Tower of Babel, it is as if the mention of Ovid would give him poetic license to tell the fantastic story of Tlacochalca's crossing the sea on top of turtles and gigantic sea snails from which they saw the water women who are half fish, 'yn acihuatl michintlaco', the sirens who drew them to

[27] Domingo Chimalpahin, *Relaciones séptima y octava*, in *Las ocho relaciones y el memorial de culhuacan*, ed. and trans. Rafael Tena, vol. 2 (Mexico, 1998), 28–9, 14–15.

[28] Ibid.

[29] All mentions of definitions by Molina refer to: Alonso de Molina, *Vocabulario de la Lengua Castellana y Mexicana y Mexicana y Castellana* (1571), ed. Miguel León Portilla (facs edn, Mexico, 1970).

[30] *Relaciones séptima y octava*, 18–19.

[31] Ibid., 21–2.

their music and lament in the middle of the water, 'oquinhuallapichilitiquizque oquinhuallatzotzonilitiquizque yn ayhtic'.[32]

Once Tlacochalca have crossed the sea, Chimalpahin proceeds to enumerate the years, the historically verifiable *xiuhtlapohualli*, that enable him to produce a total history of the Nahua. He compares and teases out the most reliable account of the years from multiple sources belonging to different locations. Thus under one year Chimalpahin might cite events pertaining to Texcoco, Tenochtitlan, and Amecamecan. This simultaneous mention of events provides a picture of the interactions between several *altepeme*, even when more attention is given to the narratives of Chalco. In the *Septima relación*, from which I have drawn the passages on the confusion of languages, the story of the Chalca is unavoidably connected to the rise of Tenochtitlan, first in flowery wars and then as subordinate tributaries, a condition Chimalpahin expresses as a form of death: 'By then it had been fifty-seven years since the Chalca had died.'[33] After Cortés's entrance in Tenochtitlan, the Tenochca lost all their lands once it was determined that they had taken possession of them by means of war. Chimalpahin provides a most gruesome picture of the *Tenochca cihuatl*, women returning to their houses in Tenochtitlan: 'They found them with bones scattered all over the ground.'[34] In addition to the simultaneous events in Mesoamerica, Chimalpahin records events in Europe, such as Charles V being crowned emperor of the Holy Roman Empire and the birth of Philip II. It hardly matters that Chimalpahin cites 1528 when in fact Charles V did not receive the crown until 1530.

We can thus situate a temporality that encompasses all events in universal history. Not only does Chimalpahin situate the events in their *anno domini*, but also in terms of biblical history of the world and major events in Europe. Chimalpahin's global history is conceptualized from the perspective of Chalco and other locations on the basin of Mexico City. It is clear to him that Mesoamerica has been incorporated into the universal history of the Catholic Church, but it is also important to understand that he uses native documentation for telling the major events in the incorporation of the Nahuas into Christianity. One may even conceive that events pertaining to European history, such as Charles V's assumption of the Holy Roman Empire, were drawn from native sources that had recorded these events decades earlier. This obviously does not mean that Chimalpahin did not have access to European sources, but that his story of the foundation of the colonial order follows native experiences and records. His references to the *huehuetque*, the ancients, include pictorial sources that established a wide range of colonial events: '2 Calli 1533. The Amaquemeca Chalca say, and left painted in their books of counts of the years [*ynxiutlapohuallamauh*], that the church of San Luis Obispo was finished on this year'.[35] Reading Chimalpahin we get the sense that the time of Christianity has been

---

[32] Ibid., 22–3.   [33] Ibid., 162–3.   [34] Ibid., 164–5.   [35] Ibid., 186–7.

incorporated into Mesoamerican time. Christianity has certainly transformed the everyday life of the Nahua; however, we do not get the impression that the use of calendrical equivalences only works in the direction of a homogeneous time, but that Christian dates now form part of Mesoamerican *xiuhtlapohualli,* count of the years.

Let us examine the recording of daily life, the history of his times, if you prefer, in the so-called *Diario.* The *Diario's* first entry for 7 House year, 1577, has an annotation indicating that 'In this year mother Teresa de Jesús . . . wrote her book named *Las moradas.*'[36] This entry corresponds to two years before Chimalpahin was born. It is not until the entry of 25 July 1594 that we have an allusion to writing in the present: 'here it is mentioned that in the year 11 Rabit in the old style was when very great misery came to us'.[37] Although the note on *Las moradas* is a marginal later addition, it is in the hand of Chimalpahin. It is as if in reflecting and revisiting entries he had realized the correspondence to Santa Teresa's writing of *Las moradas.* We know Santa Teresa, fearing the extinction of all memory of her work, wrote this book two years after the Inquisition had confiscated the manuscript of the *Libro de la vida.* Even though the *Diario* lacks the self-examination we find in *Las moradas,* one could argue that we find a critical consciousness in Chimalpahin's accounts of contemporary events. The examination of personal consciousness in Santa Teresa gives place to an examination of the consciousness of the social body: for example, the Spanish paranoia in the face of a rebellion of Black slaves, the corruptions of viceroyal authorities after an earthquake, or the hysteria among Spaniards during a solar eclipse. Let us look in some detail at the entry on the 10 June 1611 eclipse in Mexico City.

Chimalpahin juxtaposes two metaphors for the phenomenon of the eclipse, the Nahuatl *tonatiuh quallo,* 'the sun is eaten', and the analogy to a shelter that creates shade only for those standing under it. The latter simile he draws from the *Sermonario* by Juan Bautista, who derived the passage from an astrology book and translated it to Nahuatl. Chimalpahin refers to Juan Bautista's simile as *tlahtolmachiyotl,* which Molina lists as 'parabola, semejanza, or figura' (parable, simile, or figure). Rafael Tena used 'comparación', which does capture Molina's preference for a trope, but the English translators preferred 'statement', which lends it a scientific weight that the Nahuatl term does not include. The sequence

---

[36] Don Domingo de San Antón Muñón Chimalpahin Quautlehuanitzin, *Annals of His Time,* ed. and trans. James Lockhart, Susan Schroeder, and Doris Namala (Stanford, 2006), 27. There is another edition of Chimalpahin's *Diario*: Domingo Chimalpahin, *Diario,* ed. and trans. Rafael Tena (Mexico, 2001). I find the argument for titling the work as *Annals of His Time* paradoxical, given that for the most part the entries record the days and on some occaisions the hours, with the exception of a short *xiuhtlapohualli* he inserts between day entries for 15 October 1608 and 1 January 1609. I say short because of the number of pages; it actually covers the time from the beginning of the universe to the end of 1608 in twenty pages.

[37] *Annals of His Time,* 51.

of metaphors and the insistence on referring to the eclipse as *tonaituh quallo* throughout the entry, suggests an allegorization of the limits of empirical knowledge. It is indeed not inconceivable that Chimalpahin was aware of Copernicus and, given that the ignorance of the ancients was due to their being pagans, Chimalpahin would seem to suggest that the knowledge of eclipses in Juan Bautista's *Sermonario* amounts to an article of faith: 'And our forefathers, the ancients who were still idolaters, called pagans, were not able to find out anything about this because they lived in confusion.'[38] Chimalpahin qualifies this 'confusion' by noting that colonial authorities promoted fear by asking people to abstain from eating, drinking, and from leaving their house because of a malignant air (given that the astrologers were off by several hours—and people went out into the streets—these cautions proved unfounded), that Spanish women rushed to confession, and that many people died from stabbings in a generalized state of anomie that affected Spanish and Nahuas alike. But Chimalpahin's brilliant phenomenological description of the eclipse and the temporality of its experience figure even more importantly than his critique of the superiority of Spanish knowledge.

Even when God appears to clear the sky so that all the citizens of New Spain could perceive the marvels of the world that were previously hidden by the clouds covering the sun, Chimalpahin's language carries a descriptive force: 'because when the light began to fade, when the surface of the sun began to be covered by the moon, which is called being eaten, the sky was closed everywhere by clouds, only in the place where the sun was going a few thin clouds flowed by in front of the face of the sun'. The juxtaposition of God making visible the eclipse, and the description of the experience, complement each other in that the description of every detail using all his senses conveys a sense of wonder in the contemplation of the world. The clouds move slowly, the sky clears, and the sun figures alone at the centre, and gradually disappears with a gradation of dark hues, 'blackness, darkness, dark blueness'. The duration flows very slowly until it suddenly becomes dark as if it were eight o'clock at night. Chimalpahin writes *chicuey tzillini*, literally eight soundings of metal, suggesting the church bells that first introduced the Nahua to the Christian keeping of the hours. Here the concept of night is paired with an hour of the day, but the description of the eclipse follows the hours of the early afternoon. It is not only the days, but the hours that make this recording of daily life a most unconventional of annals, if that is what we should call this testimony of lived experience. Chimalpahin conveys a stoppage of time, a prolonged instant during the time the sun was eaten, 'çan niman aoctle ypan hualla, aoctle ypan oquiz' [in that instant nothing came, nothing passed by].[39] The sun might not die or be eaten but the metaphor of *tonatiuh quallo* is an apt expression for the experience of a stoppage of time, clearly much more

---

[38] Ibid., 181.
[39] Ibid., 180–3. My translations.

accurate than the simile of Juan Bautista's 'shady shelter'. Chimalpahin records a *now*, a prolonged instant, not a blink of the eye; it is the temporality of the world that stops in the instant, not a *now* that would pertain to the experience of internal time-consciousness.

As the entry progresses the discourse of science, of what cannot be known by direct observation, gives place to the experience of colours, sensations, duration, and minute details. The experience of the phenomenon partakes of the wonders of God, who works marvels so that we can appreciate his creation, and in this respect the ancestors in their gentility might have ignored what seems to be dogma with respect to the geocentric structure of the heavens, but their experience of the world was accurately captured by their metaphors.

In the *Diario* we once more find an instance of the rewriting of European knowledge, indeed of the genre of the *Diario*, in terms of the Mesoamerican institution of historical writing, which Chimalpahin summarizes in a phrase that defines his project of writing for future readers and listeners, not unlike Tezozómoc's archive for the generations to come: 'This then is what happened, so that it is said that the sun was eaten. On the said day Friday a full account of it was put in order here so that all those are born later and will live here on earth afterward, those who will not ever see the like, will see and find out about it here.'[40]

Reading Tezozómoc and Chimalpahin in the Mesoamerican archive and institution of historical writing entails paying attention to the author functions that these writers assume, to collect testimonies, to transmit them to posterity, and to negotiate the intersection of Christian and Mesoamerican temporality. I have argued that these Nahua historians assume the role of *auctor*-witness, on the basis of Agamben's definition, to collect voices that otherwise would disappear in the murmur of everyday speech. But these are not just voices but speech forms that attest to the richness of Nahuatl traditional accounts of the past. It is not just what the ancestors said, the foundational stories they told when consulting the pictographic *amoxtli*, but the preservation of the actual discourses for posterity. In fact one could say that histories written by missionaries such as Durán, Motolinía, Tovar, and Acosta, to just name those intimately related to Tezozómoc's *Chronica mexicayotl*, recorded the substance of the foundational stories of Tenochtitlan. What is unique to the Nahua historians, however, is that they preserved the speech forms as well as the historiographical genre of the pictographic accounts.

Reading Tezozómoc and Chimalpahin we have also observed how these Nahua historians insert the qualifying terms of idolatry and the devil running the risk of depleting Mesoamerican spiritual expressions of life. As they record what we may call the theogonic gests of the main supernatural protagonists in the foundational stories of Tenochtitlan, the effect is one in which the stories of old

---

[40] *Annals of His Time*, 185.

survive—as remains—resulting from the negation yet preservation of the ancient spirituality from within the Christian institutions of historical writing. The universal history of Christianity now includes, along with the Roman past, traces of Mesoamerican civilization. Tezozómoc and Chimalpahin knew all too well the secular dimension of Christianity that has as its vocation the subsumption of all history under its temporality. But, in the end, these Nahua historians preserve for posterity stories that offer us unique entries into the nature of sacrifice and the foundation of culture. In retaining Nahuatl voices, they provide the elements for tracing the limits of the Graeco-Abrahamic tradition, that is, of the 'globalatinization'[41] of all life.

In closing, let us recall that the *Historia tolteca-chichimeca* offered the unique example of an account of Quauhtinchan that included the pictographic and alphabetical texts. In the *Historia* we find no reflection of the criteria used for collecting the narratives. It is as if we were witnessing the stenographic moment that gathered elders to record their voices. In the *Historia* we trace no instances of qualifications of the gods as devils, nor of disparaging on rituals involving sacrifice or anthropophagy. These are mere facts without apology or condemnation. References to the conquest and the coming of Christianity form part of the *huhuexiuhtlapohualli*, the ancient count of the years that now includes Christian events. The mention of the reading in the eighteenth century that summons the elders to gather also bears the marks of God, the Christian God, but simply as part of the ritual. The *Historia* gathers the stories with little or no concern for what a missionary or a bureaucrat would say. These are stories to be told in the intimacy of the community. In the end, Christianity figures as one more element of the story of Quauhtinchan.

Just as one may argue that in the process of incorporating American cultures and natural phenomena Europe undergoes transformations without losing its defining identity, we may say that Mesoamerica incorporates Europe without ceasing to be its own world. In the process of incorporating alphabetical writing Mesoamerica retains its own *background*, that is, the absolute presuppositions from which and against which indigenous subjects have articulated—and continue up to our day to articulate—their own forms of life.

KEY HISTORICAL SOURCES

Anales de Tlatelolco, ed. and trans. Rafael Tena (Mexico, 2004).
Anales de Tecamachalco, ed. and trans. Eustaquio Celestino Solis and Luis Reyes García (Mexico, 1992).

---

[41] On the concept of *globalatinization*, or *mundialatinization* in French, see Jacques Derrida, 'Faith and Reason: The Two Sources of "Religion" at the Limits of Reason Alone', in *Acts of Religion*, ed. Gil Anidjar, trans. Joseph F. Graham (New York, 2002).

Buenaventura Zapata y Mendoza, Juan, *Historia y cronología de la noble ciudad de Tlaxcala*, ed. and trans. Luis Reyes García and Andrea Martínez Baracs (Tlaxcala, 1995).

Castillo, Cristóbal del, *Historia de la venida de los mexicanos y de otros pueblos e historia de la conquista*, ed. and trans. Federico Navarrete Linares (Mexico, 2001).

Cantares Mexicanos, ed. and trans. John Bierhorst (Stanford, 1985).

Chimalpahin, Domingo, *Las ocho relaciones y el memorial de culhuacan*, ed. and trans. Rafael Tena, 2 vols. (Mexico, 1998).

Chimalpahin Cuauhtlehuanitzin, Domingo Francisco de San Antón Muñón, *Memorial breve de la Fundación de la Ciudad de Culhuacan*, ed. and trans. Victor M. Castillo F. (Mexico, 1991).

——*Primer amoxtli libro, 3a relación de las Différentes histoires originales*, ed and trans. Victor M. Castillo F. (Mexico, 1997).

——*Codex Chimalpahin: Society and Politics in Mexico Tenochtitlan, Tlatelolco, Texcoco, Culhuacan, and Other Nahua Altepetl in Central Mexico*, ed. and trans. Arthur J. O. Anderson and Susan Schroeder, 2 vols. (Norman, Okla., 1997).

——*Annals of His Time*, ed. and trans. James Lockhart, Susan Schroeder, and Doris Namala (Stanford, 2006).

Códice Chimalpopoca: Anales de Cuauhtitlán y Leyenda de los soles, trans. Primo Feliciano Velázquez (Mexico, 1992).

Códice Techialoyan de San Pedro Tototepec, ed. and trans. Javier Noguez (Toluca, Mexico, 1999).

Codex Chimalpopoca: The Text in Nahuatl with a Glossary and Grammatical Notes, ed. John Bierhorst (Tucson, 1992).

Durán, Diego, *Historia de las Indias de Nueva España e Islas de la Tierra Firme*, ed. Ángel María Garibay K., 2 vols. (Mexico, 1967).

Early History and Mythology of the Aztecs: Codex Chimalpopoca, ed. and trans. John Bierhorst (Tucson, 1992).

Historia tolteca-chichimeca, ed. and trans. Paul Kirchhoff, Lina Odena Güemes, and Luis García (Mexico, 1976).

Ixtlixochitl, Fernando de Alva, *Obras Historicas*, ed. Edmundo O'Gorman, 2 vols. (Mexico, 1975–85).

Libro de los guardianes y gobernadores de Cuauhtinchan (1519–1640), ed. and trans. Constantino Medina Lima (Mexico, 1995).

Sahagún, Bernardino de, *Florentine Codex: General History of the Things of New Spain*, ed. and trans. Arthur J. O. Anderson and Charles Dibble, 13 parts (Santa Fe, NM, 1950–82).

Tezozómoc, Fernando Alvarado, *Chronica Mexicayotl*, ed. and trans. Adrián León (Mexico, 1992).

We the People There: Nahuatl Accounts of the Conquest of Mexico, ed. and trans. James Lockhart (Stanford, 1993).

BIBLIOGRAPHY

Brotherston, Gordon, *Book of the Fourth World: Reading the Native Americas through Their Literature* (Cambridge 1992).

Carrasco, David and Sessions, Scott (eds.), *Cave, City, and Eagle's Nest: An Interpretative Journey through the* Mapa de Cuauhtinchan No. 2 (Alburquerque, 2007).

Durand-Forest, Jacqueline de, *L'historie de la Vallée de Mexico selon Chimalpahin Quauhtlehuanitzin (du XIe au XVe siècle)* (Paris, 1987).

Florescano, Enrique, *Memoria mexicana* (Mexico, 2002).

—— *Quetzalcóatl y los mitos fundadores de Mesoamerica* (Mexico, 2004).

Heyden, Doris, *The Eagle, the Cactus, the Rock: The Roots of Mexico-Tenochtitlan's Foundation Myth* (Oxford, 1989).

Gibson, Charles, *The Aztecs Under Spanish Rule: A History of the Indians of the Valley of Mexico, 1519–1810* (Stanford, 1964).

Gruzinski, Serge, *The Conquest of Mexico: The Incorporation of Indian Societies into the Western World, 16th–18th Centuries*, trans. Eileen Carrigan (Cambridge 1993).

Leibsohn, Dana, *Script and Glyph: Pre-Hispanic History, Colonial Bookmaking and the Historia Totlteca-Chichimeca* (Washington, DC and Cambridge, Mass., 2009).

León Portilla, Miguel, *Aztec Thought and Culture: A Study of the Ancient Nahuatl Mind*, trans. Jack Emory Davis (Norman, Okla., 1971).

—— *Pre-Columbian Literatures of Mexico*, trans. Miguel León Portilla and Grace Lobanov (Norman, Okla., 1986).

Lockhart, James, *Nahuas and Spaniards: Postconquest Mexican History and Philology* (Stanford, 1991).

—— *The Nahuas After the Conquest: A Social and Cultural History of the Indians of Central Mexico 16th through 18th Centuries* (Stanford, 1992).

López Caballero, Paula, *Los títulos primordiales del centro de México* (Mexico, 2003).

Mignolo, Walter, *The Darker Side of the Renaissance: Literacy, Territoriality, and Colonization* (Ann Arbor, 1995).

Nicholson, H. B. 'Prehispanic Central Mexican Historiography', in *Investigaciones contemporáneas sobre la historia de México: Memorias de la Tercera Reunión de historiadores mexicanos y norteamericanos, Oaxtepec, Morelos, 4–7 de noviembre de 1969* (Mexico and Austin 1971), 38–81.

Pastrana Flores, Gabriel Miguel, *Historias de la conquista: aspectos de la historiografía de tradición náhuatl* (Mexico, 2004).

Schroeder, Susan, *Chimalpahin and the Kingdoms of Chalco* (Tucson, 1991).

Velazco, Salvador, *Visiones de Anáhuac: reconstrucciones historiográficas y etnicidades emergentes en el México Colonial: Fernando de Alva Ixtlixóchitl, Diego Muñoz Camargo y Hernando Alvarado Tezozómoc* (Guadalajara, 2003).

Wood, Stephanie, *Transcending Conquest: Nahua Views of Spanish Colonial Mexico* (Norman, Okla., 2003).

—— and Noguez, Javier (eds.), *De tlacuilos y escribanos: estudios sobre documentos indígenas coloniales del centro de Mexico* (Zamora, 1998).

Chapter 30
Inca Historical Forms

Catherine Julien

The years from 1400 to 1800 envelop almost the entire Spanish colonial era in the Andes (1532–1826) as well as the long fifteenth century, when what Spaniards knew as Peru was ruled by the Incas of Cuzco under the denomination Tahuantinsuyu. Alphabetic writing arrived with the Spaniards and quickly became a vehicle for recording a variety of forms of memory related to the Andean past. Some Spanish narratives were consciously constructed from Inca historical forms collected in Cuzco. A new genre of historical narrative written in Spanish about the events of the pre-Hispanic past imbibed rather heavily from such sources at the beginning, but in time became a textual exercise much like modern historiographical practice. Essays on Andean historiography have taken these Spanish narratives and other writings that reference indigenous history or culture as their central focus, referring to them erroneously as 'chronicles'.[1] A small group of works by indigenous authors in the Spanish language fits into this group, although it is as heterogeneous as the larger class itself.

This chapter takes Inca historical forms as a starting point and examines the creative interplay between these and European-introduced forms. Spanish narratives and other writings take centre stage after Spanish dominance was established, but other European modes of representation, including theatrical performance and painting, were important to the formation of Inca memory. Identifying the different channels for Inca memory in this period has something to tell us about the people who identified in some way with the Inca past. Everything turns on the posture we adopt. Instead of a stance that seeks to explain how alphabetic literacy came to dominate historiographical production, we will position ourselves to explore the impact of an alien tradition on historical representation in the Andes. What is important, after all, is not another iteration of European success, but rather an understanding of how historical practice changed from the time of the autonomous Inca Empire to the end of the Spanish colonial era.

---

[1] Franklin Pease, 'Chronicles of the Andes in the Sixteenth and Seventeenth Centuries', in *Guide to Documentary Sources for Andean Studies, 1530–1900* (Norman, Okla., 2008), 11–22.

Inca forms of historical representation in the pre-Hispanic period are known mainly through references to them in the Spanish narratives or through inferences based on a knowledge of their use as source materials in the construction of narratives about the Inca past. As a consequence, learning about these Inca genres is a complex historiographical enterprise that proceeds from the sixteenth century backwards in time to the fifteenth.[2] Not all Inca historical forms were apprehended by the Spaniards. After a knowledge of Inca source materials is gleaned from Spanish texts, other forms of evidence derived from material culture studies can be examined as a means of expanding what is known about an Inca historiographical repertoire. Studying later writing to learn something about earlier historical practice is not unique to the Andes. Some Roman texts (such as the Peutinger table) are known only through preservation in the work of medieval scholars. The point of view of this chapter will then shift gear, to trace the development of Inca historical forms after the arrival of the Europeans, up to the eve of independence from Spain. A knowledge of pre-Hispanic forms allows links to later forms of representation to be established, even though these are as diverse as the public performance of Inca genealogy and the re-elaboration of non-alphabetic forms of symbolic communication on such media as wooden cups inlaid with enamel.

INCA HISTORICAL FORMS AS THEY ARE KNOWN FROM SPANISH NARRATIVES

A group of Spaniards under the leadership of Francisco Pizarro arrived in the Andes and captured the Inca Atahuallpa in 1531. Thus began their campaign to overthrow the Incas and take over the territory governed from Cuzco, the Inca capital. Atahuallpa had just won a war against his brother Huascar to succeed as Inka[3] after the unexpected death of their father, Huayna Capac, on campaign in what is now Ecuador. A period of political violence and instability was unleashed by Pizarro's capture, lasting far longer than the violence that followed Hernán Cortés's earlier attack on Mexico. However, it was not until the 1540s that Spanish authors began to concern themselves with collecting information about the Incas and the creation of a large conquest state during the century preceding the Spanish arrival. This gap has led some historians and anthropologists to reject the narratives the Spaniards constructed as more faithful to their own histories of kings and events than to any Andean reality.[4] An argument can

---

[2] Catherine Julien, *Reading Inca History* (Iowa City, 2000).

[3] The spelling 'Inka' will be used in reference to the Inca rulers; 'Inca' or 'Incas' to members of the larger group.

[4] María Rostworowski de Diez Canseco, *Historia del Tawantinsuyu* (Lima, 1988), 13–14; and Franklin Pease, *Las crónicas y los Andes* (Lima, 1995), 85–120.

be made that the Spaniards used formally transmitted Inca historical forms that reflected what the keepers of these traditions knew or believed about the Inca past.[5] By comparing Spanish narratives that drew from Inca historical forms, something can be learned about their common underlying sources.

One of the forms that can be discerned is a genealogical tradition that documented the descent of the branch of the Inca line responsible for the expansion of Inca authority over the territory of Tahuantinsuyu. The dynastic Inca line traced its descent from a group of apical ancestors who had emerged from a cave at Pacaritambo, a place 30 kilometres south of Cuzco, a scant eleven generations before the time of the Spanish arrival. The dynastic line was segmented in each generation into lineages called *panacas*. The most common structuring device of the Spanish narratives is a genealogy of the dynastic line, which not only traces descent in the male line from the apical ancestors but also carefully documents the female through whom succession passed. Of the eleven Spanish narratives that drew from Inca sources in Cuzco, all trace the same or nearly the same succession in the male line: it is the identity of the female through whom descent passed that was contentious. The Incas calculated a status transmitted in the dynastic line—called *capac* status—that linked it to a solar being (hereafter, the Sun). Both men and women were conduits for it. An Inca genealogy was an argument about the purity of the lineage, and the bloodlines of the women were crucial.

Because genealogy was an important and contentious matter, a painted record was kept in a house dedicated to the Sun in Puquincancha, near Cuzco. Cristóbal de Molina, a priest and the chief catechist of the Cuzco Incas, describes the painted record as having 'the life of each one of the Inkas and of the lands he conquered, painted in their figures on some tablets'.[6] The story of Inca origins was also depicted. The Spanish term (*tablas*) implies that these tablets were made of wood. Whether they were painted or decorated in inlaid enamel—a technology used by the Incas on wooden cups when the Spaniards first arrived and afterwards—is unknown. Inca representations of human figures on ceramics are highly stylized, so the identity of the Inka may have been conveyed through conventionalized dress and pose, or other details of the representation, rather than through facial resemblance. Abstract geometric designs called *tokapu* may have been used to represent the provinces.[7]

A memory of these tablets was still evident in 1572, when Pedro Sarmiento de Gamboa composed the second part of the *Historia Indica* [Indies History] in Cuzco. To authenticate his manuscript, the history of the Incas was painted on

---

[5] For a thorough presentation of the argument see Julien, *Reading Inca History*.

[6] *Relación de la fábulas y ritos de los Ingas* (c.1576; Madrid, 1988), 50: 'la vida de cada uno de los yngas y de las tierras que conquistó, pintado por sus figuras en unas tablas y que origen tuvieron'.

[7] Catherine Julien, 'History and Art in Translation: The *Paños* and Other Objects Collected by Francisco de Toledo', *Colonial Latin American Review*, 8:1 (1999), 61–89. See the description of the design of a tapestry shirt for the meaning of its *tokapu* designs (no. 4767, p. 89).

three cloths or *paños*, each about four metres square. Full-length figures of the Inkas and portraits in medallion format of their spouses as well as an account of their origins and conquests were painted on the *paños*, with the text of Sarmiento's manuscript inserted at the margins. Representatives of the *panacas* were assembled and asked to declare that what was represented on the cloths was true. A fourth cloth, two by six metres long, was also painted to represent the descendants of the Inkas so that only they would be exempted from tribute payment. The four *paños* were taken to Spain and inventoried with the possessions of Philip II after his death in 1598, but are now lost.[8] The genealogical history painted on these *paños* may not have resembled the tablets of Puquincancha closely or at all. However, their content and the context of their creation is a clear link to an Inca painted history. Sarmiento noted in the *Historia Indica* that the Inka Pachacuti, the ninth Inka in the official genealogy, ordered the tablets to be made and appointed trained men to interpret them.[9]

A second Inca historical form—the life history—can be detected in the Spanish narratives. The life history may have been closely related to the painted history since the latter appears to have been a series of capsule life histories ordered by genealogy rather than a history of the Incas ordered by chronology. The authors who composed narratives of the Inca past had difficulty with the time of overlap between lives, indicating that the underlying genealogy did not supply this synchronization.

Compilation has its virtues, however. Once the genealogical genre and the life history are identified as sources and are set aside, the shadowy traces of other types of source materials become evident. Two other Inca forms were used by Sarmiento in his construction of a narrative of Inca history: the list of conquests of a particular Inca, recorded on a *khipu*; and stories that appear not to have been part of either the genealogical form or the life history. Sarmiento used a list of the conquests of Thupa Inka, the tenth Inca of the official genealogy. This *khipu* had been held by members of the descent group of this Inka and was presented by them to Spanish officials in 1569, just before Sarmiento arrived in Cuzco and began to collect the material for his narrative.[10] The *khipu* was read into the documentation of claims by Thupa Inka's descendants that the Spaniards had usurped lands from his patrimony. The *khipu* has the form of a list, ordered by the four *suyus* or divisions of Tahuantinsuyu. Each entry notes the place or places where fighting took place, usually indicating the names of fortresses taken, but sometimes noting the names of particular enemy lords. The Incas also negotiated peaceful annexation, but the *khipu* records only military victories. The order of

---

    [8] Ibid, 76–8.
    [9] Pedro Sarmiento de Gamboa, *Geschichte des Inkareiches von Pedro Sarmiento de Gamboa* (Berlin, 1906).
    [10] John H. Rowe, 'Probanza de los Incas nietos de conquistadores', *Histórica* (Lima), 9:2 (1986), 193–245.

the entries for each *suyu* proceeds according to the distance from Cuzco, with some indications that the sequence of conquests for each *suyu* is correct. However, the format precludes conveying any sense of an overall chronology. The *khipu* must have included signs that represented proper names of various types, and different types of names can have been segregated as a means of distinguishing between classes of names. The sheer number of signs that would have been needed to represent classes of names such as lords, fortresses, provinces, etc., indicates that the contents of a specific *khipu* had to be learned by a particular individual, even when some conventions were followed that could be read by anybody. A fairly strong degree of professionalization is indicated.

The record made of this *khipu*, like the transcription of other Inca records kept in Cuzco, tells us something of importance about how information was recorded and stored. This list is not a narrative history; it is archived information. It was used by Sarmiento and other Spanish authors to add information about military conquests that was missing in Inca narrative accounts, but what Inca purpose it might have served is unknown.

The capture of Inca historical forms as source materials for Spanish narratives is only an entrée into another world of historical practice. What we have learned from these few examples is that Inca forms involved an oral performance or learned interpretation supported by a physical record. We can also document archival practices that may not have been used as sources of narrative. Without a form of writing that reproduced or nearly reproduced speech, an Inca narrative was more dependent on interpretation or performance than Spanish narrative history. Spanish authors describe the performance of histories as being like the *cantares* of Spain, indicating that they were entoned or sung.[11] The life history form, judging by the reflection of it in Juan de Betanzos's *Suma y narración de los Incas* [Narrative of the Incas] (1551–7), is the best candidate for this sort of performance. The genealogy, on the other hand, may have been 'readable' since the figures and signs represented on the wooden tablets could have conveyed the outline of a story in and of themselves, if arranged in sequence. However, the presence of an interpreter also suggests a performance tradition of some kind. This support to Inca genealogy was private, but anyone who lived in Inca Cuzco would have seen the performance of the dynastic genealogy at various times of the year, when the mortal remains of the Inkas or their surrogates were brought to the main square of Cuzco and arranged following an established hierarchical order. When *panaca* members authenticated Sarmiento's manuscript in 1572, they may have recognized its verisimilitude as much from their memory of these events and the performances of life histories than from any direct knowledge of the privately kept genealogical tradition.

---

[11] Julien, *Reading Inca History*, 162–5.

Betanzos and Sarmiento represent the imposition of a new form of archival practice on Inca historical tradition. They captured and recorded—in the fossilized form of the written manuscript—material compiled from Inca genres. They used genres that lent themselves to their projects and almost certainly did not recognize other forms of recorded memory than those they found useful.

What can we say about other forms if they were not captured in Spanish narratives? Something can be apprehended from a close study of other types of written records, especially transcriptions made from *khipu* or from archaeological approaches. Since our understanding of the conceptual universe in which Inca historiographical practice was embedded is necessarily limited by our lack of written materials in native languages—unlike in Mexico—any description of these other forms must rely on ethnographic readings of Spanish texts. Two examples will serve to illustrate aspects of a non-European mode of historical thought.

The first involves something that Spaniards would not have recognized as a form of historical memory, though it may have been centrally important to the Incas as a representation of their past. The Incas organized a cult of sacrifice to more than 400 sacred places or objects, called *huacas*, found on the landscape of the Cuzco valley. The diverse peoples who occupied this landscape were assigned, by means of a *khipu*, to make certain sacrifices to a specific set of *huacas*, each set organized on a line called a *ceque*. A list of the *huacas*, in *ceque* order, was published in the seventeenth century, in all likelihood copied from a transliteration of an Inca *khipu* made about 1560.[12] Some of the *huacas* were durable features of the landscape, such as springs or mountains; these were likely old, or even ancient, cult sites. A fair number of these *huacas* were natural or built features associated with particular Inkas or other individuals who lived in the time spanned by Inca genealogy; some *huacas* commemorated events associated with this period. The list of *huacas* was certainly a historical representation: it reflected a particular image of the past authored at a specific moment in time. The image, in this instance, was the relationship between living people and the landscape, constructed through links to sacred sites with particular histories. A *khipu* was also a permanent record and could be read. The list of *huacas* recorded on an Inca *khipu* was a melange of history and geography, but it was also something more: if we have learned from recent ethnographic study of *khipus* in the Andes, the *khipu* was 'of' rather than 'about' what it represented.[13] It embodied a relationship that may have been beyond the power of words to express.

The second example involves objects and captives taken when an enemy was defeated. The Spaniards endowed objects with special significance (for example,

---

[12] Bernabé Cobo, *Historia del nuevo mundo*, lib. 13, caps. XIII–XVI, Biblioteca de Autores Españoles 91 (Madrid, 1956).
[13] Frank Salomon, *The Cord Keepers* (Durham, 2004), 276.

the book), and so did the Incas. Andean people took various kinds of weapons and insignia to war; these were taken as trophies by the other side following a defeat. Remember that the life history of Pachacuti transmitted by Betanzos tells us a great deal about the treatment of captives and the taking of trophies, but nothing about battle. These objects were more a potent reflection of Inca power, and hence worthy of remembrance, than stories about battle. The Incas erected something like a museum in Cuzco to house these objects. Captives taken in battle could also be treated as commemorative objects. Captives met various fates, one of which was sacrifice and display in a gruesome memorial at the battle site. The taking of insignia and captives, as well as the creation of such gruesome memorials, have a long history in the Andes.[14]

Everything changed when the Spaniards defeated the Incas. Historical narrative quickly occupied centre stage, though other forms of historical representation also flourished. The creators and receptors of Inca memory changed as much as the forms used to represent the Inca past—and became something of a moving target in the cultural maelstrom of the Spanish colonial era.

THE SHORT SIXTEENTH CENTURY

From the moment the Spaniards arrived, forces were set in motion that curbed the performance traditions associated with Inca historical forms. Rituals performed to initiate young Inca men, accession ceremonies, and funeral rites were all performed before Spaniards initially, but these activities were linked strongly to a belief system that was already attracting a fierce negative response from the Christian Spaniards. Public performances soon became impossible. No Spaniard appparently saw the wooden tablets that recorded the official version of Inca genealogy and, as mentioned above, a Spanish magistrate removed Inka mummies and the *khipu* records of their life histories from the hands of those who transmitted their contents. Both performance traditions and the unfettered access to documentary supports for Inca history came to an end within three decades or so after the Spanish arrival.

The fate of Inca history as it had been practised was inextricably linked to the fate of the dynasty itself, and the dynasty was fractured by the forces unleashed when the Spaniards arrived in Cuzco. Dynastic factionalism was nothing new, but the entry of Spaniards into dynastic politics was an important part of their conquest strategy and had predictably negative effects on the ability of the dynastic elite to reproduce itself or keep its hold on the Andean population.

---

[14] Catherine Julien, 'War and Peace in the Inca Heartland', in *War and Peace in the Ancient World* (Malden, Mass., 2007), 339–42; and Steve Bourget, 'Rituals of Sacrifice: Its Practice at Huaca de la Luna and Its Representation in Moche Iconography', in *Moche Art and Archaeology in Ancient Peru* (Washington, DC, 2001).

Francisco Pizarro began to influence dynastic succession the moment he chose to side with the Cuzco faction against Atahuallpa, after a representative of the Cuzco dynastic line—who was a viable alternative to Atahuallpa—arrived in Cajamarca. This candidate was short-lived, so Pizarro chose Manco Inca, then a teenager, whom he met just prior to arriving in Cuzco, as the next Inka. The two of them marched to Cuzco as liberators, and together began to deal with the immediate problem of defeating Atahuallpa's remaining armies. The military events of the Spanish conquest were yet to come: the Inca civil war had to be concluded first. In 1536, two years after Manco Inca accepted Pizarro's help, he tried to oust the Spaniards from Cuzco and Lima. Failing, he withdrew from Cuzco to the remote region of Vilcabamba. Because of his alliance with Pizarro, Manco Inca and his descendants were the branch of the dynastic line recognized by Spain while other Inca claimants were forced to the sidelines. Many of the latter had stronger genealogical claims to succeed than the Vilcabamba Incas; many had assisted the Spaniards during Manco's attack. Spanish narratives or testimony collected from different branches of the dynastic line reflect predictable schisms, particularly when the subject matter is the Inca civil war and the early years of the Spanish occupation. The Betanzos narrative, for example, reflects the point of view of his wife's relatives, who were the descendants of Pachacuti and Thupa Inca. Their bloodlines and prominence during the time of the Inca expansion marked them for higher status than their Vilcabamba cousins. Subtle influences are evident in Part 1 of Betanzos, which spans the period from Inca origins to the outbreak of the Inca civil war. They are much more strongly evident in Part 2, about the civil war and the first decades of the Spanish occupation.

An unusual and exceptionally important history of the years after the Spaniards arrived was authored by the Inka Titu Cusi Yupanqui, one of the sons of Manco Inca who governed the independent Inca province of Vilcabamba between 1559 and 1570. Titu Cusi kept a mestizo or mixed-blood notary with him in Vilcabamba, who had been sent with Betanzos to negotiate Titu Cusi's acquiescence to Spanish rule and return to Spanish Cuzco (Titu Cusi had spent some time in Cuzco as a boy). He authored more than sixteen letters with the aid of this notary, as well as two narrative accounts of his father's and his own dealings with the Spaniards. The second of these accounts, written as part of the instructions (*Ynstruçion*) that he gave to a Spanish governor for telling his story to King Phillip II of Spain in 1570, near the time of his death, so closely mimics the forms of Spanish narrative that scholars have been more willing to attribute the account to an Augustinian friar or the mestizo notary than to Titu Cusi himself. However, the keen intelligence of this man and his desire to communicate in writing suggest otherwise.[15]

---

[15] Diego de Castro Titu Cusi Yupanqui, *History of How the Spaniards Arrived in Peru* (Indianapolis, 2007).

A new viceroy, Francisco de Toledo, arrived in Peru as Titu Cusi was writing. He was hostile to the Incas and tried to overturn Spanish recognition of both Inca and noble status in the Andes. Oddly, he was also responsible for commissioning the Inca history of Pedro Sarmiento de Gamboa, his cosmographer, who compiled an account from various Inca historical sources, as noted above. Toledo also forced the descendants of the Incas to put testimony on record to support his case that their ancestors had conquered by force and were tyrants, not natural lords.[16] It was not Sarmiento's history (which did not circulate until the twentieth century) but the visual representation of Inca genealogy painted on the *paños*, mentioned above, that was to have a lasting echo during the colonial period. The *paños* are the first instance of a tradition of painted genealogy that was realized in various formats throughout the Spanish colonial era.[17]

Spanish narratives that drew from Inca source materials or a memory of them (such as the narratives of Sarmiento or Betanzos) were only one form of writing about the Incas that developed during the years after the Spanish arrival. Another form was based on information collected from witnesses. One such account was constructed by Pedro de Cieza de León, who travelled and collected material in the 1540s for his momumental work, the *Crónica del Perú* [Chronicle of Peru], written between 1549 and 1555. The first volume was a description of the viceroyalty of Peru, published in his lifetime and designed to appeal to the ethnographic tastes of European readers, then interested in first-hand accounts of travel and exploration. Cieza also collected an Inca history at about the same time as Betanzos was working, but from those he met on his travels, including a number of Inca governors. Since the Incas of the dynastic line knew their genealogy, these accounts were also structured by the account of the eleven Inkas descended from Manco Capac.

The largest part of Cieza's monumental work was a history of the almost constant fighting between Spanish factions (referred to as 'the Spanish civil wars') that had plagued the establishment of civil authority in Peru. Cieza had not been present for the wars he writes about (and even these accounts cannot be considered 'chronicles').[18] Other authors drafted versions of the same project, so that much of what was written during these years was not about the Incas or the Andes at all, except as a landscape for a Spanish drama. Both these histories and the kind of ethnographic writing done for European readers created problems for the Spanish Crown. Those who had served the Crown in the civil wars could claim rewards based on what was written in these narratives. Cieza's unabashed praise for the genius of the Incas simply called attention to the massive degree of destruction of life and property that had been wrought in the wake of Pizarro's

---

[16] Roberto Levillier, *Don Francisco de Toledo, supremo organizador del Perú; su vida, su obra (1515–82)*, vol. 2 (Madrid, 1935–42).

[17] Julien, 'History and Art in Translation'.

[18] Pedro de Cieza de León, *Crónica del Perú: cuarta parte*, vols. 1–3 (Lima, 1991–4).

invasion. Many works intended for publication remained in manuscript form owing to licensing requirements and censorship developed in the wake of an initial period of free expression.

THE LONG SEVENTEENTH CENTURY

In many ways the Toledan era (1569–81) marks a watershed between the old and new regimes. Toledo was not an enemy of history, as is proved by his commissioning of accounts such as Sarmiento's *Historia Indica* and the memoire of Pedro Pizarro—the nephew and page of Francisco Pizarro who had witnessed the first decades of the Spanish occupation—the *Relación del descubrimiento y conquista de los reinos del Perú* [Account of the Discovery and Conquest of the Kingdoms of Peru] (1571). But Sarmiento's collection effort marked the end of the time when direct enquiries could be made from Incas who had been adults at the time the Spaniards arrived. Histories written in the following decades were based to a much greater degree than before on textual sources. The loss of this generation did not signal the end of an interest in the Inca past, and writing about the Incas continued apace well into the seventeenth century. For instance, Bernabé Cobo's ambitious *Historia del nuevo mundo* [History of the New World] (1653) included an Inca history. Cobo said he could still collect an oral account of the pre-Hispanic past from the descendants of the Incas in Cuzco, but preferred to use authoritative written sources.

Late in the sixteenth century, and particularly in the seventeenth century, the urge to find a correspondence between a historical sequence in the Andes and a universal Christian history began to find expression in historical narrative. The Jesuit Miguel Cabello Valboa, in the *Miscelánea antártica* [Antarctic Miscellany] (1586), is the first to embed the Inca dynastic past in a universal Christian history, closely followed by Felipe Guaman Poma de Ayala, a man who claimed descent from the Incas on his mother's side and who, in the *Nueva corónica y buen gobierno* [New Chronicle and Good Government] (*c.*1615), wrote parallel accounts of Inca and biblical history. Garcilaso Inca de la Vega, born to a Spanish father and an Inca mother in Cuzco in the years after the Pizarro occupation, and writing his *Comentarios reales de los Incas* [History of the Incas] (1609–17) more than half a century after he had emigrated to Spain, adopted the novel solution of retelling the story of the Inca expansion so that it began with the first Inka and not the ninth. These solutions did not solve the basic problem, however: eleven generations simply could not be extended to the time of Christian origins. A solution emerged in the writings of the Jesuit Fernando de Montesinos (see the *Memorias antiguas historiales y políticas del Perú* [Historical and Political Remembrances of Peru], finished in Quito in 1642, Book 2 of the first part of his longer work titled the *Ophir de España* [Spanish Ophir]) and other seventeenth-century authors, who multiplied the number of Inca kings, giving Andean history the time depth it lacked.

The years of the late sixteenth and early seventeenth centuries were a time when the most important indigenous authors (Juan de Santa Cruz Pachacuti, Garcilaso Inca de la Vega, and Felipe Guaman Poma de Ayala) were writing. Juan de Santa Cruz Pachacuti Yamqui Salcamaygua wrote an account of Inca history structurally similar to the other Spanish narratives based on Inca sources, the *Relación de antigüedades deste reyno del Piru* [Account of the Antiquities of this Kingdom of Peru] (early seventeenth century). The author Pachacuti (not to be confused with the Inka Pachacuti) was not an Inca. He describes himself as from a town in the Canchis province south-east of Cuzco, the 'grandson and great-great-grandson of important people', presumably the relatives he mentions in the text who went with the Inka Huayna Capac on campaign to the northern Inca frontier. Their service may help to explain the affinity of their descendant for what was, after all, someone else's history. A Christian, as perhaps anyone who could write in Spanish must have been, the author Pachacuti uses the Inca genealogical form to deliver a message that various Incas had tried to impose monotheism, but they were succeeded by others who let the cult of the *huacas* or shrines proliferate again.[19] The repetition of this cycle as a means of stressing the point may be a feature of Andean storytelling.

Like the author Pachacuti, Guaman Poma was not an Inca. He claimed descent from a noble family from Yaros in the northern Andean highlands, resettled to the Lucanas region nearer Cuzco by the Incas. Like other noble lineages, his had been interwoven with the Inca line through marriage to an Inca daughter.[20] He included an Inca history in the first part of his *Nueva corónica y buen gobierno* [New Chronicle and Good Government] (*c.*1615), both a history and a treatise on good government represented in the form of a letter to the Spanish king. This 'letter' had 1,189 pages, including 398 full-page graphic illustrations. The size of the work, the manner of the illustrations, and other details mimetic of the printing practices of Guaman Poma's time give the manuscript the appearance of a book. The work also includes a new rendering of the Inca painted history, with full-length representations of both the Inkas and their spouses, called Coyas. A memory of a painted series is evident from Guaman Poma's description of the colours of the Inka's dress and other emblematic details in his illustrations, which were rendered in pen and ink. The page of text, which accompanies each page of illustration, bears little resemblance to the outline of Inca history found in Spanish narratives based on Inca source materi-

---

[19] Pierre Duviols, 'Pachacuti Yamqui Salcamaygua, Juan de Santa Cruz (Seventeenth Century)', in *Guide to Documentary Sources for Andean Studies*, vol. 3 (Norman, Okla., 2008), 489.

[20] See Rolena Adorno, *Guaman Poma and His Illustrated Chronicle from Colonial Peru: From a Century of Scholarship to a New Era of Reading* (Copenhagen, 2001), for a general introduction to Guaman Poma's life and work.

als, and his genealogy includes a fairly aberrant list of Coyas. Guaman Poma's real purpose was not to represent the history of others, but to tell the Spanish king that the Inca dynastic line was not the only line of kings in the Andes. A Christian who had participated in campaigns to extirpate non-Christian practices that interfered with evangelization, he nonetheless tries to explain to the king why Andean people were better off before the Spaniards came, even telling him that they were 'more Christian'.

Garcilaso Inca de la Vega, born Gómez Súarez de Figueroa in Cuzco, was the third indigenous author to craft a version of Inca history. The son of a Spanish father and an Inca mother, he inherited nothing when his father died in 1559 and departed to live out his life in Spain. Later in life Garcilaso took his father's name and added the matronym 'Inca', crafting a name in a novel way. His career as a writer included both a translation (1590) from Italian to Spanish of the *Dialoghi d'amore* [Dialogue of Love] (1535) of León Hebreo and an account of the conquest expedition to Florida by Hernando de Soto called *La Florida* (1605). The latter drew from the testimony of Spaniards who had been involved in the conquest of Peru with his father and had then gone to Florida with Soto, and from the published account of Alvar Núñez Cabeza de Vaca, popularly known as the *Naufragios* [Castaways] (1555).[21] Garcilaso turned to writing about Peru when he was more than seventy years old. The first part (1609) of the *Comentarios Reales* was an Inca history to the time of Huascar, a son of Huayna Capac. The narrative of the second part (also known as the *Historia general* [1615]) began with the Spanish arrival and covered the period to 1572, when the execution of Thupa Amaro, the last of the Vilcabamba Incas, put an end to succession in the Inca dynastic line (according to Garcilaso). The division of the work reflects a shift from Inca history to the history of the Spaniards in the Andes, but the switch to a Hispanist perspective belies the nature of Garcilaso's project, which was to put the Inca history and the history of the Spaniards who arrived with Pizarro on an equal footing—to acknowledge the glorious past of both the Incas and the conquistadores in a single chronological sweep.

Though Garcilaso praised Toledo effusively, his project in every way was to undo Toledo's argument that the Incas had recently conquered a large Andean territory and were tyrants. Garcilaso countered with its reverse. His narrative follows the general outline of Inca genealogy (though he adds an Inca between the ninth and tenth Inkas of the standard list), but he redistributes the story of the expansion of Inca power to earlier rulers, extending the life of the empire by several centuries. Garcilaso's Incas had exercised power benevolently. The *Comentarios reales* had little echo in the Andes when they were first published, but would have a remarkable impact on the Incas themselves when they were republished in 1723, a subject that will be taken up below.

---

[21] Raquel Chang-Rodríguez, *Beyond Books and Borders: Garcilaso de la Vega and La Florida del Inca* (Lewisburg, 2006).

Garcilaso lived his life in Spain, but he had not lost contact with Cuzco. In the early years of the seventeenth century, an Inca genealogy, painted on white taffeta, was sent to him in Spain from Cuzco, by Melchor Carlos Inca, son of Carlos Inca and grandson of Paullu Inca, a half-brother of Manco Inca, who collaborated with the Spaniards. Carlos Inca had been a boy in Cuzco at the same time as Garcilaso. How the Incas were represented on this taffeta is unknown, but the title page of the fifth book (*década quinta*) of the *Historia general de los hechos de los castellanos* [General History of the Deeds of the Castilians], authored by Antonio de Herrera and published between 1601 and 1615 in Spain, was apparently drawn from it. The Incas are represented as busts in medallion format, similar to the traditional representation of Spanish kings. This genealogy inserts an additional Inka between generations eight and nine of the Inca genealogies collected in Cuzco in the years before the end of the Toledo period. (Garcilaso had inserted a different Inka between the ninth and tenth Inkas, so no clear idea of any borrowing or its direction can be had.) Garcilaso's sequence of Inca rulers and painted representations of the Incas were the basis of a later Inca history written by don Justo Apo Sahuaraura, a descendant of a half-brother of Manco Inca's named Paullu (see below), and a tradition of a painted genealogy in this format appears to have been kept in Inca hands in Cuzco through this entire period.

Painting was perhaps the most important field for the fertile interplay of Inca and European historical forms. The portraits of the Inkas—either as full-bodied portraits or as busts in medallion format—had a continuing history during the Spanish colonial era. As noted above, Guaman Poma represented the Incas in a series of full-body illustrations. A related series of watercolour portraits served as illustrations in the *Historia general del Perú* [General History of Peru] (1611–16), a narrative of Inca history by Martín de Murúa.[22] Quite apart from accompanying a written history, full-figure representations or busts of the Incas could be painted as a series of portraits, the bust style enjoying particular popularity in the eighteenth century.

The painted tradition, reimagined in a new format, received popular expression in the form of cups decorated in inlaid enamel, called *keros*. While the inlaid enamel technology developed in the Andes made its first documented appearance on wooden cups at about the time the Spaniards arrived in Cuzco, its use in depicting scenes of the pre-Hispanic past in elaborate registers was something that developed afterwards, very likely in the late sixteenth century. The cups are shaped like earlier ceramic cups from Tiahuanaco (*c.*500–700), in the Lake Titicaca region, with the same concave profile. Inca wooden cups had been more nearly cylindrical. Imitations of Tiahuanaco cups were produced by the Incas in ceramics. Tiahuanaco cups from the island of Titicaca had elaborate

---

[22] Juan M. Ossio, *Los retratos de los incas en la crónica de fray Martín de Morúa* (Lima, 1985).

polychrome painting in the upper of two design registers on the exterior.[23] The scenes on both the colonial-era Inca cups and their Tiahuanaco antecedents may refer to narratives; indeed, the repetition of some themes in the case of the colonial Inca cups suggests such a tie. These themes, like the Inka seated on a traditional stool—who extends a drinking cup with one arm, denoting authority during the time of Inca rule, or the battle scene where Incas engage with people who can be identified by their dress as from the eastern lowlands, may refer to a particular story or bring a memorable activity to mind.[24] Often the cups bear a row of *tokapu* designs in the space between the two design registers. *Tokapu* were rectangular geometric designs that encoded symbolic meaning. They appear on cups and on cloth in both the pre-Hispanic and colonial eras, but no connection between the *tokapu* represented on Inca garments and colonial-era *tokapu* has yet been found.[25] Since there are no known 'readings' of the themes on wooden cups in the written record, an understanding of their narrative aspect has been elusive. They were nonetheless potent reminders of the pre-Hispanic Inca past, particularly in the eighteenth century.

Another visual form of representation, albeit one with more tenuous connections to any specific Inca precedent, was the performance of particular events from the time of the Inca Empire and, particularly, events related to the period when it came to an end. Bartolomé Arzáns de Orsúa y Vela, writing in Potosí at the beginning of the eighteenth century, describes the performance of eight short plays in 1555 in the *Historia de la villa Imperial de Potosí* [History of the Imperial Villa of Potosí] (1705–36). Four are set in the time of the Inca Empire. Arzáns is famously unreliable about dates, and his description of the particular plays belies any close connection to the stories about the Inca expansion and other events that appear in the pre-Toledan narratives constructed from Cuzco sources. The last play in the Inca series, on the encounter between Francisco Pizarro and Atahuallpa in Cajamarca and the death of the latter, is a durable theme in both painting and performance. The performance tradition can be documented for the twentieth century in a variety of locales in Peru and Bolivia, though documenting it in earlier centuries is another matter; the painting tradition may not antedate the late eighteenth or early nineteenth century.[26] From the time of Guaman Poma's *Nueva corónica y buen gobierno*, there is a confusion in iconographic treatment between the death of Atahuallpa and the death of Thupa Amaro, the last son of Manco Inca who was captured in Vilcabamba and put to

---

[23] Catherine Julien, 'Finding a Fit: Archaeology and Ethnohistory of the Incas', *Provincial Inca: Archaeological and Ethnohistorical Accounts of the Impact of the Inca State* (Iowa City, 1993), 195–7.

[24] See Jorge A. Flores Ochoa, Elizabeth Kuon Arce, and Roberto Samanez Argumedo, *Queros: Arte inka en vasos ceremoniales* (Lima, 1998), for illustrations and the presentation of various themes.

[25] Catherine Julien, 'Tokapu Messages', in *Proceedings of the Seventh Biennial Symposium of the Textile Society of America* (Earleville, 2001).

[26] Teresa Gisbert, *Iconografía y Mitos Indígenas en el Arte* (La Paz, 1980), 201–4; and Jesús Lara, *Tragedia del fin de Atawallpa* (Cochabama, 1957).

death in the Cuzco plaza in 1572. Tracing the history of the idea that the death of Atahuallpa marked the end of the Inca line is an important task for the future.

THE EIGHTEENTH CENTURY

The change of dynasty in Spain at the beginning of the eighteenth century (from Habsburg to Bourbon) ushered in a period of economic and administrative reform. The pressure to raise royal revenues had the direct effect of stimulating unrest in a population already pressed thin; and the indirect effect of exacerbating nostalgia for the time of Inca rule. This nostalgia was fed by the republication of the first part of the *Comentarios reales* in 1723 and expressed materially through painted portraits of the Incas, wooden cups decorated with Inca themes, and the revival of Inca modes of dress. Disaffection with the colonial regime also brought a rising tide of civil disturbance and led to the most serious challenge to colonial rule in the Americas in 1780, when José Gabriel Condorconqui Tupa Amaru, a native noble in the Tinta province of Cuzco who claimed descent from Tupa Amaru (executed in Cuzco in 1572), launched an armed rebellion that had the creation of a neo-Inca state as its goal.

The phenomenal echo of Garcilaso in Cuzco more than a century after he wrote has to be explained. The *Comentarios reales*—one volume on the Incas and the other taking the arrival of Francisco Pizarro as its starting point—offered the Cuzco elite a usable vision of the past. Despite very real differences in the legal status of people born Spaniards, mestizos, or Indians, the Cuzco elite could not be easily sorted into those categories. First of all, an Inca was not the same as an Indian, and descendants in the dynastic line were excused from paying tribute to the Crown, just as Spaniards were. Many of the men who arrived in Cuzco with Pizarro took Inca wives, Garcilaso's father among them. Garcilaso's history honoured both Inca and Spanish bloodlines. Overriding the breach between the two volumes—with a turn in perspective at the beginning of the second volume from Inca to Spanish, to allow the story of the Spanish conquest to be told in a positive light—is a relatively seamless history of Cuzco's elite. Descendants of the Incas could find what they needed in Garcilaso's literary narrative, despite its strict adherence to European forms.

One of these descendants was don Justo Apo Sahuaraura, a descendant of Paullu Inca, who took his Inca genealogy from Garcilaso and paired it with a portrait series of the pre-Hispanic Inkas, illustrating them as busts in medallion format, in his *Recuerdos de la monarquía peruana* [Memories of the Peruvian Monarchy] (1838). His spellings and the inclusion of an 'Ynca Yupanqui' in tenth position follow Garcilaso. The poses and paraphernalia associated with each Inka are closely tied to the series of busts that appear on the title page of Herrera's *Década quinta*, with additional portraits for Manco Inca and two of his sons, and Paullu Inca, through whom Sahuaraura traced his descent. The likeness to the busts published by Herrera is evidence that a copy of the painted taffeta sent to Garcilaso in Spain by Melchor Carlos Inca, Paullu's grandson, had remained in Cuzco and was transmitted in this family line.

Those who traced their descent exclusively or principally from Spanish blood-lines had other reasons for choosing to identify with Cuzco's past. By the eighteenth century, 'Spaniards' born in the Americas (*criollos*) and Spaniards recently arrived from Spain (*peninsulares*) were finding themselves increasingly at odds. Bourbon policies curtailed the aspirations of *criollos* to rise through church and government posts just when they were demanding more such offices.[27] Cuzco, the centre of Tahuantinsuyu and the most important Spanish city in the Andes until at least the seventeenth century, had been unmistakably eclipsed by both Lima and Potosí by the eighteenth century. If Cuzco-born Spaniards tried to build an identity based on their city of origin—as did Spaniards in Spain—they had no further to look for proof of their city's former grandeur than Garcilaso. The identification with the Incas could be taken quite far: don Diego de Esquivel, the second Marquis of Valleumbroso and a descendant of the Esquivel who arrived in Cuzco with Pizarro, called himself *apo*, the Inca title for a great lord, and wore Inca dress. His son, Diego de Esquivel y Navia, on the other hand, wrote a history of Cuzco in annals form that documented the life of a colonial city since the time of its Spanish foundation to 1750, the *Noticias cronológicas de la gran ciudad del Cuzco* [Cronological Report on the Great City of Cuzco].

Generalizations about identity formation are unwise. What can be seen in the eighteenth century are the multiple ways Inca historical forms could be used to construct a usable Inca past. An example illustrating the complexity of such projects can be drawn from narrative painting. A theme chosen for representation on at least six canvases was the marriage of Beatriz Coya to Martín García de Loyola. Beatriz was the daughter of Saire Tupa, a son of Manco Inca who had been recognized as Inca after his father's death and brought out of Vilcabamba. He had been granted a sizeable *encomienda* (a tribute right), which Beatriz inherited. This property became the basis for the Marquisate of Oropesa, the largest single property held by someone of Inca blood and the only significant piece of the patrimony in Inca hands of all that had once belonged to their forefathers. Beatriz married Loyola, nephew of the founder of the Jesuit order, Ignatius de Loyola. The only daughter from this marriage was married to a near relative of Francisco de Borja, the Spanish general of the Jesuit order at the time of Beatriz's espousal (and who was later canonized). The Jesuits founded the College of San Francisco de Borja in Cuzco in 1620, to educate the sons of native nobility from Cuzco, Arequipa, and Ayacucho. Similar institutions were run by the Jesuits in other Spanish cities. The earliest canvas, painted near the

---

[27] D. A. Brading, *The First America* (New York, 1991), 467–79.

end of the seventeenth century, depicts the two marriages in a single field, with the two Jesuit saints in the background; the painting is gigantic (more than four metres across and two metres high) and hangs in the doorway of the Jesuit church in Cuzco. The legend announces the joining of Inca and Jesuit lineages: the houses of Loyola and Borja to the Inca dynastic line. A second representation of the same theme was hung in the Beaterio of Copacabana in Lima, where elite native women were educated. The symbolism of these paintings is clear: Inca regalism was now under the tutelage of the Jesuits. A second format for narrative painting is a representation whose origins can be located in an engraving by Antonio de la Cueva, made in the first third of the eighteenth century and widely copied. The Incas of the dynastic genealogy are drawn as busts in medallion format, followed by similar representations of the succession of Spanish kings; the Inca portraits were probably drawn from a series sent by the Marquis of Valleumbroso to the Peruvian viceroy in Lima. Another format of this theme shows the current Spanish king at the centre. The secular nature of the project—in clear contrast to the argument for Jesuit tutelage—is evident from the substitution of a portrait of Simón Bolivar in similar paintings made after independence.[28] The Inca past was equally available to Enlightenment projects.

These narrative forms of painting are removed a fair distance from the Inca wooden tablets kept at Poquincancha, but the insistence on visual representation of a sequence of Inkas across the four centuries under consideration here cannot be lost on the reader. This insistence helps us to understand something important: if Garcilaso sufficed, why was Sahuaraura's history necessary? It was necessary because it married the text of Garcilaso to the visual representations of the Inkas that still meant so much. He supplied what Garcilaso lacked.

Sahuaraura helps us to understand the linkages between various modes of representation. One of the known canvases depicting the marriage of Beatriz Coya to Martín García de Loyola was in his possession. He also possessed manuscript copies of two theatrical works written in Quechua, the Inca language, titled *Ollantay* and *Uska Paucar*.[29] Both plays were set in Cuzco at about the time of the Spanish arrival. Using what is known of language change in the eighteenth century, they appear to have their origins in the first half of the eighteenth century.[30] *Ollantay*, like *The death of Atahuallpa*, includes various historical characters, but the mixing of characters, some from Cuzco and some from Quito, belies what is known about their lives. The scenarios of these plays do not square well with sixteenth-century narratives of the Inca past nor with Garcilaso. They are works of historical fiction, truer to the nostalgia of the period

---

[28] Brading, *The First America*, 467–79.

[29] Ibid, 156; and Teodoro Meneses, *Teatro quechua colonial; antología* (Lima, 1983), 177–259, 287–516.

[30] Bruce Mannheim, *The Language of the Inka since the European Invasion* (Austin, 1990), 164–5.

than to what was known about the Inca past, and by people such as Sahuaraura, for example. The plays were performed in the Inca language, so, in light of that fact, we might be able to determine who was the audience for such plays. At the end of the nineteenth century, there were no monolingual Spanish speakers living in Cuzco except for foreigners and people from other parts of the Andes. All *cuzqueños* spoke the Inca language. Some of the plays were written by priests such as Sahuaraura, and a form of 'Inca drama' continued to be written and performed into the twentieth century.[31]

A memory of the Incas fuelled more than nostalgia. It was a potent means of uniting a fairly varied cross-section of the Andean population. From the early years of Spanish colonial rule, native elites from all over the Andean region used their status under the Incas when they negotiated rights and privileges with the Spanish Crown.[32] When the increasingly oppressive economic policies of Spain began to have their effect in the eighteenth century, those who led uprisings might use a memory of the Incas as counterpoint to the current reality or even represent themselves in the role of Inka. The most successful challenge to Spanish rule in the Americas was led by José Gabriel Condorcanqui Tupac Amaru, who traced his Inca bloodline through a daughter of the Tupac Amaru executed in the Cuzco plaza in 1572. Styling himself Inka in the manner of a Spanish king, and issuing edicts modelled on royal documentary forms, Tupac Amaru enlisted support from native leaders and the disaffected in general.[33] The rebellion he launched lasted eighteen months, and at one point succeeded in detaching from Spanish authority most of the southern highlands of what is now Peru. Though his claim to kingship was argued from an Inca bloodline, the movement he led cannot be characterized as a strictly indigenous rebellion; the diverse social origins of the prisoners taken at its end suggest that this notion is wrong. Moreover, like his Vilcabamba forebears, Tupac Amaru II had very little success with his Inca relatives in Cuzco. Incas such as Sahuaraura and Mateo Puma-cahua, who would later participate in the independence movement, did not join his cause.

Tupac Amaru and his wife, Micaela Bastidas, had their portraits painted,[34] and the use of Inca symbols by this movement had its consequences. Juan Antonio de Areche, a judge sent from Spain to impose a number of administrative reforms on the viceroyalty of Peru, outlawed symbols of Inca identity following the rebellion, and specifically, the possession of portraits of the Incas and wooden

---

[31] César Itier, *El teatro quechua en el Cuzco*, vol. 1 (Cuzco, 1995), 25–42.

[32] Brading, *The First America*, 489–91.

[33] John Howland Rowe, 'El movimiento nacional inca del siglo xviii', *Revista Universitaria* (Cuzco), 107 (1954), 17–25.

[34] Leon G. Campbell, 'Ideology and Factionalism during the Great Rebellion, 1780–1782', in Steve J. Stern (ed.), *Resistance, Rebellion, and Consciousness in the Andean Peasant World, 18th to 20th Centuries* (Madison, 1987).

cups. Possession was also taken of Garcilaso's history, and like the works of Bartolomé de las Casas before him, copies of the *Comentarios reales* were collected and destroyed. José Manuel Moscoso y Peralta, the bishop of Cuzco at the time of the rebellion and a *criollo* from Arequipa who had sent parish priests into battle to crush the rebellion, later lamented that the Incas had learned what they knew about the former Inca Empire from Garcilaso.[35]

Even after the fierce repression of the Thupa Amaro movement, dreams of reviving Tahuantinsuyu were still possible. In 1805 two unlikely men tried to identify another Inka. Non-Indians born in other Spanish cities who came to Cuzco to study at the university, they somehow managed to dream of Inca monarchy. Hanged in the Cuzco plaza on 5 December 1805, the men were proclaimed 'national heroes' by the first Peruvian Congress in 1825.[36] The Inca past still had a role to play in the republican imagination.

TIMELINE/KEY DATES

*c.*1400 Beginning of the Inca expansion outside the Cuzco region

1532 Francisco Pizarro and his soldiers attack and capture the Inca Atahuallpa in Cajamarca

1533 Pizarro and his men arrive in Cuzco, the Inca capital, as allies of Manco Inca

1536–7 Manco Inca tries to oust the Spaniards from Peru

1541–63 Spanish civil wars

1570–6 Viceroy Francisco de Toledo reforms Spanish administration in the Andes

1572 Toledo executes Tupac Amaru, son of Manco Inca and last of the Vilcabamba Incas, in the Cuzco plaza

1701 Accession of Philip V, first Bourbon ruler of Spain, after the death of Charles II, the last Habsburg

1776–87 José de Gálvez serves as Minister of the Indies and implements reforms of Indian administration

1777 José Antonio de Areche arrives in Peru to implement measures to raise revenue

1780–1 Revolt led by Thupa Amaro II, a provincial noble who claimed descent from the first Thupa Amaro through a daughter

1805 A conspiracy to end Spanish rule and restore an Inca king led by two non-Indian immigrants to Cuzco

1824–5 Indepence of the central Andes from Spain

---

[35] Brading, *The First America*, 491.

[36] Ibid, 554–5; and Alberto Flores Galindo, 'In Search of an Inca', in Stern (ed.), *Resistance, Rebellion, and Consciousness in the Andean Peasant World*, 193–7.

KEY HISTORICAL SOURCES

Arzáns de Orsúa y Vela, Bartolomé, *Historia de la Villa Imperial de Potosí* (1705–36); ed. Lewis Hanke and Gunnar L. Mendoza, 3 vols. (Providence, RI, 1965).

Betanzos, Juan de, *Suma y narración de los Incas* (1551–7); ed. María del Carmen Martín Rubio (Madrid, 1987).

Cabello Valboa, Miguel, *Miscelánea antártica* (1586; Lima, 1951).

Cieza de León, Pedro de, *Crónica del Perú: primera parte* (1551); ed. Franklin Pease (Lima 1984).

Cobo, Bernabé, *Historia del nuevo mundo* (1653); ed. Francisco Mateos, Biblioteca de Autores Españoles, 91–2 (Madrid, 1956).

Esquivel y Navia, Diego de, *Noticias cronológicas de la gran ciudad del Cuzco*, 2 vols. (Lima, 1980).

Garcilaso de la Vega, Inca, 'Comentarios reales' (1609–17), in *Obras completas*, Biblioteca de Autores Españoles, 132–4 (Madrid, 1965).

Guaman Poma de Ayala, Felipe, *Nueva corónica y buen gobierno* (c.1615); ed. John V. Murra, Rolena Adorno, and Jorge L. Urioste (Madrid, 1989).

Herrera y Tordesillas, Antonio de, *Historia general de los hechos de los castellanos* (1601–15); 17 vols. (Madrid, 1934–57).

Meneses, Teodoro, 'Usca Paucar' and 'Apu Ollantay' (eighteenth century); *Teatro quechua colonial; antología* (Lima, 1983).

Molina, Cristóbal de, 'Relación de las fábulas i ritos de los Ingas' (1576), in Henrique Urbano and Pierre Duviols (eds.), *Fábulas y mitos de los incas* (Madrid, 1989), 47–134.

Montesinos, Fernando de, *Memorias antiguas historiales y políticas del Perú* (1642; Madrid, 1882).

Ossio, Juan M, *Los retratos de los incas en la crónica de fray Martín de Morúa* (Lima, 1985).

Pachacuti Yamqui Salcamaygua, Juan de Santa Cruz, *Relación de antigüedades deste reyno del Piru* (1590); ed. Pierre Duviols and César Itier (Lima, 1993).

Pizarro, Pedro, *Rekación del descubrimiento y conquista del Perú* (1571); ed. Pierre Duviols (Lima, 1978).

Sahuaraura Inca, Justo Apo, *Recuerdos de la monarquía peruana o bosquejo de la historia de los incas* (1838); ed. Rafael Varón Gabai (Lima, 2001).

Sarmiento de Gamboa, Pedro, 'Historia Indica' (1572), in Richard von Pietschmann (ed.), *Geschichte des Inkareiches von Pedro Sarmiento de Gamboa* (Berlin, 1906).

Titu Cusi Yupanqui, Diego de Castro, *History of How the Spaniards Arrived in Peru* (1570); ed. Catherine Julien (Indianapolis, 2007).

BIBLIOGRAPHY

Cummins, Thomas B. F., *Toasts with the Inca: Andean Abstraction and Colonial Images on Quero Vessels* (Ann Arbor, 2002).

Dean, Carolyn, *Inka Bodies and the Body of Christ: Corpus Christi in Colonial Cuzco, Peru* (Durham, NC, 1999).

Flores Galindo, Alberto, 'In Search of an Inca', in Steve J. Stern (ed.), *Resistance, Rebellion, and Consciousness in the Andean Peasant World, 18th to 20th Centuries* (Madison, 1987), 193–210.

Garrett, David T., *Shadows of Empire: The Indian Nobility of Cusco, 1750–1828* (Cambridge, 2005).

Gisbert, Teresa, *Iconografía y Mitos Indígenas en el Arte* (La Paz, 1980).

Julien, Catherine, 'La organización parroquial del Cuzco y la ciudad incaica', *Tawantin-suyu*, 5 (1998), 82–96.

——'History and Art in Translation', *Colonial Latin American Review*, 8:1 (1999), 61–89.

——*Reading Inca History* (Iowa City, 2000).

Mannheim, Bruce, *The Language of the Inka since the European Invasion* (Austin, 1990).

Pease, Franklin, 'Chronicles of the Andes in the Sixteenth and Seventeenth Centuries', in *Guide to Documentary Sources for Andean Studies, 1530–1900* (Norman, Okla., 2008), 11–22.

Rowe, John H., 'Colonial Portraits of Inca Nobles', in Sol Tax (ed.), *The Civilization of Ancient America: Selected Papers of the XXIX International Congress of Americanists* (Chicago, 1951), 258–68.

——'The Chronology of Inca Wooden Cups', in Samuel K. Lothrop (ed.), *Essays in Pre-Columbian Art and Archaeology* (Boston, 1961), 317–41.

——'An Account of the Shrines of Ancient Cuzco', *Ñawpa Pacha*, 17 (1979), 1–80.

——'Probanza de los Incas nietos de conquistadores', *Histórica* (Lima), 9:2 (1986), 193–245.

Salomon, Frank, *The Cord Keepers* (Durham, NC, 2004).

Chapter 31

Historical Writing about Brazil, 1500–1800

Neil L. Whitehead

This chapter examines a range of historical writings on Brazil emerging between 1500 and 1800. Although modern Brazil is a Portuguese-speaking nation, in the early colonial period both the physical geography of Brazil and its character as a Portuguese colony were unstable. French, Dutch, English, and Irish colonies challenged the exclusive occupation of both the coastal regions and the Amazon River basin, where the Spanish also vied for control. As a result, important writings on the history of Brazil exist in other languages than Portuguese while individual accounts of travel are also to be found in a range of European languages. Contemporary with the better-known Portuguese texts of discovery relating to the Atlantic coast of Brazil, there also exist sixteenth-century writings in French, German, and English on the trade there with native populations, as well as on military engagements with Portuguese colonial outposts. In particular, the French occupation of Rio de Janeiro in the mid-sixteenth century generated substantial texts on the history of the region, as did the Dutch plantations in coastal Brazil of the seventeenth century.

For the Amazon basin, the earliest writings are all in Spanish since the 1494 Treaty of Tordesillas established the limits of Portuguese right of conquest to territory east of 50 degrees longitude. This meant that until the 1640s the Portuguese presence along the Amazon River was negligible, although French, English, and Irish traders all established outposts on the river and left records of that colonial episode.[1] For the eastern coastal region of the 'Captaincies'—the system by which early colonial administration was established—the bulk of writing derives from the missionary orders. The work of José de Anchieta, Pero de Magalhães Gandavo, and Manuel da Nóbrega are important in this regard as well as other histories, such as that by the colonist Gabriel Soares de Sousa. This highly linguistically and politically diverse set of texts were extensively used in Robert Southey's well-known three-volume *History of Brazil* (1819), which marks

---

[1] Joyce Lorimer (ed.), *English and Irish Settlement on the River Amazon, 1550–1646* (London, 1989).

the termination of the period considered in this chapter but did much to establish the modern parameters of historical writing on colonial Brazil.

THE INVENTION OF 'BRAZIL'

Historical writing creates a 'Brazil'. It is through the process of codifying and reflecting on the meaning of European occupation that the notion of a place 'Brazil' was established and the heirs to that occupation, quite literally, 'inscribed' themselves as legitimate occupiers of that place. At the same time such a process of writing was not an abstract or philosophical project in the first place but rather the making of knowledge to support commercial and political ambition in the exotic space of a 'New World'. As a result, it is the ethnology and broader cultural geography of the new space of 'Brazil' that dominates its representation in the period 1500–1800 and this in turn creates the master tropes of both colonial and postcolonial Brazil as a space of luxuriant and limitless nature, causally coupled to visually dazzling, sexualized, and cannibalistic human cultures.[2] For these reasons, a necessary emphasis is given in the following discussion of historical writing to the depiction of native peoples as a cipher for 'Brazil' itself. As Janaína Amado argues concerning the legendary figure of 'Caramuru': 'narratives about Caramuru can be considered to be Brazil's myth of origin. The myth of Caramuru dramatizes some of the most fundamental historic and symbolic experiences of Brazil and Portugal.'[3] Moreover, even if there is a critical cultural difference between Europeans and native Brazilians, this does not render invalid the attempt to read others through the writings of their conquerors, though it does pose complex issues of hermeneutical approach. It is not that cultural biases in European writing on non-Europeans needs to be factored out, accounted for, or otherwise made overt—for this leaves us only with hollow texts and empty documents. Rather, given the culturally dependent nature of historical and ethnographic representation, we must also consider native social and cultural practices, particularly as expressed in native discourse.

---

[2] In a recent review article on the historiography of Brazil, Stuart B. Schwartz underscores how this writing of 'Brazil', in both the colonial and postcolonial moments, has been engaged with the idea of the indigenous. However, and contrary to the Indian's iconic status in the colonial era, scholarship on historical works of the nineteenth century has often pointed out that there was an erasure of the Indian from the national past. See Schwartz, 'Adolfo de Varnhagen: Diplomat, Patriot', *Hispanic American Historical Review*, 47:2 (1967), 185–202.

[3] Janaína Amado, 'Mythic Origins: Caramuru and the Founding of Brazil', *Hispanic American Historical Review*, 80:4 (2000), 783–811, at 786. Diogo Alvares or 'Caramuru' (electric eel) was one of Brazil's first European inhabitants, and his story is a recurring theme in Brazilian history, literature, and imagination. Diogo Alvares was shipwrecked at the beginning of Portuguese colonization. He lived in Bahia for many years, learned the native languages, and participated in native warfare. He had many children, particularly with Paragua, the daughter of an eminent Tupinambá lord in the Bahia region.

Ferocious cannibals and voracious Amazons were as much an element in existing native cosmologies and mythologies, as they are the result of European cultural projection. The presence of analogous symbolic and discursive motifs in both native Brazilian and European thought makes interpretation more difficult but simultaneously provides the hermeneutic strategy by which such histories may be written—for they are histories of the mutual, mimetic, and entangled relations of Brazil and Europe over the last five hundred years. In this way native cultural practice is itself an equally necessary and viable context for the interpretation and analysis of European texts as are the biographies and histories of their authors.[4]

COASTAL BRAZIL, 1500–1650

The Portuguese materials have a chronological priority over other sources since they include the letters of geographical discovery by Pedro Vaz de Caminha and the 'Four Letters' of Amerigo Vespucci. These texts are also amongst the earliest descriptions of the New World itself and justly famous for that reason. Some of the details given by Caminha and Vespucci also indicate that native Tupi populations were amongst the first American peoples to be described. However, this occurs in such a way as to establish a rhetorical association between Brazilian natives and the practice of cannibalism as well as exotic sexuality. Thus Vespucci writes, probably of the northern coasts of Brazil, that: 'They eat little flesh unless it be human flesh . . . they are so inhuman as to transgress regarding this most bestial custom. For they eat all their enemies that they kill or take.'[5] Vespucci also initiates a startling image of indigenous sexuality:

Another custom among them is sufficiently shameful, and beyond all human credibility. The women being very libidinous, make the penis of their husbands swell to such a size as to appear deformed; and this is accomplished by a certain artifice, being the bite of a poisonous animal, and by reason of this many lose their virile organ and remain eunuchs.'[6]

Vespucci goes on to reinforce the notion of cannibalism as a subsistence practice, rather than ritual proclivity, and in so doing indelibly carved the motif of anthropophagy into the representation of Brazil through hyperbolic forms of representation: 'I have seen a man eat his children and wife; and I knew a man who was popularly credited to have eaten 300 human bodies . . . I say further that they were surprised that we did not eat our enemies, and use their flesh as food,

---

[4] See Neil L. Whitehead, *The Discoverie of the Large, Rich and Bewtiful Empire of Guiana by Sir Walter Ralegh* (Manchester, 1997); and Whitehead and Michael Harbsmeier (eds.), *Hans Staden's True History: An Account of Cannibal Captivity in Brazil* (Durham, 2008).
[5] Vespucci, *The letters of Amerigo Vespucci and Other Documents Illustrative of his Career*, trans. Clements R. Markham (London, 1894), 11.
[6] Ibid., 46.

for they say it is excellent.'[7] Absurd and defamatory though these claims appear, the sacrifice of children or women with affinal status is thus more clearly explained in later sources, as is the accumulation, through the capture and sacrifice of enemies, of honorific names, which was indeed a way in which an individual may have claimed to have 'eaten' more than three hundred of his enemies. In the same way the 'excellence' of human flesh can be related to the importance and satisfaction of revenge through ritual sacrifice, as much as to any gustatory pleasures.

Vespucci's verifiable voyage to Brazil in 1502 was preceded by that of Pedro Vaz de Caminha, who accompanied and described Pedro Alvares Cabral's foundational discovery of Brazil in 1500. Caminha does not mention 'cannibalism'[8] but rather signals 'savagery' through the sexualized nakedness of the natives they encounter.[9] Caminha also highlighted the use of feathers among the Tupi as well as their use of lip-plugs. The sexual voraciousness and participation of women in cannibal violence is given an emphasis by Vespucci that foreshadows, along with other accounts from the Caribbean,[10] the emergence of the idea of New World 'Amazons', later fully realized in Gaspar de Carvajal's account of Francisco de Orellana's first descent of the 'River of the Amazons' in the 1540s (see below).[11]

After the period of initial discovery there is a hiatus in the Portuguese materials until the 1540s, when the first missionary writings begin to appear. The reports of Manoel da Nóbrega, head of the Jesuit Order in Brazil, written some fifty years after these first encounters, still provide some of the most extended accounts of Brazil. As a missionary resident among the natives Nóbrega was in a good position to outline some of the key features of Tupi culture and society. He duly notes subsistence practices, political and ethnic divisions, and the rules and customs of marriage and birth, the role of the *pagé* and *karai* (shamans and prophets)—but spends no less space re-inscribing the cannibal motif.[12] Accounts

---

[7] Vespucci, *The letters of Amerigo Vespucci*, 47.

[8] In fact 'cannibalism' as a word derives from the Columbian voyages to the Caribbean where the native term 'caniba' came to stand for a European notion of the eating of human flesh. See Peter Hulme and Neil L. Whitehead, *Wild Majesty: Encounters with Caribs from Columbus to the Present Day: An Anthology* (Oxford, 1992). It is notable that Amerigo Vespucci uses the term 'canibali' in his accounts of the regions to the north of the Amazon but not in regard to Brazil. See Vespucci, *The letters of Amerigo Vespucci*, 23. Hans Staden does not use the term at all, nor do other commentators on the Tupi.

[9] Pedro Vaz de Caminha, *The Voyage of Pedro Alvares Cabral to Brazil and India* (London, 1938), 15.

[10] Hulme and Whitehead *Wild Majesty*, 15.

[11] Gaspar de Carvajal, 'Discovery of the Orellana River', in *The Discovery of the Amazon According to the Account of Friar Gaspar de Carvajal and Other Documents*, ed. J. T. Medina, trans. B. T. Lee (New York, 1934), 167–235.

[12] Manoel da Nóbrega, 'Informação das Terras do Brasil' (1549), in, *Cartas do Brasil* (São Paulo, 1988), 100.

such as Nóbrega's were intended as synthetic summaries, as ethnological overviews, and so necessarily tended to erase the contingent and particular in order to arrive at a generalized statement of habits and customs. Like Caminha and Vespucci, Nóbrega also signals the erotic and bodily as part of native Brazilian identity.[13] This theme is also taken up forcefully in the French texts (see below), but the overall conjunction of the material, fleshy, and naked cannibal body with the spirituality of Eucharistic sacrifice is a theme that pervades the historical literature. In this vein, the writings of José de Anchieta, from the period of the late 1550s, broach not just sensuality but also exotic sexuality,[14] as first mentioned by Vespucci. Anchieta also widens this concern with sexuality to encompass the rules of marriage, incest, and the sexuality of sacrifice. He also hints at how the politics of leadership among the Tupi were affected by the colonial intrusion, while neatly casting suspicion on the French for having stimulated Tupi savagery:

I was told that Ambirem, a great chief of Rio de Janeiro, . . . ordered that one of his twenty wives, who had committed adultery, should be tied to a post and have her stomach cut out . . . But this appears to have been a lesson taken from the French, who are accustomed to dealing out such deaths, because no Brazilian Indian would normally inflict such a punishment.[15]

It is not for another twenty years or so after Anchieta was writing that we get further extensive reportage, this time from a secular source, Gabriel Soares de Sousa.

Sousa was writing as a Portuguese colonist resident many years in Brazil and offers a compendious description of the colony.[16] Sousa resided mainly in the region of Bahia. Like Anchieta he was alert to the politics of cultural practice in the period of his residence, and he also 'verifies' the erotic and exotic nature of cannibal sexuality:

They are addicted to sodomy and do not consider it a shame. The one who acts as the male regards himself as virile and they boast of such bestiality. In their villages in the bush there are such men who keep shop to all those who want them, like prostitutes . . . They are not satisfied with their penises as nature made them, but many of them expose theirs to the bites of poisonous animals which causes their penises to swell and they suffer for six months during

---

[13] Ibid., 101.

[14] 'The hair of others [a kind of centipede] . . . are venomous and provoke libidinous desires. The Indians are accustomed to apply them to their genital parts which incites and intensifies sensual enjoyment: after three days these hairs putrefy: sometimes the prepuce is perforated and the sexual organs infected with an incurable disease: they not only soil themselves with this foulness, but they also defile and infect the women with whom they sleep.' Ibid., 126.

[15] Ibid., 256.

[16] See John M. Monteiro, 'The Heathen Castes of Sixteenth-Century Portuguese America: Unity, Diversity, and the Invention of the Brazilian Indian', *Hispanic American Historical Review*, 80:4 (2000), 697–719, for a thorough discussion of the significance of Sousa's ethnology and its role in the nineteenth-century 'invention' of the Tupi.

which time their organs change. Their members become so monstrously big that women can hardly stand them.[17]

Paradoxically, given the negative tone of this passage, Sousa actually opens a slightly broader window on Tupian subjectivity, particularly with regard to the power of the *karai* (prophet-sorcerers), who were a constant feature in missionary accounts, since spiritual conquest was all-important to such writers. But for someone so long a resident in Brazil, the facts of Tupian war-sacrifice also loomed large and, for example, Sousa mentions details concerning the subjectivity of the sacrificial executioner; notes how individual enthusiasms cross-cut ceremonial order; and provides an extensive description of sacrificial killing, but crucially notes that gastronomic 'cannibalism' was not the purpose of such rituals.

As descriptions and commentary on the Tupi move into the latter part of the sixteenth century, further ethnological detail emerges. But as Tupian societies along the Brazilian coast faced deepening social crisis through demographic losses due to European disease and political and economic conquest, as well as through increasing dependency and entanglement with the colonial intruders, so the Tupi become a more abstract context for the philosophical and liturgical musings of the commentators. At this point in time, Gandavo makes the following statement about the 'savages' of Brazil, which has become a somewhat hackneyed statement of the colonial mentality of the time: 'It [the Tupi language] lacks three letters; one does not find in it, namely, F, nor L, nor R, a very wonderful thing, for they have neither Faith, Law, nor Ruler: and thus they live without order, counting, weights or measures.'[18] These scattered and inevitably partial accounts of the Tupi peoples found in the early Portuguese texts nonetheless often contrast favourably with the relatively brief (and perhaps derivative) French materials. The extensive and often systematic ethnology of the Portuguese missionaries, as well as the observations of long-term residents such as Sousa, combine to provide an important historical and ethnological resource. However, for various reasons, the French texts have attracted a much more substantive secondary commentary; principally because of the way in which they were seized upon by European philosophers and intellectuals, such as Michel de Montaigne or Jean-Jacques Rousseau, but also because the French missionaries evangelized the region around the Amazon to the north of Rio de

---

[17] Gabriel Soares de Sousa, *Notícia do Brasil* (São Paulo, 1974), 172.

[18] Pero de Magalhães Gandavo, 'History of the Province of Santa Cruz', in *The Histories of Brazil*, vol. 2 (New York, 1922), 85. Although in Vespucci's earliest description we are told that 'they use the same articulations as we, since they form their utterances either with the palate, or with the teeth, or on the lips, except that they give different names to things', suggesting clearly that colonial attitudes were themselves historically evolving, as was the significance of language as a comparative anthropological tool.

Janeiro in the early seventeenth century, producing very extensive descriptions of Tupi peoples there.

The early French works on coastal Brazil all date to a relatively brief period in the mid-sixteenth century, deriving from the attempt by Nicholas de Villegagnon to colonize directly the region that their traders had been regularly visiting since the 1520s. Arriving in the Bay of Guanabara (the site of the present-day cities Rio de Janeiro and Niteroi) in November 1555, the French fortified a position at the mouth of the bay and named their enclave *France Antarctique*. The nascent colony, despite the prior presence of French traders in the region, was not a success, as Villegagnon failed to negotiate the complexities of native allegiances. This encouraged rebellion from these 'Norman' traders. As early as 1503 a French trader from Normandy, Paulmier de Gonneville, spent some five to six months living among the Carijó, a coastal Tupi people, initiating a system of Norman 'interpreters' living for extended periods amongst native peoples in order to organize and promote trade. But also, according to Jean de Léry, 'accommodating themselves to the natives and leading the lives of atheists, not only polluted themselves by all sorts of lewd and base behaviors among the women and girls . . . but some of them, surpassing the savages in inhumanity, even boasted in my hearing of having killed and eaten prisoners'.[19] The rebellion of the traders was suppressed and Villegagnon sought both political and spiritual reinforcement. He wrote to Jean Calvin requesting that pastors be sent, one of whom was to be Jean de Léry. However, the Franciscan André Thévet already served the colony—and consequently the religious tensions and conflicts of Europe were transposed to Brazil, where the native practice of ritual cannibalism became the colonial mirror of theological dispute over the meaning of Christian Eucharist. Villegagnon in fact turned against the Protestant pastors and executed five of them, even as Léry was returning to France.[20] Léry and Thévet are therefore positioned very differently with regard to both the politics of colonialism in the region and the significance of Tupian sacrificial rituals.

André Thévet, in his earliest work on Brazil, *Les Singularitez de la france Antarctique* [The Singularities of Antarctic France] (1557), delineated a geography of man-eating that located the uncultured 'cannibals' to the north towards the Amazon River, and the ritualized 'anthropophages' in the orbit of French influence. The former are characterized as cruel eaters of human flesh as a matter of diet, the latter as exponents of certain elaborate rituals of revenge. Not surprisingly, this cannibal cosmography also conforms to the patterns of French trading and military alliances with the indigenous population in the region. But it is the matter of direct experience that requires special note here, since Thévet, although often lauded as the 'first ethnographer' of the Tupi, in fact composed

---

[19] Jean de Léry, *History of a Voyage to the Land of Brazil*, trans. Janet Whatley (Berkeley 1990), 128.

[20] Ibid., 218.

his account, or had others do so, from a multiplicity of second-hand sources. But both Léry and Thévet who, in the transliteration of Tupian ritual into something more akin to a witches' sabbat, suggest it is the women who are key to this ritual practice. Elaborate though anthropophagic ritual becomes in Thévet's subsequent account in the *Cosmographie Universelle* [Universal Cosmography] (1575) and his manuscript work *Histoire de... deux voyages* [History of... Two Voyages], it is clear that vengeance is the hermeneutic key for the missionary writers in understanding the meaning of the cannibal act, such that description of the careful distribution of the victim's body parts among allies and affines, as well as the embedding of the ritual in myth, becomes central to these later works. Thévet thus provides details of Tupian cosmology and mythology in the *Cosmographie* that appear nowhere else. However, the cultural importance of the sorcerer-prophets, the *Karaiba*, as well as the evil spirits, are certainly mentioned in most of the other sources, both Portuguese and French, reviewed here. Montaigne later collapses this binary geography and restricts the notion of the cannibal (as opposed to anthropophage) to the Tamoio, as constructed by Thévet twenty years earlier and as contemporaneously read by Léry.[21] Montaigne's method is to conjoin the sensationalism of cannibalism with an unexpected eulogy, mimicking another work of the period on the savageries and civilities of the Ottoman Turks, Guillame Postel's *La République des Turcs* [The Republic of the Turks] (1560). As F. Lestringant wryly notes, this particularization of the cannibal, unlike with Thévet, allows Montaigne actually to conceal the extent of his analytical and descriptive borrowing from Thévet through Léry, and directly from Léry himself.[22]

Léry's borrowing from Thévet, despite their theological differences, is very evident. In fact Léry actually adds very little new ethnographic evidence but nonetheless vastly enriches the interpretation and symbolic exploitation of that material. In his writing the cannibal becomes a universal symbolic and tropic key; the central motivation of vengeance is made systematic through an examination of various aspects of Tupi culture and he clearly allegorizes the act of eating. In this new framework of semiophagy the carnal and spiritual are expressed through the opposition of the raw and cooked. As a Calvinist pastor, Léry was also a witch-hunter of some enthusiasm in Europe, so that the imagery of life-sucking hecuba and witch cannibalism of the innocent play easily into his representation of Tupian ritual.[23] This misogyny is given further inflection through the facts of Léry's own biography since he personally encountered survival cannibalism

[21] Michel de Montaigne, *Essais* (Paris, 1580); and Jean de Léry, *Histoire d'un voyage faict en la terre du Brésil* (Geneva, 1578).

[22] F. Lestringant (ed.), *Jean de Léry: Histoire d'un voyage faict en la terre du Brésil (1578)* (Paris, 1997), 54–5.

[23] A similar transformation is evident in the reworking of Staden's illustrations for the visual compendium *Americae*, published in 1592 by Théodore de Bry.

during the siege of Sancerre, just before turning to write the *Histoire d'un voyage* (1578).

HANS STADEN, ANTHONY KNIVET, AND THE DUTCH IN BRAZIL

At the same time that Jean de Léry first travelled to Brazil, the Tupinambá captured Hans Staden, a German gunner in the service of the Portuguese. In itself this was not such a remarkable event, but in order to understand the centrality of ethnology to South American historiography, and the notion of indigenous cannibalism to the imagining of Brazil in particular, then Hans Staden's text—the *Warhaftige Historia* [True History] (1557)—is of key importance.

The *Warhaftige Historia* is a fundamental text in the history of the discovery of Brazil, being one of the earliest accounts we have of the Atlantic world from an eyewitness who was six years in Portuguese service and captive among Indians for more than nine months, as well as offering highly detailed descriptions of the nature of early Portuguese enclaves in the region of Rio de Janeiro.[24] As mentioned, the work dates to a point in time when the Portuguese presence in the region was directly challenged by the French, who had been visiting the Brazilian coast for the trade in Brazilian wood since at least the 1520s. In this context, both the French and Portuguese attempted to recruit and maintain native alliances, making knowledge of the indigenous population much more than a disinterested ethnological issue. Staden's account therefore also hinges on the way in which this inter-colonial conflict played into his situation as a captive of the Tupinambá,[25] allies to the French. In this way the work, although chiefly famed until now as a text on Tupian cannibalism, is no less important for appreciating the nature of European colonialism in Brazil and how that context was significant for the emergence of various ethnic and national antagonisms in Europe. In fact the issue of cannibalism, although obviously prominent in Staden's text and its accompanying visual illustrations (see Fig. 31.1), is by no means the only matter of contemporary interest to historians and anthropologists.

The Portuguese made every effort, not always successful, to keep out other Europeans, not least the British. Nevertheless, a number of British (and Irish)

---

[24] See Neil L. Whitehead and Michael Harbsmeier (eds.), *Hans Staden's True History: An Account of Cannibal Captivity in Brazil* (Durham, 2008).

[25] The term 'Tupi' is a collective term applied to a number of Tupí-Guarani-speaking tribes such as the Caeté, Potiguara, Tamoyo, Timino, Tupinambá, and Tupiniquin, who in the sixteenth century occupied extensive areas of the Brazilian Atlantic coast from southern São Paulo to the mouth of the Amazon River. Though now extinct, these widely dispersed tribal groups showed considerable uniformity in language and culture.

FIG 31.1 Konyan Bebe addresses Hans Staden on his capture. From Neil L. Whitehead and Michael Harbsmeier (eds.), *Hans Staden's True History: An Account of Cannibal Captivity in Brazil* (Durham, NC, 2008), 63.

sailors, adventurers, privateers, and pirates landed on the Brazilian coast during the sixteenth and early seventeenth centuries. The journals and narratives many of them wrote about what they found there are of great interest in themselves and of great value to historians of colonial Brazil. These first-hand accounts of Brazil can be found in Richard Hakluyt's *Principal Navigations* (1589), Theodore de Bry's *Grands Voyages, vol. III Americae* (1592), and Samuel Purchas's *Hakluytus Posthumus or Purchas His Pilgrimes* (1613). Among the more notable of these accounts is Anthony Knivet's story of his ten years of 'admirable adventures and strange fortunes' (1592–1601), after being captured by the Portuguese during Thomas Cavendish's attack on Santos. Thus, some forty years after Staden's captivity text was published, the *Admirable Adventures and Strange Fortunes of*

Master Antonie Knivet appeared in Purchas's collection of travel literatures, *Purchas His Pilgrimes.* The text includes the story of Anthony Knivet's voyage to Brazil, his life among the indigenous cultures there, and his eventual return to England. After shipwreck along the Brazilian coast Knivet is held captive by the Portuguese. One of his tasks under the governor is that of *bandeirante* (licensed explorer, fortune hunter). As both escapee and slave, Knivet lives among the Indians, observing their customs, language, military technique, and culture. He recounts many of his experiences, including vivid portraits of numerous Native American individuals and tribes. Knivet recounts the long march of the Tamoyo, who had captured Knivet, and the other twelve members of his *bandeira.* He witnessed the deaths by bludgeoning of all his companions. He attributed his own survival to a lie he told, stating that he was French rather than Portuguese, as had also been the case for Hans Staden. During his two-month captivity, Knivet forges a friendship with the Tamoyo. They share information on fishing, hunting, and military technique. When his military advice proves useful against the Tomomino and Tupinikin tribes, Knivet gains a position of authority among his captors. Planning to make his way to the coast in order to board a ship for England, Knivet takes this opportunity to persuade the Tamoyo chief to move his people eastward. Knivet and thirty thousand Tamoyo thus depart for the Atlantic coast and, after further tribulations, Knivet does indeed manage his return to England.

Richard Flecknoe is usually credited with having written the first separately published book by an English-speaking traveller to Brazil. Flecknoe was an Irish Catholic priest, poet, and adventurer who travelled from Lisbon to Brazil in 1648 and spent eight months in Pernambuco and Rio de Janeiro in 1649. William Dampier—pirate, adventurer, and explorer—also left a narrative of Brazil at the end of the seventeenth century in his work *A Voyage to New Holland in the Year 1699* (1729), which includes a description of a month-long visit to Bahia.

The Dutch, as with the British adventurers, also sustained important colonial connections with Brazil and between 1500 and 1610 numerous titles were published in the Netherlands, many of which contained American references. Dutch trading and trading posts in the New World led to the development of the West India Company in 1621 and Dutch pamphleteers not surprisingly represented their commercial rivals, the Spanish and Portuguese, as cruel and despotic. In particular the extended reports by Dierick Ruyters and Johannes de Laet,[26] both of whom provided important navigation information and detailed accounts of the West India Company's operations in Brazil, represent the most important of this kind of promotional literature, rich with ethnographic detail.

---

[26] Dierick Ruyters, *Toortse der zee-vaert* (1623; The Hague, 1913); and Johannes de Laet, *Nieuwe wereldt ofte beschrijvinghe van West-Indien* (Leiden, 1625).

FIRST CONTACTS ALONG THE AMAZON RIVER
AND THE CAPTAINCY OF MARANHÃO, 1540–1650

First contacts were often much later along the Amazon than the coastal regions of Brazil and the Guianas, since neither the Spanish nor Portuguese tried to settle the Maranhão region or the upper Amazon until the 1640s. Although other colonial powers were established throughout this region, their settlements were simply fortified trading posts. Notably, the first Iberian expeditions to travel the length of the Amazon departed from the Andean regions to the west. Francisco de Orellana left Quito for the 'Land of Cinnamon' in the expedition of Gonzalo Pizarro in 1541 and, although it did not represent the first European intrusion into the Amazon basin, it did signal the start of a serious interest in its exploitation and discovery. Until this point, the interior regions of the Amazon valley were not central to Spanish colonizing efforts.

The Portuguese had first sighted Brazil from the fleet of Pero Álvares Cabral in 1500; the first Spanish discovery of the Amazon had been made by Vincent Yánez Pinzón a few months earlier. The Spaniards named the channel at the mouth of the Amazon *Santa María de la Mar Dulce*, recording that the outlet that discharged so much freshwater into the ocean seemed to be a 'sea' itself. The region around the Amazon delta was difficult for sailing ships to navigate and a coastal environment of mangrove swamps made landings difficult, with the exception of the region around São Luís de Maranhão. The 'captaincy' of Maranhão, created by King João III in 1534, was the most northerly grant of land made by the Portuguese king. The Crowns of Portugal and Spain negotiated a treaty in 1494 which limited Portuguese possession in the New World to a region east of the 'line of Tordesillas' during the subsequent fifty years. Technically almost all the Amazon basin lay outside Portuguese jurisdiction and, by 1554, the Portuguese had desisted from their attempts to colonize Maranhão. Together with a lack of Spanish colonization, this situation created fertile conditions for the Dutch, English, French, and Irish trading ventures that represented the sole European occupations of the river until the 1630s.

In the European exploration of South America, the Caribbean Islands, coastal Guiana, and the Brazilian littoral south of the Amazon were the easterly starting points for journeys into the hinterland. However, Spanish occupation of the Inca Empire in the 1530s meant that the first journeys down the Amazon channel were made from the west, following the headwaters to the mouth. It is from these four regions that the first travel accounts began to emerge, all projecting different kinds of imagery of the interior, but all being simultaneously concerned with how that interior night be better known and so emphasizing the character of indigenous peoples, the ramification of their social and political systems, and the opportunities for trade and plunder that existed among them. Equally significant for these early writers was the hydrology, topography, and agricultural potential of the land—for writing about one's travels and getting it published required both a financial investment, and that such a publication had demonstrable political utility.

The first accounts of travel along the Amazon were never published by their authors. Gaspar de Carvajal's account of the journey made in 1541 by Francisco de Orellana—from the Amazon headwaters in Peru to its mouth—is nonetheless one of the most important documents of New World exploration for its description of societies of the Amazon before significant European occupation of the river in the 1630s. Carvajal also sets a tone for the way in which the river will be described in most subsequent accounts—vast, incomprehensible, filled with wonder, and rich in life and culture. For example, Carvajal writes of one of the villages they plundered: 'In this village there was a villa in which there was a great deal of porcelain ware of the best that has ever been seen in the world, for that of Málaga is not its equal . . . they are so accurately worked out that with natural skill they manufacture and decorate all these things like Roman [ware].' But this evidence of civility masks a more sinister aspect to native culture: 'In this house there were two idols woven out of feathers of different sorts, which frightened one, and they were of the stature of giants, and on their arms stuck into the fleshy part, they had a pair of disks resembling candlestick sockets', while in another landing they see: 'A hewn tree trunk ten feet in girth, there being represented and carved in relief a walled city . . . at this gate were two towers, very tall and having windows . . . and this entire structure, . . . rested on two very fierce lions.'[27]

Such marvels also implied connections both with the Inca and the walled city of El Dorado, and these connections are repeatedly evidenced in the journey through references to the presence of llamas, copper axes, clothing, and so forth. Carvajal also announces the presence of the Amazons who came to fight against the Spanish expedition with such ferocity that they clubbed any of their own warriors who turned back from the attack, and their brigantines were so stuck with arrows that they 'looked like porcupines'.[28] Carvajal also initiates an ethnological framework for understanding the great diversity of peoples whereby those upstream subtly approximate the 'civilized' Indians of Peru, while those downstream, noted for their use of poison arrows and display of severed heads, thus appear more wild and distant. The Amazonians thus occupy an ambiguous mid-point, both culturally and fluvially, as eminent women capable of brutal ferocity.

The account of Lope de Aguirre's descent of the Amazon, redacted into Pedro Simon's *Historical Notices,* followed a similar route some ten years later.[29] The

---

[27] Carvajal, *The Discovery of the Amazon*, 201, 205.
[28] Ibid., 214.
[29] Simón, Pedro, William Bollaert, and Clements R. Markham, *The Expedition of Pedro de Ursua and Lope de Aguirre in Search of El Dorado and Omagua in 1560–1* (London, 1861).

account is also charged with wonder and mystery, but as much with regard to the politics of colonialism as the environment and its peoples. Aguirre, known also as 'The Tyrant' and 'The Hooded Pilgrim', in fact mutinied against the original commander of the expedition, executed his followers, and led the survivors on a journey to establish a new empire distinct from that of Spain. Guided in part by Tupi Indian prophets searching for their own mystical 'land without evil', Aguirre's journey establishes the Amazon as a cultural site for social experiment, ethnological extremes, and mystical endeavour.

After the French Huguenots led by Nicholas de Villegagnon at Rio de Janeiro were driven out by a Portuguese attack in 1560, the French presence in Brazil persisted through numerous trading voyages. Since Portugal had not established any settlements in the Maranhão region, it was here that the French attempted another colonial venture during the early seventeenth century. In 1612 the Capuchin father Claude d'Abbeville arrived with a French expedition at Maranhão, situated along the east coast of Brazil, just south of the Amazon River. The company was headed by Daniel de La Touche and Sieur de La Ravardière and operated under a charter granted in 1610 by Marie de Medici, acting regent for King Louis XIII. Although the Portuguese presence in Brazil was dominant, French traders had operated along Brazil's coast throughout the sixteenth century. Norman French were the chief operators of an active trade in Brazilian dyewood. Members of these trading parties were frequently left to live among Brazil's natives in order to learn their language and organize the cutting and gathering of logs for the returning French ships.

Claude d'Abbeville's initial reaction to the natives of the Maranhão region was positive, and his hopes for success were great. His early letters, besides expressing his own optimism, served a propaganda purpose as well. Sustained contact with the Indians led d'Abbeville to express many doubts as to the permanent success of the Capuchin missionary effort in Brazil. Fr Claude's ideas evolved during the course of his four-month stay with the Tupinambá, which began in August 1612. His initial optimism and enthusiasm gave way to more ambivalent attitudes towards the natives and their potential for conversion. These more complex and realistic thoughts are expressed in a 381-page account that was published in 1614, one year following d'Abbeville's return to France.[30] He thus had time to reflect on his experiences. This work contains a history of the Capuchin missionary work in Maranhão, a very detailed relation of native customs and ceremonies, and information about the physical environment. Yves d'Evreux, the Capuchin cleric who continued d'Abbeville's work among the Tupinambá, contrasts his own two-year stay in Brazil with the four-month visit of d'Abbeville, but his overall attitudes are similar in seeing good possibilities for the conversion of the

---

[30] Claude d'Abbeville, *Histoire de la mission des Pères Capucins en l'Isle de Maragnan et terres circinfines...* (Paris, 1614).

natives.[31] However, Claude d'Abbeville's hopes for continued French presence in Brazil were not sustained. In 1614 the Portuguese built a fort at Maranhão and began to attack the French and their Tupinambá allies. In November of the following year, Sieur de La Ravardière surrendered. The French abandoned their colony and never renewed their efforts to establish their presence in Brazil. The Tupinambá Indians were either killed or enslaved by the Portuguese during the next decade. The French colony at Maranhão was short-lived, lasting only three years.

COLONIAL GLIMPSES INTO THE INTERIOR, 1650–1850

As the colonial regimes in South America moved permanently to occupy and expand their initial coastal enclaves, so the place of travel accounts in the cultural work of conquest changes. Although travellers coming directly from Europe are still represented, a new kind of traveller emerges—one who negotiates not so much geographical distance as cultural difference. The codification of that difference, its repeated proof and extension through journeys into the hinterland beyond administrative control, the tribal zone of anthropology, or the contact zone of literary scholarship,[32] is now the site for the production of exemplary experience and useful knowledge. The fact of encounter is itself no longer remarkable, rather specific kinds of encounter with both moral and natural phenomena provide the evidence of authentic travel. As a result, accounts of the seventeenth and eighteenth centuries move from the more general evocations to the minutiae of particular landscapes, plants and animals, or the investigation of specific cultural proclivities and practices. Writers of this period therefore tend to have clearer and more sustained identities within the colony, rather than the metropolis, and fall into two main classes, missionaries and administrators. This by no means precludes other kinds of writers, but it is striking that much of the literature was produced by such individuals.

The missionary narratives of Padre Cristobal Acuña and Padre Samuel Fritz thus return us to the sites first visited by Carvajal but narrate a loss and destruction of native culture in the intervening 130 years. This gap in writing about the Amazon was not as total as the limits of space in this chapter make it appear, since there exist manuscript accounts of individual reconnoitring and even of a journey to the palace of Coñori, Queen of the Amazons. The hiatus in published accounts was due to the fact that after Carvajal and Aguirre the only European presence in the river basin itself was provided by the existence of

---

[31] Yves d'Evreux, *Voyage dans le nord du Brésil, fait durant les années 1613 et 1614* (Paris, 1985).

[32] See Mary Louise Pratt, *Imperial Eyes Travel Writing and Transculturation* (London and New York, 1992); and R. Brian Ferguson and Neil L. Whitehead, *War in the Tribal Zone: Expanding States and Indigenous Warfare* (Santa Fe and London, 1999).

scattered trading posts manned by small companies of French, English, Irish, and Dutch adventurers. It was not until 1639 that the Portuguese actually made their first attempt at settlement of the river, and Padre Acuña was part of that armed ingress. He is therefore overwhelmingly concerned with the economic and political prospects for the river and its peoples. He also explicitly revisits many of the sites of Carvajal's narrative as if to exorcize the shadow of that Spanish emissary in favour of his Portuguese king—the Amazon basin itself having been delineated by the pope as a Portuguese territory in the Treaty of Tordesillas. In emulating the track of Carvajal, Acuña's narrative harks back to the initial metaphors of vastness and mystery, even resurrecting by allusion the conjecture of Columbus that the hydrology of the southern continent was consistent with it being the site of the biblical Eden. Acuña writes: 'if the Ganges irrigates all India . . . if the Nile irrigates and fertilizes a great part of Africa: the river of the Amazons waters more extensive regions, fertilizes more plains, supports more people, and augments by its floods a mightier ocean: it only wants, in order to surpass them in felicity, that its source should be in Paradise'.[33] The theme of an Amazonian dystopia thus becomes firmly embedded in subsequent writings, both anthropological and literary. However, it is Fritz's account that gives the more intimate picture of the Amazon since he was precisely a stationary traveller, moving in cultural rather than geographical space in the upper reaches of the river. He gives himself this kind of identity as a 'traveller', not just as an evangelical functionary, through his partial intellectual detachment from the immediate missionary project. This is signalled through nostalgia for the Amazon's native past, a sense of its destruction through disease and slavery, and ambivalence to the eradication of its superstitions.

The territorial expansion of 'Brazil' was not only taking place in the Amazon basin at this time but also along the frontier between the coastal regions and the vast hinterland that the *bandeiras* of Knivet's era had only just begun to penetrate. Histories of the Brazilian frontier experience often emphasize the contributions of both blacks and Indians as a matter of course. In Brazilian historiography the term used for this frontier hinterland is *sertão*. During the colonial era this word referred to all the unexplored and unsettled land in Brazil, and so remains evocative even today, where much still remains unexplored and the vast interior of the country remains unsettled. The *sertão* appears infrequently in histories of Brazil written during the country's first three centuries. Study of the interior did not attract much attention prior to the end of the nineteenth century, for in both countries the European heritage dominated histories of the colonies. Most chronicles of sixteenth- and seventeenth-century Portuguese America were thus limited to descriptions of the native inhabitants, the coastal environments, and settlements. An exception to this relative lack of writings on the *sertão* appeared

---

[33] Padre Cristobal Acuña, 'A New Discovery of the Great River of the Amazons', in *Expeditions into the Valley of the Amazons*, ed. Clements Markham (London, 1859), 61.

early in the eighteenth century in the chronicle by André Antonil, *Cultura e opulência do Brasil por suas drogas e minas* [The Culture and Wealth of Brazil's Products and Mines], which gave an account of the colony's economic activities, from sugar and mining to cattle. But it was quickly suppressed, probably because Portuguese authorities believed it described Brazil in terms that might prove useful and attractive to other European powers. Later in the eighteenth century the *sertão* was lauded as a unique element shaping civilization in Brazil, and local historians, such as Pedro Taques de Paes Almeida Leme and Gaspar de Madre de Deus, wrote works that intimately described the region of the Paulista plateau.[34]

'COLONIAL BRAZIL' AS HISTORICAL MOTIF

The historiography of colonial Brazil as written by its contemporary authors reflected an idea of the chronicler as recording rather than interpreting past events. The *Historia da America Portuguesa* [The History of Portuguese America] (1730) written by Rocha Pitta, a member of a wealthy family in Bahia, precisely exemplifies these characteristics but, as A. J. R. Russell-Wood notes, it 'remains worthy of consultation less as a source of factual information than for the author's perspective'. It was 'unbound by an institutional environment', since Rocha Pitta brought a perspective that revealed attitudes, values, and reflected contemporary mentalities.[35] However, neither Rocha Pitta nor his contemporary chroniclers engaged in archival research, yet chronicles of this kind had an established place in writing on Brazil.

The first history of Brazil under Portuguese colonial rule to treat the entire three centuries from the beginning of the sixteenth century to the early nineteenth century, and to be based on extensive research, was written by the English Romantic poet Robert Southey, who had also never visited Brazil. The first volume of what became a three-volume *History of Brazil* was published in 1810, two years after the Portuguese court had moved to Brazil, but Southey had begun work on the project more than a decade earlier. In 1796, aged 22, Southey spent three and a half months visiting his uncle, who was chaplain to the community of British merchants in Lisbon. He later returned for fifteen months in 1800–1. Southey wrote his *History* based on the collection of books and manuscripts on Luso-Brazilian topics that belonged to his uncle. Southey himself was a disciple

---

[34] Cited by Mary Lombardi, 'The Frontier in Brazilian History: An Historiographical Essay', *The Pacific Historical Review*, 44:4 (1975), 446, she writes: 'In the nineteenth century the *sertão* began to appear more frequently in the histories of Brazil, and its absence elicits criticism. The prize-winning essay by Karl Friedrich Philipp von Martius, 'How the History of Brazil Should be Written', for example, in addition to perceptively understanding the basic themes of Brazil's past, also suggested that the history of the *sertão* deserved to be better known.'

[35] A. J. R. Russell-Wood, 'Brazilian Archives and Recent Historiography on Colonial Brazil', *Latin American Research Review*, 36:1 (2001), 75–105, at 78.

of the political philosophy of Burke and Coleridge. His sympathies lay with humanist reformists and Liberal politics, which equated to a dogmatic conviction in the absolute superiority of English civilization. Southey's *History* is accordingly conservative in tone. Nevertheless, Southey critiqued Portuguese colonization and, although he admired racial mixing and what he saw as a policy of ethnic integration on the part of the Portuguese, he abhorred the slave-owning aristocracy and the power of the local political elites. In the *History of Brazil* Southey's defence of strengthening the state and institutionalizing paternalist social bonds (slavery) led him to welcome the arrival of the Portuguese Court in Rio de Janeiro, seeing this as a chance to found an empire whose mission would consist of adjusting the country to the civilizing benefits of English trade. Broadly speaking, Southey was interested in the nature of miscegenation between 'Indians' and colonists and understood the effects that epidemic disease, especially smallpox, had had in creating the colonial demography of Brazil, noting that 'the mixture and intermixture of three different races—European, American, and African—had produced new diseases, or at least new constitutions, by which old diseases were so modified that the most skilful physicians were puzzled by new symptoms'.[36] He was also committed to discovering the significance of religion in history: 'When America was discovered, the civilization of its different nations was precisely in proportion to the degree of power and respectability which their priests possessed; and this authority of the priesthood was not the consequence of an improved state of society, but the cause of it.'[37] Thus, Southey's historical writings reflect the idea that key individuals determined the course of historical events against the backdrop of certain political and moral certainties.

CONCLUSION

The importance of Southey's work is thus perhaps the way in which it was valued by the builders of the Brazilian Empire and by the defenders of centralized monarchy and slavery, as much for the way in which it matches modern conceptions of what 'history' should be. In this way, Southey's *History* also returns us to the first moment of writing 'Brazil' and the inception of conquest. History did not originate with the Europeans and this chapter could have also reflected further on the forms of historical 'writing' and the epistemological disjuncture between European and native forms that is thereby revealed.[38] Ironically it was an anthropologist of Brazil, Claude Lévi-Strauss, who notoriously suggested that native societies were 'cold' and European ones were 'hot' in terms of their openness to, and consciousness of, change as a means of social

---

[36] Robert Southey, *History of Brazil*, vol. 1 (London, 1819), 327.
[37] Ibid., 251.
[38] Neil L. Whitehead, *Histories and Historicities in Amazonia* (Lincoln, 2003).

progress and cultural destiny. In this view, native Brazil has 'no history' but exists in an eternal present of 'first contacts' and 'marvelous discovery'.[39] A lack of cultural significance and historical depth to native societies was, as the sources reviewed above reveal, already a historical assumption even before the pronouncements of Lévi-Strauss. As a result, historical writings about Brazil, from the sixteenth to the eighteenth centuries, are largely cast in terms of travelogues, ethnological inventories, tales of heroic evangelical redemption, or natural histories, in which the natives figure as an especially exotic form of savage wildlife. Too exclusive a focus on 'writing' also blinds us to the visual histories, contained both in the books and printed works discussed above, but also by constituting their own kinds of non-textual histories, as in the work of Albert Eckhout.[40] In just this way the archaeological record, both pre- and post-Cabral, is as yet a mute source for historiography, underlining the fundamental but unresolved historiographical issue of the periodization of the 'Native' and the 'Colonial'. As in the rest of the Americas, the stubborn persistence of the 'Native' permanently challenges the construction of the 'National' as an inclusive trope of contemporary history-writing. For all these reasons, it is to be hoped that this brief review will also function to stimulate a broader definition of what might come to constitute a more complete historiography of Brazil.

KEY HISTORICAL SOURCES

Abbeville, Claude d', *Histoire de la mission des Pères Capucins en l'Isle de Maragnan et terres circinfines*... (Paris, 1614).

Acuña, Cristobal d', 'A New Discovery of the Great River of the Amazons', in *Expeditions into the Valley of the Amazons*, ed. Clements Markham (London, 1859).

Anchieta, José de, 'Information on the Marriage of the Indians of Brazil', *Revista trimensal de historia e geographia*, 8 (1846), 254–62.

——— *Cartas, informaçoes, fragmentos históricos e sermoes* (São Paulo, 1988).

Anon., 'Enformação do Brasil, e de suas Capitanias', *Revista trimensal de historia e geographia*, 6 (1844), 412–43.

Bry, Théodore de, *Americae Tertia Pars* (Frankfurt, 1592).

Caminha, Pedro Vaz de, *The Voyage of Pedro Alvares Cabral to Brazil and India* (London, 1938).

Cardim, Fernão, 'A Treatise of Brasil and Articles Touching the Dutie of the Kings Majestie our Lord, and to the Common Good of all the Estate of Brasill', in Samuel Purchas (ed.), *Hakluytus Posthumus or Purchas his Pilgrims*, vol. 16 (Glasgow, 1906), 417–51.

---

[39] Claude Lévi-Strauss, *Tristes Tropiques* (New York, 1992).

[40] Albert Eckhout was a Dutch portrait and still-life painter. He was among the first artists to paint scenes from the New World. In 1636 he travelled to Dutch Brazil, invited by John Maurice, Prince of Nassau-Siegen. There he painted portraits of natives, slaves, and mulattos, as well as depictions of Brazilian fruits and vegetables.

Carvajal, G. de, 'Discovery of the Orellana River', in *The Discovery of the Amazon According to the Account of Friar Gaspar de Carvajal and Other Documents*, ed. J. T. Medina, trans. B. T. Lee (New York, 1934).

Evreux, Yves d', *Voyage dans le nord du Brésil, fait durant les années 1613 et 1614* (Paris, 1985).

Fritz, Samuel, *Journal of the Travels and Labours of Father Samuel Fritz in the River of the Amazons between 1686 and 1723*, trans. and ed. George Edmundson (London, 1922).

Gandavo, Pero de Magalhães, 'History of the Province of Santa Cruz', in *The Histories of Brazil*, vol. 2 (New York, 1922).

Knivet, Anthony, 'Anthony Knivet, his Comming to the R. De Janeiro and Usage Amongst the Portugals and Indians: His Divers Travels, Throw Divers Regions of Those Parts', in Samuel Purchas (ed.), *Hakluytus Posthumus or Purchas his Pilgrims*, extra series, no. 14–30 (Glasgow, 1625).

Léry, Jean de, *Histoire memorable de la ville de Sancerre* (Geneva, 1574).

——*Histoire d'un voyage faict en la terre du Brésil* (Geneva, 1578).

——*History of a Voyage to the Land of Brazil*, trans. Janet Whatley (Berkeley, 1990).

Montaigne, Michel de, *Essais* (Paris, 1580).

Nóbrega, Manuel da, 'Informação das Terras do Brasil' (1549), in *Cartas do Brasil* (São Paulo, 1988), 97–102.

Simon, Pedro, *Sixth Historical Notice of the Conquest of Tierra Firme* (London, 1861).

Sousa, Gabriel Soares de, *Notícia do Brasil* (São Paulo, 1974).

Thévet, André, *Les Singularitez de la france Antarctique, autrement nommée Amerique: et de plusieurs Terres et Isles decouvertes de nostre temps* (Paris, 1557).

Vespucci, Amerigo, *The Letters of Amerigo Vespucci and Other Documents Illustrative of his Career*, trans. Clements R. Markham (London, 1894).

BIBLIOGRAPHY

Amado, Janaína, 'Mythic Origins: Caramuru and the Founding of Brazil', *Hispanic American Historical Review*, 80:4 (2000), 783–811.

Ferguson, R. Brian and Whitehead, Neil L. (eds.), *War in the Tribal Zone: Expanding States and Indigenous Warfare* (Santa Fe and London, 1999).

Hulme, Peter and Whitehead, Neil L. (eds.), *Wild Majesty: Encounters with Caribs from Columbus to the Present Day: An Anthology* (Oxford, 1992).

Lestringant, F. (ed.), *Jean de Léry: Histoire d'un voyage faict en la terre du Brésil (1578)* (Paris 1994).

——*Cannibals* (Berkeley, 1997).

Lévi-Strauss, Claude, *Tristes Tropiques* (New York, 1992).

Lombardi, Mary, 'The Frontier in Brazilian History: An Historiographical Essay', *The Pacific Historical Review*, 44:4 (1975), 437–57.

Monteiro, John M., 'The Heathen Castes of Sixteenth-Century Portuguese America: Unity, Diversity, and the Invention of the Brazilian Indian', *Hispanic American Historical Review*, 80:4 (2000), 697–719.

Pratt, Mary Louise, *Imperial Eyes: Travel Writing and Transculturation* (London and New York, 1992).

Schwartz, Stuart B., 'Adolfo de Varnhagen: Diplomat, Patriot', *Hispanic American Historical Review*, 47:2 (1967), 185–202.

Whatley, Janet (ed.), 'Introduction', in *Jean de Léry: History of a Voyage to the Land of Brazil* (Berkeley, 1990), pp. xv–xxxviii.

Whitehead, Neil L., *Histories and Historicities in Amazonia* (Lincoln, 2003).

—— *The Discoverie of the Large, Rich and Bewtiful Empire of Guiana by Sir Walter Ralegh* (Manchester and Norman, Okla., 1997).

——and Harbsmeier, Michael (eds.), *Hans Staden's True History: An Account of Cannibal Captivity in Brazil* (Durham, NC, 2008).

Chapter 32

Spanish American Colonial Historiography: Issues, Traditions, and Debates

Jorge Cañizares-Esguerra

After many years of identifying and compiling sources, creating archives, and battling powerful enemies at the Royal Academy of History, Juan Bautista Muñoz made public in 1791 the first, and last, volume of his much awaited *Historia del Nuevo Mundo* [History of the New World]. The extreme sceptical posture assumed by Muñoz in the prologue could partially help explain the entrenched hostility he found at the Academy. This royal institution had been given the task of writing a new history of the New World since the 1760s, yet after decades of useless debates it had utterly failed on how best to proceed. Muñoz introduced his book with a lengthy critique of every single previous official chronicler of the Indies: Antonio de Herrera, Gonzalo Fernández de Oviedo, Pietro Martire d'Anghiera, and López de Gómara, dismissing all for being unreliable and even purposefully misleading. That Muñoz went after all previous 'official' historiography on the Indies was strange, for Muñoz, after all, was himself an official historian, like the sixteenth- and seventeenth-century historians he so adamantly dismissed, hired by the Crown to write patriotic defences of the monarchy against foreign historians fond of emphasizing Spanish ignorance, greed, and brutality. But the enmity between Muñoz and the leadership of the Academy, in particular its director, the Count of Campomanes, had nothing to do with any attempt on the part of the Academy to defend the soiled reputation of the Spanish chronicles, for Campomanes viewed the chroniclers with as much disdain as did Muñoz. Both parties considered that the history of Spain in the Americas needed to be entirely rewritten from scratch, avoiding rather than building on previous Spanish historians. Yet they differed on what sources and methodologies to use to rewrite the history of the continent.[1]

---

[1] On Muñoz and his debate with Campomanes, see my *How to Write the History of the New World: Histories, Epistemologies and Identities* (Stanford, 2001), 170–203. On medieval and early modern Spanish 'official' historians as 'artisans of glory', see Richard Kagan, *Clio and the Crown: The Politics of History in Medieval and Early Modern Spain* (Baltimore, 2009).

BRITISH NORTH
AMERICA
(1763)

UNITED
STATES OF
AMERICA
(1776)

Atlantic
Ocean

VICEROYALTY
OF NEW SPAIN

Mexico City •

CUBA   HISPANIOLA

JAMAICA

BRITISH
HONDURAS

Caracas •

DUTCH GUIANA
(British after 1803)

Bogotá •

Stabroek
Paramaribo
Cayenne

VICEROYALTY
OF
NEW GRANADA

Quito •

FRENCH GUIANA

DUTCH
GUIANA

Pacific
Ocean

VICEROYALTY OF PERU

VICEROYALTY
OF
BRAZIL
(1775)

Lima •

Rio de Janeiro

VICEROYALTY
OF
LA PLATA

European colonies

Spain

Great Britain

Netherlands

Portugal

France

• Seat of government

Santiago •

Buenos Aires •

PATAGONIA

1000 miles

1500 km

Map 7. Post-Conquest North and South America

The Muñoz–Campomanes debate on how to write the history of the Americas was one of many such debates in the eighteenth century. This chapter considers some of them in order to reconstruct the contours of early modern Spanish American colonial historiography.

DEBATES IN SPAIN

Campomanes and his followers thought that the Academy should simply translate with extended footnotes William Robertson's great *History of America* (1777), in which the Scottish Presbyterian minister and rector of the University of Edinburgh had managed to amalgamate the most advanced theories of the Enlightenment on political economy with meticulous critical reading of available printed and hitherto unknown archival documents. Robertson carefully weighed the evidence provided by past Spanish chroniclers. He also used the British ambassador in Madrid as an intermediary to get access to rare manuscripts. More important, drawing on the writings of Scottish writers such as David Hume, Adam Ferguson, and Adam Smith on the transformation of the passions from hunting, herding, and agriculture—in that order—to the pinnacle of civilization—namely commerce—Robertson placed the multifarious New World Amerindians and European settler-societies, from pre-colonial times to the eighteenth century, into a ranking hierarchy of progress. In short, Robertson, like Edward Gibbon, combined the best that early modern antiquarians and eighteenth-century commercial philosophers had to offer in order to create a new modern narrative synthesis of historical progress in the New World.[2] Campomanes and his followers found Robertson's moderate critical scepticism of sources, as well as his philosophical interpretation, to be most stimulating. Thus the Academy set out to translate the *History of America* with extended footnotes, correcting misrepresentations, and pointing out errors of fact.[3]

Muñoz begged to differ. He correctly understood that the Scots had used the Spanish Empire as a foil to concoct their commercial historiographical paradigm. So rather than follow the anti-Catholic Enlightenment, Muñoz embraced the techniques and methodologies first developed by Spanish antiquarians in the Renaissance and the Baroque: the collection and erudite study of primary

---

[2] On Robertson and his milieu, see Richard Sher, *Church and University in the Scottish Enlightenment: The Moderate Literati of Edinburgh* (Princeton, 1985). On Edward Gibbon and the merging of antiquarian and philosophical historiographical traditions, see J. G. A. Pocock, *Barbarism and Religion*, 5 vols. to date (Cambridge, 1999–).

[3] On the Academy of History, see María Teresa Navas Rodíguez, *Reformismo ilustrado y americanismo: La Real Academia de Historia, 1735–1792* (Madrid, 1989); and Eva Velasco Moreno, *La Real Academia de la Historia en el siglo XVIII* (Madrid, 2000).

sources. In the sixteenth century, for example, the 'artisans of glory' of Philip II had deemed necessary to create the Archive of Simancas as a repository of documents on the Spanish monarchy, which had long been scattered across the peninsula—thus creating a means to produce a tightly controlled, authorized narrative of the accomplishments of the Habsburg dynasty.[4] After scouring private and ecclesiastical repositories all over Spain and Portugal, and after ordering authorities in America and the Philippines to round up documents to be sent to Spain, Muñoz assembled some 150 volumes of choice manuscripts and created a new archive—the archive of the Indies—in Seville. Although in his own historical interpretations of the New World Muñoz did not entirely do away with Enlightenment theories of political economy and progress, he put an emphasis on the centralization of archives in order to prove through research in primary sources Spain's groundbreaking contributions to knowledge and civilization in the New World.[5]

It should be clear by now that, regardless of political ideologies or philosophical outlooks, a consensus emerged in the eighteenth century around the need to rewrite the history of the New World, for the sources and interpretations available until then were deemed either unreliable or worthless. Historians therefore embraced new forms of evidence, interpretations, and methodologies. In the following pages I explore aspects of this new historiography in order to gain a fuller sense of the range of historical thought in the early modern New World, particularly in New Spain.

LORENZO BOTURINI AND TYPOLOGICAL TRADITIONS

Although barely known outside Mexico, Lorenzo Boturini should perhaps be considered one of the most important eighteenth-century New World historians.[6] Claiming (false) Milanese noble lineage, Boturini arrived in Mexico in 1735, charged with administering the financial holdings of the Countess of Santibañez, who, although living in Madrid, was the heiress to Moctezuma, the last ruler of

---

[4] On historians as artisans of glory and the foundation of Simancas, see Kagan, *Clio and the Crown*.

[5] On Muñoz, see Nicolás Bas Martín, *El cosmógrafo e historiador Juan Bautista Muñoz* (Valencia, 2002); and ch. 4 of my *How to Write the History of the New World*. On the founding of Simancas, see José Luis Rodriguez de Diego (ed.), *Instrucción par el gobierno de Simancas (año 1588)* (Madrid, 1998). I take the term 'artisans of glory' from Orest Ranum, *Artisans of Glory: Writers and Historical Thought in Seventeenth-Century France* (Chapel Hill, 1980).

[6] On Boturini, see Giorgio Antei, *El caballero andante: Vida, obra y desventuras de Lorenzo Boturini Benaduci (1698–1755)* (Mexico, 2007); Alvaro Matute, *Lorenzo Boturini y el pensamiento histórico de Vico* (Mexico, 1976); and Miguel León-Portilla, 'Estudio Preliminar', in Lorenzo Boturini Benaduci, *Idea de una nueva historia general de la América Septentrional*, ed. Miguel León-Portilla (Mexico, 1986), pp. ix–lxii.

Tenochtitlan. She was therefore entitled to tithes in the New World.[7] Not before long, Boturini began to put together one of the greatest collections of pre-colonial and colonial indigenous writings ever assembled. Paradoxically, such an unusual collection resulted from Boturini's intense devotion to the image of Our Lady of Guadalupe.

The story of the miracle was well known: the virgin appeared in 1531 to a Nahua commoner, Juan Diego, and asked him to have the bishop build a shrine in her honour, but the prelate repeatedly dismissed the Indian. It was not until Juan Diego took flowers, which appeared miraculously on the barren hill of Tepeyac, and in front of the bishop the flowers turned into the image of Our Lady of Guadalupe, that the prelate complied. Yet such a momentous and miraculous event had seemingly passed unnoticed to contemporaries: there were no references in the archives of the cathedral, and chroniclers seem not to refer to the miracle either. When in the 1640s the story of the miracle began to gain traction, the boosters of the cult knew they had a problem.

One way of addressing the documentary gap was to maintain that the image of Our Lady of Guadalupe was itself proof: a document from the hand of God. The apparent miraculous virtues of the canvas, its extraordinary beauty, and the lack of evidence of its material decay, became proof that God himself had painted the image.[8] Along with this insistence on the preternatural aesthetic qualities of the image, cult promoters argued that God had used Mexican writing to communicate his will to the faithful. In fact the author of the first printed narrative of the miracle, Miguel Sánchez, claimed in 1648 that the image was the Mexican equivalent of Moses's tablets of the Ten Commandments, documenting Mexicans' hard-earned status as God's new Israelites. Drawing on well-established patristic and medieval typological methods of reading sacred scripture, Sánchez argued that the story of the Virgin's apparitions to Juan Diego at Mount Tepeyac was simply a fulfilment of the biblical story of Moses's encounters with God at Mount Sinai.[9]

Until Sánchez, typology had been used to justify the conquest of the Americas. Biblical passages, for example, featured prominently in the origins of the infamous *Requerimiento*, the document read aloud by conquistadores to Amerindians giving natives a choice between political subordination or war and enslavement.

---

[7] On the persistence of often powerful indigenous nobilities in Spanish America, see Carolyn Dean, *Inka Bodies and the Body of Christ: Corpus Christi in Colonial Cuzco, Peru* (Durham, NC, 1999); David T. Garret, *Shadows of Empire: The Indian Nobility of Cusco, 1750–1825* (Cambridge, 2005); and Jaime Cuadriello, *Las Glorias de la República de Tlaxcala o la conciencia como imagen sublime* (Mexico, 2004).

[8] Miguel Cabrera, the pre-eminent mid-eighteenth-century painter of New Spain, for example, wrote a treatise on the preternatural aesthetic perfection of the image. See his 'Maravilla americana' (1756), in Ernesto de la Torre Villar and Ramiro Navarro de Anda (eds.), *Testimonios históricos guadalupanos* (Mexico, 1982), 494–528.

[9] On the typological reading of the story of the miracle, see D. A. Brading, *Mexican Phoenix: Our Lady of Guadalupe. Image and Tradition across Five Centuries* (Cambridge, 2001).

Although scholars have presented it as a contrived, ludicrous Spanish strategy to cast the conquest in the legal language of the 'just war', the *Requirimiento* is better explained as part of a larger typological interpretation of colonization. For the jurists who drafted the document, the conquest was the fulfilment of Joshua 3.7–13 and 6.16–21: Israelites-Spaniards gave the Canaanites-Indians, an ultimatum to clear the Promised Land or face destruction.[10] Such biblical arguments were pervasive; they surface, for example, in the frontispiece of Antonio de Leon Pinelo's *Tratado de las Confirmaciones Reales de Encomiendas* [Treatise on the Legal Foundations of the Encomienda] (1620). This legal commentary on the laws of the Indies has the Incas as the heirs of Jacob's son, Issachar, destined to bow their shoulders 'to bear, and become a servant unto tribute' (Gen. 49.15). The frontispiece also presents the conquest of Tenochtitlan as the fulfilment of Deuteronomy 20.11: if the terms of surrender (enslavement) are refused, Israelite-Spaniards should spare no one, save women, children, and livestock. Although Sánchez was building on this tradition of typological readings of colonization, he managed to transform it into a discourse of election.

The consequence of turning the image of Our Lady of Guadalupe into a text documenting a covenant between God and the new Mexican elect was to claim that the image had been written by God using Mesoamerican hieroglyphs, for the Lord sought to accommodate to the knowledge of the Indians. Sánchez himself introduced this tradition. Again, drawing upon typology to read the canvas, Sánchez insisted that the image—a woman eclipsing the sun, wearing a shawl covered with stars, and standing on a crescent moon held by an angel—corresponded to the woman of Revelation 12. As it turns out, Our Lady of Guadalupe and the woman of the Apocalypse were one and the same; both prefigured Cortés's conquest of Tenochtitlan. The conquest of Mexico was the fulfilment of the battles in Revelation 12 between the Archangel Michael and Satan's multi-headed dragon. Sánchez paid careful attention to every detail in the image: the number of stars on the virgin's shawl corresponded through cabala to the number of soldiers in Cortés's army; the virgin stepping on the moon represented not only the preternatural powers of the Virgin over tides but also Christian *dominium* over the American tropics. Each element of the painting was a glyph demanding interpretation.[11]

---

[10] On the *Requerimiento*, see Rolena Adorno, *The Polemics of Possession in the Spanish American Narrative* (New Haven, 2007), 265; and *Colección de documentos inéditos relativos al descubrimiento, conquista y organización de las antiguas posesiones españolas de América y Oceanía*, 42 vols. (Madrid, 1864–84), i. 443–4. On typology and colonization more generally, see my 'Entangled Histories: Borderland Historiographies in New Clothes?' *American Historical Review*, 112 (2007), 787–99; and 'Typology in the Atlantic World: Early Modern Readings of Colonization', in Bernard Bailyn (ed.), *Atlantic Soundings* (Cambridge, Mass., 2008).

[11] On the demonological interpretation of the cult, see my *Puritan Conquistadors: Iberianizing the Atlantic 1550–1700* (Palo Alto, Calif., 2006).

Not even at the height of the Enlightenment would this tradition go away. Take for example the case of José Ignacio Borunda, an antiquarian whose reading of the story of the miracle caused an uproar in 1794 when his friend, José Servando Teresa de Mier—soon to become a celebrated figure in the Mexican wars of independence—made it available to the lay and religious authorities of the land during the sermon celebrating the annual feast of the cult. Unlike Sánchez, Borunda did not draw on typology and cabala to read the painting. He simply assumed the alphabet of the image-text to be syllabic. Touting great knowledge of pre-colonial classical Nahuatl, Borunda claimed that the secret historical archive of the Indies resided in the etymology of toponyms, for the natives had carefully stored the memory of the past in place names. With this basic theory in mind, Borunda set out to 'read' archaeological pieces recently dug out near the cathedral as a composite of place names, coming up with a new history of ancient Mexico characterized by sudden geological catastrophes, massive internal migrations, and early Christian apostolic visitations. Borunda read the image of Our Lady of Guadalupe to confirm his findings. A lemniscate (a horizontal eight, the mathematical sign for infinite) in the floral design in the Virgin's dress, which had long been read as God's way to communicate that the canvas was the eighth wonder of the world, became in Borunda's hand a Syriac letter. Borunda thus concluded that the image had been brought to Mexico by an oriental apostle, St Thomas, in late antiquity. The silence in the colonial archive documenting the miracle became easy to explain: the miracle had never occurred.[12]

Addressing the documentary gap in the history of the cult was clearly fraught with dangers. Thus, another strategy available for the promoters of the cult was to insist that the Amerindians themselves had recorded the events in their traditional historical annals. Boturini belonged in this second group.

Beginning in the mid-seventeenth century, the local clergy started to survey the new sacred histories of the land, drawing upon indigenous oral and written sources. One of these historians was Francisco de Florencia, a Jesuit born in provincial Florida but who in time came to represent the entire Mexican province in Rome. Florencia spent decades collecting information to write the history of hundreds of Catholic devotions in New Spain. Typical of Florencia's methods was to turn to indigenous sources to document the origins of early Catholic cults. Florencia was not alone: seventeenth-century Indian parish priests in Tlaxcala, such as Juan Ventura Zapata and Manuel de los Santos y Salazar, collected indigenous codices and calendrical wheels partly in order to write the histories of the sixteenth-century apparitions of the Virgin of Ocotlan and the Archangel Michael, and of the martyrdom of three sixteenth-century Tlaxcalan children, allegedly murdered by their elders for defending the Catholic faith.

---

[12] For a detailed study of Borunda's scholarship, see my *How to Write the History of the New World*, 305–21.

Boturini acquired large chunks of the archives of Florencia, Zapata, and Santos y Salazar.[13] Boturini, therefore, became interested in indigenous codices as he sought to find documentary proof of the historicity of the miracle.

Boturini would have perhaps remained solely a collector had his obsession with the cult not got in the way. Well connected in Rome, the Italian took the initiative to get authorization from the pope to have a feast earmarked for the Mexican virgin in the liturgical calendar, forgetting that only Crown officials could deal directly with the Vatican. Such a breach of the law of *patronato real* was compounded by Boturini's own campaign to collect gold and cash in order to have a crown made for Our Lady of Guadalupe. Arrested on charges of running a scam, Boturini had his collection impounded and was sent to Spain to face trial. It was in Madrid that he turned historian as he sought to recover his collection and to defend himself at court. His published *Idea de una nueva historia general de la América septentrional* [Sketch for a New General History of North America] (1746) and his manuscript *Ciclografía* [On Calendrics] (1749) proved both radical and controversial.[14]

Boturini claimed his history of ancient Mexico to be entirely novel, based on new sources, methodologies, and interpretations; all previous accounts were misleading and poorly documented. These claims were not well received in some quarters in Madrid that thought that by presenting himself as a new conquistador of historical knowledge the Italian was further smearing the already poor intellectual reputation of Spain overseas. Critics quickly pointed out that Boturini's alleged new methodology was, if not plagiarized, at least wholly derivative, for Boturini had taken key insights from Giambattista Vico. Despite all his efforts at collecting indigenous *written* documents, Boturini found in the etymology of words and the interpretation of tropes the crucial evidence required to rewrite the Mesoamerican ancient past. That Boturini turned to Vico and not to the written codices he had so painstakingly collected should surprise no one. Boturini was a creature of the Enlightenment, a movement that adamantly sought to do without all written sources (e.g. the Bible) to reconstruct the past.

---

[13] Florencia wrote the history of countless popular cults. He devoted, for example, a study solely to the history of Marian cults in New Spain, identifying more than one hundred images. See his *Zodiaco mariano . . .* (Mexico, 1755). For a marvellous history of eighteenth-century Tlaxcalan patriotic agendas around the cults of Ocotlan, Archangel Michael, and the three martyr children, but which unfortunately has little on seventeenth-century indigenous antiquarians, see Cuadriello, *Las glorias de la república de Tlaxcala*. On the relationship between Boturini and Zapata, and Santos de Salazar, see Boturini's 'Catálogo del museo Indiano', in his *Idea*, par. 18 sec. 2 and par. 19 (pp. 125–6); par. 27 sec. 4 (pp. 135–6); and par. 33 (p. 143). For a good survey of the massive output of sacred histories in seventeenth-century Mexico, see Antonio Rubial García, 'La crónica religiosa: Historia sagrada y conciencia colectiva', in Raquel Chang-Rodríguez (ed.), *La cultura letrada en la Nueva España del siglo XVII*, vol. 2: *La historia de la literatura mexicana* (Mexico, 2002), 325–71.

[14] Lorenzo Boturini, *Idea de una nueva historia general de la América Septentrional*, ed. Miguel León-Portilla (Mexico, 1986); *Historia general de la América Septentrional* [Ciclografía], ed. Manuel Ballesteros Gaibrois (Mexico, 1990).

The eighteenth century witnessed an explosion of interest in new forms of historical evidence, including the study of rocks (geology), grammars, alphabets, myths, and animal behaviour.[15] Boturini was not the last to consider words and vocabularies as the most important historical Mesoamerican archive. Borunda, as noted above, studied Nahuatl; and the Central American antiquarian José Ordóñez y Aguiar turned to the convoluted analysis of Mayan etymology to interpret both the ruins of Palenque and the Popol Vuh.[16]

Boturini's critics not only called into question his claims to methodological novelty but also his allegations to be the first to collect and study indigenous documents. Boturini had conveniently overlooked that in the sixteenth and early seventeenth centuries Franciscans such as Bernardino de Sahagún and Juan de Torquemada had painstakingly compiled and studied indigenous documents, putting together massive ethno-histories of Mexico. Such exaggerated statements led scholars such as the royal librarian Blas Antonio Nasarre and his party of Aragonese at court to denounce the Italian as untrustworthy and unpatriotic. Boturini, for example, had offered an evolutionary narrative of Mesoamerican history in which the natives, in complete isolation from Eurasia, went from being originally solitary mute brutes to having developed prior to the Spanish arrival astonishingly accurate calendrical systems. But such alleged final splendour, critics countered, jarred with the evidence on the ground: contemporary natives were wretchedly poor and ignorant. According to his critics, Boturini implicitly presented the Spaniards as Turkish-like barbarians who had single-handedly destroyed the dazzling civilizations of the past. But Borturini had his share of friends and admirers in Spain. The Valencian humanist Gregorio Mayans y Siscar, for example, not only helped Boturini develop an interpretation of Mexican calendrics but also became a staunch defender of the Italian against charges of unreliability and lack of patriotism. Many a Spanish scholar openly criticized his compatriots for having been incurious and uninterested in studying Amerindian antiquities.[17]

EUROPEAN NEW TRADITIONS OF READING

In Europe, sceptics questioned the reliability of Amerindian sources and doubted the credibility of earlier European observers. Abbé Guillaume-Thomas Raynal, for example, in the 1781 edition of his widely read *Histoire philosophique et politique des éstablissements et du commerce des Européens dans les deux Indes* [Philosophical and Political History of the Settlements and Trade of the Europeans in the East and West Indies], argued that all Spanish accounts

---

[15] On Vico, see Peter Burke, *Vico* (Oxford, 1985); and Paolo Rossi, *The Dark Abyss of Time: The History of the Earth and the History of Nations from Hooke to Vico*, trans. Lydia G. Cochrane (Chicago, 1984).

[16] On Ordóñez y Aguiar, see my, *How to Write the History of the New World*, 305–11, 321–45.

[17] On the critics and supporters of Boturini in Spain, see ibid., 142–8.

of the New World were 'confusing, contradictory and full of the most absurd fables to which human credulity could ever be exposed'.[18] For Raynal the conquistadores were plunderers, not reliable witnesses. In an earlier edition, Raynal had suggested that the only way to save any surviving historical records from the destruction and oblivion to which they had been subjected was to allow philosophers such as Locke, Buffon, or Montesquieu to visit the New World.[19] Clearly, by the third quarter of the eighteenth century, the sources that Europeans had traditionally used to interpret the past of the Americas—translations of documents recorded in indigenous scripts and travel accounts by conquistadores, missionaries, sailors, and colonial bureaucrats—were considered unreliable. Many intellectual and cultural developments help explain this curious burst of scepticism.

One problem presenting itself to historians of pre-Columbian America was the reliability of the Bible as a historical source. The Scriptures had long been assumed to be the sole surviving, accurate historical record of the human race. Since the second half of the seventeenth century, however, sceptics had begun to question its authority and credibility. As humanists and antiquarians unearthed ancient sources, including ancient Egyptian chronologies, and as the Jesuits made available Chinese classical texts in translation, it became clear that the chronologies of Hebrews and heathens could not be easily reconciled. Eighteenth-century conservative luminaries such as Vico and the Anglican Bishop of Gloucester, William Warburton, pursued a defensive strategy to safeguard the Bible's authority. Chinese ideograms and Egyptian hieroglyphs, long considered the repositories of ancient historical knowledge, lost their lustre and prestige. Vico and Warburton argued that non-alphabetical scripts represented a more primitive stage in the evolution of mental faculties. Thus, in the debates over the reliability of biblical chronologies, Chinese and Egyptian sources were discarded and Amerindian pictograms came to exemplify the first stage in the evolution of writing. The primitive Amerindian paintings were seen as products of a child-like mentality, the initial phase in the evolution of the mental faculties. No wonder, then, that in 1787 Warburton was so willing to dismiss documents recorded in Mesoamerican scripts.

If academic debates over biblical chronology account for the loss of credibility of Amerindian sources in the eighteenth century, the intellectual elitism that characterized the Enlightenment helps explain why earlier reports of the New World were also considered untrustworthy. When Raynal called on philosophers to visit and report on the New World in order to replace the unreliable testimony of earlier Spanish witnesses, he was simply following a convention of his time. Likewise Rousseau, in his groundbreaking 1755 study of the origins of social

---

[18] Guillaume-Thomas Raynal, *Histoire philosophique et politique des établissements et du commerce des Européens dans les deux Indes*, 10 vols. (Geneva, 1781), bk. 6, ch. 20.
[19] Raynal, *Histoire philosophique*, 7 vols. (Maastricht, 1774), bk. 6, ch. 1.

inequality, characterized the so-called European age of discovery as one of lost opportunities. According to Rousseau, missionaries, traders, soldiers, and sailors had not truly studied the foreign societies they visited and conquered, for they had failed to go beyond appearances. A new category of travellers was needed, Rousseau insisted, one whose 'eyes [are] made to see the true features that distinguish nations'.[20] Rousseau, therefore, invited the leading intellectual luminaries of his age to set sail and become philosophical travellers.

When Rousseau and Raynal called into question the reliability of typical European accounts of foreign societies, they were simply echoing the learned consensus of their age—that the observations of untrained individuals were not trustworthy: witnesses left to their own devices failed to make accurate observations. This was one of the tenets of the 'age of reason', which divided the world into two unequal parts: on one hand, the fear-stricken, deluded majority; and on the other, the reasonable few, whose minds had been trained to understand the world accurately.

Cornelius de Pauw typifies the authors north of the Pyrenees who, in the second half of the eighteenth century, sought to write histories of the New World while dismissing earlier Amerindian and European testimonies. De Pauw was a prolific author from the southern Netherlands, whose *Recherches philosophiques sur les américains* [Philosophical Enquiries on the Americans] (1768–9) proved extremely influential. The book was structured as a series of essays evaluating previous reports on the New World. Utterly sceptical of the power of the untrained mind to observe accurately, de Pauw set out to demonstrate that contradictions plagued the literature on the history of the Americas. Take for example his analysis of the Inca Garcilaso de la Vega's *Comentarios reales de los Incas* [History of the Incas] (1609–17). Owing to Garcilaso's dual heritage as the son of a Spanish conquistador and an Inca princess, which gave him access to the most learned and accurate contemporary testimonies from both European and indigenous sources, Garcilaso had enjoyed since the early seventeenth century a reputation as the foremost authority on the history of the Incas. In de Pauw's hands, however, Garcilaso's history appeared riddled with contradictions.

Garcilaso had maintained that the Inca kept their records in *quipus* (knotted strings), not alphabetical writing. He had also argued that Manco Capac, the great legislator and founder of the Inca dynasty, had turned the savages of Cuzco into civilized agriculturists and that the eleven rulers who followed Manco Capac had all been sage and prudent, spreading civilization and a humanely religious solar cult throughout an Inca Empire that expanded through gentle conquest. Finally, Garcilaso had argued that the Inca had established palaces, cities, universities, and astronomical observatories, as well as pious and prudent laws.

[20] Jean-Jacques Rousseau, *Discourse on the Origins and Foundations of Inequality among Men* (1755), in *The Collected Writings of Rousseau*, ed. Roger D. Masters and Christopher Kelly, vol. 3 (Hanover, NH, 1990–), 84–6 (note 8 in Rousseau's original).

De Pauw read Garcilaso carefully and attacked many of his premises. According to de Pauw, it was inherently contradictory to maintain that the Inca enjoyed wise laws while they lacked writing, for laws existed only when written and codified. According to de Pauw, unwritten rules were not laws—because they changed according to the whim of the times and the imagination of tyrants. He also identified other serious logical flaws in Garcilaso's narrative: for instance, he insisted that the claim that one man, Manco Capac, had single-handedly transformed highland savages into civilized creatures in one generation was outrageous. For evidence, de Pauw cited the Jesuit missions of Paraguay, the most recent example of a successful transformation of savages into settled civilized agriculturists. The achievement of civilization in Paraguay had required no less than fifty years and the imposition of harsh policies to prevent the Amerindians from escaping. Societies, de Pauw argued, are not transformed by leaps, but like nature evolve in sequential stages—evenly, harmoniously, and slowly.

Drawing upon this principle of slow social progress, de Pauw maintained that Garcilaso's chronology of the Inca did not make sense. Garcilaso had argued that forty years after the death of Manco Capac, astronomical observatories had been built in Cuzco to determine solstices and equinoxes. To evolve from a state of savagery to sophisticated astronomical knowledge required more than forty years. Finally, based on the notion of the harmoniously integrated evolution of social institutions, de Pauw insisted that the Inca could not have had an advanced agricultural society without having at the same time iron, money, and writing, all of which they lacked. Garcilaso had presented Inca rulers as patriarchal yet prudent, preoccupied with the welfare of the majority. But how could rulers have been prudent and gentle, de Pauw wondered, when the Inca had never developed institutions to check and balance the power of their monarchs? A fair, gentle patriarch was a contradiction in terms. So, too, was the idea that the Inca fought 'just wars' even as they engaged in conquest. Even if one conceded to Garcilaso that Manco Capac had in fact been fair, prudent, and gentle, what were the chances, de Pauw sardonically asked, that twelve such statesmen should appear in succession? De Pauw applied the same unrelenting critical techniques to tear apart previous versions of the history of the Americas.[21]

If the views of learned authors such as Garcilaso, who had ably synthesized the testimonies of both Amerindians and Europeans, proved untrustworthy, how then should scholars write the history of the New World? Western European authors were not merely content with dismissing as sources the translations of records written in indigenous scripts. Nor were these scholars satisfied with demonstrating logical inconsistencies in the accounts of travellers, missionaries, sailors, and colonial bureaucrats. Some philosophers, such as the Frenchman Charles-Marie de La Condamine, chose to go to the New World and study

---

[21] Cornelius de Pauw, *Recherches philosophiques sur les Américains, ou Mémoires intéressants pour servir à l'histoire de l'espèce humaine* (1768–69); 3 vols. (Berlin, 1770), ii. 195–203.

first-hand the land and its peoples, thus doing away with bothersome intermediary textual authorities. As the eighteenth century unfolded, witnesses trained in the new European sciences arrived in the Americas in ever greater numbers.

In addition to on-site research, however, another option existed for scholars who did not trust the older accounts. Some European authors set out to reconstruct the past of the New World conjecturally, using non-literary, material evidence. Rousseau, for example, tried to do away with all evidence from literary sources. Paying lip service to the reliability of the Bible as an accurate account of the past, Rousseau turned to nature for insights, drawing endlessly on evidence from animal behaviour in order to fill in the gaps in his evolutionary narrative of society and the causes of inequality. In addition, authors such as de Pauw, who found suspect all previous accounts of the past of the New World, turned to nature for evidence upon which to build alternative histories of the Americas.

De Pauw offered a new conjectural history of the lands and peoples of America based entirely on facts from geology, geography, animal distribution, and some old-fashioned medical theories. He found evidence pointing to an early geological catastrophe in America: fossil bones of gigantic animals; earthquakes and active volcanoes still rocking the earth; sea-shells strewn over all the low valleys; ores of heavy metals protruding on the surface of the land. According to de Pauw, there were also substantial indications that the New World was a humid, putrid environment: the lesser number, smaller size, and monstrous appearance of quadrupeds; the degeneration of foreign animals; the successful development of 'watery' plants from the Old World such as rice, melons, citrus, and sugar cane; the proliferation of insects and reptiles; the abundance of poisonous plants such as curare, whose virtues only the savage knew; and the American origin of syphilis (humanity's scourge). De Pauw concluded that a flood had suddenly transformed a continent of big animals and ancient civilizations into a land enveloped by miasmas. America's coldness and humidity, in turn, had emasculated its fauna and peoples. Drawing on an ancient medical tradition that assumed that males were 'drier' than females, de Pauw argued that the Amerindians were effete. The Amerindians, he claimed, were ancient inhabitants of the continent who, as a consequence of the flood that destroyed the New World, had became humid and insensitive, incapable of feeling passion and sexual urges, which, in turn, explained why upon arrival Europeans had found an allegedly sparsely populated continent.

CREATIVE ANSWERS IN NEW SPAIN

As in Europe, there was much support in Spanish America for the writing of new historical narratives. Yet these new histories of America were significantly different from those that appeared on the other side of the Atlantic. Spanish Americans tried to offer alternative accounts in which the inhabitants of the New World did not appear as degenerate and effete as conjectural historians such as de Pauw had presented them. In the process, Spanish American writers also articulated a powerful and creative critique of Eurocentric forms of knowledge. Spanish American authors, for example, exposed the shortcomings and limitations of the new European philosophical travellers, who had been arriving in ever increasing numbers to the New World. Spanish American intellectuals maintained that foreign travellers were unreliable sources because they tended to be ignorant of native languages, were gullible, and easily manipulated by savvy local informants: so much for the boasted scepticism of the observers from Western Europe.

The work of Antonio León y Gama exemplifies the distinctly patriotic scholarship that appeared in eighteenth-century Spanish America. León y Gama first articulated his views on the limited ability of outside observers to understand the past and the nature of the New World in a debate over the curative power of lizards. A flurry of speculation and clinical experimentation greeted the public of Mexico in 1782 when the leading physician of the *Audiencia* (high court and council) of Guatemala, José Flores, published a treatise claiming to have discovered that the raw meat of lizards cured cancer.[22] The discovery triggered a medical controversy in the capital of Mexico. Some physicians proved through clinical trials that the lizards were in fact poisonous, not curative. León y Gama, however, denounced these clinical trials as having either administered to patients the wrong lizards or mishandled the ones that were curative. Drawing on the works of Francisco Hernández, the sixteenth-century savant sent by Philip II to compile a natural history of the New World, León y Gama maintained that several distinct species of lizards, some of them indeed poisonous, existed in central Mexico. Yet he claimed that the physicians who conducted the trials that proved the lizards poisonous might have failed to identify the correct species or, worse, might have mishandled the right ones, turning them poisonous. Great care and great knowledge was needed to identify the correct species. Once the right lizard was caught, León y Gama argued, it had to be fed only with the appropriate local insects; all females, particularly those that were pregnant, had to be discarded; finally, the lizard had to be treated gently, for if irritated it could become poisonous. The amount of knowledge that these techniques demanded from physicians was extraordinary. Doctors needed to know the natural history of the area in order to identify, feed, and treat the curative lizards properly. The message behind León y Gama's treatise was that only those who knew the local fauna and flora in all its exquisite detail and intricacy were qualified to use the lizards. Those ignorant of the bewildering

---

[22] José Flores, *Específico nuevamente descubierto en el reino de Guatemala para la curación del horrible mal de cancro y otros mas frecuentes (experimentado ya favorablemente en esta capital de Mexico)* (Mexico, 1782).

details of Amerindian lore would never be able to master the region's curative powers.[23]

In the 1790s, in a different debate, this time over how to read Mesoamerican scripts, León y Gama maintained that outsiders had failed to understand the meaning of Amerindian sources for the same reasons that they had failed to grasp the importance of the curative power of lizards, namely, superficial acquaintance with the great complexities of Amerindian knowledge. By demonstrating the difficulty of reading Aztec documents, León y Gama set out to show the degree of linguistic and scientific knowledge required to handle this material appropriately, knowledge that only insiders could ever hope to master. He used Nahuatl documents recorded in indigenous scripts to make his case.

Nahuatl historical sources, León y Gama argued, ranged from widely accessible historical documents to arcane records that stored secret knowledge. He offered a few examples. *Codex histoire mexicaine depuis 1221 jusqu'en 1594* [Codex of Mexican History from 1221 to 1594], on the one hand, indicated that the flood of Tenochtitlan occurred in the year '8 Flint' (AD 1500). Although it located this event in equally rough fashion in the same year, the *Codex en Cruz* [Cruciform Codex], on the other hand, dated other events using a finer grid. It recorded, for example, the dates of birth of the monarch of Texcoco, Nezahualcoyotl (AD 1402), his son Nezahualpilzintli (AD 1464), and the ruler Quauhcaltzin (AD 1502). Sources such as *Codex histoire mexicaine* [Codex of Mexican History], León y Gama maintained, had been written for the masses because they required only a superficial acquaintance with writing techniques and astronomical knowledge. Sources such as the *Codex en Cruz*, on the other hand, were addressed to more knowledgeable and sophisticated audiences, for they demanded familiarity with the hieroglyphs of deities and towns as well as an exquisite command of multiple calendrical counts. A third type of source, such as the ritual calendar *Tonalamatl Aubin* [Ritual Horoscope Aubin], could only be read by highly trained religious specialists. With hundreds of symbols and obscure references to celestial phenomena and deities, sources such as *Tonalamatl Aubin* demanded from their intended audience complete command of both theological subtleties and astronomy.[24]

Complicating the picture of different documents for different audiences, there stood the additional problem of the nature of the logograms and ideograms used

---

[23] Antonio León y Gama, *Instrucción sobre el remedio de las lagartijas: Nuevamente descubierto para la curación del cancro y otras enfermedades* (Mexico, 1782). On the debate over the lizards, see also Miruna Achim, 'Making Lizards into Drugs: The Debate on the Medical Uses of Reptiles in Late Eighteenth-Century Mexico', *Journal of Spanish Cultural Studies*, 8 (2007), 169–91.

[24] Antonio León y Gama, *Descripción histórica y cronológica de las dos piedras que con occasion del Nuevo empedrado que se esta formando en la plaza principal de México se hallaron en ella en el año de 1790*, vol 1. (1792); ed. Carlos María de Bustamante, 2 vols. (Mexico, 1832), ii. 29–32 (par. 105–9). In the text, León y Gama never identified the provenance of the examples he cited. After a painstaking survey of the copies of codices he owned, I have identified the codices from which he drew most of his examples.

by Amerindians to record their annals. According to León y Gama, logograms and ideograms often alluded to local objects accessible only to a privileged few. An extensive knowledge of local natural history, León y Gama argued, was needed to understand the logograms of town names. The names of towns in such documents as the *Codex Cozcatzin* and the *Codex histoire mexicaine* could not be read without having first gained vast knowledge of the natural history of central Mexico. The name of Cimatlan, Tulan, Papatztaca, and Huexotzinca in these codices used logograms with the images of local shrubs, trees, and flowers. According to León y Gama, some logograms were simply too idiosyncratic and indecipherable, as in the case of references in the *Codez Cozcatzin* to the town of 'Teyahualco', whose rebus image León y Gama challenged anyone to explain. Even more upsetting for those who sought a shortcut to the interpretation of Amerindian documents was the fact that some towns with similar Nahuatl names were identified with the same logograms in different documents. This, León y Gama argued, was the case of 'Atempa' in the *Codex Cozcatzin* and 'Atenco' in *Matrícula de Tributos* [Tributary Rolls].

But if to read the name of towns in Aztec sources required at times knowledge beyond the reach of common mortals, the reading of the name of rulers was even more difficult. According to León y Gama, the signs used to refer to rulers did not merely allude to the sound of their names but also to some aspects of their moral character. The fact that the logogram of the ruler Quauhcaltzin in *Codex en Cruz* was a caged eagle, León y Gama argued, was of little use for those who knew that the logograms of the last Mexica monarch Quauhtemotsin, the Acolhua lord Quauhtletcohuatzin, and the lord of Coyuacan, Quauhpocatzin, were also represented as eagles in other sources. The eagles representing these rulers, however, showed subtle differences: their beaks appeared either shut, open, or giving off smoke, and their eyes were gazing up or down. According to León y Gama, such subtle distinctions were allusions to some aspect of the moral character of these rulers that had been understood only by a handful of retainers. The logic behind these correlations, therefore, was now beyond the understanding of any mortal, including any late-colonial native elites.[25]

León y Gama's reading of Mesoamerican codices was subtle and sophisticated. Notwithstanding his faith in the curative power of lizards, his insistence that there were different types of indigenous sources and that each required a vast amount of contextual information of linguistics and local natural history in order to be read, was unique for his age. León y Gama brought to bear learned humanist and antiquarian sensibilities to the reading and interpretation of sources in non-alphabetical scripts. His approach contrasts dramatically with the heavy-handed techniques of contemporary Western European conjectural historians. Radically different historiographical techniques seemed to have devel-

---

[25] León y Gama, *Descripción histórica*, ii. 41–5 (par. 117–19).

oped in each of the three areas of the Atlantic world discussed in this chapter, each paradoxically 'modern' in its own way. Although Spanish America and Spain itself are traditionally considered peripheries to an eighteenth-century North Atlantic core, the scholarship produced by authors such as Juan Bautista Muñoz and Antonio León y Gama are proof that the scepticism of the Enlightenment took on different meanings in different settings. Most studies of the Enlightenment, however, have failed to realize that the ideas produced by a handful of great French, British, and German writers were not simply 'transmitted' to the rest of the world, where they allegedly were either vigorously consumed or forcefully rejected. We have seen in the preceding pages that the same intellectual tools were used in different ways in Europe north of the Pyrenees, Spain, and Spanish America. If in the sceptical 'age of reason', non-Iberian authors created new and sophisticated forms of reading and invented the genre of conjectural history, Spanish writers anticipated the great insights of nineteenth-century German scholarship as they went about creating archives and histories based solely on primary sources. Scholars in Mexico took yet another route; they articulated a formidable critique of the limitations of knowledge that European sceptics were bound to face in the Americas. Oddly enough, it was colonial scholars such as León y Gama who put together the most sophisticated historical monographs created in the Enlightenment on the Americas.

Clearly struggles over authority and reliability had political overtones. North of the Pyrenees, enlightened scholars called into question the reliability of all written sources, because they were ultimately seeking to undermine the lasting cultural authority of traditional clerical bureaucracies, who had long had a purchase on power by claiming a sacred, privileged historiographical status for the Bible. Enlightened scholars also saw themselves actively contributing to the creation of a market-driven 'bourgeois public sphere'. In it, a new breed of male critics asserted their authority and credibility by highlighting their independence from distorting feminine emotions and powerful patrons. In the process, members of the Enlightenment went about creating new reading techniques and new conjectural reconstructions of the past that drew exclusively on new non-literary sources. Peninsular Spanish historians, to be sure, had different motivations. Their epistemological and methodological contributions came about as they sought to restore Spain's authority to determine how the colonization of the New World was to be remembered. Scholars understood that empires are lost in the struggle over naming and remembering. It is not surprising, therefore, that along with the creation of a new academy of history, archives, and new historical narratives, the reforming agenda of the Bourbon Crown also included sending dozens of cartographical and botanical expeditions to overseas territories. In addition to identifying new botanical resources for the empire, these expeditions primarily sought to challenge the power of the Dutch, English, and French to give names to new plants and old territories and to impose self-serving narratives of the history of European colonization in the New World, which had Spain as the villain. Finally historians in Spanish America had a political agenda of their own. Settlers had long envisioned their territories as 'kingdoms', loosely held parts of a much larger composite Iberian monarchy. But having kingdoms of their own, among other things, demanded scholars to endow these colonial territories with deep-rooted historical narratives and ancient dynastic genealogies. In places such as Mexico, settlers saw the ancient indigenous nobilities as their own biological ancestors and intellectuals thus turned for inspiration to the rich store of native written and oral sources.

KEY HISTORICAL SOURCES

Catálogo de la colección de Juan Batista Muñoz, 3 vols. (Madrid, 1954–6).

Clavijero, Francisco, *Storia antica del Messico cavata da' migliori storici spagnuoli, e da' manoscritti, e dalle pitture antiche degl' Indiani: divisa in dieci libri . . . e dissertazioni sulla terra, sugli animali, e sugli abitatori del Messico*, 4 vols. (Cesena, 1780–1).

—— *The History of Mexico Collected from Spanish and Mexican Historians, from Manuscripts, and Ancient Paintings of the Indians*, 2 vols. (London 1787).

—— *Historia antigua de México* (Mexico, 1964).

De Pauw, Cornelius, *Recherches philosophiques sur les Américains ou Mémoires intéressants pour servir à l'histoire de l'espece humaine*, 3 vols. (Berlin, 1770).

—— 'Amérique', in *Supplement à l'Encyclopédie*, vol. 1 (Amsterdam, 1776–7), 344–54.

—— *Recherches philosophiques sur les Grecs*, 2 vols. (Berlin, 1787).

Esteve Barba, Francisco, *Historiografía indiana* (2nd edn, Madrid, 1992).

Garcilaso de la Vega, Inca, *Comentarios Reales de los Incas* (1609–17); ed. José Durand, 3 vols. (Lima, 1959).

León y Gama, Antonio de, *Instrucción sobre el remedio de las lagartijas: Nuevamente descubierto para la curacion del cancro y otras enfermedades* (Mexico, 1782).

—— *Respuesta satisfactoria a la carta apologética que escribieron el Lic. Manuel Antonio Moreno y el Br. Alejo Ramon Sanchez. Y defensa contra la censura que en ella se hace de algunas proposiciones contenidas en la 'Instrucción sobre el remedio de las lagartijas'* (Mexico, 1783).

—— *Disertación física sobre la materia y formación de las auroras boreales* (Mexico, 1790).

—— *Descripción histórica y cronológica de las dos piedras que con ocasión del nuevo empedrado que se esta formando en la plaza principal de México se hallaron en ella en el año de 1790*, ed. Carlos Maria de Bustamente, 2 vols. (Mexico, 1832).

Muñoz, Juan Bautista, *Historia del Nuevo Mundo* (Madrid, 1793).

—— *Satisfacción a la carta crítica sobre las Historia del Nuevo Mundo* (Valencia, 1798).

Raynal, Guillaume-Thomas, *Histoire philosophique et politique des établissements et du commerce des Européens dans les deux Indes*, 6 vols. (Amsterdam, 1770).

—— *Histoire Philosophique et politique des établissements et du commerce des Européens dans les deux Indes*, 7 vols. (Maestricht, 1774).

—— *Histoire philosophique et politique des établissements et du commerce des Européens dans les deux Indes*, 10 vols. (Geneva, 1781).

Warburton, William, *Essai sur les hiéroglyphes des Egyptiens où l'on voit l'origine et les progrès du langage et de l'ecriture, l'antiquite des sciences en Egypte, et l'origine du culte des animaux...*, 2 vols. (Paris, 1744).
—— *The Works of the Right Reverend William Warburton*, 7 vols. (London, 1788).

BIBLIOGRAPHY

Ascher, Marcia and Ascher, Robert, *Code of the Quipu: A Study in Media, Mathematics, and Culture* (Ann Arbor, 1981).

Boone, Elizabeth Hill and Mignolo, Walter D. (eds.), *Writing without Words: Alternative Literacies in Mesoamerica and the Andes* (Durham, NC, 1994).

Brading, D. A., *First America* (Cambridge, 1991).

Brotherston, Gordon, *Book of the Fourth World: Reading the Native Americas Through their Literature* (Cambridge, 1992).

Carbia, Rómulo, *La crónica oficial de las Indias Occidentales: Estudio histórico y crítico acerca de la historiografía mayor de Hispano América en los siglos XVI a XVIII* (Buenos Aires, 1940).

Cline, Howard (ed.), *Handbook of Middle America Indians*, vols. 12–15: *Guide to the Ethnohistorical Sources* (Austin, 1972–5).

Florescano, Enrique, *Memory, Myth, and Time in Mexico: From the Aztecs to Independence*, trans. Albert Bork and Kathryn R. Bork (Austin, 1994).

Gerbi, Antonello, *La disputa del nuevo mundo: Historia de una polémica 1750–1900* (2nd edn, Mexico, 1982).

Herr, Richard, *The Eighteenth-Century Revolution in Spain* (Princeton, 1958).

Hudson, Nicholas, *Writing and European Thought 1600–1830* (Cambridge, 1994).

Keen, Benjamin, *The Aztec Image in Western Thought* (New Brunswick, NJ, 1971).

Lafaye, Jacques, *Quetzalcóatl et Guadalupe: La formation de la conscience nationale au Mexique* (Paris, 1974).

Lockhart, James, *The Nahuas After the Conquest: A Social and Cultural History of the Indians of Central Mexico, Seventeenth Through Eighteenth Centuries* (Stanford, 1992).

Maravall, José Antonio, *Estudios de la historia del pensamiento español (siglo XVIII)* (Madrid, 1991).

Marcus, Joyce, *Mesoamerican Writing Systems: Propaganda, Myth, and History in Four Ancient Civilizations* (Princeton, 1992).

Mestre, Antonio, *Historia, fueros y actitudes políticas: Mayans y la historiografía del XVIII* (Valencia, 1970).

Moreno de los Arcos, Roberto, 'La Historia Antigua de México de Antonio León y Gama', *Estudios de Historia Novohispana*, 7 (1981), 67–78.

Robertson, Donald, *Mexican Manuscript Painting of the Early Colonial Period: The Metropolitan School* (New Haven, 1956).

Sánchez-Blanco Parody, Francisco, *Europa y el pensamiento español del siglo XVIII* (Madrid, 1991).

Sarrailh, Jean, *L'Espagne éclairée de la seconde moitié du XVIIIe siècle* (Paris, 1954).

Chapter 33

Historical Writing in Colonial and Revolutionary America

David Read

It seems fair to say that during the seventeenth and eighteenth centuries the state of 'history' in the English-speaking North American colonies echoes, at a distance and with a certain amount of delay, the state of 'history' in England during the same period. Yet this is not saying very much. In the earlier part of the period, at least, 'history' has a notably flexible character—one that does not yet suggest the boundaries of a discipline, Sir Francis Bacon's bold efforts at definition notwithstanding.[1] While many works of the time are recognizably what modern readers would call history, quite a number of other works fit uncomfortably under a definition that, following the *Oxford English Dictionary*, understands history as, 'the formal record of the past'. A promotional tract, a political argument, a geographical or cultural survey, a collection of personal observations, or a work of fiction—any such text might include the word 'history' in the title. Since the word has always carried the broader sense of (again from the *OED*) 'a relation of incidents . . . a narrative, tale, story', it would be hard to argue with its catholic application by both writers and readers in the early modern period, but it makes the process of selecting material for a survey more challenging. For the purpose of this chapter I will restrict the discussion mainly to works that advertise themselves explicitly as projects for recording past events in the thirteen English colonies of North America that became the United States; these works in turn will be by authors who were in the colonies for at least some period of time, and will have been composed between 1607, when Jamestown was founded, and 1789, when the federal government under the Constitution officially began operations (and when, of course, another revolution of immense historical consequence also began). It would be pointless to restrict the list further to works written and published in the colonies, since a considerable number of them were actually written and published in England—though there is a noticeable shift in this

---

[1] See Bacon's important discussion of the kinds of history early in Book 2 of *The Advancement of Learning* in *Francis Bacon: The Major Works*, ed. Brian Vickers (Oxford, 1996), 175–86.

regard away from London and towards Boston and Philadelphia in the years leading up to the American Revolution.

With the field of enquiry settled in this way, one then faces some familiar historical questions. What changes can be observed in this field during the period in view? Obviously the colonial era in North America represents an extraordinarily dynamic span of time under any rubric that one cares to apply; does the historical writing of the period reflect that dynamism, and to what degree? How different is the relevant historiography of the eighteenth century from that of the seventeenth century? Is there a point (or points) where one can say that there has been a significant break with past historical practice and past historical consciousness? Finally, is there anything genuinely distinctive about history-writing in the English-speaking colonies? Can the notion of American exceptionalism be applied to early American historiography as well?

The temptation with any period that includes an event designated as a 'revolution' is to assume that the revolution is also experienced in other forms of human activity that are proximate to it. Yet to claim that the historiography of late eighteenth-century North America is 'revolutionary' in relation to what preceded it may not be the most accurate way to characterize the general state of affairs. As Michael Kammen has observed, 'Revolutionaries may subsequently write history; but historians rarely turn into revolutionaries.'[2] Still, there are noticeable shifts in the nature of historical writing in the English colonies of North America between 1607 and 1790—perhaps more incremental than dramatic, but noticeable in any case. Probably the most prominent change is the decline by the early eighteenth century of the style of history-writing associated with the New England Puritans. 'The New England Way' has long been a cliché in American history, but there is definitely such a 'way' in colonial historiography, one defined by an adherence to providentialist ideas, a rigorously delineated regionalism, and a strong sense of the sacred necessity of historicizing the deeds of the community, based on what David Van Tassel has called the New England settlers' 'passionate self-concern'.[3] One could argue that almost all early colonial history is regional history, and that historians in later periods continue to do their work with a sense of mission; what gradually fades away, however, is the idea that history exists to record a divine design. Providentialism survives as a motif, but not as a *raison d'être*. The dominant trait in eighteenth-century historiography up to the period of the revolution is a preoccupation with the archive; the historians collect and compare documents, and the focus tends to be on the deliberations of provincial government. Typically the organization of the histories is scrupulously chronological, and the overall effect can be rather dull, though there are some

---

[2] William Smith, Jr., *The History of the Province of New-York*, vol. 1, ed. Michael Kammen (Cambridge, Mass., 1972), p. lvi.

[3] David D. Van Tassel, *Recording America's Past: An Interpretation of the Development of Historical Studies in America 1607–1884* (Chicago, 1960), 10.

exceptions to the trend. The histories written prior to the revolution have remained relatively neglected, not so much because of these characteristics as because many of their authors were loyalists who were not necessarily enthusiastic about the virtues that came to be celebrated so highly in the post-revolutionary American republic. The War of Independence does prompt a shift, under the pressure of the need to make sense of (and to justify) the events of the recent past, towards thinking about causes, but the historians of the late eighteenth century are more likely to treat these causes as 'natural', as an effect of the local environment on a particular social order, than to understand them as obvious signs of divine purpose. One might still detect the shadow of divine providence in the histories of the 1780s, but it is only a shadow; the substance belongs to the previous century.

PURITAN HISTORY-WRITING IN NEW ENGLAND

In 'A General Introduction' to his most enduring work, *Magnalia Christi Americana* (1702), Cotton Mather claims that 'of all *History* it must be confessed, that the *Palm* is to be given unto *Church History*, wherein the *Dignity*, the *Suavity*, and the *Utility* of the *Subject* is transcendent'.[4] The same claim could have been made by nearly all of the early historians of New England, though few were as self-conscious in their approach as Mather. In fact, for these writers, the regional history of New England was ecclesiastical history, the development of the plantations in Massachusetts and Connecticut inseparable from the life of the churches in those places. This type of insular religious history was modelled at least in part on John Foxe's vastly popular *Acts and Monuments* (1563), but more obviously on biblical precedents in both the Old Testament and the New. Mather calls Moses '*that First-born of all Historians*', and after listing an impressive range of important classical authors, goes on to say that 'the two short Books of *Ecclesiastical History*, written by the Evangelist *Luke*, hath given us more *glorious Entertainments*, than all these voluminous Historians if they were put all together'.[5] The *Magnalia* is representative of the colonial ecclesiastical histories in being premised on the biblical notion of a chosen people, whether this people consists of suffering Israelites or post-Resurrection apostles (typologically, of course, these two groups tend to converge with each other). In another way, however, the *Magnalia*, by being so explicit about its purposes, conveys a misleadingly tidy sense of the state of history in seventeenth-century New England. It is, after all, a very late entry in the field. The earliest examples— two of the most important documents from the initial period of English

---

[4] Cotton Mather, *Magnalia Christi Americana: or, the Ecclesiastical History of New-England, From Its First Planting in the Year 1620 unto the Year of our LORD, 1698* (London, 1702), C2ʳ.
[5] Ibid., C2ᵛ.

settlement—seem to fit less easily into the category, though it would be hard to find another category more appropriate to the intentions of the authors. It is helpful in such cases to work from the idea that providentialism is not a monolithic movement in the history of thought, and that one can find obvious instances of what might be called 'loose' providentialism in contrast to the classic, 'tight' form; in a broad sense the different instances are addressing the same principle, but at varying degrees of intensity.[6]

William Bradford's *Of Plymouth Plantation* (1620–47; first pub. 1856), nicely illustrates the problem of categorizing providentialist discourse; it also presents other problems, since it is not a 'contemporary' text in the sense of appearing in print during either the seventeenth or the eighteenth century, though it was available in manuscript to Nathaniel Morton (who lifted lengthy passages of Bradford's writing more or less verbatim for his *New Englands Memoriall* [1669]), Cotton Mather, and Thomas Prince, and some of Bradford's documentary material appeared in the book commonly known as *Mourt's Relation* (1622). Though Bradford's clear intent in the relatively short First Book of his history is to chronicle the providential development of the particular community of separatists that established the Plymouth Colony, the quality of the text becomes much more mixed and uncertain when Bradford turns to an annalistic format in the Second Book, which he composed many years later, and which offers something more along the lines of a regional history of New England, taking in Plymouth's relations with John Winthrop's Massachusetts Bay Colony and with other outlying settlements. The Second Book is largely a history of conflict and struggle, but the conflict and struggle is not so much over matters of belief and ideology as it is over matters of commerce. The saints of Plymouth were part of a mercantile enterprise, after all, and needed to produce profits for investors in England in order to preserve the colony. Bradford spends a great deal of time on Plymouth's complex financial situation and the many threats to the colony's economic stability. Though there is a continuous thread of anxiety in Bradford's account about the integrity of the separatist community, this anxiety becomes inextricably tied to the overall health of the pilgrims' business enterprises in an evolving transatlantic world. As a result, *Of Plymouth Plantation* is a more outward-looking history, and one with a more obvious economic foundation, than Bradford probably ever meant it to be when he began writing his manuscript.

John Winthrop's *Journal* (1630–49) also presents a special case. Where Bradford's manuscript is carefully ruled and highly legible, as if Bradford were

---

[6] Michael P. Winship provides a useful survey of New England providentialism in *Seers of God: Puritan Providentialism in the Restoration and Early Enlightenment* (Baltimore, Md., 1996), 9–28, giving particular attention to the differences in the way that William Hubbard and Increase Mather approached providentialist history. For a discussion of the notion of 'loose' providentialism as it emerges in William Bradford's writing, see David Read, *New World, Known World: Shaping Knowledge in Early Anglo-American Writing* (Columbia, Mo., 2005), 47–51.

envisioning it as a printed book,[7] Winthrop's is very much a private journal, written in an arcane secretarial hand that has created numerous problems for editors and transcribers. Over the course of three notebooks it gradually shifts from day-to-day notation to a more deliberative and expansive style, reflecting the lengthening intervals between his entries. Winthrop's approach throughout is to record 'occasions' of all sorts, great and small. The *Journal* contains much that is invaluable to historians but even more that is merely mundane. Yet Winthrop does apparently think of himself as an historian. The heading with which he begins both the second and the third notebooks is 'A Continuation of the History of New England'. In a fascinating memorandum that Winthrop originally inserted as a loose sheet in the second notebook, he indicates at least a passing acquaintance with Sir Walter Raleigh's *A History of the World* (1614), and expresses his views on the uses of secular history: 'I deny not, but there is good use of profane histories, but only so far as they hold forth the wisdom, power justice & Clemency of this . . . supreme majesty [i.e. God] & discover the implacable malice . . . of Satan not only against the Saints . . . but against all mankind.'[8] The comment suggests that an element of cognitive dissonance exists in Winthrop's understanding of his project: the 'profane' aspects of the past should teach a lesson about providence, yet at a basic level the profane history remains what it is. Nothing in its factual content will automatically transfigure it into sacred history. The reader, then, bears the responsibility of finding the sacred in the profane. But who is the reader of a private history, other than its writer? As with Bradford's history of Plymouth, the ambiguities in the text are intimately connected to the private status of the text. Providentialism here is an attitude that threads its way through the journal rather than a fully conscious programme for interpreting historical events. Winthrop may hew strongly to the Puritan orthodoxy on providence, typology, and the coming of the millennium, but his journal acknowledges by its very character that divine illumination of ordinary events in the recent past is fitful at best.

One relatively early history of the Puritan colonists does demonstrate a high degree of historiographical consciousness and ideological coherence; unfortunately these features do not make Edward Johnson's *Wonder-Working Providence of Sions Saviour in New-England* (1654) a particularly rewarding experience for readers. It offers one of the purest instances of New English orthodoxy to be found outside of explicitly theological texts, and the overall effect is stultifying. As E. Brooks Holifield has aptly put it, the book has 'the subtlety of a recruiting poster'.[9] Johnson presents the 'wilderness-work' of the colonists, and their

---

[7] Douglas Anderson has addressed this aspect of Bradford's text in careful detail in *William Bradford's Books: Of Plimmoth Plantation and the Printed Word* (Baltimore, Md., 2003), 1–24.

[8] *The Journal of John Winthrop 1630–1649*, ed. Richard S. Dunn, James Savage, and Laetitia Yeandle (Cambridge, Mass., 1996), 769.

[9] E. Brooks Holifield, *Era of Persuasion: American Thought and Culture, 1521–1680* (Boston, 1989), 54.

continuing battles with 'erronists' on one side and Indians on the other, in a hyperbolic and admonitory style that verges on allegory and frequently blurs the distinction between past, present, and future. The events in New England (and in Cromwellian England) have for Johnson clearly been a preparation for the Second Coming, so it is perhaps no surprise that his writing shifts regularly from past to present tense and from third-person description to second-person exhortation, as he encourages his audience to hear and understand the prophetic message conveyed through the past actions of the New English saints. Occasionally, a decidedly secular interest in the specific economic circumstances of colonial life surfaces in Johnson's discussions of various towns. In general, though, *Wonder-Working Providence*—unusually for the time and place—is a history in which impersonal patterns and processes dominate over *res gestae*. In this sense, and this sense alone, it resembles histories written in much later periods.

At first glance, there appear to be many similarities, apart from length, between Johnson's book and Cotton Mather's *Magnalia Christi Americana*, published nearly fifty years later. Mather, like Johnson, intends to celebrate with all the means at his disposal the glories of Puritan orthodoxy shining in the American wilderness. Mather's prose style is as extravagant as Johnson's, but with a range of cultural reference and an attention to concrete detail that Johnson notably lacks. Yet this last monumental testament of the New England Way is significantly different in attitude from *Wonder-Working Providence*. Johnson, writing during the Interregnum, aims to persuade his readers of New England's important role in the revolution of the saints then overtaking the home country; his history anticipates better days yet to come, or at least that is the impression it seeks to convey. Mather, writing at the start of a new century and looking back over decades that included all manner of transformative events, is no such optimist. He is a conservator rather than a messenger, seeking to preserve a past that is now endangered. He claims to have 'done the part of an *Impartial Historian*',[10] by which he means that he is willing to engage in critical reflection on the deeds of the colonial leaders whose biographies take up so much of the *Magnalia*; here his model appears to be Tacitus, whose work he cites quite favourably. This suggests an important difference between Mather's historiography and that of his predecessors: his prodigious and eclectic learning. For all the exclusivity of his religious beliefs, he was one of the most erudite figures of his time on either side of the Atlantic, an extraordinarily prolific, indeed driven, reader and writer who paraded the extent of his knowledge as a matter of course.

Standing midway in the second half of the seventeenth century between the providentialist landmarks erected by Johnson and Mather, there is William Hubbard's *A General History of New England* (*c*.1682), the most obscure of the

---

[10] Mather, *Magnalia Christi Americana*, C2ᵛ.

long, ecclesiastically oriented histories of New England. It existed only in manuscript until its first printing in 1815, though it represents an important link between first-generation writers such as Bradford and Winthrop and historians at the turn of the eighteenth century. Hubbard's history has suffered not only from its lack of a public readership before the nineteenth century but from its relative proximity in time to the appearance of the *Magnalia*. In general, Hubbard's approach is providentialist, but he is much less tendentious, and frequently much more readable, than either Johnson or Mather; he writes fluently and with a certain amount of dry wit, and perhaps comes closest, given the constraints of Puritan ideology that he observes as well as his contemporaries, to producing a 'mainstream' history of New England in the seventeenth century.

An eighteenth-century outlier in the providentialist tradition is John Callender's short treatise, *An Historical Discourse on the Civil and Religious Affairs of the Colony of Rhode-Island and Providence Plantations in New-England in America* (1739), noteworthy for being a sympathetic account of a colony that the Massachusetts-based historians treated with suspicion and disdain. Though he refers regularly to the effects of divine providence in the history of Rhode Island, Callender also represents well the traditions of that colony, since he writes with great tolerance about the various sectaries and eccentrics who found a haven there.

NEW ENGLAND HISTORIOGRAPHY AND THE INDIAN WARS

An important sub-genre of history in seventeenth-century New England deals with the military activities of the settlers. The Pequot War of 1637 and King Philip's War of 1675–6 not only threatened the survival of the New England colonies but, given the relentless self-examination of the Puritan settlers, also required retrospective description, analysis, and justification. Arguably the massacre in Virginia in 1622, led by Powhatan's brother Opechancanough, was equally if not more devastating to the colony there (with roughly a third of the settlers killed), but published accounts of it are relatively few; the need to historicize the crises of the early years was simply not felt as strongly south of New England. The Pequot War, which basically ended when a Puritan militia fired a fortified Pequot settlement and massacred almost all of the inhabitants (numbering in the hundreds and apparently including women and children), resulted in a handful of short narratives by eyewitnesses in addition to the accounts that appear in Bradford and Winthrop; John Underhill's and Philip Vincent's accounts appeared in print in 1638, while the memorandum of John Mason, the commander responsible for the attack on the fort, circulated only in manuscript until Thomas Prince published it in 1736. The much more wide-ranging conflict of King Philip's War generated a number of published accounts, the most famous of which is Mary Rowlandson's memoir of her captivity among the Narragansetts, *The Sovereignty and Goodness of God* (1682). While this work had an immediate and lasting popularity, the accounts of the war that had the most contemporary prestige would have been Increase Mather's. Mather actually wrote two in close succession, *A Brief History of the War with the Indians in New England* (1676) and *A Relation of the Troubles which have hapned in New-England* (1677). The latter of these reaches back to the Pequot War, and Mather incorporates in it part of Mason's text (though he mistakenly attributes it to John Allyn, another Connecticut official).

Both books represent well the 'tight' providentialism that characterizes most Puritan accounts of the wars. In *A Relation*, Mather even arrives at the moment of original sin that allowed these wars to occur. Thomas Hunt, a ship captain with John Smith on Smith's 1614 expedition to New England, lured twenty-four Indians at Plymouth into his ship under false pretences, took them back across the Atlantic, and attempted to sell them into slavery at Gibraltar: 'Yea that inhumane and barbarous Fact was the unhappy Occasion of the Loss of many a man's Estate and Life, which the Barbarians in those beginning Times did from thence seek to destroy.'[11] If Hunt's folly engendered the initial conflict, it is the backsliding of the settlers that has led to the later one, as Mather argues in *A Brief History*: 'Nor were our sins ripe for so dreadfull a judgment, until *the Body of the first Generation* was removed, and another Generation risen up which hath not pursued, as ought to have been, the blessed design of their Fathers.' Yet the edge of providence cuts both ways: the signs of divine wrath alternate with tokens of God's benevolent guidance—tokens that can take a starkly material form. In describing the surprise attack of a militia from Sudbury on a native encampment, Mather notes that 'God so disposed of the bullets that were shot at that time, that no less than thirty Indians were wounded, of whom there were fourteen that dyed several of which had been principal actors in the late bloudy Tragedyes.'[12]

The theological reading of events tends to displace any specific concern with the identity of one's enemies, other than as perpetrators of evil deeds and recipients of just punishment. Mather displays little interest in the life ways of the 'barbarians', and certainly no interest in their history unless it happens to coincide with the history of the settlers. The same attitude prevails in a major account contemporary with Mather's, William Hubbard's *A Narrative of the Troubles with the Indians in New-England* (1677), in which Hubbard portrays the natives with a near-total absence of cultural or psychological nuance, as treaty-

---

[11] Increase Mather, *A Relation of the Troubles which have hapned in New-England, By reason of the Indians there, From the Year 1614 to the Year 1675*, under the title *Early History of New England*, ed. Samuel G. Drake (Boston, 1864), 54.

[12] *So Dreadfull a Judgment: Puritan Responses to King Philip's War, 1676–1677*, ed. Richard Slotkin and James K. Folsom (Middletown, Conn., 1978), 86, 114. The complete text of *A Brief History* is included in this anthology, 79–152.

breakers and traitors who victimized the honest and fair-dealing colonists. The lack of interest in the native side of the story is broadly typical of the other wartime histories, with the interesting exception of Daniel Gookin's *An Historical Account of the Doings and Sufferings of the Christian Indians in New England, in the Years 1675, 1676, 1677* (1677). Gookin was a secular ally of John Eliot, the famous missionary to the New England tribes, and his 1677 manuscript is a spirited defence of the allegiance of the 'Praying Indians' to the colonists during King Philip's War. It should be said that Gookin's sympathies do not extend much beyond this group of converts, but within these limits his narrative is a *cri de coeur* for the plight of a group trapped between a rock and a hard place—more specifically, trapped on Deer Island in Boston Harbour, as the first group of ethnic internees in American history. The other atypical history is Thomas Church's *Entertaining Passages Relating to Philip's War* (1716), assembled from materials left by Church's father, Benjamin, who led the expedition that killed Philip in 1676. This is very much an insider's history, reproducing the perspective of a soldier who had daily transactions with the native population. Moving forward on a steady flow of dialogue between Benjamin Church and various native interlocutors, both allies and enemies, the narrative is largely free of moralizing and theological reflection. It not only is, but reads as, a book of the eighteenth rather than the seventeenth century. The New Hampshire magistrate Samuel Penhallow's *History of the Wars of New-England with the Eastern Indians* (1726) is, on the other hand, a book that seems to belong to the seventeenth rather than the eighteenth century. A rare attempt at a comprehensive history of Queen Anne's War (1702–13), the book also includes an account of the unnamed conflict that transpired mainly in northern New England between 1722 and 1726 and concluded by treaty just a few months before Penhallow's death. The style hearkens back to the Mathers—and, like the Mathers, Penhallow displays a consistent antipathy towards the natives, whom he tags as being guilty of 'perfidy' from the title page onwards.

HISTORIOGRAPHY IN VIRGINIA

Outside of New England, efforts at any sort of systematic history-writing in the colonies are decidedly sporadic until the mid-eighteenth century, and even then there are significant gaps (no major histories of Pennsylvania, for example, until the late 1790s). Because of its originary status and steadily growing importance in imperial commerce, Virginia attracted more attention as an object of history than did the surrounding colonies—which is a way of saying that a handful is more than nothing. Of course, perhaps the most famous history of early English colonization emerges from Virginia: John Smith's *Generall Historie of Virginia, New-England, and the Summer Isles* (1624). Smith's magnum opus is not, as most of its readers will grant, a well-constructed piece of historiography. Indeed it is very nearly the opposite of that, a frequently awkward pastiche of his first-hand observations as a leader of the Jamestown colony, along with the work of several other hands, work that allowed Smith to cover the years that followed his permanent departure from Virginia in 1609 (a much longer period than the two years he actually spent there) and to address the early British colonization of Bermuda, a place he had never visited. In addition, Smith included a more descriptive and promotionally oriented section on New England based on previously published material connected with his coastal survey of that region in 1616, several years before the first waves of English settlers arrived, and on material borrowed from *Mourt's Relation.* The narrative is disjointed and episodic, with frequent and confusing shifts between the first- and third-person voice, and Smith—concerned as he is with presenting and defending his own exploits—seems constitutionally incapable of stepping back to offer a broader, more disinterested perspective.

It is probably no accident that the typical way of dealing with the *Generall Historie* is to extract historically compelling bits and pieces—the most compelling bit by far, to judge by its lasting popularity and long-since mythic stature, being Smith's account of his rescue from execution by Powhatan's daughter Pocahontas. Yet Smith's main accomplishment in the *Generall Historie* is to bring the *gravitas* of the classical historian to what had previously belonged to the modest realm of the 'report'. Both as author and historical actor, Smith casts himself in the Roman mould, emphasizing not only the deeds but also the rhetoric of individuals, presented in specific moments of conflict and negotiation. To accent the dignity of the proceedings in certain episodes, he includes both lengthy speeches by the principals and snippets of English poetry that suggest Latin epigrams, though the provenance of most of these verse tags remains uncertain. What is most striking about the book is Smith's willingness to present indigenous Americans as historical figures of roughly equivalent power and stature to the colonists, fully capable of significant action and eloquent speech (though Smith, like many colonial writers, conveniently ignores the problem of translation between structurally distant languages). For all its flaws, the *Generall Historie* is thus the most important early attempt to comprehend the encounter between the English and the natives within the conventions of a traditional historical narrative.

The next major history of Virginia after Smith's is Robert Beverley's *The History and Present State of Virginia* (1705); the fact that eight decades separate one publication from the other serves to reinforce the perception that the first few generations of Virginians, lacking any strong sense of being either alienated or exceptional in their relations with the home country, were far less interested in recounting their own past than were their contemporaries in New England. Properly speaking, the history in Beverley's *History* is limited to Part 1 of the book. Beverley's account of the colony's early years is basically redacted from Smith's *Generall Historie*; the most interesting material deals with the period from the dissolution of the Virginia Company in 1626 up to Beverley's own time. Beverley had strong opinions about the colony's recent history, evident in his criticism of its governors, most of whom he found incompetent (the exception being William Berkeley, with whom Beverley's family had had close relations), and in his deeply sceptical account of Nathaniel Bacon's motives in fomenting a rebellion against Berkeley's government in 1676. Beverley famously ties his style to the colonial place he inhabits, far from the metropolis in which his book is published: 'I am an *Indian*, and don't pretend to be exact in my Language: But I hope the Plainness of my Dress, will give him the kinder Impressions of my Honesty, which is what I pretend to.'[13] In the revised edition of 1722, Beverley decided, for whatever reason, that some of this 'Plainness' was no longer in order, for he removed nearly all of the critiques and toned down the wit; as a result the second edition has proven not nearly as interesting as the first for Beverley's more recent readers.

The last significant locally authored history of Virginia from the first half of the eighteenth century, William Stith's *The History of the First Discovery and Settlement of Virginia* (1742), is also the least, proving neither popular at the time nor influential subsequently. It is perhaps most notable for Jefferson having written dismissively about it in Query XXIII of *Notes on the State of Virginia*.[14] At the periphery of Virginian historical writing, quite literally, is William Byrd's *History of the Dividing Line betwixt Virginia and North Carolina* (c.1738), a highly personal account of the surveying expedition to set the boundary between the two colonies in 1728. Byrd's narrative is mainly famous today for existing in two versions, one of which is the rambunctious, satirical, mildly bawdy (and much shorter) 'Secret History'. In a sense, though, both versions were secret, since the manuscripts remained in private hands until the nineteenth century. Byrd refers to his work as a journal, and it is closer in resemblance to the writing of Samuel Pepys than to the more typical histories being surveyed here, but it does—at least in the 'public' version—contain useful reflections on the development of the two colonies, the rough state of the frontier communities in the border region, and relations with the native populations in the area.

HISTORIOGRAPHY BEFORE THE REVOLUTION

It may not be entirely accurate to say that all politics in eighteenth-century British America prior to 1776 are local, but to say that all histories in the colonies

---

[13] Robert Beverley, *The History and Present State of Virginia*, ed. Louis B. Wright (Chapel Hill, NC, 1947), 9.

[14] Thomas Jefferson, *Notes on the State of Virginia*, ed. William Peden (New York, 1972), 177: 'He is inelegant . . . and his details often too minute to be tolerable, even to a native of the country, whose history he writes.'

are local histories comes very close to the truth. To judge by the historiographical record, the sense of the thirteen colonies as representing a confederation with common interests, a confederation that could be described in a global if not a nationalist manner, is a relatively late development. One of the few early attempts at producing a comprehensive history roughly along the lines of the English historian John Oldmixon's *The British Empire in America* (1708) is decidedly a farrago: William Douglass's *Summary, Historical and Political, of the First Planting, Progressive Improvements, and Present State of the British Settlements of North America* (1749) is a loosely organized collection of previously published pamphlets that offer digressions and lengthy glosses on, among other things, the production of sugar, the magnetism of the mariner's compass, predestination and free will, the dangers of a paper currency, and the deficiencies of most previous colonial historians—the last in spite of the many inaccuracies that Douglass himself introduces. The majority of colonial historians in the earlier eighteenth century are primarily interested in establishing the distinctive identities and attributes of the colonies in which they happen to be living and working, and are not much concerned with placing 'their' colonies in a broader context. Thomas Prince defends the accumulation of apparently trivial details in his *A Chronological History of New-England in the Form of Annals* (1736–55) by stressing their local appeal: 'Those minute things are observed with Pleasure by the People who live in the Places where they were transacted, which are inconsiderable to Those who never saw them.'[15] This emphasis on regional individuality results, paradoxically, in a fairly homogeneous set of histories. They are long, often running to multiple volumes. They tend to be the products of the *otium*, such as it was, of extremely busy men of affairs in the colonies; they are usually rigorously chronological, and heavily concerned with the machinery of government; they are meticulous, sometimes to a fault, in collecting and presenting documentary evidence; and most of the time they are deliberately subdued in tone and style. William Smith, Jr. writes in the preface to his *History of the Province of New-York* (1757) that his book 'presents us only a regular thread of simple facts; and even those unembellished with reflections . . . choosing rather to be honest and dull, than agreeable and false, the true import of my vouchers hath been strictly regarded'.[16] Samuel Smith in his *History of the Colony of Nova-Caesaria, or New-Jersey* (1765) concludes his preface, 'To a collection principally intended to consist of a plain state of facts, much need not be premised . . . nothing is aim'd at, more than a fair and candid representation.'[17] Thomas Hutchinson, who would eventually serve as the last royal governor of

---

[15] Thomas Prince, *A Chronological History of New-England in the Form of Annals* (Boston, 1736), p. x.

[16] William Smith, Jr., *History of the Province of New-York*, 6–7.

[17] Samuel Smith, *The History of the Colony of Nova-Caesaria, or New-Jersey*, pp. ix–x.

Massachusetts, is equally self-deprecating in presenting the method of his massive *History of the Colony and Province of Massachusetts-Bay* (1765–7):

> It cannot be expected that the affairs of a colony should afford much matter, interesting or entertaining to the world in general. I write for the sake of my own countrymen, and even to many of them I expect some facts will be thought of too little importance . . . . In general, we are fond of knowing the minutiae which relate to our ancestors. There are other facts, which, from the nature of them, will afford but a dull and heavy narration. My chief design is to save them from oblivion.[18]

These remarks indicate a deep respect for the intrinsic power and authority of facts, apart from any moral, theological, or political meaning that they might convey. This attitude towards facts as being valuable simply by virtue of their truth-content is surely one of the main markers of the Enlightenment, and of Enlightenment historiography—but not necessarily of compelling history-writing.

A number of works written prior to the revolution can be highlighted for their departure from the general pattern. *A True and Historical Narrative of the Colony of Georgia in America* (1741) is a satirical attack by dissatisfied settlers on the policies of Colonel Oglethorpe and the Trustees of the colony, composed by several hands but principally assigned to the Savannah physician Patrick Tailfer. One would have to turn to Byrd's *History of the Dividing Line* to find anything remotely similar among the eighteenth-century histories.

Two books are distinctive for their concern with ethnology; both provide fuller (and fairer) accounts of the societies and cultures of the indigenous peoples of North America than were generally available in the period. Cadwallader Colden's *The History of the Five Indian Nations Depending on the Province of New-York in America* (1727) is the work of a remarkable figure, a man who could stand with Benjamin Franklin and Thomas Jefferson in terms of the range of his interests and abilities. Unfortunately for his later reputation, he was an outspoken loyalist and defender of imperial policy, and his support of the Stamp Act made him an unpopular figure in the later years of his career. Colden's book recounts the activities of the Iroquois tribal network during King William's War of 1689–97, the first of the so-called French and Indian Wars between England and France for control of the North American interior. At one level the book operates as a political tract on the colonial balance of powers: Colden is using past events to argue for the importance of maintaining a strong alliance with the Iroquois as a bulwark against New France. But the book is most noteworthy for its respectful treatment of Iroquois culture, based on the first-hand knowledge that Colden had acquired as New York's surveyor-general during the 1720s, and for its comparatively modern use of sources. The detailed accounts of

---

[18] Thomas Hutchinson, *The History of the Colony and Province of Massachusetts-Bay*, vol. 1, ed. Lawrence Shaw Mayo (Cambridge, Mass., 1936), pp. xxviii–xxix.

negotiations at Albany between colonial and tribal representatives, including lengthy speeches by various Iroquois chieftains, are drawn from transcriptions in the provincial registers of Indian Affairs, and Colden has also made heavy use of the French histories available to him. In fact, when Colden presents a particularly egregious instance of French misconduct—the sanctioned torture, execution, and cannibalization of an Indian captive by French-allied Ottawas— he pointedly says that he got his information from a French text, and cites the volume and page number.

James Adair's *History of the American Indians* (1775) also presents a strategic view of native populations—in this case the major south-eastern tribes, including the Cherokees, Creeks, Chickasaws, and Choctaws—as occupying a buffer zone between the English in the Carolinas and Georgia, the French in the Mississippi Valley and along the Gulf of Mexico, and the Spanish in Florida. Like Colden, Adair is greatly concerned with establishing British dominance in North America, and in correcting what he sees as the ineptitude of British policy towards the tribes. But Adair's history is much closer to the ground; as an Indian trader who lived among his customers for many years, Adair was in an unusually good position to observe and record native customs and traditions. His book is distinctly, if not methodically, ethnological in its approach, certainly more so than Colden's. What is perhaps most striking about *The History of the American Indians*, though, is that Adair's study is driven by a thesis that he elaborates at great length, in an argument taking up twenty-three heads and around 150 pages of text. The thesis is not in any way new with Adair, but had been circulating since the early years of European colonization in the New World: that the American natives were, as Adair puts it, 'lineally descended from the Israelites, either while they were a maritime power, or soon after the general captivity; the latter however is the most probable'. Just prior to making this claim, Adair says that 'TRUTH is my object',[19] but the prominence and baroque presentation of his *idée fixe* at the beginning of the text has at times detracted from the substantial quality of his work as an eyewitness historian among native groups that were otherwise poorly documented in the eighteenth century.

HISTORIOGRAPHY DURING AND AFTER THE AMERICAN REVOLUTION

The histories composed after 1776 inevitably reflect partisan positions, as defenders of the empire vie with defenders of independence for a sympathetic audience on both sides of the Atlantic. Yet apart from the display of political allegiances

---

[19] James Adair, *The History of the American Indians*, ed. Kathryn E. Holland Braund (Tuscaloosa, Ala., 2005), 74.

the historiography of this period is not especially distinctive. The writers are certainly aware of the lasting importance of the events they describe, but are perhaps too close to those events to provide fully formed interpretations. Their histories tend to follow the familiar European annalistic and antiquarian models. Peter Messer makes much of the emigration of educated Scots to North America and the influence of the Scottish Enlightenment (personified, at least later in the century, by David Hume) on colonial history-writing, but this influence may be overstated; it is hard to detect much in the way of a philosophical approach to historiography in the newly formed nation until the nineteenth century.[20] The interest of these histories is in their political affiliations. In this arena the loyalists are well represented, though they are little known today, since their view of events was not the one that finally prevailed. Perhaps the most imposing figure in this group is the Scottish-born George Chalmers, who spent a dozen years as a lawyer in Maryland but fled for England in 1775. His *Political Annals of the Present United Colonies* (1780), though it concludes with the year 1688, is a vast advance in terms of coherence and interest over Douglass's *Summary* of 1749 as an account of the whole group of colonies. It is marked throughout by a deep scepticism about the colonists' motives in seeking independence. Chalmers also wrote a sharply critical *Introduction to the History of the Revolt of the American Colonies* in 1782, but decided to suppress it, perhaps because he was as critical of the British government as he was of the colonists. It was not published until 1845.

Other histories in the loyalist camp include Joseph Galloway's *Historical and Political Reflections on the Rise and Progress of the American Rebellion* (1780) and Samuel Peters's *General History of Connecticut* (1781), which can be paired as contributions to a tradition of anti-Puritan polemic reaching back to Thomas Morton's *New English Canaan* (1637). Like Chalmers, Galloway and Peters fled to England during the 1770s (though Peters later returned to America). Galloway finds the sources of the rebellion in the intrinsic republicanism of the New England colonies, which he claims were pursuing independence from England by any means from the moment they were first settled. Peters similarly argues that government in Connecticut, and in New England generally, was illegitimate from the beginning, based on fraud, faulty land claims, and the settlers' wilful disregard of their obligations as British citizens. Though Peters is mainly famous for his highly exaggerated description of the 'blue laws' imposed by the Puritans on their communities, he also offers some interesting corollaries to the loyalist position: in the middle of the book he eloquently protests the decimation of the indigenous peoples and the enslavement of Africans in the name of Christianity, 'none [of these victims] seeking other happiness, than to be screened from the

---

[20] Peter C. Messer, *Stories of Independence: Identity, Ideology, and History in Eighteenth-Century America* (DeKalb, Ill., 2005). Whether or not one agrees with Messer's thesis, this book provides a valuable summary of the field of American historiography in the eighteenth century.

torture rendered necessary by that curious American maxim, that men must be willing to die before they are fit for the Kingdom of Heaven'.[21]

Another critique of slavery can be found, this time from the perspective of a southern-based loyalist, in Alexander Hewat's *An Historical Account of the Rise and Progress of the Colonies of South Carolina and Georgia* (1779). Hewat was also born in Scotland, and he too departed for England prior to the war after serving as a Presbyterian minister in Charleston. 'Can the particular laws of any country', Hewat asks, 'supersede the general law of nature? Can the local circumstances of any province upon earth be pled in excuse for such a violent trade, and for such endless slavery in consequence of it?'[22]

The two most important, and prolific, of the 'sympathetic' historians writing in the wake of the War of Independence were both deeply invested in the cause: William Gordon, an English dissenting pastor, who emigrated to Massachusetts out of his zeal for independence; and David Ramsay, a military surgeon who spent a year as a prisoner of war in the British garrison at Saint Augustine. Of the two, Ramsay has had a higher reputation in subsequent centuries, perhaps because he was the first native-born chronicler of the revolution and thus could lay claim to being among the first 'American' historians. While both were extremely active politically, they were separated not only geographically—Ramsay, though born in Pennsylvania and educated there and in New Jersey, spent much of his career in medical practice in Charleston—but also in their views about self-government. Gordon was a vociferous anti-Federalist; for fear that his work would be opposed by influential Federalists in Massachusetts, such as John Hancock and John Adams, he felt compelled to publish his sprawling, four-volume *History of the Rise, Progress, and Establishment of the Independence of the United States of America* (1788) in England. Ramsay, on the other hand, was a confirmed Federalist and supporter of the new Constitution, so his writing in the 1780s has, in the grand Whig tradition, a certain quality of the history of the victors. This writing consists of two relevant works, *The History of the Revolution in South-Carolina, from a British Province to an Independent State* (1785), an account that was too regional to attract many readers, and the much more popular *The History of the American Revolution* (1789).

As primary sources both Gordon's and Ramsay's histories have suffered a low estimation among modern historians, largely due to a series of exposés produced at the turn of the twentieth century by one of Frederick Jackson Turner's former students, Orin G. Libby, who unearthed examples of Gordon's and Ramsay's plagiarism from the British *Annual Register*, the publication so closely associated

---

[21] Samuel Peters, *General History of Connecticut*, ed. Samuel McCormick (New York, 1877), 109. Strangely, Peters was himself a slave holder, not unlike a much more famous critic of slavery on the other side of the revolution, Thomas Jefferson.

[22] Alexander Hewat[t], *An Historical Account of the Rise and Progress of the Colonies of South Carolina and Georgia*, 2 vols. (London, 1779), i. 121.

with Edmund Burke through the 1760s, and in its continuing reports of British colonial affairs a valuable and reliable source of information and documentation throughout the revolutionary period. The charge of plagiarism acted for many years, in David van Tassel's words, 'like a quarantine sticker',[23] but the onus has faded in recent years, thanks to both a growing awareness that many writers of the period unashamedly borrowed material from the *Annual Register* without attribution, and the resurgence of interest in the interpretive and rhetorical aspects of the historical writing of the revolutionary period. Gordon's political stance is more difficult to detect in his writing than is the case with Ramsay; his main concern seems to be to convey the currency and moral immediacy of the events that he describes. To this end, he frequently resorts to the relatively novel strategy of writing about past history in the present tense. Otherwise his history entails the familiar mix of annalistic narrative and transcribed documents. Ramsay's history, on the other hand, has a clearly recognizable thesis, and thus a strong affinity with the idea-driven historiography of late eighteenth-century Europe. For Ramsay, the American Revolution is an organic phenomenon, developing out of the physical as well as the social and economic circumstances of the colonies themselves. Ramsay is among the first American authors to emphasize geography as a powerful history-shaping force:

Colonists, growing up to maturity, at such an immense distance from the seat of government, perceived the obligation of dependence much more feebly, than the inhabitants of the parent isle, who not only saw, but daily felt, the fangs of power. The wide extent and nature of the country contributed to the same effect. The natural seat of freedom is among high mountains and pathless deserts, such as abound in the wilds of America.[24]

Several local items written by 'patriots', whether Federalist or not, are worth noting. Jeremy Belknap's *History of New-Hampshire* (1784–92) signals the changed character of New England historiography after Cotton Mather: though Belknap held long pastorates in Congregational churches in Dover, New Hampshire, and Boston, the historical section of the book (limited to the first volume) is largely devoid of providentialist elements, and the later volumes reflect his serious commitment to natural history and geography. Belknap is also notable for being one of the founders of history as a discipline in the new nation; the plan that he conceived for an antiquarian society in Boston coalesced some years later into the Massachusetts Historical Society. George Minot's *History of the Insurrections in Massachusetts in 1786 and of the Rebellion Consequent Thereon* (1788) is unusual for its focus on a local conflict, Shays's Rebellion, that occurred in the aftermath, and as a consequence, of the Revolutionary War. In recounting

---

[23] David D. van Tassel, *Recording America's Past: An Interpretation of the Development of Historical Studies in America 1607–1884* (Chicago, 1961), 39; (see also n. 25, which provides a good brief overview of the effect of Libby's work on the critical reception of Gordon and Ramsay).

[24] David Ramsay, *The History of the American Revolution*, vol. 1 (Philadelphia, 1789), 29.

Daniel Shays's failed effort in 1786–7 to overturn the government of Massachusetts with a force of financially strapped farmers and labourers from the western part of the state, Minot shows himself clearly on the side of established authority; even so his brief book presents a sophisticated, judicious, and even-handed analysis of the difficult economic conditions that the costs of the war imposed on a state such as Massachusetts, and he outlines the mistakes of the government as well as the misdeeds of the rebels, under the idea that 'The period of misfortune is the most fruitful source of instruction'.[25]

I will close this survey with a text that, in its way, looks forward to the next period of American history and history-writing. The significance of Jedidiah Morse's *The American Geography* (1789) is evident in the title; it is the first comprehensive geographical survey by a native of the new nation, and as such was immensely popular and influential as a textbook in the early United States.[26] Morse understands history to be a component of geographical description: the chapter on each state ends with a historical summary, and his general commentary on the United States in the first 150 pages includes both 'A Summary account of the first Discoveries and Settlements of North America, arranged in chronological order', and a considerably longer history of the War of Independence, including short biographies of Washington, Lafayette, and two other generals on the American side. It has been argued that Morse skews both his history and geography towards New England, at the expense of the mid-Atlantic and southern states that he knew less well.[27] With regard to the first edition of *The American Geography*, however, this characterization seems unfair; Morse devotes more pages to Pennsylvania and Virginia than he does to Massachusetts and Connecticut. What is notably lacking in Morse's geography is much interest in the period of British provincial government between the initial settlement of the colonies and the mid-eighteenth century. Morse's 'general view' of American history in effect begins, as he suggests, with 'the events that preceded and prepared the way for the revolution'.[28] Morse's book is probably now most famous for its remarks against slavery; he quotes at length from Jefferson's oft-cited commentary on the topic in Query XVIII ('Manners') of *Notes on the States of Virginia* (1787). As with Jefferson's discussion both there and in Query XIV ('Laws'), Morse's account combines Enlightenment notions of freedom and equity with a largely unquestioning acceptance of the tenets of biological rac-

---

[25] George Richards Minot, *History of the Insurrections in Massachusetts in 1786 and of the Rebellion Consequent Thereon* (Worcester, Mass., 1788), 3.

[26] Morse had earlier published a school primer, *Geography Made Easy* (1784), which can lay claim to being the first geographical textbook of any sort published in the United States. It circulated even more widely than *The American Geography*, going through many editions in the nineteenth century.

[27] See Joseph A. Conforti, *Imagining New England: Explorations of Regional Identity from the Pilgrims to the Mid-Twentieth Century* (Chapel Hill, NC, 2001), 79–108.

[28] Morse, *The American Geography*, 94.

ism.[29] His expression of concern is one of many over the issue that would become the central historical fact of the next century in the United States.

TIMELINE/KEY DATES

1607 Establishment of Jamestown Colony
1620 Establishment of Plymouth Colony
1630 Establishment of Massachusetts Bay Colony
1637 Pequot War
1632 Chartering of Maryland Colony
1633 Chartering of Carolina Colony
1644 Chartering of Rhode Island Colony
1664 New Netherland ceded to England, becoming Province of New York
1675–8 King Philip's War, resulting in final defeat of the New England tribes
1681 Chartering of Pennsylvania Colony
1684 Massachusetts Bay charter revoked, bringing colony under royal control
1732 Chartering of Georgia Colony
1755–63 French and Indian Wars
1773 Boston Tea Party
1775–83 War of American Independence
1776 Declaration of Independence
1786–7 Shays's Rebellion
1787 Adoption of US Constitution
1789 Election of George Washington as first president

KEY HISTORICAL SOURCES

Adair, James, *The History of the American Indians* (London, 1775).
Belknap, Jeremy, *History of New-Hampshire*, 3 vols. (Philadelphia, 1784, Boston, 1791–2).
Beverly, Robert, *History and Present State of Virginia* (London, 1705).
Bradford, William, *Of Plymouth Plantation 1620–1647 by William Bradford Sometime Governor Thereof*, ed. Samuel Eliot Morison (New York, 1952).
Byrd, William, *Histories of the Dividing Line betwixt Virginia and North Carolina*, ed. William K. Boyd, intro. Percy G. Adams (New York, 1967).
Chalmers, George, *Political Annals of the Present United Colonies* (London, 1780).
Colden, Cadwallader, *The History of the Five Indian Nations Depending on the Province of New-York in America* (New York, 1727).
Douglass, William, *Summary, Historical and Political, of the First Planting, Progressive Improvements, and Present State of the British Settlements of North America* (Boston, 1749).

---

[29] Ibid., 65–7.

Galloway, Joseph, *Historical and Political Reflections on the Rise and Progress of the American Rebellion* (London, 1780).

Gordon, William, *History of the Rise, Progress, and Establishment of the Independence of the United States of America* (London, 1788).

Hewat[t], Alexander, *An Historical Account of the Rise and Progress of the Colonies of South Carolina and Georgia* (London, 1779).

Hutchinson, Thomas, *The History of the Colony of Massachusetts-Bay* (Boston, 1765–7).

Johnson, Edward, *Wonder-working Providence of Sions Saviour in New England* (London, 1654).

Mather, Cotton, *Magnalia Christi Americana: or, the Ecclesiastical History of New-England, From Its First Planting in the Year 1620 unto the Year of our LORD, 1698* (London, 1702).

Morse, Jedidiah, *The American Geography* (Elizabethtown, NJ, 1790).

Peters, Samuel, *General History of Connecticut* (London, 1781).

Prince, Thomas, *Chronological History of New-England in the Form of Annals* (Boston, 1736–55).

Ramsay, David, *The History of the American Revolution* (Philadelphia, 1789).

Smith, John, *The Generall Historie of Virginia, New-England, and the Summer Isles* (London, 1624).

Winthrop, John, *The Journal of John Winthrop 1630–1649*, ed. James Savage, and Laetitia Yeandle (Cambridge, Mass., 1996).

BIBLIOGRAPHY

Arch, Stephen Carl, *Authorizing the Past: The Rhetoric of History in Seventeenth-Century New England* (DeKalb, Ill., 1994).

Cohen, Lester H., *The Revolutionary Histories: Contemporary Narratives of the American Revolution* (Ithaca, NY, 1980).

Colbourn, H. Trevor, *The Lamp of Experience: Whig History and the Intellectual Origins of the American Revolution* (Chapel Hill, NC, 1965).

Holifield, E. Brooks, *Era of Persuasion: American Thought and Culture, 1521–1680* (Boston, 1989).

Landsman, Ned C., *From Colonials to Provincials: American Thought and Culture, 1680–1760* (Ithaca, NY, 1997).

Messer, Peter C., *Stories of Independence: Identity, Ideology, and History in Eighteenth-Century America* (DeKalb, Ill., 2005).

Shaffer, Arthur H., *The Politics of History: Writing the History of the American Revolution* (Chicago, 1975).

Smith, William Raymond, *History as Argument: Three Patriot Historians of the American Revolution* (The Hague, 1966).

Van Tassel, David., *Recording America's Past: An Interpretation of the Development of Historical Studies in America, 1607–1884* (Chicago, 1960).

Winship, Michael P., *Seers of God: Puritan Providentialism in the Restoration and Early Enlightenment* (Baltimore, Md., 1996).

Index

Note: page numbers in *italic* refer to illustrations and maps; vital dates are normally provided only for historians and scholars in related disciplines (as well as selective political figures known to have engaged in or directly influenced historical writing). Dates are not provided for persons mentioned only incidentally. As with earlier periods, vital dates (in particular birth years) are sometimes uncertain. Where a date of birth is entirely unknown or speculative, a date of death only is given; in some instances, alternative dates of birth or death are provided. For individuals known only by years of historiographical or career activity, *fl.* (floruit) is used.

Individual historical works are normally indexed only if their authors are unknown, or if they were the product of collective authorship. For other historical works, see the entries for their respective authors.